SAMUEL RICHARDSON

A Biography

Samuel Richardson (circa 1750) by Joseph Highmore

Samuel Richardson

A Biography

BY

T. C. DUNCAN EAVES

AND

BEN D. KIMPEL

CLARENDON PRESS · OXFORD

1971

Oxford University Press, Ely House, London W.1

GLASGOW NEW YORK TORONTO MELBOURNE WELLINGTON
CAPE TOWN SALISBURY IBADAN NAIROBI DAR ES SALAAM LUSAKA ADDIS ABABA
BOMBAY CALCUTTA MADRAS KARACHI LAHORE DACCA
KUALA LUMPUR SINGAPORE HONG KONG TOKYO

PRINTED IN GREAT BRITAIN
BY WILLIAM CLOWES AND SONS, LIMITED
LONDON, BECCLES AND COLCHESTER

TO THE MEMORY

OF

GEORGE WILEY SHERBURN

1884–1962

PREFACE

IN this biography we have tried to accomplish three things which are not, we hope, incompatible. One aim has been to treat in a scholarly way, with full documentation, all of the problems, major and minor, connected with Richardson's life, to present the factual evidence and to indicate our views on what that evidence implies. In other words, we have intended to write a definitive biography. To do this, we have pursued all the lines of investigation which we could think of as far as they led us.

In addition, we wished to give a picture of Richardson as a person, using insofar as possible his own words and those of his friends and reporting any details, however minute, which might reveal his personality. As Harriet Byron says, 'The humours and characters of persons cannot be known, unless I repeat *what* they say.' We have preferred this method to the more summary one of describing Richardson in our own words or to psychoanalysis, which we believe leads to dubious results when applied to a person dead two hundred years. Our biography will, therefore, sound rather old-fashioned, and it has encountered the same difficulty Richardson himself met with, that of prolixity. We have often echoed Richardson's complaint while writing *Clarissa*, 'Length, is my principal Disgust'. Especially we have tried to portray his relationships with his friends and correspondents, which meant trying to give some picture of the people he came in contact with. For Richardson, who was much more interested in, and interesting about, human relations than abstract ideas, this emphasis seemed to us unavoidable.

Finally, we have discussed the intrinsic value of Richardson's novels. This value must be the main reason for one's interest in Richardson as a man, though we cannot claim that all of the biographical facts we discuss have a bearing on it. Again we have tended to adopt a somewhat old-fashioned approach, one more like that of Richardson's own contemporaries than like the formal or interpretative approaches popular in our century. This means not that we think our approach the only possible one to all literature but that, in our opinion, Richardson's first readers on the whole understood fairly well what he was doing and grasped his real merits.

There has been no exhaustive biography of Richardson, though there have been several good short ones. Anna Lætitia Barbauld, in her edition of Richardson's *Correspondence* (1804), recounted the main facts clearly and with considerable judgement, and no evidence discovered since her time has basically changed the picture she gave. Clara L. Thomson in *Samuel Richardson: A Biographical and Critical Study* (1900) adds a few new facts as well as some lively, if highly coloured, discussion of Richardson as a man and as a writer. The most readable life is Austin Dobson's *Samuel Richardson* (1902), which also adds a few facts but is mainly valuable for its common sense and its urbane style. Brian W. Downs's *Richardson* (1928) is primarily important for its often perceptive criticism. Paul Dottin's *Samuel Richardson* (1931) is patronizing but at least constantly amusing.

There have recently been a number of excellent serious critical treatments of Richardson's novels, the most important of which we have mentioned in our text. We have also acknowledged our indebtedness to a number of factual articles on specific topics, especially the long series of articles by Aleyn Lyell Reade on Richardson's family published in *Notes and Queries* in 1922–1923. Our indebtedness to two recent scholars is, however, too great to be acknowledged in detail. William Merritt Sale, Jr.'s *Samuel Richardson: A Bibliographical Record of His Literary Career with Historical Notes* (1936) is of primary importance for the editions of Richardson's works and of contemporary works related to him; his *Samuel Richardson: Master Printer* (1950), an exhaustive study of Richardson's business career, has been invaluable to us. Indeed the only facts connected with Richardson which we have not checked personally are some of those he gives about the books Richardson printed, based largely on the evidence of printers' ornaments—we have not thought it necessary to repeat his investigations unless the book in question had a direct bearing on the facts of Richardson's life. Alan Dugald McKillop has written a number of excellent articles about particular facets of Richardson's activities, which we have mentioned in their places, and in *Samuel Richardson: Printer and Novelist* (1936) has given a perceptive account of Richardson's writing career, with many stimulating critical insights, and of his reputation. Like all Richardson scholars we have been aided greatly by their researches; in addition, Mr. Sale and Mr. McKillop have generously made available to us various manuscripts and books in their collections. The fact that we occasionally disagree with them in no way diminishes our gratitude. We would also like to express our special gratitude to the late George Sherburn, who not only stimulated our interest in the eighteenth-century novel in the classroom but first suggested to us the need of a new biography of Richardson.

To the late Major General Henry Richardson Peck, Brigadier Oliver J. Peck, and Mr. Jasper Augustine Peck, descendants of Samuel Richardson, and to Mr. John Lucas-Scudamore and the Lady Patricia Lucas-Scudamore, the late Commander Arthur Avalon Mackinnon of Mackinnon and the Lady Mackinnon, Mrs. Alan Cory-Wright, Sir Anthony Highmore King, and Mr. F. B. Morgan-Payler, descendants of some of Richardson's closest friends, we are indebted not only for their assistance but also for their gracious hospitality.

We have received a great deal of aid from individuals, institutions, and libraries, and we regret that the following list so inadequately reflects our appreciation: Mr. John Alden; the Algemeen Rijksarchief, The Hague; the American Philosophical Society Library; Hugh Amory; the Gemeentelijke Archief Dienst, Amsterdam; the Universiteits-Bibliotheek van Amsterdam; the Reverend D. F. Andrews, Vicar of All Saints, Fulham; Commander E. B. Baker; the Universitätsbibliothek, Basel; the Bath Municipal Libraries and Victoria Art Gallery; Miss G. M. A. Beck, Archivist of the Muniment Room, Guildford, Surrey; the Bodleian Library; the Boston Public Library; Mr. Fredson T. Bowers; Mr. and Mrs. Benjamin Boyce; the Trustees of the British Museum; Brown University Library; the Library of the State University of New York at Buffalo; the Reverend H. W. R. Bywater, Vicar of St. Alkmund's, Derby; Mr. F. M. Cattell, Manager of the Gosling Branch of Barclay's Bank; the Trustees of the Charnwood Settlement; Christ's Hospital; Mr. James L. Clifford; Mr. W. B. Coley; Columbia University Library; Cornell University Library; the Corporation of London; Mr. D. M. Davin, the Clarendon Press; the Deutsches Buch- und Schriftsmuseum, Leipzig; the University of Edinburgh Library; Mr. George Eland; the Essex County Records Office; Norman Evans and the Public Records Office; the Fitzwilliam Museum, Cambridge; David Fleeman; Miss Marjorie Flint, Deputy Librarian of the British Library of Political and Economic Science; the Folger Shakespeare Library; H. B. Forster; the Freies Deutsches Hochstift, Frankfurt am Main; the Fulham Public Library; Dr. Funke, Deutsche Bucherei, Leipzig; Mr. Vedder M. Gilbert; Mr. Robert Halsband; Mr. Paul Hardacre; Mr. W. C. Hart, Clerk of the London County Council; Harvard University Library; Haverford College Library; Miss Winifred Heard, Chiswick Public Library; Peter Murray Hill, Ltd.; Mr. Frederick W. Hilles; Sidney Hodgson, F.S.A.; Mr. A. E. J. Holländer, Archivist of the London Guildhall Library; the Henry E. Huntington Library and Art Gallery; Miss Rose-Maria Hurlebusch, the Hamburger Klopstock-Ausgabe; Mrs. Donald F. Hyde and the late Mr. Hyde; the University of Indiana Library; the University of Iowa Libraries; the National Library of Ireland; Mr. Duncan E. Isles; Det Kol. Bibliotek, København; Lambeth Palace Library; the Brotherton Collection, the University of Leeds Library; the Universitätsbibliothek, Leipzig; the City of Liverpool Public Libraries; the Reverend A. Lewis Lloyd, Vicar of Chiswick Parish Church;

*a**

the London County Council; the Greater London Council; the London Guildhall Library; the Maine Historical Society; Mr. Edward L. McAdam, Jr.; Mr. Colin A. McLaren, Archivist of the Public Libraries of the Borough of Hammersmith; the Merchant Taylors' Company; the Middlesex County Records Office; W. H. Millear; the Reverend Dewi Morgan, Vicar of St. Bride's, London; the Pierpont Morgan Library; the National Portrait Gallery; the National Registry of Archives; the New York Historical Society; the New York Public Library; the Henry W. and Albert A. Berg Collection of the New York Public Library, Astor, Lenox, and Tilden Foundations; the Fales Collection, New York University Library; Mr. J. G. O'Leary, Dagenham, Essex; Mr. James M. Osborn; Mr. Stanley J. Osborne, the Stationers' Company; the Oxford University Press; the Historical Society of Pennsylvania; the Library of the University of Pennsylvania; Mr. Henry Pettit; Mr. David Piper; the late Kenneth Povey; Mr. Lawrence Fitzroy Powell; Princeton University Library; Mr. William Rees-Mogg; the Royal College of Physicians; the Royal National Hospital for Rheumatic Diseases, Bath; the Library of St. Paul's Cathedral; Mr. Charles J. Sawyer; the National Library of Scotland; Mr. John B. Shipley; Sion College; the Literary Department of the National Probate Registry, Somerset House; Mr. William C. Slattery; the Society of Genealogists; the Stationers' Company; Mr. George Stewart; C. A. Stonehill, Inc.; Nancy Ellen Talburt; Mr. Robert H. Taylor; Gordon Thomson, Deputy Director of the National Gallery of Victoria; the Board of Trinity College, Dublin; the Victoria and Albert Museum; the Reverend E. J. Walser, Vicar of Mackworth Parish Church, Derbyshire; Wellesley College Library; the Westminster Public Library; the Trustees of the Wisbech and Fenland Museum; Mr. J. F. V. Woodman, Clerk of the Chamberlain's Court; Mr. Austin Wright; and Yale University Library. Nor have we forgotten the many Derbyshire clergymen who aided us in examining the parish registers in that county or the libraries who answered negatively our inquiries about Richardson manuscripts. Juliet Eaves, in addition to other encouragement, typed our manuscript.

Of the many colleagues at the University of Arkansas who have helped us, we would like to mention especially Mrs. Harold Hantz, who has searched indefatigably for hard-to-find books and periodicals, and Dean Virgil W. Adkisson of the Graduate School, whose support has been generous and constant. We might mention also that the University's policy of encouraging research without insisting on frequent publication has enabled us to spend as much time on this book as we judged necessary.

In order to avoid at least some of the prolixity involved in an exhaustive biography, we have published a number of articles on special subjects which go into more detail than we consider desirable in this book. For further arguments about and documentation on the following subjects, we refer scholars to our articles: Richardson's town houses and the beginning of his career as a printer, 'Samuel Richardson's London Houses', *Studies in Bibliography*, XV (1962), 135–48; Richardson's family and the families of his wives, his ancestry, his birthplace, and his will, 'Samuel Richardson and His Family Circle', *Notes and Queries*, N.S. XI (1964), 212–18, 264–70, 300–4, 343–7, 362–71, 402–6, 467–9; XV (1968), 448–50; the revisions of *Pamela*, 'Richardson's Revisions of *Pamela*', *Studies in Bibliography*, XX (1967), 61–88; the composition of *Clarissa*, 'The Composition of *Clarissa* and Its Revision before Publication', *PMLA*, LXXXIII (1968), 416–28. We have not always given documentation on these subjects in this biography. Other more specific articles are referred to as the subjects arise. We have used the normal dots of omission in quotations when we have omitted only a fairly short passage; when we omit a long passage or when the quotations come from different letters or in a different order, we have closed and re-opened quotations.

'Notes are often necessary, but they are necessary evils,' Dr. Johnson sensibly observed. This biography contains frequent 'necessary evils', but since they are, with few exceptions, only citations of manuscripts and books, they can be safely ignored by the reader. In order to simplify them as well as to provide a convenient checklist, we have cited letters to and from Richardson by date only. These letters can easily be located by referring to the list of letters in our Appendix. For books printed by Richardson and for the dates of publication of Richardson's works and of contemporary works prompted by them, the reader is here referred to Mr. Sale's *Samuel Richardson: Master Printer* and *Samuel Richardson: A Bibliographical Record of His Literary Career with Historical Notes* unless we have indicated otherwise in our footnotes. Though there is no really standard edition of Richardson's novels, we have followed the usual practice of giving references to the Shakespeare Head edition, ed. William King and Adrian Bott (Oxford: Basil Blackwell, 1929–31), and for *Pamela* and *Clarissa* we have added references to the more easily accessible editions in Everyman's Library (1914, 1932).

T. C. Duncan Eaves
Ben D. Kimpel

POSTSCRIPT

I want to express my special appreciation to the John Simon Guggenheim Memorial Foundation for generously awarding me a fellowship in 1957–8 and thereby enabling me to spend an uninterrupted year in England doing some of the preliminary research for this biography and to the American Council of Learned Societies for a Grant-in-Aid in 1967. The Research Reserve Fund of the University of Arkansas has also on several occasions generously supported this work, and I am most grateful for this support.   T. C. D. E.

CONTENTS

LIST OF PLATES

ABBREVIATIONS

In citing periodicals in our footnotes we have adopted the abbreviations used in the *MLA International Bibliography of Books and Articles on the Modern Languages and Literatures*. The following abbreviations are also used in footnotes:

B.M.	British Museum
Bodleian	Bodleian Library, Oxford
EL	Everyman's Library
FM	Forster Collection, Victoria and Albert Museum
Guildhall	London Guildhall Library
P.C.C.	Prerogative Court of the Archbishop of Canterbury
P.R.O.	Public Records Office
SH	Shakespeare Head edition of Richardson's novels

CHAPTER I

FAMILY AND EARLY LIFE
1689–1721

WHETHER or not one chooses to call him the 'first English novelist' (and such titles are not very meaningful, depending mainly on definition and casting little light on intrinsic merit), Samuel Richardson wrote near the beginning of a tradition which has produced a great deal of fine work and which, though challenged for fifty years by various *avant-gardes*, is even now not dead. In spite of considerable differences in outlook, in method his books obviously belong in the same class as the great novels of the nineteenth and early twentieth centuries. More important, his major book, *Clarissa*, has the same qualities as these novels. It has recently been attracting perceptive and appreciative treatment from serious critics. We are now far enough away from Richardson to stop reacting against the often narrow moralizing which he owed to his class and time and to judge whether, aside from that moralizing, he had anything to say.

Richardson's novels are receiving their share of admiration, but Richardson as a man is still treated with hostility, scorn, or at best a rather lofty patronage. It seems that a major work, which, whatever it is, is not silly, somehow wrote itself through a silly man whose only characteristics were petty vanity and conventional propriety. The hostility to Richardson is not new. His Muse, says Thackeray, 'was attended by old maids and dowagers, and fed on muffins and bohea'.[1] (A certain animus is apparent—Richardson's female friends were almost all young girls or married women.) Coleridge was even harsher: 'I confess that it has cost, and still costs, my philosophy some exertion not to be vexed that I must admire, aye, greatly admire, Richardson. His mind is so very vile a mind, so oozy, so hypocritical, praise-mad, canting, envious, concupiscent!'[2] Later writers have treated him with at best condescension. Aside from the understandable joy of critics when they find a creative artist they may belittle, there are at least three obvious reasons for this tendency. Richardson preached too much, and not only has preaching become for many years less and less popular, but a preacher is especially vulnerable to attack, he invites attack,

[1] *The English Humourists* in *Works*, Cornhill edn. (New York, 1911), XXI, 346.
[2] *Anima Poetæ*, ed. Ernest Hartley Coleridge (London, 1895), p. 166.

which is a kind of defence against his condemnations. Worse, the tendency of Richardson's preaching is not popular today: he supported the middle-class virtues and particularly stressed the importance of chastity, a very unpopular virtue at the moment. Readers of *Pamela*, especially, are, according to temperament, either irritated by his addiction to virginity or amused by his naïveté. His works are certainly no closer to sermons than those of Henry Miller or D. H. Lawrence, but almost all modern intellectuals will regard the content of most of his sermons as false, worse as ludicrous, still worse as dull. We are not intensely interested in many of Richardson's moral pronouncements, but if a weakness for platitudes were a mortal sin, even Shakespeare would be in danger. Surely a man's character is not identical with his opinions.

A more particular reason for the condemnation of Richardson, not entirely divorced from the first, is that it has from the beginning been popular to contrast him with Fielding. Richardson himself, by his slighting and unjust remarks about Fielding, invited this contrast. The accusations against Fielding by the more pious of his own contemporaries and by the early Victorians led naturally to a reaction, and in praising Fielding many of his admirers felt called upon to lower Richardson. There is no more logical reason for not admiring both men as human beings and as writers than for not admiring, for instance, both Milton and James Joyce; but the contrast was an obvious one, and the tendency to exalt one writer by running down another seems perennial. The comparative toleration of Fielding, his openness and breeziness about sex, attracted many Victorians (always with apologies, to be sure) and continues to attract in an age when apology is no longer necessary. This is perhaps the chief reason that the more proper Richardson should be so often charged with prurience, and especially by critics who would have been willing enough to pardon or welcome in another any sign of the sexual urge, even suppressed. Richardson, according to Frederick C. Green, 'has a positive genius for disgusting the most tolerant; and could make the binomial theorem sound indecent'.[3]

Still more important, Richardson's life was that of a conventional middle-class businessman—to most intellectuals, the worst of all possible lives. His character, as R. F. Brissenden says, 'is an affront to every conception of what an artist should be'.[4] It is impossible to deny that Richardson tried (consciously at least) to preserve the conventions of his social order, or that his life fitted into that order all too neatly for modern taste. He was a poor boy who by diligence and sobriety rose to moderate wealth in business before, at about fifty, he turned to writing. And he took pride in

[3] *Minuet: A Critical Survey of French and English Literary Ideas in the Eighteenth Century* (New York, [1935]), p. 382.
[4] *Samuel Richardson* (London, [1958]), p. 9.

his success and shared the views, both ethical and social, of the puritan bourgeoisie.

The picture of Richardson's life and character has not changed much in a hundred and fifty years. And it is not our aim to change it fundamentally. We do not know the 'secret' of Richardson's character—real people are likely to have a good many secrets. Rather do we hope to fill it in, and by filling it in to remove the element of caricature which has distorted it. Richardson's character does not seem to us to have been remarkably complex, but it was too complex to pinpoint in a phrase. We do not intend to defend him any more than we intend to treat him with scorn or condescension. He was a human being, and we are therefore thankful that we are not called upon to decide his exact niche in heaven or hell. Thumbnail sketches, convenient as they may be for conversation, can never be adequate portraits of a real man, even if that man had not somehow or other got on to paper a story which, while it violates most of the preconceptions of an age in which whores are virtuous by profession and what used to be called rakes are individualists, is still capable of gripping and indeed of moving even those who hold dear the preconceptions it violates. Such a story did get written by a conventional, self-made, middle-class man who never seriously questioned the assumptions of his age and who at times made himself ridiculous.

Richardson's ancestors had been small farmers on the Royal Manor of Byfleet in Surrey since before 1572. Four successive William Richardsons held copyhold land in this manor. So far as one can judge, they were moderately prosperous yeomen, with no claims to being anything more. They seem to have been of the class which was the salt of the English earth, which kept both the gentry and the mob fed and managed to feed itself well at the same time.

The fourth William Richardson, the novelist's grandfather, was the youngest of three sons. His elder brothers, Robert and John, also held land on the manor, and Robert remained in Byfleet until his death in 1707 and was one of the overseers of his brother William's will. When their father died in 1643, he left the remainder of his property to guardians for the use of his wife, Sara, and his son William. The latter married a woman named Anne Royden, of another family of Byfleet copyholders.

William continued at Byfleet until his death in 1689 but evidently did not believe that his sons should go on being Byfleet yeomen. One son, William, became a shoemaker at nearby Weybridge. In 1683 his father agreed to leave to him when he died most of his lands in Byfleet, and he held these and other lands until at least 1692, though he did not perhaps farm them himself. Another son, Samuel, the novelist's father, was sent to London in 1667, when he was about seventeen, and was apprenticed to

B—B.R.

Thomas Turner, a joiner, for the usual term of seven years. The novelist himself says, 'My Father was a very honest Man, descended of a Family of middling Note in the County of Surrey; but which having for several Generations a large Number of Children, the *not* large Possessions were split and divided; so that He and his Brothers were put to Trades; and the Sisters were married to Tradesmen.'

Early in 1675 Richardson's father married a woman named Elizabeth Lane, who died in 1680. They had at least two daughters, only one of whom, Elizabeth, survived childhood. He soon married another woman named Elizabeth, probably the Elizabeth Hall who was married to a 'Samuell Richarson' on 2 June 1682 at St. James's, Clerkenwell. Of the novelist's mother we know only what we learn from him: that she was 'a good Woman, of a Family not ungenteel', and that her father and mother had died in her infancy, within half an hour of each other, in the Great Plague of 1665. Samuel and his new wife had a son, William, and two daughters, Mary and Anne, during the first years of their marriage, before they left London.

Evidently Samuel Richardson, Senior, at first prospered as a joiner. In 1678 he became a freeman of the Joiners' Company and of the City of London. His son tells us that 'he was a good Draughtsman, and understood Architecture'; his granddaughters, the novelist's daughters, go further and make him 'a considerable importer of mahogany', but they were inclined to exaggerate the family's importance. He did at least once advertise that he had 'the best and choicest Cedar, both for Colour and Scent', to sell. And he did well enough to take three apprentices. His home and his business were in the City, in Aldersgate Street, almost across from the Church of St. Botolph.

A year or two before the novelist's birth something happened to cause his father to leave London. To quote again his son Samuel: 'His Skill and Ingenuity, and an Understanding superior to his Business, with his remarkable Integrity of Heart and Manners, made him personally beloved by several Persons of Rank, among whom were the Duke of Monmouth and the first Earl of Shaftesbury; both so noted in our English History. Their known Favour for him, having, on the Duke's Attempt on the Crown, subjected him to be looked upon with a jealous Eye, notwithstanding he was noted for a quiet and inoffensive Man, he thought proper, on the Decollation of the first-named unhappy Nobleman, to quit his London Business and to retire to Derbyshire; tho' to his great Detriment; and there I, and three other Children out of Nine, were born.' In no other instance have we detected Samuel Richardson in a mis-statement. But the Duke of Monmouth was decollated on 15 July 1685, and Richardson's father had not left London over two years later, when he took his third apprentice between 2 August 1687 and 11 December 1688, and was evidently not planning to leave. The house he had lived in on Aldersgate Street still appears in his name, with a tenant, in lists of householders and in tax records from 1688 through 1693.

The novelist may not have been told the real reason for his father's leaving London. The Earl of Shaftesbury, when he was trying to woo the middle classes for the Whig cause, had moved to the City and indeed had an establishment in Aldersgate Ward, where Samuel Richardson, Senior, lived. They could have known each other. During 1687 and most of 1688, until the landing of the future William III in November, the Whigs, who included many of the City guildsmen, were harassed by James II. But if Richardson's father left London during this period, it would not have been much over a year before the Glorious Revolution made it safe for him to return. It may have been business difficulties that made it advisable for him to get out of London, but the reason is still uncertain.

Richardson said very little in later years about his early life. His own daughters did not even know the name of their grandmother or where their father was born or educated. Most of what they learned about his father's family and his own youth they learned from his only known excursion into autobiography, a letter which he wrote on 2 June 1753 to his Dutch translator, Johannes Stinstra, in answer to Stinstra's inquiry about his life. It is from this letter that we have quoted Richardson's remarks on his family, and we will be quoting it again. Indeed it has been almost the only basis for the biography of Richardson up to about 1720. Why he chose to break his silence to a man he had never met must remain a question, as well as whether his daughters were simply too awed by his dignity to question him about anything or whether he avoided talking about his boyhood in order not to have to reveal some fact which he wanted to hide.

At any rate, by 19 August 1689 the Richardson family was in Derbyshire. On that date the novelist was baptized in the parish church at Mackworth. From an obscure reference in one of his daughter Anne's letters, we are inclined to guess that he was born on 31 July. Samuel's elder brother, William, was buried there in September, and on 8 April 1691 another brother William was baptized.

Mackworth is a village immediately to the west of the City of Derby. It seems rather strange to find a London joiner in such a small place. Most of the land was owned by the Mundy family, which had large estates in the area, but we have been unable to find any connection between them and Samuel Richardson, though their rent rolls for this period are extant, as are accounts of receipts and disbursements by their steward. Mackworth is only a few miles from Derby, and it is possible that he worked in the city and lived in the neighbouring village.

In 1693 a Sara, daughter of Samuel Richardson, was baptized at St.

Alkmund's, the Derby parish bordering on Mackworth. If this is Richardson's sister, one more child should, according to his statement, have been born in Derbyshire—presumably a son, since Richardson once mentioned two brothers who died abroad, and we know of only one who could have done so. He was not baptized in Derby or in Mackworth or the adjacent parishes. The statement in Richardson's letter to Stinstra and these four entries in parish registers are the only records we know of connecting the novelist with Derbyshire.

Samuel Richardson, Senior, had meanwhile inherited some property. His father had died in 1689, about the time of the novelist's birth. His will, after mentioning the fact that he had already by agreement disposed of most of his land to his son William, enjoins William to see that 'my now present wife' (to judge by the urgency of his warning, she must have been William's step-mother) gets 'one Rome in the house I now dwell in with the use of ye Hall and ye Kitchin', as well as £7 a year (which William had agreed to when his father agreed to leave him the lands). This is probably a good measure of the financial status of the family. Legacies of twenty or thirty pounds go to his granddaughter Elizabeth (Samuel's daughter, who had been living with him) and to his daughters, Elizabeth Richardson, Sarah Berry, and Mary Mills. His money, corn, and cattle go to his executor and son Samuel—probably as compensation for what he had given William. He had already, in 1684, agreed that Samuel was to have after his death six acres which were still his to dispose of after the agreement with William.

In January 1698 Richardson's father appeared at Byfleet in his own person to surrender these six acres. If he had not already left Derbyshire, he returned to London to live within the next year or so. On 4 October 1699 his son Benjamin was baptized in the parish of St. Botolph, Aldgate, and on 14 January 1703 his son Thomas. If we are right in assuming that the eight brothers and sisters whom the novelist mentions in his letter to Stinstra did not include children who died in infancy before he was old enough to know them, they were his half-sister, Elizabeth, and Mary, Anne, William, Sara, a boy born in Derbyshire, Benjamin, and Thomas.

When his last two sons were baptized, Samuel, Senior, was described as living on Tower Hill. Both the southern portion of the parish of St. Botolph, Aldgate, within the City and another portion just outside, to the east, the northern part of the Liberty of East Smithfield, were called Tower Hill. His sons William and Benjamin afterwards lived in the latter district. In 1700 a Samuel Richardson was living there in a street called Mouse Alley, which ran south from the still extant street East Smithfield into what is now St. Katherine's Docks. The submerging of the novelist's boyhood home has probably not destroyed a particularly idyllic scene. Even then the district was the site of warehouses and of a large brewery.

According to the Churchwardens' Accounts, one inhabitant of Mouse Alley several times received alms, and in 1699 the parish had to pay 1*s.* 9*d.* 'to remove a Bigbellyed woman from Mouse Ally'.[5] Early in 1701 the inhabitants of the Tower Hamlets, of which East Smithfield was one, petitioned the House of Commons for a Court of Conscience, a cheap legal method of recovering small debts, because 'the said Hamlets abound very much with indigent Tradesmen, who are daily ruined, by being arrested, and thrown into Gaol, for inconsiderable Debts and Actions; whereby their Families become a Burden in their respective Parishes'. Somewhat later the officials and inhabitants asked for hospitals and work-houses or houses of correction to discourage 'Idleness and Debauchery' and render 'the able Poor serviceable to the common Good', 'setting forth, That the Poor within the said Hamlets and Liberties are of late Years become very numerous, and burdensome to the rest of the Inhabitants; and are likely to increase'.[6] According to descriptions of London later in the century, they did increase: the district between the Tower and Limehouse was long regarded as a disgrace to the city. Around Tower Hill there were 'wooden hovels, paltry erections and waste ground', 'the receptacle of whores and thieves'. Parts of this neighbourhood were regarded as dangerous, and its labyrinth of courts and alleys was mean and nasty.[7]

The appearance of Samuel Richardson's name in only one rate book of the district is probably explained by the fact that the record of 1700 is a scavenger's assessment, which all inhabitants had to pay to keep the streets clean or at least less dirty. The other records of the period are poor rates, which those inhabitants who were fairly well off paid to support the impoverished. In 1700 only one of the twenty householders of Mouse Alley who were assessed for the scavenger's had to pay a poor rate, and he lived on the corner of Mouse Alley and Swan Alley.

By 1703 the family had moved, not far from Mouse Alley but just inside the City, to Rosemary Lane, near The Minories and immediately north of the Tower. From 1720 through 1724 the house there, which Richardson's father continued to rent, had other occupants, but from 1725 into 1727 he lived there again. He was paying a respectable, medium rent. He presumably continued to practise as a joiner, since his son Benjamin was well enough trained in that profession to be admitted by patrimony to the freedom of the Joiners' Company, though he was never apprenticed. Samuel Richardson, Senior, paid his dues in the Joiners' Company through 1724, the year in which Benjamin was admitted; and after 1727 we have no record of him.

[5] Guildhall MS. 2626.

[6] *Journals of the House of Commons*, XIII, 365, 415, under dates 1 Mar. and 20 Mar.

[7] See M. Dorothy George, *London Life in the XVIIIth Century* (New York, 1926), pp. 65–9, 84, 92, 348.

Richardson never tried to conceal that his family had been poor. To Stinstra he wrote that his father wanted to educate him for the clergy but was unable to, 'while I was very young, some heavy Losses having disabled him from supporting me as genteely as he wished in an Education proper for the Function'. Referring to the education the Bath clergyman Samuel Lobb was giving his son William, he wrote, 'To My early Years Fortune was not propitious. . . . I had a very good Father; But he could not be such an Encourager—such [a] Promoter—such an Improver.'[8]

It is not, as has generally been assumed, amid the green hills of Derbyshire but in the narrow lanes to the east or north of the Tower of London that the events of his boyhood which Richardson related to Stinstra must have taken place. When he was eleven (in the year that his father was living on Mouse Alley), he wrote to a widow of nearly fifty who pretended a zeal for religion but 'was continually fomenting Quarrels and Disturbances, by her Backbiting and Scandal'; citing scriptural texts and writing in the style of an older person, he 'expostulated with her'. This first instance of his love of letter-writing and of moralizing was discovered by the handwriting, and the widow wept to his mother, who blamed him for taking such a liberty with an older person but commended his principles, 'knowing that her Son was not of a pert or forward Nature, but, on the contrary, shy and bashful'. He also repeated substantially the same story, giving his age as twelve, to Edward Young.[9]

Richardson was 'an early Favourite with all the young Women of Taste and Reading in the Neighbourhood', some of whom used to get him to read to them while they sewed, and both mothers and daughters were pleased with his observations. 'I was not more than Thirteen when three of these young Women, unknown to each other, having an high Opinion of my Taciturnity, revealed to me their Love Secrets, in order to induce me to give them Copies to write after, or correct, for Answers to their Lovers Letters: Nor did any one of them ever know, that I was the Secretary to the others. I have been directed to chide, and even repulse, when an Offence was either taken or given, at the very time that the Heart of the Chider or Repulser was open before me, overflowing with Esteem and Affection; and the fair Repulser dreading to be taken at her Word; directing *this* Word, or *that* Expression, to be softened or changed. One, highly gratify'd with her Lover's Fervor and Vows of everlasting Love, has said, when I have asked her Direction; I cannot tell you what to write; But (her Heart on her Lips) you cannot write too kindly: All her Fear only, that she should incurr Slight for her Kindness.'

Not only his ability at writing letters, but also his skill as a storyteller

<hr />

[8] [July 1746–Mar. 1750].
[9] Letter from the Rev. John Jones, Young's curate at Welwyn from 1759 to Young's death in 1765, published in the *Gentleman's Magazine*, LIII (1783), 924.

appeared, according to his letter to Stinstra, very early: 'I recollect, that I was early noted for having Invention. I was not fond of Play, as other Boys: My Schoolfellows used to call me *Serious* and *Gravity*: And five of them particularly, delighted to single me out, either for a Walk, or at their Fathers' Houses or at mine, to tell them Stories as they phrased it. Some I told them from my Reading as true; others from my Head, as mere Invention; of which they would be most fond; and often were affected by them. One of them, particularly, I remember, was for putting me to write a History, as he called it, on the Model of Tommy Potts; I now forget what it was; only, that it was of a Servant-Man preferred by a fine young Lady (for his Goodness) to a Lord, who was a Libertine. All my Stories carried with them I am bold to say an useful Moral.'

There is no reason to suppose that these anecdotes are not at least as true as most people's stories about their childhood. They are almost too illustrative of what one would expect the author of *Pamela* to have been like as a boy. His bashfulness persisted, though it later at times took its usual adult form of touchiness and an over-sensitive pride. His gravity and concern for morality also persisted. We are unable to offer our readers even a hint of scandal about Samuel Richardson. There is no reason not to believe his statement to Stinstra: 'I never, to my Know-lege, was in a vile House, or in Company with a lewd Woman, in my Life.' We can only hope that as it was possible for a Victorian to recognize that a fallen women might have a heart of gold it may be possible for a modern reader to find such a heart in a highly moral, not to say proper, businessman. It may be worth noting that his first known effort at moral improvement was directed not against the foibles of youth but against scandal-mongering.

At what school he acquired the nicknames of '*Serious* and *Gravity*' is unknown. His daughter Martha stated that he was educated at a private grammar-school near his birthplace, but her correspondence with her sister Anne shows that the family was merely guessing and did not know either his birthplace or his school.[10] Since he must have been back in London by the time he was ten, he could hardly have received much education in Derbyshire.

A Samuel Richardson entered the second form of the Merchant Taylors' School in 1701, advanced to the third form, and left the school in 1702. This could well have been the novelist. He does seem to have had a little Latin. He would have needed an elementary education to enter the Merchant Taylors' School, and there is no evidence that his formal educa-tion ever went far beyond what he might have acquired in a year there.

---

[10] This correspondence between Anne Richardson and Martha Bridgen from 18 June to 24 Aug. 1784 (frequently cited in this chapter) is owned by Professor Alan Dugald McKillop, who has generously permitted us to use it.

If he was a scholar at the school, he was just too late for the great ceremony of 11 December 1700 when the four hundred scholars marched two by two to hear a sermon at Bow Church and then to the Merchant Taylors' Hall, where they watched the gentlemen feast and were treated with a glass of canary and a roll; and one hopes he was never exposed to the school captain Samuel Phillips, who in 1703 was accused of luring a sixth-form boy to theatres, taverns, and gaming houses.[11]

Boswell, who was accompanying Richardson's old friend John Riving-ton on a tour of Christ's Hospital, noted in 1773 that 'the celebrated Richardson was brought up here'.[12] Perhaps on the basis of the same source from which Boswell got his information, a footnote was added to the letter from Edward Young's curate, the Reverend John Jones, of Welwyn, published in the *Gentleman's Magazine* for November 1783, that Richardson attended Christ's Hospital.[13] This was denied by his daughter Martha Bridgen,[14] and a search of the records of the school shows that he was not formally registered there. In fact he was ineligible if the school upheld its rule made in 1676 and still in effect in 1748 that 'no Children be taken in but such as are Orphans, wanting Father or Mother, or both'.[15] It has been suggested that Richardson may have been a private pupil of one of the masters,[16] but the financial situation of Richardson's family makes this solution dubious.

He never did receive much formal education. He wrote to Stinstra that his father was 'able to give me only common School-Learning', and everything that we know about him supports that statement. His daughter Anne remembered his talking Latin with Edward Young[17] but presumably was in no position to judge the quality of the Latin. He had to get some-one to translate the Latin letters which Stinstra wrote to him, and he told Stinstra on 6 December 1752 that his native language was 'the only one in which I have any tolerable Knowlege'. References to his ignorance of French are frequent in his correspondence. Nor does he ever display more than the most superficial acquaintance with the classics. When Edward Young wrote that the ancients put the Centaur in heaven, he so completely missed the allusion that he suggested that Centaur was an error and should be plural.[18] A good elementary-school training in reading

[11] H. B. Wilson, *The History of Merchant-Taylors School* (London, 1812), pp. 399, 401.
[12] *Private Papers of James Boswell from Malahide Castle in the Collection of Lt.-Colonel Ralph Heyward Isham*, ed. Geoffrey Scott and Frederick A. Pottle (Privately Printed, 1928–34), VI, 107.
[13] LIII, 924.
[14] *Gentleman's Magazine*, LIV (1784), 488.
[15] William Trollope, *A History of the Royal Foundation of Christ's Hospital* (London, 1834), pp. 72–4, 120.
[16] Aleyn Lyell Reade, 'Samuel Richardson and Christ's Hospital,' *N&Q*, 10 S. XII (1909), 302.
[17] Letters to Martha Bridgen, 18 June, 28 June 1784.
[18] 21 Jan. 1755; *The Centaur Not Fabulous*, 1st edn. (1755), p. 125.

and writing plus perhaps a year or so of exposure to Latin grammar would be enough to account for all the education of which Richardson is known to have been master. Even more than Shakespeare or Burns, he might be cited as an example of that untutored Natural Genius so dear to eighteenth-century Englishmen.

The first definite record of Samuel Richardson after his baptism is in the records of the Stationers' Company: on 1 July 1706 he was apprenticed for seven years to John Wilde; his apprenticeship expired on 2 July 1713, and on 13 June 1715 he became a freeman of the Company and a citizen of London.[19] He wrote to Stinstra that after his father proved unable to educate him for the clergy (a function which would have been congenial to him), he was permitted, when he was fifteen or sixteen, to choose a profession for himself (actually he was seventeen when he was apprenticed): 'I chose that of a Printer, tho' a Stranger to it, as what I thought would gratify my Thirst after Reading. I served a diligent Seven Years to it, to a Master who grudged every Hour to me, that tended not to his Profit, even of those times of Leisure and Diversion, which the Refractoriness of my Fellow-Servants *obliged* him to allow them, and were usually allowed by other Masters to their Apprentices. I stole from the Hours of Rest and Relaxation, my Reading Times for Improvement of my Mind; and being engaged in a Correspondence with a Gentleman greatly my Superior in Degree, and of ample Fortunes, who had he lived, intended high things for me; those were all the Opportunities I had in my Apprenticeship to carry it on. But this little Incident I may mention; I took Care, that even my Candle was of my own purchasing, that I might not in the most trifling Instance make my Master a Sufferer (and who used to call me The Pillar of his House) and not to disable myself by Watching, or Sitting-up to perform my Duty to him in the Day-time.'

John Wilde was in 1706 about thirty-six and was then living and lived until his death in 1720 on Golden Lyon Court in the former parish of Richardson's father, St. Botolph's, Aldersgate. By his second wife, Martha Allington, he had two children who survived infancy: Richardson's future wife Martha and his life-long friend Allington Wilde. He was apparently none too prosperous, in his late years at least, since when his mother died in 1717 he was in debt to her, and his brother Benjamin, also a printer, forgave him a sizeable debt when he died in 1718. Benjamin also left him a small legacy and his children £100 each (so that Richardson's wife had at least some dowry).

So far as one can judge, the books John Wilde printed could hardly have satisfied Richardson's desire for an opportunity to read, unless that desire was satisfied by mere quantity. One of his specialities was almanacs, and most of the other works known to have been printed by him were jest books or old-fashioned popular fiction like *The Most Pleasant History of Tom A Lincoln*. Richardson's fellow apprentices were at various times four. When he arrived at Wilde's, there was only one, Francis Clare, whose apprenticeship expired in less than a year, and it was over two years before he took another. Thomas Dewing, whom Wilde apprenticed in 1712, was later employed by Richardson; with the others he evidently lost touch.

The wealthy man, who, 'had he lived, intended high things' for Richardson remains a mystery. 'Multitudes of Letters passed between this Gentleman and me. He wrote well; was a Master of the Epistolary Style: Our Subjects were various: But his Letters were mostly narrative, giving me an Account of his Proceedings, and what befell him in the different Nations thro' which he travelled. I could from them, had I been at Liberty and had I at that time thought of writing as I have since done, have drawn great Helps: But many Years ago, all the Letters that passed between us, by a particular Desire of his (lest they should ever be published) were committed to the Flames.' Judging by the phrase 'had he lived' and by the statement later in the letter that Richardson worked for several years for other men, 'as I hinted, in a better Expectation', before '*that* failing', he set up for himself, this patron and friend from his apprenticeship days must have died before 1721. He perhaps was the gentleman who told him the story which became the germ of *Pamela*.

Whether or not this early patron was the same as the wild young friend who later fascinated Richardson's daughters Anne and Martha is uncertain. The story of this man is reconstructed largely on the basis of Anne's recollections of hearing her 'Father recount some few particulars' and fragments of her father's papers which she took to refer to him. A part of it is taken from a passage in the third volume of *Pamela* (later deleted), introducing a long poem which Richardson's daughters believed to be by the young friend and about his own love.[20] It is much wilder than anything in Richardson's sober novels.

According to the dubious evidence, this friend, who had great qualities with his many faults, got involved with two women: Marianne, a diffident young lady, and Isabella, whose father brought her up to hunt and curse and who broke into his chamber and for three nights tempted his constancy to Marianne until she finally conquered it. As a result, she had a son, whose early death prevented his being placed under Richardson's care. Meanwhile he had proposed to Marianne, but a wealthy uncle opposed the marriage and insulted the lover, who twirled him down a flight of stairs. This so offended the lady that she resolved to break with her lover, who went abroad and met a foreigner ('more extraordinary, she

[20] Correspondence of Anne Richardson and Martha Bridgen in 1784; *Pamela*, 1st edn., pp. 391-403, reprinted in McKillop, *Richardson*, pp. 108-18.

was a Jewess!'), whom he married. At this point Marianne repented her rejection and followed him abroad; he was too tender-hearted to tell her of his previous marriage, and therefore he married her also and soon afterwards went into the army. He died either on a passage to Ireland or 'of the wounds he recd. in Battle, aiding a broken heart'. The two wives then 'passed the remainder of their lives together, and loved as sisters'.

This does not sound too much like Richardson's hoped-for patron, but Martha evidently thought they were the same, and he burnt this friend's letters (though evidently not before the late 1730s), as he burnt the other's. The dates of the friend's life are quite uncertain, except that the daughter by one of his wives was old enough in 1741 to give permission for his poem to be published in *Pamela*. His planning to make Richardson the guardian of his son sounds as if Richardson was at least moderately well established. Anne's memory was shaky, and she was given to romanticizing; the more sensible Martha remembered much less of the story, which glimmers oddly in the commonplace context of Richardson's life.

To return to the less lurid life of the City, some idea of Richardson's apprenticeship can perhaps be gathered from a letter of advice he wrote his own nephew and apprentice Thomas Verren Richardson in 1732. He should study Richardson's ease and quiet; treat the journeymen with 'complaisance and decency'; contract no intimacies with 'any young man in or out of the house' without letting his master know and conceal none of his actions; avoid 'all loose words, or rash and inconsiderate expressions', though he is 'coming among a set of people of different manners and behaviour' and 'will observe greater liberties than are decent, perhaps, taken in this respect by some of the most profligate of them, (for, a printing-house is but an indifferent school for good manners)'; shun 'idleness and eye-service' and confine his reading and other amusements to his holidays or spare time; conform completely 'as to bed-time, working-time, spare-time, Sundays, &c.' to the rules of the house and to such other instructions as he receives; and speak very little.[21]

Richardson says further in *The Apprentice's Vade Mecum* (based in part on the letter he had written his nephew) that an apprentice's hours do not end until eight or nine at night, but in general an apprentice has no time he can call his own—he owes it all to his master. Gaming-houses, taverns, and playhouses should be especially avoided. In fact, most amusements are evidently eliminated since time is money, and an apprentice who shows idleness, 'that terrible Bane of Youth', is robbing his master. Respect for one's master, whether a kind or a severe one, is of the utmost importance. Poverty, chastity, and obedience seem to have been only three of the apprentice's vows.[22]

[21] Printed in the *Imperial Review*, II (1804), 609–16.
[22] London, 1734, pp. 5–9, 15, 25–6, 46–8, 50.

All the journeymen workers in a printing house were organized into a 'chapel' and were partly self-governing. Apprentices were not members of the chapel, though they had to pay 'bienvenue' to it when they began work—part of a system of fines and fees used for occasional holiday feasts. They were also initiated as 'cuz' or 'deacon'. The boy had to walk three times around the room carrying a wooden sword and preceding a procession of 'chapellonians' and then kneel while the father of the chapel exhorted him to be observant in business and not to betray the secrets of the workmen. The father then squeezed a sponge of strong beer over the head of the cuz and gave him a title such as Duke of Puddle Dock or Duke of Pissing Alley, generally some appropriately named place near his home. The chapellonians then walked round the kneeling boy singing the cuz's anthem, a nonsense succession of consonant and vowel combinations: 'Ba-ba; Be-be; Bi-bi; Ba-be-bi'. There was evidently some horseplay in a printing office, together with rare carousings; on workdays there were stringent rules, enforced by the journeymen with a system of fines, about care and disposition of equipment as well as such matters as drunkenness and swearing.[23]

In the 1750s Richardson wrote Lady Bradshaigh about several quite respectable love episodes which must have taken place during the years immediately following the expiration of his apprenticeship. 'I knew a very pious widow, a strict dissenter, who, by the way, in my juvenile days, made it a point of conscience to refuse me her niece, for no other reason but because I was a church-man.' 'The fortune of the man you hint at [Richardson himself], was very low: his mind, however, was never mean. A bashfulness, next to sheepishness, kept him down: but he always courted independence; and, being contented with a little, preserved a title to it. He found friends, who thought they saw something of merit in him, through the cloud that his sheepishness threw over him, and, knowing how low his fortune was, laid themselves out to raise him; and most of them by proposals of marriage, which, however, had always something impracticable in them. A pretty ideot was once proposed, with very high terms, his circumstances considered: her worthy uncle thought this man would behave compassionately to her.—A violent Roman Catholic lady was another, of a fine fortune, a zealous professor; whose terms were (all her fortune in her own power—a very apron-string tenure!) two years probation, and her confessor's report in favour of his being a true proselyte at the end of them.—Another, a gay, high-spirited, volatile lady, whose next friend offered to be *his* friend, in fear of her becoming the prey (at the public places she constantly frequented) of some vile fortune-hunter. Another there was whom his soul loved; but with a reverence—

[23] Ellic Howe, *The London Compositor* (London, 1947), pp. 27–9, quoting *The Life of Mr. Thomas Gent* (London, 1832), p. 16, and the *Craftsman* for 24 May 1740.

Hush!—Pen, lie thee down!—A timely check; where, else, might I have ended?—This lady—how hard to forbear the affecting subject!—But I *will* forbear. This man presumed not—Again going on!—not a word more this night.'[24]

Richardson's first biographer, Mrs. Barbauld, adds that 'this lady, from hints given in other places, and from the information of Mrs. Duncombe, appears to have been the same whose history he has delicately and obscurely shadowed out in that of Mrs. Beaumont; and never, she adds, did he appear so animated as when he was insensibly led into a narration of any circumstances in the history or description of that most revered lady.'[25] The Mrs. Beaumont to whom she refers is the subject of a letter found among Richardson's papers which at first sight appears to be a work of pure fiction. Hortensia Beaumont is a young lady of angelic virtue and beauty, daughter of a Turkey merchant, who left her an orphan at twelve years old. Robbed of her fortune by her uncle and guardian, she leaves his house but refuses to take legal steps to recover her money. In her misery she meets a man who admires her and wishes to marry her, though he is conscious of his 'Unworthiness, as well from Want of Fortune, as Merit', and will not force himself on her. She resolves neither to accept his help in starting a law case nor to marry and eventually goes to Italy as companion in an Italian family. The story is told in a letter from Dr. Bartlett to Harriet Byron, which could well be a rejected letter from *Sir Charles Grandison*, in which Mrs. Beaumont plays a minor role.[26]

The testimony of Mrs. Duncombe (the former Susanna Highmore) cannot be lightly brushed aside. In 1756 Richardson wrote to her: 'You charm me by the manner in which you mention one of the most excellent of women, Mrs. Beaumont. Mrs. Watts and *that* lady—are there in the world three such? in any one happy man's acquaintance, I mean.'[27] Since Mrs. Watts was a friend of Richardson's, the implication is that there was another real friend whom he at least called Mrs. Beaumont. Richardson's daughter Anne evidently took her to be real, for on the first of four manuscript letters (in her sister Martha's handwriting) which deal with Mrs. Beaumont's history she wrote, 'My Father was born in 1689; but from the foregoing abstract, I imagine the Lady was born later. Perhaps in 1698.'[28] Her calculation is based on the date of the letter, 1714, coupled with Mrs. Beaumont's age as given in Dr. Bartlett's letter.

The first of the four letters is from the man (later called 'Mr. R') who befriended and wanted to marry the persecuted heroine, and the second and third letters are from her to him. The man's letter is all carefully

[24] 17 Aug. 1752; [*c.* 1 Oct. 1755].
[25] I, clx-clxi.
[26] MS. in the Pierpont Morgan Library; partly printed in Barbauld, V, 301-48.
[27] [*c.* 1 Aug. 1756].
[28] MS. owned by Alan Dugald McKillop.

chastened ardour: 'It may be difficult to distinguish Love & Reverence from each other; since true Love cannot exist without a high Degree of Veneration. But a Veneration for ye Qualities of ye Mind, where those Qualities shine thro' ye Person wth. so much Lustre.—What wd. I say?— I never dared to think—What *indeed* wd. I say?' The lady is pleased with his 'Delicacy of Behavior & Sentiment' but wishes him to remain a friend. He should, however, overcome his fault of excessive modesty. Last Tuesday, in a large company, when the conversation degenerated into meaningless laughter, instead of leading the group back to sense he 'sat in smiling Silence wch: might as well have been construed Approbation as ye contrary by ye gay People'—'You have heard yr Fault, what I think yr: greatest, if not yr: only Fault—your *Diffidence.*'

The portrait of this apparently fictitious 'Mr. R' is so close to Richardson's account of himself in a letter to Samuel Lobb that autobiography seems beyond doubt. 'When I was young, I was very sheepish; (so I am indeed now I am old: I have not had Confidence enough to try to overcome a Defect so natural to me, tho' I have been a great Loser by it) but this was my Rule to get Courage, when I was obliged to go into Company I had been taught to have an Opinion of,—I let them all speak round before I open'd my Lips, after the first Introductions: Then I weigh'd, whether had I been to speak on the same Occasions, that each Person spoke upon, I should have been able to deliver myself as well, as they had done; And if I found I should have rather chosen to be silent, than to say some things they said, I preserv'd my Silence and was pleased. And if I could have spoken as well as others, I was the less scrupulous: While those who were above my Match, I admir'd, endeavour'd to cultivate their Acquaintance, by making myself agreeable to them by my Modesty, if I could not by my Merit; and to imitate them, as nearly as my Abilities and Situation would permit: Situation, I say, For Business, . . . in order, if possible, to secure my Independence, was not to be neglected; and that generally hurry'd me to my Garret, and my narrow Circle: (Printers you know must be in the uppermost Floors, for ye Light sake) and so I kept my Sheepishness, when it had given me very little Reason to be so civil to it.'[29] Writing to Miss Highmore on the advantage she has found from being 'thrown early into good and improving company,' he remarked, 'what a poor creature was I at your age!'[30]

Whether 'Mr. R's' love for Mrs. Beaumont was also autobiographical there is no way of knowing with certainty—Richardson rather liked to drop sly and mystifying hints to tease his friends. Nor is there any way of knowing just how much of Mrs. Beaumont's story is fact and how much fiction. Since this is the only romance in his life, one would like to make the most of it, but the most is not much.

[29] 4 July 1746.   [30] 31 Jan. 1754.

It is not until 1721 that Richardson's life begins to become less shadowy. 'I continued Five or Six Years after the Expiration of my Apprenticeship (Part of the Time, as an Overseer of a Printing-House) working as a Compositor, and correcting the Press: As I hinted, in a better Expectation [the hoped-for patronage]. But *that* failing, I began for myself, married, and pursued Business with an Assiduity that, perhaps, has few Examples.' This means literally that he set up for himself in 1718 or 1719, but he does not seem to have done so before 1721. Early in that year he was probably working in some capacity with the family of his future second wife, Elizabeth Leake.

Elizabeth's father, John Leake, was also a printer. In 1684 he married an Elizabeth Hurst and about that time moved to the parish of St. Botolph, Aldersgate, where Richardson's father lived and where John Wilde was soon to live. He had five children who reached maturity: John, also a freeman of the Stationers' Company, who died in 1720; Amey Langley; Mary Wright; James, a life-long friend of Richardson who later became the best known bookseller of Bath; and Elizabeth, born in 1697. In 1707 he moved to the parish of St. Vedast, where he died and was buried on 25 February 1720. One-third of his estate was divided among his children, and two-thirds went to his wife. His son James, made free of the Stationers' Company in 1709, was a printer only briefly, if at all, and by 1717 was a bookseller in Stationers' Court, in the parish of St. Martin, Ludgate, in partnership with Joseph Hazard. He was still there at the time of his father's death, and late in that year he rented a house on the corner of Blue Ball Court in the parish of St. Bride. But in April 1721, when he married Hannah Hammond, the daughter of a bookseller at Bath, he was still giving his address as St. Martin's, Ludgate. By late 1722 he was living in Bath.

The most likely explanation for James's two London addresses is that the Blue Ball Court house was used by his mother for her business. She was probably running it with the help of Samuel Richardson: when she died in April 1721, she made James and Richardson co-executors of her will and left the latter a small legacy. His address is given in the will as St. Bride's, and it is likely that he was already living in the house James had rented for his mother's printing shop, the house he later leased, and that he bought the 'Printing Presses and Letter Utensils of trade' left by Elizabeth Leake to her children and used them to set up business. He took over three boys who had been apprenticed to the Leake family, and he also used at least one of John Leake's printing ornaments.

Late in 1721 or early in 1722 the house formerly rented to James Leake was leased to Richardson. It was near St. Bride's Church on the corner of Blue Ball Court, a short lane, and Salisbury Court or Square, off Fleet Street. Richardson lived around Salisbury Court for the rest of his life, moving twice, but never out of sight of his first house there. Since the evil influence of the playhouse was removed, he wrote in 1735, Salisbury Court 'has as reputable Inhabitants as any other Part of the City'.[31] A list of the inhabitants of the precinct in 1721[32] bears him out: around the Court and on Dorset Street lived victuallers, tallow chandlers, apothecaries, engravers, bakers, glaziers, pawnbrokers, cabinetmakers, silversmiths, periwig-makers, tailors, watchcase-makers, physicians, poulterers, surgeons, and even a clergyman and two people described as gentlemen. Between it and the Thames the neighbourhood declined somewhat, to weavers, shoemakers, joiners, watermen, labourers, porters, and chimney sweepers, and the inhabitants of the far end of Blue Ball Court included a shoemaker and a mariner; but Salisbury Court itself seems to have been a stronghold of City respectability, and the neighbourhood evidently satisfied Richardson.

The first book known to have been printed by Richardson is dated 1721.[33] In March 1722 he was admitted to the livery of the Stationers' Company. And on 23 November 1721, at the age of thirty-two, he married the daughter of his former master, Martha Wilde, who was twenty-three. From this time on he ceased to be a poor and obscure but evidently ambitious and industrious aspirant and rapidly became a prosperous and respected tradesman, whose trade kept him on the fringe of English literary life until, eighteen years later, his talent plunged him into the midst of it.

---

[31] In *A Seasonable Examination of the Pleas and Pretensions of the Proprietors of, and Subscribers to, Play-Houses.*

[32] Corporation of London Misc. MS. 83.3.

[33] Jonathan Smedley's *Poems on Several Occasions.*

CHAPTER II

THE *TRUE BRITON*

1722–1724

RICHARDSON wrote to Stinstra that he 'pursued Business with an Assiduity that, perhaps, has few Examples; and with the more Alacrity, as I improved a Branch of it, that interfered not with any other Person; and made me more independent of Booksellers (tho' I did much Business for them) than any other Printer'. But that branch of his business, his printing for the House of Commons, did not begin until 1733, and in his early years he was presumably not so independent of the booksellers, who controlled what we should call the publishing trade. 'Publishing' in the eighteenth century meant something less than it does today. A publisher was rather more like what we would call a bookseller and a bookseller more like what we would call a publisher. The booksellers generally bought copyrights from authors, arranged for printing, paid costs, and took profits, in addition to distributing books. Small booksellers who sold books only and larger booksellers when they chose to distribute books printed at someone else's expense and for someone else's benefit were acting as 'publishers', that is mere salesmen of books in which they had no interest. Copyrights were retained by the authors if they were either financially independent and could afford to print at their own expense or so hard put to it to find a buyer that they had to. Their books, if ambitious enough and popular enough, were often printed by subscription—before printing they collected the cost of the book (usually a high one) from prospective buyers. This was the most profitable method for authors (Pope's small fortune came from subscription editions of his translations of the *Iliad* and *Odyssey*) and gave them the independence of booksellers which Richardson desired and obtained. But in general the large booksellers controlled the trade; when they undertook a project too large for a single bookseller, they sometimes combined in groups called 'congers'.

Richardson printed for congers and for single booksellers as well as for authors, sometimes by subscription and sometimes not; he occasionally owned a share in a copyright; and in addition he printed periodicals and later worked on government contract. But the first books he printed could hardly have made him very independent.[1] Jonathan Smedley's *Poems on Several Occasions* (1721), the first certain one, was printed for the author. Smedley, like many of Richardson's later associates, was an Irish clergyman and, also like many of them, was an enemy of Pope and Swift—rising from Fleetditch 'in majesty of mud', he triumphantly wins Pope's diving contest. Another book of 1721, a translation of Fénelon's *Éducation des filles*, is one of Richardson's first pieces of work for the booksellers. Two others were pamphlets attacking the Walpole government by a Tory member of Parliament Archibald Hutcheson.[2] Hutcheson printed at his own expense, and Richardson continued to print for him in 1722 and 1723.

Most of the works Richardson printed in the latter year are by authors more extreme and much more suspect by the government than Hutcheson: Francis Atterbury, Bishop of Rochester; his amanuensis, the Reverend George Kelly; and the Duke of Wharton. During the furor following the wild and abortive Jacobite plot of 1722, when conspirators were accused of planning to seize the important public buildings in London and kidnap George I, Atterbury and Kelly were arrested and tried in Parliament, suspected of being in correspondence with James, the Old Pretender. Atterbury was banished, and shortly after his banishment an edition of his *Maxims, Reflections and Observations*, with a preface signed J. M. and dated 24 May 1723, was published, apparently without Atterbury's knowledge. The preface calls Atterbury a 'Great Man' and indicates that the purpose of the book is to show that he is not a Papist. This volume uses three ornaments which later appeared frequently in books Richardson is known to have printed. The fourth edition (which uses the same type-pages as earlier editions) of Kelly's speech before the House of Lords in his own defence also has an ornament used by Richardson.[3] The evidence of ornaments may be questioned—they could, of course, be lent or sold; but the first subscription edition which Richardson is known to have printed is a translation of Castelnau's *Mémoires* (1724), which was made by Kelly while he was in the Tower (he escaped in 1736). There are numerous advertisements in the contemporary press stating that prospective sub-

---

[1] Sale, *Master Printer*, p. 229, lists one book printed by Richardson in 1719 and five in 1720, all politico-economic pamphlets printed at his own expense by Archibald Hutcheson. The evidence for assigning these books to Richardson's press is their use of two printers' ornaments which Richardson is known to have used later; since at least one of these was earlier used by the Leake family, it is not unlikely that both were and that the books were all printed by the Leakes, perhaps while Richardson was working for them.

[2] Hutcheson was also a contributor to the main opposition periodical, the *Freeholder's Journal*. Stanley Morison in *The English Newspaper* (Cambridge, 1932), p. [109], states that a factotum signed by Francis Hoffman used in this journal first on 3 Oct. 1722 was also used occasionally in the *True Briton*; we have not seen it in the files we have examined, though we have found a somewhat similar factotum.

[3] Sale, *Master Printer*, pp. 147, 183. Richardson also printed the fifth edition of Kelly's *Speech*.

scribers may apply to Samuel Richardson, at his house in Salisbury Court; one describes the book as published (that is distributed) by Richardson.[4] As late as 24 July 1727 Richardson was asking subscribers who had not picked up their copies to do so before the small number left should be disposed of to persons in trade.[5] It was probably Kelly's proposed translation of Cicero's letters to Atticus (never published) for which, according to advertisements, Richardson among others was accepting subscriptions in 1729.[6]

In view of these associates, it is hardly surprising that in 1722 Samuel Negus in a communication to the Secretary of State, Lord Townshend, listed 'Richardson, Salisbury-court', along with '[Allington] Wilde, Aldersgate-street', and numerous others, as one of the printers 'Said to be High Flyers', that is extreme Tories. Negus lists the printers of all the London journals, citing six of them as high flyers; he does not mention Richardson in connection with any journal. He admits that he is suffering himself from the dominance of the 'disaffected' printers, who make it hard for such loyal men as he is to get work; but his denunciation only made matters worse, since about a year later he informed Townshend that the printers had got hold of his list, printed it, and posted it in every printing house and bookseller's shop, 'desiring them not to give him any business, so that he is now with his wife and children like to be ruined' unless Townshend finds him a job.[7]

In 1782 John Nichols printed an account of Richardson which in large part came from John Duncombe, who had been a close associate of Richardson in his last years. According to Nichols: 'Dissimilar as their geniuses may seem, when the witty and wicked Duke of *Wharton* . . . about the year 1723, fomented the spirit of opposition in the City, and became a member of the Waxchandlers Company; Mr. *Richardson*, though his political principles were very different, was much connected with, and favoured by him; and printed his 'True Briton,' published twice a week. Yet he exercised his own judgment, in peremptorily refusing to be concerned in such papers as he apprehended might endanger his own safety, and which accordingly did occasion the imprisonment and prosecution of those who were induced to print and publish them.' Nichols adds that 'it appears by the original edition of *The True Briton* . . . that Mr. *Richardson* printed no more than *six numbers*; and it seems highly probable that *the*

---

[4] *Weekly Journal or Saturday's Post*, 9 Jan. 1725.

[5] *Daily Journal.*

[6] *Monthly Chronicle*, 28 Mar. 1729; *Daily Journal*, 27 May 1729. See also *Memoirs of . . . the Reverend George Kelly* (London, 1736), p. 23.

[7] John Nichols in *Literary Anecdotes of the Eighteenth Century* (London, 1812–15), I, 288–312, reprints Negus's list and dates it 1724, but Negus in his letter to Townshend dated 23 Jan. 1723 (P.R.O. S.P. 35/48, fo. 26) says that he sent Townshend the list about twelve months before. The newspapers mentioned indicate 1722 as the date.

sixth (*June* 21, 1723) was written by himself, as it is much in *his* manner'.[8] Substantially the same account is given in the biography of Richardson in the *Universal Magazine* authorized by his daughters (who probably knew no more of the affair than was contained in Nichols's account), except that the daughters consider it inconceivable that he could have written the sixth number or anything else so obnoxious to the administration.[9]

By the time these later accounts appeared, Philip, Duke of Wharton, was well known to have been a Jacobite and therefore a traitor. He was generally regarded as brilliant, though immoral and erratic—Pope's portrait of this 'scorn and wonder of our days,/Whose ruling Passion was the Lust of Praise', in the first of the *Moral Essays*, is typical of the common view. He had defended both Atterbury and Kelly in the House of Lords, and all three were working in the 1720s for the exiled Stuarts, whom they later openly joined. But when the *True Briton* began publication in 1723, he was calling himself an Old Whig, in opposition to the Walpole government but not openly to the reigning house, and he was trying to court support in the City, not altogether without success. He supported (and wrote most of) the *True Briton* until his large fortune showed signs of exhaustion, when he left for the Continent.

According to its colophon, the *True Briton* was printed 'for' T. Payne through Number 14; in Number 15 it is said to have been printed 'by and for' Payne (that is with Payne as both printer and publisher), and in later issues either 'by and for' or 'by' alone. Thomas Payne is known otherwise as a publisher; whether or not he was venturing into printing for once, he was taking all the risk. He had been apprenticed to the bookseller Thomas Shelmerdine but never made free.[10] His address is given in the colophon of the *True Briton* as 'Near *Stationers-Hall*' (as also in two other colophons of 1723, as publisher of the *Post-Boy* and the *Evening Post*): in 1722 or 1723 he had rented an establishment in St. Martin's, Ludgate, which he held until 1726.[11] Richardson could have come in contact with him through Archibald Hutcheson: an advertisement in the *Daily Journal*

---

[8] *Biographical and Literary Anecdotes of William Bowyer*, pp. 156, 306n. See also *Literary Anecdotes*, IV, 580. In *Literary Anecdotes*, IV, 584, Nichols mentions Duncombe as one of his sources.

[9] LXXVIII (1786), 18–19.

[10] 'Court Book G', p. 167, 4 July 1709; 'Apprentices' Register Book from 1666–1727', 'Master and Apprentices Calendar from October 1684 to March 1718', 'Apprentices Bound Turned Over Free and Cloathed 1640–1748', 'Freemen's Register 1688–1751', MSS. in the archives of the Stationers' Company.

[11] Land Tax Records for the City of London, Guildhall MS. 11,316/73, 76, 82; Vol. 79, for 1725, lists another name in his place, Thomas Walker, perhaps by error. Payne must have been the Thomas Payne who from 1708 through 1724 had a very modest establishment in nearby St. Faith's, Paul's Churchyard, for which he paid no rent tax but a small personal property tax and seems to have been in the house rented by Joshua Phillips (Vols. 28, 31, 34, 37, 40, 43, 46, 49, 52, 55, 58, 61, 64, 67, 70, 73, 76). A recognizance dated 5 May 1722 says Payne is of the Parish of St. Augustine and St. Faith; a search warrant dated 24 Mar. 1722 gives his address

of 24 February 1723 says that at Payne's may be purchased 'a Compleat Collection' of Hutcheson's treatises 'on the Publick Debts and South-Sea Stock', several of which Richardson had printed. He had distributed the *Freeholder's Journal*, the most important opposition organ before the *True Briton*, which after a good deal of persecution had closed in May 1723, and he had been arrested along with Thomas Sharpe, the printer, for publishing it and bound over to give evidence against Sharpe.[12]

The first issue of the *True Briton*, which came out on Mondays and Fridays, appeared on 3 June 1723. On 25 June the Lords Justices, who were ruling England during the King's absence in Hanover, heard passages from it read and ordered that it be prosecuted,[13] and on the same day Charles Delafaye, their secretary and the man usually responsible for examining persons suspected of treasonable libels, wrote to Lord Townshend that the *True Briton* was 'said to be written by the Duke of Wharton, who wants to be taken notice of. But not to give his Grace that pleasure, I am not at this time to enquire into the authors of those Libels but to fall upon printers and publishers.' Wharton, he added on 28 June, has been mortified by the results of his activities in the City sheriff's election. 'But what I believe has vext him more is, that he should not be taken notice of when the printer of his True Briton was apprehended.' The 'printer' had offered to name the author, but Delafaye refused to listen: 'I told him the Government would no longer be put off in this manner, that they, ye printers and publishers of such papers, got scoundrels not worth a Groat that lived in Garretts to write at so much a sheet, and then truly when they were taken notice of, they came off with producing the Authors.' When the 'printer' offered to produce the original manuscripts, Delafaye told him that the government 'would now fall upon printers and publishers as the more effectual way to put a stop to Libelling'. One of his aides, however, did take a look at seven papers, five of which were in the Duke's hand, and also saw a note of the Duke's saying that Walpole had desired him to write a paper in the service of the government and he had done so 'and had appointed the printer Payne to print it'.[14]

---

as 'at the Crown in Pater-Noster Row' (P.R.O. S.P. 44/80, under dates). Both would fit the St. Faith's, Paul's Churchyard, address. The colophon of the *Freeholder's Journal* gives his address at first as 'the *Crown* in *Pater-Noster-Row*' and later as the same as that of the printer, Thomas Sharpe, Ivy Lane, which runs off Paternoster Row, but unlike Sharpe he is not listed in St. Faith's, Paternoster Row.

[12] P.R.O. S.P. 44/81, p. 28 (warrant dated 27 Feb. 1722), p. 31 (order to prosecute, 13 Mar. 1722), p. 42 (recognizance for £200, 9 Apr. 1722), p. 43 (warrant dated 25 Apr. 1722), p. 59 (warrant dated 26 May 1722), p. 59 (recognizance for £100, 4 June 1722); *An Account of Persons Held to Bail to Answer in the Court of King's Bench for Libels, from 1 Anne to 57 Geo. 3. Both Inclusive* (Printed 1818), p. 8 (in P.R.O. K.B. 33/24). See also P.R.O. S.P. 44/80, under dates 24 Mar., 10 Apr., 7 June, 22 Sept. 1722; P.R.O. S.P. 44/81, pp. 39, 49, 57, 60; P.R.O. S.P. 44/123, pp. 55, 79; B.M. Add. MS. 36,134, fos. 136–7.

[13] P.R.O. S.P. 44/290, p. 22; P.R.O. S.P. 43/66, under date 28 June.

[14] P.R.O. S.P. 43/66, under dates.

The warrant to arrest him, issued on 25 June, calls Payne the 'Publisher' and authorizes the arrest of any other publishers or printers whose names are unknown;[15] but none was ever discovered, and Payne was the only person ever charged in connection with the periodical. He must on his first examination have told Delafaye that he was the printer. On 27 June Delafaye told the Attorney General that Payne 'owns himself the Printer and Publisher' of the paper and enclosed Payne's signed statement that he had published and also printed Numbers 3, 4, 5, 6, and 7, the 'Traiterous and Seditious Libels' being prosecuted, and that 'no other Person is concerned with him in ye printing & publishing of the Said Papers'. Delafaye added that the Lords Justices wanted Payne prosecuted.[16] Walpole, evidently informed by Delafaye, wrote the next day to Townshend that Wharton was 'acting the part of a Madman' and that he had 'taken up the Printer and Publisher' of the *True Briton*, 'which were very ready to have nam'd the Author, but I would not let his Grace have that Satisfaction, who seems to aim at nothing but to be taken Notice of or taken up'.[17] The plural verb indicates that Walpole thought of the printer and publisher as two men, but we hear nothing else of a second arrest. The Duke of Newcastle informed Townshend of these events on the same day: 'We have ordered the Printer to be prosecuted, and by that shall putt the D. of Wharton to some expence.'[18]

On 27 June Payne was admitted to bail on a recognizance in his own name of £500 and of £250 each in the names of two sureties, William Meers and Samuel Richardson.[19] On 25 July another warrant was issued to seize Payne for 'Printing and Publishing' the *True Briton* for 22 July.[20] The next day Delafaye wrote to Townshend that the printer had told him that the Duke 'had promised him to put nothing into that paper that might give Offense: But I told him I troubled not my head nor I believed did any body else with what the Duke of Wharton said or did; that my Business was with Him as Printer and Publisher.'[21] On 27 July Payne again gave a recognizance of £500, and again his sureties for £250 each were Meers and Samuel Richardson.[22]

On 30 July the Court of Aldermen met to consider two scandalous libels in the *True Briton*, Numbers 12 and 17, which contained 'many Scandalous Reflections Abuses and Contempts of this Court and the Magistracy of this City'. Payne 'did own himself to be the Printer and

[15] P.R.O. S.P. 44/81, p. 299.
[16] P.R.O. S.P. 44/289, p. 25.
[17] P.R.O. S.P. 43/4 and P.R.O. S.P. 43/66, under date.
[18] B.M. Add. MS. 32,686, fo. 266.
[19] P.R.O. S.P. 44/81, p. 291.
[20] P.R.O. S.P. 44/81, p. 303.
[21] P.R.O. S.P. 43/66, under date.
[22] P.R.O. S.P. 44/81, p. 315.

Publisher of the said Two several scandalous Libels', and the Court committed him to Newgate. He was bailed out on 2 August and on the following day was again seized by one of the King's messengers. On 6 August he gave another recognizance for the same amount as before, but this time his two £250 sureties were Thomas Corbet and Nicholas Langley. In reporting these events to Townshend, Delafaye remarked that 'Payne the printer and publisher of the True Briton has been pretty much visited of late'. If his papers proved to be criminal, he stood to forfeit £3,000 besides the fine imposed by the City: 'In the mean time these Seizures and Imprisonments cannot but be expensive to him.'[23] And he was not yet through. On 20 August he was arrested for the issue of the previous day and again had to give a £500 recognizance and find two sureties (Langley and Benjamin Bishop) for £250 each; in September he was seized as publisher of the *Loyal Observator or Collins's Weekly Journal* and gave a £100 recognizance, with John Bristow and James Holland as his £50 sureties—and he still had enough money to be surety for £100 for the printer of that journal, Susannah Collins.[24]

In Michaelmas Term 1723 Payne was charged with publishing four seditious libels, all in the first issues of the paper, and he pleaded not guilty.[25] The third issue of the paper, of 10 June, was alleged to be guilty of accusing the last Parliament of voting to continue itself in violation of the Triennial Act, 'which may hereafter point out to some *Future Ministry*, a Method of keeping together a House of Commons composed of their Creatures', and of passing the Riot Act (had such a law been in force in 1688, it would have made the Revolution more difficult), and of maintaining a standing army able to defend any ministers who might be inclined to commit acts of violence and oppression, and of frequently suspending the Act of Habeas Corpus—all with ironic assurances that such drastic measures were necessary in the present crisis and had not been abused by the existing government, but warning that some day 'a Parliament willing to be subservient to a Court, would not require Proofs to be made of a Conspiracy; but, on the single Word of the Ministers, would chearfully do all that should be asked of them; and it would certainly be in the Power of such a Parliament, *To offer up the Laws, Rights, and Liberties of the whole Nation, to the King*'. The fourth issue was accused of saying that a large national debt had been incurred to maintain the Mediterranean and Baltic squadrons, which were of no use to Great

[23] Corporation of London Records Office, MS. Repertory, Vol. 127, pp. 431-2; Delafaye to Townshend, 30 July, P.R.O. S.P. 43/66, under date; P.R.O. S.P. 44/81, p. 315; Delafaye to Townshend, 6 Aug., P.R.O. S.P. 43/67, under date.

[24] P.R.O. S.P. 44/81, pp. 303, 311, 315.

[25] P.R.O. K.B. 10/90 (indictments); *An Account of Persons Held to Bail to Answer in the Court of King's Bench for Libels, from 1 Anne to 57 Geo. 3. Both Inclusive*, p. 9; 'A Particular of the Causes now under prosecution with States thereof' (Hilary Term, 1724), B.M. Add. MS. 36,134, fo. 139.

Britain and not necessitated by the actions of Spain and Sweden. The fifth had blamed the extraordinary measures taken by Parliament against the Jacobite John Plunket, a mean person fitter to be in a madhouse than to threaten the country, on the grounds that he could have been dealt with according to ordinary law without establishing such dangerous precedents. The sixth (the one in which Nichols detected Richardson's manner) was sarcastic about the Bench of Bishops and especially about their abandonment of their brother the Bishop of Rochester. It does not resemble anything Richardson later wrote. It is a 'letter' (such letters were often written by the editors) warning against party spirit when it is exercised for persons and not for principles. There is much heavy sarcasm on the Whigs ('so Happy in their Governors, that they cannot follow them too blindly') and against 'our *present Happiness*', as well as the usual warning that a future corrupt government might possibly abuse the precedents set by the recent violations of liberty.

Payne was tried in the King's Bench on 24 February 1724 'for printing and publishing' the *True Briton* Numbers 3, 4, 5, and 6, which 'not only insulted every Branch of the Legislature, but manifestly tended to make the Constitution itself odious to the People'. His confession (presumably that he was printer and publisher) was read in court and he was found guilty on all indictments. On 18 May he was sentenced to a £400 fine and one year's imprisonment, 'and to find Sureties for his good Behaviour during Life'.[26] The charges against the other issues seem to have been dropped.

Meanwhile he had been indicted again, for the issues of 31 January and 3 February, which accused the South Sea Company of abusing its right to import pieces of eight from Spain and hinted that the sub-governor, Sir John Eyles, had abused his position to enrich himself. He was tried in Trinity Term, pleaded not guilty, but was found guilty by the jury.[27]

None of these charges sounds much like treason today. But in the 1720s the government was severe on criticisms of itself as well as of the established religion. It employed informers—one journeyman who had 'done very good Service to the Governmt. in discovering the Authors and Printers of certain Treasonable Libels' had lost his business and been 'reduced to very low and necessitous Circumstances' (evidently the printers stuck together against the threat of prosecution), so that Lord Townshend had to ask the Secretary of the Treasury to find him a job.[28] Messengers were charged to buy a copy of every pamphlet or newspaper,

---

[26] *Political State of Great Britain*, XXVII (1724), 205, 533; *Universal Journal*, 26 Feb.; *London Journal*, 29 Feb.; *Weekly Journal or, British Gazetteer*, 29 Feb.; *British Journal*, 29 Feb.; *Weekly Journal or Saturday's Post*, 29 Feb.; *Parker's London News*, 20 May. In reporting Payne's sentence the *Weekly Journal or Saturday's Post* of 23 May calls him 'the Publisher'.

[27] 'Controllment Rolls', P.R.O. K.B. 28/33; 'Crown Rolls', P.R.O. K.B. 10/28/90, membrane 50.

[28] 27 July 1721, P.R.O. S.P. 44/122, p. 43.

mark on it from whom they bought it for the eventuality that it might be necessary to prosecute the publisher, and turn it over to the Solicitor for the Treasury.[29] The persons whose names were listed on the colophons were generally the first to be picked up. Sometimes they implicated others and sometimes they did not.

Even an advertisement could be dangerous. The Lords Justices ordered the arrest of the printer of the *Post-Boy* for an advertisement of a book printed by Edmund Curll which stated that the book showed 'That there is neither Precept nor Example for worshiping Christ as God in the Holy Scripture'.[30] The *Daily Post* got into trouble for a mock advertisement in its issue of 6 February 1728 of a lecture on the history of synods and convocations: 'Why David used none, and Solomon imitated David: Christ crucify'd by a Jewish C——n. . . . N.B. There will be little Wit in this Essay, for Fear of the Canons.'[31] Its printer was called in again for another mock advertisement, dangerous in the days of Sir Robert, of an oration on Robin Hood (to include such information as 'the only Reason of the Navy's being at Portsmouth'), 'with a Defence of Robins, Bobs, Bobbin-lace, Bob and Touch, Bob-tail, Bob-cherry, Bob-whigs, College Bobs, and Bob-triples'.[32] John Peele, the publisher, and James Nott, assistant to the printer, of the *London Journal* were examined about an article signed 'Publicola' and directed against superstition: 'Instead of teaching us, that Religion consists in *Action*, or Obedience to the eternal moral Law of God, we have been most *gravely* and *venerably* told, that it consists in *Belief of certain Opinions, which we could form no Idea of; or, which were contrary to the clear Perception of our Minds*. . . . The only *true Divinity* is *Humanity*.' Nott disclosed the author of the article, who stated that he did not think it would give offence.[33] Several papers were cited for reprinting an article from the *Craftsman* (which was constantly in trouble) purporting to be a speech made by the Corregidor of Seville praising the King of Spain and pointing out to His Majesty that other monarchs now sued submissively to him for peace and were in 'a Kind of Dependency'.[34] The Duke of Newcastle took the matter seriously enough to write to Lord Chesterfield to get the Utrecht *Gazette*, from which it was said to be translated, reprimanded by the Dutch government.[35] Seven printers and publishers were

---

[29] 1 Mar. 1729, P.R.O. K.B. 33/1/12.

[30] Issue of 30 Nov. 1725; minutes of 9 Dec., P.R.O. S.P. 43/76, under date.

[31] P.R.O. S.P. 36/5, fos. 93–6.

[32] Issue of 5 Sept. 1729; examination of Samuel Nevill, printer, 13 Sept., P.R.O. 36/15, fo. 80.

[33] Issue of 26 Apr. 1729; P.R.O. S.P. 44/83, p. 12 (warrant dated 28 Apr.); P.R.O. S.P. 36/11, fos. 85, 89, 126 (examinations of 28 Apr. and 6 May of Nott, Peele, and James Pitt, author of the article).

[34] *Craftsman*, 12 July 1729; *Daily Post*, 17 July; *St. James's Evening Post*, 15–17 July; *Evening Post*, 15–17 July; P.R.O. S.P. 36/13, fos. 86, 102, 115, 117, 119–24, 135; P.R.O. S.P. 44/82, under dates 15 July, 18 July, 21 July, 27 July.

[35] P.R.O. S.P. 43/79 and P.R.O. S.P. 43/81, under date 22 July.

called in for questioning, and Richard Franklin of the *Craftsman* was bound over for trial. One of them, Richard Nutt, denied that he was the printer of the *Daily Post*, though he was named as printer in the colophon. Franklin also denied the evidence of the colophon and later irritated Delafaye by blandly denying that he had any knowledge of his namesake in the colophon and then refusing to sign the record of his examination.[36] He was often questioned and at least once sentenced to a £100 fine and a year in jail.[37]

The state papers are full of letters discussing whether an action may be made to lie against some newspaper. Not many of the people called in for questioning were actually prosecuted; during the reign of George I there were only thirty-six cases of people held to bail for libels.[38] But the danger was enough to give any printer cause for caution; there were several condemnations to the pillory, imprisonment, fines, and confiscation of type.[39] Espousal of the cause of the Pretender was even more dangerous: a person claiming that James III was the rightful king could be condemned to death and forfeiture of his estates for high treason.[40] In 1720 a nineteen-year-old apprentice named John Matthews was hanged at Tyburn for printing a Jacobite pamphlet.[41] It is noteworthy that Richardson's name never appears on the colophon of any newspaper, even of those he was certainly printing. The explanation suggests itself that the more solid printers used the names of less respectable men in their colophons, men who for a price were willing to accept responsibility.

In view of the evidence that Payne is constantly regarded as the printer of the *True Briton* in the state records, one might doubt the testimony of Nichols, in spite of the facts that Payne does not appear to have been a printer and that Richardson twice went bail for him. The factotums and arrangements of flowers in the periodical, however, show almost incontrovertably that Richardson was the printer not only of the first numbers but of the whole run of the periodical.[42] Ornaments could of course be

[36] B.M. Add. MS. 36,137, fo. 265, 15 Sept.; P.R.O. S.P. 36/15, fo. 82, 14 Sept.

[37] *Gentleman's Magazine*, II (1732), 584; *State Trials*, compiled by T. B. Howell, XVII (London, 1813), cols. 625–76.

[38] *An Account of Persons Held to Bail to Answer in the Court of King's Bench for Libels, from 1 Anne to 57 Geo. 3. Both Inclusive*, pp. 6–10.

[39] Laurence Hanson, *Government and the Press 1695–1763* (Oxford and London, 1936), pp. 47–58.

[40] Act of Anno Regni Annæ Reginæ Sexto, Cap. VII.

[41] *State Trials*, XV (1812), cols. 1323–1403.

[42] Sale (*Master Printer*, pp. 43, 47, 212, 214, 226, 285–6, 288) discovered that the factotum in Nos. 1, 3, 7, and 8 was used in books printed by Richardson and that ornaments known to be Richardson's appear in the fortnightly reprints of four issues of the periodical, in the two-volume collected edition, and in an anonymous memoir of the Duke of Wharton (1731). He failed to note, however, that the first two fortnightly reprints and the fortnightly reprint of Nos. 13–16 (which contains a factotum found in the first) altogether contain three factotums and two arrangements of flowers used as factotums which appear in thirty-six of the original

borrowed, but these undistinguished and frequently repeated factotums and arrangements of flowers are as conclusive as such evidence can be. The change in the colophon on 22 July, therefore, seems meaningless or to mean only that the threat of prosecution induced Payne (probably for a price) to agree to take the entire risk. The large and elaborate (and perhaps identifiable) factotums of the early issues disappear soon afterwards. The same threat may explain references in the issues of 2 August and 6 September to the sufferings of the 'Printer' of the paper at the hands of the authorities, which may have been meant to make the authorities believe they had caught the only man subject to suspicion.

The same references stress the alleged fact that the prosecution is based on '*Inuendos, Misconstructions,* and *Personal Prejudice*'—the modern Whigs, no longer interested, as their ancestors were, in the liberty of the press, are determined to misconstrue everything written by the author of the *True Briton* and if he published the Lord's Prayer would expunge it from their Bibles. This claim is hardly ingenuous, since there are a good many statements in the *True Briton* that need no misconstruction to be taken as attacks on the government, though none are in favour of the Jacobites. The periodical supports the blessed balance of power established by the great settlement of 1688. It is the government which is trying to upset the balance. The condemnation of Atterbury and Kelly is denounced as an infringement on the English liberties guaranteed by the Glorious Revolution, as are other measures which resulted from the fears aroused by the Jacobite plot. Indeed there is no evidence that there ever was a Jacobite plot.[43] The standing army, the recently burst South Sea Bubble, the use of bribery (a notoriously successful method of Walpole's), the public debt, the fact (only hinted) that English policy on the Continent is controlled by the interest not of the King of England but of the Elector of Hanover (they happened, of course, to be the same person), and especially the tyrannical methods of a Great Person (a 'Great Person' at this period was always Walpole)—all of these suggest that Englishmen would do well to beware of a 'future' possible king who, being easy and inactive, *might* 'permit every Man in his Court to be a Tyrant but Himself', with the result that the very evils the *True Briton* has been pointing out as present abuses could, in future, arise.[44]

---

issues of the *True Briton*, not counting Nos. 1, 3, 7, and 8, and that all seven small factotums in the original issues of the *True Briton* are repeatedly used in the two-volume collected edition. It is worth noting that the earliest issue containing one of Richardson's known factotums is No. 1, the latest No. 74, the last issue of the periodical. Why Nichols stated that Richardson printed only the first six numbers is unknown. Sale's explanation (*Master Printer*, p. 43) that he knew Payne had been prosecuted for Nos. 3–6 is the only suggestion so far made, but it hardly seems to account for the statement.

[43] No. 5 (17 June).
[44] No. 7 (24 June).

The fact that the Duke of Wharton was later an open Jacobite does not, of course, imply that Richardson himself was one. In the first place, he was just beginning business for himself and must have been delighted to get such a good job. The political lines were by no means clearly drawn. There was confusion between the Whigs and Tories, and both parties were split The most effective opposition to Walpole came from Whigs—Richardson's later friend Speaker Onslow at times supported the principles of 'Whiggism' against Walpole. The City was generally in opposition, partly because of the way Walpole settled the South Sea crisis; the City Bill, which was passed in 1725, giving the mayor and aldermen a veto over acts of the Common Council, aroused wide protest. All of the opposition in the early twenties was supported by the Jacobites, but it was composed of many elements, with the Jacobites becoming less and less important.[45] Opposition to Walpole was not in itself treasonable—most of the leading writers of the time, especially Richardson's later rival Fielding, were to devote their talents to attacking Walpole. The *True Briton*'s characteristic note is 'English Liberty', a note which must have appealed to many of Richardson's fellow citizens, who had no reason to suspect that it was being sounded in the interest of the royal house which the Glorious Revolution of 1688, that landmark of liberty in the eyes of many moderate Englishmen, had cast out. Even after he had left England and declared for the Pretender, Wharton continued to sound the same note, blaming the government for violating such sound Whig principles as freedom of the press, independence of the Church of England, triennial parliaments independent of the Court, and the privileges of the City.[46]

Whether the Duke of Wharton served, as he well could have, as one of the models for Richardson's later rakes is uncertain—his printer need not have known him intimately. In the 1762 edition of Defoe's *Tour thro' the Whole Island of Great Britain*, revised at the very end of Richardson's life and thirty years after Wharton's miserable and early death in 1731, is added the remark that Wharton's title is extinct 'thro' the Misconduct of the late Duke of that Name, remarkable for his great Abilities, however misapplied'.[47]

At the time of his involvement, however innocent, with the Jacobite leaders, Richardson's voting shows that he was in other ways supporting the opponents of the government. On 7 March 1724 he cast his ballot for Sir John Williams, the Tory candidate for sheriff, in a hotly contested election.[48] Walpole regarded the defeat of Williams the previous year as a

[45] Charles Bechdolt Realey, *The Early Opposition to Sir Robert Walpole 1720-1727* (Lawrence Kansas, 1931).

[46] *The Duke of Wharton's Reasons for Leaving His Native Country, and Espousing the Cause of His Royal Majesty King James III* ([c. 1729]).

[47] III, 271.

[48] *Daily Journal*, 20 Mar.

'great work'.[49] In November 1724 Richardson voted for the Tory Charles Goodfellow for Parliament.[50] In both of these elections his future brother-in-law James Leake voted like Richardson. The Leakes probably printed for Archibald Hutcheson before Richardson did, a fact which may suggest the origin of Richardson's connection with the conservative opponents of Walpole. By 1727 he had abandoned at least his support of Sir John Williams, but he voted for the other three opposition candidates for parliament, Humphrey Parsons, Richard Lockwood, and John Barnard.[51] The election involved a struggle between supporters and opponents of Walpole of 'more than ordinary Industry, Application, and Animosity'.[52] Parsons was later described by Horace Walpole as 'a Jacobite brewer'.[53] Barnard was generally admired. The 1748 edition of Defoe's *Tour* calls him 'one of the worthiest and ablest Representatives that ever the City of *London* sent to Parliament'.[54]

A much more serious charge was later made against Richardson, though on very dubious authority. On Saturday, 24 August 1728, *Mist's Weekly Journal* printed a correspondent's letter about affairs in 'Persia', giving a very bad character to Esreff, 'the present Usurper', and his predecessor, 'the old Usurper', Meryweis. No reader could have doubted that the usurpers were George I and George II, nor that their wicked Chief Scribe was Walpole. The unfortunate young Sophi, now (like the Old Pretender) in exile, is described in glowing terms—he resembles those kings of blessed memory his father and uncle—and the Persian correspondent hopes that he will soon be restored to the throne.

This is much stronger than anything in the *True Briton*. The government proceeded at once to find the culprit. On 6 September 1728 the notorious bookseller Edmund Curll wrote to John Hutchins, one of the King's Messengers in Ordinary, asking him to convince Charles Delafaye that he, with all his imprudences, had never been disaffected to the government.[55] Curll had been arrested several times during the past few years, for the politically suspect *Memoirs* of John Ker of Kersland as well as for such obscene books as *A Treatise of the Use of Flogging in Venereal Affairs* and *The Nun in Her Smock*, and had stood in the pillory in February. In 1725, thanking Delafaye for his support, he had offered to give information on those responsible for treasonable libels.[56] He told Hutchins that he had

---

[49] To Townshend, 19 July 1723, P.R.O. S.P. 43/66, under date.
[50] *Daily Post*, 7 Dec.   [51] *Daily Journal*, 31 Oct.
[52] *Political State of Great Britain*, XXXIV (1727), 358–9.
[53] *Correspondence*, ed. W. S. Lewis, XVII (New Haven, 1954), 185n.   [54] II, 136.
[55] P.R.O. S.P. 36/8, pp. 113–14.
[56] P.R.O. S.P. 44/80 (warrant dated 6 May 1724); P.R.O. S.P. 35/49, fo. 50 (letter from Curll in prison to Delafaye, 8 May 1724); P.R.O. S.P. 44/81, p. 394 (warrant dated 24 Feb. 1725); P.R.O. S.P. 44/81, p. 399 (recognizance dated 6 Mar. 1725); P.R.O. S.P. 35/58, fo. 75 (letter from Curll to Delafaye, 2 Oct. 1725); P.R.O. S.P. 43/75 (order for Curll's prosecution, 28 Oct. 1725); *Mist's Weekly Journal*, 4 Dec. 1725 (Curll tried in Court of King's Bench on

recently visited William Burton (one of those accused), but only on a friendly birthday invitation, and that Burton himself was not really guilty. 'The poor man has been inadvertently drawn into this unhappy scene, far distant from his principles, by Those who are more deeply dipt. A Printer in Salisbury-Court, & another in Jewin-Street, who are Mist's Security, are much more objects of the Resentmt. of the Govt.' Curll offered to help detect the authors of 'this unheard of attack upon the Constitution', and thus, he hoped, 'regain a remittance of all my Past Offences wh. to This are indeed but Ven[i]al'. In a postscript he added, 'Mr Richardson in Salisbury Court, & Mr. Parker in Jewin street are the men. The former I am assur'd printed the Journal of last Saturday, and the wife of the latter publish'd it.'

Unless Curll is inaccurate in his reference to 'last Saturday,' he is not accusing Richardson of printing the treasonable 'Persian' number (the evidence indicates that he did not print it), but of printing the issue of 31 August, which was not objected to. It is not improbable that Richardson did undertake this task as a favour to a fellow printer in trouble. Many of Mist's men had been arrested; the *Journal* skipped an issue on 7 September and then came out with a double issue on 14 September with a new colophon, which named J. Wilford in Stationer's Court as printer instead of J. Wolfe, whose name had appeared through 31 August, with Mist's old address in Great Carter-Lane. On 28 September the journal (still with the Wilford colophon) announced its own demise and its rebirth as *Fog's Weekly Journal*. Richardson must have known Mist at least when the latter was his Assistant Renter Warden of the Stationers' Company in 1727,[57] and he did publish several advertisements in *Mist's Weekly Journal* and its successor, *Fog's*, one of them a long series of eleven advertisements.[58] The *Weekly Miscellany*, which he printed, noticed Mist's death in a favourable manner, 'a Person very justly esteemed by all who had any Acquaintance with him, for his generous and benevolent Temper'.[59] Richardson was closely enough associated with Henry Parker of Jewin Street to

30 Nov.); P.R.O. S.P. 35/61, fo. 9 (Cracherode reports Curll's sureties inadequate, 21 Jan. 1726); P.R.O. S.P. 44/81, pp. 423–4 (order to search for John Ker and Curll, 15 June 1726); P.R.O. T.S. 11/944, No. 3430 (copy of Curll's indictment for publishing Ker's *Memoirs* with notation of evidence); P.R.O. S.P. 44/81, p. 460 (warrant for Curll for publishing Part II of Ker's *Memoirs*, 3 Feb. 1727, and order to search for his son Henry, 4 Feb.); P.R.O. S.P. 35/64, fos. 20–35 (examinations of various people, including Curll and his son Henry, concerning the printing and publishing of Part II of Ker's *Memoirs*, 3 Feb.–10 Feb., and pleas by Curll, 14 Feb., 15 Feb.); P.R.O. S.P. 35/64, fo. 42 (letter from Curll to Delafaye, 20 Feb. 1727, thanking him for his liberty and hoping for his son's); *State Trials*, XVII, cols. 153–60.

[57] 'Court Book H', p. 266, 11 Apr. 1727, MS. in the archives of the Stationers' Company.

[58] Anyone with the presentation of a living of about two hundred pounds a year in any county adjacent to London is asked to write to Richardson. See the *Weekly Journal or Saturday's Post* of 11 Jan., 18 Jan., 8 Feb., 22 Feb., 29 Feb., 7 Mar., 14 Mar., 21 Mar., 28 Mar., 4 Apr., 11 Apr. 1724.

[59] 6 Oct. 1737.

advertise with him concerning the sale of materials for a complete printing house.[60] Curll had some reason to be resentful against Parker, who had earlier testified that he had printed part of Ker's *Memoirs* for Curll.[61]

Mist was by this time used to trouble. As early as 1718 a government official had noted that the *Weekly Journals* 'do more mischief than any other Libel being wrote ad captum of the common People'.[62] Defoe's ambiguous connection with the paper is well known, and his assignment as a sort of government agent to modify it and report on it shows how closely it was being watched. Mist had often been called in for questioning. He had stood in the pillory in 1721 but had managed to avoid serving out his jail sentence; his oddly named apprentice Doctor Gaylard, who ran the paper for him in 1722, had also been prosecuted; and Mist had been arrested again when caught by accident in 1723, and again in 1727. Early in 1728 he had vanished and thus could not be arrested for the Persian number.[63]

This issue, reportedly sent from France by Wharton, immediately stimulated the government to the biggest prosecution of the press in the decade. Mist was by this time presumably at Boulogne, where he remained, and his press was being supervised (perhaps nominally) by James Wolfe, an upholsterer. The day after the paper came out, a Sunday, a warrant was issued for author, printer, and publishers, and the Attorney General was told to prosecute with severity. Mist's press was broken, and at least thirty-eight people were picked up within the next six weeks, a few of them

---

[60] *Daily Journal*, 17 Feb. 1729.   [61] P.R.O. S.P. 35/64, fo. 31, 10 Feb. 1727.

[62] P.R.O. S.P. 35/13, No. 31.

[63] In addition to *DNB*, see: for warrant for Mist, 20 June 1718, for *The Temple*, P.R.O. S.P. 44/80, under date; for Mist's examination, search, and recognizance, Oct. 1718, for the *Weekly Journal*, P.R.O. S.P. 35/13, Nos. 17, 28, 31, 32, 33, 36, and P.R.O. S.P. 44/79A, p. 230; for Mist's arrest in June 1720 for the *Weekly Journal* and for Mist in the pillory, Feb. 1721, P.R.O. S.P. 44/79A, pp. 334-8, 344, *An Account of Persons Held to Bail to Answer in the Court of King's Bench for Libels, from 1 Anne to 57 Geo. 3. Both Inclusive*, p. 8, and the *Weekly Journal or, British Gazetteer*, 25 Feb. 1721; for Gaylard's prosecution for three issues of the *Weekly Journal* in 1722 and his condemnation in Jan. 1723, P.R.O. S.P. 44/81, pp. 47, 53, 55, 57, P.R.O. S.P. 44/80, under dates 6 Aug. and 16 Aug., P.R.O. S.P. 35/41, fo. 59, P.R.O. S.P. 35/34, fos. 78-80, *An Account of Persons Held to Bail to Answer in the Court of King's Bench for Libels, from 1 Anne to 57 Geo. 3. Both Inclusive*, p. 8; for search warrant for Mist, 25 June 1723, for a new issue of the *Weekly Journal*, his accidental arrest in late June for fleeing part of his former sentence, his trial, and his sentence to one year in prison and a fine of one hundred pounds on his old charge, P.R.O. S.P. 44/81, p. 296, P.R.O. S.P. 43/66, under date 28 June, *Weekly Journal or Saturday's Post*, 6 July, B.M. Add. MS. 36,134, fos. 136-7, *Weekly Journal or Saturday's Post*, 29 Feb. 1724, *Parker's London News*, 20 May 1724; for Mist's examination for pamphlets, 23 Jan. 1725, P.R.O. S.P. 35/55, fo. 24; for Mist's arrest in Sept. 1727, *Citizen*, 25 Sept. and 29 Sept., *Weekly Journal or Saturday's Post*, 30 Sept.; for Mist's escape in Jan. 1728, leaving his corrector Bingley in charge, warrant for Bingley, 10 Mar. 1728, warrants for Wolfe, 20 July and 27 July 1728, *Weekly Journal or, British Gazetteer*, 20 Jan. 1728, P.R.O. S.P. 36/5, fos. 181-3, P.R.O. S.P. 44/81, pp. 515, 537, [547]. We have discovered no record that Richardson was Mist's security on any of these occasions.

(including Wilford) for being concerned in the issue of 7–14 September and several of them apparently for merely being around Mist's premises when the officers arrived. Of these bail was taken from twenty-four, and twelve were committed to Newgate. Some of them got into trouble for printing additional copies of the issue at the press of William Burton, who claimed that he had not known the contents and only lent his presses on request, 'as is always usual for one printer to another when they are not engaged'. Two of Mist's apprentices, with two young devils, arrived on Monday and unloaded their formes and paper from a coach and worked all evening and night, until six the next morning. Edward Farley was arrested for reprinting the issue in his *Exeter Journal*. Wolfe, one of the last to be picked up, spent at least two months in prison but somehow got away to join Mist in France, where he set up a public house. Burton, Farley, and several of the workmen were less lucky. The workmen spent some time in jail, where a special bill had to be charged for money spent on the almost naked devils, Thomas Randall and James Ford, 'or our houses would have been over run with Vermin'. There was some legal discussion about what they could be prosecuted for, and it was decided that only Farley, against whom two witnesses seemed ready to swear, could be successfully charged with high treason; the rest could at most be convicted of a misdemeanour. This was serious enough: John Clarke, the pressman, was pilloried three times and sentenced to six months hard labour in Bridewell; Robert Knell, the compositor, got pilloried only twice, but the same jail sentence; Joseph Carter, one of the apprentices identified at Burton's, in addition to a month in Bridewell, had to go round four courts in Westminster Hall with a paper on his head denoting his offence; Amy Walker, a servant maid, got six months in Bridewell and was whipped half naked. The witnesses against Farley proved to be less conclusive than was hoped, and rather than reduce the charge to a mis-demeanour (which would weaken the effect of the Grand Jury's indicting his crime as treason), the solicitors advised a *nolle prosequi*, since he had been in jail almost a year, which, as the Attorney General Yorke wrote, 'is some punishment, thô by no means adequate to so heinous a Crime'. He was pardoned on 24 July 1729, at which time Burton's case was still not settled.[64] Richardson may have been saved from the same difficulties by a mere accident.

[64] The *Bee*, I (1733), No. 1; P.R.O. S.P. 44/82, under dates 25 Aug., 30 Aug., 1 Sept., 8 Nov., 10 Dec. 1728 and 11 Feb. 1729; P.R.O. S.P. 36/8, fos. 64–7, 74–5, 107, 152, 155, 157, 165, 167, 169–70, 254; P.R.O. T.S. 11/424, No. 1290; *An Account of Persons Held to Bail to Answer in the Court of King's Bench for Libels, from 1 Anne to 57 Geo. 3. Both Inclusive*, p. 10; B.M. Add. MS. 36,137, fos. 99, 102, 176, 178, 180; P.R.O. S.P. 44/81, pp. 539, [549]; P.R.O. S.P. 44/80, under dates 18 Sept., 20 Sept., 23 Sept., 27 Sept., 25 Oct., 28 Oct. 1728; P.R.O. S.P. 36/9, fos. 60–1, 243, 247, 249; P.R.O. S.P. 44/126, pp. 37, 153; P.R.O. S.P. 43/77, under date 20 May 1729; *Weekly Journal or, British Gazetteer*, 24 May 1729; P.R.O. S.P. 36/11, fo. 176; P.R.O. S.P. 36/6,

Curll's accusation, though probably based on nothing more than Richardson's willingness to help a fellow printer, is another bit of evidence suggesting that, though he may never have got in very deep, he was involved in his early days as a printer with rather dangerous company. His later career was much safer. During the 1730s he moved out of the opposition. In 1734 he voted for a supporter of the government, William Selwin, for Chamberlain of the City.[65] By the time he wrote *Pamela* he had retired from any active participation in political matters and seems to have taken a neutral stand on politics.

Probably before Richardson had printed it, in 1722 and 1723, the *Daily Journal* mildly supported the opposition, but later it seems to have abandoned this opposition policy, and the other newspaper which Richardson printed, the *Daily Gazetteer*, was the main organ of the Walpole government. On 6 July 1738 Aaron Hill wrote to him regretting that the *Gazetteer* was 'a party paper, in that least excusable sense of the word, a professed and unconditional attachment not to things but to persons. . . . Yet I am very much pleased that the good advice you have given seems to have had its due weight in the variation of subject, which that paper appears to be opening itself into.' In 1739, in his new edition of Sir Roger L'Estrange's *Æsop's Fables*, Richardson professed the principles of the Glorious Revolution but at the same time showed a mild and tolerant spirit, distrustful of party violence. He defended L'Estrange against Dr. Croxall's attack on his Jacobite leanings, though he agreed that he was 'certainly listed in a bad Cause as to Politicks'. But perhaps if Croxall had lived in Sir Roger's day, he might have fallen into the same errors: the Restoration made 'these now exploded Doctrines as much the Fashion then, as the glorious *Revolution* under King *William* III. has made the Doctor's principles the fashion now'. Richardson, in the morals and reflections to his fables, cut L'Estrange's political remarks and substituted general ones. 'For we think it in no wise excusable to inflame Childrens Minds with Distinctions, which they will imbibe fast enough from the Attachments of Parents, *&c.* and the Warmth of their own Imaginations.' Where a political turn was necessary, Richardson 'always gave that Preference to the Principles of LIBERTY, which we hope will for ever be the distinguishing Characteristic of a *Briton*'.[66]

There is no evidence that Richardson was ever opposed to the House of Hanover: in 1740 he dedicated *The Negotiations of Sir Thomas Roe* to the King. According to the editors of *The History of the Works of the Learned* he 'declined presenting this Book in Person to his Majesty, lest it should

---

fos. 161, 163, 268; P.R.O. S.P. 36/13, fos. 78–81, 109; P.R.O. S.P. 43/79 and P.R.O. S.P. 43/80, under dates 18 July and 25 July 1729; P.R.O. S.P. 44/362, under date 24 July 1729; *State Trials*, XVII, cols. 666–8.

[65] *Daily Post Extraordinary*, 9 April.   [66] Pp. vi, ix, xi–xii.

be thought he chose the Royal Patronage merely with a View to the Royal Bounty'[67]—a typical instance of Richardson's pride and independence where money was concerned. The Dedication expresses the hope that Great Britain may be happily ruled 'by a Prince of Your Royal House to the End of Time'.

[67] I (1740), 347.

CHAPTER III

FIRST YEARS IN BUSINESS;
THE APPRENTICE'S VADE MECUM

1724–1733

AFTER 1724 the Tory tinge to Richardson's press is less obvious, and more solid books begin to appear. But the output of his press during the rest of the 1720s, so much of it as has been identified at least, is not especially distinguished. The most literary items are the works of Sir Philip Sidney (1724 and 1725); an abridgement of *Gulliver's Travels* (1727); Dennis's attack on *The Rape of the Lock*, David Mallet's *Excursion*, and a translation of *Télémaque* (1728); and Richard Savage's *The Wanderer* and James Thomson's *Britannia* (1729). He printed part of Defoe's *Tour thro' the Whole Island of Great Britian* (1724–5), as well as his *New Voyage around the World* (1725), *A New Family Instructor* (1727), and *Religious Courtship* (1729). In these early days he at times printed only parts of works: Defoe's *Tour* and *New Voyage*, for instance, Sidney's *Works*, and Nathan Bailey's *Dictionary*. Among his more substantial jobs were two books by his later acquaintance Alexander Gordon, printed for the author, *Itinerarium Septentrionale* (1726) and *The Lives of Pope Alexander VI. and His Son Cæsar Borgia* (1729); Roger Acherley's *Britannic Constitution* (1727), which was one of the first works he did for a conger and which was an ambitious, though not very successful, folio; and two subscription works for Nathanæl Salmon, *The History of Hertfordshire* (1728) and *A New Survey of Great Britain* (1728–30). During his first decade of printing Richardson had established relations with both booksellers and authors and towards the end of it was printing works of some magnitude.

Meanwhile Richardson had in all probability been printing periodicals other than the *True Briton*. The best evidence for his having printed Aaron Hill's and William Bond's short-lived biweekly the *Plain Dealer*, which ran from 23 March 1724 through 7 May 1725, is that it contains several of the same factotums as the *True Briton*[1] and that the rare advertisements in the

---

[1] Three of the eleven factotums and three of the seven arrangements of flowers used as factotums in the original issues of the *True Briton* appear in the original issues of the *Plain Dealer*. See *True Briton*, Nos. 2, 67, 71, and *Plain Dealer*, Nos. 102, 103, 104, 106; *True Briton*, No. 68, and *Plain Dealer*, No. 107; *True Briton*, No. 70, and *Plain Dealer*, No. 108; *True Briton*,

Plain Dealer include several by Richardson.[2] He was certainly concerned in the printing of the collected edition of 1730: the imprint states that it was printed 'for *S. Richardson*, and *A. Wilde*'. Since neither Richardson nor Wilde was regularly a bookseller, the fact that these volumes were printed 'for' them indicates an unusual relationship; either Hill had in some way conveyed the copyright to them (he later offered several copyrights to Richardson as a reward for the latter's services to him), or they were acting as publishers for the convenience of Hill.[3] Richardson rarely 'published' books, and it is likely that this was an act of friendship. Although the first extant letter in their correspondence is dated 6 March 1735, ten years earlier Richardson had printed a new edition of Hill's poem *The Northern-Star*, the first of many of Hill's works from his press.

The last number of the *True Briton* hints at the coming of Hill's new paper and gives it a puff: 'And whenever a Subject of PLAIN-DEALING and *Gallantry* appears in the World, many things that were incongruous to this Design, may obtain proper Place therein.' One might conjecture that Wharton had recommended Richardson to Hill as a reliable printer whose press would soon be free for a new venture in journalism.[4]

But there was no politics in the *Plain Dealer*; nor was there a great deal of the gallantry promised by the *True Briton*, nor even any unusually plain-dealing. The first number explains, in the *Spectator* tradition, that the Plain Dealer who is writing the new periodical is a quiet, eccentric unpolished, old-fashioned old bachelor, who will not meddle with Church and State, but will discourse on the passions, humours, follies, pleasures, and graces of human life. In the early numbers the bulk of the periodical usually consists of an essay, but letters to the Plain Dealer become increasingly prominent. There are occasional verses and moral or affecting tales. Like the Spectator, the Plain Dealer has a group of friends who occasionally appear, and he has a running, or rather creeping, love affair with a lady named Patty Amble. Indeed it is Miss Amble's decision to accept him on condition he stop plain-dealing that, according to the last

Nos. 12, 15, 21, 32, 35, 38, 40, 44, 48, 52, 63, and *Plain Dealer*, Nos. 33, 54, 58, 61; *True Briton*, Nos. 17, 19, 23, 26, 28, 29, 31, 34, 37, 39, 45, 46, 51, 55, 66, and *Plain Dealer*, Nos. 42, 48, 49, 52, 55, 56, 57, 59, 60; *True Briton*, Nos. 24, 25, 27, 30, 33, 36, 41, 42, 43, 47, 50, 54, 58, 59, 61, 64, and *Plain Dealer*, Nos. 39, 40, 41, 43, 45. A factotum appearing in the fortnightly reprints of the *True Briton*, Nos. 5, 13, 15, appears in the *Plain Dealer*, Nos. 32, 34, 44, 46, 47, 50, 51.

[2] In Mar. and June 1724 and again in early 1725 there are no fewer than twelve advertisements for the subscription edition of Kelly's translation of Castelnau's *Mémoires*, stating first that Richardson is accepting subscriptions and later that he is distributing copies. Another advertisement, on 12 Oct. 1724, states that persons interesting in buying the printing materials of the late Mr. Pickard may inquire of Richardson.

[3] The book, however, was sold by regular booksellers.

[4] The *True Briton* had glowingly praised Hill's *Henry the Fifth* (13 Dec., 16 Dec. 1723), and the *Plain Dealer* advertised Wharton's speech in defence of Atterbury (23 Mar. 1724), as well as several of Hutcheson's works (which were printed for J. Roberts, the publisher of the periodical).

number, forces him to cease publication in spite of the kind reception he has received. There is more or less witty satire against masquerades (one of Richardson's favourite objects of condemnation later), the eagerness of foreign nobles to be accepted as the equals of the English (the same rather exalted view of the respect mere foreigners have for the English gentry and nobility is expressed by Pamela),[5] coquettes, false wits, and ladies' love of pet animals. There is an allegorical vision and a meditation on death among the tombs of Westminster Abbey; there are serious essays on the barbarity of capital punishment for theft, on the usefulness of inoculation against smallpox, on the vanity of pride in ancient family and of nobility without accomplishment, on the cruelty of parents who force their children to marry for money, on the usefulness of planting colonies in Africa and of the slave trade, on the degeneracy of the stage, and on drunkenness; in the way of literary criticism, Pope is highly praised and Pope's enemy John Dennis equally highly (there are puffs for his *Miscellaneous Tracts* and for a performance for his benefit at Lincoln's Inn Fields), *The Universal Passion* of Hill's friend (and Richardson's later friend) Edward Young is hailed, and poems by three new Scottish writers (Joseph Mitchell, David Mallet, and the '*prodigious Young Man*' James Thomson) are welcomed and quoted.

The ballad 'William and Margaret', written or at least revised by David Mallet, is cited as 'a plain and noble Masterpiece of the *natural* Way of Writing': Marg'ret dies for love of William and her ghost returns to reproach the heartless lover:

> Why did you praise my blushing Lips,
>   Yet make their Scarlet pale?
> And why, alas! did I, fond Maid!
>   *Believe* the flatt'ring Tale?

Tortured by remorse and by these verses, William at morn seeks out Marg'ret's grave, lies down on it, and

> Thrice call'd, unheard, on *Marg'ret's* Name,
>   And thrice he wept her Fate:
> Then laid his Cheek on her cold Grave,
>   And dy'd—And *lov'd, too late.*

The poem is not an altogether unfair example of two elements which the literary histories used to call 'pre-romantic', both still in their early stages and both later developed by (among many others) Samuel Richardson: the popular style and the tender heart.

Since Aaron Hill was Richardson's most intellectual close friend before the publication of *Pamela*, the *Plain Dealer* is not uninteresting as an

[5] SH, IV, 388; EL, II, 429.

illustration of the atmosphere of a certain background. Over a decade later, Hill has all the morality of Addison combined with at least a desire to be urbane about it, while the tender emotions of Steele are perhaps even more apparent.

At the time of the *Plain Dealer* Hill was almost forty, four years older than Richardson, and had been a prominent, if not quite famous, man for over fifteen years.[6] He came of a good, though not wealthy, family and had important connections with the aristocracy; in 1710 he had married an heiress, whose wealth, though depleted by law suits and unhappy business ventures, enabled him for a time to patronize young writers and to live in at least decency for the rest of his life and bring up his children, Urania, Astræa, Minerva, and Julius Cæsar. When very young he had had an adventurous trip through the Near East, which provided the basis for his ambitious *Ottoman Empire*. He had been connected (always unsuccessfully) with a number of the 'projects' so popular in the early years of the century: making oil from beechnuts, manufacturing potash by a new method, obtaining timber from almost inaccessible areas of Scotland, colonizing Georgia. He had been concerned for a short time in managing both Drury Lane and the Little Theatre in the Haymarket, had numerous theories on acting, direction, and playwrighting, and had written some almost still-born tragedies and farces as well as the English libretto for Handel's first London opera, *Rinaldo*. As a poet he was at least both prolific and versatile, pouring out all the types of verse popular at the time in all the usual metres; his *Northern-Star*, in praise of Peter the Great, had some success, but most of the rest of his large output, including his Pindaric epic *Gideon*, suffered the usual fate of everything Hill touched—it was not quite good enough to be worth reading and was tepidly praised by his aquaintances, ecstatically praised by the poets he aided, and soon forgotten by everyone.

He carried on, at intervals, a courteous if not quite friendly correspondence with Alexander Pope, which began when Hill attacked Pope in the preface to *The Northern-Star* because of some cool remarks which he heard Pope had made about that poem and was revived when Pope made slighting remarks about Hill in *Peri Bathous* and *The Dunciad*, which he later half denied responsibility for and half apologized for. Hill's published remarks about Pope are generally full of admiration for the poet, though *The Progress of Wit* is largely a complaint about Pope's desire for praise and refusal to praise others in return; Pope's private remarks to Hill about Hill's own works are cautiously phrased, so that Hill was free to believe that Pope liked them but could never have been quite certain—at any rate

---

[6] The most detailed account of Aaron Hill is given by Dorothy Brewster, *Aaron Hill* (New York, 1913). Unless otherwise indicated, references to Hill's poems are to his *Works*, 2nd edn., 4 vols. (1754).

Pope evidently took some pains to avoid offending Hill. After Pope's death, Hill's remarks about him in letters to Richardson are more openly derogatory, not only to the man but to the writer, and probably influenced Richardson's final low opinion of Pope.

In other ways his acquaintance with Hill must have been broadening for Richardson. Hill was much more a man of the world than the middle-class citizens with whom Richardson was otherwise connected; he had a considerable share of the tolerance and largeness of view, the hostility to prejudice and narrowness, which was perhaps the most attractive side of the eighteenth century. He seems to have been generous and helpful where his self-love was not attacked and enthusiastically unselfish in advancing the many causes to which he was attached. Except about his own work, of which he had a high opinion, he showed literary taste, based on a much wider knowledge than Richardson ever had. Richardson, always likely to echo his better-educated correspondents and conscious of his own deficiencies, had (or at least expressed) great enthusiasm for Hill's writings and Hill's opinions and must have learned much from him. Pamela's unfortunate and interminable interest in Locke's theories on bringing up children may have come from Hill, who wrote a poem 'To Miranda, after Marriage, with Mr. Lock's Treatise on Education'. Richardson heartily endorsed the sentiment in *The Northern-Star*:

> Mankind's my country!—born no matter where;
> For Man's a denizen of earth and air.[7]

The international sympathies in *Sir Charles Grandison*, rather surprising in view of the fact that Richardson never left his own country and knew little about the rest of the world, may reflect Hill's views. So probably do some of Richardson's remarks about writers: his praise of Cowley is an echo of a letter Richardson had received from Hill,[8] and Lady Davers in *Pamela* is pretty certainly complimenting Richardson's friend when she endorses the sentiment of 'a Gentleman, whose Judgment, and good Heart, have hardly any Equal', that though her favourite Cowley is going out of fashion a taste for his beauties is a test of head and heart.[9] There is no doubt that Richardson prized his friendship with Hill, though there is no clear evidence that it began as early as the mid-twenties.

By 11 April 1727 Richardson was prominent enough to be elected to his first office in the Stationers' Company, that of Renter Warden, a minor office with few duties beyond collecting dues. On 2 February 1731 he was able to purchase a share in the English Stock of the company, a half-

---

[7] See R to Susanna Highmore, 4 June 1750.
[8] Hill to R, 1 June 1738; R to Susanna Highmore, 4 June 1750.
[9] SH, III, 234; not in EL.

yeomanry or £40 share. Because of its high interest, stock in the Stationers' Company was much sought after. In 1736 Richardson got a yeomanry or £80 share, in 1746 a livery or £160 share, and finally in 1751 the highest share, an assistant's, of £320.[10] The records of the Stationers' Company also reflect his prosperity in the number of apprentices he bound. As the apprenticeships of the three boys taken over from the Leakes expired, Richardson bound others to replace them, and he always kept at least three—in the forties as many as five.

A broadside headed 'Rules and Orders to Be Observed by the Members of This Chapel', dated 30 August 1734, describes Richardson's printing establishment.[11] The rules are signed by twenty compositors and pressmen, a comparatively large number, about half as many as Richardson employed in the 1750s. They impose a variety of fines, from 1d. to 6d., for such offences as failure to clear pye promptly and mixture of founts and including also fighting, breaking windows, gaming, or smoking ('except a Dispensation from the Master be obtain'd for the Sake of the Person's Health'). Differences are to be determined by the two eldest freemen or, if they disagree, by an umpire chosen by them. The master is authorized to withhold fine money out of wages if refractory workers refuse to pay. The master's influence on the chapel rules is uncertain: the chapel was, as the rules imply, a largely self-governing body of journeymen; but the rules are just such mild, sensible, and orderly rules as Richardson might have approved of. Seventy years earlier those who did not pay their fines for such offences as swearing, fighting, abusive language, being drunk, and more technical faults were 'solaced' by being laid on their bellies athwart the correcting stone and given eleven blows on the buttocks,[12] but Richardson's chapel rules mention no corporal punishments. Fines, as well as the 'bienvenues' or fees paid by new members, were spent for the good of the chapel, evidently mostly for carousing on holidays. The rules 'were as much for the protection of compositors engaged in piece-work as in the interest of their employers'.[13] Their main emphasis is on the orderly disposal of equipment, and if they were obeyed, the establishment must have been efficient and business-like.

A number of advertisements in the press of the late 1720s and early 1730s refer to Richardson's business. Most of these are of books for which he was listed among those accepting subscriptions: Castelnau's *Memoirs*,

---

[10] 'Court Book H', pp. 266, 393–4; 'Court Book I', pp. 87, 412–13; 'Court Book K', pp. 285–6, MSS. in the archives of the Stationers' Company.

[11] B.M. Add. MS. 27,799, fo. 88. Ellic Howe reprints the 'Rules' in *The London Compositor*, pp. 30–2. For the evidence that the chapel is Richardson's, see T. C. Duncan Eaves and Ben D. Kimpel, 'Two Notes on Samuel Richardson', *Library*, XXIII (1968), 242–3.

[12] Joseph Moxon, *Mechanick Exercises on the Whole Art of Printing*, ed. Herbert Davis and Harry Carter (London, 1958), pp. 323–6.

[13] Howe, *London Compositor*, p. 29.

which he is also described as 'publishing';[14] Acherley's *Britannic Constitution*, which was not in the end printed by subscription;[15] Kelly's proposed but never published translation of Cicero's epistles to Atticus;[16] *A Complete Collection of State Trials*, edited by Thomas Salmon and Sollom Emlyn;[17] *The Negotiations of Sir Thomas Roe*, which, in spite of an unusually lengthy advertising campaign, never managed to get enough subscribers and was later printed in another way.[18] He is advertised as delivering copies of subscription editions of Nathanæl Salmon's *History of Hertfordshire*[19] and of Captain James Ogilvie's translation of Giannone's *Civil History of the Kingdom of Naples*.[20]

All of the subscription editions mentioned above were printed by Richardson; several of them are rather elaborate, especially the *State Trials* in six volumes, printed in 1730. A highly successful venture of 1731 was Philip Miller's *Gardeners Dictionary*, of which Richardson also printed many editions, as he did of Miller's *Gardeners Kalendar*. Miller was a Fellow of the Royal Society, and his books had scholarly and scientific value as well as popular success. Like several of the other works mentioned, they must have given Richardson's press a measure of prestige.

Though a large percentage of the books Richardson is known to have printed were printed for the author, he seems early to have had good relations with the booksellers. Several of his subscription editions were advertised as sold by large numbers of booksellers, and of such leading booksellers as Arthur Bettesworth, John Osborn, Thomas Longman, Charles Rivington, and George Strahan. *The Britannic Constitution*, when the subscription edition failed, was sponsored by several booksellers. Some of the works from his press are handsome, even sumptuous, in format—for instance, the four folio volumes, in Latin, of the *Concilia Magnæ Britanniæ et Hiberniæ* (1737). Throughout his career his workmanship was both attractive and careful. The literary distinction of the products of his press, however, is hardly greater in the 1730s than in the 1720s.

James Thomson is perhaps the most eminent author for whom he printed. They were friendly enough so that later Thomson was among those who expressed a wish for a happy ending to *Clarissa*[21] and so that

[14] *Daily Journal*, 27 Mar. 1724; 2 Jan., 4 Jan., 14 Jan., 11 Feb., 19 Feb. 1725; 17 July, 24 July 1727; *Weekly Journal or Saturday's Post*, 9 Jan. 1725; *Plain Dealer*, 30 Mar., 3 Apr., 10 Apr., 12 June, 15 June 1724; 4 Jan., 8 Jan., 22 Jan., 12 Feb., 19 Feb., 16 Apr., 7 May 1725.

[15] *Daily Journal*, 17 June 1726.

[16] *Monthly Chronicle*, Mar. 1729; *Daily Journal*, 27 May, 29 May, 5 July, 10 July 1729.

[17] *Monthly Catalogue*, May 1729; *Monthly Chronicle*, June 1729.

[18] *Monthly Chronicle*, Oct. 1730; *Daily Journal*, 23 Oct., 27 Oct., 30 Nov. 1730; 8 Feb., 27 Feb., 20 Mar., 5 May, 22 May, 29 May, 13 July, 17 July, 27 July, 30 July, 7 Aug., 10 Aug., 6 Nov. 1731.

[19] *Monthly Chronicle*, July 1728; *Daily Journal*, 22 July and many following issues through 19 Oct. 1728; *Mist's Weekly Journal*, 3 Aug., 7 Sept., 14 Sept. 1728.

[20] *Fog's Weekly Journal*, 22 Mar. 1729; *Craftsman*, 5 Apr. 1729.

[21] R to Hill, 7 Nov. 1748.

Hill asked Richardson to thank Thomson for favours.[22] He kept in touch with David Mallet through Hill and sent Mallet a copy of the second part of *Pamela*.[23] Both Thomson and Mallet were young Scotsmen recently arrived in London, who were being encouraged by Hill. Hill had also tried in the *Plain Dealer* to support the claim of Richard Savage to being the illegitimate son of Lady Macclesfield and had written a lacrimose poem on the subject in which Savage concludes ruefully that he must pine away in silence[24]—a course he showed little indication of adopting. Richardson printed Savage's *Wanderer* in 1729, and in 1736 had some sort of dispute with him which Hill tried to patch up.[25] Savage's collection of *Miscellaneous Poems and Translations* (1726) gives some measure of Hill's group, so far as we know the first literary circle with which Richardson came in contact. Over a third of the poems in it are by Hill, and 'Hillarius' is lavishly praised in other poems. Indeed the poets devote a generous percentage of their limited talents to praising one another. Encomium appears to have been their specialty, followed at some distance by love, country life, and satiric wit. There are a good many poems by Savage, Clio (Martha Fowke Sansome), William Popple, Miranda (Mrs. Hill), and John Dyer, and two by Mallet.

With Pope's enemy, the critic John Dennis, for whom he had printed *Remarks on Mr. Pope's Rape of the Lock* (1728), Richardson was closely enough connected to lend him money on the security of manuscripts.[26] A compliment to him was added in the 1748 edition of Defoe's *Tour*.[27] Hill was also an admirer and acquaintance of Dennis and of Richardson's later friend Edward Young.

But the other authors with whom he became friendly were not exactly literary men. His connection with Philip Miller continued,[28] and with some of the other men for whom he began printing in the 1730s he later became friendly: the 'thresher poet', Stephen Duck, whose *Poems on Several Occasions* he printed in 1736; Patrick Delany, whose *Revelation Examin'd with Candour* he printed in 1732 and who later introduced Richardson to one group of the literary ladies who played so large a part in his later life; the eccentric Bath physician George Cheyne, the first of whose books known to have come from Richardson's press was *The English Malady* (1733); and the Irish clergyman Philip Skelton, whose *Some Proposals for the Revival of Christianity* appeared in 1736.

[22] 24 July 1744; 4 Apr. 1745.
[23] R to Hill, 12 Jan. 1749; two undated notes from Mallet to R, [Dec. 1741, or early 1742].
[24] *Works*, IV, 51–3.   [25] Hill to Savage, 23 June 1736, *Works*, I, 327.
[26] Note in R's hand on the MS. (in the Folger Shakespeare Library) of Dennis's 'The Causes of the Decay and Defects of Dramatick Poetry and of the Degeneracy of the Publick Tast'. See also *Monthly Magazine*, XLIII (1817), 421, and Edward N. Hooker, 'An Unpublished Autograph Manuscript of John Dennis', *ELH*, I (1934), 156–62.
[27] I, 247.   [28] Barbauld, I, clxix; Hill to R, 21 Sept. 1739.

But this hardly shows that Richardson was a member of a literary circle. Until after the publication of *Pamela*, there is no evidence that he was closely connected with any man except Aaron Hill whose primary interest was literature. His closest associates were probably the booksellers with whom he worked.

Aside from the advertisements of books which he published, other advertisements refer to miscellaneous activities of Richardson. Printing houses, like booksellers, bankers, jewellers, taverns, and coffee-houses, acted as clearing houses for various matters and especially advertised that lost articles could be left with them. Richardson advertises for the return of 'Half a Hundred Weight of Raw Coffee, in a Wainscot Box', which (in a way unaccounted for) got lost at the corner of Crooked Lane, and which is of no use to anyone except the owner, who has the permit for it; of five yards of cambric and two of muslin; of a £50 bank note; of an old blue grogram gown, in pieces, two ells of new Holland, and a red silk cloak tied in a white linen handkerchief, all left in a coach. He is also willing to accept communications from any person having a presentation to a living near London of almost £200 a year; to receive materials for Morgan's proposed *History of Algiers*; to sell the printing materials of the late Mr. Pickard and the materials of a complete printing house; and to rent a pastrycook's and confectioner's shop.[29]

A large majority of these advertisements, at least of those which have been located, as well as a heavy proportion of the book advertisements, appear in the *Daily Journal*. The advertisements make it likely that Richardson was already printing the *Daily Journal* in 1724. From 1728 to 1732 the name on the colophon was that of one of his workmen, James Purser, who presumably carried on the paper for Richardson in a house Richardson rented in 1728, across from his own dwelling. From then until its demise in April 1737 the colophon claims that it was printed by a publisher named Thomas Cooper, but there is no doubt that Richardson was printing it in 1736.[30]

The *Daily Journal* was largely a newspaper in the strict sense: most of what was not advertisement (sometimes as much as three-quarters of the

[29] *Daily Journal*, 3 Nov., 7 Nov. 1727; *Daily Journal*, 25 Mar. 1728; *Daily Journal*, 27 Mar. 1736; *Daily Journal*, 26 July 1736; *Weekly Journal or Saturday's Post*, 11 Jan. and many following issues through 11 Apr. 1724; *Plain Dealer*, 22 Jan. 1725, and *Daily Journal*, 18 Nov., 25 Nov., 3 Dec. 1726; *Plain Dealer*, 12 Oct. 1724; *Fog's Weekly Journal*, 15 Feb., 15 Mar., 22 Mar., 5 Apr. 1729, and *Daily Journal*, 17 Feb., 18 Feb., 20 Feb., 22 Feb., 24 Feb. 1729; *Daily Journal*, 13 July 1733.

[30] See T. C. Duncan Eaves and Ben D. Kimpel, 'Two Notes on Samuel Richardson', *Library*, XXIII (1968), 243–7. From 1 Feb. 1722 to 14 Mar. 1728 the colophon reads 'Printed for *T. Warner*'. There is no change in the factotum when his name first appears, and the same factotum continues to be used through 5 Dec. 1724. At least during 1722 and 1723 there are frequent advertisements for the printer John Applebee, whom Negus in 1722 listed as the printer of the paper and a high flyer. One would guess that Richardson took over the printing from Applebee during the period when Warner's name appears on the colophon.

whole) consisted of brief news items, without comment. An exhaustive analysis of these news items and of the letters, which become rather frequent in 1729 and later, might reveal some political bias, but we have been unable to discover much from a cursory examination. It was in any case not markedly opposed to the government by the time when Richardson probably started to print it; by 1734 there are advertisements of publications by Cooper attacking the opposition's *Craftsman* and signs of friendly relations with the government-supported *Daily Courant*.[31]

How much Richardson had to do with the contents of this or any other paper he printed is impossible to determine with accuracy, but such evidence as is available, mainly letters from Aaron Hill, suggests a greater influence than a modern printer would have. Stanley Morison says that 'everything points to the probability that for the first hundred years of their history, newspaper production appealed to printers who were already living on books and pamphlets and whose necessity then, as now, was to keep their plants regularly occupied. In those days the printer was the responsible head of the paper, whether he retained the services of a conductor or not; and whether he admitted anybody else to a share of the profits, the printer desired proprietary control, otherwise he might see the paper transferred to a rival office after he had invested in extra plant. Printer-control was also supported by statutes which made him personally responsible for any contravention of the licensing, libel, or stamp laws.'[32]

The letters in the paper concern such miscellaneous matters as the alleged plagiarism in *The Dunciad* from Garth's *Dispensary*, the importance for the trading part of the nation of seeing that prisoners, especially in debtors' prisons, are supported without having to pay fees, the Freemasons (would-be comical remarks), and the great aid which a receipt for curing worms printed in the *Journal* afforded to the daughter of Elizabeth Maynard.[33] There are occasional poems.

Typical enough of an issue with no letters (that is, of the majority) is the issue of 26 April 1727. The news consists of a series of very concise statements, rarely more than a sentence on one subject—journalists had not yet learned to make one sentence of news fill a column. First, under various foreign date lines, the public is informed that the Pope has arrived at Benevento, that a German officer has been beheaded for murder, that the governor of Tetuan will help the English in Gibraltar at need; then there is a good deal of shipping news; Theophilus Dillingham, High Sheriff of Bedford, has married Mrs. Faityplace, a lady of £30,000; the Garter King at Arms is not about to resign for ill health; at Edinburgh, a soldier is to be shot for desertion; —— Ross of Ireland has married Com-

---

[31] 1 May, 16 Nov. 1734 and 14 May 1736; 6 June, 26 July, 14 Nov. 1734.
[32] *English Newspaper*, pp. 143–4.
[33] 27 May 1729; 22 Jan. 1730; 18 Aug. 1730 and other issues near this date; 2 Dec. 1730.

missioner Rosse's daughter, who not only has £10,000 but is 'yet more eligible for her virtuous endowments'; John Price has been committed to Newgate for trying to palm off a piece of tin as a silver sixpence, and Standard Birch for stealing goods valued at 4s.; a sailor in liquor has fallen overboard and was drowned, Captain Whetham of Steyning has died, Colonel Stanhope has been elected to Parliament, and at Portsmouth the *Spy* is being cleaned.

After the stock quotations and a notice that the Ancient Order of GOR-MO-GON is to meet on 1 May, follow, in the middle of the second of the six columns, the advertisements: William Cheselden proposes to print *The Anatomy of Bones* by subscription; the goods of Mr. Allen, toy-man, are to be sold off cheap; the Sun Fire-Office has opened a new place of business, with an engineer in readiness and also someone to sell insurance; at Lincoln's Inn, *The Stratagem*, for the benefit of Mr. Hippisley and Mrs. Egleton—at the Haymarket, a comic opera, *La Parodia del Pastor Fido*—at the Great Room in York Buildings, a concert by Mrs. Davies, for her own benefit; a gold watch and chain have been lost from a gentleman's side; the Royal Pleasure Bath at the Prince's Bagnio in Lemon-Street is warmer than last season and has a fresh bath every day and a person in waiting to teach gentlemen to swim; a collection of paintings is to be exposed at Mr. Cock's in Poland Street; there are auctions of books, paintings, and household goods; several books have been recently published; houses are to let; Robert De Vlieger sells imported lace; the Blue Door adjoining Brown's Coffee House is open 'For the Accomodating of Gentlemen, Who are desirous at all times to appear handsomely cloathed at small Expence'; and Mrs. Freeman, formerly at the Bagnio Coffee House, 'having quitted publick Business', now lodges in Little-Bartholomew-Close, where she 'continues her Undertaking to destroy the Vermin called BUGGS, having never failed of Success. If it should happen that any Bugs appear after her Operation, which never have yet, she promises to destroy them without any Fee or Reward.'

The *Journal* got involved in a controversy in which one would not have expected Richardson to appear—it lent some support to a suspected Deist. The *Grub-street Journal* accused it of attacking priests and supporting Matthew Tindal, author of the much attacked 'Philosopher's Prayer'.[34] There were a large number of advertisements in the *Journal* for Eustace Budgell's periodical the *Bee*, in which Tindal's prayer was printed, as well as letters defending the 'Philosopher's Prayer'.[35] The *Prompter*, which Richardson was also probably printing, was similarly accused of backing

[34] 13 Nov. 1735.
[35] 12 Feb. 1733 (advertisement for the first number of the *Bee*); 15 Sept. 1733 (letter from Budgell about Tindal); 15 Sept., 2 Oct., 17 Oct., 21 Oct. 1735 (defence of the 'Philosopher's Prayer'); 27 Nov. 1735 (advertisement for the 'Philosopher's Prayer').

Tindal, whereas another of Richardson's periodicals, the *Weekly Miscellany*, attacked him.

In its last years, when the news stories seem to have been running rather thin and the advertisements, except for the publications of T. Cooper, were growing less numerous, the *Daily Journal* began to reprint various issues of the *Prompter*.[36] After the death of the *Prompter*, the *Journal* in its last days began a series called 'The Occasional Prompter', purportedly written by a man not acquainted with either of the authors of the *Prompter* but, like it, dealing largely with the theatre.[37] According to the *Grub-street Journal* of 15 January 1737, the fact that the *Journal* was thus burdened with a lame brother and afterwards with his cousin was about to cause it itself a fatal fall. Probably its reliance on this extraneous dramatic criticism instead of on news stories was rather a sign of weakness than a cause of it, but in any case the *Journal* did die on 9 April 1737—the *Grub-street Journal* was doubtful in what religion.[38]

Though by 1730 Richardson's business affairs were going well enough, his family life had brought him little but sorrow. His first child, a son named John, was born on 7 October 1722 and died of 'Convulsions' before the end of the month. A son named Samuel, born on 24 September 1723, died, also of convulsions, before the end of that year. Another Samuel, born on 18 August 1725, lived until April of the next year before he died of 'teeth'. A fourth son, William, born on 15 February 1727, did survive infancy but died shortly after his third birthday, on 10 May 1730. Meanwhile a daughter, Martha, had been born and died in the first half of 1728. His sixth child by Martha Wilde, another Samuel, was baptized on 7 April 1730, shortly before the death of his older brother; he lived for over two years and died on 3 October 1732. His mother had died before him, on 23 January 1731. Richardson wrote that one of his boys, 'a most delightful Child, carried away his most worthy Mother, at least contributed to her Death'. Judging by what he told Lady Bradshaigh in 1748, the child in question must have been William: 'By my first Wife I had 5 Sons and one Daughter; some of them living to be delightful Pratlers, with all the Appearances of sound Health, lovely in their Features and promising as to their Minds, and the Death of one of them, I doubt accelerating from Grief, that of the otherwise laudably afflicted Mother.' The marriage had been a happy one: 'I cherish the Memory of my lost Wife to this Hour.'[39]

There are several other letters which indicate that Richardson remem-

[36] See the issues of 13 Nov. 1734; 18 Mar., 17 June, 12 July, 30 July, 25 Oct., 26 Nov. 1735; 9 Jan., 28 Jan., 31 Jan., 4 Feb. 1736.

[37] See the issues of 6 Dec., 8 Dec., 10 Dec., 14 Dec., 18 Dec., 22 Dec., 23 Dec., 25 Dec., 27 Dec., 29 Dec., 31 Dec. 1736; 3 Jan., 6 Jan., 7 Jan., 11 Jan., 14 Jan., 17 Jan., 21 Jan., 7 Feb., 11 Feb., 19 Feb., 22 Feb., 5 Mar., 14 Mar., 19 Mar., 22 Mar., 25 Mar. 1737.

[38] 21 Apr. 1737.

[39] R to Mrs. Watts, [c. Aug. 1755]; R to Lady Bradshaigh, 15 Dec. 1748.

bered for the rest of his life the griefs of this decade. At least two of the children who died were old enough to have acquired personalities and to have left a strong impression on their father. Of Martha Wilde Richardson we know almost nothing. It has been hinted that Richardson married his master's daughter, like a properly ambitious apprentice, for prudential reasons. But when he married, Richardson had long ceased to be the apprentice of John Wilde. Nor is there any grounds for thinking that Martha was very wealthy. She had £100 inherited from an uncle in addition to what her father left her, but her father was himself not too well off. At any rate, there is no reason to doubt the sincerity of Richardson's attachment: a quarter of a century after her death he remembered her fondly enough to desire in his will to be buried with her. Nor, of course, is there any reason to think his was a wildly romantic love. Whatever may be the case after two centuries of hearing from the novelists, poets, and movie scenario writers that love is the only thing that counts, it was certainly possible for a man in the early eighteenth century to marry a girl whom he knew and liked and who had a small nest egg to put into his growing business without being guilty of hypocrisy or undue selfishness. And it was also possible for him to become genuinely fond of such a wife in the course of living with her. About three years after Martha's death, in *The Apprentice's Vade Mecum*, Richardson mentions among other arguments against an apprentice's involving himself in fornication or an early marriage that 'his Hopes of prefering himself, when he is out of his Time, by marrying a Person of Credit or Fortune, which joining with what he might have, or with his own industrious Improvement, might be a means to make his Life to come easy and happy, would be entirely baffled and frustrated'.[40] Such an argument would sound Philistine from a modern college boy, but the economic pattern has changed as well as the emotional. We have seen that the newspapers found it natural to refer to a bride as a lady of a certain number of pounds—though she might also have virtuous endowments. Richardson obviously did not mean to sound cynical, but only prudent— and it is impossible to believe that he was ever wilfully imprudent.

On 3 February 1733, four months after the death of his only surviving child, Richardson remarried, again the daughter of an old employer, Elizabeth Leake. He was then forty-three and she was thirty-five. We get numerous glimpses of his second wife in his later correspondence, and though they had their little quarrels and their relationship hardly seems to have been passionate, there is every reason to think of his as a happy marriage, as marriages go. They had better luck with their children. Though the first of them died within a month (Elizabeth, baptized on 23 December 1733), four other daughters survived their father: Mary (Polly), baptized on 2 January 1735; Martha (Patty), baptized on 16 July

[40] P. 4.

1736; Anne (Nancy), baptized on 16 August 1737; and Sarah (Sally), baptized on 17 July 1740. Richardson never managed to have a son and heir, however; a fourth Samuel, baptized on 26 April 1739, was buried just less than a year later—while his father was preparing to publish *Pamela*.

During all the time of his first marriage and the first four years of his second marriage, Richardson continued to live in the house he had rented in 1721 or 1722, on the corner of Blue Ball Court and Salisbury Square. In 1728 he had rented a second house, across the narrow Blue Ball Court from the first, and in 1734 he rented a third, a few doors down the court. Both of these houses were probably used for his expanding business.

Meanwhile he had begun writing, though hardly as yet anything that could be called literature. Besides the books with which Richardson is known to have been connected, Nichols mentions one item which could have been written at any period of Richardson's life, since it was one of his favourite subjects: 'He published, or rather printed, a large single sheet relative to the Married State, intituled, "The Duties of Wives to Husbands".'[41] No copy of this broadside is known to be extant. His brother printers, in January 1736, referred to the fact that 'the Publick is often agreeably entertain'd with his Elegant Disquisitions in Prose'.[42] In his biographical letter to Stinstra, Richardson mentions that the booksellers 'thought fit to seek me, rather than I them, because of the Readiness I shewed, to oblige them, with writing Indexes, Prefaces, and sometimes, for their minor Authors, *honest* Dedications; abstracting, abridging, compiling, and giving my Opinion of Pieces offered them'. Richardson later showed himself a master of index writing, if such a chore can be said to give scope for mastery, and his meticulousness and painstaking effort must have been a boon to his bookselling friends. But it is hardly likely that any of this work will be discovered. In the same letter Richardson says, 'A few other little things of the Pamphlet kind I have written; all with a good Intention; But neither are they worthy of Your Notice.' Two of these little things (one a rather sizeable thing) have been discovered.

The first known publication from Richardson's pen is a long pamphlet entitled *The Apprentice's Vade Mecum: or, Young Man's Pocket-Companion,*

---

[41] *Anecdotes of Bowyer*, p. 306. In the context, a list of Richardson's writings, Nichols surely means that Richardson wrote the work but did not offer it for public sale: he is not purporting to list books Richardson printed. If he is right, it can hardly be *The Matrimonial Mirror* sold by J. Rivington in 1742, which Sale (*Bibliographical Record*, p. xii) believes may be Richardson's broadside, though he takes Nichols as meaning that Richardson merely printed the work of someone else. *The Matrimonial Mirror* is, however, a single sheet prominently advertised from 18 Dec. 1742 through 11 Jan. 1743 in the *Daily Gazetteer*, which Richardson was printing. According to the advertisement, *The Matrimonial Mirror* (no copy of which is known) laid down the duties of both wives and husbands in extracts from the Scriptures and the Book of Common Prayer and was meant as a proper wedding present from the clergyman or a later present by one spouse to the other to be 'always carried about them' or hung in the gentleman's closet or 'the Lady's Dressing-Room, next to the Glass'.

[42] *Gentleman's Magazine*, VI, 51.

which was issued from his press in 1733. It is based on a letter which Richardson had written some two years before to his nephew, Thomas Verren Richardson, the eldest son of his most prosperous brother, William.[43] He was baptized on 18 July 1717. On 1 August 1732, at the age of fifteen, Thomas Verren was apprenticed to his uncle Samuel upon payment of the (for the Richardson of that period) large fee of £40.[44] He did not live long to enjoy his uncle's guidance, dying on 8 November of the same year.

Samuel Richardson wants to make certain that his nephew, as apprentice, does not take advantage of their relationship: when one relation works for another, the two 'frequently disagree, by reason of greater expectations, on both sides, of allowance and consideration to be had for each other, than for mere strangers'. He therefore wants his rules set down clearly he hopes once and for all, 'for, you must know, I hate repetitions in such things as this, when a person of your age is supposed to be duly apprized of his duty'. Some of these rules have been mentioned in Chapter I.

Thomas Verren is not to take advantage of his relationship to the master in dealing with the journeymen or with his fellow apprentices. 'And let it be always remembered, that no man is to be ill used by you, if he happens to be poor or low in the world; for, how can you tell what your own fate may be?' 'If you see any bad example, learn to have a proper detestation of the action, without abusing the man that sets it'—vice 'deserves the pity of a person who has not a right to upbraid, and is not injured personally'. This statement, which, though not exactly the Sermon on the Mount, is a good deal higher than most people attain to, is a fair sample of the level of the morality which, from beginning to end, Richardson preached and, insofar as one can judge, attempted to practise. Thomas Verren has 'a kind of unpolished roughness', a want of 'sweetness and complaisance of temper', which he must learn to correct in order to avoid giving pain to others. ''Tis a barbarous temper, and a sign of a very ill nature, to take delight in shocking any one: and, on the contrary, it is the mark of an amiable and a beneficent temper, to say all the kind things one can, without flattery or playing the hypocrite,—and what never fails of procuring the love and esteem of every one; which, next to doing good to a deserving object who wants it, is one of the greatest pleasures of this life.' A reader who takes such remarks as mere commonplace, to be laughed at or ignored, will never have much liking for Richardson as a man. They are ideas regarded as typically middle-class, though readers

[43] This pamphlet is dated 1734 but is advertised as early as 15 Sept. 1733 in the *Weekly Miscellany*. It was discovered by Alan Dugald McKillop and described by him in 'Samuel Richardson's Advice to an Apprentice', *JEGP*, XLII (1943), 40–54. Richardson's letter to his nephew was published in the *Imperial Review*, II (1804), 609–16.

[44] 'Apprentices and Turn Overs', MS. in the archives of the Stationers' Company.

may notice certain similarities between them and those of a man of a very different social class, the Earl of Chesterfield. They are not original, certainly, but Richardson always regarded them as important and felt them deeply. Whatever conclusion one comes to as to the validity of his moralizing and its effect, good or bad, on his art, it is necessary to understand just what that morality was—perhaps not the less because it was on the whole the morality, at least professed, of a class which in Richardson's day was beginning to dominate the country which was beginning to dominate the world; certainly the more because it is a morality which intellectuals have rejected for so long now that they can hardly understand it. It will be noted that pleasing others, though important, is a lesser pleasure than helping others.

Richardson goes on to warn Thomas Verren against a tendency to covet books more for the sake of having than of reading them; against relying on his uncle's great love for his father—Samuel Richardson will not favour a 'naughty Kinsman'; against resenting it when his uncle kindly tells him of his faults; against, of course, idleness and idle chatter; against his too great heedlessness to instructions; and above all against neglecting his duty to God: religion will 'bring down a blessing upon all your honest endeavours: and if you hope to thrive and do well in the world, your due observations of this, whatever examples you, in this bad age, may see to the contrary, will make your hope reasonable and well grounded'. This may be thought of as the religion of a tradesman—God is good business; or, with a slight twist, one might say that Richardson loved virtue so much that he found it hard to deny it any reward, even that of cash payment. The same ambiguity of religious motivation arises in his later work—only once, in his greatest novel, did he create a virtue which, in his own eyes, was too lofty to be paid for by worldly happiness.

Part II of *The Apprentice's Vade Mecum* is a revised version of this letter, with the more personal remarks removed, and the general remarks often considerably expanded and given an even more earnest tone. There is a long passage against modern foppishness and a briefer warning against the opposite vice of slovenliness. There is a caution against sordid self-interest which is hardly calculated to interfere with business—you should not centre all views in self, though you should '*principally* pursue your *own Interest*, and prefer your *self* in all *lawful* Cases, to *every one* else', not, however, to the extent of being 'incapable of a generous Action, when it would be of little or no *Prejudice* to your self'. Such moderate unselfishness will serve to gain friends and to win 'the Name of a *generous* and *Gentleman-like* Man, Epithets in no sort incompatible with Trade and Business'. We shall see later that in practice Richardson was not always so cautious or moderate in his generosity as this passage might indicate; he is not the only person who has displayed a greater mind in action than in theory.

Typically, he warns against extravagance on the grounds that it not only keeps one from helping others but forces one to seek help; he was always proud of his independence and reluctant to ask or accept favours, and there is perhaps a bitter memory beneath his admonition that waste 'sinks you to the sad Necessity of being *oblig'd*!—Of being oblig'd, or, even, perhaps, of only *vainly* hoping to be *oblig'd*, to grudging and narrow Spirits, who are incapable of doing a graceful Good, who will both in their *Manner* and their *Words* sting you to the very Soul, if your Condition has not reduc'd you beneath a Sense of *Feeling*, with the Remembrance of your Misconduct'. His advice on friendship is also prudent: since a real friend will ask nothing to hurt his friend, if you find that one of your acquaintances shows a preference for himself over you, break with him, unless, with advice, you find that you can without danger step out of your way to save him from ruin. But a wise apprentice will 'generally converse with his *Betters*, and particularly have an Eye to the Acquaintance of such Persons, as may *promote* him in his Business when he begins for himself'. One senses civic clubs in the offing.

The work is prefaced by a dedication to the Chamberlain of London, stating that it aims to combat the 'degeneracy of the Times, and the Profaneness and Immorality, and even the open Infidelity that is every where propagated with Impunity' (a favourite theme throughout Richardson's work). It is aimed at apprentices because from them are derived the most numerous and useful members of the commonwealth. The praises of the middle class are often sung in this pamphlet. Richardson then goes on to give a detailed outline of what he is going to say—he was always fond of summaries and epitomes. Part III, on religion, was added at the request of a 'judicious Friend', to 'oppose the idle Cavils and impertinent Witticisms of the Scoffers of the Age, now so frequently . . . to be met with in every Conversation'. ''Tis certain that *Morality* is an indispensable Requisite of true Religion, and there can be none without it. But it would become the Pride and Ignorance of Pagans only, to magnify it, as the Whole of what is necessary.'

Part I is a commentary on the apprentice's indentures, with excursions against gaming, fornication, taverns, and playhouses. Richardson considers the theatre harmful to apprentices in a multitude of ways, and, as it then was, hardly better for anyone else. Among other things, the dramatists make fun of citizens, 'And this in a Kingdom which owes its Support, and the Figure it makes abroad, intirely to Trade; the Followers of which are infinitely of more Consequence, and deserve more to be incourag'd, than any other Degree or Rank of People in it'. But even aside from this, the theatre has sunk low indeed: 'A good Dramatick Writer, is a Character that this Age knows nothing of; and I would be glad to name the Person living who is fit to be made an Exception to this general Censure.' There is no reason to think that Richardson knew the comedies and satires which Henry Fielding had been writing for over five years and less reason to think that *Pasquin* or *Rape upon Rape* would have made him change his mind. Part III, directed against the Deists, supports no one church but emphasizes the necessity of Christian revelation.

We do not intend to summarize all of Richardson's works at this length, since we assume that no one who has not read Richardson's novels will waste his time reading about an author who can mean nothing to him. But *The Apprentice's Vade Mecum* is hard to come by; it is typical of the ethical system which provided the background against which Richardson wrote; and it is our first glimpse into Richardson's mind, none the less interesting because the ideas in that mind resemble the ideas in many other minds of the time. What a man shares with his class and age is of course important, and at least as important are his own variations on the common theme. We hope that the reader is prepared to believe that not all bourgeois Protestants are identical, any more than all ancient Stoics or medieval Catholics or modern Flower Children, and to look for what in Richardson was peculiarly Richardson's as well as for what belonged to the context. The *Vade Mecum* gives a good picture of the context.

The other pamphlet is a slighter effort. It is called *A Seasonable Examination of the Pleas and Pretensions of the Proprietors of, and Subscribers to, Play-Houses* and was published in April or May 1735.[45] It was written in support of a bill to limit the number of playhouses and to prevent their offences against piety and good manners. Its authorship is not so certain as that of *The Apprentice's Vade Mecum*, but there is a fair probability that he wrote it. Like Richardson's known views is its lament for the 'Depravity of Manners' of the age, its luxury and 'Taste for the lightest Amusements'. It twice cites *The Apprentice's Vade Mecum* ('a little Treatise, that perhaps has done some Good as to the Case in Hand'). It takes as low a view of the state of contemporary drama as did that work and comes out especially strongly for moral censorship of the stage, for prohibiting 'any prophane, obscene, or scurrilous Passage, or any Passage offensive to Piety and Good-manners'. It stresses the middle-class tradesman's point of view: all modern and most ancient plays have been 'calculated for Persons in Upper Life'; plays make the young person discontent by giving 'a Taste for a Station *beyond his own*'. Its style is clear and forceful, and it has the tone of sarcasm for which Richardson later showed a talent, as well as the kind of cogent and sensible rationalizing (granted, of course, the premises) which characterizes his later moralizing.

[45] This pamphlet was discovered by Alan Dugald McKillop and described by him in 'Richardson's Early Writings—Another Pamphlet', *JEGP*, LIII (1954), 72–5.

CHAPTER IV

SUCCESSFUL PRINTER AND EDITOR

1733–1739

ARLY in 1736, on 17 January, was composed one of Richardson's rare poetic efforts. As stewards to a proposed feast for the printers, William Bowyer, Junior, and Edward Cave had written two couplets of invitation, to which Samuel Richardson responded with a 'humorous' answer which was judged worthy of publication in Cave's *Gentleman's Magazine*:

> To steward *St John*, steward *St John's Gate*,
> Who meet to sup on *monday* night at eight.
> Dear sons of *Phœbus*, darlings of the nine,
> Henceforth, thro' you, how will the *printers* shine,
> Who ne'er, without the muse, shall meet to sup or dine!
> Blessings, say I, attend your rhyming pen,
> No *king* John's, sure, e'er equal'd *saint* John's men!
>   But, tell me, friends, nor blush, nor be afraid
> To own the truth—had you no *third* man's aid?
> Speak out, like men—to make the verse run sweeter,
> Did not some mild-beer Bellman tag the metre?
> If so, I pray, invite the honest fellow,
> Let him partake the *praise*, and make him mellow.
> *Perpetual stewards*, may you voted be;
> No less such verse deserves—*perpetual poet* he!
>   For me, I'm much concern'd I cannot meet
> 'At salutation-tavern, *Newgate-street*.'
> Your notice, like your verse (so sweet and short!)
> If longer, I'd sincerely thank'd you for't.
> Howe'er, receive my wishes, sons of verse!
> May every man who meets, your praise rehearse!
> May *mirth*, as *plenty*, crown your chearful board,
> And ev'ry one part *happy*—as a lord!
> That when at home, (by such sweet verses fir'd)
> Your families may think you all inspir'd!
>   So wishes he, who, pre-ingag'd, can't know.
>   The pleasures that wou'd from your meeting flow.

> *S. R.*

The editor of the *Gentleman's Magazine*, judging that 'so poetical and so speedy an Answer' could have been composed only with the aid of the Muses, added a poem of praise:

> Their *Bellman*, hence, shall emulation fire,
> To raise, with grateful thanks, the metre higher,
> 'To him, whose Genius makes one printer shine,
> '*Rich*——*son* of *Phœbus*, darling, of the Nine.[']

Cave, once the stream of wit had begun to flow, responded with a longish series of Hudibrastic couplets:

> Verse can, they say, bring down the moon,
> Exalted in her midnight noon.
> Oh! could it gain your rosy face,
> How the full orb the board would grace,
> When flush'd with wine, and plump with praise!

Another anonymous bard also answered.[1] This single glimpse of Richardson in a convivial mood will have to stand for his relations with his fellow craftsmen, which were surely more intimate than available evidence indicates.

In the 1730s a new branch of Richardson's business was increasingly important, a branch which he had begun early in 1733, the printing of bills, orders, and occasional reports for the House of Commons. It must have been his government contracts which made him, as he says, 'independent of Booksellers'.[2] The first item was a 'Bill to explain ye Laws relating to ye repairing ye Highways', printed on 16 February 1733. From then on to the end of his life Richardson continued to print from four to twenty-six bills and other items a year. During the 1730s he printed from five to eight bills a year, earning amounts which varied from £81 17s. 6d. for a two-year period ending 14 September 1739 up to £171 13s. for a little over a year ending 10 August 1737. Though the number of bills printed increased in the 1740s and 1750s, Richardson rarely earned over £200 a year from this government contract; his best period was the year and a half ending 6 January 1747, when he printed twenty-one bills and made almost £600, but this was exceptional—in his second best year he made only a little over £300.[3] Clearly these sums were

---

[1] *Gentleman's Magazine*, VI (1736), 51; Nichols, *Anecdotes of Bowyer*, pp. 89-90, 160, and *Literary Anecdotes*, II, 74-9.

[2] His daughters thought so, since the biography in the *Universal Magazine*, LXXVIII, 19, says that 'this parliamentary branch of his business enabled Mr. Richardson to be more independent of the booksellers than printers commonly are'.

[3] The miscellaneous warrants of the Treasury preserve the records of payments made to Richardson for his work from 4 Feb. 1734 to 13 Apr. 1761 (P.R.O. T. 53/37-47). The sums are given by Sale, *Master Printer*, pp. 368-9. The receipt for 23 Jan. 1750 is printed by I. G. Philip in *William Blackstone and the Reform of the Oxford University Press in the Eighteenth Century* (Oxford, 1957), pp. 127-8; the order for the first payment with Richardson's receipt is in the Henry E. Huntington Library.

important for him, especially perhaps in the first years, but they were hardly as important in making him independent as his contract in 1742 to print the *Journals* of the House of Commons.

The statement that Richardson got the latter contract through the support of the Speaker of the House, Arthur Onslow, goes back, like so much other information about Richardson, to John Nichols and was accepted by Richardson's daughters.[4] Onslow may also have helped him get the contract for the bills, though Nicholas Hardinge, Clerk of the House, was probably the person chiefly responsible.[5] Perhaps it was Richardson's printing of the bills that first brought him in contact with the Speaker, of whom he later became a fairly close friend. Edward Young's curate at Welwyn, John Jones, reported that Onslow's esteem for Richardson was so great that he wanted to find him a station at Court, which Richardson refused to accept.[6] By 1750 there is ample evidence of Richardson's connection with Onslow, who is often mentioned in Richardson's correspondence with their mutual friend Thomas Edwards. The Speaker saw *Clarissa* sheet by sheet as it came from the press.[7] He and Richardson visited Edward Young together, and Richardson visited Onslow at Ember Court, in Surrey,[8] where, according to Horace Walpole, he might have admired 'a spacious wood consisting of forty fair forest trees' and, if he came on Sunday when the mill was not working, 'a noble river'.[9] Early in 1751 Onslow, writing to Thomas Edwards that he is tired of the press of business, adds that he sometimes sees Richardson, 'seldomer than I wish, and He always finds me in a hurry. We talk however of you, tho' by snatches, and endeavour to make a faint resemblance of the calm evenings you and He made happy to me.'[10] In the years following, such visits were repeated, and Onslow called on Richardson at his new house in Parson's Green.[11] All of Richardson's references to Onslow are admiring; he regrets, for instance, that '*Short Snatches* of Time indeed! are those I have had with this *truly* Great, because *Good* Man'.[12] Onslow owned a portrait of Richardson, and he and his son George received mourning rings in Richardson's will. Though their association cannot perhaps be described as close friendship, it was evidently a very cordial acquaintance, and his relations with this able and influential man should be remembered

---

[4] *Anecdotes of Bowyer*, p. 156; *Literary Anecdotes*, IV, 580; *Universal Magazine*, LXXVIII, 19.

[5] In a petition written immediately after Richardson's death asking that the contract for printing the Journals of the House be awarded to him, William Bowyer, Jr., states that Richardson obtained his contract 'by the interest of the late Nicholas Hardinge' (Nichols, *Literary Anecdotes*, II, 353–4).

[6] *Gentleman's Magazine*, LIII, 924.   [7] Edwards to R, 2 Dec. 1748.

[8] Young to R, 16 Oct. 1750; R to Young, 2 Jan. 1751.

[9] *Correspondence*, XXX (1961), 292n.

[10] 4 Feb., original in the Folger Shakespeare Library.

[11] R to Sarah Wescomb, 1 Sept. 1752; R to Edwards, 26 Nov. 1754.

[12] R to Edwards, 13 Feb. 1751.

by those who think of Richardson as surrounded by gushing females.

During the 1730s Richardson was concerned in at least two periodicals and one newspaper other than the *Daily Journal*. He printed the *Weekly Miscellany*, edited by the clergyman William Webster (a contestant in the braying match in *The Dunciad*), from its inception on 16 December 1732 through 1736. The *Miscellany* was always a financial liability to Webster— he wrote late in 1740 or early in 1741 to Dr. Zachary Grey that 'before the paper could be established, it brought me in debt to my printer 140*l*. ninety of which is still unpaid'.[13] In the last issue, 27 June 1741, he gave a fuller account: he had begun by engaging several booksellers as pro- prietors in the paper, but 'partly thro' Negligence and Ill-Management, and partly thro' the Corruption of the Age, the Design not answering their Expectations, they left me and the Paper to shift for our selves.—I then went upon my *own single Bottom*, 'till upon making up Accompts with my Printer, I found myself considerably in his Debt. I was still unwilling that the Design should sink, and agreed with another Printer, who was more at leisure vigorously to pursue the Interest of it; by which agreement *he* was to be entitled to the whole Profits arising from the Sale of the Paper, (if he could make any,) and *I* to furnish him with the Letter, *gratis*.' That the printer to whom Webster thus twice acknowledged his debt was Samuel Richardson is clear from Webster's *A Plain Narrative*, a statement of his own case, printed in 1758. After praising the generosity of one of his gentleman parishioners at Thundridge and Ware, of which he became vicar in 1740, he proceeds: 'I hope, this Gentleman, great and good as he is, will excuse me, if I distinguish another Person, not the less honourable for not being a *Gentleman*, who is absolutely the greatest Genius, the best, and the most amiable Man, that I know in the World; I mean, Mr. *Richard- son*, the Printer. When I came to *Ware*, I was £90 in his Debt, though I had clear'd off regularly, by quarterly Payments, £50, and never could save any Thing out of my Income ever since the Change of my Livings, towards getting out of Debt. As soon as I was possess'd of *Ware*, or, rather, as soon as *Ware* was possessed of *me*, he sent me a kind Letter, told me, that any Sum of Money that I wanted was at my Service; and when he saw that I liv'd as *frugally* as possible, he forgave me the whole Debt.'[14]

---

[13] Nichols, *Anecdotes of Bowyer*, pp. 543-4. In reprinting this letter in *Literary Anecdotes*, V, 164-5, Nichols inserted '[Mr. Richardson]' after 'printer'.

[14] P. ii. See also Webster's printed address to the Bishops (in the Bodleian Library), p. 66. If the coincidence of the sums mentioned is not enough to prove that Richardson was the first printer of the periodical, it is supported by the facts that letters and verses submitted by Aaron Hill to the *Miscellany* and printed in it in 1733 are now among Richardson's papers in the Victoria and Albert Museum (FM, XVI, 2, fos. 76-82); that although the *Miscellany* has comparatively few advertisements, it has, in its first four years, a good many of books which Richardson is known to have printed; and that the early colophons of the paper read 'Printed for J. Roberts', whereas from 28 Jan. 1737 they read 'Printed by C. Jephson . . . and Sold by

Webster says in the last issue that the *Weekly Miscellany* brought him only drudgery, abuse, and slights. Though Webster's corrupt age was not so averse to religious writing as later corrupt ages have been, it evidently found the *Miscellany* heavy going. It was published under the fictitious name of Richard Hooker, and soon became known as 'Old Mother Hooker's *Journal*'.[15] The first issue announces that it is going to discuss religion, morality, and government, defending in general both the establishment and the constitution, as well as comment on literature. But religion decidedly predominates.

In a typical issue (13 October 1733) the first column and part of the second are devoted to a letter from Philalethes denouncing a pamphlet by Thomas Chubb, which purports to prove that reason is a sufficient guide in religion: Mr. Chubb 'tends evidently to propagate Infidelity' and is 'a Flatterer of the human Pride'. Then follow the foreign literary articles: reviews of a life of Mahomet, published at Amsterdam (praised for opposing the Count de Boulainvilliers' too favourable life of the Prophet); of a book published in Leyden by a T. H. Van den Honert against the notion that it is not necessary to choose a particular communion; of a history of the Popes published at The Hague. Another letter denounces Budgell's compliments to Dr. Tindal, 'a publick Enemy of our BLESSED REDEEMER'. There follow verses, 'Happy's the Man, who walks before the Lord.' The news appears in a longish and rambling article, further into the periodical than in most newspapers: What is this confused situation in Poland? Will the Emperor find help against the French (who were not reduced enough after the last war)? What will Russia do? and Prussia? There is trouble with the Moors over detaining ships; Parliament has been prorogued till 15 November; Mr. Gatley, apothecary, has had a fire; there is no certainty about the whereabouts of the Spanish Flota. Six persons have been sentenced to death for robbery or coining, and Mr. Bond will be burnt in the hand for having two wives. Several preferments and deaths are noticed. Advertisements announce Dr. Cheyne's *The English Malady* and the latest issues of the *London Magazine* and the *Gentleman's Magazine*, as well as 'a Serious and Useful Scheme, to make an Hospital for Incurables'. James Royston sells old Mountain wine, from Malaga, at £14 a hogshead. Dr. Bateman's Pectoral Drops have not only effected great and wonderful cures of gout, rheumatism, jaundice, flux, stone,

J. Roberts'. Shortly before this date, on 18 Dec. 1736, a new fount and a new flower appear in the periodical. Among various persons who are listed in the early issues as accepting advertisements and letters is J[oseph] Chrichley, one of the apprentices whom Richardson had taken over from the Leake family. From 24 Feb. 1738 the colophon reads 'Printed and Sold by H. WOODFALL'. Woodfall must be the printer mentioned in Webster's letter to Grey, though the first arrangement to turn over the profits may have been made with Jephson. The *Gentleman's Magazine* for Aug. 1740 (X, 413) reports Webster's collation to the vicarages of Thundridge and Ware.

[15] Nichols, *Anecdotes of Bowyer*, p. 540.

gravel, asthma, and colic, but have 'almost incredible effects' on colds, agues, fevers, and those epidemic evils which appear in spring and fall: John Scott, a wine cooper of Cambridge, has found more ease from them than from any medicine he ever took and they have gained an unrivalled character in houses of the best rank and quality, even in that of His Majesty when Prince of Wales.

In one of its early issues (1 December 1733) the *Weekly Miscellany* printed a recommendation (perhaps the only one ever made except by its author) of *The Apprentice's Vade Mecum*. Its next issue, a week later, continued with an extract from Richardson's pamphlet, against playhouses. Certainly Richardson's remarks on Deism must have pleased Webster, even if he was not the 'judicious Friend' who induced him to write them. Richardson was always open to suggestion from friends more learned than he (on any question except how to write his novels), and printing the *Miscellany* could easily have made him conscious of the Deists —Webster strongly felt any threat to orthodoxy, announcing, for instance, on 12 July 1735, that 'the World has lately been alarmed with a new Treatise concerning the *Nature and End of the Sacrament of the Lord's Supper*'.

Several years after Richardson ceased to print it, the *Miscellany* published the first prominent notice of *Pamela*, even before the book came out: a letter from an anonymous friend (probably Webster himself) who, having read the novel in manuscript, praises it in glowing terms, especially for its morality, and urges its author to publish it. Two other articles promoting the novel appeared after publication.[16] Richardson did not lose touch with Webster when the latter gave up his thankless effort to make journalism serve religion. Webster admired *Sir Charles Grandison* and in 1754 was still in communication with Richardson.[17]

Another periodical of the 1730s was printed for a closer friend, probably Richardson's only very close literary friend until after the publication of *Pamela*, Aaron Hill. We have already mentioned the probability that Richardson printed Hill's earlier periodical, the *Plain Dealer*. The *Prompter* with Hill and William Popple[18] as its main contributors, began to appear on 12 November 1734 as a biweekly periodical essay journal. Its first number states that its title is meant to indicate a modest, humble adviser, who will give the word impartially to all performers (that is classes of

[16] The letter in the issue for 11 Oct. 1740 was later inserted in the first edition of *Pamela*. On 13 Dec. 1740 the *Miscellany* published the Editor's Preface to *Pamela*, setting forth its purpose and its qualities, and on 28 Feb. 1741 a letter from Aaron Hill printed in the second edition as well as Hill's poem on *Pamela*.

[17] Webster to R, 26 Nov. 1753. Webster was able to hint to Mark Hildesley that Richardson was hurt at Hildesley's failure to answer a letter (R to Hildesley, 13 July 1754).

[18] Richardson owned a share in Popple's play *The Double Deceit*. See 'Entries of Copies 1710-46', MS. in the archives of the Stationers' Company, under date 26 Feb. 1736.

society). It set out to deal in a light tone with all sorts of social foibles, but its title soon acquired a more specific meaning as it came to deal more and more with the stage, urging the power of good plays to reform and correct the age. It satirized absurdity, buffoonery, and acting to please the mob rather than to interpret the character—the combined avarice, ignorance, and want of talent of managers, actors, and authors have turned what should be a school of virtue into a school of vice. There are, however, other literary and non-literary subjects—praise of Thomson's *Liberty*, a defence of rhyme against blank verse, and several anti-slavery remarks. The public was treated to three instalments of Hill's epic *Gideon*.[19] One issue by Popple was devoted to a spirited defence of the notorious 'Philosopher's Prayer',[20] which had so scandalized the *Weekly Miscellany*. The *Prompter* reprints the prayer, comments on it in detail, and commends it warmly—it is 'full (examined impartially) of *noble Sentiments of the Deity* and the *profoundest Devotion* in the *Supplicator*'. Towards the end the number of letters published increases until they almost crowd out the essay. The periodical expired in less than two years, on 2 July 1736.[21]

Hill was trying to renew his connection with the stage at this period and was beginning the series of adaptations from Voltaire (*Zara*, *Alzira*, *Merope*) which were perhaps his most successful literary efforts, though hardly as successful as he thought they deserved to be. Soon afterwards, in 1738, he retired with his classical daughters, Urania, Astræa, and Minerva, to Plaistow in Essex, the scene of the last of his unsuccessful

[19] 3 June, 1 Aug., 10 Oct. 1735.

[20] 17 Oct. 1735. The issue is signed 'P.'; Popple's copy in the Bodleian Library has corrections in his hand.

[21] Richardson was by this time a friend and correspondent of Hill, and it is likely that he printed his journal. The clearest evidence that he did so is a letter from an A. B. (identified by Richardson as Eustace Budgell) concerning the publication of the letter about Tindal's 'Philosopher's Prayer' (8 Feb. 1736, B.M. Add. MS. 37,232, fos. 137–8). Richardson forwarded this letter (probably to Hill) with the notation 'You have all ye Letters that came to my Hand'. The implication is that letters for the *Prompter* were sent to Richardson. Later, on 6 Mar., Hill wrote Richardson a formal letter protesting that the *Grub-street Journal* misrepresents Hill as a defender of the 'Philosopher's Prayer' and a disliker of James Miller's *The Man of Taste*: 'As you know, that I have nothing to answer for, on either of these Two Heads, having never seen any of those Papers, till I read them in the published Prompters, I shou'd take it as a Favour, if you wou'd, immediately, find means to undeceive the Gentlemen concern'd.' On 30 June 1736 he sent Richardson the manuscript for the final number of the *Prompter*. We agree with Sale that this letter and the two letters concerning Budgell are a clear enough indication that Richardson printed the paper. We see no sign, however, that 'Richardson was assisting in outlining the kind of policy that the paper should take' (*Master Printer*, p. 71). Hill's later remark to Richardson, referring to the often-discussed but never-realized possibility of printing the *Prompters* in volume form and calling them '*your* Prompters (for I claim no Right in Any of 'em)', does not mean, as Sale says, 'that Richardson had a greater interest in this periodical than that of printer'. Richardson noted on this letter 'Copy Right' (10 July 1746). Eight years earlier Hill had told Richardson that the time and manner of printing the *Prompters* in volume form was to be decided by Richardson 'and every right, choice, and decision concerning them, I resign and submit wholly to yourself, both now and for ever hereafter' (6 July)—one of many such copyrights.

projects, an effort to produce a good English wine (even Richardson, who praised almost everything which came from Hill, was unable to wax very enthusiastic about the wine). By the late thirties his letters to Richardson show a considerable intimacy. Richardson was constantly doing favours for him, sending him books, inserting advertisements for him in newspapers, and above all encouraging him to run up a large printing bill; in return he was eager to turn over the copyrights of his works to Richardson and (probably a more acceptable and certainly at least as valuable a reward) was preparing to praise Richardson's works in the highest terms.

Hill's letters to Richardson in the last half of the thirties are among the earliest direct glimpses we have of the latter's life. There are a few letters to and from other correspondents in the same lustrum, dealing with practical matters, but the first extant letter from Richardson which can be described as personal is the one he wrote to Hill in late 1740 sending him a copy of *Pamela*.

The letters to Richardson of another correspondent of the thirties, Dr. George Cheyne, have been preserved—the first definitely dated item of Richardson's correspondence is Cheyne's letter of 21 December 1734— and are fairly constant until his death in 1743.[22]

Cheyne was over sixty when his connection with Richardson began, and was a well-known physician, settled at Bath, where he knew Richardson's brother-in-law James Leake. He had written several books arguing for his original medical theories, and in 1733 Richardson printed his *English Malady*, stressing the importance of diet (exclusively vegetable if necessary—Beau Nash 'would swear, that his design was to send half the world grazing like *Nebuchadnezzar*'),[23] of abstention from excessive alcohol, and of moderate exercise, warning against the prevalence of nervous disorders, and outlining Cheyne's own cure of himself by his own method (he had once been very fat): 'My Case was at first worse I think than any One's I think I ever read of or saw a putrified overgrown Body from Luxury and perpetual Laziness, scorbutical all over, a regular St. Anthony's Fire every Two Months, regularly the Gout all over Six Months of the Year, perpetual Reaching, Anxiety, Giddiness, Fitts and Startings. . . . Vomits were my only Relief which I continued for at least 8 or 9 Years, till of late I found out the Thumb Vomits which now the lightness of my Diet makes easy and sufficient.'[24] In 1739 Pope wrote to

[22] For Cheyne and his correspondence with Richardson, see Thomas McCrae, 'George Cheyne, an Old London and Bath Physician', *Johns Hopkins Hospital Bulletin*, XV (Mar. 1904), 1–29; Rebecca Warner, ed., *Original Letters* (London, 1817); Charles F. Mullett, ed., *The Letters of Dr. George Cheyne to Samuel Richardson 1733–1743* (Columbia, Missouri, 1943).

[23] Oliver Goldsmith, *The Life of Richard Nash* in *Collected Works*, ed. Arthur Friedman (Oxford, 1966), III, 364.

[24] To R, 23 Dec. 1741.

Lyttelton from Bath that the only object which there obliged him to smile was Dr. Cheyne, 'who is yet so very a child in true Simplicity of Heart, that I love him; as He loves Don Quixote, for the Most Moral & Reasoning Madman in the world. . . . He is, in the Scripture language, an *Israelite in whom there is no Guile*, or in Shakespear's, *as foolish a good kind of Christian Creature* as one shall meet with.'[25] From 1733 on, Richardson printed all of Cheyne's works, a demanding task: Cheyne wanted Richardson to correct the proofs himself, was particular about format and errata, made many alterations in the proofsheets, and was impatient of delays. He also undertook on occasion to be a mediator between Cheyne and his publishers, a labour involving much tact, since Cheyne was hot-headed and free in expressing his dislikes and never thought that his booksellers were doing him justice. The work which he regarded as his greatest, published in two parts as *An Essay on Regimen* (1740) and *The Natural Method of Cureing* (1742), outlining in final form his theories physical and psychological, by no means met with the reception he felt it deserved. In his letters Cheyne sounds like an improbable comic character in a Smollett novel, violent, hasty, kindly, and deeply religious, in a peculiar way of his own, as he was everything.

Aside from printing and booksellers, the correspondence concerns mainly Richardson's health. Cheyne early deplored Richardson's tendency 'to Rotundity and Liquor. Fatness is but another word for a Dropsy of Flesh which a little Time will melt into Snow-water.' He constantly warned Richardson about his diet, early urging him to abstain from animal food in warm weather and from 'fermented Liquors but on Occasitions of Gallantry Gaiety or Lowness'—Richardson was unlikely to be intemperate on at least the two first excuses. One of Cheyne's favourite remedies was a good puke: 'Your short Neck is rather an Argumt. for a Vomit now and then than against it for no long necked Animal can vomit, & Vomits are the best Preservative from Apoplexies after little Phlebotomies.' He also recommended cold baths, exercise, and chewing rhubarb, and 'a Tea Spoonful or two of the Tincture of Soot and Assa Fœtida made on Peony Water in a cold Infusion' drunk in peppermint water to make Richardson 'break Wind plentifully'. He urged the virtues of a new machine called a chamber horse—some chamber horses had springs, but the one Cheyne describes is a chair set on a long board, which must have acted like a joggling board, supported at both ends and limber in the middle, with hoops to brace the arms and a footstool to support the feet, on which Richardson was to ride while reading or dictating.[26] Richardson used this machine,[27] and it is pleasant to imagine him dropping

[25] *Correspondence*, ed. George Sherburn (Oxford, 1956), IV, 208.
[26] [*c*. Sept. 1738]; 4 Sept. 1737; 26 Oct., 1 July 1739; 20 Apr. 1740; [May 1740?].
[27] R to Lady Bradshaigh, 30 May 1754; Barbauld, I, clxxx.

Pamela's advice to her little family from this gently bouncing perch, perhaps balanced by Mrs. Richardson, since the chamber horse 'rides double better than single'.

Late in 1741 Cheyne finally induced Richardson to adopt his method of cure as the only way of preserving his life amid the sedentary but busy world of Salisbury Court: 'If indeed your Situation in Life could enable you to give up Business intirely to live in the Country and follow a Post-Boy's Life a Horse-back with a good deal of Evacuation and Apothecary's Poison perhaps you might be enabled to live on Dog's Meat some Years longer.' Until his death about sixteen months later Cheyne exhorted Richardson constantly to stick to it in spite of the very moderate success it seemed to be having ('the weaker you are the higher will be your Recovery like the Recoil of a Tennis Ball') and reproached him for his shrinking from suffering, his love of meat (Richardson is 'one of the most staunch Epicures I ever knew'), his aversion to exercise (though on one occasion, at least, Richardson did 'walk from Hammersmith to London down to Salisbury Square on a Stretch'), his refusal to abandon completely other physicians who worked with drugs and not Nature's own way ('for God's Sake have done with your dear Doctors and Apothecaries'), and his low spirits—Richardson is a 'Hyp' who increases his physical disorders with worrying and badly needs a hobbyhorse to occupy his mind.[28] Cheyne refused to accept payment for all this advice, though Richardson, who hated to feel that he was in debt, urged him, printed a few small pieces without charge, and sent him the *Weekly Miscellany* and presents of food (not always successfully: one lot of oysters was 'but absolutely stinking Garbidge'). When Richardson insisted on his debt, Cheyne, to ease his 'hyppish honest grateful Heart', suggested he might send bound copies of all of Law's works.[29]

Early in 1736 Richardson moved across the square, to a larger house on the west side of Salisbury Court, within sight of his first. This house he occupied for almost twenty years, during which he wrote his three novels. It was described by Lætitia Pilkington (whose own poverty might make her exaggerate) as 'of a very grand outward Appearance'. But it still continued to house part of Richardson's business. He gave up the first two houses on Blue Ball Court when he moved but kept the third until 1740, and the year after that he rented two small houses on Hanging Sword Alley, immediately back of his dwelling, probably as warehouses.

He must have rented his first week-end house in the country about this time. Aaron Hill, in letters of 5 July and 19 July 1736, refers to Richardson's residence at Corney House and to 'That friendly & agreeable Freedom wherein you divide & enjoy a Retreat, that carries Temptation, even

---

[28] 23 Dec., 30 Dec. 1741; 26 Apr., Feb., 5 Sept., 2 May 1742.
[29] 9 Aug. 1735; 13 Jan. 1736; 26 Apr. 1742.

in Description', hoping that it will further Richardson's health as well as pleasure, but fearing that he will 'want *Leisure*, to reap That rural Advantage, to ye full Degree requisite for the Change yt is wish'd, on your Spirits'. A letter of Richardson's in October 1736 is dated from Chiswick,[30] and there were in Chiswick some 'tenements' called Corney Houses, and a piece of land called Corney Close, adjoining the old seat of the Russell family and probably in the seventeenth century a part of the Russell estate—in 1745 they were purchased by the Honourable Peregrine Widdrington, then the proprietor of the Russell mansion, which itself was in the late eighteenth century called Corney House.[31] There can be little doubt that Richardson's first country house was one of these 'tenements'.

Between March and September 1738 Richardson first rented the country house which he was to occupy during the whole of his writing career. It was located in Fulham, then a village on the outskirts of London, on North End Road. Richardson generally calls it North End. There were two houses close together, which from the road looked like one house. They had been built in 1714 by John Smith, a former Master of the Armourers' Company, and inherited by Smith's cousin Samuel Vanderplank, who occupied one of the houses and rented the other, first to a Lady Ranelagh, then to a Mr. Sherrard, and finally to Richardson. The house which Richardson rented was of brown brick and had three floors, with three large rooms besides closets on each floor, and a cellar. It had spacious gardens, in them a grotto.[32] Richardson often refers to North End, was fond of inviting friends to visit there, spent as much time as he could spare from his business there, and seems to have appreciated his country retreat like a true city man.

Meanwhile Richardson had begun the last newspaper which he is known to have printed, the *Daily Gazetteer*.[33] He probably printed it from

[30] To Robert Dodsley?, 10 Oct.

[31] Thomas Faulkner, *The History of Brentford, Ealing, & Chiswick* (London, 1845), pp. 368-70; Daniel Lysons, *Environs of London* (London, 1795), II, 196. The rate books for Chiswick have a gap covering the 1730s.

[32] Poor Rates for 1713-39, MS. in the Fulham Public Library; W. A. Eden and Marie P. O. Draper, 'The Grange, Fulham, and Its Neighbourhood, 1713-1957', *Transactions of the Ancient Monuments Society*, N.S. VI (1958), 91-110; F. E. Hansford and G. A. C. Evans, *The Story of the Grange* (London, 1953); Charles James Fèret, *Fulham Old and New* (London, 1900), II, 289-96; 'Extracts from the Court Rolls of the Manor of Fulham' (Charles James Fèret's typescript in the Fulham Public Library), II, 592-3, 613-14.

[33] Nichols, in *Anecdotes of Bowyer*, p. 156, first connected this newspaper with Richardson, later adding in *Literary Anecdotes*, IV, 580, that Richardson printed it in 1738—probably, as Sale suggests in *Master Printer*, p. 66, because he saw a reference to it in a letter to Richardson from Aaron Hill of that year. Later letters from Hill make it clear that Richardson continued to print the newspaper until 1746; Sale's conjecture (ibid., pp. 67-8) that he printed it from 1735 rests on the evidence of advertisements—*The Apprentice's Vade Mecum* is announced (3 July 1735), persons finding a lost banknote are urged to bring it to Samuel Richardson (9 Apr., 13 Apr., 15 Apr. 1736), catalogues for sales may be obtained from William Richardson of Tower Hill (7 June and 9 June, 11 June, 24 June, 26 June, 28 June, 29 June 1736—these

its inception in 1735 and was certainly connected with it by 6 July 1738, when Aaron Hill wrote thanking him for a *Gazetteer* and expressing his pleasure in the fact that Richardson, by obtaining some 'variation of subject', had at least mitigated the purely political character of the newspaper. 'I will now and then send a paper which shall flatter no side, misrepresent no intention, nor disoblige any person; and yet may, possibly, even on politic subjects, be acceptable enough in either of the two which you, and Messrs. Peel, &c. are concerned in the success of.' This letter makes it evident that Richardson was 'concerned in the success of' the *Gazetteer* as well as of some other paper, but there is too little light on Richardson's activities at this period to allow speculation on what his other ventures may have been. The wording implies that Richardson did more than merely print the paper, that he even influenced its policy by making its contents less exclusively political. In a letter to the Bath General Hospital, on 6 February 1739, Richardson states that he has inserted an advertisement for the hospital in last Saturday's *Gazetteer* 'because of the Influence I have there'. Since he also discusses his negotiations with three other papers about the cost of inserting the advertisement in them but does not mention inserting it in another paper of his own, there is a probability that if Hill was right about Richardson's association with a second paper in July 1738 he had given it up in the interim.

On 28 June 1735 the *Daily Courant* announced the forthcoming *Gazetteer* as a union of itself, the *London Journal*, and the *Free Briton*, three defenders of the Walpole government. According to the hostile testimony of James Ralph, the Walpole government in 1735 decided to unite the talents of various writers for government organs in one paper. 'This mighty Performance came out under the Name of the *Daily Gazetteer*, and was continued, at so small a Price as four or five thousand Pounds a Year, for writing, printing, and circulating, to the End of the late Administration' (February 1742). Among its main writers at first were James Pitt (who signed himself 'Fr. Osborne') and William Arnall ('Francis Walsingham' —who almost wins Pope's diving contest in Fleetditch). After Pitt had deserted and Arnall had died, Ralph Courteville ('R. Freeman') 'seems to have been the sole Director', though many doubted his ability to write even such a paper as the *Gazetteer*.[34] According to the *Craftsman*, the

two sales are also advertised in other papers), a lost gold-headed cane may be returned to William Richardson (19 Nov. 1737); various works Richardson is known to have printed are advertised, though whether 'with greater frequency and prominence' than in other newspapers, as Sale believes (ibid., p. 367n), can only be determined by an exhaustive comparison—there are a great many book advertisements of all sorts in the *Gazetteer*, and none of Richardson's before 1738 is so striking as the long series (a round hundred between 25 Mar. 1740 and 30 Dec. 1741) announcing hopefully that the unsaleable *Negotiations of Sir Thomas Roe* is this day published.

[34] *A Critical History of the Administration of Sir Robert Walpole* (London, 1743), pp. 517–19, 346.

various writers hated one another and had to be forced to work together.[35]

Ralph further reports that over £50,000 were spent by the government during ten years on its various journalistic defenders, almost £11,000 of which went to Arnall. This sum evidently did not include the *Gazetteer*, which is not mentioned in the table printed by the parliamentary committee investigating Walpole's expenses, which otherwise gives the same figures as Ralph.[36] The Treasury records show that between 31 October 1735 and 8 March 1737 John Walthoe received £5,314 6s. 8d. from the government for copies of the *Gazetteer* sent by post to the country.[37] Perhaps he and the other proprietors, including Richardson, paid the writers, so that the government was saved additional expense beyond its sizeable indirect support. A few years later Ralph reported that this fruitful source of income for writers had been cut off, since ministers were grown too prudent to offer pleas they knew would not be admitted at the bar of prejudice and, when forced to do so, took the first person at hand in a public office or had recourse to a college.[38]

That the *Daily Gazetteer* is to be primarily a political newspaper is made clear in its first issue (30 June 1735), in an introduction signed by 'Walsingham'. The new journal is the result of an 'amicable Agreement' between several authors who, having long been working for the same cause, are resolved to unite in the same paper. They will oppose faction but will defend the Constitution and His Majesty, 'to vindicate Publick Authority from the rude Insults of base and abusive Pens'. A great deal of the space was devoted to articles answering attacks on the government by *Common Sense* and the *Craftsman*, especially by the latter journal's 'Caleb d'Anvers'. Walpole's policy was zealously defended and even his person was at times enthusiastically praised—his illness and recovery in 1738 called forth a series of effusive verses. Some effort was made to vary politics with other subjects—'Freeman', for instance, devoted leading articles to praise of Sir William Temple and to considerations on suicide. But even literary subjects were not always free of political implications. When 'a very great Writer' is censured for the praise which, in his *Essay on Man* and his *First Epistle of the First Book of Horace*, he lavishes on his 'Guide, Philosopher, and Friend', a well-known traitor and supporter of tyranny as well as of all public and private wickedness, the moral indignation against Bolingbroke must have been coloured by his opposition to the Whig administration.[39] Typical is the leading article by 'Osborne' on

[35] 2 Aug. 1735.

[36] *A Further Report from the Committee of Secrecy, Appointed to Enquire into the Conduct of Robert, Earl of Orford* (London, 1742), p. 29 and Appendix 13.

[37] *Calendar of Treasury Books and Papers* (London, 1900), pp. 55, 159, 167, 184, 193, 300.

[38] *The Case of Authors by Profession or Trade* (London, 1758), p. 20.

[39] 16 Sept., 25 Sept., 10 Oct., 28 Oct., 7 Nov. 1738 (see also the editorials of 15 Nov. 1738 and 29 Jan. 1739); 21 Sept., 17 Nov. 1738; 27 Mar. 1738.

26 July 1735, one of a series defending the modern Constitution against the invidious comparisons made between it and the Old British Constitution by the *Gazetteer*'s great enemy, the *Craftsman*: 'Osborne' lauds 'the *Progress of Liberty*, till it happily arrived at its Journey's End by the *Revolution*; or at least, approached so near, that it may take its Rest; and then travel on, by easy Stages, without *Labour* or *Anxiety*, till it reaches the *Consummation* of all its Wishes'.

After such a leading article, the journal generally prints another short article or so and then a series of the usual brief foreign news items just arrived with the various mails and of such English news as shipping, court events (the Duke of Cumberland 'rode a Fox Hunting on Banstead Downs' last Saturday), appointments, prices of bread, and bankruptcies. Finally there is a large number of advertisements, which gradually increases as the leading articles become less prominent: for the most part books, but also auction sales and sales of property, lost articles and missing persons, and such medicines as a 'Specifick Electuary' against leprosy, 'Superlative ENLIVENING DROPS' which are an infallible cure for barrenness in women and impotency in men, Dr. Newman's Famous Anti-Venereal Pill, a pleasant Electuary against hæmorrhoids, and a 'most Delightful Fragrant TINCTURE' which as soon as it is used makes 'the most offensive Breath smell incomparably fine and charming' and 'instantly makes the blackest and most foul Teeth extreamly white and delicately beautiful'.

As in other periodicals he printed, Richardson's name never appears in the *Gazetteer*'s colophon; until 9 March 1743 the paper is said to be printed 'for' Thomas Cooper and afterwards 'for' his widow, Mary Cooper, 'publishers' who distributed many of the books and pamphlets Richardson printed. Its main editor, Ralph Courteville, later sent Richardson a letter from a friend praising *Pamela* and then asked about the possibility of a continuation of that book.[40]

Writing to Pope on 21 February 1739 about attacks on that friend of Tories in the *Gazetteer*, Aaron Hill professes not to have remembered that Richardson printed the newspaper and then excuses Richardson from responsibility on the grounds that he was merely the printer and 'there should be nothing imputed to the *Printer*, which is impos'd *for*, not *by* him, on his *papers*, but was never impress'd, on his *mind*. I am very much mistaken in his character, or he is a plain-hearted, sensible, and good-natur'd, honest man: I believe, when there is any thing put into his *presses*, with a view to such infamous *slander*, as that which you so justly *despise*, he himself is the only man, *wounded*: For I think, there is an *openness*, in his spirit, that would even repel the *profits* of his business, when they were to

---

[40] Knightley Chetwood to Courteville, 27 Jan. 1741, FM XVI, 1, fo. 43; 8 June 1741.

be the *consequence*, of making war upon excellence.'⁴¹ Hill was defending a friend and may be excused a little hedging: both his earlier and later letters imply that Richardson was more than the printer of the *Gazetteer*. His statement that Richardson would rather lose profit than print something derogatory to a good man may seem exaggerated, with its implication that a printer prints only what he approves of; but as a matter of fact there is no evidence that Richardson ever did print anything he disapproved of. The known products of his press are overwhelmingly pious and are free from either scepticism or immorality.

On 25 April 1743 Hill sent Richardson some translations of Horace's odes for the *Gazetteer* and on 19 May asked if any more were wanted—Richardson knows best if they are proper for that paper, and Hill is glad to do a service, if it is one, to 'a Paper you are interested in ye Success of'. On 21 May he offered more poems, wishing to contribute any 'Service in my Power to any, Paper, Person, Purpose, or Occasion, of what kind soever, that *you* have but the least Reason to wish well to'.

Richardson's connection with the paper continued into 1746. Early in that year an account of a scandal inserted in the paper—without Richardson's knowledge—gave 'offence to several Persons of Quality'. 'I have had a good deal of Trouble about it, and perhaps shall have more', he wrote to the printer of the *London Magazine*, Charles Acres, warning him not to reprint the item.⁴² On 11 January Hill thanked him for a new instance of his 'generous and ever-friendly Propensity,—in the Gazetteers, of Saturday, and yesterday', and on 11 April sent some remarks on the drama which 'may do Service, in your *Gazetteer*—or in some Other—if there *is* Another, you have Interest in'. On 13 June Hill wrote: 'As to the *Daily Gazetteer*, since It had been thrown wholly upon your own Charge and Hazard, and wou'd have always had a *Prejudice* to make way against, from the Original partiality It was suppos'd to have *sett out* with, I am not sorry you determin'd to drop it'; the reason he had not sent anything for so long was 'a Letter from which I drew Conclusions, that your Prospect of Success in continuing that Paper, on the improv'd Addition to its Plan, was no more than a faint & a doubtful one'. Evidently Richardson had some plan for reorganizing the paper but then decided to discontinue his connection with it. The *Daily Gazetteer* continued for two more years, by which time it had 'declined', and was reorganized to become the *London Gazetteer*.⁴³ It is the last bit of journalism with which Richardson is known to have been connected.

In or before 1737 Richardson made some suggestions for a work by a French physician and protestant refugee named James Mauclerc, *The*

<hr/>

⁴¹ Hill, *Works*, II, 68–9.   ⁴² 30 Jan.
⁴³ Articles of agreement for the *London Gazetteer*, 5 Dec. 1748, B.M. Add. MS. 38,729, fos. 126–7.

Christian's Magazine.[44] The work was entered in the Stationers' Register on 8 November 1737, and an undated edition, printed for the author by 'S. Richardson', was issued soon after.[45] It is described on the title page as a collection of the most 'REMARKABLE PASSAGES' from 'Some of the Most EMINENT MODERN DIVINES', written 'AGAINST *Atheists, Deists, Socinians, Papists*, And other CORRUPT and LOOSE CHRISTIANS'. It is not exactly a collection of passages; no sources are named, and, as he explains in his preface, the author has digested his reading into method and order. He began reading the late books of eminent divines in order to strengthen his own faith and to be able to answer 'the Objections and Cavils of such prophane and Atheistical Men'. Later he copied and arranged those reasons and arguments which made the greatest impression on his mind. The book is organized in chapters by subject. The early chapters give rational proofs of the existence of God, the doctrine of immortality, and the truth of the Scriptures. The Christian religion, it is explained, is firmly grounded on Right Reason.[46] Later chapters deal primarily with piety and ethics. The Catholics are blamed for their faith in oral tradition, their claims to infallibility, and such non-scriptural doctrines as transubstantiation. Mauclerc also parts company with some Protestants in holding that though there is no merit in good works they are necessary to salvation, that predestination is not absolute, that election is conditional only, and that the will is free. In general, his religion is that of the pious but rationalistic and largely ethical middle class. He is, however, clear that it is the Christian's duty to detach himself insofar as possible from love of the world and to welcome death[47]—the attitude which turned Clarissa's death into her triumph.

Mauclerc died in April 1743.[48] In 1748 *The Christian's Magazine* was reissued with a new title page stating that it was 'Revis'd and Corrected by Mr. S. RICHARDSON, Editor of PAMELA and CLARISSA', and 'Printed for the AUTHOR', and an advertisement in the *General Advertiser* of 10 October 1748 similarly describes it. Since the edition of 1748 is, except for its title page, identical with the undated edition (the same setting of type),

---

[44] Mauclerc was educated at Montpellier and admitted to the Royal College of Physicians in 1689. He is listed as Joseph Maucleer in the published *Roll of the Royal College of Physicians of London* (London, 1878), I, 480, but according to a letter from L. M. Payne, Librarian of the College, William Munk, the editor of the *Roll*, has underlined the name Joseph in his manuscript notes and written beside it 'James?' Mauclerc is listed as a licentiate in the *Catalogues of the Fellows and Other Members of the Royal College of Physicians* from 1693 through 1742, but not in 1743; from 1722 his address was Orange Street, by Leicester Fields. He was a writer and a contributor to the *British Apollo* of Aaron Hill (William Henry Irving, *John Gay: Favorite of the Wits* [Durham, N. C., 1940], p. 46).

[45] 'Entries of Copies', under date, MS. in the archives of the Stationers' Company. *The Christian's Magazine* is listed in the Dec. 1737 register of books in the *Gentleman's Magazine*, VII, [770].

[46] Chap. XVI.   [47] Chap. XLVI.

[48] Burial under date 13 Apr. in the MS. register of St. Martin's in the Fields, in the church.

any revising or correcting by Richardson must have been done before the book was first published. It is unlikely that the claim on the title page is an outright lie, though it was certainly added in an effort to sell an unsaleable work, probably in the interest of Mauclerc's family. One might conjecture that Richardson recommended to Mauclerc books on piety and discussed with him his treatment of them, suggested changes, and as printer corrected the mechanics of the writing of his foreign-born author.

Richardson probably revised the fourth edition of Defoe's *Complete English Tradesman*, which appeared late in 1737, dated 1738.[49] This revision recommends the *Plain Dealer* ('an excellent collection of papers') and Richardson's *Apprentice's Vade Mecum*, 'a little Piece . . . which, besides some other very needful things, contain[s] general Rules and Directions for a Young Man's Behaviour in his Apprenticeship'.[50] Aside from these puffs, the revisions are the kind one would expect Richardson to make. They are typical of his fair and orderly mind; the reviser has been meticulous and conscientious. Defoe's writings, according to the Preface, have one defect—they are justly censured for being 'too verbose and circumlocutory'; the editor has therefore decided 'to pare away these luxuriencies'. The method of the book has been made uniform, chapter headings have been rewritten and expanded so that the table of contents now looks like those epitomes Richardson loved to write for his later works, and a good many passages have been added in brackets.[51]

Somewhat over an eighth of the first volume is added matter and about half that percentage of the second. Some of these additions are factual, like a whole chapter on the recent bankruptcy law and another on the genealogy of noble families descended from tradesmen;[52] others are reflections of the kind Richardson was fond of making. The present age is one devoted to unnecessary diversions: 'there never was a time when luxury and extravagance were at so great an height'; being a trading nation is England's '*principal glory*' and tradesmen here are far from being the dregs

---

[49] Alan Dugald McKillop in *The Early Masters of English Fiction* (Lawrence, Kansas, 1956), p. 53, citing the reference in it to *The Apprentice's Vade Mecum*, first suggested that Richardson may have had a hand in this revision. The third edition (of Vol. I only), dated 1732, was printed by Richardson: it contains on p. xvi Sale's ornament No. 56 and on p. [480] Sale's ornament No. 71. Both the third and the fourth editions were published by Richardson's friend Charles Rivington. The fourth edition is advertised in the *Daily Gazetteer*, 11 Nov., 3 Dec. 1737.

[50] I, 6, 83.

[51] I, x–xvi. Defoe's book was partly letters, partly chapters; the revision drops the letter form. The type, originally in three different sizes, has also been made uniform. Some chapters have been divided and others combined or transposed. Cross references have been inserted, and changes since Defoe wrote have been pointed out in footnotes. As in the second edition of Defoe's *Tour* (see note 56), added passages are enclosed in square brackets, but not at the very beginning since the editor 'did not fall upon this method, 'till after the VIIth Chapter was printed off'.

[52] Chaps. XVI, XXIV.

of the people; public houses should be more strictly licensed and licences granted only to such sober and needy persons as widows; the extravagant luxury of the fops ('our nicer Gentlemen have brought it to two clean shirts a day') should be pruned by controlling periwig-makers, pastry-cooks, and such like, and funeral pomp should also be limited—the hands thus made idle could be well used for the good of the commonwealth and in the colonies. 'Let the *French* out-do us if they wou'd, and wear the tinsel ornaments.' The reviser has corrected a hint by Defoe, contradicted else-where by that author, that he believed in the doctrine of Mandeville that private vices are public benefits.[53]

One wishes that it were certain that Richardson had the sole hand in this revision, since the Preface would then provide the only direct evidence that Richardson knew his leading predecessor in the novel—it refers to the original author, 'with whom we were well acquainted'.[54] Richardson had printed for Defoe and it is inherently likely that they were acquainted, but there is no other indication.

On 13 October 1738 appeared a second edition, revised, of Defoe's *Tour thro' the Whole Island of Great Britain*, first published in 1724–7.[55] Richardson was responsible for at least some of the revisions in this edition, as well as in the subsequent editions of 1742, 1748, 1753, and 1761–2. It is not certain whether he was sole, or even chief, editor of any of these editions. He certainly had some help and he may have had collaborators, one of them probably Isaac Kimber. The additions and changes are the kind of thing Richardson would have done. Specific additions can be assigned to him only tentatively, but since he is known to have added some things, one may go on the assumption that those things that sound most like him are his.[56]

---

[53] I, 92–4, 316–17; II, 314–17, 320–30; I, xiii.   [54] I, xiv.

[55] *Daily Gazetteer* and *Weekly Miscellany*.

[56] Knowledge of Richardson's connection with the *Tour* goes back at least to 1769, when his name appeared as continuer of Defoe's work on the title page of the seventh edition. In 1782 John Nichols, in listing Richardson's works, stated (*Anecdotes of Bowyer*, p. 158) that he 'had a share in' additions to the sixth edition of the *Tour*, and in 1786 the family-authorized bio-graphy in the *Universal Magazine* said (LXXVIII, 77) that Richardson was 'concerned in' the sixth edition, which came out in 1761, shortly after his death. But Nichols and Richardson's daughters may have known little more than the claim of the 1769 edition. There is very little external evidence to show which edition or editions Richardson was 'concerned in', or the extent of his concern.

Sale (*Bibliographical Record*, p. 41) discovered a manuscript note in a British Museum copy of the third edition of the *Tour* (1742) stating that the additions were supplied by Richardson, Kimber, and others. The copy belonged to W. Musgrave, who probably wrote the note. The only other direct external evidence is in Cheyne's letters to Richardson of 7 Nov. and 13 Dec. 1740, which show that he sent Richardson material for the third edition. Sale assumes (pp. 39–40) that Richardson was the editor of the *Tour* and wrote the preface and that he was responsible for the additions and changes in the 1742 edition and for those in the editions of 1748, 1753, and 1761–2, also extensively revised. He believes that the wording of the preface to the third edition clearly shows that a new editor (Richardson) has taken over; but this preface merely

A travel book seems an odd thing for Richardson to have worked on, since few men were less travelled. He had never, he told Lady Echlin, 'had the Opportunity of seeing Sea Prospects, and hardly any Rocks but the Inland ones at Tunbridge'. 'I know nothing', he wrote to Thomas Edwards, 'of Situations of Places, Distances, Contiguities.'[57] But as it is revised, the *Tour* becomes less and less like a travel book. Defoe gives the impression that he has seen most of what he describes; though the tour form is retained, the subsequent editions add little from first-hand knowledge except in a few acknowledged letters from friends and sound more and more like factual guide books, derived from other books. The prefaces to the various editions acknowledge aid from several worthy gentlemen, and the text quotes the letters of these gentlemen and also several times cites books from which information was taken. One of the worthy gentlemen was Dr. George Cheyne, who for the 1742 edition wrote the accounts of the waters at Cheltenham, Bath, Bristol, and

---

indicates that there has been an extensive revision and does not, in our opinion, cast any light on the person responsible for revising the second edition.

McKillop has pointed out (*Richardson*, pp. 315–17) certain similarities between the 1738 edition and Richardson's subsequently written *Familiar Letters*. He also noticed the Leake puff (quoted above) in the second edition, which of all the additions to the *Tour* is the one most likely to have been Richardson's. The second edition also adds a passage supporting the efforts of Dr. Richard Newton, whose books Richardson had printed, to get Hart Hall at Oxford made a college, and praising his 'laudable and disinterested Endeavours to serve the Cause of Learning' (II, 221). It quotes from another author Richardson had printed, Mary Chandler, in praise of Ralph Allen (II, 247–8). Defoe's statement that the increase in tea drinking has caused the sale of earthenware at Nottingham to increase, whereas the glass-houses are decaying, calls forth a reflection on one of Richardson's favourite subjects: 'a Proof, one would think, that Male Luxury is less predominant than Female' (1st, III, 18; 2nd, III, 16).

Aside from such specific additions, the nature of the changes made in the second edition suggests Richardson and is generally similar to the kind of revision in later editions. As an afterthought, square brackets were used from page 24 onwards throughout the first volume to indicate added passages (I, x), just as they were in the fourth edition of *The Complete English Tradesman*. This similarity cannot, of course, be used alone to argue that Richardson had a hand in both these works, but the method is not unlike that in the third and fourth editions of *Clarissa* (1751), where added and restored passages are distinguished by dots in the margin. Details of town government are fairly consistently added, as well as accounts of country seats and of the sights to be seen in towns (e.g. Ipswich, I, 35–8; Walpole's seat, I, 81–3; Oxford, II, 206–29; Bath, II, 243–5), and in general, later editions, especially the third, carry on this tendency. It looks as if the editor of the second edition knew what he wanted to do but did not have time or information to do it completely as yet.

Another practice carried much further in later editions but begun in the second is the citation of acts of Parliament—which Richardson was printing. They are used to give information about such things as the church and port of Yarmouth (I, 73–4), the rebuilding of Gravesend and the regulation of its watermen (I, 148), the harbour at Rye (I, 181–8), the pier at Bridport (I, 312), the docks at Chester (II, 303), and the rebuilding of Boston Church (II, 341). Many more acts are added in the third edition, including acts passed before 1738 (e.g. III, 172, 185, 188, 192, 213), and later acts are added in all of the later editions. The account of London was entirely reorganized in the second edition, and the new organization was retained with minor changes in subsequent editions. It seems to us almost certain that Richardson's connection with the *Tour* began in 1738.

[57] 20 Feb. 1756; 15 Aug. 1753.

Tunbridge, and also sketched 'a Kind of a Preface' (not asked for and not used) outlining a plan for the whole work, which was evidently not unambitious, since to answer it some person would have to draw extracts from English histories and such natural histories of the counties as were available and 'all the other memorable Incidents and natural Curiosities of the Island'. Cheyne asked Richardson to be sure to 'dilute my strong Terms and Metaphors, and to expunge my Shibboleth' (presumably the natural method of curing) in order that the doctor be not recognized.[58]

Some of the additions are gratuitous references to Richardson's friends. There is a blatant puff for the bookshop of his brother-in-law James Leake at Bath: it is 'one of the finest Bookseller's Shops in *Europe*' and a sub-scription costs only 5s. a season; 'But Persons of Quality generally subscribe a Guinea, and I think it is the very best Money laid out in the Place, for those who go for Pleasure or Amusement only.'[59] There is a compliment, also almost a puff, to 'the Reverend and Learned Dr. *Edward Young*, so famed for his excellent Compositions, that it will be as much the Honour of this Village [Welwyn] to have had him for so many Years its Minister, as it will be to the Discredit of People of Power and Interest, that he was not called forth to adorn the highest ecclesiastical Dignity'. Caius Gabriel Cibber's statues of lunatics at the gates of Bedlam ('Great Cibber's brazen, brainless brothers') call forth a compliment on the 'inimitable Performances' of the Laureate.[60] Richardson did not, however, seize every possible occasion to compliment his friends: there is no description of Speaker Onslow's house at Ember Court, Thomas Edwards's house at Turrick, or Aaron Hill's establishment at Plaistow.

Many added passages make the *Tour* less like a first-hand account and more like a methodical and complete survey of the country. Details of town government, of members of Parliament, and of titles derived from place names are added, as well as accounts of country seats and of the sights to be seen in towns. Defoe, for instance, had devoted almost ten pages to Sturbridge Fair and only three to Cambridge; the reviser expanded

---

[58] 7 Nov. 1740.   [59] Added in the 2nd edn., II, 241-2.

[60] Both these compliments were added in the 4th edn., II, 195, 136. All editions have a few new references to people or places of personal interest to Richardson. The third tells how an attempt to make potash in Scotland failed through the fault of the undertakers in London (IV, 214)—a memory of one of Aaron Hill's vain projects. The fourth quotes John Dennis on Leith-hill, adding that he 'deserved a better Fate than he met with'; Cibber is quoted describing Mary Queen of Scots at Chatsworth and again praised (I, 247; III, 97). The fifth describes Joseph Spence's improvements at Byfleet and calls him a 'Man of Taste' (I, 224). The sixth quotes a sonnet by Thomas Edwards and admires Young's generous gift of 1,000 guineas to the Society for Propagating the Gospel in Foreign Parts (III, 51; II, 150).

Evidently it was a collaborator who added, in the third edition, an unfavourable opinion of the house of Baron Onslow, cousin of the Speaker, at Clandon—it is 'indifferently situated' and 'executed in a very bad Taste' (I, 215). The fourth substitutes high praise of 'one of the finest Seats in this Part of the Kingdom' (I, 238). Richardson must here have been the corrector of such an unwary opinion.

the account of Cambridge to over twenty pages.[61] Defoe's main interest
was commercial and he often passed over ancient monuments; of Canterbury, he remarked that the 'Antiquities, and Histories of particular
Places is not my business here, so much as the present State of them'. He
passed over the town of Rochester in two lines to get to the traffic on the
river.[62] The reviser, especially in the third edition, rectified many omissions
such as the Isle of Wight, Birmingham, almost the whole of Hertfordshire,
and the Highlands and Islands of Scotland. He frequently quoted acts of
Parliament, and he added accounts of recent events—fires, wrecks, new
buildings, new charitable societies. If Richardson was responsible for all
of the latter (there is no proof that he was), he was working on the *Tour*
in the last year of his life.[63] He included a table of county statistics and lists
of members of Parliament, lords, and bishops, as well as a long account of
the Forty-Five.

Reflections that suggest Richardson often appear. A breakfasting house
in the mansion of the Earl of Ranelagh at Chelsea calls forth a disquisition
on the dissoluteness of manners and the necessity of industry. The short
skirts of the women of Edinburgh remind one of the 'monstrous Hoops'
which have made the women of England 'above Shame'—and at least
the Scots women are not idle. The Green-man at Dulwich is 'a Part of the
fashionable Luxury of the present Age'—'Diversions of no sort of Use,
but to bring the Sexes easily into each other's Company, and so to serve
for Markets, as I may say, for such young Ladies, as may be afraid of being
not enough seen once a Week at Church' (the idea of Richardson's
Rambler essay).[64]

Richardson was himself a middle-class man, interested in trade and in
making money, but Defoe's interest in these matters is more prominent
than his. The original *Tour* is thoroughly imbued with the commercial
spirit. Everything connected with commerce and industry is described
with admiration and in loving detail. Addition of other matters makes this
aspect less prominent in the revised editions, but it is still prominent
enough. A long passage on the lack of business in Galloway, the inhabitants of which have 'no Notion of being rich and populous' and do not
understand that their religion and sobriety could very well coexist with
industriousness, is reduced in size but briefly summarized in new words:
'The People of *Galloway*, especially on the Sea Coast, are much to blame
for not falling in to Commerce.'[65] There is a good deal of this sort of
reflection. A proponent of manufacture like Defoe saw nothing wrong
with child labour and indeed welcomed it. At Taunton, he rejoiced that

---

[61] 1st edn., I, 121-30, 131-3; 2nd edn., I, 101-22.
[62] I, Letter ii, pp. 38, 21.   [63] See 6th edn., I, 208; II, 23, 109-10, 127.
[64] 4th edn., II, 164-5, IV, 70; 5th edn., I, 236.
[65] 1st edn., IV, 67-73; 2nd edn., III, 249-50.

there is not a child over five who cannot earn his own bread, and at Halifax, where the manufacture of cloth in private houses called forth a glowing picture of prosperity due to industry, there is 'hardly any thing above four Years old, but its Hands were sufficient to its self'. These sentiments were preserved, and that at least one of the men responsible for revision agreed with them is shown by the addition of an approving statement that at Manchester also the smallest children are all employed and earning their bread.[66]

Richardson's responsibility for the version of _Æsop's Fables_ which was published on 20 November 1739 (dated 1740), though not acknowledged on the title page, has long been known. He acknowledged it in his autobiographical letter to Johannes Stinstra of 2 June 1753, where he said that he 'was requested to revise the numerous Editions of Æsop's Fables in English, and to give the Public one I would commend for Children'. The request must have come from the publisher, John Osborn, Junior.[67] His father had been one of the publishers of the revision of Defoe's _Tour_, and the other man who with the elder Osborn was to suggest the _Familiar Letters_ and thus provide the initiative for _Pamela_, Charles Rivington, had published the revision of _The Complete English Tradesman_, so that it is likely that most of Richardson's early ventures in writing were stimulated by his bookselling friends.

Richardson sent Stinstra a copy of the _Fables_, which Stinstra acknowledged that he would not have recognized as by the author of the novels. Richardson answered that he was not surprised. It and the _Familiar Letters_ were 'intended for the lower Classes of Persons'. The reflections, he added, 'were such, for the most part, as I found them, in one of our writers, who had some Reputation in that way, in his Day'.[68]

This is exact. The fables, with some revisions, and the morals and reflections, with more revisions, were taken from Sir Roger L'Estrange's version, first published in 1692 and long popular—an eighth edition had appeared somewhat over a year before Richardson's.[69] Richardson's Preface explained, with his usual clarity, what he had done. In addition to L'Estrange's version, he had considered that of Samuel Croxall; he had found both unfortunately extreme, on opposite sides, in politics, which he was resolved to keep out of his version. Where politics is not in question, L'Estrange shows good sense; he has humour and a lively manner; and his language is excellent. To make him acceptable, Richardson found he had only to reduce his bulk, to 'give the _exceptionable Reflections_ a more _general_ and _useful_ Turn', and to banish here and there 'a trivial or a loose

---

[66] 1st edn., II, 20, III, 101; 4th edn., III, 247.

[67] See T. C. Duncan Eaves and Ben D. Kimpel, 'The Publisher of _Pamela_ and Its First Audience', _BNYPL_, LXIV (1960), 143-4.

[68] 24 Dec. 1753; 20 Mar. 1754.   [69] _Daily Gazetteer_, 28 June 1738.

Conceit'. He also 'presumed to alter, and put a stronger Point to several of the Fables themselves, which we thought capable of more forcible Morals'. He added to his Preface four lists of the fables he had omitted or changed: fifty-eight fables dropped as repetitious or as having no suitable moral; two hundred and eight dropped as 'rather to be deemed witty Conceits, facetious Tales, and sometimes ludicrous Stories, than instructive Apologues'; ninety-five to which he had given new morals or new reflections 'in order to direct them to general Use; or to avoid Party or Political Reflections'; and thirty-four in which the fable itself had been altered.[70] Richardson included only two hundred and forty fables, whereas L'Estrange's first volume contained five hundred.[71]

Richardson discarded such fables as the pro-monarchical 'Council of Birds for Chusing More Kings' and 'A Council of Beasts', directed against the levelling of society.[72] L'Estrange had seen as the moral of 'The Frogs Desire a King' that 'The *Mobile* are uneasy without a Ruler. . . . The Multitude are never to be satisfied. *Kings are from God*; and . . . it is a Sin, a Folly, and a Madness to struggle with his Appointments.' Richardson is closer to the spirit of the fable when he cites the Israelites' desire for a king, to punish which God sent Saul as a stork, and then substitutes the unpolitical moral that God knows what is best for us. L'Estrange's moral for 'Peacock and Magpie' was that we should be careful of changing a government, and he added the reflection that popular elections are dangerous, the plurality are neither wise nor good, and elective governments are always corrupt; Richardson substituted 'a gaudy outside . . . generally indicates an empty Mind' and reflected that in elections we should reject those who boast of mere outward appearance. He cut such reflections as 'There must be no sharers in Sovereignity', 'As Government is Necessary, Sacred, and Unaccountable, so it is but equal for us to bear the Infelicities of a Male Excess of it, as we enjoy the Blessings of Authority and publick Order', that so-called Christian assemblies often pray for ability to murder their masters, that the 'licentious Multitude' are slaves, and that a plurality of voices is no eviction of right.[73]

He did a little expurgation for reasons of propriety. Among the clever sayings or funny stories he cut as not being fables were a few that were off-colour,[74] and he eliminated a few details such as the Cat's accusation

[70] Pp. x–xiv.

[71] Only five of Richardson's fables (Nos. 234, 236, 237, 238, 239) are from L'Estrange's second part, and one (No. 37) is a separate expansion of part of a L'Estrange fable (No. 167). Katherine Hornbeak in *Richardson's Familiar Letters and the Domestic Conduct Books: Richardson's Aesop, Smith College Studies in Modern Languages*, XIX, No. 2 (Northampton, Mass., 1939), pp. 30–50, has discussed Richardson's revision and summarized some of the kinds of alterations he made.

[72] Nos. 309, 399.

[73] L'E Nos. 19, 204, 206, 254, 125, 134, 122; R Nos. 19, 157, 158, 188, 97, 106, 94.

[74] Nos. 281, 283, 306, 341.

that the Cock has lain with his mother and sisters.[75] The only major change of this sort was in the fable with which Richardson decided to end the book: both fables have the moral that one should not postpone repentance, but whereas L'Estrange uses the parable of a man who seduces a girl with promise of marriage and then puts off the wedding from day to day, Richardson's story is really no fable but the tale of a profligate who proposes to mend his ways tomorrow.[76]

Richardson introduces his own ideas into the moral or the reflections on the moral: children of all ranks should be brought up to make their livings, pride should be avoided, we should keep always in mind the promise of rewards in the afterlife, respect for tutors, parents, and governors must be maintained, 'for if once undue Familiarity is suffer'd to break in upon the requisite Distinctions due from the Governed to the Governors, Contempt will be the necessary Consequence, and there will be an End of all Order, Decorum, and Improvement'.[77] He gives some fables a more earnest turn: where L'Estrange's moral for the Fox and the Grapes is that we should appear indifferent when we cannot attain something, his is that we should not repine at what is beyond our power; L'Estrange sees the Man with Two Wives as showing that one cannot please two wives, Richardson as showing that there should be no great inequality of years in marriage; L'Estrange thinks it diverting to see one rascal cheating another where Richardson finds a moral pleasure in seeing backbiters get their just dues; where L'Estrange is comparatively frivolous, Richardson reflects that we should behave well in prosperity since fortune is changeable or that we should not scoff at our age.[78] He is less cynical: the Fox's lost tail tells L'Estrange that when a man has a defect he should try to turn it into a fashion, but it tells Richardson that men try to make their companions as corrupt as they are; the Lion, the Ass, and the Fox prove to L'Estrange that we love the treason and hate the traitor, to Richardson that bad princes do so; the Dog, the Cock, and the Fox show the one that the business of the world is nothing but sharping, the other that we should turn an adversary over to his match; the Nurse and the Froward Child prove no longer that ' 'Tis Fear more than Love that makes good Men' but that ingenuous natures are best wrought on by love and perverse ones by terror (with an added reflection against frightening children); Two Friends and a Bear means 'Every Man for Himself' to L'Estrange—to Richardson it means that friendship is tried by adversity.[79]

Sometimes Richardson's moral is more useful or more general: custom is second nature and men can be turned into beasts, rather than what some

[75] L'E No. 2; R No. 2.   [76] L'E No. 495; R No. 240.
[77] L'E Nos. 345, 237, 161, 449; R Nos. 193, 180, 126, 232.
[78] L'E Nos. 129-30, 141, 156, 262, 277; R Nos. 101-2, 110, 123, 220, 223.
[79] L'E Nos. 101, 194, 143, 219, 227; R Nos. 82, 150, 112, 166, 173.

call good husbandry others call avarice; do not promise more than you intend to perform, rather than a man may lie by signs as well as by words; we should provide against all chances, rather than beasts unlike some men are not gulled by the same trick twice.[80] Richardson adds illustrative instances: an anecdote about Charles II's taking only £500 when he discovered a man prepared to bribe his minister with £1,000; as an example of an impractical league that of Russia and the Empire against the Turks; the recent use of the terms bear and bull in stockjobbing.[81] He adds details to the fables or rearranges them not only for moralistic but also for artistic effect: the Hare in his race with the Tortoise shows his contempt by skipping around and thus tires himself out, Death gives the Old Man not one but several warnings which go unheeded.[82] He assures poetic justice—the Lion that eats the Fox and the Ass is himself killed by men.[83] His sense of the sacredness of property suggests a change and an added reflection—the Ass who refuses the Mastiff a part of his load of bread points out that he does not own the bread, and where L'Estrange sees only the Ass's want of charity, Richardson sees the Ass as an honest creature who refuses to buy friendship with what is not his own to give.[84] Richardson omits a few fables for no apparent reason, including the well-known Fox and Cat, the Hen who laid the golden eggs, and the Mice who wanted to bell the Cat.[85] He omits a good many which duplicate others, or combines them. But the main pattern of his changes, aside from the elimination of politics, is to give the fables a more serious turn, as when the story of the Disappointed Milkmaid suggests to him that men 'build their sole Happiness on the transitory Pleasures or Amusements of this uncertain Life' but death cuts short all our vanities.[86]

The tendency of Richardson's fables, as indeed of fables in general, is a blend of practicality and morality, benevolence tempered with a proper regard for self: 'Tho' the Duties of Humanity oblige us to do all we can to assist a Neighbour in Distress, yet are we to take care by the Rules of Prudence not to ruin ourselves and Families for his sake', as he adds in one of his reflections. We should be energetic and help ourselves, do our part and trust Heaven. And we should learn to be content with our lot and submit without repining to the will of Heaven: 'Our Post and our Station is appointed us.'[87]

We know of no evidence that Richardson revised the fables after the first edition, though he went on advertising them and announced two new editions. He seems to have thought of them as a useful work for children

---

[80] L'E Nos. 188, 104, 119; R Nos. 144, 84, 92.
[81] L'E Nos. 272, 274, 300; R Nos. 221, 222, 225.
[82] L'E Nos. 133, 350; R Nos. 105, 196. See also L'E Nos. 219, 228; R Nos. 166, 174.
[83] L'E No. 194; R No. 150.   [84] L'E No. 491; R No. 209.
[85] L'E Nos. 374, 247, 391.   [86] L'E, Part II, No. 205; R No. 239.
[87] L'E Nos. 218, 78-80; R Nos. 165, 66.

but not one to be boasted of by a successful writer, though he did attempt to use the success of his first novel to help their sale by advertising them in 1742 as 'the Æsop quoted in Pamela'.[88]

In 1736 Richardson began to print the *Universal History*, an ambitious work by various authors in which he later acquired a sixth interest.[89] It was also puffed in the *Æsop*, where it is quoted and said to be 'now publishing with great Applause'.[90] The ancient part of the *History* was completed, except for a supplementary volume of additions which came out six years later, in 1744. Richardson's ability to buy into this venture shows his increasing prosperity. It must have been in the late 1730s that he was also able to buy a 14 per cent government annuity which paid him £115 per annum.[91]

Another publishing venture in which Richardson became involved in the late 1730s was the Society for the Encouragement of Learning. This was a group of scholars and patrons of learning, under the presidency of the Duke of Richmond, founded in 1736 to promote the printing of serious books, especially books which the usual bookseller either would not print or would not adequately reward. The Society sponsored only eleven books all told, over a period of twelve years, and was finally forced by inability to dispose of the books printed (though on three separate occasions it made agreements with various booksellers in an effort to sell

[88] There are very few extant copies of Richardson's *Fables* known and only one published by Richardson which we have located, the copy of the first edition in the Bodleian Library; the first edition was still being advertised in 1742 (*Daily Gazetteer*, 11 Dec.; *Daily Post*, 14 Dec.; *Daily Advertiser*, 22 Dec.) and in 1745 (*Daily Gazetteer*, 18 Sept.). A second edition was advertised in the first edition of *Clarissa* in Dec. 1747 (II, 309v), and in the *St. James's Evening Post* of 28 Feb.–2 Mar. 1749, where Richardson's authorship is openly stated; but we have heard of no copy of it. Sale (*Bibliographical Record*, p. 5) located a copy of an edition, seemingly the third, advertised in 1753 as a 'new edition' (*Public Advertiser*, 18 Dec.), which may be the same as the edition advertised after Richardson's death (*Public Advertiser*, 27 Oct. 1761); but we could not find the copy he mentioned as in the Bodleian. The Bodleian does have an undated York edition, which has minor changes which could be the work of a printer or publisher; and the Harvard University Library has a late eighteenth-century edition, also undated, which varies only in capitalization and punctuation.

[89] Nichols, *Literary Anecdotes*, II, 553–4. In the last folio volume Richardson is listed among those it was printed for (see also the advertisement in the *Daily Gazetteer* of 3 Nov 1744). According to entries in the Stationers' Register early in 1747, when the work was republished in octavo Richardson owned a one-sixth share, in association with his friends Thomas Osborne, John Osborn, and Andrew Millar ('Entries of Copies 1746–1773', MS. in the archives of the Stationers' Company, pp. 9–59 *passim*). Half of this sixth he later sold to the Rivington brothers for £262 10s. (receipt dated 12 Jan. 1753, MS. in the Harvard University Library).

[90] Pp. xxxii–xxxiv.

[91] Receipts dated 2 Jan. 1740 (MS. in the Haverford College Library); 13 Oct. 1741 (MS. in the Fitzwilliam Museum, Cambridge); 5 Oct. 1742 (MS. in the National Library of Scotland); 9 Jan. 1745 (MS. in the Wisbech and Fenland Museum); 10 Jan. 1748 (MS. in the Hyde Collection, Somerville, New Jersey); 11 Apr. 1751 (Bodleian MS. Autogr. B. 4. P. 28). See also receipt for another annuity for £25, 10 Jan. 1748 (MS. in the Universitaetsbibliothek, Basel).

them) and exhaustion of funds to suspend operations early in 1749.[92] Richardson was one of three printers employed by the Society—'I suppose from each Author's having had the privilege to nominate his own friend', says John Nichols,[93] in which case Richardson's being chosen would have been due either to Alexander Stuart or to Sir William Keith, whose books he printed in 1738. But perhaps he was chosen by the Secretary of the Society, Alexander Gordon, for whom he had several years before printed two books and who still owed him money in 1741.[94]

It was through this Society that Richardson came to publish *The Negotiations of Sir Thomas Roe*. Roe was a seventeenth-century statesman and British Ambassador at Constantinople, whose papers Richardson had been interested in since 1730, when proposals for issuing them by subscription were to be obtained from a large number of people—most of them booksellers, but the list is headed by the name of Samuel Richardson.[95] Evidently the subscribers were not forthcoming, but Richardson must still have thought he had on his hands a valuable literary property —he noted on the manuscript that the letters were 'excellent things'.[96] Or perhaps he was beginning to feel the scribbling fever.

On 18 March 1737 Richardson wrote to the Society making 'an humble Tender' of the Roe manuscripts and offering 'to bear any Part of ye Expence that shall be thought proper'. Thomas Carte recommended printing them with abridgements, and Professor John Ward of Gresham College was appointed chairman of a committee to supervise their editing. Carte and a Dr. Anderson were asked to digest the manuscripts and put them in order.[97] Printing of the first volume, containing Roe's correspondence from Turkey, began in early 1738 but was not finished until April 1739.[98] Meanwhile, Richardson had written to the Treasurer, Dr. Thomas Birch, to propose that Carte or someone else write a preface, with the result that he was himself directed to prepare not only a preface but a table of contents—after seeing a sample of his table the committee asked him to contract it as much as possible.[99]

[92] Nichols, *Literary Anecdotes*, II, 90–7; 'A Memorial of the Present State of the Affairs of the Society for the Incouragement of Learning', printed for the meeting of 17 April 1746, B.M. Add. MS. 6191, fos. 22–3; Clayton Atto, 'The Society for the Encouragement of Learning', *Library*, 4 S. XIX (1939), 263–88.

[93] *Literary Anecdotes*, II, 92.

[94] Sale, *Master Printer*, p. 123; Gordon to R, [c. 1 Sept. 1741].

[95] *Daily Journal*, 23 Oct.; *Monthly Chronicle*, III (Oct. 1730), 207. A copy of the Proposals is in B.M. Add MS. 4168.   [96] P.R.O. S.P. 9/207/item 33.

[97] B.M. Add. MS. 6190, fos. 34–6, 40 ('Correspondence', 20 Mar., 21 Oct. 1737); B.M. Add. MS. 6187, pp. 98, 100, 124–5 (committee meetings of 25 Mar., 1 Apr., 10 June 1737); B.M. Add. MS. 6185, p. 35 ('Minutes').

[98] B.M. Add. MS. 6185, pp. 47, 68–9, 124; B.M. Add. MS. 6187, pp. 96–7, 118, 121, 127, 153–4; B.M. Add. MS. 6186, fo. 57 ('Register').

[99] 5 Dec. 1738; B.M. Add. MS. 6185, p. 68 (meeting of 2 May 1739); B.M. Add. MS. 6187, p. 254 (committee meeting of 6 Apr. 1739).

Richardson was later to show his abundant talent for tables of contents in his novels, where he provides what amount to summaries of and commentaries on his work. The huge table of contents of the Roe papers is even more impressive. It runs to almost 90,000 words, over one-eighth the length of the letters it summarizes, and is carefully written, with cross references and explanations. He must have had help in making this epitome since some of the letters are in Latin, French, and Italian. He worked at it during the summer of 1739, a labour which aroused the admiration of Aaron Hill: 'Good God! What a Task have you had & what a comprehensive and satisfactory Abstract have you made of his Matter! It is such a *Part* of his work, as a Chymical Quintessence is of a Vegetable —It increases ye Virtue by diminishing the Bulk.'[100]

The Negotiations of Sir Thomas Roe was published in March 1740, at the impressive price of £1 7s.[101] It was perhaps the most assiduously advertised book of the eighteenth century: Richardson had a ready medium in the *Daily Gazetteer*, and the Roe advertisements run in it throughout the rest of 1740 and 1741. The reason is not far to seek: on 2 February 1741 the Society had 101 copies of the 750 published in its possession and book-sellers' receipts for 49 more; the rest 'are yet in the hands of Mr. Richardson the printer'.[102] Nor do many of them seem ever to have left his hands.

Richardson's Preface promises future volumes, containing correspondence dealing with Roe's later embassies in Poland, Scandinavia, and Germany and with his role at the outbreak of the Civil War, 'some curious detached pieces', a life of Roe, and an index to the whole. Richardson, who had not yet been paid by the Society for printing the first volume, was willing to repay its other expenses and take the remaining copies provided that the Society printed the second.[103] But when asked whether he could get the remaining papers, with a life of Roe to be written by him, into one more volume,[104] he replied that 'the execution of that affair depended upon Mr. Carte (the Editor of the first volume)'.[105] A decision was postponed until Carte's return from abroad, and it was never made.[106]

Early in 1744 the Society had recovered only a little over £70 on its £231 3s. investment for the Roe venture, a sum which seems not to have included Richardson's printing bill of £183 9s. Before the end of the year the Society paid him about a third of this sum, and probably he collected half of the total receipts, about £70 more. Three years later, pressed by the

[100] 27 Sept.

[101] B.M. Add. MS. 6185, pp. 76, 92, and advertisements in the *Daily Gazetteer* beginning 25 Mar. 1740; B.M. Add. MS. 6189, fo. 20.

[102] B.M. Add. MS. 6185, p. 107.   [103] B.M. Add. MS. 6187, pp. 305, 307.

[104] 30 Jan. 1741, B.M. Add. MS. 6187, p. 315.

[105] Richardson's letter is referred to in the committee meeting of 22 Jan. 1742, B.M. Add. MS. 6188, p. 17. See also B.M. Add. MS. 6186, fo. 57, where his letter is dated 31 Jan. 1741.

[106] B.M. Add. MS. 6185, pp. 102–3, 111, 124.

Society for some way to dispose of the unsold copies, Richardson agreed to take over those in its possession (105—the booksellers had returned 4 of the 49 they had taken, or had Richardson turned over some of his 600 copies to the Society?) and to give a discharge of all demands on his part.[107] He continued to advertise the Roe papers,[108] but several hundred copies must have continued to weigh down his attic. His long labours on the table of contents were, however, rewarded by the second known review of one of his works, a glowing notice in the periodical *The History of the Works of the Learned* for May 1740, in which he is styled the editor, his table of contents called 'an excellent Pattern, which the Publishers of such Collections will always do well to imitate', and his preface liberally drawn on to describe the interest of the work.[109]

In spite of its lack of success, Roe's correspondence is not without interest. He was ambassador to Constantinople at an important time. The Thirty Years War had broken out and the husband of King James's daughter Elizabeth had lost not only his new kingdom of Bohemia but his hereditary Palatinate. Roe was early urging on the government the possibility of creating a diversion in favour of the Queen of Bohemia by inducing Gabriel Bethlem (Bethlem Gabor, as he calls him), the warlike Prince of Transylvania, to espouse her interests. In the end the project came to nothing, mainly because the Prince was, in Roe's view, so selfish and treacherous as to prefer his own interests to those of the Queen and made a separate peace with the Empire. His letters also describe his efforts to get some redress against the Tunisian and Algerian pirates, to foster English commerce, to protect the Greek Patriarch against the machinations of Rome, to prevent a peace treaty between Spain and the Turks, to collect Greek manuscripts for the Archbishop of Canterbury and antiquities for the Duke of Buckingham (he found the fields pretty well worked over and did not locate many of either), and to defy the French ambassador, who wickedly claimed precedence at the Porte.

In the 1740s Richardson was connected briefly with another society, the Society of Booksellers, which proposed to promote learning by printing for authors on advantageous terms.[110] This Society, headed by Thomas Osborne, was even more short-lived than the Society for the Encouragement of Learning, though it did have one excellent result—its advertisements induced Parson Abraham Adams to take his sermons up to London and thus threw him in with Joseph Andrews and Miss Fanny Goodwill.[111]

107 B.M. Add. MS. 6187, p. 305 (account of 2 Jan. 1741); B.M. Add. MS. 6185, pp. 75, 153; B.M. Add. MS. 6188, p. 57; B.M. Add. MS. 6185, p. 168–70, 179–80; B.M. Add. MS. 6188, pp. 121–2.

108 *Clarissa*, 3rd edn. (1751), back of Vol. VIII.   109 I, 346–60.

110 *Daily Post*, 7 Mar. 1741; *Champion*, 7 Mar., 24 Mar. 1741. See also McKillop, *Richardson*, pp. 310–11.

111 Book I, Chap. XV.

For it Richardson printed Robert James's *Medicinal Dictionary* (1743-5), in which he was a partner.[112] It may have been this work which first introduced him to Dr. Johnson, who helped write the proposals for it and did 'a little in the Dictionary itself' as well as the dedication.[113]

What has been said about Richardson's printing ventures, in books, periodicals, and government contracts, is enough to bear out his statement to Stinstra: 'My Business, Sir, has ever been my chief Concern.'[114] That he found time to write *Pamela* in the midst of these activities is surprising enough. In addition, his health had already begun to give him serious concern. Even before the time of the writing of *Pamela* Richardson's ill health is one of the constant subjects of his correspondence. By late 1741 his ailments were severe enough for him to adopt the very strict regimen of Dr. Cheyne already mentioned, and in the late 1740s he refers to his 'nervous Complaints', which seem during the last decade of his life to have amounted to Parkinson's Disease. This malady began during the 1730s, though in what year is not so certain. Dr. Cheyne's first letters in 1734 mention Richardson's health, and so do Hill's first letters in 1736. 'I am sorry to hear your great Business and close Application sinks your Spirits often', wrote Cheyne on 21 December 1734. In 1754 Richardson wrote to Lady Bradshaigh that he should have begun his care of himself twenty years before, but 'I went plodding on in a perplexing Business . . . till a Head was gained by the Distemper that common Curatives would not subdue. I had originally a good Constitution.'[115] By 1734, then, his health had begun to decline, a misfortune which Richardson at times attributed to overwork.

He also referred several times to a more severe illness, brought on, he believed, by grief at the death of friends and relations: 'No less than Eleven concerning Deaths attacked me in two Years.'[116] What slight evidence there is points to 1737 as a likely date for this attack. Before that his complaints seem to have been mainly lethargy and low spirits; afterwards they became 'nervous', with dizziness and poor digestion. Presumably it was this illness to which he was referring when, many years later, he wrote, 'I once found great Benefit by an Excursion of some Weeks, when, overcome by heavy Family Losses (a Succession of them!) my Stomach failed me, and I digested nothing I forced down.'[117] The eleven persons whose deaths helped bring on the attack seem to have included

---

[112] See receipts of R to Osborne, MS. in the Harvard University Library.

[113] *Boswell's Life of Johnson together with Boswell's Journal of a Tour to the Hebrides and Johnson's Diary of a Journey into North Wales*, ed. George Birkbeck Hill and L. F. Powell (Oxford, 1934-1950), I, 159; III, 22.

[114] 2 June 1753.   [115] 30 May.

[116] To Lady Bradshaigh, 15 Dec. 1748. See also R to Mrs. Chapone, 6 Dec. 1750; R to Sarah Wescomb, 6 July 1752.

[117] To Lady Bradshaigh, 22 Mar. 1756.

(the wording of his letter is ambiguous) his father, two unnamed brothers who died abroad (one of them must have been Thomas), and a dear friend, quite probably the wild young friend whose improbable adventures are described in Chapter I. If, as is not impossible, the attack occurred in 1734, they may also have included two of his infant children.

Samuel Richardson, Senior, drops from sight in 1727. If he lived on into the 1730s, two of his sons, Samuel and William, were well able by that time to ease his last years. Samuel speaks of attending his father 'in every stage of his last illness' and long mourning for him. He slipped while crossing 'his own Yard', and as he tried to regain his balance, his thigh was 'snapt by a sudden Jirk', an accident from which he never recovered. His son Samuel always refers to him with love and respect, but as honest and kindly rather than as brilliant or successful. The novelist refers to his mother only once, saying that she was a 'good Woman'. She probably died around 1738. Of Richardson's sisters very little is known, except that at least two of them were still alive in 1739. His brother Benjamin, like his father a joiner, was also in poor circumstances. From 1730 he lived near his father's old house, in the vicinity of the Tower, first inside and later outside the City.

William Richardson was more successful. He lived on Tower Hill, just east of the Tower, near his brother Benjamin, where at The Star in the East he carried on business as an 'upholder' or 'upholsterer'—probably not in the modern sense, but as a dealer in household wares and second-hand furniture. He was in fairly close touch with the novelist; his eldest son, Thomas Verren, who died in 1732, had been apprenticed to his printer uncle and had been the recipient, willingly or unwillingly, of the advice which formed the nucleus of *The Apprentice's Vade Mecum*. Aside from seven half-brothers and half-sisters who died in infancy, Thomas Verren had two half-sisters and a half-brother, William Richardson, Junior, who was also apprenticed to his uncle Samuel, in 1748. Through his second wife William, Senior, had acquired land at Dagenham, Essex. The novelist's references to him are affectionate, and the two brothers, the only members of their family who are known to have been successful, seem to have been close.

Aside from these two brothers and the shadowy sisters, no other blood relatives of Richardson are known to have been living in 1739, when he began the composition of his first novel. He was always close to his brother-in-law by his first marriage, the printer Allington Wilde, and he kept up with others of his first wife's relatives—in 1738 her step-mother left him a mourning ring, and in 1742 one of her maternal aunts left him a small legacy and his daughter Patty a larger one. He was on good terms with his brother-in-law by his second marriage, the Bath bookseller James Leake, who distributed many of the books he printed. His immediate family consisted of his wife and three young daughters, Polly, Patty, and Nancy (the fourth, Sally, was born in 1740). In later life he sometimes complained about his female household, but all evidence goes to show that his women took good care of him and that he ran his household as much as a kindly man ever can.

CHAPTER V

THE COMPOSITION AND PUBLICATION OF *PAMELA* AND THE *FAMILIAR LETTERS*

1739–1741

O N his fiftieth birthday Samuel Richardson was thus a comfortable family man who from very small beginnings had worked his way up in the world until he was one of the leading printers in London, respected and by all accounts deserving of respect, honest and as kind as prudence permitted (perhaps a little kinder), amiable and hard working, ailing but still active, true enough to his own lights, which were pretty much the lights of other well-to-do businessmen, but hardly inclined to wild enthusiasms. His business had made him a competent writer and had brought him some literary acquaintances and one literary friend, none of whom, however, were among the leading writers of the time; he had written a long pamphlet about the duties of apprentices and a few other fugitive pieces, had probably helped shape the policy of some of the newspapers and periodicals he had printed and was still printing, had recently done some revising of other men's works and finished a new edition of a book of fables for children, and was on his birthday engaged in a labour of love for which his capacities were well suited, the preparing of an interminable table of contents for an edition of the papers of a forgotten diplomat of the previous century. Obviously there must have been more to his life, his inner life at least, than this, because this solid elderly citizen suddenly became in imagination a teen-aged servant girl.

The story has often been told, in his own words, which are all we have to go on. Twenty years or more before, he had heard a true story about a virtuous serving maid who had married her master, a story which had evidently appealed to him, since he had proposed it as a good subject to several writers, who considered it too humble for them.[1] There is no reason

---

[1] R to Hill, 26 Jan. 1747. See also letter from J. B. D[e]. F[reval]. in the first and subsequent duodecimo editions of *Pamela*. Since 'for twenty Years' Richardson had proposed the subject to various writers, he must have erred in telling Stinstra in 1753 that he heard the story fifteen years before he wrote *Pamela* (see above); his letter to Hill of *c*. 1 Feb. 1741 (quoted above) suggests that he heard it shortly after his friend did, around 1716.

to doubt Richardson's statement that the story was based on a real incident. Though there has been considerable speculation, the names of the real-life actors in this history have not been identified,[2] nor does it make much difference who they were. The situation itself is all that Richardson got from the story he heard, and the situation is only the starting point for *Pamela*. Aaron Hill accurately remarked 'upon how narrow and how weak a Foundation (as to matter of *Fact*), you have erected such a Temple, of Fancy and Wonder'.[3] Though Richardson as critic was perhaps naïve enough to accept the common view that a lurid event will guarantee an interesting novel, Richardson as writer instinctively knew better.

To Stinstra he wrote on 2 June 1753: 'You ask, "If I had a Model before my Eyes, in some of my Pieces"? The Story of Pamela had some slight Foundation in Truth. Several Persons of Rank were guessed at, as having in my Mind sat for the two principal Characters in that Piece: But no one Conjecture came near the Truth; nor was it likely that it should; for I myself knew no more of the Story, than what I recollected a Gentleman told me of it Fifteen Years before I sat down to write it.' Earlier, around 1 February 1741, he had written in answer to Hill's question as to 'whether there was any original groundwork of fact, for the general foundation of Pamela's story': 'About twenty-five years ago, a gentleman, with whom I was intimately acquainted (but who, alas! is now no more!) met with such a story as that of Pamela' on one of his tours. The landlord at his inn had described to him the master and mistress of a large house in the neighbourhood:

The lady . . . was one of the greatest beauties in England; but the qualities of her mind had no equal: beneficent, prudent, and equally beloved and admired by high and low. That she had been taken at twelve years of age, for the sweetness of her manners and modesty, and for an understanding above her years by Mr. B——'s mother, a truly worthy lady, to wait on her person. Her parents, ruined by suretiships, were remarkably honest and pious, and had instilled into their daughter's mind the best principles. . . .

That the girl, improving daily in beauty, modesty, and genteel and good behaviour, by the time she was fifteen, engaged the attention of her lady's son, a young gentleman of free principles, who, on her lady's death, attempted, by all manner of temptations and devices, to seduce her. That she had recourse to as many innocent stratagems to escape the snares laid for her virtue; once, however, in despair, having been near drowning; that, at last, her noble resistance, watchfulness, and excellent qualities, subdued him, and he thought fit to make her his wife. That she behaved herself with so much dignity, sweetness, and humility, that she made herself beloved of every body, and even by his relations, who, at first despised her; and now had the blessings both of rich and poor, and the love of her husband. . . .

---

[2] See Aleyn Lyell Reade, 'Richardson's Pamela: Her Original', *N&Q*, 10 S. IX (1908), 361–3, 503–5.
[3] 9 Feb. 1741.

This, Sir, was the foundation of Pamela's story; but little did I think to make a story of it for the press. That was owing to this occasion.

Mr. Rivington and Mr. Osborne, whose names are on the title-page, had long been urging me to give them a little book (which, they said, they were often asked after) of familiar letters on the useful concerns in common life; and, at last, I yielded to their importunity, and began to recollect such subjects as I thought would be useful in such a design, and formed several letters accordingly. And, among the rest, I thought of giving one or two as cautions to young folks circumstanced as Pamela was. Little did I think, at first, of making one, much less two volumes of it. But, when I began to recollect what had, so many years before, been told me by my friend, I thought the story, if written in an easy and natural manner, suitably to the simplicity of it, might possibly introduce a new species of writing, that might possibly turn young people into a course of reading different from the pomp and parade of romance-writing, and dismissing the improbable and marvellous, with which novels generally abound, might tend to promote the cause of religion and virtue. I therefore gave way to enlargement: and so Pamela became as you see her. But so little did I hope for the approbation of judges, that I had not the courage to send the two volumes to your ladies, until I found the books well received by the public.

While I was writing the two volumes, my worthy-hearted wife, and the young lady who is with us, when I had read them some part of the story, which I had begun without their knowing it, used to come in to my little closet every night, with—'Have you any more of Pamela, Mr. R.? We are come to hear a little more of Pamela,' &c. This encouraged me to prosecute it, which I did so diligently, through all my other business, that, by a memorandum on my copy, I began it Nov. 10, 1739, and finished it Jan. 10, 1739-40. And I have often, censurable as I might be thought for my vanity for it, and lessening to the taste of my two female friends, had the story of Moliere's Old Woman in my thoughts upon the occasion.

If justly low were my thoughts of this little history, you will wonder how it came by such an assuming and very impudent preface. It was thus:—The approbation of these two female friends, and of two more, who were so kind as to give me prefaces for it, but which were much too long and circumstantial, as I thought, made me resolve myself on writing a preface; I therefore, spirited by the good opinion of these four, and knowing that the judgments of nine parts in ten of readers were but in hanging-sleeves, struck a bold stroke in the preface you see, having the umbrage of the editor's character to screen myself behind.—And thus, Sir, all is out.

The similar account given to Stinstra brings out a few new facts:

Two Booksellers, my particular Friends, entreated me to write for them a little Volume of Letters, in a common Style, on such Subjects as might be of Use to those Country Readers who were unable to indite for themselves. Will it be any Harm, said I, in a Piece you want to be written so low, if we should instruct them how they should think and act in common Cases, as well as indite? They were the more urgent with me to begin the little Volume, for this Hint. I set about it, and in the Progress of it, writing two or three Letters to instruct handsome Girls, who were obliged to go out to Service, as we phrase it, how to avoid the Snares that might be laid against their Virtue; the above Story recurred to my Thought: And hence sprung Pamela. This Volume of Letters is not worthy of your Perusal. I laid aside several Letters after I had written them for this Volume as too high for the View of my two Friends.

John Osborn, Senior, and Charles Rivington had often been associated with Richardson in business, and both were close friends—Richardson was a witness to the former's will and received a mourning ring[4] and was one of the executors of the latter's.[5] In 1741 they published Richardson's *Familiar Letters*, the spur which had set him galloping off into the novel. The young lady who each night accompanied his wife to his closet to hear more of Pamela's sufferings and rejoicings was Elizabeth Midwinter, daughter of a bookseller who had died in 1736—leaving a legacy to his son by a less resistant serving maid than Richardson's heroine. Miss Midwinter was living with Richardson's family, and she later married his friend Francis Gosling.[6] Since Richardson was compiling his table of contents, or rather epitome, of the Roe papers during the summer of 1739, he must have begun work on the collection of letters in September or October and interrupted it in November to write the first version of *Pamela*.[7]

Two months is a short time to write two duodecimo volumes, but perhaps the haste helped preserve Richardson's spark. In the first edition *Pamela*, at least the first half of it, gives the impression of a book which was dashed off in a single burst, under a single imaginative vision of its main character, probably surprising the author as much as it did anybody else. Though Richardson would hardly have referred to any phenomenon so mysterious, pagan, and foreign to middle-class life as inspiration by his Muse, his account of the composition of *Pamela* in two months (over three thousand words a day, in the intervals of a busy life) sounds as if he was swept away by forces he only imperfectly understood, and one's impression on reading at least the first part of the novel is that he was indeed possessed by Pamela. His possession seems to have been good for his health, since two days after the novel's completion, on 12 January 1740, Dr. Cheyne wrote inquiring whether Richardson was better—he had not heard for some time of any new symptom or any exasperation of the old ones.

During most of the rest of the year Richardson kept the novel by him. Though he was occupied during a part of this time completing the

---

[4] P.C.C. Seymer 333, dated 1 June 1742, proved 2 Dec. 1745.

[5] P.C.C. Trenley 169, dated 10 June 1737, proved 20 May 1742. See also Hill to R, 25 Feb. 1742.

[6] Eaves and Kimpel, 'The Publisher of *Pamela* and Its First Audience', pp. 143–6; will of Edward Midwinter, P.C.C. Derby 134, dated 20 May 1736, proved 1 June 1736.

[7] Emma Danielowski in *Richardsons erster Roman. Entstehungsgeschichte* ([Berlin], 1917), pp. 48, 51, doubts the date Richardson gives for the completion of *Pamela* on grounds which are hardly convincing (Richardson could have inserted a reference to Colley Cibber's *Apology*, published in Apr. 1740, even if it is a reference, in revision before publication).

Familiar Letters, he had ample opportunity to revise and, judging by his later practice, probably did so. Richardson, who read little else, read his own works constantly and seldom read them without changing something. One would like to believe that in cold blood, after his fit had cooled, he added some of the scenes in the second volume which point up his moral, as he later in revision pointed up the morals of *Clarissa*. It was also presumably during this period that he showed the work to the two un-identified friends who offered prefaces for it which were 'too long and circumstantial' (no longer, surely, than the prefatory material he eventually included!). The world first heard of the novel on 11 October, when the *Weekly Miscellany*, edited by Richardson's friend and debtor William Webster, printed a letter from an anonymous friend to the 'Author' praising it highly for its spirit of truth and agreeable simplicity, its con-vincing suspense, and, of course, its instruction and morality. This friend urges the author to publish ('the Cause of Virtue calls loudly for its Publication') without altering its 'native Simplicity'—'should you permit such a murdering Hand to be laid upon it, to gloss and tinge it over with superflous and needless Decorations, which, like too much Drapery in Sculpture and Statuary, will but encumber it; it may disguise the Facts, mar the Reflections, and unnaturalize the Incidents, so as to be lost in a Multiplicity of fine idle Words and Phrases, and reduce our Sterling Substance into an empty Shadow, or rather *frenchify* our *English* Solidity into Froth and Whip-syllabub'. Evidently, as so often later, Richardson was asking for advice (which he rarely took), and evidently he was in some doubt about his most original trait, the natural and even low style of his heroine.

When *Pamela* finally appeared on 6 November this letter formed part of the prefatory material. Along with it was a eulogy by Jean Baptiste de Freval, for whom Richardson had recently printed a translation of Pluche's *Histoire du ciel*.[8] There was also a Preface by the Editor. Richard-son's name does not appear, even as editor or printer; Pamela's letters purport to be real letters, and de Freval's letter refers to a real story which happened within these thirty years past and to the changing of names of persons and places to avoid giving offence. The *Weekly Miscellany* letter is now addressed to the 'Editor', not the 'Author'. Under the umbrage of the character of editor, Richardson felt free to praise his work: 'An *Editor* may reasonably be supposed to judge with an Impartiality which is rarely to be met with in an *Author*', he says in the Preface; 'he can Appeal from *his own* Passions, (which have been uncommonly *moved* in perusing these engaging Scenes) to the Passions of *Every one* who shall read them with the least Attention.' The impartial editor praises, in terms which are hard to reconcile with the fiction that Pamela's letters are real, not only the

[8] See B.M. Add. MS. 6185, p. 75, and Sale, *Master Printer*, pp. 193–4.

moral benefit to be derived (religion and morality inculcated in a manner easy and agreeable, delightful to old and young; the parental, filial, and social duties from low to high life set forth in the most exemplary lights; practical examples given to the modest virgin, the chaste bride, and the obliging wife) but also the literary merit of the work—characters justly drawn and equally supported, distress raised from natural causes and compassion excited from proper motives, 'in so probable, so natural, so *lively* a manner, as shall engage the Passions of every sensible Reader, and strongly interest them in the edifying Story'.

Letters Written to and for Particular Friends, on the Most Important Occasions. Directing Not Only the Requisite Style and Forms to Be Observed in Writing Familiar Letters; But How to Think and Act Justly and Prudently, in the Common Concerns of Human Life came out on 23 January 1741.[9] To Hill Richardson mentioned 'one or two' of these letters 'as cautions to young folks circumstanced as Pamela was', to Stinstra 'two or three Letters to instruct handsome Girls, who were obliged to go out to Service . . . how to avoid the Snares that might be laid against their Virtue'. This description suits Letters 138 and 139, in which a father who has heard that a master has tempted his daughter's chastity advises her to leave the house at once, and the dutiful daughter regrets that she listened to her master's 'promises of never offering the like again' and did not depart immediately after the 'vile attempt', but assures her father that she has now done so and is on her way home. Since such a precipitate departure (obviously the correct procedure in Richardson's eyes) would have ended the novel before it began, a good deal of ingenuity is devoted in *Pamela* to explaining why the heroine stayed on in her perilous situation, though this effort to harmonize the demands of fiction with those of propriety has seemed to some readers rather strained. In any case, these two letters were presumably written before *Pamela*.

If the letters were written in the order in which they were printed, at least two-thirds of them must have been completed before Richardson interrupted them to start his novel. There is no proof that they were written in that order, though in general the earlier letters are somewhat stiffer than the later ones, which have often a more individual style and an increasing concern with matters of love and marriage. It is usually and probably correctly assumed that his work on the letters determined at least the epistolary form of Richardson's novels, and in other ways the reader of the *Familiar Letters* cannot help being reminded of *Pamela* and even of *Clarissa*.

In his letter to Stinstra, Richardson mentions two points which have a bearing on his later practice: he stresses the 'low' style of the letters and

---

[9] All quotations from the *Familiar Letters* are from the edition by Brian W. Downs (New York, [1928]).

his asking the booksellers for leave to instruct his rustic readers. This didactic aim is more apparent in the *Familiar Letters* than the low style. Collections of model letters often included letters of advice or moralizing, but Richardson emphasized this aspect at the expense of the formal rules of letter writing.[10] He must have seen one of the most popular of the letter-writers, J. Hill's *The Young Secretary's Guide*, the twenty-second edition of which was printed in 1734 for J. Clarke and Richardson's brother-in-law Allington Wilde, but he did not follow it in including long sections, amounting to almost half of the book, on superscriptions, punctuation, legal forms, Latin words, a table of interest, and a discussion of types of letters broken down into eighteen classes. Of Hill's types, Richardson is especially partial to letters of Exhortation (Hill has only two) and Remonstrance (Hill has one), whereas Hill's most common types are much less frequent in the *Familiar Letters*: letters of 'Advice' (that is information), Excuse, Consolation, and Thanks.

Richardson's double purpose, so explicitly stated on his title page, is stressed in his Preface, where he hopes that the letters 'may not only direct the *forms* requisite to be observed on the most important occasions; but, what is more to the purpose, by the rules and instructions contained in them, contribute to *mend the heart, and improve the understanding*'; he has 'endeavoured . . . to inculcate the principles of virtue and benevolence; to describe properly, and recommend strongly, the social and relative duties; and to place them in such practical lights, that the letters may serve for rules to think and act by, as well as forms to write after'. Though Rivington and Osborn probably had in mind the practical purpose of furnishing model letters, such as had been often previously published, for the use of readers too unsure of their attainments to compose their own, this courtesy-book aspect is definitely subordinated by Richardson to his didactic one. At least half the letters could serve as models only to writers who were very fond of offering advice to friends and relations; a good many of those which might be regarded as models, such as letters of condolence and courtship, have in addition a strong moral tone; and comparatively few are merely models and no more—some but not all of the business letters, five letters recommending servants, two about unanswered letters, four concerning illness, two letters from a sailor and a ship's officer abroad with replies, and twelve letters describing the sights

[10] Katherine Hornbeak, who has studied other collections of model letters and compared them with Richardson's, has shown that in Richardson's this didactic tendency is far more pronounced: Richardson omitted the theory of letter writing and rules of form which were usual, and his primary interest was 'not rhetorical but ethical' (*The Complete Letter-Writer in English 1568–1800*, Smith College Studies in Modern Languages, XV, Nos. 3–4 [Northampton, Mass., 1934], p. 104). She concludes (pp. 86–9, 97–8, 101–3) that a good many (almost a third) of Richardson's subjects appear in previous letter-writers, but many others, she says in *Richardson's Familiar Letters and the Domestic Conduct Books*, are the commonplaces of books on domestic relations.

of London.[11] Even in the last series Richardson managed to include some slighting remarks about the pride of mere aristocrats and descriptions of Bedlam and of an execution which attack vulgar curiosity about the sufferings of others and appeal to the new eighteenth-century sensibility.

Of the one hundred and seventy-three letters, no less than forty-three are letters of direct advice, reproof, or admonition, giving the writer's (often unsolicited) opinion of how his correspondent should conduct himself: a younger brother should be wary of a lady whose great charm is her gay conversation, another must learn to be more economical before he receives any more money, a son should not keep a horse until he is established in life, a kinsman should be careful of intimacy with new acquaintances, a son must guard against excessive drinking, another son should not disgrace himself by becoming an actor, a brother must guard against his fondness for ridiculing others, a daughter must not show her jealousy of her husband whether founded or not, another daughter is not to encourage a suitor who has chosen the mean and impecunious calling of a subaltern in the army, a young friend must beware of rudeness to his father, a cousin of excessive devotion to music (permissible as an occasional relaxation but a great waste of valuable time if pursued seriously), a brother of boring his friends with praises of his wife and children, a daughter of taking a 'frothy French Lover' (Richardson generally suspected the French of levity if not worse), a niece of masculine airs and modern riding-habits, a friend of neglecting the education of his children (necessary both for earning a good living and for social prestige—Richardson had had little opportunity to acquaint himself with the ideal of a liberal education), another friend of going to law (no one gains by a lawsuit except the lawyers), a daughter of talking back to her husband even if he is at times in the wrong, and a wife of scolding her servants and insisting on absolute cleanliness and rigid order in housekeeping at the expense of her husband's domestic peace.[12] The duties of apprentices are discussed in terms recalling *The Apprentice's Vade Mecum*: an apprentice has no time to call his own and should submit to his master in everything; it is his duty to reveal the dishonesty of a fellow to their master, but if he repents of a misdeed a good master will give him another chance.[13] There is throughout the *Familiar Letters* a mixture of kindness and consideration for others with sharp common sense and worldly prudence which is typical of Richardson's ethics.

In addition to these primarily cautionary letters, many others show an obvious didactic intent. Business letters about collection of rent and repayment of debt illustrate the borrower's duties of frugality and

[11] Letters 26–7, 42–3, 102–3, 117–19; 31–5; 58–9; 25, 50–2; 126–9; 149–60.
[12] Letters 9, 10, 11, 12, 36, 48, 49, 54, 63, 64, 65, 68, 70, 90, 130, 144, 146, 167.
[13] Letters 2, 5–6, 38–9.

scrupulous honesty with the money of others as well as the lender's duty of forbearance and even generosity.[14] A series of letters concerns offers of help to those in financial difficulty; though gratitude on the part of the recipient is stressed and such help is not usually given imprudently, the claims of friendship and charity are recognized and relief is offered in such a way as to spare the feelings of the man who needs it.[15] The last three letters, of consolation on the deaths of near relations, are almost sermons against excessive grief, pointing to submission to the will of God as the duty of a Christian.

Especially the many letters concerning love and marriage furnish what amounts to a summary of Richardson's views on these, his favourite, subjects.[16] Almost half of Richardson's letters touch on these topics, though not in the romantic tradition of the rhapsodic love letter—one such letter is even held up to ridicule.[17] Parents or guardians play a major role. Parents never force the inclinations of their children, though they do urge the claims of prudence and the importance of considering fortune in choosing a mate: a father presenting the advantages of an older suitor leaves the decision to his daughter, but when the daughter mildly and dutifully objects, he replies 'enforcing, but not compelling, her Compliance with his Desire'.[18] Daughters, at least, generally do not question the right of their parents to a negative voice in their choice, and when they do marry without consent, the results are disastrous, though the indulgent and heartbroken parent forgives his child at least to the extent of not allowing her to suffer great privation as the result of her imprudence.[19] Parents expect obedience but are indulgent and loving. A good many letters are models for courtship, which in the middle classes is rather formal and involves an application to the girl's father and a careful investigation of the suitor's moral and financial status before the girl will give him more than a cursory hearing; a maidservant living far from her parents need merely acquaint her father and mother with her prospects and ask their blessing when they perforce leave the matter to her discretion.[20] Suitable lovers are delicately encouraged by her relatives to speak to the girl herself; unsuitable ones are rejected politely but firmly.[21] A man who presumes to address a girl without the knowledge of her guardians receives an answer from a friend of hers informing him that she never listens to such direct proposals but, if the lover is suitable,

---

[14] Letters 109–11 and others.   [15] Letters 102–8.

[16] Miss Hornbeak has estimated (*Complete Letter-Writer in English*, pp. 107–9) that over 42 per cent of Richardson's letters concern love, far more than in previous collections in the practical middle-class tradition, and has pointed out that even in previous middle-class collections love letters are generally between the parties concerned. She could not recall a single case where the parents' consent was asked.

[17] Letter 89.   [18] Letters 91–3.

[19] Letter 67.   [20] Letters 28–30.

[21] Letters 13–20, 71–3, 95–8.

referring him politely to the guardians.[22] Several letters contain gratuitous advice to friends against remarriage to unsuitable persons, to persons younger than they are, to persons with children, or to any persons if they have children[23] (Richardson had remarried four months after the death of his last child, and his second wife was a maiden of his own social status and eight years younger than he).

The didactic letters are more rational than impassioned, and their arguments are based more on prudence and respect for public opinion than on abstract principles or on religion, a fact which need not imply that Richardson himself was moved primarily by worldly wisdom, but only that he regarded it as the safest grounds on which one could persuade others. Throughout his career as a novelist he was anxious to demonstrate that honesty is the best policy and will lead to wealth and popularity.

The Preface describes Richardson's method in terms which could apply to his later novels: 'Nature, propriety of character, plain sense, and general use' have been his chief objects, he has 'aimed to write to the judgment, rather than to the imagination', and 'would choose, that they should generally be found more useful than diverting', though 'strokes of humour, and innocent raillery' where they suit the subjects may prove that any failure to divert 'was the effect of choice, and not merely of necessity'.

The innocent raillery includes a lover's remarks on his mistress's fondness for her monkey ('Is it a recommendation in him, that he wears no breeches? For my part, I will most willingly surrender mine at your feet'), the complaint of a man mistakenly supposed to be rich at the host of flatterers that besieges him, and satiric remarks about the influence of favouritism in the promotion of clergymen and about the exaggerated and one-sided zeal of party newspapers, with Sir Robert Walpole's willingness to put up with them for the sake of holding on to office.[24] The letter in which these remarks occur is also an example of the humour. It is a description written to a bottle companion now abroad of such bits of neighbourhood gossip as unhappy marriages, bankruptcies, and numerous deaths, mostly due to drink, of old friends: 'And Ben. Tomlyns, who, you remember, would never go home sober, tumbled down stairs, and broke his collar-bone. His *surgeon* took him first, a *fever* next, then his *doctor*; and then, as it were of course, *death*: A natural round enough, you'll say, Bob. His widow made a handsome burial for poor Ben; took on grievously, and in five weeks married her journeyman.' In a manner which foreshadows Anna Howe and Charlotte Grandison, Richardson lets his wit run on happily while a young lady recounts a ridiculous scene with an unduly grave and religious lover: 'O, *ay*, madam, to be sure; every good man would contribute to such a worthy charity, to be sure.

[22] Letters 99–101.   [23] Letters 140–3.   [24] Letters 125, 168, 76.

No doubt, sir, a blessing attends upon all who promote so worthy a design. *O, ay*, madam, no doubt, as you say: I am sure I have found it; blessed be God! And then he twang'd his nose, and lifted up his eyes, as if in an ejaculation.'[25] (In the 1890s a reader who found the young lady's letter copied, without credit to Richardson, in another collection was reminded of Miss Howe.)[26] In the next letter her aunt (like Clarissa and Harriet Byron) earnestly reproves her levity. Another young lady pokes fun at her lover's hyperbolical praises of her, and a man allows himself to be severely witty against a man he barely knows who wants to borrow money: 'Surely, sir, a gentleman of your merit cannot be so little beloved, as to be forced to seek to a new acquaintance, and to have no better friend than one of *yesterday*. I will not do you the injury to suppose, that you have not *many*, who have the best reasons, from long knowledge, to oblige you: And, by your application to *me*, I cannot think *bashfulness* should stand in your way to *them*.'[27]

In a fair number of letters an effort is made to suit the style to the supposed writer. A poor tenant who needs an extension of time is more lower class (and more convincing) than most of the correspondents, as are the amorous maidservant and her parents and the sailor and his betrothed: 'John ... will bring you, too, six bottles of citron-water, as a token of my love. It is fit for the finest ladies taste; it is so good; and it is what, they say, ladies drink, when they can get it.'[28] The gentleman whose wife is too good a housekeeper, the lover whose rival is a monkey, the bottle companion, and the gay young lady with the grave lover are definite characters with a style of their own. So are a bluff, hearty wooer and his frank lady who conduct a rather unorthodox courtship and a proud young lady who resents her lover's accusation of coquetry: 'Perhaps I like to see the young fellows *dying* for me; but since they can do it without impairing their health, don't be so very angry at me. In short, sir, you are your own master; and, Heaven be thank'd, I am, at present, my own mistress; and your well-manner'd letter will make me resolve to be so longer than perhaps I had otherwise resolved. You see my *follies* in my *conduct*: Thank you, sir, for letting me know you do. I see your sex in your *letter*: Thank you, sir, for that too.'[29] One letter in which a lady describes a scene with a sincere but awkward lover whom she wants to tease without discouraging is written largely in short snatches of dialogue which look forward to the society scenes in *Sir Charles Grandison*: '*You are very busy, madam.*—Yes, sir.—*Perhaps I break in upon you.*—Not much, sir.—*I am sorry if I do at all, madam.*—You see I am pursuing my work, as I was before you came.— *I do, madam!*—very gravely, said he.—*But I have known it otherwise, when*

---

[25] Letter 83.

[26] Hornbeak, *Complete Letter-Writer in English*, p. 111n.

[27] Letters 89, 124.

[28] Letters 106, 108, 28–30, 126–7.

[29] Letters 79–82, 86.

somebody else has been here.—Very likely, sir.—But then I did as I pleased—so I do now—and who shall controul me?—*I beg pardon, madam; but 'tis my value for you*—That makes you troublesome, said I, interrupting him.—*I am sorry for it, madam!*—*Your humble servant.*—Yours, sir.—So away he went.—Well, thought I, if thou art to be lost for this, and must put me into bodily fear, every time thou hast a mind to be grave, adieu to thee!'[30]

A good many of the letters are arranged in a series which carries along a sort of narrative interest, and a few are primarily narrative: two of them are from girls deserted by false and mercenary lovers, and one tells a story, which a footnote assures the reader is a true one, about a young lady's trials in the clutches of a wicked procuress.[31] Two other situations which appear in *Clarissa* are here. A lady answers a gentleman who, after professing honourable intentions, 'proposes to live with her as a Gallant': 'Nor yet will I be an hypocrite, or deny my honest passion; for that would be to lessen your guilt. God is my witness, I lov'd you beyond all your sex; yet I lov'd you *virtuously*; I lov'd you because I thought you *virtuous*. And now, tho' it may take some time, and too much regret, to get over; yet do I hope, your behaviour will enable me to conquer my fond folly. . . . And I have one consolation, tho' a consolation I did not wish for, that I am under no obligation, but the contrary, to such a man: And am as much your superior, as the person who would do no wrong, is to one that will do nothing else.'[32] Another pleads with a suitor she does not love but who is favoured by her parents to relieve her suffering by stopping his suit.[33]

There are even hints of Richardson's later use of the epistolary form to write 'to the moment', to present events and emotions with the freshness and intensity only possible while they are still occurring or very recent. Once he uses this advantage (as often later) to obtain suspense by breaking off a letter at a crucial point, when a young lady so orders a series of three letters on her two suitors as to make her aunt think for a moment that she prefers a 'fluttering Pretender' to a sensible lover.[34] Indeed in Richardson's version of the classic mixture of *utile* and *dulce* there is much more *dulce* than one would expect. It is not surprising that the man who began the *Familiar Letters* had written a novel before he ended it. How useful his letters were as models for ignorant letter writers is doubtful, but they make surprisingly lively reading, more lively indeed than some of the novel writing in the second part of *Pamela* and towards the end of *Sir Charles Grandison*.

Richardson told Stinstra that he had 'omitted several Letters . . . as too high for the Design',[35] and the omitted letters may well include the 'Six Original Letters upon Duelling' which were published posthumously as

<hr>

[30] Letter 163.
[31] Letters 131, 166, 62.
[32] Letter 137.
[33] Letters 133–6.
[34] Letters 162–4.
[35] 20 Mar. 1754.

Richardson's in the *Candid Review* for March 1765.[36] Richardson's family denied the authorship,[37] but the *Candid Review* assured its readers that 'every word of them was written by the late Mr. *Richardson*' and that 'the originals are left in the hands of Mr. *Stuart* [the bookseller of the periodical], for public inspection'.[38] These letters are certainly in the tone of the *Familiar Letters*: Thomas Gilles writes to his two friends Andrew Crisp and John Orme pointing out what disastrous effects their fighting a duel will have in this and, more important, in the next life and induces them by his reasonable arguments to appoint him peacemaker between them. Many of the letters which were published in the *Familiar Letters*, however, seem to be too high for the use of the class of people who one would think needed a model letter-writer: it is by no means true that almost all of the correspondents belong 'to classes below the middle line of society'.[39]

[36] I, 227–31.
[37] *St. James's Chronicle*, 4–6 Apr. 1765.
[38] I, 320.
[39] Brian W. Downs, *Richardson* (London, 1928), p. 108.

CHAPTER VI

PAMELA

THERE is no reason to doubt Richardson's statement that *Pamela* grew out of the *Familiar Letters*, that the letters between the servant girl and her father reminded him of the story he had heard years before.[1] They also started him on the epistolary method which he consistently used in the rest of his novels, though in fact *Pamela* is the least epistolary of them: there is almost no interchange; most of the letters are from Pamela herself, and after her abduction, when she no longer has access to the post, they take the form of a journal for a long period. This journal, however, gives as much opportunity as letters would have for 'writing to the moment', one of the advantages which Richardson saw in the epistolary form, which meant a great gain in dramatic immediacy. Experiences written about as they happen are almost perforce more vivid to the supposed writer, and hence to the reader, than had previously been usual in the historical approach, when events were presented as if narrated years later. In addition, Richardson often used the method to obtain suspense, a device which it is easy to ridicule and which may irritate some readers: my master is coming upstairs, what will he do? I must lay down my pen, God preserve me—Break, and start again slowly without immediately revealing what has happened.

A much more important advantage in the epistolary method, especially important at a time when techniques of the novel were hardly past their infancy, is that it enables a character to present himself through his style and his thoughts and thus almost forces a writer to create a character, if at all, from inside. Recent critics have recognized the great opportunities the form offered—and Richardson seized on. Leslie Fiedler remarks that 'after abandoning the letter convention, the novel did not achieve comparable subtlety and directness in the presentation of thought until the invention of stream-of-consciousness'.[2] And Frank Kermode has said, 'By his almost fortuitous adoption of the narrative technique of "epistolary correspondencies", Richardson solved in advance (though at a cost subsequent novelists were not, on the whole, prepared to pay), the great

---

[1] For an effort to decide exactly how the *Familiar Letters* influenced *Pamela*, see Danielowski, *Richardsons erster Roman*, pp. 44–51, 67–8. Frau Danielowski seems to us somewhat too certain on the basis of inconclusive evidence, as well as too sceptical of Richardson's own statements.

[2] *Love and Death in the American Novel* (New York, [1960]), p. 41.

novelistic problem, so seriously pondered by Conrad and James, of the author's necessity to withdraw from his fiction.'[3] In the epistolary novel the problem of point of view was solved long before it was formally posed.

Of course any first person narrative can achieve the same result for one of the characters, and Defoe had already created the most lively characters in English prose fiction in this way. In *Pamela* only one of the characters has much chance to reveal herself; in his later novels Richardson tried the more complex task of letting several characters reveal themselves in interaction with each other. Those characters who do not write much (or who do not write vividly) must be seen through the eyes of others, and the reader is therefore in danger of seeing them falsely, as they appear to the main writers. It has been suggested, for instance, that our view of Mr. B. is thus distorted, that his conversion is more subtle and convincing than Pamela can know.[4] But the letters he does write do not reflect the sort of complex character who can be analysed. The same thing may be said of Sir Charles Grandison, who also writes comparatively little. Admittedly it is hard to disentangle cause and effect, but we suspect that those leading characters in Richardson who are seen mainly through others' eyes do not write because they cannot and that they cannot because Richardson had not realized them as he had Pamela and Clarissa and Lovelace and Anna Howe—and even Uncle Anthony and Mrs. Harlowe, who in their few letters speak for themselves. That they must be reported, not conveyed, is their own fault, not the fault of the epistolary method.

The combination of immediacy and subjectivity which grew out of the epistolary form undoubtedly enabled readers to identify with Richardson's characters in a way hardly possible in previous prose fiction. They saw with the eyes of the letter writers, experienced with them, thought with them, and above all felt with them. When Aaron Hill speaks of being transformed into Goodman Andrews, of striding with Colbrand the Swiss, of being kept awake at night by Mrs. Jewkes, and in general of experiencing the after-effects of the novel as of events truly lived,[5] he expresses the common feeling of a new intensity and reality. Diderot must have spoken for many readers when he said, 'O Richardson! on prend, malgré qu'on en ait, un rôle dans tes ouvrages, on se mêle à la conversation, on approuve, on blâme, on admire, on s'irrite, on s'indigne. Combien de fois ne me suis-je pas surpris, comme il est arrivé à des enfants qu'on avait menés au spectacle pour la première fois, criant: *Ne le croyez pas, il vous trompe. . . Si vous allez là, vous êtes perdu.* Mon âme était tenue dans une agitation perpétuelle. Combien j'étais bon! combien j'étais juste! que

---

[3] 'Richardson and Fielding', *Cambridge Journal*, IV (1950–1), 111.
[4] M. Kinkead-Weekes, 'Introduction' to *Pamela*, Everyman's Library edn. (London, [1965]), I, xi.
[5] 15 Jan. 1741.

j'étais satisfait de moi! J'étais, au sortir de ta lecture, ce qu'est un homme à la fin d'une journée qu'il a employée à faire le bien.'[6]

The epistolary novel did not have a great future in spite of its occasional use by able writers from Smollett to Dostoievsky and at least one brilliant success by Laclos. Its most obvious disadvantage is that it demands the assumption that all of the correspondents are able and energetic writers with a good deal of time at their disposal. But surely less likely conventions have been accepted often enough without strain. Its great advantages were the creation of a sense of reality and a personal voice for the characters hardly present in previous prose fiction. In itself it was not very important, but it was of the greatest importance in opening up new possibilities—it gave the novel a power hitherto known only in drama, it made it dramatic.

The method arose naturally enough in an age of great letter writers, when Lady Mary Wortley Montagu, Gray, Horace Walpole, and Cowper (like Byron and Keats later) exhibit themselves in much the same way that Pamela and Clarissa do, so that for us today they come through with the vividness of fictional characters. Richardson's talent has often been connected with the youthful epistolary exploits described in his letter to Stinstra. It may be that these exploits were magnified in view of his later fictional success with letter writing, but they could easily have helped him when *Pamela* called on him to reproduce the manners, the style, and the little psychological inconsistencies of a girl of about the same class as his early employers on Tower Hill. Richardson's own letters reveal a good deal about him, but they reveal a character arranged and adapted according to what his friends expected: the tone of his letters varies greatly with the correspondent, but he did not present to anyone a character as interesting, or as convincing, as Harriet and Clarissa and Pamela and Lovelace. That he did not may be regarded as not so much a sign of Richardson's own dullness as a tribute to the superior power of imaginative art.[7]

There has never been much doubt that the strength of *Pamela* is Pamela.

[6] *Éloge de Richardson* in *Œuvres complètes* (Paris, 1875), V, 213.

'Oh, Richardson! in spite of ourselves we play a role in your works, we take part in the conversations, we approve, we blame, we marvel, we are angry and indignant. How often have I surprised myself, like a child taken to the theatre for the first time, crying out: "Do not believe him, he is deceiving you... If you go there, you are lost." My mind was in perpetual excitement. How good I was! how just! how satisfied with myself! When I stopped reading, I was like a man at the end of a day which he has used to do good.'

[7] For a discussion of the relation between Richardson's own letters and his novelistic technique, see Malvin R. Zirker, Jr., 'Richardson's Correspondence: The Personal Letter as Private Experience', *The Familiar Letter in the Eighteenth Century*, ed. Howard Anderson, Philip B. Daghlian, and Irvin Ehrenpreis (Lawrence, Kansas, 1966), pp. 71–91. It seems to us that Mr. Zirker has taken some of Richardson's playful remarks to young ladies much too earnestly and that he has sometimes over-dramatized his subject by quoting remarks out of context—he might, for instance, have pointed out that the one example he gives (p. 91) of a 'catty' remark by Lady Echlin, her pity for her sister's fat, was made in a discussion of Lady Bradshaigh's health.

The morality of the book, which Richardson prized so much, has been frequently, and not unjustly, exposed not only by modern critics but even more severely by the Victorians and Edwardians. The plot has the advantage of unity and, at least for some readers, of suspense, but it is not calculated to appeal to readers today: a virtuous servant girl rejects her master's lewd advances and is kidnapped by him and confined in a lonely country house, where she continues to fight him off until he is overcome by her virtue to the extent of proposing matrimony, which is instantly accepted. The details of the plot, it is true, are well worked out and more varied and interesting than this outline suggests. In spite of Richardson's notorious verbosity the book opens swiftly (as, indeed, do all of Richardson's novels), and interest does not flag at least through the first volume.

There are a few other characters besides the heroine who have life: Pamela's jailoress, the fat and vulgar and cruel and jolly Mrs. Jewkes, is well imagined and speaks vigorously; and Pamela's proud sister-in-law, Lady Davers, though she reminds one of Restoration comedy as it would appear to a man who deplored its morality and did not understand its manners, is lively, even witty if airy and outspoken rudeness can pass for wit—as it often can. These two characters are not done from inside, but from sharp observation. But these minor successes are outweighed by Richardson's failure with the leading male figure, Mr. B. Most readers have felt that Fielding's expansion of that unfortunate initial into Booby is an apt summation. Austin Dobson points out that he is really two characters, both of them dull, a rake derived from the play-book and a reformed husband derived from the copy-book.[8] Especially in the continuation of *Pamela* the reader is often told that he is learned and intelligent and brave and high-minded, but no evidence for these virtues is ever given; his self-satisfied and punctilious demands on Pamela would be insufferable if one believed in him for a second. Of the other things which later novelists have taught the public to demand—social criticism or philosophical overtones, symbolism, atmosphere, analysis, a firmly realized setting (except that the clothes are minutely described)—there is almost nothing.

Yet in spite of almost insuperable disadvantages Pamela lives. Clara Thomson, who has been more severe than anyone on Pamela's character (a 'vulgar, practical little soul'), best explains the matter when she says that though one cannot for a moment accept her as the paragon Richardson thought he was presenting, she is a 'masterpiece of characterization', simply because she convinces us that she is real.[9] Richardson does not explain what Pamela is like—probably he did not consciously know; he *shows* her. As David Daiches says, 'He does not have to understand her

[8] *Samuel Richardson* (London, 1902), p. 35.
[9] *Samuel Richardson: A Biographical and Critical Study* (London, 1900), pp. 156, 166–7.

or to analyse her motives, any more than she understands and analyses herself.'[10] The fact that she irritates readers, that they disagree about her, that one can accuse her of hypocrisy is a sure sign of life. No one can argue about the true nature of Mr. B. If we can forget what Richardson wants us to think Pamela is, we have no trouble believing in her. For Richardson's great triumph is that he has been able to become a servant girl, to realize, in the literal sense, a character in a way that had rarely been done before except in the drama—by Lady Murasaki, by Chaucer, by Cervantes, by Mme. de Lafayette perhaps, but never in English prose fiction.

It is probably Richardson's absurd claims for Pamela that have led later critics to disparage her unduly. He makes the other characters praise her so highly that the reader is tempted to deny her the praise she deserves. If one ignores the scenes in which other characters grow ecstatic about her superhuman virtue (Richardson leads one to think that it must have been extraordinary for a servant girl in his day to keep her virginity till marriage) and almost as ecstatic about her 'ladylike' manners and her ability to carve turkey and serve cake, if one attends only to her own words (and only up to the time of her marriage, when her new propriety kills her as a character), she is consistent and not unattractive. Of course she has an eye on the main chance; of course, being an eighteenth-century servant, she has an undue respect for rank. One objection, however—that her curtsy to her master during their wedding ceremony shows too much deference—seems to arise from a misunderstanding. In a letter to Mrs. Chapone, Richardson refers to 'the assenting Bow or Courtesy, which the Minister always watches for' as if it was the normal method of saying 'I do'.[11] And in her subsequent comments on her husband's demanding rules for a wife Pamela shows that she was by no means altogether subservient—she obeyed (as in Richardson's opinion a wife should do), but she criticized the pride that could claim such obedience.

Surely Miss Thomson is taking a very high moral stand when she says that no woman can forgive her for marrying the man who so bluntly attempted to seduce her.[12] No woman or man can forgive an Ideal who would do so, and it is Richardson's great mistake that he was determined to pass off Pamela as an Ideal. But the Pamela he caused to speak and write is a real woman, and if one cannot forgive a woman for having a practical side, for respecting and desiring money and rank, and even for fooling herself into ignoring these motives in herself, then we are all in a bad way. The ambiguity of her morality 'need not spring from conscious duplicity on Pamela's part, since it is implicit in the feminine code by which

[10] *Literary Essays* (Edinburgh and London, 1956), p. 39.

[11] 18 Apr. 1752.

[12] *Richardson*, p. 164.

Morality = may lead Pamela
to opinion Hyperits

she acts'.[13] Her 'hypocrisy' is the hypocrisy of all of us: it arises from
the discrepancy between the lofty view of morality we are taught and at
times believe in and the double demand of society, for a propriety very
different from that morality and a wordly success often incompatible with
it. The severe remarks made about Pamela's morality are a tribute to her
success as a character—she is a 'hypocrite' because Richardson, consciously or unconsciously, knew her so thoroughly, with all her inconsistent motives. The Pamela he talks *about* is a puppet; the Pamela he talks
for is a fairly clever, rather pert, little girl, limited and also strengthened
by her proper upbringing, genuinely kind when it does not seriously
inconvenience her to be so, religious in a conventional but not insincere
way, who, in the usual compromise between the claims of morality as she
has been taught it and the claims of practicality as her low position in
society demands it, leans slightly towards the former and who has a
virtue, if virtue it is, which was only beginning to be cultivated by persons
of her class (and which was certainly cultivated by her creator, who
started life in a class only slightly above hers)—self-respect. She demands
to be treated as a person, when Mr. B. is treating her as a thing. One
cannot but sympathize with her demand; even today, a young girl who
does not want to be raped ought not to be raped.

How a middle-aged business man came so thoroughly to understand a
little servant girl is the usual mystery of creation. Perhaps, as has often
been suspected, Richardson had 'a deep personal identification with the
opposite sex which went far beyond social preference or cultural rap-
port'.[14] Certainly he liked the society of women and certainly most of his
successful characters are women. But there is no biographical evidence
that the feminine side of his nature was unusually prominent—no one, at
any rate, seems to have noticed it if it was. His letters to women have a
note of decorous flirtation and sound as if he was so interested in the
opposite sex precisely because it was for him the opposite sex. But we do
not intend to psychoanalyse Richardson, believing that even a trained
analyst, without getting his subject for a prolonged period on his couch,
can hardly hope to penetrate the subconscious with certainty on the
dubious evidence of the written word and such things as choice of imagery.

Nevertheless the question of how much of Pamela was Richardson's
conscious creation and how much his unconscious cannot be avoided
entirely, though the answer to such a question must be tentative. It seems
likely, for instance, that the delicate touches by which he indicates the
gradual and unconscious growth of Pamela's love for Mr. B. were on
Richardson's part conscious. She rejoices in her persecutor's safety when
he is almost drowned crossing a stream and is surprised to find she cannot

[13] Ian Watt, *The Rise of the Novel* (Berkeley and Los Angeles, 1957), p. 168.
[14] Ibid., p. 153.

hate him: 'To be sure, I am not like other People! . . . Ungenerous Master! if you knew this, you surely would not be so much my Persecutor! But for my late good Lady's sake, I must wish him well; and O what an Angel would he be in my Eyes yet, if he would cease his Attempts, and reform.'[15] Surely here Richardson meant his readers to recognize that Pamela's kind feelings are not due to gratitude towards Mr. B.'s late mother. Or her admiration of Mr. B. in his fine Sunday clothes: 'To be sure, he is a handsome fine Gentleman;—What Pity his Heart is not as good as his Appearance! Why can't I hate him?—But don't be uneasy, if you should see this; for it is impossible I should love him; for his Vices all *ugly him over*, as I may say.'[16] At the first sign that Mr. B. is becoming kinder and may consider trading, in the accepted fashion, his name for Pamela's chastity, she does not even consider rejecting the offer, though earlier she had told Mrs. Jervis that 'if I was the Lady of Birth, and he would offer to be rude first, as he has twice done to poor me, I don't know whether I would have him'.[17] He has been much ruder since, but she is not the Lady of Birth; and though she is firm enough in protecting her rights, she recognizes her place, and immediately on her master's softening she sees that 'I have now more Comfort before me, than ever I yet knew: And am either nearer my *Happiness*, or my *Misery*, than ever I was'.[18] She is nearer her misery because Mr. B.'s kindness weakens her resistance as his rudeness never can. Her conflict of feelings when Mr. B. sends her away is well presented; she is glad to be escaping from his clutches and going home, but she cannot be very happy about it:

What! when I have such Proof, that her Virtue is all her Pride, shall I rob her of that?—No, added he, let her go, perverse, and foolish, as she is; but she *deserves* to go honest, and she *shall* go so.

I was so transported with this unexpected Goodness, that I open'd the Door before I knew what I did, and I said, falling on my Knees at the Door, with my Hands folded and lifted up, O thank you, thank your Honour, a Million of times!—May God bless you for this Instance of your Goodness to me! I will pray for you as long as I live, and so shall my dear Father and Mother. And, Mrs. *Jewkes*, said I, I will pray for *you* too, poor wicked Wretch that you are!

He turn'd from me, and went into his Closet, and shut the Door. He need not to have done so; for I would not have gone nearer to him!

Surely I did not say *so much*, to incur all this Displeasure!

I think I was loth to leave the House. Can you believe it?—What could be the Matter with me, I wonder?—I felt something so strange, and my Heart was so lumpish!—I wonder what ail'd me!—But this was so *unexpected*!—I believe that was all!—Yet I am very strange still. Surely, surely, I cannot be like the old murmuring *Israelites*, to long after the Onions and Garlick of *Egypt*, when they had suffer'd there such heavy Bondage?[19]

---

[15] SH, I, 243; EL, I, 156.   [16] SH, I, 268-9; EL, I, 172.   [17] SH, I, 53; EL, I, 34.
[18] SH, I, 289; EL, I, 186.   [19] SH, II, 2-3; EL, I, 216-17.

The touches here which will strike most modern readers as ludicrous, Pamela's excessive gratitude and her offer to pray for Mrs. Jewkes and Mr. B.'s silly petulance, do not make the scene less real. They are, of course, lethal if one thinks of Pamela the Ideal of Virtue who is to be rewarded with this Egyptian garlic. But humour, even unintentional humour, does not really injure the breathing Pamela whom Richardson imagined, does not even, in the long run, make her less pathetic.

One is tempted to hope that some of the humour, especially in the seduction scenes, was intentional:

I pulled off my Stays and my Stockens, and all my Cloaths to an Under-petticoat; and then hearing a Rustling again in the Closet, I said, Heaven protect us! but before I say my Prayers, I must look into this Closet. And so was going to it slip-shod, when, O dreadful! out rushed my Master, in a rich Silk and Silver Morning Gown.

I scream'd, and ran to the Bed, and Mrs. *Jervis* scream'd too; and he said, I'll do you no Harm, if you forbear this Noise; but otherwise take what follows.

Instantly he came to the Bed (for I had crept into it, to Mrs. *Jervis*, with my Coat on, and my Shoes); and, taking me in his Arms, said, Mrs. *Jervis*, rise, and just step up-stairs, to keep the Maids from coming down, at this Noise: I'll do no Harm to this Rebel.

O, for Heaven's sake! for Pity's sake! Mrs. *Jervis*, said I, if I am not betray'd, don't leave me; and, I beseech you, raise all the House. No, said Mrs. *Jervis*, I will not stir, my dear Lamb; I will not leave you. I wonder at you, Sir! said she; and kindly threw herself upon my Coat, clasping me round the Waist: You shan't hurt this Innocent, said she; for I will lose my Life in her Defence. Are there not, added she, enough wicked ones in the World for your base Purpose, but you must attempt such a Lamb as this?

He was desperate angry, and threaten'd to throw her out of the Window; and to turn her out of the House the next Morning. You need not, Sir, said she; for I will not stay in it. God defend my poor *Pamela* till To-morrow, and we will both go together.—Says he, Let me but expostulate a Word or two with you, *Pamela*. Pray, *Pamela*, said Mrs. *Jervis*, don't hear a Word, except he leaves the Bed, and goes to the other End of the Room. Ay, out of the Room, said I; expostulate To-morrow, if you must expostulate!

I found his Hand in my Bosom, and when my Fright let me know it, I was ready to die; and I sighed, and screamed, and fainted away. And still he had his Arms about my Neck; and Mrs. *Jervis* was about my Feet, and upon my Coat: And all in a cold dewy Sweat was I.[20]

Could Richardson have missed the bathos of 'threaten'd to throw her out of the Window; and to turn her out of the House the next Morning'? or of 'expostulate To-morrow, if you must expostulate'? or of Mr. B.'s ridiculous request to Mrs. Jervis to step upstairs? Are we forced to take all of this as deadly serious if we are to adopt Richardson's official view of

[20] SH, I, 78–80; EL, I, 49–50.

Pamela's situation? Could he have been subtle enough to reproduce consciously the often absurd behaviour of excited people? Or did he get swept away—did he perhaps have a sense of the comedy in Mr. B.'s situation lurking in his mind? In any case his Pamela would certainly not have missed the 'rich Silk and Silver Morning Gown', even faced by a fate worse than death. Funny or not, the scene, with its exact detail and its simple style and breathless rhythm, shows as well as any Richardson's accomplishment.

Richardson could hardly have predicted the twentieth-century tendency to find humour in rape. Nor could he have suspected what Freudian critics could do with the two cows that Pamela mistakes for bulls possessed by the spirits of her master and Mrs. Jewkes, the fear of which prevents her making her escape, and with her being reminded of the bulls when she dreams that Colbrand and Mr. B. are 'both coming to my Bedside with the worst Designs'.[21] Her mistake and her dream may be accidental—or do they suggest that Richardson had so well imagined Pamela that he read her unconscious motives?

One dream, by Mr. B., dragged in for no apparent reason as an example of how a lady's excessive concern about a broken china dish cannot only spoil the evening but the night as well, is even more difficult to explain as coincidence: 'And it affected me so much, that when I came home, I went to-bed, and dreamt, that *Robin*, with the Handle of his Whip, broke the Fore-glass of my Chariot; and I was so solicitous, methought, to keep the good Lady in Countenance for *her* Anger, that I broke his Head in Revenge, and stabb'd one of my Coach-horses. And all the Comfort I had when it was done, methought, was, that I had not exposed myself before Company; and there were no Sufferers, but guilty *Robin*, and one innocent Coach-horse; for when my Hand was in, I might as reasonably have kill'd the other three.'[22] This odd dream was cut from his final revision of *Pamela*.[23] It is hard not to believe that Richardson had actually had it, probably stimulated by the idea of breaking arising from a real event. If so, it is an example of how he could on occasion use his subconscious mind as a source for his characters, certainly in this case without imagining the implications of the symbolism of his dream.

But such occasional and dubious plumbings of the unconscious are not the main reasons for Pamela's success as a character. Much more important is the freshness of her style. Until her elevation, when Richardson deliberately decided that it must be raised to harmonize with her new dignity (a concession to propriety, if a violation of probability), her language is that of a servant girl, homely, colloquial, even racy. Some of

[21] SH, I, 204–6, 226; EL, I, 131–3, 145.   [22] SH, II, 183; EL, I, 334.
[23] Published in 1801. For a discussion of Richardson's revisions of his novel, see T. C. Duncan Eaves and Ben D. Kimpel, 'Richardson's Revisions of *Pamela*', *SB*, XX (1967), 61–88.

Richardson's early critics blamed this novelty, and in his many successive revisions he made his heroine's writing somewhat more 'correct'. Her grammar is polished as early as the second edition, when the past tenses of 'run' and 'begin' are changed from 'run' and 'begun' and the past participles of 'break' and 'write' from 'broke' and 'wrote' to their more usual forms. Such polishing occurs in all the following editions. A few natural but inaccurate expressions are altered, and 'low' words are sometimes raised—'curchee' becomes 'curt'sy', for instance, 'my old Lady' 'my late Lady', and 'a Mort of good Things' 'a great many good Things'. But it is surprising how little Richardson changed Pamela's style even in his last and most extensive revision. When Mr. B. jokes about his knowing that 'pretty Maids wear Shoes and Stockens', Pamela is still 'so confounded at these Words, you might have beat me down with a Feather'; when in the summerhouse he holds her back and shuts the door, she still 'would have given my Life for a Farthing'; and the steward, Mr. Longman, is still 'reckon'd worth a Power of Money'.[24] The importance of Richardson's use of colloquial language can best be appreciated by comparing *Pamela* to *Moll Flanders*. Defoe's heroine and his subject could have given legitimate occasion for much more racy language than any Richardson uses, but Moll writes a comparatively colourless English. Defoe had seen his characters moving about in a world of solid details; Richardson, in addition, heard his. Chaucer, of course, had used natural language, but he was so out of date as hardly to be understood; the drama had often used it. But in prose fiction it was an innovation (for the rather pedantic jargon of the rogue novels serves a different purpose), one of Richardson's most important innovations. If readers were to find the same immediacy in another form that they had once found in the drama, rapidly dying in Richardson's day, it was necessary to let them hear a real person speaking.

Richardson's frequent mention of petty domestic detail was almost as great an innovation, though the detail in *Robinson Crusoe* was a sort of precedent. Much of the detail might seem to a hostile reader like unnecessary padding: '[My father] put on a clean Shirt and Neckcloth, (which he brought in his Pocket) at an Alehouse there, and got shav'd; and so, after he had eat some Bread and Cheese, and drank a Can of Ale, he set out for my Master's house.'[25] This is cut in the final revision, probably because it had been criticized as 'low' and trivial—Fielding had parodied Pamela's references to clothes and food in *Shamela*. But the total effect of even these superfluous details is to give a new solidity to the events described. And the details are often used to reveal character. The delicately nurtured Pamela is about to return to her parents' rude home: 'I have read of a good Bishop, that was to be burnt for his Religion; and he try'd how he could bear it, by putting his Fingers into the lighted

[24] SH, I, 13, 19, 47; EL, I, 8, 12, 31.   [25] SH, II, 67–8; EL, I, 259.

Candle: So I t'other Day try'd, when *Rachel*'s Back was turn'd, if I could not scour a Pewter Plate she had begun. I see I could do't by degrees: It only blister'd my Hand in two Places.'[26] An example of Richardson's conscious artistry is the fact that in the first edition this reads 'Tho' I blister'd'—he has made his heroine more sympathetic by a change of two words. All of the details, especially the great importance of clothes, are exactly what we would expect from Pamela.

Sometimes one feels that Richardson knew his heroine almost too well for his avowed purpose. Her sharp comments on Mr. B.'s pedantic and pompous demands on his wife would hardly augur well for their future harmony if marriage had not turned them from people into stuffed models ('That if she would overcome, it must be by Sweetness and Complaisance; *that is by* Yielding, *he means, no doubt*').[27] This was also cut in the final revision. So too are many of the details of the scene in which Pamela repeats to her husband before a large company of comparative strangers the insults which his sister, Lady Davers, has heaped on her, constantly saying that she does not want to make trouble between them and then repeating every remark that might be calculated to do so and bringing the subject up again whenever it threatens to drop, while the local gossips hang on every word.[28] Everyone behaves as vulgarly, and as naturally, as possible.

In these last two episodes, Pamela acts as a person, not a paragon. But they are exceptional in the second half of the book, which declines sharply after her return to her repentant master, and even more after their marriage.

Various causes may be suggested for the collapse of *Pamela* about half way through part one. One may simply say that Richardson's inspiration flagged; or one may point out, truly, that his moral purpose becomes more prominent: under the distorting lens of a contradictory and conventional ethics, the sharply realized character of Pamela blurs and gradually fades until we see merely a dummy through whose mouth someone else is droning platitudes. But perhaps the increasing importance of the message is as much the effect as the cause of the death of Pamela.

One not improbable cause is the somewhat mysterious but, at least in Richardson, undeniably close connection between plot and character. It is not so much that we are interested primarily in the events that are taking place as that unless interesting events are taking place there are no real people on the scene. One trend of the novel for the last fifty years has been to minimize plot, a trend which can be apparently justified by the solid reason that plot is never the most important element in a good work of fiction (what notion of *Œdipus at Colonus* or *King Lear* or *Emma* or *The*

[26] SH, I, 98–99; EL, I, 63.   [27] SH, II, 292; EL, I, 407.
[28] SH, II, 221–41; EL, I, 359–73.

Possessed or *The Charterhouse of Parma* can be conveyed by a plot summary or a comic-book version?) and the fact that the plots of many novels are conventional and mechanical devices to excuse the portrayal of character or the communication of attitude. But perhaps the matter is not so simple as it at first appears; at least it seems that the strongest characters and the most complex attitudes are often inextricably involved in a significant sequence of happenings. Character may need to be revealed in action, and attitude may be more valid when it is attitude not towards the universe and life in general but towards some particular situation. Among other things, plot in fiction may serve one purpose that sensuous imagery does in the lyric, of keeping the writer from floating off into the abstract.

However this may be, such evidence as there is suggests that Richardson's most successful works came to him at first in the form of stories. When he began with an abstract idea, as in the second part of *Pamela* and in *Sir Charles Grandison*, the result was disastrous. And the real story of the first part of *Pamela* is over when it becomes apparent that Mr. B. intends to offer Pamela his hand in exchange for her body. From then on Richardson does what he can to keep the novel moving; he tries to shift the centre of interest to Pamela's acceptance by her husband's society. But at best he discovers secondary virtues.

The most important of these is a talent for social comedy. The only successful scene in the second volume, the scene in which Mr. B.'s sharp-tongued sister, Lady Davers, and her inane nephew Jackey descend on the recently married Pamela and insult her until she is driven to flee from her own house, is successful as a comedy, almost a farce, of manners (rather bad manners). The characters, Pamela included, have the kind of reality one finds in a lively satire, where the conversation of *other* people is overheard, whereas in the words of Pamela during her trial we (contradictorily enough) seem to be hearing ourselves. Richardson reveals a surprising gift for wit, or rather for repartee. The question of whether a real lady would have been as rude and as violent as Lady Davers is today largely an academic one; so far as is known Richardson had not yet had the occasion to meet a real lady, but Lady Davers is hardly more vulgar than Lady Catherine de Bourgh and Elizabeth Elliot, whose creator did know the people she was describing. At any rate it was on sharp retort that he fell back when his intensely imagined heroines found themselves with nothing to do, and the result is a sort of social conflict with a bustling satiric surface which was to have a considerable future in the English novel.

Richardson also makes an effort to revive interest in his dying story by arousing suspense, first about how Lady Davers will affect Pamela's fortunes, then about Mr. B.'s bastard daughter, Miss Goodwin. In spite of the conscious artistry with which he carefully drops hints and prepares the way for these new plot elements, it cannot be said that his efforts are very successful: Lady Davers does flare into life of a sort in one scene, but Miss Goodwin is stillborn, like the similar vain attempts to restart the plot in the second part of *Pamela*. Aside from these two new centres of interest, the second volume of part one is taken up by the marriage itself, recounted in great detail; by Mr. B.'s demands on his wife and Pamela's resolutions to live up to them; by her thankfulness in her new glory and the acts of charity and forgiveness by which she shows herself worthy of it; and above all by the interminable praises which everyone lavishes on her.

Richardson had to show that his heroine was suited for exaltation, and he does so largely by having all the neighbours marvel at how like a real lady she is. Pamela, it appears, has all the accomplishments of the Sex. When she serves cake on a silver salver, Lady Jones declares that 'she was never serv'd with such a Grace, and it was giving me too much Trouble'.[29] There is a great deal of this, some of which Richardson had sense enough to cut in his final revision. Even her lame adaptation of the 137th Psalm must be commented on at length as an indication of her (or rather her creator's) poetic skill.[30] Pamela must tip all of her old fellow servants, and their praises of her generosity are not short of ecstatic; her condescension is almost as remarkable: 'I took each of them by the Hand, and could have kiss'd them'—but did not.[31] One must remember that servants in the eighteenth century were still servants, and a little historical perspective can prevent nausea; but it can hardly ward off ennui.

Richardson must have been thinking of this Ideal Pamela rather than of the little servant girl when he penned an unused dedication of *Pamela* to a still living lady whom he had venerated since the hour he was first admitted to her presence, 'who sat, in the Writer's Mind, for the Graces, both Personal and Intellectual, of PAMELA', 'whose Picture is attempted to be Drawn, and Excellencies delineated, in Numberless Places in the Work', and who, 'tho' neither so humble in her Birth, nor so exalted in her latter Fortunes', suffered even more than Pamela, 'with equal Fortitude, & with a Charity for her Injurers, that has met but with *one*, and that The *Divine*, Example'.[32] One immediately speculates about the mysterious Mrs. Beaumont, but one hopes that she was not such a stick as Mrs. B.

The lengthy and effusive eulogies are part of the reward of virtue, and indeed no novel ever better deserved the subtitle 'Virtue Rewarded' than *Pamela*. Western philosophy and religion have devoted a great deal of thought and effort towards proving that in one way or another honesty is the best policy. Only an atheistical immoralist like Nietzsche dares tell us that our word about virtue should be to be in our deeds as a mother is in her child. More austere and orthodox preachers prefer to demonstrate that there are good reasons why a mother *ought* to love her child—it is neces-

[29] SH, II, 60; EL, I, 254.
[31] SH, II, 315; EL, I, 422.

[30] SH, II, 105–11; EL, I, 283–7.
[32] FM XVI, 1, fos. 10–11.

sary for society, and society will help her in turn; the child will love her, even take care of her in her old age; her neighbours will praise her; God will reward her with a large income in this life and with something even better for all eternity; she will feel good inside and be able to approve of her own conduct; best of all, she may even claim to be unselfish—that is, she can demand credit for her altruism, presumably on the grounds that if she followed her own desires she would have left the child to starve. All of these advantages of virtue attend Pamela's chastity.

If Richardson had left out his moral, there would have been nothing immoral about the book. But his treating Pamela as an Ideal to be followed forces one to recognize the inadequacy of his Ideal. The independence with which she asserts her right to be treated as a person would have provided a rather effective ethical attitude, but it is forgotten in the preaching. Since Mrs. Barbauld one hundred and fifty years ago pointed out that 'the moral of this piece is more dubious than, in his life time, the author's friends were willing to allow', commentators have been fond of pointing out that Pamela's prudence, after she has hopes of marrying her master, is greater than her purity: 'We can only consider her as the conscious possessor of a treasure, which she is wisely resolved not to part with but for its just price.'[33] One does not expect a servant girl to see through the ambiguity of a code which almost identified morality, at least for a woman, with sexual morality, which put a high financial and social value on her chastity and which expected her to act and speak as though she had never been stirred by desire. One does, however, expect a professed moralist to see some of the limitations of such a code, and other novelists of the eighteenth and nineteenth centuries were capable of doing so, as Richardson himself was in *Clarissa*. A novelist who does not can be of only historical interest as a teacher of ethics, and it is therefore unfortunate that in *Pamela* Richardson devotes so much space to such teaching. In one respect, however, Richardson's moralizing certainly helped to turn the novel into a recognized literary form: it made people take his books seriously who would never have thought of earlier novels as more than popular entertainment.

It is less important that in spite of (or because of) Richardson's concern with purity there are scenes in the novel which might easily stimulate the sexually sensitive. Like a Biblical spectacular with one hundred thousand dancing girls, *Pamela* must have presented for some of its readers 'the combined attractions of a sermon and a striptease'.[34] But the pornographic aspect of the novel has already been overemphasized; only a few of the scenes are 'warm', and they are tepid. Probably Richardson's moral claims have led critics to exaggerate his prurience.

The eighteenth century took sexual propriety more seriously than the

[33] I, lxiii–vi.   [34] Watt, *Rise of the Novel*, p. 173.

Restoration had, and Richardson's class took it more seriously than did the more fashionable; but Richardson was to discover that there were still more proper men than he and must have smarted especially when his book was attacked as obscene. The Victorians were still more shocked at the outspokenness of their ancestors and often expurgated *Pamela*. Indeed it seems that even today there are men who frown at Richardson's more salacious scenes.[35] Probably he was rather more titillated by his heroine's adventures than he would have admitted to himself. If the fact that his imagination was stimulated by an approach to sex is reprehensible, then Richardson is to be reprehended.

Evidently Pamela herself, however, does not see that her story might be attended with this danger, for in the second part of her history she certainly means the reader to contrast it with the novels and romances of former days when she tells how little pleasure she could derive from such works of fiction: 'For either they dealt so much in the *Marvellous* and *Improbable*, or were so unnaturally *inflaming* to the *Passions*, and so full of *Love* and *Intrigue*, that hardly any of them but seem'd calculated to *fire* the *Imagination*, rather than to *inform* the *Judgment*.'[36] She is objecting here to a type of fiction old-fashioned but not unknown in the mid-eighteenth century, citing among absurdities tournaments, monsters, adventures of knights errant, elopements of heroines, and love at first sight (which supposes a degree of susceptibility 'which, however it may pass in a Man, very little becomes a Lady's Delicacy'). Her criticism is typical of Richardson's; he frequently mentions in various terms as the two objections which may be urged against non-Richardsonian fiction lack of realism and lack of a suitable moral. These are still the two most prominent critical canons of the middle class. That the middle class of the eighteenth century wanted a more realistic fiction is indicated in a remark in the *Weekly Journal or Saturday's Post* of 11 January 1724 that 'two Sorts of Writings which seem to be of no Use to the World' except to advance the stationers' trade are memoirs and '*Novels*, in which the Author sits down and invents Characters that never were in Nature: He frames a long Story or Intrigue full of Events and Incidents, like the Turns in a Comedy; and if he can but surprize and delight you enough to lead you on to the End of his Book, he is not so unreasonable to expect you should believe it to be true.' This description, which applies to most early eighteenth-century fiction, including much of Defoe, shows part of the originality of *Pamela*.

The inadequacy of Richardson's moral in *Pamela* has been mentioned; the adequacy of his realism is greater than one might judge from his own comments on it. Realism can mean mere surface realism, avoiding the

---

[35] For example, Bernard Kreissman in *Pamela-Shamela* (Lincoln, Nebraska, 1960), pp. 31–38.

[36] SH, IV, 426; EL, II, 454.

improbable, dealing with everyday life; this is the sense of which Richardson often seems to be thinking in his critical remarks, the sense in which his class believed in realism and still believes in it—any schoolgirl can recognize and condemn a lapse from verisimilitude. In this sense realism has probably had a narrowing effect on literature, or at least on reading. In this sense the soap opera is realistic, *King Lear* and *Lord Jim* are not. And Richardson was a realist in this limited sense, paying great attention to probability and always dealing with ordinary life.

He was fortunately also at his best a realist in another sense. He was able to conceive of real characters and situations in his imagination and to convey his conception to the reader. Though Richardson comes closest to violating probability when Pamela and Clarissa are imprisoned and persecuted, it is precisely then that he is most intensely real, whereas though nothing improbable happens in the second part of *Pamela* no one has ever been able to believe in it. All of the events could have occurred, but apparently none of them did occur in the writer's mind, and none of them occurs in the reader's.

It was this effect of reality, experienced by the reader and experienced through the mind of one of the leading characters, which impressed his audience as most original. Many contemporaries refer to it; the emotions aroused by the book depend on it. We shall leave the question of whether *Pamela* is the 'first novel' to those who believe that one can define such a literary type in some absolute sense superior to and more accurate than the rather careless sense in which human beings have used the word to describe a variety of pre-existing works. If there be, somewhere in the realm of the abstract, a Platonic Ideal of the Novel, there are enough critics to tell us what its characteristics must be.

Pamela was, at any rate, one of the first works in western prose fiction to convey a story as it happened rather than merely relate it—perhaps the very first to do so consistently, though the claims of *The Princess of Cleves*, of *Robinson Crusoe*, of *Lazarillo de Tormes*, of *Marianne*, and of others might be urged. In doing so, it helped the nascent novel to acquire the closely related virtues of psychological depth and of intensity (closely related because both arise from our seeing and feeling with the character) which had in earlier periods been the advantages of narrative poetry and especially of the drama. To these primary advantages *Pamela* added surface realism and a unified plot, two characteristics general but by no means universal in later novels. Some critics stress the combination of extension with unity of effect as Richardson's essential novelty,[37] and certainly the wealth of detail with which he elaborates a simple story is an important characteristic of later eighteenth- and nineteenth-century novels and distinguishes *Pamela* from most older prose fiction, adventurous, pastoral, or

[37] McKillop, *Richardson*, p. 35, and Watt, *Rise of the Novel*, p. 135.

picaresque, in the same way that an 'epic' like the *Iliad* or the *Nibe-lungenlied* is distinguished from a 'romance' like the *Orlando Furioso*. George Sherburn adds his 'hitherto unparalleled employment of conversation', his building up of long scenes in a style reminiscent of and probably derived from the drama.[38] He cites the scene between Pamela and Lady Davers as the first of these 'big scenes' to be fully developed by means of dialogue and stage directions, but there are earlier scenes (that in the summerhouse, for instance) which are seen and heard as if on a stage, more vividly than in most of the eighteenth-century plays Richardson might have seen.

Whichever of these elements constitutes Richardson's originality (and they are almost impossible to separate—all of them fuse into one element), that originality has generally been granted. Sources have of course been suggested. But sources of the particular story used are of little interest: Richardson himself mentioned a real event, and scholars have discovered various events; John Nichols early found a *Spectator* paper on the same subject,[39] and other accounts of the temptations of virtuous servant girls have been since discovered. None of them is strikingly similar to *Pamela* in detail, and certainly none of them accounts for its innovations in method. There are closer parallels in the plays of the Restoration and eighteenth century, which also contain characters of the same general types as those in Richardson's novels—the rake, the virtuous maiden, the gay lady.[40] It is inherently likely that the drama suggested Richardson's types, but a type is not a character: there were many sensitive young æsthetes before Stephen Dedalus, many emancipated women before Ursula Brangwen and Candace Compson, and many self-made men before Jay Gatsby. Analysis of the motifs of the plot and their parallels in other works demonstrates mainly how commonplace these motifs were.[41] Similarities in situation and character, not only to *Pamela* but also to *Clarissa*, have been found in *The Illustrious French Lovers*, Penelope Aubin's translation of Robert Challes's *Les illustres françaises*.[42] None of the similarities is striking enough to prove that this book was Richardson's 'source', though Challes was writing bourgeois (realistic and moral) fiction before Richardson.

Pamela's then unusual name goes back to Sidney's *Arcadia*, perhaps via Steele's *Tender Husband*. Its pronunciation caused some confusion:

---

[38] 'Samuel Richardson's Novels and the Theatre: A Theory Sketched', *PQ*, XLI (1962), 325–9.

[39] *Literary Anecdotes*, II, 433.

[40] Ira Konigsberg, 'The Dramatic Background of Richardson's Plots and Characters', *PMLA*, LXXXIII (1968), 42–53.

[41] See Danielowski, *Richardsons erster Roman*, pp. 69–85.

[42] Henri Roddier, 'Robert Challes inspirateur de Richardson et de l'Abbé Prévost', *RLC*, XXI (1947), 5–38.

Richardson, Sir John Hawkins tells us, 'whether through ignorance or design, and also all his female pupils, constantly pronounced it Paměla'.[43] In her verses on going away Pamela accents the first syllable;[44] Pope in his 'Epistle to Miss Blount, with the Works of Voiture' had accented the second, but Aaron Hill made all right when he followed Richardson's usage and explained to Richardson why he was correct by deriving the name from πας and μέλος:[45]—all-melody (Pope's pronunciation would have meant the use of an eta instead of an epsilon, deriving the name from all-sheep, all-apples, or perhaps all-breasts).

Sources have also been suggested for Richardson's method. Parallels between his piety and that of the Quaker journals and the Puritan conduct books have been noted, but parallels are not sources: Richardson's piety need not have been learned from any book; it was the general property of his class. We do not deny that he has much in common with this unread literature. On the other hand, what Richardson shares with it is least interesting in him. For a social historian, contemporary platitudes are undoubtedly revealing. For us, a work of literature is generally impressive not for what it has in common with its age (though of course it always does have much in common) but for what it says that no one else has said in the same way, for what it does not share with everyone else.

Two important characteristics, the deliberate cultivation of weeping on the ground that weeping indicates a tender and therefore virtuous heart and the choice of a subject from ordinary middle-class life, Richardson shares with the shortly earlier sentimental comedy of Steele and the domestic tragedy of Lillo, as well as with some of the periodic essays, which could in addition have supplied some of his reflections. That he knew these three types is certain, but it might be fairer to say that they and Richardson all illustrate the progressive embourgeoisement of the eighteenth century than that he drew directly from them. In these respects, as indeed in others, he was more a product of the *Zeitgeist* than of literary influences. And in method these types have very little in common with Richardson.

From earlier prose fiction he seems to have got almost nothing, from the picaresque tradition which influenced Fielding and Smollett as little as from the romance of adventure and marvels. Richardson, unlike Fielding, was not a learned or even well-read man. The influences on *Tom Jones* are obvious, they do not have to be sought; the influences which have been sought out for Richardson are remarkable largely because they are so distant and so minor. Richardson's freshness may have been the gift of ignorance as much as of anything else.

Only one influence on Richardson of any real importance has been

[43] *Life of Samuel Johnson*, 2nd edn. (London, 1787), p. 214n.
[44] SH, I, 116–19; EL, I, 75–6.   [45] 6 Jan. 1741.

suggested, that of Marivaux. Richardson knew no French, but a part of *Marianne* had been translated into English shortly before the composition of *Pamela*. The similarities between the two books are obvious:[46] both deal with humble heroines tempted and later rewarded, both are set in a middle-class environment, both centre on love, both use the first person narrative, both reproduce not only (not mainly) events but also mental reactions to events, both weave a basically simple pattern rich in detail, both aim at conveying the impression of events as they occur. The similarities of plot are slight, and English-speaking scholars have been inclined to deny that the similarities of method are significant enough to indicate influence. The only definite evidence available is Richardson's categorical denial to William Warburton: 'Then as to what you are pleased to hint, that I pursued in my former Piece the excellent Plan fallen upon lately by the French Writers, I would only observe, that all that know me, know that I am not acquainted in the least either with the French Language or Writers: And that it was Chance and not Skill or Learning, that made me fall into this way of Scribbling.'[47] Richardson's various vague references to writers of the French marvellous are not specific enough to belie his claim to ignorance of French writers. So far as is known he was a truthful man, at least insofar as he recognized the truth. It is therefore just as well not to question his own assertion of originality, since there is no clear proof that he had seen the parts of *Marianne* available to him. If he had not, the novels are enough alike to show that a similar environment can produce remarkably similar results, both new and new in somewhat the same way. They are also different enough to leave Richardson with a large measure of originality even if he did know Marivaux: Pamela's character and style, which constitute the real originality or at least freshness of *Pamela* and are Richardson's contribution to literature as distinguished from his contribution to literary history, do not in the least resemble Marianne's.

[46] They are well summed up by Thomson, *Richardson*, pp. 149–53, and McKillop, *Richardson*, pp. 36–40.
[47] 14 Apr. 1748.

CHAPTER VII

THE *PAMELA* VOGUE; *PAMELA* PART II

1740–1742

URING the course of the next year the authorship of *Pamela* gradually became known. In August 1741, after the publishers of the
spurious continuation took advantage of his anonymity to give
out that *Pamela* had been written by an overseer of his who had since died,
Richardson wrote to his brother-in-law James Leake that he 'did not
intend [his authorship] should be known to more than 6 Friends, and those
in Confidence'. On 3 September he wrote to Mrs. Barber that he did not
want it to be known that he was the author, but three or four friends to
whom he could not help owning it forced him to change his opinion:
'And I have suffer'd by it, as well in my own Mind, as in the Malice and
Envy of others.' Aside from his wife and Miss Midwinter and the other
two friends, de Freval and the author of the *Weekly Miscellany* letter must
have been in on the secret before publication. Dr. Cheyne was soon informed and on 13 December 1740 acknowledged the gift of the book,
which he found entertaining and hoped would 'do a great deal of Good':
'I never thought you Master of so much Wit and Gallantry as are couch'd
in it, you need not be asham'd to own it, it will do no Dishonour [to]
either your Heart or your Head.'

Soon after publication Aaron Hill discovered the truth. On 8 December
Richardson sent the two volumes for the perusal of Hill's two unmarried
daughters. Astræa and Minerva thanked him on 17 December, praising
the work in rather moderate terms, and on the same day Hill himself
wrote, much more ecstatic: 'Who could have dreamt, he should find,
under the modest Disguise of a *Novel*, all the *Soul* of Religion, Good-
breeding, Discretion, Good-nature, Wit, Fancy, Fine Thought, and Morality?—I have done nothing but read it to others, and hear others again
read it, to me, ever since it came into my Hands; and I find I am likely to
do nothing else, for I know not how long yet to come: because, if I lay
the Book down, it comes after me.—When it has dwelt all Day long upon
the Ear, It takes Possession, all Night, of the Fancy. . . . Yet, I confess,
there is *One*, in the World, of whom I think with still greater Respect,
than of PAMELA: and That is, of the wonderful AUTHOR of PAMELA.—
Pray, Who is he, Dear Sir? and where, and how, has he been able to hide,

hitherto, such an encircling and all-mastering Spirit? He possesses every Quality that ART could have charm'd by: yet, has lent it to, and conceal'd it in, NATURE.—The Comprehensiveness of his Imagination must be truly prodigious!—It has stretch'd out this diminutive mere *Grain of Mustard-seed*, (a poor Girl's little, innocent, Story) into a Resemblance of That *Heaven*, which the Best of Good Books has compar'd it to.' And much more, including his conviction that twenty ages to come would be the better for such a book and that its author must have one of 'the best, and most generous Hearts, of Mankind'—in this corrupt age, 'a salutary *Angel*, in *Sodom*'. Hill later wrote to Mallet that he had discovered the authorship 'by the resembling turn of Pamela's expressions, weigh'd with some which I had noted, as peculiar in his letters: Yet very loth he was, a long time, to confess it.'[1]

Richardson confessed it clearly enough, if not explicitly, five days after Hill's letter, when he wrote that after such high praise he could *not* in decency name the writer. Such praise from a scholar and acknowledged wit must have been heady indeed, and one can perhaps forgive Richardson for adding this letter and others from Hill in the same vein to the prefatory material in the second edition. He sent Astræa and Minerva a finely bound copy, with interleaved pages for corrections they wisely declined to make—a gift which they acknowledged with enthusiasm much greater than that in their previous letter, so great that Richardson later wrote in the margin 'Too high'. He also wrote 'Too high Praise' on a letter in which Hill, delighted to find that the author was the person he had hoped, advised against polishing the style but thought that some slight shortening might help: 'You have lent her Breadth of Wing, that will extend her from the Present to ye Future World: And brooding over both (like Miltons Image of the Holy Spirit) she will call out Virtues without Number.'[2] One cannot suspect Hill of applying his Miltonic image so pedantically as to imagine Pamela sitting dove-like over the vast abysses of the eighteenth and nineteenth centuries and making both pregnant.

On the same day Hill wrote another letter of praise recounting the story of a poor soldier's son, seven years old, who was living in his house (his name was Harry Campbell, and ten years later he was apprenticed to Richardson without paying a fee and served with him for seven years).[3] Harry, while Hill was reading Pamela's reflections by the pond where she does not commit suicide, crept under his chair and sat with his head almost touching the book and his face bowed towards the fire, until he suddenly broke out into heart-heaving sobs and his eyes were seen to be 'quite lost, in his *Tears*: which running down from his Cheeks in free Currents, had form'd two sincere little Fountains, on that part of the

---

[1] 23 Jan. 1741, *Works*, II, 159.   [2] 30 Dec., 29 Dec.
[3] 'Apprentices and Turn Overs', 7 May 1751, MS. in the archives of the Stationers' Company.

Carpet he hung over'. Since then this youngest of Pamela's converts had always insisted on being one of her auditors and had got half her sayings by heart. Richardson considered him a '*dear amiable boy*' and sent him two books with pictures in them, one of them his *Æsop*.[4]

Early in 1741 Richardson began receiving letters from unknown and often anonymous correspondents about *Pamela*. It may have been at this time that he started preserving his correspondence; so far as one can now ascertain, through 1740 Richardson saved only the letters of his two most distinguished known correspondents, Hill and Dr. Cheyne, and one letter from Dr. Delany. But he certainly saved a large number of the letters about *Pamela*, if not all, and the majority are still in existence.

Most of the letters were full of praise. Readers singled out especially the two qualities which Richardson himself mentions, the fact that a novel should be so moral and that it should seem so real. They could have found both virtues commended in the letters printed as an introduction to the book, the *Weekly Miscellany* letter stressing the former (*Pamela* will 'reclaim the Vicious, and mend the Age in general') and de Freval's the latter ('as it borrows none of its Excellencies from the romantic Flights of unnatural Fancy, its being founded in Truth and Nature, and built upon Experience, will be a lasting Recommendation to the Discerning and Judicious').

Some of the comments were ecstatic. Ralph Courteville, Richardson's associate on the *Daily Gazetteer*, sent him a letter from Knightley Chetwood saying 'if all the Books in England were to be burnt, this Book, next the Bible, ought to be preserved'.[5] Years later the Reverend Smyth Loftus wrote to Richardson that he had found in *Pamela* 'a beautiful simplicity which I never knew excelled except in the Bible'. Dr. Delany recommended the heroine to his ward as an example, and Richardson reported to Hill that Dr. Benjamin Slocock of St. Saviour's had recommended the novel from his pulpit.[6]

Many of the comments took the form of poetry, or at least of verse; Pamela awoke the Muses of a variety of persons, from a young miss not twelve years old to Aaron Hill, who regretted that so much talent and virtue came too late to save a degenerate age:

> Death has *no Cure*. Thou hast mis-tim'd thy Aim.
> Rome had her GOTHS: and all beyond was *Shame*.[7]

Hill's verses were published in the Introduction to the second edition of *Pamela*, and it was probably in repayment for them that Richardson wrote one of his rare extant poetic effusions, a series of rhymed couplets in praise of blank verse:

---

[4] Hill to R, 9 Feb., 21 Apr.   [5] 27 Jan., FM XVI, 1, fo. 43.
[6] Loftus to R, 12 Nov. 1756; Delany to R, 21 Jan.; Hill to R, 6 Jan.
[7] FM XVI, 1, fos. 51–2; ibid., fos. 40–1, and *Works*, III, 348–50.

> When noble thoughts with language pure unite,
> To give to kindred excellence its right,
> Though unencumber'd with the clogs of rhyme,
> Where tinkling sounds, for want of meaning, chime,
> Which, like the rock, in Shannon's midway course,
> Divide the sense, and interrupt its force:
> Well may we judge so strong and clear a rill,
> Flows hither, from the muses sacred HILL.[8]

There were, however, objections to *Pamela*. Several correspondents mention the 'warm' scenes as rather too warm. Isaac Watts thanked Richardson for sending him the volumes but said that the ladies cannot read them without blushing;[9] and the Dublin poetess Mary Barber (Swift's 'Sapphira'), whose verse Richardson had printed, reported that the only objection she heard in Dublin was that the second attempted rape scene was 'a little too strongly Painted'.[10] But one lover of virtue who appropriately called himself Philaretes decided that in spite of difficulties Richardson had managed to get off with modesty—the scenes between Adam and Eve in *Paradise Lost* are at least as bad.[11] Others found some of the heroine's idiomatic language lacking in propriety and even grammar. The periodical *The History of the Works of the Learned*, which had praised the Roe papers, in an otherwise favourable though not enthusiastic article pointed out that 'the Language is not altogether unexceptionable, but in several Places sinks below the Idea we are constrained to form of the Heroine who is supposed to write it'.[12] Dr. Cheyne, writing primarily about the continuation, disliked so much kissing, while some correspondents disliked so much kneeling and praying and pious ejaculation. One objected to the trivial incidents, especially to Pamela's unnecessary conversations with Mrs. Jewkes.[13] No one seems to have minded the lavish and lengthy praises heaped on Pamela, perhaps the least palatable passages to a modern reader.

Richardson evidently paid attention to these criticisms; a few of the objections led to changes in later editions. Some of the improprieties were corrected, and Pamela less often uses the name of God, though she frequently does no more than substitute that of Heaven. Most of the suggestions he rejected; it is noteworthy that the 'warm' scenes were never changed very much, though in his last revision, over ten years later, he did cut three of Mr. B.'s four attempts to feel Pamela's breasts as well as his

---

[8] Barbauld, I, 59; Hill, *Works*, II, 164.

[9] Barbauld, I, lxvii. This letter is listed in Richardson's index to his correspondence on *Pamela* (FM XVI, 1, fo. 7), but we have been unable to locate it.

[10] 26 Aug.   [11] 22 June.

[12] II (Dec. 1740), 439.

[13] Cheyne to R, 24 Aug. 1741; anonymous to Rivington, 15 Nov. 1740, FM XVI, 1, fos. 34–5; Eusebius to Rivington, 2 Feb. 1741, ibid., fos. 47–8.

breathing 'all quick and short' when he came to her bedside.[14] However, he did, unfortunately, feel strongly enough to attempt to answer all the objections in the second part of *Pamela*, which largely justifies Mrs. Barbauld's remark that that book 'is less a continuation than the author's defence of himself'.[15]

The most detailed letter of criticism was one received by Rivington shortly after *Pamela* was published.[16] The anonymous writer praised the book highly but wanted Pamela's style raised gradually along with her elevation, to accord with her new dignity; objected to the use of the word ''Squire' and suggested that Mr. B. be raised to a knighthood or baronetcy; thought that 'if she repeated the Sacred Name much seldomer, it wou'd have . . . much less the Style of Robinson Crusoe'; wished that Pamela would show more spirit with Lady Davers; felt that there was too much description of her physical charms and especially that Mr. B.'s spanning her waist with his hands would 'ruin a Nation of Women' by tight lacing; and disliked a few incorrect or low words and two possible *doubles entendres*: Pamela at her wedding should not tremble 'betwixt Fear and Delight', nor at the meal afterwards, after eating a bit of apple pie and a little custard, should she mention that she 'had no Appetite to any thing else'.[17] On 20 November Richardson advertised in the *Daily Gazetteer* thanking the anonymous gentleman for 'his *Candid* and *Judicious* Observations' and begging for further correspondence—'INSTRUCTION, and not CURIOSITY, being *sincerely* the Motive for this Request'. This letter Richardson sent to Hill for comment, and on 6 January Hill replied, disagreeing with almost all of the gentleman's objections.

It appears from Hill's letter that Richardson had also consulted Dr. Slocock, his clerical admirer, who likewise advised against altering. In enthusiasm for Dr. Slocock's enthusiasm Hill seems to have written an encomium of Slocock to which he refers in obscure terms as partial repayment of a debt, a reference possibly responsible for Brian W. Downs's unsupported statement that as a result of 'some obscure negotiations between the preacher and the novelist' the latter, in hopes of further favours, bought up half of a bad debt which Slocock owed.[18] The anonymous *Life of Pamela* is probably hinting at Slocock when it censures Pamela's language which 'must be shocking to a judicious Reader, and destroy the Character that so much Pains have been taken with, even tho' a Parson should have ten Guineas to recommend it from the Pulpit'.[19] Much later, in 1749, Richardson did pay Slocock twenty pounds, but this transaction is described in the Gosling Bank ledger as 'Mr. Leake's Bond'.[20] In 1753,

---

[14] Eaves and Kimpel, 'Richardson's Revisions of *Pamela*', pp. 81–2.
[15] I, lxxvii. [16] 15 Nov., FM XVI, 1, fos. 34–5. [17] 1st edn., II, 175, 181.
[18] Hill to R, 15 Jan.; Downs, *Richardson*, p. 48. [19] London, 1741, p. 340.
[20] MS. in the archives of Gosling's Branch of Barclays Bank, Ltd.

when Slocock died, he was a very prosperous man and left considerable sums of money and estates to various relatives, as well as ten pounds to Mr. Richardson, 'author of Pamela', as a testimony of the respect he bore him.[21] We see no convincing evidence that Richardson paid Dr. Slocock for his praise, and we are personally inclined to doubt that he would have done so.

The success of *Pamela* is undoubted. Richardson had advertised it adequately, especially in the *Daily Gazetteer*, but not as extensively as he advertised the Roe papers—the book did not need it. The later editions were also announced in the *Gazetteer*, and his friend Dr. Webster continued to give him puffs in the *Weekly Miscellany*,[22] but by then the book had caught on. As Cave's *Gentleman's Magazine* said in January 1741, it was 'judged in Town as great a Sign of Want of Curiosity not to have read *Pamela*, as not to have seen the *French* and *Italian* dancers'.[23] That country audiences were as curious is indicated by the early story, whether legendary or not (it was told of more than one village but might conceivably have happened in several) that a group of villagers who heard the novel read rang the church bells on learning that Pamela was married.[24] And that appreciation of *Pamela* was not confined to the unsophisticated is shown by Pope's enjoyment of it—he would 'not bear any faults to be mentioned in the story'—and his comment (however ironic that may be) that 'it will do more good than a great many of the new Sermons'.[25]

By the end of January 1741 a second edition was being advertised, and in mid-February it appeared.[26] To this Richardson added as further preface excerpts from Hill's letters of praise as well as a summary of the anonymous gentleman's objections and Hill's answers to them. One clergyman wrote to Osborn that, though he and his brethren of the cloth had been recommending *Pamela* on their visits, he considered that 'you were bewitched to Print that bad stuff in the Introduction', the writer of which is 'too gross in his Praises of the Author'. Besides 'a Gentleman who seems to have intended well and honestly, is very ungratefully used, and it has given Offence'.[27] And indeed Hill does handle him rather roughly.

The second edition does, however, adopt a few of the gentleman's minor suggestions, correcting the spellings of 'Curchee' to 'Curt'sy' and 'voluntierly' to 'voluntarily', dropping a few of the ''Squire's' and 'naughty's', and altering the inflammatory *doubles entendres*. And Pamela no longer drops on her knees in a corner to bless God after her wedding— even Hill had thought that her appeals to the Deity could be somewhat curtailed, and no fewer than eighty-five 'God's' were cut or changed to

[21] P.C.C. Searle 60, dated 2 Dec. 1752, proved 3 Feb. 1753.
[22] 13 Dec. 1740; 28 Feb. 1741.   [23] XI, 56.
[24] See Alan Dugald McKillop, 'Wedding Bells for Pamela', *PQ*, XXVIII (1949), 323–5.
[25] Cheyne to R, 12 Feb. 1741. See also Barbauld, I, lix.
[26] *Daily Gazetteer*, 27 Jan.–17 Feb.; *London Evening Post*, 12–14 Feb.
[27] Feb., FM XVI, 1, fo. 46.

'Heaven's'. There are a good many other verbal corrections, which raise Pamela's style slightly.

A third edition came out in March and a fourth in May, each with minor verbal changes. In the latter Hill softened somewhat his remarks about the anonymous gentleman and, at Richardson's suggestion, moderated his praises of Richardson.[28] Soon afterwards Richardson seems to have begun preparations for a more extensive revision. He must have consulted the Master of Hart Hall, Oxford, the Reverend Richard Newton, whose works he had printed and whose eventually successful efforts to have Hart Hall made a college he had supported in the revised edition of Defoe's *Tour*. On 15 May Newton wrote that he had suggested a very few alterations, though 'little Departures from Propriety out of the sweet pretty Mouth of Pamela are as natural, or more so, than Exactnesses'. Probably Richardson consulted a good many people. Hill, of course, was asked for help, though he could think of little to change.[29]

The fifth edition, which appeared on 22 September, was the most extensively revised of all those published in Richardson's lifetime. Many passages were rewritten, and there were many additions and the usual corrections in the interest of increasing propriety. A still longer addition, the expansion of the scene where Pamela, still a simple servant girl, is visited by several fine ladies who speak in Richardson's later social-comedy vein, appeared first in the French translation published on 23 October[30] and then in the de luxe octavo which Richardson released on 8 May 1742,[31] though he was planning it in October 1741.[32] The latter, though it has no special claim to textual authority, was the most sumptuous of Richardson's editions and is usually regarded as the standard. It does have the great advantage of dropping the introductory material with its effusive praise, which had been parodied in *Shamela Andrews* and probably criticized by others besides Osborn's clerical correspondent. Ralph Allen had objected to a passage in one of the introductory letters, and Richardson replied that he had been advised to omit the Introduction in future editions: 'And indeed the Praises . . . are carried so high, that since I cou'd not pass as the Editor only, as I once hoped to do, I wish they had never been Inserted.'[33]

The French translation made it possible for the Continent to know Richardson, and his reputation there, especially after *Clarissa*, was very great, perhaps as great as that of any English writer in the eighteenth century. That there were difficulties is indicated in the Preface to the translation itself: the colloquial style which bothered some English readers was even more unusual in French, and the translator felt it necessary to mention the fact that the English language is less chastened than the French (Aaron Hill hoped that it would remain so).[34]

---

[28] Hill to R, 21 Apr.   [29] Hill to R, 13 Apr., 21 Apr., 25 May.   [30] *Daily Gazetteer.*
[31] *Daily Post.*   [32] 8 Oct.   [33] Ibid.   [34] To R, 12 Nov. 1741.

In 1742 appeared with a London imprint but in French a *Lettre sur Pamela* which, if he had it translated to him, must have caused Richardson to take an even lower view of the French nation. According to this letter, though everyone is reading the book, no one speaks well of it. It moves people in spite of themselves, and they are rather ashamed of their interest. The negligence of the style is mentioned, and the gross terms which Mr. B. applies to Pamela ('salope', 'impertinente') are especially singled out as calculated to shock the delicacy of French ears, which have always been sensitive to different sorts of improprieties than those of the English. A bantering and belittling summary of the plot is given, implying that the heroine is too wise to the ways of men, that her frequent faintings indicate too ardent a sensibility which cannot sustain even the approaches to the pleasures she rejects with such horror, and that Mr. B. is inconsistent and rather foolish not to rape Pamela while she is unconscious. Much fun is made of her risking violation for the sake of staying on to finish a waistcoat, and she is also blamed for confiding in Mr. Williams—like giving her property to thieves to guard. Both Mrs. Jewkes and Lady Davers are indecent. The author hopes that the book does not give a fair picture of English manners or English conversation.

But others, even in France, were less particular, and *Pamela* had a great vogue abroad. There were theatrical versions, much altered, by such distinguished names as Voltaire and Goldoni.[35] The Continent found *Pamela* too radical in its social implications; both Voltaire and Goldoni raise the heroine's status in life and make her more decorous. But by 1793 France had outstripped England in radicalism: a French adaptation of Goldoni was censured by the Committee of Public Safety as reactionary because the heroine's father had been made a count, and her status was restored to that of a common servant. Undoubtedly a large part of *Pamela*'s popularity was due to its similarity to the *comédie larmoyante*, but it is probable that the social implications appealed to the same group which later found satisfaction in the implied satire of Beaumarchais' comedies of aristocratic lust and stupidity and of plebeian virtue and ingenuity.

Just what it was which earned *Pamela* the unusual (for an English novel) distinction of being put on the *Index* of the Roman Catholic Church is hard to understand—perhaps its popularity combined with its dubious moral. In any case, the French translation was prohibited by the Sacred Congregation in 1744 and remained on the *Index* until 1900, when the English title appeared instead.[36]

Imitations and adaptations, criticisms and panegyrics, of *Pamela* were

---

[35] See Henry Seidel Canby, '*Pamela* Abroad', *MLN*, XVIII (1903), 206–13.

[36] See Richard H. Thornton, 'English Authors, Placed on the Roman "Index" (1600 to 1750)', *N&Q*, 11 S. XII (1915), 333; Florian J. Schleck, 'Richardson on the Index', *TLS*, 25 Apr. 1935, p. 272.

not slow to appear in England. Later Richardson was able to mention, with mingled irritation and satisfaction, sixteen of them.[37] Pamela's adventures were illustrated by several prominent painters. Richardson himself commissioned Hogarth to prepare a series of illustrations for the second edition, but they were not used and are now lost. One can hardly imagine that Hogarth's style would have suited the spirit of the book; though he could have done a wonderful portrait of Mrs. Jewkes, his picture of Mr. B. dressed as the maid Nan creeping into Pamela's bed might have brought out too much humour. The octavo was illustrated by Hubert François Gravelot and Francis Hayman, and large paintings of two of the latter's designs later decorated pavilions at Vauxhall Gardens (one of them, 'Pamela Fleeing from Lady Davers', is now in Sizergh Castle). Richardson's later friend Joseph Highmore painted and sold prints of twelve scenes from the novel.[38] 'Pamela, a new Fan, representing the principal Adventures of her Life, in Servitude, Love, and Marriage' was 'design'd and engraven by the best Masters' and offered for sale by a Mr. Gamble—who did not, however, know that Pope's old pronunciation of the heroine's name should be abandoned:

> Virtue's Reward you in this Fan may view,
> To Honour's Tie, *Pamela* strictly true.[39]

Pamela's life was later even represented in 'a curious Piece of Wax-Work', 'containing above a hundred Figures in Miniature, richly dress'd, suitable to their Characters'.[40] A pirated edition of the novel appeared in London in 1741, and at least part of it was published in *Robinson Crusoe's London Daily Evening Post* in 1742.

The first of the books about *Pamela*, and the only one which still arouses much interest, is *An Apology for the Life of Mrs. Shamela Andrews*, which appeared shortly after the third edition, on 2 April.[41] It is today generally assigned to Henry Fielding, and the evidence for his authorship, though not conclusive, is considerable: its general tone as well as particular objects of satire and tricks of style can be paralleled in Fielding's works, and several well-informed people at the time assigned it to Fielding.[42] That Fielding never acknowledged it and that it was not included in Andrew Millar's 1762 collected posthumous edition of Fielding's works (though Millar owned a half share) may indicate that Fielding was none too proud of it and may even have asked Millar (a friend of both him and

---

[37] Notes on letters from Solomon Lowe to R, 21 Dec. 1741, and from R to Leake, Aug. 1741.
[38] See T. C. Duncan Eaves, 'Graphic Illustrations of the Novels of Samuel Richardson, 1740–1810', *HLQ*, XIV (1951), 349–83.
[39] *Daily Advertiser*, 28 Apr., 2 May 1741.   [40] *Daily Advertiser*, 23 Apr. 1745.
[41] *Daily Post*.
[42] See Charles B. Woods, 'Fielding and the Authorship of *Shamela*', *PQ*, XXV (1946), 248–72.

Richardson) to suppress it. In any case, Richardson, whose connection with booksellers and printers gave him opportunities to know, thought that Fielding wrote it. In 1749 he told Lady Bradshaigh so, and later, when editing his correspondence, he inserted a note in the shaking hand of his old age beside a mention of 'that vile Pamphlet *Shamela*', 'Written by Mr. H. Fielding'.[43] Perhaps the best argument for Fielding's authorship is that we do not know anyone else of that time who could have written such a well-sustained and witty burlesque. The author did not know that he was attacking Richardson, since he drops clear hints that the writer of *Pamela* was a parson-biographer who could be recognized by his '*Ciceronian* Eloquence'—probably Conyers Middleton, the author of the also recently published *Life of Cicero*.

The idea of *Shamela* is simple enough—the virtuous Pamela was not virtuous at all but the daughter of a London procuress and herself the mistress of Parson Williams, who sets out to trap her foolish master, Mr. Booby, into first a financial settlement and then, as she discovers her power, a wedding ring. Later critics have often adopted this view of Pamela's character (an indirect, if naïve, compliment to the vividness with which she is presented), and a hint of it can be found in *Pamela* itself when Mr. B. calls her 'a subtle, artful Gypsey'.[44] The writer travesties the main episodes of *Pamela* and parodies Richardson's vulnerable preface with a letter from 'The Editor to Himself' ('However you came by the excellent *Shamela*, out with it, without Fear or Favour, Dedication and all; believe me, it will go through many Editions, be translated into all Languages, read in all Nations and Ages, and to say a bold Word, it will do more good than the C[*lerg*]*y* have done harm in the World') and one from John Puff, Esq. An admirer, Parson Tickletext, quotes from Hill's letters and refers to the clergy's admiration for the book, until his friend Parson Oliver sends him the real letters written by Shamela. These catch Pamela's colloquial style and her trivial details (Shamela packs her clothes, including 'two pair of Stockings, one odd one, a pair of lac'd Shoes, a short flowered Apron, a lac'd Neck-Handkerchief, one Clog, and almost another'), as well as her writing to the moment ('Odsbobs! I hear him just coming in at the Door. You see I write in the present Tense, as Parson *Williams* says. Well, he is in Bed between us, we both shamming a Sleep, he steals his Hand into my Bosom') and her somewhat excessive preoccupation with chastity ('we sat down and talked about my Vartue till Dinner-time'). *Shamela* is a little (only a little) broader than *Pamela* in the warm scenes, and there is the healthy bawdiness one associates with Fielding. Certainly the writer was offended by Pamela's morality and by some of the absurdity of her manner. He also, as an educated man, disapproved of Richardson's

[43] R to Lady Bradshaigh, [late Nov.?]; Philaretes to R, 22 June 1741.
[44] SH, I, 27; EL, I, 17.

detailed realism and of his 'lowness' and thus can be regarded as a reactionary classicist who failed to see the freshness of *Pamela*. And he seems to have disliked the idea that a gentleman should marry his serving maid (though Fielding a few years later did just that). As a work of criticism *Shamela* is thus limited in its insight, and its seriousness of purpose has been somewhat exaggerated by Fielding's admirers. Fielding, who needed money in 1741, often produced hastily written attacks on targets which were in the public eye. But *Shamela* has the great advantage of being fun to read (ironically, partly because of the freshness of style caught from Richardson), and it was as well that someone should prick the inflated solemnity of Richardson's moralizing.

On 25 April appeared a less frivolous attack called *Pamela Censured*.[45] A dedicatory letter to Dr. Slocock states that the pulpit and press have joined in *Pamela*'s praises but that the author found passages in it inconsistent with virtue, piety, or morality. In spite of its professions, the book is not fit to be given to young girls to read. There are 'too many Scenes that directly tend to inflame the Minds of Youth', and (perhaps an echo of *Shamela*) 'instead of being artless and innocent [Pamela] sets out at first with as much Knowledge of the Arts of the Town, as if she had been born and bred in *Covent* Garden, all her Life Time'. The plot is retold with comments on (and quotations from) the objectionable passages. The grossness of Mr. B. and his sister ('little better than a downright *Billingsgate*') is blamed. The warm scenes will drive a girl too young to find a lover to 'seek Remedies which may drive her to the most unnatural Excesses'. Mr. B.'s pun on Pamela's quickness of mind, that he wished he had her quick another way, 'falls little short of the coarsest Ribaldry'. When Mr. B. looks through a keyhole and spys Pamela stretched out in one of her fits, her posture 'must naturally excite Passions of Desire' which could not be contemplated except 'by one in his *grand Climacteric* without ever wishing to see one in the same Situation'. Even the hint of lesbianism in Mrs. Jewkes is noticed.[46] The author earnestly requests Richardson to revise his novel drastically and to remove the offensive scenes. One wonders whether pain or anger predominated in Richardson's mind when he read this attack on what he regarded as his strongest point. When Aaron Hill wrote that a friend of his took it for a bookseller's contrivance to promote sales (indeed it might have made *Pamela* sound appealing to the unregenerate), Richardson understandably wrote on Hill's letter 'Quite mistaken!'[47] He never eliminated all of the objectionable scenes, but he paid enough attention to *Pamela Censured* to cut the pun about Pamela's quickness in his final revision and to specify in the fifth edition that when Mr. B. saw Pamela through the keyhole she was on her face (Richardson was presumably innocent of perversions).

[45] *Daily Post.*   [46] Pp. 19, 21–2, 24, 44, 31, 50.   [47] 25 May.

On 16 June was published a book called *Anti-Pamela: or, Feign'd Innocence Detected*, probably by Eliza Haywood.[48] It was evidently trying to capitalize on *Pamela*'s popularity, since it has little connection beyond the title, being the story of a poor young girl named Syrena Tricksy who has various love affairs and, with the help of her mother's advice, makes her beauty pay in a less respectable way than does Richardson's heroine. It is a first-person narrative, partly epistolary, written 'to the moment' like *Pamela*, though in a style that recalls *Shamela*. Like Shamela, Syrena upon occasion feigns innocence.

A book with a similar title, James Parry's *True Anti-Pamela*, also published in June, is a purportedly true autobiographical account of Parry's love affair with a Miss Powell ('Parthenissa'), who after seducing him refused to marry him.[49] It was sold by Richardson's brother-in-law James Leake,[50] who, however, can hardly be accused of family disloyalty since neither of these *Anti-Pamela*'s is a criticism of Richardson, the meaning of the titles being only that the books concern heroines as unlike Pamela as possible.

Another attempt to ride to fortune in Richardson's train was the *Memoirs of the Life of Lady H——, the Celebrated Pamela*, published in December; it is an account of Hannah Sturges, a coachman's daughter and the wife of Sir Arthur Hesilrige, Bart., one of the originals who has been suggested for Richardson's heroine. They had been married in 1725,[51] and they were both still alive—indeed they outlived Richardson. Throughout the short work the heroine is referred to simply as Pamela, though her husband is called Sir A—— H——. Her story is only in a general way similar to Pamela's. She is a poor scullery maid to whom her mistress's young son, having seen her washing dishes with a naked bosom, makes rather violent advances. Repulsed in the kitchen and in the garden, he lies in ambush for her when she is on the way to visit her parents, but her father arrives just as she is pleading for her virtue, and the young aristocrat at once declares his intention of marrying his Pamela. She learns 'the Rudiments of genteel, polite Behaviour' with such astonishing rapidity that she is soon able to impress ladies from the Court with her spinet-playing and her wit. Her story is told 'to enforce the Practice of Virtue by an Example of the Reward attending it'.

A more interesting, or at least odder, book is *The Virgin in Eden*, which appeared in November. It was written by Charles Povey, a man according

---

[48] *London Daily Post and General Advertiser.* For the attribution to Mrs. Haywood, see McKillop, *Richardson*, p. 80. A second issue, called the 'Second Edition', was published on 29 Oct. 1741 (*London Daily Post and General Advertiser*).

[49] A second edition was published on 26 September (*Daily Post*). The work was also pirated.

[50] See the *Daily Gazetteer*, 26 May 1741, where it is advertised as 'In the Press'.

[51] The social position of the partners in this marriage is reported in *Mist's Weekly Journal*, 4 Aug.

to the Preface eighty years old and according to the whole book fired by religious zeal. His novel is the story of a truly virtuous virgin, but he takes the occasion to attack *Pamela* at considerable length. A lady of piety had lent Povey the book, and from the professions of virtue in the prefatory material he conceived hopes which were sadly belied by the letters themselves. '*Pamela* is dress'd in Airs, that cannot but raise vain Desires even in Men as chaste as *Joseph*.' He dares not repeat some of the expressions, but he does mention the most objectionable scenes, the summerhouse scene and the two attempted rapes. 'Good God! Can amorous Embraces delineated in these Images, tend to inculcate Religion in the Minds of Youth, when the Blood is hot, and runs quick in every Vein? Are these Lights to direct the Soul to a crucify'd Jesus?' Pamela should have left the house at the first proposal or at least searched her room thoroughly and tried the doors—'The Maid who holds a Parley with a vicious Man a second time . . . may be compar'd to one of the fair Apples of Sodom.' As if it were not bad enough to compare the model of virtue to an apple of Sodom, Povey takes a leaf from Richardson's own book and prints letters praising his own heroine and censuring Richardson's: from a divine of the Church of England ('*Pamela*'s Letters tend more to corrupt the Morals, than refine the Mind with virtuous Ideas'), a Quaker ('Thy Manuscript wherein thou settest forth *Pamela*'s Letters immodest Romances, thou sayst well: they are profane Lessons, and shall not dwell in my House'), a young nobleman ('*Pamela*'s Romances cannot but defile the Thoughts even in advanced Years; and how much more in Youth?'), and a young lady ('*Pamela*'s Epistles I compare to the Moon in Eclipse, and the Virgin in *Eden* to the Sun at its Meridian Height').[52] When he died somewhat over a year later, Povey left, in addition to sums of money, copies of his 'treatise' to one hundred ministers' widows and one hundred tradesmen's widows. Other ministers' widows were to get the proceeds of the sale of *The Virgin in Eden*.[53]

Vice as well as virtue had its say. A poem in the *London Magazine* called 'Remarks on PAMELA. By a PRUDE' treats the heroine with levity, implying that Mr. B. was a fool not to take her by force when he could and that his failure to do so was a fault she could hardly be expected to forgive:

> In naked bed to hold her fast!
> While she did roar and bawl!
> And then to have her at the last!
> When she had ceas'd to squall!

Another says that Shamela has completely discredited the character of Pamela. These were, however, answered by a defence of the book against the libertines who laugh when they hear of virtue:

[52] Pp. 68–78.   [53] *London Daily Post and General Advertiser*, 8 July 1743.

> A *character* sets 'em a grieving,
> That excites admiration and love:
> How shou'd they be fond of *believing*,
> What serves but to *shame* and *reprove*?[54]

Two years later another poetic attack was published, *Pamela: or, the Fair Impostor*. Its author, J—— W——, retells her story in the spirit of *Shamela*: Pamela's husband, Sir Blunder, finally catches her in bed with Parson Williams. A guardian sylph named Ariel (borrowed of course from Pope) offers her advice which sums up many criticisms of her morality:

> Keep but your Honour spotless from Reproach;
> Think on the Charms of Wealth, a Title, and a Coach.[55]

A poetic effort (which seems never to have been completed) was a retelling of the novel in heroic couplets by a George Bennet, late of St. John's, Oxford. *Pamela Versified*, 'an Heroic Poem', was to have been comprised in fifteen numbers and 'adorn'd with Copper-Plate Cuts'. The first number appeared and the second was announced, but evidently the public taste did not sufficiently relish this 'curious and beautiful Versification of PAMELA'S LETTERS':

> *Fancy some sylvan nymph of ancient days,*
> *Such as inspir'd the* Latian *poet's lays,*
> *When tripping harmless o'er the verdant lawn,*
> *And from that scene let* PAMELA *be drawn.*
> *Her, thus accomplish'd, the young 'Squire beholds,*
> *And Fancy, in his arms, the nymph infolds:*
> *But Modesty wears such resistless charms,*
> *That brutal violence it soon disarms;*
> *He must enjoy her, but he fears to press,*
> *Consent would add, force make the pleasure less.*

The poet, of course, states that his effusion is written for the 'British *nymphs*' and in the cause of virtue.[56]

Pamela was also dramatized in several forms. One comedy, called *Pamela: or Virtue Triumphant*, 'intended to be Acted at the Theatre Royal in *Drury-Lane*', as it presumably never was, was published on 16 November 1741. It follows the novel very closely and includes all the familiar scenes: the summerhouse, the fine ladies, Pamela in her country habit, the first bedroom scene, Mr. Williams in the garden, Pamela by the pond, the arrival of old Andrews, Lady Davers's rudeness, even Mr. B.'s (Beaulove's) rules for a wife. The second bedroom scene and the wedding have

---

[54] X (May, June, July 1741), 250–1, 304, 358.   [55] Dublin, 1743, p. 20.
[56] Advertised in the *Daily Advertiser*, 24 July, 12 Aug. 1741. An extract was published in the *Scots Magazine*, III (Oct. 1741), 453–4.

to be related by Mrs. Jewkes. The wording of the dialogue often comes directly from Richardson.

A rival version, *Pamela. A Comedy*, rehearsed at Goodman's Fields on 22 September and performed there on 9 November, was published on 17 November.[57] Henry Giffard, manager of the theatre and author of the play, acted Mr. B[elvile] and his wife acted Pamela. Jack Smatter was acted by 'the Gentleman who performed King Richard'—David Garrick, then near the beginning of his career; the part is much longer and livelier than that of Lord Davers's nephew in *Pamela*. The two housekeepers were played by a husband and wife, the former taking the part of the suspiciously masculine Mrs. Jewkes, whose role is also enlarged by a comic affair with Mr. Colbrand. The play follows the plot of the novel fairly closely, though a good deal of farcical material is added, and the climax comes in a dramatic scene in which Parson Williams appears just in time to save Pamela from rape and to convince Belvile that she is innocent and that he should marry her. It was fairly successful, being performed seventeen times in 1741 and again in 1742.[58] In its published form it went into a second edition and was twice pirated. Garrick described it as 'very hungry & . . . chiefly lik'd by ye Middling & low Kind of Spectators'.[59] Evidently Richardson was not curious enough to go to see it—in 1748 he had never seen Garrick act.[60]

Giffard's play was in 1742 revised and published as a ballad opera. The author, a Mr. Edge, rather strangely took the occasion of his Preface to complain about the comedy which was his source—it was written in 'too great Hurry'. He admits that he himself was confined to a few days, a fact apparent enough in the text; the last three acts are squeezed into one, and the songs are uninspired. Belvile suffers for Pamela: 'I'm sad, if my *Pammy*'s not there'. Pamela scorns Smatter's gold:

> No stately Grandeur shall entice,
> Nor tempt me to do Ill-a;
> I'll shun the Great, and hate their Vice,
> To live in a Cottage still-a.

In the spring of 1742 the *Universal Spectator, and Weekly Journal* published

[57] *London Daily Post and General Advertiser*, 23 Sept., 6 Nov., 9 Nov.; *Daily Post*, 17 Nov.; *Daily Gazetteer*, 17 Nov. See William Merritt Sale, Jr., 'The First Dramatic Version of *Pamela*', *YULG*, IX (1935), 83-8. The texts of this play and of the other contemporary English dramatic versions of *Pamela* have been edited by Viralene Johnson Coleman in 'The English Dramatic Adaptations of Richardson's *Pamela* in the 1740s' (Univ. of Arkansas unpubl. diss., 1969).

[58] Arthur H. Scouten, ed., *The London Stage, 1660-1800*, Part 3: 1729-47, II (Carbondale, Illinois, 1961), pp. 929, 941-6, 948, 951-2, 971.

[59] Letter to Peter Garrick, 30 Jan. 1742, *Letters*, ed. David M. Little and George M. Kahrl (Cambridge, Mass., 1963), I, 36.

[60] R to Hill, 27 Oct. It is uncertain whether the *Pamela* presented between the acts of a concert at the French Theatre on 28 Dec. 1741 was one of these plays or a third version (see Scouten, ed., *The London Stage, 1660-1800*, Part 3: 1729-47, II, 954).

a dramatic poem on 'Pamela the Second'.[61] A reader who, being opposed to the modish gallantry of seduction, had liked the novel was still more pleased to discover that a parallel case had lately happened in Buckinghamshire and that a gentleman of that county had 'flung the Story into Dramatick Scenery'. Extracts from his effort are quoted, which are not after all altogether parallel. There are several scenes in which the Squire courts a farmer's daughter called Pamela and is repulsed by her in song. She is really waiting for her true love, William, a young miller, who for some reason does not arrive. A Mrs. Coupler urges her to take the Squire, who then tries to drag her into a summerhouse, when William opportunely enters and delivers a lecture which so impresses the Squire that he offers the couple a hundred guineas on their wedding day:

> And *Pamela* shall find, for Vice abhorr'd,
> That *Female Virtue* brings it's *own Reward*.

Also in 1742 appeared the most famous of the works called forth by *Pamela*, Fielding's *Joseph Andrews*. Richardson can claim no credit for most of the book, the account of the wanderings of Joseph and his Fanny with their friend Parson Abraham Adams. The parody is largely at the beginning, where Pamela's brother, in the service of Mr. Booby's aunt, emulates if he does not outdo his sister's feats of chastity. Even here Fielding's eighteenth-century tendency towards the new morality, which he never accepted with the enthusiasm of Richardson but was not quite free from, keeps the situation, which to a comedy writer of fifty years before would have been pure farce, from being straightforward parody. Joseph's resistance to Lady Booby, especially since it is motivated by his love for Fanny, ends by making him not ridiculous but sympathetic, and he also has some of the latent pride and resentment against the encroachments of his betters which his sister had at times shown in Richardson's novel. Pamela appears at the end of the book, proud of her new status and as stuffy as, in spite of Richardson's efforts, she is after her marriage in *Pamela*. How much Richardson at that time resented Fielding's attacks is not known: his frequent scornful or angry comments about Fielding are all several years later. He sent Dr. Cheyne a copy of *Joseph Andrews* at the latter's request, and one supposes that he was pleased when Cheyne acknowledged 'Feildings wretched Performance, for which I thank you, it will entertain none but Porters or Watermen'.[62]

One attempt to take advantage of *Pamela*'s popularity had an immediate effect on Richardson's plans. At the end of all editions before the octavo of 1742 was a long passage explaining clearly the various morals to be drawn from the book, which in the first editions began 'Here end the Letters of the incomparable PAMELA'. Between the fourth edition of early

---

[61] 24 Apr., 1 May, 8 May.   [62] Cheyne to R, Feb., 9 Mar. 1742.

May and the fifth edition of September this was changed to 'Here end, at present, the Letters of Pamela'; Richardson had decided that the letters were not to end forever. He had to decide it, because someone else had plans for continuing them. On 7 May 1741 he made an addition to his advertisement of the fourth edition: 'Certain Booksellers having in the Press a spurious Continuation of these Two Volumes (in Letters from Pamela to Mrs. Jervis her *Housekeeper*) the Author thinks it necessary to declare, that the same is carrying on *against* his Consent, and without any other Knowledge of the Story than what they are able to collect from the Two Volumes already printed: And that he is actually continuing the Work himself, from Materials, that, perhaps, but for such a notorious Invasion of his Plan, he should not have published.'[63] The fiction that the letters are real is not entirely abandoned, though the word 'Author' is used. The underlining of 'Housekeeper' is an effort to indicate that the continuers are 'low' and did not know proper social usage, a charge enlarged upon by Richardson later: he was by no means willing to draw from *Pamela* the democratic conclusion which could have been drawn from it.

Later Richardson explained to his brother-in-law James Leake that he had heard (presumably through his connections in the trade) that a book-seller named Chandler had hired 'one Kelly, a Bookseller's Hackney, who never wrote any thing that was tolerably receiv'd, and had several of his Performances refused by the Stage', to write a continuation.[64] Chandler was Richard Chandler, a bookseller not only of London but of York and Scarborough, though evidently not a very successful one, since in 1744, when faced by a debtor's prison, he shot himself. He must have been the Chandler who was one of Fielding's partners on the *Champion*,[65] since a good deal of the advertising for his continuation appeared in that paper. John Kelly was not quite so obscure as Richardson implied, having had several plays performed, though none with great success, as well as trans-lations and other works published. He occasionally styled himself (as Richardson later noted) as 'of the Temple'. Richardson remonstrated to a friend of Kelly's, and Chandler came to see him, saying he understood from John Osborn, Senior, that Richardson had not intended to pursue the story. Richardson admitted he had said as much to friends who pressed him to continue, but only 'upon a Supposition, no one would offer to meddle with it, in which Case I had resolved to do it myself, rather than my Plan should be basely ravished out of my Hands, and, probably my Characters depreciated and debased'. He said that he would still not con-tinue unless forced to do so. Chandler then 'had the Impudence' to pro-pose that Richardson join his materials to Kelly's and publish both under

---

[63] *Daily Gazetteer*. See also the *London Evening Post*, 14–16 May.　　[64] Aug. 1741.
[65] G. M. Godden, *Henry Fielding, A Memoir* (London, 1910), p. 115.

Richardson's name, and when that was rejected, he offered to lose the money he had advanced to Kelly and cancel the sheets already printed if Richardson would continue the book for him and his partners, a proposal Richardson also rejected, 'having a young Family of my own that was intitled to All I could do for them'. Evidently piqued by Chandler's saying that the continuation 'fell in nothing short of my two Volumes', he urged Chandler to publish so good a work under some other title and thought he had convinced Chandler of the baseness of his proceeding. But after offering to consult his partners, Chandler let Richardson know that he was determined to go on, boasting 'how well written their Piece was' and threatening that if Richardson advertised against them 'they had Authors who cd. give me Advertisement for Advertisement'. Through a friend, Kelly sent Richardson four half sheets of his work, 'upon full Assurance I wou'd be pleased with this Performance, and by these I saw all my Characters were likely to be debased, & my whole Purpose inverted; for otherwise, I believe I shou'd not have prevailed upon myself to continue it; for Second Parts are generally received with Prejudice, and it was treating the Public too much like a Bookseller to pursue a Success till they tired out the buyers; and the Subject to be pursued as it *ought*, was more difficult and of Consequence, my Leisure, my Health and my Capacity to do it, were all Objections to ye Attempt'. But hearing that the continuers designed a fourth volume and considering that they might go on beyond that and their volumes be issued 'by the Bookseller's Interest and Arts' with his own, reflecting moreover 'upon the Baseness of the Proceeding; they likewise giving out, that I was not the Writer of the two', he decided, in the middle of April, when the other version was well under way, to continue himself. He expected the work to require some time, since he intended to write two more volumes in order to adequately cover such material subjects as Pamela's behaviour in married life, her conversations, her 'pregnant Circumstance', her devotions, her charities, 'her Defence of some part of her former Conduct', her opinions on such genteel diversions as masquerades, operas, and plays as well as on education and friendship, and her 'relative Duties' and 'Family Oeconomy'. This is, unfortunately, a fairly complete description of the contents of the second part of *Pamela*.

By 25 May Aaron Hill knew of Richardson's plan to continue and urged him to take his time. A few days later Chandler and his partner Cæsar Ward, with three other booksellers, advertised that *Pamela's Conduct in High Life*, 'Publish'd from her Original Papers', was out.[66] The author (still unnamed) of the first part immediately advertised against this con-

---

[66] *Craftsman*, 30 May; *Common Sense*, 30 May; *Daily Post*, 3 June. Apparently it was published on 28 May, when, according to Richardson's address to the public in the *Daily Gazetteer* of 1 June, it was advertised in the *Champion*, of which no issue for this date is extant.

tinuation and 'in order to assert his Right to his *own Plan*, and to prevent such an *Imposition* on the Publick' declared that it was done against his remonstrances and promised that his own continuation would soon be printed, from materials he alone possessed, and sold by Rivington and Osborn.[67] In reply, the High-Life Men advertised that their volume was 'Printed from Original Papers, regularly digested by a Gentleman more conversant in High Life than the vain Author of Pamela, or Virtue Rewarded'.[68]

Probably Kelly's knowledge of high life was as limited as Richardson's certainly was; but this innuendo evidently stung, and Richardson was unwise enough to continue the argument on this point. On 4 June Richardson's *Daily Gazetteer* printed as its leading article a specimen of the spurious continuation 'in order to convince the Publick how well the Volume call'd *Pamela in* HIGH-LIFE, deserves that Title'. On the line 'And indeed the Knowledge of our own Ignorance is, in my Opinion, knowing a great deal' a note remarks, 'What Pity the HIGH-LIFE MEN know not thus much!' After the words 'my dear *Jervis*' the paper adds in brackets 'the House-keeper, to whom all her Letters are written, because she is now in HIGH-LIFE the Reader must remember', and after 'Thank you, Friend Jonathan', it adds 'i.e. the Butler', though Jonathan has already been identified. The specimen is well chosen to illustrate the 'lowness' of the High-Life Men. Mr. B. asks Pamela's mother how much she has earned at her wheel that day, and Pamela, with child, asks for a glass of Burgundy and proceeds to drink first a bumper and then a pint beerglass full, then finishes off two bottles and, finding that because of her condition it has no effect on her, goes off to her prayers and bed, leaving Mr. B. drinking. 'N. B. The Publick is assur'd, that the *whole* Volume is written with equal Spirit and Propriety; and if this succeeds (as who can doubt it!) the honest *High-Life* Men in their Introduction give Hopes of another Volume.' From 10 June Richardson's advertisement against the continuation added a reference to this specimen, assuring the public 'that (*bad as it is*) 'tis one of the best-written Parts of their Volume' and informing it that the specimen could be had gratis from Rivington or Osborn.[69] On 12 June Richardson printed in addition another advertisement: in order to answer 'the *scurrilous Papers* and *Advertisements* that have been scattered about the Town' to promote the sale of *Pamela in High Life*, he asserted that 'when any Person who is *above Scandal* and *scandalous Practices*, shall say any thing *worthy* of *Notice*, and set his *Name* to what he publishes, he shall receive a proper Reply'.[70] On 9 July the advertisement refers to

[67] *Daily Gazetteer*, 30 May; *London Daily Post and General Advertiser*, 30 May, 1 June; *Daily Post*, 1 June, 2 June; *Craftsman*, 6 June, 13 June; *Common Sense*, 6 June, 13 June; *London Evening Post*, 6–9 June.
[68] *Daily Post*, 3 June, 4 June; *London Evening Post*, 6–9 June.   [69] *Daily Gazetteer*.
[70] *Daily Gazetteer*. See also the issues of 15 June, 18 June, 20 June, 23 June, 25 June; *Daily Post*, 13 June; *London Daily Post and General Advertiser*, 13 June.

'fresh Irruptions of Scandal and Impertinence' from the High-Life Men.[71] An advertisement of the first volume of Kelly's continuation boasted that it was 'Published from original Papers, *without the Consent, or even Knowledge*, of the *pretended* Author of Pamela, or Virtue rewarded'. Following Addison's example with Sir Roger de Coverley, the continuers '*have been obliged to* Kill Pamela, that neither Mr. R——n or his accomplices might be guilty of Murdering Her'. '*The Proprietors of Pamela's Conduct in High Life* Think fit, once for all, to give the following Answer to the Impertinent, Vain, Self-sufficient and Scurrilous *pretended* Author of *Pamela, or Virtue rewarded*, That they have already answered him; and in that Answer, to which they defy him to reply, justified their Proceeding; and as they have Signed it, look upon his Scandalous Advertisement as pointing them out for the Persons who are not (to use his own very improper Words) *above Scandal*, by which we suppose he means what he repeats, above *Scandalous Practices* and unworthy of Notice, they think this in a most flagrant Manner striking at, and endeavouring to Stain, their Characters, which stand *at least in as fa[i]r a light* as that pretended Author's; but they don't wonder at his being *so free with them*, since, in the Work he arrogates to himself, he has *burlesqued the Scriptures* and made *Time Servers, Fools, and Fidlers*, of the Reverend Clergy.'[72]

The anonymous gentleman who had written to Rivington about the first part of *Pamela* and who had been so roughly treated by Aaron Hill wrote again in July, still admiring and still willing to offer friendly advice, 'thô I shou'd be again mistook, and have Censure instead of the contrary'; he pointed out to the author of *Pamela* that the spurious continuation did not deserve so much notice as he was giving it and urged him to take his time and to 'touch and polish his Continuation', since it was expected even to excel the first part, and to take no notice of his rival (as Cervantes had done) in the body of his work. But Richardson was already well advanced and by 13 August was able to advertise that his third and fourth volumes were 'In the PRESS, And will be Published with all convenient Speed'.[73] Kelly was just as quick, and his second volume appeared on 12 September,[74] upon which Richardson added to his advertisement a warning that the two volumes of *Pamela's Conduct in High Life* were not by the author of the first two.[75] But the High-Life Men were also advertising, and one can imagine Richardson's righteous indignation when he read in early October, in an advertisement for the second edition (of Volume I only),

---

[71] *Daily Gazetteer*. These 'Irruptions of Scandal and Impertinence' were probably published in the *Champion*, but no file of the paper for this period is known to be extant.

[72] *Common Sense*, 18 July, 25 July, 1 Aug.   [73] *Daily Gazetteer*.

[74] *London Daily Post and General Advertiser*, 12 Sept.; *General Evening Post*, 10–12 Sept.; *London Evening Post*, 10–12 Sept.; *Daily Post*, 14 Sept.

[75] *Daily Gazetteer*, 14 Sept.; *London Daily Post and General Advertiser*, 17 Sept.; *Daily Post* 17 Sept.

that their 'genuine Edition was thought Necessary to be done by another Hand, and is not by the Author of Pamela, or, Virtue Rewarded' and that Chandler's was 'the only Genuine Edition of the Continuation of PAMELA'.[76]

Though their book is hardly inspired and has none of the imaginative re-creation which gives life to the first part of *Pamela*, the High-Life Men did at least as well as Richardson in filling in the events of a situation which by its nature had to be essentially uneventful. It begins, like Richardson's own continuation, with the journey of the happy pair into Kent to set up Pamela's parents; there it is discovered that her family is really genteel and is closely related to the neighbouring squire. There is a great deal of conversation, in which a curate named Brown utters many irreproachably moral sentiments; there are several interpolated stories of the sort distantly derived from the Italian tales; there are formal characters of various admirable neighbours—everyone is admirable and amiable; there is much description of trivial occupations, of furniture, of food and drink; there are disquisitions on Biblical points in which the author displays a knowledge of Hebrew. The book picks up a little when Lady Davers arrives with her husband and Jackey and has to be humbled again. The party goes on to Tunbridge Wells, where there is an adventure with a gentleman robber, and then to Lincolnshire, where it is learned that Mrs. Jewkes has been discharged for cheating and has married a young man who beats her and that Mr. Peters, the clergyman who did not aid Pamela, has been suitably punished—his daughter has been ruined by a coachman. Such are the events possible in a happily married life in the upper circles. The author seems more interested in his discussions: scandalmongering is evil, the clergy should not be criticized, the story of the Book of Job is true, George Herbert's poetry is unjustly neglected, merchants are the props of the British nation, the doctrine of the Election of Grace is false, clerics should not hold pluralities.

In the second volume of the continuation a good many of the letters are still, as in the first, written to Mrs. Jervis, and there is a hit at Richardson's advertisement when Pamela refuses to change her sentiments towards her old friend the housekeeper 'or be laugh'd out of them by People, who, ignorant of what becomes Persons of the Rank to which Heaven has rais'd me, imagine that a haughty and distant Behaviour to their Inferiors and Dependents, are the Characteristicks of what is call'd *High Life*'.[77] Many new neighbours make their appearance and have their stories told. After the birth of her son, Pamela is presented to Queen Anne and is courted by a noble lord. Her parents die, but she is somewhat consoled by reading Marcus Aurelius. After such digressions as a description of Switzerland and of William Tell and a criticism of Lucan, the novel

[76] *Craftsman*, 3 Oct.; *London Evening Post*, 8–10 Oct.   [77] P. 2.

suddenly (a hundred pages from the end) becomes eventful: Pamela is abducted from a masquerade, her husband wounds the abductor in a duel, and the couple goes to France. Another noble lord courts Pamela in vain, but his sister is more successful with Mr. B., who, suspecting his wife, goes off to Italy with the new love. Pamela's patience in this trying situation is rewarded when Lady Frances discards Mr. B. for an Italian lover, and the couple is reunited until Pamela's death in 1730. The whole work is literate enough and at least earnest enough, with no glaring absurdities and usually enough of tepid interest to keep the reader awake.

After the first volume of *Pamela's Conduct in High Life*, was published a *Life of Pamela*, which retells her story in the third person, including her life after marriage as recounted by Kelly's continuation, indebtedness to which is twice acknowledged, once with the addition that its author 'is certainly possess'd of some authentick Memoirs of the Family, and is an ingenious Writer at least, if we do not altogether allow of the Comparison that has been made between him and the Author of *Pamela*'s Letters, viz. That the last seem to be wrote by a Girl, but the other by a Man of Sense and Learning'.[78] If this comparison was meant to be uncomplimentary to Richardson, it also indicates his great strength: he was not a man of sense and learning, but, much more important for his purpose, he was able to write like a girl. *The Life of Pamela* purports to be taken from 'original Papers now in the Hands of the Reverend Mr. *Perkins of Shendisford Abbey*', and censures Richardson's version for its departures from truth: 'We shall rectify a thousand more Mistakes that have been made in that Work'.[79] But after some introductory pages on Pamela's family and the early life of Mr. B., largely drawn from hints in *Pamela* itself, it sticks closely to its original throughout the first part, often merely turning Richardson's words into the third person. The author makes some changes in the story of both the first part and the continuation: most of the names designated by initials are given in full; the date of Pamela's marriage is given as 1726; her parents lose their money in the South Sea Bubble; and a much needed unity is given the second part by the introduction of a false friend named Sir Harry Broomstead, who eventually tries to abduct the heroine. When he finds an event improbable or improper, as when Mrs. Jervis lets Mr. B. observe Pamela in her country dress or when Lady Davers bursts into Mr. B.'s bedroom, he does not change the event but merely mentions its absurdity.[80] What liveliness the book has is a result of transcribing Richardson's scenes and conversations; it is a convincing demonstration of the advantages of Richardson's epistolary method over the conventional narrative method of the period, since its use of the factual style of pseudo-history results in a sharp loss in directness and vividness.

Notes to the narrative blame Richardson for praising himself, for the

[78] Pp. 416n, 451n.   [79] P. 2n.   [80] Pp. 68, 303.

inconsistency of Pamela's language ('talking like a *Philosopher* in one Page and like a *Changeling* the next'), for the mass of trivial details (a gentleman in a coffee house 'wondered the Author had not told the exact Number of Pins *Pamela* had about her when she set out for Lincolnshire, and how many Rows of those Pins she bought for a Penny'), for uncomplimentary remarks about Lord Davers ('this plainly betrays the Mechanick; for such, knowing nothing of the Behaviour and Conversation of the Nobility, imagine every *LORD* is a *FOOL*'), and for Pamela's readiness in conversing with her husband's friends (she 'is made to talk ... with as much Boldness as if she had follow'd the Camp with a Gin-Cog, and, like *Kate Matchlock*, had buried seven Husbands before in one Campaign').[81]

In late September still another continuation began to appear, called *Pamela in High Life: or, Virtue Rewarded*, published in instalments, which probably hoped to be taken for Richardson's own continuation.[82] It has something of the same relation to *Pamela's Conduct in High Life* that that work has to *Pamela* since it starts where the first volume of the High-Life Men ends—if a book can be said to start in which nothing with any bearing on the main characters happens. It purports to be taken from the papers of Pamela's son and is in the form of a journal written by Pamela for her parents. The heroine describes her neighbours and the long conversations she has with them, occasionally relating the tales which the various members of the company tell to while away the evenings. To fill in the vacant spaces in the conversation, the reader is given such amusements as an explanation of the office of alderman, detailed lists of Pamela's charities, the enormous bill of fare of a week-long feast (2,100 bottles of wine, 200 geese), much information about Mr. B.'s large income (he has over £15,000 a year from land and £150,000 invested), an account of the marvellous economy of ants and bees, another of the motion of the earth and of the tides of the Thames, a long discussion of the relation between natural and revealed religion which leans rather towards the former and which explains such dubious points as the cause of the old age of the antediluvians (the air was better) and whether the flood covered the whole earth (it did not), a fantasy by Mr. B. (based on an imaginary antediluvian source) of the rise in the time of Enoch of public worship and the consequent power of the priesthood, a sermon on the Gunpowder Plot, and a great deal of geographical information—brief sketches of the English cities, a thirty-seven page description of Russia and a ten-page description of the rest of Europe (a third of it devoted to the clock of Strasbourg), and short sketches of other regions. Such a partial list serves at least to illustrate the difficulty of making a novel out of Pamela's married life, a task at which the author of *Pamela in High Life* is even less successful than Kelly or Richardson. We do hear about the births of Pamela's ten children

---

[81] Pp. 185–6, 249, 340.   [82] *London Daily Post and General Advertiser*, 29 Sept.

and about Mr. B.'s gradual advance to the rank of Duke and the posts of Ambassador to France and Lord Lieutenant of Ireland. Otherwise the most momentous events are the infatuation of Charles II with Pamela, which leads to an undeveloped attempt to abduct her, and her yielding to wise advice and reducing the amount of her charities so as not to spoil the industrious poor—with unusual frankness, Lady Davers explains that 'without the Industry of the Poor we who are rich, must want a great many of the Necessaries and Conveniencies of Life'.[83] Pamela's only trouble is that one of her sons and one of her daughters are too fond of each other, but their love remains Platonic, and almost nothing is made of this promising difficulty. After fifty years of marriage Mr. B. dies, and eight years later his wife follows him, a duchess with £220,000 to bestow on her heirs. It is interesting to imagine what a reader who expected more of Pamela examining her bundles or meditating by the pond might have made of this curious conglomeration.

Richardson seems to have asked all of his friends for advice about his own continuation and, as usual, to have taken almost none of the advice he got. On 24 August Dr. Cheyne wrote that he had seen two sheets of the work, probably at Leake's, and scratched some suggestions; he urged Richardson to use as his vehicle of instruction 'many interesting Incidents, either Distresses naturally overcome or good Fortune unexpectedly happening'—for instance, a broken leg, a dangerous fever for Mr. B. with Pamela's tender nursing (her unconverted husband's weakened condition would provide a fine opportunity for noble religious sentiments), the death of a favourite child, a sudden conflagration, an epidemical distemper, a severe winter, a famine, quarrels among neighbours. Pamela should recommend the 'strongest Writers in Morality and Christianity' to Mr. B. and ultimately convert him by degrees, from a rake and pagan to a senator, a philosopher, and finally a 'true Spiritual Christian'. Her behaviour in all the duties of high life could furnish 'infinite Lessons for the Sex'. He offers to help in making out a proper library for the heroine 'of sacred History Natural Philosophy spiritual Divinity and innocent Triflers'. She should be made to 'insist with Deference' on having a room of her own, which her husband would enter only on urgent occasions, for her devotions as well as to 'keep herself clean [and] neat and do the necessary Occasions of Nature'. Fondling, clasping, kissing, and stroking are to be avoided, as is excessive humility from Pamela and her parents, creeping and holding down their heads in the dirt: 'For my own sake I should not permit it in my Wife had she been a Milkmaid', 'but avoid Drawling as much as you can and let not a long pennyfull tempt you to say low and vulgar Things Readers love Rapidity in Narrations and quick Returns keep them from doseing'.

[83] P. 305.

Incidentally Cheyne also gives advice on how to avoid the ill effects of the sedentary life induced by so much writing, having heard from their mutual friend Paul Bertrand, who had recently visited Richardson, that he is looking 'full puffed short neck't and Head and Face bursting with Blood'. About this time Richardson wrote to Mrs. Barber that he was 'sadly afflicted with the Old Complaint, bad Nerves, and Startings and Tremors, and Dizziness, and worse for the hot Weather', and was cold-bathing and coaching on the rough streets almost daily, for 'I must, as patiently as I can, bear what cannot be remedy'd'.[84]

Perhaps Cheyne's largely medical adventures were not precisely what was required, though his demand for some events points to a serious defect in Richardson's continuation. But Richardson was not inclined to follow any of these suggestions (Mr. B. is converted, but inconspicuously). An intended answer, presumably not sent, dated 31 August, is preserved among his papers. After thanking Cheyne for his suggestions and saying that he does intend Mr. B.'s conversion, he defends a certain amount of 'Matrimonial Tenderness': he was 'endeavouring to . . . catch young and airy Minds' and 'if I were to be too spiritual, I doubt I should catch none but Grandmothers'. He wishes to 'mingle Instruction with Entertainment, so as to make the latter *seemingly* the *View*, while the former is *really* the End'. The 'principal Complaints' against him 'by many, and not Libertines neither', had been that he was 'too grave, too much of a Methodist'. 'In my Scheme I have generally taken Human Nature *as it is*; for it is to no purpose to suppose it Angelic, or to endeavour to make it so.' He will not have occasion for such 'deep Scenes, as I believ'd necessary to the Story in two Places in the former'; and he mentions the anonymous defence of his warm episodes as possibly more necessary and no more inflaming than those in *Paradise Lost*. He does not think Pamela and her parents too humble under the circumstances. As for Cheyne's specific suggestions, he says only that he wishes he could 'rise to your Plan, and that the Age were fitter to receive so much more perfect and Instructive a Story'.

A franker opinion appears in a draft of a letter to the 'thresher poet', Stephen Duck, who had also seen a part of the continuation and feared that it would not live up to the first part, having too little incident. Richardson refers to an excellent physician who 'was so good as to give me a Plan to break Legs and Arms and to fire Mansion Houses to create Distresses'; he had no use for such ideas, aiming at 'instruction in a genteel and usual Married Life', hating 'the French Marvellous and all un-natural Machinery', and recognizing that his second part, a piece of natural life with its ups and downs, its stormy and sedate side, offered no scope for 'Plots, Stratagem and Intrigue'.[85] When Cheyne, after the publication of

[84] 3 Sept.   [85] Duck to R, 14 Oct.; R to Duck, [Oct.–Nov.?].

the book, reported that though he personally found the 'Moral extreemly good' critics were objecting that there were 'too few Incidents', Richardson was undoubtedly thinking of his advice when he replied, 'I must own I am so great an Enemy to the French Marvellous, that I only aimed to give the Piece such a Variety, as should be consistent with Probability, and the general Tenor of a genteel Married Life.' 'I always had it in View ... to make the Story rather *useful*, than *diverting*.' Far from needing incidents, he had to 'rein in' his 'Invention', having had as many subjects as he could possibly cover.[86]

Paul Bertrand read the first two sheets of the second part and approved the author's plan; when Cheyne showed him his letter to Richardson, he told the Doctor that such advice had not been asked for and remarked to Richardson that Cheyne's amendments were trifling. Bertrand had offered the suggestion that the book begin with letters from Lady Davers instead of with Pamela's correspondence with her parents, but he gave up his plan in favour of Richardson's. In his reply Richardson, safe with Bertrand's approval, offered to sacrifice Pamela's letters to her parents if Bertrand wished.[87]

James Leake and his family also saw two sheets and liked them better than any in the first two volumes. He sent them to 'The Man of Bath', the philanthropist Ralph Allen, who was shortly to become a valuable patron and friend of Fielding, and Allen replied approving of them and suggesting that Mrs. Jewkes be genteely and generously dismissed and that there be no affectation in Pamela's piety. Richardson answered that he had got Allen's letter too late to act on it (he had held the sheets nearly a month before printing in anticipation) and hoped that Allen would be satisfied with Mrs. Jewkes's repentance.[88]

To Mary Barber, Richardson explained that the second attempted rape scene in the first part, to which that lady had objected, was to be the subject of observation by Lady Davers which might excuse it somewhat; he had often wished for her advice on some particulars, 'I having but a poor Notion of the requisite Delicacy of our own [Sex], in relation to some nicer points'. 'I will not where the cause of Virtue is concern'd, trim one bit, in the future two Volumes, as some People expect I shd.'[89]

The notorious impostor and hack writer George Psalmanazar sent Richardson a scene in which Lady Davers, after blaming Pamela for attending her poor neighbours in their illness ('O Brother, Brother ... she'll sink you down to the very Dunghill from which you took her'), is converted and asks to assist Pamela in her charities. Though it has a few touches which suggest delicate parody and is perhaps a little heavier on tears than Richardson himself, it is not a bad effort to reproduce his tone

[86] 30 Dec. 1741; [early Jan. 1742].
[88] Leake to R, 26 Aug.; R to Allen, 8 Oct.
[87] 25 Aug., 31 Aug.
[89] 3 Sept.

and style, but Richardson did not use it and wrote in the margin such comments as 'Ridiculous & improbable, like the whole of it', 'O! Mr. Psalmanazar!!!', and simply '!!!' beside Lady Davers's remark that only Pamela's pregnancy can convince her that that paragon is really a flesh and blood creature of her own sex.[90]

An anonymous correspondent volunteered a letter from Lady Davers to Pamela, which Richardson wisely ignored. Alexander Gordon sent him remarks on the opera, which he used.[91]

Aaron Hill had of course been enthusiastic from the first, so enthusiastic that Richardson later noted on his letter that all of Hill's praises were too warm, 'Yet no Man ever had a more expanded Heart, and *truer* Friendship, nor more Sincerity'.[92] On 15 October he acknowledged two sheets: 'Where will your wonders end?' Richardson's genius rises not, like a pyramid, decreasing, but like a pillar which looks largest at its capital, 'enlarging its proportion'. 'Go on, dear Sir, (I see you will and must) to charm and captivate the world.' By 22 October he had part of volume three and was transported; he requested the 'Dear Engrosser of Whole Nature' to send him the worked-off sheets of the fourth volume and asked also that Richardson write a fifth and sixth. By 12 November he had loose sheets printed off of the third and fourth volumes, a mass of new beauties. He rejoiced that the High-Life Men had murdered Pamela so that Richardson could have no rivals in his next volumes.

By 8 October Richardson had finished writing, though the large number printed delayed publication.[93] The first part of *Pamela* had been copyrighted in the names of Richardson, Charles Rivington, and John Osborn. In his autobiographical letter to Stinstra, Richardson later reported that, when 'urged by a particular Friend to put it to the Press', he had attached so little weight to the book that he had accepted twenty guineas for two-thirds of the copyright, reserving only a third to himself. A year later he had a juster appreciation of the value of his literary property and on 4 December entered the third and fourth volumes at the Stationers' Company entirely in his own name. Early in January, with Rivington and Osborn, he took further pains to protect his interest from abridgement as well as piracy by obtaining a Royal Licence for the sole printing, publishing, and sale of the four volumes.[94]

Richardson's continuation, widely advertised, finally appeared on

[90] FM XVI, 1, fos. 27–33.   [91] 11 Oct., [summer or autumn].
[92] 29 July.
[93] R to Allen.
[94] 'Entries of Copies 1710–46', under dates 4 Nov. 1740 and 4 Dec. 1741, MS. in the archives of the Stationers' Company; John B. Shipley, 'Samuel Richardson and "Pamela"', *N&Q*, N.S. I (1954), 28–9; R. M. Wiles, *Serial Publication in England before 1750* (Cambridge, 1957), pp. 162–8. The petition for a Royal Licence is dated 7 Jan. (P.R.O. S.P. 36/58, fo. 9); on 13 Jan. the King granted Richardson, Rivington, and Osborn the sole printing and vending of *Pamela* 'within our Kingdoms and Dominions' (P.R.O. S.P. 44/367, p. 250).

7 December 1741. For the first time, his name was connected with the book, which was 'Printed for S. RICHARDSON' and sold by Rivington and Osborn. Though the continuation was not as successful as the first part, its sale must have been satisfactory, since in spite of the fact that he printed a large number,[95] he was able to publish a second duodecimo edition a little over a year later, and meanwhile the third and fourth volumes had been issued in the de luxe octavo edition along with the first two.

The continuation of *Pamela* was also valuable enough to be stolen. The best known bookseller in Dublin, George Faulkner, was able to induce someone to send him copies of the sheets as they were printed off, which he then published for his own benefit. Richardson had agreed to furnish the sheets to a Dublin coffee-house-owner-turned-bookseller named Thomas Bacon, to be reprinted there, but Faulkner got the sheets first and presumably reaped most of the profit.[96] Richardson's reaction does not seem to have been so violent as it was later, when *Sir Charles Grandison* was similarly pirated, though the publication of Faulkner's edition may have prompted him to apply for the Royal Licence to protect himself from further piracy in George II's 'Kingdoms and Dominions'. English copyrights did not apply in Ireland, and the only way to profit by a book there was to get it off the press first.

Again Richardson received letters praising and commenting on his book, from correspondents known and unknown, but (judging by those preserved among his papers) they were not so numerous as the ones about the first part, though some were as enthusiastic. Six ladies of Reading were as enchanted with part two as they had been with part one, though they had some doubts as to the authenticity of the story—how could some of the distinguished people bear to have their characters told to the public? Why does not the world recognize such prominent people and events? Why did Sir Jacob (who has dinner with Pamela thinking she is a maiden lady) not notice Pamela's wedding ring, which she never removed from her finger? If it is not true, who is the author? Suspicious, Richardson showed the letter to his landlord at North End, Samuel Vanderplank, who doubted that the six ladies were what they professed to be, and thought that if a lady did write the letter she must be a 'Bold Pullet'. After a second and more impatient letter, Richardson drafted what his index to his correspondence folder on *Pamela* describes as a letter of raillery: he must know who they are before he can answer, and besides six ladies could never keep a secret. But even these six dubious ladies were requested to give suggestions for a future edition, and he did add in the octavo that

[95] R to Allen, 8 Oct. 1741; R to Cheyne, [early Jan. 1742].

[96] See Richardson's *An Address to the Public* in the 1st edn. of *Sir Charles Grandison*, VII, 428, 441; R to Sarah Wescomb, 20 July 1753; R to Lady Echlin, 24 Nov. 1753. Faulkner had also published an edition of part one of *Pamela* in January 1741.

happily Sir Jacob stared so much at Pamela's face that he did not observe her ring.[97]

The Reverend John Swinton wrote from Oxford that 'all the Senior and more intelligent Part of the University' esteemed the third and fourth volumes highly and that the Dean of Christ Church (John Conybeare, later Bishop of Bristol), who was about to read them for the third time (in six weeks!), considered it 'the finest Picture of Nature he ever yet saw'.[98]

A writer who remained anonymous because he was under obligations to Richardson and did not want to be considered a sycophant, having heard the book 'greatly censured', read it and was inexpressibly delighted —only godless wretches can disrelish it, it is divinely inspired; it will convert the coquette, the prude, the profuse and vain, and the worn-out debauchee; the fourth volume is 'one of the most Entertaining, most Instructive Books . . . in the *English* Language'.[99]

A poor young man of about twenty-six found its morality 'severe enough for a System for Angels'. He promised that if Richardson answered, his letter should be treasured as bigots treasure amulets and relics and asked for another book portraying virtue in the lowest stations of life. Cannot the poor be benevolent? He himself had helped several people, had reclaimed a rake by writing an anonymous letter to him, and was considering giving useful hints in the same manner 'to inconsiderate People of both Sexes'. If Richardson approves, he 'shall never let slip an useless Hour after this Time'. To avoid the imputation of flattery, he found one fault—if Mr. B. had given Pamela a settlement of £100 per annum before attacking her, her indebtedness would have increased her difficulty. Richardson waited hardly a day to send his humble correspondent a relic. He was delighted with the poor man's character, specifically with his anonymous attempts at reformation (which may have reminded him of his own boyhood letter to the backbiter). He pointed out that even in her low estate Pamela did delight in her poor charities and that taking the £100 would have subjected her to the censure of the world and the disapproval of her parents. Richardson was sure that it must be a great pleasure for him to reflect on the good he had done, especially to the reclaimed rake, and approved of his plans for further anonymous reclamation 'if prudently performed'.[100]

A writer with more learning, who signed Philopamela, was so full of Pamela that he was beginning to talk like her and could hardly get to sleep for thinking of her; he found finer sentiments than in Homer or Virgil, a sublimity which completely satisfied three of Longinus's

[97] We have dated this correspondence Jan.–Mar. 1742. The passage in *Pamela* is SH, III, 316; EL, II, 163.
[98] 19 Jan.   [99] 24 Jan.   [100] 'Receivd Jany 26th. 1741/2'; 27 Jan.

desiderata and partially satisfied the other two, and an ideal example of Horace's *utile dulci*.[101]

Cheyne reported that the critics at Bath found the letters excellent but thought 'there is too much Preaching in it, it is too long too drawling and the Passions not sufficiently agitated the Booksellers here says it sells very well but not so quick as the first'.[102]

William Warburton, Pope's friend and later editor, was cautious. Richardson, having been told by Mr. Woodward that Warburton could have given hints for the continuation had he known Richardson and emboldened by 'the Approbation [of] the first Genius of the Age' (which Leake and Cheyne had told him of), sent Warburton a copy of the octavo and asked him for corrections. In acknowledging the gift Warburton avoided any expression of opinion. He did, however, say that he and Pope, discussing Pamela in high life, had thought that one excellent subject would have been her passing the judgement of simple nature on 'the follies and extravagancies of high life; which to one of Pamela's low station and good sense would have appeared as absurd and unaccountable as European polite vices and customs to an Indian'.[103] Since volumes five and six of *Pamela* were never written, Richardson had no occasion to use this suggestion—happily, since while Pope might well have written a witty satire using his heroine as a sort of English oriental or Huron traveller in the manner of Montesquieu or Voltaire, Richardson's talents hardly lay in this direction, and his knowledge of the life to be satirized was not much greater than Pamela's before her entry into it.

Evidently Richardson had considered the possibility that he might publish more works related to Pamela. An Advertisement at the end of the last volume referred to the 'Attempts of some Imitators, who, supposing the Story of PAMELA a fiction, have murder'd that excellent Lady, and mistaken and misrepresented other (suppos'd imaginary) CHARACTERS'. Lest such persons 'impose new Continuations upon the Publick', Richardson assured his readers that 'all the Copies of Mrs. *B.*'s Observations and Writings, upon every Subject hinted at in the preceding Four Volumes, and in particular those relating to *Devotion, Education, Plays*, &c. are now in *One Hand Only*'. If they should ever be published '(which at present is a Point undetermined)', it would only be after Pamela's death and at the assignment of the editor, Samuel Richardson. The list of the subjects of Pamela's observations gives some idea of what a future volume might have been and hardly makes one regret that no further volumes appeared. They would evidently have been quite unlike the continuation Pope suggested and a good deal like the last part of the extant fourth volume.

Richardson's daughters authorized the statement that though the second two volumes of *Pamela* 'did not meet with the same success' as the first, 'it is thought that the author held them in much higher estimation'.[104] If so he, with the few correspondents cited above, is in a small minority. It is hard to think of another work by a reputable writer for which there is so little to be said as for the second part of *Pamela*. It has been pointed out that there is a certain technical advance in that the correspondence is more nearly two-sided, with some interchange among correspondents,[105] but this advantage does not help the book much since in the absence of any conflict they have little to interchange. There are further signs of the talent for realistic scenes of conversation and social intercourse which had appeared occasionally in the first part. In spite of outbreaks of the rudeness which Richardson regarded as wit, they are not very lively. But developed further, such scenes do help to redeem *Sir Charles Grandison* at the frequent points when nothing is happening in that novel.

It is hard not to compare the second part of *Pamela* with *Sir Charles Grandison*. Unlike the first part of *Pamela* and *Clarissa*, which concentrate on a series of events, they concentrate on a model character, and Richardson tries to make up events to illustrate the virtues of the model. The method is not a happy one. The leading characters, because they are virtuous, can make no serious mistakes, and because their virtue has been rewarded, they can meet with no serious mishaps. The great fault of the continuation of *Pamela* is that there was nothing which could happen in it, and the best excuse that can be offered for it is that Richardson was evidently forced to write it, without any urge from inside.

Judging by the number of times Pamela apologizes for the fact that her letters contain nothing of moment, Richardson must have been conscious of a certain lack of invention. She often explains that she only dares write because her correspondent (her parents, or Lady Davers, or her new friend Polly Darnford) is interested in everything connected with her: 'Here, Miss [Darnford], I conclude my tedious Narrations. . . . To be sure, I would not have been so tediously trifling, but for the sake of my dear Parents'—her letters are made to do duty for several correspondents. 'Thus, Madam, do I run on, in a manner, without Materials'—and she does.[106]

We are well over half way through volume three before the first glimmer of a plot arises, or the first break in the uniform chorus of praise. An uncle of Mr. B.'s named Sir Jacob Swynford, who is strongly prejudiced

---

[104] *Universal Magazine*, LXXVIII, 74.

[105] McKillop, *Richardson*, p. 60. Donald L. Ball, '*Pamela II*: A Primary Link in Richardson's Development as a Novelist', *MP*, LXV (1967–8), 334–42, has shown that the continuation of *Pamela* anticipates certain characters and scenes of Richardson's later novels and, more importantly, that in it Richardson first uses several of the narrative techniques which he used later.

[106] SH, III, 334–5, IV, 8; EL, II, 174, 227.

against Pamela, arrives to visit. Briefly, there is a touch of at least comparative liveliness, but after being introduced to Pamela under an assumed name, Sir Jacob is won over with little effort. A pattern arises which is even more prominent in *Sir Charles Grandison*. Every time opposition begins, it has to subside as soon as the model character enters; the appearance of his glacial virtue freezes all conflict, and all attempts at a plot evaporate in rhapsodies at his excellence. It is the inevitable and overwhelming disadvantage of the novel of model characters combined with a morality which insists on rewarding virtue in every possible way: the model must be appreciated, even worshipped. The plot must collapse while the characters join in agreeing with whatever he chooses to say.

There are a few other faint hints that something might happen. Pamela rescues her unwilling servant maid Polly Barlow from a liaison with Lord Davers's stupid nephew Jackey. Her friend Polly Darnford has some family disagreements. Pamela finally obtains custody of her husband's bastard daughter, Miss Goodwin, the repentance of whose mother gives rise to reflections on the merits of ex-fallen women.[107] Mr. B., having been converted to morality in volume two, is converted to religion in volume four and joins Pamela in her private services. One episode which might have aroused interest and which is elaborately worked up with every trick to arouse suspense occurs well into volume four. In a letter to Stephen Duck, Richardson expressed the hope that this episode would answer Duck's objection to the lack of incident.[108] Mr. B., at a masquerade, meets and becomes fascinated by a Countess. Pamela is frantic with jealousy but controls herself; her marriage is about to be ruined, but she will submit, she knows she deserves no better. But in a highly theatrical confrontation scene she reveals her fears to Mr. B. Of course she wins him back; indeed it appears that she had really never lost him, since both he and the Countess had only the purest of motives. For by now Mr. B. is also a paragon and only by cheating the reader can Richardson make him think for a moment that the hero might waver on his pedestal.

The lack of events leaves ample room for discussion of various subjects, and the characters express their views on such matters as the importance of titles (not great), pluralities (wrong), Scots (they make good tutors, partly because of their poverty, but they need some polishing), English shipping (important), and servants (they can be kept in their places without undue asperity).[109] The ideas are sensible enough, but hardly exciting or novel.

Considerable space is taken up by Pamela's desire to nurse her own children, to which Mr. B. objects in spite of her cogent arguments in

---

[107] SH, IV, 277–8; EL, II, 359. [108] [Oct.–Nov. ? 1741].

[109] SH, III, 169–73, 270–88, IV, 326, 399–400, 332–3, 278–9; EL, II, 93–5, 147–50 (a cut version), 390, 437, 394, 360.

favour of it—which gives rise to more discussion of the extent of a husband's authority over his wife (great). Pamela, at some length, gives her views (not very favourable—they violate both morality and probability) on Ambrose Philips's tragedy *The Distressed Mother* and Steele's comedy *The Tender Husband*. At her unwary husband's request she comments at length on Locke's comments on education. By this time Richardson had abandoned all effort to begin a plot, and his heroine concludes with rather sharp remarks (her tongue never spares the weaknesses of others) on some of her neighbours whose histories serve as warnings to girls against the wiles of the other sex (one of them sketches the situation of *Clarissa*—a young lady almost elopes out of a private garden door with a dishonourable peer who intends to ruin her to take revenge on her parents) and a series of moral tales with which she is educating her children.[110]

A large part of volume three is devoted to answering criticisms of the first two volumes. Mr. B. has to retell the whole story from his point of view (Richardson's characters are always willing to discuss their most private affairs before company), making his character a bit whiter. But the opportunity thus offered to give the reader his thoughts and feelings in his own words comes to little. The passion that pervaded Pamela's account of her troubles had cooled. Lady Davers assures Pamela that none of her descriptions was calculated to shock anyone—'Lady *Betty*, who is a very nice and delicate Lady, had no Objections to any Part, tho' read before Men'; besides, it was necessary to know the full details of Pamela's danger in order to appreciate her merit. Pamela completely convinces Lady Davers that her forgiving Mrs. Jewkes was the right thing to do, for a number of reasons (Richardson often forgets that one good reason is better than ten doubtful ones): it convinced Mr. B. that she was not resentful, it was a greater triumph than revenge would have been, it led to the conversion of Mrs. Jewkes, and so forth.[111]

The author of *Shamela*, among others, had attacked *Pamela* because it gave a bad example to rich gentlemen, who might be taken in to marry their servant maids. It is difficult today to understand how distasteful such an alliance was to many people in Richardson's day. The High-Life Men emphasized their discovery that Pamela was of gentle birth. On the Continent, where family was even more important than in England, Goldoni made Pamela the daughter of a lord in disguise, a change highly lauded in a review in the *Journal étranger*. Goldoni merits praise 'for not having taken the road which Richardson had opened in his Novel. . . . He does not, to exalt the virtue of his Heroine, give at the end the example of a

[110] SH, IV, 59–78, 79–88, 305–59, 402–52; EL, II, 253–5 (a cut version), 255–6 (a cut version), 373–411, 438–71.
[111] SH, III, 43–4, 64–86; EL, II, 26–7, 39–49.

shameful misalliance.'[112] Indeed there are reflections on the gentry in Pamela's early history which might have seemed rather dangerous. A proud letter about her from Lady Davers, for instance, causes her to remark that though the proud and rich despise the poor, 'yet we were all on a foot originally: And many of these Gentlefolks, that brag of their ancient Blood, would be glad to have it as wholsome, and as *really* untainted, as ours!' All will be levelled by death and The Judgement. 'Poor Souls! how do I pity their Pride!—O keep me, Heaven! from *their* high Condition, if my Mind shall ever be tainted with *their* Vice!'[113] This was no doubt sincere; and Pamela cannot in fact be accused of becoming as proud as her namesake in *Joseph Andrews* when she is elevated. But it appears clearly that she respects and approves the way of the world as regards social classes. Her creator was also from humble condition, and there is ample evidence that he did not like being patronized by his superiors. He was always rather touchy, anxious to be independent, and hardly humble. But perhaps his resentment at the pride of his betters was, like Pamela's, more personal than general—that is, unlike Camus' Rebel, he wanted respect for himself, but he had no desire to change the situation which threatened that respect. At any rate, the second part of *Pamela* is open to no attacks on the ground of social radicalism.

Richardson was at some pains to clear his story from the charge that it might lead to social levelling. He had already printed in his preface to the second edition of *Pamela* a letter from Aaron Hill which, by a rather circuitous course of reasoning, attempted to answer this charge. In a long discussion of this matter, Mr. B. points out that his example can never lead any but a young fellow who is 'such a Booby, that he cannot *reflect* and *compare*' to do the same thing, since Pamela's resistance is almost unparalleled and her character, confirmed by the praises of all and not merely by her lover's partiality, is certainly so.[114] It is worth noting, however, that Pamela's comments on this question are more ambiguous, and imply, though they do not state, that such marriages are not undesirable. As Brian Downs remarks, 'Richardson contrives, not uncharacteristically, to "have it both ways"',[115] though the reader is left with the impression that Mr. B. is right, since the infallible Pamela has in this case expressed herself darkly. Pamela is such an exception to all rules that her story proves nothing about the desirability of marrying servant maids.

The moral of her story is made even more questionable by a remark which Richardson later made to Solomon Lowe (after his experience with Lovelace had caused him to take more serious views about marrying reformed rakes) that only Pamela's 'slavish Submission' to the 'proud and

---

[112] 1755, pp. 177–200.   [113] SH, II, 21–2; EL, I, 229.
[114] 2nd edn., pp. xxxiii–vi; SH, III, 323–9; EL, II, 168–71.
[115] *Richardson*, p. 70.

haughty' Mr. B. could have made her '*tolerably* happy'.[116] But if the reader is often tempted to agree that Mr. B., whose reform makes him pompous and demanding, is hardly a reward, nothing in the second part of *Pamela* seems consciously calculated to reinforce such a view. The morality of rewards is even more prominent than in part one. In discussing Locke's views on education, Pamela emphasizes the importance of rewards as well as punishments for the inculcation of virtue. She disagrees with her august mentor that children are not to be urged to do right by the gift of sugar plums and such things: 'I humbly think it necessary, that Rewards, *proper* Rewards, should be propos'd, as Incentives to laudable Actions: For is it not by this Method, that the whole World is influenc'd and govern'd? Does not GOD himself, by Rewards and Punishments, make it our *Interest*, as well as our *Duty*, to obey HIM?'[117] The author of *The Imitation of Christ* might question such a view of his religion, but millions of middle-class Christians will agree.

Since Pamela has been already amply rewarded in other ways, her reward in the continuation largely takes the form of praises. And these she receives unstintedly. Her ordinary politeness in saying that she forgives Sir Jacob for his earlier bad opinion, for instance, reduces that hardened old man to a state of tears at her amazing goodness: 'ANGEL did you call her?—By my Soul, I'm confounded with her Goodness, and her sweet Carriage!' She is forced several times to apologize for repeating her own praises at such length: 'Don't you think me, Miss, insufferably vain? But 'tis what they were pleased to say. 'Twas their Goodness to me, and shew'd how much they can excel in generous Politeness.' Several times these praises turn out to be praises of Pamela's creator, since one of her great accomplishments is her prose style (which unfortunately has deteriorated between the first and second parts of *Pamela*, though apparently its rise in the scale of propriety has prevented her correspondents from noticing this fact). Even Polly Darnford's shrewish sister Nancy will at any time leave her suitor Mr. Murray 'and forget to frown or be ill-natur'd, while she can hear read what you write'.[118] No author could expect a higher compliment, though it be given by one of his own characters.

In every way, the second part of *Pamela* shows Richardson at his worst —pompous, proper, proud of himself, and above all dull. A contemporary reader could have been excused for thinking that the liveliness of the first part was a fluke, and that nothing more could be expected from such a writer. But the reader who drew this almost inescapable conclusion would have been mistaken.

---

[116] 21 Jan. 1749. See also 'Hints of Prefaces for Clarissa', FM XV, 2, fo. 51.
[117] SH, IV, 306; EL, II, 377.
[118] SH, III, 320, 243–4, 97–8, IV, 31, III, 347; EL, II, 166, 133, 57, 237, 180.

CHAPTER VIII

RICHARDSON'S BUSINESS
IN THE 1740s

IN 1742 Richardson was free of the strain or the stimulus of *Pamela* and so far as is known had no new work yet in mind. Early in the year he must have been working on extensive further revisions of Defoe's *Tour* for the third edition, which came out in April, and on the de luxe octavo edition of *Pamela*. He continued to follow Dr. Cheyne's strenuous regimen, and at times there were signs of improvement, but he was never to be well again for very long. With his tendency to blame his physical ailments on mental shocks, he attributed an attack in the early spring of 1742 to the death of his friend, the publisher of *Pamela*, Charles Rivington.[1] Rivington named Richardson as one of his executors,[2] and Richardson continued to print for Rivington's son John and later for John's brother James and in 1746 took the third brother, Charles, as an apprentice. His connection with the family as well as with the business was close: he helped to arrange John Rivington's marriage, and when a question arose as to whether his mother should receive a sum of money to compensate her for leaving their house, Richardson advised the mother not to disturb family harmony by insisting on her moral, if not clearly legal, right.[3]

Throughout most of 1742 Cheyne's letters show that Richardson was often ailing, but in his letter of 5 September and subsequent ones Cheyne refers to his progressive improvement. In the fall Richardson wrote to Hill that he was considerably mended by Cheyne's remedies but was nevertheless taking preventative measures, bleeding and vomiting, against his usual autumn attack.[4] Cheyne throughout the year continued to exhort and encourage him and to advise him to get a hobby to take his mind off his hypochondria. He rejoiced when Richardson took up 'the Bowls' and suggested the 'charming manly Diversion' of billiards as well and often urged a 'Catalogue of Books for the Devout, the Tender, Valetudinarian, and Nervose', either not regarding writing novels as a proper hobby or

---

[1] Hill to R, 25 Feb.; R to Hill, 24 Sept.
[2] P.C.C. Trenley 169, dated 10 June 1737, proved 20 May 1742.
[3] R to John Rivington, 24 Apr. 1750.
[4] 24 Sept.

believing that Richardson had deserted literature.[5] In June Richardson had visited Bath, probably to consult his physician as well as to visit his wife's family and to try the waters.[6] While there he got a sheet of directions for his cure: vomits, mustard seed, Scotch pills, baths, exercise, asafœtida pills, and especially diet (milk, bread, and garden stuff); and 'He ought to avoid disagreeable melancholy vexations, and difficult Studies Ideas and Affairs as much as in his Power and indulge all light gay agreeable Studies Reflections & Ideas as far as he can.'[7]

Richardson travelled little, but he had visited Bath at least once before, and in the spring of 1742, between the two parts of *Pamela*, he had travelled to Hampshire. During the later 1740s, the time of the composition of *Clarissa*, we hear only of a trip to Hampshire and Wiltshire in the fall of 1746 and a visit to Tunbridge, for his health's sake, in July and August 1748: 'These waters were almost the only thing in medicine that I had not tried; and as my disorders seemed to increase, I was willing to try them.— Hitherto, I must own, without effect is the trial.'[8]

His business also connected him with Cheyne. That kindly but very difficult man had been disappointed by the sale of the first part of his magnum opus, *An Essay on Regimen*, published in 1740, and had been very bitter against his booksellers, Richardson's brother-in-law James Leake and close friend Charles Rivington. Though Richardson perhaps did something to soothe Cheyne's resentful feelings, he could hardly cause him to forget the fact that he had to pay £80 to the booksellers: the doctor, expecting his greatest success, had imprudently offered to guarantee their losses. Cheyne was therefore grateful for an offer from Richardson to 'take me from the Booksellers' and noted that Pope, who had also suffered much from booksellers and now dealt only with a printer, appreciated Richardson's offer. In September 1741 he sent Richardson money to clear his debt and desired him to 'publish and distribute' the second part of his great work, *The Natural Method of Cureing*, 'as your own Property for I will have no Booksellers Name to it'; presumably the doctor was to foot the bills or pocket the profits. Soon, however, George Strahan made him an offer for it, and, as he wrote, to save trouble and strain on Richardson's health, he ended by making an agreement with Strahan and others. Richardson finished printing the book late in 1741, and though in February 1742 Cheyne elatedly reported that 'it is wonderfully cried up here even by Doctors themselves, and I have already high Compliments from them and 3 Bishops', it seems to have been as much

[5] 5 Sept., 17 Sept., 26 Sept., 12 Oct., 2 Nov., 19 Nov.

[6] Cheyne to R, 22 June; Hill to R, 7 July.

[7] Dated 9 June 1742, MS. in the University of Edinburgh Library.

[8] Cheyne to R, 21 Dec. 1734; Hill to R, 25 May 1741; R to Sarah Wescomb, 15 Sept. 1746; Hill to R, 15 Sept. 1746; Sarah Wescomb to R, 4 Aug., 12 Sept. 1748; R to Sarah Wescomb, [late Aug. 1748]; R to Susanna Highmore, 2 Aug. 1748.

of a disappointment as the first part, and he probably died disillusioned with the intelligence of the British reading public.[9]

Richardson lost his friend and adviser on 13 April 1743. The fact that the doctor, an ex-invalid, died old and lively, having lost his immense fat (thirty-four stone),[10] should have encouraged his patient. Cheyne himself felt that his meat-free diet had saved his life, and the writer of some Latin elegiac couplets preserved, with an English translation, among his letters to Richardson agreed that his drinking milk and refraining 'from Carnage, & from Wine' had showed the way to health:

> Once hypocondriac, of portentous Size [pinguisque abdomine vasto];
> Since, lively, slender by his Milk's Supplies.[11]

A correspondent who sounds like Richardson's nephew James Leake informed him of the details of Cheyne's death: he was confined to his house for a few days by 'Vomiting & Purging' but was not alarmed enough to call a physician until the day before he died: 'To consider the Circumstances of your Health, and that there is taken from you by the Divine Wisdom, one, in whose Mind the Direction of it was a good deal lodged, it is impossible but we must look to the Almighty Disposer.'[12] Richardson inserted a long obituary in the *Daily Gazetteer* on that 'Learned Physician, sound Christian, deep Scholar, and warm Friend': 'Those who *best Knew him, most Loved him*; which must be the Felicity of every Man, who values himself more upon the Goodness of his Heart, than the Clearness of his Head: And yet Dr. Cheyne's Works shew how much he excelled in both.'[13]

Perhaps Richardson followed Cheyne's regimen less strictly once the director of his health was dead, since we hear no further details of the diet, but he did keep to it for over five years more. In December 1748 he wrote to Lady Bradshaigh that he had been on a regimen for seven years past;[14] he must have abandoned it soon afterwards.[15] It may have caused a considerable improvement during the 1740s, since during the time he was writing *Clarissa* there is little in his correspondence about illness. But then there is little correspondence: with Cheyne dead, Aaron Hill is the only correspondent who might have been expected to speak much of Richardson's health, and the correspondence with him is sketchy. By 1742 Richardson had the tremors which continued to plague him for the rest of his life.[16] By 20 January 1746 he was forced to apologize to Hill for using an amanuensis: 'My old Disorders will not leave me quite.' But his health

---

[9] Cheyne to R, 12 Feb., 22 Sept., 24 Oct., 15 Nov., [late Nov.], 2 Dec., 30 Dec. 1741; 10 Jan., 2 Feb. 1742.
[10] Cheyne to R, 23 Dec. 1741.
[11] Dated 16 Apr. 1743, MS. in the University of Edinburgh Library.
[12] 21 Apr.   [13] 16 Apr. See also Hill to R, 25 Apr.   [14] 15 Dec.
[15] *Universal Magazine*, LXXVIII, 20.   [16] Cheyne to R, 29 Aug.

had recently been better. In the next winter he was drinking tar water and told Edward Young that he was 'somewhat better' for it, but later stated that he was 'afraid my nerves are too much unbraced ever to be greatly bettered by human medicines. I have, however, been much worse, and so must sit down, and pray for patience and resignation; thanking God it is no worse.'[17] He was again complaining of tremors as well as headaches by November 1748 and was being bled for his expected autumn attack. Early in the next year Hill was touched to notice the shakings of so strong a hand, and in May Richardson assured him that his maladies, though new to Hill, were the same ones he had laboured under for so long.[18] The slight evidence suggests that Richardson's health was better during the mid-forties, and one might even wonder whether the writing of *Clarissa* provided the hobbyhorse Cheyne had so often urged and kept his mind off his ailments.

In spite of his intense literary activity during the years 1739–42 he was still principally a business man. His position in his profession continued to rise: on 1 December 1741 he was elected to the ruling body of the Stationers' Company, the Court of Assistants.[19] The fact that soon after his election he missed a long series of meetings, from March through August 1742, confirms the impression of Dr. Cheyne's letters that his health was especially bad at that time. By autumn he was attending the court again. In 1743 he was at about three-quarters of the meetings, but his attendance grew gradually more lax, and in 1749 he was at less than half of them.

Of course only a comparatively small percentage of the books printed by Richardson has been identified, but so far as one can judge, the quality of the output of his press in the 1740s was about the same as during the 1730s. He continued printing such ambitious, profitable, and useful works as the *Universal History* and Philip Miller's books on gardening. In 1749 came out David Hartley's *Observations on Man* and another more or less scholarly book, *An Historical View of the Negotiations between the Courts of England, France, and Brussels, from the Year 1592 to 1617*, by his former associate in the Society for the Encouragement of Learning, Thomas Birch. He continued to print many religious works—for Patrick Delany, for instance, and for Philip Skelton, and the popular *Meditations among the Tombs* of James Hervey, whose combination of gloom and moralizing in 1746 caught the taste of a public recently addicted to graveyards and long inured to platitudes. Works which can be called literary are less numerous, even if one stretches that adjective to include Mary Chandler's verse *Description of Bath*, of which new editions continued to appear, George

---

[17] 2 Dec., 24 Dec.
[18] 7 Nov., 7 Feb., 10 May.
[19] 'Court Book I', under date, MS. in the archives of the Stationers' Company.

Lyttelton's *To the Memory of a Lady Lately Deceased* (1747), which Richardson later praised,[20] and the poems of such old customers as Stephen Duck and Aaron Hill. Novels, except of course his own, he rarely printed and insofar as is known, rarely read, but he did print in 1749 the second edition of *The Governess*, by Sarah Fielding, Henry's sister and a recent friend of Richardson's. By far his most distinguished literary work during this decade was the popular *Night-Thoughts*, by Edward Young; between 1744 and 1746 he printed the last three 'Nights' of the nine comprising Young's poem and later the second volume of the two-volume octavo edition of the whole, dated 1748. Richardson still printed sometimes for booksellers and sometimes for the author. He put his own works 'into the Hands of Booksellers, allowing them their customary Rates for Selling, & taking upon myself ye Profit & Loss'.[21]

On 17 May 1742 Dr. Cheyne advised Richardson not to neglect going into 'so lucrative a Project'. He was probably referring to the proposed *Journals of the House of Commons*. On 31 May of that year the House resolved to authorize the printing of one thousand copies of its *Journals*, not to exceed thirty volumes, for the use of members. The project was under the direction of the Clerk of the House, Nicholas Hardinge, with whom Richardson had been associated for some years as a printer of bills and other official papers for the House. Hardinge had reported to a committee that some of the past journals were almost illegible and had submitted a computation of costs made by Richardson ('a Printer, in whose Skill and Integrity I can confide'). Richardson appeared before the committee and gave it his estimate on the cost of paper and printing, based on an estimate by one of Hardinge's assistants, John Grover, that the project would run to something over 26,500,000 words. The committee chose the less expensive of two formats proposed by Richardson, a folio in a smaller type which would cost more per volume but require fewer volumes; Richardson estimated that all of the journals, with an index, could be contained in twenty-three volumes of two hundred sheets a volume. At 30*s.* a sheet for one thousand copies, the printing would cost £300 a volume, one hundred of which, according to the usual custom, must have been reckoned as the master printer's share, above the wages of employees. Whoever received the job would therefore clear £2,300 to cover the cost of ink and the use of machinery and premises. Certainly the *Journals* could have been described as a lucrative project. The cost of paper was to equal the cost of printing, so that the whole cost would be £13,800 plus payment of someone to prepare and revise copy and draw up indices. Richardson's estimate was only a little optimistic, since twenty-three volumes do contain the journals up to December 1741. In 1756 the House voted to go on

[20] R to Hester Mulso, 30 Sept. 1751; 'Postscript' to the 3rd edn. of *Clarissa* (1751), VIII, 287; SH, VIII, 317; EL, IV, 556-7. [21] R to Anna Meades, 2 Feb. 1757.

and bring the *Journals* up to date.[22] It was, however, often behind in obtaining money, and the Clerk seems to have been even oftener behind in paying it out, so that it was some time before Richardson realized the advantages of this lucrative project.

There is one other project to which Cheyne might conceivably have been referring. In 1742 Richardson's friends John Osborn and Andrew Millar had acquired an interest in the *Universal History*.[23] Richardson had been printing this ambitious, if uneven and haphazardly organized, work since its inception in 1736; in the first part of Volume VII (two of the seven 'Volumes' were split, so that there were really nine), in 1744, his name still does not appear as one of those it was printed for, but later the same year it does appear on the title page of the second part. When the first volume of the octavo edition was registered at the Stationers' Company on 2 January 1747, Richardson had a sixth share in it, with Osborn, Millar, and one of the original projectors, Thomas Osborne, and for over two years they continued to register the subsequent nineteen volumes.[24]

Andrew Millar's close association with Richardson dates from somewhat later, though Richardson had already printed for him. On 12 January 1749 he highly recommended Millar to Hill as a bookseller: 'I heartily wish you, Sir, to cultivate Mr Millar's Acquaintance, and to let him, if you think fit, be your Bookseller. . . . he has great Business, and is in a Way of promoting the Sale of what he engages in. I have not been always so well acquainted with him, as I am of late. But ever had a good Opinion of him. He is a Man of Courage as well as of a handsome Spirit; and single-hearted.' Millar was one of the City's most prominent booksellers. Boswell remarks that, though no great judge of literature, he had good sense enough to choose able friends to advise him and that he acquired 'a very large fortune, with great liberality'. Johnson called him 'the Maecenas of the age': 'I respect Millar, Sir; he has raised the price of literature.'[25] He was a good friend of Henry Fielding, whose novels he published. Since he lived in London, it is understandable that there is not much extant correspondence between him and Richardson, but writing to him on business on 31 July 1750, Richardson joked about Millar's son and added a personal message to his wife, whom he had recently seen at Young's house in Welwyn, with a note of raillery which implies considerable intimacy. He mentioned both Millar's wife and his sister '(two very agreeable women)' as among the ladies he visited. And he wrote him a long letter of sympathy on a recent bereavement, inclosing a poem by a Mr. Norris: 'Take all, great God! I will not grieve.' By 1758 their association was so

---

[22] *Journals*, XXIV, 262–6; XXVII, 617 (26 May 1756).

[23] See the title page of Vol. VI of the folio edition.

[24] 'Entries of Copies 1746–1773', p. 9 and *passim*, MS. in the archives of the Stationers' Company.

[25] *Life*, I, 287–8.

close that Richardson added Millar's name to Mrs. Richardson's, Francis Gosling's, and his brother-in-law Allington Wilde's as executor of his will: their association in the *Universal History* and other concerns made such a service particularly acceptable.[26]

Francis Gosling was also a bookseller, as well as a prominent banker. His bookselling business, opposite St. Dunstan's in Fleet Street and thus near Richardson, was founded by his father, Robert Gosling, who died in 1741. In 1742 he became a partner in the bank in which Richardson since 1737 had had an account and on 12 November of that year he married Elizabeth Midwinter, daughter of a deceased bookseller, who had been living with the Richardsons; Richardson acted as a trustee for her marriage settlement, and she spent her honeymoon at North End.[27] Later it was to Gosling that Richardson turned to advise him about Sir Roger Bradshaigh's banking problems, as well as about buying stocks for a friend of Lady Echlin's: 'The Person I have always apply'd to for the Management of my little Money-Matters, is Mr. Francis Gosling, Alderman of London, and one of our present Sheriffs; a very worthy Man, and in deservedly high Reputation; joined with two Partners; one of them his Brother': 'A very prudent, a very faithful, a very prosperous Man.'[28] So prosperous was he that in 1757 he retired from bookselling and in 1760 was made a knight bachelor.

Another member of the trade with whom Richardson was for a time friendly was William Strahan, the printer. During the late 1740s and early 1750s he was living in Richardson's parish, St. Bride's.[29] In 1745, when he was 'beginning to print a little for' himself, Richardson gave him important aid: 'Mr Richardson . . . has turned out a good Friend, of which I leave you to judge, when I tell you that the work I have done within these Eight Months by his Recommendation, comes to upwards of £300.'[30] In 1749, in a series of letters written during a journey to his native Scotland, he mentions Richardson's 'long-continued friendship for me': 'I esteem you as my friend, my adviser, my pattern, and my benefactor; I love you as my father; and let me, even me also, call you my Nestor.'[31] The letters are almost equally divided between travel description and praise of Richardson (if Richardson relished this, one can perhaps

[26] R to Lady Bradshaigh, 9 Jan. 1750; R to Millar, 8 Aug. 1750, 1 Mar. 1758; Millar to R, 1 Mar. 1758.

[27] *Barclays Bank Limited: Gosling's Branch 1650–1950* ([London, 1950]), p. 4; *Register of Admissions to Gray's Inn . . . with the Register of Marriages in Gray's Inn Chapel*, ed. Joseph Foster (London, 1889), p. xlv; Anne Richardson to Mrs. Moodie, 27 Feb. 1800, MS. owned by Professor Alan Dugald McKillop; R to Hill, 29 Oct. 1742.

[28] R to Lady Bradshaigh, 9 Oct. 1756; R to Lady Echlin, 24 Jan., 23 June 1758.

[29] See the baptismal records of his children in the register of St. Bride's (Guildhall MS. 6541/1), under dates 17 Oct. 1745; 16 June 1747; 26 June 1751.

[30] Strahan to David Hill, 9 Mar., MS. in the American Philosophical Society Library.

[31] 17 Aug.

understand the amount of fulsome praise of themselves which his characters can listen to with apparent pleasure). The letters indicate great
respect and gratitude rather than intimacy on equal terms. He mentions
letters received from Richardson; he has undertaken to help Richardson
collect a Scottish debt. On 16 September he mentions a son, born yesterday (his wife accompanied him), and named Samuel, 'after you; to make
him, as it were, a living monument of your friendship'. One suspects that
this may be disingenuous, since an earlier son, who must have died, had
also been named Samuel;[32] but perhaps he also was meant as a living
monument. The fact that there is no other extant correspondence between
Strahan and Richardson does not necessarily mean much: there was probably no need for any but business letters, which Richardson did not
generally preserve, after his return to London. Strahan's ledger, which is
one of the few available records of eighteenth-century printing, shows that
he printed several works for Richardson when the latter was busy. But we
shall later mention evidence which points to a serious quarrel between the
two men.

We know comparatively little about Richardson's employees or his
relations with them. Mrs. Barbauld, on unstated authority, tells us that he
used to hide a half-crown among the letters so that the first journeyman to
arrive at work might find it, and that at other times he used fruit from his
garden.[33] The paternalistic combination of kindness and concern for
efficiency is characteristic. Consideration is shown in a letter to Thomas
Birch; Richardson, printing some work for a friend of Birch's, found the
work weary to his employees, who delayed it as long as they could, 'and
I had some Concern to oblige them to it, having chearful Service, & loth
to give them ye Trouble (tho' I paid them for it) of breaking what they
call their Measures, and setting up, and taking down their Cases, and
going off and on the other Work they had under their Hands'.[34]

That Richardson's relations were not always so harmonious, however,
is indicated in a letter from Cheyne of 4 March 1743: 'I am sorry for your
Misfortunes with your Servants your great Business is with your Principal
if he is honest serious & faithful he will make all the rest so, I think you
ought to try for such a one at any Price, for as to your Temporal Affairs I
fear not but they will come out at last beyond the most sanguin Wishes
of your Friends and Family.' Richardson must either have lost or been
dissatisfied with an overseer or have been considering for the first time
that he needed one to control unruly workmen. Late in 1744 he complained
to Edward Young that he had no overseer.[35] By 1756 he certainly did have

---

[32] Register of St. Bride's, under date 17 Oct. 1745.   [33] I, xlvii.
[34] There is no reason to date the letter 1738, as Sale does (*Master Printer*, p. 151); the only
1738 letter from Richardson to Birch refers to the Roe papers. We have arbitrarily dated it 1740.
[35] [*c.* 12 Dec.].

one.[36] Around 1 January 1751 he wrote to Lady Bradshaigh, 'I have been lost to my own wishes, till within these three years!' Since he is speaking of his lack of time, he seems to imply that after late 1748 his business was not quite so demanding. It is, therefore, likely that he hired his first overseer at about that time, perhaps as a result of his troubles with his workmen earlier in that year. By 1759 he had an 'operating compositor' (probably William Tewley) in addition to his nephew William, who had been acting as overseer, both paid, unlike his other workmen, by the year, so that he was 'entitled to their whole Service'.[37]

An overseer was not essential except in large businesses, such as Richardson's had now become; his duties might be combined with those of corrector of the press, who was paid not a salary but a percentage of the wages paid to compositors. A corrector was essential, to read proof and return it to the compositors for revision; Richardson throughout the 1740s had a good one who died in 1754, 'a Learned, diligent, worthy Man, to whom I had committed, for 15 Years past, the Care of that material Part of my Business', a man so learned that he could translate Latin correspondence for his unlearned employer.[38]

Overseer or no overseer, Richardson's misfortunes with his servants did not end quickly. On 3 April 1744 Aaron Hill referred to 'such Disorders as your Men have been drawn into', and on 4 April Richardson was glad enough to postpone the publication of Hill's *Alzira*, 'as my Workmens Defection would make it not unsuitable to do so'. Over four years later either these or new labour troubles were beginning to be ironed out: 'At present we are but just settling into a Calm with our Compositors, who have wanted to raise their Prices, and combined for that purpose, with as little Reason as Provocation—So that I, as well as others, have been forced to part with some of my Hands, and have not yet got them replaced to my Wish; and go but lamely on, with my common Business— But, as I find, we are beginning to settle.'[39]

The troubles of 1748 were due to the desire of Richardson's compositors to be paid a fixed rate of fourpence per thousand letters (often computed by 'n's'—a letter of average size, the number of which was easy to estimate from the length, height, and number of lines).[40] In the archives of the Oxford University Press there is a folio sheet headed 'For the obviating of all future Misunderstandings, or *Pretence* of Misunderstandings, the

---

[36] In advising William Blackstone to hire an overseer, at a fixed salary, for the Oxford University Press, he remarked on 10 Feb. that 'Several of us [printers in London], have such'.
[37] R to Lady Barbara Montagu, 10 July.   [38] R to Stinstra, 28 June 1754; 2 June 1753.
[39] R to Hill, 7 Nov. 1748. One might conjecture that the changes in printing style (nouns are no longer automatically capitalized, proper names italicized) which took place at about this time was one of the concessions made to journeymen.
[40] Suggested in a note by Laurence W. Hanson in I. G. Philip's *William Blackstone and the Reform of the Oxford University Press*, p. 123.

Antient RULES are particularized as follow'. It is probably Richardson's: its references to printing acts and bills as well as its tone sound like him. He must have sent it to William Blackstone in 1756, when he was advising Blackstone about reforming the Oxford University Press, but it dates from 1749.[41]

Payment to compositors varied both with the size of type (the ones most in use being English, pica, small pica, and long primer, the last and smallest type being the most expensive) and size of sheet (the '*Antient* RULES' classifies sheets as small, large, extra, and largest). In the '*Antient* RULES' there is an elaborate table comparing the sums earned by compositors according to a price fixed for type and size of sheet (evidently the system Richardson had been using) with the sums 'Come to by Letters', that is by reckoning the number of letters of average size on a sheet of the same size using the same type. This table demonstrates conclusively that Richardson's old rates to compositors are uniformly and considerably higher than what they could earn at fourpence a thousand letters. Indeed Richardson is too convincing: why, if the figures were this clear, should the compositors have ever wanted to be paid by letters? 'A great and strange Struggle', says the '*Antient* RULES', 'was begun very lately to make me a Precedent to the Trade to bring all *Work*; as a *Standard*, to be paid for by Letters, at 4*d.* a thousand, as here calculated. Could the Strugglers know what they were about? Or, did they expect, that they should be allowed the Advantage in *both Cases*; *i.e.* To bring the Price up where lower, and (*contrary to their Printed Allegations*) to keep it fixed where higher?' According to Richardson's table, his old price could never have been lower than the price by letters; perhaps he was yielding to the tendency, apparent in his novels especially when he deals with the rewards of virtue, to overstate and thus weaken his case.

Several other remarks in the '*Antient* RULES' show that Richardson regarded the subject of wages with some passion. Under his old system compositors were often paid for sheets as full when actually they were incomplete. 'All *Extraordinaries* reckon'd for (hitherto at their own Rate), and frequently Money given, besides!—What Advantage may an industrious Man, *who follows his Blows*, make of this Work!' He has hitherto trusted his workers in reckoning corrections—presumably those made at the author's request, since compositors were bound to correct mistakes discovered by the proof-reader in their own work; he now fears that he has trusted too much to their consciences and insists that corrected sheets be preserved to be produced on demand. He intends to put a stop to the '*strange* Incroachment' of putting roman numerals which ought to

---

[41] 'The *Antient* RULES' were discovered by I. G. Philip and printed by him in ibid., pp. 124–6. Some of the information in our text comes from Blackstone's 'Some Thoughts on the Oxford Press 1756', ibid., pp. 23–38.

be in the text into the margin in order to count them as notes, for which compositors were paid extra. He has often paid for heavy notes which were really light: 'In more instances than one, in the last Sessions, the Money given has exceeded the Value of the Work (yet all thought to be a Trifle).' When authors wanted work done quickly, he has paid for Sunday work even when the authors also paid extra, so that the compositors got paid double. These and other lenient practices are to cease. 'For the future, the Person I shall appoint to pay the Men, shall pay for every Jobb on the next Saturday after it is done; and keep one of them, with the Person's Name for whom done; and the Extraordinaries upon it; and see that Equity be done both to me, and the Compositor: And if any Dispute or Doubt arise, the Matter in Debate to be referred to me.' There is no mistaking the note of moral indignation in these rules. Evidently for the paternalistic Richardson, looking back to his own hard beginnings, the demands of his workers were little short of wicked.

The same note is present in the letter he wrote on 10 February 1756 to Blackstone, commenting on the latter's proposed reforms at the Oxford University Press. He states that though the prices charged by printers have not varied much during the years he has been in business, the journeymen have raised their charges—the struggle of 1748 or a later struggle had evidently ended in some gains for the workers. Workmen, he says, 'will be always for encroaching'. 'Journeymen-Printers are perhaps, the most clamorous of any Body of Men, and the most dissatisfied.' He has reduced his practice to rules but still desires to avoid trouble: 'Whenever any thing particularly troublesome, breaks into the Measures established between my Workmen and me, I choose to pay them more than they can reasonably demand, rather than break my Rule, and create a Precedent; such Occasions not often occurring.'

These prices, which had not much varied in his time, were fixed, as he told Blackstone, 'by Practice, by Example, by Custom, and by Inspection'. He had implied the same thing many years before in a letter to Alexander Gordon, saying that the prices of one printer were about the same as those of another.[42] The basic element in prices was the wages of compositors, whose job it was to set up the type, to break it and put it back where it belonged. Their wages, as stated, depended on size of type and size of sheet; for the same size page, 2s. more was paid for each smaller size type—that is a sheet paid at 6s. in English would cost 8s. in pica. These are the normal wages for octavos or duodecimos with fairly small pages.

Blackstone proposed to pay correctors one-sixth of what the compositors earned, and this is the basis Richardson had used in his 1738 letter to Gordon, which breaks down the costs of printing according to the wages it

[42] 9 Nov. 1738.

was his practice to pay at that time. Pressmen (generally, but not always, two), who were to prepare the paper and press and work off the number of copies agreed, were paid according to the number, 1s. 2d. for each 'token' of two hundred and fifty copies. The master of the press then charged, for use of his presses and for his time, half as much as compositors, corrector, and pressmen together had earned, or a 'Master's Thirds' of the total bill. If the printer furnished paper, this was of course charged for separately.

It was evidently the custom to charge higher rates to authors who printed at their own expense; Richardson states that Blackstone's figures, which follow the above scale of wages and profits, apply to booksellers, but 'the Masters generally expect something more Profit from Gentlemen of Ability, than they do from Men in Trade, who are to subsist by their Business'. Presumably this was an extra profit for the master printer.

That Richardson, who was unusually friendly with many of his authors, did not always charge them this extra rate is implied by his statement to Samuel Lobb: 'As to the Price of Paper and Printing, let That alone, till we see what ye Discourse will do towards reimbursing itself. In this I consider you as a Bookseller, as I generally do every Author, who is at his own Expence in putting his Works to ye Press:—For which the Booksellers thank me not. You would not, I dare say, have me use my Friend worse than I would use a London Bookseller.'[43] The mere postponing of payment hardly seems to justify the strength of Richardson's remarks.

Though most of Richardson's business papers are lost, a few bills for printing are extant.[44] But the bills are of little help in confirming the information on prices and wages given in Richardson's letter to Gordon and in the remarks by Blackstone on which Richardson commented in his letter. From these two sources, which are in agreement, the general rules may be determined; but those of the surviving bills which give full enough information (rate per sheet, number of copies, format, and size of type) to enable one to see how far these general rules were followed in practice are not in complete agreement. Extra charges for notes, for introductory or supplementary material in another fount, or for author's corrections are not usually mentioned in the bills. They may explain such odd rates, arrived at by figuring from the general rules, as 10s. 7$\frac{6}{7}$d. a sheet to compositors for Young's *Centaur Not Fabulous* or 8s. 8$\frac{4}{7}$d. for *The Gardeners Dictionary*. But none of these reasons would explain why in 1750 and 1751 Richardson charged 33s. a sheet for the eighth and ninth editions of Hervey's *Meditations* and in 1753 38s. for the tenth edition, in the same

[43] 4 July 1746.

[44] Ralph Strauss, *Robert Dodsley* (London and New York, 1910), p. 355 (two bills to Millar for *Night-Thoughts* and *Centaur Not Fabulous*); Bodleian Don. *c*. 66, fos. 17–20 (bill to the Rivingtons for various works, 1750–4); Records of the Treasury in P.R.O. T. 53/37–47 (printing for the House of Commons).

number of sheets—five hundred more copies were printed, but this should mean a difference of 3*s*. 6*d*., not 5*s*. Similar discrepancies may be found in the ledgers of William Strahan, as when different rates are charged for successive editions of *Joseph Andrews*.[45] Roughly, the charges in Richardson's bills and in the Strahan ledgers are similar to those which would be arrived at by using the rules which Richardson explained to Gordon or which Blackstone cited as the London practice, but they are not identical, and there were probably changes in prices or special rates of some sort, depending on agreement, of which we know nothing.[46]

A compositor was generally expected to set about one thousand letters an hour, though since he was responsible also for distribution of type he actually had to be able to set at least fifteen hundred.[47] He could earn a guinea a week or more if he worked diligently. The tables in the '*Antient* RULES' show that working at this rate steadily for six eight-hour days Richardson's journeymen could earn somewhat more than a guinea a week by Richardson's old rates, somewhat less than a guinea 'by Letters'; but of course work was probably not often that steady. At any rate, it is clear that Richardson's compositors were not always content and that he, who had himself been a compositor, was moved by their complaints to indignation and at least temporarily increased strictness. His own remarks show that he thought of himself as fair, even as generous and lenient. There is no reason to think that by eighteenth-century standards he was not so, but we do not have any record of the opinions of his workmen, except a very favourable one by his overseer William Tewley, who wrote to Young after Richardson's death that Richardson was 'highly revered and beloved by his domestics' and showed 'great condescension towards his servants'.[48]

[45] B.M. Add. MS. 48,800, fos. 38, 77.
[46] Prices are discussed by D. F. Mackenzie, *The Cambridge University Press 1696–1712* (Cambridge, 1966), I, 76–88.
[47] Howe, *London Compositor*, pp. 59, 70.
[48] *Gentleman's Magazine*, LIII, 924; Nichols, *Literary Anecdotes*, IV, 727.

CHAPTER IX

RICHARDSON AND HIS FRIENDS

1742–1748

RICHARDSON's circle of acquaintances was enlarged during the 1740s, or at least our knowledge of it is enlarged. Aaron Hill, however, continued throughout the decade to be perhaps the closest of his friends. Some of Richardson's business associates may have been even closer, but there is little extant correspondence with them, whereas the fact that Hill was still living at Plaistow made many letters necessary.

Plaistow was one of Hill's many troubles: its air disagreed with him, and he often hoped to leave it. Richardson repeatedly invited him to North End for relief. In addition to Hill's bad health, a good part of his late wife's fortune was gone, he was involved in a long and complicated law suit, and his family was far from satisfactory. His son, Julius Cæsar, was at least by his standards worthless and dissipated—he answered one inquiry of Richardson's by saying that 'for very many Months together he don't let me see him: But I *hear* of him, too many ways', that 'he is, almost every way, unhappy' and 'has run out a considerable Fortune, that was, weakly, left, to his own Early Management, by an unthinking Grandmother: And, now, he lives (if That is living) with a light young woman whome, I am told, he lends his *Name*, as well as Time, to', but 'he is not without frequent Inclination, toward a slow irresolute Repentence—so I force myself to *hope*, from That one faint Appearance—against Every Stronger Probability'. His daughter Urania had married a Mr. Warren Johnson against his wishes, and for a while he considered that he had only two daughters left. But with Urania there was a reconciliation. Though Johnson ran through both his fortune and Urania's, Hill regretted his sudden death—'a very honest, modest, and good-natur'd, Man'; 'It was a Match of Love's *rash* making, & Twas well It prov'd no other w[a]y unhappy, than Distempered Spirits & Mismanagements have left it.'[1]

In addition to his other troubles, the reception of his literary works forced Hill increasingly to worry about the declining taste and intelligence of the British public. He had long professed indifference to his contemporary reputation: 'For my part, I am *afraid* to be popular. I see so many

[1] Hill to R, 25 Oct. 1746; 27 Sept. 1739; 10 July 1746.

who write to the living, and deserve not to live, that I content myself with a resurrection when dead.' 'I mortify myself with a conscious distrust, that I think not to the taste of the public. What a monstrous new proof of it is, the reception that the Fanciad has met with!' 'I am willing to hope ye cold Regard wch, to me, seems, as yet, to have been shewn to ye Religion of Reason, by the Public, has been occasion'd by their allowing such Engrossment of Attention as you hint at. If it proves otherwise, I must either have no Power of thinking at all—or must think of this Age very despicably.' 'I almost fear to ask you, how the Public has receiv'd your Outset of the Gideon. . . . I can't forbear to say, that if a Work like Gideon meets with general Neglect, I will resign all Vanity of publishing my writings.' 'If Popularity must be the Mark of a *good* Writer, I perceive myself to be a very *bad* one.'[2]

Richardson, who had no reason to complain of the public taste, once hinted that Hill might lower his style to suit the times, as Milton or Shakespeare would be forced to do today: 'Your sentiments, even they will have it who allow them to be noble, are too munificiently adorned: and they want you to descend to their level. . . . Besides, I am of opinion that it is necessary for a genius to accommodate itself to the mode and taste of the world it is cast into, since works published in this age must take root in it, to flourish in the next.'[3] Richardson's advice was impractical—there is no evidence that Hill could have adapted his works to the taste of his or any age. Unappreciated geniuses who console themselves with the ignorance or stupidity of the average reader should avoid reading what survives of *Gideon*. The last nine books are unfortunately lost, though the preface to the three published in 1749 announces that they will appear as soon as they can be revised. The author admits that the prospects of present appreciation are dim—he writes for futurity. So far futurity has failed to recognize the greatness of this fragment of an exalted Biblical epic in Pindaric stanzas. Hill answered that Richardson's letter 'tells me nothing new, of the low estimation of my writings: I have always known them, and expected them to be, unpopular: nor shall I live to see them in another light. But there will rise a time, in which they *will* be seen in a far different one: I know it, on a surer hope than that of vanity.'[4] One could hardly laugh even if Hill had not been a kindly, intelligent, broad-minded, well-educated, and generous man. He had every qualification for a writer but talent, and there is never in his correspondence a hint of envy for the success of Richardson, who had little else.

And perhaps one can forgive Hill's lapse of generosity when he wrote of Pope after the latter's death. Pope's frequent and open resentment of insults seemed to him petty, and Pope did not write in the lofty style which

Hill, a disciple of Longinus rather than of Horace, considered proper to poetry. Even before Pope died he had been critical: 'I cannot, for my soul, help admiring him; for he out-charms even a poet, though he is none'—an anticipation of a common nineteenth-century cliché. Pope's reputation had been inflated by all sorts of tricks of puffery. 'Mr. Pope, as you with equal keenness and propriety express it, is *gone out*', he wrote to Richardson. 'I told a friend of his, who sent me the first news of it, that I was very sorry for his death, because I doubted whether he would live to recover the accident. Indeed, it gives me no surprise, to find you thinking he was in the wane of his popularity. . . . He had a turn for verse, without a soul for poetry. . . . But rest his memory in peace! It will very rarely be disturbed by that time he himself is ashes. It is pleasant to observe the justice of forced fame; she lets down those, at once, who got themselves pushed upward; and lifts none above the fear of falling, but a few who never teazed her.—What she intends to do with *me*, the Lord knows! The whole I can be sure of is, that never mortal courted her with less solicitude.' Pope's popularity was caused by the influence of his patrons and the curiosity of the public; 'the next Age will place him 3 Removes, at least, below his Last—& That was Two, below his former.' He even came to doubt the felicity of Pope's technique and had written some critical reflections showing Pope's faults—he had earlier threatened Pope with the publication of this demonstration of his incompetence. He had also undertaken to revise the *Essay on Man*, expressing Pope's meanings as Pope aimed to express them. Richardson found Hill's version 'infinitely [changed when he revised his letters to ''greatly''] amended' and gave it to Speaker Onslow to read, who commended the piece 'highly' but said that Hill undervalued 'his own Genius, by giving us any-thing of his, that is not entirely his'. Hill evidently was not happy with this remark but was willing to take it as a compliment: he had meant only to prove that 'Mr Pope was very weak and negligent (where universally suppos'd most strong) in the Significance, and Ease, of his *Expression*' and had no intention of publishing such an idle amusement—'Mr Pope's Hydropic Fame will waste too fast, without my wounding it.'[5]

All but one of the works which Hill published in the 1740s were printed by Richardson, who often gave advice of sorts and sometimes praise. He called *The Fanciad* of 1743 'the noblest, both in itself and in its End [promoting a biography of the Duke of Marlborough] that I have seen' (when Richardson was thinking of publishing his correspondence, he changed the superlative to a simple 'noble') but objected to the title as recalling *The Dunciad* and being beneath the dignity of the poem.[6] *The*

<hr />

[5] Hill to R, [Feb. ?], 10 Sept. 1744, 10 July, 29 July 1746; R to Hill, 5 Aug. 1746, 7 Nov. 1748; Hill to R, 12 Nov. 1748; R to Hill, 18 Nov. 1748.

[6] Hill to R, 2 Apr.; R to Hill, 2 Apr., 7 Apr.; Hill to R, 11 Apr.; R to Hill, 11 Apr.

Impartial, of the following year, Richardson felt lavished too high praise on Lord Carteret, who he feared would 'go all Lengths to be Sole or Prime'—he had long ago heard 'Things greatly to his Disadvantage'. Hill satisfied Richardson's doubts by explaining that he was applauding not that nobleman's 'private, or his moral, Virtues' but his public career.[7] Neither of these poems seems to have been successful, and Hill, who was constantly trying to give his works to Richardson to repay his debts, feared that Richardson would get little by them and asked to be told if he actually suffered a loss—'I shall make good, as I ought, all your Charges.'[8] So far as is known Richardson never told him; presumably he printed Hill's works and assumed the loss himself.

In 1748 he printed for Hill the also unsuccessful *Free Thoughts upon Faith: or, The Religion of Reason*, which verges on Freethinking (which Richardson was steadily opposed to), but Richardson (who did not comment) may not have read it carefully enough to understand its drift. He read too carefully *The Art of Acting*, of the same year, a description of what an actor should do to his muscles and his eyes in order to express the 'ten Dramatic Passions': 'Last Sunday I attempted to read it not as a Printer; and, was not aware, that I should be so mechanically, as I may truly say, affected by it: I endeavoured to follow you in your wonderful Description of the Force of Acting, in the Passions of Joy, Sorrow, Fear, Anger, &c. And my whole Frame, so nervously affected before, was shaken by it: I found, in short, such Tremors, such Startings, that I was unable to go thro' it.'[9]

The last two of Hill's works to be printed during his lifetime appeared in 1749. He finally decided to publish three books of *Gideon*, the great epic composed largely in the 1720s, and asked Richardson to decide how it should be published. When two months passed with no word from Richardson, he wrote inquiring why publication was delayed and wondering whether his silence meant he was angry. Richardson, pained, explained that he had been so busy for the House of Commons that even *Clarissa* had been put aside but that *Gideon* would not suffer. Two months later Hill asked again how the book was going and, anticipating the worst, offered when his affairs permitted, as they soon would, to print an edition of the complete poem at his own cost and give the proceeds to Richardson.[10]

Merope, like the earlier *Zara* and *Alzira* adapted from Voltaire, was more successful: it had been acted by David Garrick 'with great Applause' and brought Hill the proceeds of three benefit performances.[11] Hill was

---

[7] 4 Apr., 6 Apr.   [8] 22 Mar.   [9] 29 Oct.
[10] Hill to R, 8 Mar., 9 May; R to Hill, 10 May; Hill to R, 10 July.
[11] *The London Stage 1660–1800*, Part 4: 1747–1776, ed. George Winchester Stone, Jr. (Carbondale, Illinois, 1962), pp. 112–14, 118, 120.

inclined to refuse an offer from Millar for publishing, since he regarded Richardson as owning the copyright; but Richardson urged him to accept Millar's offer and even to cultivate Millar with a view towards getting a collection of his smaller pieces published.[12] The press of business kept Richardson from printing *Merope*.

If printing for Hill proved a strain and an expense, Richardson did not show it. Indeed he urged Hill to make his press 'the Vehicle' for any of his 'charming and noble Pieces', and Hill often referred to his gratitude for favours conferred. In November 1746 he asked for and received a loan of £100, and two years later he received £60 more. Richardson often sent him new books to read and helped him advertise in the newspapers he was printing; probably also he refused to accept payment for at least some of the books he printed for the author. Hill hoped to repay Richardson by giving him the copyright of his works, and Richardson thanked him for this beautiful intention of throwing his works into his lap, but 'It must not be'. Though Hill insisted, nothing formal seems ever to have been done. Later Hill sent him a blank receipt to fill in, together with the usual offer of the copyright; Richardson promised to keep accounts between them but refused to fill in the receipt and postponed consideration of the copyright.[13]

There is no doubt of the sincere mutual regard, amounting to affection, between the two friends, different as they were in education, background, and interests. Richardson once thought of leaving his writings to Hill's care and never referred to Hill with less than respect. Hill's praise of *Pamela* was not short of ecstatic and was expressed not only to Richardson himself but to David Mallet: 'such an author . . . that hardly mortal ever match'd him, for his ease of natural power'; 'I am much mistaken in the promise of his genius, or *Pamela* (all lovely as she is, in her unheeded, hasty dress) is but a *dawning* to the day, he is to give us.'[14] Hill lived to see this prediction fulfilled.

In the 1730s Richardson had also been printing for Philip Skelton, the son of an Irish farmer, who, in spite of poverty, had managed to go to Trinity and to take orders.[15] He was curate at Monagham from 1732 until 1750, when he was called to the living of Templecarn (Pettigo, in Donegal), in one of the wildest districts of Ireland, where he remained until called to Devenish in 1759. He visited London in 1748 to arrange for the publication of his attack on Deism, *Ophiomaches*, and again in 1754

---

[12] 11 Jan., 12 Jan.

[13] R to Hill, 25 June 1746; Hill to R, Nov. 1746; R to Hill, 27 Oct. 1748; Hill to R, 11 Jan. 1746, 5 May 1748, 10 Nov. 1746; Hill's promissary note dated 19 Oct. 1748, MS. in the Folger Shakespeare Library; R to Hill, 7 July 1746; Hill to R, 21 July 1746; R to Hill, 27 Oct. 1748.

[14] Hill to R, 24 July 1744; Hill to Mallet, 23 Jan. 1741, FM XIII, 3, fo. 125, and Hill's *Works*, II, 158-9.

[15] See Samuel Burdy, *The Life of Philip Skelton* (Oxford, 1914).

for the publication of *Discourses, Controversial and Practical*, both of which Richardson printed.

In 1748 Skelton saw Richardson and presented him with a copy of *Ophiomaches* as an inadequate return for *Clarissa*;[16] after he got back to Ireland he tried to help Richardson get some money from the Irish bookseller who had published the novel. He also obeyed Richardson's request to look for faults in the novel (he was 'almost blinded with gazing at the Sun in order to find out its Spots') and sent notes on a few he had found.[17] He also sent some general remarks on *Clarissa* which Richardson preserved among other suggestions for a possible preface, pointing out that since it was not a work of intrigue and adventure it was not too long—it is not a mere novel, but 'a System of religious and moral Precepts and Examples'.[18] His admiration was lasting, since in his old age he regretted that novels 'made the chief entertainment of that middle class which subsists between the court and the spade' and excepted from his censure only *Clarissa* and *Millenium Hall*.[19]

He was not too happy in his lonely parish (which he called 'Siberia'), 'peopled with the most ignorant and barbarous of all his majesty's subjects. The country is beautiful, but the people shocking.' His parishioners suspected him of being a conjurer because of his love of books; and his difficulties were increased by hypochondria and by religious melancholy. He tried to collect tithes from his parishioners, without much hope, 'for they are, in all respects, a desperate and lawless people, who are every day sending me threatening messages, by which I am to understand, that if I proceed to extremities, I may expect to have my throat cut, or the house burnt over my head'. And he was 'without a single friend, or even conversable neighbour, within less than ten long miles' (he was a bachelor). At about the same time he wrote a melancholy letter to his and Richardson's mutual acquaintance Thomas Wilson; Wilson, fearing that 'such monstrous Usage may overset a Constitution weak at ye best', asked Richardson to write him a 'comfortable Letter' and to see whether Dr. Delany (Skelton's former tutor at Trinity) might not induce some bishop to find him a new parish. Probably Skelton never ceased to want a new parish, but in 1757, during the famine, his and Richardson's friend Smyth Loftus sent Richardson very moving accounts of Skelton's efforts to help his barbarous parishioners—he had 'the extreme pleasure of not having one person lost in his parish', largely through his efforts, though he himself was always poor. He sold his books to buy meal, and his sacrifices to help his poor parishioners made him a legend. The position of a clergyman of the established Church in a Catholic land was hardly a happy one, but there were perhaps compensations. When Irish pirates

[16] FM XV, 2, fo. 35.   [17] 27 May, 10 June 1749.   [18] FM XV, 2, fo. 54.
[19] *Complete Works*, ed. Robert Lynam (London, 1824), VI, 247.

published *Sir Charles Grandison* without recompensing its author, Richardson sent Skelton a power of acting for him, and what little money was finally recovered, Richardson, always eager to claim his due but not unwilling to be generous if he got it, offered for the relief of Skelton's parishioners.[20]

Skelton had some hopes of earning money by a volume of sermons (he had made something on *Ophiomaches*). On 15 July 1752 he first proposed to send Richardson the manuscript to dispose of. A year later he was still planning to send it, proposing to print for himself. Both Richardson and Thomas Wilson tried to interest a bookseller, but without success, and as time wore on, Skelton grew bitter. He wrote imputing a part of the delay to Richardson, who was greatly grieved: 'I have not met with any thing (the whole Irish invasion was nothing to it!) that has so much disturbed me, as that my friend, Mr. Skelton, should suspect me guilty of ingratitude or indifference to him and his affairs, even had he not so warmly and kindly as he has done, engaged himself in mine.' Skelton wrote again before he received this letter, still blaming Wilson and lamenting that a further year's postponement seemed likely, 'as if I had a lease of my own life': 'If I had wrote against my Saviour, or his religion, my work would, long ago have been bought, and reprinted, and bought again.' Richardson's last extant letter to him explains that 'it is impossible that any London printer can be at leisure the moment an author wishes him to begin his work; in the winter-time especially, which is our time of hurry'. He had parted with three pieces of work, put out the new edition of *Grandison* to several printers, taken in help on the first edition of volume seven, and refused Dr. Leland's last piece, but no printer could finish two large volumes as soon as Skelton expected. 'Indeed, indeed, Sir, you have suffered your impatience to carry you too far; you have given way to your apprehensions, and have sat brooding over your anxieties; and your head has out-run the fingers of the swiftest printers in London. Forgive me, Sir, I love you; you love me, I am sure. But is there not a warmth in your temper that adds to your malady, and gives a distrust, where you (so good a man!) should place a trust?'[21] The discourses did appear in that year, and one hopes that friendship was restored.

Another Irish clergyman whom Richardson had known even before the publication of *Pamela* was Dr. Patrick Delany, who in 1744 became Dean of Down. Richardson had printed for him as early as 1732; by 1739, when Richardson printed a second edition of his *Reflections upon Polygamy*, Delany was assuring him of his life-long friendship.[22] During the 1740s he

---

[20] Skelton to R, 5 Mar. 1750, 15 July 1752; Wilson to R, 29 July 1752; Loftus to R, 20 June, 3 Aug., 18 Sept. 1757; Barbauld, V, 177n.

[21] Skelton to R, 15 July 1752, 1 Aug. 1753; R to Skelton, 17 Mar. 1754; Skelton to R, 19 Mar. 1754; R to Skelton, 3 Apr. 1754.

[22] 8 Nov.

printed his three volumes on David and editions of his sermons. The Dean's works, at least some of them, were not too successful: on 27 May 1749 Philip Skelton wrote that he had (as Richardson had evidently desired him to do when they met in London) delicately prepared the way for Richardson's sending the Dean a printer's bill, owed 'because his performances were not sufficiently called for'. Richardson sent copies of *Pamela* and of the continuation of *Pamela* to his ward, Miss Tenison.[23]

Late in 1741 Delany's wife died, and within about two years he married again. His second wife, Mary Granville Pendarves, was a widow of almost forty-three (he was fifty-eight), of some intellectual and considerable social distinction. Though fashionable, she was irreproachably virtuous, having resisted several would-be seducers (including an earl and the Hanoverian ambassador) and (like Clarissa) having missed an opportunity to marry the man she loved (Lord Baltimore) because he proposed in a place (the opera) where he could not be accepted with propriety—he seems to have reconsidered by next day. Evidently Dr. Delany was justified in hoping that she had 'seen the vanities of the world to satiety' and was ready to retire,[24] since she accepted him in spite of the opposition of some of her relations, who considered an Irish clergyman beneath her.

Judging by the extant correspondence, Richardson's friendship with the Delanys during the time of the composition of *Clarissa* was not close. By 1748 he was corresponding with the Dean's wife, who had just read part of *Clarissa*, which entertained, moved, and instructed her, though she 'was so provoked by the tyrannical Usage of the *Harlowe's* to the excellent Clarissa' that she 'detested their Company'. Her admiration for *Clarissa* was even greater when she finished the novel: 'I never had so great a Mixture of Pain and Pleasure in the Reading of any Book in my Life. I was almost broken-hearted at some Passages, and raised above this World in others. . . . it is impossible to think it a Fiction.'[25] Perhaps the situation of Clarissa at Harlowe Place recalled only too vividly the time when she was seventeen and her uncle Lord Lansdowne ('Granville the polite'), suspecting an attachment to a young man named Twyford, all but forced her to accept Alexander Pendarves, a fat, gouty, sullen man of almost sixty, for whom she had 'formed an invincible aversion'. After much weeping, Miss Granville submitted and thus made herself miserable: 'I thought that if I could convince Gromio [Mr. Pendarves] of the great dislike I had to him, that he would not persist, but I was disappointed in that view. I had nobody to advise with; every one of the family had per-

[23] Delany to R, 21 Jan. 1741; 7 Jan. 1742.
[24] Delany to Mrs. Pendarves, 23 Apr. 1743, in *The Autobiography and Correspondence of Mary Granville, Mrs. Delany*, ed. Lady Llanover (London, 1861), II, 211. For the other facts about Mrs. Delany mentioned in this paragraph, see ibid., I, 40, 50–4, 83–4, 90–6, 240–1.
[25] 18 June 1748; 25 Jan. 1749.

suaded themselves that this would be an advantageous match for me—no one considered the sentiments of my heart.'[26]

In 1749–50 Mrs. Delany was again in London, and Richardson was corresponding with her younger sister Anne Granville Dewes. Evidently Mrs. Delany, like so many of Richardson's friends, was asked to suggest corrections for *Clarissa*, since she wrote to her sister, 'As you read Clarissa, when you object to any particular expressions *let me know* the *page* and the *line*.'[27]

Through Dr. Delany, Richardson met another lady perhaps as learned but by no means as respectable. Lætitia Pilkington, the daughter of a Dutch man-midwife settled in Dublin and wife of a poor (his worldly goods when he married consisted of 'a Harpsichord . . . a Cat and an Owl')[28] but poetic Irish parson, had been a friend of Swift and was admired for her literary gifts. Her husband started a divorce suit after she was discovered by twelve watchmen conversing with a strange man in her bedroom in the middle of the night: 'I own my self very indiscreet in permitting any Man to be at an unseasonable Hour in my Bed-Chamber; but Lovers of Learning will, I am sure, pardon me, as I solemnly declare, it was the attractive Charms of a new Book, which the Gentleman would not lend me, but consented to stay till I read it through, that was the sole Motive of my detaining him.'[29] Swift said that Matthew Pilkington was 'the falsest Rogue', and his wife 'the most profligate whore in either Kingdom'.[30] She began a life of adventure which led her to London, the Marshalsea, and eventually to extreme poverty. In her *Memoirs* she explains the purity of her relations with the various men who gave her money and adds that 'Mr. P——n may rest assured, that if I would have done him the Honour to exalt his Horn like that of an Unicorn, it should, at least, have been to me a *Cornu-Copia*'.[31] Few, if any, of her contemporaries seem to have been convinced of her innocence.

Her distresses early in 1743, when she was a little over thirty, caused her to write to Ireland to her father's old friend Patrick Delany, and she was told that she would receive her answer at Mr. Richardson's, in Salisbury Court:

> As I had never formed any great Idea of a Printer, by those I had seen in *Ireland*, I was very negligent of my Dress, any more than making myself clean; but was extremely surprized, when I was directed to a House of a very grand outward Appearance, and had it been a Palace, the beneficent Master deserved it.
> I met a very civil Reception from him; and he not only made me breakfast, but also dine with him, and his agreeable Wife and Children. After Dinner, he called me into his Study, and shewed me an Order he had received to pay me

[26] *Autobiography and Correspondence*, I, 23–9.   [27] 2 June 1750, ibid., II, 550.
[28] Lætitia Pilkington, *Memoirs* (Dublin, 1748), I, 30.   [29] Ibid., I, 187.
[30] *Correspondence*, ed. Sir Harold Williams (Oxford, 1963–5), V, 95.   [31] II, 237.

twelve Guineas, which he immediately took out of his Escrutore, and put into my Hand; but when I went to tell them over, I found I had fourteen, and supposing the Gentleman had made a Mistake, I was for returning two of them; but he, with a Sweetness, and Modesty almost peculiar to himself, said, he hoped I would not take it ill, that he had presumed to add a Trifle to the Bounty of my Friend.

I really was confounded, till, recollecting that I had read *Pamela*, and been told it was written by one Mr. *Richardson*, I asked him, whether he was not the Author of it? He said, he was the Editor: I told him, my Surprize was now over, as I found he had only given to the incomparable *Pamela* the Virtues of his own worthy Heart.

When he reads these Lines, as read them, I am certain he will, even for the Writer's Sake, let him reflect, that, at least, his Bread was not scattered on the Water; but that though I have no other Way of shewing my Gratitude for his boundless and repeated Acts of Humanity to me, and my Children, but Words, mere Words; yet, if every Word of mine could charm down Blessings on him,

> *Then never shou'd Misfortune cross his Foot;*
> *But Peace shou'd be within his Walls, and Plenty,*
> *Health, and Happiness his constant Attendants.*[32]

Mrs. Pilkington's experience had not taught her to look for much kindness from the respectable: 'The cruel treatment I have received from numbers of those falsely styled virtuous, has made me fearful of applying to any of them (but such to whom my misfortunes were entirely unknown); for instead of the relief my calamities required, they were heightened by some bitter insult; and the best comfort I received, was to be informed, I deserved all that I could suffer here.' She was therefore in some dread both of Dr. Delany and of his printer. 'But how agreeably was I surprised, when, instead of an awful severe judge, I met with a gentleman truly polite and compassionate!' Richardson's first unexpected generosity led to a correspondence and to calls for further generosity. Shortly afterwards she applied for another favour, which she herself felt it was presumptuous to request: a certification of her character so that she could rent a shop in the Strand—her friend Colley Cibber had not seemed to the shop-owner to be himself of good enough character to guarantee hers.[33] How Richardson coped with this embarrassing request is not known.

There is no further extant correspondence for over a year and a half. Mrs. Pilkington kept herself alive by some means or other, though she did not get out of her troubles. She mentions applications to various eminent personages, and perhaps some of them helped, though certainly others insulted her. We next find her thanking Richardson for a paper which must have contained relief: 'How was I astonished to find you, like silent-working Heaven, surprising oft the lonely heart with good, and

32 Ibid., II, 193–5.   33 June, 15 July 1743.

bounty unexpected, unmerited, unsought!' 'But pray, Sir, why will you differ so much from the generality of mankind? a proud

> Unfeeling race! whose breasts ne'er learnt to glow
> For others' good, or bleed for others woe.

You have monopolized all the Christian, all the social virtues and graces to yourself. Sir, is this equitable; is it fair?' She agrees with a remark of Swift's that people are resentful to the same degree as they are grateful: she feels both sentiments very strongly, the latter 'winds me up even to a painful height of ecstacy'. Indeed ecstasy, either in sorrow or joy, seems to have been Mrs. Pilkington's almost constant state. Her mind is always on a lofty level, which perhaps accounts for her having recourse to Milton or to Shakespeare to express her sentiments: 'I dare say you would meet with more censure, than applause, for bestowing any favour on one who so little merits it, according to the general opinion; but you have dealt with me according to Hamlet's advice:—Use every man better than his deserts, or who shall escape a whipping? Believe me to be, with such respect as we pay to superior beings, Sir, Your ever obliged and most devoted Servant, LÆTITIA.'[34] On 16 May 1745 she recommended a poor but good servant with whom she was forced to part. During the same year she sent Richardson a set of couplets 'To a Very Singular Gentleman', singular in his benevolence and in the grace with which it was given:

> Why are th' afflicted still thy constant care?
> E'en tho' they merit all the woes they bear.
> No harsh reproach, no comment on their faults
> Wounds their pain'd ears, or shocks their nicest thoughts;
> No frown severe declares th' unwelcome guest
> Unworthy of thy converse, or thy feast.
>
> . . . .
>
> With such obliging grace thy bounties flow;
> They double all the blessings they bestow. . . .[35]

At the same time she was discussing *Clarissa*, still in its formative stages, with Cibber, who was passionately opposed to the tragic ending of the novel. Nor could she bear the thought of the heroine's being contaminated by rape: 'Spare her virgin purity, dear Sir, spare it! Consider, if this wounds both Mr. Cibber and me (who neither of us set up for immaculate chastity) what must it do with those who possess that inestimable treasure?'[36]

At one time she wondered whether Richardson's silence meant that 'I have, by any misfortune, lost the little share I once thought I possessed in your favour'. She could not dispose of any work, and her trusted maid

[34] 13 Mar., 27 May 1745.   [35] 1745.   [36] 29 June.

had robbed her of everything saleable, 'even to sheets'. In addition to poverty, she suffered from isolation: 'I am as it were cut off from human society. Mean company I cannot be pleased with; I am unable to go abroad, and have no place fit for any body to come into, so that I have no relief but a book.'[37] On 13 August 1745 she sent 'a last request', for pens, sealing wax, and 'a few sheets of gilt paper' so that she might write letters to her noble patrons for enough money to get her back to Ireland. One hopes, probably justifiably, that Richardson sent them.

At any rate she was silent for some time, till forced to write again by even greater troubles. Her daughter, following in the maternal footsteps, had arrived 'big with child, naked and desolate; and because I would not let her lye in the street, my saint-like methodist landlady has padlocked the door, and turned us both there. My own writings she has secured, as well as a few small matters, she, my child, had provided for her child. I have less authority to blame her than perhaps another mother would take. We have both been forced to sit up in a place they call a night-house, all last night, so that my head is extremely disordered; and I hope you will pity and pardon my bad writing. As I know you are a subscriber to some of the hospitals, could I but get her to lye-in in one, I should think myself happy.' Richardson sent a young gentleman, probably one of his journeymen, to her, one assumes with help, though not enough to get her out of the horrid night-house, from which she later wrote for 'a little old linen of any kind' for her daughter. The linen was sent, but new troubles arose: the parish officers threatened to send the girl, almost ready to give birth, 'from parish to parish, back to Dublin', which was responsible for supporting her. After some time Cibber got two friends to give her enough money to move into 'a very decent garret', where her family was increased not only by the birth of a grandson but by the unexpected appearance of a son, who had been rejected by his father and wanted to go on the stage. The son, John Carteret Pilkington, she sent to Richardson, who noted on her letter, probably with some displeasure: 'Ragged; destitute. I gave him a suit of clothes. He gave particular orders to the tailor to make it fashionable to the height of the mode.' The grandson's father got an aunt to put him out to nurse, the son was to be sent abroad with a young gentleman of fortune, and the former friend of Swift hoped to get bread for herself and her daughter by writing letters 'on any subject (except the law)' for those unable to write for themselves. But the son's master married and turned him off, and his mother's distresses were not lessened: 'It is my hard fate to be quite a prisoner, having nothing even decent to appear in. I have not seen a tree this season; and am as much cut off from society as the dead: but they have their advantages whose wants are ended.' 'P. S. I could not go on with the stampt paper hats, having only

[37] 1745 (two letters).

borrowed the stamps; and whilst I had it in my possession, I had no materials to proceed. All my schemes are abortive.' Mrs. Pilkington's efforts, though gallant, were indeed largely futile: 'I believe it will not greatly surprise you to hear I am quite broke: indeed, it was what I might naturally expect, having undertaken trade without any fund to carry it on; and whether I had business or not, quarter-day came.'[38]

By 1747 she was back in Dublin, where her long troubles had a moderately happy end (she died in 1750). Like more recent sinners, she found that scandal is one road to fame and fortune. With the aid of sixteen guineas from a good-natured prelate she and her son got back in time to prevent her husband's second marriage, and he had to pay her seventy pounds. Her adventures were the chief subject of talk in the Irish metropolis, and in 1748 her *Memoirs* appeared. She asked Cibber to give her respects to Mr. Richardson, but it was almost two years before she wrote to Richardson herself and then it was to recommend a printer and his wife who were going to England. She wondered about the reception of her book in London and seemed satisfied enough with her state: 'I am sure it will be agreeable to you to hear I have met with many marks of distinction in my own country.'[39] Though according to his principles she could hardly have deserved such marks of distinction, one hopes they were agreeable to Richardson. He did not, however, approve of her *Memoirs* (at least when writing to the moralistic Mrs. Chapone): he put her in a class with Constantia Phillips and Lady Vane, 'a Set of Wretches, wishing to perpetuate their Infamy'.[40]

Like most men of his time and of more recent times, Richardson can speak rather loftily of the deserving poor, and it is pleasant to find him aiding the not-so-deserving, and aiding in such a way as not to wound the delicate sensibilities of Mrs. Pilkington. Fortunately most men seem to act better when dealing with individuals than their theories demand; the world would hardly have got along even as well as it has if men lived up to their principles. A person inclined to carp might point out that Richardson's help to Mrs. Pilkington was never enough to end her distresses. But she herself had no complaint; she knew far more about the practice of charity in her own time than we can know, and Richardson's gifts, both in substance and (more difficult) in the manner of giving, evidently inspired her genuine gratitude.

Her friend Colley Cibber is famous or notorious on many counts: comic

[38] [19 Dec.?], 28 Dec. 1745; 28 Jan., [Feb.–Mar.?], 3 Apr., 6 May 1746; [late 1746]. One of her enterprises which failed must have been the bookshop in St. James's Street of which the *Dictionary of National Biography* speaks, but this failure and her imprisonment for debt in the Marshalsea took place before 1748.

[39] Mrs. Pilkington to Cibber, 18 June 1747, Barbauld, II, 159–60; Mrs. Pilkington to R, 28 May 1749.

[40] 6 Dec. 1750.

actor, theatrical manager, prolific playwright, one of the inglorious series of eighteenth-century poets laureate, Pope's King of the Dunces, and the frequent butt of Fielding. Cibber was eighteen years older than Richardson and was thus almost seventy when, in 1740, he published the much-ridiculed *Apology* for his life, which is today probably his most read and most readable work. Though toothless and weak-voiced, he was still able in 1745 to act in *Papal Tyranny*, his own adaptation of Shakespeare's *King John*. And he was still able to laugh at himself at least as wittily as his attackers (who were perhaps really attacking Walpole, who appointed him laureate) could do and still able to chase, if not to catch, a variety of pretty women.

Of her patron Cibber, the fallen but unbowed Mrs. Pilkington remarks in her *Memoirs*: 'I dare say, nobody will imagine he serv'd me from any carnal Views, since,

> *If Truth in Spite of Manners must be told,*
> *Why really Seventy-six is something old.*'[41]

Whether or not Richardson knew him already, by 27 May 1745 Mrs. Pilk-ington was sending Richardson Cibber's respects: 'He thirsts for your writings, that is his word, and hopes you will give him a morning.' And soon afterwards she found Cibber in anxiety over the fate of Clarissa; when she told him the catastrophe Richardson planned for his heroine, 'he lost all patience, threw down the book, and vowed he would not read another line. To express or paint his passion, would require such masterly hands as yours, or his own: he shuddered; nay, the tears stood in his eyes: —"What! (said he) shall I, who have loved and revered the virtuous, the beautiful Clarissa, from the same motives I loved Mr. Richardson, bear to stand a patient spectator of her ruin, her final destruction?"' 'When I told him she must die, he said, "G—d d—n, if she should; and that he should no longer believe Providence, or eternal Wisdom, or Goodness governed the world, if merit, innocence, and beauty were to be so destroyed: nay, (added he) my mind is so hurt with the thought of her being violated, that were I to see her in Heaven, sitting on the knees of the blessed Virgin, and crowned with glory, her sufferings would still make me feel horror, horror distilled."' [42] A rather interesting chapter in the history of popular reactions to the problem of evil and the rewards of virtue could be based on a comparison of Cibber's horror with the surprisingly similar horror of Ivan Karamazov.

Cibber was then one of the first to see *Clarissa* in manuscript. As Richardson wrote to Hill, Cibber, having heard of the novel and loved *Pamela*, 'was very desirous to see it; and I being put in hope, that he would not spare it, was desirous he should. Nor has he deceived me. He has had

[41] I, 246.   [42] 29 June.

Patience at his Time of Life, to go thrô it;—we have Debates upon some Places.' One of the debates was certainly over Cibber's desire for a happy ending, which he persevered in. Cibber offered some additions (probably at Richardson's request) which Richardson did not like; and (probably at Richardson's suggestion that the work was too long) he suggested cutting it drastically, taking 'away whole Branches'. But in spite of the debates, Cibber's admiration for *Clarissa* continued, though his compliments at times took peculiar forms, as when he found such lively and natural strokes in one of Lovelace's letters 'that scarce a libertine reader will forbear to triumph with him, over the too charming, and provoking delicacy of his Clarissa'.[43]

Richardson was rather inclined to make fun of his admirer. He observed him at Tunbridge, 'at seventy-seven, hunting after new faces' and thinking himself happy if he 'can obtain the notice and familiarity of a fine woman! —How ridiculous!' 'Lord, Lord! Miss Highmore! What figures do Mr. Nash and Mr. Cibber make, hunting after new beauties, and with faces of high importance traversing the walks! God bless you, come and see them!'[44] But Richardson gave Cibber a graceful compliment in print: among the 'not ill-chosen' books 'of a lighter turn' which Clarissa finds at Mrs. Sinclair's are 'that genteel Comedy of Mr. Cibber, The Careless Husband, and others of the same Author'.[45] And two compliments to him were added to Defoe's *Tour*.[46] Their relations were close enough for Cibber to visit North End with his 'female fry' and to send Richardson an invitation in his usual whimsical style: 'Though Death has been cooling his heels at my door these three weeks, I have not had time to see him. The daily conversation of my friends has kept me so agreeably alive, that I have not passed my time better a great while. If you have a mind to make one among us, I will order Death to come another day.'[47]

Cibber was also privileged to read *Sir Charles Grandison* before it was published, though his idea of a good man differed somewhat from Richardson's. In talking with Richardson about the male ideal, he proposed to give his paragon a mistress, 'another man's wife, too', in order to show the hero's virtue in parting from her when he fixed on a wife; Richardson's ideal of chastity was not calculated to impress Cibber: 'A male-virgin, said he—ha, ha, ha, hah!' According to Cibber, 'none but divines and prudes' could censure a 'moderate rake': 'Bless me, thought I! and is this knowing the world?—What an amiable man was Mr. B——, in Pamela, in this light! . . . He is as gay and as lively at seventy-nine as he was at twenty-nine; and he is a sober man, who has seen a great deal, and

[43] R to Hill, 20 Jan. 1746, 7 Nov. 1748; R to Young, 3 Dec. 1745; R to Hill, 29 Oct. 1746; Cibber to R, 30 Mar. 1748.
[44] To Sarah Wescomb, [late Aug. 1748]; to Susanna Highmore, 2 Aug. 1748.
[45] SH, III, 318; EL, II, 194.   [46] 4th edn., II, 136; III, 97.
[47] Cibber to R, 20 May 1753; 25 Dec. 1750.

always dressed well, and was noted for his address, and for his success, too, on two hundred and fifty occasions,—a little too many, I doubt, for a moderate rake: but then his long life must be considered.' The moderate rake was as much worried about the threat to Harriet Byron's virtue as he had been about that to Clarissa's: 'I have just finisht the Sheets you favour'd me with; but never found so strong a proof of your sly, ill nature, as to have hun[g] me up, upon tenters, till I see you again. Zounds. I have not patience till I know what's become of her—Why you!—I doe not know what to call you!—Ay! ay! you may laugh, if you please—but how will you be able to look me in the face, if the lady should ever be able to shew *Hers* again—What piteous, damnd disgracefull pickle, have you plung'd her in?—for Gods sake send me the sequel—or I don't know what to say!' 'The delicious meal I made of Miss Byron on Sunday last, has given me an Appetite for another Slice of her off from the Spit, before she is servd up to the Publick table', and he proposes to call on Richardson and 'nibble upon a bit more of her'. Indeed, he had never 'met with such variety of entertainment, so much goodness of heart' in any author ancient or modern: 'Can any man be a good moral writer that does not take up his pen in the cause of virtue?'[48] Perhaps Richardson did manage to convert one moderate rake, at the age of eighty-two.

Dr. Johnson, who thought Cibber 'a poor creature' and refused to let him read one of his birthday odes to the end ('I could not bear such nonsense'), says that Richardson wondered 'that I could treat him with familiarity' and was '"displeased that I 'did not treat Cibber with more *respect*'. Now, Sir, to talk of respect for a player!" (smiling disdainfully.)'[49] Perhaps Richardson showed a proper respect for the Laureate when in his presence, though he permitted himself a humourous tone in talking about him: 'Mr. Cibber (my brother elder) came to tea, by my pre-engagement: and there he read his Pindaric and Horatian Ode, and the translation of another Ode *Ad Melpomene*, and please you. Now don't you wish you had been there? It was a hot day; and he read till he was in a breathing, and wiped and acted like any thing: and every body was pleased.' When Miss Grainger described an old grandfather, 'an Old-Young Green-Grey Creature', Richardson did not hesitate to mention Cibber as fitting the description. And when Lady Bradshaigh described Cibber as a '*Shameless old Man*' ('a very poor figure wou'd he make were he to be call'd to an account even in *this* world, but in the *next*—God be merciful to him'), Richardson's comment was only 'Mr. Cibber—Poor Mr. Cibber!'[50]

A literary friend calculated to make a much better impression in the next

[48] R to Lady Bradshaigh, [Mar.? 1750]; Cibber to R, 2[9?] May, 6 June, 19 Nov. 1753.
[49] Boswell, *Life*, II, 92–3; III, 183–4.
[50] R to Susanna Highmore, 22 June 1750; R to Frances Grainger, 28 Sept. 1751; Lady Bradshaigh to R, 25 Sept. 1753; R to Lady Bradshaigh, 5 Oct. 1753.

world was Edward Young. When Richardson was just beginning work on *Clarissa*, we have the first evidence of his connection with Young, except for Dr. Johnson the most prominent literary figure with whom he was closely associated and one of his most important correspondents: if one judges by extant letters, the only people after the death of Aaron Hill who were as intimate with Richardson as Young were Thomas Edwards and Lady Bradshaigh. By the 1740s Young already had something of a name as a verse satirist, and he was making an even bigger name with his blank verse series, *The Complaint: or, Night-Thoughts*. The first thing that Richardson printed for Young was the seventh of the nine nights in this series, and except for the collected edition of the earlier nights, to which Robert Dodsley already owned the copyright, he seems to have done all of Young's printing from then on.

Young was Rector of Welwyn, in Hertfordshire, a widower, living with his step-daughter, Caroline Lee. He had written praising the continuation of *Pamela*,[51] and by the middle of 1744 the two men were writing to each other informally, with a freedom that already indicates some intimacy.[52]

[51] This letter is listed in Richardson's index to his correspondence about *Pamela* (FM XVI, 1, fo. 7) but is not now among his papers.

[52] The text of Richardson's correspondence with Young is in a confused state. All but a few of the originals are missing. Most of the extant letters were printed in the *Monthly Magazine* between 1813 and 1819; in 1804 Mrs. Barbauld had included some of the same letters and some others in her edition of Richardson's correspondence. Mrs. Barbauld's text differs considerably from that in the *Monthly Magazine*: many passages which appear in one letter in Mrs. Barbauld are scattered through several letters in the later printing, and the dates often vary widely. Probably, as Henry Pettit in 'The Text of Edward Young's Letters to Samuel Richardson', *MLN*, LVII (1942), 668–70, says, the *Monthly Magazine* version is the reliable one: the letters are more logically arranged there, and in a few cases Mrs. Barbauld's dating is clearly wrong. But so far as she can be checked, Mrs. Barbauld was not in the habit of wildly combining passages from different letters, though she did cut freely. A manuscript copy of Young's letter of 14 Mar. 1754 (in the Pierpont Morgan Library) lacks a sentence which appears in the same letter in both Mrs. Barbauld (II, 33) and the *Monthly Magazine* (XLI [1816], 231), both of which lack a postscript which is in the copy. Strangely, two passages which appear in the *Monthly Magazine* letters of 22 Dec. 1758 and 18 Dec. 1758 (XLVI [1818], 45) also appear in the *Monthly Magazine* under Jan. 1758 (XLIV [1817], 328) and 29 May 1759 (XLVII [1819], 136). They also appear in Mrs. Barbauld under the latter dates. But the text which appears under the former dates is certainly better, since in the Jan. 1758 letter both Mrs. Barbauld and the *Magazine* omit an essential 'not', and in the 29 May 1759 letter 'literally' appears in both where the 'utterly' of 22 Dec. 1758 makes a better reading, and the sensible 'hard' of 18 Dec. 1758 appears in the other *Monthly Magazine* version as a nonsensical 'want' and in Mrs. Barbauld as 'anxiety' (which could be an emendation for a shorter word which she was unable to read). The passages also fit better in the context of the Dec. 1758 letters. The introductory note to the *Monthly Magazine* letters states that they were 'from the originals in the hand-writing of the parties, as preserved by Mr. Richardson'. Richardson did have a file of letters, which Mrs. Barbauld used, but his own letters in it were generally copies, not originals. He often talked of revising it and made some cuts and changes in names and phrases. The *Magazine* probably used the same copies Mrs. Barbauld had used, with her markings on them (Richard Phillips was the owner of the Richardson–Young letters published in the *Monthly Magazine*, of which he was editor; he was also the publisher of Mrs. Barbauld's edition of Richardson's *Correspondence*). Why Mrs. Barbauld should treat the Richardson–Young letters so much more cavalierly than she did any others of which we know is a mystery unless someone else had

Young saw *Clarissa* in manuscript, heard parts of it read, and followed its progress with interest. Before its publication he wrote to the Duchess of Portland that he had already wept over it, and later he reminded her to read it: 'What a beautiful brat of the brain is there! . . . That romance will probably do more good than a body of Divinity. . . . I look on it therefore as a sort of touchstone for the readers of this virtuous age, who, while they think they are only passing their judgment on another's ingenuity, will make a discovery of their own hearts.'[53] He wrote just as enthusiastically to the Duchess's friend Mrs. Delany: it contains '*The Whole Duty of WOMAN*', 'the Bench of Bishops might go to School to the Writer of a Romance', it is by 'my Friend (Pardon the Vanity!) *my* Friend Mr. Richardson'. Young sent this letter to Richardson and told him he might read it before doing him the favour of sealing and directing it to Mrs. Delany, whose address he did not know. Richardson kept a copy among his papers and naturally enough mentioned it with pride to Miss Grainger and sent a copy to his Dutch translator, Stinstra.[54]

By the middle of 1745 Young had visited Richardson and was intimate enough to ask to be allowed to stay at North End: 'I find I thirst after you.' By 1748, at least, Richardson, for whom a trip even of twenty-five miles was an event, was beginning to visit Young at Welwyn.[55] Young seems to have stayed with Richardson almost every time he came to the city, and Richardson went to Welwyn oftener than one would have expected.

The intimacy between the two men is not fully reflected in the letters they exchanged, which are generally brief and rather factual. Richardson did not indulge in amiable nonsense with men as he did with women, and he did not so often carry on long discussions with Young as with Hill and Edwards. Their friendship comes out rather in stray remarks; perhaps they saw each other too often to need to discuss things in writing. There is a good deal of praise of each other's work. Young admired *Sir Charles Grandison* ('After *Clarissa*, you shall rise in fame'),[56] and Young was Harriet Byron's favourite writer.[57] A high compliment to Young, com-

---

earlier tampered with them. Richardson himself could easily have done so; we know that in 1758 he added notes to this correspondence (note to Letter xxxiv, 1 Jan. 1750, *Monthly Magazine*, XXXVII [1814], 327). The difference between Mrs. Barbauld's text and that of the *Magazine* may indicate that the latter's editor did a better job of piecing together a confused file.

[53] 22 Nov. 1747; 29 Jan. 1749, *Hist. MSS. Comm.: MSS. of the Marquis of Bath*, I (1904), 308, 313.

[54] Young to Mrs. Delany, 9 Feb. 1749, copy by R included in his letter to Stinstra, 2 June 1753; Young to R, 9 Feb. 1749; R's index to *Clarissa*, FM XV, 3, fo. 2; R to Frances Grainger, 28 Feb. 1750.

[55] Young to R, 2 May, 11 June, 17 Sept. 1745; Young to the Duchess of Portland, 25 Sept. 1748, *Hist. MSS. Comm.: MSS. of the Marquis of Bath*, I, 312; R to Hill, 18 Aug. 1749; R to Frances Grainger, 21 July 1750; R to Sarah Wescomb, 6 July 1752.

[56] Young to R, Apr. 1751; Lady Bradshaigh to R, 27 Nov. 1753.　　　[57] SH, II, 10.

plaining that he had not been rewarded with higher office in the church, was added to the fourth edition of Defoe's *Tour*.[58]

There is a good deal of piety. Young was sincerely devout, and people in the eighteenth century were not ashamed to mention goodness and religion. When Richardson sent Young a list of his troubles, the latter knew of but one expedient: 'that since the things of this life, from their mixture, repetition, defectiveness, and, in age, short duration, are unable to satisfy, we must aid their *natural* by a *moral* pleasure, we must season them with a spice of religion to make them more palateable; we must consider that 'tis God's will that we should be content and pleased with them'. The purchase of a pair of gilt candlesticks for his altar reminds him of death: 'I, as one going down hill, am for having all my purposes go fast, least I myself should outrun them, and leave my designs behind me.'[59]

Young has often been cited as a member of the 'graveyard school' of poets, sometimes with the implication that these poets were seeking in the graveyard the same sort of *frisson* that Poe might have sought a century later. In a day when the churches have turned to looking on the bright side of things and when many people whose beliefs, at least technically, are the same as those of Edward Young would find his consolations shallow or even hypocritical and his concern with death morbid, it is important to remember that the view that this life is meant to be a vale of tears and that death is no evil was at one time taken seriously and believed deeply. The ending to Richardson's *Clarissa* is based on the same view. It is no wonder that Young was one of those who approved of Clarissa's death; he would have regarded it as inconsistent with his Christianity to insist on the necessity of a reward on earth for her. It is even possible that Richardson's association with Young, who was devout in a way that makes the religion of *Pamela* seem superficial and merely proper, helped prepare him to write the final scenes of his novel. One may disagree with Young's religion, but it would be a mistake to sneer at it and an even greater mistake to think of it as mere verbiage. It is this pensive, melancholy, but not despairing religion which permeates *Night-Thoughts*, not a desire for a new thrill by playing with corpses.

Young tried to help Richardson in a more worldly matter. Among the young girls whom Richardson befriended was a certain 'thrice amiable Miss Parsons'.[60] She was also of concern to the Duchess of Portland. Grace Parsons, daughter of Sir William Parsons, Bart., was married in 1747 to Thomas Lambarde, of Sevenoaks, Kent.[61] Even after her marriage

[58] II, 195.   [59] 17 Aug. 1746; Jan. 1751.
[60] Sarah Wescomb to R, 3 Sept. 1746; R to Sarah Wescomb, 15 Sept. 1746. See also Young to R, 11 Nov. 1746.
[61] *Gentleman's Magazine*, XVII (1747), 247; Burke's *Landed Gentry*, under Lambarde; G. E. Cokayne's *Complete Baronetage* (Exeter, 1900–9), III, 184; Young to the Duchess of Portland, 17 July 1746, 1 June 1747, *Hist. MSS. Comm.: MSS. of the Marquis of Bath*, I, 293, 306.

Young told the Duchess that Mrs. Lambarde 'may expect to see before Christmas part of her own amiable picture in the remaining part of Clarissa'; at the same time Young reported to the Duchess that he had heard rumours that the newly married couple was not getting along well. Richardson seems to have opposed the marriage and predicted its failure, while the Duchess had favoured it; he was soon accused of doing something, probably of spreading the rumours, which caused the Duchess and Mrs. Lambarde to be seriously offended with him. On 9 September 1749 we find Richardson asking Young to set him right with Her Grace: 'I should despise myself, were I capable of the Behaviour with respect to Mrs. Lambert, that I have been accused of.' If the former Miss Parsons had equalled Richardson's love, she would have given him an opportunity to clear himself: 'My Heart is too big, obscure a Man as I am, to expostulate on this Occasion with a Lady whom I looked upon as one of my own Children.' Young informed the Duchess that 'poor Richardson's great delicacy is quite in pain about it'—'if . . . you can furnish me . . . with anything of consolation to him I shall rejoice'. The Duchess was at first 'a little on the reserve', waiting to hear from Mrs. Lambarde, but finally sent a message which Young could forward to Richardson and 'which, though very short, I hope may give you some satisfaction'. Richardson thanked him, protesting that he had never said more than that if the match were unhappy it must be the husband's fault, but took the occasion to remark that 'it is strange, methinks, that my wife . . . should never be favoured with one line, or the least notice, from Mrs. Lambard'. The friendship with Mrs. Lambarde seems never to have been re-established. There is no Mrs. L. in the list of thirty-six superior women which he sent to Miss Grainger in 1750, but there is a 'D. of P.', though he could hardly have known the Duchess well, if he knew her at all. By 1754 Richardson had recovered the Duchess's good opinion, though she was never an admirer. She gave in to the teasing of friends and tried to read Clarissa and Sir Charles Grandison, 'but I was disgusted with their tediousness, and could not read eleven letters with all the effort I could make: so much about my sisters and my brothers, and all my uncles and my aunts!'[62]

Richardson did far more for Young's works than one would expect a printer to do. He took the trouble to put the 1749 edition of Night-Thoughts to press himself, 'in hopes that it will not be the less correct for

[62] Young to the Duchess of Portland, 25 Sept., 18 Dec. 1748, Hist. MSS. Comm.: MSS. of the Marquis of Bath, I, 312–14; R to Young, 9 Sept. 1749; Young to the Duchess of Portland, 17 Sept. 1749, Hist. MSS. Comm.: MSS. of the Marquis of Bath, I, 315; Young to R, 15 Oct. 1749; Young to the Duchess of Portland, Oct. 1749, Hist. MSS. Comm.: MSS. of the Marquis of Bath, I, 317; Young to R, 28 Oct. 1749; R to Young, Oct. 1749; R to Frances Grainger, 8 Sept. 1750; Young to the Duchess of Portland, 25 June 1754, Hist. MSS. Comm.: MSS. of the Marquis of Bath, I, 321; Diary and Letters of Madame D'Arblay, ed. Charlotte Barrett (London, 1891), I, 520.

it', and to point out that the continuation made an alteration necessary in the Preface to the fourth night. When Young asked for advice about his sermon *An Argument Drawn from the Circumstances of Christ's Death* (1758), Richardson replied that he should tone down the hints in the dedication that his service at Court had not been sufficiently rewarded: 'I humbly think this part cannot be too delicately mentioned.' Young immediately decided to cut the references: 'I now see how weak myself, and what a friend is worth. I could not forbear writing to you by this post; being pained with the thought of your thinking me a fool any longer.'[63] The printed dedication has no allusion to Young's complaint.

According to Richardson's statement to Hill, the others who saw *Clarissa* in its early stages, besides Cibber, Young, and Hill himself, were 'Dr. Heylin, and his Lady; both excellent Judges, and fond of Writings of Amusement: Miss Cheyne, Daughter of my late dear Friend the Doctor; a young Lady of Taste and Reading. Mr. Freke the Surgeon, whom once I mentioned to you, who read it with a Friend of his'—all persons 'whom I could not deny'.[64] John Heylin, Rector of St. Mary-le-Strand, Prebendary of Westminster Abbey, and Chaplain in Ordinary to George II, was about sixty when he began reading *Clarissa*; his second wife, Elizabeth Ebbutt, was in her mid-forties. She died soon afterwards, on 9 June 1747, while her husband lived until 1759.[65] He was the author of religious works and had the reputation of being a 'mystic'. John Freke, born in 1688, was surgeon to St. Bartholomew's Hospital until gout and infirmity forced him to resign in 1755, the year before his death. He was a Fellow of the Royal Society and was considered a man of parts, learned in science (he experimented with electricity) and the arts. Richardson had been consulting him about his health in the late thirties. Dr. Cheyne called him a good judge when he found Richardson's 'Blood so good', but later, when he found Richardson's blood worse after entering on Cheyne's regimen, that doctor considered his opinion 'poor Ignorance'. Richardson was still consulting him in 1750.[66]

Another adviser on *Clarissa* was Solomon Lowe, a grammarian, the author of several books, and the master of Blyth House Boarding School near Hammersmith,[67] not far from Richardson's country place at North End. Their acquaintance dates at least from the time of *Pamela*: in 1741 he wrote to praise that novel and to ask for a loan of the last two volumes, as well as to express his gratitude for services rendered.[68] He was a great admirer of *Clarissa* and, when asked to discover its faults, found none of importance, but he did send Richardson a few grammatical criticisms

[63] 9 Sept. 1749; 30 Apr., 2 May, 14 May 1748.   [64] 20 Jan. 1746.

[65] *The Marriage, Baptismal, and Burial Registers of the Collegiate Church or Abbey of St. Peter, Westminster*, ed. Joseph Lemuel Chester, Harleian Society Publications, X (1876), 371.

[66] Cheyne to R, 26 Oct. 1739, 17 May 1742; Lady Bradshaigh to R, received 25 Nov. 1750.

[67] P.R.O. Privy Council 4/8, under date 3 Mar. 1725.   [68] 21 Dec.

(most of which Richardson accepted). He at least began the preparation of an index to that novel and later offered a Greek motto from Strabo to the effect that poets and lawgivers have long used fiction.[69] He died on 24 December 1750, leaving his wife, Elizabeth, and daughter in poor circumstances.[70] The daughter must be the Sarah Lowe who on 1 December 1753 asked Richardson for the loan of a copy of *Sir Charles Grandison*, which she could not afford to buy: 'I never was so much pleas'd, as at the reading of your Clarissa, nor can I believe any other, than that you were Supernaturally Assisted in the writing of it.'

One is inclined to think of the painter William Hogarth in connection with Fielding, who praised his work often and whose spirit is close to Hogarth's both in his descriptions of the seamier side of London life and in his satirical portraits of the more elegant classes. But Richardson also was an early admirer, and when in *The Apprentice's Vade Mecum* he gave a picture of a fop, he wished that 'the ingenious Mr. *Hogarth* would finish the Portrait'.[71] When Richardson decided to prefix frontispieces to the second edition of *Pamela*, he picked two scenes which he wanted to be illustrated and then chose Hogarth to illustrate them. A designer did begin work, though not upon Richardson's first choice for Volume I, the near-suicide by the pond, but upon the scene in which Pamela examines her three bundles before her expected departure; but the illustrations never appeared. In the preface to the second edition Richardson explained: 'That it was intended to prefix two neat *Frontispieces* to this Edition, (and to present them to the Purchasers of the first) and one was actually finished for that Purpose; but there not being Time for the other, from the Demand for the new Impression; and the Engraving Part of that which was done (tho' no Expence was spared) having fallen very short of the Spirit of the Passages they were intended to represent, the Proprietors were advised to lay them aside.'[72] It is not certain that it was Hogarth who, as originally planned, completed the one illustration, and in any case it is not the designer's work which is blamed but the engraver's, though it is worth noting that Richardson is perturbed because the latter has fallen short, not of the artist's sketch, but of the spirit of his own writing. Whatever happened did not cause a permanent quarrel. We learn from Boswell that Hogarth was on friendly enough terms with Richardson to pay a call on him in 1753.[73]

[69] Lowe to R, 23 May 1748; 'Scruples', dated 26 June 1748, FM XV, 2, fo. 102, and XVI, 1, fo. 90; 27 Dec. (two letters) 1748; 15 Jan., [after 1 Feb.], 5 Feb., 18 May 1749.
[70] *Gentleman's Magazine*, XX, 570. Early in 1752 Elizabeth Lowe wrote (in vain) to Professor John Ward of Gresham College for help in selling a manuscript Lowe had left of his work for a supplement to Chambers's *Cyclopædia* (B.M. Add. MS. 6210, fos. 158–9, 160–1, 165–6).
[71] P. 35.
[72] I, xxxvi–vii. See Eaves, 'Graphic Illustration of The Novels of Samuel Richardson, 1740–1810', pp. 350–1.
[73] *Life*, I, 145–7.

Among the artists who did complete illustrations for *Pamela*, the most prominent was Joseph Highmore. He was already in his fifties and well known, especially as a portrait painter, when he painted twelve pictures illustrating the novel. An advertisement of 16 February 1744 states that ten of these paintings may now be seen at Mr. Highmore's house in Lincoln's Inn Fields and that subscriptions are being taken for a set of prints from them.[74] The pictures, perhaps the best illustrations ever made of Richardson's work, are now scattered among the National Gallery, the Tate, the Fitzwilliam Museum in Cambridge, and the National Gallery of Victoria in Melbourne, but the prints may occasionally be met with. The scene with the bundles is especially successful in catching Pamela's freshness.

Highmore later painted two pictures of Clarissa, which played a major role in one of Richardson's chief friendships. Lady Bradshaigh, still anonymous as Richardson's admirer Belfour, inquired 'if there is any such Painter as Mr. Highmore or has he any Picture in his Possession which we are to suppose was taken for Clarissa'. In reply Richardson wrote: 'Mr. Highmore is an eminent Painter in Holborn-Row, Lincolns-Inn Fields, the same who published Twelve Prints of Pamela, of which he has the Drawings; and which he had finished before I had the Pleasure of knowing him. He has drawn Clarissa at whole length in the Vandyke Taste and Dress. He had finished the Piece before I saw it, or knew of it; and before Clarissa was printed, having seen only some parts of the Work in Manuscript. . . . Mr. Highmore has also drawn the assembled Harlowes, the *accusing* Brother, and the *accused* Sister on her Return from Miss Howe's as represented in the Beginning of Vol. I.'[75] The first of these Clarissa paintings has been lost, or at any rate is unidentified, but the second is now in the collection of Lord Glenconner.[76] The painting of Clarissa must have been done before April 1748, when Richardson published the third volume of his novel, which contains a reference to it, a sort of polite compliment to Highmore. A note inserted in the first edition but cut from the second makes the reference into almost an advertisement: 'This picture is drawn as big as the life by Mr. Highmore, and is in his possession.'[77] Highmore also painted Clementina, one of the heroines of *Sir Charles Grandison*, at full length and evidently during her madness: 'In her Countenance is well expressed the Dignity and Disorder of an elevated Soul.'[78]

---

[74] *London Daily Post and General Advertiser.*

[75] Lady Bradshaigh to R, 6 Jan. 1749; R to Lady Bradshaigh, [mid-Jan.] 1749.

[76] T. C. Duncan Eaves, '"The Harlowe Family" by Joseph Highmore: A Note on the Illustration of Richardson's *Clarissa*', *HLQ*, VII (1943-4), 89-96.

[77] 1st edn., III, 260; SH, III, 283; EL, II, 170.

[78] Francis Plummer, *A Candid Examination of the History of Sir Charles Grandison*, 3rd edn. (London, 1755), p. 20n.

It must have been the *Pamela* pictures which led to the enduring friendship between Richardson and Highmore. We find Highmore objecting to the fact that the rake Lovelace is not also an atheist[79] but defending the tragic end of *Clarissa*.[80] He painted the two portraits of Richardson now in the National Portrait Gallery as well as the portrait in the Hall of the Company of Stationers and that of Mrs. Richardson which hung there before it was destroyed by enemy action during the Second World War. And it is from Highmore, who happened to call for tea just before Richardson's final stroke, that we get the best description of the events leading up to his death.

Highmore's daughter Susanna, born on 5 December 1725,[81] was a correspondent of Richardson's by August 1748. Early the next year she wrote to tell him how much she and her Papa and Mamma were enchanted with *Clarissa*, and by January 1750 he was visiting her and she was one of his 'particular favourites'.[82] But she and the flock of young singing birds, male and female, which gathered around her and around her friend Hester Mulso are more closely connected with the composition of *Sir Charles Grandison*.

Richardson knew the 'thresher poet', Stephen Duck, at least by the time he finished *Pamela*. It is rather surprising that the nineteenth-century admirers of pre-romanticism did not take up Duck. He had as much right as many others to be called a natural genius: no one can deny him the right to the adjective. He began life as a farm labourer, was largely self-educated, and made his reputation with poems on country life. 'The Thresher's Labour' fairly represents the heights to which he soared:

> In briny Streams our Sweat descends apace,
> Drops from our Locks, or trickles down our Face.
> No Intermission in our Work we know;
> The noisy Threshal must for ever go.
> Their Master absent, others safely play;
> The sleeping Threshal does itself betray.
> And yet, the tedious Labour to beguile,
> And make the passing Minutes sweetly smile,
> Can we, like Shepherds, tell a merry Tale;
> The Voice is lost, drown'd by the louder Flail.

When he was still in his mid-twenties, patrons began to discover him. In 1730 there was published a pirated volume of his poems, and he was taken up by the Court and received a pension from Queen Caroline. She set him and his wife, Sarah Big Duck, to managing one of her favourite hobbies,

---

[79] [Autumn 1747].   [80] *Letters by Several Eminent Persons Deceased*, II, 148.

[81] Joseph Highmore's Bible, in the possession of his descendants the Morgan-Paylers of Cowes, Phillip Island, Victoria, Australia.

[82] R to Miss Highmore, 2 Aug. 1748; Miss Highmore to R, 2 Jan. 1749; R to Lady Bradshaigh, 9 Jan., 15 Feb. 1750.

the glory of Richmond Gardens, Merlin's Cave, a thatched cottage with Gothic windows, furnished with bookcases containing the pre-romantic Queen's 'small, but choice Collection of Books' and adorned with picturesquely displayed wax-work figures of various allegorical and historical personages, in an atmosphere of Medieval mystery. Pope and Swift, though they seem to have respected Duck's simple character, regarded the popularity of his poetry as a sign of the decline of taste:

> The Thresher *Duck*, could o'er the *Q——* prevail.
> The Proverb says; *No Fence against a Flayl*.
> From *threshing* Corn, he turns to *thresh* his Brains;
> For which Her *M——y* allows him *Grains*.
> Though 'tis confess't that those who ever saw
> His Poems, think them all not worth a *Straw*.
> Thrice happy *Duck*, employ'd in threshing *Stubble*!
> Thy Toil is lessen'd, and thy Profits double.

A later and more enthusiastic tribute, from the learned Mrs. Carter, acknowledging the gift of a volume of his verse, begins by nobly paraphrasing Pope:

> Accept, O Duck, the Muse's grateful lay,
> Who owns a favour which she can't repay.[83]

Richardson had printed for Duck since 1736 and had met him in the same year. Duck admired *Pamela* and was willing to burn all his own poems to be the author of such a work. In 1746 he was admitted to holy orders and in 1752 became rector of the parish of Richardson's ancestors, Byfleet in Surrey. His mind began to fail, and in 1756, in a fit of melancholy, he drowned himself. Richardson wrote to Thomas Edwards, 'Poor Stephen Duck. . . . I had a Value for him, and am much concerned at his unhappy Exit.'[84]

One of Duck's early patrons had been the clergyman Joseph Spence, Fellow of New College and successively Professor of Poetry and Regius Professor of Modern History at Oxford. He was a connoisseur of humble talent: in addition to Duck, he helped discover the poor, blind Scottish poet Thomas Blacklock; 'the poetic footman' (later an eminent bookseller) Robert Dodsley; and Robert Hill, 'the learned tailor of Buckingham'. But his poetic friendships also included the far from humble Alexander Pope, and indeed he is chiefly known today as the collector of anecdotes of Pope which have since been published; he relinquished his plan for a biography in favour of the claims of William Warburton.

---

[83] Montagu Pennington, *Memoirs of the Life of Mrs. Elizabeth Carter* (London, 1808), II, 24.
[84] Hill to R, 21 July 1736; Duck to R, [9 Mar. 1741?]; R to Edwards, 24 Apr. 1756. For Stephen Duck, see James M. Osborn, 'Spence, Natural Genius and Pope', *PQ*, XLV (1966), 125–32. This article also discusses others of Spence's 'natural geniuses'.

Richardson had printed one edition of his *Essay on Mr. Pope's Odyssey* in 1737, but most of the evidence for their friendship is later. On 21 January 1748 we find Spence returning with thanks Richardson's 'contents' (evidently of the unpublished volumes) of *Clarissa*, which he has read with 'those fine emotions which you know I am so fond of'. Later he sent Richardson suggestions for a preface to a new edition of the novel.[85] Richardson told Solomon Lowe that he regarded Spence highly. By 1749 the two men were intimate enough to discuss visits with each other, and Spence (like various others) was asked to 'make North-End his Town-house'.[86] In 1754 Spence numbered Richardson (along with Duck and Dodsley) 'in the little circle of my own most intimate Friends, who have been rais'd purely by their literary Merit and good Characters, from inconsiderable or no Circumstances, to considerable or at least very easy ones'.[87] Either Spence was exaggerating or he did not know Richardson very well before the publication of *Pamela*: Richardson's circumstances in 1740 were by no means inconsiderable, and his moderate affluence was due more to his industry as a printer than to his literary merit.

In 1749 Spence retired to Byfleet, but his connection with Richardson continued. Richardson praised his amiability—Miss Highmore calls him '*Gentle*, Mr. Spence',[88] an epithet confirmed by other accounts of him: he himself remarks that 'Benevolence is more of a Passion, than of a Virtue in me; & ought to be watcht, almost as much as a Vice.'[89] His notebooks of 1755, 1756, 1757, and 1758 show that he occasionally visited Richardson during those years. In 1758 he asked Richardson to observe a cousin of whose character he was in doubt and to whom he was considering leaving money: 'If I did not think that you cou'd penetrate into a man more than any other friend I know, I sd not beg this Favour of you.' Richardson also gave advice to another cousin, named Hall. Spence did not like Hall's leaving his master Whitworth but was ready to approve and to help support him if he found that Hall acted on Richardson's advice; he quoted Hall's sentiments (which may have been written with a view to pleasing his rich cousin) about 'that best of Men, dear Mr Richardson; who sure is dearer to me, than a Father! For his study, is my Welfare. Had you but seen what Goodness overspread his face, when he told me what pleasure it gave him to find I had continu'd so long, & behav'd so well at Mr Whitworth's; sure your heart wou'd have overflow'd with Joy, & the Tears stood in your eyes, as mine did.' Spence at one time considered writing an account of Richardson: Edward Young's curate, the Reverend John Jones, advised him to call on Young, who could furnish 'ample materials

[85] FM XV, 2, fos. 55–6.   [86] Lowe to R, [after 1 Feb. 1749]; R to Spence, 30 Oct. 1749.
[87] *An Account of . . . Mr. Blacklock* (London, 1754), p. 4.
[88] R to Edwards, 28 June 1752.
[89] Notebook of 1755, under Feb., MS. in the James M. and Marie Louise Osborn Collection, Yale University Library.

... relating *to ye life of his late friend Mr. Richardson, the poetical Prose writer'*.[90] But like his biography of Pope, this biography was never written.

Of the men with whom *Pamela* brought Richardson into contact, Ralph Allen was perhaps the most eminent. Though his benevolence may not have exceeded Richardson's, his reputation for benevolence—and his means of practising it—certainly did.

> Let humble ALLEN, with an aukward Shame,
> Do good by stealth, and blush to find it Fame.

The philanthropist of Bath, friend of Pope and Fielding, came as close to being universally admired as any man of his time. Richardson may have met Allen in 1739 when he was arranging advertisements for the General Hospital at Bath, of which Allen was one of the managers.[91] An account of Allen's estate, Prior Park, while it was still being built, had been added to the 1738 edition of Defoe's *Tour* with a poetic compliment to Allen by Mary Chandler; the 1762 edition of the *Tour* adds a further tribute to 'this *great* because *good* Man, who may be styled *The Genius* of Bath'.[92] It has already been said that Allen admired *Pamela* and that Richardson applied to him to help correct it. That Richardson was 'on terms of intimacy' with him, as has been asserted,[93] is not clear, unless one takes intimacy in a very loose sense, but he certainly kept up the connection. When in Bath, he dined at Prior Park; Allen called on him when in town; and Richardson's daughter Polly, when visiting her uncle James Leake in 1753, planned to call on Allen. At that time Richardson's estrangement from William Warburton, who had married Allen's niece, led Richardson to suspect that Allen was being deliberately alienated from him. He had evidently thought so three years earlier when he asked William Lobb, whose father was patronized by Allen, about a rumour that Allen 'was not permitted' to read the last volumes of *Clarissa*. But the connection was not broken by Warburton or anyone else, since as late as 1759 Allen visited Richardson at Parson's Green.[94]

Warburton, as already stated, was also asked to correct *Pamela*, and he and Pope outlined for Richardson an unused plan for continuing that work. It was after his break with Richardson that Warburton rose to be Bishop of Gloucester. When Richardson knew him, he was noted as the author of several argumentative volumes on religion and chiefly as the friend of Pope's last years, who discovered and publicized the orthodoxy

[90] Spence to R, 31 Mar., 3 May 1758, 24 July 1759; Jones to Spence, 3 Sept. 1761, MS. in the Henry E. Huntington Library.

[91] R to Bath General Hospital, 6 Feb. 1739. See also Benjamin Boyce, *The Benevolent Man: A Life of Ralph Allen of Bath* (Cambridge, Mass., 1967), p. 84.

[92] 2nd edn., II, 246–8; 6th edn., II, 292.

[93] Helen Sard Hughes, 'Richardson and Warburton', *MP*, XVII (1919–20), 45n.

[94] R to Edwards, 21 Apr. 1753; R to Lobb, 10 Apr. 1750; R to Young, 24 May 1759.

of the *Essay on Man*, and after Pope's death the self-constituted official interpreter and hierarch of the Pope cult, which was already under attack—and attack suited Warburton's combative nature well. Aaron Hill, by this time an enemy of Pope and Popites, told Richardson of his dislike of Warburton and his work;[95] but when the first two volumes of *Clarissa* appeared, Richardson was still on friendly terms with him, since we find Warburton furnishing a Preface to be published with the third and fourth volumes.[96]

This Preface begins with a brief summary of the history of fiction, which grew out of history but soon became too luxuriant in the barbarous romances of adventure. Spanish fiction is more realistic, but is dry and lacks manners; the French heroical prose romances deal with love and heroism in an artificial manner; the French amatory novels tend to corrupt the heart. At length it was discovered that the one way to make fiction 'really entertaining to an improved mind' is 'by a faithful and chaste copy of real *Life and Manners*: In which some of their [the French] late Writers have greatly excelled'. 'It was on this sensible Plan, that the Author of the following Sheets attempted to please'; his sole object was '*Human Nature*', and the reader who looks for anything but 'a *Faithful Picture of Nature* in *Private Life*' will be disappointed. But if he can find useful entertainment in a history of real life and manners, 'an idle hour or two, we hope, may not be unprofitably lost' (Warburton's style is as hasty and slipshod as his survey of literature).

On 14 April 1748, shortly before the publication of the third and fourth volumes, Richardson thanked Warburton for this Preface. His letter was polite and rather formal: 'I am infinitely obliged to you, Sir, for your charming Paper.' But he suggested two possible objections: the Preface will make even the pretence that the letters are genuine impossible, and Richardson is not acquainted with the French writers referred to. 'But these Points I absolutely submit to your Determination.' On 25 April Warburton agreed with Richardson that the proposed tragic end of the novel was proper, though perhaps Richardson did not relish the slur on his heroine's conduct implied in Warburton's statement that that end was the natural result of 'too great a sensibility & impatience under the force put on her selfe satisfaction'. In the Preface to the third edition he explained that a preface had been thought necessary to the first edition of volumes three and four because of the 'greater distance than was intended' which had elapsed since the publication of the first two volumes. 'A very learned and eminent Hand was so kind as to favour the Editor, at his

[95] 21 July, 29 July 1746.
[96] For a discussion of this preface, see Ronald S. Crane, 'A Note on Richardson's Relation to French Fiction', *MP*, XVI (1918-19), 495-9, and 'Richardson, Warburton and French Fiction', *MLR*, XVII (1922), 17-23.

request, with one. But the occasion of inserting it being *temporary*, and the Editor having been left at liberty to do with it as he pleased, it was omitted in the Second Edition, when the whole Work came to be printed together; as was, for the same reason, the Preface to the first Volume.'[97] The explanation is not entirely convincing, since Warburton's remarks would have been at least as suitable in the first volume of later editions as they were in the third volume of the first.

By the fall of 1749 either the dropping of the Preface or some undiscovered quarrel which preceded it had led to a definite break.[98] At that time Warburton revised his notes to Pope's *Epistle to Augustus*, and in 1751, when the epistle appeared in a new edition of Pope, it had a note to line 146, on the word 'Romance', which is a revised and shortened version of the history of fiction from the Preface to *Clarissa*. Warburton cut the last part, which discussed *Clarissa*, adding instead two sentences which must have seemed a direct challenge to Richardson: 'In this species of writing, Mr. De Marivaux in France, and Mr. FIELDING in England stand the foremost. And by enriching it with the best part of the *Comic* art, may be said to have brought it to its perfection.' (Fielding, incidentally, had already complimented Warburton highly in *Tom Jones*.[99])

By 1753 the quarrel between the two men was an open one. Richardson had called on Allen at Warburton's house, but when he met and addressed Warburton in the Strand, the latter snubbed him in front of Andrew Millar in a way that Richardson took as a deliberate discouragement from calling again. 'I was abundantly confirmed in this Surmize when I found that Mr. Millar had taken Notice to his Wife and Sister of Mr. W——'s Manner of Speech, and Behaviour; and when I was told, that he had designed to shew his Displeasure to me—My Crime is great—He said, that I had in a new Edition of Clarissa, reflected upon his Friend Mr. Pope, by some Passages not in the first (Which, by the Way, I know nothing of); and that I had had *the Insolence*, to present one of them to his Wife.'[100] Warburton must have been referring to a sentence, which is, however, also in the first edition, in which Miss Howe, warning Clarissa against pride, adds: 'Have we not, in the case of a celebrated Bard, observed, that those who aim at more than their due, will be refused the honours they may justly claim?'[101] Richardson later admitted that he had meant this passage as a reference to Pope.[102]

---

[97] I, x; SH, I, xvi; not in EL.
[98] Perhaps McKillop (*Richardson*, pp. 139, 164) is right in stating that Richardson never liked this Preface, especially its hint of his indebtedness to the French, but stood too much in awe of Warburton to refuse it.
[99] Book XIII, Chap. 1.   [100] R to Edwards, 21 Apr.
[101] SH, II, 12; EL, I, 247. See McKillop, *Richardson*, p. 165n, and (for another suggestion) John Carroll, 'Richardson on Pope and Swift', *UTQ*, XXXIII (1963–4), 24.
[102] Edwards to R, 19 Mar. 1756; R to Edwards, 29 Mar. 1756.

H—B.R.

Thomas Edwards's *Canons of Criticism*, a slashing, witty, and cogent attack on Warburton's editing of Shakespeare, appeared in 1748 (Richardson printed the fifth edition of 1753). By early 1750 Miss Sutton suspected that Richardson's love for Edwards made him 'think very unfavourably of another gentleman, whose first patronage was that of her late father'—Sir Robert Sutton.[103] Edwards's letters to Richardson after this date often refer in very unfavourable terms to both Pope and Warburton, and Richardson agreed that the *Essay on Man* was founded on Deism, a fact disguised by Warburton's tinkering editorship and interpretation: 'The Poet and the Parson had layed their heads together to disguise and make it pass for a Christian system.' He approved of Edwards's attack on Warburton's edition of Shakespeare; found Warburton's 'Engraftments' on Pope 'intolerable', and 'from a Christian Divine execrable'; and referred to Warburton as the huffing hero of *The Rehearsal*, Drawcansir. In 1754 Warburton neglected to send Richardson a new work of his, though he had received Richardson's novels from the author. 'His greatness', Richardson remarked, 'might well overlook my Littleness.'[104] That the break was never complete is shown by the fact that, later in the year in which Warburton snubbed Richardson in the Strand, he sent word to him through James Leake that he considered that two volumes of *Sir Charles Grandison* which Richardson had left at Prior Park 'excell his Clarissa'. Six years later, Richardson told Young that Warburton had commended his *Conjectures on Original Composition* and reported a remark on original writing which Warburton had made with 'good humour'. In a letter to Edwards, Richardson expressed the belief that Warburton was envious of Ralph Allen's regard for him: 'My Love for you, and Mr. A——n's Regard for me, of long Standing, were Faults enough in me with a Man of long Views, who wanted to engross a worthy Man.'[105]

Ralph Allen was the 'Worthy Friend and generous benefactor' of another of Richardson's friends, Samuel Lobb.[106] Lobb, a former nonconformist minister who had taken orders in the Church of England, held the living of Farley, or Hungerford Farleigh, six miles from Bath. By 1743 Richardson was intimate enough with him to be asked to serve as godfather to his son Joseph. According to a family tradition, which unfortunately cannot be confirmed, the other godfather was Henry Fielding, who could of course have known Lobb through Allen; Richardson found

---

[103] R to Edwards, 9 Jan.; *DNB*; Helen Sard Hughes, 'Richardson and Warburton', *MP*, XVII (1919–20), 45–50.

[104] Edwards to R, 15 Jan. 1755; R to Edwards, 27 Jan. 1755, 2 May, 27 July 1751; Edwards to R, 19 Dec. 1754; R to Edwards, 30 Dec. 1754.

[105] Warburton to Leake, 3 Sept. 1753, forwarded by Leake to Richardson the same day, MS. owned by Mr. Robert Hill Taylor; R to Young, 24 May, 29 May 1759; R to Edwards, 24 Apr. 1756.

[106] Will of Samuel Lobb, P.C.C. Cheslyn 62, dated 24 Feb. 1758, proved 6 Feb. 1761. For an account of Lobb, see G. Eland, *The Lobb Family* (Oxford, 1955), pp. 45–60.

Lobb's request to act as godfather especially agreeable because of 'the much-respected Persons with whom you do me the Honour to join me' and sent his respects to the gentleman.[107] There is no extant correspondence between Richardson and his godson, who went to Peterhouse in 1759, became a dealer in textiles, and lived on to 1811; but he did write to Samuel's elder son, William, a sizar at Peterhouse in 1751 and a Fellow of the college in 1758, who died in 1765.

By 1746 Lobb, accompanied by William, had visited Richardson at North End, and a correspondence between Richardson and Master Billy (aged about ten) had been proposed: Richardson, though he did not stand on the difference of age, thought that Master Billy should write first: 'I have always made the several young Ladies, who oblige me with their Correspondence, begin first. I would not, that they should put me in Mind of Sex, when I don't intend to think of it: And they may be sure, by my Earnestness in putting them upon Writing to me, that I am very desirous of their Favour: And I am not so sure that they pursue their own voluntary Option, unless they begin first:—Many a pretty Correspondent have I lost, on Account of this Presuming Nicety: But when I want Nature and Ease, not Art and Study, I persist, and put up with ye Loss; taking the Difficulty as a Test of the Delight or Reluctance to ye Correspondence, as they will or will not, get over it.' Richardson was printing a book for Lobb (probably the sermon *The Benevolence Incumbent on Us*, which was published that year) and postponed sending a bill for paper and printing until it appeared whether the discourse would pay for itself. Almost two years later he answered Lobb's request for a bill playfully: 'Lord, Sir, have you no Memory?—My Demand is long ago satisfy'd.— Don't you know, that my Godson paid it?—How can you be so forgetful?' He sent Joseph a mock-formal receipt.[108]

By 10 April 1750 the correspondence with Billy had been established, and Richardson expressed his appreciation of the fourteen-year-old boy's approbation of *Clarissa* and asked him whether either he or his father found 'any thing objectible to Manners, or in other respect'. Though William's father was afraid that Richardson might be offended by his son's neglecting to write and to call on his way to Cambridge, he did call and write at times, and Richardson seemed satisfied with his assurance 'that you would copy into your life and practice, all that was copiable (No academical word, I doubt; but it is mine, not yours.) in your different station, in Sir Charles Grandison'.[109]

We do not know who the young ladies were with whom Richardson had

[107] R to Lobb, 11 May; Lobb to R, 21 May. We are indebted to Mrs. Alan Cory-Wright (*née* Yda Lobb), a descendant of Joseph Lobb, for this family tradition.

[108] R to Lobb, 16 May, 4 July 1746; 12 Jan., 1 Mar. 1748.

[109] R to William Lobb, 29 Dec. 1755; R to Samuel Lobb, 29 Dec. 1755; Samuel Lobb to R, [1755?]; R to Samuel Lobb, 10 Nov. 1756.

corresponded before 1746, but in that year he began writing to Sarah Wescomb. He met her through his landlord at North End, Samuel Vanderplank. Vanderplank, when he died in 1750, had two daughters, one of whom, Hannah, had married a baronet (she had £20,000 dowry, enough to merit such an honour), Sir Edward Hulse, in 1742. The second, Ann, later married a Gilbert Jodrell, who was Vanderplank's heir (Hannah had already got her portion). In 1746 Ann was an intimate friend of Miss Wescomb as well as one of Richardson's many honorary nieces, though she was reluctant to write to him as he desired.[110]

Sarah Wescomb, unlike most of Richardson's young ladies, was not bookish. Her mother, Mary Page, daughter of a South Sea director, had married Daniel Wescomb, also in the South Sea Company, in 1722; he died in 1731, and early in 1737 she married James Jobson, who died before 1746, leaving her 'a widow lady of a large fortune'.[111] She lived, afflicted by gout but not by pecuniary worries, at Enfield, just north of London, with her daughter and a Miss Betsy Jobson, who must have been a step-daughter. She was to become one of Richardson's honorary sisters, but his real intimacy was with her daughter, to whom he wrote copiously throughout a period of over twelve years.

Richardson probably met Miss Wescomb during the summer of 1746 when she was visiting at North End. He urged her to correspond with him, and she dutifully began the correspondence after her return to Enfield. She was soon signing with the pet name she often used later: 'Sarh. Wescomb or Selena ad Libit[um]'. By October he had visited her '*delightful* Villa' and was sending the first volume of the manuscript of *Clarissa* in hopes that she would indicate its faults. By 5 March 1747 she was (with Mamma's approval) his daughter and soon announced her intention of directing her 'future Steps in life' by *Clarissa*. She was constantly modest and appreciated Richardson's kindness in writing to 'a Tittle-Tattle Gentlewoman that never makes any return to your condescending Goodness but an inundation of trumpery Scrible-Scrable'. But at the same time she freely obeyed his injunction to find fault with *Clarissa*, suggesting several longish cuts (like some later readers she found the Harlowes' behaviour to their daughter unnatural).[112]

[110] Will of Samuel Vanderplank, P.C.C. Greenly 98, dated 11 Jan. 1748, proved 24 Mar. 1750; burial of Vanderplank entered under date 23 Mar. in the register of St. Margaret Lothbury (Guildhall MS. 4346/2); *Gentleman's Magazine*, XII (1742), 107; Burke's *Peerage, Baronetage and Knightage*, under Hulse; MS. note by Hulse's descendant E. G. P. E[yre] in the B.M. copy of Dobson's *Richardson*; Miss Wescomb to R, 15 June, 4 Aug. 1748; R to Miss Wescomb, 5 Jan. 1747.

[111] *The Registers of St. Paul's Cathedral*, ed. John W. Clay, Harleian Society Registers, XXVI (1899), 63; MS. register of St. Catherine, Coleman (at the church), under date 14 Sept. 1731; admon. of Daniel Wescomb, 22 Sept. 1731, in P.C.C.; *Gentleman's Magazine*, VII (1737), 60, and XXIV (1754), 484.

[112] Miss Wescomb to R, 22 Aug., 3 Sept., 8 Oct. 1746; R to Miss Wescomb, 13 Oct. 1746; Miss Wescomb to R, 5 Mar., 14 Apr., 21 May 1747.

He was evidently genuinely fond of the girl, and she as evidently deserved it, in spite of or because of her utter lack of intellectual pretensions, even to correct spelling. Their correspondence is almost barren of substance and is as repetitious and trivial as possible. A letter which covers three and a half closely written pages is devoted entirely to raillery about her neglect of him while she was visiting Mrs. Jodrell: 'The agreeable Freedom, the chearful Company and Conversation [Poor N. End!] *within*; made Ankerwyke (naturally delightful) so much more so, by varying your Pleasures, by inventing every Day something new, that it was impossible to think of the poor Papa and Mamma, and Sisters, you had left.' This is a fair enough sample. And after her three-page answer to his teasing, he continued the subject for four more pages and she for still another six.[113] Much of his correspondence is taken up with praising her, especially for her devotion to her sick mother; much of hers with expressing her appreciation and hoping he will not forget her. He finds their letters 'the cement of friendship': 'A proof of this appears in the letter before me!—Every line of it flowing with that artless freedom, that noble consciousness of honourable meaning, which shine in every feature, in every sentiment, in every expression of the fair writer!' He wants to banish all diffidence—'why the diffidence to such a one as I am!—a plain writer: a sincere well-wisher: an undesigning scribbler; who admire none but the natural and easy beauties of the pen'.[114] And indeed her letters are natural and easy, so that, in spite of a certain tedium, understandable in reading someone else's purely personal letters, an impression does come through of a not unattractive relationship between a kindly old man who likes young women and a girl who can best be described as a sweet and simple gentlewoman.

She was obviously also moral. When reporting that the 'Celebrated Miss G—n——gs' (the Misses Gunning) had left Enfield for gayer society, she sarcastically hoped that 'Toupees, Powder, Lace, & Essence (the Composition of the Modern pretty Fellows)' may follow them 'to Stare, and be Stared at, till the more bashful Youths give the first Blush'. Richardson was of course pleased: 'These poor Girls seem too much in haste to make their Fortunes, to catch their Fish. When Women turn *Seekers*, it will not do. Gudgeons may bite; but not even them but by Accident, and thro' Inexperience of the Wiles of Anglers.'[115] Unfortunately, not only virtue is rewarded: Richardson may have been disillusioned when he learned that Maria Gunning married the Earl of Coventry and her sister, Elizabeth, the Duke of Hamilton and, when he died, the Duke of Argyll.

Another young lady with whom Richardson corresponded was Frances

---

[113] 1 Nov., 23 Nov, 5 Dec. 1750; 25 Jan. 1751.   [114] [Late Sept. 1746].
[115] 26 July, 6 Aug. 1750.

Grainger, whose father, Thomas Grainger, was a neighbour of his on Salisbury Court and a pawnbroker.[116] Their correspondence began in December 1748, when she was twenty-two;[117] she had naturally admired *Clarissa*, but only Richardson's assurance could induce her to prefer Miss Howe's virtuous but tame suitor Hickman to the dashing Lovelace. Richardson, who was extremely familar with his own writings and could always be counted on to quote applicable remarks from them, followed up that assurance with detailed, sensible, and proper advice on the choosing of husbands, citing passages from *Clarissa* which proved his views. Miss Grainger had been asked to offer more detailed criticism of *Clarissa* but had declined.[118]

By 9 November 1749 they were on good enough terms for Richardson to write a playful reply to a playful letter in which she reproached him for not writing. He rallied her on her over-passionate heart, joked about her laziness in writing and about her being a demanding woman, hoped her resolution to rise early might be due to his influence (Clarissa was an early riser), and praised her highly. They carried on a friendly argument about the limits of parental authority, in the course of which he held that children should submit even to bad parents but agreed that tyrannical parents are to be blamed and that government by persuasion is best—if she had attended to *Clarissa* 'as more than a Romance', she would have seen that its tenour is to warn both parents and children. But when he presented his arguments over again for three and a half pages, she was still not convinced that she could have submitted to Clarissa's parents. 'O my Miss Grainger,' he lamented, 'you have advanced strange notions, written strange things, on the subject before us, and as far as I can see are not at all changed in your sentiments for all that has been answered, though convinced of the reasonableness of the answers. This is very discouraging in our correspondence.'[119]

It seems to have discouraged her too, since a few months later they had abandoned this subject, which at one time threatened to be inexhaustible, to discuss the cultivation of women's minds. Richardson agreed that such cultivation is desirable in order that women may be '*Companions* and *Friends*, not Slaves and Servants to Men', though women should not neglect their household tasks and become mere pedants. Miss Grainger had evidently taken Clarissa's sentiments on the importance of women's domestic duties as supporting the idea that women should look no further —mistakenly, of course. But such duties are indeed woman's peculiar

---

[116] Guildhall MS. 6561, fo. 32; Corporation of London Records Office Misc. MSS. 83.3; *Daily Journal*, 13 July 1731; Guildhall MS. 3435/R51 (poor rate for 1721, assessed Mar. 1721).

[117] Frances Grainger was born on 31 July 1726. See Guildhall MS. 6550 ('Waste Book Burials and Baptisms 1709-26' of St. Bride's).

[118] R to Miss Grainger, 21 July 1750; 20 Dec. 1748.

[119] R to Miss Grainger, 5 Dec., 21 Dec. 1749; 22 Jan., 1 Feb., 28 Feb., 29 Mar. 1750.

role: 'But in another Edition of Clarissa, I shall a little enlarge upon this very Topic: And print a Number over of the Additions to perfect [the] former Impression.' This proposal not only to make his moral even clearer but to correct editions already out (carried out in *Letters and Passages Restored to Clarissa*) shows the seriousness with which Richardson took his role as preacher. A little later he lectured her on the unfortunate desire of modern girls to be seen and admired in public places: coquettes get no sincere admiration, and Miss Grainger is wrong in thinking that men of sense admire them—he himself admires thirty-six women, listed by initial and concluding with Miss Gr., who are not fools. Richardson's two subsequent letters to her are brief, and perhaps as controversial subjects ran out, their correspondence became less frequent.[120] In 1755 she married the Reverend Fifield Allen, Rector of St. Anne, Aldersgate, and Archdeacon of Middlesex, a widower of about fifty-five; she had a marriage portion of £3,000, the same as Richardson's daughter Mary later received.[121] Richardson, to judge by the variety of tone in his letters, was unusually sensitive to the characters of his correspondents and varied his own style as well as his remarks to suit their interests and capacities; his letters to Miss Grainger are among his dullest—she must have had great patience in discussing ethical issues, partly redeemed by playfulness and a humble but firm stubbornness.

Daughter of another of Richardson's neighbours was Margaret Dutton. Her father, Thomas Dutton, had died in 1741, leaving a widow and two daughters. The elder, Mary, married John Poole in 1742. Her sister, Margaret, at this time about twenty-three,[122] prepared and sold the 'Balsamick Styptick', invented by a Dr. Eaton, a remedy for vomiting, bleeding, and hæmorrhoids which Richardson advertised in *Clarissa*, where Lovelace takes it for his self-induced sickness.[123] Evidently Margaret did not get along with Poole, since towards the end of her life Richardson mentions with indignation that her 'Heart has been broken by a barbarous and most sordid Brother-in-law, with whom it was her hard Fate to live' and that it was her sister's husband who brought on her consumption—though he owed everything to her father.[124] She spent her

---

[120] R to Miss Grainger, 21 July, 6 Aug., 8 Sept., 2 Nov. 1750; 28 Sept. 1751.

[121] MS. register of St. James's, Piccadilly (at the church), under date 6 Feb. 1755; will of Thomas Grainger, P.C.C. Jenner 102, dated 3 May 1769, proved 26 Mar. 1770.

[122] Admon. of Thomas Dutton, Nov. 1741, in P.C.C. Mary's baptism is entered in the St. Bride's 'Register 1714–36' (Guildhall MS. 6540/4) and in 'Waste Book Burials and Baptisms 1709–26' (Guildhall MS. 6550), under date 9 July 1716. The marriage of John and Mary Poole is recorded in the register of St. Margaret's, Westminster (MS. at the church). Margaret's burial is recorded in the St. Bride's register on 29 Dec. 1756 (Guildhall MS. 6543/1), where her age is given as thirty-eight.

[123] SH, IV, 280, 294; EL, II, 427, 436; *Daily Journal*, 1 Sept. 1731; *Daily Gazetteer*, 3 Feb. 1739; *London Chronicle*, 8–10 May 1759.

[124] R to Sally Righton, 14 Dec. 1756; R to Mrs. Scudamore, 5 Dec. 1756; R to Sarah Fielding, 7 Dec. 1756, 17 Jan. 1757; R to Mrs. Sheridan, 19 Dec. 1756.

last months at Richardson's country retreat at Parson's Green, where she thought herself in heaven, but the air and quiet failed to cure her, and she died there. Her niece Mary Poole, born in 1743, was one of Richardson's youngest admirers, and much later gave Mrs. Barbauld some valuable reminiscences of the novelist.[125]

It seems to have been while he was composing *Clarissa* that Richardson first met Jane and Margaret Collier and their friend Sarah Fielding. Arthur Collier, father of the sisters, had been a High Church clergyman and a metaphysician whose system is said to resemble Berkeley's; before his death in 1732 he was reduced to selling the advowson of his living, Langford Magna in Wiltshire. His two daughters were childhood friends of the Fieldings in Salisbury. Sarah Fielding was in her middle thirties at this time; aside from her older brother, Henry, and a younger brother, Edmund, she had three surviving sisters, Catherine, Ursula, and Beatrice, all of whom died within a year in 1750–1. In 1744 she had published her first novel, *The Adventures of David Simple*, and in 1747 a continuation, *Familiar Letters between the Principal Characters in David Simple, and Some Others*, to which Richardson subscribed. In its epistolary form the *Familiar Letters* can be regarded as an imitation (at some distance) of *Pamela*.

In 1749 Richardson printed Miss Fielding's *The Governess*. By 1748 he was friendly enough to suggest to Jane Collier that a passage in it about severe punishment of scholars be changed to make it clear that corporal punishment was not meant. Miss Collier did not think the change should be adopted, since it might offend the Thwackums, but the author left the matter entirely up to Richardson, to change if he wished. After the publication of *The Governess* Edward Young pointed out its descent from *Clarissa*: 'I have read Miss Fielding with great pleasure. Your Clarissa is, I find, the Virgin-mother of several pieces; which, like beautiful suckers, rise from her immortal root.'[126]

Both Jane Collier and Sarah Fielding were among *Clarissa*'s defenders. The former was irritated that women seemed to be so fond of Lovelace. Richardson referred to her the Reverend Philip Skelton's objection to the fire scene in *Clarissa*, and she assured him that it was not calculated to inflame a woman, but could arouse only pity.[127] She was so vexed at some objections which appeared in the *Gentleman's Magazine* in June and August 1749[128] that she drafted an answer but thought better of sending it and sent it instead to Richardson to do with as he pleased; she cannot bear to hear Clarissa called the younger sister of Pamela, as if she should

[125] Register of St. Bride's, under date 17 Nov. 1743 (Guildhall MS. 6541/1); Barbauld, I, clxxxii–cxc; Eaves and Kimpel, 'Samuel Richardson's London Houses', pp. 144n–5n.
[126] Jane Collier to R, 4 Oct. 1748; Young to R, 5 Nov. 1749.
[127] Jane Collier to R, 13 Apr., 9 July 1749.
[128] XIX, 245–6, 345–9.

yield place to her elder, 'and if not to Her not to any one upon Earth'.[129]

Miss Fielding did even more: she wrote the *Remarks on Clarissa* published anonymously in January 1749. She told Richardson the day after its publication that she longed for his own 'easy and nervous style' in her 'daring attempt of mentioning Clarissa'. 'In short, Sir, no pen but your's can do justice to Clarissa. Often have I reflected on my own vanity in daring but to touch the hem of her garment.'[130] Another of Henry Fielding's sisters also admired *Clarissa* (as indeed Henry himself did): Ursula rejoiced to hear that the book was almost out, and wondered who could name the sweet heroine without a tear.[131]

By 1750 one of the Misses Collier was staying with Richardson as part of his family. In 1753 he printed Jane Collier's *An Essay on the Art of Ingeniously Tormenting*, a moderately witty series of instructions on how to torture husbands, wives, servants, friends, lovers, and so on. As examples of how to make children miserable she cites impartially, from her new friend and her old, old Harlowe and Squire Western.[132] The next year she and Sarah Fielding collaborated on *The Cry*. This book Richardson sent to Lady Bradshaigh as 'written by a Lady who has a good Heart as well as Head'; Lady Bradshaigh found it rather languid and objected to its defence of the author of *Joseph Andrews*, at which Richardson admired her judgement and informed her that it was written by Henry's sister. He also sent a copy to Miss Wescomb, and at her request for an opinion told her that though the book had natural strokes and a knowledge of the heart, its end was poorly managed.[133]

Miss Fielding seems to have had a less moderate admiration for *Sir Charles Grandison*, since she found that two ladies who agreed to read it together and did not take an unlawful peep between whiles made credible the fable of Patient Grizzle.[134]

Jane Collier died between the middle of 1754 and the fall of 1755. Her sister Margaret had accompanied Henry Fielding on the voyage to Lisbon on which he died and in 1755 settled at Ryde, on the Isle of Wight, in a modest cottage with a good but almost illiterate old couple, whom she entertained by reading *Clarissa* and *Sir Charles*. Her life there must have been very lonely, but it was for a while relieved by a correspondence with

[129] 19 Sept. 1749. 'June' is written by someone on the MS. of the letter, but her enclosed answer to the objections in the *Gentleman's Magazine* is dated 19 Sept. (FM XV, 2, fo. 33).

[130] 8 Jan. For the identification of Sarah Fielding as the author of the *Remarks*, see T. C. Duncan Eaves and Ben D. Kimpel, 'Richardsoniana', *SB*, XIV (1961), 232.

[131] J. Paul de Castro, 'Ursula Fielding and "Tom Jones"', *N&Q*, CLXXVIII (1940), 164.

[132] Pp. 87–8.

[133] R to Hester Mulso, 13 July 1750; R to Lady Bradshaigh, 14 Feb. 1754; Lady Bradshaigh to R, 22 Mar. 1754; R to Lady Bradshaigh, 8 Apr. 1754; Sarah Wescomb to R, 16 July, 7 Aug. 1754; R to Sarah Wescomb, 9 Aug. 1754.

[134] To R, 6 July 1754.

Richardson. She described her abode, and they discussed the charms of intellectual women. She brought up the subject by complaining that Fielding's *Voyage to Lisbon* had been ascribed to her because it was so much below his other works; Richardson blamed women for hiding 'their talents in a napkin' because they 'are afraid, lovely dastards, of shewing themselves capable of the perfections they are mistresses of', and she ended the subject with the unfortunately true remark that men do not care for intellectual rivalry in their spouses and that the 'dear uncommon geniusses' would hardly find husbands unless they had the fortune to meet with a Sir Charles Grandison. Richardson once sent her five guineas to buy a door for her room, to keep off the cold.[135] Their correspondence was, however, desultory, and her last letter is dated 4 February 1757.

Nor did his relationship with Sarah Fielding remain very close. In 1756 she went to Bath for the waters and was still seeing Richardson shortly before she left. By the spring of 1758 she had settled there.[136] There was some correspondence between her and Richardson; he printed her *Lives of Cleopatra and Octavia* in 1757 and *The History of the Countess of Dellwyn* in 1759. He and his wife subscribed for six copies of the former. Her last extant letter to him concerns the latter book: she asked Richardson to keep an eye on the printing personally if his health permitted and to alter any expressions he disliked.[137] Richardson's connection with Henry Fielding's sister and friends was fairly close for a brief period, and he never quarrelled with them, but they were not among his closest intimates.

Richardson's world, then, had grown wider when he was writing his second novel; it had expanded to include more people connected with society and with things of the intellect. This fact is reflected in the social class of his characters and may be partly responsible for a more important change, an increased awareness of the issues involved. It is hard not to smile or even laugh at Pamela's naïveté, especially when she is complacently contemplating the rewards of her chastity; but Clarissa does not allow us to laugh at her, and whatever her system of ethics may be, it is not naïve. Richardson's new friends are not sufficient to explain the great superiority of his second novel to his first, but negatively they may have helped make him too sophisticated for certain absurdities.

[135] 3 Oct., 24 Dec. 1755; 11 Feb. 1756; 24 Dec. 1755.

[136] R to Sarah Fielding, [autumn], 7 Dec. 1756; R to Mrs. Sheridan, 19 Dec. 1756; R to Thomas Sheridan, 9 Apr. 1758.

[137] 4 Dec. 1758. A letter dated 'Oct. 2 (1759)' was sold by Sotheby's on 15 Dec. 1954, item 755.

CHAPTER X

THE COMPOSITION OF *CLARISSA*
LADY BRADSHAIGH

THERE is no evidence that Richardson had a real-life story to give him the idea for *Clarissa*, as he had for *Pamela*, and he himself categorically denied having had one: 'Clarissa is a Piece from first to last, that owes its Being to Invention.'[1] He may have drawn on experience for some of his characters. Lovelace, for instance, may owe something to the wild friend whose improbable and bigamous adventures we have described in Chapter I. Richardson wrote to Hill that he had in his eye 'something that I had seen Years ago' and that in drawing both Lovelace and Mr. B. he remembered the character of a gentleman he had known, taking the best of the gentleman for the latter and the worst for the former, 'made still worse by mingling the worst of two other Characters, that were as well known to me, of that Gentleman's Acquaintance'. To Mrs. Chapone he wrote that he 'put the Iniquity of two or three bad Characters together' to make Lovelace: 'But tho I have had Ideas of this or that Person before me in *parts* no one Person Man or Woman sat before me for the *whole* of any of my Pictures.' For Mrs. Harlowe, Richardson told Hill that he had a real model. Miss Howe and Clarissa herself are, he said, entirely the creatures of his fancy. He stated that both *Pamela* and *Clarissa* are 'laid 15 or 20 Years before their respective Publication', but this does not indicate an actual history as the basis of *Clarissa*.[2]

When he got the idea for *Clarissa* is uncertain, but he had the outline of the story well in mind before 20 June 1744, when Young wrote to him defending the character of Lovelace and the proposed tragic ending of the novel against 'Your critics'.[3] More than one other person, therefore, was already familiar with Richardson's plans and had objected to the sufferings

[1] To Stinstra, 2 June 1753. McKillop (*Richardson*, pp. 108–20) believes that he sees a germ of the situation in a long passage cut from the first edition of the continuation of *Pamela*, a poem concerning a brilliant libertine who courts a lady named Maria but is repulsed by her surly uncle. The similarity to Clarissa's history hardly goes beyond this, except that the libertine, like Lovelace, is kind to his tenants.

[2] To Hill, 5 Jan., 26 Jan. 1747; to Mrs. Chapone, 25 Mar. 1751; to Lady Bradshaigh, 25 Feb. 1754.

[3] For a detailed account of the composition of *Clarissa*, see T. C. Duncan Eaves and Ben D. Kimpel, 'The Composition of *Clarissa* and Its Revision before Publication', *PMLA*, LXXXIII (1968), 416–28.

of an innocent heroine. He could hardly have begun the book before May 1742, when he finished his work on the octavo *Pamela* and on Defoe's *Tour*. During the two following years there is no evidence at all, but that period could have given him ample time to finish a first draft of *Clarissa*.

One would have expected the first comment on the new novel from Aaron Hill, and on 24 July 1744 Hill wrote: 'I have, again and again, re-perused and reflected on that good and beautiful design I send you back the wide and arduous plan of. It is impossible, after the wonders you have shewn in Pamela, to question your infallible success in this new, natural, attempt. But you must give me leave to be astonished, when you tell me you have finished it already!' What the last sentence means is open to conjecture, but on the face of it, the letter says that Richardson has finished his novel.

By November Richardson was preparing to send a part of his manuscript to Hill with the request that he try to cut it; Hill protested that he could not prune 'in Alleys wch you have yourself been trimming'. From the first Richardson was worried about the length of his new novel, though he was never able to reduce it much. Once Richardson began to send it, his manuscript reached Hill in frequent and long instalments, and from the end of 1744 on, his correspondence keeps us pretty well informed on the stages of its composition.

On 8 December Young inquired about Richardson's progress in his book ('I long to enjoy it; for I value the heart much from which it comes'). In reply Richardson said that because of the press of business 'I have not gone so far as I thought to have done by this time.—Then the unexpected success that attended the other thing, instead of encouraging me, has made me so diffident!—And I have run into such a length!—And am such a sorry pruner, though greatly luxurient, that I am apt to add three pages for one I take away! Altogether I am frequently out of conceit with it. Then I have nobody that I can presume to advise with on such a subject.—But last week, indeed, I took the liberty to send the beginning of it to my indulgent friend, Mr. Hill, whose sincerity I cannot doubt; but whose favour to me makes him so partial, that, if he approve, I shall not be without my diffidences. But if he prunes it, as I have requested he will, without mercy, then perhaps shall I have the courage to proceed with more alacrity.'

The first *Clarissa* to be submitted for Hill's criticism (perhaps the second to be written) arrived in a series of vellum volumes with blank pages interleaved for Hill's comments. By April Hill was reading in the second quarter of the novel and was ready to agree that it might, perhaps, be somewhat shorter, since Richardson had told him that these volumes admitted 'only to the Portico, or *Hall* at most, of your delightful Building'. But he himself was never tired of reading, and Richardson was not to be judged by a criticism drawn from the practice of other writers, being 'a Species, in a single Pen'. In another letter he apologized for his delay in returning the volumes but explained that his guilt was owing to the charms of the book and hoped he would not be punished by not being tempted in future: 'I will promise to *reform*;—but, for *repentance*, I disclaim it utterly.'

By June 1745 Mrs. Pilkington and Colley Cibber were discussing Clarissa's impending rape, and by the end of that year Richardson was approaching Clarissa's death. On 26 November Young wrote: 'What a heart have you to draw in *Clarissa*'s final determination! The more I think of that occasion, the more am I smitten with it.' Richardson sent him a letter between the heroine's rape and her deathbed to which Young suggested some pious additions, and on 3 December Richardson thanked him for his 'admirable additions' but proposed to 'insert them rather nearer the hour of her death, because in this letter I do not make her so fully able to die in charity with Lovelace, as she hopes she shall do'. Cibber had also submitted additions, with which Richardson was not so well pleased since they were too passionate for the comparatively cool mood he wanted Clarissa to be in above a month after the injury—he wanted her 'to touch with *warmth* the subject, but not with *passion*, that her determination may be the result of deliberation'.

By the beginning of 1746 Richardson had begun a thorough revision, trying especially to reduce the bulk of the novel. A few weeks later we find that he had done a great deal of revision of the earlier sections. It was, he told Hill, to whom he was still sending his work for suggestions, 'mostly new, or alter'd much from what you saw it before'. He had taken out the blank leaves 'that I might be less frighted at the Bulk' but asked Hill to insert loose papers with his corrections. 'Several Persons have seen them in the Interim; not always with my Inclination: Yet I hoped to benefit by them more than I have. I have run them over since any Body saw them, and alter'd again. Being extremely, yet justly diffident. But will shew them to no body after they have your Perusal; and, as I hope, Correction.— Another Parcel will be ready to attend you, if your Goodness to the Scribbler will give you Patience with his Scribble. Length, is my principal Disgust, at present. Yet I have shorten'd much more than I have lengthen'd.' Friends 'have been free upon some Parts of it', and 'where-ever my Mind was upon the *Balance*, or doubtful, I have given it against my self'. Some of his alterations, then, had been the result of criticism— but only when he was not fully decided himself. He cited Dr. and Mrs. Heylin, Miss Peggy Cheyne, Dr. Freke and a friend of Freke's, Young, and Cibber as the persons who had seen his manuscript. But nobody has seen it 'as it now stands. And they would think it a new Thing were they to see it.' Hill, as he had done in the case of *Pamela*, opposed Richardson's

tendency to over-revise, but he admired the 'new Face' of *Clarissa*—
'what an infinite Deal of charming Pains, and Patience—and self-
castigation & Humility beyond Example! are the Public in your Debt for
—if you have gone through your other Volumes, of the sweet *Clarissa*,
with the same unwearied Vigilance, of Judgment over Genius'. He found
that Richardson had '*added* Beauties' and thrown 'a *closer*, and a stronger,
Light' on previous beauties; but he could not, as requested, find any
comments to make, and he considered Richardson's design of shortening
too timorous and hoped he would use the sponge less on the rest of the
book. He thought of marking passages to convince 'your curtailing
Friends', as well as 'many Places, where the timid Care that has been
taken to *improve* a Phrase, or an Expression, substitutes, sometimes an
elegant Propriety, of Stiffness, where, before, there shone a native
Negligence of undress'd Loveliness, and picturesque Simplicity.—But,
This is almost Everywhere so frequent, (and *must*, unavoidably, be found
so, when so natural an easy Pensil as your own admits of Strokes from
a more *labour'd* Painfullness, under the Name of *Finishings*) that It were
Endless to attempt particularizing it.—Hard, well-roll'd Gravel Walks,
(it might be own'd) are necessary Ornaments in *Gardens*: But the very
best of 'em, wou'd only serve, to cover Flowers, and spoil a *Meadow*.' Hill
was probably right. Richardson's talent depended not on correctness and
care but on the vividness of his conception. His efforts to revise *Pamela*
led to minor gains in consistency and propriety at the cost of freshness and
immediacy. Hill, though himself learned and uninspired, appreciated from
the first Richardson's strong point. One would guess that during its long
revision *Clarissa* lost at least as much as it gained.

Both Hill and Young lost touch with *Clarissa* during the summer of
1746, and both expected the book to appear soon. On 15 September Hill
learned that Richardson had drawn up a compendium of the novel and on
23 October wrote that he had reperused the 'beautiful *Compendium* . . .
over and over again—With new Emotions, never felt before, from a
Compendium only!' By this time there were thirty manuscript volumes, and
Hill agreed that some cutting might be necessary, retrenching repetitions
of the same narrative and using connective notes. He also advised softening Lovelace's conduct to Clarissa's brother and wondered whether he
was wrong in wishing Clarissa in 'downright Love' before the duel. The
latter point was particularly touchy—Richardson never wanted Clarissa
clearly to acknowledge her love. Hill offered to think (not to advise) about
shortening when Richardson decided how many volumes he wanted.
Richardson showed his letter to another friend and added the friend's
comments to the manuscript of the letter. Now that Hill (with considerable urging) had yielded to suggest changes, the friend assumed Hill's
former role of enthusiastic opposition to any alteration. Hill, it seems,

would substitute another character for the author's Lovelace, and making Clarissa in love with him would equate her with any giddy girl who runs away with her father's footman. The advice of abridging is fatal—what beauties do such hewers not despoil us of?

On 29 October Richardson thanked Hill for his suggestions. He had already greatly shortened, though not half enough. He was perplexed by the contradictory advice of his advisers. Dr. Heylin thought that if anything must be cut it should be sweated out of the whole, whereas Cibber was for taking away whole branches—the very branches Young would not part with. He had already tried Hill's plan of putting 'many of the Repetitions of the same Facts, as Lovelace, and as the Lady gave them, by way of Notes', but had altered them back again since Lovelace's 'wicked Levity' turned 'into a kind of unintended Ridicule half the serious and melancholy Reflections, which she makes on her Situation'. But he had preserved 'only those Places in his, where his Humour, and his Character are shewn, and his Designs open'd', and had 'put many others, into a merely Narrative Form, referring for the Facts to hers, &c. So of some of hers, vice-versâ'. He had tried to make the unyielding opposition of Clarissa's family more credible, he had made Lovelace's conduct in his duel with Clarissa's brother more moderate, but he did not intend Lovelace to be amiable. He had read Lovelace's death to a young lady of seventeen and was so upset at her tears for the villain that he had resolved to 'make him still more and more odious, by his heighten'd arrogance and Triumph, as well as by vile Actions'. He changed Lovelace's first letter to make it clear that his love was never honourable but that from the beginning he thought of seduction. He did not agree with Hill about Clarissa's being in downright love but accepted Hill's offer to help abridge.

On 5 November Hill replied, agreeing to Richardson's views on Lovelace and Clarissa and making another suggestion: if the title were simply *Clarissa*, readers would think that the heroine, like Pamela, was meant for an example; he suggested 'The Lady's Remembrancer: Or, The Way of a YOUNG MAN, with a MAID'. Richardson's comment on this, written in the margin, was '!!!' Richardson often said that he wanted Clarissa to have faults, but he never wanted her to be criticized. On 20 November Hill, hesitantly and with many words of praise, suggested that Richardson might send him one of his written copies, which he could try, on separate papers, to amend according to Dr. Heylin's plan; if Richardson approved of his beginning, he would then go on with the rest.

In the fall of 1746 and early in 1747 Richardson was also sending instalments of *Clarissa* to his new friend Sarah Wescomb, asking her to return the manuscript with 'some pinn'd-on pieces of paper, of corrections and observations'. She reported that Clarissa's arguments in her afflictions were soothing to her own mother in her gout and hoped that the book 'may ever bear upon my Mind direct my future Steps in Life show what is truely comendable for our imitation'. Timidly and humbly, she obeyed Richardson's request to find some faults. 'The story is pretty long', she wrote, and among the scenes which might be cut are Lovelace's courting Clarissa's sister Arabella (which is improbable in view of his dislike of marriage), some of the impertinence of the servant Betty, and Lovelace's abortive and rather absurd scheme of abducting Miss Howe and her mother on their way to the Isle of Wight and raping both of them. And is not the heroine too lofty to Lovelace after she is in his power? In a later letter she had more cuts to suggest: some of the rather trifling conversation at Hampstead, the brother and sister there 'coming in on her shrieking out', and the multitude of mourners at Clarissa's funeral—'dont you think as there is so many Characters all in the same turn of Thought, that Mrs. Hervey at least might have been left at home, since without her their seems (I believe) enough to compass this Tragical End?' And the infatuation of all members of Clarissa's family seems to her unnatural. Perhaps Richardson should have let Selena play the role of Molière's old woman.

Meanwhile, on 22 December 1746, Hill wrote that he was almost ready to send a cut version of the first letters as a specimen of the best he could do in shortening. If he had hit Richardson's purpose, he would go on.

Hill claimed that 'there was nothing in these *Transcrips* but what was literally *your own*' except a few connective phrases, and though he did add a little more than he said he had, his abridgement gives us a measure of how much Richardson's draft differed from his published version. The language is hardly ever exactly the same and several scenes are almost unrecognizable. The wording of the draft was less elevated—Richardson polished, sometimes at the cost of colloquial freshness, as he had in *Pamela*. In the interest of propriety, he softened Miss Howe's and Clarissa's remarks against the latter's family and removed a passage in which Clarissa feared that her unwelcome suitor Solmes was coming to her chamber. The first two letters were completely rewritten and a letter between them, from a surgeon describing the duel between Lovelace and Clarissa's brother, was cut.

Richardson's reaction to the abridgement was polite but unhappy. He was amazed at Hill's pains, but it would be a waste of time and effort to go on much further in 'an Undertaking so groveling and puerile' for Hill's great pen, since *Clarissa* is '*principally* suitable to the Years and Capacities of Persons under Twenty of the one Sex, and under Thirty of the other'. Hill would surely not be displeased if he used the abridgement only as a guide and did not copy it. Richardson objected specifically to a change making Lovelace more gentlemanly, which implied a different concept of the character than the one Richardson had formed; he was always most unwilling to accept any suggestions about his characterization. Lovelace was an original type: 'I intend in him a new Character, not confined to usual Rules.' But he would welcome some more specimens of Hill's cutting, which might be of use. 'If the Piece, after all, should be too unconscionably long; and if I should, nevertheless, ever resolve to put it to the Press my self, and not rather leave it to the Determination of my Executors, as I early intended', he would publish only one volume at first and wait to see how it was received. In the context of Richardson's hurt feelings, there is no reason to take this hesitation to publish very seriously.

Hill was perplexed and concerned and answered that he had only tried to carry out Richardson's intention: Richardson should now see by the sample that Hill was right, that *Clarissa* could not be shortened. He could not go on with his abridgement—everything he tried to cut was beautiful; he had thrown away almost twice as much of the altered *Clarissa* as he had sent. He still disagreed, however, with Richardson's intention to blacken Lovelace's character—a completely black Lovelace would ruin the moral effect, since no young lady would think herself in danger of such a wretch—each would think *her* Lovelace too different. And Lovelace must not be too bad for Clarissa to love—only love could justify her going away with him.

This last objection brought up two points always most delicate for Richardson, Clarissa's guilt in running away and the degree of her love for her ravisher. Richardson answered that he was sorry Hill had destroyed an abridgement which could have proved useful to him as a model, though he might have restored some passages which other friends liked. He would consider the advice about Lovelace—doubtless Hill was right. But he had in mind men he had known, and 'aimed at an uncommon' though 'not quite unnatural Character'. He had already revised in an effort to clarify Clarissa's motives for running away with Lovelace and was considering further revision in this connection. He obviously did not want anyone to think that she was at fault in the elopement. Two very delicate females whom he had consulted had said they themselves would have been '*tricked off*' by such a determined 'Contriver'. And he *did* intend Clarissa as an example—her only voluntary fault is that of meeting Lovelace, and in her preparations for death he had hoped to make this a much nobler and more useful story than Pamela's. 'But since I find my principal Design and End so liable to be misapprehended; and the Story so likely to be thought *Inferior*, which I thought *Superior*, bating the supposed Tragical (tho' I think it *Triumphant*) Catastrophe, which cannot recommend it as to Sale, as a prosperous and *rewarded Virtue* could (In the one I looked principally to Happiness with respect to the Enjoyments of this Life; in the other, beyond them, and to which all should aspire, and the more for their Calamities) since this, I say, is the Case, I think to sit down where I am: And at present, my natural Diffidences being so much and so justly augmented, I have no Intention to trouble the World for its Opinion; and am only sorry for the Trouble and Perplexity I have given by it to a Gentleman to whom I wish to be able to give Pleasure, and nothing else.' He proceeded to discuss the printing of Hill's own pieces: 'And now, Sir, if you will look upon me in the Light I ought only to wish or aim to appear in, that of a Printer (A Business more than sufficient to take up all my Time and Attention).' He would go on through his present reading of *Clarissa*, being already in 'the 4th. Century of Letters (Monstrous Number!); and then shall let the poor Unhappy sleep!' Richardson's hurt feelings are obvious, but anyone whose own work has been criticized or who has seen the effect of his criticism of someone else's work may be indulgent enough not to laugh much.

Hill replied that he was now convinced 'that nothing *should be* shorten'd, further than you have already marked the Places (and in some of those, I think, not quite so much)', and later wrote hoping that Richardson had not mistaken his meaning. But he continued to urge that Clarissa must *not* meet Lovelace privately; her going to him voluntarily (as of course she does in the final version) would injure the book's moral effect. And Lovelace must be made less profligate, less indelicate—when Richardson said that new characters are not confined by rules, he surely did not mean by 'the Rules of *Nature*, or of Reason'.

No answer to these last two letters is extant. There is a gap in the correspondence of almost nine months. Perhaps letters have been lost and there was no real quarrel. But Hill was evidently no longer consulted on *Clarissa*, since when he wrote in November to inquire about the book's progress, Richardson promptly sent him the first volumes in print. There had been many more alterations since Hill had seen the manuscript; he commented on the 'many beautiful, and finely-judged, *Increases*, and *Subtractions*, you have made, in these two Leading Pieces'.

Young, who happily avoided giving adverse criticisms or suggestions, continued to urge that the book be completed and regretted the multiplicity of affairs which distracted Richardson from it: 'Though we are told that Venus rose from the sea, yet I do not remember that it was from the sea in a storm; which seems to me no unapt resemblance of your London life.' On 17 May 1747 he wrote: 'As for the request you are pleased to make me, about Clarissa, if I am better qualified for it than yourself, you may command my utmost in it.' Perhaps Richardson had asked him for a preface, for more pious reflections, or for a justification of the tragic ending such as was later included in the Postscript to the last volume.

Highmore sent some notes on the Preface, most of which were not used. Specifically Richardson did not adopt Highmore's suggestion that

Lovelace be made an atheist. Heylin suggested a minor change in the title page, which was adopted.

By November Richardson was finally ready to publish. It had been well over three years since he had begun, possibly a good deal longer. For at least a year and a half the first version of the novel had been complete. For two years Richardson had been mainly occupied in revising, in seeking criticism and aid, and in trying to shorten. He had made at least two thoroughgoing revisions and had cut a number of letters (or parts of them) that covered the same events as others as well as some scenes, poems, and meditations, but the book was still longer than he wished. He had asked many people for advice, but he had adopted advice only on minor matters. From the first mention of the novel he had had its general plan firmly in mind, and he held to his own conception of the story and especially of the characters. He may well have written his first version rapidly, as he had *Pamela*, before consulting anyone; but he thought about the novel carefully and took great pains with it before publishing.

On 19 November Richardson wrote to Young that the beginning was printed: 'What contentions, what disputes, have I involved myself in with my poor Clarissa, through my own diffidence, and for want of a will! I wish I had never consulted any body but Dr. Young, who so kindly vouchsafed me his ear, and sometimes his opinion. Two volumes will attend your commands, whenever you please to give me your direction for sending them. I think I shall publish in about a fortnight.' 'Miss Lee', he added, 'may venture . . . to read these two to you. But Lovelace afterwards is so vile a fellow, that if I publish any more I don't know (so much have some hypercritics put me out of conceit with my work) whether she, of whose delicacy I have the highest opinion, can see it as from you or me.—And yet I hope, at worst, there will be nothing either in the language or sentiments that may be so very censurable, as may be found in the works of some very high names.'

On 1 December 1747 the first two volumes were advertised in the newspapers, for sale at six shillings bound, and sold by J. Osborn, A. Millar, J. and J. Rivington, R. Dodsley, and J. Leake. At the end of Volume II the heroine was left at St. Albans, in the power of Lovelace, having just abandoned her house and family.

In his Preface to these volumes Richardson anticipates objections to the immorality of his leading male correspondents, Lovelace and Belford, by pointing out that these two gentlemen are not 'Infidels or Scoffers', that Lovelace 'preserves a Decency' in his language 'not always to be found in the Works of some of the most celebrated modern Writers' whose subjects might give less warrant to such liberties, and that his friend repents, 'antidoting the Poison'. He justifies the length, which he had struggled so hard to correct, on the grounds that letters written 'while the

Hearts of the Writers must be supposed to be wholly engaged in their Subjects' must abound with 'what may be called *instantaneous* Descriptions and Reflections' and with 'affecting Conversations', and that 'the Lives, Characters, and Catastrophes' of others besides the heroine are included. But, he adds, the editor 'was so diffident in relation to this Article of *Length*' that he submitted the letters to 'the Perusal of several judicious Friends'. One of these friends advised him to turn the letters into a narrative and to cut the secondary characters and collateral incidents. This was probably, as Aaron Hill guessed, Colley Cibber,[4] since Richardson mentions his age as a reason which might make his 'half-tired Mind' aim 'at little more than *Amusement*' and therefore not value the instructive passages so important to youth. But the others 'insisted, that the Story could not be reduced to a Dramatic Unity, nor thrown into the Narrative Way, without divesting it of its Warmth; and of a great Part of its Efficacy; as very few of the Reflections and Observations, which they looked upon as the most useful Part of the Collection, would, then, find a Place'. These friends were of the opinion that in such works the story should serve as a '*Vehicle* to the more necessary INSTRUCTION'; but their interest was not entirely moral, since they also saw that making the scenes 'less busy' would make them languid and deprive the work of variety. 'Others, likewise gave *their* Opinions. But no Two being of the same Mind, as to the Parts which could be omitted, it was resolved to present to the World, the Two First Volumes, by way of Specimen.' If they met with a good reception, two others would follow. The purpose of the book, which was to be made clear in the future volumes, was twofold: to 'caution Parents against the undue Exertion of their natural Authority over their Children, in the great Article of Marriage' and to warn 'Children against preferring a Man of Pleasure to a Man of Probity, upon that dangerous, but too commonly received Notion, *That a Reformed Rake makes the best Husband*'. Richardson never tired of quoting this maxim (which *Pamela* had certainly not helped to discountenance) to his friends, always with detestation.

In his second volume Richardson had made his heroine, in her melancholy, set to music a 'charming ODE to WISDOM, which does honour to our Sex, as it was written by one of it':

> Beneath Her clear discerning Eye
> The visionary Shadows fly
>   Of Folly's painted Show.
> She sees thro' ev'ry fair Disguise,
> That All but VIRTUE's solid Joys,
>   Are Vanity and Woe.

---

[4] 3 Dec. 1747.

He printed the ode as well as the music, evidently contributed by a friend. The ode was written by Elizabeth Carter, the 'celebrated' Mrs. Carter, learned spinster of Deal and future translator of Epictetus. She was not pleased at seeing it in public and wrote to Richardson to that effect: 'To print any thing without the consent of the person who wrote it, is a proceeding so very ungenerous and unworthy of a man of reputation, that, from the character I have heard of you, I am utterly at a loss how to account for it.' Richardson replied at once: 'a worthy Kinswoman, Miss Elizabeth Long her Name', had showed him the poem 'as a Piece she knew I should admire'. She had seen it on a visit to Wiltshire and had had a copy sent her. Richardson 'wanted not Matter for the Piece I had then ready for the Press'—he had indeed 'a Redundance of it' and had already parted with 'several beautiful Transcripts from our best Poets' which he had inserted to enliven a work 'which perhaps is too solemn'. But he was so pleased with the ode that he asked his kinswoman to write to Wiltshire to see if anyone would object to his inserting it. She could not discover who the authoress was, but as she had seen several copies without restriction, she assumed that no offence could be given. Having the work set to music and engraved caused him trouble and expense and brought no profit, so that he was not 'govern'd by any low or selfish Views'. He sent her the two volumes so that she might see how the poem was introduced and offered whatever satisfaction or atonement she might require.[5]

Mrs. Carter had indicated to Edward Cave that she was 'much vexed' and asked him 'to inform her how she should properly express her dislike of it'. He had advised her to let him publish the ode in his *Gentleman's Magazine*, with an introduction 'yt it being wrong printed & without ye leave & contrary to ye *declard* Intention of ye Author, we had obtained a genuine copy'. She wrote to her friend Catherine Talbot that she 'received so civil an answer' from Richardson 'that I knew not how to be angry with him', especially since 'it appeared in a book which I greatly esteem'. After Richardson's apology Mrs. Carter informed him that Cave was to print the ode. 'But I have taken care the manner in which it is introduced shall cast no reflection upon you; though I think there should be great caution used in publishing any thing where there is not the highest reason to believe it would not be disagreeable to the author.' After this last echo of her displeasure, she acknowledged that he had 'introduced the Ode in a way that does it honour, and in a work with which I am greatly pleased'. There was, however, a reflection on Richardson, though a mild one, when the *Gentleman's Magazine* printed the ode, with minor variations: 'We have had the following beautiful ODE above a year, under an injunction, which was general on all the copies given out, not to print it; but as it has appeared in *Clarissa* with several faults, we think ourselves

[5] SH, II, 52–7; EL, I, 274–8; 13 Dec., 18 Dec.

at liberty to give our readers so agreeable an entertainment, from a corrector copy.'[6]

A year later Richardson sent her the last volumes of *Clarissa*, and she wrote thanking him for the 'very high Entertainment' she had received and praising in formal terms the conduct of the story and its 'very judicious Conclusion'. Richardson expressed his appreciation of this letter, after which their correspondence seems to have languished for well over four years.[7]

In the second edition of *Clarissa*, in 1749, Richardson cut all but the last three stanzas of the 'Ode', which were engraved on a special sheet with the music, and explained that he did so because the authoress had complained, but 'it is hoped, that the Lady will not be displeased with the continuing of those, for the sake of the Music, which we will venture to say is set in so masterly a manner as to do credit to her performance, admirable as that truly is'.[8] When contemplating a third edition, however, he asked Miss Highmore to get from Mrs. Carter her consent to insert in it her ode. At about this time William Duncombe informed Mrs. Carter that Richardson planned to print the whole ode, 'as he believes you are quite reconciled to him'.[9] Evidently she was. The third edition, of 1751, contains the ode. It was not until 1753, however, that Mrs. Carter became friendly with Richardson, partly through Miss Talbot, who had met him in the meantime. And though Mrs. Carter had a high admiration for his character and his talents, she never became an uncritical worshipper or a really intimate friend.

The reception of the first two volumes probably soon convinced Richardson that he would be justified in publishing their successors, but it was almost five months before he did so. The rest of the novel must have been substantially ready, and he probably spent a good part of this time going over and revising it.

In January 1748 Joseph Spence read and returned the 'contents' of the book (probably the same as the compendium which so delighted Hill). He proceeded to give Richardson the excellent (but never taken) advice not to consult others, or distrust himself, so much. 'I have a moral feeling for you, of another sort; on seeing how much you suffer from the contrariety of advices that have been given you. Such a multitude of opinions can only serve to confuse your own judgment, which I verily believe would direct you better, without any help, than with so much.' The

---

[6] Cave to Thomas Birch, 12 Dec., B.M. Add. MS. 4302, fo. 121; Mrs. Carter to Miss Talbot, 20 Jan. 1748, *A Series of Letters between Mrs. Elizabeth Carter and Miss Catherine Talbot* (London, 1808), I, 164; Mrs. Carter to R, 31 Dec.; *Gentleman's Magazine*, XVII (Dec. 1747), 585.

[7] Mrs. Carter to R, 16 Dec.; R to Mrs. Carter, 17 Dec.

[8] II, 48.

[9] 4 June 1750; Duncombe to Mrs. Carter, n. d., Pennington, *Memoirs of the Life of Mrs. Elizabeth Carter*, I, 146.

opinions of bad judges 'will only be so much lumber in your way' and even those of good judges are much to be suspected in the case of *Clarissa*, since not only can they not know Richardson's exact scheme, but 'those that are called the best judges . . . generally go by rules of art; whereas your's is absolutely a work of nature. . . . A piece quite of a new kind must have new rules, if any; but the best of all is, following nature and common sense.'[10] The originality of Richardson's genre struck many readers at the time, and of course the age was ready for a 'natural genius'— by 1750 a fairly large and vocal body of critics were tired of even such limited adherence as England had given to the 'rules'.

It must have been at about the same time that Warburton agreed to write a Preface for the forthcoming volumes. Richardson's difficulties with regard to this Preface may be another instance of the unfortunate results of his asking for too much help. He was unsure enough of himself to want the approval of men more learned and more polished than he (and indeed of everyone, even Miss Wescomb and Master Billy Lobb); but about the basic purposes and methods of his craft he was always ultimately sure. He would at most correct a social slip or elevate a phrase.

The third and fourth volumes of *Clarissa* appeared on 28 April 1748. They left the heroine in obvious danger from her by now determined seducer, who had learned of her retreat to Hampstead and was about to pursue her thither. Richardson promised that 'the Remainder of this Work will be published at once [that is all together]; and that as soon as indispensable avocations will permit'. They had, like the first two, been heavily revised. Young acknowledged the gift of the volumes: 'I have read your two volumes through, and am much pleased, nor less surprized, at the many alterations you have made for the better.'

Aaron Hill was more profuse in his praise. He was especially amazed at such breadth of knowledge in a man apparently bound to the daily round of business and could think that Richardson verified the story of the Wandering Jew and had throughout the world gathered the fruits of seventeen ages. As to the effect of his writings, they produced the opposite enchantment from Circe's—Richardson turned beasts into men. In reply Richardson wrote, 'You will observe . . . by the innumerable Variations, from what it was when you saw it that I was strengthen'd, guarded, and obliged infinitely, by your Observations.' The sale had been 'pretty quick'. Yet 'I know not whether it has not suffer'd much by the Catastrophe's being too much known and talked of. I intend another Sort of Happiness (founded on the Xn. System) for my Heroine, than that which was to depend upon the Will and Pleasure, and uncertain Reformation and good Behaviour of a vile Libertine, whom I could not think of giving a Person of Excellence to. The Sex give too much Countenance to Men of

[10] 21 Jan.

this vile Cast, to make them such a Compliment to their Errors. And to rescue her from a Rake, and give a Triumph to her, over not only him but over all her Oppressors, and the World beside, in a triumphant Death (as Death must have been her Lot, had she been ever so prosperous) I thought as noble a View, as it was new. But I find, Sir, by many Letters sent me, and by many Opinions given me, that some of the greater Vulgar, as well as all the less, had rather it had had what they call, an Happy Ending. This will be of Prejudice to me in the Sale, and has been. But, as I had an Ambition to attempt what I have the Vanity to think was never yet attempted; and as I think, if Health be spared me, that I shall be able to give an uncommon Turn and Appearance, to common Calamities, which, at one time or other, in every Person's Life, may be of some Use, I am not at all concerned about the Sale; I mean as to the Profits of it; tho' neither in Circumstance nor Philosophy absolutely above attending to that Part.' He had never intended the catastrophe to be known. 'But one Friend and another got the MS. out of my Hands', and some of them 'most indiscreatly' talked of it. He needs time to prepare the rest of the novel. Aside from his business and his 'constant Disorder' (his 'Paroxysms'), 'I have so greatly alter'd the two last Volumes, that one half of the Sequel must be new written: And I am discouraged with the Prospect.' He asked, of course, whether Hill or his daughters see any improvements which should be made. 'My Girl is thought overnice by many, I find: But I think I could defend her in all her Delicacies—And yet, I would that she should have some little things to be blamed for, tho' nothing in her Will; and that Lovelace should have something to say for himself to himself, tho' not to the rest of the World.'[11]

Soon afterwards, Solomon Lowe sent suggestions for minor corrections and proposed that *Clarissa* should have an index, like the *Tatler* and *Spectator*.[12] To treat a novel as the works of Addison and Steele had been treated was to take it with unusual seriousness. *Clarissa* never got a regular index, though *Sir Charles Grandison* had one from the first. But Richardson later collected, at the end of *Clarissa*, the most notable 'sentiments' in the book and provided a brief index of them.

During the late spring and summer of 1748 Richardson must have been going over the last part of his novel. In it there is a pedantic clergyman named Elias Brand, a petty-minded man who is misled by trying to be too clever; among other things he is used as a vehicle for satirizing affected style, pompous and irrelevant learning, and worship of the ancients as against the moderns. His three letters, especially the last, are larded with lines from the Latin poets, dragged in unnecessarily though not inappropriately. Richardson certainly needed help in finding suitable quotations,

[11] 5 May, 10 May.
[12] 23 May; 'Scruples', dated 26 June, FM XV, 2, fo. 102, and XVI, 1, fo. 90.

though the tone and style of the letters themselves almost guarantee that they were composed by Richardson.

Mrs. Barbauld has suggested, in our opinion on insufficient evidence, that the man who helped Richardson draw his pedant was John Channing. We believe that he was probably a certain R. Smith, who may well have been Richardson's learned corrector of the press.[13] At any rate there was a brief correspondence between Channing and Richardson in the fall of 1748. He was an apothecary and a friend of Heylin.[14] Late in October he was reading the sheets of volumes six and seven, which led up to and described the heroine's death. Just before publication he read the ending. His disagreement with 'your bookselling curtailers' indicates that among the advisers who wanted *Clarissa* shortened were business associates, perhaps Millar or the Rivingtons. He hinted that the flippant letter from Lovelace's friend Mowbray, which follows immediately the announcement of Clarissa's death and which is one of Richardson's most unconventional strokes, is rather hard to swallow after the long agony of the deathbed. But otherwise he was full of praise, and especially for the tragic ending. Clarissa's death reminded him of the pious death of his own father. He could find no blemishes worth mentioning, having been 'too earnestly engag'd, to stop to look out for trifles, or pick little faults, as subjects for dull criticism'. And he considered the Postscript, in which Richardson defended the poetic justice of the heroine's death, 'unnecessary, and too great a deference paid to the opinions of many of your friends'.[15]

Richardson sent Johannes Stinstra copies of several of Channing's letters and also quoted his remarks to one of the staunchest supporters of a happy ending, Lady Bradshaigh, who found one sentence from his letter of 31 October a 'mortifying stroke': 'The desire of having your piece end happily (as 'tis called) will ever be the test of a wrong head, and a vain mind.'[16]

By the middle of September, Richardson was able to advertise that the rest of *Clarissa* was in 'great Forwardness at the Press' and that he hoped to finish it by the middle of November. This was a little optimistic, but by 1 October he had sent Edward Moore the fifth volume and by 15 October Henry Fielding had read it. Volumes five and six were ready by 7 November, when Richardson sent them to Hill; he explained that he had crowded what should have been eight volumes into seven by a smaller type, feeling that because of his prolixity he owed the public the contents

[13] T. C. Duncan Eaves and Ben D. Kimpel, 'Richardson's Helper in Creating the Character of Elias Brand', *N&Q*, N.S. XIV (1967), 414–15.

[14] In his will (P.C.C. Arran 270, dated 8 Mar. 1759, proved 17 Aug. 1759) Heylin leaves Channing £50. The will of Heylin's daughter Elizabeth (P.C.C. Arran 131, dated 1 May 1758, proved 3 Mar. 1759), leaves 'Mr. John Channing Apothecary' £100.

[15] 5 Sept., 26 Oct., 29 Oct., 31 Oct., 28 Nov.

[16] R to Stinstra, 2 June 1753; Lady Bradshaigh to R, 3 June 1750.

of eight volumes at the price of seven. By 29 November Hill was reading the ending, needless to say with frequent tears ('enough to swim the Volumes that excited 'em'). On 6 December 1748 volumes five, six, and seven were available to the public.

The elaborate pretense that the letters are real ones which Richardson had maintained in *Pamela* is dropped, but his name is not given as the author: the book is '*Published by the* EDITOR *of* PAMELA' and 'Printed for S. Richardson'.

A Postscript to the last volume refers to the 'many anonymous Letters' expressing various wishes as to the ending, which the author had received. 'Most of those directed to him by the gentler Sex, turned in favour of what they call a *Fortunate Ending.*' Richardson defends the heroine's death with considerable warmth. He quotes the *Spectator* on poetic justice, as expressing the views of Aristotle ('the greatest master of reason, and the best judge of composition, that ever lived') on this subject. The demand for poetic justice is a modern engraftment on Aristotle. Richardson certainly knew Addison, but there is no other indication that he was much inclined to subscribe to the authority of Aristotle, and both the paragraph introducing the *Spectator*'s remarks and two long footnotes added to them sound as if he was aided in composing the Postscript by one of his more learned friends.[17] Young would have approved the sentiments and could have suggested the quotation from Rapin's discussion of Aristotle which is included. But the main justification of the ending is based not on critical theory but on Christian theology, 'since the notion of *Poetical Justice*, founded on the *modern rules*, has hardly ever been more strictly observed in works of this nature, than in the present performance', if any regard at all is paid to 'the *Christian System*' on which it is formed. The wicked are all punished; the few good characters aside from Clarissa herself are rewarded in this life; and she is rewarded in the Heaven to which she herself looked for reward. The Postscript also defends the great length of the piece, as necessary to the moral ('the Story . . . was to be principally looked upon as the Vehicle to the Instruction') and to the maintenance of an 'Air of Probability'. These seem to have been the two main objections to the novel which Richardson had heard.

Two months before the last volumes were ready, one of the 'greater Vulgar' whom Richardson had mentioned to Hill found herself unable to appreciate the tragic ending and was enough moved by what she feared the heroine's fate was to be to protest. Dorothy Bradshaigh was a woman of about forty and of a good family. She and her sister, Elizabeth, who

---

[17] For a contrary view 'that Richardson had consciously written his masterpiece according to a certain conception of tragedy' and that Rapin was 'an important source' of this conception, see John A. Dussinger, 'Richardson's Tragic Muse', *PQ*, XLVI (1967), 18–33. In our opinion neither these ideas nor the idea 'that Richardson was indebted to post-Restoration tragedy for the basic conception of his heroine' is supported by convincing evidence.

married Sir Robert Echlin, Bart., were the daughters and heiresses of William Bellingham of Levens, Westmorland. Her half-sister, Elizabeth Hesketh, was married to Edward Stanley, eleventh Earl of Derby, so that she was closely connected with one of the oldest noble families in the kingdom. In 1731 Dorothy Bellingham had married Roger Bradshaigh of Haigh, near Wigan, in Lancashire, who in 1747 had inherited his father's baronetcy.[18]

Lady Bradshaigh had been much moved by the first four volumes of Clarissa's sufferings, and when she heard the report that these sufferings were to end with the heroine's death, she wrote, signing her name 'Belfour' and asking about the truth of the rumour. It was probably this letter which she left in Andrew Millar's shop: 'I . . . was frightened out of my wits, for fear of being detected in the fact I there committed. A large sheet of paper lying upon the counter, I very dexterously conveyed my parcel under it, and run out of the shop as if I had stole something out of it, rather than left any thing in it, waded across the street up to my ancles in dirt, and got, well pleased (though in a flurry), to my party, who were waiting for me in an adjacent street.'[19] Richardson answered, as she requested, by an advertisement in the *Whitehall Evening Post*.[20]

She then wrote directly to Richardson, pleading that 'after you have brought the divine Clarissa to the very brink of destruction, let me intreat (may I say, insist upon) a turn, that will make your almost despairing readers half mad with joy'. She even admitted that she was not motivated only by her affection for Clarissa, 'but you must know, (though I shall blush again,) that if I was to die for it, I cannot help being fond of Lovelace'. 'If you disappoint me, attend to my curse:—May the hatred of all the young, beautiful, and virtuous, for ever be your portion! and may your eyes never behold any thing but age and deformity! may you meet with applause only from envious old maids, surly bachelors, and tyrannical parents! may you be doomed to the company of such! and, after death, may their ugly souls haunt you!—Now make Lovelace and Clarissa unhappy if you dare.' All this, though she was no 'giddy girl of sixteen' and 'past my romantic time of life'.[21]

Richardson's answer is lost. It did not satisfy Lady Bradshaigh, but she did not quite give up hope: 'If you should think fit to alter your

---

[18] Cokayne, *Complete Baronetage*, under Bradshaigh and Echlin; John Bernard Burke, *Extinct and Dormant Baronetcies of England*, 2nd edn. (London, 1844), under Bradshaigh; Burke's *Peerage, Baronetage, and Knightage*, under Derby and Echlin; will of Edward, Earl of Derby, P.C.C. Bellas 172, dated 21 June 1771, proved 2 Apr. 1776; 'Betha' (probably Joseph Budworth, the husband of Lady Echlin's granddaughter Elizabeth Palmer) in the *Gentleman's Magazine*, LXXIV (1804), 899–900, and LXXXIII (1813), ii, 307 (for Lady Bradshaigh's relation to the Countess of Derby).

[19] To R, 28 Jan. 1750.

[20] Barbauld, IV, 177.

[21] 10 Oct.

scheme, I will promise to read your history over, at least once in two years, as long as I live; and my last words are,—be merciful!' Richardson's first extant letter to his incognita Belfour is his answer to this. He is already calling her the daughter of his mind. He is sympathetic but adamant. Others have also wished for a happy ending, in vain; it seems he has drawn his girl 'too amiable'—'nor can I go thro' some of the Scenes myself without being sensibly touched (Did I not say, that I was another Pygmalion?)'. But his purpose is too firmly fixed to be swayed by such emotions; he wants to show the nothingness of 'temporary Happiness' in this world. 'Religion never was at so low an Ebb as at present: And if my Work must be supposed of the Novel kind, I was willing to try if a Religious Novel would do good.' He points out that Lovelace's unworthiness of her regard should have been clear from the first. If he married Clarissa to him, he would do no more than he had done in *Pamela*. He has a great deal to say against marrying reformed rakes. Besides, 'another of my great Ends' was to familiarize the reader with death, which has become too terrible—since it is our common lot, we must be led back to it as (to quote Clarissa) a starting steed is led back to the object it starts at.[22]

Lady Bradshaigh admits much of what he says, but still—Lovelace is, of course, wicked, but may he not be gradually reformed? She knows the rest of the book will be well executed, 'too well for such tender and foolish hearts as mine'—'Would you have me weep incessantly? I do assure you, nothing can induce me to read your history through. Do not wonder or take it amiss, for I cannot, indeed I cannot.' As she is about to post the letter, the fifth volume arrives. 'I long to read it—and yet I dare not. But I have a kind friend who will first look it over; though, God knows, he has a heart tender as my own, but is willing to save me pain, though at the expence of suffering it himself. If I find the dreaded horrid act is not perpetrated, I will promise to read it.' But she is prevailed upon to read a part of it—she discovers that Clarissa has been raped. 'Dear Sir, if it be possible—yet, recall the dreadful sentence; bring it as near as you please, but prevent it. . . . Blot out but one night, and the villainous laudanum, and all may be well again.—I opened my letter to add this, and my hand trembles, for I can scarce hold my pen. I am as mad as the poor injured Clarissa; and am afraid I cannot help hating you, if you alter not your scheme.'[23]

In her next letter she has one last desperate scheme—let Lovelace, overwhelmed by Clarissa's refusal to marry him, be thrown into a dangerous fever; at his dying request, urged by her favourite clergyman, Dr. Lewen, Clarissa may visit him, may finally, to enable him to die with greater resignation, suffer their hands to be united or at least promise to

[22] [*c*. 20 Oct.], 26 Oct.   [23] [17 Nov.].

marry him—which promise would aid his recovery, and after many tender scenes marital bliss would reward sinner and saint.[24]

By her next letter Belfour has lost all hope: she knows that Clarissa is to die. 'Had you been so long expecting a history, which you had set apart for the amusement of your life, and had, like me, been disappointed, would it not have been a vexation to you? O what pleasure I proposed! Now shall I never look on the outside without a sigh, and, I fear, a harsh thought of the author.' She even doubts whether a tender heart could draw such shocking scenes. Richardson had mentioned to her several tragedies as precedents for his ending, and she owned that she had been moved by the approach of their catastrophes and 'been forced to talk all the ridiculous things I could think of, in order to conceal my weakness'. But such pains were nothing to what she felt for Clarissa: 'I am not affected, in the same sensible manner, by distresses in unnatural heroines, as I am when they appear purely in nature.' Richardson had written that if Lovelace did reform, he should marry not Clarissa but one of the girls he had previously seduced, a point of morality with which she can in no way agree, having a low opinion of those 'who are so weak as to be tempted by such an old bait as a promise of marriage'. 'Will you not take it amiss, Sir, if I beg you will not send the remainder of your volumes? Pray think me unworthy of such a favour, though I should be sorry to know you thought so. I cannot promise to read them, but will endeavour. I shall not want the encouragement of my affectionate partner, who is your sincere admirer, but in my way of thinking as to your catastrophe.' Later in the letter she is even firmer: 'I have been sometime *thinking* your History over, and I find I cannot read it. Good Sir, do not send it, do not compel me to be ungrateful.' Perhaps at seventy she may have different notions, but by that time she will have given up novels for books of devotion and thus will never get to finish *Clarissa*.[25]

Richardson's answer to this was, as he himself said, a monstrous long letter. His catastrophe is the 'only natural one', and he is sorry that 'it was supposed that I had no other End in . . . so large a Piece . . . but the trite one of perfecting a private Happiness, by the Reformation of a Libertine'. 'Indeed, Madam, I could not think of leaving my Heroine short of Heaven.' Suppose her married to Lovelace, reconciled to her foolish and obstinate relations, a happy wife and mother: 'What is there unusual in all this . . . worth troubling the World about. How many are the Infelicities, how many are the Drawbacks upon Happiness, that attend upon even what is called a happy married Life? Indeed the best of our Happiness here is but Happiness by Composition, or Comparison. A becalmed Life, is like a becalmed Ship.' Children often bring new griefs. Perhaps stung by her remarks on his lack of tenderness, he recounts his own griefs, the

[24] 20 Nov.   [25] [Early Dec.]

loss of a dear wife, of all six of his sons and two of his daughters, and of many others. Such sorrows are the common lot. Thinking he had made Lovelace 'too wicked . . . to obtain the Favour and good Wishes of any worthy Heart of *either* Sex', he tried out his character on a young lady, whose pity for the wretch induced him to throw 'into his Character some deeper Shades. And as he now stands, I verily think that had I made him a worse Man, he must have been a Devil.' Perhaps Lady Bradshaigh was convinced, since she never again defended Lovelace warmly. He has sent Belfour the last volumes—if she will not read them, let her at least accept them. They may after all be suitable for her at seventy, 'since they appear in the humble Guise of a *Novel* only by way of Accommodation to the Manners and Taste of an Age overwhelmed with a Torrent of Luxury, and abandoned to Sound and Senselessness'.[26]

Her resolution was too weak for his insistence. On 6 January 1749, having returned home from an excursion, she retired to read 'with Attention would I could say Pleasure' the ending. Her pain was great: Richardson should have curbed his genius, since few have like him 'the Art to make their Readers see and feel every thing they represent'. 'I verily believe I have shed a Pint of Tears.' 'When alone in Agonies would I lay down the Book, take it up again, walk about the Room, let fall a Flood of Tears, wipe my Eyes, read again, perhaps not three Lines, throw away the Book crying out Excuse me good Mr. Richardson, I cannot go on. It is your Fault you have done more than I can bear, threw myself upon my Couch to compose, recollecting my Promise (which a thousand Times I wished had not been made) again I read, again acted the same Part. Sometimes agreeably interrupted by my dear Man, who was at that Time labouring through the Sixth Volume with a Heart capable of Impressions equal to my own, tho' the Effects shewn in a more justifiable Manner, which I believe may be compared to what Mr. Belford felt when he found the beauteous Sufferer in her Prison Room. "Something rose in my Throat, I know not what; which made me guggle as it were for Speech."— Seeing me so moved, he beg'd for God's Sake I would read no more, kindly threatened to take the Book from me, but upon my pleading my Promise, suffered me to go on. That Promise is now fulfilled, and am thankfull the heavy Task is over, tho' the Effects are not. Had it been as I wish'd instead of being thankfull or impatient for the End, how should I have dwelt with Pleasure upon every Line, and dreaded to come to the Conclusion.—My Spirits are strangely seized, my Sleep is disturbed, waking in the Night I burst into a Passion of crying, so I did at Breakfast this Morning, and just now again. God be merciful to me, what can it mean?' 'I must lock up such a History from my Sight, *never more* to be look'd into.' 'I fancy, Sir, you found yourself remarkably easy, when you had

[26] 15 Dec.

sent him [Lovelace] to Destruction both of Body and Soul. It seemed to
be a favourite Point with you. After all I believe you are of a cruel Disposition.' But she ends on a friendly note. She is made proud by Richardson's saying that he will consult her if he writes again. And she asks
whether there is such a painter as Mr. Highmore and whether he has a
picture of Clarissa. She will be in town before she is a year older and would
like to see it—and to see Richardson too, though unknown to him.[27]

Richardson told her about Highmore's pictures of Clarissa and her
family, as well as about a head of Clarissa in crayons belonging to Dr.
Charles Chauncy. He evidently felt their argument on *Clarissa* had been
exhausted and wanted to continue the correspondence, since he devoted
most of his letter to the discussion of old maids and of a house for repentant fallen women.[28] Though there is a gap of nine months in their
extant correspondence following this letter, they evidently continued to
write to each other.

Richardson was not a little pleased with his correspondence with Belfour and lent it to several of his friends, including Hill's three daughters,
Miss Talbot, Miss Grainger, Mrs. Dewes, and Mrs. Delany.[29]

By October 1749 she and Richardson had begun discussing his next
work, which was to portray a good man. They also discussed a question
arising from *Clarissa*, the married as against the single state, and in this
connection she mentioned a girl who 'obstinately refused her lover for
nine years, and was prevailed upon to alter her condition in the tenth, (no
Clarissa neither).'[30] In later letters it came out that she was describing her
own courtship by Sir Roger.

Clarissa has already affected her life: she now emulates the heroine in
rising early and in trying to budget her time. She describes the history of
a Magdalen, now repentant, whom she is endeavouring to place in some
suitable family. Both she and Richardson had a constant, lively, and not
unsympathetic interest in the sufferings of fallen women. She is intimate
enough with Richardson to give some description of her youth, with a
reserved and rather frightening father and a mother whose only fault was
an inclination to suspiciousness. She was far from a model daughter,
though she has improved since: 'I am going to tell you, Sir, (with all my
faults) I reckon myself amongst the middling sort, tho' far from the best.'
'I was what a fond parent calls a very comical girl.'[31]

They had begun to consider the possibility of an interview. She was no
longer bitter about the cruel murderer of Clarissa, but the 'impudent
things' she had written on that subject make her shy of a meeting at which

[27] She finished her letter on 11 Jan.   [28] [Mid-Jan.]
[29] Astræa and Minerva Hill to R, [1750?]; Urania Johnson to R, 5 Apr. 1750; Catherine
Talbot to R, [Dec. 1750]; R to Frances Grainger, 28 Feb. 1750; Mrs. Delany to Mrs. Dewes,
30 Nov. 1750, *Autobiography and Correspondence*, II, 620.
[30] 29 Oct.   [31] [Early Nov.]

she would 'shew you a countenance more stupid than saucy'—'the oftener I think of it, the more terrible it appears'. She would like to know what church he goes to or whether he ever walks in St. James's Park; after a glimpse of him, she can better judge whether she can dare to face him. She promises in her next letter to give a new address, that of a friend in London (a transparent disguise for herself); she must have gone up to town before the end of 1749.[32]

She and Sir Roger soon followed Richardson's suggestion and went by Highmore's studio to see his paintings of Clarissa. While there she also saw Highmore's portrait of Clarissa's creator. Highmore, curious to know who his anonymous visitors were, sent his French servant down to their landau to make inquiries. Unfortunately he was not familiar enough with English to get the name right and could only report that the gentleman was 'Sir Roger somebody, with a B.' from Lancashire. This fact, together with the lady's familiarity with *Clarissa* as evidenced by her pointing out the various persons in the painting of the Harlowe family, as well as a remark she made about Richardson's portrait, led Highmore to guess that she was the incognita of whom Richardson had spoken. He passed this information on to Richardson, describing her husband, who 'appeared to be very much a gentleman; was dressed plain', and herself: 'You were of a good stature, he told me, rather plump than otherwise; lively; good humoured, he dared to say; great politeness between you and the gentleman, yet great ease and unaffectedness; sound health promised by your complexion, and looking as a lady accustomed to reside in the country.'[33]

It may have been on the same visit to town that she stopped by Rivington's shop and asked him for the contents to *Clarissa* (published in June 1749); he did not have it, and 'seemed very short in his answers. Oh! thought I, friend, if you knew me, perhaps you would ask me to sit down.'[34]

Richardson is willing to fall in with any proposal she makes which may lead to an interview. He wishes especially that she would visit him at North End, where 'I have common conveniences, tho' not splendid ones'; but he will allow her, if she insists, to preserve her anonymity. He walks through St. James's Park once or twice a week on the way to North End; if she commands, he will spend three or four hours a day in it, for a week together. And that she may recognize him, he gives a description of himself.[35]

In her reply Lady Bradshaigh had recourse to an innocent deception. She has no hopes of taking so long a journey this winter but has sent his description to a friend, whose desire to see him is as great as hers. This

---

[32] [Early Nov.]
[33] Lady Bradshaigh to R, 28 Jan.; R to Lady Bradshaigh, 15 Feb. 1750.
[34] 28 Jan.   [35] [Late Nov.]

friend will go to the Park every fine, warm day between one and two. The friend has almost visited Richardson once already. About three weeks ago she was in the neighbourhood of Salisbury Square and had to do 'the greatest violence to her inclination' to avoid calling on him—she feared she might, if she called, say more than Belfour would wish, 'for you must know she is not remarkable for keeping a guard upon her tongue, especially in company she likes'. She walked around the court, 'she had her foot upon your steps, and almost the knocker of your door in her hand; but so it was, when she found that to advance was impossible'. But she will try to see Richardson and will not dare to appear in an immoderate hoop. 'I am of opinion, should she meet and know you, she will, in surprise, make a full stop, perhaps a courtesy; and should you turn back, it is not unlikely she may ask—is it because you like or dislike, Sir? not knowing at the time that she speaks at all. In surprise or eagerness, she is apt to think aloud; and since you have a mind to see *her*, who has seen the king, I give you the advantage of knowing she is middle-aged, middle-sized, a degree above plump, brown as an oak wainscot, a good deal of country red in her cheeks; altogether a plain woman, but nothing remarkably forbidding.'[36]

Richardson did not receive this letter until 30 December 1749.[37] The following day was a Sunday and fine, and he walked in the Park—in vain—'contenting myself with dining, as I walked, on a sea biscuit which I had put in my pocket; my family at home, all the time, knowing not what was become of me. A Quixotte!' The next Saturday, 6 January, on his way to North End, he walked backwards and forwards in the Mall until after two and was again disappointed. On 9 January he wrote her, hinting that he suspected that she was herself her friend and that he was rather tired waiting for her to appear: he related a story of how the Pope used to honour princes with the gift of a consecrated rose, which they prized highly; the Elector of Saxony was especially eager to receive a consecrated rose—and the Pope finally did send him one, but not until after his conversion by Luther, when he no longer looked upon the rose as more than a common flower.

On 28 January she as much as admitted that she and her friend were the same. She was still too sensible of the things she had written him to look forward to the interview: 'I have so terrified myself with the thoughts of it, that, at this moment, I tremble, supposing myself before you.' She could not bring herself to appoint a meeting, to 'come plump upon you with a full face (broad too by nature), and begin talking, as to an indifferent person'. She had been frequenting the Park on most warm days;

---

[36] 16 Dec., 28 Jan.

[37] The following account of the events leading up to their first interview is put together from their correspondence of 9 Jan. to 24 Feb.

once she thought she saw him, and 'I gave a sort of a fluttering start, and surprised my company' before she found she was mistaken. And now she must fear 'being looked upon as the long expected, slighted, consecrated rose'. 'I do not expect or desire to be taken for a rose in June, and to be looked upon as a common flower, is all I can hope for. If that is too much, I'll condescend to be put down a thistle, if you please.' Whenever there was a fine Saturday, she would look for him in the Park.

On Saturday, 3 February, Richardson tried again, though the day was not fine. 'Up the Mall walked I, down the Mall, and up again, in my way to North End. O this dear Will-o'-wisp, thought I! when nearest, farthest off! Why should I, at this time of life—No bad story, the consecrated rose, say she what she will: and all the spiteful things I could think of, I muttered to myself.'

He also tried to lure her to his house by telling her that a head of Clarissa in crayons, which he had already once mentioned, belonging to Dr. Chauncy had been lent to him and that she might choose to send someone of her acquaintance to see it. She did not rise to that bait, and he returned the picture to Chauncy: 'I was in hopes my Lancashire Lady would have had an Opportunity to see it; but she plays fast and loose with me so idly, that I have some Pleasure in considering the Opportunity she has lost, as a Punishment to her.'[38]

On 7 February Lady Bradshaigh half apologized for her neglect on the grounds that she was forced to go much into company. Richardson answered with an enigmatic and irritated little note: 'You are pleased to tell me, Madam, that you often go out to oblige other people, when your inclinations and whole heart are at home! Often did you say, Madam, with deliberation say?'

But on the day this note was written, Lady Bradshaigh took a step which led to a confrontation. On Thursday, 8 February, she went again, as she had hinted she would, to see Mr. Highmore's pictures. He had promised to bring out his illustrations of *Pamela*. She was in some fear, or hope, of finding Richardson himself there, and indeed Highmore had suggested as much to Richardson, who had preferred to let the lady have her own way and not to surprise her. But Highmore himself challenged her as the incognita. 'But, Sir, at this time, the devil forsook me; no evasion, no white fib, or the least falsehood could I utter.' 'I felt like an idiot.' She trembled all the time she was there, 'and indeed the whole day after'— perhaps the flutter she was in was due to an earth tremor which was felt

---

[38] [12 or 19 Feb.]. Charles Chauncy was a medical doctor and a Fellow of the Royal Society, known as a collector. His collection, sold in 1790, included a picture of Clarissa Harlowe, 'after Angelica [Kaufmann], by Read, *very fine*' (*A Catalogue of the Extensive, Valuable, and Superb Collection . . . of Those Well-Known Connoisseurs Charles Chauncy . . . and Nathanael Chauncy, Esq., His Brother*, under date 7 May). He was a close enough friend of Richardson to be shown later the sheets of *Sir Charles Grandison* (Chauncy to R, June 1753; 10 Mar. 1754).

that day in London, though at the time she had not noticed the shock. Everything came out. The next day she wrote regretting that she had disclosed herself first to someone else and not to Richardson directly, that she was now so poor that she had not even the favour of her name to bestow on him. She signs herself 'your obliged and faithful (O! that I could say) INCOGNITA'.

And soon after sending this letter she had a further blow, Richardson's puzzling note of the eighth, which she took as a reproach for gadding about. She wrote again on the same day: 'My spirits were sunk sufficiently with what had happened yesterday, and I am now overwhelmed with your severe reprimand. Shall I tell you (being in bad spirits) it even drew tears from me.' Richardson answered in haste the next day that he had heard nothing from Highmore and that he had not meant the note as censure but only as a hint that she was 'a little unkind to make such difficulty of favouring me'.

On the same Saturday, 10 February, she did go to the Park and walked there for an hour, 'but then you were in the height of your spite. At two o'clock, I said to myself, Worse than the consecrated rose!' She proposed to go again on the seventeenth. Her letter announcing this was the first she signed with her own name.

It was Sunday evening, 11 February, before Richardson saw Highmore and finally learned the name of his incognita. When he received her letter describing her vain walk in the Park, he answered it the next day (15 February), in a much better humour, explaining that Highmore had challenged her without his knowledge.

On Friday the sixteenth she went with Sir Roger into the City. 'As we crossed the end of Salisbury-court, it was proposed to turn a certain imaginary scene into reality. The coach being ordered to turn, I screamed so, that you might have heard me, and pulled the check-string with such violence, that I believe the coachman's thumb suffered a good deal; for all which I was laughed at, and made believe they were only in joke.'

He did go to the Park on Saturday the seventeenth, and so did she. She passed him four times, 'knew you by your own description, at least three hundred yards off, walking in the Park between the trees and the Mall; and had an opportunity of surveying you unobserved, your eyes being engaged amongst the multitude, looking, as I knew, for a certain gill-o'-th'-wisp, who, I have a notion, escaped being known by you, tho' not your notice, for you looked at me every time we passed; but I put on so unconcerned a countenance, that I am almost sure I deceived you. Tell me, Sir, if I am mistaken. I must own to you, that I was terribly apprehensive of finding something in your person stern and awful—but quite the contrary. Nothing appeared but what I told Mr. Highmore I saw in your picture, together with a mildness and good-nature, which bid me banish fear, and venture to see you. And yet—O that this first meeting was over!' Richardson's irritation was renewed—her curiosity had been satisfied, but not his. He had been indisposed but had nevertheless walked with Miss Collier and his daughter Patty to North End. They stopped by the Park, the girls waiting at a distance in order not to give umbrage to the incognita, and Richardson walked up and down looking for his gill-o'-th'-wisp. But he saw no one who gave 'the least intimation of herself (for I imagined not, that it was either in your ladyship's intention . . . or in your power, to put on such an unconcerned countenance, and on purpose to deceive me). Yet, she cannot be come, thought I—nor yet—nor yet—And so continued walking, expecting, and sometimes fretting, till the Mall was vacant of ladies. I gave this lady an honest description of myself, thought I—And after the young lady and my daughter then walked I, extremely tired and fatigued, and joined them on the upper part of Constitution Hill; made my five miles at least nine; the sauntering four fatiguing me twice as much as the five. I was so ill, that tho' I had very agreeable company there, I was obliged to retire some hours sooner than otherwise I should have chosen. Am now but indifferent.' 'You must be a cruel lady!'

Richardson again asked the no-longer-unknown to visit him at North End. This she was not ready quite to do. She pointed out in her answer that Richardson had had as fair a chance of guessing at her description as she at his; and she explained that having seen him first at a distance, she was forewarned when he came nearer, so that she did not start but was able to go on talking with great composure to her companion. Finally, 'all animosity apart', she said that she and Sir Roger would have accepted his invitation, except that she had another plan: she would, if she lived and had health and eyesight, see him, but at her lodging. This invitation was written on 24 February. It took Richardson still some time to accept it, but the correspondents did finally meet, on 6 March 1750.[39]

The interview removed any lingering irritation and any fears on Lady Bradshaigh's part. She saw she had no cause for apprehension so far as Richardson's character went—indeed she had worried mainly about her own impertinent writing, and his lack of severity gave her new reason to fear on this score: 'Your looks are so of a piece with your indulgent words, that I greatly fear they will not give a check to the saucy freedoms and impertinences with which I am too naturally inclined to treat my best friends, when I think I have their license for so doing; and yet, Sir, I am a little afraid to your face.—No—I am not afraid neither—it is not that—but it is something that reigns in my freedom of speech.—Oh! I believe, I fancy, I shall talk like a fool—that is it.'[40]

[39] Lady Bradshaigh to R, 5 Mar. 1751.
[40] 27 Mar.

At their last interview before she left London, Mrs. Richardson was present, and Lady Bradshaigh liked her at once. 'I must say, never did I see more good temper, mildness, and compliance, appear in any body, than in her.' There had been another earth tremor, and Richardson was trying to get his wife to move for a while to North End for safety. Her refusal caused some argument, and Richardson as usual said that his mild wife always insisted on her own way, but Lady Bradshaigh remembered her real reason. 'I heard her say, and with truth say, "Why will not I go to North-End?—Because, Mr. Richardson, you will not go with me. Do you think I can enjoy the least satisfaction, though I was to think myself in safety, when I thought I had left you in a place of danger?"' [41]

In March 1750 Richardson asked Lady Bradshaigh to be allowed to take a copy of a picture of her and Sir Roger in front of Haigh, which he had seen over her chimney in town. She answered that she agreed, except that the copy must be a present from her; and not long afterwards Richardson had it in his house. In return, she asked Richardson to let Highmore do another portrait of him, which she had by the end of the year. [42] She changed the name under it to Dickenson and hung it in her dressing room. [43] 'The first time my friend saw your picture, he asked, "What honest face have you got there?" And, without staying for an answer, "Do you know, I durst trust that man with my life, without farther knowledge of him." I answered, I do know you might do so with safety. And I put you down for a judge of physiognomy.' [44]

Lady Bradshaigh's letters give an agreeable picture of her life in the country. What with reading and writing, with domestic duties and walking, and with chatting, joking, and social amusements she found her time well filled. Fine ladies might complain of having too much time on their hands, but she did not feel the need of more distractions. And she was willing to turn her hand to any useful work, even cow doctoring, let the fine ladies think what they might. [45]

Haigh was located 'one mile North from Wigan in ye County Pal[atine] of Lancaster, A large & handsome Building with fine Gardens & Plantations about it, & is reckon'd one of ye best Situations in ye North of England, where from ye Top of a large Mount in ye Park are seen 13 Countys and ye Isle of Man. In this Lordship are ye finest Works of Coale call'd Cannell, in England wch: is so much admired for it's heat & brightness as well as ye extraordinary Curiositys made of it nowise inferior to Jett in colour & hight of Pollish, they are inexhaustible mines &

[41] 25 Mar., 3 Apr.
[42] R to Lady Bradshaigh, 31 Mar.; Lady Bradshaigh to R, 3 Apr.; R to Lady Bradshaigh, [Jan. 1751]; Lady Bradshaigh to R, 3 June, [27–8 Dec.].
[43] Barbauld, VI, 72n; Lady Echlin to R, 13 Dec. 1759.
[44] [27–8 Dec. 1750].
[45] Ibid.

produce a very considerable yearly Income to this Family.'[46] Mining was already beginning to change Lancashire, and there were local textiles, samples of which Lady Bradshaigh later sent Richardson. But as yet the future of the Midlands cast only a faint shadow, and Haigh was still primarily a country seat and its life a country life.

Lady Bradshaigh also made visits to other country houses, especially to Knowsley, the estate of her brother-in-law, the Earl of Derby, who had been 'not only a Brother, but a Father' to her.[47]

Her married life seems to have been as smooth as possible. After her nine years' hesitation, she had given her 'yes' at last with all her heart, and for twenty years she and Sir Roger had been inseparable. They were a regular Darby and Joan, and she could only pity the poor souls who needed routs and drums to amuse them.[48] A letter to the *Gentleman's Magazine* in 1804 speaks of her 'prudent œconomy', 'good sense', and 'sound integrity', and remarks that 'she *managed*, indeed, to make an appearance proper to her station upon a straitened income, till the debts of Sir Roger Bradshaigh's father, incurred by a parliamantary *mania*, were paid to the uttermost farthing, though not subject to those debts by any law but the law of conscience'. She was 'eminent in every Christian and moral virtue; above all, "in *the greatest of these*," in Charity, which she practised in its most extensive sense, and in all its various meanings.'[49]

She must have spent a good deal of her time helping others. There are further references to her efforts to help a Magdalen, either her previous one or another. The girl seems to have had few talents even as a servant, but Richardson offered to let her (or another penitent) come to him to 'do just what she can, and stay till she is otherwise provided for'. Lady Bradshaigh's behaviour to another fallen woman, who was not educated enough to know that she was fallen, shows a typical combination of morality and kindness: 'A poor ignorant, that I was lecturing after a slip of this kind, said, "to be sure she had been faulty; but, she thanked God, Thomas had made her an honest woman; and, if *I* would forgive her, she had nothing now to answer for." The extreme simplicity of her words turned all my anger to compassion: I made her sensible whose forgiveness she ought to seek for, gave her a good book, and sent her to preach to Thomas.' She got Richardson to find a lawyer to help a Mrs. Strangeways, who was in some sort of trouble, and asked him to help apprentice two young boys, natural geniuses as painters; but when he expressed his willingness to try and asked what schooling they had had and wished to

---

[46] B.M. Add. MS. 24,120, fo. 141 (the MS. is dated *c*. 1728–30). See also Defoe's *Tour*, 1st edn., III, 218.

[47] Lady Bradshaigh to R, 25 Nov. 1750.   [48] [Mid-1751], 11 Dec. 1753.

[49] Letter signed 'BETHA', LXXIV, 899–900.

have some drawings to show, she reconsidered and decided that the boys did not have enough education.[50]

She followed closely, as we shall see, the progress of *Sir Charles Grandison*. To one character in that book she felt an especial kinship, Sir Charles's sharp-tongued and self-willed but humourous sister Charlotte. She admitted her similarity to that lively but hardly model lady.[51] She referred not without complacency to her 'wild' youth; at twenty she was 'a strange unthinking girl'. The wildness seems to have been confined to comical pranks. When Richardson came to correspond with her more earnest sister, Lady Echlin, one of their favourite subjects was the lively youth of the comical 'Miss Do'. Once, it appears, she 'scrupled not (tho' younger Sister, if I remember right) to pull Caps, in good-humoured Roguery'. Her sister had found her hard to manage; 'we always were affectionate sisters, although her over-hasty disposition, did not altogether please my graver turn'. In his letters to Lady Bradshaigh, Richardson rather encouraged her Miss Do side to come to the fore, though to her sister he professed, not very seriously, to deplore it: 'Strange! that so excellent a Lady as Lady B. your Ladiships Sister, should be so misled by such a Gilflirt as Miss Do—— Yet, not so very strange neither; for, I know not how it is, but I myself, tho' I could sometimes beat her, see something to be pleased with, in that lively Girl. Favour me, dear Madam, with the History of this young Lady, and her Airs, that I may either like her more or less.'[52]

Her love of fun was by no means dead, though it was combined with strict propriety. She had in the country a young male friend who was a 'wicked madcap'; she enjoyed his company, lectured him on his morality, hoped for his reformation, and laughed at him in spite of herself. She had laughed also at Lovelace, for all his wickedness, and we have seen that she could not altogether hate him—'never any thing equall'd the Humour of that Man'. And though she agreed with Richardson on the immorality of *Tom Jones*, she did not miss its humour: 'There are very different kinds of laughter: you make me laugh with pleasure; but I often laugh, and am angry at the same time with the facetious Mr. Fielding.' She even laughed sometimes in reading *Tristram Shandy*, though it was 'mean *dirty Wit*'. A good deal of her correspondence with Richardson consists of badinage and playful raillery. 'I *will* call you names,' she wrote, 'for you are I sincerely think, the most indulgent, unprejudiced humblest, bearing, and

[50] Lady Bradshaigh to R, 25 Nov., [27-8 Dec.] 1750, [mid-1751]; Barbauld, I, clv; Lady Bradshaigh to R, [May–Nov. 1751], 1 June 1755; R to Lady Bradshaigh, 28 June 1755; Lady Bradshaigh to R, 5 Sept. 1755, 31 Mar. 1758; R to Lady Bradshaigh, 4 Apr. 1758; Lady Bradshaigh to R, 21 Apr. 1758.

[51] 30 June 1754.

[52] Lady Bradshaigh to R, 16 Apr. 1751; R to Lady Echlin, 12 Sept. 1754; Lady Echlin to R, 27 Sept. 1754; R to Lady Echlin, 10 Oct. 1754.

forebearing correspondent that ever saucy woman was favoured with.' She was glad that they quarrelled and always would, but regretted that he had grown so cool it gave her no pleasure. 'I love to argue with your Ladiship, and hardly with any-body else', he later wrote.[53]

Shortly before his death Richardson asked for her comments on *Pamela* and *Clarissa*, and she sent him the volumes with her marginalia.[54] The *Clarissa* is still extant, in the possession of her collateral descendants, and shows the careful love with which she read the book.[55] Richardson devoted some of his last days to reading her comments and to making his own comments on them. She had largely come around to Richardson's views on the subject of Lovelace. When she remarked that, knowing Lovelace's 'wicked end, how every good thing he says, raises my Indignation against him, a deceitful, practiced vilain', Richardson wrote, 'Now, Madam, at last you see him!'[56] And at the conclusion of the fifth volume she wrote: 'Did I ever wish Clarrissa to marry Lovelace? How I hate myself for it. I was set upon a reformation. What a childish Notion? A Clara. never cou'd have been happy with a Lovelace, tho' he had in time reform'd. Her reflections on what was pass'd, must have riveted an everlasting hatered towards him.' To this comment Richardson replied with '!!!!' But she could not quite resist Lovelace's humour: 'I wish I cou'd help laughing at him. I often check myself, as if he cou'd see me.'[57] And she still did not approve of the ending: Lovelace should have attempted, but not executed, the 'last outrage', and Clarissa, after reaching the brink of death, should have recovered to live on unmarried, edifying her neighbours, rearing her wicked brother's worthy son, cheering her widowed mother, advising Mrs. Hickman (*née* Howe) on family matters, and even evincing 'a sort of distant friendship with Lovelace, to his *Soul*, I mean'.[58]

[53] Lady Bradshaigh to R, 9 Oct. 1750, 6 Jan. 1749, 25 Mar. 1750, 23 Aug. 1760, 23 Dec. 1753, 14 Jan. 1754, 25 Sept. 1753; R to Lady Bradshaigh, 4 Jan. 1754.

[54] Martha? Richardson to Lady Bradshaigh, [early Mar. 1761]; Lady Bradshaigh to Martha? Richardson, 13 Mar. 1761.

[55] We are indebted to the late Commander Arthur Avalon Mackinnon of Mackinnon and to Lady Mackinnon for their kindness in permitting us to quote from the marginalia in these volumes.

[56] III, 169.   [57] III, 177.   [58] At the end of Vol. VII.

CHAPTER XI

CLARISSA

NOTHING that we know of Richardson's life or of his character and nothing we find in his letters or his earlier books adequately prepares us for *Clarissa*. Its plot, except for the ending, is rather commonplace; its sentiments are, as has been pointed out, the sentiments of many conduct books and of the middle class in general. It is not hard to find sources for Richardson's characters and situations—Nicholas Rowe's tragedy *The Fair Penitent* and Charles Johnson's *Cælia* have often been cited and may conceivably have given him the germ of his intrigue and of the character of Lovelace. Other works built, as *Clarissa* is, around the seduction of a virtuous girl have been discovered, especially in the drama,[1] though the closest parallels suggested so far lack the distinctive feature of Richardson's conception of Clarissa's tragedy, the reversal in which she rises above her seducer by refusing to marry him. It is easy to find parallels to Richardson's 'ideas', about parents and children, for instance, or about marrying rakes. But these are rather the things which limit *Clarissa* than the things which make it important. If there are any literary critics left of the school of Taine, they will have no difficulty in explaining many things about *Clarissa* by the background of its author. If one is interested in those things that Richardson had in common with his milieu, it is no trouble to find them; if one is interested in why Richardson and not another product of the same milieu wrote *Clarissa*, one had perhaps best wait until psychology becomes more nearly a science. One might not expect to find a powerful novelist in a conventional, poorly educated printer. But if one seeks the ideal background for a powerful novelist, one is driven to conclude that he should be either a Jew early impressed with the importance of æsthetic snobs and of Parisian aristocrats, or a Polish exile who has spent much of his life on the sea, or a half-educated but well-to-do Russian count, or an impecunious member of a Russian liberal circle converted by political prison to reaction and jingoism, or a vicar's daughter who has never spiritually left the world of the vicarage, or an ex-officer of Napoleon and would-be dandy, or a lower middle-class and Jesuit-educated Irish exile, or the scion of a wealthy Mandarin family which has been ruined, or a lady of the minor nobility

---

[1] Konigsberg, 'The Dramatic Background of Richardson's Plots and Characters', pp. 48-52.

who has been confined most of her life by the rigid etiquette of the Japanese court.

The only way to get to know Richardson at his best is to read *Clarissa*, and to read it unabridged. There has never been much disagreement about the fact that his reputation rests primarily on this work. In *Pamela* one can find at times a freshness and liveliness greater than in *Clarissa*, and in *Sir Charles Grandison* Richardson displays a wider range and an increased skill in the portrayal of manners. But neither of these novels is likely to add significantly to the reader's sense of Richardson's greatness—they may, in fact, decrease it.

And *Clarissa* is not a novel to race through. Its length has undoubtedly kept off many readers, a fact which may be deplorable but is inevitable. The prolixity of *Clarissa*, as Hester Mulso early pointed out to Elizabeth Carter, is necessary: its minute strokes are the principal beauty which distinguishes it from other works of its kind. One may not be able to follow Miss Mulso when she says that she would not quarrel with twice as many volumes.[2] But the book could hardly be a short one and do what it does. It must be lived with for a while. Like *The Remembrance of Things Past*, it creates its own atmosphere, its own world, and this world must be experienced, unless of course you are looking merely for remarks for literary cocktail parties. In that case the less reading you do the better, and the following plot summary will serve your purpose.

Clarissa, a young girl of virtue and good family, is courted by a rake named Lovelace. Her family quarrels with him and tries to force her to marry Mr. Solmes, a suitor she detests. Lovelace tricks her into his power, tries to seduce her, and after her resistance has been convincingly shown, rapes her while she is drugged to sleep. She refuses to marry him, goes into a decline, and dies; he is killed in a duel by her cousin Morden. The telling of this story takes well over a million words. As Balzac says, '*Clarissa* is a masterpiece, it fills fourteen volumes, and the dullest writer of vaudevilles will tell you the story in one act.'[3] Dr. Johnson called it 'a prodigious Work—formed on the stalest of all empty Stories'.[4]

Obviously such an outline gives little idea of the book. Yet Richardson sticks very closely to his plot. He truly claimed that 'long as the Work is, there is not one Digression, not one Episode, not one Reflection, but what arises naturally from the Subject, and makes for it, and to carry it on'.[5] His invention goes into creating an immense number of incidents which elaborate his theme or reveal his characters while advancing the action—slowly, it is true, but inevitably. If unity is the test of a good structure, Richardson's is almost perfect. He never loses sight of his main story. We

---

[2] 18 May [1751], *The Posthumous Works of Mrs. Chapone* (London, 1808), I, 30.
[3] *La Maison Nucingen.*   [4] James L. Clifford, *Hester Lynch Piozzi* (Oxford, 1941), p. 437.
[5] 'Hints of Prefaces for Clarissa', FM XV, 2, fo. 52.

have seen what a poor job Richardson made of it in the continuation of *Pamela*, where he had no plot at all. But he did not need a complicated plot or one involving many adventures and surprises. The history of Clarissa, simple as it is, was ideal for his purposes.

And yet in spite of this simplicity the book runs to a length which has frightened off many readers and which worried Richardson himself. He had tried to shorten but had only partially succeeded. He had tried to avoid repeating the same incidents and, considering the fact that two sets of correspondents (Clarissa and her friend Anna Howe, Lovelace and his friend Belford) are writing about most of the events, there is surprisingly little repetition. There are long periods when the situation does not change much. After the eighth letter there is no important new development until almost the end of the second volume, but Clarissa's conflicts with the various members of her family and her efforts to avoid the odious Solmes keep the action moving. Here, however, some cutting might be possible; one uncle, for instance, is enough, and Uncle John could be spared. The third and fourth volumes consist almost entirely of Lovelace's increasingly determined designs against the heroine and of his offensive behaviour to her, his explaining it away and making up and then beginning again in a more virulent form. Richardson displays great invention in the incidents which illustrate this central conflict, and all of them add to our knowledge of the leading characters. Taken together, they make the involvement of the reader grow constantly more intense. Very little could be eliminated in these volumes. Even after the rape, when it would appear that the crisis is past, Richardson preserves the interest through most of the remaining two and a half volumes. Length is necessary, since Clarissa's reaction to the rape is all-important. Perhaps some of her reflections would not be much missed, and such artificial efforts to preserve suspense as her ambiguous allegorical letter and the misleading hints that she may be pregnant add little. But her constant state of mind and Lovelace's changing one give a centre of interest, and many details are there to illustrate them. It is only after her death that interest definitely lags; the repentance of her family may be necessary to poetic justice, but it is a bore and is dragged out at great length. Only at the end is interest revived, when Lovelace dies. Here the action moves swiftly, as it does elsewhere when Richardson wanted it to.

Some cutting (perhaps a fifth or a sixth) would certainly be possible. But drastic abridgements have never been very successful. Richardson's strength is in characterization by a series of small details and scenes and in gradually creating an atmosphere. There are people who have found an abridgement dull and have later been moved by the complete novel. The most recent person to attempt a shortened version, and certainly one of the best qualified to do so, George Sherburn, writes in a private letter, 'I think *Clarissa* is one of the very greatest novels ever written. It cannot be improved by any sort of *abridgment*. I don't believe you can like what I have done: I don't myself, but I have cut out two-thirds and more of it, and still her skeleton is there.'

At first glance, Dr. Heylin's advice to Richardson to reduce his novel's excess weight by sweating it out of the whole rather than by lopping off whole branches sounds plausible. But the result of such an abridgement can be seen by comparing the two English translations of Tsao Hsueh Chin's *Dream of the Red Chamber*, by Chi-Chen Wang and by Florence and Isabel McHugh from Franz Kuhn's German version. The former reduces each episode by cutting dialogue, description, and detail, with the result that, while it contains many scenes the loss of which one regrets in the other version, few scenes are solidly built up and few characters are allowed to present themselves completely. It is extended too thin; the air of reality vital to one kind of fiction (a kind to which *The Dream of the Red Chamber*, for all its religious allegory, belongs) is lost.

Arnold Bennett has called *Clarissa* 'the greatest realistic novel in the world'.[6] The story is thoroughly realistic if one can believe in the existence of such a character as the heroine. Fault might be found with a few of the details. The universal harshness of Clarissa's family needs some explaining, as Richardson himself felt when he added or increased the role played by Lovelace's 'and their own corrupted Agent, Joseph Leman', in working them up 'to continue their Inveteracy': 'I was afraid, I had hardly made it credible enough.'[7] It has been pointed out that it is improbable that Clarissa could have been held in a bawdy house against her will.[8] But these details are hardly more improbable than many which actually take place, and, more important, Richardson presents them in such a way as to make them real to the reader. Richardson practised the art of making his events convincing in terms of the fiction itself, though he also adhered to the more conventional doctrine of realism, portraying only events which could easily have occurred in everyday life.

In avoiding inconsistencies Richardson was very careful, and his many reperusals of his own works (aided by the fact that he had a printing press at his disposal) enabled him to correct in future editions such slips as did occur. The time sequence of *Clarissa* is meticulously worked out. The events take up less than a year; the first letter is dated 10 January and the last 18 December (7 December, English style). At the beginning and end, letters are dated only by the day of the month; throughout most of the novel, days of the week are included, and they are all consistent. It may be that because the earliest and latest letters are more widely spaced Richardson did not bother to work out the days of the week, whereas

[6] *Books and Persons* (New York, [1917]), p. 139.   [7] To Hill, 29 Oct. 1746.
[8] Thomson, *Richardson*, p. 188.

during the more thickly crowded happenings he knew what his characters were doing almost every hour. It is also worth noting that the first letter for which the day of the week is given is that of Wednesday, 1 March, a fact which prevents the reader from finding out whether the year of the action is a leap year or not. Richardson wanted his readers to think of the time as some years ago, and later pointed out in footnotes certain changes which had taken place since the time of the action; but he did not want to commit himself to any one year. The action of the novel takes place after 1720.[9] In 1721, 1727, and 1732, 1 March fell on a Wednesday. This example is only one of many which show his care in minutiæ.

But this attention to detail is only one cause of the impression of reality in *Clarissa*. That such an impression was a strong one is apparent from many comments; as with *Pamela*, this reality and the moral virtue of the heroine seem to have been the two things which most struck Richardson's contemporaries. 'One can scarce persuade oneself that they are not real characters, and living people', wrote Richardson's future friend Catherine Talbot.[10] We have seen how real they were to Lady Bradshaigh. This sense of reality is built up by a mass of detail, by the same sort of familiarity, acquired over a long period, which one has with real people. That Richardson himself felt it is apparent in his almost personal hatred when he speaks of Lovelace and in the tenderness and admiration with which he always mentions his heroine. 'Poor Cl!' he wrote years later in Lady Bradshaigh's copy, 'how much I pity thee! Whenever I think of thy Character as a real one!' And in the same copy he underlined Clarissa's spoken reflection 'But now I am poor myself!' and commented, 'Who can stand this, if he thinks he sees and hears her say it.'[11] 'Indeed I suffer'd much in writing the distressful Parts,' he wrote to Lady Barbara Montagu.[12] That he was conscious of the importance of this air of reality is shown by a letter to Warburton, in which he opposes anything in the preface which would *prove* the letters not to be genuine, though he does not want them to be *thought* genuine, not only to avoid weakening their force as moral examples but 'to avoid hurting that kind of Historical Faith, which Fiction itself is generally read [with], even tho' we know it to be Fiction'.[13]

Many readers today are not interested in the air of reality in a work of fiction, or at least believe that the realistic surface is unimportant relative to a reading on a deeper level. There is no evidence that Richardson was

---

[9] SH, V, 176; EL, III, 101. See Arthur Sherbo, 'Time and Place in Richardson's *Clarissa*', *Boston University Studies in English*, III (1957), 139–46, and John Samuel Bullen, *Time and Space in the Novels of Samuel Richardson*, Utah State University Press Monograph Series, XII, 2 (Logan, Utah, 1965), pp. 12, 14, 21.

[10] 28 Dec. 1747, *Letters between Mrs. Elizabeth Carter and Miss Catherine Talbot*, I, 161.

[11] 1st edn., III, 168; VI, 223.   [12] 5 Jan. 1759.

[13] 14 Apr. 1748.

an author who consciously wrote on several levels, but of course we are
no longer bound by the author's conscious intentions or concerned, as
Swift was, that many books 'have met with such numberless commentators, whose scholastic midwifery hath delivered them of meanings, that
the authors themselves never conceived'. The most consistent attempt to
read *Clarissa* on various levels is that of Dorothy Van Ghent.[14] The novel
is built around Jungian myths. 'Though absurd, Clarissa has an archetypal
greatness and a secret, underhanded, double-dealing association with the
seeds of things, for she takes upon herself a social dream: the sterilization
of instinct, the supremacy of the "Father," the consolidation of society
in abstraction, the cult of death. . . . Her classic significance as love-
goddess lies in the fact that she dies to promote not fertility but sterility.'
On one level, she is 'the love-goddess of the Puritan middle class', with
its mercantile values, 'an expensive chattel'. Since this class mistrusts sex
and worships money, its values are sterile and its code is 'a cult, in short,
of death'. Psychologically, Clarissa's 'perverted sexuality' identifies sex
and death: her passion, as well as Lovelace's, 'symbolizes gratification,
not of sensual life, but of a submerged portion of the emotional life whose
tendency actually opposes gratification of the senses—the death wish, the
desire for destruction'. On both levels, therefore, *Clarissa* may be read as
'an idealism of death as against the threats and delights of vitality'.
Possible surface inconsistencies and improbabilities are irrelevant, since
'the novel that is myth deals in "realities" of a different kind, those of wish
and fear and desire and dream'. Mrs. Van Ghent finds most of the evidence
for her view in an analysis of the imagery, a kind of evidence which is not
subject to proof or disproof. We suspect, however, that her method could
be used just as convincingly to 'prove' the greatness of *Pollyanna* or *Little
Lord Fauntleroy* or *Peyton Place* or *Valley of the Dolls*.

In our opinion a more persuasive use of the fashionable archetypal
terminology is that of Leslie A. Fiedler in *Love and Death in the American
Novel*.[15] Mr. Fiedler also sees in the novel a 'mythos' of the struggle
between classes, with Clarissa of course representing the bourgeoisie and
Lovelace the aristocracy; such an interpretation is, indeed, hard to escape
and might occur to even a literal reader. In addition, Mr. Fiedler sees
Lovelace as the male tempter, the Seducer, and Clarissa as the female
saviour, the Pure Maiden. That is what they are, and Mr. Fiedler is convincing when he shows how these types persisted in later British and
American fiction. His identification of Lovelace with the head, the Enlightenment, and of Clarissa with the heart, the sentimental view of
Christianity threatened by reason, is not so easy to see—it is, after all,

---

[14] *The English Novel: Form and Function* (New York, [1953]), pp. 45–63, 307–22, and 'Clarissa
and Emma as Phèdre', *Partisan Review*, XVII (1950), 820–33.
[15] Pp. 29–42.

Lovelace who, like a romantic hero, follows his passions. But if one ignores some of the ingenuity and forgets Mr. Fiedler's rather slapdash way of rising above mere accuracy in the details of the plot, there is some truth in his idea that the conflict between the characters represents 'a psychological division in the soul of man itself'; such an idea may even be helpful in reading the novel. Mythos (with its tendency to return to allegory by a side door) apart, even the most realistic works must, if they are to be of more than mild interest, appeal to something more general than the individual situation. Mr. Fiedler, in our opinion, does, unlike Mrs. Van Ghent, grasp the effect of the book: 'The myth of Clarissa's immolation represents archetypally that victory which can only be wrung from defeat and which lifts up the heart in exultation above merely human notions of success and failure.' And he also recognizes that *Clarissa* 'achieves its mythic resonance without sacrificing verisimilitude', that essentially Richardson's art creates ' "character" in the full modern sense, that is . . . fictional actors at once complexly motivated and consistent, highly individualized and typical'. So long as one remembers this reservation, the dangers of the mythological approach are minimized.

Readers who find abstract statements about social relationships or illustrations of the doctrines of psychoanalysis of primary interest may read *Clarissa* in the light of one of these myths or, if they are clever enough, make up their own. We will discuss the novel, as Richardson's simple contemporaries (including Diderot and Johnson) read it, in terms of its realistic surface, of its characters and of the emotions they feel and inspire and the attitudes they embody and convey. These emotions and attitudes do, in our opinion, have a wide application to many human situations and thus may not illegitimately be called 'archetypal' or 'mythical'. But in this sort of novel the wide application arises from and cannot be divorced from the specific events because it depends, as Mr. Fiedler realizes, on the effect which the experience of reading has on the reader, not on extraneous doctrines or morals which can be thought up *about* the events—and Richardson as well as Mrs. Van Ghent was able to think up several such morals. Realism, in the sense of that air of reality which is the result of solid and vivid imagination, is not in conflict with the general, it embodies and conveys the general.

Richardson's letters show that he was no accidental artist when he wrote *Clarissa*. We do not mean to imply that a part, perhaps the most important part, of his work was not due to a side of himself of which he was not altogether conscious, a side which ran away with him, to use a convenient if vague phrase. But he thought a good deal about what he was doing. The reception of *Pamela* must have made him recognize, if he had not already done so, that his genre was original. We have seen that he protested to Hill that Lovelace is not to be bound by the usual rules. He was

reminded of his originality fairly often—for instance, by the author of a
poem called 'Apollo's Court', which he kept among his correspondence,
in which the god of poetry complains that the author of *Clarissa* does not
obey his laws:

> He charms a new invented way,
>   Regardless of the Lyre;
> Bows not beneath our sovereign sway,
>   Nor asks our aid t'inspire.[16]

One of the inventions of which he was proudest was that writing to the
moment which often arises naturally from the epistolary method, but
which Richardson sometimes forced. Lovelace is conscious of its advantages: 'Thou'lt observe, Belford, that tho' this was written afterwards,
yet (as in other places) I write it as it was spoken and happened, as if I had
retired to put down every sentence as spoken. I know thou likest this
lively *present-tense* manner, as it is one of my peculiars.' Richardson compliments himself again when he has Belford tell Lovelace of the 'melancholy pleasure' he promises himself from the perusal of Clarissa's
voluminous papers: 'Such a sweetness of temper, so much patience and
resignation, as she seems to be mistress of; yet writing of and in the midst
of *present* distresses! How *much more* lively and affecting, for that reason,
must her style be; her mind tortured by the pangs of uncertainty (the
events then hidden in the womb of Fate) *than* the dry, narrative, unani-
mated style of persons, relating difficulties and dangers surmounted; the
relator perfectly at ease; and if himself unmoved by his own Story, not
likely greatly to affect the Reader!'[17]

At times he rather abuses this method, as he had in *Pamela*, to obtain
suspense, having a letter-writer break off in midstream to meet new perils.
He was certainly interested in suspense and several times uses the devices
of only half revealing an event in one hurried letter and then allowing a
digression to intervene before the event is fully described. This is most
effective in the letter which concluded the second volume, and his first
instalment, in which the bare fact of Clarissa's flight with Lovelace is
revealed, without the details which explain it.

But the most important use of the present-tense method is in building
up scenes. Richardson generally alternates passages of reflection with
lively descriptions of action. The latter, especially when described by
Lovelace, often read like drama. It is apparent that Richardson had
visualized his people and their movements. Lovelace, for instance, describes an early-morning interview with Clarissa after he has highly
offended her by his nicely calculated advances the night before; she enters,

---

[16] Dated 15 Apr. 1751, FM XV, 2, fos. 91–2. A second copy is in FM XVI, 2, fos. 15–16.
[17] SH, V, 312, VII, 77; EL, III, 195, IV, 81.

ready to go out, and answers him curtly, and he urges her to breakfast
first:

Yes, she would drink one dish; and then laid her gloves and fan in the
window just by.

I was perfectly disconcerted, I hemm'd, and was going to speak several times;
but knew not in what key. Who's modest now, thought I! Who's insolent
now!—How a tyrant of a woman confounds a bashful man!—She was acting
Miss Howe, I thought; and I the spiritless Hickman.

At last, I *will* begin, thought I.

She a dish—I a dish.

Sip, her eyes her own, she; like an haughty and imperious sovereign, conscious of dignity, every look a favour.

Sip, like her vassal, I; lips and hands trembling, and not knowing that I
sipp'd or tasted.

I was—I was—Iffp'd—(drawing in my breath and the liquor together, tho'
I scalded my mouth with it) I was in hopes, Madam—

Dorcas came in just then.—Dorcas, said she, is a chair gone for?

Damn'd impertinence, thought I, thus to put me out in my speech! And I
was forced to wait for the servant's answer to the insolent mistress's question.

William is gone for one, Madam.

This cost me a minute's silence before I could begin again.—And then it
was with my hopes, and my hopes, and my hopes, that I should have been
early admitted to—

What weather is it, Dorcas? said she, as regardless of me as if I had not been
present.

A little lowering, Madam—The sun is gone in—It was very fine half an
hour ago.

I had no patience. Up I rose. Down went the Tea-cup, Saucer and all—
Confound the Weather, the Sunshine, and the Wench!—Begone for a devil,
when I am speaking to your Lady, and have so little opportunity given me.

Up rose the saucy-face, half-frighted; and snatched from the window her
gloves and fan.

You must not go, Madam!—Seizing her hand—By my soul, you must not—

Must not, Sir!—But I must—You can curse your maid in my absence, as well
as if I were present—Except—Except—you intend for *me*, what you direct
to *her*.[18]

Richardson's scenes are rich in brief and telling descriptions of gestures,
expressions, and movements.[19] As Clarissa says, 'Air and manner often
express more than the accompanying words.'[20] He wrote before the vogue
of long descriptions of nature, which began later in the century in novels
like *The Spiritual Quixote* and *John Buncle* and fascinated Gothic writers

[18] SH, IV, 213–14; EL, II, 381.

[19] See George Sherburn, '"Writing to the Moment": One Aspect', *Restoration and Eighteenth-Century Literature: Essays in Honor of Alan Dugald McKillop*, ed. Carroll Camden (Chicago, 1963), pp. 201–9.

[20] SH, I, 8; EL, I, 5.

from Mrs. Radcliffe to Poe. Nor did he have the nineteenth century's love of detailed descriptions of rooms and costumes, though Lovelace does describe Clarissa's dress in some detail on the crucial occasion of her abduction.[21] In order to make Lovelace more acutely conscious of the enormity of his treatment of Clarissa, Belford minutely describes her bed-chamber at the bailiff's,[22] but such physical descriptions are rare and usually brief. Where they occur, they almost always serve to illustrate the reporter's state of mind.[23] And most of Richardson's lengthy descriptions are directly of motives and states of mind.

There are a good many effects which betray conscious artistry. In the first volume Lovelace is talked about by the other characters well before he enters the stage with a letter of his own. And this letter, though it contains warnings of Lovelace's true character which Richardson was able to point out to Lovelace's admirers, is ambiguous enough for a reader not on the alert to consider him an over-passionate but rather amiable man. His next letter, in which he resolves not to seduce Rosebud, the innocent daughter of his innkeeper, is even more sympathetic; and the only other letter from him in the first two volumes still leaves his character in doubt. Rather theatrical, perhaps, but effectively theatrical, is the brief letter in which Lovelace announces the long-awaited rape: '*Tuesday Morn. June* 13. And now, Belford, I can go no farther. The affair is over. Clarissa lives. And I am *Your humble Servant,* R. LOVELACE.' A similar effect is aimed at in the letter informing Lovelace (and the reader) that Clarissa is at last dead: '*Seven o'Clock, Thursday Evening, Sept.* 7. I have only to say at present —Thou wilt do well to take a tour to Paris; or where-ever else thy destiny shall lead thee!!!—JOHN BELFORD.'[24] And this is followed by a flippant letter from their rakish friend Mowbray. The first part of *Pamela* may have been a lucky hit, but throughout *Clarissa* Richardson knew exactly what he was doing.

This conscious artistry may not do much to recommend Richardson to an age that seems to prefer the semi-articulate and the unfinished, the rough rhythm and the off-rhyme. Today Richardson is usually praised, when he is praised, for the psychology of his characters. By this, it is not always meant that his characters can be analysed in Freudian or other modern terms, though such analysis has, of course, been attempted, and has been about as successful with Richardson as it has with most writers. The force of Richardson's characterization was recognized long before Freud. It can best be summed up in E. M. Forster's term: Richardson's characters are round characters. 'Richardson is the least flat, the most stereoscopic novelist of an age which ran the plain or formal statement to

---

[21] SH, III, 27–9; EL, I, 511–12.   [22] SH, VI, 296–8; EL, III, 444–5.
[23] Bullen, *Time and Space in the Novels of Samuel Richardson,* p. 35.
[24] SH, V, 314, VII, 464; EL, III, 196, IV, 342.

death in the end.'[25] The distinction between round and flat characters is not simply synonymous with good and bad. Many excellent characters, especially in heroic poetry and in early tales, are flat. Chaucer's characters in the Prologue to the *Canterbury Tales* are flat, though the Wife of Bath begins to take on some rotundity in her own Prologue. Homer, the Icelandic sagas, and the *Nibelungenlied* contain first-rate flat characters. They are flat in that we never get into their minds (we are often even in doubt about their motives) and in that they are one-sided, or at most two-sided. We do not experience with them. But we see their experiences sharply, and we hear their voices. They are striking, lively, memorable representations of some important aspect of human nature.

The modern novel, at least until recently, has preferred on the whole more complex characters and characters seen from inside. There are brilliant exceptions; in spite of the recent tendency to prefer the later novels of Dickens, in which one finds such more-or-less round characters as Bradley Headstone and Arthur Clennam, it is still possible to believe that nothing in *Our Mutual Friend* and *Little Dorrit* quite consoles us for the loss of Mrs. Nickleby and Dick Swiveller and Sarah Gamp, who are as two-dimensional as possible. Of Richardson's contemporaries, Fielding rarely (perhaps only in *Amelia*) strives for a round character and Smollett seems never to have dreamed of one. Richardson was one of the first to give the novel this direction, though Mme. de Lafayette, at least, preceded him. But Richardson did more than any other to form the taste for round characters. This taste was not an unmixed blessing. In the analysis of motives and the examination of mental states, a certain sharpness of outline is often lost, a symbolic impressiveness, a generality. Just as the flat character can degenerate into a wooden type unless the author breathes intensity into the trait he represents, so the round character can slop over and spread out until he is little more than a formless series of emotional exclamations unless the author is able to keep his outlines clean. The round character, seen from inside, can easily lapse into 'lyricism' in the sense of expression of personal feeling; and his many-sidedness, if his traits fail to coalesce into the molecule of a new compound with a unity of its own, may result in his remaining a mere mixture. When these dangers are avoided, the round character may take on the generality and grandeur, the symbolic quality, of the best of the flat characters. Shakespeare had already united the advantages of the two types in the drama; and few people will doubt that there are characters in novels who unite them, Raskolnikov, for instance, and Julien Sorel, and Leopold Bloom. If Richardson ever united them, it was in Clarissa and in Lovelace.

One is not supposed to use the word 'sincere' in criticism any more, since it is impossible to be *certain* that any author was sincere, and of

[25] V. S. Pritchett, *The Living Novel* (London, 1946), p. 15.

course the reader is interested not in the state of the author's mind but in what that state of mind has produced. But it is hard not to believe that Richardson, aside from the obvious but less interesting sincerity of his moral purpose, had sincerely imagined his characters. He had 'got inside them' and they often 'ran away with him'. The easiest, and probably truest, interpretation of these phrases is that an author may intensely imagine a character by embodying in that character one aspect of his own nature. Round characters are not complete people. It might be clearer to think of them as being not round like a statue but shaded into perspective like a painting. A novel which tried to portray a whole person would have to be many times as long as *Clarissa* and would be so dull that no one could read it; and it would still select and omit. A round character does not portray the author, but something, or some things, in the author which he has managed to conceive of as separate from the rest of himself and to fuse into a dramatic unity. The variety within any mind should be great enough for a writer to discover a large enough number of round characters to people more novels than he has time to write. This variety may be one reason why psychological studies which purport to give us an author's 'real' character on the basis of an analysis of one of his characters usually seem as oversimplified as the 'humours' in comedies. Perhaps the greatest richness of which the novel is capable comes when an author manages to embody several important sides of himself in different characters, each complex and yet fused so that he gives an impression of unity and of generality, and all in conflict with one another. At least the interaction of the three Karamazov brothers, perfect types and yet supremely individual, and of the many other round characters who support them would lead one to think so.

The epistolary method, to be successful, demands that an author 'live' his characters at least to the extent of being able to write in their names and not in his own. And since style is an important element of characterization, this extent is a large extent. The first part of *Pamela* is not really an epistolary novel, since most of it (and all the best of it) is written by one person; the second part is more nearly epistolary, but unsuccessfully so—none of its characters has any style, much less a personal style. That Richardson was conscious, at least after the fact, of having made an effort in *Clarissa* to suit the style to the character is apparent from a letter in which he explained to Lady Bradshaigh the importance of distinguishing characters by the way they write and told her that he had been 'complimented wth: giving a Stile to each of my various Characters, yt: distinguishes *whose* from *whose*, ye Moment they are entred upon'. His style, he said, was determined by the 'supposed Characters of ye writer & written to' and by the occasion and the moral effect desired.[26]

[26] 12 July 1757

In the novel itself, Belford thinks that Clarissa's 'allegorical' letter, in which she leads Lovelace to imagine that she may marry him by speaking of a journey to her father's (God's) house, where she hopes he may join her, cannot be a forgery of Lovelace's because of its style, 'tho' thou art a perfect Proteus too'. And indeed Lovelace's style is varied, and he shows that he has thought about style. He prefers the familiar style (*'familiar writing* is but *talking*, Jack'); 'the little words in the Republic of Letters, like the little folks in a nation, are the most significant. The *trisyllables*, and the *rumblers* of syllables more than *three*, are but the good for little *magnates.*' He loves, like his creator, to coin words. Clarissa's style is less varied and less full of strong effects and surprises, but she too prefers the familiar style, in which women can excel, and makes fun of the style of scholars, whether they affect a 'masculine' style as rough as their manners which aims at the sublime but rumbles into bombast, or by 'aiming at *wit* . . . forfeit all title to *judgment*', or fall into the '*classical pits*' where they 'poke and scramble about', priding themselves only on their knowledge of the 'beauties of two thousand years old in *another* tongue, which they can only *admire*, but not *imitate*, in their own'.[27]

Richardson, then, had ideas about style. Like many later novelists, he discovered how well characters may be presented through their ways of speaking. His dialogue is often typical and lively. There is, however, some indication that he made it less lively in revision, as he did in his successive revisions of *Pamela*. His various drafts are lost, but Hill's abridged version of Richardson's first or second revision preserves much of Richardson's wording.[28] In Hill's version, Clarissa's sister, Arabella, when she looks on Lovelace as her suitor, praises his manly beauty:

Let me see! she cried, (and danced up to the Looking-glass—) In truth I have not a *quite bad* Face neither! Many Ladies had done Mischief, with inferior Force of Features for it!—Her *Eyes* at least, she could not think were much amiss (and truly I had never seen 'em shine so brilliantly!)—Nothing here perhaps too flamingly transporting; and yet nothing neither to find fault with— *Is* there, Clary?

In the earliest published version, this passage reads:

But then, stepping to the glass, she complimented herself, 'That she was very *well*: That there were many women deemed passable, who were inferior to herself: That she was always thought comely; and, let her tell me, that comeliness having not so much to lose as beauty had, would hold, when that would evaporate and fly off:—Nay, for that matter,' (and again she turn'd to the

---

[27] SH, VII, 210, V, 397, IV, 293, VIII, 224–5; EL, IV, 171, III, 241, II, 435, IV, 495. Clarissa's remarks were added in the third and fourth editions.

[28] See Eaves and Kimpel, 'The Composition of *Clarissa* and Its Revision before Publication', pp. 422–3.

glass), 'her features were not irregular; her eyes not at all amiss.' And I remember they were more than usually brilliant at that time.—'Nothing, in short, to be found fault with, tho' nothing very engaging, she doubted—Was there, Clary?'

After she no longer has hopes of marrying him, Arabella belittles Lovelace's claims:

As for the Estate he had pretended to, she knew it must be dipped—How could it possibly be otherwise? A Man so given to his Pleasures!—He kept no House: Displayed no Equipage: And since no-body pretended they could reckon *Pride* among his *Wants*, it was an easy thing to guess at the true Reason.

This appears, more elegantly, in the novel as:

'His estate was certainly much encumber'd: It was impossible it should be otherwise; so intirely devoted as he was to his pleasures. He kept no house; had no equipage: Nobody pretended that he wanted pride: The reason therefore was easy to be guessed at.'

However much the elegance fits in with Clarissa's character, and with her and Arabella's class, something has been lost. But even in the final version the dialogue is not commonplace.

Richardson took pains that the epistolary style of even his minor correspondents should reveal their characters. Occasionally the methods are not very subtle. Lovelace's servant, Joseph Leman, writes to him: 'Be pleased, howsomever, if it like your Honner, not to call me, *honnest Joseph*, and *honnest Joseph*, so often. For, althoff I think myself very honnest, and all that; yet I am touched a little for fear I should not do the quite right thing: And too—besides, your Honner has such a fesseshious way with you, as that I hardly know whether you are in jest or earnest, when your Honner calls me honnest so often.' Clarissa's business-man Uncle Antony is broadly but sharply distinguished by his middle-class wit and his love of proverbs: '*If there were no such man as Lovelace in the world, you would not have Mr. Solmes.* [He is answering Clarissa's plea, in which she made this statement.]—You *would not*, Miss!—Very pretty, truly!—We *see* how your spirit is *embittered* indeed.—Wonder not, since it is come to your *will not's*, that those who have authority over you, say, *You shall have the other.* And I am one. Mind that. And if it behoves You *to speak out*, Miss, it behoves US not to *speak in*. What's *sawce for the goose is sawce for the gander*: Take That in your thought too.' (The trick of repeating his correspondent's phrases and exclaiming on them is one which Richardson used in his own letters.) Lovelace's uncle Lord M. also loves proverbs, but in a way which is appropriate to his higher social standing as well as to his prosy, weak, and kindly character: 'I never was offered a Place myself: And the only one I would have taken, had I been offered it, was *Master of the Buckhounds*; for I loved hunting when I was young; and it carries a good sound with it for us who live in the country. Often have I thought of that excellent old adage; *He that eats the King's goose, shall be choaked with his feathers.* I wish to the Lord, this was thoroughly considered by Place-hunters! It would be better for them, and for their poor families.' Miss Howe's would-be strict but ultimately indulgent mother writes to her daughter's unwelcome suitor: 'I cannot but say, Mr. Hickman, but you have cause to be dissatisfied—to be out of humour—to be displeased —with Nancy—But, upon my word; But indeed—what shall I say?—Yet this I will say, that you *good* young gentlemen know nothing at all of our Sex. Shall I tell you—But why should I? And yet I will say, That if Nancy did not think well of you in the main, she is too generous to treat you so freely as she does.' Even the rhythm of the parallel phrases in the first sentence reflects her good-humoured helplessness under a show of strength. Mrs. Harlowe, torn between her habitual subservience to her husband and her love for her daughter, writes to Mrs. Norton, who has a letter from Clarissa, which her mother dares not receive:

She has made my Lot heavy, I am sure, that was far from being light before!— To tell you truth, I am enjoined not to receive any-thing of hers, from any hand, without leave. Should I therefore gratify my yearnings after her, so far as to receive privately the Letter you mention, what would the case be, but to torment myself, without being able to do her good?—And were it to be known—Mr. Harlowe is *so* passionate—And should it throw his Gout into his Stomach, as her rash Flight did—Indeed, indeed, I am very unhappy!—For, Oh my good woman, she is my Child still!—But unless it were more in my power—Yet do I long to see the Letter—You say it tells of her present way and circumstances.—The poor child, who ought to be in possession of thousands!— And *will!*—For her Father will be a faithful Steward for her.—But it must be in his own way, and at his own time.

And is she *really* ill?—so *very* ill?—But she *ought* to sorrow.—She has given a double measure of it.[29]

These are among Richardson's flat characters, though there may be a touch of the author in Uncle Antony, Lord M., and Mrs. Howe. They are largely drawn from observation, not from participation. They are, however, drawn from close and keen observation; they are not incredible caricatures, they are not dull, and they each have more than one trait. Even the pedant Brand, whom Richardson drew as a more conventional type, is convincing. Such characters are almost necessary in a novel about round characters. Proust, for instance, who was certainly not lacking in psychological penetration, has a great many, some of them among his most brilliant creations. Richardson's flat characters are not so memorable as Mme. Verdurin, but most of them are individualized and lively, and they give the impression of being true.

[29] SH, II, 371, I, 240–1, IV, 259, II, 143, VII, 35; EL, I, 492–3, 164–5, II, 412, I, 336–7, IV, 53.

Even the lower-class, disreputable characters, though they are probably not drawn from any close observation but are based on convention, are vivid enough. Here is Lovelace describing Mrs. Sinclair, the madam to whose house he has brought his unsuspecting victim: 'The old dragon straddled up to her, with her arms kemboed again—Her eye-brows erect, like the bristles upon a hog's back, and, scouling over her shortened nose, more than half-hid her ferret eyes. Her mouth was distorted. She pouted out her blubber-lips, as if to bellows up wind and sputter into her horse-nostrils; and her chin was curdled, and more than usually prominent with passion.'[30] The description is not exactly convincing; but it makes an impression. The very fact that it is exaggerated, and yet not so exaggerated as to stretch a heightened imagination, provides the proper note of horror in this scene, where Clarissa, with all her delicacy and all her pride, is exposed to this creature shortly before she loses the virginity which has been, to her, the epitome of delicacy and the justification of pride. A more extended bravura piece in the Hogarthian tradition of 'low' grotesque is Belford's description of Mrs. Sinclair in her last illness. It is, to underline the moral, made as disgusting as possible: 'Behold her then, spreading the whole tumbled bed with her huge quaggy carcase: Her mill-post arms held up; her broad hands clenched with violence; her big eyes, goggling and flaming-red as we may suppose those of a salamander; her matted griesly hair.'[31] Unfortunately Mrs. Sinclair, unlike most of the characters in *Clarissa*, does not speak very convincingly. She does not seem to be someone Richardson had seen and heard: Mrs. Jewkes in *Pamela* can move and talk, whereas Mrs. Sinclair can only look. She is one of Richardson's weaker flat characters, but she is adequate to her role.

A more serious weakness is that of Clarissa's father. Richardson's story demanded that the heroine's family be all but monsters. Uncle Antony, with his petty-minded, money-loving propriety and his tradesman's practicality and wit, is more than adequate. So is the timid mother, whose habit of subservience to her husband has made her unable to defend her own child. Clarissa's brother, James, is carefully motivated, though he remains a stage villain. Her sister, Arabella, is little but spiteful, but Richardson had a talent for reproducing the language of spite.[32] Yet a selfish brother and envious sister could have done nothing if their father had defended Clarissa. Perhaps a high idea of the parental prerogative combined with Mr. Harlowe's gout and general bitterness might have been a sufficient motivation for his driving her to desperation by insisting on her marriage with Solmes. Undoubtedly eighteenth-century fathers were often high-handed. But the novel needs not a logical, realistically probable motive, but a motive which the reader is made to believe because

[30] SH, V, 313; EL, III, 195-6.   [31] SH, VIII, 57; EL, IV, 382.
[32] See, for example, SH, I, 345-6; EL, I, 235-6.

of the force with which it is presented. It is not that we are not intellectually convinced that Mr. Harlowe's anger is possible; it is that Mr. Harlowe himself, on whom Clarissa's fate largely depends, makes only brief appearances, and colourless ones. He was necessary to the plot, but Richardson had not created him as a character, had not imagined him. His motives may be explained, but they do not exist so far as the novel is concerned. Clarissa can come in conflict with a vivid flat character like Bella, but not with a cipher. The father is the only character in *Clarissa* who is entirely inadequate for the role he has to play, and the fact that he is present largely in name leaves a serious gap in the first two volumes.

In having his story told mainly by means of letters between Lovelace and his friend Belford and between Clarissa and her friend Anna Howe, Richardson ran the risk of falling into the trap into which so many plays have fallen, the undue prominence of the confidant. Since there is a real exchange in the letters, not a mere narrative to a shadowy listener, a dangerously large portion of the book depends on two characters who must usually be outside the action, since they have to be told about it. Belford is not so lively a character as Miss Howe, though his early letters, while he is still a rake, have a certain wit. In the central part of the book he becomes more and more earnest, until he begins to plead for Clarissa against his friend. He serves as a foil, to whom Lovelace can say anything, but who is likely to argue against what he says and so to provoke further argument. He becomes the voice of common sense and good feeling. In the last volumes, the events leading up to Clarissa's death are mostly narrated by Belford, who by this time has become somewhat sentimental. Analysis and reproof of Lovelace come better from him than they could from anyone else. It cannot be said that he is memorable as a character, but neither is he a clog on the book. He is all that he needs to be and at times more. That Richardson not only keeps him from getting in the way but makes him perform several necessary functions is a tribute to the technical skill of the writing, if not to the writer's imagination.

Miss Howe is still better. Each of Richardson's novels has a basically good but sharp-tongued, hot-tempered, and determined woman. One might speculate on why the mild-spoken printer was so fond of drawing viragos. He seems to have had no difficulty in thinking of nasty remarks which might be made to people, though so far as one can judge he rarely made them. At most, in his correspondence with ladies he occasionally became rather arch, with a touch of vinegar. The letters which we have quoted about his meeting with Lady Bradshaigh show that he could be cutting at times. If he did frequently think of unkind remarks which he would not allow himself to make, he let his strong-minded women have free reign in expressing what he judged it best not to express. Charlotte

Grandison, particularly, often goes beyond the limits of permissible rudeness.

Miss Howe is not so violent as Charlotte, but she is sharp and witty enough to hold the reader's attention. Since she is the main admirer and supporter of the heroine, there was a great danger of her becoming cloying —as she does become, after Clarissa's death, in her excessive praises. Throughout most of the novel her outspoken and wilful nature saves her; she is able to be entirely loyal to Clarissa and yet independent, good-hearted without sentiment, kind without sugariness. She analyses Clarissa's motives, especially her love; she explains with realism and common sense the necessities of Clarissa's situation. While the main action takes place in an isolated, unusual, and intense world, Miss Howe moves in normal society, visits and receives visitors, is properly courted and goes to balls. Though she is not earthy like Sancho Pança, her role is not unlike his: she responds to Clarissa's idealism with the voice of ordinary life. Indeed it is in large measure owing to Miss Howe that we are able to believe in so much idealism. She admires it and yet criticizes it. Clarissa herself is at times fairly sharp-tongued, but she can never be allowed to go as far as Miss Howe. She must forgive, being a Christian heroine; her friend can refuse forgiveness and thus serve as the mouthpiece of indignation.

Miss Howe's treatment of her dull and virtuous suitor Mr. Hickman sets off Clarissa's experiences. She is by no means under the thumb of her Mamma, and she is allowed to make remarks on the abuse of parental authority which the virtuous Clarissa cannot make but which help us to sympathize with Clarissa's much milder resistance. She does finally accept Mr. Hickman. Clarissa thinks she should and sees no parallel between him and Solmes, since Miss Howe does not loathe him, she only makes fun of him. Whether the reader can agree with Clarissa on this point is doubtful. Richardson would never have wanted to state that a girl should not marry unless she is passionately in love, nor that a suitor whose only drawbacks are meekness and dullness is an unsuitable husband. Indeed Richardson later tried to convince some of his female readers that they should be more attached to Mr. Hickman than to Lovelace. Richardson the moralist thought so. But it is doubtful if any reader has ever felt that Miss Howe was lucky in her conquest. Before he draws the moral, Richardson permits Miss Howe to torture and laugh at Mr. Hickman in a way that makes it hard to accept the moral once drawn.

We have seen the effect Lovelace had upon Lady Bradshaigh. And she was not the only person to admire him. We have also seen that Richardson even before publication of the first volumes began blackening his character, pointing out that such admiration was misplaced. He later added notes which underlined Lovelace's wickedness. Years later his indignation against his own creation is apparent in his comment on Lady Bradshaigh's note in her copy of *Clarissa* that the heroine is too violent against Love-lace: 'O let her, let her, use her own Discretion in her Treatment of such a teazing Villain, as he opens to her!'[33]

Sir Leslie Stephen, in a remark often echoed, considers that Lovelace is very animated and at the same time a 'fancy character': 'When we coolly dissect him and ask whether he could ever have existed, we may be forced to reply in the negative. But whilst we read we forget to criticize; he seems to possess more vitality than most living men.'[34] The conception of a convincing character who never existed may not be so clear as it appears to be at first sight. In an obvious but not unimportant sense no character in fiction ever existed, not even one who has been drawn from a friend of the author or from the author himself. If Sir Leslie meant merely that no real man ever acted as Lovelace acted, we suspect that he was wrong, but the question is not so important as whether Richardson was able to put into Lovelace characteristics which the reader can recognize, on the basis of his own experience, as human. We cannot prove that he did—each reader must decide for himself. Perhaps readers as virtuous as Sir Leslie will continue, luckily for them, to find him incredible. We are more inclined to agree with Frank Kermode that he is 'not merely a "round" character but a moral being'.[35]

The indebtedness of Lovelace's character to the ranting hero of the heroic play of the Restoration has been noted.[36] And indeed Lovelace does rant at times. But surely he has a reality far beyond that of Almanzor and his brothers. Dryden could hardly have imagined himself, or anybody, ranting in Almanzor's style, whereas Lovelace, though he may exist only in fantasy (as did, for instance, the Rousseau of Rousseau's *Confessions*), at least exists there. It might be truer to say that Lovelace frequently quotes the Restoration heroes because he likes to think of himself as a protagonist of a heroic play to feed his insatiable vanity by comparing himself with ranting kings and princes. Brian Downs comes close to the truth when he says that Lovelace 'is not Lucifer, but a type as perennial and common and odious as Pamela's, that of the over-grown schoolboy: a schoolboy soaked in the lust of adolescence, intoxicated with the sense of power and of immense intellectual superiority (*soi-disant* genius) which a careful preference for the society of inferiors confers and which in his eyes invests all that he does and thinks with a sheen worthy of the best effects of Covent Garden or Drury Lane.'[37] The schoolboy rants as much as Almanzor (whom he greatly resembles), he exists in part in the atmos-phere of the theatre. But he does exist. It might even be asked how much more theatrical his life is than that of other men, though his is a

[33] 1st edn., III, 163.   [34] 'Richardson's Novels', *Cornhill Magazine*, XVII (1868), 66–8.
[35] 'Richardson and Fielding', p. 110.   [36] McKillop, *Richardson*, pp. 149–52.
[37] *Richardson*, p. 116.

melodrama and theirs a rather dull soap opera. At any rate, though we do not agree with Mr. Downs that lust is a major element in Lovelace's make-up, we do agree on the intensity of his desire to assert his own superiority.

The excellence of his portrait is shown by the fact that for several generations Lovelace was a familiar figure, whose name was so well known as to become almost a common noun. Baudelaire, in 'Danse macabre', warns the 'lovelaces chenus' that, like other devotees of pleasure, they will vanish into the unknown. One of Hazlitt's reasons for admiring Napoleon was that he, on meeting a young English officer named Lovelace at his levée, remarked, 'I perceive your name, Sir, is the same as that of the hero of Richardson's Romance!'[38] Whether or not Napoleon had read *Clarissa*, he knew of the type—as did everyone.

A large part of Lovelace's appeal is, as one would expect, his style. Here he is training the maid Dorcas to act surprise and terror when he takes ipecacuanha and feigns sickness:

Come hither, Toad [sick as a devil at the instant]; Let me see what a mixture of grief and surprize may be beat up together in thy pudden-face.

That won't do. That dropt jaw, and mouth distended into the long oval, is more upon the Horrible, than the Grievous.

Nor that pinking and winking with thy *odious eyes*, as my charmer once called them.

A little better *That*; yet not quite right: But keep your mouth closer. You have a muscle or two which you have no command of, between your cheek-bone and your lips, that should carry one corner of your mouth up towards your crows-foot, and that down to meet it.

There! Begone! Be in a plaguy hurry running up stairs and down, to fetch from the Dining-room what you carry up on purpose to fetch, till motion extraordinary put you out of breath, and give you the sigh-natural.[39]

He has a constant flow of wit, which it is hard not to think that his creator enjoyed as much as Lady Bradshaigh did. Even when he is becoming somewhat gloomy, after his rape of Clarissa is beginning to turn into a disaster for him as well as for her, Belford's solemn statement that he considers Clarissa as a beatified spirit sent from Heaven to draw him, Belford, out of his miry gulf reminds Lovelace of Dame Elizabeth Carteret's monument in the Abbey:

If thou never observedst it, go thither on purpose; and there wilt thou see this Dame in effigie, with uplifted head and hand, the latter taken hold of by a Cupid every inch of stone, one clumsy foot lifted up also, aiming, as the Sculptor designed it, to ascend; but so executed, as would rather make one imagine, that the Figure (without shoe or stocken, as it is, tho' the rest of the body is robed) was looking up to its Corn-cutter: The other riveted to its native earth, bemired,

---

[38] *Complete Works*, ed. P. P. Howe (London and Toronto, [1930–4]), XII, 227n–8n.
[39] SH, IV, 292; EL, II, 435.

like thee (*immersed* thou callest it) beyond the possibility of unsticking itself. Both Figures, thou wilt find, seem to be in a contention, the bigger, whether it should pull down the lesser about its ears—the lesser (a chubby fat little varlet, of a fourth part of the other's bigness, with wings not much larger than those of a butterfly) whether it should raise the larger to a Heaven it points to, hardly big enough to contain the great toes of either.[40]

Richardson certainly regarded this levity as wicked; yet he did not take any less pains in phrasing it.

After Clarissa's death Lovelace does at times become very solemn. He has serious reflections on the afterlife and on his wickedness. It is perhaps well for the maintenance of his character that Richardson was not one of the newfangled sentimental moralists who would have insisted on the clear repentance of Lovelace. Perhaps his last words, 'LET THIS EX-PIATE!', are meant to leave the way open so that the reader can believe in his repentance if he chooses.[41] But Richardson's comment to Edward Moore shows that he did not consider Lovelace as saved: 'And at last with his wonted haughtiness of Spirit—LET THIS EXPIATE all his apparent Invocation and address to the SUPREME. Have I not then given rather a dreadful than a hopeful Exit, with respect to Futurity, to the unhappy Lovelace!'[42] Richardson did not mean Lovelace to be a Charles Surface, a rake with a heart of gold. However unhappy this fact may be for Lovelace in the afterlife, it means that he never loses his character. His letter written in delirium after hearing of Clarissa's death is still, in spite of his self-reproaches (rather, in the very violence and exaggeration of those self-reproaches), in character:

My brain is all boiling like a caldron over a fiery furnace. What a devil is the matter with me I wonder! I never was so strange in my life.

In truth, Jack, I have been a most execrable villain. And when I consider all my actions to this angel of a woman, and in her the piety, the charity, the wit, the beauty, I have *helped* to destroy, and the good to the world I have thereby been a means of frustrating; I can pronounce damnation upon myself. How then can I expect mercy any-where else!

I believe I shall have no patience with you when I see you. Your damn'd stings and reflections have almost turned my brain.

But here Lord M. they tell me, is come! Damn him, and those who sent for him!

I know not what I have written! But her dear heart and a lock of her hair I will have, let who will be the gain-sayers! For is she not mine? Whose else can she be? She has no Father nor Mother, no Sister, no Brother; no Relations but me. And my Beloved is mine; and I am hers: And that's enough.—But Oh!

She's out! The damp of death has quench'd her quite!
Those spicy doors, her lips, are shut, close lock'd,
Which never gale of life shall open more!

[40] SH, VII, 331–2; EL, IV, 252–3.   [41] SH, VIII, 277; EL, IV, 530.   [42] [Jan.? 1749].

And is it so! Is it *indeed* so?—Good God!—Good God!—But they will not let me write on. I must go down to this officious Peer—Who the devil sent for him?[43]

This letter is certainly rather theatrical, but it is Lovelace as Richardson had imagined him. When he thinks of reforming, like Belford, he still has his reservations: 'That I will not take a few liberties, and that I will not try to start some of my former game, I won't promise—Habits are not easily shaken off—But they shall be by way of weaning.' And even towards the end his humour crops up from time to time, as when he imagines Belford living a virtuous life with his respectable old housekeeper: 'But what a pretty scheme of life hast thou drawn out for thyself, and thy old widow! By my soul, Jack, I am mightily taken with it. There is but one thing wanting in it; and that will come of course: Only to be in the Commission, and one of the Quorum. Thou art already provided with a Clerk, as good as thou'lt want, in the widow Lovick; for thou understandest Law, and she Conscience: A good Lord Chancellor between ye!—I should take prodigious pleasure to hear thee decide in a bastard case, upon thy new notions, and old remembrances.'[44]

Lovelace has one characteristic which foreshadows the hero of the romantic poets: he does not try to control his passions. One might say that he follows his heart, though his heart leads him into cruelty rather more often than into benevolence. For a modern reader, the fact that Lovelace's heart is selfish, ruthless in pursuit of its desires, eager above all for subservience in others to gratify its own pride, need not make him incredible. To Richardson, as an old-fashioned moralist, the heart was anything but a sure guide. He was no more sympathetic to Lovelace because he occasionally felt kindliness (when it did not inconvenience him) and could be good-natured (to those who did not cross him).

Richardson was right, Lovelace is a villain, insofar as a person not incredible can be a villain. Sentimentalists in Richardson's day, and even more since, have tended to think of the wicked as incomprehensibly malevolent; they have turned them into abstractions—the Western 'bad guy', the cruel Nazi, the evil Communist or capitalist. Then, when it is shown that a person who does wicked things has motives which we can recognize as not dissimilar to our own, that his mind works in a way which we can understand, by an obvious reaction they will find that he is 'good at heart'. Shylock speaks very well for himself: therefore, Shakespeare, according to one Victorian interpretation, must have meant him to be a hero in disguise. Milton knew better: when he needed a devil who was a genuine temptation to evil, he endowed him with Miltonic traits and made him tempting to Milton. He had no intention of damning sins he had no mind to.

---

[43] SH, VIII, 51; EL, IV, 378.   [44] SH, VIII, 212–13, 163; EL, IV, 487, 454.

The resemblance between Richardson and Lovelace, however, is not at first sight striking. It might be held that Lovelace embodies Richardson's secret sexual cravings. Ian Watt, among others, has emphasized Lovelace's sexuality.[45] He sees Lovelace as representing the eighteenth-century view of the masculine role as that of a hunter, as ultimately sadistic, and as leading directly to the protagonists of the Marquis de Sade and the brutal heroes of the Brontë sisters. Clarissa's desires are masochistic; she unconsciously 'courts sexual violation as well as death'. Richardson was exploring 'the frightening reality of the unconscious life' and felt a much deeper identification with Lovelace than he knew. One might add that if this view is true, since several of the 'unconscious' symbols Mr. Watt sees in the book arise from Clarissa's mind, Richardson must have felt at least as deep an identification with her masochism as with Lovelace's sadism. Indeed, when one considers merely the outline of the story, in the light of modern preoccupations such an interpretation is likely to suggest itself.[46]

Dorothy Van Ghent also finds a great deal of sexual symbolism in *Clarissa*.[47] The novel is a wish-fulfilment dream, with the usual 'distortion' caused by dream censorship. Since she can hardly mean that Richardson was consciously adopting Freudian techniques, we assume that the book is a fulfilment of Richardson's own unconscious wishes, although she does not elaborate on the implications of this fact. Or perhaps it is merely that *Clarissa* can be best read as a mythological fulfilment of the wishes of the reader. Lovelace is 'a woman's dream, the infantile imago of the male, the appealing figure of the sex-murderer'. Clarissa equates death with the sexual experience, in accordance with the familiar seventeenth-century pun on 'dying', and longs both to be killed and to be violated—hence her 'typical gestures with sharp instruments', which are, of course, phallic symbols.

The main objection to Mr. Watt's theory and to Mrs. Van Ghent's, in

---

[45] *Rise of the Novel*, pp. 231–5.

[46] A less Freudian reading has been suggested by Norman Rabkin in '*Clarissa*: A Study in the Nature of Convention', *ELH*, XXIII (1956), 204–17. Mr. Rabkin sees the battle as a struggle between extremes, neither of which is right. Lovelace is a kind of D. H. Lawrence hero, the 'natural' man, following the free force of instinct; Clarissa lives solely by decorum, which man has invented in order to live in society, and wants to deny the animal. Both are to blame for the tragedy, because neither alone is fitted for life in this world. The solution is implicit—compromise, represented by Belford, Lovelace's family, and especially Miss Howe, who represents flexibility, a convincing norm. Mr. Rabkin is swept away by his thesis into ignoring the facts of the novel: Lovelace's pride is by no means altogether resentment against social restrictions, nor is his temptation motivated by a desire to liberate Clarissa's sexual instincts. Richardson's letters show that he, at least, did not regard Lovelace as fundamentally amiable, with only one vice, sexual passion. It is possible that Richardson did not know what he really wanted to imply, so that Mr. Rabkin could be right about his unconscious perception; but it is harder to see how the unconscious self could create such a neat scheme of social ethics than how it could betray the writer's secret sadism.

[47] *English Novel: Form and Function*, pp. 315–16; 'Clarissa and Emma as Phèdre', pp. 823–6.

our opinion, can only be felt after reading the whole novel. We see very little sex in it, surprisingly little considering the story. If, as Leslie Fiedler suggests, the pornography of the book is the reward for enduring the piety, there is very little reward.[48] It has been a commonplace of Richardsonian criticism to emphasize the sexual aspect of his work, often with implications about his character. As good a judge as Mr. McKillop speaks of Richardson as verging on 'the weak and prurient side of sentimentalism'.[49] 'Clarissa', says V. S. Pritchett, 'is a novel written about the world as one sees it through the keyhole. Prurient and obsessed by sex, the prim Richardson creeps on tip-toe nearer and nearer, inch by inch, to that vantage point.'[50] Walter Allen sees Lovelace as coming 'straight out of the depths of his creator's unconscious': 'I doubt whether it is possible for the critic who comes to *Clarissa* after reading Freud to deny that the novel must have been written by a man who was, even though unconsciously, a sadist in the technical sense.' Mr. Allen also finds 'an element of quite inescapable pornography compared with which the obscenity of Smollett and the indecency of Sterne . . . appear innocent'.[51]

Perhaps the situation itself inevitably suggests prurience. But one would expect far more prurience in the details than we can find—far more than a scattering of veiled and minor Freudian symbols, unless one assumes that such things as daggers and penknives and white lilies with broken stalks and tumblings into open graves must necessarily have had buried associations with sex in the mind of even a pre-Freudian. If so, the fact that there is a very large number of longish-shaped objects used in everyday life makes it extremely hard to avoid sexual symbolism, unless one has been warned by reading Freud. Mr. Watt might have pointed out that Clarissa is unduly fond of writing and must have used a pen. But perhaps it would have posed troublesome problems if he had noticed that Lovelace deliberately courts the duel with Colonel Morden, that both men prefer the short rapier, 'a gentleman's weapon', to the pistol, and that Lovelace 'repeatedly told him' that he valued himself much on his 'skill in that weapon'.[52]

We are not, of course, denying that Richardson had unconscious sexual urges and that these urges might have influenced some of the imagery in the novel, but we do not believe that the heavy emphasis on sexual imagery so popular with many modern critics is of much help in reading *Clarissa*. As to the biographical implications, psychoanalysing a man on the basis of his writings is in our opinion not an illegitimate occupation but a very dangerous one. Biographically the important question would be how much of Richardson's unconscious life was expressed through the

---

[48] *Love and Death in the American Novel*, p. 31.   [49] *Richardson*, pp. 143–4.
[50] *Living Novel*, p. 10.   [51] *The English Novel* (London, [1954]), p. 46.
[52] SH, VIII, 270–2; EL, IV, 526–7.

character of Lovelace. But Lovelace's 'sadism' is not so much a desire to torture as a desire to dominate; it is more closely related to pride than to cruelty. Perhaps most people have at least this much sadism lurking in their unconscious minds.

If one is to adopt the assumption that Richardson released his own unconscious urges through Lovelace, we are inclined to prefer Morris Golden's development of Mr. Watt's reading. Mr. Golden is, in our opinion, somewhat too free with the word 'sadism', blurring its meaning by finding evidence of it in any feeling which might bolster a person's sense of superiority (Richardson's desire for posthumous fame, for instance) or in the mild jokes with which Richardson liked to tease his female correspondents. With such a lax definition, it is hard to think of any action of one person towards another which could not be described as either sadistic or masochistic, and Mr. Golden does find what to him is convincing evidence of masochism also in Richardson's correspondence. But he emphasizes not the overtly sexual aspect of sadism but the 'dominance fantasies' to which it gives rise. At times he seems to us to press his thesis too far, as when he thinks that Clarissa's loss of 'animal energy' as a result of her trials is 'part of the expression of his [Richardson's] own sadistic tendencies' or sees in Lovelace's occasional recognition of his inferiority to Clarissa masochistic tendencies ('androgynous male–female urges') which prefigure Leopold Bloom. But such statements are probably no more than the reflection of the modern feeling that all human motives are more meaningful if expressed in sexual terms, and our disagreement with Mr. Golden is therefore more in vocabulary than in substance. We thoroughly agree that Lovelace succeeds because Richardson projected into him his own imaginative life. Mr. Golden calls him 'Richardson's best-realized character'; our only reservation in agreeing with this judgement is that Clarissa is just as well realized. Lovelace's primary motivation is, as Mr. Golden says, a desire to dominate. Richardson realized Lovelace and therefore to a degree he was Lovelace, but he was not only Lovelace. He opposes to Lovelace a sense of integrity and independence as powerful as Lovelace's passion, and as fully realized. 'Clarissa', Mr. Golden justly concludes, 'does not impress because she is good, but because she exerts for goodness a strength and passion that can match those of its antagonists.' Her victory is not merely a tacked-on moral—it is part of the artistic conception of her character. 'The pervasiveness of fantasy in the creation of character is, I believe, Richardson's pre-eminent contribution to the novel; and the fantasies are mainly of dominance and subordination, as seem to have been those of the author himself.'[53] We would not, as Mr. Golden does, phrase it so that Richardson's conception seems to be the fulfilment of a sexual daydream. Richardson's intellect and his spirit

[53] *Richardson's Characters* (Ann Arbor, 1963), pp. 17, 6–11, 25–6, 66, 23–5, 5, 192–3, 17.

endorsed the defeat of the Lovelace he had imagined. But perhaps we are not entirely in disagreement when we say that Richardson's greatness in *Clarissa* is the result of his having found in himself two basic drives which he projected in a thoroughly realized conflict.

All of these sexual interpretations assume a certain amount of sympathy on the part of Richardson with his villain, which it is hard to deny in view of the fact that Lovelace expresses himself in a natural and lively way which would be impossible if the creative part of Richardson's mind disapproved of the character as thoroughly as the moralistic part did. Lovelace is to some degree a precursor of the hero-villain, the glamorous criminal so popular in the Gothic novel and its successors. But in our opinion Richardson has successfully controlled his unconscious sympathies. Lovelace is thoroughly realized and is to that extent appealing, but the feelings of the reader about him are not, or at least in our opinion should not be, ambiguous, as they usually are with the later hero-villains. Whatever of himself Richardson put into Lovelace, he rejected, and not merely in a conventional moralistic way, but with a side of his mind as deep and at least as important as the side which was able to realize Lovelace. As we see it, the battle of the pride that needs to dominate against the pride that desires independence need not be presented only in terms of sadism. It is one of the commonest patterns in history and is copiously illustrated in everyday life. The motives of both contestants can be found in any human mind. They provide the basis of a tragedy, not of an exposé. And they can be found in *Clarissa* on much surer evidence than ambiguous imagery.

Lovelace describes to Belford a good many of his fantasies about Clarissa. They are never concerned with the seduction itself but always with her submissive attitude after she has been seduced:

> Let me perish, Belford, if I would not forego the brightest diadem in the world, for the pleasure of seeing a Twin Lovelace at each charming breast, drawing from it his first sustenance. . . .
> I now, methinks, behold this most charming of women in this sweet office: Her conscious eye now dropt on one, now on the other, with a sigh of maternal tenderness; and then raised up to my delighted eye, full of wishes, for the sake of the pretty varlets, and for her own sake, that I would deign to legitimate; that I would condescend to put on the nuptial fetters.[54]

He speaks fairly often of Clarissa's physical charms and of his desires, but in our opinion never very glowingly. Once he kisses her breast, but in a very different spirit from that with which the impetuous Mr. B. had groped in Pamela's bosom. In one of their rare periods of quiet agreement the two are sitting side by side on a sofa, and it appears that they will actually be married—Clarissa is willing and so, temporarily, is Lovelace. But he cannot be satisfied without another attempt:

[54] SH, IV, 355; EL, II, 477.

Now surely, thought I, is my time to try if she can forgive a still bolder freedom than I had ever yet taken.

I then gave her struggling hands liberty. I put one arm round her waist; I imprinted a kiss on her sweet lips, with a *Be quiet* only, and an averted face, as if she feared another.

Encouraged by so gentle a repulse, the tenderest things I said; and then, with my other hand, drew aside the handkerchief that concealed the Beauty of beauties, and pressed with my burning lips the most charming breast that ever my ravished eyes beheld.[55]

Clarissa immediately jumps up, and the battle begins again. Lovelace, as usual, uses the language of the romances and the plays ('burning lips'), but his spirit can hardly be described as the spirit of a lover.

Belford, in his first letter, tells Lovelace that 'a mere Sensualist' would be made 'a thousand times happier' by one of the ladies of easy virtue whom Lovelace knows than by a girl like Clarissa. It is noteworthy that during his whole pursuit of the heroine Lovelace, to all appearances, is living a life of complete chastity. His taste in the object of his desire is always delicate. In his answer to Belford, he emphasizes his 'sportive cruelty': what he longs for is a girl who will struggle but '*consent in struggle*', who will finally be brought to willingness. In a vivid description, he compares what he wants Clarissa to become to a captive bird, which at first fights its fate but gradually acquiesces in it.[56] His references to animals show, certainly, a delight in cruelty, but perhaps even more a delight in power: 'When a boy, if a dog ran away from me thro' fear, I generally looked about for a stone, or a stick; and if neither offered to my hand, I skimmed my hat after him to make him afraid for something. What signifies power, if we do not exert it?'[57] As Belford says, '"Tis a seriously sad thing, after all, that so fine a creature should have fallen into such vile and remorseless hands: For, from thy Cradle, as I have heard thee own, thou ever delightedst to sport with and torment the animal, whether bird or beast, that thou lovedst, and hadst a power over.'[58] In many other places Lovelace makes it clear that what he most desires is to conquer Clarissa's mind, to make her submit willingly, eagerly, to what she at first loathed. Whether such a desire for domination is a sublimated form of sadism, we leave to the psychologists to decide. Indeed such a question may be largely a matter of phrasing—the sexual vocabulary seems today to have more meaning than, say, the religious vocabulary, which often says the same thing. One could also call the desire to dominate another's mind, to reduce him to inward dependency, a form of spiritual pride, the sin of Satan. We do not intend to argue about words. But it is clear that pure physical satisfaction, if there be such a thing, is not uppermost in

[55] SH, IV, 353; EL, II, 476.
[57] SH, IV, 135; EL, II, 328.

[56] SH, IV, 10, 12–14; EL, II, 244–6.
[58] SH, IV, 363; EL, II, 483.

Lovelace's thoughts: 'What, as I have often contemplated, is the enjoyment of the finest woman in the world, to the contrivance, the bustle, the
surprizes, and at last the happy conclusion, of a well-laid plot?—The
charming *roundabouts*, to come the *nearest way home*;—the doubts; the
apprehensions; the heart-akings; the meditated triumphs—These are the
joys that make the blessing dear.—For all the rest, what is it?—What but
to find an Angel in imagination dwindled down to a woman in fact?'[59]

One thing Richardson does seem to have experienced along with Lovelace is the delight in cleverness, the invention of devices. 'Lord, Jack, so
much delight do I take in my contrivances, that I shall be half-sorry, when
the occasion for them is over; for never, never, shall I again have such
charming exercise for my invention.'[60] Many authors seem to participate
in the cleverness of their villains—indeed, if they do not, their villains
will not be very clever. Richardson enjoys Lovelace's intrigues as
Thackeray enjoys Becky Sharpe's, though he is more earnest about their
consequences. The fact that Lovelace also enjoys them fits in well enough
with his character: they prove his superiority, they enable him to look
down on his victims.

One of many clear examples of this is the scene in which Lovelace
pursues Clarissa to Mrs. Smith's shop, where she has escaped to die after
the rape.[61] Lady Bradshaigh in her copy of *Clarissa* objected to the scene
and thought Lovelace's 'Ill-tim'd gayity' showed him as a madman: 'The
whole is an absurdity.' Below her comment Richardson wrote, 'A characteristic one, however!' Lovelace bullies Mrs. Smith and her husband,
forces his way in, tries to overawe them with his superior social position,
and playfully decides to wait on their customers and to insult or flatter
them as his whim moves. It is a funny scene, but its humour is essentially
the humour of a wealthy juvenile delinquent throwing his weight around.
At this time Lovelace does want to marry Clarissa—because she has got
away from him and has not yielded after losing her virginity, as according
to his notions she should naturally have done. He is even in a sense heartbroken: that is, he wants very much something he cannot have. His joking
partly serves to cover his concern. Everything he does in this rather complex scene is understandable; yet Lovelace is no less cruel for that. Failing
to dominate Clarissa, he demonstrates that he can dominate other people
easily enough. He never tires of demonstrating how easy it is for him to
dominate people; he has a very high opinion of himself throughout, but
the opinion needs to be constantly fed by subservience. Richardson seems
to have understood the workings of this passion very well—a fact which
is not surprising if one considers how easily introspection can discover a
model for self-assertiveness and its usual concomitant, sensitiveness and

[59] SH, VI, 8; EL, III, 248.   [60] SH, IV, 282; EL, II, 428.
[61] SH, VII, 142–54; EL, IV, 124–33.

yearning for approval. We do not mean to imply that Richardson was an unusually proud man, though he often showed signs of sensitiveness and resentment of neglect. But by isolating his own feelings of pride and letting them guide him when he wrote as Lovelace, he was able to give him a reality far superior to that of the would-be rake, Mr. B.— or of the good man, Sir Charles.

For instance, it is typical that Lovelace, especially when he himself has just done something wicked, loves to become satiric on the wickedness of generals, lawyers, doctors, all the world. After the rape Clarissa is trying to escape and Lovelace thinks of bribing a new helper to recapture her; he immediately reflects on how easy it is to find people who can be bribed to do anything: 'How else could the Princes of the earth be so implicity served as they are, *change they hands ever so often*, and be their purposes *ever so wicked*?'[62] He has, at this time, been moved by her delirium and her suffering into wanting to marry her—two or three times during his long pursuit he feels real affection or pity for Clarissa and sincerely desires her happiness. But on this occasion, as before, his feeling for her passes quickly. His new contrivance suggests again, as he has often suggested to himself before, that he will make one last trial of her virtue—if she resists *this* trial, he assures himself (as he has before assured himself) he will submit to marriage. In the next letter, Clarissa is very ill—no, he reflects, she must be pretending, in order to escape from his prison. When *he* needed to pretend illness in order to surprise her love for him, *he* was not deceitful—he really made himself ill, by taking ipecacuanha. 'But here to pretend to be very ill, only to get an opportunity to run away, in order to avoid forgiving a man who has offended her, how unchristian!'[63] One must, of course, read this reference to forgiveness in the light of Lovelace's new plot to catch Clarissa's virtue; and one is supposed to remember Clarissa's behaviour on Lovelace's pretended illness, her sincere concern, her pity which is almost love. Richardson expected his readers to notice things. These little touches show how completely Richardson knew his character. Immediately after his indignation against Clarissa (Lovelace is much given to moral indignation) he gets news which furthers his new plot and is all bustle and frivolity again. It is hard to see how anyone could have seen Lovelace as an amiable good-hearted rake; Richardson gives enough indications of his lack of compassion to convince even an age which tends to identify rakishness with 'feeling' and propriety with coldness. Lovelace has enough feelings, even violent feelings, but very rarely and very briefly are they feelings for anyone else.

Earlier, when Clarissa plans to get away from him, he is indignant that she is 'impudently [Yes, I say, *impudently*, though she be Clarissa Harlowe] contriving to rob me of the dearest property I had ever purchased'.[64] He

[62] SH, VI, 14; EL, III, 252.   [63] SH, VI, 15; EL, III, 252.   [64] SH, V, 17; EL, II, 518.

always tends to regard her as a property, a precious object which, if he gains it, will prove his worth. His feeling towards her is not unlike that of a Texas millionaire towards a private submarine. But there is the added pleasure that the property has a mind to conquer, an even greater proof of superiority if it is conquered. 'Miss Howe says, that my Love is an *Herodian* Love: By my Soul, that Girl's a Witch!—I am half-sorry to say, *that I find a pleasure in playing the Tyrant over what I love.*'[65] Lovelace would be quite capable of wanting his Mariamne to die if he should die and could no longer possess her; indeed what he does do amounts to as much. He always sees their relationship as a battle for mastery. In the end it is Lovelace himself who loses his freedom, whereas Clarissa retains hers: 'As I hope to live, I am sorry (at the present writing) that I have been such a foolish plotter, as to put it, as I fear I have done, out of my *own power* to be honest. I hate compulsion in all forms; and cannot bear, even to be *compelled* to be the wretch my choice has made me!—So now, Belford, as thou hast said, I am a machine at last, and no free agent.'[66]

Lovelace is determined to subdue Clarissa. At times he is even willing to marry her to do so. Sometimes he feels genuine sympathy for her, generated by her influence over him—an influence which later he regrets. At least once (at Widow Sorlings's) this sympathy leads to a sincere offer of marriage.[67] At other times, he considers marrying her only because he sees no other possibility of getting her. Or he will marry her later, when he has first tamed her: when his hireling, the pretended Captain Tomlinson, asks him shortly before the rape if he has thoughts 'of marrying this wonderful Lady', Lovelace replies: 'Yes, yes, Patrick, but I have. But let me, first, to gratify *my* pride, bring down *hers*. Let me see, that she loves me well enough to forgive me for my *own* sake.'[68] After he has raped her, he is moved by her delirium; and he is even more moved, in a different way, when he finds that, contrary to all his expectations, the loss of her virginity has not subdued her. He offers marriage again and is upset and even angry when she refuses it; but as soon as her allegorical letter leads him to hope that she may accept, he has doubts: 'And, 'egad, Jack, I know not what to say to it, now the fruit seems to be within my reach—But, let what will come, I'll stand to't: For I find I can't live without her.' He is distressed by her death, certainly. The passion of his regret sounds like the wildness of some of the romantic heroes. He even anticipates Byron's 'And if I laugh at any mortal thing,/'Tis that I may not weep . . .': 'I am forced, as I have often said, to try to make myself laugh, that I may not cry; for one or other I must do.'[69] This regret is exactly what one would

---

[65] SH, V, 123; EL, III, 65.   [66] SH, V, 241; EL, III, 146.

[67] In the 'Table of Contents' added to the second edition, Richardson, underlining Lovelace's falsehood, stated that only on this one occasion was '*he absolutely in earnest in those vows*'. See SH, III, 393; EL, II, 530.

[68] SH, V, 220; EL, III, 132.   [69] SH, VII, 201, 346; EL, IV, 165, 262.

expect from Lovelace. It does not imply that he would have treated Clarissa differently if she had lived. Perhaps it is, in the romantic sense, 'true love'. At least he *wanted* Clarissa badly enough.

Clarissa's struggle against Lovelace's physical domination is paralleled by his struggle against her moral domination, against a recognition which at times threatens to force itself upon him that she is the superior being. 'I protest I know not how to look up at her! Now, as I am thinking, if I could pull her down a little nearer to my own level; that is to say, could prevail upon her to do something that would argue *imperfection*, something *to repent of*; we should jog on much more equally, and be better able to comprehend one another: And so the comfort would be mutual, and the remorse not all on one side.' He hopes to gain a superiority by forcing her to speak out, to plead with him to marry her: her embarrassment will lend her additional charms in his eyes—only silly rogues will spare a lady in such circumstances. 'Still I will be all silence—her eyes fixed upon my shoe-buckles, as I sit over-against her—Ladies, when put to it thus, always admire a man's shoe-buckles, or perhaps some particular beauties in the carpet.' *After* she has been humiliated, he will be generous, even lavish in the settlements he is willing to make on her—for this sort of generosity to a vanquished foe is another proof of superiority. 'If I marry her [And I have no doubt but that I shall, after my Pride, my Ambition, my *Revenge*, if thou wilt, is gratified] I will do her noble justice. . . . But, by my soul, Belford, her haughtiness shall be brought down to own both Love and Obligation to me.' When she is dying, he resents the fact that she is still superior: 'O the triumphant subduer! Ever above me!—And now to leave me so infinitely below her!' And after she is dead, he is forced to see that her superiority is now assured, that he can no longer hope to overcome it: 'But the generosity of her mind . . . is what stings me most. And the more still, as it is now out of my power any way in the world to be even with her.'[70]

He is not only afraid that Clarissa will scorn him; he is even worried that the whores he has employed will think him weak and will laugh at him.[71] Such a character, determined above all not to recognize the superiority of anyone else and eager to humble any person whose claims to superiority might be urged, is familiar enough today. The great fear of being laughed at, perhaps the strongest fear of those persons today who have been freed from physical danger, is typical. 'Je ne vois de réel qu'une peur abominable du ridicule,' says Julien Sorel. Lovelace later goes so far as to blame the rape on the women whose scorn he fears: 'O that cursed, cursed house! But for the women of that!—Then their damn'd potions! But for *those*, had her *unimpaired* intellects, and the *majesty of her*

---

[70] SH, III, 135, IV, 115–16, VII, 435, VIII, 248; EL, II, 69, 314–15, IV, 323, 511.
[71] SH, IV, 118; EL, II, 316.

virtue, saved her.'[72] Like the narrator of Orwell's 'Shooting an Elephant', he must maintain his 'image' before his own creatures: the white man has to shoot the elephant if the people expect it, because 'it is the condition of his rule that he shall spend his life in trying to impress the "natives".' Lovelace is worried about his 'reputation'; if he marries Clarissa, 'what a figure shall I make in Rakish Annals?' He, like Clarissa, has an image of himself to maintain: 'At this silent moment, I think, that if I were to pursue my former scheme, and resolve to try whether I cannot make a greater fault serve as a sponge to wipe out the less; and then be forgiven for that; I can justify myself to *myself*; and that, as the fair Invincible would say, is all in all.'[73] There is a subtle irony in Lovelace's thus applying to himself Clarissa's renunciation of public approval in favour of self-justification. Lovelace's justification of himself depends much more than hers on the image others have of him. There are conventions for rakes at least as rigid as the conventions of virtue.

Lovelace does at times pay tribute to Clarissa's virtue. 'For what a mind must that be, which tho' not virtuous itself, admires not virtue in another.' Her chastity several times, notably in the fire scene, causes him to retreat. 'Once or twice (to say nothing of her triumph over me on Sunday night) I was prevailed upon to fluster myself, with an intention to make some advances, which, if obliged to recede, I might lay upon raised spirits: But the instant I beheld her, I was soberized into awe and reverence: And the majesty of her even *visible* purity first damped, and then extinguished, my *double* flame.' Her very excellence makes Clarissa the best possible object of his stratagems, since in subduing her he might well feel that he had subdued the highest claims of female excellence. 'All that's excellent in her Sex is this Lady!—Until by MATRIMONIAL, or EQUAL intimacies, I have found her *less than angel*, it is impossible to think of any other. . . . What a triumph!—What a triumph over the whole Sex!'[74] The desire for such a triumph is thoroughly in keeping with Lovelace's character, and with a little ingenuity we might use it to justify psychologically Lovelace's awe before Clarissa's virtue. But we suspect that Richardson let his desire for an acceptable moral take over when he emphasized this characteristic: virtue *should* be able to tame the savage breast, to impose itself. In Richardson there is always the double aim, to convey a character as he has understood him and to make a proper ethical point. In *Clarissa*, especially when the main characters are speaking for themselves, the first aim is generally in the ascendancy, but the second, though not so prominent and so deadening as in his other two novels, is never quite forgotten. It may, at times, deform the characters.

And there is another possible source of deformation, the conscious

---

[72] SH, VII, 88; EL, IV, 88.   [73] SH, V, 238; EL, III, 144.
[74] SH, I, 212, IV, 241, I, 220; EL, I, 145, II, 400, I, 150.

desire for probable and logical motives, for motives his more realistic readers will recognize as adequate. This desire leads to over-motivation, to additions and explanations which rather weaken than strengthen the inherent credibility of Lovelace's actions. The credibility of a character presented from inside depends on the author's feeling his motives, not on 'giving' his motives. Such gratuitous motivation, where the author seems to explain too much, and from outside, is seen in the passage last quoted, from Lovelace's first letter, and there is every reason to believe that it was an addition made after readers of the novel in manuscript were too attracted to Lovelace.[75] In addition to his desire for triumph, Lovelace also explains to Belford how his project will stimulate his love of contrivances and will get revenge on Clarissa's family. It is, of course, impossible to prove that what we have taken as the main element in Lovelace's character, the yearning for superiority, was the element which Richardson worked at from inside. Any reader will notice that it is referred to constantly; but the tone in which Lovelace speaks of it, the little touches which make it real, are more important than the number of references. Richardson may have seen more than one of Lovelace's characteristics from inside, as he seems to enjoy with him his cleverness. But we believe that if Lovelace is thought of as a sensualist and rake he will fail to carry conviction, whereas a reader who concentrates on his pride will be swept along with him.

Clarissa is also a proud character. Lovelace is not altogether wrong when he says: 'Don't tell me, that Virtue and Principle are her guides on this occasion!—'Tis *Pride*, a greater Pride than my own, that governs her.'[76]

Clarissa is quite aware of Lovelace's pride: 'Mr. Lovelace is a proud man. We have both long ago observed, that he is. And I am truly afraid, that his very Generosity is more owing to his *Pride* and his *Vanity*, than to that *Philanthropy* (shall I call it?) which distinguishes a beneficent mind.'[77] In speaking of his desire for admiration even from his rakish companions, who are obviously his inferiors in every way, she gives him a character not unlike that which Pope gave the Duke of Wharton,[78] one of the men who might conceivably have been used by Richardson as a model: 'But it is amazing to me, I own, that with so much of the gentleman, such a general knowlege of books and men, such a skill in the learned as well as modern languages, he can take so much delight as he does in the company of such persons as I have described, and in subjects of frothy impertinence, unworthy of his talents, and of his natural and

---

[75] See Eaves and Kimpel, 'The Composition of *Clarissa* and Its Revision before Publication', pp. 420-1.

[76] SH, V, 284; EL, III, 175.   [77] SH, IV, 337; EL, II, 465.

[78] In the first of the *Moral Essays*, ll. 180-207.

acquired advantages. I can think but of one reason for it, and that must argue a very low mind; his VANITY; which makes him desirous of being considered as the head of the people he consorts with. A man to love praise; yet to be content to draw it from such contaminated springs!'[79]

She comes to see her own pride just as clearly. She is, it is true, rather sharp-tongued and critical of others at the beginning. Richardson was prone to make even his virtuous characters sharp-tongued and critical. She speaks up readily enough to both Arabella and her brother. When she is being pressed by her sister, who, as she is quite aware, would be glad to marry Solmes or any other suitor, she asks 'if Mr. Solmes had such merit in every-body's eyes, in *hers* particularly, why might he not be a *Brother* to me, rather than a *Husband*?' And when Bella thinks that Clarissa's feeling for Lovelace makes it necessary to marry her to the first man who opportunely offers, she does not scruple to remind her that Lovelace has thrown her over: 'And, as to *opportune* offers, would to Heaven some one had offered *opportunely* to somebody! It is not my fault, Bella, the *opportune* gentleman don't come!'[80] She is free enough in resenting her family's pressure and firm enough in resisting it and has great faith in her own judgement. 'I thought I could *proceed*, or *stop*, as I pleased. I supposed it concerned *me, more than any other, to be the arbitress of the quarrels of unruly spirits*—And now I find my presumption punished!—Punished, as other sins frequently are, by *itself*!'[81]

Her misfortunes make her conscious of her pride. 'But oh, my dear! my calamities have humbled me enough to make me turn my gaudy eye inward; to make me look into myself—And what have I discovered there? —Why, my dear friend, more *secret* pride and vanity than I could have thought had lain in my unexamined heart.'[82] In view of the degradation suffered by the word 'humility' since the romantic period, such statements may be overlooked as mere pious platitude, but Richardson was conscious enough of the earlier tenets of Christianity to take humility seriously. Clarissa is gradually forced to give up many of the bases of her former pride. 'Let me *but* get from him!—As to my reputation, if I leave him—That is already too much wounded for me, now, to be careful about any-thing, but how to act so, as that my own Heart shall not reproach me. As to the world's censure, I must be content to suffer that—An unhappy composition, however.—What a wreck have my fortunes suffered, to be obliged to throw overboard so many valuables, to preserve, indeed, the *only* valuable! . . . What a pride did I take in the applause of every one!— What a pride even in supposing I had *not* that pride!—Which concealed itself from my unexamining heart under the specious veil of *Humility*, doubling the merit to myself by the *supposed*, and indeed *imputed*, graceful-

[79] SH, III, 371; EL, II, 230.   [80] SH, I, 313-4; EL, I, 213-4.
[81] SH, II, 361; EL, I, 486.   [82] SH, II, 264; EL, I, 420.

ness in the manner of conferring benefits, when I had not a single merit in what I did. . . . So desirous, in short, to be considered as an *Example*! A vanity which my partial admirers put into my head!—And so secure in my own virtue!'[83]

One must understand, though one need not agree with, the importance which the eighteenth century attached to woman's chastity in order to understand the effect of the rape on Clarissa. *Clarissa* is not a novel *about* seduction and sex, any more than *Antigone* is a play about burial rites. A moderate degree of historical imagination should enable a reader to see that a similar issue to the one which arose for Antigone because her brother was denied burial could arise today for different reasons; the importance of interment depended on a transient custom, but Antigone's feelings about it and the conflict in which it involved her are by no means transient. The rape is, in a sense, a symbol which depends on convention, for Lovelace as much as for Clarissa. His theory leads him to believe that a woman once conquered, even by such means, must be always dependent on him, must beg for his favours, must admit her inferiority by submitting to his will. 'She will not refuse me, I know, Jack; the haughty Beauty will not refuse me, when her pride of being corporally inviolate is brought down.'[84] It is for this reason that he hopes she is pregnant: that, he thinks, would both make her helpless and publish her humiliation. Perhaps the most surprising thing about *Clarissa* is that Richardson, conventional as he had always seemed, was willing to subject his heroine to what in his day was a final humiliation and to draw her triumph from the humiliation itself.

Her reflections in her delirium following the rape are not mere moral platitudes. She recognizes that she can now be sneered at by anyone. She had been brought up on admiration; she had had great faith in her own virtue and judgement—not altogether without justification; she had tried to avoid conceit, but she had had every reason to think herself superior; she had been independent, even to the extent of being self-willed. 'How art thou now humbled in the dust, thou proud Clarissa Harlowe!' 'I never shall be myself again: I have been a very wicked creature—a vain, proud, poor creature—full of secret pride—which I carried off under an humble guise, and deceived every-body—My sister says so—And now I am punished.'[85] This theme is mentioned again and again. Not that her pride is quite lost. Her refusal to accept money from Belford or Lovelace's family or Lovelace himself or even Miss Howe, her insistence on giving Mrs. Lovick a diamond ring as security for the three guineas she borrows from her, and her refusal to admit Dr. H.'s visits unless he will accept his fees show a dislike of being under obligation in money matters which

[83] SH, IV, 209–10; EL, II, 378. This passage first appears in the third and fourth editions.
[84] SH, V, 305; EL, III, 190.   [85] SH, V, 329, 337; EL, III, 206, 212.

reminds one of Samuel Richardson. 'If I am poor, Sir, I am proud. I will not be under obligation. You may *believe*, Sir, I will not', she tells Belford.[86] One reason, and undoubtedly a sincere one, which she gives Miss Howe for her refusal to marry Lovelace is that her pride, 'altho' a great deal mortified, is not *sufficiently* mortified'. 'Yes, I warrant, I must *creep* to the violator, and be thankful to him for doing me poor justice!—Do you not already see me (pursuing the advice you give) with a downcast eye, appear before *his* friends, and before *my own* (supposing the latter would at last condescend to own me) divested of that *noble confidence*, which arises from a mind unconscious of having deserved reproach?'[87] In answering her Uncle Harlowe's cruel letter, she must 'leave off several times—To struggle . . . for an humble temper. "My heart . . . is a proud heart, and not yet, I find, enough mortified to my condition; but, do what I can, will be for prescribing resenting things to my pen." '[88] After her humiliation, her main effort is directed towards attaining humility.

She also comes to recognize that it is towards God she should be humble, and to a certain extent this makes her more independent of the world, since she is no longer so dependent on its opinion. Lovelace's pride, and to a lesser extent Clarissa's former pride, is not freedom but dependence. The superiority in which such pride rejoices must be constantly confirmed by the opinions of others. Before her flight Clarissa thinks a good deal about her reputation: one important reason which she urges against leaving her family is that the world would blame her, and she will not accept Miss Howe's offer to accompany her because it would '*double* and *treble* my own fault in the eye of the world . . . which, cruelly as I am used (not knowing all) would not acquit *me*'. The fact that Lovelace does not value his reputation she cites as one of his worst qualities. But she is conscious that the world's opinion is not the most important consideration. In her behaviour to Lovelace she will follow her own heart, and 'answer *for* myself *to* myself, in the *first* place; to *him*, and to the *world*, in the second only'.[89] That the word pride can be applied both to this ultimate independence and to a desire for approval which would make such independence impossible is a result of our inadequate and inaccurate vocabulary of the passions. Clarissa's pride is a complex feeling, much more complex than Lovelace's. But the aspect of it that longs for admiration is less strong than the aspect that needs self-approval.

Regret at the loss of her reputation is not her strongest feeling after the rape, and it is this fact which enables her to triumph in humiliation. If she had wanted above all reputation, she would have grasped at the offer of marriage which Lovelace dangles before her.

[86] SH, VI, 355, VIII, 93, VI, 373–4, 330, 356, 330; EL, III, 484, IV, 92, III, 496, 467, 484, 467.
[87] SH, VI, 408; EL, III, 519–20.   [88] SH, VII, 99; EL, IV, 95.
[89] SH, II, 318, III, 112, IV, 102; EL, I, 457, II, 54, 306.

I renounce thee for ever, Lovelace!—Abhorred of my Soul! for ever I renounce thee!—Seek thy fortunes wheresoever thou wilt!—Only now, that thou hast already ruin'd me——

Ruined you, Madam—The world need not—I knew not what to say.

Ruined me in my *own* eyes; and that is the same to me, as if *all the world* knew it—Hinder me not from going whither my mysterious destiny shall lead me.[90]

Her refusal to be made honest in the eyes of the world is an unconventional, though a Christian, decision. And though she recognizes that pride has a part in it, pride in the usual sense is not its main motive. She does truly abhor Lovelace. He has treated her as a thing, he has seen in her only his own desires: in Kant's terms, he has treated her not as an end but as a means. If the feeling which has been violated is pride, it is simply the pride which leads a human being to demand that he be treated as a human being.

Clarissa is frank in admitting her loss of 'honour'. 'Why should I seek to conceal that disgrace from others, which I cannot hide from myself?'[91] 'As to the *world* and its *censures*, you know, my dear, that however desirous I always was of a fair fame, yet I never thought it right to give more than a *second place* to the world's opinion.'[92] Clara Thomson finds in Clarissa's final independence of public opinion 'the salutary moral effect of the book': 'Clarissa, the slave of convention, suddenly revolts against its tyranny, and vindicates her claim to liberty.'[93] The English novel of the eighteenth and nineteenth centuries, with a few exceptions like *Wuthering Heights* and some of Hardy's work, assumes that it is highly desirable for the main characters to find a place in organized society. *Clarissa*, for all the conventionality of its author, is curiously modern in portraying a heroine whose triumph depends on her becoming an outcast.

One might cynically say that Clarissa is unconventional in taking seriously the doctrines that her society professed to believe. Christopher Hill, in a good analysis of the economic background of the novel, concludes that Clarissa is doomed by following a Puritan ethic no longer applicable (or applied) in an age when money was all-important: 'Richardson pressed the logic of the situation (and of the Puritan conception of virtue) a stage further than most of his contemporaries would have dared.' After she is raped, 'the goods, from the point of view of the market, were irreparably damaged'. 'Clarissa's standards, however, are those of the Puritan ideal, not those of conventional market morality. . . . She had no sense of guilt: her conscience was clear. But she knew what society's verdict would be. Its standards are those of the market: justification by faith was for Sundays only. Society judges by events, not by motives. Clarissa knew it, and it was this that

---

[90] SH, V, 366; EL, III, 232.
[91] SH, VI, 138; EL, III, 336.
[92] SH, VI, 456; EL, IV, 26.
[93] *Richardson*, pp. 196-8.

made her death inevitable. How could she have lived? There was no room in a commercial society for flawed goods.'[94]

To consider Clarissa as merely proper is to miss the quality of her character entirely. She is 'proper' in the importance she attaches to chastity, but one could no more have expected her not to be than one could have expected a saga hero to ignore the code of the blood feud. The historian may legitimately find most interesting the fact that a character illustrates the mores of his time; but if literature is to be read as relevant in any but a historical light, the ways in which characters differ in their reactions to accepted mores must often be more significant than the mores themselves. Pamela and Clarissa are no more alike in their feelings about woman's honour than are Gisli and Gunnar in their feelings about the feud.

Clarissa has been accused of losing the opportunity to marry Lovelace after her flight from home through mere punctilio. Their relations during this period, the third and fourth volumes of the first edition, are perhaps the most interesting thing in the novel. They are worked out with great care and deserve to be read with care. From the beginning Clarissa and Lovelace are both inclined to see the relationship as a battle: 'We are both great watchers of each other's eyes; and indeed seem to be more than half-afraid of each other', writes Clarissa.[95] Lovelace enjoys the battle; for Clarissa it is intolerable, since the only satisfactory way out of her predicament is by marriage and yet with her sensitivity she can hardly want to marry a sparring partner. Lovelace wants to subdue a woman; Clarissa wants neither to subdue nor to be subdued.

In the beginning, Clarissa, although or because she is dependent on Lovelace, stands on her dignity and insists on being treated with at least as much respect as she would have received at home. Her remarks to him are frank to the point of rudeness: 'I . . . told him, that I was every hour more and more dissatisfied with myself, and with him: That he was not a man, who, in my opinion, improved upon acquaintance.'[96] Her demand for respect aids Lovelace in his effort to avoid marriage, but even without it he could have succeeded. Clarissa, at the beginning of the novel, explains how Lovelace had proposed to her sister in a way which even the insensitive Bella could not accept: he has worked up a quarrel and at the height of it mentioned marriage and urged it in a way which made it impossible for her immediately to accept—and he had given her no time to cool down. He now does the same thing with Clarissa herself. Miss Howe has warned her that she must now marry Lovelace, and Clarissa herself realizes it. She tries her best to forget her dignity. But Lovelace is clever enough to know how far she can lower herself without giving up all self-respect. Richardson

---

[94] 'Clarissa Harlowe and Her Times', *Puritanism and Revolution* (London, 1958), pp. 384–6.
[95] SH, III, 169; EL, II, 93.   [96] SH, III, 71; EL, II, 26.

never showed greater knowledge of his characters than in these proposal scenes. Lovelace provokes her into resentful remarks and then mentions marriage in such a way as almost forces her to do half the proposing.
A woman today could probably, without loss of self-respect, do more than
half; but for Clarissa to have done so, in view of the conventions of the
time, would have meant that she threw herself entirely on Lovelace's mercy
at the same time that she gave up all claim to his regard. 'Would he have
had me catch at his first, at his *very* first word?—I was *silent* too—And do
not the bold Sex take silence for a mark of favour?' Lovelace sees clearly
enough that she is ready to accept him and hastens to accept her silence as
refusal: 'Charming creature, thought I [*But I charge thee, that thou let not
any of the Sex know my exultation*] Is it so *soon* come to this?—Am I *already*
Lord of the destiny of a Clarissa Harlowe!' Richardson later added a rather
bitter note to the word 'exultation': 'Mr. Lovelace might have spared his
caution on this occasion, since many of the Sex [we mention it with
regret] who on the first publication had read thus far, and even to the
Lady's first escape, have been readier to censure her for over-niceness . . .
than him for artifices and exultations not less cruel and ungrateful, than
ungenerous and unmanly.'[97]

Clarissa agrees with Miss Howe that she must accept Lovelace; but she
cannot do it—not because of a foolish attachment to etiquette but because
of her own character. 'O my dear! if this be right to be done, how difficult
is it, where Modesty and Self (or where Pride if you please) is concerned,
to do that right?' 'And then must I be very humble, very submissive, and
try to insinuate myself into his good graces: With downcast eye, if not by
speech, beg his forgiveness for the distance I have so perversely kept him
at!—Yes, I warrant!—But I shall see how this behaviour will sit upon
me!—You have always rallied me upon my meekness, I think: Well then,
I will try, if I can be still meeker, shall I!—O my dear!—.'[98] Clarissa's next
letters describe another proposal scene, which is too long to quote, but
which illustrates clearly her efforts to lower herself to her situation. One
can certainly accuse her of standing so much on dignity that she misses her
opportunity—another girl might have improved the occasion better. But
one must remember that Lovelace gives the occasion knowing Clarissa.
'At the very Altar, our hands joined, I would engage to make this proud
Beauty leave the parson and me . . . and this only by a single word.'[99] Her
inability to accept him shows pride, proper pride or not the reader may
judge, but it is not dictated by propriety. She is throughout uneasily conscious that something is lacking in his proposals; and indeed his apparent
warmth of manner is carefully calculated. Looking back over the scene,
one can see that she has brought on her own troubles by too much

[97] SH, III, 75, 82; EL, II, 28–9, 33. The footnote was added in the second edition.
[98] SH, IV, 89, 91; EL, II, 297–8.   [99] SH, IV, 116; EL, II, 315.

dignity, by demanding the kind of respect with which a lady in her day was normally treated. But in each individual speech her motives are clear, and she would not have been the Clarissa Richardson had imagined if she had answered otherwise.

There is not much to be gained by asking whether Clarissa 'really' loved Lovelace. Miss Howe early guesses that she is attracted by him. She is attracted by him. But she also distrusts him and never greatly respects him. There are clear indications that if his behaviour had ever given her an opportunity to relax her guard she could have loved him enough to marry him. After his feigned illness she virtually admits her love to herself. 'One cannot, my dear, hate people in danger of death, or who are in distress or affliction. My heart, I find, is not proof against kindness, and acknowledgement of errors committed.'[100] 'Nevertheless let me tell you (what I hope I may justly tell you) that if again he give me cause to resume distance and reserve, I hope my reason will gather strength enough from his imperfections (for Mr. Lovelace, my dear, is not a wise man in all his ways) [the mildness of this statement is the best of all the demonstrations of her love and shows how well Richardson understood her] to enable me to keep my passions under.' For the third edition Richardson expanded Clarissa's reflections on love: 'If Love, as it is called, is allowed to be an excuse for our most unreasonable follies, and to lay level all the fences that a careful education has surrounded us by, what is meant by the doctrine of subduing our passions?—But, O my dearest friend, am I not guilty of a punishable fault, were I to love this man of errors? And has not my own heart deceived me, when I thought I did not? And what must be that Love, that has not some degree of purity for its object?'[101] Some readers may be offended by the added moralizing. Love (perhaps today one should say sex) should overcome all obstacles, even the unworthiness of its object. But those who hold to such a view must at least recognize that Clarissa does her best to forget her scruples and could have done so if Lovelace had not taken her behaviour as a sign of his triumph over her and an invitation to further plots. Clarissa is even willing to admit that such has been the case. At Hampstead she tells Captain Tomlinson: 'Mr. Lovelace's conduct has made me appear, perhaps, *over-nice*, when my heart wanted to be *encouraged* and *assured*; and when, if it had been so, my whole behaviour would have been governed by it.'[102] Though she is the one who believes in prudence (that virtue so unpopular, in theory at least, since the romantic period) and he is the one who urges the claims of the heart, it is she who is sincere, unguarded, and even eager to surrender and he who uses her love as an opportunity to deceive her.

When she thinks of the differences between them, it is not on his past

[100] SH, IV, 296; EL, II, 437. [101] 1st edn., IV, 210; SH, IV, 297–8; EL, II, 438–9.
[102] SH, V, 230; EL, III, 138–9.

escapades that she concentrates but on his lack of consideration and lack of honesty with her, and especially on his lack of generosity: 'Ungenerous, ungrateful Lovelace!—You know not the value of the heart you have insulted!' That there is a fundamental difference, she early recognizes and can only partially forget. And when she is angry, she is open enough in expressing to him her sense of the difference: 'My Mind, I believe, is superior to yours, debased as yours is by evil habits: But I had not known it to be so, if you had not *taken pains* to convince me of the inferiority of yours.' 'Urge me not to tell thee, how sincerely I think my soul above thee!—Thou hast, in mine, a proud, a too proud heart, to contend with!' Lovelace later remembers this statement, as well as the distrust which he has kept alive by never dealing with her truthfully or openly: 'She will not confide in my honour. Doubt, in this case, is Defiance. She loves me not well enough to forgive me generously. [Her previous forgiveness has recently emboldened him to attempt to rape her in the fire scene.] *She is so greatly above me!* How can I forgive her for a merit so mortifying to my pride!' Their long duel does not afford an atmosphere which allows her love to crystallize: 'O Mr. Lovelace, we have been long enough together, to be tired of each other's humours and ways; ways and humours so different, that perhaps you ought to dislike *me*, as much as I do *you*.'[103] To argue about whether either of them is in love with the other would be to argue about a mere word: 'Si on juge de l'amour par la plupart de ses effets, il resemble plus à la haine qu'à l'amitié.' But there can be no doubt that she is right when she tells Miss Howe, 'Mr. Lovelace's mind and mine are vastly different; different in *essentials*.'[104]

She states clearly that her decision not to marry him after the first attempted rape is owing above all to the fact that she cannot love him. She honestly admits that she once had a '*byas*' in his favour; and she reminds him that the fact that she put herself into his power was caused by her refusal to marry a man she could not love. 'The more I *think*, the less can I forgive an attempt, that I am convinced was intended to *destroy* me. . . . My heart is not *with* you—It is *against* you, Mr. Lovelace.'[105] Between this statement and the rape itself, she does again give signs of yielding slightly. After the rape she is unwavering. Some readers have seen Clarissa's death as the result of a foolish conventionality or an even more foolish pique. So acute an analyst of love as Stendhal must have been betrayed by his memory: 'I have not read the boring *Clarissa* for a long time; however, it seems to me that it is through feminine pride that she lets herself die and does not accept the hand of Lovelace.'[106] Above all else

---

[103] SH, V, 137, 252, IV, 215–16, V, 13, IV, 225; EL, III, 74–5, 153, II, 382–3, 515, 389.
[104] SH, IV, 268; EL, II, 418.
[105] SH, V, 199, 215; EL, III, 117, 128.
[106] *De l'amour* (Paris: Éditions de Cluny [1938]), p. 103.

she is offended by the dishonesty and selfishness which have used her own feelings to entrap her. 'And yet,' she writes to Mrs. Norton, 'I will own to you, *that once I could have loved him—Ungrateful man!—had he permitted me to love him, I once could have loved him.*'[107]

We have described her behaviour and Lovelace's in such detail because we think it is important that the novel be read as a struggle between genuine and human passions, not as an allegory or a historic curiosity. Much of what we have said is obvious to any careful reader, but in our day of ingenious interpretations the obvious has to be constantly repeated.

Richardson's own view of Clarissa is a little ambiguous. It is clear that he wanted her to be a model character, though not a perfect one. He wanted her to 'have some little things to be blamed for' 'that I might not seem to have aimed at drawing a perfect Character'. He had no fear as great as making her too perfect to be natural. Against Miss Mulso and Mrs. Chapone he maintained that all her calamaties arose from continuing to correspond with Lovelace after her father had forbidden her to. In spite of her possible faults, Clarissa (unlike Sophia Western) was too good to serve as a model for his depraved age, though he hoped that the next would be sufficiently amended to attempt to imitate her.[108]

Modern critics are less likely to worry about Clarissa's flaws of character than about her flaws as a character. Helen Sard Hughes expresses a typical view when she indicates that Richardson weakened his book because he wanted his heroine to be a model and 'is not drawing from life but from an ideal'.[109] Miss Howe, in *Clarissa*, anticipates such an objection: 'But one observation I will add, that were *your* character, and *my* character, to be truly drawn, mine would be allowed to be the most natural. Shades and Lights are equally necessary in a fine picture. Yours would be surrounded with such a flood of brightness, with such a glory, that it would indeed dazzle; but leave one heartless to imitate it.' She also expresses Richardson's desire to make his heroine a model: 'You will be as excellent an Example, as ever you hoped to be, as well as a Warning: And that will make your story, to all that shall come to know it, of double efficacy.'[110] Her list of her friend's accomplishments is an example of Richardson's weakness, so deadly in the continuation of *Pamela* and in *Sir Charles Grandison*, for having his characters praised effusively and indiscriminately. But there is surprisingly little of this sort of thing. The nature of the plot forced Richardson to put most of his praises in the mouth of Miss Howe; up to the very end most of the other people in the novel happily are hostile to the heroine.

[107] SH, VI, 151; EL, III, 345.

[108] To Hill, 10 May, 18 Nov. 1748; to Mrs. Chapone, 2 Mar. 1752; to Frances Grainger, 22 Jan. 1750.

[109] 'Characterization in *Clarissa Harlowe*', *JEGP*, XIII (1914), 110–23.

[110] SH, III, 226, IV, 63; EL, II, 131, 280.

One might make the distinction that in Clarissa Richardson draws a virtuous character, whereas in the later Pamela and in Sir Charles he only draws a model character. The model character is simply a list of abstractions which the author considers desirable, like Miss Howe's anticlimactic list of Clarissa's accomplishments. But a character may be admirable by bringing to life the author's own most admirable feelings. Dostoievsky manages this successfully in Sonia Marmladova and in Alyosha Karamazov, perhaps also in Prince Myshkin. Balzac at least aimed at it, and he cited Clarissa as the kind of character he had to produce a hundred times. Such a character, he says, is much more difficult than a wicked one: 'Lovelace has a thousand forms, since social corruption takes on the colours of all the environments in which it develops. Clarissa, on the contrary, that lovely image of ardent virtue, has lines so pure as to make one despair [Au contraire, Clarisse, cette belle image de la vertu passionnée, a des lignes d'une pureté désespérante].'[111] Virtuous characters are not in demand today, and we will not stress Clarissa's claims to the dangerous honour of being one. But Balzac is surely right when he points out how hard they are to bring off. There are not many of them in the history of the novel. No reader today is likely to use Clarissa as a model; but a reader might well ask himself as he reads whether he is not caught up in Clarissa's reality to see through her eyes and whether as he does so he is not moved to a sort of admiration, a sense of the possibilities and powers of the human spirit.

Admittedly this is not what Richardson said that he intended. When he described his purpose in writing the book, he thought of his moral in the most conventional terms. He wanted to show that prudence should prevail over passion, to admonish parents not to force their daughters into marriages, to explode the pernicious notion that reformed rakes make the best husbands, to make his readers look to rewards in the afterlife, to show that young girls should marry Hickmans and not Lovelaces and that saucy girls like Miss Howe who make fun of their dull Hickmans must be a little punished, to advise young ladies to obey their parents and to keep early hours, to combat the notion that women cannot have true friendships, to enforce the duty of children to obey parents whatever the parents may do.[112] Some of these opinions were probably stimulated by his correspondent of the moment: he liked to underline the demands of propriety to Miss Grainger, and with Mrs. Chapone he tended to be very strict in his moral views.

These subsidiary morals, though Richardson seems to have considered them important (at least after the fact), have little to do with the quality of

[111] 'Avant-propos' to Comédie humaine.
[112] R to Hill, 29 Oct. 1746; R to Frances Grainger, 20 Dec. 1748, 21 Dec. 1749; R to Mrs. Chapone, 25 Mar. 1751, 2 Mar. 1752; R to Susanna Highmore, 26 Nov. 1749.

the book. Mrs. Barbauld long ago asked the puzzling question: 'That
Clarissa is a highly moral work, has been always allowed; but what is the
moral?' It cannot be that a young lady should not place her affections on
a libertine: 'Such a maxim has not dignity or force enough in it, to be the
chief moral of this interesting tale.' The author, according to Mrs. Barbauld, is even to blame for implying that his heroine's resistance to a trial
on her chastity 'had any thing in it uncommon, or peculiarly meritorious.
But the real moral of Clarissa is, that virtue is triumphant in every situation.'[113] As she phrases it, such a notion sounds as contrary as possible to
twentieth-century views; yet one could, with some ingenuity, rephrase it
in a jargon which might be acceptable. Even in this century there are
figures in fiction who rise above the most miserable circumstances to
assert human dignity and worth. Malraux, for instance, is hardly a writer
one associates with virtue triumphant, and yet the behaviour of Kyo
Gisors and of Katov in their prison is not entirely unlike the behaviour of
Clarissa in hers, if one allows for a difference of idiom.

The phrase 'intentional fallacy' has been used somewhat loosely, to
express a variety of meanings not necessarily connected. We see no harm
in taking the trouble to find out what an author thought he was doing.
Writers sometimes do do what they set out to do, and at other times what
they intend to do affects what they accomplish. In *Sir Charles Grandison*,
for instance, what Richardson intended was pretty much what he did—
with results that are none too happy. What he said he intended to do in
Clarissa does not adequately explain the quality of the book. The subsidiary morals, about reformed rakes and parental authority and so on,
hamper him a little, but not much. They account for a few uninteresting
passages and they may at times have reigned in his free course. The main
moral he never phrased clearly, unless it be that one should look to a
future state for rewards and punishments.

Brian Downs has emphasized the fact that such a religion of rewards
and punishments after death is not really different from the shallow
'virtue rewarded' of *Pamela*.[114] From the point of view of the twentieth
century (not, of course, from that of the eighteenth) such a religion is still
'practical' and selfish. We do not believe that we are guilty of being over-
ingenious when we say that it is our impression, both from the novel itself
and from Richardson's letters about it, that his concept, his attitude, in
Clarissa is that virtue does not need rewards but that his conventionality
forced him to emphasize the rewards. It would not be the first time that a
selfish motive has been made up to justify unselfish conduct. The notion
of rewards and punishments, of inducements and motivations, is firmly
fixed in the western middle-class mind. But rewards in heaven are different
in one vital way from rewards on earth: few people really believe in them.

[113] I, xcix, ci.   [114] *Richardson*, pp. 75–6.

If they have rarely been sought with impatience since the days of the Christian martyrs and Moslem conquerors, it is hard to see how they can be called selfish. A young girl who believed in the joys of heaven in the same way that she believed in those of a happy marriage would see how much better they must be and would regret every day they were postponed for such inferior toys as houses and balls and husbands and children. Some refined Christians have felt that future rewards should not be our motive for religion; more ordinary ones have felt that they *should* be but rarely are. Rewards in heaven are often mentioned in *Clarissa*, especially towards the end, when the life is beginning to ebb from the novel. We cannot 'prove' that they were not Clarissa's main motive for virtue, but we do not believe that a reader who sees events through her eyes will feel that they were. They give a 'logical' reason for her doing what she was going to do anyway.

A good description of Clarissa's religion has been given by John A. Dussinger.[115] We cannot quite see *Clarissa* as 'a parable illustrating the fundamental doctrine of the cross', since it seems to us much richer than a parable, but we do agree that it emphasizes the imitation of Christ and the internal spiritual experience. Richardson, says Mr. Dussinger, 'attempted to portray the nature of sin and guilt under the operations of conscience and to represent in his heroine the ultimate refinement of sensibility as the condition of salvation'. Whether or not he attempted consciously to do so, he did. The vital element in Clarissa's religion is her sensibility, and thus her religion is one well adapted to fictional presentation. Mr. Dussinger shows that the emphasis on the freedom of Clarissa's will, on her personal conscience and her intense self-scrutiny, on her purification through suffering and her acceptance of affliction as a means of expiating her former pride, is in line with the doctrine of the atonement as interpreted by many Protestant writers. It is also perfectly adapted to a novel which emphasizes the analysis of character; such a novel is ideally suited to portray a religion which depends more on experience than on doctrine, which is and should be internal and emotional. The acceptance of suffering and of individual responsibility sounds a keynote which in our opinion can legitimately be called tragic.

Shortly after the publication of the first edition Richardson commented to Solomon Lowe on an opinion of Thomas Cooper's that the moral against marrying reformed rakes could have been more clearly drawn had Clarissa married Lovelace.[116] His main point was that, though Cooper was perhaps correct about the moral, such an ending would not have answered his design. It would have robbed Clarissa of her triumph. And it is clear

---

[115] 'Conscience and the Pattern of Christian Perfection in *Clarissa*', *PMLA*, LXXXI (1966), 236–45.
[116] 21 Jan. 1749. See also 'Hints of Prefaces for Clarissa', FM XV, 2, fo. 51.

that Clarissa's 'triumph' was the one thing Richardson would not sacrifice.

In imaginative literature one must distinguish between the 'moral' of a book and its effect. The moral or meaning is drawn *from* the book, the effect is *in* it. Diderot, speaking of Richardson, saw the great advantage of this sort of fiction: 'I felt that I had gained experience [acquis de l'expéri-ence].'[117] It is our opinion that the 'meaning' of *Clarissa* is the experience which the reader has while he reads the book. Richardson had various not altogether consistent ideas about what he was doing, but he also had a concept which he could not express adequately in abstract terms but which he conveyed in his characters. Fiction is a poor way to 'prove' something, but it is an excellent way to convey an attitude. Zola, for instance, set out to illustrate a theory of heredity in which no one is any longer interested and to 'prove' scientifically a deterministic theory of human behaviour. Since he was free to make up his facts, he proved nothing. Fortunately he had attitudes which are more interesting than his theory: the Rougon-Macquart series is a classic illustration of an author's accomplishing more than he intends. It seems to us that much the same can be said of *Clarissa*.

Many critics have noted that the effect of *Clarissa* is something altogether different from the 'morals' which Richardson discusses. As Ian Watt puts it, 'If the need arises, Richardson the novelist can silence Richardson the writer of conduct books.'[118] As we read the book, the effect is something not unlike the effect of the classical tragedy. We do not intend to try once again to define a 'true' tragedy. What seems to us important is that *Clarissa*, in its realistic setting, succeeds in catching some of the same grandeur, the same heroic quality that pervades Greek tragedy and Shakespearean tragedy, as well as the best of the Greek and Germanic epics.

It would not be difficult to show that Clarissa qualifies as a tragic hero if all that a tragic hero needs is a tragic flaw. Richardson makes Clarissa in the preface of her volume of *Meditations* compare herself with Job: '*His* afflictions were from GOD, and *mine*, in a great measure, from myself.'[119] She herself repeatedly points to her early pride and exagger-ated self-confidence as faults which, appropriately, are punished by the consequences of the actions which they motivated. Like Oedipus and Lear, she learns to see herself as a result of her suffering. Aristotelian critics should keep reminding themselves that the tragic flaw is not part of Aristotle's definition of tragedy and that it is closely connected with the concept of poetic justice: our pity is excited by misfortunes un-deservedly suffered. Divorced, however, from the invidious distinctions of poetic justice, the tragic flaw does have the advantage that it keeps the disaster from appearing as a meaningless accident; if it does not

---

[117] *Œuvres complètes*, V, 213.   [118] *Rise of the Novel*, p. 213.   [119] London, 1750, p. vi.

itself give significance, it enables us to find significance in misfortune. It also lends itself to the kind of enlightenment through failure which perhaps exalts our conception of humanity as high as poetry has ever succeeded in exalting it.

The ending of *Clarissa* sounds another note frequent in tragedy, that acceptance of destruction and ruin which purifies us of bitterness and repining and which may (or may not) be what Aristotle meant by his mysterious 'catharsis'. The ending of, say, *Oedipus at Colonus* leaves us in a satisfied tension between the wrong and injustice which are never denied or glossed over and the submission, not forced but willed, which overcomes a part of the wrong by consenting to it. To borrow Joyce's terms, the catastrophe is static, not kinetic: we do not want to *do* anything about it, we see it and we are content. In *Clarissa* this effect is marred by the fact that Richardson drags out the ending. During Clarissa's funeral we do want to do something—we want to get it over and close the book. But the note of acceptance is sustained over many pages before the heroine's death, and it is sounded again, this time briefly and conclusively, when Lovelace dies.

There are even hints in *Clarissa* of hybris and of a pursuing fate— shifted to a Christian context, of course. Even before her flight Clarissa suspects that the attempt to reconcile Lovelace with her family which first leads her into trouble may be an interception 'perhaps of the designs of Providence, which may intend to make these hostile spirits their own punishers.—If so, what presumption!—Indeed, my dear friend, I am afraid I have thought myself of too much consequence. But, however this be, *it is good, when calamities befal us, that we should look into ourselves, and fear.*' 'We have been till within these few weeks, every one of us, too happy. . . . Surrounded by our heaps and stores, hoarded up as fast as acquired, we have seemed to think ourselves out of the reach of the bolts of adverse fate. . . . *Strange*, I may well call it; for don't you see, my dear, that we seem all to be *impelled*, as it were, by a perverse fate, which none of us are able to resist?'[120]

The simplicity of the story, its concentration on one conflict, also resembles that of the classic tragedy. The outlines are as clear and sharp as those of a folk tale. In a discerning comparison of Richardson and Fielding, Frank Kermode describes Richardson's manner as 'mythopoeic': 'The aspect of Richardson's novel technique which may legitimately be called Shakespearian, is his refusal to allow the primitive nature of this simple situation to be obscured, and his willingness to let it talk and talk and talk for itself. . . . *Clarissa* is complex by reason of the infinity of moral overtones which radiate from the central choice and dishonouring. . . . It was a sound instinct that led the older critics to associate Richardson

[120] SH, II, 255, 263-4; EL, I, 413, 419.

with Shakespeare; both these writers had the great gift of being aware of
the unfathomable significance of simple and time-honoured story.'[121]

Unlike Fielding, Richardson was not steeped in the classics. So far as
we know, he had never read the Greek plays. There is certainly no
evidence that he was trying to imitate them and to write a tragic prose
epic as Fielding set out to write a comic one. The similarity is largely in a
similar view of mankind. Aristotle says that the aim of comedy is to exhibit men as worse than they are, that of tragedy to exhibit them as better.
'Greater' might be a more exact word for the tragic view than 'better', if
one thinks of 'better' with its ethical Christian associations. One can
hardly avoid the outmoded word 'noble'. Clarissa understands her fate
and accepts it; though she does not overcome it, she overcomes herself.
If she is not the master of her fate, she is the captain of her soul. Much of
modern literature has been devoted to making such words sound silly.
Yet one can find something of the same inherent dignity in Leopold Bloom
and in Camus' Joseph Grand, among others. Richardson would hardly
have dared permit his heroine to suffer the ignominy of being ridiculous,
as Bloom and Grand are. The situation of man did not seem so desperate
in the eighteenth century that dignity had to be rescued from such depths.

But he did humiliate her. At the beginning of the book she has every
external advantage which society can give her, and it is by losing this
social and external dignity that she gains a more reliable dignity. The
position of women in the eighteenth century, with its concomitant the
battle of the sexes, is not the important theme of *Clarissa*, but it gave an
excellent opportunity for developing the important theme. So long as they
were chaste (or had the reputation of being chaste), women who were at
the same time 'ladies' (rich and well-connected) were at least nominally
idealized. They were not, in the long run, either free or secure, but the
poetic clichés encouraged them to think of themselves as goddesses.
Chastity was their honour; loss of chastity was their ruin. Clarissa's
triumph (and Richardson's triumph) is that she loses chastity and rises in
the loss.

In *Pamela* and in *Sir Charles Grandison* Richardson is both frivolous and
solemn. In *Clarissa* he is serious. That is, he takes his characters seriously,
he takes human nature and the human situation seriously. Inevitably he
connected this seriousness with his religion. *Clarissa* is one of the rare
novels which take Christianity at its face value. If one looks over the works
of the major English novelists of the eighteenth and nineteenth centuries,
most of them orthodox, it is surprising what a small part Christianity plays
in them. The characters, of course, go to church; if they are clergymen,
they are concerned with the organization and ritual of the church; some
of them even argue about doctrine. They are generally ethical. But their

---

[121] 'Richardson and Fielding', pp. 110–13.

ethics is the ethics of their class and time, not of the Sermon on the Mount. Today there is a tendency to think of religion as always mystical. Clarissa is no mystic. Her religion is the religion of the seventeenth century, of right reason supported by revelation. And towards the end of the book she takes it literally, and she dies by it. It is hard to deny respect to a person who lives up to the highest ideal he can conceive of. Whether or not she was factually right in her belief, Clarissa is 'right' as Antigone was right, and Prometheus and Njal and Roland and Dr. Stockmann and Nekhludov and Captain MacWhirr. So in a way she is after all a model character. Not quite in the way Richardson thought, perhaps. She raises our conception of the capabilities of human nature; she makes men greater, it may be, than they ever are, but not greater than they can imagine themselves as being.

This may seem to be claiming a good deal for the heroine of a domestic mishap. But in the realistic details of his domestic situation Richardson found materials to exalt his heroine. Clarissa is involved in a conflict suitable to realistic treatment but also to noble emotions. She has a pride which demands to be treated as an independent person, to be respected; Lovelace's pride can only be satisfied by seeing other people as his own reflections, by dominating and humiliating them and so raising himself by lowering them. Clarissa needs to feel equal to anyone, Lovelace needs to feel superior. She loses all the external props of her pride and discovers at last that she does not need them.

It is for this reason that Richardson was right in resisting any suggestion that some friend or relative be allowed to attend Clarissa's deathbed. It is, to be sure, rather improbable that all of her old friends are kept from her. Lady Bradshaigh could not understand this deprivation: 'Surely it is a wrong thing to make every body unable to stir from home, who cou'd be of any comfort to her. I cannot see why. I feel at this moment, as if I was just going to write privately to enforce the necessity of Mrs Nortons attendance.' 'Excellent Lady B!' replied Richardson. 'But of what service woud the Interview be now? Had they met, I must have drawn a Scene that every Reader could not have stood. I believe I have made ye excellent Creature give a better Reason for dispensing with their Visits than seeing them. If I have not, I could.'[122] The 'better Reason' is doubtless Clarissa's thought that 'the sight of one I so dearly love, so happily fraught with good news, might but draw me back to wishes I have had great struggles to get above. . . . *God will have no rivals in the hearts of those he sanctifies*. By various methods he deadens all other sensations, or rather absorbs them all in the Love of Him.'[123] Richardson's conception required that Clarissa be abandoned by all but friends whom she had found after her humiliation.

[122] Marginalia in Lady Bradshaigh's copy of *Clarissa*, 1st edn., VI, 366–7.
[123] SH, VII, 404; EL, IV, 301–2.

Only when abandoned by everyone can she learn to look at herself. Her integrity has been frivolously and selfishly violated and she recovers it. She is no longer self-assured or self-approving: in humiliation she has learned (what humiliation rarely teaches) humility. But she trusts herself because she has nothing else to trust. Ian Watt is correct in calling her a heroine of Puritan individualism, of 'the new and inward ethical sanction which an individualistic society requires'.[124] Propriety, that parody and heir of the Puritan conscience which Richardson, like the Victorians, was in his other works all too likely to mistake for morality, is not the final guide of Clarissa. Very early in the novel she begins to look beyond it to her sincerity, to 'the integrity of my heart'.[125]

[124] *Rise of the Novel*, p. 225.   [125] SH, I, 150; EL, I, 103.

CHAPTER XII

THE RECEPTION OF *CLARISSA*
RICHARDSON AND FIELDING
1748–1750

EVEN before the publication of the final volumes of *Clarissa* Richardson began to receive letters about it. He preserved them, as he had the *Pamela* letters, in his correspondence, which was by this time growing to a considerable bulk. Some of the letters were from acquaintances. Other writers became acquaintances: Richardson wrote to Stinstra that *Clarissa* had brought him many friends and greatly enlarged his correspondence with both sexes. He could, he said, quote testimonials of regard from 'some of our gravest Divines and finest Writers'. His novel had obtained for him the acquaintance of five bishops, one of whom declared that he had read it eleven times already and proposed to re-read it every two years as long as he lived.[1]

One of the new friends made by *Clarissa* may have been John Read, at this time of King's College, Cambridge. Read wrote on 5 December 1748 praising the novel for its new plan, not subject to Aristotle's rules. Shortly over a year later he was friendly enough to introduce a young friend who wanted to meet the author of *Clarissa*, and to visit Richardson in town. He later became a clerk assistant of the House of Commons, where he would naturally have been thrown much with Richardson, who planned to leave him a mourning ring but was prevented by Read's untimely death.[2] Another may have been James Harris of Salisbury, to whom he sent a copy of the second edition of *Clarissa*.[3] Harris seems to have been of a rather heavy and pedantic turn of mind. He was a classical scholar of some note—Dr. Johnson said 'a sound sullen scholar' and added that he was 'a prig, and a bad prig'.[4] When Richardson expressed his admiration for his *Hermes*, he acknowledged Richardson's taste, in spite of his lack of the learned languages and his business: 'The sordid views of trade have not (as usual) been so far able to engross you, as to withdraw you from the contemplation of more rational, more ingenuous, and (what perhaps may

---

[1] 6 Dec. 1752.
[2] Read to R, 2 Feb. 1750; R to David Graham, 3 May 1750; Eaves and Kimpel, 'Samuel Richardson and His Family Circle', p. 303.
[3] Harris to R, 13 June 1749.　　　　[4] Boswell, *Life*, III, 245.

sound strange to many of your neighbours) more interesting subjects.'
Richardson knew him at least well and long enough to send him a copy of
Sir Charles Grandison.[5]

Susanna Highmore wrote that though she could not regret so noble a
death as Clarissa's, her heart had been almost broken; she and her Papa
and Mamma 'each read to ourselves, and in separate Apartments wept'.[6]
Mrs. Delany and her husband had been so moved they had to throw down
the book; the Dean had declared that it was the most valuable work the
age had produced and touched the heart more than his sermons could.[7]
Edward Moore, who once planned to dramatize *Clarissa* with Garrick as
Lovelace,[8] reported that three fair ladies had ordered him to scold the
author because Clarissa shows up all women by showing what a woman
ought to be and because the book's tendency is to put people out of
conceit with all other reading. If these girls could see Clarissa's creator,
'perhaps your Turn of Ravishment might be next'; they say they 'would
give a Hundred Pound for an Hour with Mr Richardson'.[9] Presumably
Richardson avoided his heroine's fate by not meeting these dangerous
ladies. Philip Skelton was pleased at the passions aroused only because
they were used to such good purpose: while the heart is stirred up and laid
open, Richardson pours in lessons of morality and religion. Others can
create a whirlwind, he directs the storm. It is lucky that the 'Author proposed to himself so noble an End as that of rectifying the Heart thro' its
Passions; and not like other Novel-Writers, that only of amusing it's Cor-
ruptions; happy indeed! because he can do what he will with the Heart'.[10]
Edward Young called *Clarissa* '*The Whole Duty of WOMAN*' and said
that 'the Bench of Bishops might go to school' to the writer of this
romance.[11] Miss Wescomb reported that a friend considered *Clarissa*, next
to the Bible, the best of all books.[12] Others held similar views: Miss Frances
Cotterell (who disliked Richardson's works) later remarked that 'when
she was a young woman one might as well have said one had not read the
Bible as Clarissa Harlowe'.[13]

Thomas Edwards, soon to be a close friend of Richardson's, received
the last three volumes from the author soon after they came out: 'I was
never so moved with any thing in my life, and was obliged frequently to
throw away the book to give vent to those passions which that great

[5] Harris to R, 19 Jan. 1752; 10 Nov. 1753.   [6] 2 Jan. 1749.
[7] Mrs. Delany to R, 25 Jan. 1749.
[8] Barbauld, I, cvii; Mrs. Delany to R, 24 Apr. 1751.   [9] 1 Oct. 1748.
[10] 10 June 1749.
[11] To Mrs. Delany, 9 Feb. 1749, copy sent by R to Stinstra, 2 June 1753. See also R to
Frances Grainger, 21 Dec. 1749; 28 Feb. 1750.
[12] 3 July 1752.
[13] Letter from Elizabeth Smart Le Noir to Cuthbert Sharp, 22 Aug. 1831 (Sharp MS. 28
in the Chapter Library of Durham Cathedral), quoted by Arthur Sherbo, 'Anecdotes by Mrs.
Le Noir', *DUJ*, LVII (1965), 166.

Master of the heart has raised. He seems to me, at lest next to Shakespear, to have more of that Magical Power which Horace speaks of than I ever met with. . . . To me it will be a Touchstone, by which I shall judge who of my acquaintance have hearts, and who have not.'[14] Edwards was somewhat given to gushing about the heart, but he, like Young, Skelton, and Delany, was an educated man, and he was not stupid. The great appeal which *Clarissa* made to those who were at the same time tender-hearted and sympathetic towards virtue can hardly be demonstrated more strongly. Edwards used *Clarissa* as 'a Criterion of Sensibility'. Two years after his first reading he had read the novel for the fifth time, 'with almost the same eagerness, and with an equal concern as I did at first, but with more pleasure because I every time observe more of those fine touches, those minute strokes of the pencil which give his works a beauty unknown to most if not all others'. The book, he believed, 'will last as long as our English language'.[15]

Lady Bradshaigh, like Edwards, used *Clarissa* as a touchstone. When feeling the pulse of the young, gay, and fashionable, she would ask them if they had read the novel; 'if the answer is, as it has been, D——n it, I would not read it thro' to save my life,—I put that youth down as an incurable'. A young friend, on the contrary, who gave as his excuse for not visiting her for several days his pleasure in and instruction from the divine Clarissa was fully absolved and assured 'that had he changed the conversation of Clarissa for any other, my good opinion of him would have been much weakened'. She also reported an anecdote: 'A lady was reading to two or three others the seventh volume of Clarissa, whilst her maid curled her hair, and the poor girl let fall such a shower of tears upon her lady's head, that she was forced to send her out of the room to compose herself, asking her what she cried for; she said, to see such goodness and innocence in distress; and a lady followed her out of the room, and gave her a crown for that answer.' A woman whom she knew equalled Edwards's record and in 1753 was reading *Clarissa* for the fifth time.[16] An even more sincere compliment came later from Sarah Chapone, who in describing her husband's death told how he was helped to die by the example of Clarissa; shortly before he died he pronounced the novel the best tragedy since Adam.[17]

There were, of course, those who found fault. On 6 April 1748 a violently indignant lady wrote to berate Richardson for disclosing her story—she had never told a word of it to anyone. He noted on the letter that the lady flattered herself. A later correspondent also thought he knew

---

[14] To Daniel Wray, 16 Jan. 1749, Bodleian MS. 1011, pp. 95-6.

[15] To Philip Yorke, 19 Jan. 1749; to the Rev. Lewis Crusius, 3 May 1749; to Speaker Onslow, 16 Feb. 1751, Bodleian MS. 1011, pp. 97, 130, 229-30. The original of the letter to Yorke is in B.M. Add. MS. 33,605, fo. 336.

[16] 16 Dec. 1749; 25 Sept. 1753.   [17] 20 June 1759.

the original of the heroine, since he wrote sarcastically expressing his concern that *Clarissa* should be so generally condemned and that the once-celebrated author of *Pamela* should thus fail in his object—libelling a private family. Richardson found this 'an unaccountable Letter'.[18]

There were also sincere objections to Richardson's handling of his story. Mrs. Chapone herself, though generally admiring, found the heroine short of her feminist ideal—she is too submissive to her father. Earlier a Mr. Bennet had objected on the opposite grounds: the Harlowe family was right in endeavouring to force Clarissa to marry Solmes to keep her out of the arms of Lovelace, since her correspondence with the latter showed that she was not to be depended on. David Graham could himself find nothing to censure in the heroine but reported that while some blamed her for her opposition to her father, others thought she was not independent enough; some called her a prude, others a coquette. He found this lack of appreciation not surprising in an irreligious age: those 'who can listen to the dissonant Jingle of Tom Jones, woud for ever be deaf to the Music of your Charmer'.[19]

Probably more usual was the objection of an anonymous correspondent that in spite of the suspense, the knowledge of the human heart, and the excellent observations, he like all of his friends resented the author's 'tedious Repetitions'; the book was entirely too long. A man who signed himself Philaretes agreed that it needed shortening and objected so much when he heard that the ending was to be unhappy that he resolved to read no more; he found many gentlemen of his mind and predicted that it would sell badly unless the catastrophe were changed. But Edward Moore wanted it lengthened by more details of Lovelace's remorse and death and objected only to the postscript justifying the ending, as entirely unnecessary—though he shed tears, they were joyous ones, and he could not wish her to live but was rather inclined to 'exult in the Loss of her'.[20] Another learned man, George Jeffreys, former Fellow of Trinity College, Cambridge, and author of sorts, was by no means willing to exult. Though after reading the book he revised his earlier opinion that it violated the principle of poetic justice, since the heroine was rewarded in heaven, he wrote to Richardson's friend William Duncombe that after all he found the work too melancholy for him. How many are there who would wish themselves in her place? 'What I mean by this is, that the work can be of no general use, as the majority of readers (not excepting the clergy themselves,) can never be reconciled to the sufferings of Clarissa in this life, by the prospect of her happiness in another; though there may be many, both among the clergy and laity, who are hypocrites enough to pretend

---

[18] Jan. 1749.
[19] Mrs. Chapone, 22 Feb., [Mar.], 1752; Bennet, [1746-1747?]; Graham, 22 Apr. 1750.
[20] Anonymous, 20 May 1748; Philaretes, [early 1748?]; Moore, 23 Dec. 1748.

the contrary.' Jeffreys also thought Lovelace a greater accomplishment than Clarissa: 'By what I have heard of the author's station in life, one would wonder how he could enter so well into characters so much above it, and support that of Lovelace, for instance, with so much wit and humour, such spirit and gaiety throughout.'[21] Being a cousin of the Duke of Chandos and a member of his household, Jeffreys may be considered an authority on elegant rakes.

The also learned Elizabeth Carter was of another opinion. Her intimate friend Catherine Talbot was one of *Clarissa*'s warmest admirers (the character of the strong-minded Anna Howe reminded her of Mrs. Carter), and she responded warmly if not enthusiastically to Miss Talbot's praises. But when Miss Talbot wrote of her detestation for *Tom Jones*, which increased her admiration for *Clarissa*, Mrs. Carter could not agree. 'I am sorry to find you so outrageous about poor Tom Jones; he is no doubt an imperfect, but not a detestable character, with all that honesty, goodnature, and generosity of temper. Though nobody can admire Clarissa more than I do; yet with all our partiality, I am afraid, it must be confessed, that Fielding's book is the most natural representation of what passes in the world, and of the bizarreries which arise from the mixture of good and bad which makes up the composition of most folks.' Clarissa, she continued, is an entirely credible character, but Richardson's vicious characters have 'a strange awkwardness and extravagance': 'To be sure, poor man, he had read in a book, or heard some one say, there was such a thing in the world as wickedness', but being ignorant how it operates on the heart, in attempting to portray it he drew a monster.[22]

A criticism which must have disturbed Richardson was that of indecency. The same charge had been made, with more reason, against *Pamela*. In *Clarissa* only one scene was singled out as objectionable, the 'fire scene', in which Lovelace, with the excuse of a conflagration he himself has had set, invades the heroine's bedroom in the middle of the night, finds her in undress, and attempts unsuccessfully to overcome her resistance. Richardson wrote Stinstra that friends had rallied him on this scene. He took the matter seriously enough to print an *Answer to the Letter of a Very Reverend and Worthy Gentleman*, an eleven-page pamphlet defending the fire scene, dated 8 June 1749, and directed (as he told Stinstra) to 'two particular Divines'.[23] One of them was probably the virtuous Irish clergyman Philip Skelton, who had recently returned from London to Ireland. On 10 June he wrote that he could find few spots on the sun of *Clarissa* but thought the fire scene should go—an opinion he may well

[21] 21 Sept. 1749, n. d. [29 July 1750], *Letters by Several Eminent Persons Deceased*, II, 149, 157. A dated extract of Jeffreys's second letter is in FM XV, 2, fo. 89.

[22] Miss Talbot, 28 Dec. 1747, 22 May 1749; Mrs. Carter, 20 June 1749, *Letters between Mrs. Elizabeth Carter and Miss Catherine Talbot*, I, 161, 206-8.

[23] 6 Dec. 1752.

have expressed earlier. Richardson respected him and submitted his remark to some of his friends for comment. Jane Collier reassured him: she respected the honest heart of his friend in Ireland, but she herself had been warmed only in the cause of injured innocence. Aaron Hill found the parson horrid and the scene wonderful. Richardson explained to him that the parson was a good man and that in addition he wanted to show two or three ladies of his acquaintance who had been attacked about the scene and wanted to defend him how they might modestly own him. To save transcribing he had printed a few copies of his answer for particular friends.[24] He justifies the scene both on artistic grounds (the description was in accordance with Lovelace's character, and it had to be vivid to justify Clarissa's flight to Hampstead) and on moral grounds (it would serve as a warning to young ladies; the detail in it would prevent even grosser things from being imagined). He cannot believe that the scene can be inflaming: in writing it 'the Passion I found strongest in me, whenever I supposed myself a Reader only, and the Story real, was *Anger*, or *Indignation*: I had too great an Aversion to the intended Violator of the Honour of a CLARISSA, to suffer any-thing but alternate Admiration and Pity of her, and Resentment against him, to take place in my Mind, on the Occasion.'[25]

A good deal less was printed about *Clarissa* than about *Pamela*, but the comments were generally favourable. A mock letter from a fashionable young man who signed himself Charles Easy appeared in the *Gentleman's Magazine* for December 1748. The length of the book had frightened him, but once he began, he sat up repeatedly till morning, and in spite of his levity and indifference at the destruction of armies, the swallowing of cities, the oppression of nations, 'and my steady resignation at the loss of dear relatives', he wept. This pleasant puff was followed by a sample letter from the novel. The next month the magazine carried an elegiac couplet, purportedly by Pamela B. Junior: 'Scire hominum mores varios, bene scribere, si vis:/Perlege Clarissam; mente fruare tuâ.'[26]

A more ambitious criticism, also published in the *Gentleman's Magazine*, was a translation of an article by Albrecht von Haller which had appeared in a French periodical in Amsterdam.[27] The first instalment was almost entirely laudatory—the book is generally assigned 'the first rank among romances'. The author ('S. Robinson') has avoided the 'tiresome gravity' of the last volume of *Pamela*; *Clarissa* has more variety than the earlier

---

[24] Miss Collier, 9 July 1749; Hill to R, 10 July 1749; R to Hill, 12 July.

[25] For a description of this rare pamphlet, see Eaves and Kimpel, 'Richardsoniana', pp. 232–233.

[26] XVIII, 548; XIX, 38.

[27] XIX (June and Aug. 1749), 245–6, 345–9; *Bibliotheque raisonnée des ouvrages des savans de l'Europe*, XLII (1749), 324–36. The article is included in *Sammlung Kleiner Hallerischer Schriften*, 2nd edn. (Bern, 1772), I, 293–315.

novel and deals with a higher class and hence has more elegant, cultivated, and useful reflections. It is a story of private life, far better than the French romances, better even than Marivaux, who lacks 'the minutiæ of *Virtue*'. In addition, it shows in the heroine duty to God, to parents, to relations, to friends, to servants, and to herself. '*Marianne* amuses, *Clarissa* not only amuses, but instructs.' The second instalment also begins with praises. The epistolary method lends warmth and probability. The characters are excellent, and the style is well adapted to them. The descriptions are particularly good. There are, however, a few minor faults. Clarissa should have broken off correspondence with Lovelace when her mother forbade it; she should not have made assignations with Lovelace or taken his part against her relations; she was disrespectful to Solmes; she was too delicate with Lovelace after the abduction. More serious, Lovelace is often indecent, and the house of ill repute is coarse. It is improbable that in England, jealous of law and liberty, a lady should be confined in a brothel. Belford paints an offensive scene of common women (Mrs. Sinclair's deathbed). The heroine's ravings in her delirium are trifling. And Lovelace is not criminal enough in the way he dies. The criticisms, in short, are almost all on ethical grounds.

After the adverse criticism, the magazine printed, in brackets, an answer, possibly by Richardson himself.[28] Clarissa must have some faults; she had 'no reason to apprehend any ill consequences from these assignations', and the only time she actually kept an assignation was to pacify Lovelace on her resolution not to leave her father's house; Lovelace appeared to her 'in the light of a persecuted man'. Solmes is odiously persistent, and Clarissa frank. Many English readers have thought Clarissa too delicate, but Lovelace's letters and the author's notes in the second edition should be read carefully. Lovelace's manner is never coarse. The appearance of the bawdy house was specious until Lovelace had gone too far to retreat. Belford's description was designed to be shocking. Lovelace's crime did not consist in the manner of his death.

The most ambitious defence of *Clarissa* was written by Sarah Fielding. Her anonymous *Remarks on Clarissa*, a small pamphlet of fifty-six pages, came out soon after the last volumes of the novel, in January 1749. Richardson said that he did not see the pamphlet before it was in print.[29] Miss Fielding attempts to answer the objections made against *Clarissa* and thus gives a good summary of the various kinds of unfavourable comments which were being made. She analyses the book's virtues in some

[28] McKillop (*Richardson*, p. 252) has pointed out that in Richardson's index to his *Clarissa* correspondence (FM XV, 3, fo. 2) there is an entry: 'Observations on ye Amsterdam Critic, by Mr R: for ye Magazine. Aug. 1749'. It may well be, as he conjectures, that this indicates that Richardson himself wrote the answers; the entry in the index must refer to them, though Richardson was not the only 'Mr R:' in London, and his wording in the index is often careless.
[29] To Stinstra, 6 Dec. 1752.

detail and with a good deal of perspicacity. Though she emphasizes the noble moral, the model character of the heroine, and the true Christian philosophy of the ending, she devotes at least as much space to purely literary virtues.

She imagines a series of three conversations, one after the publication of the first two volumes, one after the second two, and one when the last volumes had appeared. A Miss Harriote Gibson defends the book against all objectors. The first criticisms are of the book's length and tedium. The length enables us to know the characters, to see and hear them, and the study of the human heart justifies it. There are some trifling objections to motivations, and one gentleman blames the newly coined words. Clarissa is called a prude and a coquette, too obedient and too undutiful to her family, too fond of Lovelace and too harsh to him. Miss Gibson points out that such contradictory faults cancel each other out and, more cogently, that the fact that they can be made proves that the character is real, since people talk of her as real. A newly entered character named Bellario feels that the heroine wants passion, that she is cold; he also has doubts about the advisability of the unhappy ending which he has heard that the novel is to have. But in the last conversation he has been completely convinced. Clarissa is love itself, the ending is the only possible one. Minor objections are still made by some of the interlocutors to impropriety and to 'cant'—too much religion. The pamphlet concludes with two letters, from Bellario to Miss Gibson and her answer. The beauties of *Clarissa* are analysed in detail. The method is new, the author may make his own laws; the vast design is revealed gradually and is worked out with justice and proportion; the styles fit the characters. Many particular scenes and details are singled out for praise: Clarissa's madness is compared to Lear's. Lovelace's humour is quoted with appreciation. In short, the reader of Miss Fielding's pamphlet was well prepared to appreciate *Clarissa*.

We have mentioned that several readers were led to compare *Clarissa* with the new novel by Miss Fielding's brother, and comparisons have been made from that day to this. *Tom Jones* appeared shortly after the last volumes of *Clarissa*, at the end of February 1749. Fielding was, of course, already known as a writer, but his reputation was greatly increased by the popularity of this new book. For the first time England had two contemporary writers of prose fiction whom the public could discuss seriously, two writers whose merits were almost entirely different. Comparison was inevitable.

Very little is known of Richardson's relations with Fielding before the publication of *Clarissa*. The two men must have known of each other in 1740, when Richardson was printing the government organ, the *Daily Gazetteer*, and Fielding was writing for its opponent, the *Champion*. The contributors to the *Champion* were attacked by the *Gazetteer* in the no-holds-barred political style of the day. The issue of 30 July 1740 clearly refers to Fielding when it sketches the character of a '*foul mouth'd Farmer*', 'the CHAMPION of our Village', who began life as a wrestler and quarreller, member of a band of drunkards and roisterers. He amused the mob by singing 'Ballads about *Tom Thumb*' and giving pieces of his own invention 'where *Abuse* went for *Wit*, and nothing that wanted *Decency* passed unapplauded'. Vexed with the interposition of the Justices (the Licensing Act), he talked of turning solicitor but instead became secretary of the Crabtree Club, a group of enemies of all people of note and especially of one Friendly, Steward of Squire King. As their Champion, he now delivers invectives against innocent Mr. Friendly (Walpole). The *Gazetteer*, in turn, was often the object of the *Champion*'s satire: 'By the Translation of a certain Speech in Yesterday's Gazetteer, we learn, that one, at least of the Legion, who have so *uniformly* kept up the Spirit of that *egregious* Paper for so many Years, can make a Shift to *construe Latin*, tho' it has been often affirmed, they could not *read*, and is every Day manifest they cannot *write English*.' The newspaper is 'the Quintessence of Falshood, Dullness, Baseness and Malevolence'; its writers are 'a Set of men *hired* to do the *Drudgery* of your *Patron*; and abuse the People at their *own Expence*'.[30] That will give an adequate sample. Richardson's connection with the *Gazetteer* was not of a nature likely to call for particular notice, but he must have heard from his colleagues a good deal of adverse comment on Henry Fielding. There may be no significance in the fact that the *Champion* was the favourite advertising vehicle for the rival continuers of *Pamela*.

It is unlikely that Fielding knew that Richardson was the author of *Pamela* when he burlesqued that novel in *Shamela*. Richardson did believe that Fielding was the author of *Shamela*, but it is not known when he came to believe it —both his statements to that effect are later than the publication of *Clarissa*.[31]

Mrs. Barbauld, who did possess letters lost to us and also had an

[30] Issues of 15 May, 21 June, 5 July 1740.
[31] See p. 128. Owen Jenkins in 'Richardson's *Pamela* and Fielding's "Vile Forgeries"', *PQ*, XLIV (1965), 200–10, sees the second part of *Pamela* primarily as an answer to *Shamela*, and it is true that some of Fielding's objections are answered; but then so are the objections of others. Jenkins's suggestion that the minor character Turner is a caricature of Fielding would be more convincing if the similarities were less general—both are lawyers and wits and both disguise themselves as clergymen (Fielding writes in the character of Parson Oliver). But Turner's worldly position could hardly have reminded a contemporary reader of Fielding—he is not a writer and is financially above the need to work. Nor is his role in the story (he tries to make Pamela jealous of Mr. B. and the Countess) such as to cause readers to think of the attacks on Pamela's character in *Shamela*. A satire which cannot be deciphered until over two hundred years after its object is dead is rather too subtle to be effective. One could make at least as good a case for Sir Jacob Swynford as a caricature of Fielding. The detailed description of him resembles Fielding, he suspects Pamela's virtue, and Lady Davers says that 'he's more of a Hostler than a Gentleman' (SH, III, 304; EL, II, 156), a remark which, according to Dr. Johnson, Richardson made about Fielding (see p. 303).

opportunity to speak with some of those who knew Richardson, says that he was much hurt by *Joseph Andrews*, 'the more so, as they had been upon good terms, and he was very intimate with Fielding's two sisters'.[32] But she may well have been guessing about his probable reaction to *Joseph Andrews*: there is no extant evidence to support her statement, nor is there any evidence of Richardson's friendship with Sarah Fielding or her three sisters before 1747.[33] There is no sign of a quarrel before the publication of *Tom Jones*, and we do not know what the earlier relations between the two authors may have been. Fielding may or may not have meant the reader to think of Richardson when, in his Preface to Sarah's *Familiar Letters between the Principal Characters in David Simple*, he remarked that 'no one will contend, that the epistolary Style is in general the most proper to a Novelist, or that it hath been used by the best Writers of this Kind'.[34] There are some signs of friendliness during the publication of *Clarissa* and many signs of enmity, on Richardson's part at least, after the publication of *Tom Jones*.

Richardson's most complimentary reference to Fielding is in a letter to Edward Moore of 3 October 1748: *Clarissa* is designed only 'to fill a Gap in the Reading World, while Mr Moore and Mr Fielding are . . . reposing their Understandings'. Soon afterwards, Fielding sent Richardson a much more glowing compliment. On 15 October he wrote one of the warmest letters of praise ever written by one author to a rival.[35] The first two volumes of *Clarissa* had been very favourably noticed in his *Jacobite's Journal*: the author showed 'deep Penetration into Nature'; he engaged the affections and made one eager to read the rest; the snarling critics are blamed who make all sorts of contradictory remarks against the heroine— she is undutiful and too dutiful, too cold and too fond, she uses her parents too well and too ill.[36] By October Fielding had just finished the fifth volume, evidently sent to him in advance of publication, and he outdid these earlier praises. He found the 'true Comic Force' in the Widow Bevis, and he lauded the character of Lovelace: 'His former Admirers must lose all Regard for him.' But his highest praises are reserved for the heroine and for the emotions she arouses; surely few of Richardson's readers gave clearer signs of reading with the 'heart':

Shall I tell you? Can I tell you what I think of the latter part of your Volume? Let the Overflowings of a Heart which you have filled brimfull speak for me.

[32] I, lxxix.

[33] See p. 202. Alan Dugald McKillop in 'The Personal Relations between Richardson and Fielding', *MP*, XXVIII (1930–1), 423–33, believes that Richardson's hostility began because he was galled by the praise of *Tom Jones* even among his own circle.

[34] London, 1747, I, ix.

[35] This letter is discussed by E. L. McAdam, Jr., in 'A New Letter from Fielding', *YR*, XXXVIII (1948), 300–10. Mr. McAdam has generously allowed us to quote from the manuscript in his possession.

[36] 2 Jan., 5 Mar. 1748.

When Clarissa returns to her Lodgings at St. Clairs the Alarm begins, and here my Heart begins its Narrative. I am shocked; my Terrors ar[e ra]ised, and I have the utmost Apprehensions for the poor betrayed Creature.—But when I see her enter with the Letter in her Hand, and after some natural Effects of Despair, clasping her Arms about the Knees of the Villain, call him her Dear Lovelace, desirous and yet unable to implore his Protection or rather his Mercy; I then melt into Compassion, and find what is called an Effeminate Relief for my Terror. So I continue to the End of the scene. When I read the next Letter [Lovelace's brief announcement of the rape] I am thunderstruck; nor can many Lines explain what I feel from Two. . . . [Clarissa's] Letter to Lovelace is beyond any thing I have ever read. God forbid that the Man who reads this with dry Eyes should be alone with my Daughter when she hath no Assistance within Call. Here my Terror ends and my Grief begins which the Cause of all my tumultuous Passions soon changes into Raptures of Admiration and Astonishment by a Behaviour the most elevated I can possibly conceive, and what is at the same time most Gentle and most natural. This Scene I have heard hath been often objected to. It is well for the Critick that my Heart is now writing and not my Head. During the Continuance of this Vol. my Compassion is often moved; but I think my Admiration more. If I had recd no Hint or Information of what is to succeed I should perceive you paving the way to load our admiration of your Heroine to the Highest Pitch, as you have before with wonderfull Art prepared us for both Terror and Compassion on her Account. This last seems to come from the Head. Here then I will end: for I assure you nothing but my Heart can force me to say Half of what I think of *the* Book. And yet what hinders me? I cannot be suspected of Flattery. I know the Value of that too much to throw it away, where I have no Obligation, and where I expect no Reward. And sure the World will not suppose me inclined to flatter one whom they will suppose me to hate if the[y] will be pleased to recollect that we are Rivals for that coy Mrs. Fame.

And he signs 'Yrs. most Affectionately', which implies friendship between the two men.

Even later, after he had written many bitter things against Fielding, Richardson forwarded this letter to Stinstra among other letters in praise of *Clarissa*, adding that Fielding 'had been a zealous Contender for the Piece ending, as it is called, happily'.[37] He also told Hill and Young that Fielding was among those who wanted a happy ending to *Clarissa*.[38] There must, then, have been other communication between Richardson and Fielding about the novel; indeed the fact that Fielding read the fifth volume so early indicates as much.

Richardson's sudden outburst of bitterness against Fielding in 1749 has done as much as anything to injure his reputation as a person. It is hard to

[37] 2 June 1753.
[38] R to Hill, 7 Nov. 1748; Young to the Duchess of Portland, 29 Jan. 1748 [1749], *Hist. MSS. Comm.: MSS. of the Marquis of Bath*, I, 313.

justify, especially in view of Fielding's letter on *Clarissa*. Richardson may well have heard unfavourable reports of Fielding's personal life, and he was undoubtedly legitimately shocked by what he knew of his work. But of course he knew some rather shocking things about his friend Colley Cibber. Still, if he had been inclined to look for them, he could have found enough things about Fielding which violated his code of morality to make him feel justified in moral indignation. Dr. Johnson, according to Dr. Charles Burney, disapproved: 'Johnson's severity against Fielding did not arise from any viciousness in his style, but from his loose life, and the profligacy of almost all his male characters. Who would venture to read one of his novels aloud to modest women? His novels are *male* amusements, and very amusing they certainly are.—Fielding's conversation was coarse, and so tinctured with the rank weeds of *the Garden*, that it would now be thought only fit for a brothel.'[39]

Richardson's dislike of Fielding's improprieties, whether personal or in print or conversation, is not likely today to make his hostility more acceptable. A little charity might remind us that human motivations are complex and tricky. If Richardson was stung by envy, he was not the first man to feel that passion, or the first to hide it from himself when he found what according to his lights was a perfectly good excuse for moral indignation, a much more comfortable feeling. We do not intend to justify Richardson, certainly not to justify him against Fielding. His remarks about *Tom Jones* and *Amelia* are not admirable. But we do believe that these remarks, one incident in his career, have been given too prominent a place in accounts of his character and that few men can bear to be judged by the worst incidents in their lives. Envy is not now regarded as so amiable a feeling as lust, but it is no less natural and perhaps as widespread. Richardson undoubtedly regarded his books as serious and Fielding's as frivolous; intellectual modern writers have been known to make bitter remarks about popular successes in the lighter vein.

Solomon Lowe was praising Richardson at Fielding's expense by 10 July 1749: 'all Europe will ring of' *Clarissa* 'when a Cracker, that was some thous[an]d hours a-composing, will no longer be heard, or talkt-of'. On the back of this letter Richardson wrote 'Cracker, T. Jones'. Two days later Richardson himself made the comparison of the two books to Aaron Hill. When the taste of the age can be gratified by *Tom Jones*, he cannot expect the world to bestow two readings, or even one attentive one, on a grave story like *Clarissa*, which makes those think of death who do all they can to banish it from their thoughts. Has Hill read *Tom Jones*? 'I have found neither Leisure nor Inclination yet, to read that Piece, and the less Inclination, as several good Judges of my Acquaintance condemn it, and the general Taste together.' What do Hill's daughters say? 'If

[39] Boswell, *Life*, II, 495.

favourable, they would induce me to open the Six Volumes; the rather, as they will be so soon read.'

Astræa and Minerva took Richardson's request seriously. Overcoming an initial reluctance caused by the coarseness of the title (Foundling!), they had gone through the volumes and found 'much (masqu'd) merit', both of head and heart. They recommend them to Richardson's close attention. Fielding's bantering levity often spoils the effect of his good sense; and they believe they are right in thinking that, however well meant his motive, his execution was distasteful—virtue cannot be treated with too much respect. But they praise the design and structure, the just and pointed satire. Sincerity is rewarded, virtue is made attractive and vice unattractive. 'In every Part It has Humanity for its Intention.' In spite of its bold, shocking pictures, it 'woud . . . *deserve* to please,—if stript of what the Author thought himself most sure to *please by*'.[40]

Richardson's answer to this innocent attempt at a balanced critique is hard to excuse. 'I must confess, that I have been prejudiced by the Opinion of Several judicious Friends against the truly coarse-titled Tom Jones; and so have been discouraged from reading it.' His judicious friends have, it seems, found no virtues in the book: it is rambling, it is improbable, and above all it has a bad tendency, so that he has been forced to conclude that the author's second view '(His *first*, to fill his Pocket, by accommodating it to the reigning Taste)' was 'to whiten a vicious Character, and to make Morality bend to his Practices'. Why else should he make Tom illegitimate and make him 'a common—What shall I call it? And a Kept Fellow'. And the foolish, fond, insipid heroine who leaves her father's home to go traipsing after him—there is only one excuse: 'He knows not how to draw a delicate Woman—He has not been accustomed to such Company.' He takes the bias which 'a perverse and crooked Nature has given him; or Evil Habits, at least have confirm'd in him'. 'But, perhaps, I think the worse of the Piece because I know the Writer, and dislike his Principles, both Public and Private, tho' I wish well to the *Man*, and Love Four worthy Sisters of his, with whom I am well acquainted. And indeed should admire him, did he make the Use of his Talents which I wish him to make; For the Vein of Humour, and Redicule, which he is Master of, might, if properly turned, do great Service to ye Cause of Virtue.' The favourable report he has had from the Misses Hill may, if he has leisure, tempt him to read the book. His judges may have been too severe, and he is sure that 'I am disinterested enough, if I do read it, to give it (to the best of my Judgment) its due Praises, as well as Censure'.[41] The unusual heat of Richardson's expression in the middle of this letter makes one hope that since Fielding's letter in praise of *Clarissa* some event, of which we know nothing, had supervened to confirm Richardson's low view of Fielding's character.

[40] 27 July.   [41] 4 Aug.

Hill informed Richardson that his daughters had wept, as well they might on reading Richardson's letter, that he should think they approved of a work with evil tendencies. They still believed that when he had had time to read it he would disapprove of the judgement of his over-rigid friends. Richardson half apologized. The ladies had mistaken him; he had not meant to hurt their feelings. He wrote only what others had told him. 'I said, that, knowing the Man, I had the more Suspicion; for he is a very indelicate, a very impetuous, an unyielding-spirited Man, and is capable of forming a Morality to his Practices.' But he has undertaken, on their recommendation, to read the book.[42]

Lady Bradshaigh also drew on herself a mild rebuke in connection with *Tom Jones*. Some months before their first meeting she mentioned the great popularity of the book among her acquaintance; all the ladies talk of their Tom Joneses and the men of their Sophias, till she is 'fatigued with the name'. Richardson's answer may be guessed from Lady Bradshaigh's reply: 'The girls are certainly fond of Tom Jones, as I told you before, and they do not scruple declaring it in the company of your incognita; for, alas! I am no awful body to them; they just say the same before me as if I were but twenty; tho' I give you my word, I never let a faulty word or action pass me without a visible disapprobation; and many a round battle have I had with them concerning Tom Jones, as soft and as gentle as you seem to think my blame; and you repeat my pretty words with a sort of contempt. Now, if you would only lay a little stronger emphasis upon those words, you would not find them so gentle; at least, I did not mean them to be so; for I designed the condemnation strongly from my heart.'[43]

At about the same time, he was discussing with her the possibility of a novel about a good man. But would the world be interested in such a man?

How tame a character? Has not the world shewn me, that it is much better pleased to receive and applaud the character that shews us what we are (little of novelty as one would think there is in that) than what we ought to be? Are there not who think Clarissa's an unnatural character?

I will only say, that when the world is ready to receive writings of a different cast, I hope writers will never be wanting to amuse, as well as instruct. Nor perhaps may the time be very far off. So long as the world will receive, Mr. Fielding will write. Have you ever seen a list of his performances? Nothing but a shorter life than I wish him, can hinder him from writing himself out of date. The Pamela, which he abused in his Shamela, taught him how to write to please, tho' his manners are so different. Before his Joseph Andrews (hints and names taken from that story, with a lewd and ungenerous engraftment) the poor man wrote without being read, except when his Pasquins, &c. roused party attention and the legislature at the same time, according to that of Juvenal, which may be thus translated:

---

[42] 11 Aug., 18 Aug.   [43] [Early Nov.], 16 Dec. 1749.

Would'st thou be read, or would'st thou bread ensure,
Dare something worthy *Newgate* or the *Tower*.

In the former of which (removed from inns and alehouses) will some of his next scenes be laid; and perhaps not unusefully; I hope not. But to have done, for the present, with this fashionable author.[44]

Before the end of 1749 Richardson had evidently heard about Fielding's plans for *Amelia* from his bookselling friends.[45]

Lady Bradshaigh had, like the Hill girls, urged Richardson to read *Tom Jones*, but it seems that by the end of the year he had still not read it and did not intend to. His remarks are lost but can be partly reconstructed. 'I shall not say a word more', wrote Lady Bradshaigh, 'toward persuading you to read Tom Jones, and beg pardon for having done it; but I meant not to compel; how could you insinuate such a thing? You really seem not only grave, but angry with me.' She approves some things in the book, but disapproves many more, and would have liked to have Richardson's opinion. 'I do assure you, Sir, Mr. Fielding's private character makes him to me appear disagreeable; so I am no ways prejudiced in his favour, I only impartially speak my opinion.'[46] Since she would have had few possibilities of hearing of Fielding's private character, it is not reading too much into these lines to assume that her information on this head came from her correspondent.

In reply Richardson took yet another fling: 'As to the list of Fielding's performances, I have seen at least twenty of them; for none of which, before Joseph Andrews (except for such as were of a party turn), he gained either credit or readers.'[47]

He wrote to Miss Grainger that he was pleased with her remarks on the weakness of ladies in their degenerate age. 'This is the very Reason by which I have taken the Liberty to account, elsewhere, for the good Reception the Character of the weak, the insipid, the Runaway, the Inn-frequenting Sophia has met with [Richardson evidently considered his heroine on such a different plane that he was not afraid Miss Grainger might remember that Clarissa had, after running away from her family, spent a good deal more time in the inn at St. Albans with Lovelace than Sophia spent in that at Upton without Tom]: In that, as in the Character of her illegitimate Tom, there is nothing that very common Persons may not attain to; Nothing that will reproach the Conduct or Actions of very ordinary Capacities, and very free Livers: While Clarissa's Character, as

[44] [Late Nov.?].

[45] Wilbur L. Cross in *The History of Henry Fielding* (New Haven, 1918), II, 311, must have been incorrect in assuming that Fielding began *Amelia* early in 1751, after the composition of his *Enquiry into the Causes of the Late Increase of Robbers*; F. Homes Dudden in *Henry Fielding* (Oxford, 1952), II, 798, follows Cross.

[46] 16 Dec.   [47] 9 Jan.

it must appear unattainable by them, must be supposed Prudish, too delicate, and a silent Reproach to themselves. Had I been at Leisure to examine the History of Tom Jones—But I must have been at Leisure indeed to set about such a Task! And yet I am sure I should have been able to do the Author impartial Justice.' We have seen that others besides Richardson were inclined to contrast the books on the grounds that Richardson painted an ideal, Fielding a flawed reality. A little later, in discussing with Miss Grainger the faults of Whitehead's *Roman Father*, he told her that to speak of simplicity and nature and to show none of either, to boast of dispensing golden laws and to dispense leaden ones, and to discard sentiment because one has none to bestow is (according to the printed version) 'T——ng' style.[48] Richardson's 'F's' and 'T's' are enough alike to be easily confused.

He evidently resented a reference to the two authors in the novel *Charlotte Summers*, which he supposed compared him unfavourably with his rival, since Lady Bradshaigh assured him that she found only a harmless statement that could be taken as a compliment to both.[49] The remark was meant as a compliment—Richardson and Fielding are 'two inimitable Moderns' who move us more than do the ancients. *Clarissa* and *Tom Jones* are 'two wonderful Performances' by 'brother Biographers'. Each writer, ignoring artificial laws, followed his own nature, and *Tom Jones* is, therefore, full of laughter, whereas *Clarissa* moves to tears. Its author has 'such a peculiar melancholy Cast in his Temper, that it is very rare that he can be prevailed on so much as to smile'. His strength is tender sympathy for imaginary distress.[50] Richardson may have resented this slur on his capacity for humour, or he may have been prejudiced by the fact that the author of *Charlotte Summers* acknowledges Fielding as his own literary father.

These references are sufficient to show that *Tom Jones* was much on Richardson's mind. And time did not make him altogether forget it. Early in 1751 he wrote to his friend de Freval in France, 'Tom Jones is a dissolute book. Its run is over, even with us. Is it true, that France had virtue enough to refuse a licence for such a profligate performance.' His brief hopes of England's frivolous neighbours proved unfounded: de Freval assured him that *Tom Jones* was not only published there, but had 'a vast run'. Soon afterwards he regretted again that his picture of a good woman had drawn half her sex to oppose him: 'Mr. Fielding's Sophia is a much more eligible character.'[51] But he was right about the run in England being over—after the first four editions, in its first year, a new edition of *Tom Jones* was not called for until 1762.

There were, of course, a good many people through whom Richardson could have met Fielding—the latter's sisters, the Lobb family, or Ralph

[48] 22 Jan., 29 Mar. 1750.   [49] 25 Mar. 1750.
[50] London, [1750], I, 220-2.   [51] 21 Jan., 17 Apr.; to Lady Bradshaigh, [Feb.-Mar. 1751].

Allen, for instance. But shortly after the publication of *Tom Jones* Richardson became a close friend of the publisher of that novel, Fielding's friend, the bookseller Andrew Millar.[52] One would think that from Millar he must have received a more favourable report at least than from his old associates on the *Gazetteer*.

Late in 1751 Richardson informed Edward Young that Millar was unable to defer to another date a meeting the three had projected, since 'he was preparing the publication of a new piece of Mr. Fielding'.[53] The new piece was of course Fielding's last novel, *Amelia*, which came out in December 1751. Though more obviously moral than *Tom Jones* and certainly not deficient in sentiment, *Amelia* hardly softened Richardson's harsh judgement.

Richardson apparently sent Thomas Edwards a copy soon after publication, and Edwards told him that it was 'Dead small-beer'. 'Go on my good Friend to shew these [pe]ople how they ought to write.'[54]

Amelia is not so lively as *Tom Jones*, and Fielding in two issues of his *Covent-Garden Journal* defended it against readers who found it boring. Counsellor Town brings *Amelia* to the bar of the Court of Censorial Enquiry, 'indicted upon the Statute of Dulness'. The heroine is considered 'a *low* character, a *Fool*, and a *Milksop*'. Her father, 'a grave Man', can only answer that she is his favourite child, that he took more than ordinary pains with her education, and that he followed the best rules and models. But he submits to compromise and 'will trouble the World no more with any Children of mine by the same Muse'.[55] Though Fielding was suffering in the cause of morality, from criticism similar to what Richardson himself had received, Richardson was not mollified. He wrote to Edwards: 'Mr. Fielding has met with the Disapprobation you foresaw he would meet with, of his Amelia. He is in every Paper he publishes under the Title of the Common Garden Journal, contributing to his own Overthrow. He has been over-matched in his own Way, by People whom he has despised, and thought he had Vogue enough, from the Success his spurious Brat Tom Jones so unaccountably met with, to write down. But who have turned his own Artillery against him, and beat him out of the Field. And made him even poorly in his Court of Criticism give up his Amelia, and promise to write no more on the like Subjects.'[56]

Mrs. Donnellan, urging Richardson to continue with his good man, asked him whether the world was to be left with Captain Booth as an example. 'Now, perhaps, you have not read this stuff, but I desire you will, and then I think your conscience must make you publish. Poor Fielding, I believe, designed to be good, but did not know how, and in the attempt

[52] R to Hill, 12 Jan. 1749.
[53] 18 Dec.
[54] 2[3] Dec.
[55] 25 Jan., 28 Jan. 1752.
[56] 21 Feb.

lost his genius, low humour.' Richardson in reply was willing to agree
with this very moderately charitable judgement, but he took the occasion
to go back over Fielding's past errors and was by no means displeased at
his recent failure:

Will I leave you to Captain Booth? Capt. Booth, Madam, has done his own
business. Mr. Fielding has over-written himself, or rather *under*-written; and in
his own journal seems ashamed of his last piece; and has promised that the same
Muse shall write no more for him. The piece, in short, is as dead as if it had been
published forty years ago, as to sale.

You guess that I have not read Amelia. Indeed I have read but the first
volume. I had intended to go through with it; but I found the characters and
situations so wretchedly low and dirty, that I imagined I could not be interested
for any one of them; and to read and not to care what became of the hero and
heroine, is a task that I thought I would leave to those who had more leisure
than I am blessed with.

Parson Young sat for Fielding's parson Adams, a man he knew, and only
made a little more absurd than he is known to be. The best story in the piece, is
of himself and his first wife. In his Tom Jones, his hero is made a natural child,
because his own first wife was such. Tom Jones is Fielding himself, hardened
in some places, softened in others. His Lady Bellaston is an infamous woman
of his former acquaintance. His Sophia is again his first wife. Booth, in his last
piece, again himself; Amelia, even to her noselessness, is again his first wife.
His brawls, his jarrs, his gaols, his spunging-houses, are all drawn from what
he has seen and known. As I said (witness also his hamper plot) he has little or
no invention: and admirably do you observe, that by several strokes in his
Amelia he designed to be good, but knew not how, and lost his genius, low
humour, in the attempt.[57]

He was even more outspoken to Lady Bradshaigh: 'I have not been able
to read any more than the first volume of Amelia. Poor Fielding! I could
not help telling his sister, that I was equally surprised at and concerned for
his continued lowness. Had your brother, said I, been born in a stable, or
been a runner at a sponging-house, we should have thought him a genius,
and wished he had had the advantage of a liberal education, and of being
admitted into good company; but it is beyond my conception, that a man
of family, and who had some learning, and who really is a writer, should
descend so excessively low, in all his pieces. Who can care for any of his
people? A person of honour asked me, the other day, what he could mean,
by saying, in his Covent Garden Journal, that he had followed Homer and
Virgil, in his Amelia. I answered, that he was justified in saying so,
because he must mean Cotton's Virgil Travestied; where the women are
drabs, and the men scoundrels.'[58] In view of Richardson's own lack of
what was then called education and of Fielding's familiarity with the
classics, the condescending 'some learning' is really rather strong, even

---

[57] 11 Feb., 22 Feb.   [58] 23 Feb.

under the circumstances. But he was not the only one to see autobiography in Captain Booth's history—Lady Mary Wortley Montagu, for instance, says the same thing.[59]

The comparative failure of *Amelia* may have removed some of the bitterness from Richardson's feelings, but it did not change his opinion. In 1753, writing to Lady Bradshaigh about her wild young friend, he considered that it was little excuse for his conduct that he loved his wife: 'Mr. Fielding loved his Wife, and hated to contradict his Children— Tender-hearted Man!' A little later he reminded her that Fielding had found the public capricious.[60]

He was obviously thinking of the old comparison between *Clarissa* and *Tom Jones* when he wrote in the Concluding Note to *Sir Charles Grandison*: 'It has been said in behalf of many modern fictitious pieces, in which authors have given success (and *happiness*, as it is called) to their heroes of vicious, if not of profligate, characters, that they have exhibited Human Nature as it *is*. Its corruption may, indeed, be exhibited in the faulty character; but need pictures of this be held out in books? Is not vice crowned with success, triumphant, and rewarded, and perhaps set off with wit and spirit, a dangerous representation? And is it not made even *more* dangerous by the hasty reformation, introduced, in contradiction to all probability, for the sake of patching up what is called a happy ending?'[61] There is no doubt that Richardson believed this as firmly as his friend Dr. Johnson, who in the fourth *Rambler* had objected strongly to the portrayal of characters in whom virtues and vices were so mingled that the reader is led to admire the vicious: 'Vice, for vice is necessary to be shown, should always disgust.' Both Johnson and Richardson were probably thinking of Fielding's defence, in the introductory chapter to Book X of *Tom Jones*, of characters in whom a great measure of good is set off by little blemishes. Indeed Fielding may there have been thinking of Richardson (or at least Richardson may have believed that he was thinking of him) when he wrote that there are 'books enow written' to gratify any taste the reader may have for models of perfection, but that he doubts whether either 'this consummate degree of excellence' or men of 'diabolical depravity' have ever existed. Whatever his personal motives, Richardson had also a motive for disliking Fielding's work which he regarded as a serious one and was surely serious, if misguided, in telling Dr. Johnson 'that the virtues of Fielding's heroes were the vices of a truly good man' and 'that had he not known who Fielding was, he should have believed he was an ostler.'[62]

---

[59] *Complete Letters*, ed. Robert Halsband (Oxford, 1965-7), III, 66. See also Lady Orrery to Lord Orrery, 6 Jan. 1752, *The Orrery Papers*, ed. Countess of Cork and Orrery (London, 1903), II, 285-6.

[60] 5 Oct., 12 Nov.   [61] SH, VI, 329.   [62] Boswell, *Life*, II, 49; III, 174.

A few months after the publication of the last volume of *Sir Charles Grandison*, Fielding, broken in health, left for Lisbon, where he soon died, in October 1754. Early in the next year appeared his last work, *The Journal of a Voyage to Lisbon*. In the Preface to that work is a passage which Richardson's friends, probably with reason, considered a hit at Richardson: 'I might now undertake a more pleasing task, and fall at once to the direct and positive praises of the work itself; of which indeed I could say a thousand good things: but the task is so very pleasant that I shall leave it wholly to the reader; and it is all the task that I impose on him. A moderation for which he may think himself obliged to me, when he compares it with the conduct of authors, who often fill a whole sheet with their own praises, to which they sometimes set their own real names, and sometimes a fictitious one.' (*Shamela* had years before made fun of Richardson's self-praises in *Pamela*.) Just below this passage, Fielding refers, apparently in another connection, to Richardson's opinion that entertainment should 'be but a secondary consideration' in a work of fiction. If, he continues, a critic should censure his vanity in hoping to convey useful instruction, 'I answer with the great man, whom I just now quoted, that my purpose is to convey instruction in the vehicle of entertainment; and so to bring about at once, like the revolution in the rehearsal, a perfect reformation of the laws relating to our maritime affairs: an undertaking, I will not say more modest, but surely more feasible, than that of reforming a whole people, by making use of a vehicular story, to wheel in among them worse manners than their own.'[63]

Whether Fielding wrote to his friends about Richardson in anything like the same tone which Richardson used in talking of Fielding is not known. The references in the *Voyage to Lisbon* are his only certain hits at Richardson after *Joseph Andrews*; they may indicate that he knew what Richardson was saying of him and had noted the remark in *Sir Charles Grandison*.

Thomas Edwards was not touched by the stoically-borne sufferings described in the *Voyage*: 'I have lately read over with much indignation Fielding's last piece, called his Voyage to Lisbon. That a man, who had led such a life as he had, should trifle in that manner when immediate death was before his eyes is amazing; but his impudence, in attributing that to your works which is the true character of his own which are the reverse of yours, is what puts me beyond all patience. It seems to me as if conscious that the world would not join with Warburton in transferring the palm from yours to his desertless head, he envied the reputation which you have so justly gained in that way of writing. From this book I am confirmed in what his other works had fully persuaded me of, that with all his parade of pretenses to virtuous and humane affections, the fellow

---

[63] 1st edn., London, 1755, pp. xv–xvii.

had no heart. And so—his knell is knoll'd.' To his friend Daniel Wray he wrote of his indignation at Fielding's slur at Richardson in the book: 'Fielding's malevolence against our friend was the more unpardonable as the Good Man had once by his interposition saved his bones and at the very last by his correspondence at Lisbon had procured him accommodations which he could not otherwise have had.'[64] We know nothing more of Richardson's services to Fielding. He did have connections in Lisbon, and one hopes that he used them for Fielding. Edwards should have known: he must have had his information from Richardson, who is not likely to have lied outright. At least this is an indication that the two men were not openly quarrelling at the time of Fielding's death.

After Fielding died we find no more hits at him in Richardson's letters except one remark to Henry's sister Sarah after a reperusal of her *Familiar Letters*: 'What a knowledge of the human heart! Well might a critical judge of writing say, as he did to me, that your late brother's knowledge of it was not (fine writer as he was) comparable to your's. His was but as the knowledge of the outside of a clock-work machine, while your's was that of all the finer springs and movements of the inside.'[65] The comparison is so much like Dr. Johnson's famous comparison of Fielding and Richardson that one wonders whether Johnson had heard of Richardson's image or whether (more probably) the image was originally Johnson's.

His remarks about Fielding show Richardson at his least amiable: if we were trying to present our hero as a model character, on the order of Sir Charles Grandison, they would have to be regarded as a black mark against him. In view of the disagreement between the two, about both morals and art, they are, however, hardly surprising. The difference which most struck contemporaries was clearly expressed in an anonymous letter to Richardson about *Sir Charles Grandison*. The writer must have pleased Richardson when he stated that he much preferred his pure characters to those in certain recent novels, which seem to think all men a mixture of virtue and vice.[66] There was, however, a wider area of agreement between the two novelists than is always recognized. As often happens, the points of difference most struck Richardson's contemporaries; recently it has been shown that their basic assumptions were in many ways similar—their ideals of human behaviour, their moral purpose, their essentially conservative social and religious attitudes.[67] Both of them put reliance on the heart, without, however, being more than very mildly anti-rational. In any case, it is surely high time to stop treating them as rivals and taking sides with one or the other.

It is possible that Richardson's bitterness against Fielding was somewhat

[64] To R, 28 May 1755; to Wray, 16 June 1755, Bodleian MS. 1012, p. 212.
[65] 7 Dec. 1756.   [66] 'Recd.' 17 Apr. 1754.
[67] William Park, 'Fielding and Richardson', *PMLA*, LXXXI (1966), 381-8.

intensified by disappointment at the public reception of *Clarissa*. Several of the remarks quoted above deplore the bad taste of the public, and the public had demanded four authorized editions of *Tom Jones*, a total of ten thousand copies, within a year.[68] Certainly Richardson's second novel did not cause as much stir as his first, nor does it seem to have sold quite so well. 'It is not relished here so much as his *Pamela*', wrote Thomas Birch.[69] The first part of *Pamela* had gone into its sixth edition within two and a half years. Comparisons may be misleading because we do not often know the number of copies printed, but *Clarissa* called for only five editions during the thirteen remaining years of Richardson's life.

Shortly after the fourth volume had been published and before the last three were nearly ready, Aaron Hill hinted his disappointment at the sale. In response Richardson wrote that the sale had been 'pretty quick' for an uncompleted work, but that perhaps it had suffered by the ending's being known.[70] He did, however, print more copies of the last three volumes than of the first four,[71] so the sale cannot have been too bad. On 10 May of the next year he wrote to Hill that the novel had been out of print for over two months: the first volumes, that is, since for the second edition of June 1749 he used the extra copies already printed of the last volumes. By 3 May 1750 this edition was 'near sold off' and by 21 January 1751 not a copy was left 'out of near 3000'—'it rises in reputation'.[72] It was not until April 1751 that he issued two new editions, a third in eight volumes duodecimo and a fourth, slightly more expensive, in seven volumes octavo. Almost three years later he was still advertising both of these editions.[73] The only other edition which appeared before his death was also called the fourth, a duodecimo edition in 1759.

Obviously the number of editions does not imply that *Clarissa* was a failure, but it may nevertheless have been a disappointment. Richardson knew that he had created a work more ambitious than *Pamela*. He may not have recognized how much its novelty and its simple, lively story had helped his first novel. Besides, *Clarissa* was lengthy and earnest, two qualities which probably helped the sale of elaborate subscription editions designed to rest unread on library shelves, but not a recommendation for a novel in a day when novels did not yet have the prestige to be purchased primarily for showing off to acquaintances. A good many of the remarks by Richardson and his friends indicate that the gay world found *Clarissa* very solemn and very moral and very long and was not inclined to welcome novels with unhappy endings. Under the circumstances, Richardson had no reason to complain of the reception of his book.

---

[68] William Strahan's Ledger, B.M. Add. MS. 48,800, fos. 64, 70.
[69] To Lord Orrery, 19 Jan. 1748, *Orrery Papers*, II, 14.   [70] 5 May, 10 May.
[71] R's 'Alterations in *Clarissa*', FM XV, 2, fo. 43.   [72] To Graham; to de Freval.
[73] *Public Advertiser*, 19 Mar. 1754.

Very soon after the publication of the last volumes of *Clarissa* Richardson was planning a new and revised edition. One day before the last volumes went on sale we find John Read writing about his request that he look for faults. The chief objection he had heard was to the length of the novel, but he did not want anything struck out. 'But is there not here & there a Nursery-Phrase, an ill-invented, uncouth Compound, a Parenthesis which interrupts, not assists the Sense?'[74] This was a direct challenge to Richardson's love of minute revision.

He already had a short list of minor suggestions which Solomon Lowe had sent him soon after the publication of the third and fourth volumes, some of which he adopted into the second edition. Lowe remarked, for instance, in connection with Lovelace's word '*phil*-tits' (used to indicate the victims on which he as an eagle preyed), that 'of all the *New Words and Phrases*, with which you have enrich'd our Language, more than any Writer I ever read', he objected only to 'podagra-man' (to describe Lovelace's gouty uncle) and hesitated about 'excurse' (for digress). Richardson cut 'podagra-man' but left 'excurse', and he added a note explaining that 'phyl-tits' were the female of the species ('Phyllis-tits' as opposed to Tom-tits) and took the occasion to point out Lovelace's fondness for coining new words. He did not adopt Lowe's later suggestion that the wrens (also among Lovelace's victims) be described as 'Jinny wrens'. But he did cut one item of a series of three so that he could refer to it with the word 'neither'. He evidently did not appreciate the grammarian's fine point in suggesting that 'to see, if I were to be denied' be changed to 'was', but he obeyed him in changing 'and' (for 'if it') to 'an't' and 'younger brother of three' to 'youngest'. Of Lovelace's remark that he 'never brought home from my voyages and travels, a worser constitution that I took out with me', Lowe (whose interest in grammar did not blind him to naturalness of speech) remarked that '*Worser* seems to suit him better than *Worse*.' Richardson retained the ungrammatical form.[75] Such meticulousness and such independence are typical of Richardson's method of revising.

On 27 December 1748 Lowe promised to send Richardson further suggestions, in compliance with his request, 'as you are re-considering ye whole, while the impressions are recent, with a view of improving it . . . ag:st another edition'. Shortly afterwards he forwarded a remark by a former scholar of his named Thomas Cooper that the moral against marrying rakes would have been much better illustrated if Clarissa *had* married Lovelace. Richardson agreed as to the moral but pointed out that

[74] 5 Dec.
[75] Letter of 23 May 1748; 'Scruples', dated 26 June, FM XV, 2, fo. 102, and XVI, 1, fo. 90. 1st edn., III, 352, 349, 91, IV, 82, 97, 105, 136, 108, 109; 2nd edn., III, 366, 360, 91, IV, 83, 99, 107, 138, 110, 111; SH, IV, 24, 7, III, 69, IV, 135, 152, 165, 199, 168, 169; EL, II, 253, 249, 24, 328, 339, 348, 371, 350, 351.

he would have had to write a different story; when Cooper sent another letter politely enforcing his view, Richardson, though he obviously could not have adopted Cooper's plan even for the sake of a moral, took the matter seriously enough to ask his friend R. Smith to comment on Cooper's letter and used part of Smith's comment in an argument against Cooper's plan in the Postscript to the third edition. Both Lowe and Smith also suggested classical mottoes for the novel,[76] but Richardson decided against a motto.

One suggestion which he did adopt came in a letter signed John Cheale, Norroy King at Arms—it was actually written as a joke by the Duke of Richmond.[77] The letter is in a mock-severe tone and points out an 'egregious Blunder' which has 'highly affronted all the Dukes, Marquisses, and Earls Daughters, in England, Scotland, and Ireland': Clarissa's mother, daughter of a mere viscount, is called Lady Charlotte. Richardson recognized Cheale's authority and his own ignorance (Cheale wondered why his 'Brother Booksellers of the genteel Side of Temple-Bar did not inform' him of his mistake), and the offending lady became Mrs. Harlowe in the second edition.

Richardson must have been considering a preface for his second edition, though at last it contained only a short Advertisement and the preface was postponed to the third. Among his papers are several sheets called 'Hints of Prefaces for Clarissa'.[78] One of these sheets refers to 'this Second Publication'. Two of the prefaces were by Richardson's friends Philip Skelton and Joseph Spence: the rest seem to have been put together by Richardson, using the remarks of various people. Skelton hinted that readers might find the novel rather tedious if they looked on it as a romance, but that they were not to expect wild adventures but scenes of common life embodying moral and religious precepts. In his Preface to the third edition Richardson did warn readers that the book 'will probably be thought tedious to all such as *dip* into it, expecting a *light Novel*, or *transitory Romance*: and look upon Story in it (interesting as that is generally allowed to be) as its *sole end*, rather than as a vehicle to the Instruction.' Spence also emphasized the fact that the book was no romance and that it followed Nature and had a highly moral aim. The Preface to the third edition takes from one of Richardson's drafts the idea that even the rake Lovelace expresses himself with great decency, but other matters stressed in these prefaces were later taken up in the Postscript: justification of the

[76] Lowe to R, 15 Jan.; R to Lowe, 21 Jan.; Cooper to Lowe, 1 Feb., FM XV, 2, fos. 110–11; Smith to R, 3 Feb.; Lowe to R, 18 May; Smith to R, 20 May.

[77] 9 Feb. 1748. For the Duke of Richmond's authorship of the letter, see Charles H. G. Lennox, Earl of March, *A Duke and His Friends: The Life and Letters of the Second Duke of Richmond* (London, 1911), II, 636–8.

[78] FM XV, 2, fos. 50–8. See also *Samuel Richardson, Clarissa: Preface, Hints of Prefaces, and Postscript*, Augustan Reprint Soc. Pub. No. 103 (Los Angeles, 1964), pp. 1–14.

ending by a general opposition to sudden conversions of rakes and an answer to the objections that Clarissa is cold and too delicate. Other objections are answered in the drafts: that Lovelace could not be so wicked and so generous, that the Harlowe family is improbably bad, that the story is too minute (it is no mere novel but a history of life and manners), and that Clarissa could have saved herself by going to Lovelace's kinswoman Lady Betty Lawrance. In general, the draft prefaces stress the difference between *Clarissa* and the ordinary romance of adventure, as regards both its superior realism and its moral aim.

On 10 May 1749 Richardson wrote to Aaron Hill that business (including Hill's epic *Gideon*) had forced him to have one volume of the new edition printed by two other presses and that all of his vacant hours were taken up with the infinite labour of writing a detailed table of contents. On 10 June Skelton sent him a few suggestions, all minute except for Skelton's desire that the fire scene be omitted. But they must have arrived too late, since the second edition appeared on 15 June 1749.

The brief Advertisement which introduced the book pointed out that the prefaces had been omitted but that a table of contents had been added 'which will not only point out the principal Facts, and shew the Connexion of the Whole; but will enable the *youthful Readers* of both Sexes to form a judgment as well of the *blameable* as of the *laudable* Conduct of the principal persons'—and there follows Richardson's by now familiar statement that the work is not to be considered 'a *mere Amusement*' but, 'by a seeming accommodation to the Taste of the Age, is intended to inculcate the HIGHEST and *most* IMPORTANT *Doctrines*'.

The table of contents covers forty-three closely printed pages. It tells the story in detail and informs careless readers what to look for as well as how to judge. Italics emphasize the points most important to Richardson's understanding of his story or of his various morals. After the rape, for instance, but for the stimulus of the vile women of the house '*the majesty of her virtue* he [Lovelace] says, *would have saved her, as it did once before*'. Miss Howe 'acquits Clarissa of *Prudery, Coquetry*, and *undue Reserve*'.[79] When Hill pointed out the danger of such a detailed account of the work, since 'Book-poachers' could satisfy a 'superficial Curiosity' without purchasing, Richardson answered that his observation was just. 'But as I had not a View principally to my Profit, but hoped to do some good by my Clarissa, I chose in my Second Edition to give a little Abstract of the Story, that it might be clearly seen what it was, and its Tendency; and to obviate as I went along, tho' covertly, such Objections as I had heard (as I have done by the Italicks) altho' I made many Persons Masters of the Story to my Detriment, as to Sale. And I thought this necessity also for the Sake of those who had read it, at the distant Periods in which it

79 Vol. VI, Letter cii; Vol. IV, Letter, liv; SH, VII, 474, V, [383]; EL, IV, 570, III, 527.

was published . . . and would not chuse to read 7 tedious Volumes over again, as a Help to their Recollection, and to their Understanding.'[80] So many people since the time of *Clarissa* have objected almost equally to the mercenary motives and the moralizing tendency of the middle class that it is at least useful to remember that these two dominant traits could at times conflict, and there is no reason to doubt that whenever they did Richardson was guided by the latter.

Only the first four volumes of the second edition were revised, a larger number having been printed of the first edition of the last three. Richardson preserved among his papers a list of the most important alterations, including a good many of such minor importance that he did not later include them in his separate publication *Letters and Passages Restored from the Original Manuscripts of the History of Clarissa*. In the one of his draft prefaces which mentions the second publication Richardson wrote that 'the Author has in this Edition *restored* several Passages, which, for Brevity, were omitted in the former', such as Lovelace's comic instructions to his friends about to meet Clarissa. 'Several other Inlargements and Alterations there are, which tend further to illustrate his Design.'[81] All this at no extra price. Aside from Lovelace's instructions, the only passage of any length which seems probably to be a restoration of a passage cut from the original manuscript is an exchange of letters between Lovelace and the servant Joseph Leman, summarized in the first edition and now given in full.[82] Most of the other changes serve to underline those points in the characters of Clarissa and Lovelace which Richardson thought had been misread.

Richardson had been upset that some readers found Lovelace too sympathetic and Clarissa too cold and too delicate. He added footnotes to emphasize Lovelace's villainy and to explain why Clarissa had to hold him at arm's length and could not accept his offers of marriage. He evidently felt that such misreadings were due to hasty and careless reading, and at times he came close to scolding his audience. 'Surely those who have thought her to blame on this account, have not paid a due attention to the Story.' 'The particular attention of such of the Fair Sex as are more apt to read for the sake of amusement, than instruction, is requested to this Letter of Mr. Lovelace.'[83] A hint that Clarissa might feign illness to avoid her parents' importunities is removed.[84] The scenes in which Lovelace deliberately proposes in such a way as to make it impossible for Clarissa to accept are carefully rewritten to make it clear why she cannot. Cross references in footnotes point forward or backward to statements the reader might have

[80] 10 July, 12 July.
[81] FM XV, 2, fos. 43–4, 56–7.
[82] SH, III, 349–55, 243–57; EL, II, 215–19, 143–53.
[83] SH, III, 13, 85; EL, I, 501, II, 35.
[84] 1st edn., II, 259; SH, II, 290; EL, I, 438.

forgotten, especially when such passages show that Lovelace was no mere amiable rake. One added passage shows Lovelace wishing for his uncle's death. Two long passages make clear his desire to dominate Clarissa. In both he imagines the joy of having her under his control, pleading and humiliated; in the first he goes on to justify his actions to her by man's cruelty to animals: 'By my Soul, Jack, there is more of the Savage in human nature than we are commonly aware of.'[85] These two passages especially are written in Richardson's best manner, imaginatively re-creating the mood of the character, and most of the added touches are well done. They do not basically change the characters; they serve mainly to make them clearer. A modern reader, however, can hardly welcome the footnotes, and Mr. M. Kinkead-Weekes is not wrong in holding that Richardson's changes move in the direction of moralizing and over-simplifying and reflect 'a cruder analysis than the novel originally contained.'[86] Richardson was becoming more interested in his fable and in his model characters. But in the second edition he does not move far in this direction or falsify in any important way his original concept.

Other changes are in the interest of propriety or serve to increase slightly the vividness of the book. Indirect discourse is occasionally turned into direct. A letter of Lovelace's uncle, Lord M., is expanded to underline his love of proverbial wisdom. A letter from Clarissa's cousin Dolly is entirely rewritten to elevate her language—in the first edition she wrote rather like a servant girl.[87] Grammar is corrected; 'Mamma' and 'Papa' are changed to 'Mother' and 'Father'. This is the same sort of change which Richardson had made in successive editions of *Pamela* and shows his desire to write in a way worthy of his new characters, who were decidedly above him in class.

In her will Clarissa leaves to Mrs. Norton 'my book of *Meditations*, as I used to call it; being extracts from the best of books . . . suited particularly to my own case'.[88] Late in 1749 the still unknown Belfour wrote urging Richardson to publish 'the meditations you design to print'. They were printed soon afterwards, since Richardson sent a copy to Edward Young and another to Young's housekeeper, Mary Hallows, as a New Year's present. A note later made on Richardson's letter forwarding the volumes identifies the book as 'Clarissa's Meditations; a little piece, hitherto (July 30, 1758,) unpublished'. 'It is strictly true that I had no intention of printing it', wrote Richardson. 'But reading it to a little assembly of female friends one Sunday night, one of whom was labouring under some distresses of mind, they were all so earnest with me to print it . . . that I

---

[85] SH, IV, 138, 13–17, 20–3; EL, II, 330, 246–8, 251–2.
[86] '*Clarissa* Restored?' *RES*, N.S. X (1959), 169.
[87] SH, IV, 126–30, II, 327–8; EL, II, 322–5, I, 463–4.
[88] SH, VIII, 119–20; EL, IV, 423.

could not resist their entreaties; and, as they were all great admirers of Clarissa, I thought I could not do better than, by historical connexion to the piece, point the use of them in a distress so great as my heroine's is represented to be.—I have printed but a small number. Your approbation, or the contrary, will give me courage to diffuse it, or to confine it to the few hands for which it was designed; notwithstanding the booksellers' names in the title page.'[89]

Young approved, as Richardson must have expected, and in thanking him for the book urged him both to publish it and to include it in the next edition of *Clarissa*.[90] Nevertheless Richardson never did diffuse it. Very few copies are extant, and these must be the copies sent to friends. Young's remark that 'now her [Clarissa's] character is established, your reason for not inserting it at first ceases' implies that the meditations were composed before the publication of the first edition and were probably cut to avoid excessive length.

Meditations Collected from the Sacred Books contains thirty-six passages, or combinations of passages, from the books of Job, the Psalms, the Wisdom of Solomon, and Ecclesiasticus in which Clarissa is supposed to have found consolation at various stages of her tragedy after the rape. Most of them are introduced by a description of the circumstances under which Clarissa found the passages applicable to her situation and state of mind, though in some cases the situation is left vague and the last seven are said to have been used by her on different occasions as her 'heart was elevated, or touched, on contemplating the Mercies, the Wisdom, the Goodness, the Might, the Majesty of the ALMIGHTY'. An Advertisement states that four of the meditations have appeared in the novel—actually five of them are there. The Advertisement goes on to stress the moral aim of *Clarissa* (as usual, it is no mere '*Novel* or *Romance*') and explains that the editor has omitted most of them lest 'an Age so deeply immersed in the pleasures of sense, and which gives so much countenance to works of froth and levity' as his be put off by such solemnity and thus not derive the desired benefit from Clarissa's history. He is still conscious of length, and (perhaps with a glance at Fielding's recent 'bill of fare to the feast') asserts 'that the whole compass of human nature, as far as *Capacity would allow*, or the *Story admit*, was aimed to be taken into' *Clarissa*. At the end of his Advertisement he drops his pose as editor: 'We shall only add, that it cannot but be thought proper to preserve, in the little historical connexions prefixed to each Meditation (as is also done in the following Preface ascribed to Clarissa) all those marks of genuineness which are necessary to give the greater efficacy to the Example proposed to be set by the Heroine; and which are carefully endeavoured to be preserved in the History itself.' In her 'Preface' the heroine explains her changing states

[89] 16 Dec., 1 Jan.   [90] 7 Jan.

of mind 'from *impatience* and *despair*, to *resignation* and *hope*, and from thence to *praise* and *thanksgiving*' and indicates the usefulness of her meditations.[91]

As usual, Richardson began revising again soon after the publication of the second edition of *Clarissa*. In September 1749 he wrote to Dr. John Conybeare that for a possible third edition he had considered his advice that the anguish of the Harlowe family should be given 'a sharper Point' by their learning more about their daughter's excellencies. He sent an addition, which he proposed to insert in Belford's concluding letter. The Conclusion in the third edition does contain a long addition, at the place which Richardson indicated to Dr. Conybeare, in which the guilt feelings of the family are stimulated by reading some of Clarissa's letters.[92]

In the spring of 1750 David Graham, the student of King's College whom John Read had sent to Richardson with a letter of introduction, apologized for his delay in beginning a correspondence he himself had desired and made up for his neglect with lengthy and ecstatic praises of the morality of *Clarissa*. In reply Richardson praised his good heart and added: 'The last Impression being near sold off, I have been preparing a new Edition for ye Press. I intend at the Desire of several Friends, to print an Octavo one; a small Number, however; for ye Work is too voluminous to be every one's Price. You will greatly oblige me, Sir, in transmitting to me any Objections that you shall think of Weight, and any Corrections either in Style or Expression. The very great Advantage of an Academical Education I have wanted.' He also declared his intention to 'restore a few Letters, and not a few Passages' 'by particular Desire'; to print the contents at the end of each volume, instead of all together at the beginning; and to add at the end a collection of 'the Moral Sentiments scatter'd thro' the Volumes'. This collection had been begun by a gentleman to whom Richardson was at the time unknown, and he intended to enlarge it, 'that so, on a general Retrospection of the whole, it may appear to be, what I had the Presumption to design it, a History of Life and Manners, and not a mere Novel or Romance'. We have already seen that the latter distinction had become a favourite of Richardson's; he often used the phrase 'History of Life and Manners' as the most accurate description of *Clarissa*. He went on to suggest that in spite of their short acquaintance Graham might write a preface for the new edition—the earlier ones were 'temporary', and he did not love preface writing.[93]

There is no evidence that Graham did try his hand at a preface, which would probably not have been used. Their friendship seems to have been short lived. The rest of Richardson's plans were carried out, though not for almost a year.

[91] Pp. 65, i–iii, v, viii.   [92] 12 Sept.; SH, VIII, 278–81; EL, IV, 532–4.
[93] 2 Feb., 22 Apr., 3 May.

On 4 June 1750 he wrote asking Susanna Highmore to get Mrs. Carter's permission to insert the complete 'Ode to Wisdom' in 'the new edition, now printing'. At the time he was discussing with Miss Grainger the amount of learning proper for ladies and proposed to add some thoughts on this interesting topic—as he did, in Miss Howe's description of her late friend, which became a kind of catch-all for earnest reflections and model attributes.[94] By the end of the year he had sent to Miss Talbot the lives of the two fallen women Sally Martin and Polly Horton which were later inserted in the Conclusion. They may have been among the passages restored from the first version, though their moralistic tone would fit in well with Richardson's additions. Miss Talbot, of course, urged him to be sure to insert them. She also mentioned that Lady Sophia E[gerton] had been shown the exchange of letters between Mrs. Howe and Mr. Hickman, also to be inserted in the new edition.[95]

Late in 1749 Thomas Edwards sent Richardson a sonnet on *Clarissa*: 'Were the Sonnett worthy of the Subject, it would be the best I ever wrote.' Early in 1751 Richardson sent Edwards printed copies of his 'charming sonnet' on *Clarissa*. By 8 February Edwards had evidently received an advance copy of the new edition—he found the heroine 'a Witch' and approved of the restored passages. 'You do me great Honour in approving of my Additions to Clarissa, so far as you have gone', Richardson replied. 'Tho' too late, freely blame me, dear Sir, when you do *not* approve.'[96] In addition to Edwards's prefatory sonnet, the third and fourth editions contain a longer set of verses at the end of the book, written by John Duncombe.[97]

On 21 January Richardson described the new editions to de Freval much as he had earlier described them to Graham. 'I have been prevailed upon to restore several passages, and some few letters, which I omitted, because of the length of the piece.' These statements would seem to disprove the contention that the word 'restored' used in the printed editions to describe the added passages was simply part of Richardson's pose of being an editor[98]—that pose was by now very thin, and he was certainly not posing as editor to his friends. We do believe, however, that the restorations were probably fewer than the additions. Richardson went on to tell de Freval that he had 'taken much pains' with the table of moral sentiments; many friends wished to see it printed separately.

[94] 6 Aug.; SH, VIII, 226–7; EL, IV, 496–7.

[95] [Dec. 1750?].

[96] Edwards to R, 28 Dec.; R's index to the Edwards–R correspondence, FM XII, 1, fo. 184; R to Edwards, 9 Jan.; Edwards to Speaker Onslow, 19 Jan., Bodleian MS. 1011, p. 208; Edwards to R, 24 Jan., 8 Feb.; Edwards to Speaker Onslow, 16 Feb., Bodleian MS. 1011, p. 229; R to Edwards, 13 Feb.

[97] Nichols, *Literary Anecdotes*, IV, 584; R to Susanna Highmore, 22 June 1750; R to Hester Mulso, 13 July 1750.

[98] Kinkead-Weekes, '*Clarissa* Restored?', p. 157.

Dr. Johnson approved of the more expensive octavo and of the restored passages: 'Though Clarissa wants no help from external Splendour I was glad to see her improved in her appearance but more glad to find that she was now got above all fears of prolixity, and confident enough of success, to supply whatever had been hitherto suppressed.' The seriousness with which so serious a man took *Clarissa* is shown by his desiring an *Index Rerum*, in order that 'this Edition by which I suppose Posterity is to abide, may want nothing that can facilitate its use'. 'Clarissa is not a performance to be read with eagerness and laid aside for ever.'[99]

By 20 April 1751 there were advertised both the third edition in duodecimo and the fourth edition in octavo, as well as a volume of *Letters and Passages Restored from the Original Manuscripts of the History of Clarissa*. The latter contained the more important passages added to the second edition as well as those added to the third, the poems, the new Preface, and the sentiments. Purchasers of the first edition could now take advantage of the new material, an extraordinary example of Richardson's earnest care when his novel was concerned and also of his commercial fairness: no one was forced to buy a new edition because he had bought early.

The new Preface pointed out the advantages of the epistolary form and included sketches of the principal characters. The various morals to be derived from the book were also pointed out: it warned thoughtless girls against the arts of men, cautioned parents against undue exercise of authority and children against preferring a man of pleasure to a man of probity, and investigated 'the highest and most important Doctrines not only of Morality, but of Christianity, by shewing them thrown into action in the conduct of the *worthy* characters; while the *unworthy* ... are condignly ... punished'. Indeed it was not 'designed *only* to divert and amuse'. Rarely has there been a happier example of the intentional fallacy. The restorations were mentioned. There was a rather weak apology for dropping Warburton's Preface. The utility of the new collection of 'Moral and Instructive Sentiments' was emphasized. Finally readers were referred to the Postscript for answers to objections.

Of the additions we would claim only three with any confidence as restorations from the original version, one scene between Clarissa and her sister, two letters from Elias Brand, and Lovelace's abortive scheme for raping Miss Howe and her mother on the way to the Isle of Wight.[100] Miss Wescomb had objected to the last when she saw the novel in manuscript. Perhaps Richardson allowed one of his least intellectual friends to influence him in dropping it; at any rate, someone or something unfortunately influenced him to restore it—probably the fact that it increased Lovelace's wickedness. A great many of the other additions are designed

[99] 9 Mar.
[100] SH, I, 326–34, VII, 414–34, IV, 268–78; EL, I, 222–8, IV, 308–22, II, 418–25.

to increase Lovelace's villainy as well as to answer objections to Clarissa's excessive delicacy and to underline the various morals. The sizeable additions to Miss Howe's character of Clarissa are especially unfortunate; they tend at the very end to make the reader forget that the heroine has been a woman, as she has been, and to suggest that she is a wooden model on the order of Sir Charles Grandison.

Not all of the additions are this bad. Several long scenes between Clarissa and Lovelace may be designed to make their relations, and thus the book's moral, clearer, but the characters are well maintained and the dialogue is lively; they may be cuts from the first version. In general, the larger additions show Richardson at his best. As in the second edition, there are also small additions and deletions and minute revisions, correcting grammar, tightening or clarifying or elevating language.[101] Most of the minor changes are made in the interest of correctness or elegance (removing colloquialisms, avoiding ending a sentence with a preposition). Others, however, heighten the drama and elaborate the characterization. Several alterations in the last volume emphasizing that Clarissa's fear of her father's curse arises partly from her weakened mental state and that she fears more for her father than for herself may be the result of the objections of his new friend Hester Mulso.[102] In spite of Richardson's moral concerns, many of the additions in his two extensive revisions improve the novel. Except at the end, which even in the first edition was by far the dullest part of the novel, most of the additions seem to have been written by the Richardson who created Clarissa and Lovelace, not by the Richardson who later discussed them.

The Postscript was greatly expanded, to answer the objections to which Richardson was so sensitive. Many ideas, and even phrases, came from the first of the draft prefaces preserved among Richardson's papers. First, much was added to the existing defence of the ending. Then Clarissa is defended from the charge of coldness: 'We may presume to say, that this objection has arisen from want of attention to the Story, to the Character of Clarissa, and to her particular Situation.' This counterattack against his readers, which was becoming frequent with Richardson, is not altogether convincing; a reader might answer that it is the author's business to convey the impression that Clarissa is not cold and that logical reasoning has little to do with such an impression. However that may be (and readers can indeed be careless), Richardson's flat denial that Clarissa was in love and his moralizing against uncontrolled love were more likely to increase than decrease the impressions of her coldness. Highmore's objection that

---

[101] See the unpubl. diss. (University of Arkansas, 1970) by William Booth Warde, Jr., 'Revisions in the Published Text of *Clarissa*'.

[102] SH, VI, 25, 123–4, 143, 206, 213–14, 255; EL, III, 260, 326, 340, 382, 387, 416; Miss Mulso to R, 12 Oct., 10 Nov. 1750.

Lovelace should have been an atheist is answered; Mr. Hickman is defended; Haller is quoted in defence of the epistolary method ('Some have wished that the Story had been told in the usual narrative way'); and the probability that the four principal correspondents could have written so much is defended. Some have objected that the heroine is too excellent to be true—'It must be confessed, that we are not to look for *Clarissa's* among the *constant frequenters* of Ranelagh and Vaux-hall, nor among those who may be called *Daughters of the Card-table.*' The many letters of commendation are mentioned, and the Postscript closes with the statement that the principal objection has been to the length of the book.

These two editions of 1751 contain the last major revisions known of the text of *Clarissa*, but in his usual way Richardson did go on tinkering with the text. Another edition in duodecimo, described as the fourth, was published in 1759, which followed the third edition closely except that the sentiments were omitted. On 26 November 1755 Richardson wrote to Stinstra that he had made his final revisions to *Clarissa* and that they varied little from the last edition. But he probably continued to make further changes. Almost the last thing he did was to go over a set of *Clarissa* marked by Lady Bradshaigh, agreeing with her remarks in some places and disagreeing in others and making a few minor revisions. In the spring of 1761 one of Richardson's daughters informed Lady Bradshaigh that her father's health was a little better and that he would like to see her comments on *Pamela* and *Clarissa*; in reply she sent him her marked copies, which were returned to her after Richardson's death.[103] When Lady Bradshaigh objected to events or details of characterization, Richardson generally argued against her view, but it is likely that he would have accepted some of her suggested verbal changes and especially those of her remarks which affected propriety: she pointed out that he often overdid his elegance and gentility, made garments too rich and language too courtly. On 12 April 1792 Richardson's daughter Anne wrote to her niece Mrs. Moodie about the possibility of corrected editions of her father's works. Evidently she herself was suggesting some changes in the text of *Clarissa*: 'I know not yet whether the Clarissa's will be in time: But the little alterations I have presumed to make in them, are not very important, only changing a word or phrase; for I have no altered Copy of my Father's for my guide in that work; as I have in Grandison.'[104] Whether anyone else had such a copy is unknown. The title page of the edition of 1792 claims that it contains the author's last corrections. A few of the changes are of the sort Lady Bradshaigh suggested and could have been

---

[103] Martha? Richardson to Lady Bradshaigh, [early Mar.] (the draft of the letter is in Richardson's hand); Lady Bradshaigh to Martha? Richardson, 13 Mar.; Lady Bradshaigh to Martha Richardson, 19 Mar., 25 Apr. 1762, FM XI, fos. 279, 281.

[104] MS. owned by Alan Dugald McKillop.

made by Richardson, but they could also be almost anybody's: minor deletions and small revisions in the interest of correctness. Style is often elevated. There are many misprints, and a few changes are clearly made to bring the work up to date.

It is not our intention to trace Richardson's reputation in England or abroad except insofar as he himself knew of it and was affected by it. One foreign translation which he certainly knew was the work of a novelist almost as celebrated as he was, the Abbé Prévost. When *Clarissa* appeared, Prévost was already well known as the author of *Mémoires et avantures d'un homme de qualité* (in which his most famous work, *Manon Lescaut*, was included), *Cleveland*, *Le Doyen de Killerine*, and other works. He had spent a good deal of time in England and is sometimes said to have been the translator of *Pamela*, though the translation is almost certainly not by him.[105]

The first French *Clarissa* was apparently published without consulting Richardson. It appeared in 1751. There were considerable cuts, mostly in the last two volumes. Prévost thought it necessary to adapt the novel to French taste. 'Low' scenes such as the death of Mrs. Sinclair and extravagant scenes such as Clarissa's temporary madness after the rape were ruthlessly toned down. 'Par le droit suprême de tout Ecrivain qui cherche à plaire dans sa langue naturelle', states the introduction, 'j'ai changé ou supprimé ce que je n'ai pas jugé conforme à cette vûe. Ma crainte n'est pas, qu'on m'accuse d'un excès de rigeur. Depuis vingt ans que la littérature Angloise est connue à Paris, on sait que pour s'y faire naturaliser, elle a souvent besoin de ces petites réparations.'[106] In other words, English writers could not be counted on for the propriety necessary to please a French public. As Frank Howard Wilcox has shown, Prévost weakened the impact of the book somewhat by over-refinement, by watering down Richardson's realism, and by omitting many of the minute details which are essential to Richardson's method of characterization.[107] Perhaps even worse from Richardson's point of view, he cut out a good deal of the moralizing and drastically shortened the tedious final scenes.

Richardson had hoped that a French translation would be made by his old friend Jean Baptiste de Freval, who had written one of the laudatory

---

[105] For a discussion of Prévost's possible connection with the translation of *Pamela* and of his translations of *Clarissa* and *Sir Charles Grandison*, see Frank Howard Wilcox, 'Prévost's Translations of Richardson's Novels', *University of California Publications in Modern Philology*, XII (1925–6), 341–411.

[106] *Lettres Angloises, ou Histoire de Miss Clarisse Harlove* (Dresden, 1751).

'By the sovereign right of every Author who tries to please in his native language, I have changed or suppressed whatever I did not judge compatible with this aim. My fear is not that I will be accused of being too severe. During the twenty years that English literature has been known in Paris, we have learned that to be naturalized it often needs these little repairs.'

[107] 'Prévost's Translations of Richardson's Novels', pp. 395–6.

introductory letters to *Pamela*. He wrote to de Freval expressing his regret that he had been 'prevented in your intended translation' and asking how far along the French edition was. He hoped that the additions he was making in the new English version could be included in the French: 'When a writer is living, methinks it is pity he should not be consulted whether he has any assistances or alterations to contribute, for the translator's own sake.'[108]

Far from seeking new material, Prévost had omitted much of the old, and Richardson, who was unlikely to appreciate the delicacy of the French taste, was not pleased with the result. Among his papers is a translation of the introduction and of the reasons Prévost gives for cutting various scenes.[109] Presumably Richardson was interested enough to get a friend who understood French to write this account. Prévost, he wrote to Lady Bradshaigh, 'has thought fit to omit some of the most affecting parts . . ., with some apologies, that, a lady, who understands the language, says, imply a reflexion on his nation. He treats the story as a true one; and says, in one place, that the English editor has often sacrificed his story to moral instructions, warnings, &c.—the very motive with me, of the story's being written at all.' He also complained to Alexis Clairaut that the Abbé had 'left out in his Translation of Clarissa, some of the most useful and pathetic Parts of the Piece; and those among us, who have read both Editions, are greatly disgusted with the French one on that Account. I knew not, that such Mutilations were allowable, except the Translation had been called an Abridgment.' And to Johannes Stinstra he made the same complaint: 'He has given his Reasons for his Omissions, as he went along; one of which is, The Genius of his Countrymen; a strange one to me!'[110] Prévost was, it is true, regretful and half apologetic about some of the omissions: 'Ces suppressions sont autant de sacrifices, que le Traducteur est obligé de faire au gout François, qui n'est pas pour les détails sans action; car la plus inutile de toutes ces lettres a des beautés de caractère & de sentiment qui méritent d'être regretées.' At other times he was less complimentary to Richardson. 'Ceux que le sujet de cette lettre n'a peut-être pas moins ennuiés que sa longueur', he remarks after translating the beginning of Lovelace's description of his interview with Col. Morden, 'se pleindroient beaucoup de la suivante ['would have much more cause to complain of the following' was the translation Richardson read], qui contient le reste de cette conférence & qui est plus longue du double. Passons sur un détail inutile.' Of the death of Mrs. Sinclair, he writes, 'Ce tableau est purement Anglois; c'est-à-dire, revêtu de couleurs si fortes, & malheureusement si contraires au goût de notre Nation, que

[108] 21 Jan. 1751.
[109] FM XV, 2, fos. 62–72.
[110] To Lady Bradshaigh, 24 Feb. 1753; to Clairaut, 5 July 1753; to Stinstra, 2 June 1753.

tous mes adoucissemens ne le rendroient pas suportable en François.'[111] Richardson, who shared his countrymen's belief that neither earnestness nor honest good feeling was to be expected on the other side of the Channel, was hardly likely to become a greater Francophile after reading the translation of these remarks.

The German and Dutch translations were more satisfactory. Richardson mentioned to Lady Bradshaigh receiving the first from 'the celebrated Dr. Haller, Vice-Chancellor of the University of Göttingen', and the first volumes of the latter done into Dutch 'by an eminent hand, M. Stinstra, of Haarlingen'.[112] Albrecht von Haller, the Swiss physiologist and later the author of philosophical romances, was an early admirer of Richardson.[113] He had written a generally favourable review of the novel which evidently was the subject of correspondence with Richardson, since, speaking of the answer in the *Gentleman's Magazine* to the faults he had mentioned in it, his editor later wrote that 'Mr. Richardson himself has also since then remembered them in a way certainly not disagreeable to Herr von Haller.'[114] His *Göttingische Zeitungen von Gelehrten Sachen* had welcomed Richardson's first two volumes in March 1748 and had promised a translation.[115] His exact connection with the translation is uncertain, but he at least encouraged it; he must have been the man who 'is regarded by the largest and best part of Germany as the greatest judge of art of our time in belles lettres', whose praise of *Clarissa* especially influenced the publisher to have it translated and who advised the publisher in choosing the translator.[116] It was published at Göttingen, where he was teaching. The first volumes were translated by the Hebrew scholar Johann David Michaelis, also a professor at Göttingen.[117]

[111] VI (Dresden, 1752), 106, 525, 629.

'These suppressions are so many sacrifices which the Translator is forced to make to French taste, which does not relish details without action; for the least useful of these letters has beauties of character and sentiment which deserve to be regretted.'

'Those who have been as bored by the subject of this letter as by its length would complain much of the following which contains the rest of this discussion and which is twice as long. Let us omit going into useless detail.'

'This picture is purely English; that is, clothed in colours so strong, and unfortunately so contrary to the taste of our Nation, that I could not tone it down enough to make it bearable in French.'

[112] 24 Feb. 1753.

[113] Lawrence Marsden Price, 'On the Reception of Richardson in Germany', *JEGP*, XXV (1926), 16–22.

[114] *Sammlung kleiner Hallerischer Schriften*, 2nd edn. (Berne, 1772), pp. 293n–4n.

[115] Pp. 274–5.

[116] 'Vorrede', *Die Geschichte der Clarissa, eines vornehmen Frauenzimmers*, 2nd edn. (Göttingen, 1749).

[117] *Lebensbeschreibung von ihm selbst abgefasst, mit Anmerkungen von Hassencamp* (Leipzig, 1793), p. 296. *Letters and Passages Restored* was added as an eighth volume (*Göttingische Zeitung von gelehrten Sachen*, 1752, pp. 550, 1047).

Stinstra sent Richardson the first two volumes of his translation on 14 September 1752, with a letter in Latin praising Richardson and expressing the hope that the next two volumes would be ready by the next spring.[118] Richardson had to get both the Latin letter and the Dutch preface translated. He must have been pleased with the latter; it concentrates especially on the ethical qualities of the novel, which are such as to make it worthy of a clergyman translator, and goes on to praise Clarissa's characterization and general air of probability. As in the usual English comments, the two aspects of the book which are most strongly stressed are its naturalness and its morality.

Richardson asked William Duncombe to find out something about Stinstra. Duncombe replied that Stinstra must be the author of *A Pastoral Letter against Fanaticism* and of five sermons on liberty of conscience and, after further investigation, that the former tract, written against the Moravians, had been honoured by the approbation of the Archbishop of Canterbury.[119] Stinstra, who was born in 1708, was a learned man and a Mennonite. He had, however, been accused of Socinian views and in 1742 forbidden to preach, though he went on performing his other functions and wrote many theological works. He was not fully reinstated until 1757, and it is perhaps this partial enforced leisure which gave him time for translation. Judging by his letters and his preface to *Clarissa*, he was a man of great piety and earnestness, not without breadth of view.

Richardson answered his letter on 6 December, reporting what Duncombe had told him and enclosing his defence of the fire scene, Miss Fielding's *Remarks on Clarissa*, and the privately printed *Meditations*. He asked Stinstra to correspond with him and hoped that if he got to England he would visit North End. In his reply Stinstra explained that the fact that he supported an aged mother would prevent his coming to England, a country he greatly admired. He gave a long account of his life, especially of his persecutions by the rigidly orthodox, and asked in return for information about Richardson.[120] It was in answer to his questions that Richardson wrote on 2 June 1753 his fullest extant account of his life. On 30 April Stinstra had been able to send the third and fourth volumes, with another preface using some of the remarks Richardson had made to him and including a translation of the defence of the fire scene. His translation of the novel was not completed until 1755. Meanwhile he and Richardson had become warm correspondents, though they were never to meet.

---

[118] See the unpubl. diss. (University of Arkansas, 1962) by William Carlin Slattery, 'The Correspondence between Samuel Richardson and Johannes Stinstra, the Dutch Translator of *Clarissa*' and Mr. Slattery's *The Richardson–Stinstra Correspondence and Stinstra's Prefaces to Clarissa* (Carbondale and Edwardsville, [Illinois], London, and Amsterdam, [1969]).

[119] R's letter to Stinstra of 6 Dec. 1752 quotes both letters. Duncombe to R, 18 Nov. 1752.

[120] 2 Apr.

CHAPTER XIII

RICHARDSON AND HIS FRIENDS

1750–1754

RICHARDSON did not begin a new novel immediately on the publication of *Clarissa*, but it was not long before he began to think about one. It was to have as its main purpose the description of a good man, a kind of counterweight to his two good women. He had doubts about his ability to treat the subject adequately and also about whether he would be physically able to finish the task. 'To say the Truth', he wrote to young Billy Lobb in April 1750, 'I am afraid Time of Life, Business, and, for these 6 Weeks past very severe Paroxysms of my Nervous Disorder, together with the Difficulty of drawing a good Man, that the Ladies will not despise, and the Gentlemen laugh at, will, and must set me down where I am.'[1]

Richardson's old illness may have been relieved by Dr. Cheyne's rather violent method of curing, but it was by no means cured; indeed it was growing worse. Complaints are heard regularly throughout the rest of his life, though there were periods of relief. Spring and fall were the worst times; during one bout of illness he comforted himself with the thought that 'the time of year, the vernal equinox (as well as the autumnal), generally most distresses me.'[2] But they were not the only times. On 6 August 1750 he told Miss Grainger, 'I am, indeed, and have been, very much out of Order, with an Increase of my Nervous Symptoms.' In February of the next year Thomas Edwards inquired whether the nervous disorders were better since he had seen him and closed his letter with a half-apology: 'But I must dismiss you or I shall bring Dr. Heberden upon my Back. Yet he does not say that you must not read Letters? No—but he will say that I write with a wicked Design to provoke you to write again.'[3] Obviously Heberden had warned his patient against writing too much.

Dr. William Heberden was a celebrated physician who had settled in London in 1748 on the advice of Sir Edward Hulse, the son-in-law of Samuel Vanderplank, Richardson's landlord at North End. Dr. Johnson

[1] 10 Apr.
[2] To Sarah Wescomb, 2 May 1753.
[3] 8 Feb.

called him '*ultimus Romanorum*, the last of the learned physicians',[4] and another patient, William Cowper, addresses him as

> Virtuous and faithful HEBERDEN! whose skill
> Attempts no task it cannot well fulfil. . . .[5]

Heberden was Richardson's physician during the rest of his life, and they often visited each other.[6]

In March Mrs. Chapone regretted to hear that Richardson was ill, and Edwards voiced his hesitation about urging him to continue with the novel because of health. But Richardson, in spite of his difficulties, was feeling the call of his new novel: 'To have Soul and Body pull Two Ways, is a grievous thing. But in spite of Dr. Heberden and Mr. Watson, I must at last let go.' In July he was again complaining of 'increased Malady in the Nervous Way', which had robbed him 'of the Inclination, and almost of the Capacity of Reading and Writing'. Soon afterwards, Mrs. Chapone got a bad report on his health from her daughter. And Edwards lamented to Speaker Onslow, 'I am very much concerned that that good Man has so ill a state of health, which I hear more of from my other friends than from him, but the variation in his writing discovers what he in tenderness would concele from me.' Edwards was not hinting at any decline of Richardson's literary abilities; he was referring to his handwriting, which from this time on is often very shaky. Richardson wrote to Miss Grainger that he had 'had one of the most unhappy Summers, in my Nervous Way, that I have known a great while, tho' always complaining, as you know, and always must expect to have Cause of Complaint. Nervous Maladies are in one particular English Bull-dogs or Mastiffs, which you please: When once they seize, they never quit their Hold.'[7]

Richardson hinted that he might meet Edwards at Bath, and Edwards assumed that this intended trip was for his recovery.[8] But he did not go then. Travelling was becoming more and more difficult. He made a few visits to persons who lived not far from the capital: to Miss Wescomb at Enfield, just north of London, in 1750; to Speaker Onslow at Ember Court, in Surrey, in January 1750 and again in December and again in the fall of 1752; to Young, at Welwyn in Hertfordshire, in 1752 and again in 1754.[9] And there were other visits. But most of his life was spent between

---

[4] Boswell, *Life*, IV 399n.
[5] 'Retirement', ll. 279–80.
[6] R to Susanna Highmore, [c. 1 Aug. 1756].
[7] Mrs. Chapone to R, 20 Mar.; Edwards to R, 9 Mar.; R to Edwards, 19 Mar., 27 July; Mrs. Chapone to R, 5 Aug.; Edwards to Onslow, 13 Aug., Bodleian MS. 1011, p. 285; R to Frances Grainger, 28 Sept.
[8] 27 July, 26 Aug.
[9] R to Susanna Highmore, 4 June 1750; R to Young, 2 Jan. 1750; Edwards to R, 24 Jan. 1750; R to Sarah Wescomb, 1 Sept., 6 July 1752; R to Lady Echlin, 24 July 1754.

Salisbury Court and North End. Miss Wescomb was always urging him to come to her, and so was Thomas Edwards; Lady Bradshaigh hardly even hoped for a visit in distant Lancashire. In the summer of 1752 Edwards talked of a possible trip of Richardson's to Gloucestershire, probably to see the Chapones, where Edwards hoped to meet him and take him to see an admirer of his at Cirencester. Richardson, though 'so bad a Traveller', considered the Gloucestershire trip not impossible, though at the moment he could not manage Turrick, Edwards's home in Buckinghamshire, being 'so little my own Master'. Edwards wanted Richardson to join him on a visit to the Speaker and discuss the trip and baited him with more admirers at Cirencester: 'You . . . are the constant toast of a Club of young Gentlemen, who have virtue enough to prefer Clarissa to Tom Jones.' But Richardson replied that, unlike Edwards, he had '*Women* to consult' and was still uncertain when he could travel—his 'increased Tremors' did not even permit him to come to Ember—he would be too much trouble with his '*ineffectual* Armour (after all) of Hartshorn, Palsie-Drops, my Pockets a little Apothecary's Shop'. When Edwards did get to Gloucester, he did not find Richardson, though the latter still gave hope that he might make the trip in the spring, or at least come to Turrick.[10]

Early in 1753 he was again in indifferent health. By spring he was very ill. He noted on a letter from Miss Wescomb that when her messenger arrived he had pled a nervous paroxysm, as well he might, and he answered the letter by saying that he had 'indeed been extremely ill'. In July he reported to her that he had 'so wretched a pain in one side of my face, and which aggravates my old maladies, that I can hardly hold a pen'.[11]

He did, however, take what for him was a long trip in the late summer of 1753. He set out on 21 August for Bath, where his wife's brother, James Leake, was living and where his eldest daughter, Polly, had been visiting. After picking up Polly he went on to Cheltenham to take Sally Chapone, who had been staying with his family, back to her mother and to drop his second daughter, Patty, for a visit with the Chapones. On the way home he was in a hurry to get back but took time to stop in Oxford, where he saw the Reverend Benjamin Kennicott, the Hebrew scholar and Fellow of Exeter College, and to go on to nearby Cuddesdon, where the Bishop of Oxford, Thomas Secker, was residing—Richardson's new friend Miss Talbot was a member of his household. He meant only to eat his midday meal there, but Miss Talbot was away for dinner, and he

[10] Edwards to R, 24 June; R to Edwards, 28 June; Edwards to R, 9 July, 20 Aug.; R to Edwards, 21 Aug.; Edwards to R, 23 Oct.; R to Edwards, 25 Oct.
[11] R to Edwards, 20 Feb.; R to Sarah Wescomb, 8 Feb.; Sarah Wescomb to R, 13 Apr.; R to Sarah Wescomb, 2 May, 31 July.

ended by spending the night. The next day he dined with Miss Lintot at Dorton, Buckinghamshire ('27 Gates to open in our Way thither from Cuddesden'), and the following day, 7 September, hurried back to his business. Edwards had hoped to persuade him to make his long-promised visit to Turrick when he was so close and tried to waylay him on the road but missed him.[12] He wrote to Miss Wescomb that though his twenty years' malady would not yield to a three weeks' excursion, he found himself no worse.[13] But next spring he was writing again of an increase in his nervous disorders, which Young was blaming on over-work. He was still promising to visit Edwards at Turrick but was unable to join him at Speaker Onslow's, though the Speaker proposed to send a post-chaise to North End.[14]

Health, as Miss Mulso wrote, was often unkind to the good and blind to merit:

> Hast thou not left a Richardson unblest?
> He wooes thee still in vain, relentless Maid!
> Tho' skilled in sweetest Accents to persuade,
> And wake soft Pity in a savage Breast:
> Him Virtue loves, & brightest Fame is his,
> Smile thou too, Goddess, & compleat his Bliss![15]

Aaron Hill died early in 1750, and Richardson wrote to Philip Skelton: 'I have just lost my dear and excellent-hearted friend, Mr. Hill, author of Gideon. I was present at some of his last scenes: my nerves can witness that I was. I am endeavouring to find opportunities to shew my regard to his memory, by my good offices to three excellent daughters, who, for their filial piety, merit all praise, and for their other merits, deserve to be the care of all who know them.'[16] A few months later Hill's brother Gilbert was thanking Richardson for his generosity to Aaron and to his family.[17] He continued to shower his benefactions on Hill's daughters and visited them at Plaistow, and they visited him at North End.[18] He was delighted to accept Urania as the daughter of his mind. But the intimacy languished. In 1753 he sent her and her sisters a copy of *Sir Charles Grandison*

[12] R to Edwards, 15 Aug.; R to Sarah Wescomb, 15 Aug.; R to Lady Talbot, 16 Aug.; R to Elizabeth Carter, 17 Aug.; Edwards to R, 21 Aug.; Edwards to Daniel Wray, [10 Sept.], Bodleian MS. 1012, pp. 113–14; Edwards to R, 14 Sept.; R to Edwards, 19 Sept.; R to Elizabeth Carter, 2 Oct.; R to Lady Bradshaigh, 5 Oct., 8 Feb. 1754.

[13] 11 Sept.

[14] R to Sarah Wescomb, 22 Mar.; R to Edwards, 5 Apr.; Edwards to R, 7 Oct., 17 Oct.; R to Edwards, 18 Oct.

[15] 'An Ode to Health', Stanza 6, FM XVI, 2, fo. 64.

[16] 10 Feb.

[17] 22 May.

[18] Urania Johnson to R, 29 June, 23 July 1750; R to Urania Johnson, 24 July 1750; Astræa Hill to R, 9 July 1750; Gilbert Hill to R, 17 Aug. 1750.

and in 1755 a copy of his *Moral and Instructive Sentiments*, but the fact
that she thanked him and his wife for the latter in a third-person note does
not indicate that she had continued to be the daughter of his mind—his
many other honorary daughters were not formal. He advised her on a
building for a proposed business and recommended her as a person worthy
of help, of which she was evidently in considerable need. 'Cruelty, and
unkind Fortune' pursued her, she wrote, but 'tho I am too low, alas! I
am not yet, beneath the Favour, of a wish'd-place, in Mr Richardson's
Reflection!' She was low enough in 1756 to be thankful for some pens and
paper which Richardson sent her. In 1758 she apologized for not having
visited him and his wife because of 'a Mind *Oer-charg'd* with *Trouble* into
an Incapacity of being pardonable Company' and asked for 'a single
Frank'. In the same year she sent him a work of fiction called 'Almira',
written 'long since', hoping he would touch it up and convert its lead to
silver or gold. He did suggest improvements and offered detailed criticisms:
the characters are exaggerated ('Need Brutus be made so very a Brute?
And withal so shockingly silly?'), the plot is improbable ('Crudelia's false
Letter, not sufficiently clear'd up'), Cleone is a prude in not visiting
Samander in his rooms when he is wounded, 'a Lady writer, shoud not,
I think, be so particular in describing Florello's Disposition to retire on
the Wedding Night', 'thou' should be changed to 'you'. Urania in her
humbler way reacted somewhat as her mentor had reacted to her father's
advice about *Clarissa*. She recognized the faults of the book, but she
justified some of the supposed improbabilities on the grounds that the
stories were real ones (her father had evidently not thoroughly grounded
her in Aristotle) and defended herself against some of Richardson's particular criticisms. She pointed out that in one scene where Richardson
mentioned eleven characters there were only ten. Richardson's note on this
letter, the last memorial of a long friendship, is 'I might be mistaken. But
surely, the Unwelcome Observations I made, show that it was not for
want of Pains and Attention—At a time too—but I will only say, I truly
meant Service, not Criticism. Who but the Lady was to see what I wrote?'[19]

Of the new friends whom Richardson made at about the time of the
composition of *Sir Charles Grandison*, Thomas Edwards was probably the
closest. He had only a few years to live when Richardson began corresponding with him, but their intimacy ripened fast. He was a gentleman,
who had inherited a good estate and who since 1740 had lived, in the
intervals of visits to town and to friends, on an estate he had purchased,
Turrick, near Ellesborough in Buckinghamshire. He was an enthusiastic
landscape gardener and had adorned his own estate and the estates of

[19] Urania Johnson to R, 28 Oct. 1753, 6 Mar., 26 Mar. 1755; R to Mr. Scott, 18 Apr. 1755;
Urania Johnson to R, 16 Aug. 1756, 18 July, 16 Aug., 19 Aug., 9 Sept. 1758. Richardson's
observations on her novel are in FM XIV, 1, fos. 15–19.

others.[20] In spite of poetic and scholarly interests and a penchant for praising the beauties of Nature, he seems to have been rather lonely at Turrick; he was a bachelor and was not in very good health (though ten years younger than Richardson) and was a gentle, melancholy, and somewhat timid man, with a tendency towards enthusiasm, not to say gushing. He is usually accorded a small place in literary histories as a reviver of the sonnet. He wrote a good many sonnets, most of them addressed to friends, though a few are on such subjects as a family picture ('only I survive of all that band,/Which one chaste bed did to my Father raise . . .; Amidst our House's ruins I remain/Single, unpropp'd, and nodding to my fall'), the lost cantos of the *Faerie Queene*, false patriotism ('O Sacred Love of Country! purest flame'), Shakespeare, God, and the edition of Pope by Edwards's enemy William Warburton.[21]

Edwards was a close friend of Speaker Onslow, and it may have been through Onslow that he met Richardson. The first evidence of their acquaintance is a letter from Edwards to Richardson, dated 2 December 1748, thanking him for the present of the last volumes of *Clarissa* and praising the work highly. He had already praised it to his friend John Clerke: Richardson 'has as good a heart, and as clear an insight into human nature as ever any had'. 'I am very much obliged to that best of Creatures, as you justly call him', he wrote to Daniel Wray of Richardson's gift. 'I never was so moved with any thing in my life.' 'I look upon this work as a Criterion of Sensibility', he told the Honourable Philip Yorke, 'which I think it is almost as dangerous to be without, as Dr. South thought it was to have no ear for music.' To the Reverend Lewis Crusius he wrote that he could find no important faults in *Clarissa*, but 'perhaps I am not a competent judge of them, for I own I look on her with a Lover's eye'. Even before he read *Tom Jones* he was convinced from what he knew of its author and of his former works that it would be admired by those 'who look more to the head than the heart' and who do not relish *Clarissa*.[22] From then on, Edwards was a steady opponent of Fielding, in whom he could find no good at all.

Many of his praises Edwards repeated to the author himself: 'It is well for us that you are of a Humane and gentle disposition, for you are so absolute a Master of the Heart, that instead of swelling it with a noble grief, you could in numberless instances have torn it with intolerable

---

[20] See Vedder M. Gilbert, 'Thomas Edwards as the Wooden Inigo', *N&Q*, N.S. II (1955), 532–5.

[21] *The Canons of Criticism, and Glossary; The Trial of the Letter Y, alias Y, and Sonnets* (London, 1755), pp. 307–51. Quotations from Edwards's works, unless otherwise indicated, are from this edition.

[22] To Clerke, 31 Aug. 1748; to Wray, 16 Jan. 1749; to Yorke, 19 Jan. 1749; to Crusius, 20 Jan., 3 May 1749, Bodleian MS. 1011, pp. 51, 95, 97, 100–1, 130. The original of his letter to Yorke is in B.M. Add. MS. 35,605, fo. 336.

anguish.'[23] By the end of 1749 he had sent Richardson the sonnet later printed in the third edition of *Clarissa*:

> O Master of the heart! whose magic skill
> The close recesses of the Soul can find,
> Can rouse, becalm, and terrify the mind,
> Now melt with pity, now with anguish thrill;
>
> Thy moral page while virtuous precepts fill,
> Warm from the heart, to mend the Age design'd. . . .[24]

Richardson had made Edwards a present of a print of himself; Edwards wanted his sonnet put under it, and Richardson therefore planned to have his daughter Anne's writing master copy it and then decided to have it printed.[25] The sonnet appeared in *Clarissa* anonymously, to Edwards's disappointment: 'I heartily wish my Name had been printed to the Sonnet, that I might have the Honour of its being joined to a Work of yours, which must live as long as our Language.' Richardson replied that he did not dare to ask for Edwards's initials to it, but everyone who knew his manner would recognize it.[26] By this time the two men were good friends. By April 1750 Edwards was visiting at North End. By June he had visited North End again and Salisbury Court several times. He notified Onslow of his receipt of a gift of the new edition of *Clarissa* from 'Good Mr Richardson, whose friendship I shall reckon an honor to the last day of my life'.[27]

Edwards was soon introduced at the houses of Richardson's friends Mrs. Donnellan and Miss Mulso. He agreed with Richardson (and with many other men in their century and before and since) in the pleasures of female admiration: 'There is, and I doubt not but that you have felt it, there is something more deliciously charming in the approbation of the Ladies than in that of a whole University of He-Critics.'[28] In Miss Mulso he found a kindred soul, a fellow warbler. She greeted his sonnets in the manner of Spenser with an ode in which she compared herself to a young linnet who 'Tries her weak Voice, and, twitt'ring, aims to sing':

> But most thy Strains my raptur'd Spirit raise,
> When Love of Virtue prompts thy tuneful Tongue,

[23] 26 Jan. 1749.

[24] 28 Dec. Richardson's index to his correspondence with Edwards (FM XII, 1, fo. 184) identifies the sonnet mentioned in this letter as the one on *Clarissa*.

[25] R to Edwards, 9 Jan. 1751; Edwards to R, 24 Jan. 1751; Edwards to Onslow, 19 Jan. 1751, Bodleian MS. 1011, p. 208.

[26] 8 Feb., 13 Feb. See also Edwards to Speaker Onslow, 16 Feb. 1751, Bodleian MS. 1011, p. 229.

[27] Edwards to R, 28 Apr.; R to Susanna Highmore, 22 June; Edwards to Onslow, 16 Feb. 1751, Bodleian MS. 1011, p. 229.

[28] 24 Jan., 30 Mar. 1751.

When R——n's lov'd Name adorns thy Song,
What honest Heart but Echoes back his Praise!
Sing on, sweet Bard! prolong the darling Theme:
Hush'd be the Breeze! and mute the babling Stream![29]

In return, Edwards foretold the linnet's welcome among the Muses:

Thee *Polyhymnia*, in the roseate bowers
Of high *Parnassus*, 'midst the vocal throng,
Shall glad receive, and to her tuneful sire
Present; where, crown'd with amaranthine flowers,
The raptured choir shall listen to thy song.[30]

Miss Highmore was also a friend, and an enthusiastic one, since she thought that Edwards 'could equal Spenser'—a judgement from which even Richardson dissented, except as regards the sonnet: 'There he may undoubtedly, I think, rival that prince of English poets.'[31] 'Why, *Every-body*', Richardson quoted Miss Highmore as saying, 'loves Mr. Edwards.'[32]

Edwards sent Richardson a manuscript copy of a new work, a little discussion of spelling reform, later published as *An Account of the Trial of the Letter Υ, Alias Y*. It urges a more consistent and logical spelling, one which indicates derivations, in the form of a legal argument among the various letters as to their just rights. An American will welcome his rejection of the 'u' from 'honour', 'labour', and similar words, but so far no one has agreed with him to banish the 'g' from 'foreign' and the 'a' from 'lease'. Richardson urged him to complete it, and a year later, in March 1752, Edwards was planning to have it printed, but it was not until late in that year that he sent Richardson a preface to the work, in preparation for publication.[33] The little book came out in 1753, printed by Richardson, who in the same year printed a new edition, the fifth, of *The Canons of Criticism*.

First published in 1748 as *Supplement to Mr. Warburton's Edition of Shakespear, The Canons of Criticism* is a sensible, generally sharp, and often witty attack on Warburton's practices as an editor, which others also deplored. Warburton had struck back at his too cogent critic in 1751 in the notes of a new edition of the works of Pope. His attack was more virulent than Edwards's, but a good deal less clever. In a note on line 463 of the *Essay on Criticism* he goes out of his way to call Edwards a critic

[29] R to Edwards, 19 Mar. 1751.
[30] 'Sonnet XXIV. To Miss H. M.'
[31] 'Sonnet' by Susanna Highmore, FM XVI, 2, fo. 45; R to Susanna Highmore, 22 June 1750.
[32] To Edwards, 21 Aug. 1752.
[33] Edwards to R, 8 Feb. 1751; R to Edwards, 13 Feb., 19 Mar. 1751; Edwards to R, 20 Mar., 23 Oct. 1752.

with neither parts nor learning. He ever forced Pope to attack him, by applying to him line 568 of the fourth book of *The Dunciad*. Edwards, he explains in his note, 'early retained himself in the cause of *Dulness* against *Shakespear*, and with the wit and learning of his Ancestor *Tom Thimble* in the *Rehearsal*, and with the air of good nature and politeness of *Caliban* in the *Tempest*, hath now happily finished the *Dunce's progress*, in personal abuse'. In both places the abuse in his footnotes overshoots the mark and becomes simply name-calling, so that while it may have irritated Edwards, it could hardly have hurt him. He sensibly, on second thoughts, asked Richardson to delete a fling at Warburton in *The Trial of the Letter Y*.[34] But there are a good many references to Warburton in his letters at this period. Richardson, at least in his letters to Edwards, seemed sympathetic with the latter's battle and indeed helped him in it. In the spring of 1751 Edwards wrote mock proposals for editions of Chaucer, Gower, and Daniel, to be done according to the canons which he had accused Warburton of basing his edition of Shakespeare on. He asked Richardson to help him get them published in some periodical.[35] Richardson, 'with some Difficulty', got Dr. John Hill to include them in the new *London Daily Advertiser, and Literary Gazette*, for which Hill wrote a periodical letter, 'The Inspector'.[36] Richardson regretted that Edwards's satire was so subtle: 'You are too modest in these Proposals. I wish they had been more pointed'. But other papers had refused the proposals even in their veiled form. In thanking Richardson for taking 'more Trouble about the Proposals than they were worth', Edwards added that 'there is such a Combination among the Booksellers, that it is impossible to get any thing into the public Papers whereby their Craft may be in danger'.[37]

Edwards was lonely in winter—'the badness of the weather makes Turrick a very desolate place'. Richardson, always hospitable, had already invited Edwards to stay at either of his two houses and now urged him to make North End his winter home. Edwards gratefully refused on the grounds of health and 'other affairs'. 'I know not how I came to be so simple as to complain of the desolateness of my situation, which gave you this kind concern for me. . . . It is my duty however to reconcile my self to it as well as I can since it is too late for me to think of changing either my place or condition.'[38] To Daniel Wray, who wondered at his not accepting, he explained that the invitation had been tempting. 'He is one of the most generous and friendly men living, but would it be *reasonable*, would it be decent, would it be just, for me to come and bring my acquaintance with me, and live upon him who has a wife and a family of

---

[34] 1 Jan. 1753.   [35] 8 May.

[36] Issue of 22 May.   [37] 27 May, 19 June.

[38] Edwards to R, 23 Dec. 1751; R to Edwards, 13 Feb., 30 Dec. 1751; Edwards to R, 10 Jan. 1752.

children? If such a scheme could be so adjusted as to suit my circumstances and not injure his family, there is no place where I could with more pleasure spend that part of the year when if my health would permit I should be in London, since thus I should be next door to it, and have a good deal of the company of that worthy man.' The invitation was repeated for the next winter and again refused for the same reason.[39]

Richardson often pressed Edwards to use his talents for the public good. *The Trial of the Letter Y* made him desire a definitive work on spelling, which Edwards felt he had neither the time nor the learning to attempt. He hoped that Edwards would 'vindicate Pope and Milton from their Editors', as he had Shakespeare. When Edwards feared that in a forthcoming edition Spenser would 'be even worse treated than either Milton or Shakespear', Richardson naturally expressed the wish that Edwards himself would edit his favourite, but Edwards, though he did do some work on Spenser, again declined.[40]

Edwards had long been interested in the progress of *Sir Charles Grandison*. 'The greatest part of it', he told his friend the Reverend Peter Hervey, 'I saw in Manuscript.' Early in 1752 he sent Richardson a poem for Miss Mulso, urging her to sing and inspirit the '*Good Man*' to new heights.[41] But he evidently was no more sure how it would end than were the rest of Richardson's friends, since early in 1754, during the interval between the publication of the sixth and seventh volumes, he worried a little, though he believed that Harriet was not to die and hoped for a happy end —*Clarissa* had made Richardson's admirers a little fearful. His letters at this time are full of admiration for the novel. Richardson's works 'touch the heart in such a manner as no one I know does since Shakespear'. *Sir Charles Grandison* and *Clarissa* are 'the two greatest works that any Modern has produced'.[42] He was surprised that the Reverend John Lowry, once he started *Grandison*, could postpone finishing it: 'I was angry at every thing that gave any interruption to my enjoyment of so exquisite a mental feast.'[43] When Richardson sent him the last volume, he was pleased with the conclusion. He objected only to the four pages of selected similes at the end of the volume, which he said looked 'like affectation'—as they do; but though Richardson agreed that the similes were a mistake and blamed them on the corrector of his press, they were

[39] Edwards to Wray, 14 Feb. 1752, Bodleian MS. 1011, p. 333; Edwards to Joseph Paice, 28 Dec. 1752, Bodleian MS. 1012, p. 56.

[40] Edwards to R, 9 Mar., 30 Mar. 1751, 20 Mar. 1752; Edwards to Wray, 23 Mar. 1752, Bodleian MS. 1012, p. 9; Edwards to R, 30 Mar., 8 May 1751; R to Edwards, 27 May 1751; Edwards to R, 19 June 1751.

[41] 30 Mar. 1754, Bodleian MS. 1012, p. 163; 28 Feb.

[42] To Joseph Paice, 28 Feb.; to Peter Hervey, 7 Feb.; to George Onslow, 22 Feb., Bodleian MS. 1012, pp. 155–6, 146, 149. See also to Isaac Hawkins Browne, 1 Feb., and to John Lowry, 5 Feb., ibid., pp. 135–6, 140.

[43] 27 Feb., ibid., pp. 151–2.

not cut in the later editions issued during his lifetime. He hoped that writing it had not injured Richardson's health, but even if it had, it was a 'glorious kind of Martyrdom'. *Clarissa* and *Sir Charles Grandison* had improved his character, though he could not rise to the height of Sir Charles's attitude towards death.[44] He immediately began to read through the whole book for the third time, and, echoing Young on *Clarissa*, was ready to call it 'The whole duty of Man'. A year later, imprisoned at Turrick by the weather, he was going through all of Richardson's works again and finding 'very great relief'.[45]

Edwards wrote a sonnet to the author of *Sir Charles Grandison*:

> Sweet Moralist, whose generous Labors tend
>   With ceaseless diligence, to guide the Mind,
>   In the wild maze of error wandering blind,
> To Virtue, Truth, and Honor, glorious end
>
> Of glorious toils!

This sonnet he sent to Richardson, 'which if it should be thought worth publishing I desire may be inscribed to the Author of Grandison . . . and subscribed T. E. You see how ambitious I am.' The sonnet, signed with its author's initials, was prefixed to the second edition, thus fulfilling Edwards's longing to 'go down to Posterity in an advantageous light, and be read by the Fair and the Good'.[46]

It is not certain when Richardson first met Dr. Johnson, but by the time he was composing *Sir Charles Grandison* the two men, who were so similar in morals and so dissimilar in manners and education, were good friends. There are only nine recorded letters from Johnson to Richardson and one from Richardson to Johnson;[47] but since they were living in London, not far from each other, there was not much reason for them to write. The first evidence of their friendship is a letter of 9 March 1751, welcoming the new edition of *Clarissa*. Six years before, Richardson had hesitated to send Aaron Hill a copy of the *Life of Savage* because he believed that Hill might be displeased with it.[48] It would, of course, have been easy for Richardson to meet Johnson during the 1740s or even before.

In one of the first *Ramblers* Johnson wrote about fiction in terms which informed readers would take as implying praise of *Clarissa* and censure of *Tom Jones*.[49] Richardson returned the compliment by telling Cave, who

[44] Edwards to R, 29 Mar.; R to Edwards, 5 Apr.

[45] To Peter Hervey, 30 Mar. 1754; 20 Feb. 1755, Bodleian MS. 1012, pp. 163, 195.

[46] 6 Feb., 1 Mar.

[47] For Johnson's letters to Richardson, see T. C. Duncan Eaves, 'Dr. Johnson's Letters to Richardson', *PMLA*, LXXV (1960), 377–81. For Richardson's letter to Johnson of 2 Nov., [1751], see Duncan E. Isles, 'Unpublished Johnson Letters', *TLS*, 29 July 1965, p. 666.

[48] Hill to R, 4 Apr., 10 Apr.   [49] No. 4 (31 Mar. 1750).

had sent him the first numbers, that he was 'inexpressibly pleased with them' and with the later ones, which he had been buying. He remembered nothing in those *Spectators* he had read which half so much struck him. He could only guess at the author but thought that there was but one man who could write them. In answer, Cave told Richardson that Johnson was 'the *Great Rambler*, being, as you observe, the only man who can furnish two such papers in a week'. He added that in spite of high praise by the judicious the sale had been somewhat disappointing and that the author thought highly of Richardson's writing.[50]

This exchange sounds as if Richardson's friendship with Johnson could not have been close in 1750. Their acquaintance may well have grown when early in 1751 Richardson contributed one of the rare numbers of the *Rambler* which were not written by Johnson himself.[51] It was introduced as by 'an author from whom the age has received greater favours, who has enlarged the knowledge of human nature, and taught the passions to move at the command of virtue'. Richardson's only known excursion into the periodic essay was on one of his favourite subjects, the modern woman. The women of today are too much given 'to idle amusements, and to wicked rackets'; they neglect their domestic duties. Richardson gives a picture of the ideal courtships of old days, which were arranged through parents and with reserve and modesty on the part of the bride. 'Oh Mr. RAMBLER! forgive the talkativeness of an old man! when I courted and married my *Lætitia*, then a blooming beauty, every thing passed just so!' This statement cannot be strictly accurate, since both Richardson's wives were orphans when he married them, but perhaps Martha Wilde had been as cautious, proper, and retiring as the women of the good old days. The modern coquettes only bring contempt on themselves by 'rendering themselves so impolitickly cheap'—a favourite subject of Richardson in his letters to young ladies. The essay hardly teaches the passions to move at all, but it does teach the virtues to move at the command of prudence. John Nichols reported on the authority of John Payne, the publisher of the *Rambler*, that Richardson's was the only paper 'which had a prosperous sale, and may be said to have been popular'.[52] Perhaps its success was responsible for the fact that Richardson was asked to contribute to John Hawkesworth's *Adventurer*, to which Johnson contributed, but Richardson 'never found Leisure' to write for that periodical.[53] The only book which Richardson is known to have printed of Johnson's was the fourth volume of the first collected edition of the *Rambler*, early in 1752.[54]

[50] 9 Aug., 23 Aug. 1750.

[51] No. 97 (19 Feb. 1751). See Boswell, *Life*, I, 203.

[52] *Literary Anecdotes*, V, 39; see also Alexander Chalmers, *The British Essayists* (London, 1802–3), XIX, xiv.

[53] R to Lady Bradshaigh, 9 Oct. 1754.

[54] Eaves, 'Dr. Johnson's Letters to Richardson', pp. 379–80.

Dr. Johnson was at about the same time reading the manuscript of *Sir Charles Grandison*. He was eager for the next instalment: 'To wish you to go on as you have begun would to many be a very kind wish, but you, Sir, have beyond all other men the art of improving on yourself.' In the spring of 1753 he expressed the hope that the new novel was printing and in the fall, well over a month before the first four volumes appeared, thanked Richardson for volumes of the printed work: 'But it is a kind of tyrannical kindness to give only so much at a time as makes more longed for.'[55] But Johnson never praised *Sir Charles* in the high terms he used for *Clarissa*.

In 1755, in his *Dictionary*, he gave that novel a compliment of another sort. In his preface to that work he stated that he had not intended to cite living authors as testimony for words and had departed from this policy only 'when some performance of uncommon excellence excited my veneration, when my memory supplied me from late books with an example that was wanting, or when my heart, in the tenderness of friendship, solicited admission for a favourite name'.[56] An example of the last sort may be his citing four lines by Miss Mulso under 'quatrain'. Richardson might fall into either the last or the first category. At any rate, he cited *Clarissa* ninety-seven times and *Pamela* three. The living author cited most often after Richardson is Johnson himself, over fifty times; next come Charlotte Lennox (eighteen) and Young (thirteen).[57] Richardson is then an easy favourite. The number of unusual or new words he used made him an obvious author to quote. The *Oxford English Dictionary* finds no earlier source for several of the words under which he is cited: 'disavowal', 'domesticate' in the sense of 'to make domestic', and 'alive' in the sense of 'sprightly', for example. A few of the words are said to be from 'somewhere in *Clarissa*' and are probably cited from memory. Most of them, however, come from the 'Moral and Instructive Sentiments' added to the end of the fourth edition of *Clarissa*. Johnson's choice, which emphasizes words dealing with morality, such as 'seduction', 'rakish', 'profligate', 'hardheartedness', 'modesty', 'giddy', 'dishabille', 'encroacher', 'suicide', and 'violator', may well be a sign of his desire to bring morality even into the *Dictionary*: 'When I first collected these authorities, I was desirous that every quotation should be useful to some other end than the illustration of a word.'[58] When Garrick objected that Johnson had cited authorities like Richardson, beneath the dignity of his work, Johnson is said to have answered, 'Nay . . ., I have done worse than that: I have cited *thee*, David.'[59]

---

[55] [Early 1752?], 17 Apr., 26 Sept.   [56] *Works* (Oxford, 1825), V, 39.
[57] See William R. Keast, 'The Two *Clarissas* in Johnson's *Dictionary*', SP, LIV (1957), 429-39.
[58] *Works*, V, 38.   [59] Boswell, *Life*, IV, 4.

Richardson's opinion of Johnson did not have much occasion to get recorded, but one can assume that he was impressed with his intellectual friend. Johnson's opinions of Richardson, somewhat conflicting as they are, have often been quoted and some of them have probably done much to influence the picture usually given of Richardson as a man of almost childlike vanity. Johnson's slighting remarks on Richardson's circle of admiring females will be discussed later. Some light on them may be cast by a remark of Miss Frances Reynolds that though Johnson was a great admirer of Richardson's works, especially *Clarissa*, 'yet of the Author I never heard him speak with any degree of cordiality, but rather as if impress'd with some cause of resentment against him; and this has been imputed to something of jealousy, not to say envy, on account of Richardson's having engross'd the attentions and affectionate assiduities of several very ingenious literary ladies, whom he used to call his addopted daughters, and for whom Dr. Johnson had conceived a paternal affection (particularly for two of them, Miss Carter and Miss Mulso, . . .) previous to their acquaintance with Richardson; and it was said, that he thought himself neglected by them on his account'.[60] It would be a mistake to take this anecdote, and indeed any of Johnson's unfavourable remarks, too seriously. Some irritation on Johnson's part is not unlikely, and the rather gushing admiration of his favourite Hester Mulso for Richardson was probably not too welcome. But there are other remarks about Richardson as a person, made after the latter's death, which should correct the impression that there was ever anything amounting to a quarrel. Boswell mentions Johnson's boast that William Duncombe used to come to him: '"I did not seek much after *him*. Indeed I never sought much after any body." BOSWELL. "Lord Orrery, I suppose." JOHNSON. "No, Sir; I never went to him but when he sent for me." BOSWELL. "Richardson?" JOHNSON. "Yes, Sir."'[61] Boswell's question implies that he would have expected Johnson to seek out Richardson—indeed it may imply a twinge of Boswell's not unusual jealousy of his hero's friends. James Northcote reports that 'Dr. Johnson had a great desire to cultivate the friendship of Richardson . . . and with this view paid him frequent visits. These were received very coldly by the latter; "but," observed the Doctor (in speaking of this to a friend), "I was determined to persist till I had gained my point; because I knew very well, that when I had once overcome his reluctance and shyness of humour, our intimacy would contribute much to the happiness of both." The event verified the Doctor's prediction.'[62] Johnson late in life regretted his narrow circle of enjoyment, as compared

[60] 'Recollections of Dr. Johnson', *Johnsonian Miscellanies*, ed. George Birkbeck Hill (Oxford, 1897), II, 251-2.

[61] *Life*, III, 314.

[62] *Memoirs of Sir Joshua Reynolds* (London, 1813), p. 46.

to the pleasant neighbourhood he once had, with Richardson, Dr. Lawrence, Mrs. Allen, Miss Williams, and Levet near at hand. And again, 'The black Dog I hope always to resist, and in time to drive though I am deprived of almost all those that used to help me. The neighbourhood is impoverished. I had once Richardson and Laurence in my reach. Mrs. Allen is dead. My house has lost Levet. . . . Mrs Williams is so weak that [she] can be a companion no longer.'[63]

We have several pictures of Johnson seeking out Richardson at his house and, one hopes, driving the black dog away with his company. He used to be a pretty frequent visitor. An anecdote recorded by Boswell, who did not like Richardson as a writer and did not know him personally but is probably reliable, shows Johnson mildly ridiculing the uneducated printer. In connection with Sir Joshua Reynolds's statement that Richardson had little conversation except about his own works, about which he was always willing to talk (a statement abundantly illustrated in Richardson's letters), Boswell tells how Johnson took Mr. Langton to see Richardson, saying that he could make him talk: 'Sir, I can make him *rear*.' But on that occasion Richardson did not *rear*: he 'said little else than that there lay in the room a translation of his Clarissa into German'.[64]

Johnson first met Young at Richardson's, having been sent for to hear him read his *Conjectures on Original Composition*. One day, not long after the execution of Dr. Archibald Cameron in June 1753, when he was at Richardson's, Hogarth, whom he did not know, came in and began to justify Cameron's execution. Johnson, standing in a window, began to shake his head and roll himself about so that Hogarth decided he was 'an ideot, whom his relations had put under the care of Mr. Richardson, as a very good man'. When Johnson came forward and began eloquently to denounce the harshness of George II, Hogarth 'imagined that this ideot had been at the moment inspired'.[65] Richardson, describing a visit of Miss Mulso to North End, wrote to Mrs. Carter that 'Mr. Johnson *rambled* thither, principally on her Account, last Sunday. He is in Love with her.' On another occasion Johnson addressed most of his discourse to the lovable and intellectual Hester, who had the temerity to argue against his view of the natural depravity of mankind.[66]

This second time he brought with him Anna Williams, and Miss Mulso was charmed with his behaviour to his blind friend. Miss Talbot and her mother also met Miss Williams at Richardson's and were charmed with

[63] Letters to Mrs. Thrale, 8 May, 28 June 1783, *Letters*, ed. R. W. Chapman (Oxford, 1952), III, 24, 41.

[64] *Life*, I, 145; IV, 28.

[65] *Boswell's Journal of a Tour to the Hebrides*, ed. Frederick A. Pottle and Charles H. Bennett (New York, [1961]), p. 234; Boswell, *Life*, I, 145-7.

[66] 2 Oct. 1753; Hester Mulso to Elizabeth Carter, 10 July, [1753?], *Posthumous Works of Mrs. Chapone*, I, 73.

her.[67] She wrote some verses about Richardson which were published in the *Gentleman's Magazine*, praising all three of his novels, especially for their morality, and contrasting him with Fielding:

> In distant times, when *Jones* and *Booth* are lost,
> *Brittania* her *Clarissa*'s name shall boast.[68]

Later Johnson wrote to convey her thanks for a present, probably the last volume of *Sir Charles Grandison*, and to ask Richardson to take a share of the copy of a dictionary she was planning to do with the help of an amanuensis and to induce his friends to take the rest.[69]

These anecdotes are enough to show the close relationship between Johnson and Richardson. In addition, Johnson gave Richardson a copy of *Rasselas* and sent him a pheasant presented by Bennet Langton.[70] They were still seeing each other as late as the spring of 1759, when Richardson passed on a comment Johnson had made on Young's *Conjectures on Original Composition*.[71]

On at least one occasion Richardson helped Johnson with money. He wrote, from his own house, that he was 'under an arrest for five pounds eighteen shillings'; Strahan was not at home, and he was afraid Millar would not be, and if Richardson would send the sum, he would 'gratefully repay' him 'and add it to all former obligations'. Richardson's nephew William noted on the letter that six guineas had been sent, and Johnson thanked Richardson with a book, Sir Thomas Browne's *Christian Morals*.[72] George Steevens gives an anecdote which is either a garbled version of this or another instance of Richardson's aid: 'Dr. Johnson confessed himself to have been sometimes in the power of bailiffs. Richardson ... was his constant friend on such occasions [the mention of Strahan and Millar in Johnson's letter makes this statement dubious]. "I remember writing to him," said Johnson, "from a sponging house; and was so sure of my deliverance through his kindness and liberality, that, before his reply was brought, I knew I could afford to joke with the rascal who had me in custody, and did so, over a pint of adulterated wine, for which, at that instant, I had no money to pay."'[73]

Johnson's compliments to Richardson's work are numerous. Once indeed he compared the character of Clarissa unfavourably with that of Amelia: 'You may observe there is always something which she [Clarissa]

[67] Miss Talbot to Mrs. Carter, 24 Feb. 1756, *Letters between Mrs. Elizabeth Carter and Miss Catherine Talbot*, I, 394.
[68] XXIV (Jan. 1754), 40.
[69] 28 Mar. 1754.
[70] *The Library of Jerome Kern* (New York, 1929), p. 236; Johnson to Langton, 9 Jan. 1758, *Letters*, I, 114.
[71] 24 May.
[72] 16 Mar., [19 Mar.] 1756.
[73] *Johnsonian Miscellanies*, II, 323.

prefers to truth.'[74] Though it is dangerous to ignore Johnson's views, he said so many things that he must have said some things rather hastily—as he himself said, 'Nobody talks more laxly than I do.'[75] Sir John Hawkins says that Johnson 'was inclined, as being personally acquainted with Richardson', to favour the opinion which celebrated Richardson 'as a writer similar in genius to Shakespeare, as being acquainted with the inmost recesses of the human heart, and having an absolute command of the passions, so as to be able to affect his readers as he himself is affected, and to interest them in the successes and disappointments, the joys and sorrows of his characters . . ., but he seemed not firm in it, and could at any time be talked into a disapprobation of all fictitious relations, of which he would frequently say they took no hold of the mind'.[76] It is not unexpected to find that Johnson was occasionally inconsistent, but in general his recorded opinion of Richardson's work is very high. When Richardson forwarded to Edwards Johnson's comments on *The Trial of the Letter Y*, he also forwarded a copy of Johnson's accompanying letter, 'notwithstanding the very high and undeserved Compliment he makes me in it' (he had referred to Richardson as 'adorning' the English language).[77] Anna Seward quotes Johnson as having called *Clarissa* 'not only the first *novel*, but perhaps the first *work* in our language, splendid in point of genius, and calculated to promote the dearest interests of religion and virtue'.[78] Miss Frances Cotterell disputed with Johnson about *Clarissa*, 'which he warmly patronised': '"No man could have written such a book," she said, "who was not nervous." "No Madam, nor any man that was, excepting Richardson."'[79] According to Mrs. Piozzi, he 'used to say that he believed no combination could be found [for fiction] and few sentiments that might not be traced up to Homer, Shakespeare & Richardson'.[80] Comparing French novels with those of Richardson, reported the Reverend Dr. William Maxwell, he once said 'they might be pretty baubles, but a wren was not an eagle'.[81] Hannah More said that she saw Johnson really angry with her only once, when she mentioned a witty passage in *Tom Jones*: '"I am shocked to hear you quote from so vicious a book. I am sorry to find you have read it: a confession which no modest lady should ever make. I scarcely know a more corrupt work." . . . He

[74] Hester Lynch Piozzi, *Anecdotes of the Late Samuel Johnson* (London, 1786), p. 221. For a milder version of this statement, see James L. Clifford, *Hester Lynch Piozzi* (Oxford, 1941), p. 437: 'The Heroine sometimes justified her Parents at the Expense of Truth.'

[75] *Boswell's Journal of a Tour to the Hebrides*, p. 350.

[76] *Life of Samuel Johnson*, p. 217.

[77] R to Edwards, 21 Apr. 1753; Johnson to R, 17 Apr. 1753.

[78] *Variety: A Collection of Essays* (London, 1788), p. 215.

[79] Elizabeth Smart Le Noir to Cuthbert Sharp, 22 Aug. 1831, quoted by Sherbo, 'Anecdotes by Mrs. Le Noir', p. 167.

[80] Marginalia in her copy of Boswell's *Life*, quoted by Powell in his edition, IV, 524n.

[81] Ibid., II, 125.

went so far as to refuse to Fielding the great talents which are ascribed to him, and broke out into a noble panegyric on his competitor, Richardson; who, he said, was as superior to him in talents as in virtue; and whom he pronounced to be the greatest genius that had shed its lustre on this path of literature.'[82]

Johnson's two most famous pronouncements on Richardson were also made in contrasting him to Fielding. '"Sir, . . . there is all the difference in the world between characters of nature and characters of manners; and *there* is the difference between the characters of Fielding and those of Richardson. Characters of manners are very entertaining; but they are to be understood, by a more superficial observer, than characters of nature, where a man must dive into the recesses of the human heart."' But, says Boswell, 'It always appeared to me that he estimated the compositions of Richardson too highly, and that he had an unreasonable prejudice against Fielding. In comparing those two writers, he used this expression; "that there was as great a difference between them as between a man who knew how a watch was made, and a man who could tell the hour by looking on the dial-plate".' Boswell, who did not agree at all on the relative merits of the two writers, adds that 'Johnson used to quote with approbation' Richardson's saying 'that the virtues of Fielding's heroes were the vices of a truly good man'. But, says Boswell (who was more an authority on men like Tom Jones than either Johnson or Richardson could be), 'He who is as good as Fielding would make him is an amiable member of society, and may be led on by more regulated instructors, to a higher state of ethical perfection.' 'Fielding being mentioned, Johnson exclaimed, "he was a blockhead;" and upon my expressing my astonishment at so strange an assertion, he said, "What I mean by his being a blockhead is that he was a barren rascal." BOSWELL. "Will you not allow, Sir, that he draws very natural pictures of human life?" JOHNSON. "Why, Sir, it is of very low life. . . . Sir, there is more knowledge of the heart in one letter of Richardson's, than in all 'Tom Jones'. I, indeed, never read 'Joseph Andrews'."'[83]

A friend of Johnson's whom Richardson knew at least by 1753[84] was the Italian author Giuseppe Baretti, who arrived in London in May 1751 and lived there until 1760. Later, when Johnson sent him news of Richardson's

---

[82] William Roberts, *Memoirs of the Life and Correspondence of Mrs. Hannah More*, 3rd edn. (London, 1835), I, 169.

[83] *Life*, II, 48-9, 173-5. We can see no merit in Robert Etheridge Moore's contention in 'Dr. Johnson on Fielding and Richardson', *PMLA*, LXVI (1951), 162-81, that Johnson's principles are better illustrated by Fielding's novels than by Richardson's. Mr. Moore supports this stand by such dubious methods as implying that all of Johnson's *Rambler* No. 4 can be paralleled in Fielding, whereas actually Johnson's main point about characterization is altogether different, and as quoting Johnson's statement that 'Clarissa is not a performance to be read with eagerness, and laid aside forever' without the last four words.

[84] Anna Williams and Mary Masters to R, 30 Oct.

death, Baretti recalled him as one of the best friends he had had in England: 'I still grieve at losing him; such a man and such a friend is not soon recovered.'[85] It has been suggested that Baretti may have helped Richardson with the Italian background of *Sir Charles Grandison*.[86] Wherever he got it, Richardson surely needed help in describing a background he had never seen. He even dragged into the novel unnecessary local colour like a note on the splendid Casino at Bologna and a suggested visit to the antiquities at Herculaneum, and the long, dull, and irrelevant letter from Mr. Lowther describing his crossing of the Alps must have come in substance, if not in its entirety, from a friend.[87]

During the years between *Clarissa* and *Sir Charles Grandison* Richardson continued to make new friends, largely in more elegant circles than he had hitherto moved in. Even in his first novel Richardson had described a society above his own walk in life. After the publication of *Pamela* he had enlarged his horizon, and Clarissa moves in a still more elevated sphere. The hero of *Sir Charles Grandison* is a baronet, and he is intimate with lords. Some of Richardson's new friends could have made him more conversant with the manners of the nobility, though he never seems to be altogether at ease in writing about them. Lady Mary Wortley Montagu, to be sure, exaggerated when she said that she believed Richardson was never admitted into higher company than the lowest class of people, 'and should confine his Pen to the Amours of Housemaids and the conversation at the Steward's Table, where I imagine he has sometimes intruded, thô oftner in the Servants' Hall'.[88] But his aristocrats are rather middle class. In *Clarissa*, where passions are far more important than manners, this fact hardly matters; but social customs are more prominent in *Sir Charles Grandison*.

Clarissa had brought him, as he proudly told Stinstra, 'the Honour of a personal Acquaintance with Five of those Prelates who have done, and do, most Honour to the Bench of Bishops'.[89] Two of these were the Bishops of Bristol and Oxford. John Conybeare, who had given him advice about revising *Clarissa*, was made Bishop of Bristol in 1750. Richardson had printed for him as early as 1732, was still sending him greetings and compliments after the completion of *Sir Charles Grandison*, and in 1757, after his death, undertook a subscription edition of his *Sermons* for his widow.[90] Richardson was connected with Thomas Secker, Bishop of Oxford and from 1750 also Dean of St. Paul's,[91] through

[85] 20 July 1762, *Letters*, I, 139; Baretti to Francesco Carcano, 29 Dec. 1770, *Lettere instruttive descrittive e familiari* (Messina, 1825), p. 186.

[86] McKillop, *Richardson*, p. 212.   [87] SH, IV, 148, 357, 106-12.

[88] *Complete Letters*, III, 96.   [89] 6 Dec. 1752.

[90] R to Conybeare, 12 Sept. 1749; *Gentleman's Magazine*, XX (Nov. 1750), 526; R to Kennicott, 26 Nov. 1754; Sale, *Master Printer*, pp. 116-17.

[91] *Gentleman's Magazine*, XX (Nov.), 526.

Catherine Talbot, who was a member of the Bishop's household. A third bishop may have been Secker's brother-in-law, Martin Benson, Bishop of Gloucester, who (William Duncombe reported to Mrs. Carter) called on Richardson at North End with Secker and Mrs. and Miss Talbot around the middle of 1750.[92]

Apparently Duncombe's friendship with Richardson was at this time growing rapidly. 'I am much more intimate with him now than I was when you were in town. The more I know, the better I like him', he also told Mrs. Carter. He was almost Richardson's age and had been a gentleman of 'literary leisure' since his retirement from the Navy Office in 1725.[93] The intimacy continued, and in 1757 and 1759 Richardson printed for him and his son John their translation of Horace.[94]

John, born in 1729 and a student of Corpus Christi, Cambridge, and later a clergyman, was a leading member of the circle of young people who gathered around Richardson during this period. He wrote verses which were published in the third edition of *Clarissa* and at least by the fall of 1751 had begun a correspondence with Richardson. He had already heard part of the new novel and regretted the distance which kept him from peeping at the manuscript to learn more of the fates of its characters, especially of 'your fair Italian': 'I indulge the pleasing, but painful reflection, of the wound which Clementina so lately gave me, which now, on recollection, bleeds anew.' Richardson must have told him, as he told his father, that he could not because of his health decide whether to continue, since Duncombe replied that his health must not be endangered, and 'if you find writing inconsistent with it, for God's sake throw away your pen'. When the novel appeared, he admired it enough to let its poor reception at Maidstone lower his opinion of that city.[95]

Meanwhile Richardson had been the confidant of both parties during his long-drawn-out courtship of Susanna Highmore. One of his poetic efforts, called 'Ode to Content', is preserved among Richardson's papers. He envisions a future of wedded bliss with Stella when they see their friends assembled at Friendship's 'social Board':

> Thou too, Palemon, often there,
>   Smiling on the happy Pair,
>   To thy Daughter and thy Friend
>   Thy Converse and thy Counsel lend. . . .

[92] N. d. [1750], Pennington, *Memoirs of . . . Mrs. Elizabeth Carter*, I, 146.

[93] Nichols, *Literary Anecdotes*, VIII, 265–78.

[94] Sale, *Master Printer*, p. 168; Charles Ryskamp, *William Cowper* (Cambridge, 1959), pp. 12, 112.

[95] John Duncombe to R, 15 Oct.; R to William Duncombe, 22 Oct.; John Duncombe to R, 17 Nov.; John Duncombe to the Rev. John Deane, 30 Mar. 1754, in John Nichols, *Illustrations of the Literary History of the Eighteenth Century* (London, 1817–58), VI, 798.

Stella replied in another poetic effusion that love must be deferred—neither Innocence nor Stella,

> Where Love and Duty disagree,
> Can ever deign to bless the Lover's Choice,
> The Sanction wanting of the Parent's Voice.

Meanwhile,

> Let Corydon to Cam remove,
> Try Learnings Pow'r to cure his Love;
> Stella the Force of Friendship try;
> To good Palemon's Grotto fly;
> For all distress'd, Asylum kind,
>   Where ev'ry Sickness of the Mind
>   Sage Palemon knows to heal,
> And soothing Counsel to reveal;
> Advice in Fancy's Garb arrays,
> Instruction with Delight conveys;
> Mends ev'ry Heart that hears his moral Page,
> Adapted well to ev'ry State and Age.[96]

There can be no doubt that Palemon's grotto was the one at North End. The lovers appear to have been patient under parental disapproval, and one can be sure that sage Palemon urged patience. He also teased Miss Highmore about her lover: he wrote her a long and lively account of a dinner at North End and a boating party the next day, the main point of which was to defer satisfying her curiosity about whether the younger Mr. Duncombe had been present.[97] They were finally rewarded in April 1761,[98] two and a half months before Richardson's death.

Duncombe's patient fiancée was the centre of one of the interconnected circles of women who played a large part in Richardson's life at the time of the composition of *Sir Charles Grandison*. She often visited North End with pleasure, where she met 'with the instructive, though at the same time paternally tender and indulgent, conversation of the generous patron of that happy mansion'.[99] It was Susanna Highmore who drew the sketch of Richardson in the grotto at North End, reading the manuscript of *Sir Charles* to a group of young friends.[100] The three girls and three young men in Miss Highmore's sketch are Miss Highmore herself, Mary Prescott, Hester Mulso, her brothers Thomas and Edward, and John Duncombe.[101]

[96] FM XVI, 2, fos. 10-11; index to the poetry, ibid., fo. 3.   [97] 22 June 1750.
[98] 20 Apr. See *Gentleman's Magazine*, XXXI, 188.
[99] To Hester Mulso, 18 July 1751, Barbauld, II, 264.
[100] The original drawing is in the Pierpont Morgan Library; an engraving of it is reproduced in Barbauld, II.
[101] McKillop, *Richardson*, p. 194, incorrectly identifies Thomas Mulso as his father, also named Thomas.

Richardson had, of course, enjoyed the company of women earlier; the ladies who read and gave advice about *Pamela* have been mentioned, as have various girls he met and corresponded with in the late 1740s, notably Sarah Wescomb. But except for the Collier sisters and their friend Sally Fielding, none of these women seems to have had intellectual pretensions, and all were more or less middle class. Nor is there any sign that Richardson's friendship for them played as prominent a part in his life as his friendship for such men as Hill and Young. In 1750 he finally unmasked Lady Bradshaigh, who as the years passed became his closest female friend. Around the same time he met a good many more women and became more friendly with some whom he had known only slightly in the 1740s, like Elizabeth Carter and Mrs. Delany. In general his new friends came from a somewhat higher social or intellectual level than Miss Grainger and Miss Dutton. The success of *Clarissa*, less popular but more critical than that of *Pamela*, probably attracted many of them.

On 8 September 1750 he sent Miss Grainger a list of thirty-six examples of superior women (to disprove the contention of men who consider women an inferior breed), 'almost all of them of my intimate Acquaintances'. He used only initials or first and last letters: 'A Mrs. D——n,' 'A D. of P.' Over half of the names can be identified with some certainty, and a few more conjecturally. They do not include such unassuming ladies as Miss Dutton or Mrs. Gosling (the former Miss Midwinter)—Miss Grainger's name, of course, does occur, but she is the recipient of the list. Some of the more distinguished, like Lady Anson and the Duchess of Portland, were at most acquaintances, hardly intimate. Miss Wescomb is there, and the two Misses Collier with their friend Miss Fielding, and Lady Bradshaigh. The three young friends of the sketch, Miss Highmore, Miss Prescott, and Miss Mulso, are included; so are Mrs. Delany and the new friends to whom she had directly or indirectly introduced Richardson, Mrs. Dewes, Mrs. Donnellan, Mrs. Chapone, and Miss Sutton; and Elizabeth Carter and her closest friend, Catherine Talbot. The latter three groups all knew each other, though the intimacy was greater within each group than between the groups. Unlike Miss Wescomb and Lady Bradshaigh, who remained somewhat off to one side, they were all to a greater or lesser degree bluestockings, interested in conversation and art and literature. The two latter groups were definitely genteel, with aristocratic as well as clerical connections, and had pretensions to being a part of 'Society', though a society perhaps more intellectual than fashionable. All of the ladies were pious and were supporters of virtue.

Richardson was a friend of Susanna Highmore's father and had been corresponding with the daughter for two years. It was probably through her or the Duncombes that he met Hester Mulso, who later, as Mrs. Chapone, became a rather celebrated bluestocking. It was at Richardson's that she met her future husband, John Chapone, in the early 1750s; after the long engagement which was the fate of most of Richardson's young friends, they married in December 1760, but nine months later she was a widow.[102]

Richardson wrote to her first on 13 July 1750, a rather formal note on a blank page of a letter William Duncombe was writing her. She answered and thus began a correspondence which, a year later, had assumed the bantering, gay, affectionate tone which Richardson liked to adopt with young ladies.

Her eldest brother, Thomas, and her youngest, Edward, had already called at North End with William and John Duncombe and Mary Prescott. After Richardson's first note, Hester recommended her second brother, John, to Richardson's acquaintance.[103] By fall John was writing that 'My Sister & ye Family are got into the Acquaintance of Richardson ye Author of Pamela & Clarissa, in which they take great Delight, for the Man is a Sort of an Original for Goodness & Sensibility. He has got a new Plan to work upon, so that we may hope for more Reason to admire Him.' A year later he wrote that Mr. Richardson had called Hester 'a charming child', '& all that Mr R—— says is with us oracular'.[104]

He himself had met Richardson in December 1750 and had been very favourably impressed: 'Mr Richardson very well answers ye Prejudice which his Works raise in his Favour, & therefore is indeed an extraordinary man. He is in Person a short fat man, of an honest Countenance, but has ill Health & shatter'd nerves. But his gentle Manners, his generous Charitableness, his Studiousness to oblige & improve without ye air of Superiority, his extreme Tenderness to every proper Object of it that comes within his Notice, make Him infinitely dear to those who know Him, and studiously sought after by those who do not. Rara Avis in Terris.' His sister, with her two brothers and Miss Prescott, 'are much with Him, & have spent some Days at his Country House'. And Hester had already begun her interchange of letters on the subject of parental authority, 'occasioned by her thinking Clarissa's apprehensions of her Father's malediction too strong'. According to John, such great men as the Bishop of London (Thomas Sherlock) and the Speaker, who had seen the dispute, thought Richardson 'hard pressed, & Heck has gained great Honour. Old Cibber swore to her Face She would never be married.'[105]

The brothers, as well as the sister, were literary. John, who became a prebendary at Winchester and Salisbury, wrote some verses on Clarissa in

---

[102] The Life and Correspondence of Mrs. Chapone (London, 1807), I, 1–11; Registers of Marriages of St. Mary le Bone, Middlesex, Harleian Society Registers, LXVIII (1918), 30, under date 30 Dec. 1760; Gentleman's Magazine, XXXI (Jan., Sept. 1761), 43, 430.

[103] R to Miss Mulso, 20 July.

[104] To Gilbert White, 6 Oct., 4 Nov., The Letters to Gilbert White of Selborne from ... the Rev. John Mulso, ed. Rashleigh Holt-White (London, [1907]), pp. 43, 55.

[105] To Gilbert White, 5 Dec., ibid., pp. 45–6.

which he compared Richardson to Ezekiel in his use of moving stories to reform the age.[106] Thomas wrote an ode to Highmore 'On Mr. Richardson's sitting to him for his Picture': 'O Skilful Highmore! can thy noble art/Express the beauties of a worthy heart?' The answer is no; the pencil can trace 'The comely features of his honest face', 'suffuse his eye/With sense and soft humanity', and make 'the dimpled cheek' bespeak good humour, but it is inadequate to reproduce Richardson's 'restless zeal for doing good', 'His ardent love for all mankind', his sorrow 'For the poor wretch his charity maintains', and the 'eloquence divine' which we expect to pour from his mute lips. Fortunately for us and for posterity, his own works can succeed in portraying where the artist fails.[107]

Miss Mulso's three letters to Richardson on parental authority[108] cover well over a hundred pages in her works, and since she wrote to Mrs. Carter that his side of the correspondence was very long and that his argument would have been better had his letters been shorter, the mind boggles at imagining how many words of his the world has lost on this subject.[109] The argument about Clarissa's being too fearful of the curse of an unjust father began at North End. Miss Mulso's tone is quiet and reasonable; she allows that parents should have a veto power in their daughters' marriages and that in general (there are exceptions) women should submit to the authority of the superior sex even in wedlock. She concludes that they are not too far apart. Throughout her letters she seems to be trying to force Richardson to make clear distinctions, which he avoids doing. Insofar as one can judge from one side of a controversy, she seems to have been the more logical and cool-headed, and the Bishop and Speaker may well have been right, though Richardson accused her of tenaciousness.

Mrs. Carter, whom Miss Mulso had met at about the same time, without having read the letters decided that Richardson was in the wrong: Mrs. Carter was not one to put up with slurs against her sex. Miss Mulso defended Richardson against her own defender: 'I declare I will be angry with you, for he deserves that even his failings should be respected.' She granted that the stories with which he illustrated his arguments were 'not much to the purpose', but Richardson 'never . . . wrote any thing that did not shew an excellent heart and a very uncommon understanding'.[110] Richardson, however, evidently thought that he had had the best of it. Two years later he wrote to Mrs. Chapone, Miss Mulso's future mother-in-law, that his young friend was wrong principally in making the duty of the child depend on the kindness of the parent and that he had also given her over twenty reasons why wives should submit to husbands. He

---

[106] FM XV, 2, fos. 59–60.
[107] Barbauld, V, 286–8.
[108] 12 Oct., 10 Nov. 1750; 3 Jan. 1751.
[109] 18 May, [1751], *Posthumous Works of Mrs. Chapone*, I, 31.
[110] 25 Mar., 18 May, [1751], ibid., I, 27–8, 32.

remarked to Mrs. Carter that Miss Mulso, who had argued so strenuously against the authority of parents, was herself the most dutiful of children.[111]

Miss Mulso tried poetically to console Miss Highmore in her desperate but patient love by offering the joys of friendship:

> But join the Sports of Dian's careless Maids
> And Laughing Liberty's triumphant Train.

Stella answered her Aspasia, in worthy verse, that she would turn from the 'enchanted Bow'rs' of love and that the prospect of Aspasia's friendship made her bosom glow with hope.[112]

Hester's friendship with Mrs. Carter was somewhat cooler but seems to have lasted longer. It is apparent that in their relationship Miss Mulso at that tender age (she was twenty-three when they met in 1750), was dealing with a firmer, more rational, and better informed mind than her own. By the end of 1750 Mrs. Carter was charmed with her and found her possessed of 'uncommon solidity and exactness of understanding' and had begun a correspondence. She found Miss Mulso unaccountably severe on *Amelia* and called both her and Miss Talbot 'arrant enthusiasts' in their admiration for Harriet Byron.[113] Many years later Hester's enthusiasm had simmered down, and her opinion of Richardson was more like that of Mrs. Carter: when she re-read *Pamela*, 'which I had not read since my enthusiasm for the author', she found it 'somewhat different from what I thought of it thirty years ago', but still found in Richardson 'amazing genius, unpolished indeed, either by learning or knowledge of polite life, but making its way to the heart by strokes of nature'.[114]

Mary Prescott is often mentioned in connection with the Mulso–Duncombe–Highmore group in the early 1750s. She was Pressy; the other two girls were Sukey and Hecky. She also must have had a long engagement, since in 1752 Edwards called her Miss Mulso's brother's Miss Prescott and four years later, when John Mulso married, wondered when his brother and Miss Prescott would do likewise.[115] It was over four more years before they did so, shortly after Thomas Mulso's sister married John Chapone.[116]

There are several references to visits of the three girls to North End in the early 1750s, and Miss Prescott, at least, was still visiting after Richard-

---

[111] 2 Mar. 1752; 17 Aug. 1753.

[112] 'Ode to Stella' and 'To Aspasia', FM XVI, 2, fos. 67–9.

[113] John Mulso, 6 Oct., *Letters to Gilbert White*, p. 43; Mrs. Carter to Miss Talbot, 28 Dec. 1750, 30 Mar. 1752, 18 Mar. 1754, *Letters between Mrs. Elizabeth Carter and Miss Catherine Talbot*, I, 246, 296, 356.

[114] To Elizabeth Carter, n. d., *Posthumous Works of Mrs. Chapone*, I, 175–6.

[115] To R, 29 Sept., 2 June.

[116] *Registers of Marriages of St. Mary le Bone, Middlesex*, Harleian Society Registers, LXVIII (1918), 30, under date 8 Jan. 1761; *Gentleman's Magazine*, XXXI (Jan. 1761), 43.

son moved to Parson's Green.[117] But the intimacy of the group was over. 'I believe Miss M., Miss P., and that more than agreeable set of friends, and we, love one another as well as ever', wrote Richardson to Mrs. Dewes; 'I can answer, I am sure, for our side; but we meet not near so often as we used to do. The pen and ink seems to have furnished the cement of our more intimate friendship; and that being over with me, as to writing any more for the public, the occasion of the endearment ceases. If this be not the cause of the distance, I know not to what to impute it, for I, and all mine, love them dearly; and whenever we see them, let them know that we do.'[118] Miss Highmore, at least, looked back with pleasure to 'the hours that we have so agreeably spent in the delightful retirement of North End':

> For while this pleasing subject I pursue,
> The grot, the garden, rush upon my view;
> There, in blest union, round the friendly gate,
> Instruction, Peace, and chearful Freedom wait;
> And there, a choir of list'ning nymphs appears
> Oppress'd with wonder, or dissolved in tears;
> But on her tender fears when Harriet dwells,
> And love's soft symptoms innocently tells,
> They all, with conscious smiles, those symptoms view,
> And by those conscious smiles confess them true.[119]

Another poetic effusion which is in part a memorial of this flock of singing birds, and a worthy reflection of its talents, is John Duncombe's poem *The Feminiad*.[120] Duncombe asks 'the sex's friend and constant patron', Richardson, to attend to his 'weak strains' in praise of female genius. In opposition to the proud masculine claim of intellectual superiority, he extols 'The various graces of the female lay'. It is not necessary to go back to Sappho and her Lesbian grove in search of genius: Britain has ample evidence in the works of such writers as the Matchless Orinda, the Countess of Winchelsea, and Molly Leapor. Even today, the Kentish strand has its Eliza:

> Hail, Carter, hail! your favourite name inspires
> My raptur'd breast with sympathetic fires. . . .

A comparison of Duncombe's lines with Mrs. Carter's own poem to Duck supports the poet's contention that the male and female genius are indeed on a level. Finally are celebrated the twin muses Delia and Eugenia, who

[117] R to Lady Bradshaigh, 20 Nov. 1752; R to Elizabeth Carter, 2 Oct. 1753; R to Edwards, 12 July 1756; R to Susanna Highmore, [c. 1 Aug. 1756]; R to Hester Mulso, 2 Aug. 1757.
[118] 15 Dec. 1756.
[119] Barbauld, I, clxii–iii.
[120] Written in 1751, published in 1754, and reprinted with revisions and notes in the 1783 supplement to Dodsley's *Collection of Poems*, IV, 176–91.

are identified in notes as the pupil of Spenser and Thomas Edwards, Miss Mulso, and the author's future wife, Miss Highmore.

> And, hark! what songstress shakes her warbling throat!
> Is it the nightingale, or Delia's note?

Dr. Johnson playfully suggested to Mrs. Thrale a motive for Richardson's coolness towards Miss Mulso: 'You make verses, and they are read in publick, and I know nothing about them. This very crime, I think, broke the link of amity between Richardson and Miss Mulso, after a tenderness and confidence of many years.'[121] It seems rather to have been the lady who neglected him. In 1756 he was hurt by her failure to answer a long letter. As late as 1758 he called Miss Mulso a favourite and wished she would write to him; though his hand was by that time very shaky, he was still ready to try his pen in another exchange with Hester. He seems also to have been neglected by Hester's future husband, since in 1756 he regretted not having seen that 'worthy young man' and mentioned 'his seemingly studied, at least wilful slights'.[122] But they were not permanently alienated—Richardson left John Chapone a ring in his will.

Ten years earlier, however, Miss Mulso and the rest were eagerly following the progress of the Good Man. Mrs. Donnellan hints that Hester may have served as model for the elegant characters in the new novel—whether for Harriet or the shrewish Charlotte or both is not clear: Mrs. Donnellan 'commends Miss Mulso's letters' but 'does not so well like the young woman, that is, she admires her sense and ingenuity, but thinks her only *second rate* as to *politeness of manners*; and that Richardson's *high admiration for her* has made him take her *as a model* for his genteel characters, and that is the reason they *are not* so really polished as he thinks them to be'. Perhaps she unconsciously recognized herself in the heroine —at least, after she had met her but not the hero, she did not see how Richardson could draw a man who would appear to advantage beside her.[123]

Miss Mulso expected the new work to be '(if possible) superior to Clarissa'. Richardson asked her to set her 'charming imagination' to work, and give him a few scenes. Later he asked her and Miss Highmore for prefaces: 'I will take liberties with both. You must not praise much, promise much.—But as it will be said, "preface by a friend," you may say more than it will become the writer of the piece to say.' Miss Highmore wrote her preface, but Miss Mulso refused.[124]

---

[121] 18 Apr. 1780, *Letters*, II, 343.

[122] To Susanna Highmore, [*c.* 1 Aug. 1756]; to Mrs. Chapone, 30 Aug. 1758.

[123] Mrs. Delany to Mrs. Dewes, 16 Nov. 1751, *Autobiography and Correspondence*, III, 60; R to Lady Bradshaigh, 24 Mar. 1751.

[124] Miss Mulso to Elizabeth Carter, 31 July [1751], *Posthumous Works of Mrs. Chapone*, I, 33–4; R to Miss Mulso, 27 July 1751, 20 June 1752; Susanna Highmore to Miss Mulso, two undated letters [July and Aug. 1752], Barbauld, II, 314–15, 318.

Richardson enjoyed making fun of what he considered Miss Mulso's over-exalted sentiments on the subject of love: 'But the love you describe "cannot be call'd selfish, because it must desire the happiness of its object preferably to its own." Fine talking! Pretty ideas!—Well; and where this is the case we will not call it selfish, I think. And yet what means the person possessed, but to gratify self,—or self and proposed company?' Later, in 1752, he enjoyed a controversy with her as to whether the Lady Clementina, having lost her first love, should submit to parental authority and marry Count Belvedere, whom she only liked. 'I want to have young people think, there is no such mighty business as they are apt to suppose (and so never struggle against a bias) in conquering a first love. If there were, God help ninety out of an hundred, that marry not their first flames!' He finally convinced the young lady that such a marriage was fitting, though at one time she had preferred to have the heroine die and look down from heaven with pity on her successful rival.[125]

We hear of a few other young ladies whom Richardson counted among his friends—a Miss Allen, the daughter of Dr. Allen of Sion College, a Miss Bull, a Miss Bundy, probably the daughter of Richard Bundy, the late vicar of Richardson's parish, St. Bride's—but they are shadowy figures.[126] More is known about the group of women, most of them older, whom Richardson met through Mary Delany. Around 1750 or shortly before, he became more intimate with Mrs. Delany and with her sister, Mrs. Dewes. He even found a governess for Mrs. Dewes's children.[127] At the recommendation of Mrs. Delany, a friend of hers called in June, 1750, at North End to take breakfast. She was Anne Donnellan, 'a woman of fine parts, and great politeness'. With her, she brought her young friend Isabella Sutton. Both knew *Clarissa*, and both were 'extremely earnest' with Richardson to give them the projected and already much discussed Good Man. Richardson sent them a copy of Clarissa's *Meditations*.[128] They soon became correspondents of Richardson's, and Mrs. Donnellan became a rather close friend for the rest of his life: she received a mourning ring in his will, as did Patrick Delany, though his wife and her sister did not.

Mrs. Donnellan, like Mrs. Carter, was *Mrs.* by virtue of dignity and accomplishments. She was middle-aged and still unmarried in 1750. Her father, Nehemiah Donnellan, had been Lord Chief Baron of the Exchequer in Ireland. Her friendship with Mary Delany had begun in 1729, when the latter was impressed with her 'sensible soul' and touched 'prodigiously' with the strength of her feelings for a departed friend—all Richardson's female friends seem to have felt strongly the force of friendship. Together

[125] 30 Sept. 1751; 20 June, 5 Oct. 1752; 24 Sept. 1754.
[126] To Hester Mulso, 13 July 1750; to Edwards, 27 July 1751; to Susanna Highmore, 22 June 1750.
[127] Mrs. Delany to R, 24 Apr., 15 June 1751.
[128] R to Susanna Highmore, 4 June; Anne Donnellan to R, 14 July.

they visited Mrs. Donnellan's sister, the wife of the Bishop of Killala and Achonry, for two and a half years, where they met Swift. He called Mrs. Donnellan '*the syren*', and both women became his friends and correspondents.[129] Mrs. Donnellan was noted as a singer, and back in London she went to Handel's rehearsals and frequently had the master himself to her musical evenings—she had a miniature of him, and he left her fifty guineas in his will.[130] Richardson could have met Handel at her house, but his compliments to him in *Sir Charles Grandison* were probably a tribute to Mrs. Donnellan's enthusiasm.[131] Mary Poole Way, writing to Mrs. Barbauld, remembered her as a frequent visitor at Richardson's 'house in town and country'—'a venerable old lady, with sharp-piercing eyes'.[132]

In the summer of 1750 Mrs. Donnellan and Miss Sutton went to Epsom, and Richardson's correspondence with her had a chance to ripen. By fall he had shown her his correspondence with Belfour, one of his prize possessions. By 1752 we find her visiting North End.[133]

Miss Sutton was the daughter of Sir Robert Sutton, a well-known diplomat; in 1750 she was an orphan, living with Mrs. Donnellan, who commended 'her understanding and great genius for reasoning on religious subjects', but thought her 'not acknowledging nor affectionate enough'. Her mother, the Countess of Sunderland, had been an old friend of Mrs. Delany.[134] Her father had been a patron of William Warburton, and she was still connected with Richardson's former friend and Edwards's enemy. She was also a friend of the learned Mrs. Carter. She was somewhat backward about entering into a correspondence with Richardson and about giving her advice as to what his Good Man should be like, but when Richardson seemed to set store by it, she did enclose a letter with one of Mrs. Donnellan's—still with no opinion on the future Sir Charles. She visited North End in the spring of 1751 and spent a week there in 1752. But the tone of their correspondence is never as playful as that of Richardson with his other young ladies; she is always formal, not to say stiff. After 1753 their friendship seems to have languished. Perhaps the reason was that which Richardson hinted to Mrs. Dewes: 'Miss Sutton is very well. You have an high opinion of her: but I persuade myself that you know not fully her endowments and abilities. She is prudent above

[129] Mrs. Pendarves to Ann Granville, n. d. [1729], 8 June 1731; to Swift, 21 July 1733 *Autobiography and Correspondence*, I, 223, 276, 417.

[130] Ibid., I, 457–8, 532–4, III, 383; will of Anne Donnellan, P.C.C. St. Eloi 192, dated 12 Nov. 1758, proved 22 May 1762; will of Handel, P.C.C. Arran 132, codicil dated 11 Apr. 1759, proved 26 Apr. 1759.

[131] SH, I, 158, 366–7; VI, 215.   [132] I, cxc.

[133] R to Susanna Highmore, 20 July; R to Lady Bradshaigh, 25 Nov. 1750, 20 Nov. 1752; Mrs. Delany to Mrs. Dewes, 14 Oct. 1752, *Autobiography and Correspondence*, III, 163.

[134] Will of Sir Robert Sutton, P.C.C. Edmunds 749, dated 4 Feb. 1744, proved 3 Sept. 1746; Mrs. Delany to Mrs. Dewes, 7 Nov. 1751, *Autobiography and Correspondence*, III, 56; Mrs. Delany to R, 24 Apr. 1751.

her years, but is too industrious to conceal her talents. I too seldom see
her. I live in the city; and my side of Temple-Bar abounds with nuisances.'[135]

A more congenial connection was another friend of Mrs. Delany and
Mrs. Dewes, Sarah Kirkham Chapone. Her husband, John Chapone
(originally Capon), was a clergyman who lived near Cheltenham, and her
friendship with Richardson was, therefore, almost purely epistolary, but
since she was a fluent writer, as copious as Richardson himself, this perhaps made little difference. Before making her acquaintance through the
pen Richardson during the summer of 1750 read in manuscript and possibly printed her anonymous *Remarks on Mrs. Muilman's Letter to the Right
Honourable The Earl of Chesterfield*, a polite but firm reproof of a fallen
woman, whose apology had, in Mrs. Chapone's view, not shown humility
and true penitence and who, in addition, had shown Deistic tendencies. In
it she complimented Richardson as 'the most masterly intellectual Painter,
that has adorn'd this Age and Nation'.[136] In her first letter she admitted
her authorship of this pamphlet, since he must recognize the handwriting.
On the basis of this and, one should hope, other of her writings, Richardson called her one of the best of female writers. Later she wrote a discussion of the sense in which God created man in His image, a problem
on which she wanted Richardson's opinion.[137]

Mrs. Chapone and Mrs. Delany had been friends when both were girls,
and according to Mrs. Delany she 'had an uncommon genius and intrepid
spirit, which though really innocent, alarmed my father, and made him
uneasy at my great attachment to her'; but she was a 'perfect creature'.[138]
In 1750, when her correspondence with Richardson began, she had two
sons and two daughters living. The eldest, John, was destined to be briefly
the husband of Hester Mulso. Mrs. Dewes had sent him to Richardson in
July 1750 with a letter of introduction, praising him as 'a remarkably
sober, good young man', and Richardson was 'greatly taken' with him
and found him sensible, ingenious, and modest.[139] He became an attorney.
The youngest boy, only twelve, never grew to manhood. The two girls
were Sally, her 'Brown Maid', and Catherine, the future lady of Sir John
Boyd. Perhaps they had tamed her, since from her correspondence with
Richardson one would not imagine that she had ever alarmed anyone's
father. She is pious, earnest, verbose, and rather gushing.

She had long been anxious to meet Richardson when he sent her a copy

---

[135] Anne Donnellan to R, 14 July 1750; R to Anne Donnellan, 20 July 1750; Anne Donnellan
to R, 17 Aug. 1750; R to Edwards, 27 May 1751; Anne Donnellan to R, 26 Mar. 1752; R to
Mrs. Dewes, 21 June 1752.
[136] P. 19.
[137] Mrs. Chapone to R, 12 Oct. 1750; R to Mrs. Chapone, 19 Oct. 1750; R to Sarah Wescomb,
11 Sept. 1753; Mrs. Chapone to R, 3 June 1758; R to Mrs. Chapone, 27 June 1758; Mrs.
Chapone to R, 23 Aug. 1758.
[138] *Autobiography and Correspondence*, I, 15-16.   [139] 8 July, 20 Aug.

of Clarissa's *Meditations*: her heart had 'talk'd of him for years', and *Pamela* had helped mould the tender years of her children—'the blooming Virgin, replete with every Grace, entered their ductile Hearts, and diffused a faint Resemblance of her Sweetness of Manners, and gave some small Tincture of the Justness and Solidity of her Sentiments to their puerile Thoughts and Performances'. Her youngest boy had written a sermon on a text from Parson Williams, 'The liberal Soul shall be fat', but it had unfortunately been eaten by rats. 'Vile Vermin', wrote Richardson. 'I ever had a kind of natural Aversion to that Species of Animals. I shall now hate them worse than ever.' Sally was accustomed to meeting any unusual situation by asking what Clarissa would do. Richardson, Mrs. Chapone soon found, was like a lodestone—all lovers of God clung to him. She was in ecstasies when he sent her two daughters and a friend copies of Clarissa's *Meditations*— indeed she was usually in ecstasies when she thought of that heroine. Richardson's portrait was even more warmly welcomed: 'such Doves Eyes—such a sweet Benevolence in the Countenance'.[140]

Richardson suggested that she write a denunciation of Lady Vane's memoirs, but when she hesitated to soil her fingers with such filth, he agreed that the woman was unworthy of her pen. He soon invited her daughters to visit him, and in June 1751 the Brown Maid accepted and set out. Sally was evidently popular in the Richardson household, and though after a decent interval her mother suggested she go on to Mrs. Dewes, Richardson pressed for a longer visit, and Sally stayed on. She stayed on until October 1752 and in her sorrow at parting with the Richardson family had a hysteric fit at Bush Hill. She left for only a few months and then returned. Mrs. Chapone herself feared that she would never meet Richardson 'below the Stars' but would have to wait until the next life, but as we have seen, she did not have to wait quite so long, since Richardson stopped in Cheltenham when he brought Sally back in the summer of 1753 and left his daughter Patty with the Chapones, where his visit 'guilded the Roof as with the Gold of Opher' and revived the dimly burning flame of 'the dusky Torch of Life'. Patty stayed for several months, went on with Sally to Mrs. Dewes for a while, and when Sally accompanied Mrs. Delany to Ireland, returned to the Chapones and was finally delivered to her aunt and uncle Leake in late July 1754.[141]

---

[140] Mrs. Chapone to R, 12 Oct., 24 Nov., 15 Dec. 1750; R to Mrs. Chapone, 6 Dec. 1750; Mrs. Chapone to R, 21 Jan., 20 Mar. 1751.

[141] R to Mrs. Chapone, 6 Dec. 1750; Mrs. Chapone to R, 15 Dec. 1750; R to Mrs. Chapone, 11 Jan. 1751; Mrs. Chapone to R, 25 Feb., 20 Mar. 1751; R to Mrs. Chapone, 25 Mar. 1751; Mrs. Chapone to R, 17 June, 18 Nov. 1751; R to Mrs. Chapone, 22 Nov. 1751; Mrs. Chapone to R, 9 Dec. 1751; R to Isabella Sutton, 24 July 1752; Mrs. Chapone to R, 23 Oct. 1752; R to Mrs. Delany, 14 Mar. 1753; Mrs. Chapone to R, 9 Dec. 1751; Mrs. Chapone to R, 8 Sept. 1753; R to Mrs. Chapone, 19 Sept. 1753; Mrs. Chapone to R, 21 May 1754; R to Mrs. Chapone, 28 May 1754; Mrs. Chapone to R, 8 June, 15 June, 31 July 1754.

Mrs. Chapone was no more entirely submissive than Richardson's other female correspondents. She found that he took too strict a view on the submission of women: Clarissa should not have been so meek in allowing her father to keep the estate her grandfather had left her. Richardson seemed to her to have promulgated the harsh idea that women should never be independent and thus to have denied that they are members of society and free agents. Nor was she convinced by his unanswerable arguments on this subject to Miss Mulso. She clearly contradicted his hints that she had not attentively enough read his letters. In one respect she dared to prefer Anna Howe even to Clarissa—Miss Howe is more simple and does not reflect so much when she does right. Richardson's answer to her arguments was rather lacking in clarity and cogency, but as usual he enjoyed the exchange—he loved 'to stimulate a Genius'. He found that she had not read him carefully enough and that she and Miss Mulso, two of his most ingenious readers, had mistaken his drift. They were, he decided, in substantial agreement, though against her hint that he took rather a bargaining view of marriage, he reaffirmed the necessity of prudence and the justice of a girl's marrying a man she does not love if her family insists—not that he was in favour of compulsion in such matters, either.[142]

Like the young songstresses, Mrs. Delany and her friends followed the progress of *Sir Charles Grandison* with interest, and both Mrs. Delany and Mrs. Donnellan gave advice.

Late in 1751 Mrs. Donnellan arrived in Ireland and brought Mrs. Delany news of the Good Man. At about the same time Sally Chapone sent her mother an account of the hero, and Mrs. Chapone urged Richardson not to hide him from the world.[143] Early in 1752 Mrs. Donnellan also urged him to publish, especially to counteract the bad example of Captain Booth in *Amelia*,[144] and Richardson responded by again asking for her help and that of Mrs. Delany 'in describing a scene or two in upper life. Miss Sutton is so intent upon *practising* (at least I tell her so) the racketting life, that she cannot give me one line of the *theory*.' Mrs. Donnellan suggested an episode showing how contemptible old people are when they try to imitate the frivolity of youth, and she thought that the hero might properly expatiate on the exaggerated modern admiration in high life for fashion and taste.[145] By 9 November 1752 she had read more of the book, and in response to Richardson's desire 'for correction, not praise', she suppressed her admiration and pointed out a few faults: she was not fond of

[142] Mrs. Chapone to R, 22 Feb., [Mar.], 1752; R to Mrs. Chapone, 18 Apr. 1752.
[143] Mrs. Delany to Mrs. Dewes, 7 Nov., *Autobiography and Correspondence*, III, 54; Mrs. Chapone to R, 18 Nov.
[144] 11 Feb. See also Mrs. Delany to Mrs. Dewes, 18 Jan., *Autobiography and Correspondence* III, 79.
[145] 22 Feb., 26 Mar.

the idea of a double love, though Richardson had managed that 'unnatural affair' as well as it could be managed; she found that the glorious Clementina 'annihilated' the merely mortal heroine Harriet. 'I have but one fault to find with Sir Charles; and that is, he has no fault, no passions; indeed, Sir, you have a charming hand at drawing angels, how dare we poor mortals converse with you, and let you see our weaknesses?' Sir Charles's sister Charlotte was too unlike her brother, too ill-natured—especially in her humourous remarks about old maids, a question in which Mrs. Donnellan admitted she had a personal concern.

By September 1753, two months before Richardson published the first four volumes of his novel, Mrs. Chapone had read some of it, and Richardson promised to send her the third and fourth volumes, which no one else had, and did so. Shortly after the publication of the first volumes Richardson promised the Reverend John Chapone that he would send him and his wife the next two volumes, in hopes of her suggestions and judgement. Mrs. Chapone had two objections, to the compromise with Catholicism which Sir Charles was willing to make in view of his marriage with Clementina and (a minor objection, delicately hinted) to his being so perfect as to excite despair rather than emulation—but then 'whoever found fault with the Exactness of a Geometrical Rule?' After the publication of the last volume she indicated another objection, a renewal of her old argument: Sir Charles's views on the authority of the family in marital arrangements and on the inferiority of women. If she had been his sister Charlotte, 'he should have lower'd his top-sails'.[146]

Most of the women we have mentioned knew the celebrated Mrs. Carter, who was to become still more celebrated in 1758, when her translation of Epictetus appeared. Up to that time her celebrity was based mainly on a small and not distinguished body of poetry, her translations of Crousaz's *Examen de l'Essay de Monsieur Pope sur l'homme* and Count Algarotti's *Newtonianismo per le dame*, and her unusual linguistic abilities: she knew Latin, Greek, Hebrew, French, Italian, Spanish, and German and later learned some Portuguese and Arabic.[147] She educated her half-brother Henry for the University, to the surprise of his friends. But she was a housekeeper as well as a scholar, skilled with ladle, needle, and pen. She was not devoid of independence in her judgement of the classics, since she found the *Odyssey* tedious and low and was prevented from liking Pindar by her lack of interest in races.[148] She was born in 1717, in Deal, which was her home all of her life, though from 1757 on, especially after the success of the Epictetus made her independent, she spent a good deal

---

[146] Mrs. Chapone to R, 8 Sept.; R to Mrs. Chapone, 19 Sept.; the Rev. John Chapone to R, 3 Oct.; R to the Rev. John Chapone, 26 Nov; Mrs. Chapone to R, 10 Dec., 21 May 1754.
[147] Pennington, *Memoirs of the Life of Mrs. Elizabeth Carter* I, 12–14, 16.
[148] *Letters between Mrs. Elizabeth Carter and Miss Catherine Talbot*, I, 110, 240–1.

of time in London. Her father was a clergyman, and she lived with him until he died in 1774. Though she is said to have been somewhat of a romp when young (she went to dances), she was, by the time she knew Richardson, settled in her ways, pious, and earnest, though not without humour. She could defend heathen morality and Henry Fielding, but she refused to read authors whose personal characters were not good, who were likely to injure the cause of religion and virtue, or who had 'the least tendency towards levelling and democratic principles'.[149] Among the works she would not read were Sterne's *Sentimental Journey* and the later books of Voltaire, and she found nothing good to say of Rousseau, Hume, or Chesterfield's *Letters to His Son*: 'Never listen to the half learning, the perverted understanding, and pert ridicule of French philosophers, and beaux esprits.'[150] She is said to have devoted herself to the maiden state early in life, though she once had a suitor, whom she refused because he had 'published some verses, which, though not absolutely indecent, yet seemed to show too light and licentious a turn of mind'.[151] Miss Mulso hoped that 'armour-proof against the "frivolous bolt of Cupid"' as she was, with her low opinion of the lordly sex, she would approve of Miss Mulso's particular choice—'if you *can* love a *man*, I expect you will love him'.[152] The tone of her correspondence with females, especially with Catherine Talbot, her most intimate friend from 1741 on, might have given rise to another sort of gossip had she lived in a later age, and there might even have been references by amateur psychologists to her frequent and severe headaches; but no one in her time doubted her strict virtue, nor is there any reason to doubt it. She was an early friend of Dr. Johnson, and she wrote two of the five numbers of the *Rambler* which, according to Johnson, were not his own (the others were by her friends and his, Miss Mulso, Miss Talbot, and Richardson).[153]

Her resentment at Richardson's publishing her 'Ode to Wisdom' has been mentioned, as well as the amicable outcome of that little dispute. She had little connection with Richardson until *Sir Charles* was almost completed, and her connection then was largely the work of her friends Miss Mulso and especially Miss Talbot. As early as 1750 she sent the latter a little advice, undoubtedly at Richardson's request, about the Good Man: he must be superior to false glory and false shame and show 'a steady opposition to the false maxims of the world in essential points, and a perfectly good-natured compliance in trifles'. On first reading, she did not like Richardson's *Rambler* essay—one would think him in one respect a

---

[149] Ibid., I, 400, 403, 16, 207, 295, 245–6; Pennington, *Memoirs*, I, 444.

[150] *Letters between Mrs. Elizabeth Carter and Miss Catherine Talbot*, II, 166, 272; Pennington, *Memoirs*, II, 156, 163; *Letters between Mrs. Elizabeth Carter and Miss Catherine Talbot*, II, 146, 274, 312.

[151] Pennington, *Memoirs*, I, 29.

[152] *Posthumous Works of Mrs. Chapone*, I, 90, 121.   [153] Boswell, *Life*, I, 203.

Mahometan for his supposition 'that Providence designed one half of the human species for idiots and slaves'; when Miss Talbot argued her into a second reading, however, she was less unfavourable. In 1752 Miss Talbot was still reproaching her for not loving Richardson as she ought, 'but when Sir Charles appears, he will make you pay for all'. For robbing Clarissa of her 'delightful owl', she owes Sir Charles or one of his friends a poem. Miss Talbot hoped that when they met Miss Mulso would convert her to Richardson; after the meeting Mrs. Carter referred to Richardson as 'her friend and your friend, and I am sorry I have no pretensions to say my friend, though we are upon mighty civil terms, and write very handsome postscripts about each other'. But in May 1753 they did see each other. He 'heartily abused and perplexed' her, but they arranged that she was to visit North End. She stayed two days, and though she much regretted not going there in company with Miss Talbot, she was sociable and good-humoured and on the whole enjoyed herself.[154] The visit led to a little flurry of correspondence between her and Richardson during the rest of 1753, a correspondence much less formal than their earlier one—there are even jokes.[155] Richardson's opinion of her learning and genius was high: she is, he reported, ranked among the English classics, on what basis is not clear.[156]

After her first bit of advice, Mrs. Carter seems to have lost touch with Sir Charles until after her visit to North End, but she evidently heard or read of him there, since soon afterwards she wrote, 'I am undone for Sir Charles Grandison. A hundred questions have been asked me about him, to which I make no other answer but that I am in love with him, and shall have a very bad opinion of every lady who is not in love with him too, as soon as he makes his appearance.'[157] Richardson sent her four volumes in September and two of them in half binding shortly before publication, which she promised not to let out of her hands, for her own sake as well as his, since, to the honour of Deal, the ladies there were so impatient for the hero that 'I apprehend there would be so much scratching & clawing that it would be impossible to keep him in my possession & he would run some Hazard of being scattered to the four Winds of Heaven'. Though she defended Charlotte Grandison (who made a vain effort to resist the masculine superiority of her brother), she admired the work highly, especially the character of Clementina. But she still preferred *Clarissa*— an opinion with which the more enthusiastic Miss Talbot was forced to agree.[158] It has been suggested that Richardson, who did occasionally slip

---

[154] Mrs. Carter, 28 Dec. 1750, 4 Mar., 24 Mar. 1751; Miss Talbot, 22 Apr., n. d. [answered 12 Aug.], 1752; Mrs. Carter, 12 Aug. 1752, 13 May, 17 May 1753, *Letters between Mrs. Elizabeth Carter and Miss Catherine Talbot*, I, 246–7, 254–5, 258, 298, 304, 307, 324–6.

[155] 9 June–13 Oct. 1753.   [156] To Edwards, 25 July 1754.   [157] 22 June.

[158] Mrs. Carter to Miss Talbot, 21 Sept., *Letters between Mrs. Elizabeth Carter and Mis Catherine Talbot*, I, 342; R to Mrs. Carter, 2 Oct.; Mrs. Carter to R, 6 Oct., 13 Oct.; Mrs. Carte

private allusions into his books, was pointing at Mrs. Carter when he had Harriet remark: 'Who, I, a woman, know any thing of Latin and Greek! I know but one Lady who is mistress of both; and she finds herself so much an owl among the birds, that she wants of all things to be thought to have unlearned them.'[159] The allusion is highly probable, but we know of no evidence that Richardson was right—Mrs. Carter seems to have been content enough as an owl.

Richardson was never intimate with her, but they remained friends. He printed her Epictetus, by subscription—he even felt that the men and women of Kent would be shamed if they did not make her list of subscribers a county cause.[160] The edition was a success—more copies had to be printed, and there were later editions. Mrs. Carter made a thousand pounds.[161] Shortly after Richardson's death she was planning to have her complete poems printed by his widow.[162] Mrs. Barbauld prints an epitaph on Richardson which she says was written by Mrs. Carter, and though her nephew and biographer doubted the attribution and found it 'very inferior to her usual style', so far as we can tell it is worthy of her Muse.[163]

Mrs. Carter's friend Catherine Talbot was a good deal closer to Richardson, especially during the time of the composition of *Sir Charles*, than she herself was. She was thirty in 1750. Her father, Edward Talbot, was the son of the Bishop of Salisbury (later of Durham); he had died young and on his deathbed had recommended to his father's notice three young clergymen, all of whom were aided by Miss Talbot's grandfather, all of whom became bishops, and all of whom were close friends. They were Thomas Secker, who became Archbishop of Canterbury in 1758, Martin Benson, Bishop of Gloucester, and Joseph Butler, Bishop of Durham. With Secker, Miss Talbot's relations were almost those of a daughter. Mrs. Talbot, who outlived her daughter, had been a close friend of Secker's wife, Benson's sister, and during her lifetime Miss Talbot and her mother lived with Secker's family; they continued to live with him after her death in 1748. Secker had been Bishop of Oxford since 1737; in 1750 he was made Dean of St. Paul's but remained Bishop of Oxford; the family divided their time between the Deanery in London and the Bishop's seat at Cuddesdon, near Oxford.[164]

---

to Miss Talbot, 10 Dec. 1753, 18 Mar. 1754; Miss Talbot to Mrs. Carter, 4 Apr. 1754, *Letters between Mrs. Elizabeth Carter and Miss Catherine Talbot*, I, 346-7, 356, 358.

[159] George Birkbeck Hill in *Johnsonian Miscellanies*, II, 11n. The passage is in SH, I, 69.

[160] To Hester Mulso, 2 Aug. 1757.

[161] Pennington, *Memoirs*, I, 159, 203-4, 207-8.

[162] Mrs. Carter to Miss Talbot, 26 Sept. 1761, *Letters between Mrs. Elizabeth Carter and Miss Catherine Talbot*, I, 506.   [163] I, ccxii; Pennington, *Memoirs*, II, 119.

[164] See Montagu Pennington, ed., *The Works of the Late Miss Catherine Talbot*, 7th edn. (London, 1809); Beilby Porteus and George Stinton, eds., *The Works of Thomas Secker*, 3rd edn. (Dublin, 1775).

Miss Talbot had connections in a world more exalted than that usually frequented by Richardson's friends. Lady Anson and Jemima, Marchioness Grey, were close friends, and in 1752 she became a friend of the Duchess of Somerset, Thomson's 'blooming and benevolent' Hertford. She herself was a very pious young woman, not so learned as her friend Mrs. Carter but sufficiently aware of books. She read and wrote French and Italian with fluency, though not with complete accuracy. The family at Cuddesdon generally read some solid work, often a history or memoir, in the evening, and Miss Talbot also had a broad taste in *belles lettres*: Pascal was a favourite, but so was Montaigne, and she read with delight Ariosto, Molière, Cervantes, Mme. de Sévigné, and a good many others.[165] She was not, like her friend, invincibly averse to matrimony from an early age and argued with her on the subject.[166] She was inclined to resignation and gentle melancholy. 'Apres tout je n'aime pas trop les Tragedies', she wrote after seeing Edmund Smith's *Phædra and Hippolitus*, 'elles donnent trop aux Passions, elles les representent trop importantes—elles alterent la belle Tranquillité—elles font resouvenir des plus desagréables Momens de la Vie.' Such books as sermons 'refresh my Mind vastly more than all the French Amusing ones'.[167] She gradually became more listless and at last sickly, so that after forty she was an invalid, though she lived on to 1770. She wrote essays, poetry, and imitations of Ossian, but was known especially for her religious *Reflections on the Seven Days of the Week*, which was quite popular and ran through many editions.

She had evidently been an admirer of *Pamela*, though a rather condescending one, since she wished its author would compile a book of useful sentiments 'in an amusing and lively way' for the benefit of farmers and spinners. She was delighted by *Clarissa* before she was a friend of its author. 'Are you so happy as to be acquainted with these Richardsons?' she wrote to Mrs. Carter in 1747. 'I am sure they must be excellent people, and most delightful acquaintance.' She had met him at least by early 1750, when she and her mother called to see a portrait of Clarissa. By December Richardson was calling on her, and she was asking Mrs. Carter to send her hints for his Good Man. The friendship grew rapidly, and by the end of the year she had read the first volumes of his correspondence with Belfour. By the middle of 1753 Richardson called Miss Talbot 'the Queen of all the Ladies I venerate'.[168]

She took her duty of giving advice on the Good Man more seriously

---

[165] *Letters between Mrs. Elizabeth Carter and Miss Catherine Talbot*, I, 184, 191, 26–8, 47, 51.
[166] 8 June 1751, ibid., I, 267–8.
[167] 'Journal', 3 Dec., 17 Dec. 1751, B.M. Add. MS. 46,690.
[168] Miss Talbot to Mrs. Carter, 6 Jan. 1745, 28 Dec. 1747, *Letters between Mrs. Elizabeth Carter and Miss Catherine Talbot*, I, 58, 161; R to Chauncy [12 or 19 Feb. 1750]; Miss Talbot to Mrs. Carter, 17 Dec. 1750, *Letters between Mrs. Elizabeth Carter and Miss Catherine Talbot*, I, 244; Miss Talbot to R, [Dec. 1750?]; R to Mrs. Carter, 4 July 1753.

than the many other ladies who were asked for suggestions. Bishop Secker
evidently also promised to help, but there is no sign that he did so:
Edwards speaks of the bishops, Sir Charles's godfathers, and proceeds,
'Your silence about my Lord of Oxford makes me fear that you are not
yet much the better for his neighborhood [he had recently moved to his
new Deanery]; . . . and yet were it otherwise, you would surely have mentioned some of your frequent interviews.'[169] But Miss Talbot had been
more obliging. By the end of 1751 she had been favoured with a sight of
parts of the book. On 20 November Richardson called in the evening and
stayed for three hours ('I was really ashamed of having tied down . . . so
remarkable a Genius to sit Tete a Tete with poor Me'), and she noted that
his Harriet had been their 'amusement a day or two'. Secker read the novel
while she and her mother worked; 'Harriet Biron even now is a most
agreeable Companion, tho not by any means I imagine & hope what she
will be.' Her hopes were justified. She had, of course, been expecting the
entrance of the hero, and he came: 'And now what shall I say of Sir
Charles—My long sought & never to be found, Ideal.—The World of
Angels is made up of Sir Charles's.' From then on, her enthusiasm knows
no bounds. She must indeed have been waiting for someone to love, since
she fell in love with Sir Charles Grandison. 'C'est mon Idéal. Enfin le
Voilá. Il n'y a Compagnie ni Amusement dont Je me soucie quand nous
avons cette Lecture qui nous plait également à Tous. J'y trouve pour mon
particulier mille instructions—L'Excellent Auteur etoit avec moi asséz
longtemps hier Matin.' Charlotte Grandison reminds her of 'our Dear
Lost Friend', probably Mrs. Secker. 'What Publick Gayety would I not
give up for my own dear Fireside & Sir Charles!' When she finds herself
in low spirits in company, she reasons herself into a good humour by the
thought that 'Harriet's Soul . . . would have been above them Sir Charles
out of the Case, & so I who have no Sir Charles made an effort & got
above them'. Richardson has called after church and she has done all the
talking and thus missed the profit of his conversation: 'Passe pour les
Gens de Commun, mais un homme tel que lui—Fi Parleuse, Babillarde!'
But after supper Sir Charles (and Fontenelle) put her in 'un Dolce Oblio
de toute Tristesse'. She is keeping her knowledge of *Sir Charles* secret.
'Oh! Miss Carter did you ever call Pigmalion a fool, for making an image
and falling in love with it—and do you know that you and I are two
Pigmalionesses? Did not Mr. Richardson ask us for some traits of his good
man's character? And did not we give him some? And has not he gone
and put these and his own charming ideas into a book and formed a Sir
Charles Grandison?'[170]

---

[169] 8 May 1751.
[170] 'Journal', 20 Nov., 22 Nov., 3 Dec., 8 Dec., 9 Dec., 18 Dec., 20 Dec.; Miss Talbot to
Mrs. Carter, 23 Dec., *Letters between Mrs. Elizabeth Carter and Miss Catherine Talbot*, I, 291.

Her reading was not merely passive rapture. Early in 1752 we find her at work on the manuscript, 'looking over correctly the 5th of the admirable Books. They improve on every Review. Oh Sir Charles! My Idol before I knew Thee! My Almost Adorable *Idæal*! Charming Excellent Author. Him I shall see to Morrow—Marcus [Bishop Benson] is here all today. Is not this Happiness enough? Does not my Cup run Over? How shall I deserve it!' On 4 January she saw Richardson for an hour and a half and did much reading and criticizing, and though 'some bewitching Old Mss stole away' three-quarters of an hour she should have employed more usefully, she felt that Sir Charles '(Idolo Mio!)' would not have much disapproved of most of her employments. There are many more records in her journal of visits from Richardson and readings of *Sir Charles* about this time. On the eighteenth of January she was reading 'the 10th No of our Incomparable Manuscript which I am reviewing as carefully & I could almost say as conscientiously as I can. Never did I spend in Town so agreeable a Winter as this has been.' Four days later her occupations were agreeably interrupted by Richardson: 'Javois beaucoup sur le Cœur touchant son Livre. Cetoit une belle Querelle.' She had learned to love solitude and looked back 'with Wonder & Pity on those Giddy Years (those Harriet Byron Years)' when fine company was necessary to her. Her task of correcting the manuscript seems to have been a real joy, a significant occupation in an age when ladies were permitted very few significant occupations, and she took it seriously: 'I am sure I owe him all the pains I can take for his goodness in consulting me.'[171] One hopes she never knew how many ladies he had consulted.

During the summer two close friends, Bishops Butler and Benson, died, and she returned to town in a depressed mood, but in spite of loss of appetite and sleep, nervous headaches and cold feet, she enjoyed an agreeable party at North End. Addressing her friend 'Angelina' (Lady Grey), to whom much of her journal is written, she mentions a call on Mr. and Mrs. Richardson: 'That is a Friendship Dear Ang: that you know nothing of, it is a great good to us, but I have no mind you should know of it till I have heard your unprejudiced Opinion of Sir Charles—I wish one could have it Now, when it might be of use *indeed*.' On 14 October her family went with 'le bon Ami R:' as far as Kensington and 'Eugenius' (Secker) gave him 'Les meilleures Avis du Monde sur son Ouvrage, & lui les recevoit avec un bon sens & une bonne humeur qui lui est particulier parmi tous les Auteurs. Il sçait si bien deffendre ses opinions sans jamais s'opiniatrer. Il est si docile aux Avis ou il y à lieu d'en donner et si ferme dans son jugèment quand des sottes gens le critiquent mal à propos.' On the twenty-third she dispatched four volumes in an uninterrupted evening. On the last day of the year she noted among the blessings of 1752

171 'Journal', 2 Jan., 4 Jan., 18 Jan., 22 Jan., 17 Feb., 21 Feb.

(along with a new friendship and a new taste for music) that it had engaged her 'in I hope a very useful employment'.[172]

Early in 1753 a proposal for Miss Talbot's hand, by a man she had never met, was made through her friends, who persuaded her that he would make an eligible husband; but his father would not guarantee enough money, and her friends changed her mind.[173] But in the middle of the year she met another man, thirteen years younger than herself, who evidently did make a strong impression on her sensitive heart. He was George Berkeley, son of the philosopher-bishop, who was then at Oxford. His mother and his fifteen-year-old sister, Julia, visited Cuddesdon late in June,[174] and the brother soon followed. 'Ce que Sr Charles etoit a 18. G[eorge] l'est. Il est tout a fait aimable.' He has all the virtues of the Good Man: he is kind to his sister, he is pious, he worries about the religion and morals of his servants, he is a good student yet gay and diverting, he never speaks ill of people. She is soon referring to him as 'Sir G:'.[175] To Mrs. Carter, who might not have appreciated such raptures, she says little about her new friends, but she does mention that they fixed their whole attention on Mrs. Carter's *Rambler*, 'and if any person would have been pleased to fix the attention of Sir Charles Grandison, when he was about eighteen [George was two months short of twenty], they need not be mortified at engaging Mr. Berkeley's'.[176] Her journal at this time is full of flutterings, vague regrets, mild panics, even a sort of resigned bitterness—her only happiness is to bury herself in solitude. George is her brother. The Berkeleys go to Oxford, and she is sad; but they return. Soon she is reading '*The Book*' to them. They do not know her connection with it: Eugenius makes a mystery of the matter, which adds much to the amusement. 'Je suis charmée pour mes Enfans du bien que leur fera cette Lecture. Je me rejoüis de les voir applaudir ce que m'a fait tant de Plaisir & a quoi Je m'interesse tant. J'ecoute J'observe avec les emotions d'une Mere, d'une Amie. Cest un vrai Charme.' Miss Talbot's motherliness towards her new *enfants* leads to moods of gaiety and to moods of gloom. The reading continues. One evening they are all longing for the book but are too delicate to ask Eugenius to bring it out, and he punishes them by saying nothing and condemning them to an evening of ennui and fretting. But there are other charming evenings. 'Yet I feel too much anxiety about this Book to have the happiness unmingled. So formed to do good! So liable to petty Criticisms!'[177] She hates to leave the country scenes, the

---

[172] Ibid., 6 Oct., 9 Oct., 14 Oct., 23 Oct., 31 Dec.

[173] Ibid., 'From Decr to June'.

[174] Miss Talbot to Mrs. Carter, 19 June, *Letters between Mrs. Elizabeth Carter and Miss Catherine Talbot*, I, 332.

[175] 'Journal', 15 July, 27 July.

[176] 21 July, *Letters between Mrs. Elizabeth Carter and Miss Catherine Talbot*, I, 335.

[177] 'Journal', 30 July, 27 Aug., 28 Aug., 6 Sept., 8 Sept.

charming weather, and the hour's reading every evening to go to the races at Chipping Norton and turn her mind to dances, dresses, and idleness.[178] And in October she is forced to go up to the empty town. Her journal breaks off, to resume in wearisome London.[179] George's sister, Julia, is now the friend to whom it is written.

That her friendship for her new-found brother lasted longer and was a serious one is shown by a note which George Berkeley's wife, Eliza Frinsham, the learned heiress whom he married in March 1761, wrote on a set of verses Miss Talbot wrote 'just before her only Love as she told me married me'.[180] George, by this time Vicar of Bray, would not permit Miss Talbot to visit his betrothed before their wedding, though Eliza languished to meet one of whom she had heard so much. 'I knew not until after I was married the tender attachment that had subsisted between that by me tenderly beloved pair.' They had loved for six years before their parents became aware of it and forbade the match. When her angelic friend Miss Talbot asked the new wife how she had learned of the attachment, 'I replied Myself the first time I ever saw you together—I asked her how she liked me. She replied I thought I must have fainted at your feet when saluting you as his bride. . . . She used frequently to say—that from the day she was obliged by *Parental* Authority to give him up for herself— she never ceased to Pray that God wd vouchsafe to send him the woman in the world the most calculated to render him happy—adding then and when she was dying—If ever any Prayer was answered by God that has been.' The verses are a defiance of the tyrant Cupid—she will not give in to the black despair he leads but will find patience in wisdom and cheerfulness in duty:

> Think'st thou blind boy my stubborn heart
>   Will e'er of thee complain?
> Or *own* it *drags in reason's Spite*
>   An Heavy, Hopeless Chain.

In the fall of 1753 Miss Talbot visited her new friend, the Duchess of Somerset, and that family also began reading *Sir Charles*, which had now started to appear. She wondered if it was right to conceal the fact that she was already well acquainted with the novel, but she did so. The distinguished company found objections to make—Harriet was too talkative and too vain; but on the whole they were pleased. The Duchess herself owned that if Charlotte Grandison's letter had not relieved her anxiety

---

[178] Miss Talbot to Mrs. Carter, 8 Sept., *Letters between Mrs. Elizabeth Carter and Miss Catherine Talbot*, I, 340. See also 'Journal', 6 Sept.

[179] 10 Sept.; letter to Julia Berkeley, 30 Oct. This letter and the remainder of her extant 'Journal' are in B.M. Add. MS. 46,689.

[180] B.M. Add. MS. 39,316, fos. 41-4. See also Mrs. Berkeley's letter in the *Gentleman's Magazine*, LXVI (1796), ii, 631-2.

about the almost ravished Harriet 'She could not have eat a bit of supper'. So much for those who think the aristocracy heartless. Indeed the Duchess was so tender-hearted that it was a recommendation with her that the novel was not quite so moving as its predecessor: 'The D[uche]ss like Mrs B[erkeley] thinks it the most pleasing & most useful Book she ever read. Clarissa she admired but was too much affected with it.' But she was not to be spared all suffering: 'The Scenes of Clementina's Madness &c were so affecting I could scarce see through my Tears to read, & we both went in to Supper with hearts so heavy that we were forced to have recourse afterwards to some silly Riddles to make us laugh.'[181]

Mrs. Carter hints at Miss Talbot's role in revising the novel when she says, 'Every body I am sure will be struck with the advantageous difference of the language, though but few can observe it with the peculiar pleasure that I do.' It must then have been irritating to Miss Talbot to hear her work criticized: 'What particular fault do you think I have heard found by some top beaux esprits with Sir Charles? That the language is low, stiff, and vulgar, and much worse than Clarissa.'[182] She was well qualified to help Richardson in one area where he was conscious that he was weak and ready to accept help: she did know the conversation and the manners of the more pious and moral wing of the upper classes. There is no reason to doubt that a good many of her painstaking corrections were accepted. Miss Talbot, though she had agreed with Mrs. Carter that *Sir Charles* was not equal to *Clarissa*, could find few faults with its hero, to judge by a paper headed 'Spots Observed by the Purblind in the Sun' which Richardson preserved and marked 'Miss T.' She merely suggests mildly that the paragon was too submissive to his wicked father, an 'Excess of a Virtue', and was not bound to wait for years on the decision of the proud Porretta family.[183]

We have seen that Richardson visited Cuddesdon in 1753. The period when he was writing *Sir Charles* was the height of his friendship for Miss Talbot and her mother; but the friendship continued. Richardson wrote that knowing Bishop Secker and Mrs. and Miss Talbot had been 'one of the principal Pleasures of my Life'. He induced Lady Bradshaigh to stop off at Cuddesdon, but the visit was a disappointment to everyone—the two ladies did not get close to each other in the company and both were too shy to make a point of starting a conversation, though Richardson had praised each highly to the other. He scolded Lady Bradshaigh for not making the first advances to a single lady and took the liberty also to blame Miss Talbot. In 1756, while visiting Edwards, Richardson planned

---

[181] 'Journal', 10 Nov., 12 Nov., 15 Nov., 19 Nov., 28 Nov.
[182] Mrs. Carter to Miss Talbot, 21 Sept. 1753; Miss Talbot to Mrs. Carter, 19 Jan. 1754, *Letters between Mrs. Elizabeth Carter and Miss Catherine Talbot*, I, 342, 350.
[183] FM XV, 4, fos. 49–50.

to go on with his host to Cuddesdon, but the roads were so bad that he gave up the visit. He rejoiced in Secker's appointment as Archbishop of Canterbury: 'There has not been a more justly-applauded Promotion in this Kingdom.'[184] After 1757 there are fewer references to him in Miss Talbot's correspondence, but he was still visiting her in his last years.[185] 'I hear poor Mr. Richardson is ill,' she wrote to Mrs. Carter in 1758, 'but have not seen him this age'; but she did see him in October. Just before his death she announced his last stroke to Mrs. Carter: 'How many good hearts will be afflicted by this, in many more countries than England! To how many will he be an inexpressible loss!' She remembered with pleasure that their last morning together, on 28 May, 'was particularly friendly, and quiet, and comfortable'.[186] Richardson left her a mourning ring. She was a friend after his heart, with her resigned melancholy, her calm but firm piety, her quiet refinement, and her modest intelligence.

[184] R to Lady Echlin, 19 Apr. 1755; Lady Bradshaigh to R, 1 June 1755; R to Lady Bradshaigh, 28 June 1755; Lady Bradshaigh to R, 25 July 1755; R to Miss Talbot, 25 Oct. 1756; R to Mrs. Klopstock, 23 June 1758.

[185] Miss Talbot to Young, 3 Sept. 1761, Bodleian MS. Engl. Lettr. c. 209.

[186] Miss Talbot to Mrs. Carter, 15 Aug., 22 Oct. 1758, 2 July 1761, *Letters between Mrs. Elizabeth Carter and Miss Catherine Talbot*, I, 433, 436, 493-4.

CHAPTER XIV

THE COMPOSITION OF
SIR CHARLES GRANDISON

B UT if Miss Talbot was the corrector of *Sir Charles Grandison*, Lady
Bradshaigh was more than anyone else responsible for its inception.
Richardson had promised to consult the still unknown Belfour if he
should write again. In late October 1749 a 'Scotch gentleman' had given
Richardson a plan for a new work, which Belfour conceded might be useful and instructive, 'but I am sure you know it will not answer my
wishes'. Mrs. Barbauld says that the gentleman's plan was 'something like
that of "The Beauties of History," afterwards published'; but Lady
Bradshaigh seems to be referring to a proposal made by Henry Home,
later Lord Kames, for a series of stories to be used in educating the youth
of the land. He had discussed such a collection with Richardson and later
written to him about it. There were to be several classes of stories, all of a
moral cast. As Home describes them, they sound remarkably like the
realistic, socially useful, and boring stories which some educators now
consider helpful in winning the young away from the dangers of the
imagination implicit in Andersen and the brothers Grimm (Home deplores
the tales nurses tell about hobgoblins) and which often do succeed in
winning them away from books altogether. Richardson was not to write
all of them but was evidently to oversee the work. In his answer to Home,
Richardson sounded interested and asked for further suggestions and
copies of any suitable material he might have; it was possible, he said, that
his direction might enable him to enter into the plan with the necessary
warmth.[1] But either Home's direction or Richardson's warmth was insufficient. The plan would have had only moral utility to recommend it,
and though Richardson was never a man to ignore such an aim and did not
ignore it in his next novel, a series of tales of the kind which Pamela told
her children could hardly have inspired the author of *Pamela*.

'As to my Scottish friend's plan', Richardson replied to Lady Bradshaigh, 'had I freedom of spirits, or inclination to set about that, and to
trouble the world again, I might as well pursue the other, that I once had
thought of pursuing. The gentleman is an exceedingly worthy, sensible

---

[1] Lady Bradshaigh to R, 11 Jan., 29 Oct. 1749; Barbauld, IV, 259n; Home to R, 30 June
1749; R to Home, 11 July 1749.

and learned man, and fain would I have obliged him, if I had thought I could execute his scheme to the purpose. Indeed I have some degree of pain in refusing or declining to answer the wishes of any one for whom I have something more than an indifference. ''Why then, (will you ask) do you not set about obliging me, for whom you express a high value?''— Health! business! Madam. But for what should I set about the work I had once in view?—To draw a good man—a man who needs not repentance, as the world would think! How tame a character? Has not the world shewn me, that it is much better pleased to receive and applaud the character that shews us what we are (little of novelty as one would think there is in that) than what we ought to be? Are there not who think Clarissa's an unnatural character?' Lady Bradshaigh encouraged him to pursue the project, but he found the preference given to Lovelace over the virtuous Mr. Hickman discouraging for the prospects of a good man. He later acknowledged to her that the novel was 'owing more to you, than to any other one Person', and the lady several times mentioned her pride in her influence.[2]

Richardson's reference to a plan which he once thought of pursuing implies that he had already mentioned his Good Man to Lady Bradshaigh. She evidently spurred him on to carry out an earlier project of his own. As early as 2 February 1741 an anonymous correspondent had asked the author of *Pamela* to write 'the History of a Man, whose Life would be the Path that we should follow'. There is a cryptic statement made late in 1745 by Aaron Hill, after having read about half of *Clarissa* in manuscript: 'I am greatly pleas'd at the small Hint you give, of a Design, to raise Another Alps, upon this Appenine!—we can never see too many, of His Works, who has no Equal, in His Labours.'[3] This could refer to future instalments of *Clarissa*, but if so Hill's language is at least strained. It would more naturally refer to a project for a successor to *Clarissa*.

There is an even more tenuous hint which may have a bearing on the original project for *Sir Charles*. When urging Richardson to go on with his new novel, Lady Bradshaigh asks for 'a Letter from Harriot Reeves'.[4] In Richardson's copy of this letter 'Harriot' has been crossed out and 'Anna' written above it. The reference must be to the heroine of *Sir Charles*, whose final name was Harriet Byron but who has cousins named Reeves, whom she visits in London. Years later Richardson's daughter Anne, writing to her sister Martha, quotes from a 'little book' of her father's, 'filled in general with transcripts from the poets':

[2] R to Lady Bradshaigh, [late Nov.] 1749; Lady Bradshaigh to R, 16 Dec. 1749; R to Lady Bradshaigh, 9 Jan. 1750, 5 Oct. 1753, 13 Aug. 1755; Lady Bradshaigh to R, 14 Oct., 27 Nov. 1753, 14 Jan., 22 Mar. 1754.

[3] Eusebius to R, 2 Feb. 1741; Hill to R, [late 1745].

[4] 25 Nov. 1750.

Diffidence, too easy a persuadeableness, the property of the last adviser; being influenced by judgements weaker than her own. Slighting when in her power, what her Heart was most set upon when out of it. Character of the fair Diffidence (Lady Mary) in 20 instances to be produced and interspersed in Miss Reeves &c—

And in the Baron of his Imperiosity and blended good & faulty disposition—The fruits of an unsuited education—of a violent and Headstrong Wife in his Mother—of a meek & contemplative Father, whose authority, loving his own quiet, being impugned by his Lady, made his Son, who saw the foibles of both, unmanageable by either.

Lady P. a farther Instance of bad education and an atheistical Father.—Her History—why & how unhappy.[5]

The reference to Miss Reeves leads one to think that these must be notes for a novel, and Lady Bradshaigh's reference to the heroine of *Sir Charles* by the same name is an indication, though hardly a conclusive one, that the novel may have been the germ of *Sir Charles*. But there is no similarity between the characters sketched here and those of the novel. Harriet is not a fair diffidence. Anne takes these notes to refer to Richardson's wild young friend. Mr. McKillop has surmised that Richardson used a part of his wild friend's story in *Clarissa*.[6] The fact that the friend married two women, one of them a foreigner, is rather more similar to the double love of Sir Charles. The lady who played such a flamboyant role in the friend's story suggests in her mannishness Miss Barnevelt and in her amorous designs Lady Olivia. We have no desire to press these similarities very far. Certainly the coincidence of the name 'Reeves' is not enough to build a firm case on. We would only suggest the possibility that even while he was composing *Clarissa* Richardson was toying with the idea of working over the story of a wild but well-meaning man who gets involved with at least two women and loves both. Both *Pamela* and *Clarissa* arose from similarly simple situations, and such a story seems to have led Richardson to do his best work. Later, either at his own or at Lady Bradshaigh's suggestion, he substituted his Good Man for the rake, with necessarily major alterations, but kept the germ of the plot. Some such history might account for the rather uneasy relationship between the story of the novel and the character of its hero, who is never credible in his double love—or in any love. Wherever it came from, the idea of the Good Man proved fatal to the novel. The evidence is not sufficient to assert even with probability, much less with certainty, that he is an afterthought; one can only say that Richardson had considered a new novel before 1749, that by the fall of that year Lady Bradshaigh was urging him to write it, that by then it was to be primarily a novel about a Good Man, and that by early 1750 he was seriously considering the idea.

[5] 10 July 1784, MS. owned by Alan Dugald McKillop.
[6] See Chap. I; McKillop, *Richardson*, pp. 118–19.

The wild friend certainly did not provide a source for the character of Sir Charles. Dr. Johnson is reported to have supposed that Richardson was thinking of the non-juror Robert Nelson, who died in 1715, when he drew his hero.[7] Benjamin Boyce has recently suggested that Richardson's conception of Sir Charles might owe something to the character of Ralph Allen.[8] The Reverend John Newton wrote that he had heard that when asked about the original of Sir Charles, Richardson 'said, he might apply it to Lord Dartmouth, if *he was not a methodist*'.[9] But William Legge, second Viscount Dartmouth, was only twenty when the novel was begun, and in any case Richardson's words do not imply that he used Lord Dartmouth as a source. Nor is any source either probable or necessary. In character, Sir Charles is not a person but a collection of virtues, some of which may have been suggested by the various women whom Richardson asked to help him but none of which is distinctive enough to call for any special explanation. The name Grandison may possibly have been suggested by that of Irish Viscounts who were friends of Mrs. Delany and Mrs. Donnellan.

Two characters were drawn partly from life. Sir Charles's maiden aunt Nell got at least her fondness for pink and yellow ribbons from a maiden lady named Catharine Warren who lived with the Bradshaighs and who many years later was still referred to as Aunt Nell.[10] Lady Bradshaigh recognized some of her own traits in Sir Charles's sharp-tongued sister Charlotte.[11] Lady Echlin also thought that she recognized her sister in Charlotte Grandison and even suspected her of writing some of Charlotte's letters. Richardson wrote to Lady Echlin that he had put touches of her sister into Charlotte and had deliberately made Charlotte make fun of old maids in order that Harriet might correct her and thus correct the same fault in Lady Bradshaigh.[12] Another private joke was Charlotte's satiric remarks on Lady Bradshaigh's favourite occupation, shell-work.[13]

By 10 April 1750 Richardson was asking for help in drawing his Good Man—he wrote to young William Lobb that he would like William's

---

[7] William Seward, *Anecdotes of Distinguished Persons* (London, 1798), II, 91; see also *Johnsonian Miscellanies*, II, 305.

[8] *Benevolent Man: A Life of Ralph Allen of Bath*, p. 210n.

[9] To Hannah More, 7 Apr. 1799, Roberts, *Memoirs of the Life and Correspondence of Mrs. Hannah More*, III, 78. In announcing the forthcoming marriage of Lord Dartmouth to Frances Nicholl, Mrs. Delany wrote to Mrs. Dewes on 6 July 1755: 'I would have had *my Sir C. Grandison* have a Harriet Byron' (*Autobiography and Correspondence*, III, 283). Perhaps Richardson had heard her (and possibly others) compare Dartmouth to his paragon.

[10] Lady Bradshaigh to R, 11 Dec. 1753, 5 Feb. 1754; R to Lady Echlin, 11 Sept. 1758; Lady Bradshaigh to R, 8 June 1760.

[11] R to Lady Bradshaigh, 4 Jan. 1754; Lady Bradshaigh to R, 5 Feb., 22 Mar. 1754.

[12] Lady Echlin to R, 12 Aug. 1754; Lady Bradshaigh to R, 30 June 1754; R to Lady Echlin, 12 Sept. 1754.

[13] Lady Bradshaigh to R, 27 Nov. 1753; R to Lady Bradshaigh, 8 Dec. 1753; Lady Bradshaigh to R, 14 Jan. 1754; R to Lady Bradshaigh, 8 Feb. 1754.

father to give a sketch from his own heart. He was not sure that he could proceed, but 'if I see Materials rise upon me, they may encourage'. About the same time Mrs. Dewes and Mrs. Delany read 'two or three letters' together.[14] By June he was asking Miss Highmore to help him to a Good Man: 'He must be wonderfully polite; but no Hickman! How can we hope that ladies will not think a good man a tame man?' The next month Mrs. Dewes hoped that he would continue the work, though not if it would injure his health, but was unable to contribute. In August he reported to Mrs. Dewes that he had 'not been able to add a line': he had been prevented by business, by his brother Benjamin's death, by his advanced age, and by the difficulty of drawing 'a man that *good* men would approve, and that young ladies, in such an age as this, will think amiable'. He asked Mrs. Donnellan and Miss Sutton for help: 'Will she, or will you, Madam, be so good as to acquaint me what he *is* to do, and what he is *not* to do, in order to acquire and maintain an exemplary character?' Specifically, how is he to deal with challenges? He must, 'to make *sport* for the *tender-hearted* reader', have great distresses—and then be made happy, in this life, 'for few, very few, care to pass to another, if they can help it'. Mrs. Donnellan offered advice, which Richardson took no more to heart than he took most of the advice he asked for. It is easy, she sensibly pointed out, to think of a man with all good qualities, 'but to work these up into a story, to produce these into action—I know nobody who is capable of doing it but Mr. Richardson'. Perhaps the hero may have fought his duel before the reader meets him. His distress could be owing to his love for a woman whose affections are already engaged 'to one of a more modern cast', and his winning her at last could, 'to the credit of my sex', show the triumph of virtue over the man of mode. But a man can hardly be engaged in situations so moving as Clarissa's. There must be a friend to sing his praises and thus avoid the odium of self-praise. He must have some faults, 'some sallies of passion; the best *man's* character will bear it, tho' a Clarissa's would not'. He may then be 'recovered by reason and religion'. But he must be in need of being set right and therefore cannot be as perfect as Clarissa—he must have more of Miss Howe in him.[15] Unfortunately Richardson saw no more necessity of a man's falling and then returning to virtue than of a woman's doing so.

In September Thomas Birch wrote to Philip Yorke that Richardson was employing himself on 'the Subject, which you heard him mention at your own House, of the virtuous & generous Gentleman. He complains to me

[14] Mrs. Dewes to R, 8 July 1750; R to Mrs. Dewes, 20 Aug. 1750. The reading must have taken place before 4 May, when Mrs. Delany left for Ireland (*Autobiography and Correspondence*, II, 542).
[15] R to Susanna Highmore, 4 June; Mrs. Dewes to R, 8 July; R to Mrs. Dewes, 20 Aug.; R to Anne Donnellan, 20 July; Anne Donnellan to R, 25 Sept.

of the Difficulty of enlivening it with proper Incidents: But we may safely trust to his Invention, which is inexhaustible upon all Occasions. He has desir'd me to give him an Hour or two's Attention in the reading of his plan.'[16] Probably by that time a good many more people had been consulted. Unlike *Pamela* and *Clarissa, Sir Charles Grandison* was composed in the full view of Richardson's friends, which may account for some of its weaknesses.

On 25 November Lady Bradshaigh felt a '*conscientious* Pang' when Richardson complained of writing as one of his grievances: 'For is it not barbarous to put you upon any-thing which may add to your Uneasiness? However, I do not forget, that I heard you say, History-writing gave you Pleasure.' And she sends him a present, hoping for one in return, 'Neither Gold, Silver, nor Diamonds; but something much more valuable—No less—than a Letter from Harriot Reeves'. She was to get no repayment for some time: on 5 March 1751 she was still hoping for something from Clarissa's 'young Sister'. Nine days later she returned from a visit to find the first instalment of Harriet. Sir Charles does not enter until well along in the novel, and she was still wishing for 'just [a] peep at the good man'. Richardson was not to expect correction and amendments from her. In reply Richardson explained that the Good Man had 'not peeped out yet': 'He must not appear till, as at a royal cavalcade, the drums, trumpets, fifes and tabrets, and many a fine fellow, have preceeded him, and set the spectators agog, as I may call it.' In his new heroine he was trying to steer a middle course between Pamela and Clarissa, between Miss Howe and Clarissa—a Clarissa without persecution. And he begged her to find faults. How could he, an obscure business man, draw characters from upper life, scenes 'of busy and yet elegant trifling?'[17]

Edwards had met Harriet Byron even before Lady Bradshaigh did, having heard some of her letters read in January. He even found something to censure in her character: she does not seem to demand absolute chastity in her future husband. Richardson promptly took his heroine to task and cut the offending sentence from Harriet's speech: 'It may not be thought absolutely necessary perhaps to make very nice Scrutinies into the past Life and Actions of the Man to whom we have no very material Objections: But I will be for ever single, rather than marry a Man who is avowedly a Libertine, and who continues to hold bad Principles.' He desired to give Harriet 'a livelier Turn than Clarissa . . ., to reign her in, when the good Man appeared, as she is to be but the second Character: But not to be in the least wanting, as to Purity of Manners: No vile Accommodation to the Times!' He was still in doubt about his new work: he had not mentioned it to the Speaker, though he would have done so

[16] 29 Sept., B.M. Add. MSS. 35,397, fo. 299.
[17] Lady Bradshaigh to R, 5 Mar., 17 Mar.; R to Lady Bradshaigh, 24 Mar.

had he thought of proceeding. Edwards was hesitant to urge him to proceed, because of his health and his business, but pointed out that he needed amusement: 'Play with her only, and "*as she pulls, do you let go*," and see what will come of it.' 'Harriot has pulled: And I have let go, a little', Richardson answered. 'But if one aims at Warmth, according to the Scenes to be represented, is it possible to affect without being affected?— Yet, as you observe, I *must* do something. I cannot be idle.'[18]

By this time a good many people were eager for the new work. In January he wrote to de Freval that he had been 'teazed by a dozen ladies of note and of virtue, to give them a good man', but that his nervous infirmities and the press of business made him hesitate; in the same letter, however, he went on to ask what a good man might be expected to do or see in Paris and what were the French laws on duelling. Miss Talbot was one of the ladies who urged him 'to comply with ye repeated Requests of his Agreeable Incognita, and shew the World such a Man as would neither have been unworthy of a Clarissa, nor unagreeable to a Miss Howe'.[19]

By late March Miss Mulso had met the heroine. By mid-April Lady Bradshaigh had received another instalment, still without the Good Man. The date she met him is uncertain, but it must have been soon afterwards; she made the hero one of her 'very best courtesies' at the long-awaited introduction. Edwards learned early in May that the hero was almost ready for the world: 'After long, long Travelling I think I have found ye good Man; just found him: But you, Sir, & an auxiliary Lady or two must correct, adorn & finish him.'[20] But we still hear of doubts and hesitations.

He was getting some advice from his often-consulted friends. Lady Bradshaigh advised him that July was not the time for a young lady to go up to London, and he moved the opening of the novel to January.[21] Edward Young sent him a prayer which Richardson asked leave to give to Sir Charles's adviser, Dr. Bartlett, but Young found it unsuitable and promised a better one.[22] Skelton advised him to make his hero 'as good a Christian, as a fine gentleman can be', but not quite so given to devotion as Pamela: 'rather a Christian hero than a saint'. He must be persecuted, else he can be no very good man (advice which Richardson would have done well to heed—Sir Charles has things decidedly too much his own way). There must be plenty of adventures for the bulk of readers. And a bad woman ('expensive, imperious, lewd, and at last a drammer') would be both fruitful and entertaining. Richardson asked Skelton to assemble the traits of the bad women he knew, to serve as models, and he would try

[18] Edwards to R, 24 Jan.; R to Edwards, 13 Feb.; Edwards to R, 9 Mar.; R to Edwards, 19 Mar.

[19] R to de Freval, 21 Jan.; Catherine Talbot to R, [Dec. 1750?].

[20] R to Lady Bradshaigh, 24 Mar.; Lady Bradshaigh to R, 16 Apr., [mid-1751]; R to Edwards, 2 May.

[21] Barbauld, I, ccvii–viii.   [22] 30 July, 1 Aug., 7 Aug.

to 'ingraft them in my story'. But the bad women in the book are minor characters and very pallid ones at that—perhaps neither the clergyman nor the printer knew enough models. Skelton considered that most men find nothing more unpalatable than morality and religion and that for its moral to go down the book must be 'either well peppered and salted with wit, or all alive from end to end with action'. Mrs. Delany and her husband agreed that the novel should have a bad woman to serve as a foil, though not as a principal figure. And she suggested that he again show, as he had in *Clarissa*, but in a milder way, the dangers of parents' inducing their daughters to marry men they dislike (her own first marriage had been the result of such pressure).[23] One lady showed Richardson some 'pretty observations on the education of women', which he appropriated and put into the mouth of Mrs. Shirley.[24] Miss Mulso was asked to help but seems never to have complied: 'But set your charming imagination at work, and give me a few scenes, as you would have them, that I may try to work them into the story. You will be in time: for I am not likely to proceed soon with the girl. . . . But difficulties must be thrown in. Give me half a score of them, Miss Mulso: look but among your female acquaintance, and you will be able to oblige me.' And Richardson teased her about the ending: 'But will you have the story end with a fiddle and a dance: that is to say with matrimony; or will you not? If you will, Harriet must have her difficulties.'[25]

Miss Mulso was unfortunately absent from town during the early summer and missed the satisfaction of a reading from the novel which rejoiced the heart of Miss Highmore: 'Oh! my dear, Sir Charles will be all we wish him.' John Duncombe was also forced to leave the characters in an interesting situation, and in October he regretted from Cambridge that he was no longer able to satisfy his curiosity. He had met the Lady Clementina, so that by this time Richardson had got into his main plot, the double love of Sir Charles. 'Clementina's Fate is not yet come to my knowledge', Richardson wrote to John's father. 'I have been hinder'd from enquiring after her; in other words, from pursuing her story. But I think she rises upon me. . . . I want more time than my Business will allow me, now her story is become arduous, to adjust, reconcile, retrospect, connect, etc. I have half a Mind to lay by the Work for ever. A very little inducement will make me resolve to do so. Do you think it right at my time of life, and shook by maladies, that affect me mentally as well as corporally, to write Love Stories, and fill my head with Nugatories of Boys and Girls?'[26]

[23] Skelton to R, 10 May 1751; R to Skelton, 19 Feb. 1752; Skelton to R, 28 Dec. 1751; Mrs. Delany to R, 16 Aug. 1751.

[24] Barbauld, I, cxl; 1st edn., VI, 354-6; SH, VI, 406-7.

[25] 27 July 1751.

[26] Susanna Highmore to Hester Mulso, [*c.* 1 July], Barbauld, II, 259; John Duncombe to R, 15 Oct.; R to William Duncombe, 22 Oct.

In December 1751 he complained that Harriet suffered from his avocations: 'I have lost my thread, and know not where to find it.'[27] The progress of *Sir Charles* was often marked by doubts and delays. 'Could I have proceeded with Harriot and *your* good man (your's he is—he owes the existence he has to you)', he wrote to Lady Bradshaigh, 'I should have been better.' But he has passed through 'more than a month of grievous and incapacitating suffering'. 'I have no thoughts, were I to finish this new piece, of having it published in my life-time. The success of a writer's work is better insured, when the world knows they can be troubled with no more of his.'[28] Perhaps Richardson's health and business are enough to explain the irregular course the novel ran. But Richardson's remarks to Duncombe also imply that the plot did not develop itself in his mind in any inevitable way. In the first part of *Pamela* and in *Clarissa* the whole book is implicit in the opening letters, and the movement is unified and straightforward. In *Sir Charles* Richardson often seems to be inventing incidents, even straining for them, padding, striving to fill out his paragon's portrait and to think up an interesting story.

'I fear it will be a long time, if ever, before Mr. Richardson's "*good man*" is produced,' Mrs. Delany wrote to her sister, 'and I am afraid his health will suffer from his too close attention to it; he has undertaken a *very hard task*, which is to please the *gay and the good*, but Mrs. D[onnellan] says, as far as he has gone he has succeeded wonderfully.' Mrs. Chapone was upset by Richardson's harsh plan to publish only on his death, and he replied that it would be time enough to think about publishing when he had finished—he lacked still a great deal. Mrs. Donnellan urged him not to be so cruel to his own generation as to leave the novel to be published after his death. Shall the world have only Captain Booth as an example? 'Mr. R. indeed sometimes talks as if it should not be published during his life,' Miss Mulso informed Mrs. Carter; 'but I am very sure he will change his mind as to that particular. He can't be insensible to fame: I believe nobody that could deserve it ever was.'[29]

At the end of 1751 he reported to Edwards that he had made 'a very little Progress' since they had last seen each other. Soon the work was going on very fast. As we have seen, Miss Talbot had begun reading the manuscript in November 1751; by the beginning of January she was in the fifth manuscript volume and later in the month the tenth,[30] so that in spite of all his hesitations Richardson was well along. In early February

[27] To John Duncombe, 12 Dec.

[28] [April–Oct. 1751]. See also R to Frances Grainger, 28 Sept., and R to Lady Bradshaigh, 26 Dec.

[29] Mrs. Delany to Mrs. Dewes, 7 Nov., *Autobiography and Correspondence*, III, 54; Mrs. Chapone to R, 18 Nov.; R to Mrs. Chapone, 22 Nov.; Anne Donnellan to R, 11 Feb. 1752; Hester Mulso to Mrs. Carter, 11 Feb. [1752], *Posthumous Works of Mrs. Chapone*, I, 44–5.

[30] 28 Dec.; Catherine Talbot, 'Journal', 2 Jan., 18 Jan.

Miss Mulso hoped it would appear before long.[31] But later that month Richardson told Lady Bradshaigh that he was at a very difficult part: 'Entanglement, and extrication, and re-entanglement, have succeeded each other, as the day the night; and now the few friends who have seen what I have written, doubt not but I am stuck fast. And, indeed, I think so myself.' By June he had overcome further difficulties: 'But what shall I do, they multiply upon me!' The Good Man 'from a thin gentleman, as I designed him', had grown 'to a gigantic bulk'. 'I knew not what the task was which I undertook.' He was still doubtful of his ability to handle such subjects, 'a very ordinary man, unlearned, all my early years employed to get a mechanic business for a livelihood'. 'There are so many things that may be done, and said, and written by a common man that cannot by a good man, that delicacies arise on delicacies.' He still threatened that if the book seemed likely to disgrace him it would never see the light.[32]

In the summer of 1752 he was again teasing Miss Mulso about the ending. 'And you really expect no back-stroke of fortune? All to be halcyon to the end of the chapter?' Sir Charles might die gloriously, and Harriet appear 'in her vidual glory'. A murder on the very day of the nuptials? What scenes it could give rise to! And ladies like surprises. Hecky, Pressy, and Sukey made what Richardson considered 'charming Expostulations' at this grim prospect. But neither Miss Highmore nor Miss Mulso was really much alarmed.[33]

In the middle of 1752 Edwards had no recent news about the novel and was eager to hear about it. Nor could Lady Bradshaigh have seen a great deal of the book: she bounced off her chair on reading Richardson's statement that two girls were in love with his hero and he was in love with both. In September Edwards was still envying those who had seen more of the manuscript than he had and hoping for a full draught rather than the mere taste he had had.[34] Since Edwards and Lady Bradshaigh were among those most likely to have seen the manuscript, it appears that after the beginning Richardson was not so free in showing it to his friends.

By August Richardson was writing what he hoped was his last volume. By 25 October he was able to write, 'I think I have come to a Period of my Story: Except I change the Catastrophe on going over it again. Which I am busying myself about. I want to reduce. I shall reduce. But this is Labor, Drudgery! I don't love it.'[35] He later wrote to Stinstra that he had struck out two volumes, suppressing answers to letters, but as it is *Sir Charles* is almost as long as *Clarissa* and at least in the last two of its seven

[31] Hester Mulso to Elizabeth Carter, 11 Feb., *Posthumous Works of Mrs. Chapone*, I, 44–5.
[32] To Lady Bradshaigh, 23 Feb., 24 June; to Mrs. Dewes, 21 June.
[33] R to Hester Mulso, 20 June; R to Edwards, 21 Aug.; Susanna Highmore to Hester Mulso, two letters [July–Aug.], Barbauld, II, 315–16.
[34] Edwards to R, 9 July; Lady Bradshaigh to R, [Aug.–Oct.]; Edwards to R, 29 Sept.
[35] To Lady Bradshaigh, 17 Aug.; to Edwards, 25 Oct.

volumes still appears capable of considerable reduction. When Stinstra feared (unnecessarily) that this shortening might crowd events too closely and give the book the air of a romance, Richardson explained that he hoped it would not have that appearance since 'in many Places, I omitted some Busy Scenes, as well as the Parts that connected them with ye Story, and the Sentiments that accompanied them'.[36] In November he was still trying to cut. Mrs. Donnellan had read through the sixth manuscript volume and had made minor corrections and suggestions for shortening; she found but one fault with the hero: 'He has no fault, no passions.'[37]

Meanwhile he had a new motive for hurrying: another writer had offered to Andrew Millar, among other booksellers, a novel which Richardson heard had a similar plan and even characters with the same names as his own.[38] This novel was *Sir Charles Goodville*, which was published on 20 February 1753.[39]

Except for the name of the hero and the moral tone of the book, there is little that anticipates Richardson's *Sir Charles*. The announced aim would have fitted *Grandison* well enough: 'to promote every social Virtue, and to prove that there only wants the Countenance of Persons of Rank and Fortune, to render them universally extensive'.[40] But Sir Charles Goodville, unlike Richardson's model, has very little to do in his novel; we are informed that he is virtuous, but he shows his virtue only in an occasional lecture reprehending female frivolity, defending country sports, or proving that a fine gentleman may be learned. He seems almost an afterthought. The main plot concerns his poor but virtuous clerk Melfort, subjected to persecution because of a forged signature, and Melfort's equally virtuous wife Sophy, ex-maid of Lady Goodville. Sir Charles's sister Mrs. Frankly, a vain, sprightly, and light-minded widow, is the centre of another series of incidents and the occasion for many scenes of small talk. A good deal of the novel consists of conversation. The book is only nominally in epistolary form, since the letters are a straightforward narration, written fifty years after the events they describe. The letter writer moralizes frequently on such subjects as the dangers of passion and the virtues of the poor and was evidently especially interested in the theatre, which he and the characters he describes often discuss. *Sir Charles Goodville* reads as if it were hastily thrown together by a man who had thought of a little tale about honesty in distress but, unable to make it stretch over two thin volumes, had tried in vain to pad it out with other characters and with miscellaneous talk and had finally injected into it a

[36] R to Stinstra, 2 June 1753; 28 June 1754.

[37] R to Lady Bradshaigh, 20 Nov.; Anne Donnellan to R, 9 Nov.

[38] Thomas Birch to Philip Yorke, 18 Nov., B.M. Add. MS. 35,398, fo. 113.

[39] *Public Advertiser*, 12 Feb., 13 Feb., 14 Feb., 20 Feb.

[40] *Memoirs of Sir Charles Goodville and His Family* (Dublin, 1753), I, iii. We have not had access to the London edition.

virtuous baronet with no role to play, hoping to capitalize on the rumours about Richardson's forthcoming work.

In order to warn readers against his rival, Richardson inserted an advertisement to the effect that *Sir Charles Grandison*, 'by the Editor of PAMELA and CLARISSA', would not appear until the following winter.[41] He was, however, trying to get his work in shape for the public as quickly as possible; when Edwards inquired about Miss Harriet, about whom he had heard nothing for a long time, Richardson answered that 'the bold Hussey is intending, to steal into Public, even in an Undress. These Vaux-hall and Ranelagh Frequenters have ruined her. Harriet is but a Woman.' Seeing so many bold ones in her 'Age of Tastelessness; and Audacity', she wanted to make one of the crowd, though her story was not yet concluded. Edwards inquired about the advertisement that *Sir Charles* would not appear till next winter, and Richardson explained that it had been necessitated by *Sir Charles Goodville*, which he had found out about when booksellers, thinking it was by him, sent to him for it.[42]

In June Richardson told Stinstra that he had had considerable trouble in building his plot around a good man, that the book had cost him more pains than *Clarissa*. The Good Man must 'have his Trials, his Perplexities —And to have them from good Women, will require some Management.' It was to be his last work. The whole story had been his invention, 'entirely new and unborrowed, even of my self'. He was uncertain whether to publish in parts or not; his French and German translators, Prévost and Haller, had asked for sheets as the parts were published, but he was afraid to send them lest if he waited to publish all together his translators might reach the public ahead of him.[43] Early in July he wrote that he had decided to publish the first two volumes in October or November, the second two about the middle of December, and the last three (in duodecimo—the last two in a six-volume octavo edition) about February 1754.[44] He had received an application for Irish rights, offering him a premium, and was planning to send the sheets of the first volumes to Ireland soon.[45] Printing had evidently begun. Before the end of May, Colley Cibber had read seven sheets (through the abduction of Harriet) and on 3 June had visited Richardson for the sake of Miss Byron's conversation and proposed to return to hear more of it.[46] Before the end of

[41] *Public Advertiser*, 17 Feb., 20 Feb.

[42] 15 Feb., 20 Feb., 5 Mar., 21 Apr.

[43] 2 June. See also R to Mrs. Dewes, 21 June 1752.

[44] See also R to Elizabeth Carter, 4 July; R to Clairaut, 5 July.   [45] 4 July.

[46] 22 or 29 May, 20 May, 6 June. Sale (*Bibliographical Record*, pp. 76–7) says that Cibber was one of the first to see *Sir Charles Grandison* in manuscript, but he bases this statement on two letters which Barbauld prints, II, 172–4. The first (16 Jan. 1750) asks for an unidentified transcript, which may or may not be the manuscript of *Sir Charles*; the second is about *Sir Charles*, and Barbauld dates it 27 May 1750. But the original, which must have been the one Barbauld saw, has part of the date torn off: 'May 2[ ] 17[ ]'—on the latter is the tail of the

June Dr. Chauncy had seen ten sheets which included the death of Sir Charles's mother, and Miss Talbot's cousin-in-law Lady Talbot had been sent the first volume. In early July Richardson sent her the second volume.[47] In answer to Edwards's hope 'that now your fatigue is lessened your health amends; that Sir Charles is returned, or at lest upon his return out of Oxfordshire, and that I shall soon hear you are quite rid of that burthen, which has so long laid heavy on your mind', Richardson replied that he was 'pretty forward'. 'But am perplexing myself with extracting Sentiments, &c. which I once thought I could have left to another hand. —Ah, Sir! I never shall be able to tell you, that I am not a Burthen to myself—I will, God favouring, as soon as I can, try what Recess and for-bearing the Pen will do; but when these Mastiffs fasten, they never quit hold, till they have one under their Feet. I find this to be the Case with many who never trouble themselves with Scribbling.'[48] He had already written the conclusion defending the character of his hero, and the book, large as it was, had been 'much abridg'd'.[49]

Just when he seemed in sight of a calm haven, he heard news which caused him to try to hasten publication and which, though it did little real damage, caused him a great deal of annoyance. He had sent Miss Wescomb 'some of the first Sh[ee]ts' in July, with the warning not to let them out of her hands and to return them—he had only 'three Setts going, as printed', so that his 'Workmen may not give them out to Pyrates', as was done with the last two volumes of *Pamela*.[50] But his precautions were in vain. He had been pretty free in sending sheets to his friends: in addition to Miss Wescomb, Cibber, Dr. Chauncy, and Lady Talbot, Miss Talbot had a copy in August, and even a friend of the Chapones named John Birkbeck had received part of the book.[51] But it was his own journeymen who betrayed him. In early August he received news that four Dublin booksellers had got hold of a copy from his workers.[52] By that time he had printed five complete volumes, most of the sixth, and several sheets of the seventh.[53] He stopped his presses on or before 10 August, but his

---

'5' and the tail of something that is not a 'o' and could be a '3'. Barbauld's date is clearly wrong, since the letter is also dated 'Tuesday', and 27 May 1750 was Sunday. The letter should be dated 22 or 29 May 1753.

[47] Chauncy to R, June; Lady Talbot to R, 23 June, 6 July.

[48] 6 July, 16 July.

[49] Thomas Birch to Philip Yorke, 7 July, B.M. Add. MS. 35,398, fo. 129.

[50] 20 July. See also *The Case of Samuel Richardson, of London, Printer; with Regard to the Invasion of His Property* (dated 14 Sept. 1753), in which he says that he had had all sheets locked up in his warehouse except three copies of the duodecimo and one of the octavo.

[51] Catherine Talbot, 'Journal', 27 Aug.; Birkbeck to R, 1 Aug.

[52] R to George Faulkner, 10 Aug.; R to Sarah Wescomb, 15 Aug.; R to Edwards, 15 Aug.; R to Lady Talbot, 16 Aug. For an account of the piracy, see William M. Sale, Jr., '*Sir Charles Grandison* and the Dublin Pirates', *YULG*, VII (1933), 424-42.

[53] R to Lady Bradshaigh, 5 Oct., 12 Nov.; *Case*.

early printing and delayed publication enabled the Irish pirates to get ahead of George Faulkner, the Dublin bookseller through whom he had arranged to publish *Sir Charles*.

Richardson had already had dealings with Faulkner, and none too pleasant ones. It was Faulkner who, according to a report from an English printer whom Richardson considered reliable, had pirated the second part of *Pamela*. In spite of this fact, Richardson had been induced to give him the rights to *Clarissa* in Ireland but had with great difficulty collected the full seventy guineas which he promised for that work—Faulkner tried to pay only forty.[54] But in July 1753 he made another agreement with him for *Sir Charles*, again for seventy guineas. Faulkner had warned him that Irish booksellers boasted of being able to procure the sheets of any book being printed in London, and indeed Richardson had already heard of this boast. He therefore cautioned his journeymen to be on their guard—cautioned them not only orally, but also by means of a printed warning: 'I hope I may depend upon the Care and Circumspection of my Friends, Compositors and Pressmen, that no Sheets of the Piece I am now putting to Press be carried out of the House; nor any Notice taken of its being at Press. It is of great Consequence to me.' He had taken the further precaution of having the sheets wrought off at three separate presses in his three workhouses, by different workmen, and then locked in a warehouse under the care of a proofreader whom he thought he had special reason to trust, Peter Bishop.[55]

On 4 August 1753 Faulkner wrote to Richardson that he had just received four sheets of the novel from Richardson but that four other booksellers had received by the same post much more, sheets of both the duodecimo and octavo editions. They had shown their sheets to Faulkner, who though indignant at 'the villainy and fraud of your Journeymen, who have *robbed you*, and *injured me*', considered it useless for Richardson to send him any more of the work, since the pirates claimed the whole property and Faulkner could only hope to get even a fifth share by dealing with them. Three of the booksellers advertised *The History of Sir Charles Grandison*, and one added ('Vile Artifice!') 'printed for *S. Richardson*'.[56] Richardson answered Faulkner's letter on 10 August by inquiring whether 'he was to conclude that all dealings between them were absolutely at an end'. In reply Faulkner informed Richardson that the pirates had determined to get hold of the work when they saw Richardson's advertisement directed against *Sir Charles Goodville*. A bookseller named Peter Wilson had managed to get the first two volumes of the octavo; two others named John Exshaw and Henry Saunders had got those of the duodecimo.

[54] Richardson, *Address to the Public*, reprinted in *Sir Charles Grandison*, 1st edn., VII, 428–9; Skelton to R, 27 May 1749; R to Lady Echlin, 24 Nov. 1753.
[55] *Address*, p. 426; *Case*.   [56] *Case*.

Faulkner had had to show them the sheets he had received (with some corrections by Richardson) to induce them to go shares with him. He was ready to pay Richardson a part of the stipulated seventy guineas proportional to the share he got from the pirates and could only advise Richardson to write the pirates for the rest. Richardson answered 'that he never could consent to propose terms to men who had bribed his servants to rob him; and who were in possession of the stolen goods' and cautioned 'him to consider how far his own honour was concerned in the engagements he had entered into with them'.[57] Faulkner does not seem to have felt that honour was much involved in such cases. Irish booksellers took English books as they could get them, and Richardson's strong righteous indignation at the violation of the sacred rights of property does not appear to have been shared by the Dublin trade.

He tried to get help in Ireland. On 4 September Garrick wrote to thank him for the first two volumes, which would not leave his hands, and to forward a letter from Lord Orrery promising to extend his influence against the pirates. Richardson had earlier met the friend of Swift in Andrew Millar's shop and had received from him a compliment on *Clarissa*.[58] But Lord Orrery found it impossible to help him. Through Miss Grainger he sought the advice of a Mr. Sharpe. Dr. Johnson also offered to help. He was willing to go to considerable effort: 'I am not cool about this piracy. Suppose instead of this edition you should print three or four thousand in brevier [2]4to and sell them first in the remoter parts, every printer and Bookseller in the town will help you. I will correct a volume or more, and every body will do what they can.'[59]

On 8 September Faulkner wrote again: he had tried to convince Wilson, Exshaw, and Saunders of the wickedness of their actions, but not only had he met with no success, he had even heard it hinted that they planned to send the sheets to Scotland and to France and thus to forestall Richardson in those kingdoms. Had they done so, Richardson would have stood to lose more than he lost by the Irish piracy. Richardson prevented them 'by putting a stop to Printing what remained of it unprinted' and sent his clerical friend Philip Skelton a power of acting for him in Ireland.[60] He also printed for free distribution a statement of his grievances, *The Case of Samuel Richardson, of London, Printer; with Regard to the Invasion of his Property*, dated 14 September. He summarized the actions of the pirates, naming them, and also expressing his suspicions of two of his journeymen, Bishop and Thomas Killingbeck, a compositor. Undoubtedly they were the two men whom he told Lady Bradshaigh he had discharged, being

[57] 14–16 Aug., 24 Aug.
[58] R to Lady Bradshaigh, 23 Feb. 1752.
[59] Lord Orrery to R, 9 Nov.; R to Frances Grainger, 16 Oct.; Johnson to R, 26 Sept.
[60] R to Lady Echlin, 24 Nov.

sure they were guilty;[61] Bishop had been working for Richardson at least since 1748, when he several times withdrew money from Richardson's bank account.[62] In a quotation from Richardson's *Case* in the *Public Advertiser* are the statements, not in the London edition, that the pirates have made no less than forty of the editor's workmen uneasy and some of them suspected and have caused the ruin of any who might be discharged, since no other master would care to employ them.[63] The *Public Advertiser*'s quotation occurs in a news story about the Dublin version of the *Case*, published as a half-sheet (with great difficulty, 'almost all the Presses having been shut up against it'). The *Advertiser*'s article strongly supported Richardson's side, praising him both as a man and as an author, denouncing the wickedness of the pirates, and urging all honest Irishmen to buy Richardson's edition. This edition, we learn, could not be printed in Dublin because the influence of the pirates had closed all presses against him, and he was forced to send over an edition printed in England. The Irish were able to print more cheaply and had no payments to make to authors and were able to undersell the English edition by two shillings for the first six volumes.[64] In London, the *Gentleman's Magazine* took up the cudgels for Richardson,[65] and *Gray's Inn Journal* denounced the 'vile Act of Piracy'.[66]

The Irish, to Richardson's bewilderment though perhaps not to the bewilderment of those better acquainted with that nation, seemed inclined to make a national cause of what in London looked like a plain theft. The public there does not seem to have been open to Richardson's moral argument. The Irish view was fervently argued by the *Dublin Spy*. It referred to Robert Main, the distributor of Richardson's edition, as a Scottish peddlar who had come to Dublin to encourage the importation of English editions: 'If such practices as these are permitted, fare well to all printing in *Ireland*.' Richardson was told to keep his complaints and his editions at home; the Dublin Society had encouraged the making of good types and paper 'to keep the business of printing among ourselves' and thus prevent money from going over to England. A few days later it devoted its leading article to Richardson's 'invasion of the press' and consequent 'invasion of our civil libertys and propertys'. In attempting 'to obstruct this choicer Palladium [the press] of our state than blood, or treasure', he had threatened a worse danger than the copper chains of Wood. He had already, with *Pamela*, tried 'to carry his black designs against this kingdom, into execution' by sending over fifteen hundred sets

---

[61] 19 Oct. [62] Gosling's Bank Ledger.

[63] 30 Oct. (under the dateline '*Dublin, Oct.* 18, 1753'). Probably Richardson wrote this before he discharged Bishop and Killingbeck and revised his *Case* after sending the earlier version to Dublin.

[64] *Address*, p. 439. [65] XXIII (Oct.), 465–7.

[66] 13 Oct.

with a man named Bacon. '*Richardson* has had this execrable design of ruining our printing business in his head many years since.' With all England, 'nay the whole world', to range in, he is cruelly and covetously determined 'to improvish poor *Ireland*'. All printers have a right to his work, and it is his own fault that the 'eminent stationer' to whom he had sold it did not publish first: he had probably purposely delayed sending over the sheets, 'while by such delay he might publish himself and send over his complete edition here as he has done to one *M——n*, a stationer from *Scotland*, who joins him in this injurious confederacy'. The public is vehemently urged not to purchase books printed in England.[67]

Faulkner got a mutual friend named Johnson to write to Richardson defending at least Faulkner's role, but in a reply to Faulkner Richardson described his actions in bitter terms and implied that he was almost as guilty as the pirates: 'What can I think *of*, what can I say *for*, Mr. Faulkner; but this—That he has given a proof, that it must be an ingenuous mind only, that, having made a false step, will choose to own the fault, as the best method of extricating itself.'[68] Faulkner was in no mood to own his fault, however. He wrote to Richardson, in a letter which must have crossed Richardson's, that he proposed to break off negotiations with the pirates.[69] But on 3 November, perhaps irritated by Richardson's high moral stand, he printed an announcement in his *Dublin Journal* giving an account of the affair as he saw it: immediately after he had posted his title to the work, on 3 August, the other three booksellers had posted theirs, and the invariable custom among the booksellers of Dublin was 'that whoever gets any Books or Pamphlets, or any Part of them, by the same Post, shall, or may join together, if they think proper'. Faulkner, therefore, asked Richardson to send no more sheets, offering to pay in proportion to the share he might have, and 'in two or three Letters following, he told Mr. Richardson, that notwithstanding the Neglect and Delay, in not sending him the Sheets directly from the Press, which he ought to have done, and not have stayed for the finishing of five or six Volumes, it might have prevented what hath happened to all Parties, and hindered the reprinting of any other Edition, but that designed by the Author for Mr. Faulkner; yet Mr. Richardson might draw upon him for any Sum not exceeding the Contract, and he would pay it; and further, that if Mr. Richardson would acquit him of the Contract, or desire him to withdraw from his Partnership with the Booksellers, he would do it.' Richardson had 'delayed answering these Letters for some Time', and Faulkner had declined the partnership and did not intend to have any share in *Sir Charles Grandison*.[70] This announcement inspired Richardson with great indignation and was the

---

[67] 29 Oct., 5 Nov.
[68] 16 Oct. The letter is quoted in R to Lady Echlin, 24 Nov.
[69] 20 Oct.   [70] 30 Oct.–3 Nov., 3 Nov.–6 Nov.

immediate occasion for the *Address to the Public* which he later printed, denouncing Faulkner even more bitterly than he denounced the pirates.

Richardson, having broken with Faulkner, made arrangements with Main to publish the novel in Dublin. Main's edition was announced on 1 November, as emanating from one 'who has kindly undertaken to do the Proprietor that Justice, which almost all the Booksellers and Printers of Dublin have refused him'.[71] But the pirated edition was advertised soon afterwards: six volumes of seven were ready, reprinted from the octavo, which had the advantage of many corrections.[72]

Richardson did not cease to worry about the pirates after the first volumes of *Sir Charles Grandison* were published. Among his papers is a notice which Skelton proposed to insert in the Irish press, denouncing the pirates and urging the public to buy Main's edition as an act of probity.[73] Perhaps untactfully, Skelton countered the argument that to buy the Irish edition was more patriotic by asserting that English and Irish interests were one, that Ireland had a great debt to England, and that, besides, the latter country was more powerful and should not be irritated. He ended by claiming that to buy a stolen edition of such a work as *Sir Charles* was as dishonest as stealing a Bible. Richardson worried because Skelton's intervention had made him such enemies among the Irish booksellers as to injure the sale of Skelton's own works.[74] Lady Bradshaigh appealed to her sister Lady Echlin, who was living in Ireland, and the latter wrote to Richardson offering to help; in reply he sent her a full account of the case.[75] He drew up his case against Faulkner,[76] which was published on 1 February 1754, as *An Address to the Public*. It was distributed gratis and was inserted in the last volume of the novel.

The pirates, Richardson informed Edwards, met with success. Something should be done for the security of authors, but he did not expect to live to see it. Faulkner had half-heartedly offered to pay Richardson the whole of the seventy guineas promised, but Richardson refused and did not repent his refusal.[77] Nor did he have reason to be pleased with his new Dublin bookseller. Main kept eighty-one pounds, eighteen shillings which he had received for Richardson 'and had a large Profit allowed him besides'; he gave Richardson a note for his debt early in 1755, but since he went bankrupt, Richardson had no way of collecting and feared he had

---

[71] *London Evening-Post.*

[72] *Pue's Occurrences* (Dublin), 13–17 Nov.

[73] FM XV, 4, fos. 45–8.

[74] R to Lady Echlin, 24 July 1754.

[75] R to Lady Echlin, 24 Nov. See also Lady Bradshaigh to R, 27 Nov.; R to Lady Bradshaigh, 8 Dec.

[76] R to Lady Echlin, 30 Jan.

[77] R to Edwards, 16 Feb.; R to Skelton, 17 Mar. On 24 July Richardson asked Lady Echlin for a line to tell him whether the pirates had reprinted the last volume, what their success had been, and whether they or Faulkner had answered his *Case*.

'been guilty of a premeditated Baseness'.[78] Richardson was bitter about the Irish experience for years. He must have been thinking of Main in 1758 when he referred to 'the very Man I trusted to, running away with the chiefest Part of the Money that came into his Hands; and one of the once active Friends I had in Dublin, obliging me to interest a Stranger to me, to bring him but to *Composition-Justice*'.[79]

Although forced temporarily to stop his presses, Richardson went forward with plans to publish. On 11 September 1753 he sent Stinstra the first four volumes, and on 19 September he sent the third and fourth to Mrs. Chapone, telling her that no one had yet seen them. Soon afterwards Mrs. Carter and Dr. Johnson had received a part of the novel.[80] Sir Roger and Lady Bradshaigh received the first four volumes on 13 October,[81] and on 4 November he wrote that they and two 'hitherto contented old virgins' who were with them were dying with impatience for the two last volumes.[82] Lady Bradshaigh noticed 'many alterations from the manuscript', and Richardson explained that what she had seen 'was immediately transcribed from the first Running' and that he had had a second copy on which he had made corrections, some of them suggested by her.[83]

On 1 October Richardson registered the first two volumes of the octavo with the Stationers' Company, to secure copyright, on 7 November the third and fourth, on 5 December the fifth, and on 11 March 1754 the last.[84] He wrote to Lady Bradshaigh early in October that he was waiting to publish until the town filled and also because he did not want to give the Irish a chance to complete their edition. He explained that his plan to publish duodecimo and octavo editions simultaneously was owing to his belief that it was unfair to the public to publish first an expensive edition and later a cheaper one.[85]

On 13 November the first four volumes appeared, in both the cheaper and the more expensive editions. Richardson had published four, instead of two as originally planned, evidently in order to forestall the pirates. The next two duodecimo volumes were promised for about 11 December and the final volume with all convenient speed. Several booksellers were listed, most of them Richardson's old friends (Millar, Rivington, Dodsley, Leake), but also Main in Dublin and two partnerships in Edinburgh.[86] But Richardson told Lady Bradshaigh that Rivington had taken the whole bookselling part on himself—presumably the responsibility for distribution—and that the booksellers had already 'subscribed for the whole

---

[78] R to Lady Echlin, 28 May, 7 July 1755.
[79] To Mrs. Chapone, 27 June.
[80] See pp. 356, 334.
[81] Lady Bradshaigh to R, 14 Oct.
[82] Postscript to Lady Bradshaigh's letter of 4 Nov.
[83] 27 Nov., 8 Dec.
[84] 'Entries of Copies 1746–73', pp. 132, 134, 136, 139, MS. in the archives of the Stationers' Company.
[85] 5 Oct.
[86] *Public Advertiser*, 9 Nov., 10 Nov., 12 Nov., 13 Nov.

Impression in Twelves, and a considerable Number in Octavo'. By early December the booksellers were almost out of the duodecimo, and a new edition was being planned. Three thousand copies of this cheaper edition had been printed; of the more expensive octavo one thousand had been printed, but they evidently went more slowly. Richardson was disappointed only in the sale in Ireland, and there because of the lower price of the pirated edition.[87]

On 11 December volumes five and six were offered to the public, along with the fifth volume of the octavo.[88] Soon afterwards Miss Talbot wrote to Julia Berkeley that the first edition 'has sold off much faster than the first of Clarissa did, & there will soon be a new one'; 'everybody' was discussing *Sir Charles*. Of adverse criticism, she (in her clerical circles) had heard only that some people disliked the Catholic compromise, the offer that the hero made to the family of Clementina that if he married her he would allow their female children to be brought up as Catholics.[89] By 4 January the new duodecimo (sometimes called the second edition, but really the third) was being printed at several different presses, for the sake of haste, but the publication of the last volume had been delayed—presumably by the difficulty of printing fast enough. Richardson told Philip Skelton that the press of business had forced him to give the new edition to several printers and to take in help for the last volume of the first edition. In mid-February Richardson was regretting further delay and hoping for publication of the last volume by early March.[90]

The delay in publishing the last volume gave Richardson a chance to tease Lady Bradshaigh about the ending, as he had earlier teased Miss Mulso and Miss Highmore. But Lady Bradshaigh, the strongest opponent of the tragic end of *Clarissa* and the godmother of *Sir Charles*, took the teasing more seriously than they had done. On 5 October Richardson hinted that his novel might have a 'strange, perhaps, unnatural Catastrophe', and Lady Bradshaigh took the hint: 'But how you frighten me Sir? the *strange* perhaps *unnatural* Catastrophe. What or how can it be? *Polygamy* once popt into my head.' Richardson encouraged her misconception and hinted that Harriet might even make the proposal to give up her husband for half of each year to the Lady Clementina: 'If I resolve, never fear but I make it probable, and glorious for both Ladies.' Lady Bradshaigh did not find this solution 'in *nature*'—'but what a fool I am, I know you are only allarming me, and you did allarm me'. Richardson then asked her advice about the ending—his own family did not know it, though one other family and two people besides did. How was he to dispose of Clementina—marriage to the Count of Belvidere, death, seclusion in a

---

[87] R to Lady Bradshaigh, 12 Nov., 8 Dec.
[88] *Public Advertiser*, 7 Dec., 11 Dec.   [89] 19 Dec., B.M. Add. MS. 46,689.
[90] R to Lady Bradshaigh, 4 Jan.; R to Skelton, 3 Apr.; R to Sarah Wescomb, 17 Feb.

nunnery, polygamy, or marriage to Sir Charles after the death of Harriet? Lady Bradshaigh was hardly pleased with the two last alternatives—she wished all happiness to Harriet's rival, all happiness except Sir Charles; Harriet had already married the hero, and Lady Bradshaigh, who decidedly preferred the English to the Italian heroine, saw no need for further complications.[91] On 14 January she added a note to a letter begun on 23 December: 'If anything is to happen to obstruct the happyness of Sr Charles & Lady Grandison, why I shall have a fine flameing Bone-fire, that's *all*, except that I shall wish you in the midst of it.'

Richardson was enjoying the exchange too much to let it languish. 'Dear Madam,' he wrote on 8 February, 'permit me to . . . make a glorious Exit for Harriet [I never yet killed a Woman in her *Regal* Month] and bequeath her Husband, and her surviving Child to Clementina. . . . I can draw, I fancy, a charming Child-bed Death.' And he gave her a sample of a deathbed scene proving that he could. 'There, Madam! Do you like me *now?*—No *Bonfires* I hope; no *Faggot* to be made of your Admirer and humble Servant, to augment the Blaze.' Before she received this letter, Lady Bradshaigh reported that she had heard a lady say that Sir Charles was to be drowned, 'at which I laugh'd and look'd wise, holding the Lady's knowledge very cheap, but who knows? You are a very surprizeing man. And this wou'd be a *master* stroke. Suppose Hero, Heroines, with the most valuable friends on both sides, shou'd all sink in the same bottom, in passing to, or from Italy? Good Heavens! What a shocking thought? I *hate* myself.' As to the fate of Harriet and the Lady Clementina '(O—dose that savage *live* who wou'd *kill* either of them. He *shou'd not* if I cou'd come at him)', Clementina should marry the Count of Belvidere, Harriet should keep Sir Charles, and all should remain friends, she argued for three pages. In reply Richardson dropped an ominous hint: Sir Charles was not to be drowned. 'In such a death he could not be great. He must struggle and resist like a common man. Such a hero cannot fall alone, that's certain—But you will soon see what I have done.' He wishes that he had read her argument for the marriage of Clementina to the Count of Belvidere sooner—'But what is done, is done.' Lady Bradshaigh took the threat of death for Harriet seriously: 'Wou'd I had *never* re'd Clarissa, wou'd I had *never*, officiously (and to please my own ridiculous humour,) wrote to its author, wou'd he had *never* wrote, the long expected Grandison, once my *delight*, now my *Torment*.' His second letter arrived while she was writing her answer to the first (Lady Bradshaigh often wrote her letters, like Richardson's characters, journal-wise, over several days) and only confirmed her fears. 'I wish I cou'd raise my passion a little, it wou'd do me good, but no,—I am at present a piece of *Still Life*. Very small indeed. . . . I will only add, (if I can for Tears) that I have done with

[91] 27 Nov., 8 Dec., 11 Dec., 4 Jan.

what I propos'd to be the entertainment of my *Life*, my long *expected*, and much *admir'd*, Sr Charles Grandison. May you be happy, with the applause of your more judicious readers, and may I be a *single* Mourner, and dis-approver of your scheme' (she had been made to understand that the judicious approved of the ending of *Clarissa*, but she had no ambition to be considered judicious). She was 'far from well'.[92]

Richardson was touched. 'What a Wretch am I!' He hastened to assure her that he had been joking and that she would not be 'much displeased' with the ending. 'God allmighty bless you Dear Sir', was her response. 'I wish you had seen me open your letter, *trembling*, laying it *down*, takeing it *up* again, unresolv'd whether to look at the *begining*, or *conclution* first. At last, I ventur'd to unfold it *partly*, and with a *side* glance, read a few words, which instantly produced, the *happiest* tears I ever shed.' How could she guess he was teasing? 'There is no knowing when you *grave* men joke.' Sir Roger had known all along he was teasing, she wrote a few days later.[93]

Richardson started to send the last volume to Thomas Edwards on 7 March but had to add in a postscript that it was not yet ready. It finally appeared, in both duodecimo and octavo, on 14 March.[94] Lady Bradshaigh received it on 18 March, and it excelled all—she '*laugh'd* and *cry'd* thro the whole, but when I came to the *last* word, I even sob'd again. Is this the *last*, the *last work* of this Inimitable Author?' But she dried her tears in thankfulness for knowing him. 'What charming thoughts! O Sir! you ought to have been a Bishop.'[95]

---

[92] 5 Feb., 14 Feb., 22 Feb.
[94] *Public Advertiser*, 13 Mar., 14 Mar.
[93] 25 Feb., 1 Mar., 22 Mar. (begun on 3 Mar.).
[95] 22 Mar.

PLATES

PLATE 2

I. Van Diest pinx.

I. Faber fecit.

Georgius Cheynæus. M.D.
et Societatis Regiæ Socius.
Ætat: 59. 1732.

Sold at the Great Toy Shop in Bath.

George Cheyne by John Faber after J. Van Diest

PLATE 3

Samuel Richardson
and his family
with Elizabeth
Midwinter (circa
1741) by Francis
Hayman

PLATE 4

Sarah Wescomb

PLATE 5

Sir Roger and Lady Bradshaigh on the lawn at Haigh

PLATE 6

Samuel Richardson (1750) by Joseph Highmore

PLATE 7

Elizabeth Leake Richardson by Joseph Highmore

PLATE 8

Edward Young by Joseph Highmore

PLATE 9

THOMAS EDWARDS ESQ.

Author of the Canons of Criticism.

Ob. Jan 3, 1757. Æt. 58.

Engraved by W. Holl from the original painting in the Possession of Mr J. H. Burn, Bookseller.

London Pub.d by. J. Wivell, Castle Street East, 1828.

Thomas Edwards by William Holl

PLATE 10

Susanna Highmore by Joseph Highmore

PLATE 11

Richardson Reading *Sir Charles Grandison* in his grotto to Thomas Mulso, JR.,
Edward Mulso, Hester Mulso, Mary Prescott, John Duncombe, and Susanna
Highmore by Susanna Highmore

CHAPTER XV

SIR CHARLES GRANDISON

*S*IR *Charles Grandison* has found admirers—notably Jane Austen and George Eliot, who found the morality perfect and was sorry it was not longer.[1] Unlike the second part of *Pamela*, it has virtues. But it is not a good novel. Richardson shows that he has learned a great deal about the technique of writing fiction, and he takes pains to keep up the interest, especially by arousing suspense. His conscious artistry is apparent; it keeps the novel from being boring, at least through the first five of the seven volumes; but it does not do more than that. Brian Downs is perhaps correct in calling *Sir Charles* Richardson's best book in a technical sense (though *Clarissa* has a technique which, though it calls less attention to itself and was probably less conscious, is at least as effective); he is certainly correct in concluding that on the whole it is 'a poorer thing' than *Clarissa* or the first part of *Pamela*[2]—if it offends less, it also gives less delight.

The first volume is the most interesting. It shows the structural skill which Richardson had mastered. The appearance of the hero is delayed while interest is built up around the heroine, or one of the heroines, Harriet Byron. She emerges, in a series of lively scenes of realistic social comedy, as a charming if rather sharp-tongued young lady, well able to take care of herself. When her character is well established, the plot thickens: one of her many admirers, Sir Hargrave Pollexfen, abducts her from a masquerade and attempts to force her to marry him. Enter the hero. He hears her screaming from a coach and, after cautiously and correctly assuring himself that she is not Lady Pollexfen, rescues her.

From then on, the novel never allows one to forget for very long that it is about Sir Charles Grandison. If Richardson is correct in saying that there are no episodes,[3] it is because all of the various events and characters are used to illustrate the Good Man's virtues. There is, to be sure, a main plot thread: Sir Charles loves Harriet but is loved by and half committed to the aristocratic and loftily virtuous Italian, Lady Clementina della Porretta. But there are many subsidiary threads. The structure is less like

---

[1] *The George Eliot Letters*, ed. Gordon S. Haight (New Haven, 1954–5), I, 240; II, 65; VI, 320.

[2] *Richardson*, pp. 98, 89.　　　　　　　　[3] In the Preface to *Sir Charles Grandison*.

that of *Clarissa* than that of *Tom Jones*, which also has inserted into the main plot various episodes designed to illustrate moral issues connected with the character of the hero. Sir Charles must be shown (in a flashback) as an ideal son to a difficult father; as an ideal brother to his two sisters, one of whom, Charlotte, furnishes a good deal of the liveliness of the book; as an ideal guardian to his young ward, Emily Jervois; as an ideal friend to young Edward Beauchamp. His conduct is perfect in dealing with his father's housekeeper and former mistress, his sister Charlotte's youthful infatuation, his ward's mercenary and dissipated mother, his immoral tutor, his rakish old uncle, his scatterbrained cousin Everard, his passionate admirer Lady Olivia.

The variety of stories necessary to show all of Sir Charles's virtues somewhat dissipates the interest. The novel does not have the single-minded concentration of *Clarissa* or the early part of *Pamela*, and Richardson resorted to the same sort of tricks for maintaining suspense which he used in the latter part of *Pamela*. Throughout most of *Clarissa* there is only one thing for the reader to think about. In *Sir Charles Grandison* his interest shifts. In the second volume interest is centred on Harriet's growing love, with digressions on the hero's past history and little incidental mysteries— why does Sir Charles slip off to Canterbury? By the end of that volume Harriet has been overcome by the splendours and virtues of the Good Man; her struggle is over, and throughout the rest of the novel she has nothing important to do except to hope that her love will be returned and to confess her feelings with remarkable frankness to almost all comers. Interest shifts to Sir Charles's Italian *innamorata*, whose history is recounted, partly in the past tense and partly to the moment in excerpts from Sir Charles's and Mrs. Beaumont's letters to Dr. Bartlett, throughout most of the third volume. In volume four Charlotte's marriage with Lord G. and her shrewish treatment of her meek husband occupy the centre of the stage for a good deal of the time. A weaker effort to arouse interest is made with the introduction of Lady Olivia. Sir Charles returns to Italy to make one more try to win Clementina; he loves Harriet, but duty tells him that his first loyalty is in Bologna, where the woman to whom he had once felt bound to offer his hand has run mad at being deprived of him. Luckily Clementina overcomes herself and prefers her religion to her love for a Protestant, and by the end of the fifth volume everything is really settled. The last two volumes, as has been recognized, are 'quite superfluous'.[4] Frances Grainger, though charmed herself, reported to Richardson that most readers failed to appreciate the 'almost passive beauties' of the final volume.[5] Richardson tried hard to keep something going: Harriet's suitor Greville tries to make trouble, she herself is unexpectedly and belatedly afflicted with delicacy and cannot bring herself to name the day, Emily

---

[4] Thomson, *Richardson*, p. 241; Dobson, *Richardson*, p. 136. [5] 23 May 1754.

evinces innocent love for her guardian, Charlotte is partially tamed by her
brother, finally Clementina and her family arrive in England. But nothing
really happens; most of volumes six and seven are as tedious as the second
part of *Pamela*. One can understand why the venerable old lady of Scott's
acquaintance chose to hear *Sir Charles Grandison* read to her in preference
to any other work, '"because," said she, "should I drop asleep in course
of the reading, I am sure, when I awake, I shall have lost none of the
story, but shall find the party, where I left them, *conversing in the cedar-
parlour*."'[6]

Though *Sir Charles Grandison* is in the epistolary form, it only occasionally takes full advantage of the form. A good deal of the early part is
straight narrative by Harriet. But it is done 'to the moment'. The first
Italian episode, like a good deal of the rest of the book, takes in part the
form of past narrative and thus misses the full advantage of Richardson's
characteristic method. Dr. Bartlett, for instance, tells us much of what has
happened in Bologna; we hear the voices of Sir Charles and Clementina
only occasionally. And, unlike Lovelace's and Clarissa's, their voices have
no distinctive tone. Nor do we often see through their eyes. Whether the
narrative method, which Richardson never mastered, keeps us out of the
minds of his characters or whether his failure to imagine those characters
led him to resort to the method might be argued.

Throughout his work, Richardson reinforces the effect of reality with
minute details. *Sir Charles Grandison* is even more fully documented than
the earlier novels. Richardson had never seen Italy, yet Mrs. Piozzi,
visiting Bologna, was constantly reminded of the Porretta family: 'Dear
Richardson at Salisbury Court Fleet Street, and Parson's Green, Fulham
[Mrs. Piozzi did not know when Richardson changed his country house],
felt all within him that travelling can tell, or experience confirm.'[7] And the
solidity of Richardson's Bologna is remarkable. Hazlitt reports that he at
first considered the full description of Harriet's wedding dress tedious,
'till I was told of two young ladies who had severally copied out the whole
of that very description for their own private gratification'.[8] 'We get the
same sort of elaborate familiarity with every aspect of affairs that we should
receive from reading a blue-book full of some prolix diplomatic correspondence', says Sir Leslie Stephen. 'The result of all this is a sort of
Dutch painting of extraordinary minuteness. . . . We are gradually forced
into familiarity with them [the characters] by a process resembling that by
which we learn to know people in real life.'[9] Sir John Everett Millais
enthusiastically called the novel 'pure pre-Raphaelitism'.[10]

[6] 'Memoir' of Richardson, *Ballantyne's Novelist's Library*, VI (1824), xlvi.

[7] *Observations and Reflections Made in the Course of a Journey through France, Italy, and Germany*
(London, 1789), I, 265–6.   [8] *Works*, VI, 118.   [9] 'Richardson's Novels', pp. 55–6.

[10] Letter from John Ruskin to his father, 3 Oct. 1853, quoted by Mary Lutyens, *Millais and
the Ruskins* (New York, [1967]), p. 94n.

The cast of characters in *Sir Charles* is large. Hazlitt remarks that 'the effect of reading this work is like an increase of kindred. You find yourself all of a sudden introduced into the midst of a large family, with aunts and cousins to the third and fourth generation, and grandmothers both by the father's and mother's side;—and a very odd set of people they are, but people whose real existence and personal identity you can no more dispute than your own senses,—for you see and hear all that they do or say.'[11] The effect of reality is undoubted and is probably the greatest strength of the book. There is something of the same effect that one gets in the detailed and solidly drawn country-club scenes of John O'Hara. One is *there*, certainly; but one would rather be somewhere else. Horace Walpole's interest in this domestic realism gave out in the fourth volume: 'I was so tired of sets of people getting together, and saying, "Pray, Miss, with whom are you in love?"'[12] In volume six, especially, one has the impression of actually being at a house-party with a lot of sufficiently individualized but very dull people, who have nothing stimulating to say and nothing at all to do. Yet there is no doubt that the realism of presentation is worthy. And an authority with whom one hesitates to disagree did not find it boring. Henry Austen, in the 'Biographical Notice' to the posthumous edition of *Northanger Abbey* and *Persuasion*, tells us how much his sister enjoyed this novel: 'Richardson's power of creating, and preserving the consistency of his characters, as particularly exemplified in "Sir Charles Grandison," gratified the natural discrimination of her mind.'[13] As to whether the minor characters are better drawn than those in Richardson's earlier novels, there seems to be room for a difference of opinion. Miss Thomson, for instance, holds that they are.[14] Our opinion is that while there is no doubt of their reality there is a good deal of question as to how interesting that reality is.

Thrown back on subjective judgement, we can only say that for us some of the characters never have any life at all: Beauchamp, Mrs. Shirley, Dr. Bartlett, Mr. Deane, Clementina's parents, Fowler, Orme, Lord and Lady L., Mrs. Beaumont merely repeat the lines Richardson thinks they ought to repeat. Others show signs of life, only to subside into ecstatic praises when exposed to the Good Man: Lord W., Sir Hargrave, Lady Beauchamp, Jeronymo. Olivia is a rather half-hearted attempt at a woman of wild passions and demonstrates pretty clearly that Richardson's experience with her type was confined to hearsay. Uncle Selby and Sir Rowland are not unworthy attempts at the quaint old character so dear to the

[11] *Works*, VI, 118.

[12] Letter to Richard Bentley, 19 Dec. 1753, *Letters*, ed. Mrs. Paget Toynbee (Oxford, 1903–5), III, 202.

[13] Oxford Illustrated Edition, ed. R. W. Chapman (New York, London, Toronto, 1954), p. 7. See also E. E. Duncan-Jones, 'Notes on Jane Austen', *N&Q*, CXCVI (1951), 15–16.

[14] *Richardson*, p. 233.

Victorian novel, though it is hard to avoid thinking how much better Dickens would have handled them. The adolescent Emily is, when her guardian is absent, an appealing combination of simple sweetness and simple jealousy, with some unconscious lust in the background. It is hard to believe that any woman of her class was ever so rude as Charlotte Grandison, but Lady Bradshaigh, who knew more about her own century that we can know, was delighted with her and even saw herself in the character. Probable or not, she is lively. Richardson's enjoyment of sharp-tongued women had already created Lady Davers and Anna Howe, and before her love for a good man Harriet shows the characteristics of the type. But Charlotte is his most elaborate treatment of it.

Harriet is also drawn from inside, at least during much of the book. Her gradually dawning love is analysed in much the same way as that of Pamela and Clarissa had been. She shows the pride and jealousy natural in her position; she struggles against her attachment; she even tries (in vain) to find faults in her idol. If her role after the second volume had been a more active one, the novel might have had a great deal more life.

Clementina, on the other hand, is only occasionally allowed to speak or think for herself. The letter she writes to Sir Charles resigning her love for him while admitting that she does not dare to argue with him in person, that she would be convinced at the time only to suffer again from doubts when he was absent, that it is still in his power to force her to break her resolution, makes her briefly convincing as a person.[15] But generally she is convincing in another way, as a character in melodrama. Without believing in her, we are at times swept along until we forget that we do not believe in her. Of all Richardson's characters, she owes most to the stage. If she is not Shakespearean, she is worthy of comparison with the best of Otway or Nat Lee or Rowe. She is what some people like to call 'good theatre'. And though Richardson at his best could do better than 'good theatre', Clementina's scenes do serve to keep the novel moving. Their quality is best recognized in volume six, when they are over and nothing has taken their place.

It is, however, unfortunately, the third of the principal characters who dominates the book. Ruskin's hesitation as to whether Sir Charles or Don Quixote was his favourite character in romance must be regarded as simply odd, like his reaction to re-reading the Clementina scenes: 'At present I feel disposed to place this work above all other works of fiction I know. It is very, very grand; and has, I think, a greater practical effect on me for good than anything I ever read in my life.'[16] The trouble with *Sir Charles Grandison* is Sir Charles. When he is absent, the novel stirs to life. When he appears, it freezes. And he is never long absent after the first volume. He touches the other characters with the icy finger of death. Indeed, one

[15] SH, V, 292–6.   [16] *Works* (London, 1903–12), XXXVI, 193; XXXV, 308.

is reminded of the 'Dance of Death': when he enters, they all stop whatever they are doing. But instead of being whisked off to sing praises to the Supreme Deity, they break out in a chorus of praise for this merely mortal one. They are always stunned into admiring silence by the platitudes and the long familiar reasoning of the paragon. Over and over again, a group of people will begin to speak and act in a natural way, to develop a conflict, even to rebel and disagree with the hero. They cannot hold out—one reasonable speech from Sir Charles, explaining clearly, calmly, and firmly the demands of virtue, and they collapse. The riotous companions of Sir Hargrave lapse into reverential nonentity; the Porrettas are bludgeoned kindlily into submission; Greville and Lady Beauchamp and Emily's mother and step-father endeavour to resist—in vain. Against Lady Beauchamp, Sir Charles even uses the weapon of banter, with chilling effect. All are crushed—for their own good, of course, but hardly for the reader's. Only Charlotte rises again after her moral defeat, but she does so only to subside again. The result, as William Henry Hudson has pointed out, is 'a demonstration rather than a story'.[17]

Mrs. Barbauld, who so often anticipated the discoveries of later critics, early saw Sir Charles's main faults. He is afflicted with 'a certain stiffness'; he is too often '*proné*' by the other characters; and he is too successful: 'Prosperous perfection does not greatly engage our sympathy.'[18] Philip Skelton had warned Richardson that his hero must be persecuted; but he was determined, even after the loftier morality of *Clarissa*, to see virtue triumphant, and he could not bear to make it wait long for its triumph. 'How shall we call virtue by its name, if it be not tried', writes Harriet.[19] But she is writing of Sir Charles's trial in being loved by Clementina, which is the best trial Richardson managed to invent for him. That might be enough if he ever made us believe that Sir Charles was really in love with two women. But his morality prevented him from exposing his hero to such a genuine trial. He hedged. 'I own to you, Ladies,' says the hero of his sublime Italian, 'that what was before *honour* and *compassion*, now became *admiration*; and I should have been unjust to the merits of so excellent a woman, if I could not say, *Love*.' This is Sir Charles in the grip of passion. One of his views, Richardson wrote to Lady Bradshaigh, was 'to shew the Vincibility of' love.[20] Sir Charles's love is convincingly vincible. Later, to save Harriet from the impropriety of loving a man who did not love her, he tells her (and he is always truthful) that he would have proposed to her early if he had not been bound by honour to Clementina.[21] Were one to take this literally, one would conclude that he loved Harriet at first sight, then went unwillingly to renew his proposals

---

[17] *A Quiet Corner in a Library* (Chicago, [1915]), p. 212.
[18] I, cxxxix.   [19] SH, IV, 16.
[20] SH, V, 111; 14 Feb. 1754.   [21] SH, VI, 42.

to Clementina because he felt constrained to do so by a nice sense of honour and admired and almost loved her in turn, only to return when free to Harriet.

But it is futile to think about Sir Charles's 'real' passions. We are never at any time allowed inside his mind—indeed his mind has no inside, because he must do what virtue requires. This fact is the most damning comment possible on the kind of virtue presented in Sir Charles Grandison —it cannot be imagined as existing in a person, it has no relation to the human mind. In order to illustrate it, Richardson was forced to give us a character whose feelings and motives had to be slurred over. We can never press his author as to his motivations, or speculate as we can speculate about Lovelace and Clarissa and even Pamela and Harriet. He cannot struggle mentally because he can never fail to overcome any desire for what is improper. Therefore he cannot be in love with two women, and his trial with Clementina is rather an embarrassment—an over-eager woman has thrown herself at him and he is willing to do the right thing and marry her. Fortunately she herself saves him from having to. The other trials are still more easily overcome, and his virtue never has to be put to any test.[22]

Mr. Downs and Mr. McKillop have compared Sir Charles with Meredith's egoist, Sir Willoughby Patterne: 'His benevolence is part of a system and is inseparably connected with his control of property and with the policies determined by his reason and his will.'[23] Hazlitt, even more severe, calls him 'the prince of coxcombs,—whose eye was never once taken from his own person, and his own virtues'. He cites with approval the remark of an acquaintance that 'Richardson would be surprised in the next world to find Lovelace in Heaven and Grandison in Hell!'[24] More reasonable is Sir Leslie Stephen's view that Sir Charles's morality has no heights but is 'compounded of common sense and a regard for decorum' —'not a very exalted ideal'.[25]

We may be unduly irritated today with virtue based on a system. We are, after all, still in the shadow of the movement which followed closely on Richardson's heels and to which he even contributed, which holds that the true morality is that of feeling. Richardson even tried to give his hero this sort of morality; Sir Charles asserts that he suffers from a feeling heart, and at least he is not bound by public opinion when he thinks it wrong—he does not confuse morality and propriety as so many middle-class model characters have done: 'Great God! I thank thee, thought I, that thou enablest me to do what my conscience, what humanity tells me, is fit and right to be done, without taking my measures of right and

---

[22] See McKillop, *Richardson*, p. 209.

[23] *Richardson*, p. 118; *Richardson*, pp. 210, 207.

[24] *Works*, VI, 120; XVII, 249. [25] 'Richardson's Novels', p. 61.

wrong from any other standard.' Harriet seems to be suspecting her lover of coldness when she wonders what he would have done if he had been Adam and his Eve had tasted the forbidden fruit. He could not, surely, share in the fault. 'No; it is my opinion, that your brother would have had gallantry enough to his fallen spouse, to have made him extremely regret her lapse; but that he would have done *his own duty*, were it but for the sake of posterity, and left it to the Almighty, if such had been his pleasure, to have annihilated his first Eve, and given him a second.'[26] Milton's Adam would have done the same thing, if he had followed Milton's advice. Probably no Adam since 1790 would have felt justified in doing so, but it is not yet a settled question, whatever the assumptions of our age may be, whether an Adam led by passion is better than an Adam with a system of ethics. Sir Charles, at any rate, has a system of ethics.

Austin Dobson is just enough to Sir Charles when he decides that he is 'not really so unsupportable'.[27] He seems more repulsive than he is because Richardson tried to make us believe that he is a great deal better than he is. Judged as a prosperous and respectable middle-class man (for his aristocracy is never very convincing), Sir Charles is well above the average. Judged, as he is meant to be, as an ideal, he is not good enough. Except for his preservation of his chastity and his refusal to fight a duel, nothing that he does is beyond the powers of an ordinary man of good will. Like Pamela, he is endowed with unconvincing and unnecessary accomplishments: he is 'a Library of gardening', he plays the violin and the harpsichord like a master, he is 'one of the finest dancers in England'.[28] Richardson, by praising him too much, did him the same sort of injustice he did Pamela. Mrs. Andrew Lang's reaction is, if unfair, understandable— she found the admirers of Mr. B. and Sir Charles 'so servile, and the admired so odious, that I, for my part, am lashed into an absolute frenzy of annoyance'.[29] The other characters are in constant ecstasies about his virtues. They fall into raptures at the slightest civility; Harriet's rejected suitor Mr. Orme, for instance, needs only to exchange a few words with him after his marriage, in which Sir Charles politely tells him he will be welcome to visit him and his wife as their brother, and Mr. Orme gushes into tears and runs into the house crying, 'Good God! Good God! . . . He is all I have heard of him. Happy, happy Miss Byron!' When the wedding party alight from the coach to enter the church, Sir Charles devotes his attention to Harriet's lame grandmother, Mrs. Shirley, an example of common courtesy which is sufficient to charm the populace: 'He deserved to live to be old himself, one said: They would warrant,

---

[26] SH, II, 345; IV, 169, 362.   [27] *Richardson*, p. 157.
[28] SH, VI, 45; III, 412, 333.
[29] 'Manners and Morals in Richardson', *Littell's Living Age*, CLXXXIII (1889), 776.

others said, that he was a sweet-tempered man; and others, that he had a good heart.'[30] This sort of absurdity is not uncommon and makes one wonder what manners were generally expected in the eighteenth century.

Clementina's brother, a Catholic bishop, judges that 'were he *one of us* [he] might expect Canonization'.[31] The Marquis d'Argenson went even further when he agreed with those who called the book 'un second Nouveau Testament, et le Christ réapparu sur la terre'.[32] But Sir Charles's religion is obviously the sincere but moderate religion of an Anglican with a stake in his country and thus in his church. He is as far from being a saint as he is from being a martyr. He would have been justly admired as a bright light of the Sadduccees, he would have considered the Pharisees rather Methodistical, and he would certainly never have associated with those radical enthusiasts in Palestine who were likely to end on the gallows.

If one can forget the praises, Sir Charles is decent enough. He is apt to lay down the law and to be sure he is right; but one might speculate, if one could escape from the standards of a democratic age in which everyone is equally right, whether self-assurance has not generally been the mark of a superior man. Some of his laws are obviously laws that Richardson believed in himself. He rises early, for instance, like Clarissa—Richardson shared the middle-class notion that evening activities are suspect, whereas morning activities are bound to be moral (sin, for him, was committed at masquerades, not in countinghouses). He would have agreed with Dr. Johnson's opinion (with which today many would disagree violently) that 'there are few ways in which a man can be more innocently employed than in getting money'. Sir Charles dines earlier than most people in his condition—he will, 'in things he thinks right, be govern'd by his own rules, which are the laws of reason and convenience'.[33] But he is well-bred enough not to insist on such petty matters. He is always reasonable, using logic rather than emotion to support his ethical code. He is genuinely charitable. His charity is not, of course, the charity of St. Francis; it is more like the charity of his creator. But he gives up the bulk of an inheritance left him by his friend Mr. Danby to help Mr. Danby's relations. He is both considerate of and helpful to his father's former mistress and housekeeper, Mrs. Oldham. He takes frequent thought of the deserving poor. These are not the qualities of a saint; Sir Charles is never likely to suffer by his kindness. But if Sir Charles's charity is below the highest human ideal, it is above the common human practice.

In his chastity, also, Sir Charles probably resembled his creator, at least so far as we know. For a modern taste there is perhaps something a little

---

[30] SH, VI, 3–4; V, 366–7. [31] SH, IV, 228.

[32] *Mémoires*, ed. René d'Argenson (Paris, 1825), p. 437.

[33] Boswell, *Life*, II, 323; SH, I, 207.

ludicrous in his reflecting with joy that he did not take advantage of the favour shown him by Olivia, when he was '(shall I say?) the *sole* guardian of Olivia's honour!'[34] He says that he felt an almost irresistible temptation, but he necessarily left the nature of the temptation too vague to be convincing. Balzac, in *Le cousin Pons*, was one of the first to find that this characteristic of Sir Charles was not that of a proper hero of fiction: 'Sur terre, le juste, c'est l'ennuyeux Grandison, pour qui la Vénus des carrefours elle même se trouverait sans sexe.' Charlotte Grandison anticipated such an objection when she desired to keep Sir Charles's chastity from the ladies: 'I would not have my brother made the jest of one Sex, and the aversion of the other; and be thought so singular a young man.'[35]

Richardson said, as he said of *Clarissa*, that he did not mean any of his good characters to be absolutely faultless.[36] Writing to Miss Mulso of Sir Charles, he remarked, 'Well, but, after all, I shall want a few unpremeditated faults, were I to proceed, to sprinkle into this man's character, lest I should draw a *faultless monster*. . . . I would draw him as a mortal. He should have all the human passions to struggle with; and those he cannot conquer he shall endeavour to make subservient to the cause of virtue.'[37] Harriet does have some faults, because Harriet is at times done from the inside; she can be petty, malicious, jealous. Richardson says that Sir Charles has faults, but he only says it, he cannot show it.

Harriet, when she is still only in process of being overcome by Sir Charles's virtues, tries to discover faults in him. He seems to be too reserved, not quite frank. He savours of singularity in not docking his horses' tails (she later discovers that this is not singularity but sensible kindness to dumb brutes). Later she thinks him too calm and prudent for not coming to her at the hour he promised, only to find that he had an excellent reason for his delay. She resents his going off to town so soon after she had accepted him, again to be silenced when she hears his motive. He stays too long at dinner with Mr. Greville—and of course was quite right in doing so.[38] Richardson is chiefly bringing his heroine to life, but at the same time he teases the reader with the hope that something may be wrong with his hero. Nothing is. In his Concluding Note he is indirectly defending his presentation of a perfect character, as well as hitting at Fielding, when he mentions that many modern fictions in which 'heroes of vicious, if not of profligate, characters' have been crowned with success are defended on the grounds that 'they have exhibited Human Nature as it *is*. Its corruption may, indeed, be exhibited in the faulty character; but need pictures of this be held out in books?'[39] Whatever Richardson said

---

[34] SH, IV, 416.
[35] *La comédie humaine* ([Paris]: Bibliothèque de la Pléiade, [1955]), VI, 536; SH, IV, 186.
[36] To Stinstra, 28 June 1754.   [37] 11 July 1751.
[38] SH, I, 280, 278; V, 95, 215, 240.   [39] SH, VI, 329.

in general about his characters having faults, Sir Charles is, and is meant to be, free even from foibles.

Richardson presents his hero's perfection as the result of a successful struggle of principle against inclination. Sir Charles often tells us that he is a passionate man, choleric, rash, proud, imperious.[40] There is even some effort to convey the fervour of his love for Harriet, after they have been correctly engaged: 'And, dear Lady G. he downright kissed me—My lip; and not my cheek—and in so fervent a way—.' It is a measure of the ardour of Sir Charles's courtship that one of the most surprising and moving passages in the sixth volume is the scene in which instead of taking a seat he throws himself at the feet of Harriet and her aunt and sits on the floor. In context, it seems dashing, almost exciting. No, Sir Charles did not disown the passions; he even, like earlier moralists, found them useful in their place: 'I never am severe on Lovers foibles. Our passions may be made subservient to excellent purposes. Don't think you have a super-cilious brother. A susceptibility of the passion called *Love*, I condemn not as a fault; but the contrary. Your *brother*, Ladies . . . is no Stoic.'[41]

The above may serve as a fair sample not only of Sir Charles's passionate nature but of his conversational style. In some of the minor characters, in Harriet, and in Charlotte, Richardson shows his ability to write breathing, fast-shifting dialogue. But Sir Charles cannot speak. Richardson has to speak for him, and not in his own person, as he wrote to Lady Bradshaigh or Miss Wescomb, but as he felt an elegant paragon should speak.

Nor does Sir Charles write very much. Most of his story is told by others. Of course Richardson wanted to preserve the suspense of the double love and could not have his hero too early give away his secret (indeed, having no secret, he never gives it away). But he was technically skilful enough to have overcome this difficulty if he had wanted Sir Charles to speak and write, if he had had anything for him to say as he had for Lovelace and Clarissa. Sir Charles cannot write because there is no Sir Charles. His great fault is not his tendency to pomposity nor his lack of passion. It is that he is not realized. He is a collection of characteristics gathered around a name.

It is sometimes said that virtuous characters are never successful, and convincing good men are less frequent in fiction than vicious or fallible ones. But they are not lacking. One might contrast Sir Charles, for instance, with Alyosha Karamazov or with Prince Myshkin. Dostoievsky's characters are a good deal closer to canonization than Sir Charles. But, more important, they are real; they are a part of the author's mind imagined, embodied, and conveyed. Their goodness existed (along with a good deal else, it is true) in Dostoievsky before it passed to the char-acters. It is quite possible to create a virtuous character, but Sir Charles

[40] SH, I, 315, 392, 401; II, 373; III, 11, 388.   [41] SH, V, 182, 247, 169; II, 194.

is not that—he is merely a character who illustrates all the virtues. Richardson was a good man, and very much the same sort of good man as Sir Charles; but he has not succeeded in incorporating his goodness in Sir Charles, he has only told about it. Perhaps that sensible charitableness is not the kind of goodness which can be imaginatively realized, perhaps it did not lie in the level of the mind from which poetry comes, as the goodness of Clarissa (and the vice of Lovelace) did. Much of the novel seems designed to be read in the spirit with which one reads a sermon. Sydney Smith's praise sounds rather ambiguous today: 'Sir Charles Grandison is less agreeable than Tom Jones; but it is more agreeable than Sherlock and Tillotson; and teaches religion and morality to many who would not seek it in the productions of these professional writers.'[42]

Richardson did not understand that if an author is to convey a quality, a feeling, a value, he must infect the reader, to use Tolstoy's phrase. Clarissa does infect us. And her virtue is most successfully conveyed when there is least 'reason' for us to want to emulate her, when she is suffering and despised. In *Sir Charles Grandison*, as in *Pamela*, we have reasons for being virtuous. Too many reasons. Virtue is good policy, it is always admired, it is always successful, it brings joy to one's friends and honour after death, it brings riches at the same time that it gratifies the generous impulses of the heart.[43] In short, it does far too much. Richardson always points out that it is best to be virtuous on principle alone, and he himself was probably sincere in his principles, but he cannot bear that all the rest shall not be added. So though Sir Charles is a good enough man, he is also a correct man and a successful man, a man admired by the world— and a rich man. Verily he has his reward.

There are a good many incidental morals in *Sir Charles*. Richardson took up subjects he had discussed with his female correspondents, such as marriage with reformed rakes, parental authority, the vincibility of love, the proper difference between women and men.[44] At the end of the last volume, an 'Index Historical and Characteristical' of over a hundred pages contains '*A few only of the* SENTIMENTS *with which this Work abounds*'. A few samples will show the quality of Richardson's mind when he was moralizing, not creating. '*Apologies* uncalled for, are tacit confessions.' '*Attachments*, guilty ones, the inconvenience of pursuing them, politically as well as morally considered.' '*A Clergyman*, who is an honour to his cloth, may be said to be an ornament to human nature.' '*Disappointment* in Love is one of those cases in which a woman can shew fortitude.' '*Genius's*, different, given by Providence for different ends, and that all might become useful links of the same great chain.' '*Humanity* inseparable from true

---

[42] Review of Hannah More's *Cælebs*, *Edinburgh Review*, XIV (1809), 146.
[43] SH, II, 281, 342; III, 240, 354–5; IV, 71; VI, 48.
[44] SH, II, 80, 90, 218–19, 46; VI, 220–1; V, 406–8.

bravery.' '*Vice* is a coward, when it knows it will be resolutely opposed.' '*Virtue*. The cause of Virtue, and that of the Sex, can hardly be separated.' '*Virtuous Love* looks beyond this temporary scene.'[45] Richardson made *Sir Charles* the vehicle for the platitudes, undoubtedly sincere and invariably worthy, of a lifetime.

If one judges a book by its contribution to literary history, one can see the importance of *Sir Charles Grandison* as an ancestor of the realistic social novel, leading to Jane Austen.[46] There are several lively scenes when the hero is absent. The realistic surface is well maintained even when it is not very interesting—and it sometimes is interesting. A large cast of characters is manipulated with plausibility and consistency. The first volume promises a work of well-observed social comment, and though the promise is not fulfilled throughout the later volumes, it is never entirely neglected. This realistic, comic aspect gives the book a considerable historical importance and is also responsible for a large part of its intrinsic interest.

There is also some interest in the female characters, especially in Harriet and Charlotte. They are imagined from inside, as Pamela and Clarissa are imagined, though they are not so fresh as the former nor by any means so impressive as the latter. Their little foibles show Richardson's often-praised knowledge of women, and their wit is genuine and not always correct.

Clementina, with everything that pertains to her, is harder to assess. She was a new experiment on Richardson's part, a lofty theatrical character. She aims at tragedy—the tragedy of the Restoration and eighteenth century. And she has succeeded in moving. It must have been over Clementina that Stendhal wept so copiously in his garret, when he stole *Sir Charles* from his father's bookcase.[47] Any judgement of how successful she is will remain a matter of taste. We would say that though she is only convincing at the moment, she is not flat; she is a *tour de force*, but not a failure.

The three virtues mentioned above are not compatible ones. Clementina does not belong in a comedy of manners. *Sir Charles Grandison* lacks the unified tone of *Clarissa*, the concentration. It has qualities, but they are attached to it, not in it. There is no centre of interest, since if Sir Charles is the centre, he is not interesting. We are inclined to think that the great falling off, in spite of its technical skill, in Richardson's third novel was caused by its central plan. His earlier works (except the continuation of *Pamela*) seem to have sprung from a character conceived in a situation. Their basic plots are simple, and Richardson could elaborate at great

---

[45] The 'Index' is not reprinted in SH.
[46] See McKillop, *Richardson*, pp. 213, 242.
[47] *Henri Brulard*, Chap. 32.

length without losing touch with the thread of the story, filling in character and building up scenes. If *Sir Charles Grandison* did begin with the
idea of a plot about a man's double love, that plot and the hero of it must
have been entirely remade when the novel became the portrait of an
exemplary man. As it stands, the motive force of *Sir Charles Grandison* is
not a story or a realized character, or better the story of a realized character, but an ethical idea. In spite of its virtues, it leaves one with the
impression of its hero. And that hero has been cruelly but aptly summed
up by Taine: 'He is great, he is generous, he is refined, he is pious, he is
irreproachable; he has never done a mean action nor made a false gesture.
His conscience and his peruke are intact. Amen. We must canonize him
and stuff him [Il faut le canoniser et l'empailler].'[48]

[48] *Histoire de la littérature anglaise* (Paris, 1899), IV, 120.

CHAPTER XVI

THE RECEPTION OF
SIR CHARLES GRANDISON

THE Preface to the first edition of *Sir Charles Grandison* maintains the fiction that the letters are real letters, and the novel is said to be 'By the Editor of PAMELA and CLARISSA'. But the editor does not take much trouble to maintain the fiction: 'How such remarkable Collections of private Letters fell into his hands, he hopes the Reader will not think it very necessary to enquire.' The present work is owing to the insistence of 'several of his Friends', who wanted him to give 'the Character and Actions of a Man of TRUE HONOUR'. It is 'not published ultimately, nor even principally, any more than the other two [novels], for the Sake of Entertainment only'. Dr. Johnson objected to that part of the Preface which seemed 'to disclaim the composition': 'What is modesty if it departs from truth? Of what use is the disguise by which nothing is concealed?'[1] And Richardson, in the third edition, sensibly became less modest and dropped the sentence.

The last volume contains a copious illustration of one of Richardson's earliest talents, a detailed index, which he had prepared almost at the last minute: 'Worn out am I with Index-making', he told Miss Highmore on 10 January. 'The worst Work I can do; and the least regarded it will be, tho' the most troublesome. But it will be a great Help to such as will like to join in Talk on the Story, without giving themselves the Trouble of reading the Book.'

The new duodecimo edition appeared on 19 March 1754. Twenty-five hundred copies of this third edition were printed.[2] Early the next month Richardson was able to report to Lady Bradshaigh that the new novel was more widely read than *Clarissa*, that it was much borrowed. The first edition had been temporarily out of print, and seven printers had worked to assist him in rushing with the third. Of the twenty-five hundred copies of that edition, only one thousand were sold by the end of June; two-thirds of the one thousand copies of the octavo had been sold.[3]

[1] 26 Sept. 1753.
[2] William Strahan's Ledger, B.M. Add. MS. 48,800, fo. 3 (under Mar. 1754, account for printing Vol. V).
[3] R to Lady Bradshaigh, 8 Apr.; R to Stinstra, 28 June.

Shortly before publication Richardson wrote to Stinstra that he was sending a complete set of the new duodecimo and wanted the translation made from it, since there were several corrections, 'of Nicety, rather than of Need'. The octavo, he said, was correct; but soon afterwards he wrote that the seventh volume in the new duodecimo was somewhat more perfect than the sixth octavo and was the more proper to be translated.[4] In spite of the fact that they had been printed simultaneously, there are almost a thousand corrections between the first duodecimo edition and the octavo. Most of them are minor, but they are in line with Richardson's usual practice—addition of italics in conversation, clearer punctuation or word order, more correct grammar and in a few cases more formal phrasing, two corrections of wrong dates and another of an error in etiquette.[5] There are about the same number of changes between the octavo and the third edition, mostly of the same minor nature. Richardson took account of Dean Delany's objection to Harriet's rather flippant remarks on the learned and deleted a few of them. He changed the words 'stare' and 'leer', to which Delany had also objected.[6] And he added a passage further explaining Sir Charles's excessive submission to his father, one of the few spots Miss Talbot had found 'in the Sun'.[7] He added a few explanatory phrases and pruned a good many unnecessary ones. He made several changes in the interest of propriety. Some of the praises of herself which Harriet reports are cut, though not nearly enough; and some of the dropping on knees, the tears, and the other affectedly emotional behaviour is omitted. But on the whole the changes in both editions are minor.

Sir Charles Grandison found admirers. Cowper wrote an ode in praise of it.[8] Gibbon thought it superior to *Clarissa*.[9] Most of Richardson's friends wrote to him expressing admiration. Edwards considered it 'The whole duty of Man'. Young received a gift of the first volumes in September and before the end of the year was reading them for a second time and liking them better than before. After he had received the last volume he looked on Richardson as 'a peculiar Instrument of Providence' to show the age what the phrase 'fine Gentleman' really meant: 'Joy to you, dr Sr, & Joy to the World.' The book assured Richardson of a double immortality—one immortality would last till the language should fail, the other beyond the failure of the heavens and the earth. William Webster wrote to Richardson that he could find no faults in the first four volumes; at first

---

[4] 12 Mar., 20 Mar.

[5] For a discussion of the text of *Sir Charles Grandison*, see Robert Craig Pierson, 'The Revisions of Richardson's *Sir Charles Grandison*', *SB*, XXI (1968), 163–89. Pierson's unpubl. diss. (University of Arkansas, 1965), 'A Study of the Text of Richardson's *Sir Charles Grandison*', contains a complete collation.

[6] Delany to R, 20 Dec.; R to Delany, 22 Dec.

[7] See p. 363.   [8] See p. 454.

[9] To Catherine Porten, *c.* 15 Nov. 1756, *Letters*, ed. J. E. Norton (New York, [1956]), I, 37.

he had thought that the hero might be *too* courageous and *too* generous, but 'found that the *presumption* was not *yours* in Going so near the Borders of *Quixotism*, but mine in Imagining that I could Judge better than *you* of the just *Boundaries*'. Urania Hill Johnson was given the first volumes and wrote in October that she had to throw down the book three times before she could get through the letter on the death of Lady Grandison.[10] She later celebrated in verse the ascension of Harriet's star to join the stars of her two sisters in the firmament and the rise of a male comet to flash through this constellation.[11] Miss Grainger thought *Sir Charles Grandison* 'ye most complete system of life & manners, & ye best calculated for ye amendment of head & heart, that ever has been exhibited in Prophane writing'. John Chapone's praises were the most lavish of all; his enthusiasm was unbounded, ecstatic, and copious. His 'Faculties' were 'all oppress'd and dazzl'd with beholding the bright and glorious Offspring' of Richardson's 'creative Hand'. Sir Charles was 'the noblest Representation, that ever did Honour to Human Nature'; for the first time he was proud of being a man, and yet at the same time he was humbled: 'Who but must fear and tremble, lest the Blandishments of Hell and the Witchcraft of Sin cast my own proper Lot in so deadly an Heritage? God forbid! that *Clarissa* shou'd have dy'd, and Sir Charles *Grandison* shod. have liv'd in vain for *my* Sake!'[12]

Richardson, as usual, also received anonymous letters in praise of the novel. Several of them asked for another volume: Richardson had left several of his characters in suspense; Clementina should be married off, and Emily. One lady, plagued by all of her acquaintance to urge Richardson to continue the work and not knowing him or any of his friends, left a card for Mrs. Richardson asking her to intercede with her husband.[13] One ex-libertine who signed himself B. F. wrote from a debtors' prison, overflowing with gratitude to Richardson 'for effecting in a few hours by yr. Sr. Charles Grandison wt. five years Imprisonment wth. all the Want & Indigence imaginable annex'd to it coud not'.[14] He had been converted by Richardson (as Captain Booth was by Isaac Barrow). Sir Charles had made him in love with virtue, and he would always deem Richardson the source of every good that might accrue to him. This letter must have warmed Richardson's heart—the reform of the B. F.'s of the world was exactly the kind of end he most desired. He mentioned the letter with pride to Lady Bradshaigh, but must have forgotten it when, a few months later,

[10] Edwards to Peter Hervey, 30 Mar. 1754, Bodleian MS. 1012, p. 163; Young to R, 20 Sept., 18 Dec., 14 Mar.; Webster to R, 26 Nov.; Mrs. Johnson to R, 28 Oct.

[11] FM XV, 3, fos. 14-16. It was enclosed in her letter of [Dec.? 1753].

[12] Frances Grainger, 23 May 1754; Chapone, 2 Dec. 1753.

[13] N.d. [mid-1754?], FM XV, 3, fo. 59.

[14] 2 May 1754.

he told Lady Echlin that 'instantaneous, or sudden, Conversions are not very natural'.[15]

Not all of the letters he received were so gratifying. One K. L. made no bones of it: 'My first wish is, that you had never commenc'd Author, my next, that you will let Sir Charles Grandison's History be the last of the kind you trouble the Public with; and I do assure you, whatever some of your friends may tell you to the contrary, these are the wishes of Numbers besides.'[16] Richardson sent a copy of this note to Lady Bradshaigh, commenting that he would follow the advice as well as he could.[17] Another writer was disgusted at the whole Italian episode; Sir Charles should have put his love of religion and country first and not courted a foreign lady, especially since the French and 'Foreign Fashion' are ruining the morality of the English and even their teeth—a 'Foreign Operator in Old Bond-street' has offered for thirty pounds to file and set a friend's teeth in order and all know then 'what will happen to the Teeth'. 'The general cry among the Men is, how much they despise a Man who could be in love with two Women at once.'[18] Richardson complained that many 'very excellent Women' did not like the hero's double love and was inclined to ascribe it to the fact that women are 'Enthusiasts in the Theory of Love; tho' *but* in the Theory'.[19] Others resented the compromise under which Sir Charles had reluctantly agreed, if he should marry Clementina, to let his daughters be brought up Papists. It was a 'wicked absurd Supposition', wrote one, to think that 'a true Englishman' could make 'a zealous Papist' 'a Part of himself!' A postscript is, however, appreciative of Sir Charles's kindness in not docking his horses' tails: 'If my Mind was not filled with those odious Particulars I would have express'd how grateful the merciful Hint about Horses was to me.' Richardson should continue to write, wrote another, but should beware: 'Great will be your Account at the last day, If *you*, who know so well your Duty in every Various Circumstance that life affords, are not extremely carefull in the performance of it.'[20]

Mrs. Chapone did not like the compromise either, nor did Mrs. Delany, who thought it 'the only blot in Sir Charles's character' and threatened to tell the author so. She found a few faults in the other characters: Emily, young as she was, should not have loved her guardian; Charlotte was diverting, 'but considering her heart is meant to be a good one, she too often behaves as if it were stark naught'; Harriet told her love to too many people. Otherwise Mrs. Delany was charmed with the novel and even used its charms to threaten her sister: until Mrs. Dewes hurried to London she

[15] To Lady Bradshaigh, 9 July 1754; to Lady Echlin, 14 Feb. 1755.
[16] 'Recd.' 28 Mar. 1754.
[17] 30 May 1754.   [18] 26 Jan. 1754.
[19] To Mrs. Chapone, 29 Dec. 1753.
[20] 11 June 1754; 23 May 1754. See also 'about' 26 Dec. 1753, and Cox Macro, [Mar. 1754].

would not receive the last volume.[21] Miss Sutton and Mrs. Donnellan had already urged on Richardson the objection to Harriet's frankness in telling her love, and the latter had sent him the verses from *Paradise Lost* describing the modesty and reluctance of Eve—verses which Richardson made Sir Charles cite as an example of female affectation.[22] Richardson was, as he frequently did, answering in the book the criticisms of his friends. Mrs. Donnellan also admired with reservations. She warned Mrs. Montagu that she might find the book too delicate and fine-spun for her taste; 'the great fault of my friends writings, there is too much of every thing', but 'I dont know how it is but his tediousness gives one an eagerness to go on, one wants events & they come slow'.[23]

Lady Bradshaigh reported that a very near female relative of Miss Sutton thought that Richardson did not know '*how* to *tell* a Story' and that Sir Charles was 'wholy *ungenteel*', and that a gentleman had sent her word 'it was *damn'd stupid*'—she sent *him* word that she 'knew it was a *moral* piece', and one hopes he was duly chastened.[24] Lady Bradshaigh was of course enthusiastic. She took sides for and against the characters, had decided opinions about how they should act, often changed her mind about them, was eager to see what they might do next—she was, in short, a story-teller's ideal audience, and read with full participation.[25]

Richardson for some reason sent Lord Chesterfield a copy of the book and received a letter from his brother-in-law James Leake expressing the Earl's pleasure, which has been lost but which undoubtedly contained polite and tactful commendation.[26] Just before *Sir Charles* was published Lady Bradshaigh had reported that Chesterfield had said that 'he cou'd not suppose there ever was such a Character as Lovelace, but if the author wou'd say he took it from *real Life*, he shou'd think himself oblig'd to believe it, otherwise he cou'd never forgive him' ('These old Rakes', she remarked, 'do not love to be told, that such villainous Arts are a part of their Character'). Richardson answered that he had not heard that remark. 'Yet something buzzes in my Head, that he did say, that was brilliant.'[27] Perhaps the Earl's brilliant remark was an encomium on *Clarissa*; if so, Richardson's sending him a copy is explicable. So far as we know, they never met. Chesterfield's comment to David Mallet on Richardson's gift was mixed. He thought the novel too long and too talky. 'Whenever he

---

[21] Mrs. Chapone to R, 10 Dec. 1753; Mrs. Delany to Mrs. Dewes, 21 Dec., 3 Dec. 1753, 21 Jan. 1754, *Autobiography and Correspondence*, III, 257, 251–2, 265.

[22] R to Isabella Sutton, 7 Nov. 1751; SH, II, 427.

[23] To Mrs. Elizabeth Montagu, 10 Nov. [1753] (misdated 1754), MS. in the Henry E. Huntington Library.

[24] 21 May, 14 Jan. 1754.

[25] See her running letters of 28 Oct.–27 Nov., 30 Nov.–11 Dec., 23 Dec.–14 Jan. 1754.

[26] Listed in Richardson's index to letters relating to *Sir Charles Grandison*, FM XV, 3, fo. 1.

[27] 25 Sept., 5 Oct.

goes *Ultra crepidum*, into high life, he grossly mistakes the modes; but, to do him justice, he never mistakes nature, and he has surely great knowledge and skill both in painting and in interesting the heart. He has even coined some expressions for those little secret movements that are admirable. He would well have deserved a higher education than he has had; however, he deserves well of mankind, the object of all his writings being virtue.'[28]

The first printed criticism of *Sir Charles*, an anonymous letter to the *Gentleman's Magazine*, on the other hand, singled out the author's knowledge of the polite world for commendation: 'Such a knowledge of the polite world, of men and manners, may be acquired from an attentive perusal of this work as may in a great measure supply the place of the tutor and boarding school.' It also praised and printed the dull and unnecessary description of the crossing of Mount Cenis. According to the letter, though some readers may complain of the descriptions and conversations, they are the most valuable part of the book. '*Horace's* rule of *utile dulci* was never more happily executed.' *Sir Charles Grandison* 'resembles a *great drama*'.[29] Miss Mulso sent Richardson a copy of this letter and may have had a hand in it.[30]

In 1755 Bowyer printed two books of remarks on *Sir Charles*, one by Dr. Free (eighty copies) and one by Mr. 'Plumer' (twenty-six copies).[31] The first seems to be lost, but the second is probably the second or third edition of *A Candid Examination of Sir Charles Grandison*. This short anonymous pamphlet, which originally appeared on 15 April 1754, was by Francis Plummer.[32]

A Candid Examination is a letter 'to a Lady in the Country', written 'without any Intention of publishing it', on the first six volumes of *Grandison*; a postscript considers the seventh. Plummer begins by attacking Richardson on what was undoubtedly a tender spot: at the end of the fifth volume 'it seems as if Mr. R——n begun to consider himself as a *Bookseller* as well as an *Author*', just as he had in publishing *Pamela* and *Clarissa*, 'or he could not, in writing for Reputation only, have surfeited us so much with tedious Repetitions and very trifling unentertaining Circumstances'—it is wrong to multiply volumes in order to get more money. But the novel does contain many good scenes and excellent conversations;

---

[28] See *The Letters of Horace Walpole*, ed. Peter Cunningham (Edinburgh, 1906), IV, 305n–6n.

[29] XXIII (Nov. 1753), 511–13.

[30] FM XV, 3, fos. 61–2.

[31] Nichols, *Literary Anecdotes*, II, 277.

[32] A copy in the British Museum is bound with several other pamphlets, one of which is by F. P—— and another a letter to a brother at Lilling Hall, where Francis Plummer had a brother; on the flyleaf of the volume is the note: 'I give to my Son my Picture in Oil, and I have printed these few Letters for him: that he may have some Knowledge of his Father's Person & Mind. Fr: Plumer.'

there is 'a Profusion of Wit and Fancy in Lady *G*——'s Conversation and Letters', and the madness of Clementina and the scenes in Italy are 'inimitably fine'. It abounds with 'good Language' and 'noble Sentiments', and Sir Charles himself is 'greatly good', 'the Character . . . very imitable: imitable by a *Christian*'. Plummer also commends Richardson's coining of words and his 'pathetic Manner of moving the Passions'. 'No Man goes beyond him in Descriptions. You see every Scene as if present in real Life.' He anticipates much that later readers have found absurd: Sir Charles is 'insufferably vain' in his courtship and '*loves to hear himself talk*', and his courtship with its divided love is 'the most awkward and unbecoming Courtship, that ever was put in print'. 'The Praise of Sir *Charles Grandison* is a Note too often touched.' It is indelicate to have Lady G. 'insinuate that her Brother still kept his Maidenhead', and 'it has hurt his Character a good deal with the Ladies'. Richardson 'has introduced such whining, and crying, and kneeling, as is very absurd, and no where in practice, except amongst the *Pamelas* and *Clarissas, &c.* of his own making. Then so many *sweet blessed Words*—Language that would better become an old Nurse than any of the Parties that use them: And so much of *God be thank'd*, and *God Bless*, and *God* reward, that I think it is quite taking the Name of *God* in vain.' He has heard 'People of Distinction' say that they like a good deal of the book, '*But I don't know what: it is low.*'[33]

Richardson was not pleased. He wrote to Lady Bradshaigh that where the writer's 'Blame seems most plausible, he is most mistaken, not having comprehended, or at least, not attended to the Delicacy of the Situations', particularly when he censures the hero for proposing to the Porrettas without first consulting his father. *A Candid Examination*, he concludes, is 'a little complicated Piece . . . of Pride, Conceit, Arrogance; his very Praise not always given in the right Place. Yet I could *almost* wish (I would say *quite*, if I were better in Health) for a *really* candid Examiner to call me forth to vindicate some of those Scenes, which some may think censurable; as it would give me an Opportunity, not only to point out those Delicacies of Situation, which the Hero is involved in; and which, from the Nature of the Writing, cannot be easily seen by hasty or common Readers; but ingenuously to own those Faults which ought not to be defended; and to shew, that I am not so *extremely* tenacious, but that I could be thankful for just Castigation.'[34] The small, dry bones of grammar and propriety were all that the tenacious Richardson had been willing to grant her in six years of exhaustive argument—she must have wondered what castigation he would consider 'just'.

Even earlier, before the appearance of the last volume, was published another short work, *Critical Remarks on Sir Charles Grandison, Clarissa and*

---

[33] Our quotations are from the 3rd edn. (London, 1755).
[34] 30 May 1754.

Pamela, 'By a LOVER of VIRTUE'.[35] The writer finds some virtues in *Clarissa,* but is on the whole hostile. Richardson receives condescending praise and outspoken scorn; he is accused of ignorance and vanity; it would take a 'bulky volume' to do justice to his 'innumerable faults' and 'some few shining beauties'. The author admits that he might have been less severe if Richardson had not constantly endeavoured to make those who questioned Christian orthodoxy 'the objects of public hatred and detestation', a sign of the weakness of a head which retains all the prejudices imbibed 'from the old women in the nursery' and of the badness of a heart that imagines that speculative differences of opinion 'can give just occasion to an unfavourable distinction among members of the same society, partakers of the same human nature, and children of one common indulgent Parent, the almighty and beneficent Creator of all things'. Though obviously an *esprit fort,* the author states that he does not want to bring religion into disrespect, since it is socially useful in restraining the vicious: 'the commonly received doctrine of rewards and punishments in a future state', for instance, is highly useful as an incentive and deterrent and 'can never be too sedulously inculcated on the minds of the people by their public teachers'. He even blames Richardson for letting his characters criticize the clergy. But to determine whether or not 'there was ever a divine revelation given . . . requires more learning and judgment than you are possessed of'.[36]

He is an extremely moral freethinker and a classicist in literature. Richardson is unfavourably compared to Homer as to both his characters and his morals. Mr. B., whom Fielding properly named Booby, 'is indeed one of the greatest bubbles, and blunderers that one can meet withal'. Lovelace is an inconsistent blend of the characters of Achilles and Ulysses. Sir Charles has too many discordant virtues; he is represented as at once learned and bigoted (in being reluctant to marry a Catholic), whereas 'universal learning naturally leads to scepticism'; 'his benevolence has something showy and ostentatious in it; nothing in short of that graceful and beautiful nature which appears in Fielding's Allworthy'. Pamela's chastity was never properly tempted and 'she was not of that rank or situation in life which could entitle her to those notions of honour and virtue' proper to Clarissa and Harriet. Only Clarissa is 'admirable throughout the whole', but even she 'is rather too good, at least too methodically so'.[37]

The moral of *Pamela* is 'very ridiculous, useless, and impertinent'—that a young gentleman ought to marry a handsome servant girl who resists

---

[35] London, 1754. It was published on 21 Feb. (*Daily Advertiser*). It has been reprinted with an introduction by Alan D. McKillop by the Augustan Reprint Society, No. 21 (Los Angeles, 1950).

[36] Pp. 54–5, 58–9, 35, 8–9.   [37] Pp. 21, 18, 20, 23–4, 35, 24.

him. *Sir Charles* is not only devoid of 'the least shadow of either plot, fable, or action' but has no moral, 'unless it be this, that men and women, old and young, after a certain ceremony is performed, may go to bed together'. *Clarissa* indeed does, like the *Iliad*, inculcate two good morals, 'the bad consequences of the cruel treatment of parents towards their children' and 'the pernicious effects of a young lady's reposing confidence or engaging in correspondence with a man of profligate and debauched principles'. But even it is weakened by the fact that Clarissa is unique and therefore rakes need not dread such another catastrophe.[38]

Chastity is treated in the spirit of cultural relativism—Richardson's heroines would have been quite different in the position of Nausicaa or among the Hurons. But Richardson's greatest guilt is in encouraging indulgence in the passions. 'Love, eternal Love, is the subject, the burthen of all your writings; it is the poignant sauce, which so richly seasons Pamela, Clarissa and Grandison, and makes their flimsy nonsense pass so glibly down.' Writings 'which heighten and inflame the passions, which paint in lively colours the endearments between the sexes, are of a bad and pernicious tendency'. Like later critics, the author sees Richardson as encouraging a romantic temperament he would by no means consciously have approved of but probably did do much to further. Of all novel writers, only 'the moral and ingenious authoress of David Simple', 'perhaps the best moral romance that we have', is guiltless in this respect. Richardson is responsible for a bad vogue: 'Your success has farther corrupted our taste, by giving birth to an infinite series of other compositions all of the same kind, and equally, if not more, trifling than your's.'[39]

In addition to corrupting taste, he has corrupted the language with his new-coined words: 'Our language . . . has, I imagine, been for some time on the decline, and your works have a manifest tendency to hasten that on.' He repeats the same characters from one novel to the next. His epistolary form has great advantages, but Richardson's length in it is intolerable—like Plummer, the author accuses him of padding to increase his profits. He is totally ignorant of the necessary 'art of blotting judiciously'. Fortunately such productions as novels are by their nature short-lived, though *Clarissa* perhaps deserves a better fate. The author wonders at the patience of the public and admires the 'contexture' of the author's brain 'which can weave with unwearied toil such immense webs of idle tittle-tattle, and gossipping nonsense'.[40] In short, there is little to be praised in Richardson's latest work. Which one of the supporters of the Fieldings in this mid-century battle of the books wrote the pamphlet has not been determined. Mrs. Chapone suspected Fielding himself.[41]

Richardson answered two of the least important objections urged

[38] Pp. 13–14, 12–14, 52.
[39] Pp. 27–9, 38–9, 19, 4.
[40] Pp. 4, 25, 56–7, 5, 56.
[41] To R, 6 Apr. 1754.

against *Sir Charles* in the form of two letters, printed together and given to all who were interested. On 5 April 1754 he had written to Edwards about the letters he received from those who wanted further details of Clementina, Emily, and the new parents and also from those who objected to the Catholic compromise. He was printing 'to give away to select Friends and the Discontented, who may ask for them, two Letters which I have written in Answer to Objectors on these two Subjects'.

One of the letters asking for another volume had made several specific inquiries about the fates of the characters and had hoped for a view of the hero fulfilling in his usual exemplary fashion his duties as a tender father. The letter was signed Julia. Richardson responded quickly, and two weeks later 'Julia' wrote another letter, this time signed Julian Bere, thanking him for his satisfactory answers to the queries.[42] On 10 April Richardson wrote again (in some perplexity as to the sex of his correspondent), explaining that he had made additions to his first reply and had had it printed to deliver gratis to anyone who wanted to know more about the Lady Clementina and her friends. He enclosed a copy, offered to send more if desired, and hoped for the honour of meeting his perhaps-fair unknown.

The *Letter to a Lady Who Was Solicitous for an Additional Volume* is dated 15 March 1754. Richardson points out that whereas the stories of Pamela and Clarissa are supposed to have taken place about thirty and twenty years respectively before the publication of their letters, the events of *Sir Charles Grandison* are recent history—the rebellion of 1745 took place during the hero's first visit to Italy—and there is not therefore much time for further developments, especially as Harriet's lying-in and the subsequent nursing (which she would of course give her child personally) would not allow her and her husband to go off to Italy for some time. Most of the characters are suitably settled, the good happily, the bad as they deserve. Nothing further can be supposed to happen to them ('Miss Orme is a good girl, and must be happy'—Clarissa seems forgotten). Olivia is not worth the trouble of continuing, nor are some of the minor characters. As to Clementina, he has 'been very complaisant to my Readers to leave to them the decision of this important article'. Some of his correspondents want her to marry the Count of Belvedere, others do not; she herself may decide. He has already shown the ideal parental character in *Pamela* and has avoided in his latest history touching on those topics he had dealt with in the others. Besides, one can assume that Sir Charles would shine as a father. He might have given his opinion on the education of children, but 'the lovers of Story would have found fault with me for it, as they have done with the few independent conversations that appear in the book, however useful others have thought them'. In short, a book

[42] 14 Mar., 29 Mar.

must end somewhere, though a life goes on. 'All that can be expected therefore in such a work . . . must be to leave the principal characters happy, and the rest with fair prospects of being so.'

When Sir Charles proposes to the Porretta family that he will marry the Lady Clementina on condition their sons are brought up Protestant and their daughters Catholic, he makes it clear that his proposals are a compromise, not what he could wish: 'I would not have begun an address upon these terms with a Princess.' By the time he makes his offer, he is already deeply involved. 'I had in my thoughts', he later explains, 'this further plea, that our church admits of a possibility of salvation out of its own pale.—God forbid but it should!—The Church of God, we hold, will be collected from the sincerely pious of all communions. Yet, I own, that had the intended honour been done me, I should have rejoiced that none but sons had blessed our nuptials.' And in other places he takes pains to explain the hero's unwillingness. But in his Concluding Note, arguing against those who think Sir Charles too perfect, he mentions the fact that many look upon this compromise 'as a blot in the character'.[43]

Among the letters written on this subject was one by the Reverend Cox Macro. It is extremely polite, speaking of the honour Richardson's three novels had done himself and his country and singling out the propaganda against duelling for special praise. But the writer feels that in view of the fact that such agreements as Sir Charles's compromise had almost become a matter of course, 'if you had pleased to have made use of that Handle to expose the Iniquitys of such a Practice, and that poor Girls Souls were as much to be regarded as Boys, some few of those Reasons which you would have then brought might have done more Service towards putting a stop to so wicked a practice, than the best set Discourses upon it could have done'. Richardson in reply pointed out various passages in the novel dealing with the compromise and stressed the delicacy of Sir Charles's situation, which forced him to make some concessions, though they had been a severe trial to him. He did not defend the compromise as such and pointed out that in his Concluding Note he had refrained from 'contending with such of my Readers, whose laudable Zeal for the true Faith, led them to consider this Compromise as a Blemish in Sir Charles's Character'. His defence is based on the circumstances of his story and on the nature of the characters concerned.[44] The second of the two printed letters is an *Answer to a Letter from a Friend* who had also objected to the compromise and consists largely of quotations from the letter to Cox Macro.

Richardson sent these printed letters both to anonymous correspondents

[43] SH, III, 134, IV, 373, VI, 326.

[44] A copy of Macro's letter in his own handwriting is preserved among his papers, n.d., B.M. Add. MS. 32,557, II, fo. 175; the letter is also in FM XV, 3, fo. 57, forwarded with a letter from W[illiam] S[mith], received 17 or 18 Mar. 1754. A draft of R's answer, 22 Mar, is in FM XV, 4, fo. 23; R's letter is in B.M. Add. MS. 32,557, II, fos. 176–7.

and to friends. One of the friends was Lady Echlin, who, as Richardson says, had blamed the compromise 'with a laudable Zeal for the purest Religion on Earth'. He had, he told her, sent copies to Main to give away to those who had bought the book from him in Dublin. 'This Effect they will have, if no other, To shew the World, that I was willing to lay aside the Pen, before I had quite tired its Patience.' As to the fate of Clementina, he mentioned the fact that half a dozen of his female correspondents could not bear the thought of her marriage to the Count of Belvedere, which was the most probable subject of a further volume. He also, incidentally, sided with Lady Echlin and her sister Lady Bradshaigh in decidedly preferring his English heroine to his Italian one.[45] Over a year later he explained to Clairaut that he had thought it best to leave Clementina's fate undecided: 'Readers were so divided and so very earnest in relation to *her*, some putting an End to her Life, some marrying her to the Count of Belvedere; others destining her to the single Life that I thought it was best, to leave the Readers to make it out as they pleased. . . . And have I not been a profuse Scribbler? But do you, my dear Sir, give me your Opinion, should the Humor return, as to proceeding or closing, as at present.'[46] Even this late, Richardson was not willing entirely to rule out the possibility of a continuation. Or perhaps he wanted to be coaxed a little. Few modern readers will see any reason for another volume of *Sir Charles Grandison*.

Richardson had, during the latter part of 1754, been playing with a very odd idea for a continuation. An ingenious gentleman, he told Lady Bradshaigh, made a proposal: 'That every one of my Correspondents, at his or her own Choice, assume one of the surviving Characters in the Story, and write in it; and that out of more than Half an hundred, as he supposes will be sent me, I shall pick and choose, alter, connect, and accommodate, till I have completed from them, the requested Volume. Will your Ladi-ship, who would make a most charming Lady G. contribute to the Tempta-tion?—I think myself absolutely worn out.' Or would Lady Bradshaigh prefer to begin the volume as Harriet? 'I hope you will write in more Parts than one.' 'I am in Earnest.'[47]

It is hard to believe that he was. Certainly Richardson liked to cor-respond with his female friends about his work—perhaps he missed that more than the work itself. Lady Bradshaigh did not approve of the suggestion—the result would be 'a piece of patch-work'. But she did end by contributing to it, the only friend who did. In August she sent a long letter in the character of Lady G. (Charlotte).[48] She railed about children and about female hunters and about bustling housewives and maintained the character, though not the style, fairly well. The letter contributes nothing to a story, nor could it of course; it is mainly a discussion of

---

[45] 17 May 1754.   [46] 12 Sept. 1755.   [47] 30 May.
[48] 6 Aug. Charlotte's letter is in FM XI, fos. 116–19.

Charlotte's character. Lady Bradshaigh wanted her name kept secret. Richardson found the letter 'very *Charlottish*', though he did not think Lady G. should have boxed her husband's ears. No one else had sent a letter, though one young lady had promised to be Harriet and he hoped that Miss Mulso, 'who has charmingly chalked out a Path for Clementina at the Year's End, to walk in, . . . will be dutiful'.[49]

He had asked Hester for a letter from Clementina to Harriet and as a bribe offered to let her marry Clementina to the Count, as she had agreed Clementina should: she could unfold all the emotions of her soul either on her deciding to marry or after she had done so. 'You know not what use I may make of such a letter.' Miss Highmore, he told her, was inclined to write a letter in the character of Harriet. Perhaps the British Minerva (Mrs. Carter) would assume Mrs. Shirley, or even make Sir Charles shine in some new acts of beneficence. Miss Mulso did not comply. 'What a proposal!' was her answer. And she persuaded Miss Highmore not to comply. Nor was Mrs. Carter more agreeable. 'Well, I can't help it. I was very much in earnest in my request to you all three. Another trial!—I will see, thought I, if they value the poor story so much, as to wish it to be continued for one volume more? If they do, surely they will contribute each one letter. "You cannot write like Clementina." Have you try'd? You would, on either of the occasions I hinted to you, write better than she. You must needs think—but I will say no more; so flatly denied, and your example so influential. Go, naughty girl, I wish I could avoid loving you. I should not have dared to hope for Miss C. in Sir Charles's character; but that I wanted to make him rise in it, were I to have proceeded. Particularly I wanted a better hymn for him than he had before given us.'[50] He also asked his newly recovered friend Mrs. Watts and her friend Miss Mogg to help,[51] but there is no evidence that they complied. Lady Bradshaigh prophesied that when he got all the letters he would lock them up, 'but the duce a word shall we ever see in print'.[52] Richardson answered that most of his girls had refused him, but he still asked her for another Lady G. letter.[53]

Richardson was considering the possibility of translating *Sir Charles Grandison* before the first volumes had been published in English. On 24 February 1753 he told Lady Bradshaigh that the German, French, and Dutch translators of *Clarissa* had all asked him 'to furnish them with sheets as printed, of my new piece'. He was afraid that if he sent the sheets they might publish ahead of him.[54] In July he informed Alexis Clairaut that he could not oblige Prévost with the sheets because he had not determined

---

[49] 28 Aug. [50] 21 Aug., 24 Sept.
[51] 27 Sept. [52] 27 Sept.
[53] 9 Oct.
[54] To Stinstra, 2 June. His letter to Stinstra of 4 July also mentions an application from de Freval from The Hague.

about the manner and time of publishing. He had hoped that his brother-in-law James Leake, then on the Continent, would see Prévost, but had since learned that Leake was in Italy and asked Clairaut, if he knew Prévost, to tell him his intentions as to publication. Since he went on to tell Clairaut of his dissatisfaction with the heavy cuts which Prévost had made in *Clarissa* ('I knew not, that such Mutilations were allowable'), one can assume that he would have been as glad to find another translator for his new work. He also mentioned that in addition 'Dr. Holler of the University of Gettingen' and a M. 'Lormell' had asked Leake to request the sheets, that his old friend de Freval from The Hague had applied to him for them, and that he had heard of an Amsterdam bookseller who also wanted them.[55] De Freval had applied much earlier, asking for the sheets before the book was well under way: 'I cannot, with God's grace, fail getting an estate by publishing at my own cost a book of your's upon such a subject [as a good man], or rather upon any subject whatever.'[56] But de Freval was not given this opportunity to get his estate; Richardson must have considered him unworthy and very wisely set limits to charity to a friend. Shortly afterwards Charles Kaiser, who had recently visited Richardson in England, wrote from Hanover asking when *Sir Charles* was to appear: 'Every body here wishes, soon to see him. . . . I intend to publish a German Translation of these Memoirs with Your Approbation and Assistance, which I hope You will not refuse me. Give me Leave to send for the Sheets, as they are publishing.'[57] Surely he had every reason to be satisfied with the growth of his Continental reputation.

In the fall he told Lady Bradshaigh that he had friends in Paris, Göttingen, and Holland 'to whom I have left it to oblige any Friends of theirs, who are likely to do Justice in the Translation'. Clairaut was probably the friend in Paris, since Richardson told Stinstra that he felt 'under an Obligation of Civility to M. Clairaut', who wanted the book for someone else.[58] Haller must have been the man in Göttingen. The Dutch friend was Johannes Stinstra, who translated *Clarissa*.

Stinstra wrote to Richardson in August 1753 that an Amsterdam publisher named Isaac Tirion had already announced a Dutch translation of the new work; Stinstra hoped to persuade him to defer it until his own rather slow translation of *Clarissa* was completed, and Stinstra's publisher Folkert van der Plaats himself agreed to announce a translation. Richardson informed him that a minister of Amsterdam had, in Richardson's absence, recommended Tirion to William Richardson, his nephew and assistant. But he sent the first four volumes to Stinstra, telling him that he might do as he wished about translating them and that neither he nor the friend he got to do the translating would owe Richardson anything.

[55] 5 July.
[56] 17 Apr. 1751.
[57] 10 July.
[58] 19 Oct., 11 Sept.

Stinstra accepted the direction of the translation, regretting that he had no time to do it himself. He was applying to a Mr. Pieter Verwer.[59] In March he received the corrected duodecimo, from which Richardson wanted the translation done.[60] But Verwer did not like the idea of Stinstra's reviewing his work, and Stinstra had trouble in finding another translator. He rejected an English teacher after reading a specimen of his Dutch writing, a second man because his English was inadequate, and another because he wanted to cut the work; but after negotiating with at least two more, he at length settled on a group of Amsterdam writers, who were so good that Stinstra no longer felt bound to insist on his right to review the work, which seems to have been the main cause of the delay.[61] It appeared in 1756–7.

The German translation had gone more rapidly. For some reason, perhaps at Haller's recommendation, Richardson had sent a copy of the novel to Erasmus Reich, a bookseller at Leipzig, who gave it to the distinguished writer Christian Gellert, 'the only Man in Germany fit for such a task'.[62] Gellert's reaction to the novel was as enthusiastic as any author could wish. At the parting of Grandison and Clementina he tasted again (as he had when he read the end of *Clarissa*) the greatest satisfaction of life—tears: 'Habe ich geweinet ... mein Buch, mein Pult, mein Gesicht, mein Schnupftuch durch—durchgeweinet, laut geweinet, mit unendlichen Freuden.' He would have given up his fortune rather than not read on and was inclined to agree with a friend who said that if he had written *Grandison* he would be certain of salvation.[63] Gellert set about translating it, saying that '*nothing could put him to that, but such a Man as Mr. Richardson, and the friendship he has for me* [Reich]'. There is some evidence that Gellert did not personally complete the translation,[64] but in any case it was carried on fairly rapidly, and by 24 July 1755 Richardson had five volumes of it.[65]

At the same time he informed Stinstra that the firm of Weidmann, in Leipzig, who was publishing it, had engaged to do a French translation, which unlike Prévost's *Clarissa* was to be unmutilated, to be printed in Holland, by Luzac of Leyden. Richardson gave Luzac a list of subjects which might furnish suitable illustrations. This translation did not appear promptly; before it did appear, Clairaut wrote again, evidently now in touch with Prévost. Richardson seems to have been embarrassed about Prévost. It is obvious from his many resentful remarks about Prévost's alterations in *Clarissa* that he was not anxious to have him translate *Sir*

[59] 11 Aug., 11 Sept., 24 Dec.
[60] William Richardson to Stinstra, 12 Mar.
[61] Stinstra to R, 8 Apr., 23 May 1754; 13 June, 23 June, 17 Sept. 1755.
[62] Reich to R, 10 May 1754.
[63] Gellert to Graf ?, 3 Apr. 1755, MS. in the Yale University Library.
[64] Reich to R, 10 May 1754; R to Reich, 5 Aug. 1754.
[65] R to Stinstra.

Charles Grandison. On the other hand, he seems to have been unwilling to offend so prominent a writer (he thinks himself happy in 'Such a Translator of the Piece, as M. Provost'), and probably he had committed himself both to and through Clairaut. 'Ought I not here to acquaint you, Sir,' he says hesitantly, 'that a French Edition of Grandison is actually in the Press in Holland?' He had 'thought the Abbé had dropt his Design of proceeding with his Translation. No wonder if such a fine Genius for *Original* writing had.' He hopes he is not to blame in regard to the Abbé in writing to Luzac. 'The Case is nice.' At least it should be hinted to Prévost that he should regulate the number printed in expectation of a French edition in Holland.[66]

Prévost did proceed with his translation, and again he cut heavily and made the work suitable to French taste by omitting uncomplimentary references to that nation as well as other offences against good taste.[67] According to his introduction, Richardson's novel was one of those works which enclose superior beauties 'sous une rude écorce . . ., avec de grands défauts dans la forme', and he therefore retrenched 'des excursions languissantes, des peintures surchargées, des conversations inutiles & des réflexions déplacées' and suppressed those English customs ('ces restes de l'ancienne grossièreté Britannique') which shock other nations. By reproducing Richardson in his entirety the other French translation was 'un des plus singuliers monumens que soient jamais sortis de la presse'.[68] We have no record of Richardson's comments, but surely he was not pleased. Nor was he pleased with the other French translation. 'I am told, yt ye French Translation is as ill performed, as ye German is well. Pity, that ye Translator of it, was not as well acquainted wth ye English as wth: ye French.' In 1758 Reich informed him of a new edition of *Grandison* in German which was being printed.[69]

Richardson was constantly revising his novels. He asked Stinstra on 28 June 1754 to correct in translation 'any great Slips' he saw. 'If I know what you do in this particular, I will amend by your Judgment, should there be a *Fourth* Edition.' In 1755 he told Stinstra that he had made his last revisions to his novels (*Clarissa* and *Sir Charles Grandison* 'vary but

[66] 12 Sept. 1755.
[67] See Wilcox, 'Prévost's Translations of Richardson's Novels', pp. 353–60.
[68] Prévost's translation, *Nouvelles lettres angloises, ou Histoire du chevalier Grandisson*, was published in Amsterdam in 1755–6. Our quotations are from the Amsterdam edition of 1784. The other French translation (by Gaspard-Joël Monod), *Histoire de Sir Charles Grandison*, was published in Göttingen and Leiden in 1756.

'under a rough rind . . ., with great defects in the form.'
'languid excursions, overcharged pictures, useless conversations, and misplaced reflections.'
'these remains of the ancient British coarseness.'
'one of the strangest monuments which have ever issued from the press.'

[69] R to Reich, 2 Apr. 1757; Reich to R, 12 June 1758.

little from ye last Editions of those Works').[70] In the spring of 1754 Lady Bradshaigh told him that she had taken the liberty of making alterations in her copy of *Sir Charles*, which she would be glad to explain to him when they met, though she could hardly read them herself. She did, however, send the volumes to him, and he was grateful for her suggestions: 'I shall be greatly improved by them & corrected in another edition, should the work come to another.'[71] He kept her copy until early in 1758 and, when he sent it back, told her that he had taken her advice in some places and that she could see 'what I thankfully allow'd, & humbly disallow'd of them'.[72]

But there were no further editions of the whole of *Sir Charles Grandison* during his lifetime. There is a copy of an edition of the last volume dated 1756 which has a good many revisions. They seem certainly to be by Richardson, since they not only follow his general practice in revising but often follow Lady Bradshaigh's specific suggestions, especially in matters of genteel speech and behaviour. In one place she pointed out that he had incorrectly hung portraits on a tapestried wall, and he thanked her for noticing this slip; the portraits are in 1756 hanging elsewhere.[73] The year after his death there was a fourth edition, also with changes. The revisions in the last volume, like those in the 1756 edition, follow Lady Bradshaigh's suggestions and Richardson's practice.[74]

In 1792 Richardson's daughter Anne mentioned to her niece Mrs. Moodie that she had in her possession a copy of *Sir Charles Grandison* with her father's alterations.[75] In 1810 an edition was published which claimed, on the title page, to contain the last corrections of the author.[76] Anne, who had thought of issuing corrected editions of her father's works, had died in 1803. There are about six hundred revisions in the 1810 edition which are enough like Richardson's to lend credence to the claim on the title

---

[70] 26 Nov. [71] 21 May, 9 July. [72] 2 Jan.

[73] Vol. VII of Lady Bradshaigh's copy of *Sir Charles Grandison* with marginalia by her and by Richardson is in the Henry E. Huntington Library. The copy of Vol. VII dated 1756 is in the Brown University Library.

[74] The two editions of Vol. VII should be regarded as one, since only certain gatherings were revised in 1756 and these were used again in 1762, whereas the gatherings not revised in 1756 (undoubtedly because enough sheets were left from the earlier editions) were revised in 1762. The changes in the first six volumes are minor and show no clear pattern; it is not necessary to assume that they are Richardson's, though they could be. This confused situation was probably the result of the printing of the earlier editions at various houses and in a hurry. Gatherings of the first and third editions are also often mixed in the same copy. By 1756 sheets for some gatherings of the last volume must have been exhausted. Richardson probably printed the whole volume with his revisions and used only the sheets he needed; the others were used in the fourth edition. In all probability, then, this edition is not to be considered as embodying Richardson's revisions except insofar as it first issued sheets of Vol. VII printed earlier. See Pierson, 'The Revisions of Richardson's *Sir Charles Grandison*', pp. 174–8.

[75] 12 Apr., MS. owned by Alan Dugald McKillop.

[76] For a discussion of this edition, see Pierson, 'The Revisions of Richardson's *Sir Charles Grandison*', pp. 178–88.

page. A few of the corrections follow Lady Bradshaigh's suggestions; several dates are readjusted with great care; and there is one rearranged letter with an added paragraph by Charlotte which is too 'Charlottish' to have been written by anyone but her creator. None of the changes, however, are major. Indeed only a few of those in the earlier editions are of much moment. Aside from verbal alterations, often in the interest of clarity but often also for no apparent purpose, most of the changes in all of the editions seem designed to make the novel more proper, more suitable as a presentation of Sir Charles's class. Exaggerations, affectations, and simple oversights are corrected, sometimes in accordance with Lady Bradshaigh's suggestions. All of the revisions together, even including the few longer ones, do not materially alter the novel. But it is probable that Richardson did go on correcting, even after he told Stinstra he had made his final corrections, and that most of the alterations in the last volume were printed by him in 1756 while those in the other volumes remained on his corrected copy in Anne's possession, to be published after her death, in 1810. The revisions of *Pamela* and *Clarissa* often sought correctness at the cost of Richardson's original conception of his characters; those of *Sir Charles Grandison* were less extensive and also less damaging, since the original conception was so correct that the elevation of language and removal of improprieties harmonized well enough with the tone of the book.

CHAPTER XVII

RICHARDSON'S LAST
LITERARY ACTIVITY

IN the Preface to *Sir Charles Grandison* the 'Editor' announces that he has 'in this Publication, completed the Plan, that was the Object of his Wishes, rather than of his Hopes to accomplish'.[1] Even before ending the novel, he informed Mrs. Chapone, he had resolved to make it his last work—'the Indifference to the Pen, which I had at first struggled to obtain, has grown upon me to an Averseness to it; so that now Writing, even to my chosen Friends, is generally an irksome Task to me.' Well before the publication of the first volumes he had informed Stinstra that in future he would write only letters. Age, poor health, and the press of business were reasons he often gave for his unwillingness to write more. Two correspondents who wanted another novel were informed that he would consider it when 'the many delicate situations that this piece, as well as Clarissa, abounded with, were generally understood and attended to!' Like other writers, Richardson often felt that the public did not quite understand him. He was also somewhat embarrassed about the length of what he had already written: '19 Volumes in Twelves, close Printed—In Three Stories—Monstrous!—Who that sees them ranged on one Shelf, will forgive me?'[2] But it is probably unnecessary to search farther for Richardson's resolve than his weariness and his lack of any compelling idea for another novel. In any case, he announced firmly in the advertisement for his new edition of *Sir Charles Grandison* that it and his two previous works 'complete the Editor's Design in publishing these Collections' and at about the same time repeated to Miss Wescomb that he had done with the pen: he proposed to make some excursions, to visit friends, and to heed Young's advice that he needed to take care of his health and to find some rational amusement.[3]

We have described his abortive plan of continuing *Sir Charles* with the help of letters written for him by his correspondents. Evidently already by the summer of 1754 he was beginning to tire of his leisure, though he

---

[1] SH, I, vii.
[2] To Mrs. Chapone, 28 May 1754; to Stinstra, 2 June 1753; to Susanna Highmore, 31 Jan. 1754; to Lady Echlin, 17 May 1754.
[3] *Public Advertiser*, 19 Mar.; to Sarah Wescomb, 22 Mar.

still did not want to start a new book. 'Nineteen volumes', he wrote to Lady Bradshaigh; 'the Subject one: Human nature, as many thousand times varied, is no easy task to be pursued, with variety still; and at an advanced time of life; Twenty years of infirmity to have laboured with—I really do think myself in a manner worn out; and as one proof, begin to loath the pen; yet know not how well, such is the Mill-horse habit, to employ my supererogatory Time; for I am a bad Sleeper of nights, tho', of late I am ready to doze all day.'[4]

But he had found a new task, though not a creative one. We have described how an unknown gentleman had sent Richardson a collection of the moral sentiments in *Clarissa*, which he had enlarged and inserted in the third and fourth editions of that novel—Benjamin Franklin thought well enough of them to borrow over twenty for Poor Richard.[5] Even before the completion of *Sir Charles Grandison* he began collecting such sentiments himself, perhaps only for that novel: on 15 July 1753 he wrote to Miss Highmore that he was 'involved in sentimentalizing' and complained that none of the 'charming girls' he knew would help him. 'Go, naughty, idle chits—to pretend to approve what I am about, as if it would be promotive of the public good; and yet, when I hoped a finger from every one of you, to find no aid—not so much as extracts from a work ready written to your hands!' On 28 June 1754 he told Stinstra that he was engaged in collecting the sentiments in his novels. In July he asked Benjamin Kennicott for a preface to a volume of sentiments: 'I hate to think of prefaces; for I have an aversion to all parading.' The implication seems to be that he preferred to have friends do the parading for him, as they had done for *Pamela*. Late in the fall he told Kennicott that the volume might steal out after the election: 'It is a dry Performance—Dull Morality, and Sentences, some pertinent, some impertinent, divested of Story, and Amusement; I cannot expect much from it, tho' enliven'd by your kind and friendly Preface. There are who think I should have been otherwise employ'd: And these, Persons of the highest Consideration with me for their Judgment.' When it was about to be published, however, he was inclined to brag of it mildly; it would show 'that there are not many of the material articles that may be of use for the conduct of life and manners unattended to in one or other of them [his three books]; so that all together they complete one plan, the best I was able to give.'[6]

The volume appeared in early March 1755 under the title of *A Collection of the Moral and Instructive Sentiments, Maxims, Cautions, and Reflexions, Contained in the Histories of Pamela, Clarissa, and Sir Charles Grandison*, 'printed for S. Richardson'. It contains the Preface 'By a Friend' and (as

[4] 9 July.

[5] See pp. 313–15; Robert Newcomb, 'Franklin and Richardson', *JEGP*, LVII (1958), 27.

[6] To Kennicott, 15 July, 26 Nov. 1754; to Mark Hildesley, 21 Feb. 1755.

an appendix) 'By Desire' the two letters Richardson had printed on *Sir Charles Grandison*. Kennicott praises highly the 'modestly *anonymous*' author. He compares Richardson with Plutarch: his works 'will perhaps last as long, probably be as much admired, and certainly prove much more extensively beneficial'. 'The *Histories* may be considered as the LIVES of so many eminent persons, and this collection of *Maxims*, as the MORALS.' The volume was originally to have contained a picture of Richardson, which was so poorly done that it was not used—Richardson consoled himself that it would be more modest not to publish his own portrait.[7]

Richardson was not content merely to extract sentiments from his novels. He often rewrote them thoroughly, adding new ideas and pointing up the moral; or he wrote sentiments which had not been expressed in so many words but had been implied by the characters and situations. The sentiments are arranged alphabetically under each novel by some key word, such as 'Friendship', 'Platonic Love', 'Conjugal Piety', 'Duelling', and 'Libertines'. He apologized to Edwards for not having alphabetized the three novels together: to do so would have meant three columns in the margin containing volume and page references, which would have taken up a third of the page and swelled a volume already more than large enough for the price. He also asked Edwards to notice that he had chosen the sentiments from the three books so as not to repeat himself: 'Perhaps I had some Vanity in giving a *comparing* Reader an Opportunity of discovering, that I have not, in many of them, borrow'd from myself; yet ye Subject ye same (viz. Men & Women).' The volume, he recognized, would not be saleable. 'But as they [the novels] were all written for ye Sake of Instruction to young People; who are apt to read rapidly wth. a View only to Story; I thought my End wou'd be better answer'd, by giving at one View ye Pith & Marrow of what they had been reading, perhaps with some Approbation; in order to revive in their Minds ye Occasions on which ye Things were supposed to be said & done, ye better to assist them in ye Application of ye Moral.' Similarly, he repeated to Lady Echlin that some of his best friends wished he had bestowed the time on another story and added sarcastically that they declared they would not read the sentiments, though they claimed that they read for instruction; he had published more to do good than to make a profit, 'though it is the Pith and Marrow of Nineteen Volumes, not unkindly received'.[8]

Nothing could more clearly show Richardson's conscious views about the aim of his novels than such statements. He obviously believed that a collection of moral platitudes could sum up the effect he hoped to create, that the moral could be detached from its fictional setting without losing its force or changing its meaning. He was even inclined to think that

[7] To Edwards, 23 Feb. 1755.
[8] To Edwards, [c. 1 Aug. 1755]; to Lady Echlin, 7 July 1755.

readers who did not admire the sentiments were frivolous, lovers of amusing stories only. In this mood, he subscribed to the old idea of fiction as the gilding on a philosophic pill. Miss Hornbeak considers the *Collection of Moral and Instructive Sentiments* as 'the final flower of Richardson's literary activity'.[9] It is indeed the final flower of one aspect of that activity, though it is hardly the aspect that accounts for Richardson's enduring reputation. Evidence has been cited to prove that the sentiments are similar to those in many didactic handbooks.[10] There is no reason to doubt it. They are undoubtedly also similar to the moral commonplaces which Richardson had heard in many conversations. This hardly means, however, that Richardson's novels arose from 'the great literature of edification of the old protestant time, approaching its end'. His moral sentiments arose, if not from that literature, at least from the atmosphere which produced it and in which Richardson grew up. The novels arose from another layer of Richardson's mind altogether, though they were strongly coloured by his Protestant ethics. The *Collection of Moral and Instructive Sentiments* contains that part of Richardson's novels which was not his but his time's. That he regarded the volume as the pith of what he had said shows how little one Richardson was able to appreciate the work of the other. The volume does contain the pith of the continuation of *Pamela* and of much of *Sir Charles Grandison*. And it explains certain features of the first part of *Pamela* and of *Clarissa*—the rather silly moral of the first book and the religious intensity of the second, when for once Richardson was able to fuse his imagination and his traditional morality. But the morality even of *Clarissa* is poor and dry when it is torn out of its context and divorced from the character of the heroine, and the volume of *Sentiments* is at best a curiosity of literature.

Richardson must have spent a good deal of time choosing and rewriting his sentiments, but for such a prolific writer they could hardly have been a full-time occupation—or a full-time avocation, rather, since throughout the decade he continued to be an active printer. Even before the publication of the *Sentiments* Miss Talbot had worried about his inactivity: 'It would be great charity in you', she wrote to Mrs. Carter in December 1754, 'to think of half a dozen subjects for plays, and notify them to Mr. Richardson; for I am clear in it that a play must be his next undertaking, and some undertaking he must have to keep him in tolerable health and spirits.' Mrs. Carter agreed that writing might help Richardson's health, 'for I remember when I was in London to have heard somebody say, that whenever Mr. Richardson thought himself sick it was because he had not a pen in his hand'. Several months later Miss Talbot was still worried:

---

[9] *Richardson's Familiar Letters and the Domestic Conduct Books*, p. 28.

[10] Miss Hornbeak, ibid., p. 28, cites Herbert Schöffler's *Protestantismus und Literatur* (Leipzig, 1922), pp. 166–7.

Richardson 'would give a good deal, I believe, if he was fairly got into the midst of a new work, though he has not resolution enough to venture on the beginning'.[11]

Early in 1755 Richardson mentioned Miss Talbot's desire to Thomas Edwards and evidently also hinted that he was considering the history of Mrs. Beaumont, his name for the much-suffering female friend of his early years. Edwards replied that her story would be 'both entertaining and instructive, but after what we have been favored with would, I doubt, seem cold and uninteresting'. Richardson must have only toyed briefly with the idea since he replied that the quarrel between him and the pen would never be made up.[12]

He had also been asked to write the life of a good widow and at least half hinted to Lady Echlin that he might attempt it.[13] In the fall of 1755 Lady Bradshaigh suggested another subject, which she had previously discussed with Miss Talbot, the history of his own life. She feared only that the writing might affect him too much and that he was too modest. Richardson, ever fond of teasing her, gave vague hints of his early life and of the women who figured in it. She was excited and wanted Miss Talbot and Miss Mulso to help her 'fix the pen' in his hand and reminded him that Dr. Young had told him that he could not sit inactive. But Richardson wrote that he could not do as she asked: 'I have, or seem to have, an unconquerable Aversion to the Pen! My Imagination on which you kindly compliment me, seems entirely quenched.'[14] At about the same time Lady Echlin wrote that she would like to see him portray the good widow. She received a similar refusal: 'I think the little Spirit I once had, of that Kind, is departed from me.' Should the spirit, however, 'offer again to irradiate my heavy Mind', her subject would be given due attention. But he could not quite make up his mind. Perhaps he would write again if Lady Bradshaigh and Miss Talbot should act as flint and steel to 'strike up a Spark in the dying Tinder'. 'I seem to be getting fast into a State of Supineness, for want of Employment to carry myself out of my Self', he wrote to Samuel Lobb. 'Well but, my good Friend, let the Impulse return, and if God give me Ability, it shall be obeyed. Mean time, do you be so kind as to think for me, and if any Subject further offers, suggest it to me; as you have heretofore done some. Yet, I fear, as I said before, the Spirit of Scribbling, is extinguished. Nevertheless, I am not in ye least apprehensive of a narrow Spirit taking place of a more dilated one, tho' I were to make the Care of my Family my *whole Study*.' He has not long to live and finds no diminution in his good will towards his fellow creatures.

[11] 27 Dec., 11 Jan., 14 May, *Letters between Mrs. Elizabeth Carter and Miss Catherine Talbot*, I, 374, 376, 383-4.
[12] 4 Feb., 23 Feb.   [13] 24 July 1754.
[14] Lady Bradshaigh to R, 5 Sept.; R to Lady Bradshaigh [*c*. 1 Oct.]; Lady Bradshaigh to R, 18 Oct.; R to Lady Bradshaigh, 21 Oct.

'My Dislike to the Pen continues. It encreases', he informed Lady Echlin in February. Still he begged her, as one of the four ladies he especially honoured, 'to suggest to me any Plan or Subject, as it rises to your Mind'. If health permitted, he might be able 'to obey the Inspiration'.[15]

Clearly he was not quite ready to give up all idea of writing another novel and vaguely hoped that Lady Echlin or Lady Bradshaigh or Miss Talbot or Miss Mulso or Mr. Lobb would get him started. But just as clearly, his urge to write had left him. Richardson was referring, as distinctly as a respectable printer could refer in sober prose, to his Muse. Whatever level of his mind had suggested the characters of Pamela, Clarissa, and Lovelace was making no more suggestions. He was of course busy, and his health was poor; but he had been busy and ill long before, and yet he had written. On internal evidence, one might judge that the Muse deserted him not after but during the composition of *Sir Charles Grandison*. That book might have taught him not to woo inspiration by asking his friends to suggest subjects; but Richardson seems never to have been entirely conscious of what it was that took over when he wrote *Pamela* and *Clarissa*.

He felt an aversion even to correspondence, yet at the same time he missed his writing and found no suitable substitute: 'How irksome to me now is the thought, the obligation of writing! I said, on finishing Grandison (ashamed, and tired, at the thought of the many volumes I had scribbled), that I would write no more for the public; but confine myself to the favours of my correspondents. Stupidity, even to dozingness, has seized me; and, let me tell you, that they are not many with whom I wish to correspond: yet, at the same time, I regret, as I ought, the painful indifference; and the more, as no eligible engagement offers in its place; and I am nothing but supineness and wearisomeness.'[16]

He continued to play with the idea of another novel into 1757, and after that we hear no more about further writing. He found many reasons for not writing. To Mrs. Dewes he mentioned not only age, illness, business, and the length of what he had already written, but also his bitterness about the Irish pirates and his disillusionment with the moral effect of his books—good people did not need them, 'and what bad ones have they converted?' At the same time, while mentioning some of the same reasons for not writing, he was asking the Reverend Smyth Loftus to find him a plan in case he should resume the pen. He told Lady Bradshaigh about the suggestion that he describe a widow and pointed to his handwriting as evidence that his staggering hand would no longer permit him to write ('My Pen sometimes will not stay in my Fingers'); neverthe-

---

[15] Lady Echlin to R, 2 Sept.; R to Lady Echlin, 15 Dec.; R to Lady Bradshaigh, 17 Dec.; R to Lobb, 29 Dec.; R to Lady Echlin, 20 Feb.

[16] To Hester Mulso, 30 Aug. 1756.

less he would like to know what she thought of the subject. Lady Bradshaigh believed that she saw in this letter signs of an inclination to take
up the pen again, and she did not disapprove of the subject—indeed it
might be well to show two widows, one of a good and the other of a bad
husband. 'I own the *Life* of a *certain person*, was what I had set my heart
upon. I thought it might be form'd into a story, partly True, partly Fictitious, and yet there are objections. I am affraid you wou'd be rein'd in
too close by families now in being, fearing to give offence.' Richardson
answered that the idea of two widows was a good one, but his mention
of a possible new subject 'is to be looked upon but as ye Effort of a
dying Taper'. '*O that I were as in the Days past*', he quoted from Job.
Yet less than two months later he hinted that had he ever started writing
again Mrs. Beaumont would have been much in his thoughts. 'O that
I could carry myself out of myself, into *other* Characters, as in Times past!
I am not pleased with *my own*; and want Amusement that I could be
fond of.'[17]

Just when he wrote the fragments of the history of Mrs. Beaumont
which are still extant is not clear.[18] We have discussed this mysterious
lady in our first chapter. It is not certain that the character was based upon
a person he had known in his youth, but there is fairly good circumstantial
evidence that it was. She is a minor character in *Sir Charles Grandison*,
and Dr. Bartlett had promised to give Harriet her history but deferred
doing so and never did. Some of Richardson's correspondents had looked
forward to it.[19]

The longest letter relating to Mrs. Beaumont's history is probably the
letter he promised. Though usually described as a fragment, it is a complete letter from Dr. Bartlett to Harriet and relates as much of her history
as a reader of *Sir Charles* could possibly want to know. Richardson may
have rejected it because his novel was too long or because he was already
considering greater things for Mrs. Beaumont. Four shorter letters connected with her story could have been written when Richardson first mentioned the subject of Mrs. Beaumont to Edwards or later. None of the
fragments shows clear signs that the Muse was very active. Dr. Bartlett's
letter is largely past narrative, which gave Richardson little chance to
write to the moment. What conversation there is is lacking in life. Nor
is the lady herself realized; she is described, and since she is entirely
virtuous, the description is tame. The other four letters approach the
subject differently. They are obviously meant to be part of an epistolary

[17] To Mrs. Dewes, 15 Dec. 1756; to Loftus, 13 Dec. 1756; to Lady Bradshaigh, 27 May
1757; Lady Bradshaigh to R, 25 June 1757; R to Lady Bradshaigh, 12 July, 2 Sept. 1757.
[18] MS. in the Pierpont Morgan Library, partly printed in Barbauld, V, 301–48; four MS.
letters owned by Alan Dugald McKillop.
[19] SH, III, 41, 223, 231; James Fitzgerald to R, 17 May 1754; Frances Grainger to R,
23 May 1754.

novel in which the lady's history was to be treated at much greater length than in Dr. Bartlett's narration. One is from a timid young friend expressing his intense but pure admiration for the lady. He is later referred to as 'Mr R', and he may well be meant to portray the artist himself as a young man. Two are from Hortensia Beaumont to the young friend, largely discussing his excessive diffidence. The last is from Mrs. Beaumont to their mutual friend Mrs. Winwood and concerns the main plot of Mrs. Beaumont's story, her struggle with her wicked uncle and the attempt of a pretended protector to seduce her. The four short letters, possibly because they are using his distinctive method, are more like Richardson at his best. Both writers manage to reveal their characters. They do not lead one to expect that if it had been continued the history would have rivalled *Clarissa*, but they do show some of the mastery of the epistolary technique apparent in *Sir Charles*. It is probable that these four letters represent Richardson's only attempt to write another long novel. Whether he wrote other letters as part of the same plan we have no way of knowing.

As we have said, Richardson made minor corrections and changes in *Clarissa* and *Sir Charles Grandison* during the 1750s. He did a much more elaborate revision of *Pamela*. After the de luxe octavo edition of 1742, Richardson printed two other duodecimo editions during his lifetime, each of which contains minor corrections. Soon after his death, an eighth duodecimo edition appeared, with more important changes, especially in the interest of propriety and manners. It is likely that some of these changes were the result of his examining, during the last months of his life, a copy of *Pamela* with corrections by Lady Bradshaigh. A much more extensive revision he left in manuscript. His daughters Martha and Anne considered publishing it, but it was not until 1801, after Martha's death and shortly before Anne's, that it finally saw the light.[20] Richardson was considering such a thorough revision as early as 1753. By that time he had learned to be a little ashamed of his first daughter, who in more ways than one belonged to a lower class than her younger sisters. His revision must have been substantially completed by 1758.

The final revision of *Pamela* certainly occupied a good deal of his time. Hardly a passage in the novel is untouched. Some scenes are cut, especially in the continuation, and one rather long scene is added, as well as a good many shorter passages. This revision shows the tendency, apparent already in the second edition, to elevate the style of the book, but it is to Richardson's credit that he recognized, as Aaron Hill had told him and as he told Lady Bradshaigh, that at least before her elevation Pamela's way of writing should not be too much tampered with. In each revision of the book, some of her homely language is lost, but even in the last one she remains in her early letters a simple and credible servant girl. Richard-

[20] See Eaves and Kimpel, 'Richardson's Revisions of *Pamela*', pp. 70–88.

son tried to clear up her motives in such a way that she would not be open to the cutting criticisms that had been directed against her, as a deceitful and self-seeking little minx. He rewrote even more thoroughly Mr. B.'s letters, evidently conscious that something was wrong with him; but he never succeeded in making him either lively or credible. Some of the added passages show considerable skill at social comedy; they are the best evidence that if Richardson's Muse had flown, his technique at least remained. There are lively flashes of conversation throughout the revision. It provides clear evidence, if any is needed, that though in his best writing Richardson may have been possessed by a force beyond his conscious mind, he was by no means lacking in conscious artistry and especially when writing the novel of manners knew exactly what he was doing. The other chief influence of his conscious art, the heavy moralizing, is surprisingly not prominent in the final revision of *Pamela*.

There are three literary works by other people in which Richardson has been supposed to have had a hand during the last years of his life, *Balbe-Berton*, *Sir William Harrington*, and *Conjectures on Original Composition*; he certainly had a hand in a fourth, Young's *Centaur Not Fabulous*. A little over a year before his death appeared a translation of Marguerite de Lussan's *Vie de Louis Balbe-Berton de Crillon*, 'Translated from the FRENCH by a LADY, And revised by Mr. RICHARDSON, Author of CLARISSA, GRANDISON, &c'.[21] Lady Bradshaigh read about fifteen pages of it and told Richardson that she did not like it: 'Warriour Hero's are not my Favourites. Did Mr Ricn. open the Book?' Richardson in reply said that he did not wonder she could not read the book. 'I was drawn in, against my Will, to give the Translation a Reading, by the Lady who render'd it into English, of French I know nothing; and advised some Notes of the Massacre of Paris, and Assassination of Henry IV. Cotemporary Transactions. This brought upon me the Application to have my Name mentioned to the Public as the *Reviser*. My Kinsman [William Richardson] printed it. I was willing, little as he deserved Favour from me, to promote his Interest. Yet my Compliance, made with great Reluctance, was wrong.'[22] Who the lady was who translated the book, we do not know.

The book is a life-and-times of a late sixteenth-century soldier and gentleman. A part of Lady Bradshaigh's displeasure may have been caused by remarks early in the biography rejoicing at the fact that the English were driven out of Calais and approving the stern anti-Protestant measures of Henri II; if she read so far as the high praise given the Duc de Guise, she must have been even less pleased. But the French author is on

---

[21] The *London Chronicle* of 17–19 Apr. 1760 advertises that it will be speedily published; of 26–9 Apr. 1760, that it is published (VII, 379, 410).
[22] 8 June, 20 June.

the whole moderate and fair; Crillon (or Grillon, as he is called in the English) condemns the St. Bartholomew's Day Massacre[23] and is an early adherent of Henri IV.

The English translation follows the French fairly closely up to the end, when it cuts some poems in honour of the Chevalier and a long genealogy. In return, it adds a good many notes on contemporary events, largely derived from French historians—generally on events either of special interest to Englishmen or appealing to Protestant sentiment.[24] Towards the end are a very long note on the murder of Henri IV and an appendix on the Massacre.[25] These also are drawn from a variety of French writers, whose works are cited. The appendix is followed by a second account of the Massacre 'given by a very worthy writer'.[26] It is much warmer and more anti-Catholic than the notes, though it also draws copiously on French writers. A note at the end says 'Considerations upon war, upon cruelty in general, and upon religious cruelty in particular'—presumably the source of the account. References to religious rage and over-zealousness sound faintly anti-clerical. In any case, the style in no way resembles that of Richardson, nor does it seem at all likely that he could have called upon so many French authorities, though the fact that he had many years before printed a translation of Castelnau's *Mémoires* may have given him some knowledge of the period. It has been suggested that he wrote at least this second account,[27] but to us his authorship appears highly improbable, and we are inclined to believe that his connection with *Balbe-Berton* was limited to the suggestion of which he told Lady Bradshaigh, a suggestion which the translator obviously followed.

Another attempt to take advantage of his reputation to sell a book was made ten years after his death. In 1771 was published *The History of Sir William Harrington*, which is described on the title page as 'revised and corrected By the Late Mr. RICHARDSON'.[28] On 19 January 1757 an unknown young lady who signed herself Cleomira wrote to Richardson that, having heard he planned to write no more, she had attempted a novel in his manner, which she would like him to publish. She asked him to correct 'any very gross error, or striking faults', to print the book, and

[23] I, 152.

[24] The negotiations between Condé and Queen Elizabeth (I, 58), the St. Bartholomew's Day Massacre (I, 151), the remorseful death of Charles IX (I, 175), the honours paid by certain Catholics to the monk who murdered Henri III (II, 54), and the relations between Henri IV and Queen Elizabeth (II, 128, 132, 145), among others.

[25] II, 160–73, 193–209.   [26] II, 210–16.

[27] Sale, *Bibliographical Record*, p. 99.

[28] The authorship of this book and its connection with the correspondence between Richardson and the author which is preserved in the British Museum (Add. MS. 28,097) were discovered by William Merritt Sale, Jr., and discussed by him in *TLS*, 29 Aug. 1935, p. 537. For a discussion of Richardson's influence on this novel, see T. C. Duncan Eaves and Ben D. Kimpel, 'Richardson's Connection with *Sir William Harrington*', *Papers on Language & Literature*, IV (1968), pp. 276–87.

to take half of the profits. She described herself as 'a little turn'd of twenty' and as having partaken for the past eight years of all the diversions of Bath and London. Though she did not need money, she would not object to making some. It later developed that her real name was Anna Meades and that she had previously written and was just publishing anonymously a work called *The History of Cleanthes, an Englishman of the Highest Quality, and Celemene, the Illustrious Amazonian Princess*. The book is all that the title promises, a generous helping of shipwrecks, rapturous love, Moslem slaves, and other ingredients of the kind of romance which Richardson had from the first set his face against. A preface admits that it was written to kill time and to revive the manner of such 'Ancient Writings' as *Cassandra* and *The Grand Cyrus*.

Richardson replied that he was not a bookseller, and was both ill and busy, but hoped he could help; Cleomira still hoped that he would print the work at her risk, give it to booksellers he approved of, and take half the profits.[29] She mentioned her former excursion into literature ('an inoffencive unexceptionable thing'); but her new work was quite different: it was '*A description of Modern life*' and was perhaps not altogether unexceptionable, since though her women were good, the letters of the men, modern life being what it was, must contain 'many passages not altogether free from what might be stiled improper to flow from ye. Pen of a Woman.' On 28 March she wrote again: *Cleanthes* having been published, she was sending Richardson a copy with the request that he give his real opinion and point out the faults of the work, that she might avoid similar faults in future. Richardson did not answer until 16 May, excusing himself on the ground of health; he had still not quite finished the adventures of the Amazonian Princess, but, judging by what he had read, he praised her 'fine Imagination' but ventured to state that 'a due Attention is not always given to Nature & Probability'. He hoped for the pleasure of a visit from her: 'I am often honoured wth: ye Visits of very worthy young Ladies.' Cleomira found his reproof just; she had been only nineteen when she wrote *Cleanthes* and was now four years older and hoped to do better, especially since she had studied Richardson's works with great care. She hoped to visit him in July.[30] And on 8 July she wrote again asking whether she might call next Monday (the eleventh), and bring her new work, now completed.

Evidently Richardson welcomed her call, since in her next letter she is '*your Anna*' and mentions his kind reception. Richardson had looked just as she had expected: 'Ye. eyes with a charming Benignity, diffusing a mixture of ye. Parental, ye. Friendly, ye. gentle Admoniter, & ye. able Teacher, over ye. whole countenance. . . . I could converse with you without Fear, so obligingly did you in ye. course of our conversation

[29] 2 Feb., 12 Feb.   [30] 28 May.

submit to talk with me upon a level—What a kind condesension!' She would rise to him, so that he would not have to stoop. Richardson found that her work showed 'a Knowlege of Men and Manners' surprising in one so young. He had made a few observations as he read, which he could best give her in person. She proposed to call again on her way to her father's home in Cambridgeshire and to hear his remarks on her work '& most readily submit to whatever you lay down, for by your advice & direction I am determined [to] be guided in every particular relating to this work'.[31] On 20 September she wrote proposing to call on Friday the twenty-third. In the only other extant letter from her to Richardson we learn that she had begun a correspondence with his daughter Martha and that he had promised when he returned the manuscript of her novel to send some written remarks.[32] The manuscript had long since arrived, with Richardson's handwriting 'in many parts to ye. very great amendment of all ye. passages [whe]re it is found'. But still she hoped for the promised remarks.

Sir William Harrington has the slow-moving but on the whole realistic tone of *Sir Charles Grandison*, though Sir William himself is a Lovelace without wit. The slight plot is elaborated with much polite conversation and detailed description of clothes and houses. There is a group of rakes, including Sir William; at least one of them, Renholds, does write letters which Richardson must have thought odd coming from the pen of a lady, even one used to the diversions of Bath. Sir William tries to seduce Letitia, the daughter of a clergyman, and even weakly attempts to rape her but finally has a change of heart and marries her. His sisters have very mild adventures and after very mild courtships marry very mild men. Renholds is induced to take Letitia's sister Charlotte, and all five couples end in very mild bliss. All the characters frequently refer to Richardson's novels, especially *Sir Charles Grandison*.

A manuscript containing Richardson's remarks on the work is extant, but neither Miss Meades nor the editor who published the book appears to have used it.[33] They probably had the other remarks which were written in the margin of the manuscript; what these were we have no way of knowing, and therefore no way of determining the extent of Richardson's influence on the novel. Most of the extant comments, including all of the

---

[31] 18 Aug., 5 Sept., 15 Sept.   [32] 17 Aug. 1758.

[33] Richardson's remarks are preserved with his correspondence with Miss Meades, which apparently was originally a part of his file of correspondence. Shortly after the publication of the novel in 1771 Richardson's widow and daughters published a denial that it had been revised by him and claimed that all of his manuscripts were in their hands. However, in the second edition (1772) the editor reasserted his claim and said (I, iiin) that Richardson's 'notes and emendations, in his own hand-writing, were left for many months with Mr Bell the bookseller, for general inspection'. See Eaves and Kimpel, 'Richardson's Connection with Sir William Harrington', pp. 278-9.

major ones, are divided almost equally between matters of propriety and matters of consistency of character and probability, faithfully reflecting the double concern of Richardson whenever he talked of prose fiction. They show him as a meticulous reader and painstaking corrector, conscious of minute detail and extremely careful both as craftsman and as moralist.

When Edward Young met Richardson, he already had a considerable reputation; he was a clergyman, with a much better education than Richardson's. It is therefore rather surprising that he asked Richardson's advice about his compositions, just as Richardson was constantly asking the advice of his friends—and accepted much more advice than Richardson ever accepted.

In 1754 he was preparing a moral prose work called *The Centaur Not Fabulous*—the centaurs of the title are men of pleasure, in whom the brute runs away with the man. On 14 July he wrote to Richardson that he would like to show him his latest work, which he planned to print at his own expense; a week later, evidently after having discussed it with Richardson, he wrote, 'Blot, add, alter, as you please; and, if then you approve it, print it; if not, lay it by.' If any evidence is necessary of Young's high regard for Richardson, this unusual scope given to a printer provides it. Richardson found nothing to change in the dedication, which seems to be all he had yet seen, and asked for instructions on the format, to which question Young replied that he should decide the manner in which it should be printed, 'in which I shall thankfully acquiesce, for I understand nothing at all of it'. He was sending Richardson the work a letter at a time; it was at first to consist of four letters in all. He repeated his request that Richardson correct: 'If you see any thing wrong in the [first] letter, please to dele it, or let me know it'; 'if any thing occurs that will mend the letter, by your own pen, or a hint to me, deny not the favour to one that will much thank you for it'. Richardson made various suggestions about publication and sale and, at Young's request, offered to find an artist to improve the frontispiece which Young had sketched, a fantastic and allegorical picture of an elegant centaur surrounded by men and women of pleasure.[34]

After reading the whole, Richardson wrote asking that Young 'excuse the liberty I have presumed to take with his dedication' and suggesting many more changes in a second edition. 'I am apt to think that the reader is not sufficiently prepared in that dedication for the solemn and elevated subjects of the following letters, and that a few pages cancelled will answer a good end, after some such manner as I have presumed to offer in a waste sheet of the print; which I enclose.' The original version is not extant, but

[34] R to Young, 24 July; Young to R, 28 July, 1 Aug., 5 Aug.; R to Young, 5 Aug.; Young to R, 12 Aug.; R to Young, 14 Aug.

Young accepted Richardson's cuts with thanks: 'I . . . beg that so much may be cancelled and destroyed as both your very kind and most judicious insertions require; and that they may instantly be put in the press.' He also proposed to consult with Richardson to see whether the other corrections he had suggested could be made in the first edition: 'Expence, if that is all, shall not hinder it.' 'All your remarks are most just. I find that I am safer in your hands than my own; I beg you, therefore, to blot, add, alter, as you think good; and let not *delay* or *expence* be any objection to any thing *now* practicable, and you kindly wish to be done.'[35]

The Centaur Not Fabulous is a satire of modern morals, with an earnest intention but not without humour, and Richardson evidently did not relish some of the humour, mixing noble emotions with the ludicrous or treating ethics with levity. Some of the changes he suggested are merely verbal or correct matters of fact; others eliminate phrases which might be considered improper or too frivolous for the context. The dedication is still largely a series of humourously fanciful interpretations of ancient myths, but the original version must have contained more misplaced levity. A postscript, justifying the mixture of levity and seriousness, was probably suggested by Richardson's reaction. Some of the detailed changes Richardson suggested were made in the first edition and others were adopted later.[36] They are not extensive enough to justify one in saying that Richardson had an important hand in the work, though his influence on *The Centaur Not Fabulous* was greater than on *Balbe-Berton* and probably at least as great as that on *Sir William Harrington*. On receiving a copy of the second edition Young wrote: 'Till I looked over the copy you sent me I knew not how much I was obliged to you; accept my sincere thanks for your many excellent alterations.'[37]

Richardson's influence on a later and better-known work of Young's was greater. *Conjectures on Original Composition* has been cited as a precursor of Romantic criticism, and if this view is somewhat exaggerated, the book is at least an attack on imitation of other writers, ancient or modern, and

[35] R to Young, 21 Jan. 1755; Young to R, [26 Jan.], [29 Jan.].

[36] At Richardson's suggestion the fifth letter (added to the original four) was split into two. In the first edition Young accepted two long cuts (pp. 161–3) and wrote new material to fill in the gap, resulting in the cancellation of signatures N1 and N2. Two more of Richardson's suggestions were included in the errata (pp. 24, 92), and Young paid to have two words accidentally omitted written in by hand (p. 131). In addition to signatures N1 and N2, signatures R1, R2, and U1 are cancels, and perhaps sheets E, T, 2A, and 2C contain several more cancels or were completely reset, since these deviate from the pattern of one press figure for each sheet (see William B. Todd, 'Observations on the Incidence and Interpretation of Press Figures', *SB*, III [1950–1], 193, who fails to note the irregularity in sheet 2A). Three pages of the dedication (iii, viii, xi) were certainly reset since they are short by one or two lines. Of Richardson's thirteen suggestions made in his letter of 21 Jan. and not acted on in the first edition, nine were accepted in later editions (1st, pp. 158, 172–3, 207, 225, 291, 307, 314, 323; 3rd [1755], pp. 114, 125 [2], 149, 163, 216, 227, 233, 240).

[37] 23 Mar.

a defence of originality. Richardson, who in his own writing was about as close to being original as a writer can be, might have been expected to sympathize with Young's main aim. He is certainly the unnamed friend who is complimented for combining originality with morality and for making 'a convert to virtue of a species of compositions, once most its foe'.[38] It is not, however, the theme of originality with which most of his comments deal; like his comments on *The Centaur Not Fabulous*, they are largely concerned with morality, not so much this time with mere propriety as with ethics and the religion behind ethics.[39]

Young sent Richardson his manuscript on 21 December 1756: 'If it has merit I beg you give it more. How much does the *Centaur* owe to you?' A few weeks later he sent Richardson more of the book, hoping 'you may favour it with some strokes of your pen'. The deaths of Thomas Edwards and Miss Dutton, together with illness in his own family, prevented him from giving Young's work his immediate attention,[40] but on 14 January he sent a letter full of detailed and copious suggestions. It is not always possible to identify the passages to which Richardson refers, especially since the text of the *Conjectures* was extensively revised by Young after Richardson first saw it, but insofar as we can judge, most of Richardson's suggestions were adopted. The idea of enjoying a common prostitute is no longer found in the same context as the Sacred Name; Pallas springs adult from Jove's head, but her birth is no longer improperly coupled with the sacred creation of Adam; Lucretius is no longer praised (the Epicurean 'need not be set up for an example, however original'). Young, at Richardson's suggestion, adds, almost in Richardson's words, a two-page digression warning that genius does not take the place of divine revelation and that the 'self-taught philosophers of our age' may be dangerous when they toy with religious subjects or set aside divine truth. He did not, however, drop a statement that Shakespeare, Bacon, and Newton were great men.[41] Richardson had been willing to call them only great originals and suggested that 'though Shakspeare as an *author* was so far *greater* than Addison, as more an *original*, yet was he inferior to him as a man; because, in his best writings, *less useful*—for *man* to *man* is only *great* with respect to his fulfilling the important purposes for which man was made'. Young did moderate his praises of Pope: Richardson argued at length that Pope's genius could never have lifted souls to Heaven, 'since it soared not in the Christian beam'—besides 'an *heroic* poem ought not to be mentioned in these terms, which so exactly belong to a *divine* one'. (Young had evidently regretted the loss of Pope's pro-

[38] London, 1759, pp. 77–8.
[39] See Alan D. McKillop, 'Richardson, Young, and the *Conjectures*', MP, XXII (1925), 391–404.
[40] Young to R, [2 Jan.]; R to Young, 7 Jan.   [41] Pp. 31, 37–8, 79.

jected epic.) Richardson asked Young to reconsider the question of Pope's originality, and Young must have done so, since in its published form the *Conjectures* stresses the fact that Pope was a confirmed imitator.[42] One long paragraph suggested by Richardson, on the hardness of our hearts and our blindness to God, was not used.

Originally Young meant to name Richardson as the person who had requested him to write on original and moral composition, but Richardson objected to being thus named, since the fact that the work is written in a letter to the author of *Sir Charles Grandison* and the compliment paid him in it might lead the public to think that he had proposed the subject in hopes of praise. He suggested that 'some powerful and deserving friend' be substituted for himself, and Young changed the passage as he requested: 'your worthy Patron, and our common Friend' asked the questions which induced Young to write.[43] How Richardson liked this is not on record— since he became successful, he had never had a patron, worthy or otherwise, and there is no reason to think that he would have welcomed one.

The second subject, moral composition, was to form the theme of a second letter; by May 1757 it had been written, but it did not please the author—'the subject is too common'.[44] The end of the printed book promises a continuation; but the moral comments he added at Richardson's request may have led Young to think the second letter unnecessary, and it never appeared.

Young welcomed Richardson's pains and his 'masterly assistance', and in February 1757 he proposed to call on Richardson to 'read the letter, as now, by your assistance, amended'. In May Richardson had the manuscript again, in a revised form, and was ready to return it with two or three small observations pasted on it.[45] The book was not, however, published for two more years. In October 1758 Young sent Richardson another revision, again asking him to correct or to mark what needed correction. He had added several things, including, as Richardson desired, a passage describing Addison's pious death. Richardson was charmed with the addition. By the end of the year, however, Young had decided to alter his scheme and asked Richardson to return the manuscript with whatever corrections he had made. Richardson decided that his few corrections could not be read, written as they were in his shaky hand, and that he would therefore wait for the return of the manuscript. He did suggest that since the end of the work (Addison's death) made 'such mere nothings of all human attainments and genius' and therefore weakened the plea for originality in the first part, two distinct pieces should be made of the work, 'one for the delight of learned men; the other, and, doubtless, the most eligible, for the sake of true piety and our

----

[42] Pp. 65–9.   [43] P. 3.   [44] 12 May.
[45] 20 Jan., 24 Feb., 10 May.

everlasting welfare'. He also wondered if Addison's death should not be shortened; it might discourage the friends of those who had no opportunity to die with such piety. Soon afterwards, he did send more detailed suggestions.[46]

On the basis of these new suggestions, Young added, almost in Richardson's words, a passage promising that after the lighter matter of the first part of the book the reader could look forward to a monumental marble (Addison's death) in the pleasure garden which would call forth more serious reflections.[47] He cut a phrase referring in favourable terms to censorship of the press which Richardson though might offend the 'liberty-mad'; Richardson, in commenting earlier on the passage in which the phrase occurred, had regretted that since legal authority does not stand 'centinel', 'the press groans beneath infidelity, indecency, libel, faction, nonsense'. In this passage, as in others, Young added Richardson's own words to his text.[48] He took from Richardson, for instance, some reflections on writing in old age: 'Shall they be less esteemed [than old soldiers], whose unsteady Pen vibrates to the last in the cause of Religion, of Virtue, of Learning?'[49] The 'cause of Learning' was appropriate to Young's old age, but the 'unsteady Pen' was surely Richardson's. Another of Richardson's additions pointed out that the ancients, with no models, could not help being originals—there is more merit in an original modern, since he has a choice. Another is a comparison of learned men proud of their hard-learned rules to beauties who owe their charms to art and denounce natural, unstudied graces.[50] Almost all of Richardson's new suggestions, great and small, were adopted; on the whole, they were less exclusively moralistic than the earlier suggestions. Young was admiring and thought that he was now ready to begin printing; he also sent Richardson the rest of his book, which Richardson had evidently not yet seen in its final revision, in hopes that it would receive the same sort of corrections. Richardson promptly answered with still more suggestions. Perhaps Young's mood had changed; at any rate he adopted fewer of this last group of revisions and was more independent in changing the wording of those he did adopt. He had 'profited much' by Richardson's remarks, 'but as I have added much of my own, some of yours I have omitted. . . . Where I have not taken you at length, I have often taken the hint, and made the best use of it that I could.'[51] He did accept a passage censuring Pope's idolatry of canonized writers,[52] a fault natural to one of Pope's religion. But he did not use a severe denunciation of Pope's harshness to

[46] Young to R, 8 Oct.; R to Young, 11 Oct.; Young to R, [17 Dec.]; R to Young, 18 Dec., 26 Dec.

[47] Pp. 2–3. [48] P. 4; R to Young, 14 Jan. 1757.

[49] P. 8. [50] Pp. 18–19, 27.

[51] Young to R, 7 Jan., 11 Jan.; R to Young, 24 Jan.; Young to R, [late Jan.].

[52] P. 67.

other writers or a paragraph on the Augæan ordures of the modern stage. An addition pointing out that even unlettered Christians are immortal was modified and watered down,[53] and the account of Addison's death was somewhat shortened.

The *Conjectures on Original Composition* was published soon afterwards, in May 1759. On 24 May Richardson reported that Speaker Onslow, Warburton, Ralph Allen, and Dr. Johnson were all pleased with it—the latter promised Richardson to commit a few observations on it to paper, to send to Young. Surely Johnson did not propose to ask Richardson to pass on to Young the comments which Boswell reports: 'He was surprised to find the Doctor receive as novelties, what Mr. Johnson thought very common thoughts. He said he believed Young was not a great scholar, nor had studied regularly the art of writing.'[54] The first part of Johnson's statement might be pondered by those who consider him a 'neo-classic' critic and the idea of originality distinctively Romantic. Young hoped to have Johnson's comments to use for the second edition, which was published the next month, and Richardson tried to get them for him but urged him not to wait for them.[55]

By this time he regretted that Addison's death scene, which he had suggested, should have assumed such prominence as to be 'made the sole end of your writing it'. He praised the subject of originality and referred to 'three good judges of my acquaintance, and good men too, [who] wish, as I presumed formerly myself to propose, that the subject had been kept more separate and distinct. They think the next to divine vehemence (so one of them expressed himself,) with which original writing is recommended, suffers some cooling abatement.' The three judges were undoubtedly right. Richardson had been largely responsible for turning Young's critical piece into a moral tract, and he was regretting too late his own influence.

There was one more literary labour of sorts with which Richardson, during the seven years he had still to live after the completion of *Sir Charles Grandison*, occupied a part of that free time which Miss Talbot, probably with reason, feared might prove burdensome to him. He worked over his correspondence, preparing it for possible eventual publication. Even before he began to write *Pamela* he had saved the letters of such correspondents as Aaron Hill and Dr. Cheyne. During the 1740s he began to keep copies of some of the letters he wrote. Especially after the publication of *Clarissa*, when he was making new friends and probably writing and receiving more letters than before, he made a more or less systematic effort to preserve his correspondence. That part of it which is still extant

---

[53] P. 99.
[54] *Boswell's Journal of a Tour to the Hebrides*, p. 234.
[55] 25 May, 29 May.

shows that he went over it late in life, arranging it in volumes, sometimes with indexes, deleting passages he did not consider suitable for publication and disguising names.[56]

Early in 1755 Richardson wrote Thomas Edwards that he was sorting his correspondence and intended to destroy much of it so that his executor's work would be easier; 'if any of my Friends desire their Letters to be return'd, they will be readily come at for that purpose. Otherwise they will amuse & divert my Children, & teach them to honour their Fathers Friends, in their Closets, for the Favours done him.'[57] A little over two years later he was toying with the idea of taking at least some of them out of his closet: he had received an application from Erasmus Reich, at Leipzig, for a volume or two of selected letters, to be printed in German, and had replied that if his correspondents should apply to *him*, not he to them, an anonymous volume or two for Germany might not be altogether impossible.[58] Though a few months later, on 14 October, he wrote Reich that since he had no way of making an application to his correspondents Reich's wish 'must only remain a Wish', the idea evidently still appealed to him. The following month he consulted Lady Bradshaigh, who was inclined to allow her letters to be published, provided, of course, that the names were disguised. 'But pray, my *nice* friend, which of your Correspondents do you think, will apply to you to publish their letters? I am afraid, it will hang upon the point of this *lancet*.'[59] Mrs. Scudamore, recently Miss Wescomb, was told of the plan and wrote that she would

---

[56] Most of the extant correspondence which was in his possession is now in the Forster Collection in the Victoria and Albert Museum. It is arranged in volumes which are not identical with the volumes in which Richardson kept it and has a foliation which does not correspond to his pagination. But his own arrangement can be in part determined by indexes which he prepared for such sections of letters as those to and from Thomas Edwards (XII, 1, fos. 184-92) and the correspondence about his novels (XVI, 1, fo. 7; XV, 3, fos. 1-2). Richardson notes on prefatory sheets to the Hill correspondence (XIII, 2, fo. 1; XIII, 3, fo. 1), for instance, that the letters should be arranged in two volumes, that although some of the letters had been printed in Hill's *Works* (1753) they should nevertheless be retained, and that the letters would have to be reconsidered for reduction since Hill's warm heart was inclined to overflow in praise of those he loved. One of the notes is dated 13 June 1758. The Hill correspondence also has marginal remarks in Richardson's hand, made presumably as he read the letters again after his friend's death; and like most of the correspondence, it shows many passages struck through, some of them lightly, some of them so heavily as to be illegible, or almost so. A note in front of the Edwards correspondence (XII, 1, fo. 1) states that the letters might be of interest to several 'excellent Persons' whose names are listed, all friends of Edwards and a few, such as the Onslows and Miss Mulso and Mrs. Donnellan, also friends of Richardson, but that nothing is to be copied from it and that it is to be returned to his family 'with whom it must ever be private'. On the letters from Dr. Cheyne, which are not with the bulk of the correspondence but are in the University of Edinburgh Library, there is a note by Richardson: 'This Book, and the Letters in it, on no Terms, or Consideration whatever, to be put, (or lent) into such Hands, as that it may be printed, or published. Aug. 11. 1744.' Cheyne had asked Richardson to burn his letters (2 May 1742). [57] 27 Jan.

[58] Reich to R, 11 June; R to Reich, [July?]; Reich to R, 7 Sept.

[59] 19 Nov., 24 Jan.

like, even more than Lady Bradshaigh, to see such a volume but wanted her 'poor Stuff' burned. Richardson answered that he had reluctantly marked her letters never to appear and had altered his to her (Enfield was changed to Epping, Wescomb to Warner, for instance). Other ladies, he added, were grateful for similar alterations he had made in his letters to them.[60] By the following May he had abandoned the project. He wrote Lady Bradshaigh that he would go over his collections of correspondence cursorily and would destroy 'great Numbers' of the letters to save his survivors trouble. But should calamities befall his daughters 'and *proper Leave be obtained*, the Daughters of a Father, who never troubled the Public with levying a Subscription upon it, and has been so shamefully invaded in a Property so *singularly* his own [years later, the Irish pirates still rankled], may perhaps, if any thing be deemed worthy in his Part of the Collection, meet with Favour'.[61]

So far as we know, Richardson never considered the matter again and left the volumes of correspondence to his daughters, probably with the thought that they might be published posthumously. About 1780 his nephew William issued proposals for a new edition of the novels with anecdotes of the author, a critique, and 'a collection of letters written by him on moral and entertaining subjects, never before published.'[62] This edition never appeared, and it is impossible to determine what these 'letters' were. The correspondence with Lady Bradshaigh was left by Martha Richardson's husband, Edward Bridgen, to Richardson's surviving daughter, Anne.[63] The long delay in publication was explained in 1804. Shortly before many of the letters finally were published, an article in the *Monthly Magazine* stated that, since the correspondence related chiefly to living characters, Richardson in his last illness had enjoined that his papers not be published during the lifetimes of his daughters, 'unless either of them should by accident be reduced in circumstances, when he trusted the publication would prove a fortune to them'.[64] Anne was now dead, and his grandsons Samuel Crowther and Philip Ditcher had sold the manuscripts to the publisher Richard Phillips, who had arranged for their publication. They were published in July,[65] edited by the poetess and bluestocking Anna Lætitia Barbauld.[66]

[60] Mrs. Scudamore to R, 15 Apr. 1758; Mrs. Scudamore to Martha Richardson, 27 Aug. 1758; R to Mrs. Scudamore, 1 Sept. 1758.

[61] 30 May. See also his letter to her of 27 June.

[62] Nichols, *Anecdotes of Bowyer*, p. 157; *Literary Anecdotes*, IV, 581.

[63] P.C.C. Major 355, dated 30 Apr. 1787, proved 8 Aug. 1787. The original is also preserved at Somerset House.

[64] XVII (1 Mar. 1804), 158–9.   [65] Ibid. (1 July), p. 600.

[66] Mrs. Barbauld was given letters in the possession of Mrs. John Duncombe (formerly Miss Highmore), including some from Miss Mulso, and Mrs. Scudamore's son John sent her some (ibid. [1 June], p. 466, and Barbauld, I, iv–vi). Mrs. Barbauld did not publish nearly all the letters which Phillips had acquired, though her edition runs to six volumes. Some of the

letters must have been missing when she got them—it is hard to believe, for instance, that she would have omitted James Leake's letter on the Earl of Chesterfield's pleasure in reading *Sir Charles Grandison*, which is listed in Richardson's index to the *Grandison* correspondence. She herself says (I, cxcviii) that Miss Mulso's letters were 'withdrawn from the collection after Richardson's death'. Mrs. Barbauld modernized spelling and punctuation and cut freely, but where her versions can be checked against a manuscript, most of them are fairly accurate except for the cuts, generally made with good judgement. The letters to Young, however, and some of the letters to Lady Bradshaigh, especially during the time of the composition of *Grandison*, seem to be much more confused than the others. The manuscripts of a great many of the letters she published are now missing; perhaps she sent some of them directly to the printer's, where they vanished. Some of the markings on the extant manuscripts must be Mrs. Barbauld's, since they indicate cuts which she made.

What remained of Richardson's volumes after Mrs. Barbauld got through with them was sold by Southgate in 1828 (*Catalogue of Manuscripts . . . Which Will Be Sold by Auction . . . on Monday 21st, and Tuesday 22d, of January, 1828*). A large number of the letters were bought by William Upcott, including all of those later acquired by John Forster and now in the Forster Collection. In bulk, the letters in this collection far outweigh all of the others at the sale. Other letters bought by Upcott have appeared in other libraries or private collections, like the long letter on Mrs. Beaumont and the correspondence with Lady Barbara Montagu. Still others we have been unable to locate, though some of them have since been mentioned or quoted in sales catalogues. A good many individual letters or groups of letters were bought by other collectors, and though we have located some of these (the letters to Anna Meades, for instance, are now in the British Museum), there can be little doubt that many of the letters in Richardson's carefully prepared volumes are now scattered in private collections unknown to us.

CHAPTER XVIII

RICHARDSON AND HIS FRIENDS

1754-1761

Insofar as one can judge by the evidence of the extant correspondence, those of Richardson's old friends who remained closest to him during his last years were Lady Bradshaigh, Miss Wescomb, Edwards, and Young. His correspondence with Lady Bradshaigh continued until the end of his life, though it became shorter and somewhat rarer towards the end. Among other things, they ran out of topics to argue about. Richardson told her sister Lady Echlin that 'we have worn out our Subjects of Disputation. Cannot your Ladiship set us into an innocent Quarrel? Write something to her ag[ains]t me, that I may see if she is as good to me, as she used to be, and will offer any thing in my Vindication.' One typical little contretemps concerned some checks, textiles of Lancashire manufacture, which she proposed to send for Richardson's new town house. Richardson, who never much relished receiving favours, at first declined—he had enough furniture. She replied rather angrily that she *would* send the checks; Richardson rather grudgingly accepted, but she then wrote that her pleasure in the gift was lost, they would be a mere encumbrance. And then she decided that she would send them, though they be made into rubbers. Richardson finally received the checks, with thanks.[1]

Her formerly robust health began to deteriorate—in one bout of illness she lost fifty-four pounds. Richardson's suggested remedy, a drink made with brandy, together with riding, helped somewhat.[2] But her complaint kept returning—though she outlived Richardson by twenty-four years. Her relationship with Richardson seems to have meant a great deal to her —perhaps a sign of times to come, that a definitely genteel lady with excellent connections, though living a rather retired life, could be so impressed with a middle-class tradesman, famous author though he was. And Richardson's regard for her was also steadily high and was by no means

---

[1] R to Lady Echlin, 7 July 1755; Lady Bradshaigh to R, 23 Jan., 22–4 Feb. 1756; R to Lady Bradshaigh, 22 Mar. 1756; Lady Bradshaigh to R, 29 Mar. 1756; R to Lady Bradshaigh, 4 Apr. 1756; Lady Bradshaigh to R, 23 Apr., 23 May, 26 June 1756; R to Lady Bradshaigh, 10 July 1756.

[2] Lady Bradshaigh to R, 5 Sept. 1755; 23 Jan. 1756.

stimulated altogether by her social position. One can see in her letters the mixture of kindliness and high spirits which attracted him. We hope it is true that Lady Bradshaigh 'carried a dash of Miss Do' until her death in 1785.[3]

His correspondence with Miss Wescomb also went on, punctuated by occasional visits, largely with teasing, joking, and affectionate name-calling. By 1753 her letters became increasingly sombre. She was leading a gloomy life nursing her mother, who grew more seriously ill, and had few diversions. She reminded Richardson to write to her: 'What! am I quite forgot by my Dear Papa? not so much as one Line, message, or enquiry after his once favourd Daughter for the space of several Months? shall I say tis hard? no! I will not, for that would look like a reproach. . . . what am I? not a bare acquaintance, not friend, but a *Child*, tho an adopted one whch is too tender a name to be easily dropt, or given up, either on the side of the Parent, or Child.' A little over a year later she again wrote: 'A Carte Blanche signd with your name and directed to me would at any time be sufficient, & give me the highest satisfaction; of which I'd be bound by Promise not to make an ill use, for I wou'd only write upon it the Words, I love you still my Dear Daughter, dont be uneasy [I h]ave not forgot you, or something to the same purpose.'[4] Both times he replied immediately.

In the fall of 1754 Mrs. Jobson died, and Richardson invited the orphan to come to him. She appreciated but did not accept the invitation. She promised to consult him in any important matter which might come up and urged him often to visit Enfield. Again we find her, in October 1755, complaining of neglect from Mr. Richardson ('I must no longer say Papa'), and Richardson immediately promised her a visit. His visit, delayed by the press of business, was brief, but his daughter Polly stayed longer and evidently helped cheer up the too calm and peaceful retreat.[5]

On 26 August 1756 Sarah Wescomb married, and married well (after her mother's death, if not before, she must have been 'of a large fortune'), John Scudamore of Kentchurch Court, Hereford. He was almost twenty-nine and of an old county family.[6] Samuel Richardson, in spite of the 'trembling Figure' he made, gave her away.[7] For some time their correspondence continued. She even accepted his offer of a loan of four

[3] Letter signed 'BETHA', *Gentleman's Magazine*, LXXIV, 900.

[4] 7 Feb. 1753; 16 Feb. 1754.

[5] R to Miss Wescomb, 2 Oct. 1754 (the printed version in the *European Magazine*, LIV [1808], 97, is dated 3 Oct.); Miss Wescomb to R, 9 Oct., 23 Oct. 1754, 1 Oct. 1755; R to Miss Wescomb, 3 Oct. 1755; Mary R to Miss Wescomb, 13 Nov. 1755, *European Magazine*, LIV (1808), 191–2.

[6] Scudamore family records in the possession of John Lucas-Scudamore, Esq., of Kentchurch Court; *The Register Book of Marriages Belonging to the Parish of St. George, Hanover Square, in the County of Middlesex*, Harleian Society Registers, XI (1886), 66; MS. register at the church.

[7] R to Mrs. Scudamore, 12 Sept. 1757.

hundred pounds, which was lent and promptly repaid. But Mrs. Scudamore went to Herefordshire and soon was fully occupied in raising a
family. Her son John was born in June 1757, and for a while her children
came almost as fast as Pamela's—by whose comments on Mr. Locke's
theories of education she proposed to guide herself in raising them. A
little over a year later her family had become 'all so much of one Mind,
such strange domestick creatures, without (I believe) one spark of the
modern Spirit', that she would never want to return to London except to
see her friends there. It was surely a sign of friendship for Richardson
that she agreed to subscribe to Mrs. Carter's translation of the works of
Epictetus: 'I am apprisd they are upon very important, & agreable,
Subjects.'[8] Their correspondence gradually grew less frequent and more
formal; the last extant letter is one from her on 10 May 1760, asking him
to accept three hampers of cider. He noted on the back, 'Answered,
May 27th'. There is no known quarrel, and it is surprising that she was
not left a mourning ring in Richardson's will. Perhaps there was some
fancied slight from her during the last year of his life; she had married
into a class which he was apt to suspect of looking down on the City.
She had been a friend for many years, closer than most of his more
literary ladies, and only a confirmed intellectual, puritan, or Freudian
could fail to find a certain charm in their innocent, uneventful, affectionate,
and generally pleasant relationship.

In 1754 Richardson induced Young to sit for his portrait for the first
time, a portrait which Richardson wanted for himself and which his
daughter Anne left to All Souls, Oxford.[9] Their visits continued through
the 1750s, and Richardson's daughter Nancy stayed some time at Welwyn.
When excusing himself for not calling on Mark Hildesley, the future
Bishop of Sodor and Man, Richardson cited as evidence of his extreme
busyness that 'I never, in two or three Years could make a Visit to Dr.
Young of more than three or four Days out and in'. On a visit to Welwyn
in 1759 Richardson found the twenty-five miles too much for him; in
apologizing in 1760 to Lady Bradshaigh for not writing, he mentioned
that he could not write even to Dr. Young. The two old men were both
in bad health: on hearing that young Major Hohorst had died of a fever,
Young exclaimed, 'And, am I, still alive? I pity the dying, & envy t[he]
Dead.'[10] There is no extant correspondence after August 1759 except
one letter dated 8 September 1760; Young was having trouble with his

[8] Mrs. Scudamore to R, [c. Dec. 1756]; R to Mrs. Scudamore, 22 Mar. 1757; Mrs. Scudamore
to R, 12 Mar., 10 Dec., 15 Apr. 1758.
[9] R to Joseph Highmore, [Oct. or Nov. 1754]; Anne's will is in P.C.C. Heseltine 133, dated
6 Oct. 1802, proved 11 Feb. 1804. See also T. C. Duncan Eaves, 'Joseph Highmore's Portrait
of the Reverend Edward Young', *SP*, XLIII (1946), 668–74.
[10] R to Lady Echlin, 10 Jan. 1757; R to Lady Bradshaigh, 2 Aug. 1759, 10 Aug. 1760;
Young to R, 27 Sept. 1757.

eyes and Richardson with his staggering hand. But they remained fast friends.

A few months after Richardson's death, Lady Bradshaigh was moved to an unusual poetical effort in her friend's memory, which she sent to Richardson's daughter Martha:

> Why sleeps the pen of Young! the friend profess'd,
> The known abillities, the knowing best
> That heart, which few can equal, none excell,
> That heart which lov'd thee and thou lov'd'st so well.
> His humb'ler friends expected, wish'd, and waited
> To hear from thee his character compleated.

Her next letter shows that she had been informed that Young had commemorated his friend.[11] He included a passage on Richardson in his poem *Resignation*, which Richardson was already beginning to print when Young received the news ('Which strikes me to the heart!') of his friend's death:[12]

> To touch our passions' secret springs
>   Was his peculiar care,
> And deep his happy genius div'd
>   In bosoms of the fair;
>
> Nature, which favours to the few,
>   All art beyond, imparts,
> To him presented, at his birth,
>   The key of human hearts.

One stanza is typical of Young's piety and especially indicative of his true regard for Richardson:

> When heaven would kindly set us free,
>   And earth's enchantment end;
> It takes the most effectual means,
>   And robs us of a friend.

In 1755 Richardson again urged Edwards to relieve his loneliness by spending the winter at Parson's Green, his new country house. Edwards at first refused on the grounds that an invalid should not inflict himself on others; but later he visited the new retreat to discuss the matter and evidently fell ill there, since he apologized for encumbering Richardson with an invalid. He ended by making Parson's Green his headquarters for the season.

In the summer of 1756 Richardson again gave hopes of a long-deferred excursion to Turrick, and Edwards pressed him more strongly for a visit

---

[11] 19 Mar., 25 Apr. 1762. The letters and the poem are in FM XI, fos. 279-81.
[12] Stanzas 72-83.

than ever, 'which I beg for other reasons beside the uncertainty of life, but which I cannot at present mention in a letter'. Two months later, he again mentioned that he had a special reason for wanting to see Richardson, and Richardson finally made definite plans and did in fact come, for four days in late September, bringing his wife with him; he had to hurry back much more quickly than Edwards wished.[13]

In the fall of 1756 Richardson again invited Edwards to Parson's Green, where Mrs. Richardson and her eldest daughters, Polly and Patty, would be present to attend him and where Richardson himself would be coming often. By early December he was there and was gravely ill, unable to leave his chamber; Dr. Heberden gave little hope of his recovery. He had caught cold at a friend's house where he stayed for a week on his way to Parson's Green and could not be moved; Mrs. Richardson and her daughters tended him, and he called it cruel in himself that he 'should add to our Concern for his Sufferings, by dying with us'. Miss Dutton was at Parson's Green at the same time, in the last stages of consumption, and Richardson's niece and three of his daughters were ill.[14] Early in the morning of 3 January 1757 Richardson began to write to Mrs. Scudamore, 'Poor Mr. Edwards! Rich Mr. Edwards! I should perhaps rather say, since I left him Yesterday Evening in a dying State, quite insensible, knowing not any-body'—he had not recognized his old friend Speaker Onslow when the latter called on New Year's Day. And at ten that morning Richardson added a postscript—a messenger from Parson's Green had just arrived with the news that 'good Mr. Edwards commenced Immortal this Morning at 5 o'Clock!'[15]

In 1753 Richardson was for some reason offended by the neglect of his former favourite Sally Chapone; her brother tried to excuse her, since she herself was awed into silence by her fears of and reverence for Richardson, and asked that she be forgiven. A year later, however, Sally was still, or again, in disfavour; she had neglected to write to Mrs. Richardson and her daughters. Sally had been carried off to Ireland by Mrs. Delany while she and Patty Richardson were visiting Mrs. Dewes, and Patty had returned to the Chapones in June 1754. Sally wrote from Ireland to Miss Mulso and Miss Prescott, but not to Patty—or at least Patty did not get her letter soon enough. 'I hope', Mrs. Delany wrote to her sister, 'to find

[13] R to Edwards, 12 July; Edwards to R, 30 July, 13 Sept., 15 Sept; R to Edwards, 18 Sept., 24 Sept., 28 Sept., 1 Oct.; Mrs. Scudamore to R, 3 Oct.; Edwards to John Lowry, 8 Oct., to Peter Hervey, 8 Oct., to Daniel Wray, 14 Oct., Bodleian MS. 1012, pp. 277-81, 283-4; R to Catherine Talbot, 25 Oct.

[14] R to Edwards, 28 Sept.; R to Mrs. Scudamore, 5 Dec.; R to Sally Righton, 14 Dec.; R to Mrs. Dewes, 15 Dec.; R to Sarah Fielding, 7 Dec.; R to Mrs. Sheridan, 19 Dec.; R to Miss Pennington, 23 Dec.

[15] See also R to Sarah Fielding, 17 Jan. Edwards's will is in P.C.C. Herring 11, dated 1 June 1754, proved 4 Jan. 1757.

Mr. Richardson when I see him more reasonable; . . . we have not yet seen him: in short, that *fiend jealousy* goes about destroying all the delight of friendship!' When Richardson did see Mrs. Delany, she 'expostulated with him on Sally's account: he is really *very angry*, but *kindly* so, and if she writes a kind letter of excuse to Mrs. Richardson, (it must be to *Mrs. R.*, not Mr. R.) and soon after to *Miss Patty*, all will be well. It is only a kind *jealous fit*'. Soon afterwards Sally was 'quite in favour again', but a year later he was angry again—she had gone to visit Miss Mulso instead of coming to him. By 1758 she was his Sally again.[16]

In 1755 Mrs. Chapone's youngest son died. Her correspondence with Richardson grew less frequent but was not broken off. Once, when she took almost two months in answering one of his letters, his sensitivity appears in his noting on his copy of it that it was not yet answered, but when she explained that various friends and relatives had been ill and went on to tell him how much good his works had done her children and how she tested her friends by their reception of *Sir Charles Grandison*, he noted that it was an answer worthy of the lady. Late in 1758 he pressed her again to visit him so that they could discuss female delicacy and the meekness of women: 'Hasten to me your salutary Presence, and shine upon me, Sun of my terrestrial Hope!' This phrase is, incidentally, an excellent illustration of Richardson's at times unfortunate habit of catching the style of his correspondent. In 1759 the Reverend John Chapone died, and at his widow's request Richardson disclosed that he had supplied her husband with money but he did not press for payment. Mrs. Chapone was in some financial difficulty, and he asked her again to come and stay with his family. The death of Clarissa was often in the mind of the dying clergyman and had a happy effect on him at the last. He had been re-reading Richardson's works with his wife during his last months and on finishing *Clarissa* pronounced that since Adam no man or set of men had 'ever produced so noble—so just, so instructive and so fine a Tragedy!'[17]

Richardson also asked Mrs. Donnellan to stay with him while she was looking for a house, but after trying it, she found the situation of North End too low.[18] Later Patty Richardson visited her and acted as her amanuensis.[19] In 1756 she was still calling at Parson's Green, and Richardson was still delighted with her: 'Mrs. Donnellan is an excellent Woman,

[16] John Chapone to R, 2 Dec. 1753; Mrs. Chapone to R, 8 June, 15 June, 31 July 1754; Mrs. Delany to Mrs. Dewes, 5 Nov., 10 Nov., 18 Nov., 1754, 24 Jan. 1756, *Autobiography and Correspondence*, III, 298–9, 304, 403; R to Mrs. Chapone, 27 June 1758.

[17] Mrs. Chapone to R, 22 Sept. 1755; R to Mrs. Chapone, 27 June 1758; Mrs. Chapone to R, 23 Aug. 1758; R to Mrs. Chapone, 11 Sept. 1758, 26 June 1759; Mrs. Chapone to R, 20 June 1759.

[18] Anne Donnellan to Mrs. Elizabeth Montagu, 10 Nov. [1753] (misdated 1754), MS. in the Henry E. Huntington Library. See also R to Mrs. Delany, 29 June 1754.

[19] R to Benjamin Kennicott, 26 Nov. 1754; Mrs. Delany to Mrs. Dewes, 11 Dec. 1754, *Autobiography and Correspondence*, III, 310–11.

greatly respected by all who know her, for her good Sense, sound
Principles, and Politeness.'[20] They evidently remained friends till the end,
since there are legacies to Richardson and Mrs. Richardson in her will,
though he did not live to receive his.[21] Her old friend Mrs. Delany was
not quite so pleased with her, and found her dis-improved and likely to
be jealous of Mrs. Delany's other friends.[22] But Richardson was friendly
with both. He admired the excellent way Mrs. Dewes performed her duties
as a mother, though he wondered whether she was not giving her daughter too much wisdom too early. Mrs. Delany and Mrs. Dewes were also
still visiting Parson's Green in 1757.[23]

His relations with Miss Mulso grew cooler during his last years, and
he must have seen less of most of the literary ladies who surrounded him
at the time he wrote *Sir Charles Grandison*. In 1757, of the thirty-five people
he listed in his original will as the recipients of mourning rings, only eight
were women: Mrs. Mary Wright (his wife's sister), Miss Talbot, Miss
Lintot, Mrs. Donnellan, 'my dear Lady Bradshaigh', Lady Echlin, Sarah
Lewis, and Mrs. Gosling. Miss Mulso, Miss Highmore, Mrs. Chapone, and
Mrs. Delany are not mentioned. Aside from four names crossed through,
of people who had died between the writing of the will and Richardson's
death, about five names have been so thoroughly erased that they cannot
be made out.[24] 'Many other Friends', he wrote in his will, 'would I, in
like manner, have remembered by the small Bequests of Rings; but having
been bless'd with great Numbers, whom I think of with great Gratitude,
as such, I shall be excused. To all of them, occasionally, my most grateful
and most respectful Thanks for their Favour to me: And Wishes for a
happy Meeting in a better World. Had I bequeathed a Ring to each of the
Ladies I was honoured by, as Correspondent, and truly venerate for their
Virtues and amiable Qualities, the List of their Names, would, even in this
solemn Act, have subjected me to the Charge of Ostentation.'

Of his literary friends, Dr. Delany, John Chapone, and Young appear,
as does Young's bachelor neighbour Mr. Shotbolt, with whom Richardson
had stayed while visiting Young.[25] Both Arthur Onslow, his old friend the
Speaker of the House of Commons, and Onslow's son are included. A
large number of the men are business associates, many of them officers
of the House of Commons. The booksellers John Peele, John Osborn,
and John Rivington are listed and his wife's brother, James Leake. The

[20] To Lady Echlin, 22 June.
[21] P.C.C. St. Eloi 192, dated 12 Nov. 1758, proved 22 May 1762.
[22] To Mrs. Dewes, 21 Dec. 1756, *Autobiography and Correspondence*, III, 456.
[23] R to Mrs. Chapone, 15 Aug. 1755, 11 Sept. 1758; R to Lady Bradshaigh, 27 May 1757.
[24] P.C.C. Cheslyn 266, dated 13 Nov. 1757, proved 18 July 1761. The original will is also
at Somerset House. For a discussion, see Eaves and Kimpel, 'Samuel Richardson and His
Family Circle', pp. 300–4.
[25] Nichols, *Literary Anecdotes*, IV, 727; *Gentleman's Magazine*, LIII (1783), 924.

nature of that part of Richardson's correspondence which has been preserved has undoubtedly given a somewhat one-sided view of his associates.
His business friends are scarcely represented in it, and friends who lived
in London did not, naturally, write to him often. Though the list of
recipients of rings is probably also one-sided in its own way (it was hard
to know where to stop in leaving rings to the officers of the House), it
may serve as a corrective to the view that Richardson was surrounded
almost exclusively by literary females.

Among the new friends of his last years, probably the most important
was Lady Bradshaigh's sister Lady Echlin; though they perhaps never
met, he carried on a regular and increasingly intimate correspondence
with her from late in 1753. Even before that date he had heard from his
former Incognita of her earnest sister, who (in contrast to Lady Bradshaigh herself) before she was twenty 'read divinity, and all grave books;
remembered what she read, lectured me for saying short prayers, and
talked like a sage old woman'.[26] Elizabeth Bellingham had married in 1725
Sir Robert Echlin, second baronet, whose seat was located near Dublin.
Their two sons had died young, and their only daughter and heiress,
Elizabeth, had in 1747 married Francis Palmer of Palmerston, County
Mayo.[27] Lady Bradshaigh sent Lady Echlin a copy of Richardson's *Case*
against the Irish pirates, and she offered him help. She sent Richardson a
copy of Faulkner's defence, and he answered her in November 1753 with
a long account of his side.[28] Evidently Lady Bradshaigh did not altogether approve of her writing to Richardson—she told Richardson that
Lady Echlin had meant well but that she hoped he was not to have the
trouble of another correspondent.[29] He, however, was by no means averse
to the trouble; he even informed Lady Echlin that he had already thought
of applying to her (as he had applied to so many others) for advice about
and correction to *Sir Charles*, but 'the kindly-intended, but naughty
Interposition of dear Lady B. has discouraged me from such an Application'.[30]

Richardson and Lady Echlin devoted a good portion of their correspondence to joking about the whims of her wild sister Miss Do.
'Does not naughty Lady B—— say her loving sister is a bold intruder',
the lady wrote; 'but, this dear, cross creature shall not discourage me
from returning thanks for your last obliging favour.' Lady Bradshaigh
'has almost scolded her sister', wrote Lady Echlin, 'for troubling Mr.
Richardson with her scribble: but I have desired her to be quiet, promising that I would not be very troublesome to her worthy friend'. 'She

---

[26] 16 Apr. 1751.
[27] Cokayne, *Complete Baronetage*; John R. Echlin, *Genealogical Memoirs of the Echlin Family*,
2nd edn. (Edinburgh [1881]).   [28] 24 Nov.
[29] Lady Bradshaigh to R, 27 Nov.; R to Lady Bradshaigh, 8 Dec.; Lady Bradshaigh to R,
11 Dec.   [30] 30 Jan. 1754.

has threatened me', replied Richardson, 'on our Correspondence. And I have taken the Liberty to threaten her. She says, she knows how to set us together by the Ears, and perhaps will do it. I have boldly returned her Menaces.'[31] Thus the correspondence was established. She described herself as 'perhaps the oldest woman of my years, in this genteel town [Dublin]'; she was no 'modish fine lady' who amused herself with cards. She was a lover of solitude and often repeated Young's lines on those 'Who think it solitude to be alone' when 'a mistaken civility, or real good nature' forced her into company. Her health was not so good as her high-spirited sister's, and she had a religious turn of mind—fine ladies would call her a Methodist if she recommended to them one of Dr. Skelton's 'instructive discourses', 'and I should be as little affronted with that, as I am at their thinking me a strange, old-fashioned, hum-drum creature'. She loved especially her retreat by the sea, Villarusa, of which she sent Richardson long and glowing descriptions; she built there a 'rock-savage hive, grot, or hermitage', adorned with curious stones and natural shells, a 'humble cell' under a high rock near the sea, a romantic situation in which she could indulge her taste for simplicity and Nature.[32]

She could not undertake to offer corrections to *Sir Charles Grandison*, though she did report that some people in Ireland complained of prolixity and were disappointed in the ending: 'These complainers have neither taste nor judgment, I am sure.' She herself approved of the novel; her only adverse criticism was that Harriet's friendship for her rival, Clementina, was rather overstrained. As for those 'fine polite gentlemen' who dislike Sir Charles 'because he is much too religious and virtuous'— 'Alas! Sir, you have thrown away pearls upon brutish mortals.'[33]

She was perhaps more critical of *Clarissa* than even her sister had been. The novel contained 'many excellent things', but it was by no means 'a faultless piece'. Her chief objection was to some of the 'shocking Circumstances leading to the Catastrophe'. 'I felt Emotions not to be describ'd; and was too much oppresst, or distracted, to admitt a rational sensibility to take place—but my heart fired with indignation at those passages so horribly shocking to humanity.' Morden ought not to kill Lovelace—'no good instruction, either moral, or Religious, can be drawn from any thing so contradictory to Christianity—besides a breach of promise to the dead'. Instead, Lovelace, whose morals had been 'corrupted, and vitiated by wicked Communication', should be 'reformed by Clarissas virtuous Conversation' and die 'a sincere Convert'. 'To please and amuse' herself, she wrote a new ending to the novel along these lines,

---

[31] 23 Feb., 12 Aug., 12 Sept. 1754.

[32] 23 Feb., 12 Aug., 27 Sept. 1754; 22 Jan., 2 Sept. 1755; 7 Feb. 1756.

[33] Lady Echlin to R, 23 Feb. 1754; R to Lady Echlin, 24 July 1754; Lady Echlin to R, 12 Aug. 1754.

in which the rape never takes place. Lovelace's conversion is instantaneous when he sees Clarissa a 'meer shadow' of herself—a sort of living death's head, which brings him to a sense of his own guilty soul. Clarissa dies of a broken heart at the usage of her family. Lovelace then dies, leaving his large estate to charitable uses.[34]

Richardson was greatly honoured by her pains but thought that since no harm after all had been done to the heroine she might 'have been spared to ye World' and be 'the Cause of every one's Happiness'. He also thought that her Ladyship was somewhat too hard on Arabella (she elopes with 'a Lousey Taylor—and Cabbage is his name' and returns home in a beggarly state 'despised by every mortal, but her compassionate Father') and too generous in giving Mrs. Norton most of Clarissa's effects and her entire estate ('A happy Competency was all that that good Woman could wish for')—in short had rather overdone poetic justice. Half-mockingly, he suggested to her an even more happy ending, with Lovelace shining as a governor of one of the American colonies, 'as a Man you had reformed, by giving an Example of Piety and Enacting . . . Laws promotive of Religion and good Manners'. His criticism of her performance, though very polite, could hardly have given her a high opinion of her literary talents, though he wrote that he saw 'Reason to admire your Religious Sentiments, and the Excellency of your Heart'.[35]

Richardson and Lady Echlin found a good deal to write about. She asked him for an inscription, 'a serious moral sentence', to place on the wall of her cell at Villarusa, and he, sacrificing his modesty to show his obedience, proposed one from Ecclesiasticus, one from *Night-Thoughts*, and two which seem to be his own compositions:

> Tho' in this little Cell the Body seems confin'd,
> Nor Earth, nor Seas, nor Skies, can bound th' outsoaring Mind.

> Sacred to Meditation be this humble Grot!
> My Heav'nly Hope enlarg'd; my Earthly Cares forgot!

Lady Echlin chose his four excellent lines: 'Nothing can be more proper', she wrote, 'than the two first.'[36] Richardson hinted that he would like a sketch of her rural retreat to place near his view of the Bradshaighs' Haigh—always punctilious in money matters, he intended to pay the artist; Lady Echlin hired a young lady, whom she insisted on paying herself. He insisted on some acknowledgement to the fair artist, 'tho' but a Pepper-corn one, compared to the Value of her Piece, in Books, &c.' The lady refused even a pepper-corn, but Richardson continued to insist.

[34] MS. (166 pp.) in the Henry W. and Albert A. Berg Collection of The New York Public Library, Astor, Lenox and Tilden Foundations.
[35] 14-18 Feb. 1755.   [36] 20 Feb., 2 Aug. 1756.

He did, however, accept the two pictures which she sent and hung them at Parson's Green.[37] And Lady Echlin accepted his offer to do her some service in London. She asked for his advice in the investment of money, and he consulted his friend Francis Gosling in her behalf.[38]

Sir Robert Echlin died on 13 May 1757, leaving his title and estate to his nephew Henry, a young orphan whom he put under his wife's guardianship. She soon sent him over to England, and in 1759 she herself went over. She declined Richardson's offer of the use of Parson's Green, where she could live privately and in her own way while she looked for a house. He evidently made some modest remark about its location, since she replied, 'Don't talk of a genteel neighbourhood to Dame Echlin; she has nothing to say to such fine people, for you are to know, and I hope you will see, that she is not at all genteel, in the fashionable sense of that expression. . . . I only desire to live quiet in this pleasure-mad world.' For about a year, before renting a house near Waterstock, she wandered rather restlessly around England. She spent several weeks with her sister at Haigh, where there was much talk of Richardson and where she first saw her friend, in effigy, on the wall of her sister's dressing room.[39] Lady Bradshaigh wrote to Richardson on 18 September that after Lady Echlin's arrival and 'our first carresses and tears of joy were over, now said she, "Introduce me to Mr R."; in which I imediatly obliged her, "Why said she shou'd I have given him the complexion of a Black Man? in that alone I am mistaken, but there I see, the very same Heart, with which I have been so long acquainted." And so our Chimes rung in exact concord.' She seems to have been travelling incognita in order to avoid her nephew Henry's requests for money—Henry later dissipated most of his estate.[40] She announced her intention to pay Richardson and his wife a visit in April 1760, though she wanted her name to remain unknown and assumed that of Dame Roberts: 'Dear Sir, you will shortly see, I hope, what sort of a body your humble servant is; the most unfashionable plain country body you can imagine—uncouth at least.' But in August they still had not met, and three months before his death he was still hoping for a visit from her.[41]

Even closer to Richardson for a brief period, though she does not seem to have been altogether a new friend, was a woman named Mary Watts. On the manuscript of one of her poems which Richardson preserved

[37] R to Lady Echlin, 3 Dec. 1757; Lady Echlin to R, 5 Jan. 1758; R to Lady Echlin, 24 Jan. 1758; Lady Echlin to R, 6 Apr. 1758; R to Lady Echlin, 11 Sept. 1758, 29 Feb., 20 May 1759.
[38] R to Lady Echlin, 24 Jan. 1758.
[39] Lady Echlin to R, 31 July 1757, 6 Apr. 1758; R to Lady Echlin, 20 May 1759; R to Lady Bradshaigh, 2 Aug. 1759; Lady Bradshaigh to R, 18 Sept. 1759; R to Lady Echlin, 2 Aug. 1759; Lady Bradshaigh to R, 8 June, 23 Aug. 1760; Lady Echlin to R, 13 Dec. 1759.
[40] Letter signed 'BETHA', Gentleman's Magazine, LXXIV, 900.
[41] Lady Echlin to R, 28 Mar. 1760; Lady Bradshaigh to R, 23 Aug. 1760; R to Lady Echlin, 5 Apr. 1761.

among his papers a note (not in Richardson's hand) describes her as 'The lady of Mr Watts an English Merchant at Lisbon, and was Richardson's adopted sister'.[42] She was a Mary Shewrin of Bristol who, in 1737, married James Watts, of a family who had lived at Westcombe near Shepton Mallet, Somerset, for at least sixty years.[43] The couple had four children in Lisbon between 1738 and 1744, two of whom died there in infancy.[44] She and her husband appear in Richardson's life rather suddenly in the summer of 1754, but they must have been back in England for some time, since another child, James, was baptized in Somerset in January 1752.[45]

There are a good many references in the four extant letters from Richardson to Mrs. Watts to friends of hers. A 'younger brother' (in the usual figurative sense) to her and to Richardson was called Jeronymo, after the brother of the Lady Clementina. He seems to be the Mr. Lefevre who is also referred to. In 1754 he was involved with a love-lorn maiden, and Richardson, though he sympathized, was afraid that Mrs. Watts had been too tender to the unhappy pair and offered to help the young lady (evidently to overcome her love or at least to learn patience) if she would apply to him as Emily in *Sir Charles* had applied to Dr. Bartlett. Mrs. Watts later informed Richardson, always eager for the life-histories of his acquaintances and their acquaintances, of his story, and Richardson concluded him to be 'one of the worthiest of men'.[46] John Lefevre was left a mourning ring in Richardson's will.

Another favourite, at least at first, was Miss Mogg, also called Arabella, a young lady of extraordinary delicacy with whose merits Mrs. Watts was in love and who was considered as one of Richardson's many daughters. Miss Mogg's delicacy seems eventually to have palled, and she and Mrs. Watts had a serious argument which led Richardson also to have second thoughts: she was still a daughter, but a trying one, and he considered Mrs. Watts entirely right in her altercation and called Miss Mogg a 'dear Visionary', a contradiction between 'strange Tenacity' and 'imaginary Diffidence', a girl of 'invincible Foibles, and Lady Errantry' and of 'proud and more than princely Notions of Independence'.[47]

Richardson must have known Mrs. Watts before she went to Lisbon. Immediately on her appearance she was a 'long-lost Sister'. He seems to

---

[42] FM XVI, 2, fo. 84.

[43] MS. register of St. Mary the Virgin, Batcombe, under date 22 Aug. We want to thank the Reverend Fabian Jackson, Rector of the church, and Commander E. B. Baker for examining the register for us.

[44] Diocese of London, Foreign Registers, Lisbon Factory, Guildhall MS. 10,446/1. The four children were John, baptized 25 Sept. 1738; Charles, baptized 3 Apr. 1740, buried 16 Feb. 1742; Mary, baptized 11 Feb. 1742; James, baptized 21 Oct. 1744, buried 22 Aug. 1745.

[45] Register of St. Mary the Virgin, Batcombe, under date 28 Jan.

[46] R to Hester Mulso, 21 Aug. 1754; R to Mrs. Watts, 9 Apr. 1755.

[47] To Mrs. Watts, 27 Sept. 1754; 13 May 1756.

have known little of her life, since he was eager to learn 'all that is material to know of my long-lost Sister, now she has been so happily restored to me'. Nor did she know so much as the first name of his eldest daughter. She passed through London and saw Richardson and his family briefly in the summer of 1754.[48] Richardson's letters to her are full of affection and enthusiastic admiration; she had been through severe trials, had passed through 'the furnace of affliction' and come out pure gold, for which reason, Richardson told Miss Mulso, he gave her 'the first place among the women I have the honour to be acquainted with'. She was even compared to the mysterious Mrs. Beaumont—there cannot be three such women. She was 'a most excellent lady, and I think one of the most perfect women, as a Christian, an economist, a wife, mother, mistress, friend, and neighbour, that I know and have heard of'.[49] Like so many others, she was asked to point out the faults of *Sir Charles Grandison*, and she did mention a few minor ones ('all the faults' she found), including the fact that Charlotte's baby 'crowed' when only a fortnight old, a fault that Richardson admitted was a pure oversight and corrected in the posthumously published 1810 edition.[50] He sent her his books and asked her for a picture of herself, which he insisted on paying for, a picture which his daughter Anne later possessed.[51]

In the summer of 1756 Mr. and Mrs. Watts again visited London and spent four or five days at Parson's Green. Richardson lost not a quarter hour of the short stay.[52] It was arranged that his daughter Anne should visit her in Somerset, and before the end of September Anne was with her and was still there early in February 1757 when Mrs. Watts died in childbirth.[53] Her daughter Mary Anne, evidently named for Richardson's daughter, was baptized on 16 February.[54] Richardson wrote an epitaph for her, which must have been glowing indeed.[55] There is no other example known to us of such sudden and steady enthusiasm on Richardson's part as that for Mrs. Watts, though their recorded friendship was so brief—a little over two years of correspondence, with two short visits. She must have reminded him of some episode in his early life, and one would like to know more about this paragon among women.

One of the many admirable friends she mentioned to Richardson was

---

[48] To Mrs. Watts, [Aug.?], 27 Sept. 1754.

[49] To Hester Mulso, 30 Aug. 1756; to Susanna Highmore, [c. 1 Aug. 1756]; to Mrs. Dewes, 15 Dec. 1756.

[50] 9 Apr. 1755. See Pierson, 'The Revisions of Richardson's *Sir Charles Grandison*', pp. 187–8.

[51] 13 May 1756. The portrait is mentioned in Anne's will.

[52] R to Hester Mulso, 30 Aug.; R to Susanna Highmore, [c. 1 Aug.].

[53] R to Edwards, 28 Sept.; R to Sarah Fielding, 7 Dec.; R to Mrs. Dewes, 15 Dec.; Anne Richardson to her parents, 6 Feb.; R to Mrs. Sheridan, 11 May.

[54] Register of St. Mary the Virgin, Batcombe.

[55] Mrs. Sheridan to R, 24 July 1757.

'your worthy Mrs. Bennet',[56] whom Young described as being 'of the first form' in Richardson's 'school'.[57] Little with certainty is known about her, though she was probably Jane Bennett, the sister of Richardson's future son-in-law Edward Bridgen.[58] Just as shadowy is Mrs. Sarah Lewis of Kensington, to whom Richardson meant to have left a mourning ring had she not died before him. Her own will tells us little more than that she was a well-to-do widow who left Richardson half of her estate and his wife and daughters various articles of furniture, porcelain, and silver. She had intended to make Richardson her sole executor but, because she was 'fearful it should be too great a fatigue to him in regard to his present ill State of Health', she made him joint executor with her other principal legatee, Daniel Chinn, a surgeon.[59] That we learn only by accident of a woman in whose life Richardson played such a large role may serve as a warning against relying too much on his correspondence for a picture of his associates.

A little more is known of E[lizabeth?] Pennington, daughter of the Reverend John Pennington, Rector of All Saints', Huntingdon, poetess of sorts (she is praised in John Duncombe's *Feminiad*) and an occasional visitor at Parson's Green. She started corresponding with Richardson in 1756. Like many of his young friends, Miss Pennington had 'not yet got over that time of life when the Heart, spite of sense & Virtue is liable to weaknesses it doesn't care to own' (she was in her early twenties), and in 1757 their mutual friend Frances Sheridan hoped that he could bring her into his confessional, discover her secret, and cure her heart: 'No body like you has the art to penetrate into the secrets and unwind the Mazes of a female heart.' But the awe which he inspires tends, at the same time, to discourage confidences. 'You once observed to me that you coud never get some of your young folks to be as open & ingenuous before you as you coud wish: I know Penny loves as well as esteems & honours you more than any body & yet I fear she woud not open her Heart to you freely.' People do not like to feel inferior to those to whom they confide their foibles. 'This way of thinking in respect to you Sir must lock up the mouths of almost every body, except those who by years & experience have subdued that sense of Pride or false shame which I suppose implanted in all our natures.'[60] We do not know whether Richardson ever wormed out of Miss Pennington the secret yearnings of her heart. She died two years later, in 1759.[61]

[56] R to Mrs. Watts, 13 May 1756.   [57] Young to R, [22 May?] 1759.
[58] Aleyn Lyell Reade, 'Samuel Richardson and His Family Circle', *N&Q*, 12 S. XII (1923), 410, 446-7; Dodsley's *Collection of Poems* (London, 1782), V, 316.
[59] Eaves and Kimpel, 'Samuel Richardson and His Family Circle', pp. 302-3. Mrs. Lewis's will is in P.C.C. Hutton 337, dated 14 May 1758, proved 3 Nov. 1758.   [60] 24 July.
[61] Note to John Duncombe's *Feminiad* in the supplement to Dodsley's *Collection of Poems*, IV, 188.

One of Miss Pennington's close friends was Mary Unwin. Miss Pennington told Richardson of her piety, reading, taste, and judgement, and he sent Mrs. Unwin his most particular respect. She in return sent 'her admired' Mr. Richardson her respect and hoped to visit him when in town, 'a visit she has so long been desirous of'.[62] Her future friend William Cowper was already acquainted with Richardson (probably through the Duncombes) and had sent him, directly or indirectly, a copy of his ode to the author of *Sir Charles Grandison*.[63]

An even closer friend of Miss Pennington was Frances Sheridan, mother of the future dramatist and wife of Thomas Sheridan, the theatrical manager and actor. 'Was he of any other profession', Miss Pennington told Richardson, 'I should with great pleasure think of going to spend a few months with them in Ireland.'[64] She later lived with them and died in Mrs. Sheridan's arms.[65] By early 1756 Richardson had honoured Mrs. Sheridan's romance *Eugenia and Adelaide* with his approval, and she asked him to dispose of it in any way he saw proper and, probably gently hinting that he himself might take the trouble to make some corrections, hoped his daughter Patty would polish it a little.[66] Encouraged and inspired by Richardson, she went on to try her powers in a more ambitious work, *Memoirs of Miss Sidney Biddulph*, which late in the same year she left with him to read.[67] The Sheridans visited Parson's Green, with their son Charles, in 1756, and Richardson thought the husband 'equally ingenious, learned and worthy' and the wife 'for Patience, Equanimity, good Sense, an excellent Woman'.[68] The intimacy must have grown rapidly if, as Mrs. Sheridan's granddaughter states, their daughter Ann Elizabeth, born in 1756, was named for Richardson's third daughter.[69] When, in the fall of that year, Sheridan returned to his post as manager of the Theatre Royal, Dublin, a correspondence began between Richardson and his wife, which was rather desultory, with apologies on both sides for delay in answering, and was largely taken up with news of family and friends. Sheridan also wrote Richardson, asking 'the best Man and the greatest Genius of the age' to aid him in his struggles with an opposition

[62] 31 Oct., 10 Nov., 2 Dec. 1756.

[63] T. C. Duncan Eaves and Ben D. Kimpel, 'Cowper's "An Ode on Reading Mr. Richardson's 'History of Sir Charles Grandison'"', *Papers on Language & Literature*, II (1966), 74–5.

[64] 2 Dec. 1756.

[65] Alicia Lefanu, *Memoirs of the Life and Writings of Mrs. Frances Sheridan* (London, 1824), pp. 90–1.   [66] 5 Feb.

[67] Lefanu, *Memoirs*, pp. 86–7, 108–9; R to Mrs. Sheridan, 19 Dec.

[68] Mrs. Sheridan to R, 20 Nov. 1756; Thomas Sheridan to R, 16 Mar. 1758; R to Lady Echlin, 22 June 1756.

[69] Lefanu, *Memoirs*, p. 88. Mrs. Lefanu is confused when she states that Anne Richardson married Mr. Ditcher and that Ann Sheridan was born while Miss Pennington was living with the Sheridans (p. 89). The baptism of Ann Elizabeth Sheridan on 15 July is recorded in *The Registers of St. Paul's Church, Covent Garden, London*, Vol. II: Christenings 1752–1837, Harleian Society Registers, XXXIV (London, 1906), p. 13.

theatre which was threatening to corrupt Dublin and divide it by feuds, motivated purely by a factious party spirit.[70] Richardson put Sheridan's case before Speaker Onslow, who did not want to put himself under obligation to John Ponsonby, Speaker of the Irish House of Commons, by intervening in this virtuous cause. He also tried to help Mrs. Sheridan by interesting Dodsley in her first novel but was told that the demand 'for Writings of Entertainment and Fancy' was over.[71] In 1758 the Sheridans returned to London. *Sidney Biddulph* was published by Dodsley in March 1761 and was dedicated to Richardson as a 'tribute due to Exemplary Goodness and distinguished Genius'.[72]

Another intimate friend of Miss Pennington, who, like her, also tuned her lay by the slow Ouze, was Martha Ferrar, who married the Reverend Peter Peckard. Richardson already knew her by 1756 when Peckard started using his press for his various religious works.[73] The two men had met by the end of the year, but they seem never to have been close.[74]

Richardson had already a good many clerical friends and was, as one would expect, sympathetic to the clergy and well liked by them. One clergyman with whom he began a cordial correspondence after the publication of *Sir Charles Grandison*, though they seem never to have met, was Smyth Loftus, an old friend of Philip Skelton and, like Skelton, an Irish clergyman. It must have been Skelton who induced Loftus to help Richardson in his struggles against the Irish pirates.[75] Richardson sent him his argument against continuing *Sir Charles* and later copies of his works—a present which caused him to be 'sadly rated' by the women of his family when he neglected their company to read again about the trials of Pamela. Loftus's letters were earnest and full of feeling: he wrote of his love of birds, his sympathy for the poor Irish, and his alarm at the inroads of the Catholics and at the growth of irreligion.[76] Richardson agreed with him in deploring 'the spirit of irreligion that has so visibly gone out'.[77]

More difficult were Richardson's relations with the Reverend Mark Hildesley. Hildesley was, as he says himself, 'a little obscure man, wholly unknown to the literary world: a country vicar' (of Hitchin, Hertford-shire) when, moved by his admiration for *Clarissa*, he called on Richardson at his house in order 'to obtain a sight of the external form of a person, whose inward qualities had afforded me so much entertainment'. Though he intruded without introduction, he had an 'unaffectedly easy and agreeable reception'. Some years later, hearing of Richardson's troubles with the Irish pirates, he asked his friend Lady Lambard, then in

---

[70] 16 Mar. 1758.   [71] 9 Apr. 1758.   [72] Lefanu, *Memoirs*, pp. 85-6, 110.
[73] R to Miss Pennington, 4 Apr. 1756; Peckard to R, 5 Feb. 1756. For the Ferrar family, see the preface to Peckard's *Memoirs of the Life of Mr. Nicholas Ferrar* (Cambridge, 1790).
[74] R to Peckard, 16 Feb.; Peckard to R, 19 Feb., 14 May; R to Miss Pennington, 15 Oct.
[75] Barbauld, V, 171n, 177n.
[76] Loftus to R, 12 Nov. 1756; 20 June, 3 Aug. 1757.   [77] 25 May 1758.

Dublin, to help expose their iniquities and wrote his first letter to Richardson to express his sympathy and report what he had done, 'not in the hopes of serving you, which I am as incapable of, as I am of claiming any sort of title to your friendship or acquaintance. To admire your talents is sufficient honour to me, as I thereby manifest some degree of taste.'[78] All of Hildesley's letters to Richardson are written in this courtly and modest style. Richardson answered his letter 'in grateful terms', but Hildesley's extreme humility, or perhaps sensitivity, evidently kept him from continuing the correspondence. Richardson complained to Lady Echlin that though he revered Hildesley, 'to the Answer I wrote to a very kind Letter he favoured me with, in which I requested the Favour of his Friendship and Correspondence, he has not, and it is a great while ago, returned me one Line in Reply. A Slight from a good Man, who had warmly professed himself (and spontaneously too), one's Friend, must be a little (*not* a little) mortifying.'[79] Richardson mentioned that he might complain to Lady Lambard, and Lady Echlin evidently took the hint and wrote to her, since Hildesley quoted 'A slight from a good man' in his second letter to Richardson, who had also voiced his complaint through William Webster. Hildesley apologized ('overpowering me with his Humility', Richardson remarked)[80] for the apparent neglect: 'I could by no means look upon myself either by abilities or station qualified (notwithstanding his condescending invitation) to continue a correspondence with so great a genius.' It was Richardson's turn to be apologetic: 'What pain have I given myself in the pain I have given to a most worthy heart!'[81]

Hildesley's parish was not far from Edward Young's, and it was in company with Young that Richardson for the second time met Hildesley, at the inn at Barnet.[82] At Richardson's desire he sent him a few critical remarks on *Sir Charles Grandison*, made with his usual effusive professions of humility, as timid suggestions from 'a little Country Vicar, who, I'm sure, has nothing more to recommend him to your Notice & good Graces, than a well meaning Heart' (Hildesley makes one believe in the plausibility of Uriah Heep). Except for two minor objections to details and a wish that Richardson had denounced the 'hainous Sin of *Suicide*' (Richardson answered that he had already done so in *Pamela*), they are confined to high but vague praise, with, however, the conclusion that the new work was 'by many degrees *not comparable* to Clarissa'. Hildesley regretted that he would never be able to preach so effectively as Richardson and half wished that Richardson had entered the ministry.[83] The

[78] 20 Dec. 1753.   [79] To Lady Echlin, 19 Mar., 17 May 1754.
[80] To Lady Echlin, 24 July 1754.   [81] 11 July, 13 July.
[82] R to Hildesley, 22 Oct. 1754; R to Lady Echlin, 10 Jan. 1757, 24 July 1754.
[83] Hildesley to R, 8 Feb. 1755; R to Hildesley, 21 Feb. 1755.

acquaintance remained formal, and in April 1755 Hildesley was made Bishop of Sodor and Man and left for his new see.

Lady Echlin knew Hildesley and admired him as a primitive Christian.[84] Richardson agreed with her that he had all the merit necessary for his promotion, but he complained that Hildesley had neither called to take his leave, 'tho' he made me hope he would', nor written. 'Shall I be allowed to say', he wrote to Lady Echlin, 'that I expected other Things from ye good Vicar of Hitching?'[85] Lady Echlin offered to have a letter conveyed from him to the Bishop, but he only thanked her and added, 'I may one Day accept of the Favour.'[86] To Lady Bradshaigh he expressed his admiration for Hildesley: 'He is a good Man . . . Chearfully pious too; and so humble, that in the few Letters he favoured me with, the undue Preference he paid me, always made me blush.' But, he added, 'I have . . . some Negligence . . . to accuse him of, since his Arrival in the Isle of Man. . . . Surely the truly good Man was not disobliged with me for telling him, as I once did, that I thought he would not, admired as he was in his very large Parish, both for his Doctrine and his Example, have accepted of the Bishopric of Man. Yet, I remember, he turned quick upon me, on the Occasion; He assured me at the same time, that his secular Profits were not increased by the Exchange. And I verily believe his chief Motive for the Acceptance was, the Enlarging of his Power of doing good. I have a very proud Spirit; and think I cannot write to him, on his long Silence. But had I been the promoted, the Titled Man, and he what he was, I would have called upon the Worthy, the Pious Vicar of Hitching, with the first, for his Felicitations and Notice.'[87]

Lady Echlin's intervention brought out the fact that relations were indeed strained. 'I am very sorry', Richardson wrote to her, 'that the Bishop says, He dare not call me his Friend. No one living could value the good Vicar of Hitchin more than I did. . . . To myself, in the Letters he favoured me with, I always thought him too condescending, too humble.' Hildesley had evidently complained that Richardson had never visited him; Richardson explained how busy he had been, but if he had known that the Vicar of Hitchin had had 'but half a Wish to see me there', he would have gone. He repeated his respect for the Bishop and rejoiced 'in his kind Promise not to *free* me in future, occasionally, from what he calls his Intrusions. . . . I should take it for a Favour to be considered by so worthy a Divine, as more than an *Acquaintance*.' Hildesley did visit Richardson in 1758; the misunderstanding caused by the touchiness of two sensitive men was at an end.[88] But not until 26 August 1760 was their correspondence revived.

[84] 23 Feb. 1754.   [85] 28 May, 15 Dec. 1755.   [86] 20 Feb. 1756.
[87] 6 May 1756.
[88] R to Lady Echlin, 10 Jan. 1757; 11 Sept. 1758.

Hildesley wrote to ask Richardson to send a copy of a new book and hoped that time and distance would be no bar to his request 'to be retained in, or restored to, the roll, of those you call your friends'. Richardson rejoiced in being allowed to rank himself among the Bishop's friends, 'a liberty I shall be proud of taking to the last hour of my life'. When Hildesley replied, Richardson's weak health kept him from answering for several months, but a brief respite enabled him to write some of his last letters to Hildesley.[89] Their correspondence, finally established after so many delays, came too late to continue long. Hildesley expressed his regret (in cool and measured words) for the death of 'the worthy and ingenious Mr. *Richardson*'.[90]

In one of his last letters Hildesley asked Richardson the question, 'Pray, who is this Yorick?'[91] Richardson, of course, knew who was meant. The first volumes of Sterne's novel had made a sensation early in 1760, and in June of that year Richardson had used the word '*Shandying*' to Lady Bradshaigh, asking her if she knew the word. She answered that all the world knew it.[92] Praising the people of Manchester for their observance of the Sabbath, the 1761 edition of Defoe's *Tour* adds: 'God continue to the Inhabitants of this noble Town their Prosperity for the Example they set in such a *Shandy*-Age as this!'[93] Richardson answered Hildesley's inquiry: 'You cannot, I imagine have looked into his books: execrable I cannot but call them; for I am told that the third and fourth volumes are worse, if possible, than the two first; which, only, I have had the patience to run through. One extenuating circumstance attends his works, that they are too gross to be inflaming.' And he added the more extensive sentiments of a young lady: the town is forced to read the book because it is the fashion and there really is 'subject for mirth, and some affecting strokes', but the author's 'character as a clergyman seems much impeached by printing such gross and vulgar tales', and 'by another season, this performance will be as much decryed, as it is now extolled; for it has not intrinsic merit sufficient to prevent its sinking, when no longer upheld by the short-lived breath of fashion'.[94]

One does not think of Richardson as being an especially literary man, as writers go; he was a business man, with middle-class connections. Yet he was acquainted to some degree with most of the leading authors of

[89] R to Hildesley, 10 Sept. 1760, [*c.* Mar. 1761]. Barbauld, V, 145, dates this second letter 24 Sept. 1761, but it is answered by Hildesley's letter of 1 Apr. 1761. In a letter to the Rev. Mr. Hatfield, 26 Aug. 1761 (B.M. Add. MS. 19,686, fo. 33), Hildesley refers to a May letter from Richardson. A letter from Richardson to Hildesley, 4 May 1761, is listed in Sotheby's sale catalogue of 22–3 Oct. 1956, item 444. We have been unable to trace it.

[90] To Dr. Cornewall Tathwell, 22 Aug. 1761, B.M. Add. MS. 19,685, fos. 14–15; to the Rev. Mr. Hatfield, 26 Aug. 1761, B.M. Add. MS. 19,686, fo. 33.

[91] 11 Nov. 1760.   [92] 20 June, 23 Aug.

[93] III, 249.

[94] [*c.* March].

the mid-eighteenth century; he knew some of them more as a printer than as a fellow writer. Two of the leading intellectuals, Young and Johnson, and one lesser light, Edwards, were close friends. Walpole, Gray, and their friends probably did not consider Richardson up to their level, though Gray, unlike Walpole, admired *Clarissa* greatly.[95] Most of the rest, he had at least met.

Richardson printed for William Law, the author of *A Serious Call*, and for his friend John Byrom, Manchester's religious poet, with whom he was on friendly terms—in a poem criticizing Hill's *Art of Acting* Byrom mentions what he would say if he were speaking frankly to Richardson or Freke, and he addressed a poem on *Gideon* to Richardson.[96] He also printed for John Shebbeare, whose works he found occasionally lively, but he considered the man vain, pretentious, impertinent, scurrilous, and bad.[97] Mark Akenside passed at least one evening with Richardson at Dr. Heberden's and monopolized the conversation so that no one else had a chance to be heard,[98] but the only extant letter from Akenside to Richardson is a business letter concerning the correction of an erratum in an article written for the *Philosophical Transactions* of the Royal Society.[99] The author of *The Schoolmistress* sent Richardson hints for illustrations to *Pamela* in 1741, or so he wrote to his friend Richard Jago in a letter imitative of Pamela's style: 'Well! and so I sat me down in my room, and was reading *Pamela*—one might furnish this book with several pretty decorations, thought I to myself; and then I began to design cuts for it, in particular places. . . . So I just sketched them out, and sent my little hints, such as they were, to Mr. R[ichardso]n.' He admired *Pamela* and *Clarissa*, though he considered them too long. *Grandison*, he thought, was not 'equal to Clarissa; though, were merit in this age to be preferred, the author of it deserves a bishopric'.[100] He must have expressed some of these sentiments to Richardson's friend Mrs. Bennett, since in her poem on the alcove at Parson's Green she asks Shenstone's Muse to sing 'The Author's seat whom SHENSTONE loves'.[101] While he was a student at Cambridge, Christopher Smart called on Richardson in 1750 and was rewarded by

---

[95] 'Norton Nicholl's Reminiscences of Gray', *Correspondence of Thomas Gray*, ed. Paget Toynbee and Leonard Whibley (Oxford, 1935), III, 1298.

[96] Sale, *Master Printer*, pp. 126–7, 154, 183; *The Private Journals and Literary Remains of John Byrom* (London, 1857), II (Part II), 520–1, 543. Byrom's poems are in FM XVI, 2, fos. 55–7.

[97] Lady Bradshaigh to R, 23 May; R to Lady Bradshaigh, 29 May 1756.

[98] Miss Pennington to R, 2 Dec. 1756.

[99] 25 Jan. 1759. Sale in *Master Printer*, pp. 73, 264, identifies the article and doubts Charles Bucke's claim, in *On the Life, Writings, and Genius of Akenside* (London, 1832), p. 25, that Richardson printed *The Pleasures of Imagination*.

[100] To Jago, 22 July 1741; to Richard Graves, 1743; to Lady Luxborough, 23 Mar., 6 May 1750; to Richard Graves, 19 Apr. 1754, *Letters of William Shenstone*, ed. Duncan Mallam (Minneapolis, [1939]), pp. 24, 68, 199, 202, 290. See also to Thomas Percy, 16 May 1762, ibid., p. 444.

[101] Dodsley's *Collection of Poems* (London, 1782), V, 316.

being introduced to the poems of Molly Leapor. Richardson got Smart to promise to write an epitaph on the poetess, but the performance of this promise was delayed—Smart first sent word that he had been ill and then sent no word.[102]

Miss Leapor was a young natural genius of poor family who had died in 1746. Richardson was promoting the second volume of her poems, edited by Isaac Hawkins Browne, and feared that there would not be enough material, but was unwilling to fill in with Miss Leapor's letters until he knew whether there would be more verses—'More Rhymes I was going to say; but even that I cannot always say—And I am afraid, if we are not choice in the rest of the Volume, that this second Publication will do no great Credit to the Author, and depreciate the first.'[103] The number of subscribers did fall short of that for the first volume, though Richardson subscribed for four copies and got a good many of his friends to subscribe.[104]

The proposals for the volume were drawn up by David Garrick.[105] Richardson had no close connection with the theatre and seems to have attended rarely—so far as we know, not at all during the last years of his life, when his activities are easiest to follow. In 1748 he wrote to Aaron Hill that he had never seen Garrick on the stage, 'but of late I am pretty well acquainted with him'.[106] He tried to soothe Hill when he was irritated at Garrick's delay in acting his *Merope*; at one time it was planned to have a reading of the play at Richardson's, on which occasion Garrick expressed his esteem for Richardson.[107] Richardson sent him a copy of the last three volumes of the first edition of *Clarissa*, which Garrick acknowledged by proposing to visit him—he had not seen him for some time.[108] The gift was particularly welcome because Richardson had gone out of his way to pay a compliment to the great actor-manager of the day in his Postscript: in making a plea for the production of *King Lear* with Shakespeare's rather than Tate's ending, Richardson remarked that '*Now* seems to be the Time, when an *Actor* and a *Manager*, in the *same person*, is in being, who deservedly engages the public favour in all he undertakes'.[109] He later sent Garrick a copy of the third edition, in which Garrick wrote some verses in praise of the novel, 'Of *Nature* born, by *Shakespeare* got'.[110]

---

[102] R to Isaac Hawkins Browne, 10 Dec.

[103] Alexander Chalmers, *Biographical Dictionary* (London, 1815), under Molly Leapor; R to Browne, 10 Dec.

[104] Edwards to R, 8 May 1751; list of subscribers to the second volume of Miss Leapor's *Poems* (London, 1751).

[105] Chalmers, *Biographical Dictionary*, under Molly Leapor.   [106] 27 Oct.

[107] Hill to R, 4 Jan. 1749; R to Hill, 6 Jan. 1749; Hill to R, 9 Jan., 11 Jan. 1749; R to Hill, 12 Jan. 1749; Hill to R, 16 Jan. 1749; R to Hill, 17 Jan. 1749; Hill to David Mallet, 12 Jan. 1749, *Works*, II, 336.   [108] 12 Dec. 1748.   [109] VII, 428n. Not in SH or EL.

[110] McKillop, *Richardson*, pp. 160-1; *A Catalogue of the Library . . . of David Garrick . . . Which Will Be Sold by Auction . . . on Wednesday, April 23d, 1823*, item 2029.

Garrick told Edward Moore that he would have great pleasure in acting Lovelace in the dramatization of *Clarissa* which Moore thought of writing.[111] Richardson later sent him two volumes of *Sir Charles Grandison* before publication, and Garrick tried to enlist the help of Lord Orrery against the Irish pirates.[112] Richardson knew him well enough to ask him for a performance of *Every Man in His Humour*.[113]

At her request Dr. Johnson took Charlotte Lennox to see Richardson.[114] By November 1751 the two friends were co-operating in trying to get her *Female Quixote* published. Richardson liked the novel, gave Mrs. Lennox some criticisms of it, persuaded the reluctant Andrew Millar to publish it, and printed it.[115] He was repaid by a passage of high praise, which, he told Lady Bradshaigh, he 'was very desirous ... should be omitted'.[116] He may have printed her later novel *Henrietta*,[117] and he recommended her to Robert Dodsley to do a translation from the French.[118]

Around 1756 Richardson met Oliver Goldsmith, who began his career as a literary hack in London in the last years of Richardson's life but was not known as a writer until after his death. Boswell reported that for a time Goldsmith had served as a 'corrector of the press'.[119] Sir James Prior, so far as we can determine on his own authority, added that 'there seems no reason to doubt' that Goldsmith acted occasionally in this capacity for Richardson and that 'we may believe that he shared the hospitality and society of his employer' and at Richardson's met Edward Young. There seems to be no better authority for Goldsmith's having worked for Richardson, but they were acquainted. Miss Milner, daughter of the dissenting minister in whose school Goldsmith worked, reported that Goldsmith came to the school from Richardson, 'with whom he had some, she knew not what, connection, and of whom he spoke in terms of

[111] Barbauld, I, cvii. [112] Garrick to R, 4 Sept. 1753.
[113] This letter is dated 'Tuesday morng'. David M. Little and George M. Kahrl in their edition of *The Letters of David Garrick* (Cambridge, Mass., 1963), I, 191, date the letter '*post* November 20, 1752', because of their belief that Richardson's fire took place around 20 Nov. 1752. Since the fire was on 28 Sept. (see p. 495) and *Every Man in His Humour* was performed on 30 Nov., Oct. is the probable date for the letter.
[114] *Diary and Letters of Madame D'Arblay*, I, 45.
[115] See Eaves, 'Dr. Johnson's Letters to Richardson', pp. 579-81; Duncan S. Isles, 'Other Letters in the Lennox Collection', *TLS*, 5 Aug. 1965, p. 685; and R to Johnson, 2 Nov. [1751]; R to Mrs. Lennox, [late Nov. or Dec. 1751]; Mrs. Lennox to R, [late Nov. or Dec. 1751]; R to Mrs. Lennox, 13 Jan. 1752; Johnson to Mrs. Lennox, 4 Feb. 1752, MS. in the Harvard University Library.
[116] 24 Feb. 1753. He also suggested to Mrs. Lennox that she remove it (unsigned sheet of criticisms, probably forwarded with his letter of [late Nov. or Dec. 1751], MS. in the Harvard University Library).
[117] Sale, *Master Printer*, pp. 119, 185. In 1769 Richardson's nephew William, who had taken over his business, owned a share in this novel (B.M. Add. MS. 38,730, p. 148).
[118] R to Mrs. Lennox, 6 Apr. 1752.
[119] *Life*, I, 411.

regard'. Bishop Percy, on the authority of Goldsmith's old classmate at Edinburgh, Dr. William Farr, reports that in 1756 Goldsmith called on Farr with a manuscript of a partly written tragedy which he wanted him to read and correct: 'I . . . pressed him not to trust to my judgment', said Farr, 'but to the opinion of persons better qualified to decide on dramatic compositions, on which he told me he had submitted his production, so far as he had written, to Mr. Richardson, the author of *Clarissa*, on which I peremptorily declined offering another criticism on the performance.'[120] The tragedy is not extant, nor is Richardson's opinion of it known. Nor is there any further record of their acquaintance.

Richardson's charitable instincts were fully exercised by one of the correspondents of his last years, Lady Barbara Montagu, daughter of the first Earl of Halifax, who had squandered much of his estate and left his daughters only a moderate fortune. Lady Barbara lived at Bath with her friend Sarah Scott, the novelist, who was separated from her husband. Mrs. Scott was a sister of the bluestocking Mrs. Elizabeth Montagu, who visited her and Lady Barbara in 1755 and has left a vivid description of their 'convent', as she calls it. Lady Barbara and Mrs. Scott lived a life devoted to good works, 'a manner of life', says Mrs. Montagu, 'which most people will approve, but very few will commend'. They educated twelve poor girls and twelve boys, not neglecting their religious instruction, and put the girls to work 'making childbed-linen and clothes for poor people in the neighbourhood'. 'These good works are often performed by the Methodist ladies in the heat of enthusiasm, but thank God, my sister's is a calm and rational piety. Her conversation is lively and easy, and she enters into all the reasonable pleasures of society; goes frequently to the plays and sometimes to balls, &c.' The convent, Mrs. Montagu reports, was 'really a very chearful place, and the two ladies lived in harmony and contentment'.[121]

Lady Barbara had met Richardson by November 1753, when she wrote asking him to call on her in London. Her health did not permit her to call on him, and she was 'well acquainted' with his 'generous and humane disposition'—she needed his friendly advice in order 'to serve persons in distress'. In the fall of 1758 she had another charitable project, which called forth an extensive though rather formal correspondence between her and Richardson. In order to aid a poor and aged gentlewoman, Elizabeth Pattillo of Bath, a set of educational and amusing cards had been designed, to teach painlessly geography, chronology, and history —her original plan called also for cards on geometry, astronomy, and

[120] Prior, *The Life of Oliver Goldsmith* (London, 1837), II, 211-17; Percy's memoir in *The Miscellaneous Works of Oliver Goldsmith* (London, 1801), I, 39; Katherine C. Balderston, *The History and Sources of Percy's Memoir of Goldsmith* (Cambridge, 1926), p. 56.

[121] To Gilbert West, 16 Oct. 1755, *The Letters of Mrs. Elizabeth Montagu* (London, 1813), III, 335-7.

philosophy.[122] The cards contained maps of the ancient and modern world; brief accounts of soil, climate, government, and manners; the chronology of England, France, Germany, and Turkey from the eleventh century; and short histories of these four kingdoms.[123] Lady Barbara paid Richardson £56 to print the cards, which appeared in April 1759. This undertaking, about which both Richardson and Lady Barbara took a great deal of trouble, does not seem to have answered its purpose, since over four months later very few sets had been sold.[124]

Meanwhile, Lady Barbara had another protégée, a neighbour of fortune inferior to her birth and education, who had written a novel for which she hoped that Richardson would find a bookseller.[125] Richardson did not know the name of the author.[126] This novel was *The Histories of Some of the Penitents in the Magdalen House*. The Magdalen House was a hospital for repentant prostitutes, and the writer believed that 'the Title wou'd greatly forward [the] Sale of it, as it may encline People to buy it from various motive[s,] and tho' many perhaps may be disappointed of what they expect, yet [the Bo]okseller will receive the benefit, of their Curiosity'. Lady Barbara approved of this pious fraud. Richardson submitted the novel to Andrew Millar, who was not eager for it: 'He says, that the Demand for that Species of Writing is over, or nearly so. Other Booksellers have declared the same thing. There was a Time, when every Man of that Trade published a Novel, 'till the Public (in this Mr. Millar says true) became tired of them.' But Richardson himself, so far as he had read, was enthusiastic: 'It *must* appear, for Virtues sake.' Richardson had submitted it to Millar because of his generosity to authors and asked Lady Barbara to get her friend to name a price, one for a first edition of 1,000 copies and another in case of a second edition. If Millar should refuse, he would try Dodsley, himself 'one of those Booksellers, who think the Day of Novels is over', but 'an ingenious Man, a Writer himself, and no indifferent Judge of Writing'. Should Dodsley also refuse, Richardson would 'put her in the best way I can, to usher it into the

---

[122] On 14 Dec. 1757 the Crown granted her permission to print these cards for fourteen years. See P.R.O., S.P. 44/371, pp. 369–70.

[123] *Public Advertiser*, 28 Apr. 1759.

[124] Lady Barbara to R, 2 Nov. 1758; Mrs. Scott to R, 16 Nov. 1758; R to Mrs. Scott, 21 Nov. 1758; Lady Barbara to R, 23 Nov. 1758; R to Lady Barbara, 5 Jan. 1759; Lady Barbara to R, [16 Jan. 1759]; William Richardson to Lady Barbara, 27 Jan. 1759; Lady Barbara to R, 31 Jan. 1759; R to Lady Barbara, 17 Feb., 8 Mar., 27 Mar. 1759; Lady Barbara to R, 31 Mar. 1759; William Richardson to Lady Barbara, 3 Apr. 1759; Lady Barbara to William Richardson, 7 Apr., 22 Apr. 1759; William Richardson to Lady Barbara, 25 Apr. 1759; Lady Barbara to William Richardson, 29 Apr. 1759; William Richardson to Lady Barbara, 1 May 1759; Lady Barbara to William Richardson, 8 May 1759; Lady Barbara to R, 28 June 1759; R to Rivington, 31 May 1759 (with statement); R to Lady Barbara, 10 July, 2 Sept. 1759; Lady Barbara to R, 16 Sept. 1759.

[125] Lady Barbara to R, 31 Jan. 1759.

[126] R to Lady Bradshaigh, 18 Oct. 1759; 20 June 1760.

World for her own Benefit; she finding Paper only; we will leave the Printing to be paid from the Sale. . . . But this Offer need not be mentioned to Booksellers, or their Friends. Those Gentlemen have been often displeased with me for the ready Help I have been used to give to Author's at their setting out.'[127]

Millar did refuse the book, on the grounds that he had his hands full, and Dodsley also returned it, having 'left off Business to his Brother'. Richardson suggested a subscription edition. The author of *The Brothers*, Miss Smythies,[128] had met with no encouragement from booksellers; Richardson had 'advised her to try her Friends by a private Subscription', and she had 'succeeded beyond her Hopes'. Lady Barbara asked Richardson to print the novel for the author, offering to pay for it. Early in the fall Richardson was printing it and admired the lady's stories of repentant prostitutes more than ever: 'What Instructions, what Warnings do they abound with! How pathetically are the Distresses of unhappy Sufferers described! The Histories of poor Wretches, of which Virgin Modesty would be apprehensive in entering upon, are given with so much true Delicacy, that Parents of the strictest Virtue need not be afraid of their being read by their Daughters in their Closets.' He was a little irritated when, after all his pains, the lady sent him a very long list of errata; he suggested that some of the corrections were mere variant spellings and others were trivial, whereat Lady Barbara's friend left the whole matter to him.[129] The book was dated 1760 but was out before the end of 1759 and was well received, according to Richardson.[130] The preface, suggested by Richardson, is a plea for penitents and admits that the book is fiction—with a moral purpose 'where precept is enlivened by examples'. The book contains four histories of girls who are misled by wicked men and rescued by the Magdalen House. For all his pains Richardson received some venison from Lady Barbara's brother, Lord Halifax, and undoubtedly he was richly repaid in other ways by this correspondence with a pious and charitable aristocrat.[131]

When Richardson received this account of the inmates of the Magdalen House, he was already interested in that institution, though it was a very new one. It had been founded in 1758 'for the reception, maintenance, and employment, and with a view to reclaim penitent prostitutes', and the first eight 'unhappy objects' were admitted in that year. The originator

---

[127] 17 Feb.

[128] See Frank Gees Black, 'Miss Smythies', *TLS*, 26 Sept. 1935, p. 596.

[129] R to Lady Barbara, 8 Mar., 27 Mar.; Lady Barbara to R, 31 Mar., 28 June; R to Lady Barbara, 2 Sept., 27 Sept.; Lady Barbara to R, 11 Oct.; R to Lady Barbara, 15 Oct., 3 Nov.; Lady Barbara to R, 23 Oct.

[130] R to Lady Barbara, 12 Dec. See also Lady Bradshaigh to R, 2 Dec.

[131] Lady Barbara to R, 14 Jan. 1760; Mrs. Scott to R, [Nov. 1760]; Lady Barbara to R, 28 June 1759; R to Lady Barbara, 2 Sept. 1759.

of the idea was Robert Dingley, who was treasurer of the institution. Girls who had been seduced by promise of marriage were preferred. The authorities tried to reconcile the girls and their families; if they could not, they found them honest employment. No young woman who behaved well was discharged unprovided for. The girls were instructed in the principles of Christianity, in reading, and in various kinds of work; they were daily visited by a chaplain. They were to 'be cloathed and fed meanly, though with cleanly and healthful provision', and those who behaved best were to be given preference in food and clothing. They wore a uniform of light grey. For board and lodging the penitents agreed to pay £10 a year; they were not permitted to leave without permission.[132]

Sir Charles Grandison had several years before proposed the establishment of a hospital for female penitents who, betrayed by the perfidy of men, would gladly return to the paths of virtue if enabled to; 'these . . . are the poor creatures who are eminently intitled to our pity, tho' they seldom meet with it'.[133] Richardson contributed ten pounds, ten shillings, to the Magdalen House, and a good many of his friends also gave. Lady Bradshaigh was interested in the project, having penitents of her own to take care of, and visited the Hospital in the spring of 1759. She was charmed by the behaviour of the inmates and especially by the psalms sung by them. 'I thought myself in a congregation of saints', she wrote to Richardson. He replied that he himself could not have stood to visit the house. But he was friendly enough with Mr. Dingley to be visited by him and to show him the histories written by Lady Barbara's friend; in return, Dingley showed Richardson some letters from genuine prostitutes. Both were charmed. Richardson suggested that a second edition of the novel might appropriately be dedicated to Dingley.[134] In 1760 he was one of the annual governors of the charity.[135]

It was his charitable nature which got Richardson involved with one further correspondent of his last years (who can, however, hardly be described as a friend); and it was his practical business sense and middle-class notions about money which made this correspondence end in bitterness and recrimination. A good deal of Richardson's character, his kindness as well as his touchiness and his trader's morality, comes out in his

[132] *Proposals for Establishing a Public Place of Reception for Penitent Prostitutes* (London, 1758); *The Plan of the Magdalen House* (London, 1758); *The Rules, Orders and Regulations, of the Magdalen House* (London, 1760); William Dodd, *An Account of the Rise, Progress, and Present State of the Magdalen Charity* (London, 1761); Antony Highmore, *Pietas Londinensis* (London, 1810), I, 215–23; *A Short Account of the Magdalen Hospital* (London, 1822); *The Origin of the London Magdalen Hospital* (Wellington, [Somerset], [1893]). [133] SH, III, 384–5.
[134] Dodd, *Account of the Rise, Progress, and Present State of the Magdalen Charity*, p. 151; Lady Bradshaigh to R, 22 May; R to Lady Bradshaigh, 5 June; R to Lady Barbara Montagu, 15 Oct., 3 Nov., 12 Dec. 1759.
[135] *Rules, Orders and Regulations, of the Magdalen House*, p. 32.

relations with Eusebius Silvester. Silvester wrote first on 22 August 1754 to express his admiration for *Sir Charles Grandison*: 'None surely but that All-perfect Being who made us can conceive so just and extensive ideas of Humane Perfections.' He described himself as an attorney of Warwick, and when Richardson (after inquiry) found that his correspondent was real,[136] he replied, asking him to call if he should be in town.[137]

In reply, Silvester was again enthusiastic about Richardson's virtues, but no less so about his own. He had lived in perplexity from his cradle and had been practising at Warwick for ten years under adverse circumstances, such obsolete qualities as beneficence, the desire of self-knowledge, rational tastes, and a desire to control his passions having brought him no worldly advantages. His refusal to ruin the opponents of his clients or to tamper with evidence prevented success in his profession. And he posed a question for Richardson to answer, though he must have been pretty sure what answer he would get—is it lawful, in order to gain the favour of mankind, to put on the semblance of folly and vice? He proposed to accept Richardson's invitation and visit him soon.[138] He did so early in 1755, and Richardson noted, 'His seeming Modesty, good Behaviour, and specious Address confirmed in me the high Opinion which his Letters and Professions gave me of his Integrity and Worthiness of Heart.'[139]

Silvester wrote again in late autumn, apologizing for negligence and enraptured by *Pamela*. He had a manuscript on agriculture which should be of great benefit to the nation. Would Richardson undertake to print it—and to correct it? Richardson agreed to undertake the printing, and again Silvester was full of praise. He would like to live in harmony in a villa with a little 'Knott of Worthys', Richardson, 'The real Sr. Chas: Grandison at their Head', and contrive plans for the universal betterment of mankind. And if his great expectations were realized (vague reversionary hopes from a family which, when alive, had been hostile; success in his profession; his book on agriculture) he would share everything with his chosen companions. Meanwhile he sent a haunch of venison.[140]

He again visited London and, after his return to Warwick, wrote in February 1756, crushed by a horrible blow: worn out by adversity and the promotion of the wicked, he had reached a crisis in his fortunes and was about to fall forever for want of a small assistance, an assistance which would be both safe and advantageous to the giver. He knew not how to raise friends by 'sycophant Arts'. Richardson not unnaturally inquired what his embarrassments were. Perhaps his hopes were too high? His scheme for improving all the unused land in the kingdom was charming, it would make him the richest man in England, but he should not

[136] R's note on Silvester's letter.
[138] Received 12 Oct.
[140] 12 Nov., 24 Nov., 15 Dec.

[137] 24 Sept.
[139] FM XIV, 4, fo. 6.

count on it. But Richardson concluded by asking whether he could help. He could. Silvester urgently needed £100 to keep up his credit while he matured his projects (land reclamation was not the only one). He had no security except his character, but he could easily repay with interest: most of the leading men of Warwick were his clients (evidently the wicked were coming round). Silvester found comfort in thoughts of a future life, but his mortal part longed for enjoyment (Richardson later noted here, 'What flighty, contradictory Nonsense!'). Besides, he had a helpless mother and sister. He had no other friend to turn to but Richardson. But he would not have Richardson prejudice his family—'No, This might kindle such Apprehensions in Me, as might be a check on my Endeavours!' Perhaps the numerous persons of fortune whom Richardson knew could make up the sum between them?[141] Richardson could spare only £25, which he sent.[142] Silvester sent him a bill of sale on his furniture as security, which Richardson returned.[143]

In July Silvester wrote that he was in hourly expectation of 'an Overwhelming Storm'. But Richardson was not to worry about it: 'I wou'd rather cease to live, tha[n] exist at the expence of anothers Welfare!' Richardson, moved, offered to apply to a friend who had had a recent accession of wealth and to join with the friend in another loan. Silvester was to send a full account of his affairs but to omit his great project, which the friend would consider romantic.[144]

Silvester answered that he would soon be in London about another project, to obtain from the crown the grant of hundreds of thousands of acres of forests, chases, and commons in England and Ireland, which he proposed to rent out to be farmed by a new method, invented by him and his father. Richardson showed him some sensible comments on his financial situation: Silvester disliked the profession on which his success depended, and Richardson could have no opinion of his grandiose project; his hopes from a rich relative were based merely on the civility she had shown him on a chance visit; Silvester owed between £300 and £400, though he had earlier claimed that £100 would make him entirely easy— a further loan of £75 could only stop a few gaps, and the creditors he did not satisfy would resent his satisfying the others. Richardson's friend would lend money only if Richardson would be bound for it, and only at five per cent. Richardson sensibly saw nothing to be gained from a new loan under present circumstances and advised Silvester to compound with all of his creditors at once. Silvester replied to Richardson's comments in a paper which displayed more heat than light; he hoped that Richardson did not share the common prejudice against 'projects', and he had a new

[141] 15 Feb., 22 Feb., 28 Feb.   [142] 16 Mar.
[143] Silvester to R, 20 Mar.; R to Silvester, 24 Mar.; Silvester to R, 3 Apr.
[144] 13 July, 20 July.

plan—he had become 'so sour'd with Adversity' that he felt he could never be really happy in marriage and would therefore be justified in marrying a wealthy woman (he had several in view) and accepting the inferior happiness of money.[145]

Richardson's answer of 12 August shows that he was hardly satisfied with Silvester's reasoning. Silvester's warmth on the subject of projects led him to apprehend 'a Flightiness bordering on Romance': 'Can this be from you, and to me! . . . To be able to write thus on this Occasion, must be owing to some Fault in your Temper, which, were I writing to my Son, I would wish him to correct.' The best way to wealth was through his profession. But Richardson did not disapprove of his plan of marrying for money; he had long ago thought it the best solution but had hesitated to recommend it. Richardson had already done much to aid other people, beyond most men in his station, having lost or expended sums nearly equal to what he had left for his family. Yet he concluded by offering another loan of £25. Silvester answered that he had three women in mind, 'not very young', who he thought would accept him and with whom he could be more happy than most of his married acquaintances. He dropped another hint about voluntary contributions by Richardson's rich acquaintances, but Richardson firmly replied that such a proposal showed little knowledge of the world or of Richardson, who possessed 'the Favour of Persons of some Consequence, because I am not troublesome to them'. Marriage was the best scheme. And he sent a draft for £25, for which he desired Silvester's bond for £50 (including the former loan) for one year, at 4 per cent. Silvester sent him the bond.[146]

Four months later, at the end of 1756, Silvester wrote again, sending some letters on a subject (corn) now before the legislature which, if they would help the public and oblige Dodsley or some other bookseller, were at Richardson's service. He also sent some more venison. William Richardson replied for his uncle that the venison had been put into a pasty but that it did not suit Richardson to print the piece. After that cool answer Silvester was silent for many months. When the year stipulated in the bond was up, Richardson wrote a brief note inquiring why he had heard nothing from him.[147] Silvester's answer, if there was one, is not extant. But in March he wrote that he could not yet repay the loan—his prospects had improved, but his difficulties more than kept pace with them.[148]

Perhaps Richardson was irritated by Silvester's neglect and thought

[145] 26 July (and R's note on the letter); R's observations, FM XIV, 4, fo. 28; Silvester's answers, 10 Aug.

[146] R to Silvester, 12 Aug.; Silvester to R, 12 Aug.; R to Silvester, 13 Aug.; Silvester to R, 15 Aug. Richardson's account in Gosling's Bank Ledger records a payment of £25 to Silvester on 14 Aug.

[147] 27 Dec., 31 Dec., 28 Aug.   [148] 20 Mar.

that his former admirer, having milked him for all he could get, was dropping him. In his last years he lapsed easily into bitterness, and he had waited eight months after Silvester's bond fell due. In April he wrote again: he needed his money. 'Am I, at last, Mr. Sylvester, to depend for Justice from you, upon Projects and Moonshine?' Since this note was not answered, he wrote again in July. He had been turning over his correspondence and had happened to dip into Silvester's letters. 'How I blushed for You and for Myself!' He had an immediate call for his money. This note caught Silvester in another crisis; a few weeks would determine his fate, which, however, was now almost indifferent to him. Richardson hoped that Silvester would not force him to take measures he would find painful. Silvester replied in his old tone of persecuted virtue: from birth he had 'been pinion'd down to the Earth', but he would still climb. He hoped that in a month or six weeks a favourable turn would enable him to repay the money. If he had thought that Richardson would have such need for his money, he would never have accepted it, 'and if I remember right I intimated as much'—Richardson noted that Silvester had given no such hint. In November he asked him to wait a few weeks more, and Richardson answered that he hoped Silvester would be able to pay by 1 January.[149] Silvester had another project. He was sending a memorial to the Lords Commissioners of the Treasury, pointing out that tanners were partially evading the duty on hides; by drying the hides too long, they reduced their weight and thus defrauded His Majesty of over a sixth of his just revenues. By adding a clause limiting the time of drying, His Majesty could at the same time improve the quality of leather and gain, in England alone, £27,632 15s. 8d. Silvester hoped that His Majesty would remember the trouble and expense he had gone to to make this calculation.[150] His Majesty, however, seems to have forgotten.

In February and again in April 1759 Silvester informed Richardson that he still could not pay 'the most Generous & perhaps only Disinterested Friend I ever met with'. In June Richardson, who was collecting all the money he could get to purchase the law patent, threatened to take measures. Silvester, in a discouraged tone, informed him that he could not be surprised at any measures he might take. He was ill-qualified to obtain the favour of the world and had 'hardly any Heart or Spirits left to struggle any longer with it'. He hoped only that he would not forfeit, 'even in appearance only, that Veracity & Integrity which, however appearances may be construed, I hope I shall live no longer than I shall hold most sacred'. Particularly he did not want to suffer in the esteem of 'The Man, whose Esteem wou'd be of greater Value & Consolation, than that of the greatest part of the World besides'. Richardson was no longer

---

[149] 6 Apr., 18 July, 31 July, 5 Aug., 17 Aug., 2 Nov., 9 Nov.
[150] Dated 27 Nov. 1758, B.M. Add. MS. 32,886, fos. 92-3.

to be won by flattery. His reply was very severe. Silvester had hoped to excite his vanity by 'undesired and officious' praise of his writings, which he had attributed more to the goodness of Silvester's heart than to his own merit. 'This wounds me not a little', remarked Richardson, 'when I think of it, and look back upon the Beginning of our Correspondence!' Silvester replied on 21 July with one of his most moving letters. The accusation of insincerity and ingratitude had caused him great anguish—had he only been less sincere, he would be living in affluence. If Richardson had given £100, as requested, he might have succeeded. He had no security, no friends. He was in Richardson's power, but he would be unable 'to support life long, after a reduction to the last extreme'.[151]

Richardson was not moved. He did not write again himself. Silvester next received a letter from a John Douglas saying that Richardson was too ill to reply and that Silvester's 'Behaviour to him' and the 'surprizing Contents' of his last letter had contributed to his indisposition. The concluding letter in the correspondence is also from Douglas. Richardson was making a collection of the letters 'for a *Warning Piece* to Posterity', to be joined to those concerning another imposition put upon him by an attorney a number of years before. Silvester, said Douglas, copying a letter which Richardson had written out, abounded in 'gross Pretensions to *Integrity* of *Heart*', but appearances were against him. His letter of 21 July had been 'astonishingly ingrateful', especially in view of his statement that he 'cou'd wish that the most inward recesses of my heart were exposed to the whole World; this may perhaps seem like boasting'. Above this claim Richardson wrote, 'No, no! It cannot look like that. It is capable of a much worse Look!'[152]

Silvester, who bore a remarkable resemblance to Mr. Micawber, surely remained in debt until the end of his life. Judging by Douglas's final letter, Richardson never took measures to reduce him to the last extreme but contented himself with an outburst of moral indignation. Silvester had indeed been guilty of deceit in the sacred matter of pecuniary obligations, obviously because he was unable to avoid deceiving himself. The only wonder is that his transparent projects and promises, all of them vague, ever deceived Richardson. When he made the loan, which for him was not a large one, he could hardly have had high hopes of seeing his money again. Perhaps Silvester's neglect, combined with a growing tendency in his last years to worry and to resent imposition, gradually led him to see a primarily charitable action as a business deal; and then Silvester had not shown much gratitude, a feeling on which Richardson set great store.

[151] 24 Feb., 21 Apr., 25 Apr., 26 June, 30 June, 17 July, 21 July.
[152] 11 Aug., 21 Aug.

CHAPTER XIX

RICHARDSON AND HIS FAMILY

IN 1748 Richardson lost 'an excellent sister'. 'We loved each other tenderly!' he told Aaron Hill.[1] But there is little evidence about Richardson's relationship with his brothers and sisters. Two of his brothers, and probably two of his sisters, were already dead. His brother Benjamin died in August 1750, 'a dear, but unhappy brother', Richardson called him. He was 'an honest, a good-natured, but a careless man; of late years careless, so that his affairs were embarrassed, and he has left six children, five of them small and helpless'.[2] Shortly before his death Richardson had paid him almost £80, presumably to help him out.[3] Benjamin's eldest daughter, Mary, was the widow of a Moses Gentleman; four other daughters and a son were minors. Mary Gentleman renounced Benjamin's estate, for herself and the other children, in favour of Benjamin's principal creditor, his brother William. William and Samuel Richardson shared responsibility for the children, and Samuel took the youngest daughter, Susanna or Sukey, aged fourteen, to live with him, 'a good Girl; for whom we intend to provide as Prudence mix'd with true Love shall direct'. She was afflicted with rheumatic disorders.[4] Richardson left her £50 and hinted in his will that she might later get more from his family. If by any unexpected accession of fortune or the death of one of his unmarried daughters, 'any Room for Kindness to my Relations should fall into the Power of my Relict or Daughters, at their respective Demises', he recommended the two daughters of his brother William and 'the not happy Daughters' of Benjamin, 'Sukey most particularly; whom my Wife has in a manner adopted, and who has been always dutiful to her, and obliging to all her Cousins'.[5] Mrs. Richardson left her £200.[6] Richardson left three guineas each to Benjamin's other children, and Mrs. Richardson left John, the son, twenty guineas and ten guineas each to two of the daughters. After Mrs. Richardson's death Sukey continued to live with her cousin Nancy.[7]

[1] 27 Oct.; see also to Lady Bradshaigh, 15 Dec.

[2] To Mrs. Dewes, 20 Aug.; Barbauld, I, clvi.

[3] Gosling's Bank Ledger, under dates 6 Jan. and 17 Mar. 1750.

[4] To Mrs. Watts, [Aug.? 1754]; to Isabella Sutton, 20 Aug. 1750; to Sarah Fielding, 17 Jan. 1757.   [5] Codicil dated Apr. 1760.

[6] P.C.C. Stevens 444, dated 18 Oct. 1773, proved 16 Nov. 1773.

[7] Martha Bridgen to Anne Richardson, 4 Aug. 1784, MS. owned by Alan Dugald McKillop.

Richardson's last surviving brother, William, died in 1755. He seems to have been more prosperous than Benjamin and left a freehold estate in the Parish of St. Botolph, Aldgate, in addition to other possessions. But towards the end of his life he must also have had difficulties, since in 1756 Richardson mentions lending £450 'to a dear Friend & Relation, about a Year ago, to make his last Hours easy', and we know of no other relation who might have received such a large loan at this time.[8] William left a son, William, and two daughters, Mary Howlatson and Elizabeth, unmarried. Richardson seems to have been closer to William than to any other member of his family. He called William's death a 'very great Grief'.[9] 'We were dear friends as well as brothers. My cares for his relict and family, the nephew with me, and his two sisters (who have a title to them) will be increased. Excuse me, Madam, I hardly know what I write. He died but this morning (9 April). Adieu and adieu', he wrote to Mrs. Watts.

At about the same time as William's death Mary Gentleman and Joseph Howlatson, the husband of William's daughter Mary, died.[10] William's widow died in the fall of 1757, and her brother-in-law was enough afflicted to use mourning wax and paper.[11] In 1759 Richardson lost another sister, presumably the last surviving one, since no other sisters are mentioned in his will. What her first name was, we do not know; she was married to a man named Warburgh—the name is so unusual that it is hard to avoid speculating about the facts that one of the parishes in Derby near which the Richardsons had lived is St. Werburgh's and that bastards were generally named after the parishes in which they were baptized. The Warburghs were evidently poor. In the first version of his will Richardson had asked his executors to secure to 'my worthy Sister Warburgh instead of the Quarterly Allowance I have made her, Ten Pounds every Quarter, for her Life. She is far advanced in Years. My Family I am sure will not let her want any Comfort they can give her. If her Husband survives her, I bequeath to him a Legacy of Five Pounds.' Mrs. Warburgh died on 9 May 1759 after a long illness; her husband, whom Richardson described as 'helpless from Years, and Grief at her Illness', dropped down dead on 19 May as he was looking out of his chamber window. Richardson buried them both. 'Dear sir,' Richardson wrote to Young, 'what awful Providences! In the past two years, (to go no farther back,) what have I not suffered!'[12] One other poor relation whom he had been supporting was his wife's sister Amey Langley. In his will he left her 'the Six Guineas a Year I have long paid her; that is to say', he added with what must be a reflection on James Leake, 'if her Brother and Nephews, who are of ability, choose not to take this Payment on them selves'.

[8] To Eusebius Silvester, 16 Mar.   [9] To Lady Echlin, 19 Apr.
[10] To Edwards, 30 May 1755.   [11] To Lady Echlin, 24 Jan. 1758.
[12] To Lady Bradshaigh, 5 June; to Young, 24 May.

In 1754, when he finished *Sir Charles Grandison*, Richardson's daughters were growing up. Mary (Polly) was nineteen, Martha (Patty) was seventeen, Anne (Nancy) was sixteen, and Sarah (Sally) was thirteen. They and their mother spent much time at North End or Parson's Green, which Richardson visited on the weekends and more in winter than in summer.[13] Richardson has left one picture of domestic evenings: 'It is a Custom with my Wife and Daughters in long Evenings to sit round a Table employ'd in Needleworks; while some one of them, in Turn, reads to the rest.'[14] Mary Poole Way, who visited the family when she was very young, described the same evening scene and added that 'as soon as Mrs. Richardson arose, the beautiful Psalms in Smith's Devotions were read responsively in the nursery, by herself, and daughters, standing in a circle: only the two eldest were allowed to breakfast with her, and whatever company happened to be in the house, for they were seldom without. After breakfast we younger ones read to her in turns the Psalms, and lessons for the day. We were then permitted to pursue our childish sports, or to walk in the garden.'[15]

Even by eighteenth-century standards Richardson was rather reserved as a father, though there is ample evidence that he was also loving. Edmond Malone, evidently on the authority of Dr. Johnson, reported that 'to acquire a facility of epistolary writing he would on every trivial occasion write notes to his daughters even when they were in the same house with him',[16] but by the time Richardson's daughters were growing up he hardly needed to cultivate his epistolary skills. Sir John Hawkins, a hostile witness, says that those who expected his 'temper and domestic behaviour' to correspond with the 'refined morality' inculcated in his novels were deceived. 'He was austere in the government of his family, and issued his orders to some of his servants in writing only. His nearest female relations, in the presence of strangers, were mutes, and seemed to me, in a visit I once made him, to have been disciplined in the school of Ben Jonson's Morose, whose injunction to his servant was, "Answer me not but with your leg." In short, they appeared to have been taught to converse with him by signs; and it was too plain to me, that on his part, the most frequent of them were frowns and gesticulations, importing that they should leave his presence. I have heard it said, that he was what is called a nervous man; and how far nervosity, with so good an understanding as he is allowed to have possessed, will excuse a conduct so opposite to that philanthropy which he laboured to inculcate, I cannot say.'[17]

[13] R to Edwards, [*c.* 1 Aug. 1755].
[14] To Anna Meades, 5 Sept. 1757.
[15] Barbauld, I, clxxxvi–vii.
[16] Sir James Prior, *Life of Edmond Malone ... with Selections from His Manuscript Anecdotes* (London, 1860), p. 439.
[17] *Life of Samuel Johnson*, pp. 385–6.

Richardson does not seem to have been, by the standards of his day, unusually stern, but evidently he was too dignified to be very close to his daughters. His natural shyness may have had more to do with his aloofness than his theories of parental authority. He agreed with Miss Grainger that children should be governed by persuasion—he did not love a tyrant. 'I often complain that my own Girls seem more to fear me, to keep Distance to me, than I wish them to do. My dear Girls, I often say, let me have nothing but your Love. Open to me all the Secrets of your Hearts. I will be favourable and kind even to your Faults. All that you say to one another, that say to me. Ask me Questions: My Answers shall be encouraging. Yet the dear Creatures will have more Awe than I wish them to have.'[18] He deplored the reserve of his girls to him again to Mrs. Chapone, partially addressing his daughter Patty, who was visiting her. Evidently sparing Patty's reserve, he told Mrs. Chapone that if she needed money she had only to write to him or, if she found it easier, to her sister—Patty wrote to him.[19]

Lady Bradshaigh found his idea of the relations between parents and children somewhat stiff. In praising a letter to him from one of his daughters, she said that it 'shew'd an excellent and an humble mind, and consistant with her duty to you, & to her self. . . . The stile, was the stile you like, and now I have so fair an opportunity, shall I resume my old spirit of *sauciness*, and find some faults with the stile you generally make use of from children to their parents? Is not the repetition of so many respectful words rather overdoing it? Is it not somthing too *formal* and seems to throw a child, at too great a *distance* from an object, whom I think, ought to be approach'd with an *easie familiarity*, tho' with Love and *respect*. . . . I have heard you complain of the want of freedom in your good, your amiable children. Their high notions of your superiority, and their great Reverence for you, must be the reason, and I love and value them for it.' The letters of Richardson's heroines, she had often thought, were 'too much crouded with these Reverential Expressions'. Richardson welcomed her criticism—he was 'more than half sorry' he had not written 'every Word of it' himself. But 'as *Stiffness*, as you call it, as *too much* Reverence is not ye Vice of ye Age, I had rather, lay down Rules yt shd: stiffen into apparent Duty, than make ye pert Rogues too familiar wth: Characters so Reverend yt: it can never be thot: Want of Breeding to demonstrate a Reverence for them in all Companies, in all Conversations: While I Wd: have ye Parent so behave to ye Child, as to shew yt: he or she, was above ye Pride & Stiffness of exacting ye Reverence.' He approved a middle course; they were really in agreement. But he had rather his published children should be guilty of too much reverence than

18 1 Feb. 1750.
19 R to Mrs. Chapone, 19 Sept., 29 Dec. 1753; Mrs. Chapone to R, 2 Feb. 1754.

of too little. Perhaps he was the cause of the want of freedom in his daughters: 'I have been always ready to blame myself, as if there appear'd to them in my Behaviour, a Stiffness, yt I was willing to correct in myself, if found guilty of it. I have rallied them all in turn, I have jested wth: them, I have freely spoken my Mind before them on every Occasion; & I hope they are come off a good deal of ye Distance, I have sought to make them break thro'.' Patty, he boasted, had once written him a very free letter preferring Mrs. Watts's opinion to his and even to Sir Charles's (free indeed!); and he had 'applauded her Frankness, & let her go away wth: a Palm in her Hand'. But she had 'stuck in ye Words *Hon[oure]d*: & *Duty*, & Dutiful, oftener' than he desired, and 'than was necessary perhaps, in order to soften (for her own Heart's Sake) ye Preference she gave to Mrs. Watts's Argument'.[20]

The correspondence, after his death, between his daughters Anne and Martha shows great respect, even love, for him, but it also shows that they did not feel entirely free with him. Martha regretted the veil Richardson had drawn over his early life, and Anne agreed that she was sorry they could not venture to ask their father more questions.[21]

'Most of the ladies that resided much at his house', Mary Poole Way told Mrs. Barbauld, 'acquired a certain degree of fastidiousness and delicate refinement, which, though amiable in itself, rather disqualified them from appearing in general society, to the advantage that might have been expected, and rendered an intercourse with the world uneasy to themselves, giving a peculiar air of shiness and reserve to their whole address, of which habits his own daughters partook, in a degree that has been thought by some, a little to obscure those really valuable qualifications and talents they undoubtedly possessed. Yet, this was supposed to be owing more to Mrs. Richardson than to him; who, though a truly good woman, had high and Harlowean notions of parental authority, and kept the ladies in such order, and at such a distance, that he often lamented, as I have been told by my mother, that they were not more open and conversable with him.'[22]

He had little to complain of in his daughters' behaviour. He found fault with them for not making extracts from their reading and for copying their mother's example ('ye only Fault yr. Sister has', he told Mrs. Watts) and shamefully indulging 'their Love of their Beds on Morngs., ye Pride of ye Day, notwithstanding my Expostulations & Example'.[23] Mrs. Barbauld quotes him as calling them 'shy little fools'.[24]

The most glowing description of the girls we have seen is by Erasmus

[20] 25 June, 12 July 1757.
[21] 7 July, 10 July 1784, MSS. owned by Alan Dugald McKillop.　　[22] I, clxxxviii–ix.
[23] Lady Bradshaigh to R, 28 July 1752; R to Lady Bradshaigh, 17 Aug. 1752; R to Mrs. Watts, [Aug.? 1754].　　[24] I, cli.

Reich, who was more than a little gushing in his description of Richardson's home and family: he saw in them 'beauties without affectation; wit without vanity; and thought myself transported to an inchanted land. . . . The harmony of this charming family furnished me with many reflections on the common ill-judged methods of education, whence springs the source either of our happiness or misery. The ladies affected not that stiff preciseness peculiar to coquettes.'[25] 'They are good Girls,' Richardson wrote to Edwards, 'that's true—But I am afraid are neither rich enough, nor handsome enough, to attract Lovers. How should I rejoice to see my Eldest happily married!' 'Children are careful comfort', he later wrote, 'tho' good; Daughters when marriageable, especially.'[26]

He described his eldest, Mary, to Mrs. Watts: 'A goodnatur'd, honest hearted Girl, lively, modest, & bless'd with good Health: A generous disposition'd young Creature; rejoicing to hear her Sisters prais'd, & disclaiming any Pretensions herself to ye Praise she, occasionally, hear[s] given to them.'[27] Polly was the only one of the four whom he described as having good health. In 1757 plans were being made for her marriage to a surgeon of Bath, Philip Ditcher: 'The Girl is to be removed 100 Miles off; and yet the Mother is prepossessed in favour of the Proposal [rather more, let me own, than the Father; tho' he *dis*likes not.] Ah, my Miss Mulso! You know I was always a *meek* Husband; but now, I am quite a *tame* one.'[28]

Mrs. Richardson's nephew James Leake had come up to London with Ditcher, and the courtship was somewhat rushed on the plea that Ditcher had to return to his business.[29] Richardson, who was much absent on business and in addition was 'Very much indisposed thro' the whole Treaty', thought that Ditcher might properly return to Bath so that he and Mary could get to know each other's hearts through correspondence. But he found that his wife and Leake had already carried matters too far for that course.

When he asked Mrs. Richardson whether anything was intended by Ditcher's visit, she answered 'that if there were, she hoped I would not be against it'. Thus apprised that a proposal had been made, he drew up in writing some objections to it. A surgeon can only live on the interest of capital, not 'turn and wind' his money as a tradesman can. The pro-

---

[25] Ibid., I, clxvi–vii.

[26] 30 Dec. 1754; 29 Mar. 1756.   [27] [Aug.? 1754].

[28] 2 Aug. See also to Lady Bradshaigh, 2 Sept.

[29] The following account of the events leading up to Polly's marriage is taken from a manuscript in Richardson's hand headed 'Private Thoughts on a certain Proposal and Narrative of the Transaction consequent'. We want to thank Mr. William Rees-Mogg, the former owner of the manuscript, for making it available to us and the Yale University Library, the present owner, for permitting us to quote from it. The manuscript is printed by Joseph W. Reed, Jr., in 'A New Samuel Richardson Manuscript', YULG, XLII (1968), 215–31.

fession could be of no service to a widow. 'Bath, a gay, sauntering good-for-nothing Place for a young Woman to live in. The Town's People, tho' ever so genteel, even the Wives of the *Physicians*, despised by the Guests of ye Place.' It was prudent and just for him to give with each of his daughters only such a sum as could well be afforded and to let the husband wait for the rest of his wife's fortune; otherwise national calamities or business reverses would fall on his wife and unmarried daughters only.

On the Sunday morning when he bespoke his wife's attention to these remarks, he discovered that Leake was that day to make him a formal proposal; and his wife had already made up her mind about it. 'But will it be believed from such a Characteristic Gentleness that she should leave me before I had read them half thro', abruptly, and with an Air of Dis-pleasure, go down Stairs.' 'It will be, I find, as much Happiness as I can hope for, if I can judge by ye Proposals of Marriage hitherto made me, and—[but my Wife means well]—that I am not absolutely to *dislike*. My Choice, my Wish, my preferable Option I am not to expect will be given me. Nor might it be more happy, perhaps, if it were.' Neither his own character in the world nor the merits and fortune of the bride seemed to him to have 'due Weight given them by *Ourselves*'. Leake seemed to be acting more in his friend's interest than in his cousin's.

Ditcher's proposal called for a dowry of £3,000 to be given to Mary, obviously more than Richardson had expected to give and more than he thought Ditcher's own fortune justified him in asking. Ditcher's business brought in upwards of £300 a year, and he had an estate of over £100 a year. Either Mary's own portion or Ditcher's estate, at the option of the suitor, was to be settled on her and her children. Richardson was not pleased. 'Great Honour is often done to my Judgment—when it coincides with ye Consulter's own', he wrote. 'Acquiescence is not Approbation. My Infirmities will not allow me to contend—with *Prepossession* especi-ally.' He asked the opinion of a counsel, who answered that more settle-ment might reasonably be expected and that the gentleman should declare his option as to whether the estate or the dowry was to be settled.

This opinion was shown to Ditcher, who opted for settling the estate and agreed that if Mary got further money it should be settled on her and her children. Richardson put Ditcher's agreement in writing, for his formal consent, adding that he proposed to give the dowry in bank annuities, at that time low, and to pay in cash the difference for the last thousand pounds' worth, which he had recently bought at £891 5s.[30] 'Mistress Richardson thinks that her Daughter, whose Moderation in Expences, &c. she and every one who knows her, can answer for, should have some

[30] Gosling's Bank Ledgers show that Richardson had £2,000 in annuities when on 16 May 1757 he bought £1,000 for £890 and that on 5 July 1758 he bought another £1,000 and on 25 Oct. 1758 had only £1,000, which he sold on 3 Nov. 1758.

certain Quarterly Allowance stipulated for her. I, who never was, for making a Wife in the least manner independent of her Husband, and believing that Mr. Ditcher, far from being of an illiberal Disposition, will take pleasure even in anticipating the Wishes of an obliging and reasonable Wife, am for leaving this Article intirely to his Kindness and Generosity.' Mrs. Richardson and Ditcher could talk the matter over. In a note not altogether consistent with his high view of the prerogatives of husbands, but quite consistent with his usual generosity where his prerogatives were acknowledged and with his expectation of generosity from others, Richardson added: 'Had Mr. Ditcher's Case been mine, I know how I should have answer'd to a Point thus generously put, and insisted upon to me, by ye Girl's Mother, to be proposed by me to Mr. Ditcher, tho' she herself gave it up to his Will and Pleasure afterwards.'

Ditcher was now puzzled by the article that any further money his wife might acquire should be added to her settlement. He hinted that Mrs. Richardson might agree to leave him her daughter's share in her estate even if that daughter should predecease her or bind herself to leave a fourth of her estate to his wife. 'A Proposal', Richardson noted, 'of a strange *indicative* Nature, regarding my Wife's own Option as to a second Choice &c. &c. Indeed he never mentioned this twice. But this gave me— equal Surprize & Alarm.'

Ditcher agreed to all of Richardson's articles. One article, that Richardson would trust Ditcher to take care of the children, he said required no answer. 'Except Thanks he might have said', Richardson noted. Nor did the request that Mary receive an allowance require comment. 'Yet let me here say that I hardly ever met with the Treatment I gave. There is a great Difference between my giving up, and his declining to consent to Articles that would have shewed his Affection to and Confidence in my Daughter's good Dispositions, and Politeness to my Wife; Gratitude I might say; as she was so much prepossessed in his Favour; and who had it in her Power to insist upon them as she desired she might when she talked of them to me, and to another Friend who was entirely of her Opinion—Strange her Complaisance to Mr. D!— . . .—Strange, Strange, Strange, the whole Conduct every Point in his Favour, that he could insist upon!'

Ditcher made another remark which displeased Richardson, that he intended to bar from the settlement any further purchases he might make as additions to the estate—a possibility suggested by Richardson's counsel. Richardson, being indisposed, though surprised, said nothing. 'Surely we have *all* behaved to Mr. D. in this Treaty, as if all the Credit and Advantage lay in his Favour; and that we were infinitely obliged to him for condescending to accept of our Child; and he has behaved to *us*, as if he were entirely of our Opinion.'

In discussing the articles with their mutual friend, the surgeon Stafford Crane, Ditcher had indicated his fear that any additional money Mary might inherit would be settled on the younger children of the marriage, not left to Ditcher or his wife. Richardson noted that this fear was groundless. 'Let not Mr. Ditcher be apprehensive, that I will do my Child Injustice either living or dying.' Ditcher could easily have cleared the matter up with the counsel, 'nor would he have thought it necessary for himself to guard my Daughter against the Unnaturalness of her Father'. When the settlement was drawn up, nothing was said about strengthening it if Mrs. Ditcher's fortune was later increased, or about the allowance. 'God Bless the Man? He must dearly love Power', Richardson wrote. 'May he make a good Use of it!' He wished that he had seen all the preliminaries settled before permitting 'so inchanting a Man' to visit Parson's Green.

The articles were signed on 31 August. When it was to be specified that one-third of the dowry be returned if Mary died within a year, Francis Gosling, who seems to have been the counsel consulted, proposed to write £1,000. Ditcher, 'that his Behaviour might be all of a Piece throughout the whole Transaction', wanted to write a strict one-third of the current price of the bank annuities, £933 6s. 8d. 'To shame him, and set him an Example he had not the Spirit to object to, I ordered it to be put 900 l. only; for which he, and his Friend for him, tho' but a Contingency, and what I hope will never happen, were as thankful, as if I had put 33 l. 6s. 8d. in his Pocket.'

The whole transaction shows Richardson not as a hardheaded business man but as a man desiring to deal with some nobility. What he resented most in Ditcher was that he did not meet with an answering nobility. 'By all that passed in this Treaty, I am convinced that Mr. Ditcher is not ye Man he has had to deal with in me. He has a Sovereign Regard to himself. . . . I am sure he has a Hand ever open to receive.'

Richardson had planned to call Mary's attention to the self-partiality of her suitor and to question her about her affection. But precipitation, he wrote, deprived him of an opportunity—perhaps he was also rather timid about speaking with his daughter, since he did after all have two months to do so. The articles were signed. 'The dear Girl, I am sure, meant not either Disregard or Slight: But was hurried only by her Timidity. But what a Wasp's Nest did I disturb, by mentioning what I had expected and desired, when we were retired among ourselves, that Night of Signing!— from Hysterical Girls, Polly, Miss Lintot, &c. the Paroxysm catching, one from the other—and unkind Reflexions—from—But, die, Remembrance, on the last-hinted at Occasion.' Those who can be cruel enough to gloat over the poor man, whose theories about the sovereign rights of husbands and fathers had been so often and so firmly expressed, may say that he had been weak in not expressing his objections in time and foolish in bringing them forward too late.

Mary Richardson and Philip Ditcher were married at Fulham on 6 September 1757.[31] Richardson gave her away, though he had objected his trembling nerves as an excuse: 'It was not admitted; and very Nervously affected for many Weeks before, I have been grievously ill ever since', he told Mrs. Scudamore.[32] On 14 September Richardson wrote in his almanac that he had had an explanation with Ditcher. In reviewing the particulars of the treaty 'in order to my making a new Disposition of my Affairs', he had remembered Ditcher's hint that he would, if he increased his estate, bar the increase from forming part of his wife's settlement, as well as other disagreeable circumstances. He had then expressed himself warmly to Leake, who had informed Ditcher of Richardson's continued anger. Confronted by Ditcher, Richardson admitted that he was not satisfied. And 'one Word brought in another, so that some unwished-for Warmth passed on both Sides'. Ditcher promised to do 'generous Justice' and appealed to his future behaviour. But what room had been left for misconceptions? 'There was no need to buy an Husband for such a Girl. . . . How was a Mother so fond, ever so fond, of that Daughter, prepossessed, that my Reasonings were not to be attended to.' Their warmth led to no permanent quarrel. On that very day Richardson paid Ditcher £105[33]—perhaps the father-in-law ended his expostulations with the final dowry payment. The next day, evidently in milder mood, he added that 'Mr. D. avowing to do his Wife Justice in his Will, and disclaiming the Barring Scheme; I hope that Generosity and Love will cement the Alliance so lately enter'd into'. Polly soon set out for her new home. Mrs. Richardson, in anticipation of the parting, 'begins to breath in Sighs, poor Woman—Yet all her own Doings!—Had I been ye Proposer, Distance would have been an insuperable Objection.'[34]

Early in 1758 Richardson wrote Lady Bradshaigh that 'however indelicately treated in ye Progress of ye Affair, I was not a little comforted in ye good Acct: I have from every Mouth of my Girl's Happiness, & ye Man's Behaviour to her, & good Character, upon ye Whole'.[35] A few months later he wrote to Mrs. Chapone that he found Mr. Ditcher worthy, but his task was easy, 'Too easy, I think, between you and me, considering another Affair was so recently gone off'.[36]

And he left a full account of the affair, transcribed from a pocket almanac kept at the time, for the guidance of his executors, 'for advising my Wife that Mr. D. has had *full* Justice already done him, *till* my other

[31] Fulham Register of Banns and Marriages 1754–8, MS. at Fulham Parish Church. See also Reade, 'Samuel Richardson and His Family Circle', N&Q, 12 S. XII (1923), 248.
[32] 12 Sept.   [33] Gosling's Bank Ledger.
[34] To Mrs. Scudamore, 12 Sept.
[35] 2 Jan.   [36] 27 June.

Girls may have the like done for them, by Her and Me'. 'My Wife, tho' very worthy, and intentionally just, being *too open to Persuasion* where she has an Opinion; and being *too apt* to sacrifice *Possession* to *Hope*, and to be captivated by *Speciousness*, and by *Adulation*, where not too gross; and having a great Notion of doing what she calls *handsome Things*.' 'Having by my Writings made my self a Sort of *Public Man*, it may be the rather forgiven me, that, in Support of the Prudential Doctrines I have advanced in them, that I set down the Particulars of a Transaction, which respecting the Welfare of my whole Family, make me chargeable in my own Judgment with Indiscretion. But I wish the following Pages to pass only the Eyes of three of my Executors [Mrs. Richardson was the fourth]; and not to be read by my worthy Wife, whom I too dearly and deservedly love, to give her the least Uneasiness that can be avoided, in recollecting an Affair, that hurt me (ill and low-spirited as I was) throughout its whole Progress, to its Completion.'

In his will, written a few months after Polly's marriage, on 13 November 1757, he left Mrs. Richardson a third of his estate, and out of the remaining two-thirds his three unmarried daughters were to receive 'a Portion equal to what I gave with my Daughter Mary on her marriage with Mr. Ditcher, if the same Two Thirds shall be sufficient'. If not, the unmarried daughters were to get the whole two-thirds; if the two-thirds more than sufficed, the surplus was to be divided among all four daughters. Later, in a codicil of 6 November 1758, Richardson reminded Mr. Ditcher that he 'can have no further Expectations till my other Children have been equally consider'd with their beloved Sister, his Wife'. Ditcher did eventually get £90 more when his wife's sisters had received their shares.[37]

In the fall of 1758 Mrs. Richardson and Patty went to Bath to be with Polly at the birth of her first child.[38] Richardson's first grandchild, Elizabeth Ditcher, was baptized on 9 October. He lived to see the birth of a grandson, Philip, who was baptized in August 1759 and died young. The Ditchers, after his death, had three more children, another Philip, Maria, and Mary. The last, who married the Reverend Kenrick Peck, was the only one to leave children whose descendants are still living.[39] Mrs. Richardson and Patty returned late in 1758, and in the spring of 1759 Polly brought her daughter to visit her family at Parson's Green.[40] Richardson's impressions of being a grandfather are not recorded.

Patty, Richardson informed Mrs. Watts, 'has a Taste for Drawing— My Dear, said I, to Polly, I have given a Master to Patty, to direct her in her Taste for Drawing—Don't think I wd. deny to my Elder Girl, wt. I

[37] Gosling's Bank Ledger, under date 25 Aug. 1772.
[38] R to Mrs. Scudamore, 1 Sept.; to Lady Echlin, 11 Sept.
[39] Reade, 'Samuel Richardson and His Family Circle', *N&Q*, 12 S. XII (1923), 287–9, 329–30, 366–8.
[40] R to Young, 11 Oct.; Young to R, 6 Dec.; R to Lady Bradshaigh, 5 June.

allow to my Younger—Thank you, Sir—I delight in my Sister's Improvements, & in ye Opportunities you give her for them—But I have no Genius—My Dear, replied I, you have Qualities much more laudable than Genius, where Genius is destitute of them. . . . Patty has a pretty Universal Taste; Drawing, Music, Needle-Works, Writing Letters, one of wch. you have seen, & kindly approve.'[41] She was the only one of the girls 'that has any thing like a Voice'. Patty was obviously the talented daughter; her father feared, indeed, 'from the sort of Universality of her Taste . . . that she will get a Smattering in several Qualifications; but not be eminent in any'.[42] Richardson sometimes used her as an amanuensis.[43] She was presumably named after Richardson's first wife, Martha Wilde, and Martha's sister Sarah Sprigg left her £100, which amounted to over £175 by the time Allington Wilde turned it over to Richardson.[44] By 1758 she was in poor health. It was thought that after visiting Polly in Bath she might go on to Bristol for the waters, but her doctor advised that it was not necessary.[45] Miss Talbot reported to Mrs. Carter that she planned again in 1760 to go to Bristol and should have gone before.[46] Evidently her illness was not too serious: the year after Richardson's death she married Edward Bridgen, a widower and a merchant. She died childless in 1785.[47]

Nancy, Richardson told Mrs. Watts, was a good girl, but sickly, and 'indulg'd because of her heavy Maladies'. 'She has a worthy a grateful Heart: Great Sensibility. A great Reader, & digests well, & remembers wt. she reads. We reckon her a fine Needle-Woman too: Has Patience, Perseverance; & when much Younger than she is, I saw ye Seeds of Judgment begin to germinate, & have often to try her, desired her to give me her Opinion of Passages, wch. she has heard observ'd upon in my Writings, unbiassed & free from partiality to a Father: & I have always had Reason to be pleas'd wth her. She spells well, endites well . . . [her Hand-]writing bears no Proportion to her Sense.'[48] This last opinion was repeated to Mrs. Chapone, with the addition that her early disorders had prevented her improving her penmanship.[49] She never did improve it. One of the opinions on his works which Richardson mentioned is extant; she informs him that she has come to agree with his reasons against continuing *Sir Charles*, since if the reader went on for four years he would still be curious about the hero's heir. She only dreaded that someone else might finish the book.[50]

[41] [Aug.? 1754].
[42] R to Mrs. Chapone, 19 Sept., 29 Dec. 1753.
[43] R to Lady Bradshaigh, 23 May 1758.
[44] See Eaves and Kimpel, 'Samuel Richardson and His Family Circle', pp. 216, 302.
[45] R to Mrs. Chapone, 27 June, 30 Aug.; to Mrs. Scudamore, 1 Sept.
[46] 31 Jan., *Letters between Mrs. Elizabeth Carter and Miss Catherine Talbot*, I, 456.
[47] Fulham Parish Register, under date 24 Apr. 1762. See Reade, 'Samuel Richardson and His Family Circle', *N&Q*, 12 S. XI (1922), 506–8.
[48] [Aug.? 1754].   [49] 30 Aug. 1758.   [50] [Late May 1754].

In 1751 she was very ill. 'We are apprehensive of the worst. We indulge her in all her wishes, and even humours, as a valetudinarian. She is excessively fond of North-End. But when, at the latter end of the week, worn out with business, I fly thither for recess, the dear child's illness, and my indifferent prospects as to her, sit heavy upon me. Yet she lives in hope of seeing me, as usual, every week.—Children, good children, are not always comforts.'[51] In 1752 she was sent to Southampton for the sea bathing—though her parents had little hope that it would help, her heart was set on it because a friend was going there for another malady. 'I have long resolved,' Richardson told Miss Hallows, 'by way of mitigating her sufferings, to deny her nothing.'[52] In 1756 she visited her Uncle Leake at Bath and from there went on to visit Mrs. Watts, who died during her stay.[53] The next year Edward Young invited one of Richardson's daughters to stay with his housekeeper, and Richardson sent Nancy, who made a good impression and was urged and permitted to stay on.[54]

'She has more ear than tongue', Richardson told Mrs. Dewes of Nancy. 'I wish she would be a little less reserved, when she finds herself called upon, and encouraged; but it is a fault on the right side in young people. . . . I, who observe upon the natural tempers of my children, can see, that Nancy, with all her silent meekness, wants not a consciousness, that she is somewhat more than a quite common girl.'[55] In his will he commended her to such favour in his wife's will 'as may consist with her Maternal Love', Nancy 'not having high Health and Spirits, from Delicacy of Frame and Constitution'. Mrs. Richardson did leave Anne her household goods and furniture—Anne had been living with her after the other girls were married. But soon after making his will Richardson was able to report that Anne was the stoutest of his three unmarried daughters,[56] and indeed she outlived her sisters by a good many years. After her mother's death she moved to St. Mary Stratford, Suffolk, where she died in 1803.[57] Her correspondence with her sister Martha and with her niece Sarah Crowther Moodie shows her as a lively, sharp-tongued old maid.[58] She held the family together, though sometimes distrustful of the Ditchers. Her nephews and nieces, both Ditchers and Crowthers, visited her, though she was inclined to be resentful about their (and everyone's) neglect and to prophesy disaster for all. To Mrs. Moodie, she criticized everyone except Mrs. Moodie's own immediate family and especially disliked

[51] To Lady Bradshaigh, 24 Mar.
[52] 4 July. See also to Sarah Wescomb, 6 July, and to Edwards, 21 Aug.
[53] See p. 452; R to Hester Mulso, 30 Aug.; Mrs. Delany to Mrs. Dewes, 27 Sept., *Autobiography and Correspondence*, III, 444.
[54] Young to R, 22 May, 29 May; R to Young, 19 July; Young to R, 21 July; R to Young, 26 July; R to Lady Bradshaigh, 12 July; R to Hester Mulso, 2 Aug.
[55] 4 June 1755.   [56] To Mrs. Scudamore, 1 Sept. 1758.
[57] Reade, 'Samuel Richardson and His Family Circle', N&Q, 12 S. XII, 44-7, 83-5.
[58] See the MS. letters owned by Alan Dugald McKillop, 1780, 1783-4, 1792, 1796, 1800-2.

children; she was interested about equally in money and in gossip; and family feeling ran so high that she got quite indignant with a Dr. Meek of Portsmouth, whose succession Dr. Moodie had bought and who in spite of his advanced age refused to retire.

Sally, the youngest, Richardson told Mrs. Watts, was 'a good-natur'd well inclin'd Girl . . . an inoffensive Rogue & Mimic: But not overfond of Work; Yet had rather do little playful Mischiefs, than be quite idle'. Though at times the 'Picture of Health', at others she was 'unhappily afflicted with Rheumatic Disorders'.[59] She had a bout of rheumatism in 1756[60] and again in 1758, and her lungs were affected.[61] Though a fine, jolly girl when well, Richardson wrote to Mrs. Chapone, she was sometimes ill for weeks together—girls, he reflected, seemed to be more ailing in 'these my *Evil Days*' than they had been in his youth.[62]

Like her sister Martha, Sally married fairly soon after Richardson's death, in 1763.[63] Her husband was a surgeon named Richard Crowther. She was the first of the sisters to die, in 1773, leaving two sons and a daughter. Richardson seems to have worried needlessly about whether his daughters would find husbands. In his will he hoped that some worthy person could be found for them who would be willing to take part of their dowry in business assets. 'Nor may it perhaps be easy to find a young Man of Qualities acceptable, and Fortune so ample, as to justify his Pretensions to a more than common Portion'. Mary, however, had already done well enough, as Martha and Sarah did after her; and Anne lived out her life in genteel comfort.

Their mother, Richardson's second wife, Elizabeth Leake, was a plain, pleasant woman, with no pretensions to intellect or elegance. Mrs. Delany warned Mrs. Dewes that Mrs. Richardson was hardly the proper person to find a servant for her: 'She is a retired quiet sort of woman, who I believe cannot have had any opportunity of knowing of a suitable servant of that sort.' Mrs. Carter made gentle fun of her, describing to Miss Talbot a woman of Deal who 'makes curtesies *qui ne finissent point*, and at least as many in number as good Mrs. Richardson'.[64] Indeed Mrs. Richardson must have been unable to contribute much beyond curtsies to the entertainment in those days during the composition of *Sir Charles* when so many bluestockings were visiting at North End. But she got along with them well enough. 'My Wife', Richardson told Lady Echlin, 'is a very worthy Woman: But I cannot prevail upon her to be, where she ought, a

---

[59] [Aug.? 1754].　　　　　　　　　　[60] R to Sarah Fielding, 7 Dec.

[61] R to Lady Bradshaigh, 23 May; to Mrs. Chapone, 27 June; to Mrs. Scudamore, 1 Sept.

[62] 30 Aug. 1758.

[63] Fulham Parish Register, under date 28 May. See also Reade, 'Samuel Richardson and His Family Circle', *N&Q*, 12 S. XII, 126-30.

[64] 8 Nov. 1750, *Autobiography and Correspondence*, II, 611; 1 May 1760, *Letters between Mrs. Elizabeth Carter and Miss Catherine Talbot*, I, 463.

Visitor; But she rejoices in the Visits of her and my Friends, and adopts all my adopted Daughters, as hers, with an Openness and Unreserve, and Affection, that has not many Examples.'[65] One lady who knew them, probably Miss Highmore, told Mrs. Barbauld that the formality of the family was to be attributed rather to Mrs. Richardson than to her husband. 'She was, by all accounts, a formal woman, but with a very kind heart.'[66] At any rate, she probably appeared rather stiff in company.

Richardson married her somewhat late in life, and their union can hardly have been a romantic one, but it appears to have been solidly affectionate, with no more rubs than can be expected in any marriage. There is extant an inscription he wrote to her in a volume of *Clarissa*: 'Do you know, that the beatified CLARISSA was often very uneasy at the Time her Story cost the Man whom you favour with your Love; and that chiefly on your Account?'[67] He told Lady Bradshaigh that he had been 'twice married, and both times happily' and later repeated this sentiment and added, 'You will guess so as to my first when I tell you that I cherish the Memory of my lost Wife to this Hour, and as to the second, when I assure you that I can do so without derogating from the Merits of, or being disallowed by my present; who speaks of her on all Occasions as respectfully, and as affectionately, as I do myself.'[68] He praised her highly for her nursing of the various invalids at Parson's Green in the winter of 1756-7: 'Good wife did I say? she behaved throughout the whole trial like an angel; but sometimes I was afraid would have sunk under it.'[69] He described to Edwards a little scene in which Mrs. Richardson modestly desired to send greetings to Speaker Onslow: 'Will so honourable and honoured a Man, says she, allow of such a Person as me, presenting my dutiful Respects to him and his Lady?—Will he, Bett? Yes, He is all Goodness: So is his Lady—He will. They regard the Heart—I have said, You have a good Heart.'[70] A modern wife might not be quite pleased by such praise, but one assumes that Mrs. Richardson was satisfied.

Though so far as we know she was not a romantic woman, she probably contributed one trait to one of Richardson's heroines. Pamela is superstitiously insistent on being married on a Thursday, a day for which she has an especially high regard. This was also one of Mrs. Richardson's two lucky days.[71] Richardson fairly often made private references in his works, and it is likely that he was permitting himself a little fun with his wife's superstition.

[65] 12 Sept. 1754.   [66] I, clii–iii.

[67] Dated 1 Dec. 1748. Her copy of *Clarissa* is owned by her descendant Jasper Peck, Esq., who has kindly permitted us to examine it.

[68] 26 Oct., 15 Dec. 1748.

[69] To Sarah Fielding, 17 Jan.   [70] 21 Aug. 1752.

[71] SH, II, 118; EL, I, 292; Hester Mulso Chapone to Mrs. Carter, 14 Dec. [1773], *Posthumous Works of Mrs. Chapone*, II, 170–1.

Like her three youngest daughters, she was none too healthy, and in 1749 we find Richardson regretting the illness of 'as good a wife as man ever had'.[72] She was ill in the summer of 1752 and again in that of 1753 and in 1756.[73] In 1753 physicians prescribed the air of North End, but she put off removing to the country. She had gone down and then come up again and with no business to detain her stayed on and on in town. She 'knows not her own Mind', Richardson told Mrs. Carter, '—because—because—she has been used to her own Will'. And it was too late to put her right, especially when she was ill. 'But to be serious—My Wife, tho' an exceeding good Woman, is one of the most procrastinating of her Sex.' Women, he added in a later letter, always govern 'poor silly Men'. 'Men in general are contented with the Sound; Women have the Substance.' His wife, having her own will, was puzzled what to do with it.[74]

His wife's obstinacy was a theme of which Richardson never tired—perhaps occasionally he was almost in earnest on it. Lady Bradshaigh, who liked her, joked soon after their first meeting about Mrs. Richardson's '*sternly* commanding' countenance—the opposite of her real appearance: 'I verily believe she would suffer greatly herself, rather than ask you to do any thing contrary to your inclination; for, I must say, never did I see more good temper, mildness, and compliance, appear in any body, than in her; and I doubt not, that appearances speak her mind. Govern *you*—a likely story!—and yet she does, for you have not a heart to contradict so much goodness!' Richardson read his wife the joke without the explanation, and reported the scene between them: '"*Sternly*! said she: I was in hopes nobody could think I looked *stern*. But I am sorry for it. I am sure I was extremely pleased with Lady B. and am sorry she thought me—. But did you think, Mr. R. that I looked *stern* in her presence? Silly and bashful I might look; but I think I had no *sternness* in my countenance."—"Ah! Betsy: we sheepish people always look worst when we mean to look best. We know not how either to look or to act with a grace.—But, when her Ladyship returns, we must both try to mend, I think."—"Mend! said she: impossible I should mend. I must look as I am. I may be aukward; but I thought I looked pleased; for I was so, I am sure: and am sorry Lady B."—"Well, come, my dear, interrupted I, I will amuse you no longer."' 'You good women', he added, 'compliment one another; but, upon my word, an honest man, who loves his quiet, has a hard task to persuade you to do any thing you do not incline to do.'[75]

'I have as good a wife', he wrote later, 'as man need to wish for. I believe your Ladyship thinks so.—Yet—shall I say, O Madam! women

[72] To Susanna Highmore, 26 Nov.
[73] R to Edwards, 28 June 1752, 16 July 1753; R to Hester Mulso, 30 Aug. 1756; R to Catherine Talbot, 25 Oct. 1756.   [74] 4 July, 17 Aug. 1753.
[75] 25 Mar., 31 Mar. 1750.

love not King Logs!—The dear creature, without intending contradiction, is a mistress of it. She is so good as to think me, among men, a tolerably sensible one; but that is only in general; for, if we come to particulars, she will always put me right, by the superiority of her own understanding. But I am even with her very often. And how, do you ask, Madam? why, by giving up my will to her's; and then the honest soul is puzzled what (in a doubtful case) to resolve upon. And, in mere pity to her puzzlings, I have let her know my wishes; and then, at once, she resolves, by doing the very contrary to what she thinks them to be. And here, again, I am now and then, but not often, too hard for her.—And how?—You guess, my Lady.—Need I say, that it is by proposing the very contrary to what I wish;—but so much for King Log and his frog.' 'And when I have mentioned my wife and *her myself*, it is not that I would reflect upon her, as either designing to be contradictory, or as being unusually so. No, Madam, she falls into it naturally, as I may say, and as if she could not help it.'[76] She would let him use up all of his arguments and then a day or two later bring up the matter again, and Richardson, who could not bear to repeat all his reasonings, let her carry the point.[77] Mrs. Richardson furnished copious material for the bantering arguments Richardson and Lady Bradshaigh both loved.

As soon as the law against buying tea and cambrics was repealed, Mrs. Richardson, against her husband's convictions, began buying these luxuries; her persistence provided another occasion for Lady Bradshaigh to smile and for Richardson to rail at meek wives who always get their way: 'I wish she would set me at Defiance; I then should know what she would be at.' Again when reporting that Mrs. Carter had advised him to assume the role of tyrant and send Mrs. Richardson with Patty to Bristol for the latter's health, he pointed out his helplessness: '*I* a Tyrant!'[78] His complaints were probably about as serious as such joking complaints usually are: that is, not entirely jokes.

Mrs. Richardson outlived her husband for over twelve years. Joseph Highmore described her in the early days of her widowhood: she 'behaved with propriety, grave and silent as usual, rather dejected, but not more than I had apprehended, and seemed less perplexed on account of the particular circumstances in which you [his daughter] imagined she must be involved, than was feared'. When he mentioned a matter of business, she said that such matters were left to the executors, 'in whom she appeared to have a confidence sufficient to ease her of the burden and anxiety'.[79] Her confidence was apparently justified. As Richardson had

[76] 26 Dec. 1751; 23 Feb. 1752.   [77] Barbauld, I, cliii–iv.
[78] R to Lady Bradshaigh, 2 Sept. 1757; Lady Bradshaigh to R, 2 Oct. 1757; R to Lady Bradshaigh, 19 Nov. 1757, 5 June 1759.
[79] 18 July 1761, *Gentleman's Magazine*, LXXXVI (1816), i, 578.

planned, the executors conducted his printing business for her and her unmarried daughters, but only for a few months. She and Nancy continued to live at Parson's Green after the marriages of Patty and Sally.

Mrs. Richardson's death was brought on by the death of her daughter Sally Crowther. Sally came to Parson's Green to pay her mother 'a morning visit, was taken with violent fits, which flung her into labour, was brought to bed at Parson's Green, and seemed in a good way for a fortnight, when one night Mrs. R—— was waked with the news that her fits had returned, and that she was dying.—The poor mother got up in time to see her die, and immediately said she had taken her death's wound, and should not long survive. She died within a fortnight.'[80] In a sense, then, Richardson's prosaic wife, like Clarissa, died wilfully of a broken heart; it is indeed, as Gertrude Stein remarked, as roses that cows commit suicide.

[80] Hester Mulso Chapone to Elizabeth Carter, 14 Dec. [1773], *Posthumous Works of Mrs. Chapone*, I, 170.

CHAPTER XX

RICHARDSON'S LAST YEARS

1754–1761

ALTHOUGH there was not so much excitement about Richardson's novels during the years after *Sir Charles Grandison* as there had been when *Pamela* was fresh off the press, there is no sign of a serious falling off in his reputation. An abridgement of *Clarissa* was published in Dublin in 1756.[1] The year before his death there appeared 'an entire new Set of Entertaining Cards, neatly engraved on Copper-Plates. Consisting of moral and diverting Sentiments, extracted wholly from the much admired Histories of PAMELA, CLARISSA, and SIR CHARLES GRANDISON. The whole designed, while they amuse and entertain, to establish Principles of Virtue and Modesty in the Minds of both Sexes.'[2] Even Clarissa, who generally had more useful things than card-playing to do with her time, might have agreed to pass an hour in such improving diversion.

Richardson could have found public compliments to read. In 1754 *The Book of Conversation and Behaviour*, by 'A PERSON of DISTINCTION', was dedicated 'To the AUTHOR of the HISTORY of Sir *Charles Grandison*'. It consists largely of discussion between various genteel characters on such subjects as card-playing, duelling, true politeness, and of course the relations between the sexes. According to the dedication, it is 'a Work formed on the same Model with your own', with the same intention: 'to establish Morality upon the Foundation of good Sense; and to fix the wavering Notions of good Manners'—another indication that many of his contemporaries were most impressed by Richardson's professed moral purpose. The author hopes that his dedication will 'prompt you to continue your own Labours'.[3] In Maryland, an American admirer, James Sterling, addressed to Richardson, 'Author and Printer of Sir *Charles Grandison*, and other works, for the Promotion of Religion, Virtue and polite Manners, in a corrupted Age', his 'Poem on the Invention of Letters and the Art of Printing'.[4] He began with the statement that his

[1] The dedication to this two-volume edition is signed 'W. M.'
[2] *London Chronicle* for 22–4 Apr., VII, 394. [3] Pp. iv–vi.
[4] *American Magazine and Monthly Chronicle for the British Colonies*, I (Mar. 1758), 281–90. This tribute was discovered by Albert H. Smyth, *The Philadelphia Magazines and Their Contributors 1741–1850* (Philadelphia, 1892), pp. 35–7.

lays belonged to Richardson, 'the friend and patron of mankind'—'His *Arts* and *Virtues* have inspir'd the song.' He ended by advising the Genius of Albion that Richardson asserted her rights in 'impious days':

> His *Virgin-sheets* no prostitution stains,
> His moral ink no venom'd gall profanes.

Richardson is not only the 'first printer' but is revered by all as 'the good man and author', who 'lives himself the *Grandison* he paints'.

> See him, like censer'd Aaron, dauntless stand,
> 'Twixt wrath divine and a devoted land!
> From his pure *Press*, see, hallow'd incense rise,
> As from an altar grateful to the skies!

In 1760 he must have been pleased to read Lord Lyttelton's compliment in *Dialogues of the Dead*. Plutarch having explained the usefulness of characters exemplary of quiet, domestic virtues, a modern bookseller tells him that writers in both English and French have recently been doing what he suggests. Fielding and Marivaux are both praised, but first place goes to Richardson.

BOOKSELLER. In the supposed Character of Clarissa, (said a Clergyman to me a few days before I left the world) one finds the dignity of Heroism tempered by the meekness and humility of Religion, a perfect purity of mind and sanctity of manners. In that of Sir Charles Grandison a whole Pattern of every private Virtue, with sentiments so exalted as to render him equal to every public Duty.

PLUTARCH. Are both these Characters by the same Author?

BOOKSELLER. Aye, Master Plutarch, and what will surprise you more, this Author has *printed* for me.

PLUTARCH. By what you say, *it is pity, he should print any works but his own.*[5]

There were few new editions of Richardson's novels after the publication of *Grandison*. The octavo *Pamela* was not sold out during his lifetime, but there was a seventh duodecimo edition in 1754 and an eighth, prepared by Richardson, published after his death, in 1762. A fourth duodecimo edition of *Clarissa* appeared in 1759. After the first three editions, in quick succession, there seem to have been enough copies of *Sir Charles Grandison* to satisfy the demand, though volume seven was reprinted and partially issued with sheets from earlier editions in 1756, and a fourth edition appeared in 1762. The copyrights to the three novels were still valuable enough in 1766 so that that of *Pamela* was priced at £288, that of *Clarissa* at £600, and that of *Sir Charles Grandison* at £480.[6] In spite of

---

[5] Pp. 316–19.

[6] William H. Peet, 'Booksellers' Sales in the Eighteenth Century', *N&Q*, 7 S. IX (1890), 301–2. In 1772 the copyright of *Sir Charles Grandison* was still worth £554 8*s*. (Lowndes receipt for 1/48 of *Grandison*, £11 11*s*., from William and John Richardson, B.M. Add. MS. 38,730, fo. 149).

objections and a decline in interest natural once their novelty had worn off, Richardson in his last years had no reason to be dissatisfied with the reception of his works.

Undoubtedly there were contemporaries who agreed with Horace Walpole about 'those deplorably tedious lamentations, *Clarissa* and *Sir Charles Grandison*, which are pictures of high life as conceived by a bookseller, and romances as they would be spiritualized by a Methodist teacher'.[7] But one can hope that Richardson never learned of their opinions.

The spread of his reputation on the Continent made several new friends for him. Though he seems never to have been in direct communication with his French translator, Prévost, he carried on a warm correspondence with the Dutch translator of *Clarissa*, Johannes Stinstra. In Germany he had many admirers. Erasmus Reich visited England in 1756, as he said, purely in order to know Richardson, whose country house recalled his idea of the Golden Age. He kissed the ink horn in the author's grotto. When at last it was necessary to leave England and 'that divine man', Reich wrote, 'he embraced me, and a mutual tenderness deprived us of speech. He accompanied me with his eyes as far as he could: I shed tears.'[8] Richardson informed Lady Bradshaigh that his works were 'read wth: strange Approbation' in Germany.[9] A striking instance of this admiration among earnest and moral Germans was the desire of the sect of the Moravian Brethren that Richardson write something for them and the invitation from the secretary of their leader, Count Zinzendorf, to go to Germany, 'solely, it should seem, from their high opinion of the moral tendency of his writings'.[10]

Charles Kaiser, of Göttingen, had paid Richardson a visit while he was in England in 1753[11] and at one time hoped to translate or have translated *Sir Charles Grandison*.[12] Kaiser also sent to Young through Richardson a translation of *Night-Thoughts*. In Germany Young and Richardson attracted the same admirers, and it was natural that when Major Bernhard von Hohorst of the King of Denmark's Grenadier Guards visited Richardson he should want also to visit Young. Richardson sent him with a letter of introduction.[13] Hohorst gave Richardson great joy by telling that his works were used in Germany as a moral system and had the pleasure of having read to him selections from the bound volumes of Richardson's

---

[7] Letter to Sir Horace Mann, 20 Dec. 1764, *Correspondence*, XXII (New Haven, 1960), 271.

[8] Barbauld, I, clxv–xx. The visit can be dated by Reich's references to Antoinette Sack and Richardson's desire to add her to his collection of 'adopted daughters'. Miss Sack's first or second letter to Richardson is dated 8 Jan. 1757.   [9] 19 Nov. 1757.

[10] Lady Bradshaigh to R, 21 Aug. 1756; Barbauld, I, clxxv.

[11] R to Mrs. Klopstock, 7 Apr., 22 Dec. 1757; Mrs. Klopstock to R, 6 May 1758; R to Mrs. Klopstock, 23 June 1758.

[12] Kaiser to R, 10 July 1753.

[13] R to Young, 7 Jan. 1757; Young to R, 13 Jan. 1757.

correspondence with the ladies ('Was waren das für schöne Briefe').[14] Through Hohorst, Young became a correspondent of the author of the *Messias*, Friedrich Gottlieb Klopstock.[15] It is to be hoped that he appreciated Klopstock's ode to him, which begins 'Stirb, prophetischer Greis, stirb!' Hohorst himself wrote an ode on the enthusiastic welcome Clarissa received in heaven, a translation of which Richardson kept among his papers.[16] Richardson was afflicted to learn of Hohorst's death of fever and considered him a true hero, pious and brave, 'respected by all mine, as well as by me!'[17]

Reich was responsible for a brief correspondence between Richardson and Antoinette Sack, daughter of a chaplain of the King of Prussia.[18] He greeted her as a new daughter, invited her to visit him in England, and (because of his shaking hand) tried to get her to continue the correspondence with his daughter Patty.[19] But the new kinship seems soon to have languished.[20]

A more lasting epistolary friendship was formed with Meta Klopstock, the wife of the author of the *Messias*. She had long admired *Clarissa* and had recently enjoyed the history of her male counterpart; she had suggested to an engraver who liked to engrave great men gratis that since he was going to England his first duty was to engrave Young and Richardson; she had heard about Richardson and his family from Hohorst. And she took the opportunity of a letter to Young to address one (her first letter in English) to Richardson. Richardson replied by asking her for her history, a request which she promptly granted: 'You will know all that concerns me. Love, dear Sir, is all what me concerns! And love shall be all what I will tell you in this letter.' She described how on reading the *Messias* and hearing an account of its author, she began to think only of him; how when he visited Hamburg she sent him word that she wished to see him; how their three-day acquaintance on that occasion led to a serious correspondence, which after eight months became so warm that Klopstock admitted that he was in love, 'and I startled as for a wrong thing'; she replied that she was sure it was only friendship, but when he visited Hamburg again a year after his first visit, she soon admitted that it was love, on both sides; her mother's opposition to her marrying a stranger had caused some delay, but they had been married for four years, 'and still I dote upon Klopstock as if he was my bridegroom'. Richardson was

[14] Franziska and Hermann Tiemann, *Geschichte der Meta Klopstock in Briefen* (Bremen, [1962]), pp. 473-4.

[15] *Auswahl aus Klopstocks nachgelassenem Briefwechsel und übrigen Papieren* (Leipzig, 1821), I, 237-9.

[16] FM XVI, 2, fo. 85; printed in Barbauld, V, 288-9.

[17] Mrs. Klopstock to R, 29 Nov. 1757; R to Mrs. Klopstock, 22 Dec. 1757.

[18] Miss Sack to R, 8 Jan. 1757.   [19] R to Reich, 2 Apr. 1757.

[20] Mrs. Scudamore to R, 12 Mar. 1758; R to Mrs. Scudamore, 6 Apr. 1758.

charmed with this account, as one might expect. 'Happy, thrice happy Pair!' The more he read the story, the more delighted he was. He was especially charmed with Mrs. Klopstock's broken English and quoted much of it back to her with approval of her words and sentiments. 'Angelic Pair!—A Love begun in Mind, as yours was, and meeting with a Return so grateful; the Gentleman, the Author of *The Messiah*, who can wonder?' And he asked for an account of that poem, as well as of two sisters and five female friends whom she had mentioned among her blessings.[21]

In reply she offered to send him a translation of the arguments of the ten books of her husband's poem which had been published, but she hinted that her friends were not quite worthy of the honour of being described to him: 'Though I love my friends dearly, and though they are good, I have however much to pardon, except in the single Klopstock alone.' Richardson's answer was filled almost entirely with admiration of her character and rejoicing at her happiness. He hoped that she would continue writing, and at length, 'as if of one Family'. Her next letter acquainted him with the fact that she was soon to know the only blessing she had lacked—she was to be a mother in November.[22] But the crowning of Meta's happiness proved the end of it, since she died in childbirth.[23]

Like most Englishmen of his class and time, Richardson had no high opinion of the French.[24] Mrs. Klopstock's remark that their language was *fade* confirmed his own opinion, though he did not know the language.[25] But when the mathematician Alexis Claude Clairaut visited England in 1753, Richardson entertained him and told or read him enough of his new novel to make Clairaut anxious about the hero's duel—he 'would fain have been his second had I known the Rendezvous'.[26] He later communicated through Clairaut with Prévost about the French translation of *Sir Charles Grandison*. The naval warfare which led up to the Seven Years War had begun, and Richardson regretted the 'National Misunderstandings, which divide Lovers and Friends of different Countries from one another. But *we* will be Friends to the End of our Lives, whatever may be the National Enmities. . . . And now, what a grievous thing would it be to me, if the Events of War and Hostility, between our two Nations, should make it culpable to pursue a Correspondence so innocent as ours! Be this as it may, continue to love me, as (I repeat) I will you to the End of my Life. . . . Adieu, and Adieu, my dear M. Clairaut!'[27] Though

[21] 29 Nov., 22 Dec. 1757; 14 Mar., 7 Apr. 1758.

[22] 6 May, 23 June, 26 Aug. 1758.

[23] Richardson was informed of that fact in a letter from Hanover (21 Dec. 1758) by a writer whose name Mrs. Barbauld (III, 158) gives as L. L. G. Major, but who, since as she says he continued to write to Richardson, is probably the Mr. Majes of Hanover who sent Richardson some inquiries about the obscure meaning of *Night-Thoughts* (R to Young, 24 May 1759; Young to R, 25 May 1759).

[24] R to Edwards, 27 Jan. 1755.   [25] 6 May, 23 June 1758.   [26] 6 Apr.

[27] 12 Sept. 1755.

Richardson may well have guarded these exalted sentiments throughout the war, which broke out formally the next year and lasted the rest of his life, his Adieu to Clairaut was, so far as we know, a permanent one.

In 1758 the Swiss geologist Guillaume Antoine de Luc visited England and met Richardson. Jean André, de Luc's elder brother, later said that they had been 'very intimate',[28] and though their extant letters lead one to think that 'intimate' is an exaggeration, Richardson obviously found in de Luc a young man of religious and ethical principles and exalted sentiments after his own heart. The brothers de Luc had defended in their scientific studies the Mosaic account of the origin of the earth. Richardson's first letter rejoices in de Luc's pious education and requests a further account of his family. He was especially charmed with de Luc's portrayal of his 'pathetic Aspirations after the wedded State'. In his next he has hopes through de Luc of initiating a correspondence with a Mme. d'Epinay (apparently Rousseau's friend), a hope which, because of that lady's illness, was not realized. He received the history of de Luc's family with delight: 'How greatly do I venerate your Father. . . . Why did I not know there was such a living Character, when I undertook the History of Sir Charles Grandison? What an Increase of public and private Virtues might I not have given my Hero!—Had I only made Sir Charles, or Dr. Bartlett for him, have set forth the great Qualities of a truly good, great, and wise Man, they must have said that such a one, they found in their Way to Italy, at Geneva.' Evidently de Luc's morality was an enthusiastic one: 'I love you', wrote Richardson, 'for your beautiful Apostrophe to Virtue.' He was charmed by de Luc's history of his first love, to a lady married to an older man. His cautious English printer's morality must have been momentarily swept aside by a burst of Gallic sentiment, since such a situation was hardly one which Richardson in cold earnestness would have advised toying with, though everyone involved acted with virtue and nobility—lover, lady, and husband alike. The latter had complete confidence in the youthful admirer of his wife. Richardson advised de Luc, who distrusted his English, to go on writing without recourse to the dictionary: 'Dictionaries would not have enabled you to write *from* the Heart and *to* the Heart, which is your Excellence.' Richardson hoped to see again before he left England 'a Youth I so greatly respect'. He chided him gently for his intrepidity in exploring volcanoes: 'And had you any Call but that of Curiosity? One should not tempt Providence by rushing into needless dangers in one's reliance on it.'[29]

While he was writing *Sir Charles Grandison*, Richardson lived, as he had

[28] Letter to Richard Phillips, 18 Oct. 1813, MS. in the Yale University Library.

[29] 25 July, 26 Aug., 7 Nov. 1758; 17 Feb. 1759. Later in 1759, when de Luc was back in Switzerland, Richardson sent him a complete set of his novels, and de Luc replied with a silver medal of Geneva (see G. A. Bonnard, 'Samuel Richardson and Guillaume-Antoine de Luc' MLR, XLVI [1951], 441).

been living since 1736, in the large house on the west side of Salisbury Court. His business was carried on partly in his dwelling house, partly in two small buildings immediately behind it, on Hanging-Sword Alley. In addition he was renting a house on the edge of London, on North End Road in Fulham, as a kind of country retreat for himself and his family.

On 28 September 1752 a fire broke out in Richardson's printing establishment. At about seven in the evening, a boy folding sheets in the back room accidentally set them on fire with his candle. Sheets hanging from 'Poles' near the ceiling were set ablaze. The boy tried to put out the fire himself, but Richardson fortunately felt it in the room above, where he was drinking tea with two young ladies. The heat of the floor became 'scarce tolerable'. Richardson 'had Presence of Mind to give the necessary Orders: But twice I gave up all for lost. Had any Main Beam taken fire, the Weight of Metal on the Upper Part of the House, would have sunk the whole.' The fire was kept from spreading beyond the room, and the water did more damage than the fire. A good many books, especially copies of the *Journals of the House of Commons* and of Chambers's *Cyclopædia*, were destroyed: the damage was early estimated at £600, but Richardson was insured.[30]

Richardson's landlord at North End, Samuel Vanderplank, had died in 1750, and his son-in-law Gilbert Jodrell sold the house to a Mr. Pratt. In the summer of 1754 Richardson was told that if he wished to stay on after Christmas his rent would be increased from £25 to £40 a year. According to Richardson, Jodrell had told Pratt that Richardson was 'a Tenant proper to be raised', that the house had previously been rented for £50 a year, and that Vanderplank let Richardson have it for £25 'in stark, staring Love' of him. 'But the Truth of the Matter is this—After Lady Ranelagh left the House I live in, Mr. Vanderplank lett it to one Sherwood an Attorney, for 30 Pounds a Year; and laughing told me, that that fantastic Woman of Quality would have thought herself disgraced, had she lived in an House under 60 l. a Year; and that they made her (besides paying 50 l. a Year) build the Coach-house and Stables; and having done so, she thought she had a Bargain at 50. I was an absolute Stranger to Mr. Vanderplank when I treated with him for the House. He *pretended not* to do me Favour. I *expected* none from him. He asked me 30 l. a Year. I said, The Stables and Coach-house would be useless to me. If he could employ them, I desired he would; and in that Case, proposed to give no more than 20; the highest I then thought to go to. He said, He had no Occasion for them: But as he had two Girls that were growing up, and would have handsome Fortunes, and was cautious of whom he admitted

[30] Thomas Birch to Philip Yorke, 7 Oct, B.M. Add. MS. 35,398, fo. 102; Mrs. Delany to Mrs. Dewes, 14 Oct., *Autobiography and Correspondence*, III, 163; Edwards to R, 15 Dec.; R to Edwards, 23 Dec.

into so near a Neighbourhood, and liked my Character and Family, he would take 25 l. a Year instead of 30. . . . I had improved the House and Ground I rented: Had joined other Parcels to it.' He did not think Jodrell had properly protected him, particularly in view of the improvements—'I hate Imposition', he told Lady Bradshaigh. After looking for a month at other houses, by 25 July he was in treaty for a new house, at nearby Parson's Green, and by 9 August he had rented it. The garden was neglected and the house needed repairs, and Richardson did not expect the landlord to do much towards putting them in order. But the new house was more convenient and 'genteeler'.[31]

It was also nearer the water, an easy quarter mile from the Thames, and was located on the King's Road, between Fulham and Chelsea. Parson's Green, named for the old rectory, formed a pleasant little village; it was surrounded by good houses, and the house Richardson rented faced the Green. According to tradition, it had been the dower house of Katherine of Aragon. It was pulled down early in the nineteenth century. Nearby was Fulham Church.[32] 'There is', Richardson told John Duncombe, 'a porch at the door (an old monastery-like house) in which my friends, such even as will not come on purpose, will find it difficult, as they pass by, to avoid seeing the old man, who, if he lives, proposes, often in it to reconnoitre the Green, and watch for them.'[33]

Richardson moved to Parson's Green at the end of October 1754. Repairing and removing to the new country house cost him over £300. Within a month his lookout for friends had been rewarded by calls from Speaker Onslow, the Bishop of Oxford, Mrs. Talbot, and Miss Talbot; Miss Mulso and Miss Highmore had also come and stayed for two or three days. His wife and daughters immediately made it their home, and Richardson went out at weekends, as he had gone to North End. His family liked the place, and there were always some of them there. Miss Talbot visited Parson's Green in the summer of 1756 and found it very agreeable, though not in every particular according to her taste: 'There we sat together for an hour in an Arbour as pleasant as a Yew Arbour can be, that is besides decorated with indifferent Shells & bad Paintings, but the Air was sweet, the Garden gay with Flowers & the Company Agreeable. What need one wish for more?' 'I wished you there,' she wrote to Mrs. Berkeley, 'because those who only know Mr. Richardson as an Author do not know the most amiable part of his Character. His Villa is

[31] Vanderplank's will, P.C.C. Greenly 98, dated 11 Jan. 1748, proved 24 Mar. 1750; R to Edwards, 25 July 1754; R to Sarah Wescomb, 9 Aug. 1754; R to Lady Bradshaigh, 28 Aug. 1754.
[32] R to Lady Bradshaigh, 9 Oct. 1754; T. Faulkner, *An Historical and Topographical Account of Fulham* (London, 1813), p. 283; Charles James Fèret, *Fulham Old and New* (London, 1900), II, 126-7.
[33] 24 Aug. 1754.

fitted up in the same Style his Books are writ. Every Minute detail attended to, yet every one with a view to its being useful or pleasing. Not an inch in his Garden unimproved or unadorned, his very Poultry made happy by fifty little neat Contrivances, his House prepared not for his Family only but for every friend high or low to whom Air & Recess may be of Benefit. One always sees there a succession of Young Women & exceedingly elegant well-behaved sensible Young Women, who improve & entertain his Daughters, at the same time that their health is mended or their distress assisted by being there, & every one (in the book style again) calls him Papa. Walking round all the Offices with him I could see every domestic Countenance brightening up as he came near them with Unaffected Joy, while he asked every one en passant some kind question.'[34]

The summer after he moved to Parson's Green, Richardson also moved his house in town, though not far. In 1752 he had rented, and used as a warehouse and a dwelling for his workmen, a second house in Salisbury Court, two doors down from the first, set back on the northwest corner of the Square. His former dwelling was larger than the new one, but it was old, and the 'very great Printing Weights at the Top of it' made it dangerous for him to renew his lease, which was about to expire. To compensate for the fact that the new house was less roomy and less handsome, Richardson managed to remove his business altogether from his dwelling. He rented eight small houses along White Lyon Court, which ran north into Fleet Street and on to which the north side of the new house opened. He pulled them down and 'built a most commodious Printing-Office', 'distinct from, tho' adjoining to, the Dwelling-Part'. In spite of this advantage, Mrs. Richardson took some time to accept the loss of the more elegant house. 'Every-body is more pleased with what I have done than my Wife', Richardson wrote Lady Bradshaigh. 'But that, I flatter myself, is because she has not seen either the Offices or the House she is to live in, *since* the former were little better than a Heap of Rubbish . . . and the latter was a dirty Warehouse.' 'I have a very good Wife', he wrote Edwards. 'I am sure you think I have: But the Man who has passed all his Days single, is not always and in every thing, a Loser.' Mrs. Richardson's dissatisfaction continued even after she had moved into the new house: 'She must stay till the new one becomes an old one; and then she will—Such is the Force of *Constancy* with her. . . . She *intends* not now, she says, to be perverse. I believe not, I tell her: But must conclude in her Favour, that it is natural to—and she can't help it.' But she soon began to get used to the change: 'My Wife says, she begins to be reconciled to her new Habitation. I think,

---

[34] R to Thomas Newcomb, 24 Oct. 1754; Mrs. Delany to Mrs. Dewes, 30 Oct. 1754, *Autobiography and Correspondence*, III, 296; R to Silvester, 16 Mar. 1756; R to Edwards, 26 Nov. 1754, [*c.* 1 Aug.] 1755; Catherine Talbot to Mrs. George Berkeley, 9 Aug. [1756], B.M. Add. MS. 39,311, fos. 83–5.

if she hasten not her entire Reconciliation I have a Way to effect it. It is but hinting to her, that we must probably leave it in a very little Time for some other [My Tenure *is* precarious, as to the Dwelling-Part I mean,] she will then see all its Conveniences at once.'[35]

Richardson's move cost him £1,400, much more than he had expected. He had begun reconstruction by the summer of 1755, and for a while he was completely taken up with it. He watched the carpenters at work through a 'spy window' in his old house and was by no means satisfied with their progress. He tried to get the builders to keep the cost within the estimated £500. Once he sent for the master carpenter to complain of the slowness. The carpenter arrived while he and his wife were at dinner and immediately appealed to Mrs. Richardson, asking her if she did not think they were making good progress. 'Indeed you do, Mr. Burnell, answered, promptly, the good woman. I did not expect to see the building so much advanced.—I was forced to pull in my horns, as the saying is. The charge of unreasonableness seemed to be implied on the husband, who knew something of the matter; and the wife, who knew nothing at all of it, went off, at her honest man's expense, with the character of a very reasonable, courteous, good sort of a woman.' He could not, as Miss Mulso suggested, simply go away and take his ease at Parson's Green, leaving the workers to their own devices. 'I am not a woman, child. I do not think the whole world made for me: and I have no mind, were I to fly to Parson's-Green, to find the men employment on my return, by altering what they had done in my absence.'[36]

In spite of the delays, the building was completed by December, and his printing materials were in their new quarters. He was prevented from changing his dwelling at the same time by his wife's objections, but by early April 1756 he moved to the new house while she was at Parson's Green.

Poor health probably combined with new interests and with a prosperity which put him above the necessity of drudgery to induce Richardson in his last years to relax somewhat in his business. He had worked hard all his life; he could afford to take life a little easier. The biography approved by his daughters speaks of his activity: 'He generally rose at five in the morning, and retired to rest about eleven. His first business, at that early hour, was to walk through the different rooms of his printing office; but, in the latter years of his life, he sometimes indulged in bed till seven, and was very rarely seen among his workmen, sometimes not twice in a year; his writings and correspondence engaging his whole attention. His overseer and journeymen, in course, generally received his directions by notes or letters.'[37]

---

[35] See Eaves and Kimpel, 'Samuel Richardson's London Houses', *SB*, XV (1962), 145-8.
[36] 15 Aug. 1755.   [37] *Universal Magazine*, LXXVIII, 20.

His business was by this time a large one. At the time of the publication of *Sir Charles Grandison* he speaks of employing thirty or forty men; his weekly payroll 'to Journeymen &c.' ran from £30 to £40.[38] He left each of the journeymen working for him at the time of his death 'as a small Token of my friendly Esteem for them, half a Guinea for a Pair of Gloves'. He was prominent enough to be chosen first Upper Warden and then Master of the Stationers' Company and served a year in the latter office in 1754–5.[39] In short, he was one of the leading members of his profession, and he could justly congratulate himself on having risen to the top by his own efforts.

His overseer in his last years was a man named William Tewley, who had been working for him over ten years at the time of his death. Tewley had been a compositor and had acted as Richardson's foreman; he must have been made overseer in 1759, when Richardson's nephew William left him to set up for himself.[40] Richardson wrote in June of that year of breaking in a new overseer and a new corrector of the press as well.[41] The learned and diligent corrector who pleased Richardson so well had died in 1754,[42] and his replacement went into business for himself. Tewley wrote a letter to Edward Young praising his late master: 'He was always very sedulous in business, and almost always employed in it; and dispatched a great deal by the prudence of his management.'[43]

A man who does not seem to have been an employee but who was very helpful during Richardson's last years was James Bailey. Perhaps he was Richardson's legal adviser. Lady Bradshaigh, urging Richardson in 1759 to spend as much time as possible in his country retreat, assured him that 'Good Mr Baily will be your deputy in Town to the utmost of his power. What a friendly creature that is? I love him for his good dispositions, especially for those towards you.' Richardson replied: 'Mr. Bailey, worthy and obliging Man! has left me for some of the Summer-Months, to be the Guest of a Brother of his good Wife in Buckinghamshire.'[44] In a codicil to his will dated 5 July 1760 Richardson made 'my kind Friend Mr. James Bailey of St. John's Square, Clerkenwell', a co-executor, giving as his reason the law patent in which he had recently acquired an interest, along with Catherine Lintot. Bailey had been 'equally intrusted with the Management of this Affair by both Parties, and has Skill and Knowlege of

[38] *An Address to the Public* in *Sir Charles Grandison*, 1st edn., VII, 432; R to Silvester, 16 Mar. 1756.

[39] 'Court Book L', pp. 68–9, 116, under dates 30 June 1753 and 6 July 1754.

[40] In his affidavit attached to Richardson's will Tewley says he had worked for him for ten years. Richardson's first payment to him in the Gosling's Bank Ledgers is on 3 Mar. 1750. For his having been Richardson's compositor, see John Jones's account of Richardson in the *Gentleman's Magazine*, LIII, 924.

[41] To Lady Bradshaigh, 5 June.

[42] R to Stinstra, 28 June; R to Edwards, 25 July.

[43] *Gentleman's Magazine*, LIII, 924.   [44] 22 May, 5 June.

all Particulars relating to it'.[45] Knowing Bailey's kindness, impartiality, and justice, and knowing that he would spare no trouble to aid the other executors, whose own great affairs would hinder their attending to all the details of the trust, Richardson asked that Bailey be given 'grateful, that is to say *genteel* Amends for all the extraordinary Trouble, and Loss of Time he may be at'. He was later executor of Mrs. Richardson's will.

At one time Richardson had great hopes of his brother's son, William Richardson, Junior. He had evidently forgotten Pamela's sensible advice to her parents against employing their cousins Thomas and Roger: 'I think it would be better to have *any body* than Relations. . . . One is apt to expect more Regard from Relations, and they more Indulgence, than Strangers can have Reason for.'[46] William was apprenticed to his uncle in 1748 and was made free, after the usual seven years, in August 1755, and admitted to the livery on the same day.[47] At the time of his freedom Richardson looked forward to passing most of his days at his new retreat, Parson's Green, were it but to try William's management and 'wean my Business, if I may so express myself, from me'. He had made William his overseer, was taking him into the business by degrees, and was getting his accounts in order for his use.[48] During his last years he worried a good deal about the future of his family,[49] and he must have thought that William offered an ideal solution when he was 'proposing to have the Business carried on, after my Decease, for the Benefit of my Wife and Girls, for their more commodious Maintenance'.[50] William was still working for Richardson in May 1759,[51] but he left his uncle before 15 July, when Lady Bradshaigh wrote: 'The additional trouble by the loss of so near a relation, I know will sit heavy upon you.' By the end of that year he had set up a printing business for himself in Castle Yard, Holborn, and had taken his first apprentices.[52]

[45] See also R to Miss Lintot, Oct. 1760.   [46] SH, III, 20; EL, II, 12.

[47] 'Court Book K', p. 407, under date 5 July 1748, 'Court Book L', p. 80, under date 5 Aug. 1755, 'Apprentices Bound, Turned Over, Free and Cloathed', 'Freemen's Book', 'Master and Apprentice Calendar', MSS. in the archives of the Stationers' Company. J. F. V. Woodman, Esq., Clerk of the Chamberlain's Court, writes us that he was admitted to the freedom of the City in Aug. 1755.

[48] R to Edwards, [c. 1 Aug. 1755]; R to Lady Bradshaigh, 13 Aug. 1755; R to Hester Mulso, 15 Aug. 1755. Even during his apprenticeship Richardson must have used William at least to withdraw from his bank the money needed for the operation of his business. Beginning on 19 June 1749 there is a long series of frequent payments to William Richardson (Gosling's Bank Ledgers). Since these payments run on unchanged after the death of Richardson's brother William, they must have been made to the son. They generally are from £15 to £50, though a few are larger. They are frequent through 13 Jan. 1759, and there are two later ones: 25 Oct. 1759 and 5 Apr. 1760.

[49] R to Lady Bradshaigh, 4 Apr. 1758.

[50] R to Samuel Lobb, 29 Dec. 1755.

[51] On 1 May he wrote for Richardson a letter to Lady Barbara Montagu.

[52] 'Court Book L', p. 381, under date 4 Dec., 'Master and Apprentice Calendar', MSS. in the archives of the Stationers' Company.

Richardson felt some distrust of him as early as November 1757, when he wrote his will. He hoped that William would assist his executors, but if he should not behave as worthily as those executors might expect and should not make up true accounts, 'which I am willing to think impossible to happen', the executors may do such justice as the case requires. If William does proceed with the 'Integrity, Punctuality, Diligence, and Obligingness, which I have Reason to hope for from him', he is recommended to the favour of the executors. On 11 September 1759 a codicil cancelled these references to William, since he has 'begun for himself—To whom I cordially wish Success'. Another codicil, dated April of the next year, is less cordial. In recommending the daughters of his brother William, Richardson added that 'the Son has shewn such a strong Disposition to take Care of Himself, that He wants not the Recommendation, and I hope never will'. 'I mean that Son well, and wish him Success. But the Letters that have passed between him and me will manifest, that he *will* have Success if it can be obtained, and I doubt not that after my Death, my Family will be made as sensible, as I am sorry, for his Sake, to say, I have been on every Occasion, that has offered. If any Difficulties attend him, they must arise from his unprecedented Rashness in two Steps of his Life.—God amend his Heart, and give him to overcome them and their natural and almost unavoidable Consequence!—I mean this only for Caution and Warning to my Family with regard to this partial and selfish young Man; that he may not, at its *Expence*, and to its *great Detriment*, get from it, the means he will undoubtedly get, if he can, to repair the exceeding rash Steps he has taken.' A bequest to William in the original will is blotted out and above it Richardson wrote that William was to receive 'Three Guineas: When he reflects, he will allow that he merits not, from me and mine greater Distinction.'

One might guess that William's two rash steps were marriage and setting up his own business. Charles Pooley, an executor of the husband of Richardson's granddaughter Sarah Moodie, once owned the manuscript of a 'noble poem' which he thought was by Richardson, called 'The Choice of Hercules' and dedicated to his nephew.[53] The poem may well have been the poem of the same title by Bishop Lowth, published in Dodsley's *Collection of Poems* and in Spence's *Polymetis*. Its moral Richardson would certainly consider appropriate to inspire a nephew inclined to sloth and pleasure. In any case, William does not seem to have felt the gratitude for Richardson's favours which his uncle considered proper, and his defection must have been a further trial at a time when he was obviously tired and anxious to get rid of some of his burdens. William may have been selfish, as the codicil indicates—at least more attached to his own interests than to those of his uncle; but he was not quite so rash as

[53] Charles Pooley, 'Richardson's "Choice of Hercules"', *N&Q*, 1 S. VI (1852), 485.

Richardson thought, since in 1761 he found himself in a position to take over, with Samuel Clarke, Richardson's former business and even to move into his house on Salisbury Court—Clarke's share of the business cost him £1,125.[54] Whatever his feelings towards his uncle, he hoped to make money from his reputation, since he issued proposals for an edition of his novels with anecdotes of the author, a critique, and some never before published letters on 'moral and entertaining subjects'.[55] He could hardly at this time have expected aid from Richardson's family: Anne Richardson in 1784 mentioned to her sister Martha her fear of her cousin, 'O that he had no title to our name, or to be considered as one of our Family!'[56] She was probably echoing her father's sentiments. Two months after the codicil about William's rashness was written, Richardson referred to his kinsman as deserving little favour from him—though typically his rancour did not keep him from helping William by allowing him to use his name on the title page of a book he was printing.[57]

Richardson's will provided that his business be carried on in his wife's name for her benefit and that of his three unmarried daughters, under the direction of his executors: his wife, Allington Wilde (the brother of his first wife), and his old friend the bookseller and banker Francis Gosling. Early in 1758 he added the bookseller Andrew Millar to the list of executors and in 1760 James Bailey. He had in 1756 bought some land adjoining the estate of his late brother William near Dagenham, Essex.[58] But according to his will, 'the Chief of my Worth lies in Stock, Copies [copyrights], and Printing-Materials, Household Goods, &c.' This worth was sufficient to enable his wife and their daughter Anne, who never married, to live out their days in comfort, as well as to provide the other daughters with marriage portions. The three younger daughters eventually got as much as Polly had received, £3,000, and there was a little money left over to divide among the four girls. Mrs. Richardson got half as much as the three together, so that Richardson left in all about £14,000.[59] Richardson pre-

[54] Richardson's account in Gosling's Bank Ledger, 29 Sept. 1761.

[55] Nichols, *Anecdotes of Bowyer*, p. 157; *Literary Anecdotes*, IV, 581.

[56] 31 July, MS. owned by Alan Dugald McKillop.

[57] *Balbe-Berton*. See p. 427.

[58] On 12 May 1756 £450 were paid to Alexander Hill and Michael Tovey (Gosling's Bank Ledger). This estate was sold by Richardson's executors on 12 Apr. 1763 for £450, paid by 'Messrs Sumpners for the Essex Estates' (ibid.). Richardson refers to this purchase in his letter to Silvester, 16 Mar. 1756. See also Eaves and Kimpel, 'Samuel Richardson and His Family Circle', pp. 301-2.

[59] The records of Richardson's bank account in the Gosling's Bank Ledgers show the settlement of a part of his estate. There was a partial settlement in 1763 (under dates 20 May and 25 May), when Mrs. Richardson got £750 and her three youngest daughters £500 each. In 1764 (22 June) Mrs. Richardson received £300 more and the three youngest daughters £200 each. In 1765 (12 June) Mrs. Richardson received £150 and the three youngest daughters £100 each. By 1772 the three youngest daughters must have received a share equal to Polly's dowry, since Ditcher was paid £90, as were Edward Bridgen, Richard Crowther, and Anne Richardson

sumed that his wife would not 'think of keeping on the House at Parsons-Green' but would put the rent from it and the saving which accrued from giving it up into the business. Mrs. Richardson evidently did not consider that her situation made it necessary to follow this advice—she was living at Parson's Green when she died. In spite of his worries, Richardson left his family well provided for.

Illness and lack of mental occupation may have contributed to give Richardson during his last years a tendency towards gloominess. Mrs. Sheridan's granddaughter Alicia Lefanu, who got her anecdotes at third hand through her mother and is therefore not an unimpeachable witness but who must indirectly echo her grandparents, describes his moodiness: 'He was not only an improving, but occasionally, a very agreeable companion. Like most persons of genius, however, his spirits were unequal.—Mr. Sheridan has sometimes called, and found poor Richardson (to use his own expression) dull "as a drowning fly," and vainly struggling with the oppressive weight of melancholy that oppressed him. On those occasions, the best way to rouse his spirits was to divert his attention from the unpleasant object that might happen to engross it. When this was judiciously effected, Richardson would gradually become animated, cast off his mantle of gloom, and display in his conversation all the whim, point, and humour that guided his pen, when pourtraying a Lovelace, or a Charlotte Grandison.'[60]

Like other ageing men, he may have had a tendency to see persecution all around him, or at least to devote an undue amount of attention to the persecution he actually saw. He told Lady Bradshaigh that 'the Baseness and Ingratitude of more than one or two whom I have benefitted in a high manner' contributed to his sleeplessness.[61] 'I have suffered within these very few Years past', he wrote to Mrs. Klopstock on 7 April 1758, 'by the Defection and Ingratitude of more than one, from whom Charity made me hope better Things.' In Richardson's day it was expected that persons who received benefits should repay with gratitude. We have no intention of presenting Richardson as paranoid, but he did resent the dishonesty of the Irish pirates long and bitterly, and as far as we can tell, the sins of his nephew William were not so great as to justify the tone of his remarks.

In 1757 he mentioned the 'Detection of a false & ungrateful Friend'

—Mrs. Richardson received £140 (25 Aug., 26 Aug., 15 Sept.). The estate was finally closed on 12 Aug. 1777, when there was a balance in the bank of a little over £50.

£2,500 of Sally's portion was settled on her children (will of Richard Crowther, P.C.C. Macham 18, dated 1 Sept. 1787, proved 21 Jan. 1789); when her husband was planning to marry again after her death, her sister Martha calculated that Sally had 'brought him, first & last, what may justly be reckon'd £4000. Happy was it that her fortune was settled on her children' (letter to Anne Richardson, 28 Dec, 1780, MS. owned by Alan Dugald McKillop).
   [60] Memoirs of Mrs. Sheridan, pp. 197-8.   [61] 4 Apr. 1758.

among the troubles which had increased his nervous disorders.[62] This man may have been the same as the false Scotsman of whom he complained over a year later, who, after professing friendship for years and acknowledging obligations, went on visiting Richardson for almost a year after he had secretly tried to circumvent him by underpricing him in a principal part of his business, attempting at Richardson's expense to deal with a man he had met through Richardson. When finally detected, he had admitted his guilt and attempted to justify it by falsehood, having become an implacable and gossiping enemy. Richardson had written his side of the case but had exposed the treacherous Scot only to himself and to the friend he was dealing with. He had been forced to lower his already low prices in a branch of his business which he hoped would help support his family when he was dead. The Scotsman, though prosperous, pleaded self-interest in justification of his baseness. Richardson identified neither the Scot nor the branch of business threatened, though he did say that he had 'lately laid out great Sums of Money in Building for its better Conveniency of carrying on this particular Branch of Business, improved and, as I may say, established in my Self and Family, by my honest Care and Industry'.[63] Unless he was exaggerating, the branch of business must have been an important one, since he could think that the improvement of his workshops was made for the convenience of carrying it on. The most important branch of his business was his work for the House of Commons, and it is therefore probable that that was the branch in which the false Scot tried to cut him out. Nor is it unlikely that the false Scot was Richardson's old protégé William Strahan.[64] The friend to whom Richardson had introduced him could have been Jeremiah Dyson (then Clerk of the House). What is clear is that Richardson had been underbid in a printing contract which he regarded as virtually a monopoly, had had to save the contract by lowering his own prices, and regarded this kind of competition as highly unethical, and, in a friend, treacherous.

Nor were his troubles over. The year before he died, he told Lady Bradshaigh that he had been having law troubles and was afraid of leaving his women involved in two or three cases with very difficult people, 'vigorously attack'd as I am, by several unprovoked Enemies in the most valuable of my Interests in Business, to the probable disconcerting of all my honest views for my Family's creditable Subsistence, when I cease to be'.[65]

Those of the books Richardson printed in the last decade of his life which have been identified do not show that the nature of his business

---

[62] To Reich, 2 Apr.   [63] To Mrs. Chapone, 27 June, 30 Aug. 1758.

[64] For this conjecture, see Sale, *Master Printer*, pp. 84–5.

[65] 12 Mar. Richardson's executors did get involved in at least one law case and collected an old debt of £192 from an attorney named John Burke (P.R.O. K.B. 122/308, membrane 176: Pleas, Michaelmas Term, 2nd George III).

had changed much. A great many of them are the works of friends: Young, Edwards, Skelton, Delany, Spence, Sarah Fielding, Mrs. Carter. It is not always possible to determine whether they became friends because he printed for them (as Delany did) or whether he printed for them because he already knew them (as he did Mrs. Carter). Except for Young's works, Charlotte Lennox's and Sarah Fielding's novels are about as literary as any books he printed—except of course his own. Dyer's *Fleece* and Lord Lyttelton's *Dialogues of the Dead* perhaps lie within the boundaries of literature. But there are more works on religion, such as John Conybeare's *Sermons* and various treatises of John Leland—Richardson must have approved of his *Reflections on the Late Lord Bolingbroke's Letters* and *A View of the Principal Deistical Writers*. There were practical works like a new edition of the ever-popular *Gardeners Dictionary*. More profitable probably than these miscellaneous books were several government contracts or monopolies.

In the most lucrative branch of his business, his printing the *Journals of the House of Commons*, Richardson was having some trouble. Ample sums were advanced at various times to the Clerk of the House, Nicholas Hardinge, to pay the cost of the original estimate. On 25 June 1748 Richardson deposited in his account at Gosling's Bank £1,000 'By Harding's Note',[66] but by 12 January 1749 he was complaining that the House owed him upwards of £1,500 for ten volumes already printed: 'A thousand times have I wished, that I had never been concerned in that Work!—Before that, I had always been within my Compass—And I sought them not—I have no grasping Mind.' On 10 May 1749 he regretted (as he often did) his too busy life—'the hurrying Life of a Man of such a strange Variety of Affairs (Worthless half of it too, but confined to Time) as mi[ne] has been for the past Four Months. . . . Half a Day every Day obliged to be thrown away on a personal Attendance at Westminster. Five o'Clock in the Morning my Hours, till Eleven at Night.'[67] Though this probably refers primarily to the printing of bills, the slow payment for the *Journals* must have increased his bitterness. The debt to Richardson for the *Journals* at one time reached £3,000.[68] His ability to wait so long for such large payments is a further measure of his prosperity.

On 22 May 1755 Hardinge paid Richardson £250 and apparently on

[66] Gosling's Bank Ledger.

[67] To Hill. Sale (*Master Printer*, p. 82) identifies Hardinge as the man to whom Philip Skelton referred on 27 May 1749, offering to go to the Isle of Man to recover money from someone who, according to Skelton, was in 'very good circumstances', though he 'hath a great deal of other men's effects in his hands' and who habitually hides out in the Isle of Man between sessions of Parliament. Hardinge had resigned his clerkship and been elected to the House as a member for Eye, Suffolk, but it seems unlikely that Skelton's description could apply to a man as prominent as he was.

[68] Barbauld, I, xlvi.

23 October gave him a mortgage.[69] But on 22 February 1756 Richardson complained to Thomas Edwards of 'Mr. H.' He had recently spoken to Speaker Onslow and desired him to be 'very tender' in this matter; the Speaker had said that he might mention it to Jeremiah Dyson (who in 1748 had succeeded Hardinge as Clerk of the House), but Richardson doubted that this would induce the 'unkind Man' to keep terms and was inclined to think that the only method would be for some member to ask a question in the House about the money paid by the Treasury for printing the *Journals* over such a long period of years: only such an action could make 'this careless, this promising Man' do justice. Five or six weeks before, Richardson had written pressingly to him, and he had promised to give a satisfactory answer in a week or two, but no answer had yet been received. On 16 March he mentioned the debt to Eusebius Silvester, stating that the gentleman owed him over £1,500 for printing the *Journals* and had been putting him off but had promised to settle soon. On 29 March he again wrote to Edwards that he still had no answer from 'Mr. H.' The Speaker, having heard of Richardson's idea of a motion in the House, had 'approved of the Method; and said, It *would* be done'. Richardson also told Edwards that he had made 'Mr. H.' a proposal, and on 15 April Edwards wrote that he did not favour the proposal because Richardson would be too honest to be a match for him at a treaty. On 24 April Richardson reported to Edwards that 'Mr. H.' had given two notes for £500 payable in a month and promised security for the rest ('I hope he will discharge them when due'), but he was far from reassured. By 25 May he had received—'with Difficulty (too much!)'—£500, and the debt had been reduced to £1,100, for which he had refused 'Mr. H.'s' note at hand for six months and was continuing to press. Speaker Onslow had engaged Jeremiah Dyson to help him to collect it. His relations with Hardinge were either more cordial than the letters to Edwards suggest or their differences were patched up, perhaps when the money was paid, since when Richardson made his will in November 1757 he left Hardinge a mourning ring.[70]

Presumably Richardson did eventually get most of his money. This should have amounted to almost £7,000, due him according to his first estimate, as well as the money for supplemental volumes later voted to bring the *Journals* up through the Session of 1755-6.[71] The total amount which the House owed him for his government contracts, both bills and

[69] Gosling's Bank Ledgers record the payment on 22 May 1755 and on 28 July 1757 a payment of £60 by Hardinge on account of a mortgage. After this last entry is written in red the date 23 Oct. 1755.

[70] He later struck through his name, presumably when Hardinge died on 9 Apr. 1758. On the debit side of Richardson's account in Gosling's Bank Ledger under date 13 Apr. 1758 is the entry: £1,000 and £38 5s. interest 'to full of Hardinge's Mortgage and his Bond dated 24 Octr. 1757'.   [71] *Journals*, XXVII, 617.

Journals, cannot have been far short of £12,000. This must have been some consolation when his work for the House kept him very busy, as it often did, and even in urgent cases almost absorbed the facilities of his press.[72]

Richardson had also obtained the contract to print for the Royal Society, possibly through the Secretary, Thomas Birch, former Treasurer of the Society for the Encouragement of Learning, for whom Richardson had printed and with whom he corresponded.[73] He was printing the *Philosophical Transactions* of the Society by 1753,[74] but whether he had this contract before that date, when the *Transactions* began to be published under the supervision of a committee, is uncertain. One volume appeared yearly during the rest of Richardson's life. 750 copies were printed for the benefit of the fellows, and all copies exceeding the number of fellows were sold to the Society's booksellers. If he looked at the volumes in his press, he could in 1753 have read Franklin's account of his kite experiment along with ninety-six selected letters on scientific subjects.

At the very end of his life Richardson entered into a new branch of business. A codicil to his will, dated 5 July 1760, mentions that 'I have engaged in an equal Partnership in the Law-Patent, as it is called with my dear Miss Catherine Lintot, to commence June 24, 1760; and have, with her Consent, removed the Printing-house belonging to her in the Savoy to my own Printing-house in White-Lyon Court, Fleet Street, subject to Articles of Copartnership agreed upon between her and me'. His half must have cost in the neighbourhood of £1,250, which was the amount William Strahan paid in 1762 for a half share.[75] This law patent gave exclusive rights to print books dealing with the common law, though there was some dispute about what rights it gave to print those dealing with statute law.[76] Miss Lintot had inherited it from her father, who died in 1758.[77]

---

[72] R to Lady Bradshaigh, 12 Nov. 1753; R to Skelton, 3 Apr. 1754. Even after Hardinge's death Richardson seems to have been having trouble collecting from the government, if, as seems likely, he was referring to this contract when he told Young on 24 May 1759 about his difficulties with an account of sixteen years' standing. He had put some papers relating to this 'troublesome account of long standing' into the hands of the attorney Robert Richardson in an attempt to 'prevent future trouble from base and designing parties to my family, when I am no more'. After Robert Richardson's death the papers had come back into his hands, and he was 'very unhappily engaged' in trying to settle the matter, since no one else could do so. 'How has this undelightful task affected me.'

[73] *An Historical View of the Negotiations between the Courts of England, France, and Brussels from the Year 1592 to 1617* in 1749 and another work in 1744 (R to Birch, 21 Dec., 28 Dec. 1744, 12 Feb. 1745).

[74] For his bill for £76 11s. for printing the volume published that year, see Charles Richard Weld, *History of the Royal Society* (London, 1848), I, 523n. The imprint of all volumes names other men as 'Printer to the Royal Society', but Richardson's bill and a letter at the time of his death from William Bowyer, Jr., asking for the contract (Nichols, *Literary Anecdotes*, II, 352-3) leave no doubt that Richardson did the actual printing.

[75] J. A. Cochrane, *Dr. Johnson's Printer: The Life of William Strahan* (London [1964]), p. 123n.

[76] Sale (*Master Printer*, pp. 136-44) gives a long discussion of these rights.

[77] Will of Henry Lintot, P.C.C. Arran 24, dated 20 June 1753, proved 10 Jan. 1759.

Richardson had been a friend of hers at least as early as 1753, when he dined with her at Dorton on his way back from Bath.[78] A letter to her in September 1759 shows that they were then on intimate terms: he is her Papa, he runs little errands for her while she is out of town, he is affectionate and joking.[79] By that time he was considering the purchase of part of the patent and was trying to collect his debts to get together the necessary money.[80] His relation with Miss Lintot continued to be warm and friendly. In October 1760 he wrote to his daughter, friend, and partner, regretting that he could not make the thirty-mile journey into Hertfordshire to visit her ('Young Ladies can do any thing. Old Men must not forget they are Old Men'). He and James Bailey were trying to put her affairs in order: she was planning to make further sales and probably wanted to get rid of as much of her business as possible, since, judging by Richardson's letter, she was a young lady primarily interested in social pleasures. She was a witness to Richardson's will and was left a mourning ring.

Richardson's share in the law patent got him into another controversy during the last months of his life. Early in April 1761 an advertisement appeared that in a few days proposals were to be issued for a new edition of the Statutes at Large, to be published by subscription and printed by Mark Baskett and the Assigns of Robert Baskett and for C. Lintot and S. Richardson, Statute and Law Printers to his most excellent Majesty. The price was to be £5, and the patentees proposed to finish publication no later than Michaelmas Term 1763.[81] The proposals actually appeared on 30 May.[82] Just before they did, another edition of the Statutes was announced, edited by Danby Pickering of Gray's Inn and printed for Charles Bathurst of Cambridge, to be finished by the same date, but at the price of £6.[83] On 3 June the advertisement for the Pickering edition was enlarged by a statement that the publisher hoped that the fact that he was 'the first who attempted to reduce the great Price of the Statutes at Large, will engage the Public to favour him rather than his Opposers': for thirty years the Statutes had cost 'from twelve to twenty Pounds and upwards with a Prospect of growing dearer', and far from having intended to lower the price, the patentees had maintained a sixteen-year suit in chancery to prevent the University of Cambridge from competing.[84] Richardson and his partners were not slow to reply: 'Mr. Bathurst having inserted, in several of the Papers, an Advertisement equally disingenuous and untrue (as he must know) relating to the Folio Edition of the Statutes, the candid

---

[78] R to Edwards, 15 Aug., 19 Sept.   [79] 24 Sept.
[80] R to Silvester, 21 Apr., 26 June, 17 July.
[81] *Public Advertiser*, 7 Apr., 8 Apr., 10 Apr.; *London Chronicle*, 4–7 Apr., 7–9 Apr.
[82] *Public Advertiser*, 28 May, 29 May, 30 May, 1 June, 3 June; *London Chronicle*, 26–8 May, 28–30 May; *Lloyd's Evening Post, and British Chronicle*, 3–5 June.
[83] *London Chronicle*, 26–8 May, 28–30 May.   [84] *Public Advertiser*.

Reader is referred to our Quarto Proposals for an Answer to it.' They also denied a groundless report that they did not intend to publish a quarto edition.[85] Both editions did appear, but by that time Samuel Richardson was dead.

Richardson's part in publishing the ambitious *Universal History* has been described. By 1750 publication of the edition in folio and of the twenty-volume edition in octavo of the ancient part of the *History* was completed. Meanwhile plans were being made for the modern part of the *History*. On 12 December 1751 Richardson asked John Duncombe whether he knew anyone at Cambridge 'who would be willing to engage in writing any part of the modern history, which is now pursuing; and several hands employed in it!' He had owned a sixth share in the *History*, but he sold half of it in 1753 to John and James Rivington for £262 10s.;[86] he retained a twelfth share in both the already published ancient part, in folio and octavo, and in the forthcoming modern part, towards which £1,190 10s., had already been advanced by the patrons.

One of the authors of the ancient part was the Reverend John Swinton of Oxford. In 1754 a dispute arose between Swinton and the proprietors about the modern part. Richardson tried to keep out of the argument— 'It was unhandsome in him [Swinton]', he wrote to Benjamin Kennicott, 'to endeavour to draw me into it.' Swinton evidently tried to use the *History* for religious polemic; he was writing a life of Mohammed and wanted to denounce the impostor in no uncertain terms. 'I was very far from wishing to restrain a Christian Writer, from doing Justice to the Cause of Christianity, in a decent, *scholar*-like (that is to say, a *Gentlemanly*) manner, in the Notes', Richardson wrote; but Swinton's manner was furious. Furthermore the two volumes he was supposed to write, and which were to begin the modern part, were running into three large ones, and he often neglected to follow the forms agreed on for reference. Swinton had been reproved, evidently by George Sale, in what Richardson thought a rather rough manner; but Richardson and the other proprietors agreed that Swinton had not followed the rules laid down for writers. Swinton accused his opponents of not being Christians—'calling Deists and Atheists, Persons absolutely unknown to him'; Richardson referred to 'the Vehemence, the Puerilities, and Insults' of his last letter. A learned 'revisor' had been engaged to whom all the writers were supposed to submit, who in his desire to preserve his anonymity called himself 'Eusebius'—only Richardson and one other knew his identity. Eusebius, however, was not much help, since in his desire to remain behind the curtain he insisted on staying aloof from the dispute, though he too disagreed with Swinton.[87] The dispute evidently blew over.[88]

On 30 November 1758 proposals for 'the Modern Part of the Universal History' were issued. It was to extend to twenty-five volumes, the first eight volumes octavo (and three volumes folio) to appear on 1 January 1759, and one volume to follow each month.[89] The *History* ran much longer than was proposed, and the final volume (the forty-fourth octavo) did not appear until 1766. The planning of the modern part must have been rather haphazard, or perhaps all of the writers were as hard to control as Swinton; at any rate the contents of the various volumes are somewhat miscellaneous, poorly ordered and even more poorly balanced.

Whoever Eusebius may have been, one of the general editors of the *History* by the time of its publication was Tobias Smollett. One would hardly expect Richardson to admire Smollett's novels, and indeed he called the story of Lady Vane in *Peregrine Pickle* 'that Part of a bad Book which contains the very bad Story of a wicked Woman'.[90] He may have had a higher opinion of others of Smollett's works, since he sent Young a copy of the *History of England*[91] and Margaret Collier a copy of *The Regicide* ('by what I have read of it,' she wrote, 'I think Mr. Garrick is very much obliged to the author for shewing the world how much he was in the right for refusing it').[92] Smollett's considered opinion of Richardson's novels was more favourable, though hardly so favourable as Richardson could have wished: in the *Continuation of the Complete History of England*, which appeared in the year of Richardson's death, he praised Richardson for enlisting the passions on the side of virtue in 'a species of writing equally new and extraordinary, where, mingled with much superfluity and impertinence, we find a sublime system of ethics, an amazing knowledge, and command of human nature'.[93]

Smollett was already engaged as an author and possibly as an editor of the *Universal History* when we have our first positive evidence that he and

[87] [Mid-Nov.], 26 Nov.

[88] On 11 Apr. 1758 Richardson sent Swinton a letter he had received from George Psalmanazar (dated Monday [10? Apr.]) suggesting that an apology be added for repeating in a list of dynasties in the third volume information already given.

[89] See also *London Evening-Post*, 16–18 Nov. Richardson's name does not appear on the proposals. On 1 Jan. 1759, however, it was listed first when the first eight volumes were entered at the Stationers' Company ('Entries of Copies 1746–73', p. 189), as it was when subsequent volumes were entered: Vols. IX–XXXIX, between 30 Aug. 1759 and 29 June 1763 (ibid., pp. 197, 199, 203–5, 207–8, 210, 212–16, 221, 223, 230–1, 236). When Vol. XL was entered on 31 Oct. 1763, the name 'E. Richardson' appears instead of his (ibid., p. 240).

[90] To Mrs. Chapone, 11 Jan. 1751.

[91] R to Young, 19 July 1757; Young to R, 21 May 1758.

[92] Margaret Collier to R, 13 Apr. 1749. McKillop (*Richardson*, p. 180n) identifies the work.

[93] IV, 128.

Richardson knew each other.[94] In 1756, in his anonymously published *Critical, Satyrical, and Moral Maxims, Characters, and Reflections*, Fulke Greville had included a passage about Richardson which mingled high praise with severe blame. This passage was quoted in full in a review of the book in the April 1756 number of the *Critical Review*, which Smollett was editing, as one 'of the most striking observations and characters in this performance'. 'There is a certain author', wrote Greville, 'who produces perpetual paradoxes in my mind; I am at a loss to decide whether he charms or offends me most, whether to call him the *first* of writers or the *last*. . . . It is his great praise, his honour, that he is condemned by sensible men, and applauded by weak women; for the first are often as ignorant of the powers of the heart, as the last are of those of the understanding.' Richardson (for no one could fail to guess the author who was meant) is praised for his minute observation and his refined and just sentiments, 'but he often carries that refinement into puerility, and that justness into tastelessness; he not only enters upon those beautiful and touching distinctions which the gross conceptions of most men are incapable of discerning, but he falls also upon the trivial silly circumstances of society, which can have attractions only for a nursery'. In short, he lacks taste, 'he has neither from nature nor education the kind of intelligence, which should guide him in the pursuit he attempts . . .; his men of the world are strange debauchées, his women ridiculously outrées, both in good and bad qualities'. In spite of his merits, you see plainly that he is not a master: 'Deficiencies, stiffness, improprieties, break in upon you at times, and shock you: and you grieve that he does not please you more—or less.'[95]

Richardson was evidently hurt by the remarks. He told Lady Bradshaigh that he had written to a lady who feared they might vex him that 'there may be Justice in the most unfavourable Part of it', that perhaps Greville was 'as much too high-bred, as the other [Richardson] was too low: But that, with his Superior Advantages, it is as much a Wonder, that he wrote no better, as that the other wrote no worse'.[96] He expressed the same sentiment in a letter to Samuel Lobb, whose son William had tried to answer Greville's objections.[97] Greville's remarks, by implying that he lacked education and breeding, hit him where he was most sensitive. Among his papers he kept a letter inquiring whether a poetic epigram written against the *Critical Review* was really by Richardson:

> That the Monthly Review has condemn'd what I writ,
> Does not alter the Case of that writing, one Bit:
> Usurping to judge, periodical Haste,
> To be sure, would give Sentence that suited its Tast.

[94] Louis L. Martz, *The Later Career of Tobias Smollett* (New Haven, 1942), pp. 7–8.
[95] Article IV, I, 224–5. Alan Dugald McKillop comments on this article in 'Notes on Smollett', *PQ*, VII (1928), 369–71.   [96] 10 July 1756.   [97] 10 Nov. 1756

> They do not like mine; and I do not like theirs;
> But I leave the free Judgement to them and their Heirs:
> I my self had condemn'd it without more ado,
> Had it been to the Tast of a Monthly Review.[98]

Though he had not written the poem (a note on the manuscript says it is 'By Sir Charles Hanbury Williams'), Richardson apparently approved of the sentiments.

Smollett wrote a letter of apology to Richardson: 'I was extremely concerned to find Myself suspected of a silly, mean Insinuation against Mr. Richardson's Writings.' He had already asked Andrew Millar to assure Richardson that he knew nothing of the article, and Richardson had accepted his explanation. He has never mentioned Richardson's name with disrespect, and 'it is impossible I should ever mention him either as a Writer or a Man, without Expressions of admiration and applause'—and he includes a tribute to Richardson's 'amiable Benevolence, Sublime morality & surprizing Intimacy with the human Heart'. The letter shows no great degree of intimacy, but it concludes with thanks for Richardson's judicious remarks on the plan of Smollett's *History of England*. Richardson answered that he had never imagined that the passage in the *Critical Review* was Smollett's. He had not even seen it; the author was welcome to censure what he had written, but he might have forborne to do so if he had reflected that prolixity cannot be avoided in writing to the moment. He would not have offered his little hints about Smollett's history if he had not been greatly pleased with his plan.[99]

In 1759 and 1760 Richardson and Smollett exchanged several letters, mainly about the *Universal History*. They are businesslike in tone and show no signs that the two were close friends. In 1759 Richardson sent him eight sheets on the history of Ansiko and of the Hottentots for his opinion —he was afraid they would have to be reprinted because of Mr. Shirley's 'barrenness both of style and compilation'. Smollett was worried because he was left to fill up fifteen or sixteen sheets on Antarctica—the only thing he could think of was to include various accounts of voyages in the southern seas.[100] Smollett was an accomplished hack writer, but even he must have been baffled by the haphazard method of composing the modern history. In 1760 he sent back part of the copy on France with his revisions but was at a loss to cut it effectively since its bulk 'arises, not from a great multiplicity of incidents and variety of matter, but from a spunginess of expression'. He himself was at work on the history of Sweden. In a postscript he asked Richardson to 'favour our Magazine with any loose essay lying by you'. He was soon forced to leave Sweden for Holland because he could not get hold of the necessary books.[101]

---

[98] FM XVI, 2, fo. 48.   [99] 10 Aug., 13 Aug. 1756.
[100] Smollett to R, 4 Apr.; William Richardson to Smollett, 5 Apr.   [101] 1 May, 31 May.

Smollett's last letter to Richardson shows that the *Universal History* was in considerable difficulties. Some of the proprietors evidently wanted to discontinue the project—Smollett warned against any who might have an interest in doing so to encourage a rival performance. He himself had no interest in the matter: 'I can always employ my time to much greater advantage than I could possibly reap from the completion of this work.' And he complained in vague terms of his literary slavery ('an author of genius and reputation must, it seems, be a journeyman for life, and be obliged to subsist by the labour of his own hands'). He enclosed some thoughts on the *History*: 'The public have been disgusted and cloyed by the bad execution, as well as the enormous extent, of the first part of the Modern Universal History, and by the frequent publication of the volumes.' They had no time to read one volume before another appeared. However, once it was finished, it would be welcomed as a complete and authentic history in all public and almost all private libraries, and it would be a pity to leave it unfinished, 'because, in that case, there could not be the least prospect of indemnifying the proprietors for the loss they have already sustained'.[102]

The account of Richardson approved by his daughters, which in this part is almost identical with the earlier account which had appeared in John Nichols's *Anecdotes of William Bowyer*, describes his last years: 'By his writings [Nichols adds "by many family misfortunes"], which in a manner realized every feigned distress, his nerves naturally weak, or, as Pope expresses it, "tremblingly alive all o'er", were so unhinged, that, for many years before his death, his hand shook, he had frequent vertigoes, and he would sometimes have fallen, had he not supported himself by his cane under his coat. His nerves [Nichols speaks of his "paralytic disorder"] were affected to such a degree, for a considerable time before his death, that he could not lift the quantity of a small glass of wine to his mouth, without assistance, although put into a tumbler. This disorder at last terminated in an apoplexy. . . . During seven years of the time, in which he was thus afflicted, he never tasted any animal food; but lived chiefly upon vegetables [Dr. Cheyne's regimen]. Finding, however, no benefit from this kind of diet, he resumed his former mode of living, which had ever been regular and somewhat abstemious'.[103] Richardson had often been ill from the 1730s on, so that his writings could hardly have been the first cause of his malady. But after the publication of *Sir Charles Grandison* his references to his poor health are even more frequent than before, and his disorders, already considerable, certainly increased during his last years.

The record of the meetings he attended at the Company of Stationers

[102] 12 Oct.
[103] *Universal Magazine*, LXXVIII, 19–20; *Anecdotes of Bowyer*, p. 157.

probably reflects his state of health. From 1747 through 1752 he was at about half of the meetings. From 1753 through 1755, when he was Upper Warden and then Master of the Company, he attended almost invariably, and he kept going to most of the meetings through 1756. After that he attended about a third of the meetings in 1757, only one in 1758, less than a third in 1759, and just over a fifth in 1760; but he was still going in the year of his death, when he was present at the meetings of 3 March and 5 May.[104]

Lady Bradshaigh was constantly concerned about his health. Soon after the completion of *Sir Charles Grandison* she offered to order him a wooden horse so that he could get his much needed exercise, but he replied that he had long ago furnished himself with a chamber horse, which yielded 'really pretty Exercise'.[105] 'I really do think myself in a manner worn out', he wrote shortly afterwards.[106] He was ill in the fall of 1754 and the late spring of 1755.[107] Earlier in that year he had begun a very painful bout with a dentist named Galloni or Galleni, who was also treating Young—in neither case with success. A year later Richardson was 'still under those cruel hands' but without improvement. He inquired about Young's teeth: 'Mine are leaving me apace. O this Galeni!' He had found only suffering and loss of time and money.[108] At the same time he was 'in ye Old Way; full of Tremors and convulsive Startings'.[109] There was a new siege of illness in the fall of 1756: 'Nervous disorders mend not by added years. My hands shake more and more. What will be must.'[110] And in the next spring he was 'much indisposed': 'Writing has been painful to me; & too often have I been unable to write at all.' 'I make but few visits, by reason of my bad Nerves.'[111] His pen, he told Lady Bradshaigh, would not stay in his fingers.[112] He wrote in July 1757 that Dr. Heberden had told him many months before that no physic would help him, but his apothecary had put him back on bark, valerian, and Sir Walter Raleigh's cordial mixed, which he had continued until within the fortnight.[113] He had recently begun to take only tar water. 'God only can be my Physician.' 'I have left off Physic', he wrote to Miss Mulso in August. 'Good Dr. Heberden . . . told me, that I must not expect Relief from it. And I am got deep into Tar-Water. Three or four times a Day, by Entreaty of an

[104] 'Court Books K and L', 1742-51, 1751-63, MSS. in the archives of the Stationers' Company.

[105] 21 May, 30 May 1754.   [106] To Lady Bradshaigh, 9 July 1754.

[107] R to Thomas Newcomb, 24 Oct. 1754; Edwards to R, 18 June 1755.

[108] Young to R, [27 Feb.], 6 Mar., 30 Mar. 1755, 30 Mar. 1756; R to Young, 23 Apr. 1756; Young to R, 27 Apr. 1756.

[109] R to Edwards, 22 Feb. 1756.

[110] R to Mrs. Scudamore, 4 Oct. See also to Sarah Fielding, 7 Dec.

[111] To Anna Meades, 16 May.

[112] 27 May 1757. See also R to John Duncombe, 14 July 1757; R to Lady Echlin, 12 Aug. 1757.   [113] To Lady Bradshaigh, 12 July.

experienced, tho' not medical, Friend. I am sure I have better Spirits for it—and, do you see else! Can hold a Pen, pretty tolerably. God be praised, say I, twenty times a Day, as I look back on my afflicting Debility. But as to *quite recover'd*, that never can be. I must expect Plunges, till the last Plunge will set me free.'[114] In November we find him again in poor health.[115] Miss Talbot reported in December to Mrs. Carter that she did not 'think Mr. Richardson near so well this winter as he was last'.[116]

In January 1758 he was unable to join Young at Bath—he had never received any benefit from the waters there anyway. His acquaintances, he told Lady Bradshaigh in February, were beginning to visit him less frequently, because they thought he was slighting them: 'My Disorders have been so troublesome, and have so fast increased upon me, that I have been very sparing of my Visits, & Communications for a Twelve Month past.' In April he reported to her that he had been unable to walk for several weeks because of a swelling caused by a cold in the 'Great Tendon' of his left leg. He was stupid and dozing during the day, yet 'more easy up than in Bed', which made him 'impatient of Bed'. A few days later he could not write clearly but had to get his daughter Martha to transcribe what his paralytic fingers had traced 'in this almost incapacitating Evening of my Life'.[117] By 23 May he was enough improved to be able to get some exercise in a coach.[118] And soon afterwards he was on rare occasions able to write with a somewhat steady hand, but he had to change his habits: 'My Nervous Disorders are so much increased', he wrote to Mrs. Chapone in June, 'that in a Morning especially, which used to be my chosen, and most capable time, I cannot some times hold a Pen. Evenings, if I have a quiet Afternoon (as now, I make the Attempt very promisingly) I do what I can. Bad Rest is my Misfortune; and makes my Days unhappy, and increasing Tremors.' By August he could write better, and was pleased with a 'rare Instance' of his steadiness.[119]

Late in the year he was 'unhinged' by being the witness of an accidental death. On 28 November an attorney of Fleet Street named Robert Richardson was standing at the corner of Hartshorn Lane and the Strand talking to his friend Samuel Richardson when a nearby dray got into a dispute with a passing carriage as to which should give way. The carriage drove the dray on to the pathway and its wheel gave Mr. Richardson such a blow on his chest that he was killed on the spot.[120] One can imagine the

---

[114] 2 Aug.   [115] R to Lady Bradshaigh, 19 Nov.
[116] 20 Dec., *Letters between Mrs. Elizabeth Carter and Miss Catherine Talbot*, I, 422.
[117] To Young, Jan.; to Lady Bradshaigh, 11 Feb., 4 Apr.; to Thomas Sheridan, 9 Apr.
[118] To Lady Bradshaigh.   [119] To Mrs. Chapone, 27 June, 30 Aug.
[120] Young to R, [17 Dec.]; R to Young, 18 Dec., 24 May 1759. See also Mrs. Delany to Mrs. Dewes, 27 Jan. 1759 (*Autobiography and Correspondence*, III, 535), where the dead man is called Richardson's 'relation'. The accident is reported in the *Whitehall Evening Post*, 28 Nov.; *Public Advertiser*, 30 Nov; *London Chronicle*, 28-30 Nov.; *London Evening-Post*, 28-30 Nov.;

effect on the quiet and gentle printer, who even in his novels avoids almost entirely physical violence. He was troubled by 'wicked Sleepless-ness' and when Young wrote that he suffered from the same affliction, Richardson replied, 'But, when you sleep not, you are awake to noble purpose: I to none at all; my days are nothing but hours of dozings, for want of nightly rest; and through an impatience that I am ashamed of, because I cannot subdue it'.[121]

In January 1759 he was so ill that his nephew had to write for him.[122] The amount of his extant correspondence begins to decline in 1759 and declines sharply in 1760. In the summer of 1759 he regretted being unable to court a correspondence with Lady Barbara Montagu and Mrs. Scott— undoubtedly, for him, a real deprivation. 'Too, too often my Pen will not touch the Paper,—nor stay in my Fingers', he wrote to Lady Barbara in October. 'One of my Paralytic Fits seems hastening on.'[123]

Richardson had never been a great traveller. After the completion of *Sir Charles Grandison* he seems to have gone almost nowhere. A two-day visit to Young at Welwyn, twenty-five miles on a fine road, in the summer of 1759 left him 'so shatter'd, that I find I must give up all Excursions above 10 Miles out and in'.[124] A journey of fifteen or twenty miles some-times 'made it difficult for me to keep my Seat, when I have alighted, unless supported by a Chair on each hand'.[125] He never got so far as Lancashire, to visit Lady Bradshaigh—he did not even manage to carry out a project of meeting her in Oxfordshire.[126]

On 10 March 1760 Lady Bradshaigh was so worried about a silence of over three months that she wrote an alarmed note asking what the matter was. He replied that he had been so much worse 'in the Paralytic way' that he could not even write to Young, to his daughter in Bath, or to the 'most beloved and revered of my Correspondents'. Nor could he walk to take exercise.[127] Richardson was seventy years old and had little more than a year to live. In the summer he wrote her again after a long and enforced silence.[128] There are no extant letters from him during the last two months of 1760 or the first two of 1761. In early March in an increasingly shaky hand he wrote a draft of a note for one of his daughters to write to Lady Bradshaigh: after three months of silence Richardson had been able to answer a letter from Mark Hildesley and he hoped 'that he shall one Day

Owen's Weekly Chronicle, 25 Nov.–2 Dec.; *Universal Chronicle*, 25 Nov.–2 Dec.; *Lloyd's Evening Post, and British Chronicle*, 1–4 Dec.; *Gentleman's Magazine*, XXVIII (Dec.), 611. Robert Richard-son's will is in P.C.C. Arran 32, dated 4 Mar. 1748, proved 29 Jan. 1759.

[121] 22 Dec.   [122] To Lady Barbara Montagu, 27 Jan.
[123] 10 July, 15 Oct. See also to Lady Bradshaigh, 18 Oct.
[124] To Lady Bradshaigh, 2 Aug.
[125] To Lady Echlin, 4 May 1756.
[126] Lady Bradshaigh to R, 30 June 1754; R to Lady Bradshaigh, 9 July 1754, 22 Mar. 1756.
[127] 12 Mar.   [128] 10 Aug.

be able to write to his ever-to-be-esteemed Correspondent Lady B. and to her beloved Sister Lady Echlin'.[129] If he did write to Lady Bradshaigh, the letter is lost; he did write to Lady Echlin on 5 April. But even in his last days Richardson was still interested in revising his novels—the main reason for his daughter's note to Lady Bradshaigh in early March was to ask for her marked copies of *Pamela* and *Clarissa*.

Richardson died of a stroke, the outcome of his old paralytic disorder, which attacked him on Sunday, 28 June 1761. Miss Talbot wrote to Mrs. Carter on 2 July that she had seen him on 28 May and that he then looked well, though a stroke had long been feared: 'The disease made its gradual approaches by that heaviness which clouded the cheerfulness of his conversation, that used to be so lively and so instructive; by the encreased tremblings which unfitted that hand so peculiarly formed to guide the pen; and by perhaps the querulousness of temper, most certainly not natural to so sweet and so enlarged a Mind, which you and I have lately lamented, as making his family at times not so comfortable as his principles, his study, and his delight to diffuse happiness wherever he could, would otherwise have done. Well, his noble spirit will soon now, I suppose, be freed from its corporeal incumbrance—it were a sin to wish against it, and yet how few such will be left behind!'[130] Joseph Highmore, at Richardson's invitation, was drinking tea with him at the time of his stroke. 'But, after he had drunk one dish or two, Mrs. Smith brought him another; he would not or could not drink it, and immediately faltered in his speech, and from that time spoke no more articulately. . . . Mr. Richardson continued speaking, or rather attempting to speak; but no one . . . could understand one word distinctly.' Dr. Heberden was sent for, as well as Richardson's family—Nancy was the only one in town. On 1 July Highmore wrote to his daughter that Patty had sent word Richardson recognized no one;[131] on 4 July he died, happily, as Patty wrote to Lady Bradshaigh, released 'from a World wch. had long ceased to give him Pleasure'.[132] He had left instructions in his will that his funeral was not to cost more than £30; he was buried at St. Bride's, the church near his town house, in the centre aisle, beside his dead children and his first wife. His second wife joined them there later, to rest together for 180 years, until German bombs brought the family again to the light of the world.

[129] The draft is undated, but the letter is answered by Lady Bradshaigh's letter to Richardson of 13 Mar.
[130] *Letters between Mrs. Elizabeth Carter and Miss Catherine Talbot,* I, 493.
[131] *Gentleman's Magazine,* LXXVI (1816), i, 577–8.
[132] [Mid-July], FM XI, fo. 277.

CHAPTER XXI

PERSONALITY

WE hope that Richardson's personality has already appeared from his words and actions, like that of a character in one of his novels. It may, however, be useful to discuss some of his more prominent traits, especially those which have been most often condemned or made fun of. Some of Richardson's contemporaries found him lacking in elegance, and others found him lacking in education; but no one, so far as we know, found him ridiculous or cruel or hypocritical. Our century, however, is clever enough to follow the faintest of scents in ferreting out secret shame and wise enough to laugh, patronizingly or scornfully, at most of the men of the past. No one has been more often laughed at than Richardson. The different periods of his life are not always distinguished. His closest association with literary ladies (as well as with Dr. Johnson) was during the early 1750s; his irritability and touchiness increased greatly in the late 1750s, when he was often ailing.

A typical view is that presented under slight fictional guise in Katharine Tynan's short story 'The Romance of a Bookseller'.[1] She portrays Mr. R., the author of *Clorinda*, as a silly and rather pitiful lower middle-class man who falls sick with love when a fine lady named Dulcinea writes to him about his novel and talks of meeting him in the park. In the end Dulcinea deserts poor R. for his manly and magnanimous rival F., and the whole town recognizes its mistake in having admired *Clorinda* and also decides to follow Mr. F. Those who admire Fielding (as we do) seem almost forced to belittle Richardson. Such an attitude has been strengthened, though it is not logically justified, by Richardson's savage attack on Fielding, of all his actions the one which has done most to injure his personal reputation.

This age can hardly condemn Richardson for being less aristocratic than Fielding or for lacking Fielding's classical education. Its condemnation is generally aimed at Richardson's vanity or at his attitude towards sex. Not that the two writers were in complete disagreement about sex. Both prized female chastity highly—as everyone in their day did; and neither was as open in describing the physical aspects of sex as we are today, though both were more frank than the Victorians, who preferred to forget 'unpleasant' subjects. But Fielding laughs about the subject and is tolerant of male lapses, in youth at least.

[1] *Cornhill Magazine*, N.S. XXII (1907), 678–89.

For a long time it has been accepted by Fielding's adherents that Richardson is 'prurient'—indeed in circles of literary criticism this word seems to be applied exclusively, but inevitably to Richardson. 'Fielding's sexual comedy is free and open and hearty, unlike the pornographic melodrama of Richardson's bedroom scenes.'[2] We have discussed this cliché already. Though we would not be upset to discover that Richardson was more easily stimulated to lust than most men, we have found no evidence that he was. He enjoyed the company of young ladies, and he perhaps added a few unnecessary touches to the warm scenes in *Pamela*. That seduction formed the plot of two of his novels is hardly surprising—it was one of the most popular subjects of his day (as of most days). In our opinion, the main impression left by the novels is not of the attempted seductions but of the emotions (not sexual) they gave occasion for.

It is quite likely that Richardson, like other men, felt sexual drives and not improbable that they were at least partly repressed. But the violent reaction of, for example, Frederick C. Green is, in our opinion, silly: 'One can visualize Richardson licking his lips as he dwelt over the account of B.'s abortive attempt to rape Pamela in the presence of his housekeeper. He really enjoys writing these scenes and, having absolutely no sense of humour, contrives to invest them with a sliminess of which he and Pamela, in their self-righteousness, are blissfully unaware. To make matters worse, his strange and twisted imagination is ever coiling back on itself, harking back to these erotic moments. . . . Mr. B. is quite obviously invented in order to allow Richardson to indulge his penchant for smug salaciousness.' 'We know from his biography that, in his quiet way, this fat little sultan of North End was a tyrant of the worst description.' 'He was still [in *Clarissa*] the frustrated romantic, absorbed in the contemplation of emotional experiences which he was never to know save through the medium of a vivid and erotic imagination.'[3] Presumably, in spite of his twelve children, Richardson had no 'emotional experiences' with his two wives. So good a judge as D. H. Lawrence takes almost the same view as Mr. Green when he speaks of Richardson's 'calico purity and his underclothing excitement'.[4] For what it is worth, one might admit that Richardson was rather more concerned with sex than befitted such a strict moralist. As to the recently fashionable accusations of sadism, we do not think that the slight and ambiguous evidence on which they are based, being interpretative only, can be refuted or needs refuting. We leave it to the amateur psychologists to decide whether teasing young girls is necessarily a sadistic diversion and to decipher the intricacies of Richardson's

[2] Martin C. Battestin, 'Introduction' to the Riverside Edition of *Joseph Andrews* and *Shamela* (Boston, [1961]), p. xvi.

[3] *Minuet*, pp. 381–2, 386, 401.

[4] *Phoenix*, ed. Edward D. McDonald (New York, 1936), p. 552.

repressed sexual urges. In view of the fact that he identified more with his persecuted heroines than with his seducers or his all-conquering paragon, a much better case could be made for his masochism, but we have no intention of making it. Nor do we intend to probe for 'the feminine element in Richardson's character', which the pre-Freudian Sir Leslie Stephen found 'a little in excess',[5] and thereby discover strong latent homosexuality.

As far as his conscious actions went, Richardson seems to have been free of what Gibbon calls 'the most amiable weakness of human nature'. He explained to Stinstra that he drew his bawds and rakes entirely from his imagination: 'I never, to my Knowlege, was in a vile House, or in Company with a lewd Woman, in my Life.' Boswell reports that he made a similar claim to Johnson.[6] 'Drunkards & such were always odious to me', he adds, in giving the same assurance to Mrs. Chapone; the knowledge of such wicked diversions as masquerades shown in his novels was altogether from second hand, as was his knowledge of sinners.[7] Perhaps he had forgotten Mrs. Pilkington; but in any case their companionship seems to have been quite innocent. We have no reason to doubt his word and know of no evidence of extra-marital sexual activity, unless one considers it reprehensible that he enjoyed the company of young girls.

A description of Richardson by an unnamed acquaintance probably gives a good idea of the way he impressed those who knew him, largely as a simple businessman, with a good share of the artist's vanity but without intellectual pretensions: 'Richardson . . . was a silent plain man, who seldom exhibited his parts in company, and above all things avoided those oddities and peculiarities of character and behaviour upon which his rival [Rousseau] seems to pride himself. Richardson heard the sentiments of others sometimes with attention, and seldom gave his own; rather desirous of gaining your friendship by his modesty than his parts. He either had no learning, or never shewed any: he was equally ignorant of French and Latin, and seldom seemed to enjoy that conversation which sprung from erudition. In his latter years he appeared almost buried within himself; and if ever he was alive, it was when his own works were the subject of applause. Upon such a topic he seemed to dwell with delight: this turn of temper led him to improve his fortune with mechanical assiduity; he was by trade a printer, and having no violent passions, nor no desire of being triflingly distinguished from others, he at last became rich, and left his family in easy independence.'[8]

[5] 'Richardson's Novels', p. 55.
[6] R to Stinstra, 2 June 1753; Boswell, *Journal*, 21 Sept. 1777, *Private Papers*, XIII, 50.
[7] 11 Jan. 1751.
[8] 'A Critical Examination of the Respective Merits of Voltaire, Rousseau, Richardson, Smollett, and Fielding', *Universal Museum*, N.S. II (1766), 392. The article was reprinted in the *Royal Magazine*, XV (1766), 146–9, and Nichols quotes from it in *Anecdotes of Bowyer*, p. 310.

Aaron Hill, writing to David Mallet and not to Richardson, could find but one fault in him—modesty: 'And to say the least I can of qualities, which he conceals, with as much fear, as if they were *ignoble* ones, he is so honest, open, generous, and great a *thinker*, that he cannot in his *writings* paint a virtue that he needs look farther than his *heart*, to find a *pattern for*.'[9] Probably we have all by now learned too much psychology to see any conflict between the modesty Hill stressed and the vanity others found in Richardson. An over-lively sensitiveness could account for both. Hill was, to be sure, a close friend to whom Richardson had been generous, and the praise of Richardson as a great thinker may make his testimony suspect. Closer to the truth is his praise two years before, in 1739, when he was trying to convince Pope that Richardson, then only a printer, was not responsible for a slur in the *Gazetteer*: 'I am very much mistaken in his character, or he is a plain-hearted, sensible, and good-natur'd, honest man.'[10] No one seems to have accused him of dishonesty, in financial or in any other relationship.

A man's view of himself always casts light on his character, though not always directly. One trait which he repeatedly stressed was his bashfulness, 'a bashfulness, next to sheepishness', he called it in a letter to Lady Bradshaigh. He associated it, in this letter and elsewhere, with the very modest circumstances in which he passed his early years and with his strong desire to make himself independent. 'How shall a man obscurely situated,' he wrote to her at another time, 'never delighting in public entertainments, nor in his youth able to frequent them, from narrowness of fortune, had he had a taste for them; one of the most attentive of men to the calls of his business; his situation for many years producing little but prospects of a numerous family; a business that seldom called him abroad, where he might in the course of it see and know a little of the world, as some employments give opportunities to do; naturally shy and sheepish, and wanting more encouragement by smiles, to draw him out, than any body thought it worth their while to give him; and blest, (in this he will say blest,) with a mind that set him above a sought-for dependence, and making an absolute reliance on Providence and his own endeavours. How, I say, shall such a man pretend to describe and enter into characters in upper life?'[11] Since the great bulk of Richardson's extant correspondence was written after the publication of *Pamela*, after the author was over fifty, it is easy to forget his youth, though Richardson never forgot it. Even his vanity must be viewed against this background—he was quite conscious of the fact that till late in life he had been the social inferior of the people who sought him out when he was famous and that he remained the inferior in education of at least the men. And he never tried to conceal

[9] 23 Jan. 1741, *Works*, II, 158.   [10] 21 Feb., ibid., II, 68.
[11] [*c.* 1 Oct. 1755]; 24 Mar. 1751.

either fact, though social classes were far more important in his day than in ours and the day when intellectuals were to envy those of their colleagues who had a proletarian background was in the distant future.

He often mentioned his inadequacy in society. He wrote to Miss Mulso that he feared his 'native awkwardness' might make him seem guilty of faults his heart was clear of: 'Never was there so bashful, so sheepish a creature as was, till advanced years, your paternal friend; and what remained so long in the habit could hardly fail of shewing itself in stiffness and shyness, on particular occasions, where frankness of heart would otherwise have shone forth to the advantage of general character.' Or to Samuel Lobb: 'When I was young, I was very sheepish; (so I am indeed now I am old: I have not had Confidence enough to try to overcome a Defect so natural to me, tho' I have been a great Loser by it).' He repeated to Stinstra that he was a 'bashful and not forward Boy', adding that his schoolfellows called him '*Serious* and *Gravity*'. To Mrs. Chapone he said that the reason was his tendency to introspection: 'You are undoubtedly in the right in supposing I think too much. From Boyhood, when my Schoolfellows used to call me *Gravity* and *Serious*, oftener than by my own Name, this was my Fault: And what Cure is there for it?' His sense of inadequacy in conversation he expressed clearly to Lady Bradshaigh in explaining, with his usual sensitiveness to personal slights, why a man he had recently met (Eusebius Silvester) had not written to him: 'I suppose I answered not, on a personal Acquaintance, the *too* high Ideas he had of me from what I had published. I am always jealous of suffering in the Opinion of my Readers, when we come into personal Conversation—And why?—Because the Simplicity of my Character (I hope I may say so) and the Frankness of my Communicativeness, lay me open all at once, and must convince the new Acquaintances that they had thought too highly of me, by their Reading. I design not either Affectation or Reserve; and if I appear to have Shyness, it is owing more to my native Awkwardness, than to Design.'[12] There is probably a touch of mock-depreciation; Richardson had reason to hope that Lady Bradshaigh had not been disappointed on meeting him and might protest. But he was undoubtedly conscious of the deficiency.

John Whiston, the bookseller, noted another fault, though he considered Richardson a 'worthy man altogether': he was so 'liable to Passion' that he directed all his employees by letter, 'not trusting to reprove by Words which threw him into hastiness & hurt him, who had always a Tremor on his Nerves'.[13] John Nichols, quoting Whiston for the fact of Richardson's notes to his employees, added that he had heard nearly the same account

[12] 15 Aug. 1755; 4 July 1746; 2 June 1753; 30 Aug. 1758; 13 Aug. 1755.
[13] MS. note in the British Museum copy of *A New and General Biographical Dictionary*, X (London, 1762), 142, under Richardson.

from some of Richardson's workmen but offered a different motive, 'for convenience, to avoid altercation, and going up into the printing office' and because William Tewley was 'remarkably deaf'.[14] But there is other evidence that Richardson was not free of strong attacks of moral indignation—witness the Irish pirates.

Richardson gave two long descriptions of himself, one to Miss Highmore and the other to Lady Bradshaigh when she was still the unknown Belfour. The first was written while he was at Tunbridge Wells in 1748: 'I will shew you a still more grotesque figure than either [Beau Nash or Cibber]. A sly sinner, creeping along the very edges of the walks, getting behind benches: one hand in his bosom, the other held up to his chin, as if to keep it in its place: afraid of being seen, as a thief of detection. The people of fashion, if he happen to cross a walk (which he always does with precipitation) *unsmiling* their faces, as if they thought him in their way; and he as sensible of so being, stealing in and out of the bookseller's shop, as if he had one of their glass-cases under his coat. Come and see this odd figure!' Hoping to meet Belfour, he wrote in November 1749: 'My countenance, I dare tell you, from the opinion of my favourers, (confirmed by unreasonable applications from some, who have beheld somewhat soft and weak in it) and have demanded of me what they would not have hoped for from any other, has nothing in it severe or forbidding. . . . I go thro' the Park once or twice a week to my little retirement; but I will for a week together be in it every day three or four hours, at your command, till you tell me you have seen a person who answers to this description, namely, Short; rather plump than emaciated, notwithstanding his complaints: about five foot five inches: fair wig; lightish cloth coat, all black besides: one hand generally in his bosom, the other a cane in it, which he leans upon under the skirts of his coat usually, that it may imperceptibly serve him as a support, when attacked by sudden tremors or startings, and dizziness, which too frequently attack him, but, thank God, not so often as formerly: looking directly foreright, as passers-by would imagine, but observing all that stirs on either hand of him without moving his short neck; hardly ever turning back: of a light-brown complexion; teeth not yet failing him; smoothish faced, and ruddy cheeked: at sometimes looking to be about sixty-five, at other times much younger: a regular even pace, stealing away ground, rather than seeming to rid it: a gray eye, too often overclouded by mistinesses from the head: by chance lively; very lively it will be, if he have hope of seeing a lady whom he loves and honours: his eye always on the ladies; if they have very large hoops, he looks down and supercilious, and as if he would be thought wise, but perhaps the sillier for that: as he approaches a lady, his eye is never fixed first upon her face, but upon her feet, and thence he raises it up, pretty quickly for a dull eye; and one would

[14] *Anecdotes of Bowyer*, p. 157; *Literary Anecdotes*, IV, 597.

think (if we thought him at all worthy of observation) that from her air and (the last beheld) her face, he sets her down in his mind as *so* or *so*, and then passes on to the next object he meets; only then looking back, if he greatly likes or dislikes, as if he would see if the lady appear to be all of a piece, in the one light or in the other. Are these marks distinct enough, if you are resolved to keep all the advantages you set out with? And from this odd, this grotesque figure, think you, Madam, that you have any thing to apprehend? Any thing that will not rather promote than check your mirth?'[15]

That Richardson's plumpness was not of recent date in 1749 is evident from the poem written in January 1735 by Edward Cave, urging him to appear at supper and promising:

> I'll place two seats, whene'er you come,
> This for your arms—and that your bum.

If his verse gains the attendance of Richardson's 'rosy face':

> How the full orb the board would grace,
> When flush'd with wine, and plump with praise![16]

Over twenty years later Major Hohorst described Richardson to Klopstock: 'Richardson is a man about sixty-four years old, as tall as you, but fairly stout and sedate [ziemlich stark und gesetzt]. He has light brown hair and a pair of large, blue, fiery, roguish, witty eyes [grosse blaue feurige schalkhafte geistige Augen]: Has a friendly gentleness and agreeableness in his bearing [Ist sehr freundlich sanft und angenehm in seinen Wesen], in short he has a heart full of true love of mankind, which any man who is good himself must recognize and honour.'[17] He estimated Richardson two years younger than he was. As a stranger who knew Richardson from his novels, he may have been looking for the philanthropic heart, but he must have seen the friendly, mild, and pleasant manner; the stout, sedate figure; the light brown hair; and the large blue eyes which struck him as fiery, roguish, and witty. A former friend told Mrs. Barbauld about the amiable features and sparkling eyes and added that Richardson was 'slow in speech, and, to strangers at least, spoke with reserve and deliberation'.[18] Miss Frances Cotterell reports that at their first meeting he was just as she had pictured him, 'short and tun-bellied, with his hands joined over the protuberance and twirling his thumbs'.[19]

The extant portraits of Richardson bear out, as well as portraits are

[15] 2 Aug.; [late Nov.].

[16] Nichols, *Anecdotes of Bowyer*, p. 89; *Literary Anecdotes*, II, 77.

[17] 29 Oct. 1756, *Geschichte der Meta Klopstock in Briefen* (Bremen [1962]), p. 473.

[18] I, clxxvi.

[19] Elizabeth Smart Le Noir to Cuthbert Sharp, 22 Aug. 1831, quoted by Sherbo, 'Anecdotes by Mrs. Le Noir', p. 167.

likely to, these descriptions. None of them is youthful. The earliest is a
family group of Richardson, his wife, his four daughters, and a girl who
is probably Miss Midwinter, painted in the early forties, possibly by
Francis Hayman.[20] It shows the same light wig, the same smooth, white,
round face with large blue open eyes, full nose, slightly smiling mouth,
and double chin, the same sort of plain costume (a snuff-coloured coat,
steel-blue waistcoat, and dark blue small clothes) and calm, settled pose
as the more familiar later portraits. A portrait by Mason Chamberlin,
presented to Speaker Onslow, cannot be later than 1754, when Edwards
saw it at Ember Court.[21] It shows Richardson wearing a cap and a red
coat and breeches, seated with his legs crossed, and holding a pen and a
manuscript.[22] Joseph Highmore's half-length now in the National Portrait Gallery must be the one Lady Bradshaigh saw and liked before she
asked Richardson to get him to paint another for her; it is therefore
probably of the late 1740s. In 1750 she described to Richardson the portrait she wanted, drawn in his study, 'a table or desk by you, with pen,
ink, and paper; one letter just sealed, which I shall fancy is to me'.[23] Her
instructions were followed exactly in the full-length portrait now in the
National Portrait Gallery—there is even a 'B' visible on the letter. And as
an added compliment Richardson had painted in the background the
picture Lady Bradshaigh had given him of herself and Sir Roger, with
Fanny the fawn, on the lawn of Haigh House.[24] Judging by its appearance,
the third portrait by Highmore, in the Hall of the Company of Stationers,
must have been painted at somewhere near the same date.[25] It shows
Richardson, against a conventionalized outdoor background (trees, a
balustrade, the bottom of a statue), three-quarter-length, holding a book.
It was probably the 'portrait de grandeur naturelle et à l'huile' which
Mme. de Genlis saw and admired at Edward Bridgen's, though she must
have been using her knowledge of the novels when she saw that 'sa
physionomie et ses yeux étoient remplis de douceur'.[26] In 1902 G. K.

[20] It is now in the possession of Richardson's descendant, Brigadier Oliver Peck.

[21] To R, 7 Oct.

[22] This portrait was engraved for the Reverend Edward Mangin's edition of Richardson's
novels in 1811. It was later in the Earl of Rosebery's collection and around 1939 was advertised
for sale by Charles J. Sawyer, a London bookseller, who has kindly sent us a photograph of it.
We do not know its present location. A copy is owned by Richardson's descendant, Mr. Jasper
Peck.

[23] 3 June.

[24] R to Lady Bradshaigh, 31 Mar. 1750. Lady Bradshaigh left this portrait of Richardson to
his daughter Polly (P.C.C. Norfolk 139, dated 22 July 1780, proved 11 Mar. 1786), but it was
apparently never delivered, since the National Portrait Gallery acquired it from Lady Bradshaigh's collateral descendant, I. W. A. Mackinnon.

[25] On 16 June 1750 Richardson paid Highmore £42 and on 28 Nov. 1750 £24 18s. 6d.
See Gosling's Bank Ledger.

[26] *Mémoires* (Paris et Londres, 1825), III, 292–3. Bridgen sent her a miniature of the precious
portrait. The original was left by Bridgen to his sister-in-law Anne Richardson (P.C.C. Major

Chesterton, looking at the very similar half-length by Highmore, decided that Richardson looked 'as if he had composed his features systematically all his life to such an extent that normal human nature might strongly be tempted to discompose them with a brickbat'[27]—surely a reflection of the change in what people expected to see in Richardson.

We have a few glimpses of Richardson's personal habits. Dr. Cheyne reproved him for his love of good living and for his excessive worries about his health ('you are a true genuine Hyppo now with all it's plainest Symptoms').[28] Cheyne himself was hipped on the subject of diet, but he must have known what he was talking about, though his idea of high living need not have been very high. And at least in his later life Richardson's maladies were not imaginary. From Hill we learn that in 1738 Richardson drank wine two or three times a week, 'a moderate Glass . . . in an Evening'.[29] Later he was on Cheyne's wineless diet, and after he abandoned it his health was so weak that his eating and drinking must have been very moderate. As a poor apprentice, he could hardly have been brought up to high living; but whatever abstinence he practised was probably due to necessity or prudence rather than principle. He was able to walk from Salisbury Court to North End, no mean achievement by modern American standards. He informed Smyth Loftus that he never could ride,[30] nor do we hear that he took any other exercise except on his chamber horse.

From his biography in the *Universal Magazine* we learn that he was plain and unaffected in his dress (as his portraits show) and manners and that until late in life he usually rose at five and went to bed at eleven.[31] When in town he was 'very seldom abroad in a Morning',[32] presumably because he was kept busy in his own establishment. From Saturday to Monday he was usually at North End or Parson's Green.[33] There, he wrote in 1755, his leisure was generally in the morning. He complained half-humourously that between their late rising, their writing and dressing

---

355, dated 30 Apr. 1787, proved 8 Aug. 1787), with the desire that after her death it be 'delivered to the Company of Stationers to be fixed up in their hall'. Anne left it to her nephew Philip Ditcher (P.C.C. Heseltine 133, dated 6 Oct. 1802, proved 11 Feb. 1804), but it did eventually get to the Stationers' Company. The companion portrait of Mrs. Richardson, which also hung in the Hall of the Company of Stationers, was destroyed during the Second World War.

Richardson had this portrait of himself engraved in mezzotinto by James MacArdell at a cost of £15 15s. (Gosling's Bank Ledger, under date 3 Oct. 1750). In sending a copy to Stinstra (2 June 1753), Richardson mentions that it was 'done at the Command of a Great Man'— presumably Onslow. He gave prints to various of his friends and even sent four copies for distribution to Edwards's admiring female friends (Edwards to R, 8 Feb., 9 Mar. 1751; R to Edwards, 19 Mar. 1751).

[27] 'England's Novelists in the National Portrait Gallery', *The Bookman*, XIV, 472.
[28] See p. 64 and Cheyne to R, [July–Aug. 1742].
[29] To R. 26 Dec.   [30] 13 Dec. 1756.   [31] LXXVIII, 20.
[32] R to Lady Echlin, 22 Sept. 1755.
[33] *Universal Magazine*, LXXVIII, 19.

and walking, he saw little of the girls that visited the house. At dinner the conversation was agreeable but, because of the servants, consisted largely in 'prattlings on vague subjects'. If the day was fine, the girls went for a walk and nobody could read or be read to till they returned. After giving directions to the gardener, he went upstairs 'to his writing- (I should *now* rather say reading-) desk'. When the girls returned, he had to go down, because they were 'at *leisure* to expect him'. But he had the mortification of hearing that the neighbouring fields and lanes lacked variety and that other situations were better than his. He was asked to read to them 'by-and-by' and bowed acceptance, the opportunity being still distant. At last they assembled around a large table and 'the passive man' was 'called to his lesson'. But the girls were making ruffles or flowering muslin or drawing, and he was often interrupted by preparations for supper. After supper, 'as paradeful a one as if it were a less frugal meal than it always is at Parson's Green', the business of the day was concluded, but the girls were 'as loth to retire to rest' as they were 'to get together in the morning'.[34]

We have a few glimpses of Richardson's writing habits. He wrote himself—'I never could dictate', he told Edward Young at a time when his hand was even more trembling than it was when he was composing *Sir Charles*.[35] He told Lady Bradshaigh that he was forced to write at 'Intervals and Snatches of time . . . now perhaps, at one House, now at another'.[36] Mme. de Genlis, when she visited the Bridgens after Richardson's death, sat in Bridgen's garden on Richardson's bench, a bench the right arm of which opened to reveal an escritoire. She was told that Richardson composed and wrote there during a part of the morning, though the garden in which she was sitting cannot have been the one in which *Sir Charles* was composed.[37]

He was primarily a city man, with a city man's enjoyment of his rural retreat in a convenient suburb. His residence as a boy in Derbyshire must have been brief and left no traces. When Edwards suggested that after the hay harvest would be a convenient time for him to visit Turrick, Richardson had to ask the Talbots when the hay harvest took place: 'I am a very Cockney.'[38] Few men have ever been more thoroughgoing Londoners than Samuel Richardson, who seems to have shared his friend Dr. Johnson's feelings about the advantages of the metropolis. He made few trips beyond what is now greater London, and so far as is known, he never left England.

In 1750 he paid a good many visits to ladies: 'My acquaintance lies chiefly among the ladies; I care not who knows it.' But by that date his nervous malady had already begun to force on him a more retired life. 'I

[34] To Hester Mulso, 15 Aug.   [35] 18 Dec. 1758.
[36] 5 Oct. 1753.   [37] *Mémoires*, III, 292.   [38] To Edwards, 12 July 1756.

have forborn going to public diversions, and even been forced to deny myself (what I used to be delighted with) opportunities . . . to hear the debates of both houses of Parliament.' He had also long given up going to church: 'My nervous malady . . . will not let me appear in a crowd of people.'[39] Six years later he told Mrs. Watts almost the same thing: 'I, who cannot bear a Concourse of People: Who have been obliged to deny my self the being present at the rational Amusement of a good Play; of hearing Debates in either House of Parliament; which was a favourite Diversion to me; and even, till within a Year or two past, attending at the Public Worship; the most indispensable of all Duties.'[40] This implies that he had begun again to attend church, probably when he moved to Parson's Green.[41]

Most of the people who knew Richardson mention his friendliness and benevolence. Among other things, these must have arisen from his strong interest in people. He was always eager to listen to a personal history. Even towards the end of his life we find him asking de Luc for the history of his family and that of the French lady he had praised (Mme. d'Epinay).[42] And after having got from Mrs. Klopstock her own story, he wanted to hear that of her two sisters and five intimate friends—it was always a joy to hear of virtue.[43] He seems, at least as far as the evidence goes, to have much preferred stories about the virtuous to spicy gossip, of which there was an abundance at the time.

He occasionally mentioned his love of solitude and retirement.[44] But so far as we know, he was almost constantly surrounded by people and was constantly urging others to visit him. Even people who cannot bear to be alone are apt to fancy they would like to be if the occasion ever offered itself. We suspect that Richardson, though not well suited for the conversation of strangers or of persons with social or intellectual pretensions, needed to have people around him when he was not working. In her copy of *Sir Charles* Lady Bradshaigh noted, when Charlotte reported that most of the Grandison family's guests had just departed, that she rejoiced the company had left. Richardson's brief comment implies that he believed that the departure of guests was a cause of selfish pleasure which should not be indulged in: 'Right, Lady B. But a little too regardful of Self. I myself, never part with those I value, but I look after them, as far as I can see them.'[45] Erasmus Reich wrote that when he last left Richardson 'he

---

[39] To Lady Bradshaigh, 9 Jan., [late Nov.].   [40] 13 May.

[41] The Churchwardens' Accounts of Fulham Parish Church for 1761 include a sum received 'of Mr. Richardson for seating him and his wife in Mrs. Putland's pew'. We want to thank Mr. Colin A. McLaren, Archivist of the London Borough of Hammersmith, for sending us this information.

[42] 25 July 1758.   [43] 7 Apr. 1758.

[44] To Hill, 4 Apr. 1744; to Lady Bradshaigh, 9 Oct. 1754.

[45] VII, 37. Her copy of this volume is in the Henry E. Huntington Library.

accompanied me with his eyes as far as he could',[46] and we imagine that he always thus followed his departing guests.

He was eager to meet new people—especially if they had admired his works. When an anonymous letter about *Pamela* arrived, he advertised in the newspapers that he earnestly desired to correspond with the writer.[47] A. B. was forced to decline Richardson's invitation to visit him, after having written to him anonymously about *Sir Charles*.[48] After a similar letter from Julian Bere, Richardson hoped he could acknowledge the honour in person.[49] We have described how he induced Anna Meades to disclose her name and to make his acquaintance. Most important of all, he overcame the shyness of his incognita Belfour to make a lifelong friend. Aside from the anonymous admirers, his correspondence is full of pressing invitations to friends and friends of friends. Only repeated insistence induced Thomas Edwards, for instance, to make Richardson's house his own for the winter. Edwards explained to Speaker Onslow that the generosity of Richardson's temper 'makes me afraid of employing him in any commissions as he has often kindly pressed me to do'.[50] Young visited him so frequently that Mrs. Delany, hearing Young was in London in the winter of 1753, supposed him at Richardson's and sent her compliments to him there.[51] At his own suggestion he acted as Sir Roger Bradshaigh's London agent.[52] It would be easy to multiply instances of his obligingness to friends and his hospitality. The biography in the *Universal Magazine* says that North End and Parson's Green were seldom without visitors.[53]

The favourable comments by people who knew Richardson stress largely the kindness of his heart. 'A Sort of an Original for Goodness & Sensibility', John Mulso called him. After his death his overseer, William Tewley, mentioned his goodness, piety, generosity, and love of helping the distressed 'and relieving many without their knowledge'.[54]

He was liberal not only in social intercourse. As one of his obituaries states, 'His humane and compassionate disposition was constantly displayed in various acts of benevolence and uncommon generosity.'[55] When John Grover, Clerk of the Ingrossments in the House of Commons, died, Richardson wrote to Young: 'I have all his very greatly disordered Affairs likely to be upon me. He was the Support of a Maiden Sister, as he had been of a decayed Father, Mother, and Family. I have got her (a worthy

[46] Barbauld, I, clxx.

[47] *Daily Gazetteer*, 20 Nov., 26 Nov. 1740; *London Evening Post*, 11–13 Dec. 1740.

[48] 21 July 1754.   [49] 10 Apr. 1754.

[50] 19 Jan. 1751, Bodleian MS. 1011, p. 208.

[51] To Mrs. Dewes, 9 Dec., *Autobiography and Correspondence*, III, 253.

[52] R to Lady Bradshaigh, 21 Oct. 1755.   [53] LXXVIII, 19.

[54] 6 Oct. 1750, *Letters to Gilbert White*, p. 43; *Gentleman's Magazine*, LIV (1783), 924–5, and Nichols, *Literary Anecdotes*, IV, 727.

[55] *London Chronicle*, 2–4 July 1761.

Creature) to N. End to my good Wife. He was too much regardless of
Money to leave her very happy in that Particular. I am endeavouring to
get those who valued him, to be kind to her.'[56] Richardson had, of course,
a respect for prudence in money matters and exercised it even in his
charities—he did not sell all and give to the poor. Those who have done
so may, if they choose, censure his lukewarm benevolence.

Since he seems never to have boasted of his charity, we learn of it largely
by chance, yet the list of those we know he helped is a fairly long one.
Early in his career as a printer he lent John Dennis money. In 1744, when
a liveryman named Thomas Brown was in danger of being turned out
of his house with his wife and children, the Stationers' Company chose
Richardson to take the ten guineas it voted and see them 'applyed as Mr.
Brown's occasions shall apply'.[57] His generosity to William Webster, forgiving him a large debt and offering to give more help, has been mentioned, as has his sending Margaret Collier five guineas for a door to keep
her cottage bedroom warm. Aaron Hill often mentions his obligations to
Richardson. Sir Charles, noted for his charity, is anxious to help *worthy*
objects—maidens in need of a dowry, young people of both sexes about to
begin in the world, 'The industrious poor, of *all* persuasions, reduced
either by age, infirmity, or accident; Those who labour under incurable
maladies'.[58] Richardson, less strict in practice than in theory, helped Mrs.
Pilkington, though she could hardly be described as one of the deserving
poor. Sir John Hawkins was 'a witness to his putting into the hand of Mr.
Whiston the bookseller, ten guineas for the relief of one whom a sudden
accident had made a widow'.[59] He took Harry Campbell, the juvenile
admirer of *Pamela*, as apprentice without a fee. He lent money to Dr.
Johnson. Thomas Edwards states that he helped Fielding. He offered to
help Philip Skelton's poor Irish flock. His name headed the list of those
who would receive contributions in aid of Spence's protégé, Robert Hill
of Buckingham,[60] and there can be little doubt that he contributed to help
that self-educated paragon. James Hervey sent five guineas for a poor but
deserving woman whom Richardson was evidently helping at the request
of Spence and asked Richardson if he knew any other 'virtuous and
valuable person in distressed circumstances, to whom a few guineas might
be a seasonable and acceptable present'; at some unknown proof of
Richardson's generosity he said that, knowing his worth, he begged 'leave
to regard him, not as a printer whom I employ, but as a choice friend,
whom I highly honour, cordially love, and for whom I shall frequently

[56] 9 Sept. 1749. Administration of Grover's estate was granted in P.C.C. on 16 Sept. 1749,
to Mabella Grover.
[57] 'Court Book K', p. 226, 4 Sept., MS. in the archives of the Stationers' Company.
[58] SH, II, 291-2.
[59] *Life of Samuel Johnson*, p. 386.
[60] Spence, *A Parallel in the Manner of Plutarch* (Strawberry Hill, 1758), p. 104.

pray'.[61] He helped a poor schoolmaster of Hertfordshire, James Bennet, a 'worthy man under difficulties for his worthiness', publish a subscription edition of Ascham.[62] It must also have been charity which made him subscribe for copies of Miss Smythies' *The Brothers* for himself, his wife, and all four of his daughters.[63] We have described how Lady Bradshaigh appealed to him to help her fallen women and her other poor. He induced Young to try to find a position for a young clergyman named Forester.[64] He lent over £70 to Mr. Chapone. We have described his early generosity to Silvester, as well as the unfortunate consequences when Richardson came to believe that Silvester did not deserve such generosity, and the agent employed to collect that hopeless debt informed Silvester that Richardson had some years before been imposed upon in a similar way by an attorney. He was also sensitive to the feelings of the needy and could disguise his charity, as when he employed an 'honest Man, not high in Circumstances' to translate from the German a work he wanted to read in order 'to be kind' to him 'in his own way'.[65] The year before his death he tried to use his influence with Onslow and another, unnamed, great man to get employment for a lame and needy man of learning named Mills. He helped his brother-in-law James Leake.[66] From his will we learn that he had lent ten guineas to otherwise unknown cousins named Jane and Elizabeth Lindsley; that he made a quarterly allowance to his sister Warburgh; and that he paid six guineas a year to his wife's sister Amey Langley. We have mentioned his connection with the Magdalen House; in 1754 he was elected as one of the governors and guardians of the Foundling Hospital and contributed over £5 yearly to it.[67]

William Merritt Sale, Jr., has discussed several printing jobs which Richardson undertook evidently only to help the author: Hill, Mary Barber, Molly Leapor, George Kelly, Mary Porter.[68] We have seen that he also went out of his way to help Charlotte Lennox and the writer of *The Histories of Some of the Penitents in the Magdalen House* and that in connection with the latter he told Lady Barbara Montagu that the booksellers were displeased with him for helping authors at their setting out by printing books for their benefit. He also read and offered suggestions

---

[61] R's note on an envelope dated 29 Feb. 1748, MS. in the Pierpont Morgan Library; 3 Nov. 1747.

[62] Joseph Spence, *Observations, Anecdotes, and Characters of Books and Men*, ed. James M. Osborn (Oxford, 1966), I, 433.   [63] London, 1758.

[64] R to Miss Colborn, 21 Feb. 1756; R to Young, 23 Apr. 1756; Young to R, 27 Apr. 1756.

[65] R to Erasmus Reich, 2 Apr. 1757.

[66] R to Mills, 18 Mar.; Leake to R, 3 Sept. 1753.

[67] Foundling Hospital Vols., under date 8 May. We would like to thank Mr. W. C. Hart, Clerk of the London County Council, for arranging with Miss Marjorie Flint, Deputy Librarian of the British Library of Political and Economic Science, to have made for us a photostat of this entry.

[68] *Master Printer*, pp. 90-1, 114-17.

for manuscript novels by Anna Meades, Mrs. Sheridan, and Urania Hill
Johnson.

There is every reason to believe that he was telling the exact truth when
he informed Silvester that he had, by helping others, found himself 'a
Loser and Expender of Sums nearly equal to what I have left for a Wife
and 4 Children, and other very near Relations, who expect from me, more
than they otherwise would, by Reason of my Kindness to Persons unally'd
by Blood'.[69] His combination of practical attention to money and
generosity is well illustrated by one of his comments on *Sir William
Harrington*. The hero's penniless friend Renholds is about to marry
Charlotte Randall, whose sister Sir William has just married, and the
bride's father, a clergyman with only a small living, offers the couple a
rent-free house and four thousand pounds after his death: 'What Occasion
has the Clergyman Randall for the 4000 l. he intends at his Death for
Charlotte, tho' his living is a small one; both his Daughters disposed of.
2000 l. of it given up by Sir W.—A bad Oeconomist, I doubt, if he had
saved nothing out of 4000 l. Interest, besides his Living—Sir W's
Generosity to his Lady would not suffer Renholds his dear Friend, and
who wanted Money, to trust till old Mr. Randall's Death.'[70] In editing
Æsop's *Fables*, he revised the fable of the Bull and the Goat to make the
Goat remark, when the Bull chased by a lion seeks admittance, that it
would be imprudent to let him and his pursuer in, and he pointed out in
the moral that we are not to ruin ourselves and our families to help others;
but he left the substance of L'Estrange's reflection on that favourite
middle-class fable of the Ant and the Grasshopper, that the Ant was also
to blame: she was right to reprove the Grasshopper, 'but she did ill after
that to refuse her a Charity in her Distress'.[71] Richardson's practice was
perhaps a little better, but these two morals aptly summarize his theory.

Mrs. Barbauld, evidently on the authority of one of his surviving
friends, records that he was 'familiarly kind' to young children, and they
were very fond of him; 'he generally carried sugar-plumbs in his pocket
to make his court to them'. Mary Poole Way recalled that 'as a playful
child' she was admitted into his study, where she 'was generally caressed,
and rewarded with biscuits or *bonbons* of some kind or other, and sometimes with books'. When late in the evening he used to drop in at her
father's to supper, after 'he had worked as long as his eyes and nerves
would let him' and wanted to relax, she 'used to creep to his knee, and
hang upon his words' and was reluctant to leave him for bed. She frequently visited at North End, sometimes with her mother but often, for
weeks, without her; and when Richardson came down for the weekend,

---

[69] 12 Aug. 1756.
[70] Eaves and Kimpel, 'Richardson's Connection with *Sir William Harrington*', p. 284.
[71] L'E Nos. 218, 217; R Nos. 165, 164.

'he used to like to have his family flock around him, when we all first asked and received his blessing, together with some small boon from his paternal kindness and attention; for, he seldom met us empty-handed, and was by nature most generous and liberal'.[72]

His eighteenth-century sensibility is shown in the *Familiar Letters*, where he censures the habit of laughing at the inmates of Bedlam and the levity and curiosity shown at public executions.[73] Much later he sent Lady Bradshaigh a grim account of the mismanagement of debtors' prisons. His comment on it is a typical mixture of the gentle heart and the cautious head, unwilling to urge anything to undermine financial stability: 'How slightly are we accustomed to hear mentioned the jail distemper as an usual thing! and yet have we not had instances, though not so many [as] at one time, of like fatal effects from it? It is pity, me thinks, that some other means, than that of depriving our fellow-creatures of the common blessings of air and sunshine, could not be thought of, for doing justice to creditors, and for punishing delinquents; for prisons must not be made palaces neither. Could not the careless, the idle, the extravagant debtor, be made to work for a certain number of years, in proportion to the value of his debt, and according to his demerits in contracting it?—the debt first reduced to a probably payable sum, as mercy and justice should direct: and this (there are wastes enow every where) in places clean and comfortable, erected at the public expense, or by every parish, precinct, &c. What great and good things might not the poor's rates, taken into the hands or direction of the legislature, rightly administered, do!'[74]

Mrs. Barbauld, in her introduction to Richardson's correspondence, wrote the first full-length study of him, and by no means one of the worst. She admired his general character, especially his kindness and friendliness, but criticized, mildly it is true, several traits: his envy of Fielding, his stiffness with his daughters, his touchiness and pride towards the upper classes, and above all his vanity and his dependence on a circle of female admirers.[75] The vanity and the female admirers have caused much harsh comment. Byron (certainly an authority on vanity) called Richardson the vainest of writers.[76] Dr. Johnson's statements have been often quoted. Boswell informs us that, though Johnson admired Richardson's talents and virtues, he observed that 'his perpetual study was to ward off petty inconveniences and procure petty pleasures; that his love of continual superiority was such that he took care to be always surrounded by women, who listened to him implicitly and did not venture to controvert his opinions; and that his desire of distinction was so great that he used to give large vails to the Speaker Onslow's servants that they might treat him

[72] I, clii, clxxxii–v.   [73] Letters 153, 160.
[74] 22 July 1750.   [75] I, lxiii, lxxix, cl–cli, clvii–viii, clxx–xxi.
[76] *Letters and Journals*, ed. Rowland E. Prothero, in *Works* (London, 1898–1924), V, 148–9.

with respect'.[77] The account of Richardson written with the approval of his daughters shows how much Richardson's family resented this passage, but in spite of their bias, their answer is perhaps more sensible than the condescension with which some scholars, presumably exempt from vanity, have quoted Johnson's remarks: 'Of this last circumstance it may be asked, (admitting, for a moment, the representation to be just) where exists that transcendent, that superhuman character, which is in *every* respect uninfluenced by the littleness of Vanity? And with regard to the motives to which Mr. Richardson's desire for the society of women is imputed, it may be questioned whether this observation is so much a satire upon that great man, as upon the sex in general.' We hope that we have presented enough evidence that Richardson's female admirers frequently ventured 'to controvert his opinions' and that he enjoyed arguing with them. But there is no need to share the indignation of the writer of the article when he adds: 'But to insinuations so uncandid and illiberal, we are enabled, by authentic information, to give an answer still more satisfactory. A gentleman, who was very intimate with Mr. Richardson, has observed to us, that he has no reason to question the accuracy of Mr. Boswell's Journal. It must be a subject of concern, he thinks, to all the admirers of Dr. Johnson's writings, that his grateful feelings toward Mr. Richardson, who was his *friend* and *benefactor*, and whose purse often made him happy, were not more lasting in their duration, nor more honourable in their influence. He has frequently been in company with Mr. Richardson and Dr. Johnson, at the house of the former, when several ladies of great character and understanding were present. In their conversation, which was generally directed to Mr. Richardson, they would often attack some part or other of his writings, which he always defended so well, as to convince his fair opponents that they were wrong. If the ladies did not begin with him, he would artfully lead them to the subject himself; for female opposition animated him most, and seemed a greater cordial to his spirits than any flattery which they could bestow upon him and his works. In Dr. Johnson's company, on other occasions, Mr. Richardson has been observed to be more silent than in any other, if a third person were present; so that it has been a doubt with his friends, whether his silence in the Doctor's company proceeded from respect or fear: for Mr. Richardson was naturally very modest and well-bred.' The same gentleman wondered how Johnson knew what went on at the Speaker's house, Ember Court, where, 'he has reason to imagine, [Johnson] was never admitted'. 'Mr. Richardson was ever generous to excess; a circumstance with which Dr. Johnson was well acquainted, and which he ought to have noticed in a very different manner; especially, since he himself, as before observed, had been so much the object of his liberality.'[78]

[77] *Boswell's Journal of a Tour to the Hebrides*, pp. 386–7.   [78] *Universal Magazine*, LXXVII, 20–1.

All of Johnson's public remarks about Richardson were complimentary, and everyone knows what a sharp tongue he had in private conversation— we can hardly wish that it had been less sharp. Mrs. Piozzi recorded that Johnson once said 'that if Mr. Richardson had lived till *I* came out, my praises would have added two or three years to his life: "For," says Dr. Johnson, "that fellow died merely for want of change among his flatterers: he perished for want of *more*, like a man obliged to breathe the same air till it is exhausted."'[79]

Boswell relates an anecdote he had learned from a literary lady and which Johnson, who was present, 'appeared to enjoy' very much. A gentleman just returned from Paris told Richardson that he had seen a copy of *Clarissa* lying on the table of the king's brother. 'Richardson observing that part of the company were engaged in talking to each other, affected then not to attend to it. But by and by, when there was a general silence, and he thought that the flattery might be fully heard, he addressed himself to the gentleman, "I think, Sir, you were saying something about,—" pausing in a high flutter of expectation. The gentleman provoked at his inordinate vanity, resolved not to indulge it, and with an exquisitely sly air of indifference answered, "A mere trifle, Sir, not worth repeating." The mortification of Richardson was visible, and he did not speak ten words more the whole day.'[80]

Sir John Hawkins also gives us a picture of Richardson's vanity, as well as of his inadequacy in general conversation: 'Richardson's conversation was of the preceptive kind, but it wanted the diversity of Johnson's, and had no intermixture of wit and humour. Richardson could never relate a pleasant story, and hardly relish one told by another: he was ever thinking of his own writings, and listening to the praises which, with an emulous profusion, his friends were incessantly bestowing on them, he would scarce enter into free conversation with any one that he thought had not read "Clarissa," or "Sir Charles Grandison," and at best, he could not be said to be a companionable man.'[81]

There is no reason to doubt any of this. One would not have expected Richardson to be witty in conversation; he certainly had not an intellect like Johnson's. But Johnson was for some time his close friend and remembered him with affection. Boswell, who did not like Richardson's novels, for all his extraordinary memory for the great man's words, forgot almost all of the character of Richardson which Johnson, 'with a strong yet delicate pencil', drew at the house of Mr. Nairne, remembering only in general that Johnson 'expressed a high opinion of his talents and

[79] *Autobiography Letters and Literary Remains*, ed. Abraham Hayward (London, 1861), I, 311.
[80] *Life*, IV, 28n–29n.
[81] *Life of Samuel Johnson*, p. 384.

virtues', but he recalled in detail the remarks about Richardson's vanity and love of female admirers.[82]

Miss Frances Cotterell, who had never seen Richardson and was employed by a female friend to get a book printed, waited a long time in his parlour and found the bookcases 'entirely filled with Richardson's own works translated into most of the European languages', which she took as 'parade'.[83] As to his love of his own written words, Isaac Disraeli says that Mrs. Lennox, 'a regular visitor at Richardson's', told him that 'she could scarcely recollect one visit which was not taxed by our author reading one of his voluminous letters, or two or three, if his auditor was quiet and friendly'.[84] Hazlitt records an evening party at Lamb's when the subject of discussion was 'Persons One Would Wish to Have Seen': ' "Richardson?"—"By all means, but only to look at him through the glass-door of his back-shop, hard at work upon one of his novels (the most extraordinary contrast that ever was presented between an author and his works), but not . . . to go upstairs with him, lest he should offer to read the first manuscript of Sir Charles Grandison, which was originally written in eight-and-twenty volumes octavo, or get out the letters of his female correspondents, to prove that Joseph Andrews was low." '[85] It is this love of admiration, together with the female worshippers, which Thackeray stresses in his brief sketch of Richardson in *The Virginians*.[86]

That Richardson set some limit to the amount of adulation he was able to swallow, at least in public, is shown by the fact that in revising his correspondence, with possible publication in his mind, he noted on some letters from Aaron Hill and his daughters that the praise was too high and cut in others a few of the compliments. When, for instance, Hill wrote that one of his daughters was 'awe'd, by your vast Genius', Richardson struck out the word 'vast'.[87] He was upset by some of the compliments in Stinstra's introduction to the Dutch translation of *Clarissa*, especially by the mention of five bishops, friends of his, who had praised it, and offered to pay for altering the preface in as many copies as possible. When he found that most of the copies were sold, he mentioned that one of the bishops might resent it if he discovered that Richardson had reported his sentiments, so that his offer probably does not show that he had learned much from the ridicule that had been heaped on the praises published in the introduction to *Pamela*. But later, when reporting that the two eldest princes were reading *Sir Charles*, he cautioned Stinstra not to repeat the fact. And he also cautioned him against printing the admiring letters he

[82] *Boswell's Journal of a Tour to the Hebrides*, pp. 386–7.

[83] Elizabeth Smart Le Noir to Cuthbert Sharp, 22 Aug. 1831, quoted by Sherbo, 'Anecdotes by Mrs. Le Noir', p. 167.

[84] *Curiosities of Literature* (New York, 1877), II, 227.

[85] *Works*, XVII, 129.

[86] Chap. xxvi.

[87] 29 July, 8 Dec. 1741.

had sent him—though he added that if Stinstra wanted to use them, he would ask the writers' permission.[88]

Richardson was undoubtedly naïve in the openness with which he showed his pride in his achievement and in the recognition it gained for him. Whether his pride was really greater than that of other writers can be questioned. Much fun has recently been made of the frankness with which Norman Mailer brags about himself, but one might hold that it is his frankness rather than his self-assurance that is remarkable. And Richardson, after all, had some reason, considering his opportunities, to be proud of his achievement. When one remembers the poor apprentice from Tower Hill, it is hard to blame Richardson for wanting others to know that he was going to dine with Ralph Allen at Prior Park: 'Twenty years ago', he is reported to have added, 'I was the most obscure man in Great Britain; and now I am admitted to the company of the first characters in the kingdom.'[89] This seems to us to show lack of sophistication, but nothing much more reprehensible. Even Dante admitted (with some reason) that he would have to pass a considerable time in the circle of pride. And he surely has much literary company there. Unless one is to judge Richardson by the standard of the saints, we think that his vanity may well be forgiven him—at least that it is high time for it to be forgotten, since it has certainly received enough attention and to spare. One of the few who does not sneer at Richardson for it is Augustine Birrell, who admits it but adds that it 'afforded nobody anything but pleasure. The vanity of a distinguished man, if at the same time he happens to be a good man, is a quality so agreeable in its manifestations that to look for it and not to find it would be to miss a pleasure.'[90]

As for the circle of females, Richardson obviously enjoyed associating with admiring women and was proud of the ones his talents had attracted to him. Even in his will he mentioned the many ladies who had honoured him with their friendship. To Stinstra he wrote, 'I am envied Sir, for the Favour I stand in with near a Score of very admirable Women, some of them of Condition: all of them such as would do Credit to their Sex, and to the Commonwealth of Letters, did not their Modesty with-hold them from appearing in it. Yet with Several of them, I have charming Contentions, on different Parts of what I have written.'[91]

Yet it seems to us that the picture of Richardson as the happy centre of a group of admiring (and rather silly) women has been over-emphasized.

[88] R to Stinstra, 12 June 1753; Stinstra to R, 23 June 1753; R to Stinstra, 4 July 1753, 28 June 1754.

[89] Richard Graves, 'Trifling Anecdotes of the Late Ralph Allen, Esq. of Prior Park, near Bath', *The Triflers* (London, 1806), p. 68. Graves dates this incident 'about the year 1752'; it must have taken place in the summer of 1753, when Richardson was in Bath with Sally Chapone.

[90] 'Samuel Richardson', *Res Judicatæ* (New York, 1892), p. 36.   [91] 2 June 1753.

Typical is the statement of Mr. McKillop: 'Incapable as he was of meeting men like Garrick, Fielding, and Johnson on equal terms, Richardson preferred, in the years after *Clarissa*, to withdraw into his own little world of cotton-wool and compliments. . . . He was uneasy in the presence of scholars and wits. . . . He was now happiest in his own circle of admirers—mostly women, but with a few docile and complaisant men as well—discussing questions of propriety and principle in endless correspondence and conversation, and inhaling any quantity of incense smoke.'[92]

There is certainly some truth in the portrait of Richardson among the ladies. But we know of no evidence that he was unable to meet Garrick, say, on equal terms. His quarrel with Fielding can be explained without assuming a subconscious sense of inferiority on Richardson's part. Undoubtedly he recognized that he was inferior to Dr. Johnson in wit and learning—as he was; but this recognition did not prevent their intimacy, which contributed 'much to the happiness of both'.[93] Young was a wit and a scholar with whom Richardson was intimate long before and long after the composition of *Sir Charles Grandison*; Aaron Hill and Thomas Edwards were at least scholars, and they were not stupid. The latter was a new and close friend at this time, and there was no reason for him to be docile or complaisant unless it was his genuine feeling of admiration and liking. Nor did Joseph Spence have to truckle to Richardson, nor Benjamin Kennicott, nor Philip Skelton, nor Patrick Delany, nor Colley Cibber. Of his female admirers at least two, Mrs. Carter and Miss Mulso, had qualities which won the admiration of Dr. Johnson. Mrs. Delany and Mrs. Donnellan and even Lætitia Pilkington had earlier charmed Swift, and Mrs. Delany was later praised highly by Burke.[94]

In addition, the picture of Richardson drawn from his correspondence is necessarily one-sided. It does not reflect, for instance, his fast and enduring friendship with the Speaker of the House of Commons, who mentions enjoying his company, or with the various civil servants mentioned in his will and in passing elsewhere, or with such colleagues in the trade as the Rivingtons, the Osborns, Millar, and Gosling. All through his life a great deal of his time was devoted to business, and apparently the men with whom he associated respected him highly. He wrote mainly to people outside London, and he wrote many of his longest and chattiest letters to women—who, among other things, had more time to write. With these qualifications, it is quite true that Richardson enjoyed talking and writing to women.

He was sensitive with people who might think themselves above him. Lady Echlin was anxious for her daughter, Mrs. Palmer, to meet her

[92] *Richardson*, p. 189.   [93] Northcote, *Memoirs of Sir Joshua Reynolds*, p. 46.
[94] Mrs. Delany, *Autobiography and Correspondence*, ed. Lady Llanover, 2nd Series (London, 1862), II, 12; *Diary and Letters of Madame D'Arblay*, III, 421.

epistolary friend, but their acquaintance never ripened. Mrs. Palmer called once, with Lady Bradshaigh. Richardson wrote to her mother: ' "You kindly hope that I will not drop my new Acquaintance, your beloved Daughter, on Lady B's leaving London." I drop Mrs. Palmer!—Alas! I never had the Pleasure of seeing her but once—I am very shy of obtruding myself on Persons of Condition,—The Favour of a repeated Visit must proceed from her, as she only before accompanied Lady B. And then the Condescention will be acknowleged as such, with all due Gratitude. But Temple-Bar is looked upon as a Bar indeed, that divides the two Ends of the Town. Mrs. Palmer, with all her Goodness, might be reproached for passing it, in favour of a Citizen.' Lady Echlin replied with the hope that Mrs. Palmer could not be so unlike her mother as to be 'so foolishly courtly', and Richardson retreated somewhat: 'I was very far from imputing the Dislike of City *Visits*, merely *as such*, to the amiable young Lady I so much admired at her *first*. What I wrote on that Subject respected generally the Fashion, and not that particular Lady. I owe the Misfortune of not being better known (I dare say) to Mrs. Palmer rather to Lady B's much regretted Illness of so long Duration, than to Mrs. Palmer's want of Condescention.' 'I have the Vanity to hope, that did I endeavour personally to cultivate ye Favour of this fine young Lady, as her good Mamma and Aunt encouraged me to do, and as the Man, in such a Case, should think it his Duty to do, I should not have been repulsed, *so* recommended and favoured. But in Cases where the Favour must be done me, from Condescention, on Acct. of our different Stations in Life, I cannot help being backward.'[95] Richardson later saw Mrs. Palmer more than once at Mrs. Donnellan's, and the two ladies called at Parson's Green when he was not there.[96] When Mrs. Palmer's husband died, he so far forgot his pride (he was always willing enough to do so with those who were unfortunate) as to invite her through Lady Bradshaigh to stay at Parson's Green, an invitation she did not accept.[97]

Two years before Mrs. Palmer's appearance he had written to Mrs. Delany that there was a bar between him and Mrs. Donnellan, 'Temple-bar—ladies who live near Hill-street, and Berkeley and Grosvenor squares, love not to pass this bar.'[98] And he feared that Miss Sutton would be deterred by the nuisances east of Temple Bar; 'as her acquaintances are in the upper life, that upper life is low enough to despise the metropolis, which furnishes them with all their beloved luxury'.[99] Of an acquaintance of Lady

---

[95] 28 May, 20 June, 7 July, 15 Dec. 1755.

[96] R to Lady Echlin, 22 June 1756; Lady Echlin to R, 2 Aug. 1756.

[97] R to Lady Bradshaigh, 4 Apr. 1756; R to Lady Echlin, 4 May 1756.

[98] 14 Mar. 1753. The original of this letter is lost. Barbauld (IV, 79) gives the name as 'Mrs. Desbrough', the name for Mrs. Donnellan in Richardson's revision of his letters for possible publication (see R to Lady Bradshaigh, 29 May 1756).

[99] R to Mrs. Dewes, 21 June 1752.

Bradshaigh's who did not like *Sir Charles*, he wrote that if she had thought him from her side of Temple Bar she would have thought his hero more genteel.[100]

His hurt reaction to Fulke Greville's criticism was at least partly stimulated by his knowledge that Greville came from a class above his: Greville, he said, was perhaps 'as much too high-bred' as he himself was too low. But his sensitiveness was not directed only towards the upper classes; it appears clearly in his early dealings with Hildesley, for instance, and probably in the fact that, as he told Samuel Lobb, he always made his young ladies begin the correspondence.[101] And Greville's criticism stung him little more than Hill's well-meant and polite efforts to revise *Clarissa*, as Richardson himself had asked, which called forth an effusion of self-depreciation, a (temporary) resolve not to publish his novel, and an almost bitter request that Hill look on him only as a printer. There is no doubt that Richardson was generally sensitive to slight and criticism.

He always recognized himself as a member of the middle class and congratulated himself on having risen from its lower fringes almost to its heights. Perhaps it was his low origin combined with pride that made him stress his desire for independence. 'I never sought out of myself for patrons', he informed de Freval, apparently truly. 'My own industry, and God's providence, have been my whole reliance. The great are not great to me, unless they are good. And it is a glorious privilege, that a middling man enjoys who has preserved his independency, and can occasionally (though not Stoically) tell the world, what he thinks of that world, in hopes to contribute, though but by his mite, to mend it.'[102] He told Stinstra that though he had gained the favour of several persons of rank and fortune he had never courted it by flattery. There were no dedicatory epistles, he boasted, in his works. 'I will be bold to say, that never Man of a small Fortune, and obscure Birth and Station, was more independent. God and my own Diligence were ever my chief Reliance.'[103] A good middle-class sentiment, but not necessarily for that reason an insincere one. Ideally one might regret that he mentioned with such satisfaction the persons of rank who had, uncourted, befriended him. But he was, after all, living in the eighteenth century. There are a few letters to great personages couched in terms of the politeness of his day, which may seem servile to us; but they are brief and restrained. His manner to those members of the gentry he knew personally—Lady Bradshaigh, Miss Talbot, and Young, for instance—was not at all servile.

He disliked being under an obligation, though he loved to confer obligations. 'You love to give as much as a Miser does to receive', wrote Dr. Cheyne, who had a long friendly struggle with Richardson about

[100] 30 May 1754.
[102] 21 Jan. 1751.

[101] 4 July 1746.
[103] 2 June 1753.

which was under obligation to the other. 'Peggy [Miss Cheyne] says you are the perfect original of your own Pamela, and that Generosity and Giving which in others are only acquired Virtues are in you a natural Passion and as others (the best) only like to give as much as to receive, you only like to give.'[104] There is a touch of the older middle-class commercial pride in this trait, as well as of Richardson's love of independence.

We know of only one bit of evidence that he tried to rise above his own class. On at least one letter, to Samuel Lobb, and on his will, he used a seal with arms similar to those rightfully used by several genteel families of Richardsons, but not identical with any. The arms had never been granted him by the College of Arms, and the seal was evidently a result of mild vanity.[105] When Mrs. Donnellan asked him whether he was related to Sir Thomas Richardson (as he was not) he 'replied with a smile "He believe[d] He was"—or to that purpose'—or so his unreliable daughter Anne remembered being told.[106]

Richardson's leading characters rise in rank from *Pamela* to *Sir Charles*. He objected to the fact that one of the heroines of *Sir William Harrington*, Miss Randall, who was to be introduced to genteel company, should lodge with a haberdasher in the Strand.[107] But there is no adulation of the aristocracy in his novels. In the *Familiar Letters* he had made slighting remarks about mere aristocrats,[108] and there is no reason to think that he changed his mind, though he was willing enough to show the usual respect for the aristocracy, from a distance. Perhaps he would have liked to lessen the distance, but if so his pride or his discretion kept him from showing it. His daughters, he wrote to Miss Highmore, were not to expect the diversions proper to 'girls of fortune and fashion': 'Girls of middle families, middle life, such as my own in particular, I would only indulge in seeing every thing, and partaking in every thing innocent, in the public diversions, once, twice, thrice in the season; and not so often as *thrice*, if I saw that they were likely to be drawn from domestic usefulness by the indulgence.'[109]

---

[104] 27 Jan., 14 Jan. 1743.

[105] Eaves and Kimpel, 'Samuel Richardson and His Family Circle', p. 347.

[106] To Martha Bridgen, 10 July 1784, MS. owned by Alan Dugald McKillop.

[107] Eaves and Kimpel, 'Richardson's Connection with *Sir William Harrington*', p. 280.

[108] Letter 155. [109] 26 Nov. 1749.

CHAPTER XXII

RICHARDSON'S GENERAL IDEAS

RICHARDSON was certainly not consciously in favour of any major changes in society as he knew it, though some of the implications of his novels may have led others to be so. Several of L'Estrange's versions of Æsop's *Fables* had pointed out the necessity of social classes, so obvious to everyone in his day, and Richardson, while revising other kinds of political reflections, left these little changed. 'What would become of the Universe, if there were not Servants as well as Masters? . . . If there were not Instruments for Drudgery, as well as Offices of Drudgery? If there were not People to receive and execute Orders, as well as others to give and authorize them?'[1] 'Surely he had a vested interest in trying to preserve those conventions of the social order in which his own small authority rested', says Mr. Brissenden.[2] Surely he did. But in Richardson's day people were not conscious of the influence of vested interests on their opinions and did not know that they should feel guilty about profiting from the social order.

He several times expressed his view of the high value of the trading class in Great Britain. Early, in *The Apprentice's Vade Mecum*, he said that tradesmen 'are infinitely of more Consequence, and deserve more to be incourag'd, than any other Degree or Rank of People' in the kingdom.[3] Twenty years later Sir Charles Grandison, aristocrat that he is, encourages the young Danby family as they go into business: 'The merchants of Great Britain are the most useful members of the community.' 'But what', he says in speaking of the genealogical table of his cousin Grandison, 'in a nation, the glory and strength of which are trade and commerce, is gentility!'[4] In a nation fast becoming a nation of shopkeepers, this was almost a statement of fact.

Clarissa has been read as, on one level, 'a lengthly parable on the anti-thesis of the aristocratic and familiar [middle-class] codes, to demonstrate the superiority of the latter'.[5] Even without subscribing to allegorical

---

[1] L'E No. 191; R No. 147. [2] *Richardson*, p. 9.
[3] P. 11. [4] SH, II, 259; VI, 143.
[5] Downs, *Richardson*, p. 182; Van Ghent, *English Novel*, pp. 56–7. Mrs. Van Ghent sees the book as a mythical fulfilment of 'the wish to embody in the middle class itself the universal order, both divine and social', thus counteracting the middle-class wish to become aristocratic: 'What Richardson tells his readers is that the middle class, to see an image of what is socially

interpretations, one can agree that the values in Richardson's novels are the values of his class. At times, as in Lovelace, the aristocracy is immoral in the style of the Restoration immorality which Addison and Steele had attacked; more often, as in Lovelace's uncle, Lord M., and in Sir Charles, the aristocracy itself accepts middle-class morality—as it was doing in reality. Richardson thus typifies the English middle class, which did not so much rebel against the aristocracy as absorb it, even while reserving for it a measure of cautious respect.

David Daiches has justly emphasized the importance of society in Richardson's novels, not so much in the class struggle as in the conception that inner struggles are not merely private but are 'carried out in full view of society and conditioned by the structure of society'—'Richardson was the first important English writer to deal with basic moral problems imaginatively in a detailed social context.'[6] Certainly Richardson saw his characters in complex association with a wide circle of relations, friends, and acquaintances; both their stories and their values are largely determined by that circle. But this is not to say that his novels are interesting primarily for what they tell us about the social structure—only that they are inconceivable except in terms of that social structure.

The poor, Richardson seems to have felt, will always be with us, and therefore we need not worry too much about them, though we should of course treat them kindly. In an age of increased social consciousness, Mrs. Andrew Lang found Richardson's 'views about the inferior classes . . . altogether so singular that one would think that he, like Marie Antoinette, had never crossed the path of any but the well-to-do'.[7] As Grandmother Shirley sagely observed to Harriet Byron, 'The honest poor . . . are a very valuable part of the creation.' Sir Charles has a library for his servants, divided into three classes: divinity and morality; housewifery; and history, true adventures, voyages, and innocent amusement. But much education is not necessary for the poor unless they display special talents. 'I could be glad', Sir Charles writes to Dr. Bartlett, 'that only such children of the poor as shew a particular ingenuity, have any great pains taken with them in their *books*. Husbandry and labour are what are most wanting to be encouraged among the lower class of people. Providence has given to men different genius's and capacities, for different ends; and that all might become useful links of the same great chain.'[8] He is, of course, expressing the opinion of his time. So is Clarissa when she says that she pities Dorcas for her neglected education only because Dorcas regrets it, 'Else, there would not be much in it; as the Low and Illiterate are the most useful people in the commonwealth (since such

and morally desirable, need not look beyond itself, but will find that image in what it already is.'   [6] *Literary Essays*, pp. 27–8, 35.

[7] 'Morals and Manners in Richardson', p. 775.   [8] SH, I, 144; VI, 45; IV, 156.

constitute the labouring part of the public); and as a Lettered Education but too generally sets people above those servile offices, by which the business of the world is carried on. Nor have I any doubt, that there are, take the world thro', twenty happy people among the Unlettered, to one among those who have had a School Education.'[9] The superior happiness of the poor as well as their superior goodness (what Bertrand Russell calls 'The Superior Virtue of the Oppressed') is a comforting belief. 'I have sometimes thought', writes Clarissa, 'that (even take number for number) there are more *honest low people*, than *honest high*.'[10] Perhaps universal education is still too new for us to decide whether Sir Charles and Clarissa were right about the need of the common man for book learning.

The poor most likely to be brought to the attention of the writing classes in the eighteenth century were servants. Richardson's heroines urge that they be treated considerately, as human beings, and there is no reason to think that their creator did not live up to their precepts, though undoubtedly he was strict by modern standards. Clarissa shows delicacy when she says that she would not lock everything away from the servants, since she would not keep servants she had reason to suspect: 'People in low station have often minds not sordid.' Pamela tells Miss Goodwin that good servants deserve civil distinction, and 'so long as they were ready to oblige her in every thing, by a kind Word, it would be very wrong to give them imperative ones'. She also believes that servants should be made to understand that 'Sobriety of Manners, and a virtuous Conversation' are demanded of them, that their masters should not only make it clear that no breaches of this kind will be tolerated but should themselves educate their servants in virtue by their example.[11] It is easy to see why Richardson admired the strict and pious, but not unkind, rules which Lady Bradshaigh drew up for her women. Among other things, they were to attend church regularly, weather permitting; 'Never tell a *Lye* upon any account'; perform orders without grumbling, for 'willingness, & good nature, are half a servant'; not be fond 'of gadding abroad, Tattleing, Gossiping, private Feasting or junketing'; not take snuff or drink tea, 'Two very pernicious & expensive things'; dress plainly and neatly; beware of the men, and not keep company unless, at a proper age, they intend to marry; avoid quarreling and scolding; have due respect to superiors; rise at six and go to bed at ten, and breakfast, dine, and sup regularly and all together at fixed hours and in the places appointed. 'But above all things,' she exhorted, 'keep yourselves *Honest*, for your souls sake in the next world, as well as for your reputation in This.'[12] To his

[9] SH, IV, 157–8; EL, II, 343.   [10] SH, II, 159; EL, I, 348.
[11] *Clarissa*, SH, II, 159, EL, I, 348; *Pamela*, SH, IV, 278–9, 329, EL, II, 360, 392.
[12] These rules were dated by Richardson 2 Oct. 1757, FM XI, fos. 219–20. For Richardson's approval, see his letter to Lady Bradshaigh, 19 Nov.

own maidservants, Richardson left three guineas each for mourning, which they probably thought generous enough.

It is evident Richardson had no intention of changing the class structure of England. Yet *Pamela* seemed to point the moral that under certain conditions a man might marry his servant girl. Richardson took considerable pains to show that this apparent moral was illusory, that Pamela's case was so exceptional that no one else could take it as an example. Nor did he ever clarify the implications of *Clarissa* about the limits of parental authority and the position of women, though Miss Mulso and Mrs. Chapone tried to get him to do so. It is clear that insofar as these books might have an effect on readers they would weaken the rigidity of the class structure and cause readers to doubt whether parents should have absolute control over children or men over women; the emotions roused work in this direction, whatever logical or illogical intellectual arguments Richardson might use. When he wrote as Pamela or Clarissa, Richardson must have shared the feelings he roused; but when he reflected, he had no desire to follow through.

Richardson's political views do not seem to have played a large part in his life. We have described how when he first set up as a printer he got involved with the 'high flyers', the Tories suspected of favouring the Pretender. But there are no signs of Jacobite leanings in his later life. The account of the '45 added at the end of the 1748 edition of Defoe's *Tour*, though factual and moderate in tone, shows no sentiment but loyalty to the House of Hanover and is especially warm in its praise of the conduct of the Duke of Cumberland. Before the composition of *Pamela* he was printing the leading journal of the Walpole government. There is no proof that he was an ardent supporter of either side. In the *Familiar Letters* he satirized the one-sided virulence of party newspapers and took the occasion to have a very mild fling at Sir Robert Walpole.[13]

There are few political remarks in Richardson's novels. *Pamela* has more than the others, but they are rather conventional: there is much knavery in courts, kings should be subject to law, and party labels are odious; titles of nobility are at best but shadows and should not be highly prized; London is inadequately represented in Parliament (a sentiment also expressed in the revision of Defoe's *Tour*);[14] a member of Parliament should neither clog the wheels of government by unreasonable opposition nor be willing to do the dirty work of the administration, and his only party should be that of his country. Lord M. in *Clarissa* cites with approval two sayings he attributes to Richardson's early customer, Archibald Hutcheson, to the effect that a member of Parliament should vote for the administration whenever he conscientiously can and not 'needlessly put

[13] Letter 76.
[14] 2nd edn., II, 186.

Drags upon the Wheels of Government' and that since neither an opposition nor a ministry can be always wrong, a man who is 'a plumb man' with either is suspect. That perfect representative of English gentry Sir Charles Grandison avoids a public life, though he is willing to employ his advantages of rank and education for the service of his fellow-men by serving as a magistrate, and may, when somewhat older and less warm-natured, agree to represent his county in Parliament if he can do so without engagements to either party.[15]

Richardson agreed with Aaron Hill's unqualified censure of the political opinions found in Milton's prose writings: 'Indulging a licentious Independency, on Religion, on Manners, or Policy, [Milton] was for pulling down Authority, till it came to *His* Level, that his Anger might have Nothing to fear nor his Pride a Superior, to flatter.'[16] But this is probably no more than a sign of his moderation. He seems in later life to have kept himself carefully detached from either party and to have expressed only opinions which most Englishmen would have shared.

A slight Whig bias is possibly shown by his high praise of the Duke of Marlborough[17] and by his irritation at the opposition of the extreme Tories of Oxford to the government and the royal house during and after the election of 1754, which the Whigs won against violent opposition by the right-wing Tories. One of the leading Tory speakers, Dr. William King, Principal of St. Mary Hall and known for his Jacobite sympathies, was denounced by Richardson in a letter to one of King's strongest opponents, Benjamin Kennicott: 'Old, yet so abandoned of decency! So much a reviler of the powers that be! Such a rebel, as I may call him, to the doctrines of Christianity, and so great a stranger to that meekness and submission, which are its characteristics! . . . Do you think any other government, but that of the present family, would not have given active tokens of their resentment against a body under its protection, who, forty years ago, chose a chancellor [the Earl of Arran, brother of the Duke of Ormonde] in despight of it, whose whole merit was, that he was the brother of a perjured, yet weak, rebel . . .? . . . But what am I about? Running into politics! I have long laid aside so contemptible a subject.'[18] He wished, however, that the election 'had never been so warmly contested,' since if the 'Loyalists' won, 'the Feuds raised will not so soon subside, as to give any Hope of the University's Reformation'.[19] To Thomas Edwards he wrote on 30 May 1755, congratulating him on the results of the election: instead of Whigs and Tories, he would call the two

---

[15] *Pamela*, SH, II, 229–30, III, 171, IV, 4, 140, EL, I, 365, II, 93, 225, 281; *Clarissa*, SH, IV, 257–8, EL, II, 411; *Grandison*, SH, VI, 287–8, V, 179.

[16] Hill to R, 29 May, 1 June 1738.

[17] To Hill, 2 Apr., 7 Apr. 1743; to Susanna Highmore, 4 June 1750.

[18] 15 July.

[19] To Edwards, 23 Feb. 1755.

parties in that election Loyalists and Faction and thus turn the tables on 'ye Tories, & perjur'd High Churchmen: And let us not humour them wth: ye Distinctions of *Old & New Interest*; for is not ye latter [the Whig or Loyalist interest] ye Constitutional Interest; ye Interest of ye Country?' He is here blaming the principles upheld by Bishop Atterbury and the Duke of Wharton, praising the Hanoverians as guardians of liberty (if anything, of too much liberty), and recommending submission to the government as a proper Christian virtue. Whatever his early ties with the Jacobites, by 1751 he was undoubtedly sincere when he exclaimed to Edwards, 'God long preserve the invaluable Life of our Patriot King.'[20]

His patriotism is occasionally apparent, though not obtrusive. He added to Æsop's fable of a Lion and Bulls the example of the Grand Alliance, when a separate peace made by one power enabled the King of France to bring the rest to terms and afterwards 'in some sort, to give Laws to the rest of Christendom'.[21] Pamela travels abroad with her husband for nearly two years, but she is happy to get back and to end her rambles for life, to bring back 'an Heart as intirely *English* as ever'. She discovered on the Continent that 'an *English* Gentleman is respected, if he be any thing of a Man, above a foreign Nobleman; and an *English* Nobleman, above some petty Sovereigns'. Sir Charles is 'in the noblest sense, a Citizen of the World'; but 'his long residence abroad, has only the more endeared to him the Religion, the Government, the Manners of England'. He wants to encourage the trade and manufacture of his own country by buying English and discourages the aping of foreign fashions, which 'carries Wealth and Power to those whose National Religion and Interest are directly opposite to ours'.[22] Nevertheless, throughout the novel Richardson is remarkably fair to the Italian Catholics and shows that he himself, though nationalistic as a tradesman, was more a citizen of the world than one would have expected.

Though he supported his country in the Seven Years' War, he was anything but an ardent militarist. Sir Charles will not fight, 'even in a national cause, without examining the justice of it'—a measure of the change during the past two centuries, since such a stand could now land that model of propriety in jail. He has made one campaign abroad, as a volunteer, and felt the ardour roused by martial movements; but he would not again undertake foreign service or engage unless his country were unjustly invaded. He dislikes the life of a soldier, 'whose trade is in blood' and who is a slave to his superiors. As for military glory: 'The word and thing called *Glory*, what mischief has it not occasioned!'[23] Homer's *Iliad*, Richardson wrote to Belfour, has 'done infinite mischief

[20] 2 May.   [21] L'E No. 236; R No. 179.
[22] *Pamela*, SH, IV, 382–8, EL, II, 425–9; *Grandison*, SH, VI, 11.
[23] SH, I, 403–4; II, 195–6.

for a series of ages', since to it 'and its copy the Eneid, is owing, in a great measure, the savage spirit that has actuated, from the earliest ages to this time, the fighting fellows, that, worse than lions or tigers, have ravaged the earth, and made it a field of blood'.[24] Soldiers, says Sir Charles, value themselves too highly 'on their knowledge of what, after all, one may call but their trade'.[25] The old Romans, Richardson told Miss Highmore, from whom 'our university-men, and dramatic-writers' borrow their heroes, were 'abominable fellows, thieves, robbers, plunderers', who proceeded 'from robbery to robbery' to conquer most of the known world—the Turks are 'a much better people'. And he subscribed to Aaron Hill's sentiment 'Mankind's my country'; 'nobody can have more universality of love to the whole human species than myself'.[26]

When, in 1755, rumours of war with France began to spread, Richardson was ready to call the French 'a Nation of mischievous Monkeys' and to wish that their kingdom were split into three: 'How often am I ready to execrate our Utrecht Negotiators!'[27] But in the same year he wrote to Clairaut regretting the 'National Misunderstandings': 'To what narrow bounds do those confine their Love, their Humanity, let me say, who make it merely *National*. An *Universal* Philanthropy (a Ray of the Divine Nature!) can be only worthy of an enlarged Mind.'[28] He refers several times to his worry about public affairs during this period. In 1755 he wrote to Edwards about his alarm that the British coast might be invaded or the Papists in Ireland aroused and added that he regretted the impressment of seamen, torn from their families and left to the prey of wretches in offices—surely they could be recruited voluntarily. The next year he wrote to Lady Echlin, 'What a *Situation* are we in as to our Public Affairs! God Almighty amend *Us*, and *That*!' Shortly afterwards he wrote to Miss Talbot that he was disheartened by the public prospects but added, 'What *aduce* has such an obscure Mortal as I am, to do with Public Affairs!'[29] In 1757 he told Lady Bradshaigh that he was so upset at the dearth of corn and the avarice of wealthy corn dealers that 'I have sometimes, on this Occasion, been ready to suspend all my Patriotick Notions; & to wish for a temporary Despotism, a kind of Dictatorship, wch: shd: leave it in ye Royal Power, to punish or compel a few Private Wretches for ye Sake of ye Public'; but ministers will be men, and 'we are best as we are'.[30]

Early in 1758 he was worried about events in Germany and wondered what could save the 'bravest of Princes'.[31] He again complimented Frederick the Great when he wished that the English would follow a

[24] [Late Nov. 1749].   [25] SH, III, 187.   [26] 4 June 1750.
[27] To Edwards, 27 Jan.   [28] 12 Sept.   [29] 23 Feb., 25 Aug., 25 Oct.
[30] 27 May.
[31] To Lady Bradshaigh, 2 Jan.

policy in Ireland more like that of the King of Prussia in Silesia, one of moderation and harmony towards the Catholics. He was agreeing with a treatise written by Smyth Loftus urging that the Irish Catholics be won over to the English cause (the nation was at war and needed volunteers) by a more humane and tolerant treatment: 'Cannot we . . . make such a brave and sturdy people, if not immediately protestants, patriots; and active in behalf of those who pay them, and give them protection in their civil concerns?'[32]

He was certainly no proponent of the freedom of the press: he regretted to Young that no legal authority stood sentinel over it, to prevent 'infidelity, indecency, libel, faction, nonsense'.[33] He evidently favoured the act permitting persons professing the Jewish religion to be naturalized by Parliament and deplored 'the foolish, the absurd Cry' against it; but he thought that the Jews themselves would be well advised to ask for its repeal, since they got little by it and it excited popular prejudice against them 'in a Country which they honour for the Liberty of Conscience and the Safety of Property given them in it'.[34]

As early as 1739, when he was working on the Roe papers, he was clearly in favour of moderation. His preface praises Roe's role during the Civil War, when Sir Thomas stood 'in an unexceptionable light with both parties' until 'the publick distempers of the nation grew too violent and raging to be assuaged by his moderate counsels'. It would have been happy, Richardson adds, for king and for nation had his 'wise and healing measures' been followed. Richardson's compendium comments favourably on a letter dissuading Sir Maurice Berkeley from engaging 'in the cause of the malcontents against the court'. 'We are by nature prone enough to liberty', Richardson summarizes, 'and every suggestion of that should be suspected to us.' And Richardson adds that this letter 'will give the reader a beautiful foretaste of the honest part this able minister acted in the following times of confusion'.[35] He was, above all, in favour of peace. 'I am no politician, but I cannot help thinking that we feel so many blessings, which must be the effect of an easy good government, that I am always shocked at any attempt to sow sedition and discontent among the people.'[36] This pretty well sums up his political stand, at least during his last years.

---

[32] 25 May.

[33] 14 Jan. 1757. One of the strangest readings of *Pamela* and *Clarissa* interprets them as allegorical attacks on the Licensing Act of 1737 (R. Baird Shuman, 'Censorship as a Controlling Theme in "Pamela" and "Clarissa"', *N&Q*, N.S. III [1956], 30–2).

[34] To Elizabeth Carter, 17 Aug. 1753. See also his letter to her of 13 Aug. 1753.

[35] Letter CDLXXIII, p. xlv.

[36] When we copied this quotation, we carelessly neglected to note its source, and we cannot now locate it; but we are reasonably certain that we did not dream it. It will be a considerable relief if anyone can tell us where in Richardson's letters or works it occurs.

On religion he undoubtedly had stronger convictions, but in his non-fictional utterances he rarely reached the high, unworldly view of Christianity expressed by Clarissa. Presumably Richardson was born and brought up in the Church of England—at least he was baptized in it and adhered to it in later life. We hear very little, however, about his connection with the church. For many years his nervous malady forced him to forego attendance at divine services because he could not appear in crowds (he was not prevented from mixing freely in more private society). Even before his illness he does not, judging by the Vestry Minute Books of St. Bride's, seem to have played an active role in his parish—he did serve as questman in 1726–7, but he paid the usual fines to avoid serving as collector of rates or as church warden.[37] We find no mention of any relations with the various incumbents of St. Bride's, his own parish, except that he knew the daughter of one of them, Richard Bundy.

At least as early as 1733, when he printed his *Apprentice's Vade Mecum*, he was earnest enough about religion to add, at the request of a friend, a section on religion, asserting confidently that morality without true religion is insufficient. Part III is directed against the 'Scoffers of the Age', that is the Deists, who 'bring down to the Level of their short-sighted Reason' the awful points of Faith. It avoids theology or the doctrines of any special church but is a strong argument in favour of Christian revelation, largely in the form of copious quotations from such authors as Jeremy Collier, Locke, and Addison. The mysteries are necessary and are kept dark by God to exercise our faith and reverence; science has as many mysteries of its own. Revelation is proved by the uniqueness of the Christian ethics, by the consistency of the Bible and the probability of its accounts, by the blood of the martyrs, and by the testimony of the heathens. Even if the Deists themselves are moral, how can they be sure the multitude will be? What can they hope for? Why, professing doubt, do they speak so certainly? The result of their efforts would be to loosen the bonds of human society, confound right and wrong, take away the terrors that hold back evil doers, 'tear up the Fences that inclose and preserve Property', and leave the weak to the mercies of the strong. The age is overrun with atheism, Deism, and infidelity—even morality is under attack, so that only the civil magistrates can protect our sisters and daughters from the lewd attempts of the modern sceptics.

Richardson printed a large number of religious books; whether it was unusually large for his time can only be decided after a general statistical study of the kinds of books then printed. He had several good clerical friends, at least one of whom, Young, can be called an intimate. There are a good many references to religion in his letters, especially in those to

[37] Guildhall MSS. 6554/4, under dates 19 Dec. 1726 and 30 Nov. 1725, and 6554/5, under date 10 Apr. 1735.

Young, but most of them are general and tell us little except that he was not a sceptic. Richardson has been accused of 'apathy towards religious matters' and of being 'strangely indifferent to religion except as a supernatural sanction of Morals'.[38] *Clarissa* itself, however, shows his deep concern with religion, as do his suggestions for revising Young's *Conjectures on Original Composition*.

It would be fairer to say that he was not much concerned with doctrine, though he undoubtedly thought of himself as orthodox. In the third edition of *Clarissa*, for instance, he added that in order for a rake to reform, 'a portion of divine *Grace*' is necessary and that a rake's attitude towards Grace is the shibboleth to test whether there is hope of his reformation—a remark he thought important enough to add in his own hand in the margin of a presentation copy of the first edition.[39] He once stated that if Lady Bradshaigh commanded he would 'give Swift's Sermon on the Trinity, a reading. But, as I hinted in my last, I have no notion of men's attempting to explain a mystery. In short, I am afraid of raising doubts in my own mind, which I cannot, from the nature of the subject, lay. All that concerns us to know for the conduct of our life, in order to fill us with a blessed hope, is plain and easy.'[40] Mr. Downs interprets this as an ingenuous admission that he would not risk losing his complacency.[41] One could as logically conclude that he knew himself to be an uneducated man, unfit to cope with such subtleties, and was content to confine himself to the simple, clear essentials of religion. Milton himself, though as a learned man he felt it his duty to work out his own theology, did not consider it necessary for every Christian to do so and held that the essential doctrines of Christianity are easy to grasp, so that no higher education is required even for a minister of the gospel. Richardson kept among his papers an extract from a letter of Mrs. Carter's to the effect that most religious controversies are 'wicked unchristian things': scripture alone should be consulted, and each Christian should interpret it as he sees fit.[42] 'The things we *must* believe, are *few* and *plain*', wrote Dryden before his conversion to Catholicism. And since Dryden's day Europe has continued to move away from polemic theology. It is hardly surprising that Richardson, who never considered himself an intellectual, avoided such matters.

One result was that he was comparatively tolerant. We have seen that he favoured the naturalization of the Jews; a long account is added to the

[38] Downs, *Richardson*, p. 58; Hornbeak, *Richardson's Familiar Letters and the Domestic Conduct Books*, p. 6n.

[39] SH, VIII, 67; EL, IV, 389. The 1st edn. (VII, 267) in the Widener Collection, Harvard University Library, contains the handwritten addition.

[40] 2 June 1753.   [41] *Richardson*, p. 58.

[42] FM XVI, 2, fo. 70. On the back of the extract is written 'Mr. Duncombe's from Miss Carter'.

1742 edition of Defoe's *Tour* of medieval persecution of the Jews of York, obviously disapproving.[43] Sir Charles, who may safely be assumed to express Richardson's own ideas, is of course religious, indeed a model of piety, though 'no bigot, no superstitious man'; he reflects that his piety should not be sunk 'in the boast of Benevolence, my Love of God in the Love of my fellow-creatures'. In other words, ethics without religion is not enough. He believes firmly in the church of his own country, but 'good manners will make me shew respect to the religion of the country I happen to be in, were it the Mahometan, or even the Pagan; and to venerate the good men of it'. He firmly refuses to join the Catholic Church for the sake of winning Clementina, but he will not interfere with her religion—he will even permit and respect her confessor, provided that when in England he does not try to convert others ('had I not insisted on it, I should have behaved towards my country in a manner for which I could not answer to my own heart'). When reminded of the disqualifications under which Catholics lie in England, he sidesteps an argument but in such a way as to imply that he does not favour the disqualifications: 'A great deal . . . may be said on this subject. I think it sufficient to answer for myself, and my own conduct.' And he reminds the Catholics that the Church of England does not confine salvation within its own pale. In addition to respecting the Catholics, he does not lecture on religion to the frivolous, 'he never frights gay company with grave maxims.'[44] The zealous may well consider him, and Richardson, lukewarm; modern liberal Christians may find them still too narrow. Perhaps all men of the world are Laodiceans; or perhaps all believing Christians are intolerant in holding that their belief is true, which implies that other beliefs are false. But many men in Richardson's day reconciled to their own satisfaction the claims of the world and those of God and felt no inconsistency. And many thought that tolerance means putting up with doctrines one disagrees with, not, as some people today assume, putting up with all doctrines because one disagrees with none. In other words, Richardson's religion, though not saintly or original, was more than enough to satisfy his times, and there is no reason to question his sincerity. He justifies in *Sir Charles* a comparative silence about religion: Harriet reminds Sir Hargrave that the future life 'is a very material consideration with me, tho' I am not fond of talking upon it, except on *proper* occasions, and to *proper* persons'.[45]

Richardson prided himself on his religious impartiality in *Sir Charles*. In July 1753 he wrote to Alexis Clairaut: 'I shall think myself unhappy, and shall be greatly disappointed, if I have not done as much Honour to the Lady [Clementina] for her Zeal and Stedfastness, and that from motives that could not be found fault with at Rome; as to the Gentleman; for to

---

[43] III, 152-5.
[44] SH, VI, 55-6; III, 71; IV, 238-41, 4.   [45] SH, I, 142.

both, and to all her Friends, I give equal Piety and Goodness: In short, this Part is one of those that I value myself most upon, having been as zealous a Catholic when I was to personate the Lady, and her Catholic Friends, as a Protestant, when I was the Gentleman.' A clergyman had told him that some would think him more a Catholic than a Protestant.[46] When he answered those who objected to the compromise by which Sir Charles agreed to let his daughters be brought up as Catholics, he avoided committing himself on Catholic marriages in general by stressing the peculiarity of Sir Charles's situation. In his history of Mrs. Beaumont even the most zealous Romans admire that lady for her moral virtues, and she lives on good terms with a Catholic family.[47] Among Richardson's papers is a poem called 'A Catholic Christian's Dying Speech'; the speaker belongs to the Church of England but holds that there is truth in all creeds and addresses the 'God of all Churches'.[48]

One other sect is mentioned several times in *Sir Charles*, the Methodists. Thomas Birch called Archbishop Tillotson Richardson's 'favourite',[49] and in the 1738 edition of Defoe's *Tour* is added a compliment to Tillotson, 'the Model of true rational Preaching'.[50] In 1742 is added the reflection that 'a new Sect, lately sprung up, called *Methodists*, with great Pretences to *Meekness*, and intolerable *Conceit* and *Vanity*, at present seek publicly to depreciate the Memory and Works of that truly great Man'.[51] The flippant Charlotte considers them '*overdoers*' who 'make religion look unlovely, and put *underdoers* out of heart'. But when they convert Mrs. O-Hara, she is ready to find great merit in them: 'I am sorry that our own Clergy are not as zealously in earnest as they. They have really . . . given a face of religion to subterranean colliers, tinners, and the most profligate of men, who hardly ever before heard either of the word, or thing.'[52] Richardson had printed William Law's *The Oxford Methodists* as early as 1733, and he also printed two of Whitefield's sermons. He must have heard Whitefield and been less than carried away with his emotional style of oratory: Lovelace speaks of an enthusiastic preacher whom he heard 'declare himself to be a *dead dog*; when every man, woman, and child, were convinced to the contrary by his howling'. In a note in Lady Bradshaigh's copy of *Clarissa* Richardson identified the preacher as Whitefield, which sounds as if he was drawing on his own reminiscence.[53] He blamed the Reverend James Hervey as 'too mystic', 'inclined to the

---

[46] 5 July.
[47] MS. in the Pierpont Morgan Library.   [48] FM XVI, 2, fo. 47.
[49] To Philip Yorke, 7 July 1753, B.M. Add. MS. 35,398, fo. 129.
[50] III, 83.   [51] III, 131.
[52] SH, IV, 187; V, 58. See also H. G. Ward, 'Samuel Richardson and the Methodists', *N&Q*, 11 S. III (1911), 124.
[53] 1st edn., VI, 283, copy owned by the late Commander Arthur Avalon MacKinnon of MacKinnon. The passage is in SH, VII, 5; EL, IV, 33.

enthusiastic part of Methodism'.[54] Insofar as the evidence goes, it appears that Richardson admired the piety and sincerity of the Methodists but thought that they went a little too far. His own religion was not 'enthusiastic': Sir Charles regrets that love or religion 'should ever run the human heart either into enthusiasm, or superstition; and thereby debase the minds they are both so well fitted to exalt'.[55] Sir Charles himself is certainly guilty of enthusiasm in neither love nor religion—indeed he may well be literature's least enthusiastic hero.

An orthodox eighteenth-century Christian could hardly deny that non-Christians might be damned, whatever their merits. But Richardson did not rejoice in their damnation, or in anyone's. When Sir John Stanley asked him to read a translation of Pierre Cuppé's *Le ciel ouvert à tous les hommes*, he replied that he 'had but little time to read any thing that I thought controversial, or shocking to fundamentals' but agreed to read it if Young considered it not heterodox.[56] He was interested in Hartley's doctrine of ultimate, unlimited happiness to all and hoped one day to read all of his *Observations on Man* (which he had printed), though he felt he could not hope to understand 'the abstruser Parts'. He could hope that the doctrine is true, but did not dare to decide, 'so fearful am I, of weakening Foundations', 'and the less, as I am interested to wish it to be so, as well as inclined to that Side from Principles, that I could flatter myself are those of universal Benevolence'.[57] In short he did not want to see anyone damned but feared that the concept of damnation is an integral and necessary part of Christian doctrine—as most Christians until recently thought it. Sir Thomas Browne was tempted to almost the same heresy for similar reasons. Belford, who is not, to be sure, a guarantor of orthodoxy, thinks a world beyond this one necessary to reward merit, else Clarissa and the 'divine SOCRATES' will have suffered in vain.[58] It is doubtful that in his own person Richardson would so confidently have placed Socrates in heaven, but he would surely have liked to. It is probable that he agreed with the orthodox but hopefully charitable views of Mauclerc in *The Christian's Magazine*: the good and pious heathens may well win salvation by special revelation (like Dante's Rifeo)—God will hardly condemn invincible ignorance. But it would be 'one of the absurdest Things in the World, to imagine that God should grant to Men Forgiveness of Sins, and eternal Life, let them behave themselves as they will'. Yet Mauclerc concludes his chapter on hell by saying that though sinners can have no reasonable hope of a relaxation of their eternal torments, God is not restrained from doing whatever he pleases.[59] In other words, like many

---

[54] To Lady Bradshaigh, 31 Mar. 1750.   [55] SH, III, 173.
[56] Young to R, 8 Dec. 1744; R to Young, [*c*. 12 Dec. 1744].
[57] To Lady Bradshaigh, 30 May 1754.
[58] SH, V, 316; EL, III, 198.   [59] Pp. 204–6, 236, 245.

men of their time, Mauclerc and Richardson were by no means sure that God would be as lenient as they would have been in His place. Richardson wrote to Miss Grainger that he hoped God will not damn hard hearts but feared that he will.[60]

One of the most obvious contrasts between *Pamela* and *Clarissa* is that in the latter novel virtue is not rewarded on earth. Modern writers have sometimes felt that this fact makes little difference since she is to be rewarded in heaven. Brian Downs, for instance, finds that Richardson 'was in effect merely post-dating the Reward and paying it in a different currency from that in common use at B—— Hall. He substituted a trans- cendental for a sublunary audit: and that was all.'[61] The idea that con- sideration of the after-life is as selfish, as unworthy of a great mind, as consideration of worldly profit is common enough today, and Shaftesbury had already suggested it in Richardson's day. But such a view was hardly conceivable to most of the orthodox. Besides, insistence on Clarissa's reward in heaven is especially prominent only in the Postscript, where Richardson is speaking in terms of non-fiction, arguing that his novel has poetic justice. It is not emphasized in the novel itself as Clarissa's main motive. The emotional richness of Clarissa's, and of Richardson's, Christianity goes far beyond a mere calculation of future rewards. But there is no doubt that Richardson thought the good will be rewarded. At the end of his history of Mrs. Beaumont he saw to it that the evil were punished in some degree in this life but added, in the person of Dr. Bartlett: 'I am not . . . for inferring temporal Judgments upon Evil- doers from every unhappy Event that befalls them. This Life is not the Life of final Rewards and Punishments. The Righteous as often suffer in it as the Wicked: Perhaps more frequently. And it is no bad Proof of another, a better, that they do.'[62] A similar argument was offered to Belfour for the sufferings of Clarissa; it was one of his 'great Morals' in his novel to show that there must be a world beyond this to reward merit and punish wickedness. And yet, though this life should be a vale of tears, Richardson was not often gloomy about it; religion, he told Belfour, 'is the cheer- fulest thing in the world'.[63]

The only religious group towards whom Richardson showed constant hostility, from *The Apprentice's Vade Mecum* on, were the Deists. *The Christian's Magazine* was written against atheists, Deists, Socinians, and Papists. That Richardson had no doubt of Bolingbroke's damnation is implied by his remark to Edwards, 'Poor Man! He is not a Doubter now!'[64] When he suggested that Peckard cut out his attacks on Boling- broke and Hume, he made it clear that he did not defend these sceptics ('I

[60] 21 July 1750.
[62] MS. in the Pierpont Morgan Library.
[64] 30 Dec. 1754.

[61] *Richardson*, p. 76.
[63] 15 Dec. 1748; [late Nov. 1749].

despise the one, for his absurdities and contradictions of himself, as well as for his presumption and evil intentions; and very much dislike the other, for his attempts to sap the foundations of our common Christianity'). But he thought that a pious divine should hardly recommend Mr. Hume to go hang himself, in spite of his defence of suicide, or call Bolingbroke 'what yet he is, an impudent liar'.[65] He printed several of John Leland's works against Deism and suggested that de Freval translate *Deism Revealed* into French.[66] Towards the end of his life he described at length to Miss Talbot, evidently with approval, a letter which Young planned to write to (and against) Voltaire.[67] He obviously deplored the sceptical spirit of the age as one sign of its decline.

That the age was a bad one Richardson had long been convinced. In *The Apprentice's Vade Mecum* he cited as a chief cause of the present depravity of servants 'the Degeneracy of the Times, and the Prophaneness and the Immorality, and even the open Infidelity, that is every where propagated with Impunity'.[68] Later references to the age stress especially 'the growing Depravity of the better Part of the Creation'—indeed he informed Miss Grainger that one purpose of *Clarissa* was to correct this decline in the standards of the female sex. Later he treated Miss Grainger to a picture of the modern woman, her boldness, her extravagance, her enormous, indecent, unnatural, and expensive hoop skirts, her love of vain amusements, her chasing the men—Miss Grainger had said that men often prefer a 'pretty Fool', but Richardson, who could not believe or admit that he believed that virtue and reward could be separated, insisted that coquettes win no sincere admirers. Miss Wescomb and Miss Highmore received satiric pictures of the centres of current diversion, such as Vauxhall and Tunbridge Wells, and of the women who went to them to make themselves cheap: 'Modesty, humility, graciousness, are now all banished from the behaviour of these public-place frequenters of the sex— Women are not what they were.'[69] His essay for the *Rambler* compares his period with that of the *Spectator*. Then, it is true, women went to church to attract lovers, and were thus 'Seekers'—a mark of infamy for their sex, since women should wait to be sought. But at least they and the men did go to church, and their object was matrimony; now he would be glad to call them by no worse name than seekers. Women are given to expense and idle amusement, to the neglect of their domestic business. In Addison's day, modesty, diffidence, gentleness, and meekness were at least looked on as virtues appropriate to the sex; now the ladies are so impudent as to frighten the men off by their shamelessness. Their settlements are too

[65] 16 Feb. 1756.   [66] 21 Jan. 1751.

[67] Catherine Talbot to Young, 3 Sept. 1761, Bodleian MS. Eng. Letts. c. 209.

[68] In his Dedication to the Chamberlain of London.

[69] To Frances Grainger, 22 Jan., 8 Sept. 1750; to Sarah Wescomb, late Aug. 1748, 2 July 1750; to Susanna Highmore, 2 Aug. 1748.

large; their pin money puts it out of the husband's power to lay an obligation on them; they are devoted to cards and to the company of foplings. They make themselves so cheap that the men need not even be complaisant; they have no lovers, for love is respectful and timorous—the gay coquettes soon pass and are forgotten.[70]

This essay summarizes several themes which Richardson never tired of repeating. The ideas he loved to discuss were not about politics, religion, or philosophy, but about the family, the relations between women and men, the position and proper conduct of women.[71] In this he was wise: he was certainly better qualified to discuss such questions. They are also closer to the themes of his novels; and aside from the implications about them which arise from the plots and characters of *Pamela* and *Clarissa* and *Grandison*, Richardson inserted in these books (especially in the second part of *Pamela* and in *Grandison*, where the story and characters are least compelling) numerous asides on these subjects. Such asides, though they may be spoken by Pamela or Mr. B. or Sir Charles, are not spoken as part of their characters—they are Richardson seizing the occasion to have his say. In general, the effect of the first part of *Pamela*, of *Clarissa*, and of those sections of *Sir Charles* where Harriet and Charlotte are able to forget the shadow of the overwhelming hero is liberalizing. The disquisitions of the model characters who speak for their author are sensible enough but timid, conventional, and restraining.

The *Rambler* essay had given a sketch of a modest and proper courtship, as it was in the old days. In it the family played a large role. Richardson described a similar courtship, as a model unfortunately neglected, to Miss Grainger: the young lady 'is *wholly* . . . at her Parents Disposal'.[72] The question of parental authority in marriage was one which concerned Richardson often and which had a direct bearing on his major novel. It is therefore especially striking that in spite of his numerous lectures on it he never managed to be altogether clear. It would, of course, be silly to blame him for not foreseeing that in the twentieth century parents were to be given no role at all in the choice of mates for their children. But it was not unusual in his age to claim that children should have at least a negative voice, that they should not be *forced* to marry a person they disliked. A century before, Milton, in *The Christian Doctrine* (which Richardson of course could not have seen), had concluded that though the consent of parents, if living, should not be wanting, 'the mutual consent of the parties themselves is naturally the first and most important requisite'.

The tone of the first volumes of *Clarissa* strongly supports a similar

[70] No. 97.

[71] See Nancy Ellen Talburt, 'The Use of Family Relationships for Dramatic Effect in the Novels of Samuel Richardson', University of Arkansas unpubl. diss., 1967.

[72] 8 Sept. 1750.

doctrine, which, though not universally accepted, was hardly revolution-ary. But Richardson was unwilling to state it unequivocally in the terms of non-fiction. The notion that *Clarissa* endorses a mercenary middle-class view of marriage seems to us to rest on no evidence. It has been claimed that the idea that child and parent should both have a negative voice is like 'a sign at a railroad crossing [which] decrees that neither vehicle, car or train, can go ahead until the other one has started'.[73] It does, however, appear to have been Richardson's idea, and one might more aptly compare it to a contract which cannot take effect until it is signed by both parties or to an aeroplane which cannot take off until both pilot and control tower are ready. He never made it clear whether Clarissa's running away from her parents was to be regarded as a flaw in her character or a result of highly peculiar circumstances—many readers must have felt that neither justification is necessary. It is even less clear what she should, or could, have done to avoid marrying Solmes had she not run away. For the pur-poses of the novel it is hardly important to settle this ethical issue, but it is typical that Richardson the lecturer never did settle it.

In the *Familiar Letters* parents are usually indulgent and generous; daughters are not forced to marry and are forgiven when they marry against their parents' wishes; good children are loving and obedient.[74] Such mutual good feeling was undoubtedly Richardson's view of the proper relationship. No question need arise if both sides do right. He was opposed to corporal punishments for children. He was upset when Miss Highmore suggested that their parents' admonitions never have as much influence on young people as the examples of those near their own age. 'Never, Miss H——! where the parents are companionable to their children; and can allow for the foibles of youth—such as your's, suppose! . . . I have . . . taken notice in print, that young people, in certain cases, should never be determined by the advice of young people.'[75] Richardson was not the last understanding parent to repine at Miss Highmore's sad truth. He himself was a reserved and moderately strict but loving father, and he ended by having no decisive voice in the marriage of his eldest daughter.

Harriet Byron does not see how children are to be allowed to decide which commands of their parents they are to obey: 'I am apprehensive . . . of Children's *partiality* in this respect: If they make themselves their own judges in the performance or non-performance of a duty, *inclination* I am afraid, will too often be their guide, rather than right reason. They will be too apt, perhaps, to call those commands unnatural, which are not *so* unnatural as this seems to be.'[76] A large part of his correspondence with

[73] Van Ghent, *English Novel*, p. 58.   [74] Letters 64, 66–7, 69, 91–3.
[75] Jane Collier to R, 4 Oct. 1748; R to Susanna Highmore, 31 Jan. 1754.
[76] SH, II, 46.

Miss Grainger concerned parental authority—he even tried to convince her that Clarissa should have submitted to her parents. Not that he justified tyrannical parents: 'I would have them [children] complied with in every reasonable request, only that parents should be the judges, not the children, of the fit and reasonable.'[77] He had argued the question in a series of letters with Miss Mulso, and though only her side of the correspondence is extant, one can guess from it that, though he avoided taking a clear-cut stand on the exact limits of parental authority, his leaning, at least when arguing with a young girl, was towards the side of the parents. Just as he had avoided the obvious implication of *Pamela* by claiming that only under the unique circumstances in that novel was a man justified in marrying his servant girl, so he told Miss Mulso that a daughter may disobey her parents on the important article of marriage only if she had all of the reasons which Clarissa had. Richardson agreed that a daughter should at least have a negative voice in choosing her future husband and might even, if force were attempted, escape from her parents' power. According to Richardson, parents will agree to the reasonable passion of a grown child who is prudent and docile 'unless they can give superior reasons'.[78] But evidently, as Harriet says, it is the prerogative of the parent to decide which passions are reasonable. Miss Mulso's future mother-in-law also felt that Richardson was too strong an advocate of parental authority; she got him to agree that parents should never force their children to marry, though he also maintained that no amount of unkindness from the parents can dissolve the duty of the child.[79] Miss Highmore got a milder lecture than Miss Grainger or Miss Mulso; she argued that young ladies should be permitted to associate freely with young persons of both sexes and induced Richardson half to agree, so far as regarded 'girls of fortune and fashion'. Again he was not willing to allow that want of duty on the part of parents excused want of duty on that of children.[80] He wrote and sent to Lady Bradshaigh a dramatic sketch in which a kindly but indignant father gives his daughter good reasons why she should not marry the man of her choice: when she is swept away by unwise passion and does marry against her father's command, she repents too late, though the father is not stern and unforgiving. The scene is meant as a protest against the romantic view: 'Arguments of this nature, in books, dramatic stories, &c. always turn in favour of the amorous girl, and against the supposed tyrannical parent.'[81]

It is clear enough that young ladies should heed their parents' negative voices. It is also clear that Richardson did not approve of parents who

[77] 29 Mar. 1750. On 22 Jan. 1750 he had sent her a long diatribe on the duties of children.
[78] Hester Mulso to R, 12 Oct., 10 Nov. 1750; 3 Jan. 1751.
[79] R to Mrs. Chapone, 2 Mar., 18 Apr. 1752.
[80] 26 Nov. 1749.   [81] 1 Aug. 1750.

forced their children to marry: 'Shall not parents', says Sir Charles, 'who hope to see their children happy, avoid compelling them to give their hands to a man who has no share in their hearts?' If both sides do right, there will be no problem. It is not so clear how far girls are justified in resisting the commands of parents unwise enough to give such commands or how far parents should pay attention to their daughters' inclinations. When asked whether young ladies are to be allowed to be their own choosers, Sir Charles avoids the issue: 'Daughters . . . who are earnest to choose for themselves, should be *doubly* careful that prudence justifies their choice.'[82]

Richardson's view of love was somewhat cool by romantic standards. He saw no reason why a person in love should forget prudence. Clarissa never forgets it and has been blamed accordingly by those who see passion as justifying all. Nowhere in Richardson is passion presented as a safe guide. In *The Apprentice's Vade Mecum* he had even recommended a poor man's marrying a woman of credit or fortune, who might contribute to making his future life easy and happy, and to the project-mad and impecunious lawyer Silvester he recommended marriage to a wealthy woman as the only solution to his financial problems.[83] There are no such mercenary motives in his novels, but neither do the admirable characters get swept away by romantic love. Young people who are so swept away repent as they grow wiser, like Charlotte Grandison, who lives to be happy that she was not allowed to marry the man of her first choice. But his own leading characters are again exceptions to the general rule. Sir Charles and Harriet themselves do marry the object of their first choice, and the reader is led to think that in this special case true love has been a safe guide and has been properly rewarded. When Charlotte argues that love should be vincible, Harriet cannot quite agree: 'Love merely *personal*, that sort of Love which commences between the years of fifteen and twenty; and when the extraordinary *merit* of the object is not the foundation of it; may, I believe, and perhaps generally *ought* to, be subdued. But Love that is founded on a merit that every-body acknowleges—I don't know what to say to the vincibility of *such* a Love.'[84] Hers is a love-match, and she could never have given her affection to another after knowing Sir Charles. But Richardson's heroines are too exceptional to be safe guides on delicate moral issues—at least his opinions in sober non-fiction never endorsed all the implications of their actions. When Mrs. Chapone denounced low bargaining in marriage, Richardson agreed that sordid proposals should not be encouraged but insisted that proper prudence should not be ridiculed.[85] Mrs. Barbauld, citing a letter from Miss Mulso and perhaps relying also on the memories of those who had known Richardson, says

[82] SH, III, 385.
[84] SH, V, 72.
[83] P. 4; to Silvester, 12 Aug. 1756.
[85] 18 Apr. 1752.

that 'he was in the habit of inveighing to his young friends against romantic ideas of love, and particularly the notion that a first passion could not be conquered, and he feared it would have a bad effect if he represented the contrary in his works'.[86] He certainly tried to laugh Miss Mulso out of her high-flown notions of the unselfishness of romantic love. When she was offended at his calling love 'a little selfish passion', he answered, 'Now, Madam, if that passion is not little and selfish that makes two vehement souls prefer the gratification of each other, often to a sense of duty, and always to the whole world without them, be pleased to tell me what is?' 'Love is a blazing, crackling, green-wood flame, as much smoke as flame; friendship, married friendship particularly, is a steady, intense, comfortable fire. Love, in courtship, is friendship in hope; in matrimony, friendship upon proof.' Love 'is really made too generally, nay almost universally, the sanctifier of bad actions'.[87] It goes without saying that it did not, for him, justify unchastity, though he was not harsh to fallen women. Sir Charles proposes the foundation of a 'Hospital for Female Penitents',[88] and when such a hospital was actually founded, Richardson supported it. Indeed he had much earlier pointed out to Lady Bradshaigh the need for such a refuge,[89] and still earlier Pamela had expatiated on the merits of Magdalens: 'Must not such a Lady as this . . . have as much Merit, as many even of those, who, having not had her Temptations, have not fallen?'[90]

The authority of husbands over their wives was another question on which Richardson's theory was somewhat higher than his practice. At least he was fond of claiming that his wife always managed to get her way. Again the question was best solved by mutual love and respect. Or, as he less romantically put it to Lady Bradshaigh, the partners must get used to each other. 'I have compared Marriage, even where not unhappy, to a Journey in a Stage Coach; Six Passengers in it. Very uneasy sit they at first, tho' they know by the Number of Places taken, what they are to expect; one wishing another to take up less Room; the slender intituled as they think to grudge the more bulky their very Size and Shape. But when the Vehicle moves on, a hearty Jolt or two, in a rugged Way, settles them: Then they begin to open Lips and Countenances, compare Notes, tell Stories, assume Consequence, and endeavour placidly to keep up to the Consequence they assume, and are all of a Family. I believe no two ever came together who had not each (however pleased in the Main) some little Matter they wished to be mended, altered, or yielded up; that had not some fine *Jolts* as I may call them. The first Six, Eight or Ten Months, may probably pass in

---

[86] I, cxxii.
[87] 11 July, 3 Sept., 30 Sept., 1751; 20 June, 5 Oct. 1752.
[88] SH, III, 384-5.   [89] [Mid-Jan. 1749].
[90] SH, IV, 277-8; EL, II, 359.

settling each to the other their Minds, and what the one, or what the other shall or will give up, or insist upon. When this is found out, it ends in a Composition, a tacit one at least, and then they settle tolerably together. Then Love (the *intenser* the *truer* Love) increases if each be satisfied in each others Love—Yet a dangerous Illness, a Fever suppose on the Man's Side; the parturient Circumstances, on the Womans, keep Hope and Fear alive; and the well Party will not be able to forbear looking out for *what* is to be chosen (were the dreaded worst to happen, tho' not wishing it should happen) and perhaps for whom. But both arrived at the good old Age, which you would have had afford[ed] to Clarissa and her reformed Lovelace, their Minds weakened, both domesticated, their Views narrowed; Company *principally* for each other, and looking not out of themselves, or their own narrow Wicket for Comfort—must not a parting then be very grievous?—Bodies may be sundered in Youth, may be torne from each other, and other Bodies may supply the Loss: For the Loves of Youth have more in them of *Body* than of Mind, let Lovers fancy what they will. But in Age a Separation may be called a Separation of Souls.'[91] This picture will give as good an idea of what marriage meant to Richardson (at least in his later years—he was not young when he wrote his novels) as any we can cite. It may serve as counterweight to his views of a husband's proper authority. 'No Man', he told Miss Grainger, 'can be worth providing for or thinking of, who talks of his Prerogative when it is not called in question. If he be wiser than his Wife, let him shew his Wisdom (and let that be his Prerogative) by Acts of Kindness, Compassion and Forbearance, if she be obliging modest and kind, and willing to be taught. Prerogative enough in doing that.'[92]

In 1757 John Duncombe asked Richardson to give advice to a lady, referred to as Sylvia, who had borne patiently for eighteen years the ill-usage and unfaithfulness of a husband she had married initially at the urging of friends. Sylvia was finally considering the advisability of a separation from her Dorastus. Without entirely rejecting the possibility of separation, Richardson emphasized the merit acquired by her long sufferings and the glorious reward awaiting her if she persisted in it ('This Life if a Life of Probation'). At most, she might draw up her reasons for desiring a separation and show them to Dorastus; if he really wanted the separation himself, she could agree to it as a temporary measure with no fixed period, gently and without injuring his reputation, and could still try to redeem him by correspondence. Evidently Sylvia felt the force of Richardson's urging her not to lose any of the merit she had gained with such difficulty: she took a 'noble Resolution' to 'return Good for Evil' and presumably remained with her unworthy mate, heaping coals of fire

[91] 15 Dec. 1748.
[92] 6 Aug. 1750.

on his head.[93] Richardson must indeed have believed, as he says, that 'Meekness, Gentleness, Susceptibility, are the true Feminine Graces'.[94]

We have seen that in the *Rambler* essay he disliked the idea of pin money for wives because it made them independent of husbands, or rather made it harder for husbands to be generous. He had also disagreed with his wife about stipulating for pin money in the settlements of his daughter Polly, though he had agreed to ask for it at her request. A similar sentiment was expressed to Miss Grainger—if a wife has pin money, her husband can lay her under no obligation as a sign of his love.[95] Richardson loved to be generous—and loved having the opportunity to be generous. A wife, he wrote to Mrs. Chapone, should never be independent of her husband.[96]

Like several others of his female friends, Mrs. Chapone did not quite agree, though she admitted that a husband has authority. Richardson became involved in a long argument with her on the subject. At one point he cited the example of Eve to prove that women are naturally dependent since they make no right use of independence. The real argument was over the question of woman's inferiority to man. Richardson admitted exceptions: Mrs. Chapone and some others were superior, certainly; but perhaps even they were not among the first geniuses. Mrs. Chapone and Clarissa and a few others whose names he had forgotten were not guilty of obstinacy and perverseness. But men do not want to violate their wives' consciences—'We love our Wives so well, that we could eat them and drink them.'[97]

Though of the women Richardson knew probably only Elizabeth Carter could be considered learned, a good many were 'accomplished'—that is, they read and often did some writing and had wider interests than the home. Of these Hester Mulso, the future Mrs. Chapone, was one of the most accomplished. In her correspondence with Richardson about parental authority she felt called upon to defend women against what she considered Richardson's low opinion. In 'A Matrimonial Creed', addressed to Richardson, she defends herself against a charge which, judging by the tone and context, could only have been made, in jest or half-jest, by him: 'Being told one evening that I could not be quite a good girl, whilst I retained some particular notions concerning the behaviour of husbands and wives;—being told that I was intoxicated with false sentiments of dignity; that I was proud, rebellious, a little spitfire, &c.', she resolved to examine herself—and acquitted herself. She did not want to rule her husband. But she could not agree with Richardson's statement that women 'never can be in a state of independency'. They seldom are; but naturally they are rational and accountable beings as well as men. She agreed with him that 'the law of God and their own choice and consent make them dependent on their husbands'; but they may nevertheless be superior to those husbands. And God and Nature made daughters no more dependent on parents than sons are, though the customs of people of fashion do make a distinction.[98]

Richardson evidently loved to argue with women about the position of women. When Lady Bradshaigh, who did not pride herself on being one of the accomplished, wrote that she did not approve of learning in women beyond 'what would enable them to write and converse with ease and propriety', he was willing temporarily to take the feminist side—cautiously. 'If a woman has genius, let it take its course, as well as in men.' Not, however, that they can 'be trusted to be sent abroad to seminaries of learning'. They must learn their domestic duties. But enough learning to keep them out of mischief till they have taken on enough ballast for the voyage of life is no bad thing. The argument went on and on, though the contenders were not after all far apart: whenever Richardson appears as a favourer of women's genius, which, 'as a ray of the divinity', should not be suppressed, he quickly adds that a woman who neglects her domestic tasks is good for nothing.[99] Probably the rays of divinity vouchsafed to the young poetesses of Richardson's acquaintance were not so warm as to be distracting. Indeed one can see what Richardson meant by genius in a woman from Clarissa, who had all sorts of accomplishments herself, though she never allowed them to interfere with any of her actions, and who could read French and Italian and had even begun Latin, but who, like her creator, warned against neglecting 'the *Useful* and the *Elegant*, which distinguish *her own Sex*, for the sake of obtaining the learning which is supposed more peculiar to the *other*'. She even was known to say 'that it was no great matter whether the Sex aimed at anything but excelling in the knowlege of the beauties and graces of their mother-tongue; And once she said, that This was field enough for a woman; and an ampler was but endangering her family usefulness'.[100]

'I agree with you', he wrote to Mrs. Watts, 'that there is no Sex in Souls, when divested of Bodily Organs. But, *generally* speaking (Mrs. Watts, Miss Mogg, Miss Mulso, &c. &c. out of the Question) I am apt to think—Yet let Sir Charles Grandison speak for me.'[101] Sir Charles had indeed spoken. He was giving the final word in a debate in which Harriet's venerable grandmother, Mrs. Shirley, had pointed out that though women ought not to invade the men's province, any more than the men theirs, they 'are generally too much considered as a species apart'. They should not engage in learned disputes; but in common conversation 'why are we to be perpetually considering the *Sex* of the person we are talking to?'

[98] *Posthumous Works of Mrs. Chapone*, II, 147–56. Hester Mulso to R, 3 Jan. 1751.
[99] Lady Bradshaigh to R, 28 Dec.1750; R to Lady Bradshaigh, [Jan. 1751], [Feb.–Mar. 1751].
[100] SH, VIII, 225–7; EL, IV, 496–7.   [101] 27 Sept. 1754.

They have little opportunity for sounding the depths of science and polite literature; but then many men have as little—merchants for instance. Sir Charles does not disagree, but he silences the company, as usual, with ease, when he asks why, if no differences in temperament were intended, 'nature made a difference in the beauty, proportion, and symmetry, in the *persons* of the two Sexes', why the one had 'delicacy, softness, grace', and the other strength and firmness. At any rate he detests masculine women and effeminate men, as well as married women who relieve their husbands of the reins. But he also is a friend to the accomplishments, in their place. He does not want his ward Emily to pride herself on the name of poetess (she has written a sonnet): 'The titles of *Wit* and *Poetess*, have been disgraced too often by Sappho's and Corinna's ancient and modern.' But he means 'no check to liveliness and modest ingenuity. The easy productions of a fine fancy, not made the business of life, or its boast, confer no denomination that is disgraceful, but very much the contrary.'[102] And surely Richardson's friends Miss Highmore and Miss Mulso were safe—they meant no more and were in no danger of sharing the disgrace of Sappho.

Within these limitations Richardson defended the literary women. Let them go on writing, he wrote to Edwards. Even University men praise such geniuses as Miss Highmore, Miss Mulso, and Mrs. Carter—'I mean, Women of real Genius; not little Poetical Dabblers.'[103] Pamela, over a decade younger than Sir Charles and perhaps therefore, as well as because of her sex, more liberal, had insisted that in spite of their cramped education the ladies 'make *more* than an equal Figure with the Gentlemen in all the graceful Parts of Conversation' as well as in other ways; among her acquaintance there is 'more than Parity in the Genius of the Sexes', and Mr. B. is almost the only gentleman who excels every lady she has seen.[104] Margaret Collier, therefore, had reason to look to Richardson to defend the sex against their unjust detractors, 'as the only candid man, I believe, with regard to women's understandings; and indeed their only champion, and protector, I may say, in your writings; for you write of angels, instead of women.'[105] Richardson's novels do give a higher idea of women than his letters, and the imagined parts of the novels than the inserted opinions. Anna Meades called him 'Guardian to ye Female Sex', and he proved it when he warned her against letting one of her heroines speak slightingly of the girls: 'The Sex it is a kind of Fashion to depreciate. Let not a Lady Author do it.'[106] In spite of his insistence on the husband's prerogative and on the priority of domestic duties, he had some grounds when he wrote, 'The Tendency of all I have written is to exalt the Sex.'[107]

[102] SH, V, 406–7, 413–14; II, 220–1.
[103] 25 July 1754.
[104] SH, IV, 365–7; EL, II, 414–16.
[105] 3 Oct. 1755.
[106] 19 Jan. 1757; remarks on her novel, B.M. Add. MS. 28,097.
[107] To Lady Bradshaigh, 15 Dec. 1748.

In one respect he strongly agreed with Mrs. Shirley, and he cited her authority to Lady Bradshaigh for the doctrine 'that the two sexes are too much considered as different species'. The relevance of this idea to his own writing is apparent. 'A tolerable knowlege of men will lead us to a tolerable knowlege of women. . . . He or she who aims to understand nature, and soars not above simplicity, is most likely to understand the human heart best in either sex; especially if he can make allowance for different modes of education, constitution, and situation.'[108] The same idea, in reverse, he imparted to Johannes Stinstra. His early opportunities to observe young women led his 'Enquiries, as I grew up, into the Knowlege of the Female Heart. And knowing something of that, I could not be an utter Stranger to that of Man. Men and Women are Brothers and Sisters: They are not of different Species.'[109] And Harriet Byron shared his view: 'Men and women, I believe, are so much alike, that, put custom, tyrant-custom, out of the question, the meaning of the one may be generally guessed at by that of the other, in cases where the heart is concerned.'[110]

Though these various pronouncements could, with ingenuity, be reconciled, we have not tried to reconcile them, because we do not think that there is any point in trying to form Richardson's 'ideas' into a system. Often his statements are the result of the situation when he writes or the character of the person to whom he is writing. With the possible exception of the practicability of knowing the hearts of women from a knowledge of the hearts of men (which directly concerned his art), they are all commonplace. Some come from the conservative puritan tradesman's tradition, some from the upper middle-class female society of his later years. They can be found in books, in many books, but we do not believe that there is any necessity for assuming that Richardson got them from his reading. It is the fact that such attitudes are breathed in with the air of the times that gives them their historical interest. A more original thinker would have been less typical. Since these ideas were the ones Richardson most loved to discuss, they give a fair enough measure of his mind and of his position in the history of ideas. Yet in his imaginative writing Richardson was one of the most original of authors. Few men have done more to forge their own literary forms than he, few men have been so little indebted to their predecessors. The very fact that those who point out influences are likely to cite conduct books, early eighteenth-century plays, or periodical essays, all of which had some influence on him but none of which had an important bearing on what he was doing, is a tribute to his originality. On one level, we are left with the vexed question of the relation between originality in imaginative art and originality in abstract thought, a question which must be answered differently for different writers. In Richard-

[108] 14 Feb. 1754.   [109] 20 Mar. 1754.   [110] SH, II, 211.

son the relation was negligible. On another level, one can point out that the very lack of literary education which helped make his ideas those of the great middle class also helped free him from the example of earlier writers who might have cramped his own talent.

CHAPTER XXIII

RICHARDSON'S READING
AND CRITICISM

R ICHARDSON, says Mrs. Piozzi, 'had seen little, and Johnson has
often told me that he had read little'.[1] He must have had a decent
elementary education, and perhaps he had a year or so at a good
secondary school. He himself says that he had 'only common School-
Learning', and it is certain that he did not have the regular classical
education which led to the University. He had probably less Latin than
Shakespeare, and no Greek. He says that he had no 'tolerable Knowlege'
of any language except English, and all the evidence shows that he was
not being modest. 'The very great Advantage of an Academical Education I have wanted', he wrote to Dr. Graham.[2] Young spoke of Richardson as a 'natural genius' who with a moderate education had conquered
a new province of writing.[3]

He was a little inclined to disparage the learned, though usually with
qualifications. Like the women and merchants whom Mrs. Shirley cites,
he had had no opportunity for learning, and no need of it. But he always
admitted the usefulness of true scholars who were not 'mere pedants'. He
had a good many friends and a few close friends (Hill, Edwards, Johnson,
Young) who, if not scholars in the technical sense, were men with sound
classical backgrounds. He often made a distinction against 'that Learning
which is denominated so, merely from a Skill in Languages'; that, he
wrote Edwards, he could dispense with—it is 'not absolutely necessary to
Genius'.[4] He introduced in *Clarissa* a pedant, Elias Brand, who is not only
ridiculous but rather vicious as well. Brand loves Latin references;
Clarissa, though she has read 'in the English, French, and Italian Poets'
and 'the best translations of the Latin classics', avoids quoting them as an
affectation; Lovelace, who had a good education, says that 'in a language
so expressive as the English, I hate the pedantry of tagging or prefacing
what I write with Latin scraps'. Clarissa also speaks slightingly of '*mere*

---

[1] *Observations and Reflections Made in the Course of a Journey through France, Italy, and Germany,*
I, 265.
[2] To Stinstra, 2 June 1753, 6 Dec. 1752; to Graham, 3 May 1750.
[3] *Gentleman's Magazine*, LIII (1783), 924; Nichols, *Literary Anecdotes*, IV, 726–7.
[4] 25 July 1754.

scholars', who know only the parts of speech and the dead languages.[5] Harriet Byron makes similar belittling remarks about the merely learned, which Richardson modified slightly when Dr. Delany objected to them. He explained to the Dean that he was not at all opposed to the learned languages or to the classics, though 'I always thought, that the Cause of the Christian Religion was sometimes far from being strengthened by the implicit Regard that is paid to the Pagan Antients, however, in the main, admirable.' 'It was incumbent upon me to assure you, that I meant not to cast Dishonour on Learning', he added. 'Far otherwise. I ever honoured it; and have ever regretted my own want of it.'[6]

Not only did Richardson have little acquaintance with the classics, his reading in modern literature was limited. In a study of Richardson's reading made over half a century ago in Germany, Erich Poetzsche found that Richardson's knowledge of books was 'relatively great': 'it is clear from the preceding survey that into extreme old age Richardson was industrious in a course of study which deserves our full recognition.' 'He used every opportunity that offered itself to extend his literary knowledge.'[7] We do not wish to deny that Richardson's reading was 'relatively' great, if one means relatively to the average middle-class tradesman's. For the other statements we see no evidence; indeed there is positive evidence that Richardson did not pursue his studies into his old age. Perhaps he did seize every opportunity that offered itself to extend his literary knowledge, but because of his fully occupied life not many opportunities seem to have offered themselves. Dr. Poetzsche bases his conclusions on citations and references in Richardson's works and in his letters; but even if one adds to his list various references which he did not find, the list is still not very impressive. Most of them are either mentions of the productions of Richardson's personal friends or vague statements which could easily have been based on common knowledge, without Richardson's having read the book referred to. One cannot conclude, for instance, that because Hill, through Richardson, sent his thanks to the author of *The Seasons* 'for his remembering an old friend'[8] Richardson had necessarily read Thomson's work. And his high admiration for *Myra. A Pastoral Dialogue Sacred to the Memory of a Lady*, by Dr. William Oliver of Bath, over which he wept and was charmed[9] was not unconnected with the fact that he knew 'good Dr. Oliver', who had been enthusiastic about *Sir Charles Grandison*.[10]

We do not mean to imply that Richardson read nothing. Probably he read more in his youth, when little evidence is available, than in his later

[5] SH, VIII, 238, 247, 225; EL, IV, 504–5, 511, 496.
[6] 22 Dec. 1753. See Pierson, 'The Revisions of Richardson's *Sir Charles Grandison*', pp. 167–8.
[7] *Samuel Richardsons Belesenheit* (Kiel, 1908), pp. 80, 88, 5.
[8] 24 July 1744.   [9] R to Sarah Fielding, 7 Dec. 1756.
[10] Oliver to R, 12 Aug. 1754. In his letter of 5 Dec. 1758 Oliver thanks Richardson for a gift of a copy of *Sir Charles*,

years. He told Johannes Stinstra that he chose the profession of printing 'as what I thought would gratify my Thirst after Reading' and went on to describe how he stole 'my Reading Times for Improvement of my Mind' from his hours of rest and relaxation.[11] He must have read a good many of the works that came from his press. In the 1730s, if one may judge by the evidence of his 'Rules and Orders to Be Observed by the Members of This Chapel', he sometimes acted as his own proof-reader,[12] and as such he could have read *The Seasons* and some of the poetry of Pomfret and Cotton and Hill and others. But most of the books he is known to have printed were not what we today think of as literary. His style itself is proof of more than casual exposure to good writing: he is always able to express himself with the ease and accuracy usual in the eighteenth century. He was not, considering his background and education, ignorant. Neither was he an habitual reader or a great lover of books.

Reading is recommended in one of the *Familiar Letters*, from an uncle to an apprentice nephew, who has fallen into bad company: 'Would it not be much better to choose the silent, the sober conversation of books, than of such companions as never read or think? . . . By applying yourself to books, instead of such vain company, you will be qualified in time for the best of company, and to be respected by all ranks of men.'[13] Dr. Cheyne considered Richardson qualified enough to compile a catalogue of virtuous and amusing books for the relief of the ill and the nervous,[14] but Richardson does not seem to have been tempted by the idea. Soon afterwards, in April 1743, he wrote to Aaron Hill, 'I seldom read but as a Printer, having so much of that, and a Head so little able to bear it.'[15] And by this time, aside from the demands of his business and poor health, he had his own writing to exhaust his time and energy.

Lady Bradshaigh, in asking Richardson to recommend books, added, 'I do not hope for your recommendation of Books, from your *own* reading but I know you converse with those who read.' In reply, Richardson admitted the implication: 'What have I lost, by writing so much, and reading so little! Now I have done Writing . . ., I must endeavour to recover the Power of Reading: Yet, what will be the End of it, if I do, but to shew me that I ought to have read more, and writt less?' And towards the end of his life he did inform her that because of his painful and staggering writing he was obliged to read more for entertainment.[16] Evidently during the time when he was an active printer and active writer Richardson read few books but his own except when business or friendship forced him to.

---

[11] 2 June 1753.
[12] Dated 30 Aug. 1734. B.M. Add. MS. 27,799, fo. 88.
[13] Letter 2.   [14] 5 Sept. 1742.   [15] 2 Apr.
[16] 25 Sept., 5 Oct. 1753; 18 Oct. 1759.

Richardson and Lady Bradshaigh joked a little about a friend of hers who collected risqué works: 'I wish I had a Catalogue of a certain Lord's Shelf of Books of the lively Sort', he wrote.[17] There is, however, no reason to think that he would have read them. The books he did recommend to her were *The Adventurer*, Sarah Fielding's *The Cry*, some books about Pope, Johnson's edition of Browne's *Christian Morals*, and an old book of advice by the Marquis of Argyll, *Instructions to a Son*.[18] In mentioning the latter, he gave a good indication of his taste in literature: 'I believe, Madam, that if such a low-classed scribbler as he is, who is now addressing himself to the Lady of Haigh, could but bend his mind to reading, he would better employ his time in collecting the wisdom of past times, than in obtruding upon the world his own crudities. He has, for a trial, classed under particular heads, alphabetically, the Proverbs of Solomon, Ecclesiastes, the Books of Wisdom, and Ecclesiasticus, and called it (though he has not yet taken it into his head to publish it) *Simplicity the True Sublime*. Those books are a treasure of morality.' His knowledge of the Bible is also evident in Clarissa's *Meditations* as well as in many passages in his novels. In *The Apprentice's Vade Mecum* he quotes from and relies heavily upon a number of recent religious writings.[19] Twenty years later, Lady Bradshaigh complained that she could not get him to read even religious writings: 'Not a *single* sermon, cou'd I ever prevail with you to look into, nor my good uncle Howes Meditations, nor in short any thing that woud give you pleasure.' In answer, he hinted a half-hope of reading some sermons and her uncle Howe (Charles Howe's *Devout Meditations*)—and also the Lord's lively books.[20]

He had some knowledge of the English philosophers,[21] though probably not a very deep one. He used Locke's theories on education as a basis for Pamela's comments on that subject, and had obviously read them carefully and critically. His other references—to Shaftesbury, Mandeville, Bolingbroke, Hartley, Hume, and Bishop Berkeley—show that he knew something of the general tenor of their work.

There are quotations from and references to several of the Classic writers in his novels, generally for dramatic effect, as when his pedant, Elias Brand, cites liberally from the Latin poets. At least for Brand's letters, he evidently sought and got help from more learned friends. In his letters there are very few references to the Greek or Latin writers. Homer

[17] 5 Oct. 1753.
[18] R to Lady Bradshaigh, 14 Feb. 1754; Lady Bradshaigh to R, 21 May 1754; R to Lady Bradshaigh, 10 July 1756, 24 Feb. 1753.
[19] John A. Dussinger, in 'Conscience and the Pattern of Christian Perfection in *Clarissa*', pp. 236–45, has shown considerable similarity between Richardson's attitudes in *Clarissa* and those of other writers, especially William Law.
[20] 27 Nov., 8 Dec. 1753. See also Lady Bradshaigh to R, [Jan.–Feb. 1753].
[21] H. G. Ward, 'Samuel Richardson and the English Philosophers', *N&Q*, 11 S. III (1911), 5–6.

he cites for his unfortunate effect in promoting the ideal of military glory.[22] He once thanked Miss Highmore for some transcriptions and observations from Pliny: 'As you say, I should never find time to read the book. What stores of knowlege do I lose, by my incapacity of reading, and by my having used myself to write, till I can do nothing else, nor hardly that. Business too, so pressing and so troublesome.'[23]

His knowledge of English literature was more extensive. He used quotations from the English poets and playwrights also largely for the purposes of characterization—Lovelace, especially, likes to quote. But even here one cannot altogether rely on quotations in his novels as implying first-hand acquaintance. Three quotations in *Pamela*, five in *Sir Charles*, and no less than forty-three in *Clarissa* are to be found in Bysshe's *Art of English Poetry*.[24]

Shakespeare is, as one would expect, often mentioned. Poetzsche's opinion that this demonstrates unusual critical acumen on Richardson's part ('steht er weit über seiner Zeit')[25] reflects the curious opinion of the Victorians that the age of Pope and Johnson failed to recognize Shakespeare's greatness. But Richardson's admiration is warm. Harriet Byron prefers to all the other amusements of the town 'a good Play of our favourite Shakespeare'.[26] Shakespeare, Richardson wrote to Lady Bradshaigh, knew the characters of women best of all writers[27]—a knowledge for which Richardson himself had often been praised. He could quote Juliet's speech just before she takes the opiate to justify to Belfour the horror in *Clarissa* and cite Edgar's description of the cliffs of Dover as the height of the 'terribly descriptive', so vivid that it makes him dizzy to read it—a statement which also appears in a description of the cliffs added to the 1748 edition of Defoe's *Tour*, where Shakespeare's lines are quoted.[28] Sir Charles offers one mild reservation, which, as the author of *Grandison* must have reflected, might apply to himself: 'Surely, our Shakespeare himself, one of the greatest genius's of any country or age (who, however, is an adept in the superior learning, the knowledge of nature) would not have been a sufferer, had he had that greater share of human learning which is denied him by some critics.'[29] A limitation more important for Richardson was suggested in his remarks to Young on the *Conjectures on Original Composition*—though Shakespeare is greater as an author than Addison, he is inferior as a man, as being '*less useful*'. Shakespeare has always been

[22] See pp. 547–8 and Ian Watt, 'Defoe and Richardson on Homer', *RES*, N.S. III (1952), 325–40.   [23] [1753–4?].
[24] A. Dwight Culler, 'Edward Bysshe and the Poet's Handbook', *PMLA*, LXIII (1948), 870–1.
[25] *Samuel Richardsons Belesenheit*, p. 82.
[26] SH, I, 26.   [27] 14 Feb. 1754.
[28] To Lady Bradshaigh, 15 Dec. 1748; to Lady Echlin, 4 May 1756; *Tour*, I, 185–6.
[29] SH, V, 410.

difficult to fit into a moralistic view of literature. He subscribed to Theobald's 1733 edition, but a measure of the breadth of his reading is that he had not read by any means all of the works of this favourite. Referring to Charlotte Lennox's *Shakespear Illustrated*, which, as he says, attempts 'to rob Shakespeare of his Invention' (it studies his sources and often finds fault with his changes in them), he remarked, 'Methinks I love my Shakespeare, since this Attack, better than I did before. Great, injured Shade, I will for ever revere Thee, for what I have read, and, many Years ago, seen acted of thine; and hope to live to read the rest of Thee, the far greater Part; which has been postponed, as the Reformation of the Roman Governor of Judæa was in hopes of a more convenient Season, than yet I have found.'[30]

Richardson printed an edition of the Prologue to *The Canterbury Tales* and 'The Knight's Tale', with a modernization of the former and Dryden's version of the latter, which gave him at least enough knowledge of Chaucer to refer to a passage from Dryden's 'Palemon and Arcite' in *Clarissa*.[31] Thomas Edwards had a great enthusiasm for Spenser, and it was undoubtedly from him that Richardson caught his own admiration: 'The Prince of Poets in his Time, says his Monument—The Prince of Poets in *any* time, I had almost said.' 'What an imagination! What an invention! What painting! What colouring displayed throughout the works of that admirable author! and yet, for want of time, or opportunity, I have not read his Fairy Queen through in series, or at a heat, as I may call it.'[32] His admiration for Cowley was probably a similar gift from Aaron Hill, since he repeated Hill's sentiments in his own praises.[33]

If one may judge by the frequency of quotations, the earlier poetic work with which he was most familiar was *Paradise Lost*. He at least knew well the sections on the relations between Adam and Eve, and both Clarissa and Lovelace can quote appropriate passages.[34] Sir Charles expounds Milton to the Porretta family and thus wins their admiration. Though Sir Charles admires Milton and doubts that he wants perspicuity, as some critics have charged, he does find one little fault: 'that he makes a greater display of his reading, than was quite necessary to his unbounded subject'.[35] Earlier Richardson had agreed with a much more violent attack by Hill on Milton's prose works; Hill, like Johnson, admired *Paradise Lost* but detested the prose, both for style and matter: like his own Satan, Milton was rebellious, a hater of power, licentiously independent on

---

[30] To Lady Bradshaigh, 8 Dec. 1753.
[31] Sale, *Master Printer*, p. 189. SH, VIII, 46; EL, IV, 375.
[32] To Lady Bradshaigh, 5 Oct. 1753; to Susanna Highmore, 22 June 1750.
[33] To Susanna Highmore, 4 June 1750; cf. Hill to R, 1 June 1738.
[34] *Sir Charles Grandison*, SH, II, 427, IV, 362; R to de Luc, 25 July 1758; *Clarissa*, SH, III, 369, V, 88, EL, II, 229, III, 41.
[35] SH, III, 20, 54; V, 411.

religion and manners, malignant, depraved.[36] Richardson's agreement
need not mean much—he was likely to agree with his better-educated
friends on such matters. That he knew at least something about the prose
is shown by his teasing Lady Bradshaigh about Milton's views on
divorce.[37] Another criticism was expressed to Young, who had compared
the birth of Pallas with that of Adam, that 'Milton too often mingled the
Christian and Pagan theologies', an idea he may have imbibed from
Addison.[38] And he informed Edwards that in *Sir Charles* he intended to
'be even more pure than Milton, since he, in one Place, mentions the
amorous Disport of the First Pair: In a word, I would be as pure as Mr.
Edwards.'[39] In spite of these reservations, he regretted the poor edition
by Dr. Thomas Newton of the 'glorious Milton' and wished that he and
Spenser and Shakespeare might be 'handed down in their own unborrowed Lights to latest Times'.[40] And Milton is 'almost equally-inspired'
to the writer of the Psalms.[41]

Most of Richardson's remarks on Pope are much less favourable,
though he did express some admiration for Pope as a writer.[42] Even Pope's
praise of *Pamela* did not raise him permanently in Richardson's esteem.
Again it is probable that Richardson was influenced by his more literary
friends, especially by Hill and Edwards. But for various reasons he was
unlikely to admire more than the surface of Pope's writing.

Like everyone else, he had of course ample opportunity to hear Pope
decried. He printed works by many of Pope's detractors, including John
Dennis's *Remarks on Mr. Pope's Rape of the Lock* and *Remarks upon Several
Passages in the Preliminaries to the Dunciad*. The *Daily Journal*, which he
printed, had carried attacks on Pope,[43] and it, as well as the *Weekly
Miscellany* and the *Prompter*, had been mentioned without honour in *The
Dunciad*.[44] Richardson was also associated with others of the dunces and
may well have shared their resentment. One of the attacks in the *Daily
Journal* he echoed when, in conversation with Nathaniel Hooke, he preferred *Cooper's Hill* to *Windsor Forest* and *Alexander's Feast* to Pope's *Ode
for Musick, on St. Cecilia's Day*. He went on to express the opinion that
Theobald ('and no great Glory to the Person preferr'd I thought') would
do a better edition of Shakespeare than Pope, 'who I presumed to think
undervalued his Genius to stoop to the Drudgery of being an Editor; I
offended the Gentleman, and have Reason to think, inconsiderable as I
am, Mr. Pope too, tho' I never had the Honour to be known to him

[36] Hill to R, 29 May, 1 June 1738.   [37] 24 June 1752.
[38] 14 Jan. 1757; *Spectator* No. 297.   [39] 13 Feb. 1751.
[40] To Edwards, 19 Mar. 1751.   [41] To Lady Echlin, 20 May 1759.
[42] See John Carroll, 'Richardson on Pope and Swift', *UTQ*, XXXIII (1963–4), 19–29.
[43] Sale, *Master Printer*, p. 129. Examples are in the issues of 18 Mar., 29 Mar., 3 Apr.,
6 Apr., 16 Apr., 23 Apr., 11 May, 28 May 1728.
[44] II, 280n, 258n; III, 152n.

personally: And I have never since had the Favour of Mr. Hook's Conversation.'[45]

Pope was a frequent target of attack in the *Daily Gazetteer*, though generally the attacks were restrained and were partially balanced by praise of his skill as a poet. His praise of Bolingbroke ('*B——ke* was canoniz'd by *Pope Alexander*') was often—and bitterly—mentioned, a fact not surprising if the *Gazetteer* believed its own accusation that there is 'too much Reason to suspect, that the *Man*, who . . . subscribes himself *Caleb D'Anvers* [of the *Craftsman*, the *Gazetteer*'s chief opponent], is Viscount *Bol——ke* in his own proper Person'. Freeman even speculated that one of d'Anvers' papers 'might have come from *Twickenham*'. Pope's espousal of the Patriot cause was the subject of sarcasm, as were his pretensions to reward virtue and punish vice, his conceit and his lofty claims, and his jealous attacks on other writers:

> A Traitor's Fame *Rome*'s Poet sings,
> And pleads for Guilt—and libels Kings.

The collected edition of the *Craftsman* will have at least one defender:

> 'Tis Great, — 'tis Heavenly, P— will cry;
> And, if P— praises, all must buy!

Early in 1739 two letters, which, not being signed by the regular writers for the paper, may possibly in Pope's eyes have seemed the responsibility of the printer, opened a more direct attack, and on a very sore subject and one not connected with politics. They answered 'W. W[arburton's]' defence of Pope against Crousaz's accusations against the heresies of the *Essay on Man*. YZ found many learned Englishmen scandalized by the notions of the poem, 'Notions! only worthy of the bad Heart of that Man whom our Poet hath unhappily chosen for his *Guide* and *Philosopher*'. M. P. was even more open. Pope's satires (libels and '*Billingsgate*') were written only for money and to vent his gall against the world. His lines

> Laugh where we must, be candid where we can;
> But vindicate the ways of God to Man

demonstrate that for him '*Ethicks* are *Jokes* and *God* himself a *Jest*'. His refusal to take the oath disqualifies him from discussion of politics.[46] It was probably this letter of which Pope complained to Aaron Hill, who assured him that the printer of the paper was not to blame for its contents and that Richardson was above slander.[47] But the day before Hill's answer

---

[45] *Daily Journal*, 11 May 1728; to Hill, [11 Apr. 1743].
[46] See the issues for 27 Nov. 1738; 6 Jan. 1739; 15 Sept. 1738; 24 Aug. 1738 (and also 26 Aug., 12 Oct., 19 Oct., 9 Nov., 10 Nov., 27 Nov., 19 Dec., 30 Dec. 1738, and 15 Feb. 1739); 27 Dec., 1738; 8 Jan., 9 Jan. 1739.
[47] 21 Feb. 1739, *Works*, II, 68-9.

a little play, in dog Latin, describing a meeting of supporters of sedition, showed the journal unrepentant. Poet Major bears in the close-stool of the President (Bolingbroke), when the President sits on it stands behind 'with a large Parcel of his *own Writings* in his Hand, ready to apply them to a proper Use', and when he rises '*wipes his P——s, with the last leaf of the Essay on Man*'. Perhaps Hill saved Richardson from becoming a dunce—by 17 May Pope had added the *Gazetteer*'s writers to the diving competition in Fleetditch.[48]

The first edition of the *Familiar Letters* had two slightly derogatory remarks about Pope (his verses on Kneller are 'not very extraordinary', and his praises of James Craggs are higher than anyone else gives him), which were cut in later editions.[49] The month after the publication of the *Familiar Letters* Richardson was told of Pope's 'warm Compliments' on *Pamela*.[50] Cheyne offered to introduce Richardson to Pope when he came to London, but so far as we know the introduction never took place. In writing to Warburton in 1742 to ask for corrections to *Pamela* he referred to Pope's 'Approbation' and called him 'the first Genius of the Age',[51] but two months later he was much more critical in a letter to Cheyne: 'Methinks, Sir, Mr. Pope might employ his Time, and his admirable Genius better than in exposing Insects of a Day. . . . A Quarles and a Bunyan may be of greater Use to the Multitude who cannot taste, or edify by, the Superlative, than Mr. Pope's Writings.' The reference to Quarles and Bunyan, since they are obviously cited as writers of morality and piety but lacking in literary talent, is an example of Richardson's ethical bias. 'Some of the Pieces of Pope, of Swift, & other eminent Authors, of the Poetical Tribe especially, ought to be called in, and burnt by the Hands of the common Hangman.' Were Pope to give a translation of the Psalms, as Cheyne had reported he was considering doing, 'how much more noble a Work would that be, than any he has been employ'd in?'—to glorify God, 'who gave him Talents which adorn and distinguish him above all his Cotemporaries'.[52] In short, Pope's genius, or rather his literary skill, is undoubted, but Richardson does not approve of his subject matter. Richardson's brief connection with Warburton brought him into the outer orbit of the admirers of Pope, but other influences, as well probably as his own tastes, kept him from circling in it.

Aaron Hill had, in spite of quarrels, been a friend of Pope, but by the 1740s he was in writing to Richardson openly critical of him. But so far as their extant correspondence shows, Richardson's criticisms to Hill anticipated Hill's to Richardson. On 2 April 1743 he told Hill that he in

---

[48] Pope to Swift, *Correspondence*, IV, 178–9; *Dunciad*, II, 305–14.

[49] Letter 156. See Downs's edition, pp. 249, 252.

[50] See R's index to the *Pamela* correspondence, FM XVI, 1, fo. 7; Barbauld, I, lix; Cheyne to R, 12 Feb. 1741.   [51] 17 Nov.

[52] 21 Jan. See also Cheyne to R, 12 Feb. 1741.

his satires could not 'be guilty of that Fault, which I always lament in another Great Genius who hardly writes but to Persons, rather than Things, and who chuses to irritate rather than amend; and therefore generally, I doubt, loses the good Effects that would otherwise attend his fine Satirical Vein' (the word 'fine' was cut when Richardson went over his letters with an eye on publication). He went on, in a pointed contrast, to praise William Whitehead's *Essay on Ridicule*, which shows goodness of heart, 'so much preferable to that of the Head alone'. A few days later he found Hill's *Fanciad* superior to *The Dunciad*, which was unworthy of the genius of its author, who might better employ himself than in immortalizing dunces. Early the next year he wrote that he was tired of buying new editions of Pope, citing the new version of *The Dunciad*. He admired Pope's genius and versification but was 'Scandaliz'd for human Nature, and such Talents, sunk so low. Has he no Invention, Sir, to be better employ'd about? No Talents for worthier Subjects?—Must all be personal Satire, or Imitation of others Temples of Fame, Alexander's Feasts, Coopers-Hills, Mac Flecknoe's? Yet his Essay on Man convinces one he can stand upon his own Legs. But what must then be the Strength of that Vanity and of that Ill-nature, that can sink such Talents in a Dunciad, and its Scriblerus-Prolegomena-Stuff?' But, he concluded, this is impudent from me to you.[53] Hill did not find it impudent; indeed he was charmed 'by the generous truths'. Richardson was very kind to consider the *Essay on Man* as evidence of genius.[54] And after Pope's death Hill's severity was not lessened. Richardson seems to have urged him to publish his correspondence with Pope, which Hill claimed would do the dead poet great harm.[55] He sent Richardson an 'amended' version of the *Essay on Man*, which Richardson found infinitely improved—he had always thought less of Pope than some of his readers but had not known him to be so faulty as Hill's corrections showed him to be.[56] Richardson agreed with Hill that Pope's reputation had been greatly inflated 'by so many mean Arts, and by so much insolent Terror' that no one dared receive other men's works (like Hill, Richardson must have thought especially of Hill's works) according to their merits.[57]

Thomas Edwards, one of Richardson's closest friends after the death of Hill, also had a low opinion of Pope. Unlike Hill, Edwards was inclined to that vague enthusiasm for the heart, for Nature, and for the older verse forms which used to be called pre-romanticism. But he also professed to admire Pope 'as a Poet', though in no other light—how can an ill-natured person be a good man? His morality is faulty, in spite of

[53] 7 Apr., 19 Jan.   [54] [Feb.?].
[55] Hill to R, 10 July, 21 July 1746.
[56] Hill to R, 29 July 1746; R to Hill, 5 Aug. 1746.
[57] 7 July 1746.

Warburton's endeavours to make it look orthodox.[58] Edwards was engaged in a quarrel with Warburton, and much of his criticism of Pope is primarily an attack on Warburton's effort to make Pope's system appear Christian. Richardson had quarrelled with Warburton about a passage in *Clarissa* which was taken as a slur on Pope. Richardson admitted that the bard who, by aiming at more than his due, will be refused the honours he may justly claim was no other than Pope and went on to denounce Pope for his animosity towards Theobald and for taking money for an edition of Shakespeare to which he had contributed only his name and a preface.[59]

When Lady Bradshaigh wrote that Pope's letters show him to be a good man, Richardson took exception. He later recommended to her a book about Pope's writings, warning her that she would not approve of everything in it—presumably because of her admiration for the poet. It was Joseph Warton's *Essay on the Genius and Writings of Pope*, and he assured her that in spite of her reluctance she would 'read the Piece quite through' if she read but six pages.[60] He induced Young to moderate his praises of Pope in *Conjectures on Original Composition* and even to adopt a hit at Pope's Catholicism. 'Pope's, sir', he argued, 'I venture to say, was not the genius *to lift our souls to Heaven*, had it soared ever so freely, since it soared not in the Christian beam. . . . Indeed, sir, I cannot imagine that Pope would have shone in blank verse; and do you really think he had invention enough to make him a great poet? Did he not want the assistance of rhyme, of jingle? [Young had written his chief work without its assistance.] What originality is there in the works for which he is most famed?'[61] Pope not only lacks religion, morality, heart; he is imitative, lacking in invention, and by now even his versification is propped up by rhyme. Very little is left of 'the first Genius of the Age'. Evidently Richardson's initial doubts, largely on moral grounds, had been fortified by Hill and Edwards, until he saw almost nothing good in Pope.

Most of the poets for whom Richardson expressed admiration were his friends. Hill and Edwards were enthusiastically praised. The poetesses of his circle were admired. The collection of verse preserved among his papers is largely by Edwards and by such songbirds as Miss Mulso and Miss Highmore, though it does contain one poem by Addison and one by Pope.[62] Richardson occasionally praised a new poem, such as *Amyntor and Theodora: or, the Hermit* by David Mallet and *Elfrida* by William Mason, though he found Mason's effort '*too* poetical'—too lavish in poetical talents, not regardful enough of probability, and wanting in pathos (Mason 'knew little of the hearts and Characters of Women').[63]

[58] To R, 20 Mar. 1752.
[59] Edwards to R, 19 Mar. 1756; R to Edwards, 29 Mar. 1756.
[60] 25 Nov. 1750; 10 July, 9 Oct. 1756.
[61] 14 Jan. 1757.   [62] FM XVI, 2.
[63] To Lady Bradshaigh, 14 Feb. 1754.

Richardson, in short, had little taste for poetry—one might say he had little taste for literature or, in any case, in it. When he criticized poetry, he criticized it as prose with versification. Among his contemporaries he usually managed to single out the third rate. He did mention honourably one poet of merit, but even here his opinion is not certainly a purely literary one. Miss Highmore asked him for his opinion of Gray's *Odes*, and in reply he wrote: 'You know I admire ye Author. I have heard that you and Mr. G[odshall] have both studied them together, and have found out all their Beauties. I have no doubt but they are numberless. But indeed have not had Head clear enough to read them more than once, as yet.'[64]

The prose writers he mentions most often are, not surprisingly, Addison and Swift. Swift is almost always mentioned with great reservations. Various passing references do show that Richardson had at least read Swift with some attention, not only *Gulliver* but some of the poems and *A Tale of a Tub* and the *Battle of the Books* as well. Pamela censures his low opinion of women. In *Clarissa*, Lovelace finds the Yahoos 'abominable', and Richardson in a footnote censures the indecency of *The Lady's Dressing-Room*. Clarissa herself 'often pitied the celebrated Dr. Swift for so employing his admirable pen, that a pure eye was afraid of looking into his works, and a pure ear of hearing any-thing quoted from them. "Such authors," she used to say, "were not *honest* to their own talents, nor grateful to the God who gave them." Nor would she, on these occasions, admit their beauties as a palliation; on the contrary, she held it as an aggravation of their crime, that they who were so capable of *mending the heart*, should in any places shew a *corrupt one* in themselves; which must weaken the influences of their good works; and pull down with one hand what they built up with the other.' Harriet Byron is the most severe of all. In speaking of the fact that wickedness and libertinism are often called knowledge of the world and of human nature, she adds that 'Swift, for often painting a dunghil, and for his abominable Yahoe story, was complimented with this knowlege: But I hope, that the character of human nature, the character of creatures made in the image of the Deity, is not to be taken from the overflowing of such dirty imaginations.'[65]

When Lord Orrery's *Remarks on the Life and Writings of Dr. Jonathan Swift* appeared, with their biographical anecdotes largely to Swift's disadvantage, Richardson found them greatly to his liking. 'I join with your Ladyship', he wrote to Lady Bradshaigh, 'most cordially in all you say of the author, of the Dean, and of the Dean's savage behavior to his unhappy wife, and Vanessa; as it is of a piece with all those of his writings, in which he endeavours to debase the human, and to raise above it the

---

[64] 19 Sept. 1757.

[65] *Grandison*, SH, I, 74–5; *Pamela*, SH, IV, 367, EL, II, 416; *Clarissa*, SH, VII, 265, VIII, 56, 237–8, EL, IV, 208, 381, 504; *Grandison*, SH, II, 89.

X—B.R.

brutal nature. I cannot think so hardly as some do of Lord Orrery's observation; that the fearful deprivation, which reduced him to a state beneath that of the merest animal, seemed to be a punishment that had terrible justice in it.' Lady Bradshaigh agreed, and Richardson in reply continued his attack on Swift and his praise of Lord Orrery. Swift, 'whatever his head was', had not nearly so good a heart as Lord Orrery. Richardson had heard that Sir William Temple 'never favoured him with his conversation, because of his ill qualities, nor allowed him to sit down at table with him. Swift, your Ladyship will easily see by his writings, had bitterness, satire, moroseness, that must make him insufferable both to equals and inferiors, and unsafe for his superiors to countenance. Sir William Temple was a wise and discerning man. He could easily see through a young fellow taken into a low office, and inclined to forget himself. Probably, too, the Dean was always unpolite, and never could be a man of breeding.'[66]

Lord Orrery was answered by Swift's and Richardson's old friend Dr. Delany with some *Observations* on his observations,[67] in which Richardson also took a lively interest. He called the attention of Edwards and of Lady Bradshaigh to the volume.[68] When Mrs. Delany expressed her joy at the approbation the book had met with in Dublin, Richardson answered circumspectly, in language that could be taken as entirely favourable to Swift. The book has been commended also in London, though not many buy it. 'I am confident that the Observations must be extremely approved, when known and read. But yet, from Ireland, I expect the greatest demand: for Swift is not so much a favourite with *us* as with the *Irish*. The men of wit and taste will always admire him, and in every country—but they are few.'[69] Richardson may well have made the mental reservation that wit and taste are not the highest of all possible qualities. They were certainly not those he most often praised or illustrated. His opposition to Swift was no doubt due in part to what he would think of as Swift's coarseness but even more to the low opinion of human nature expressed in *Gulliver*. Richardson was too tender-minded to stomach the Dean or his frankness. The virulence of his remarks could hardly have been due to personal hostility and might be remembered by those who think his remarks on Fielding are altogether a result of envy. Surely Richardson was genuinely shocked by the tone of Swift's writing.

The mild Addison was much more to his taste. But he admitted to Cave that he had never had time to read all of the *Spectator* papers.[70] He cited Addison, 'an excellent Judge, and sound Christian', as authority for the

[66] 23 Feb., [March], 22 Apr. 1752.
[67] *Observations upon Lord Orrery's Remarks on the Life and Writings of Dr. Jonathan Swift* by 'J. R.' (London, 1754).
[68] 25 July, 9 July 1754.   [69] 29 June.   [70] 9 Aug. 1750.

doctrine that books may have unhappy endings. Addison was a more useful writer than Shakespeare and greater as a man; he was even 'sometimes *original*, and, in his Sir Roger, as much so as Shakespeare'.[71] Richardson's greatest tribute was indirect, and typically was made not to the writer but to the man: he got Young to make Addison's death the pivot of the last part of *Conjectures on Original Composition*.

Richardson rarely referred to Continental literature, and when he did so rarely showed more than the most general knowledge. An exception is the *Orlando Furioso*, a poem which he must have read with some enthusiasm in his youth: he remembered it well in later years. One reference, to Angelica's ring of invisibility, gives us an unexpected picture of Richardson glowing with romance: 'I remember when I first read of it, having then more faith in romance than I had afterwards, I laboured under a real uneasiness for a whole week, from the strong desire I had to be master of such a one. I was a very sheepish boy, and thought I should make a very happy use of it on a multitude of occasions.'[72] When Margaret Collier expressed her admiration for Ariosto, he soon found an apt reference to the shield of Ruggiero, remembering one of the cuts in Harrington's translation; and Lovelace appropriately cites Astolfo's trip to the moon to recover Orlando's lost wits and the off-colour anti-feminist fabliau in Ariosto's twenty-eighth book.[73] Tasso he remembered well enough to refer to Armida in *Sir Charles Grandison* and in a letter to Young.[74] And making fun of William Whitehead's play *The Roman Father*, he was able to compare it unfavourably with *Horace* by 'the great Corneille', who at least avoids a scene which shows the heroine 'when her country is in the utmost danger, running about complaining that her man may have his crown cracked, that she is in love up to the ears and cannot *bear it*; deafening the ears of her *father* as well as *brothers*, zealous as they are for the public safety, with the confession of what she suffers from the stings of a private passion'— in Corneille the lovers 'poured out their silly souls into each other's bosoms' in private.[75] It was perhaps their opposition to the high-flown view of love as a sublime and uncontrollable passion that made him admire the *Letters of Ninon de Lenclos, to the Marquis de Sévigné*, in spite of the fact that it was not 'chaste enough' to recommend to a young lady, or even to Lady Bradshaigh. Yet 'for the knowlege of the hearts of people given up to what is called Gallantry, particularly French, I have not seen its equal.' He also admired the letters of Mme. de Sévigné and wished he had seen her daughter's letters.[76]

[71] To Lady Bradshaigh, 26 Oct. 1748; to Young, 14 Jan. 1757.
[72] To Elizabeth Carter, 12 June 1753; see also his letter to her of 4 July 1753.
[73] 3 Oct. 1755; 5 Jan. 1756; SH, VIII, 147, V, 373; EL, IV, 443, III, 236.
[74] SH, III, 415; 14 Jan. 1757.
[75] To Frances Grainger, 29 Mar. 1750.
[76] To Lady Bradshaigh, 14 Feb. 1754; 12 July 1757.

Richardson referred to the stage enough to show that he had attended a fair number of performances, though during the latter part of his life, when we know most about his activities, he went rarely if at all. He had seen some Shakespeare and probably some of the later tragedians, such as Otway and Rowe; he had seen at least enough comedy to know that he disapproved. In *The Apprentice's Vade Mecum* he had gone out of his way to warn apprentices away from the theatre, though 'under proper Regulations, the *Stage* may be made subservient to excellent Purposes, and be an useful Second to the *Pulpit* itself'. As it is, 'the Stage may be a tolerable Diversion to such as know not how to pass their Time, and who perhaps would spend it much worse', but for a young tradesman to haunt the playhouse must be 'of very pernicious Consequence'. Most plays are calculated for those in upper life; they waste time and money; lewd women go to the playhouses; most modern plays treat men of business as dupes and fools; and the contemporary stage is even more debased than that of the Restoration—it has not even wit to recommend its infamy, but 'the horrid Pantomime and wicked Dumb Shew, the infamous Harlequin Mimicry', and the exploits of rogues. The only play useful to a city youth is Lillo's *George Barnwell*.[77] Richardson was probably the author of the similar remarks in *A Seasonable Examination of the Pleas and Pretentions of the Proprietors of, and Subscribers to, Play-Houses*, written to support a limitation in the number of playhouses, and urging strict moral censorship.

In the *Familiar Letters*, Richardson was somewhat milder. One female writer enjoys a comedy and commends the decency of the audience, though she finds some of the speeches put into the mouths of women hardly consistent with the modesty of the sex and wonders any woman would choose to be an actress, though she has been assured that several of them are strictly virtuous. She is later greatly moved by *Hamlet* but detests the harlequinery which followed it. A father strongly urges his son not to become an actor, partly because of the undesirable company he will have to keep but even more because of the servility and dependence in which actors live, fearing the hisses of the audience and urging acquaintances to attend their benefits: 'A thought the most shocking to a free and generous mind!'[78] Pamela finds little good in *The Distressed Mother*, Ambrose Philips's adaptation of *Andromaque*, and much bad in even such a sentimental comedy as Steele's *Tender Husband*; and she likes an Italian opera even less.[79] Clarissa has better luck; she attends *Venice Preserved*, 'a deep and most affecting Tragedy in the reading', and is greatly moved.[80] Richardson, justifying the ending of *Clarissa*, urged on Lady Bradshaigh the virtues of tragedy in softening and mending the heart: 'If Warning and

[77] Pp. 9–13, 16.   [78] Letters 158, 159, 48.
[79] SH, IV, 59–93; EL, 253–8. The discussion in EL is heavily cut.
[80] SH, IV, 201; EL, II, 372.

Example be not meant in Public Representations, as well as Entertainment and Diversion, what wretched Performances,—what mere kill-time Amusements must they be to thinking Minds.' Good comedies are few, and even those that are tolerable are 'mixed with indecent Levities', so that a modest young creature can hardly bear them.[81] It is, then, hardly surprising that, in spite of his admiration for a few plays, towards the end of his life Richardson suggested (in vain) that Young add to his *Coniectures on Original Composition* a passage on the ordures of the stage: 'To our stage in its present state (and yet its present state is much better than it hath been in some former times,) the stables of Augæus were a place of safety and neatness. In those stables men were devoured by horses: in our licentious comedies, how often does the brute devour the nobler man; devour him body and soul too? What a mass of corruption? Were there an Hercules to extirpate the wild beast, who is often too rampant, even in our tragedies, the theatre might easily become again a temple sacred to virtue and improvement: but, till then, what do we more in bringing on now and then a play, be it ever so correct and blameless, than endeavour to sweeten a pestilential vault by pouring in, once a twelvemonth, a pint of rose-water?'[82]

Richardson refers in a general way to French romances. But when William Warburton hinted that before *Clarissa* the French had found the way to realistic fiction, Richardson took the reference as implying that he had pursued their plan: 'All that know me, know, that I am not acquainted in the least either with the French Language or Writers: And that it was Chance and not skill or Learning, that made me fall into this way of Scribbling.'[83] He could have read some of Marivaux in translation, but there is no evidence that he ever did so or that he knew the work of his own translator, Prévost. He had read one of the most distinguished of the earlier French novels, *The Princess of Cleves*, but though he praised its 'dangerous elegance', he did not approve of its moral tendency. Harriet Byron's grandmother, Mrs. Shirley, cites it to illustrate one of Richardson's favourite texts, that Love is not 'a blind irresistible Deity, whose darts fly at random, and admit neither defence nor cure'. In youth she had been given to the reading of the then-fashionable romances: 'You, my children, have, in that respect, fallen into happier days. The present age is greatly obliged to the authors of the Spectators.' She had refused to marry the man with whom she was later happy, simply because she felt no love for him, until a wise friend pointed out that a 'preferable inclination' was quite sufficient. And when the future Mrs. Shirley mentioned her fear that she might after marriage meet a man she could have loved, her friend picked up from her table Mme. de Lafayette's work and called the heroine 'a silly woman', whose distresses had an idle foundation: 'To fansy herself

---

[81] 15 Dec. 1748.   [82] 24 Jan. 1759.   [83] 14 Apr. 1748.

in Love with a mere stranger, because he appeared agreeable at a Ball, when she lived happily with a worthy husband, was mistaking mere *Liking* for Love, and combating all her Life after with a chimera of her own creating.'[84] With one sentence Richardson rejects almost the whole French novel and confirms the worst French suspicions of the cold and hypocritical islanders.

He very seldom mentions other novelists and when he does so is inclined to deny that he has read them. Though he revised Defoe's *Tour*, there is no proof that he had read any of his fiction. He denied that he had read *Tom Jones* or more than the first volume of *Amelia*. Though he knew Smollett, there is only a single reference to one of his novels: he calls the story of Lady Vane 'that Part of a bad Book which contains the very bad Story of a wicked Woman'. And he said that he had only 'run through' the two first volumes of *Tristram Shandy*. On the other hand, he praised Sally Fielding and Charlotte Lennox and the *Histories* of the Magdalen House penitents.

It is natural enough that his profession of ignorance of his rivals has been suspected. Surely, one thinks, his taste cannot have been *that* bad. Yet we have never found any evidence of Richardson's telling a deliberate lie. There is not evidence enough for any certain conclusion—our conjecture is admittedly based mainly on our impression of Richardson's often narrow but honest character. We suspect that he did like the idea of being first in the field and did not want anyone to think him indebted to the French or anyone else. Also there was probably lurking just out of sight in his mind a tinge of envy at the popularity of *Tom Jones* and of *Tristram Shandy*, though we have found no signs that he was much subject to envy in non-literary matters. And undoubtedly he was willing enough to praise the female novelists who could hardly have been thought of as serious rivals. We doubt that this ever led him so far as deliberate hypocrisy—rather it gave a bias which found ample re-enforcement in his moral principles. He was undoubtedly sincerely shocked at Fielding and at Sterne. Their popularity was a clear indication of the baseness of popular taste. He told the Misses Hill that he 'should admire' Fielding if he would use his talents as he wished him to—'the Vein of Humor, and Redicule, which he is Master of, might, if properly turned, do great Service to ye Cause of Virtue.' Virtue was always dearer to him than talent. It is virtue, not genius, that demands the appearance of the stories of the Magdalen penitents. If one is to blame his taste in novels, it should not be for the all-too-human touch of vanity that contributed to it but for the blind morality, or rather propriety, which made his judgement so fallible as soon as he got beyond the code of his age and class.

Aside from morality, he had one other critical principle which applied

[84] SH, VI, 223–6.

to novels. He objected to Anna Meades's first novel on the grounds that 'a due Attention is not always given to Nature & Probability'. He disliked the 'French Marvellous'. Both of these principles appear in Pamela's discussion of prose fiction: 'There were very few Novels and Romances, that my Lady would permit me to read; and those I did, gave me no great Pleasure; for either they dealt so much in the *Marvellous* and *Improbable*, or were so unnaturally *inflaming* to the *Passions*, and so full of *Love* and *Intrigue*, that hardly any of them but seem'd calculated to *fire* the *Imagination*, rather than to *inform* the *Judgment*. Tilts and Tournaments, breaking of Spears, in Honour of a Mistress, swimming over Rivers, engaging with Monsters, rambling in Search of Adventures, making unnatural Difficulties, in order to shew the Knight-Errant's Prowess in overcoming them, is all that is requir'd to constitute the *Hero* in such Pieces. And what principally distinguishes the Character of the *Heroine*, is, when she is taught to consider her Father's House as an inchanted Castle, and her Lover as the Hero who is to dissolve the Charm, and to set her at Liberty from one Confinement, in order to put her into another, and, too probably, a worse: To instruct her how to climb Walls, drop from Windows, leap Precipices, and do twenty other extravagant Things, in order to shew the mad Strength of a Passion she ought to be asham'd of: To make Parents and Guardians pass for Tyrants, and the Voice of Reason to be drown'd in that of indiscreet Love, which exalts the other Sex, and debases her own. And what is the Instruction, that can be gather'd from such Pieces, for the Conduct of common Life?'[85]

Pamela is stressing Richardson's two main critical principles, the two main critical principles of the middle class even today, surface realism (avoidance of the obviously improbable) and moral purpose:

> But play, you must,
> A tune beyond us, yet ourselves,
>
> A tune upon the blue guitar
> Of things exactly as they are.[86]

In other words, the facts of ordinary life must be made themselves to yield an ideal. Richardson was untouched by the scepticism of Stevens about the possibility of reconciling these two demands. The preface to the second part of *Pamela* states that he hopes that work 'will be found equally [with the first part] written to NATURE, avoiding all romantick Flights, improbable Surprises, and irrational Machinery; and that the Passions are touched, where requisite, and Rules, equally *New* and *Practicable*, inculcated throughout the Whole, for the *General Conduct of Life*'.[87] As an

---

[85] SH, IV, 426; EL, II, 454.
[86] Wallace Stevens, 'The Man with the Blue Guitar', i. Reprinted from *The Collected Poems of Wallace Stevens* (New York, 1955), p. 165, copyrighted by Alfred A. Knopf, Inc., and Faber and Faber Ltd., by permission of the publishers.   [87] EL, II, v. Not in SH.

illustration of such literature in its simplest form, Pamela's last letter describes the nursery tales she tells her children—tales with no knights or dragons or fairies or witches, but with young ladies 'just like' those around us, Coquetilla, Prudiana, Profusiana, and Prudentia. It needs hardly be said that only the last comes to a good end, but Prudentia is happy enough for any four people.

Pamela inculcates another critical principle, closely related to her dislike for romantic flights, when she undertakes to cure a Miss Stapylton, who 'is over-run with the Love of Poetry and Romance, and delights much in flowery Language, and metaphorical Flourishes'. Pamela composes a 'poetic' disquisition: 'While the *Banks* of *Discretion* keep the *proud Waves* of *Passion* within their natural Chanel, all calm and serene, glides along the silver Current, enlivening the adjacent Meadows, as it passes, with a brighter and more flow'ry verdure. But if the *Torrents* of *sensual Love*—' and so on. Miss Stapylton, whose notions of poetry seem to be elementary, is pleased; but she is then informed that the ex-chambermaid, now mentor, does not approve of these high flights of fancy, 'for I am convinc'd, that no Style can be proper, which is not plain, simple, easy, natural, and unaffected'.[88] If one takes Pamela's prose poem as an example of the fancy style, one sees why she and her century preferred the plain. The plain style was certainly the best adapted to Richardson's purposes, and he consistently held to it.

When Miss Highmore wrote that rural scenes and pleasures are more delightful in the poets than they are in reality, Richardson answered, 'Have you not found it so, in every thing that these madmen touch upon? If you have not, in every thing you will.' He had once, he told her, written a letter in the person of a girl 'mad after arcadian scenery', who teased her mother into letting her leave her 'charming Greenwich residence' for a country cousin's. She soon begged to be allowed to return and raved at the poets for deceiving her.[89] Certainly they never deceived Richardson into seeking pleasures more rural than those of suburban Fulham or into any but the most moderate love of scenery.

Similar critical pronouncements appear throughout Richardson's novels. In the heading to the table of contents of *Clarissa* he summarized the two aspects, realistic and moral, of that novel in terms similar to those he often used in his letters: it is 'a HISTORY of LIFE and MANNERS' which 'is designed for more than a transitory Amusement'. Lovelace criticizes the drama not for immorality but for unnaturalness: servants in plays are either too wise or too foolish or both at once, often wittier than their employers, and sometimes used, 'like the *machinery* of the antient poets (or the still *more* unnatural Soliloquy) to help on a sorry plot, or to bring

[88] SH, IV, 403, 415–17; EL, II, 439, 447–8.
[89] 22 June 1750.

about a necessary eclaircissement, to save the poet the trouble of thinking deeply for a better way to wind up his bottoms'. Sir Charles also damns asides and soliloquies, 'very poor (because unnatural) shifts of bungling authors, to make their performances intelligible to the audience'.[90]

He instructs the Lady Clementina about poets, who speak 'to their *feeling*'. 'Poets have finer imaginations, madam, than other men: they therefore feel quicker: But . . . they are not often intitled to boast of judgment (for imagination and judgment seldom go together).' Harriet has also heard her grandfather say that 'to be a poet, requires a heated imagination, which often runs away with the judgment'. And Charlotte, who is allowed to hold her tongue on a very loose rein and to exaggerate everything, is even more severe, hating the whole 'poetical tribe', who inflame 'the worst passions'. Homer made Alexander a madman, and the epic poets have propagated 'false honour, false glory, and false religion'. 'Those of the *amorous class* ought in all ages (could their future genius's for tinkling sound and measure have been known) to have been strangled in their cradles. Abusers of talents given them for better purposes (for, all this time, I put Sacred poesy out of the question); and *avowedly* claiming a right to be *licentious*, and to overleap the bounds of decency, truth, and nature.' Mr. B. thinks that to soften and polish his manners the Scot needs 'a Taste of Poetry; altho' perhaps it were not to be wish'd he had such strong Inclinations that way, as to make that lively and delectable Amusement his predominant Passion: For one sees very few Poets, whose warm Imaginations do not run away with their Judgments.'[91]

It is hardly surprising that Richardson thought that Pope would have been more nobly employed in versifying the Psalms and that some of his pieces should be burnt by the common hangman. The poets, if they were not very religious, were in grave danger of breaking both of Richardson's principles, of being unnatural and immoral. True, Richardson had praised a few of established reputation, Shakespeare, Milton, Spenser; and he admired the elegant versifying of Edwards and the female songbirds, which was in no danger of either immorality or excessive imagination. His conception of poetry was that of a successful businessman. It was all right in its place, but—. There is little use trying to make his remarks consistent; poetry was one of the accepted things, and Richardson was not a man to deny that what was accepted must have something to be said for it. Homer, the inspirer of madmen, is praised by Harriet 'because he writes to nature': 'And is not the language of nature one language throughout the world, tho' there are different modes of speech to express it by?'[92] Of course what Harriet says need not be consistent with what

[90] *Clarissa*, SH, I, 351, VII, 199, EL, I, 517, IV, 163; *Grandison*, SH, II, 425.
[91] *Grandison*, SH, III, 63–4, II, 30, V, 354; *Pamela*, SH, IV, 326, EL, II, 390.
[92] SH, I, 282.

Charlotte says. But her praise indicates more admiration for the language of nature than for Homer.

Charlotte also echoes a frequent complaint of Richardson's when she remarks that 'the French only are proud of sentiments at this day; the English cannot bear them: Story, story, story, is what they hunt after, whether sense or nonsense, probable or improbable.'[93] He did not want to be read merely as a storyteller; he was proud of his sentiments, and Dr. Johnson paid him the high compliment of saying that there are 'few sentiments that might not be traced up to Homer, Shakespeare & Richardson'.[94] All of his works, but especially the second part of *Pamela* and *Sir Charles Grandison*, are full of such sentiments, which he collected into one unreadable volume of *Moral and Instructive Sentiments*.

Richardson, as early as *The Apprentice's Vade Mecum*, had complained that 'even in the best Plays, the Moral lies so deep and hidden, as if the Play were not written for the Sake of it'.[95] He slightly watered down the impropriety of Young's *Centaur Not Fabulous* and late in life saw that a large dose of morality was mixed into the *Conjectures on Original Composition*. There was some reason for Lady Bradshaigh to suggest that he ought to write a volume of sermons, of which she offered to buy a thousand copies.[96] Moral improvement had from the beginning been a chief aim. In addition to their obvious purpose as models, the *Familiar Letters* had aimed at being 'more useful than diverting', at giving rules 'to *mend the heart, and improve the understanding*'.[97] *The Apprentice's Vade Mecum* was praised in the *Weekly Miscellany* for mixing pleasure with profit, the old Horatian formula.[98] A variation on the same formula, in almost the words later used by Jack Point, serves as a justification to Lady Echlin for writing so much about love: 'Instruction without Entertainment (were I capable of giving the best) would have but few Readers. Instruction, Madam, is the Pill; Amusement is the Gilding. Writings that do not touch the Passions of the Light and Airy, will hardly ever reach the Heart.'[99]

That for a long time Richardson's morals were an important reason for his popularity could be demonstrated from many sources, but Macaulay will suffice. He praises Richardson for raising 'the fame of English genius in foreign countries', for originality, for pathos, for 'profound knowledge of the human heart', and concludes by praising his moral tendency, citing two morally unimpeachable witnesses: 'My dear and honored friend, Mr. Wilberforce, in his celebrated religious treatise, when speaking of the unchristian tendency of the fashionable novels of the eighteenth century, distinctly excepts Richardson from the censure. Another excellent person

---

[93] SH, V, 383.

[94] Marginalia in Mrs. Piozzi's copy of Boswell's *Life*, quoted in Powell's edition of Birkbeck Hill, IV, 524n.

[95] P. 11.   [96] 27 Nov. 1753.   [97] P. xxvii.

[98] 1 Dec. 1733.   [99] 22 Sept. 1755.

whom I can never mention without respect and kindness, Mrs. Hannah More, often declared in conversation, and has declared in one of her published poems, that she first learned from the writings of Richardson those principles of piety by which her life was guided.' It is sad to have to report that he goes on to say that one of Richardson's grandsons, a clergyman (Samuel Crowther), had 'conceived a strong prejudice against works of fiction', thought all novel reading sinful, and 'had never thought it right to read one of his grandfather's books'.[100] Some early Victorians were too moral even for Richardson. But generally he was admired by the regenerate.

One method of improving humanity was by the creation of model characters. Pamela, Clarissa, and Sir Charles are all treated, at least at times, as models. The poor waiting maid is not sturdy enough to bear such a burden and collapses under it well before the end of her story. Clarissa bears it triumphantly during her lifetime, though her poor corpse is buried under the half-acre tomb of her friend's praises. Sir Charles complacently shoulders the load, having been made for it; and though he is unable to move under it, he suffers little, since he prefers in any case to stand in monumental pose. Richardson was somewhat inconsistent when his virtuous characters were accused of slight imperfections; on the one hand he admitted that characters of human beings should not be perfect, while on the other he liked to defend his people from any particular charge. When, for instance, Lady Bradshaigh wrote that Harriet Byron was too frank about her love, Richardson replied, 'Some Imperfections I intend in my best Characters, and must leave it to my Sovereign Judges the Readers, to agree as well as they can, which to blame, which to acquit.' Only a few months previously, however, he had told her that he meant Harriet as a model: 'I wrote not *from* Women; but *for* them—In other Words, to give them, not to take from them, an Example—There was Boldness!'[101]

---

[100] 'Speech on Copyright', 5 Feb. 1841, *Complete Writings* (Boston and New York [1899–1900]), XVII, 247–8. Perhaps Macaulay mistook Crowther's motive: Daniel Wilson reported that Crowther considered himself 'an unworthy grandson, never to have read those celebrated works' (*A Sermon Occasioned by the Death of the Rev. Samuel Crowther* [London, 1829], p. 43n).

[101] 8 Feb. 1754; 5 Oct. 1753.

CHAPTER XXIV

RICHARDSON'S ACHIEVEMENT

SUCH statements as those given in the preceding chapter would lead one to expect nothing from Richardson's characters. Fortunately they give us little idea of the best of them. There are other statements which better help to explain how he managed to create Pamela and Harriet and Charlotte and Anna Howe and above all Lovelace and Clarissa. In justifying the fire scene in *Clarissa* he mentioned that the strongest passion he experienced when he imagined himself as a reader was indignation: 'You know, Sir, what is required of Writers, who aim at *personating* (in order to describe the more naturally) a particular Character, whether good or bad.' '*Just* and *natural* Description', he added, 'is a great Part of the Writer's Aim throughout the Piece. And if that be allowable, are not the different Persons to write *in Character*? And *To the Occasion*?'[1] He several times mentioned his emotional involvement with his people. While writing *Sir Charles*, he told Edwards that 'if one aims at Warmth, according to the Scenes to be represented, is it possible to affect without being affected?' When Lady Bradshaigh humourously remonstrated with him for letting Charlotte make fun of her Aunt Nell's pink and yellow ribbons, he answered that the raillery was Lady G.'s, not his: 'Here I sit down to form characters. One I intend to be all Goodness; All Goodness he is. Another I intend to be all Gravity; All Gravity he is. Another *Lady G—ish*; All *Lady G—ish* she is—I am all the while absorbed in the character. It is not fair to say—*I*, identically, am any-where, while I keep within the character.' 'It is, I believe, very difficult for such a character [as Charlotte] to keep within proper bounds', he told Mrs. Watts. 'I am apt to be absorbed in my characters when I write for them, and the reader that is not, as he or she reads, must be too often alarmed, I doubt, especially by the things put into the mouths of the freer characters.'[2]

It is not so fashionable now as it once was to speak of characters who run away with their writers, but we must express our conviction that such a method of writing is at least one very good one. By putting one part of himself, conscious or unconscious, into a character and then letting that part write the character's role, a novelist is able not only to convince but,

---

[1] *Answer to the Letter of a Very Reverend and Worthy Gentleman*, pp. 7, 9.
[2] 19 Mar. 1751; 14 Feb. 1754; 9 Apr. 1755.

still more important, to convey insights which are often far more important than his ostensible moral. The person who is writing is not the person who has miscellaneous ideas on a variety of subjects which he expresses in society but a personality often far more alive than the public one.

We have indicated that we consider Richardson interesting as a thinker only historically, but we do not think that this much matters in his best writing. The novels are Richardson's; the ideas are those of his class and time. When they become obtrusive, as they do in the continuation of *Pamela* and in *Sir Charles*, they get in the way; but when Richardson is writing as a novelist, when he is speaking through his characters, his ideas fade into the background, perhaps to be brought forward later when he wants to show that he did not really say what he obviously did say. We do not mean to draw any general conclusions that novels should not deal with ideas—some very good ones have done so. But it might be shown that even writers whose ideas were more original, more consistent, and more penetrating than Richardson's were not always able to embody them in characters and situations. Dostoievsky, for instance, honest as a thinker but also honest as a novelist, stopped short before completing the regeneration of Raskolnikov and never afterwards carried out his idea for a story about the redemption of a great sinner; and in his last novel he left many readers in doubt whether Ivan, who represents all that the author of *Diary of a Writer* ought to loathe, is not the hero. He expressed his ideas clearly enough in non-fiction form, and these ideas do appear as themes in the novels; but they never, even in *The Possessed*, manage to shape the novels or control the characters. Norman Mailer has recently stated that he did not succeed in making *The Deer Park* prove what he wanted it to prove: it turned out as if the author who planned *Anna Karenina* had surprised himself by writing *Crime and Punishment* instead. We cite these out of many possible examples only to underline what has often been said, that a work of imagination has its own kind of truth, which may not be the truth the writer believes when his imagination is not acting. Richardson, of course, would have had no sympathy for such a theory, probably no comprehension of it. Most of his comments on his works try to point the correct morals. Nevertheless, in the first part of *Pamela* and, more importantly, in *Clarissa* he did write imaginatively, throwing a part of himself (which was not the part that argued about parental authority) into characters who showed what they showed, not what Richardson wanted them to show—in the case of Clarissa, at least, showed something a great deal loftier than anything the non-fiction Richardson who wrangled in a friendly fashion with Lady Bradshaigh and Miss Mulso was able to express.

It must have been partly the tendency of his characters to take over which caused Richardson to be at times uncertain what he would do next—

at least the phrase 'rises upon me' in a letter he wrote to William Dun-combe while in the midst of *Sir Charles* implies a sort of imaginative stirring in his depths: 'Clementina's Fate is not yet come to my know-ledge. I have been hinder'd from enquiring after her; in other words, from pursuing her story. But I think she rises upon me. And as I know not what is to offer next; being too irregular a scribbler to be able to write by a plan, I seem to be at a loss, to know what to do with her, or to fetch up Harriet again, and make her the principal Female character. Compassion, Sir, for people in calamity.'[3]

Richardson several times mentioned his inability to write according to a plan. Hill referred to a 'wide and arduous plan' for *Clarissa*, but his exact meaning is uncertain.[4] And if there was such a plan, there is no evidence as to whether Richardson followed it. One of the causes of mis-takes about titles in *Pamela* and *Clarissa*, he told Lady Bradshaigh, besides his ignorance of the proprieties of the upper classes, was that 'writing without a Plan, I more than once changed the Qualities and Degrees of my Characters'.[5] He told Stinstra that he was a man 'who never was regular enough to write by' a plan 'and who when he ended one Letter, hardly knew what his next would be'. When Stinstra expressed his astonishment, Richardson answered, 'There are many Discouragements and Incon-veniences, which attend the Man who has not Regularity enough to write by a Plan. I mentioned my Inability in this Particular, as a Defect.'[6] In difficulty over *Sir Charles* he asked for Lady Bradshaigh's help: 'I am a very irregular writer: can form no plan; nor write after what I have pre-conceived. Many of my friends wonder at this: but so it is. I have not therefore that encouragement to proceed, that those have, who, forming an agreeable plan, write within its circle, and go on step by step with delight, knowing what they drive at. Execution is all they have to concern themselves about, having the approbation of their friends of their plan, and perhaps helped by those friends to incidents or enlargement. But I often compare myself to a poor old woman, who, having no bellows, lays herself down on her hearth, and with her mouth endeavours to blow up into a faint blaze a little handful of sticks, half green, half dry, in order to warm a mess of pottage, that, after all her pains, hardly keeps life and soul together. This stick lights, that goes out; and she is often obliged to have recourse to her farthing candle, blinking in its shove-up socket; the lighter up of a week's fires. Excellent housewife, from poverty!——And do not you think, Madam, that invention, execution, expression, are too much to be left to the moment? And will you refuse me the help of your waxen taper, when my candle is just burnt out?'[7]

In spite of his protests that he did not write by a plan, Richardson was

---

[3] 22 Oct. 1751.   [4] See p. 206.   [5] 5 Oct. 1753.
[6] 2 June, 24 Dec. 1753; 20 Mar. 1754.   [7] [Apr.-Oct. 1751].

not unconscious of his artistic effects. The history of the composition of *Clarissa* shows how much pains he took and how often he rewrote. He had the outline of his story, if not a completed first draft, over three years before the publication of the first volumes, and at least the last two of these years were mainly devoted to extensive revisions. His first version of *Sir Charles Grandison* was greatly altered, 'whole Papers' were cut and others substituted, 'but not near the Quantity omitted'.[8]

He was always ready to comment in detail on his works, to quote from them, or to justify them. To Edward Moore, for instance, he wrote at length explaining the appropriateness of the last letter in *Clarissa*, in which the servant De la Tour forcefully and succinctly describes the death of Lovelace.[9] The letter could not have been written by someone else, as Moore had suggested—it would, for instance, have been out of character for Lovelace's friend Mowbray, whose earlier letter describing Lovelace's temporary fit of madness shows that he would have given a brutal or farcical account. As often, Richardson is especially concerned with pre-serving consistency of character. Lovelace's brief statement on being wounded, 'The luck is yours, Sir', shows, Richardson correctly points out, the pride typical of him, as does his final 'LET THIS EXPIATE!' Obviously Richardson's characterization was by no means entirely uncon-scious. Lovelace's cry on his deathbed, 'Take her away', allows the reader to imagine the appearance of Clarissa's ghost, but it can just as well be attributed to delirium. The contrast with the death of Clarissa, Richardson said, was deliberate. He wanted an effect of terror. The whole explanation demonstrates how clearly Richardson understood what he had done in this concluding letter, which is itself one of the best proofs that he did not lack art as well as a demonstration that he could, on occasion, achieve strong effects with surprising economy of means.

In *Sir Charles Grandison*, he said that he deliberately tried to provoke disagreement about his characters and to shift the reader's sympathies. 'I intended to raise little amicable Debates on their Characters', he wrote of Harriet and Clementina, 'as well as on those of others; And to leave it to the Readers to decide upon them, as they pleased.' 'I have lost a great Part of my Aim, if I do not occasion many Debates upon different Parts of my Management.' Perhaps he was merely forestalling criticism, but there is every reason to believe him when he goes on to say that he hopes for the pleasure of 'turning my Readers Hearts now one way, now an-other'. 'I have designedly play'd the Rogue with my Readers'—by making them first like Charlotte and then despise her and then be diverted by her, by making them sympathize alternately with Harriet and with Clementina. About his hero, he added, they can think only one way—unfortunately a true remark. He was, therefore, not speaking of any fundamental ambiguity

<hr />

[8] To Lady Bradshaigh, 8 Dec. 1753.   [9] [Jan. 1749?]

in the book when he said that it was 'not an unartful Management to interest the Readers so much in the Story as to make them differ in *Opinion* as to the Capital Articles'.[10]

One indication of how consciously he wrote, a rather unfortunate one, was the frequency with which he asked for advice. Surely no other author ever asked so many people for suggestions—though he rarely adopted such suggestions, except on minor matters of propriety. We have no evidence before the publication of *Pamela*, but the author of the letter '*To my worthy Friend, the Editor of* PAMELA' (probably William Webster), printed at the beginning of the first edition of the novel, demands '*Pamela* as *Pamela* wrote it; in her own Words'. The implication is that he (and doubtless others) had been consulted at least as regards Pamela's style of writing. After the publication of the novel many people were asked to help revise it. Aaron Hill was a regular consultant, as might have been expected. But correspondents as casual as six anonymous ladies from Reading were asked to comment.[11] The one known letter containing detailed, and unsolicited, comments which Richardson received was treated rather roughly—Aaron Hill's answers to its suggestions were included in Richardson's preface to the second edition. For the continuation Richardson asked for suggestions from Dr. Cheyne, Paul Bertrand, Mary Barber, Ralph Allen, George Psalmanazar, and Stephen Duck.

Edward Young and Aaron Hill were consulted about *Clarissa* early and often; the latter made the mistake of taking Richardson at his word and trying to do a real revision. Before publication began, Sarah Wescomb, Colley Cibber, Peggy Cheyne, Dr. John Heylin and his wife, and Dr. John Freke also saw the manuscript—the first was told that since the novel was written for the youthful, the criticism of young ladies was better than that of learned men.[12] Among those asked to suggest revisions were John Read, Solomon Lowe, Philip Skelton, Dr. John Conybeare, David Graham, Mrs. Delany, and Mrs. Dewes. Even the fourteen-year-old Billy Lobb was asked for his own and his father's suggestions, 'if there be any thing objectible to Manners'.[13]

Lady Bradshaigh and Miss Talbot were perhaps the chief advisers on *Sir Charles Grandison*, but by no means the only ones. Thomas Edwards, the Delanys, Stinstra, Miss Wescomb, Dr. Charles Chauncy, James Leake, Thomas Birch, Mark Hildesley, Mrs. Donnellan, and the female songbirds were asked to comment, either before or after publication, or both. Indeed Richardson's entire circle of acquaintances seems to have followed this novel from its inception. As late as 1758 he returned her copy to Lady Bradshaigh, with her comments in the margin and his comments on her comments, and at the very end of his life he asked for her marginal com-

---

[10] To Lady Echlin, 24 July 1754; to Lady Bradshaigh, 8 Dec., 12 Nov. 1753, 25 Feb. 1754.
[11] [*c*. Mar. 1742].   [12] 13 Oct. 1746.   [13] 10 Apr. 1750.

ments on *Pamela* and *Clarissa*. He informed Mrs. Watts in 1755 of 'the reason why I am solicitous to have the faults in my printed writings marked by my kind friends. It is this: I have laid by a copy of each, with such corrections in them as my friends, or my own reperusal, have suggested to me, in case, after my demise, new editions should be called for: and, as any thing of this sort occurs, I put it down in its proper place.'[14] We have seen that during his last years he made a thorough revision of *Pamela*. He was evidently constantly making smaller revisions.

It is clear that Richardson was anything but unconscious of his own literary reputation, that he took his writings seriously and worked over them carefully. He evidently read them aloud to friends, with expression—Paul Bertrand, who had recently visited Richardson, on receiving the first sheets of the continuation of *Pamela* wrote of his pleasure in having the opportunity of reading them, 'I say of reading, divested of the Pathetic Accents of the Author'[15] (it is hard to see how even Richardson could have been pathetic over the beginning of that novel, or rather discourse). There are numerous references to his reading *Grandison* aloud, and Miss Highmore has left us a picture of Richardson thus entertaining his friends. Probably his increased use of italics for dramatic effect in the revised *Clarissa* and in *Sir Charles* was in part the result of these performances. Richardson constantly quoted his novels in his letters and obviously knew where to put his finger on whatever sentiment he wanted.[16] Indeed few writers can have been so thoroughly acquainted with their own works. He discussed them at length in many letters, and they were evidently his favourite reading. He even had an idea that posterity would be interested in them. In 1748, when Aaron Hill was complaining that his age was unable to appreciate him, Richardson advised him that 'it is necessary for a genius to accommodate itself to the mode and taste of the world it is cast into, since works published in this age must take root in it, to flourish in the next'.[17] Later he himself, though not by any means so unappreciated as Hill, was also inclined to look to the future: 'There will come a time, when some People (O my Vanity!) will think better of my Writings than they do at present. A living Author, and one from whom they may perhaps dread to have more dull Morality, must not expect to be encouraged—Yet I am contented with the Approbation I have already met with.' 'A living Author', he wrote to Lady Echlin in connection with those who found fault with the character of Sir Charles, 'who succeeds tolerably, will have more Enemies than a dead one. A Time will come, and perhaps it is not far off, when the Writer of certain moral Pieces will meet with better Quarter from his very Censurers. His Obscurity, a Man in Trade, in

[14] 9 Apr.   [15] 25 Aug. 1741.
[16] See, for instance, his letter to Frances Grainger, 21 Dec. 1749.
[17] 27 Oct.

Business, pretending to draw Characters for Warning to one Set of People, for Instruction to another—Presumptuous!'[18]

That Richardson was conscious of style is shown by several remarks in *Clarissa*. He generally praises simplicity and the familiar style, though he was by no means unconscious of the need for liveliness and loved coined words and picturesque phrases. According to Lovelace, '*Familiar writing is but talking*',[19] and Richardson certainly strove for a conversational effect. Harriet Byron points out the importance of reporting conversations justly: 'The humours and characters of persons cannot be known, unless I repeat *what* they say, and their *manner* of saying.'[20] He was conscious of varying his style to suit the character. In reference to Anna Howe he mentioned the importance of distinguishing the characters and boasted that he had been 'complimented wth: giving a Stile to each of my various Characters, yt: distinguishes *whose* from *whose*, ye Moment they are entred upon'.[21] The English-speaking novel has achieved some of its best effects by giving each character a voice of his own. Such individuality may be merely the effect of some trick of speech or of speech peculiar to a class or region or trade. Lord M.'s proverbs and Joseph Leman's grammatical mistakes are examples of such relatively easy tricks. The most important characters in *Clarissa* have such fluent, varied, and adaptable individual styles as to indicate a full imaginative identification, for the moment, of author and character. In Lovelace and Clarissa, especially, style and characterization are inseparable.

In sending advice about letter writing to Billy Lobb, who he hoped would begin to correspond with him, Richardson pointed out that the young boy should not have his genius suppressed when he writes to his elderly friend. 'He should, therefore, be only told, to write free, easy, and familiar, as if to his most intimate Friend, of like Age.' 'Familiar Writing no one obtains a mastery in, who begins not [y]oung.'[22] Unless carried away by his own preaching, in his novels Richardson generally succeeds in maintaining the conversational tone very well. His style is not so highly wrought, so precise and balanced, as that of the best non-fiction writers of his age; but for its own purposes it is well adapted, perhaps the better for being less literary. One suspects that he most enjoyed writing in the persons of those characters who were allowed a more colourful expression, Lovelace and those outspoken females Anna Howe and Charlotte Grandison. The light, quick, sharp style of Lovelace, with its wit and its extravagance of fancy, entirely unlike anything one would have expected from Richardson, is in our opinion his great triumph in writing. The fancy style

---

[18] To Lady Bradshaigh, 9 Oct. 1754; to Lady Echlin, 10 Oct. 1754.
[19] SH, V, 379; EL, III, 241.　　　　　　　　　　　[20] SH, I, 44.
[21] To Lady Bradshaigh, 12 July 1757.
[22] To Samuel Lobb, 4 July 1746; to William Lobb, [July 1746–Mar. 1750].

he consistently disliked, as when he objected to James Hervey's *Meditations among the Tombs* as 'too flowery for prose, too affected: a judicious friend of mine calls it *prose* run mad.'[23] On the other hand, he loved the German English of Meta Klopstock, with its incorrect but striking phrases.[24] And he warned de Luc not to worry about correctness or to consult dictionaries: 'for such is the Perspicacity of your Stile, such the Propriety of your Language, that all ye Help you could have received from Dictionaries, would have served only to perplex your Sense, and stiffen your Expression. Dictionaries would not have enabled you to write *from* the Heart and *to* the Heart, which is your Excellence, and the Excellence of all Writing. To give yourself so much Pains in Writing to *me, of all Men*, who know nothing of good Writing, but what is easy and familiar in it; who cannot *study*, who cannot even *transcribe* what I write; but send to my Friend, infirm and ill as I am, the first Runnings of my Pen; how unnecessary, my good M. de Luc!'[25]

One device of which, as we have seen, Richardson was not only conscious but evidently proud was 'writing to the moment'—describing events, in the letters and journals which constitute his novels, as they happen, not retrospectively. Charlotte Grandison emphasizes the virtues of the method: 'I love, Harriet, to write to the moment; that's a knack I had from you and my brother: And be sure continue it, on every occasion: No *pathetic* without it!'[26] The method had its disadvantages, at least for inattentive readers. Justifying the compromise which Sir Charles made with the Porretta family, allowing the future daughters to be raised as Catholics, Richardson explained that he had carefully shown that Sir Charles was unwillingly forced to make such concessions by special circumstances. But because of his manner of writing to the moment, the observations on this subject are scattered—one of the inconveniences of the method. Its great convenience, he added, is that it permits immediate descriptions of the agitations of the heart.[27]

Richardson often complained that his readers did not judge his characters correctly—notably, many of them were inclined to admire Lovelace. Had he been writing today, he might have plumed himself on the ambiguity which permitted such varied judgements; but he tried to prevent it as far as he could. He loved, he told Lady Bradshaigh, to see how his readers judged his characters. 'But a great deal in charity to them, I attribute to their inattention. Ye world is not enough used to this way of writing, to the moment. It knows not that in the minutiæ lie often the unfoldings of the story, as well as of the heart; & judges of an action undecided, as if it were absolutely decided.' How few, like Lady Bradshaigh, would read a second time in order to judge properly! 'But when

[23] To Lady Bradshaigh, 31 Mar. 1750.   [24] To Mrs. Klopstock, 7 Apr. 1758.
[25] 7 Nov. 1758.   [26] SH, V, 61.   [27] To Cox Macro, 22 Mar. 1754.

this hasty-judging world will be convinced that they have seen the *last work* of this too-voluminous writer, they will give what he has done, more of their attention—*perhaps*—Especially when they are convinced that his own interest has been less his motive for writing, than that of their children, in the most dangerous part of their lives. Then, madm. will be discovered and approved, if I am not a false prophet, and deceive not myself, or am not deceived by my vanity, those delicacies occasioned by the difficult Situations of my principal Characters, to which now they will not attend.'[28] Richardson's hope that posterity would have more time for careful reading than his contemporaries was naïve, and he could hardly have demanded that posterity would take his motive for writing into account. But his remark shows that he did not think of his own writing solely in moralistic terms. He obviously took his characters seriously, and his attention to detail is a purely artistic consideration. He was not an accidental genius, at least by the end of his career.

The minutiæ, important as they were, had the disadvantage of caus-ing Richardson to run into great length. He himself wondered at his 'enormous Luxurience'—'the new Manner of Writing—to the Moment—betray'd me into it.'[29] His efforts to shorten *Clarissa* and *Sir Charles* have been described. In the latter novel he several times apologized directly or indirectly for his prolixity. 'The Nature of Familiar Letters, written, as it were, to the *Moment*, while the Heart is agitated by Hopes and Fears, on Events undecided, must plead an Excuse for the *Bulk* of a Collection of this Kind. Mere Facts and Characters might be comprised in a much smaller Compass: But, would they be equally interesting?' As many letters as could be spared have been omitted. 'There is not one Episode in the Whole; nor, after Sir CHARLES GRANDISON is introduced, one Letter inserted but what tends to illustrate the principal Design.' 'How does this narrative letter-writing', says Harriet, 'if one is to enter into minute and characteristic descriptions and conversations, draw one on!' 'Two sheets!' she exclaims at the end of her next letter, 'and such a quantity before! Unconscionable, say; and let me, Echo-like, repeat, Unconscionable HARRIET BYRON.'[30]

The length of his novels has probably done Richardson's reputation even more harm than his moralizing. It has kept *Clarissa* from being read. Or it has caused it to be read in a version which curtails those minutiæ which, Richardson rightly pointed out, are the strength of his method. Or it has caused readers to sample *Pamela* and reject Richardson on the basis of that book. One of the most often quoted remarks about Richard-son is Johnson's answer to Erskine's charge of tediousness, that 'if you were to read Richardson for the story, your impatience would be so much

[28] 14 Feb. 1754.   [29] To Lady Bradshaigh, 9 Oct. 1756.
[30] SH, I, ix, 86, 94.

fretted that you would hang yourself'.[31] And yet the impassioned reaction of some of Richardson's contemporaries shows that they did read him for his story, and it has been our experience that at least some modern readers can still do so. It is not enough to read, as Johnson urges, 'for the sentiment'—whatever he meant by that ambiguous word. Any work of fiction must be interesting as fiction. It would be more accurate to say that if you read *Clarissa* only in order to see how the plot turns out you will hang yourself. But this remark would apply to all good fiction. The interest must lie not solely in the outcome but in the details along the way towards that outcome, and the final impression must be gradually built up by the details. If one likes to read, there is no necessary assumption that the sooner one gets through reading a book the better. In spite of Poe, it is our opinion that neither poetry nor prose need aim exclusively at sharp, simple effects—length itself, if the details are not dull and are so organized as to support each other, may contribute to an effect unified in complexity and gaining cumulative impact. Whether Richardson succeeds in making his details interesting and in unifying them, each reader must decide. Tennyson, speaking of *Clarissa*, told FitzGerald that he loved 'those large, still, Books'.[32] It does not seem to us that 'still' is quite the right adjective, since almost every episode in *Clarissa* is written with considerable intensity. 'Slow' might be more accurate. *Clarissa* is long not because, like *War and Peace*, it is rich and varied in incident and character, but because, like *The Remembrance of Things Past*, it wrings the utmost possible out of the incidents and characters it has. If this be tedium, Richardson is lost. Desmond MacCarthy has pointed out that 'Richardson performed in his day much the same service for his contemporaries and successors as Proust has done for us', the service of conveying a type of sensibility through a manner 'detailed, long-winded, exact'.[33] In any case, we doubt that FitzGerald was right in saying, 'I . . . am sure I could (with a pair of Scissors) launch old Richardson again.'[34] Prolixity is the inevitable result of Richardson's method, as he himself saw.

The English novel has traditionally relied heavily on humour, which is admittedly not Richardson's strong point. Such humour as he has comes largely from the sharp-tongued remarks of his secondary female characters, Lady Davers, Anna Howe, and Charlotte Grandison, who often do not know the bounds between witty comment and insult. Lovelace has a more ambiguous and subtle humour. He has a good deal of wit and can describe scenes in a lively and ludicrous way; but there is generally some cruelty in his descriptions. He is funny only so long as one can forget his

[31] Boswell, *Life*, II, 174–5.

[32] FitzGerald to C. E. Norton, 4 Apr. 1878, *Letters and Literary Remains* (London, 1902–3), III, 321.

[33] *Criticism* (New York and London, [1932]), pp. 212–13.

[34] To W. F. Pollock, 9 Jan. 1868, *Letters and Literary Remains*, II, 247.

motives. One of the reasons Lady Bradshaigh liked him was that she laughed at him. She also laughed at Charlotte Grandison till tears ran down her cheeks.[35] One of Richardson's anonymous correspondents was 'excessively diverted at Charlotte'. Even the moral William Webster laughed as well as cried at *Sir Charles* and remarked that on looking at 'That *sober, serene* Countenance of Thine' it was a riddle how Charlotte's letters got written. Fielding thought the fifth volume of *Clarissa* preserved 'the same Vein of Humour which hath run through the preceding Volumes' and that the Widow Bevis showed the 'true Comic Force'.[36] We do not think that Richardson is a serious rival to Fielding among the English humourists; but neither is he altogether solemn. He himself appreciated the importance of humour, 'one of the finest flowers of English Growth'.[37] His letters show a rather avuncular and old-fashioned type of humour, a love of teasing, which caused one commentator to take a mock-angry, joking reply to Miss Grainger as an 'indignant composition . . . of the little apoplectic moralist and printer'.[38]

The traditional remark to make about Richardson is that he was the first English novelist. This in itself need be no great claim to attention except in literary histories. But his originality was recognized early. Edward Young called him a 'natural genius', as great in his way as Shakespeare and Milton in theirs, who struck out at once 'into a new province of writing' and succeeded so well that he left no room for followers.[39] This is, of course, the praise of a friend. But Richardson is no bad claimant for the title 'natural genius', that concept so dear to an age which is supposed to have admired imitation. Few writers have been less influenced by their reading.

We have already speculated a little on the nature of Richardson's originality. Much might be urged for unity of plot and effect. The first part of *Pamela* is closely knit, and *Clarissa* is even more so. In our opinion Richardson was almost entirely justified in claiming for *Clarissa* that 'long as the Work is, there is not one Digression, not one Episode, not one Reflection, but what arises naturally from the Subject, and makes for it, and to carry it on.'[40] Frederick S. Boas has described the organic unity of *Clarissa*: 'There is a constant interlacing of phrases and of ideas throughout the work which reminds us of the repetition of the theme in a fugue.'[41] It is the structure of the book which Thomas Hardy singles out

[35] To R, 9 Oct. 1750; 27 Nov., 11 Dec. 1753.
[36] To R, received 17 Apr. 1754, 26 Nov. 1753, 15 Oct. 1748.
[37] To Lady Bradshaigh, 9 July 1754.
[38] F. W. C., 'Richardson's Novels', *N&Q*, 4 S. I (1868), 285, commenting on Richardson's letter to Frances Grainger, 9 Nov. 1749.
[39] *Gentleman's Magazine*, LIII, 924; Nichols, *Literary Anecdotes*, IV, 726–7.
[40] 'Hints of Prefaces for Clarissa', FM XV, 2, fo. 52.
[41] *From Richardson to Pinero* (New York, 1937), pp. 21–2.

for special praise: 'No person who has a due perception of the constructive art shown in Greek tragic drama can be blind to the constructive art of Richardson.'[42] In spite of Coleridge's often-quoted praise of the story of *Tom Jones*, the structure of that book seems to us, as compared with *Clarissa*'s, contrived. We do not mean to imply that the novel as a whole is inferior; *Tom Jones* has many virtues, and important ones, of a kind that Richardson never even aimed at or conceived of. But Fielding can intervene as he pleases in the fortunes of his hero and especially at the end does so in a way that the modern reader can only forgive. *Clarissa* from the beginning has an inevitability, a logical and single-minded movement towards the only possible ending, which we consider the best of all possible structures, a structure so perfect as almost to conceal itself. Frederick W. Hilles has demonstrated how carefully Richardson echoes sentences and images to tie together widely separated episodes, how he changes the predominant viewpoint from that of Clarissa, to that of Lovelace, to that of Belford, and how he obtains contrast by balancing scenes in various tones.[43] Ian Watt considers that Richardson's most important contribution to the novel is probably plot, concentration on a single action.[44] Insofar as we disagree, it is only because we think that a writer's most important 'contribution', if he is a writer of any real merit, is his own works, not what he enables other men to write, and also think that structure, though undoubtedly a respectable minor virtue, has been somewhat overstressed of late, as if it were an end in itself. But if Richardson did indeed write *Clarissa* without a detailed plan, his imagination must have been working at white heat when he chose his various scenes and episodes. Except at the end they are all fused into one homogeneous material. In *Sir Charles*, on the other hand, the various parts can be justified only in that they generally serve to build up the virtues of the hero. But such a unity is merely logical. Many, if not most, of the scenes must have been not imagined but thought up.

We cannot agree that Richardson's originality arose primarily from his subordination of story to moralizing.[45] Undoubtedly Richardson did consciously regard his moral as the most important part of his work. But not only is his conscious moralizing of little but historical interest today, the moralizing itself was conventional even in his day, and his personal contribution in this respect is limited to putting so much of it in a work of prose fiction—in our opinion a minor claim to fame, though it helped to win an audience for the novel.

Mario Praz gives Richardson an important place in the history of the

---

[42] 'The Profitable Reading of Fiction', *The Forum*, V (Mar. 1888), 67.
[43] 'The Plan of *Clarissa*', *PQ*, XLV (1966), 236–48.
[44] *Rise of the Novel*, p. 135.
[45] See, for instance, Danielowski, *Richardsons erster Roman*, pp. 148–51.

novel of passion, considering him primarily important as a precursor not only of Diderot and Laclos but of the Marquis de Sade. He sees Richardson as 'at bottom a supporter of the instinct against whose manifestations he preached in the name of a virtue which he estimated also by materialistic standards' and his moralizing as 'little more than a veneer'.[46] If this is true, one must assume that, as Blake said of Milton and Satan, Richardson was on Lovelace's side without knowing it. The idea has a certain attraction, and we cannot claim to be intimate enough with Richardson's unconscious motivations to disprove it. But we cannot manage to read *Clarissa* from Lovelace's viewpoint—not because of Richardson's moralistic statements, which we find it easy enough to ignore in *Pamela* and in *Sir Charles Grandison*, but because in the fiction itself it seems to us that Clarissa, not Lovelace, is sympathetically conceived. Richardson himself must have felt for her when, re-reading a passage of his novel at the end of his life, he was moved to write at the bottom of a page in Lady Bradshaigh's copy, 'Poor Cl! how much I pity thee! Whenever I think of thy Character as a real one!'[47] To prove our view of the book is hardly possible without quoting hundreds of pages of it. We can only ask the reader to form his own impression, without preconceptions.

Though we do not see that Richardson was, even unconsciously, a 'supporter of the instinct', of the violent and uncontrolled passions he so often denounced, it is certainly true, as Morris Golden has amply demonstrated, that Richardson does not present such moral milksops as Hickman with much sympathy and that his main characters are all masterful individuals who in crises follow their own inner light. Mr. Golden, who sees 'the conflict . . . of reason and the passions' as the 'central issue' for Richardson, holds that Richardson, though he did not accept the 'cardinal rule of sentimentalism' that human nature is fundamentally good and consequently felt that the 'urges of the ego' need restraint, 'always implied, in a split that goes through his life and all of his writings, that the restraint must cover, or preferably not quite cover, something extremely dangerous. And he implies, as a consequence, that violent passions are in themselves a mark of admirably strong character.'[48] We do not see much evidence of this split in Richardson's life, except insofar as his inner life can be deduced from his writings; as regards the writings, Mr. Golden's statement seems to us exaggerated but not altogether untrue. Richardson's most thoroughly realized characters, Lovelace and Clarissa, are both passionate, though Clarissa's passions are generally under firm control. The effect of the novel is neither to make one trust to the guidance of passion nor to be content with the guidance of the social conventions. Strong

[46] *The Romantic Agony*, 2nd edn. (London and New York, [1951]), pp. 95–107, 442n.

[47] 1st edn., III, 168. Copy owned by the late Commander Arthur Avalon Mackinnon of Mackinnon.　　　　　　　　　　　　　　[48] *Richardson's Characters*, pp. 182, 192.

passions are made to seem dangerous, but they are also made to seem admirable—perhaps more important, they are made moving.

Mr. Praz does give a true picture of one side of Richardson's influence, of his place in one stream of literary history. The Marquis de Sade himself says that it was the English novel, as exemplified by Richardson and Fielding, which taught the French how to succeed in this genre. He praises both novelists for their knowledge of the human heart in all its variety, but what he says about the superiority of the novel in which virtue does not triumph hardly applies to Fielding, all of whose works have happy endings. Although his praise of the end of *Clarissa* cites the delicious tears it arouses, it might perhaps be legitimate to wonder whether he is not cautiously hinting at the kind of pleasure stimulated by his own novels of virtue unrewarded—the 'Idée sur les romans' was published under his own name, and in it he specifically denies the authorship of *Justine*.

C'est Richardson, c'est Fielding qui nous ont appris que l'étude profonde du cœur de l'homme, véritable dédale de la nature, peut seule inspirer le romancier, dont l'ouvrage doit nous faire voir l'homme, non pas seulement ce qu'il est, ou ce qu'il se montre, c'est le devoir de l'historien, mais tel qu'il peut être, tel que doivent le rendre les modifications du vice, et toutes les secousses des passions; il faut donc les connaître toutes, il faut donc les employer toutes, si l'on veut travailler ce genre; là nous apprîmes aussi, que ce n'est pas toujours en faisant triompher la vertu qu'on intéresse; qu'il faut y tendre bien certainement autant qu'on le peut, mais que cette règle, ni dans la nature ni dans Aristote, mais seulement celle, à laquelle nous voudrions que tous les hommes s'assujettissent pour notre bonheur, n'est nullement essentielle dans le roman, n'est pas même celle qui doit conduire à l'interêt; car lorsque la vertu triomphe, les choses étant ce qu'elles doivent être, nos larmes sont taries avant que de couler; mais si après les plus rudes épreuves, nous voyons enfin la vertu terrassée par le vice, indispensablement nos âmes se déchirent, et l'ouvrage nous ayant excessivement émus, ayant, comme disait Diderot, *ensanglanté nos cœurs au revers*, doit indubitablement produire l'intérêt, qui seul assure des lauriers.

Que l'on réponde: si après douze ou quinze volumes, l'immortel Richardson eût *vertueusement* fini par convertir Lovelace, et par lui faire *paisiblement* épouser Clarisse, eût-on versé à la lecture de ce roman, pris dans le sens contraire, les larmes délicieuses, qu'il obtient de tous les êtres sensibles? C'est donc la nature qu'il faut saisir quand on travaille ce genre, c'est le cœur de l'homme, le plus singulier de ses ouvrages, et nullement la vertu, parce que la vertu, quelque belle, quelque nécessaire, qu'elle soit, n'est pourtant qu'un des modes de ce cœur étonnant, dont la profonde étude est si nécessaire au romancier, et que le roman, miroir fidèle de ce cœur, doit nécessairement en tracer tous les plis.[49]

[49] *Les Crimes de l'amour*, *Œuvres complètes*, III (Paris, [1961]), 26–8.
'It is Richardson and Fielding who have taught us that only the profound study of the heart of man, that veritable maze of nature, can inspire the novelist, whose work should make us see man, not only what he is or what he appears to be (that is the duty of the historian) but as he can be, as he will be made to be by the alterations of vice and all the shocks of the passions;

It is not an accident that Pushkin lists Richardson's novels among the favourite reading of Tatyana, who imagines herself to be Clarissa as well as Julie and Delphine and sees her Onegin not only in that 'rebellious martyr' Werther but in the 'incomparable Grandison, who puts us to sleep'.[50] She was certainly not the only girl, in an age when the choice of fiction was limited, who found nourishment for her passion in Richardson's passionless moral model. The enthusiasm for Richardson seems to have lasted longer on the Continent than in England and to have affected especially writers of whom Richardson would not have approved. Voltaire, it is true, says that he could not have taken any interest in the characters of *Clarissa* even had they been his relatives and friends: 'Il est cruel . . . de lire neuf volumes entiers dans lesquels on ne trouve rien du tout.'[51] Laclos, who called *Clarissa* 'le chef-d'œuvre du roman', 'celui des Romans où il y a le plus de génie', is perhaps the happiest example of Richardson's direct influence. Valmont, in his love of stratagem as well as in his libertinism, owes much to Lovelace; he refuses to commit rape on a sleeping woman and make her a new Clarissa because the method is not his own—'me traîner servilement sur la trace des autres, et triompher sans gloire!' he exclaims, with a pride in his own wit which in its very determination not to copy Lovelace is worthy of Lovelace.[52] Later Barbey d'Aurevilly, in 'La Vengeance d'une femme', a story which we are not hardy enough even to imagine Richardson reading, cites Lovelace as his example of the fact that a fictitious character can last longer than the portrait of an actual person in a history because the novel digs deeper than history.

Diderot's 'Éloge de Richardson' contains praise as ecstatic as any

---

one must then know them all and use them all if one wishes to work this genre; there we have also learned that it is not always by making virtue triumph that one is interesting; that one must admittedly lean in this direction as far as one can, but that this rule, which is neither in nature nor in Aristotle but is only the rule to which we would like all men to subject themselves for our happiness, is not at all essential in the novel, is not even what makes it interesting; for when virtue triumphs, things being as they ought to be, our tears are dried up before they flow; but if after the hardest trials we finally see virtue crushed by vice, our souls are necessarily torn, and the work, having greatly moved us (having, as Diderot said, *stained our hearts with blood at the defeat*), must without doubt create interest, which alone assures laurels.

'Answer: if after twelve or fifteen volumes the immortal Richardson had *virtuously* ended by converting Lovelace and having him *peacefully* marry Clarissa, would you, in reading this novel taken in the opposite sense, have shed the delicious tears which it won from every feeling reader? It is, then, nature one must capture in working this genre, it is the heart of man, the strangest of its products, and not at all virtue, because virtue, however beautiful and necessary it may be, is still only one of the modes of this amazing heart, the profound study of which is so necessary to the novelist and which the novel, faithful mirror of this heart, must necessarily map out in all its windings.'   [50] *Eugene Onegin*, III, ix–x.

[51] To Mme. La Marquise du Deffan, 12 Apr. 1760, *Œuvres complètes* ([Paris], 1785), LVI, 259–60.

[52] *De l'Éducation des femmes*, 'Sur le roman "Cecilia"', *Les Liaisons dangereuses*, Chap. cx, in *Œuvres complètes*, ed. Maurice Allem, Pléiade edn. ([Paris], 1959]), pp. 454, 521, 262.

author could desire: if he had to sell all other books, he would keep Richardson with Moses, Homer, Euripides, and Sophocles and read them turn and turn about. He uses admiration for Richardson as a touchstone of people and tells of a woman who quarrelled with a friend who did not admire *Clarissa*; he always asks those who return from England first 'Avez-vous vu le poëte Richardson?' next 'Avez-vous vu le philosophe Hume?' (Richardson would have been surprised at the association.) But his praise is not merely exclamatory. He justly points to the skill with which Richardson distinguishes his characters from each other ('Quelle immense variété de nuances!') and to the importance of his apparently commonplace details. Before Richardson the word 'novel' has meant merely 'un tissu d'événements chimériques et frivoles, dont la lecture était dangereuse pour le goût et pour les mœurs'. Richardson would have been at least as shocked by *La Réligieuse* as by *Les Liaisons dangereuses*, but Diderot's novel shows how much he had learned from the effect of solid reality in his favourite *Clarissa*. In *Jacques le fataliste*, making fun of the absurdities of the romances, he adds, 'Je n'aime pas les romans, à moins que ce ne soient ceux de Richardson.'[53]

Rousseau refers to Diderot's praise of Richardson's variety only to say that this variety is hardly a sign of superiority: 'Il est aisé de réveiller l'attention, en présentant incessament et des événements inouïs et de nouveaux visages . . .; et si, toute chose égale, la simplicité du sujet ajoute à la beauté de l'ouvrage, les romans de Richardson, supérieurs en tant d'autres choses, ne sauraient, sur cet article, entrer en parallèle avec le mien' (the version in the Paris manuscript is even stronger: 'les romans de Richardson, quoique M. Diderot en ait pu dire, ne sauraient . . .'). But before he had written his own superior novel, Rousseau was as enthusiastic as anyone: 'On n'a jamais fait encore, en quelque langue que ce soit, de roman égal à Clarisse, ni même approchant.'[54] *Julie, ou la Nouvelle Héloïse*, as has often been pointed out, owes not only its method but even some of its characters and something of its tone to Richardson. Richardson, as might have been expected, was nevertheless not enthusiastic. An English translation appeared only a few months before his death, but he is said to have written to a friend in Germany that 'it was impossible for him to read the Julie of Mr. Rousseau.'[55] According to John Nichols,

[53] *Œuvres complètes*, V, 212–27; VI, 239. The 'Éloge' was first published in *Journal étranger*, 1761.

[54] *Confessions*, ed. Louis Martin-Chauffier, Pléiade edn. (Paris, [1933]), pp. 537–8; *Lettre à M. D'Alembert*, *Œuvres complètes*, 2nd edn. (Paris, 1826), II, 125n.
'It is easy to awake the attention by constantly presenting both extraordinary events and new faces . . .; and if, other things being equal, the simplicity of the subject adds to the beauty of the work, the novels of Richardson, superior in so many other things, cannot, in this respect, be compared with my novel.'

[55] *Briefe, die neueste Litteratur betreffend*, 18 June 1761, No. xix, collected edn. (Berlin, 1763), X, 287.

however, he did manage to read Rousseau's novel but was 'so much disgusted at some of the scenes and the whole tendency of the new *Eloisa*, that he secretly criticized the work (as he read it) in marginal notes, and thought, with many others, that this writer "taught the passions to move at the command of Vice."'[56] Rousseau, like so many of the French novelists, would have been guilty in Richardson's eyes of overestimating the force of passion. Richardson evidently found the urge to adultery easy to control, and his remarks on *The Princess of Cleves* show that he did not want to dignify it even by allowing it to be overcome in dubious battle.

Richardson's suspicions of romantic love have been mentioned. In his novels he makes it clear that a first love may be overcome and that proper prudence should be exercised.[57] But Sir Charles is not against love—he is, as he says, no stoic: 'Our passions may be made subservient to excellent purposes. . . . A susceptibility of the passion called *Love*, I condemn not as a fault; but the contrary.' And Harriet cannot agree with her sister-in-law Charlotte, who has overcome a first passion, that love matches are foolish things—she has just been rewarded with a love match of her own.[58] In Charlotte's slighting remarks on girls, Richardson wrote in his comments on *Sir William Harrington*, he 'had a view to shame the *Romancings of Girls*'.[59] Harriet's efforts to reconcile the love proper to the heroine of a novel with the sensible attitude generally urged by her creator are not altogether convincing. There is generally some ambiguity in Richardson's treatment of love. He often warned against it, and yet he could not deny its importance for even his most virtuous characters.

It is, however, worth noting that in his most successful work Richardson is in one way closer to the French than to the English tradition. *Clarissa* is primarily the story of a conflict between two lovers. Until the time of Hardy and Henry James, in those English novels which were written by men the young lovers are generally an unfortunate convention. The main interest is in the older characters or in the comic characters or in the hero's struggle with economic or social forces—the relationship of the hero and heroine is often mechanical and at most provides a plot framework. Perhaps Richardson's concentration on the conflict of Lovelace and Clarissa is one reason why the French continued to rank the novel so very high and to praise, more than the English ever did, the character of Lovelace, who seemed improbable to some nineteenth-century English critics. *Clarissa* is a love story in a sense in which no novel by Scott, or Dickens, or Thackeray is.

Shortly after Richardson's death, even in England, writers are found

---

[56] *Anecdotes of Bowyer*, p. 158; *Literary Anecdotes*, IV, 598.
[57] *Clarissa*, SH, I, 67, 275–6, EL, I, 46, 188; *Grandison*, SH, VI, 39, 220–7, I, 96.
[58] SH, II, 194; V, 72.
[59] See Eaves and Kimpel, 'Richardson's Connection with *Sir William Harrington*', p. 281.

exalting 'sensibility' to a position far above any Richardson would have allowed it.[60] Sir John Hawkins early accused him of fostering the cult of sentiment: 'The words *sentiment* and *sentimentality* became, not only a part of the cant of his school, but were adopted by succeeding writers, and have been used to recommend to some readers sentimental journies, sentimental letters, sentimental sermons, and a world of trash, which, but for this silly epithet, would never have attracted notice.'[61] Some of the tearful reactions to *Pamela* and *Clarissa* show that the accusation was not altogether unjust. We do not hear quite so much about the value of weeping from Richardson as one might expect, but certainly he aimed at the feelings in the last volumes of *Clarissa*. And he believed it is good to show the tender emotions. When Lovelace tries to conceal the fact that he is affected, Clarissa reflects, 'But why ... should these men ... think themselves above giving these beautiful proofs of a feeling heart? Were it in my power again to chuse ..., I would reject the man with contempt, who sought to suppress, or offered to deny, the power of being visibly affected upon *proper* occasions.'[62] Sir Charles does not offer to deny it. He weeps over his dying mother, much to her gratification ('These are precious tears—You embalm me, my son, with your tears'), and thus causes Harriet to weep much later when she hears of the scene ('Tears, when time has matured a pungent grief into a sweet melancholy are not hurtful: They are as the dew of the morning to the green herbage'). In tribute to his dead father, he more discreetly retires to his apartment, where in half an hour he gives grief its due and changes his clothes.[63] Through Edwards, Richardson sent his compliments to some ladies who had been affected by the sufferings of Clarissa: 'Beauty in Tears is Beauty heightened, especially when their Tears are Tears of Humanity and Tenderness; and are shed for the Calamaties of others. Did you never observe, dear Sir, that the silent Gushings of a compassionate Heart at the Eyes, made even the brightest Eyes still brighter?'[64]

Brian Downs correctly says that Richardson was 'a sentimentalist of the older school', not affected by Shaftesbury's doctrines that man's fundamental nature is benevolent and craves virtue and that we need only allow the real self free play to realize the Harmony of Nature.[65] 'You call the maxim cruel,' he told Miss Highmore, 'which teaches to act against inclination, and call it my maxim. I am far from thinking it a maxim that is always to be followed; though too generally, I believe it is a safer rule than to pursue an inclination.'[66] Richardson was not exempt from the new spirit of his age; and we have quoted many remarks in which he adopts

[60] See James R. Foster, 'The Abbé Prévost and the English Novel', *PMLA*, XLII (1927), 452–63.

[61] *Life of Samuel Johnson*, p. 384.   [62] SH, IV, 338; EL, II, 466.   [63] SH, II, 37–8, 108.

[64] 13 Feb. 1750.   [65] *Richardson*, p. 179.   [66] [1753–54].

the popular dichotomy between the head and the heart, always favouring
the latter.[67] He evidently meant, however, something quite harmless—
that clever men like Pope are likely to be immoral, that learned philosophers like Hume and Bolingbroke come up with some dangerous
doctrines, and that a good cry is a sign of benevolence. He is never very
clear about the 'heart', and it is useless to try to extract from him a
consistent belief. Clarissa and Sir Charles both follow the dictates of their
hearts as against the dictates of the world. Though Sir Charles's heart
leads him consistently in the proper paths, Clarissa's is not so conventional, and a case could be made for her as a mild example of the individualistic rebel. But in them 'heart' comes closer to the Christian conscience, to Milton's Holy Spirit, than to the urgings of passion. Both are
guided not by emotions but by principles. Clarissa says that 'the *Heart* is
what we women should judge by in the choice we make, as the best
security for the party's good behaviour in every relation of life'. And she
fears that Lovelace 'wants a *heart*: And if he does, he wants everything.
A wrong *head* may be convinced, may have a right turn given it: But who
is able to give a *heart*, if a heart be wanting?'[68] This very insistence on the
necessity of a *good* heart implies a contradiction to the full-blown Romantic
ethics of emotion, according to which all hearts, if uncorrupted, are good.

Clarissa has been thought to be cold. She has, it is true, a regard for the
claims of prudence—when they do not conflict with something more
important. Her actions at times are anything but prudent. But few concepts have been so ambiguous, used in so many conflicting connections,
as the concepts of 'head' and 'heart'. Melville, a 'heart' man certainly,
had doubts of the whole dichotomy: 'But it's my *prose* opinion that in
most cases, in those men who have fine brains and work them well, the
heart extends down to the hams.' In Richardson's day the 'heart' stood
mainly for the softer passions, tenderness and pity. Slightly later, Rousseau
shifted its meaning towards following the passions, but he speaks generally as if all true passions are tender. The Marquis de Sade took Rousseau
at his word and at the same time showed that passions are by no means
universally tender: Nature is the best guide, and Nature stands for a
ceaseless round of lust and destruction.

There are a few other tentative signs in Richardson of the impending
spirit of Romanticism. He followed Thomas Edwards in admiring
Spenser and the sonnet form, and he occasionally mentioned a love of
solitude. He waxed enthusiastic over Lady Echlin's rustic grotto and
wished he could rejoice with her in her 'romantic Situation'.[69] But one
doubts if he would have cared very long for it. His 'nature' was suburban
Hammersmith. The only extended attempt in his novels at nature descrip-

[67] See Edwards to R, 28 Dec. 1749.
[68] SH, I, 290, 296; EL, I, 198, 202.   [69] 20 Feb. 1756.

tion is the crossing of the Alps in *Sir Charles*. It may well be from another hand; it has no merits as description; and it presents the Alps as horrible and uncouth, as they appeared before two generations of poets had deluged the world with odes on crossing Mont Blanc. One can assume that Richardson's attitude towards wild scenery was the same as Defoe's— at least he never altered the remark in Defoe's *Tour* that Westmoreland is 'a Country eminent only for being the wildest, most barren, and frightful, of any that I have passed over in *England*, or even in *Wales* it self', though there 'are some very pleasant, populous and manufacturing Towns'.[70] As Mr. E. R. A. Temple has shown, the nature imagery of *Clarissa* is not only largely conventional but usually has unpleasant implications. The frequent animal imagery, especially, is generally used to debase man by his similarity to the brutes and shows no affection or admiration even for the horse or the dog.[71]

A more important foreshadowing of the future, in our view more basic than Richardson's toying with sentiment, has been pointed out by Ian Watt.[72] Richardson re-oriented narrative to get inside human minds and thus was part of 'the transition from the objective, social and public orientation of the classical world to the subjective, individualist and private orientation of the life and literature of the last two hundred years'. His novels encourage subjectivity and self-analysis and in this way, more than in any other, helped usher in the Romantic Movement.

Frederick Boas may be right in saying that through Rousseau 'the electrical spark lit in Richardson's back-parlour helped to kindle the conflagration in which the Bastille disappeared'.[73] But that result, and the more likely relaxation of sexual and other moral restraints, would have seemed to the author of *Sir Charles Grandison* an outrageous perversion of his good intentions. If he was in any way responsible, it was in helping to provide a superior method for the presentation of human emotions. In imagining characters and letting them speak for themselves in credible and solidly built situations, he showed the later proponents of the morality of feeling how to be more convincing. The method itself naturally leads to the danger Richardson wished to preach against. In presenting his characters Richardson inevitably described their passions. Judged by later standards, they are not very passionate characters, and Richardson tried to warn the reader against such passions as they did possess. But such added warnings rarely make much impression—the effect of his work was necessarily to involve sympathetic readers with the feelings of Pamela and Clarissa and Clementina. To the degree that he aroused feelings, helped train an audience for them, and showed other writers how to stimulate

---

[70] SH, IV, 106–12; 1st edn., III, 223.
[71] 'The Somber World of *Clarissa*', University of Arkansas unpubl. diss., 1970.
[72] *Rise of the Novel*, pp. 175–6, 190.   [73] *From Richardson to Pinero*, p. 44.

them, Richardson did lead towards the logical conclusion of the morality of emotion in the Marquis de Sade, who, adopting a view of Nature at least as probable as Rousseau's, came to conclusions about following Nature which would have horrified Rousseau as much as Richardson and consistently enough claimed that though the cold law has no privilege to claim a person's life, individuals may justly do so, since their murders are legitimized by passions. Most writers of sensibility, of course, stopped a long way short of de Sade. They shut their eyes to the more inconvenient passions.

The fact that Richardson was read enthusiastically by writers of passionate novels was certainly not the result of any conscious glorification of passion, nor was it even the result of any strong strain of romance or emotion in his work. Other writers were far more emotional. But Richardson made the emotions he aroused seem real. Frank Howard Wilcox has concluded that the changes Prévost made in translating Richardson's novels show the difference between them and the earlier French tradition, the tradition of the memoir: the translations disguise Richardson's innovations, his accurate eye for character and his immediate contact with events. Richardson's realistic detail was new: he 'was the first really to see his characters on the stage'.[74]

So competent a judge as William Dean Howells is enthusiastic over the 'conviction of life and truth' in Richardson's novels and finds 'a fullness and perfection of portraiture and self-portraiture which you will hardly find in any novel again till you come to Tolstoy's'.[75] Richardson's 'realism' is compounded of several elements, which need not necessarily go together but which did, in many nineteenth-century novels (and notably in Tolstoy's), go together. There are the detailed surface realism, the subjects from everyday life, the strict attention to probability (a classic concern), the little traits which merge into a psychologically believable character; and, probably most important of all, there is what one might call the realistic (perhaps better, the realized) imagination, which creates a picture of characters and events in the mind of the author which has its own life and its own truth.

One might debate about how 'true to life' Richardson's novels are. Few readers, probably, will go so far as William Lyon Phelps: 'His realism was bolder and more honest than Fielding's and shrank from nothing that might lend additional power to the scene, or that might deepen the shades of character.'[76] 'Boldness' (a popular word today in jacket blurbs, though a rather strange one at a time when a writer risks nothing) is usually taken to refer to outspoken sex, or at any rate insistence

[74] 'Prévost's Translations of Richardson's Novels', pp. 382–4, 395–6.
[75] 'Editor's Easy Chair', *Harper's Monthly Magazine*, CV (1902), 483.
[76] 'Richardson', *Essays on Books* (New York, 1914), p. 113.

on what used to be thought of as the seamy side of life. One might cite the vivid description of Mrs. Sinclair and her whores, but such boldness is rare in Richardson.

Richardson idealized his main characters—they are larger than life. The same thing might be said of Tolstoy's main characters; though recognizable, they are larger than life, possibly because Tolstoy himself was larger than ordinary life. Yet this magnification of characters, this presentation of individuals who are at the same time types, does not work against the realistic effect so long as the magnified characters were born, like Lovelace and Clarissa, in the imagination and not, like Sir Charles Grandison, compounded from maxims of morality. There is nothing paradoxical in the harmony between realism and this kind of idealization—after all, imagination is at least as real as observation.

Richardson's influence in England, unlike his influence in France, was largely on the realists—his important influence, that is; we are not much concerned with his influence on a few second-rate sentimental females. His successor in the comedy of manners was Jane Austen, who singled out *Sir Charles Grandison* for special praise. It is in that novel that Richardson's surface realism and his analysis of social situations are at their height.

The realistic surface does not seem to have been the result, as it has been in some novelists, of a close copy of environments or events which Richardson had experienced. He boasted that he had had no firsthand knowledge of rakishness or of loose women. He had had little of the well-to-do country-house life in the midst of which most of his characters move. He wrote almost nothing of his own class. 'I never wrote from what I saw by the bodily eye', he told John Duncombe.[77] What sources are known for the plots of his novels are mere general suggestions which have little effect on the tone or quality of his work. Nor did he attempt the elaborate portrayal of background, which is the strength of many novelists of the next century.

Hazlitt, who has made subtle remarks about Richardson's artificiality, singles out his characters for special comment. He considered himself 'a thorough adept in Richardson' and found 'no part of them [the novels] tedious; nor should I ask to have any thing better to do than to read them from beginning to end, to take them up when I chose, and lay them down when I was tired, in some old family mansion in the country, till every word and syllable . . . were once more "graven in my heart's tables"'. Yet he decided that Richardson was neither 'an observer of the characters of human life' like Fielding nor 'a describer of its various eccentricities' like Smollett. Richardson 'seemed to spin his materials entirely out of his own brain, as if there had been nothing existing in the world beyond the

[77] 24 Aug. 1754.

Y—B.R.

little room in which he sat writing. There is an artificial reality about his works, which is no where else to be met with. They have the romantic air of a pure fiction, with the literal minuteness of a common diary.'[78]

This need not necessarily be taken as an adverse criticism. It is accurate, however, in pointing out that Richardson's realism is not so much a matter of reporting what he saw as of reporting what he imagined. He did 'spin his materials . . . out of his own brain'. But then, his brain was not unreal. It even worked generally on the events of common life. Henry James has argued convincingly that the 'experience' from which the novelist writes need not be altogether external to him: 'Experience is never limited, and it is never complete; it is an immense sensibility, a kind of huge spider-web of the finest silken threads suspended in the chamber of consciousness, and catching every air-borne particle in its tissue. It is the very atmosphere of the mind; and when the mind is imaginative—much more when it happens to be that of a man of genius—it takes to itself the faintest hints of life, it converts the very pulses of the air into revelations.' 'A novel is in its broadest definition a personal, a direct impression of life: that, to begin with, constitutes its value, which is greater or less according to the intensity of the impression.'[79] The words 'personal' and 'impression' stress the major importance of the imaginative power of the writer's mind. In a sense, those uneducated readers who say that they do not want to read about the dull events of their everyday lives are right. No one wants to read a succession of meaningless facts, no matter how real.

James adds that 'the air of reality (solidity of specification) seems to me to be the supreme virtue of a novel'.[80] This air of reality is not the same thing as realism, since one finds it in fantastic or even allegorical fiction; it comes when an author has 'realized' his scenes, whether or not they are intrinsically 'life-like'. Howells and Galsworthy, for instance, are certainly life-like, and their stories are probable and well contrived, but they rarely convey the conviction of reality that is almost always felt in Jane Austen or Flaubert; similarly, whatever their other virtues, a reader is not swept along, as in an experience of his own, by Faulkner's *A Fable* or Hofmannsthal's *Die Frau ohne Schatten* as he is in the concluding scenes of *Moby-Dick* or in *The Trial*. *The Trial* is not realistic in most of the received senses of that vague word, and *Their Wedding Journey* is; but *The Trial* is realized as *Their Wedding Journey* is not. *Clarissa* is realistic in most senses, but more important it is almost constantly realized. There are failures, especially towards the end, but the total effect is convincing, because the author saw and felt all of what he described.

[78] *Works*, XII, 226–7; VI, 117–18.
[79] 'The Art of Fiction', *Partial Portraits* (London, 1899), pp. 388, 384.
[80] Ibid., p. 390.

Many of the comments made at the time on Richardson's work show that it was the 'air of reality' which made the deepest impression. Lady Mary Wortley Montagu, who had many harsh things to say about Richardson and did not regard his work as worthy of serious consideration, could not help weeping over *Clarissa*.[81] A Frenchman visited Hampstead to find out the house where Clarissa lodged and 'was surprised at the ignorance or indifference of the inhabitants on that subject'.[82] A 'romantic young lady . . . arriving for the first time in London, asked to be shown the street where Miss Clarissa Harlowe died'.[83] André Chenier imagines the 'ami des champs' dreaming in rural solitude of his favourite heroines, Julie, Clarisse, and Clémentine:

> Avec vous
> Il est dans vos foyers, il voit vos traits si doux.
> A vos persécuteurs il reproche leur crime.
> Il aime qui vous aime, il hait qui vous opprime.
> Mais tout à coup il pense, ô mortels déplaisirs!
> Que ces touchants objets de pleurs et de soupirs
> Ne sont peut-être, hélas! que d'aimables chimères,
> De l'âme et du génie enfants imaginaires.
> Il se lève; il s'agite à pas tumultueux;
> En projets enchanteurs il égare ses vœux.
> Il ira, le cœur plein d'une image divine,
> Chercher si quelques lieux ont une Clémentine. . . .[84]

Chénier is conscious that his heroines are ideals—ideals that are real to him. A good many of Richardson's minor characters are accurately observed and reported without exaggeration, often with humour. But precisely those characters who are allowed to speak most freely for themselves, Lovelace and Clarissa, embody attitudes rarely found in life, perhaps never in their pure form. We do not think that this means that they are less 'real'. They are, in our opinion, Richardson's greatest triumph. They embody something that must have been in Richardson's mind, though we can find no clear evidence for it in his life or in his letters, something at once loftier (for Lovelace has his own loftiness) and more intense than we expect to find in him, something that the reader in turn can recognize as real because he (perhaps quite as unexpectedly) finds it

[81] *Complete Letters*, III, 8–9, 90.   [82] Barbauld, I, cix.

[83] Alfred de Musset, *Œuvres complètes en prose*, ed. Maurice Allem and Paul Courant, Pléiade edn. ([Paris, 1960]), p. 944.

[84] 'Elégies, II', *Œuvres complètes*, ed. Gérard Walter, Pléiade edn. ([Paris, 1950]), p. 58.

'With you, he is in your homes, he sees your sweet features. He reproaches your persecutors for their crime. He loves those who love you, hates those who oppress you. But suddenly he thinks—Oh, miseries of mortality!—that these touching objects of tears and sighs, alas! are perhaps only lovable chimeras, imaginary children of the mind and of genius. He gets up, walks about stormily; he lets his wishes wander in enchanting projects. He will go, his heart filled with a divine image, to search whether there is anywhere a Clementina. . . .'

in his own mind. The enthusiastic contemporaries who compared Richardson with Shakespeare were not entirely mistaken: Clarissa and Lovelace are comparable in kind with Lear and Falstaff. Their quality of feeling is discovered in the mind and given solidity through the realizing imagination.

Brian Downs, who considers characterization Richardson's greatest virtue, has pointed out that he cannot be said exactly to possess psychological insight.[85] His characterization does not explain human conduct or teach us how the mind works. But it might be held that such explanations are a matter best left to scientists. The artist needs to feel how the mind works, but he does not need to understand it. Freud has not notably improved characterization in fiction; rather those characters in modern fiction who most obviously show his influence are incredible puppets, a fact which need not cast doubt on either psychology as a science or fiction as an art, but does underline their difference.

Hazlitt has made a more serious charge against Richardson's characters: 'He furnishes his characters, on every occasion, with the presence of mind of the author. He makes them act, not as they would from the impulse of the moment, but as they might upon reflection, and upon a careful review of every motive and circumstance in their situation.' 'Every thing is too conscious in his works. Every thing is distinctly brought home to the mind of the actors in the scene, which is a fault undoubtedly: but then it must be confessed, every thing is brought home in its full force to the mind of the reader also; and we feel the same interest in the story as if it were our own.'[86] Richardson's characters are highly conscious—perhaps too conscious to convince an age like ours, inured to characters who often have no consciousness at all but drift through uncontrollable events in a dream or, like the people of Robbe-Grillet, see only with their physical eyes. But this is merely to say that they are a particular kind of character—as are the characters of all the individual novelists. Richardson's mind worked logically, within the limits of his premises, and so do the minds of his characters. His is one way of looking at people, a way which tells a truth about human nature—not *the* truth, which has yet to be told.

Richardson, as we have seen, in his own comments about literature stressed morality and realism. In one sense, though not quite in the sense he meant, these are the great virtues of his fiction. His professed morals are at most of historic interest. They are commonplace and often dubious; they are sometimes, because of his habit of avoiding clear issues, ambiguous. One might, with about equal justice, say, as Yeats says of Wordsworth, that Richardson is 'always destroying his poetic experience, which was of course of incomparable value, by his reflective power. His intellect was commonplace, and unfortunately he has been taught to respect nothing

---

[85] *Richardson*, p. 125.   [86] *Works*, VI, 119.

else.'[87] But he succeeded best when he failed in providing clear rules for conduct.[88] The moral effect of *Clarissa*, at least, is something quite different from the moralizing. Diderot pointed out that Richardson furthered virtue by embodying it, by making the reader experience it, feel it. Who, he asks, would wish to be Lovelace with all his advantages? Who would not wish to be Clarissa in spite of her misfortunes? If this is true, and we think that it is, Richardson's insistence on the rewards of virtue was one of his great mistakes, even in the interest of his own morality. Pamela loses our sympathy when she succeeds in life; Sir Charles, who always succeeds, never has it. Richardson thought, as many men have thought, that it was important to *prove* that we should be virtuous—for all sorts of contradictory reasons. Fortunately, in his major work he did much better —he showed how it feels to be virtuous. His morality in *Clarissa*, though he occasionally weakened it by preaching, was the morality of a novelist, of an imaginative writer.

Richardson's conscious morals were conventional and professed to be useful. The morality of *Sir Charles Grandison* is proper and social; the effect of *Clarissa* is religious and individual. Morris Golden exaggerates his favourite theme of wish fulfilment, in this case fulfilment of the death wish, but is otherwise accurate enough when he says that 'Richardson speaks with two voices—the irrational self, seeking freedom, exaltation, and death, and the social self, the spokesman for an orderly, pragmatic morality that wants life to run along with as few rubs as possible. Like every man he is both Apollo and Dionysos; but unlike most writers, he is often both in extreme form at the same time.' 'In the conflict between the ego and society, whatever his professed attitudes Richardson gives the victory to the ego.' Even without the aid of psychoanalytical interpretations one can agree that Richardson was most successful in realizing exceptional persons, not in the typical or average demanded by the 'rules of moralizing'.[89] Whether or not Richardson repressed, and released in his fiction, strong antisocial drives we do not know. But when he is writing at his best, he does give the victory to the ego in the sense that the important thing for the reader is the intense emotion within the individual, not the social situation which may partly have given the occasion for that emotion. In about half of Richardson's fiction, as in almost all of his letters, he concentrates on the conventions that make societies jog along smoothly. But one need not have violent 'dominance fantasies' to feel that it is not quite enough for society to jog along smoothly, that a more intense quality of emotion, a more meaningful experience is necessary if one is not to grow weary of the jogging. And the successful printer

---

[87] *Letters*, ed. Allan Wade (London, 1954), p. 590.
[88] See Charlotte Lefever, 'Richardson's Paradoxical Success', *PMLA*, XLVIII (1933), 856–60. [89] *Richardson's Characters*, pp. 119, 186, 190.

and family man who seems to have jogged smoothly enough through his own life found that experience somewhere in himself in rich enough variety to endow with it both Lovelace and Clarissa.

The difference between the morality of *Clarissa* and the morality of *Sir Charles Grandison* is the same as the difference between the 'realism' of the two novels. The realism of *Sir Charles* depends on accurately observed manners; its morality is based on maxims about what human conduct should be, approved by Richardson's class and by his own conscious mind. These maxims are grouped together and given the name of Grandison, and various actions are devised to illustrate them and are then reported with due attention to plausibility. The actions are 'true to life', but one can never be allowed to imagine the feelings of the man who performs them. The maxims do not depend on feelings but on rules, and these rules demand that the embodiment of the maxims even *feel* correctly—that is not feel in any way which another human mind can recognize. The realism must remain on the surface or the morality will become ambiguous. In *Clarissa* the morality *is* the feelings, and the surface realism is subordinated to the imagined characters. If the reader tries to identify with Sir Charles, realism and morality both evaporate; if he does not identify with Clarissa, the impression of reality is impoverished and the moral effect is reduced to a series of platitudes.

It is, of course, possible to read Richardson's novels as allegories or myths. Like all the major realistic novels, they embody an outlook on life, a set of values, which can be stated in abstract, general terms. We might even suggest a 'mythos' for *Clarissa*, the perennial conflict of the demands of the ego—its desire to assert itself at the expense of others against its desire to remain independent of others. The Lovelace part of our minds can fulfil itself only by dominating our fellows and lowering them in order to put us on at least a relative height; the Clarissa part can learn to be independent of the invidious comparison and to assert its independence even when violated and humiliated. Such a conflict lends itself very well to the 'determining emotional pattern' which, according to Maud Bodkin, 'corresponds to the form of tragedy'. If the tragic archetype is 'an ambivalent attitude toward the self' arising from the contrast between 'a personal self' and 'a self that is free to range imaginatively through all human achievement', then this archetype is built into *Clarissa* both in the conflict between the two main characters and in the development of the heroine. Lovelace throughout, and Clarissa to a lesser degree at first, can be taken as embodying 'the self of imaginative aspiration', 'the power-craving'; Clarissa's final mood is an ideal example of the other pole of tragedy which 'satisfies the counter movement of feeling toward the surrender of personal claims and the merging of the ego within a greater power'. The story itself thus gives us that 'organization of the tendencies of self-assertion and submission' which according to Miss Bodkin creates the tension which gives rise to 'the distinctive tragic attitude'.[90] Whether or not such a mental conflict is seen as an archetype in the Jungian sense, it is certainly one of the most general of experiences and accounts better than secret sadism for the success of Lovelace, who embodies basic human drives just as Clarissa does. Some readers find more significance in the abstract than in the concrete, and they have a right to describe the general assumptions beneath the fictional surface. But even when it avoids over-ingenuity (the interpreter is always tempted to read himself and not his author), such speculation tends to substitute a pallid essay for a complex work of fiction. We would only insist that in a realistic novel the reader should first read the surface, participate in the events, feel with the characters. The 'meaning' should come to him as he reads, not as he speculates afterwards about the book.

It is our contention that Richardson's main achievement, historically and more important intrinsically, was the realism—not primarily the realism of everyday probability, though he had that, but the realism of completely imagined events, described dramatically in such a way that the reader can share the imagined reality. We think that his first readers were right about the nature of his greatness and that Dorothy Bradshaigh was a better reader of *Clarissa* than Dorothy Van Ghent. This kind of writing demands most of all that the reader become involved in it and participate with the characters in the scenes. As Dr. Johnson advised, 'Let him, that is yet unacquainted with the powers of Shakespeare, and who desires to feel the highest pleasure that the drama can give, read every play, from the first scene to the last with utter negligence of all his commentators. When his fancy is once on the wing, let it not stoop at correction or explanation.'[91]

In Richardson the embodied morality is inextricably mixed with the imagined character and situation. Together they constitute his claim to a place in the 'Great Tradition'. In our century many writers have turned away from the 'air of reality' and have tried to convey truth not through embodying it in characters who interact on each other but (when not preaching directly, like the lesser Richardson) through symbol, myth, or (more convincingly) lyric suggestion. Perhaps it is high time for a change, lest one good custom should corrupt the world. We have no desire to limit the novelist to one method. When the 'air of reality' is mere plausibility, illusionistic realism, as it has often been in inferior writers, it leads naturally to a reaction. In the best novelists from Richardson through Joyce and Proust it was something much more than plausibility. The novel became real to the reader because the writer had imagined it as real, had put his attitude towards life (or his attitudes) into his people and had

[90] *Archetypal Patterns of Poetry* (Oxford, [1968]), pp. 22–3.
[91] 'Preface to Shakespeare', *Works*, V, 152.

let them act out the results. We are not suggesting that Richardson is the equal of Stendhal or Dostoievsky or Conrad. His view of life was less rich, his conscious mind was conventional, his characters and situations were comparatively limited. But in *Clarissa* he did have a lofty view to convey, and he conveyed it through two characters who were imagined in the same way as the best of those of the later novelists.

Richardson is one of the clearest cases in literature of the difference between the imaginative mind and the speculative mind. Few writers have led less interesting lives and had less interesting 'ideas'. His life and his ideas have historical interest as revealing the best side of an important and often maligned class, because he sincerely tried to live up to what that class was supposed to stand for. Richardson was narrow, but he was not hypocritical. He was a businessman, but he was not ruthless or exclusively selfish. In the descent of the 'protestant ethic', which has been blamed indiscriminately for all the ills of western society, from Milton to Samuel Smiles, he was below the former but above the latter. Quite aside, however, from his historical position is his position as a writer of fiction. In *Clarissa* he realized a Christianity older and more internal than that which supported business ethics. He also dramatized aspects of his mind which he was unable to describe in terms of non-fiction, or rather which he would never have thought of trying to describe. For anyone interested in literature, the apparently complete divorce between the author of *Clarissa* and the kindly but slightly ridiculous printer who collected the *Moral and Instructive Sentiments* makes Richardson an especially good example of the creative mind at work, unsupported by learning, analytic intelligence, or even much experience, and thus thrown back on its own native strength.

For a biographer, it is rather disappointing that so little of the Richardson that went into Clarissa and Lovelace shows in his life. His letters show Clarissa's charity and many of her conscious ideas, it is true, but not her intensity or her nobility. Even if it could be shown that he was a suppressed seducer, he would still be no Lovelace—seducers are common enough, but Lovelace's wit and pride are by no means common. The details of Richardson's life and background tell us much more about what limited his work than about what makes it important. Proust attacks Sainte-Beuve because his biographical method of criticism 'méconnaît ce qu'une fréquentation un peu profonde avec nous-même nous apprend: qu'un livre est le produit d'un autre *moi* que celui que nous manifestons dans nos habitudes, dans la société, dans nos vices.' The man who appears in conversation and drawing-room essays is the product of a superficial self, not of 'le moi qui a attendu pendant qu'on était avec les autres, qu'on sent bien le seul réel, et pour lequel seuls les artistes finissent par vivre'.[92]

---

[92] *Contre Sainte-Beuve* (Paris, [1954]), pp. 137, 141.
'fails to recognize what a moderately profound acquaintance with ourselves teaches us: that

Sir Charles Grandison was the product of Richardson's social self, the Richardson who wrote to Mrs. Chapone or, in its best passages, the Richardson who wrote to Lady Bradshaigh. But it is the Richardson who wrote *Clarissa* who is most interesting, and this Richardson hardly appears in his biography. One might conclude that if this is true literary biography is useless. At least it should make biographers modest. But Proust has not discouraged his own biographers. A biographer can give the context out of which a book came. The book itself must give the rest.

---

a book is the product of another "me" than the one we manifest in our habits, in society, in our vices'.

'the "me" who has waited while we were with others, which we feel is the only real "me," for which in the end only artists live'.

RICHARDSON'S CORRESPONDENCE

THIS list contains all of the letters we have located to or from Richardson, including a few written for him by others, or to others for him. We have always quoted from the first listed manuscript version and have indicated ellipses within quotations though not at the beginning and end. We have listed printed versions when (1) they are the only ones extant; (2) they contain significant variations; (3) they are contained in whole or in part in Anna Lætitia Barbauld's *Correspondence of Samuel Richardson* (London, 1804) and John Carroll's *Selected Letters of Samuel Richardson* (Oxford, 1964), abbreviated as B and C. The following abbreviations are also used:

Amsterdam   Gemeentelijke Archief Dienst, Amsterdam
Berg   Henry W. and Albert A. Berg Collection of the New York Public Library, Astor, Lenox, and Tilden Foundations
B.M.   British Museum
Edinburgh   University of Edinburgh
EM   *European Magazine and London Review*, LIII (1808), 370–2, 429; LIV (1808), 10–13, 94–8, 190–2; LV (1809), 101–4
FM   Forster Collection, Victoria and Albert Museum
Hill   *The Works of the Late Aaron Hill*, 2nd edn. (London, 1754)
Huntington   Henry E. Huntington Library and Art Gallery
Hyde   Hyde Collection, Somerville, New Jersey
Klopstock   *Auswahl aus Klopstocks nachgelassenem Briefwechsel und übrigen Papieren* (Leipzig, 1821)
MM   *Monthly Magazine*
For correspondence with Elizabeth Carter, XXXIII (1812), 533–43
For correspondence with Tobias Smollett, LXVIII (1819), 326–8
For correspondence with Edward Young, XXXVI (1813), 418–23; XXXVII (1814), 138–42, 326–30; XXXVIII (1814), 429–34; XXXIX (1815), 230–3; XL (1815), 134–7; XLI (1816), 230–4; XLII (1816), 39–41, 331–5; XLIII (1817), 327–9; XLIV (1817), 327–30; XLV (1818), 238–9; XLVI (1818), 43–5; XLVII (1819), 134–7
Morgan   Pierpont Morgan Library
Morrison   *Catalogue of the Collection of Autograph Letters . . . Formed . . . by Alfred Morrison* (Privately Printed, 1883–92)

Osborn   James Marshall and Marie-Louise Osborn Collection, Yale University Library

For ease in reference we have added the numbers given the letters in the Young correspondence in the *Monthly Magazine*, the Wescomb correspondence in the *European Magazine*, and the Cheyne letters in the University of Edinburgh Library. In justifying our dates we have given only brief indications but will be glad to explain further to anyone interested.

DATE	CORRESPONDENT	REMARKS	LOCATION
		1732	
[*c.* 1 Aug.]	R to Thomas Verren R	Written about the time of TVR's apprenticeship	*Imperial Review*, II (1804), 609–16
		1734	
21 Dec.	Cheyne to R		Edinburgh 2
		1735	
9 Aug.	Cheyne to R		Edinburgh 3
		1736	
13 Jan.	Cheyne to R		Edinburgh 4
8 Feb.	R to Hill	Note on a letter from Eustace Budgell	B.M. Add. MS. 37,232, f. 138
6 Mar.	Hill to R	Dated 1735, but refers to *Prompter*	FM XIII, 2, f. 3
30 June	Hill to R		FM XIII, 2, f. 4
2 July	Hill to R		B, I, 5–7
5 July	Hill to R		FM XIII, 2, f. 5
8 July	Hill to R		FM XIII, 2, f. 8
19 July	Hill to R		FM XIII, 2, f. 7
19 July?	Hill to R	Date in another hand, but reference to *Alzira* fits this time	FM XIII, 2, f. 9
21 July	Hill to R	Awaiting sheets of *Alzira*	FM XIII, 2, f. 10
Thurs. Morning [22 July]	Hill to R	Receives sheets of *Alzira*	FM XIII, 2, f. 6
10 Oct.	R to Robert Dodsley?		Wisbech and Fenland Museum
		1737	
18 Mar.	R to Society for the Encouragement of Learning		B.M. Add. MS. 6190, f. 32

DATE	CORRESPONDENT	REMARKS	LOCATION
14 Apr.	Hill to R		B, I, 9–10
4 Sept.	Cheyne to R		Edinburgh 5
7 Sept.	Cheyne to R		Edinburgh 6
Oct.	Hill to R		B, I, 11–13
28 Oct.	Hill to R		FM XIII, 2, f. 11
13 Dec.	Hill to R	P.S. 14 Dec.	FM XIII, 2, ff. 12–13
		1738	
[1738?]	Hill to R	B dates 1736, but refers to North End	B, I, 7–9
4 Jan.	Cheyne to R		Edinburgh 7
10 Feb.	Cheyne to R		Edinburgh 8
20 Feb.	Ralph Allen to R	Dated 1737, but concerns publication of a letter which appeared in the *Daily Gazetteer*, 1 Mar. 1738	Royal National Hospital for Rheumatic Diseases, Bath
29 May	Hill to R		FM XIII, 2, ff. 14–15
1 June	Hill to R	B dates 1730, but letter refers to *Merits of Assasination* (1738) and Milton's prose, referred to in H's 29 May	B, I, 1–3
22 June	Cheyne to R		Edinburgh 9
6 July	Hill to R		B, I, 13–18
18 Aug.	Cheyne to R		Edinburgh 10
23 Aug.	Cheyne to R		Edinburgh 11
29 Aug.	Hill to R		FM XIII, 2, ff. 16–17; B, I, 19–22
31 Aug.	Hill to R		FM XIII, 2, ff. 18–19
[Late Aug. ?]	Cheyne to R	Sends proof as he had promised 23 Aug.	Edinburgh 12
[3 Sept.?]	Cheyne to R	Dated Saturday, n. y., but receives more proofs	Edinburgh 12 *bis*
30 Sept.	Cheyne to R	N. y., but sends proofs of *Natural Method of Cureing*	Edinburgh 13

DATE	CORRESPONDENT	REMARKS	LOCATION
[*c.* Sept.?]	Cheyne to R	Sale, *Master Printer*, p. 157, takes this, evidently because it is first letter in file, to refer to *English Malady* (1733), but remarks about proofs are like those on *Natural Method of Cureing*	Edinburgh 1
4 Oct.	Cheyne to R		Edinburgh 14
14 Oct.	Cheyne to R	N. y., but refers to *Natural Method of Cureing*	Edinburgh 15
9 Nov.	R to Alexander Gordon		B.M. Add. MS. 6211, ff. 51–2
18 Nov.	Cheyne to R		Edinburgh 16
29 Nov.	Cheyne to R	N. y.; refers to printing	Edinburgh 17
5 Dec.	R to Birch		B.M. Sloan MS. 4317, f. 172
18 Dec.	Cheyne to R		Edinburgh 18
20 Dec.	Cheyne to R	N. y.; receives sheets asked for on 29 Nov.	Edinburgh 19
26 Dec.	Hill to R		FM XIII, 2, ff. 20–1
		1739	
3 Feb.	Cheyne to R	Dated 1738; refers to sheets and booksellers	Edinburgh 21
6 Feb.	R to President of Governors of Bath Hospital		Royal National Hospital for Rheumatic Diseases, Bath
28 Feb.	Cheyne to R	Dated 1738; discusses *Essay on Regimen*	Edinburgh 20
[Mar.?]	Cheyne to Mr. 'Motte' [William Mole]	Printing of *Essay on Regimen*	Edinburgh 22
27 Mar.	Cheyne to R	Dated 1738; discusses booksellers of *Natural Method of Cureing*	Edinburgh 23

DATE	CORRESPONDENT	REMARKS	LOCATION
12 Apr.	Hill to R	End missing	FM XIII, 2, f. 22
12 Apr.	Hill to R	May be end of above	B, I, 22–3
May	Hill to R		B, I, 24–7
13 May	Cheyne to R	Note at end on bleeding dated Tuesday, 18 May, but Tuesday was 15 May	Edinburgh 24
4 June	Cheyne to R	N. y.; referred to in next	Edinburgh 25
7 June	Cheyne to R		Edinburgh 26
20 June	Cheyne to R		Edinburgh 27
1 July	Cheyne to R	Dated 1738, but remarks on Leake and Strahan fit June 1739 letters	Edinburgh 28
16 July	Cheyne to R		Edinburgh 29
6 Aug.	Cheyne to R		Edinburgh 30
29 Aug.	Cheyne to R		Edinburgh 31
[Early Sept.]	Cheyne to R	Sends dedication mentioned in 29 Aug. letter	Edinburgh 32
12 Sept.	Cheyne to R		Edinburgh 33
21 Sept.	Hill to R		B, I, 28–31
27 Sept.	Hill to R		FM XIII, 2, ff. 23–4
6 Oct.	Hill to R	Breaks off	FM XIII, 2, f. 25
12 Oct.	R to John Ward		B.M. Add. MS. 6211, f. 53
16 Oct.	Hill to R		B, I, 32–3
26 Oct.	Cheyne to R	N. y., but refers to *Essay on Regimen*	Edinburgh 34
8 Nov.	P. Delany to R		National Library of Ireland; B, IV, 1–3
19 Dec.	Hill to R		B, I, 33–6
21 Dec.	C. Marsh to R		FM XIII, 2, f. 26
23 Dec.	Hill to R		FM XIII, 2, ff. 27–8
		1740	
[1740s??]	Birch to R	Friday morning; the date of this letter is quite uncertain; R	B.M. Sloan MS. 4317, f. 181

DATE	CORRESPONDENT	REMARKS	LOCATION
		is printing some book for a friend of Birch	
3 Jan.	Hill to R		B, I, 37–41
12 Jan.	Cheyne to R		Edinburgh 35
20 Apr.	Cheyne to R		Edinburgh 36
[May?]	Cheyne to R	Remarks on *Essay on Regimen* fit between preceding and following letters	Edinburgh 37
6 June	Cheyne to R		Edinburgh 38
Sept.	John Windus to R?	No day; concerns Hill's wine-making —may be to Hill	FM XIII, 2, f. 29
17 Sept.	Hill to R		B, I, 41–53
1 Oct.	Hill to R		FM XIII, 2, f. 30
[Before 11 Oct.]	William Webster? to R		*Weekly Miscellany*, 11 Oct.; *Pamela* Introduction 1st edn.
[Before 6 Nov.]	de Freval to R		FM XVI, 1, f. 13; *Pamela* Introduction, 1st edn.
7 Nov.	Cheyne to R		Edinburgh 39
8 Dec.	R to Hill		FM XIII, 2, f. 32
13 Dec.	Cheyne to R	Rebecca Warner in *Original Letters* (Bath, 1817), p. 63, dates this letter 18 Dec., but the MS. has clearly 13 Dec.	Edinburgh 40
17 Dec.	Hill to R	B has cut	Hill, II, 114–19; B, I, 53–5; *Pamela* Introduction, 2nd edn.
17 Dec.	Astræa Hill to Mrs. R	Thanks for copy of *Pamela* R sent with 8 Dec. letter	FM XIII, 2, f. 31
22 Dec.	R to Hill		FM XIII, 2, f. 33
23 Dec.	R to Allington Wilde	Note written on the bottom of a notice of payment of dividend of stock in the Stationers' Company	John Johnson Collection, Bodleian Library
29 Dec.	Hill to R	Hill may have mis-	FM XVI, 1, ff.

DATE	CORRESPONDENT	REMARKS	LOCATION
		dated—answers R's disclosure (22 Dec.) that he is author of *Pamela*, which one would have expected Hill to answer at once; a second letter of this date (see below) reinforces this view	37–8; Hill, II, 128–31 (cut); *Pamela*, Introduction, 2nd edn.
29 Dec.	Hill to R		B, I, 55–8; *Pamela* Introduction, 2nd edn. (cut)
30 Dec.	Astræa and Minerva Hill to R		FM XIII, 2, f. 34
		1741	
6 Jan.	Hill to R		FM XIII, 2, ff. 36–9, and (end) FM XVI, 1, f. 39; *Pamela* Introduction, 2nd edn. (cut)
15 Jan.	Hill to R	Four missing pages	FM XIII, 2, ff. 40–4; *Pamela* Introduction, 2nd edn. (cut)
[Jan.?]	Hill to R	Only letter in *Pamela* Introduction not located in MS.; may be missing pages of 15 Jan. letter	*Pamela* Introduction, 2nd edn., I, xxxiii-xxxvi
21 Jan.	P. Delany to R		FM XVI, 1, f. 43
27 Jan.	Ralph Courteville to R		FM XVI, 1, f. 43
30 Jan.	'Philo-Paideias' to R		FM XVI, 1, ff. 44–5
[*c.* 1 Feb.]	R to Hill	Answers Hill's inquiry (15 Jan.) about basis of *Pamela*	B, I, lxix-xxvi; C, pp. 39–42
9 Feb.	Hill to R	FM copy breaks off (index to *Pamela* correspondence indicates 8 pp.; only 2 are in FM). B dates Dec. 1740 and in-	FM XIII, 2, f. 45; Hill, II, 161–166; B, I, 59–66

DATE	CORRESPONDENT	REMARKS	LOCATION
		cludes paragraphs not in FM or Hill, but these cannot be Dec., since they concern Harry Campbell, first mentioned by Hill 29 Dec., and index says these parts answer R's answer to Hill's 14 Jan. Part of B overlaps Hill, and part of that overlaps FM version	
12 Feb.	Cheyne to R		Edinburgh 41
[*c.* 20 Feb.]	Hill to R	Refers to 2nd edn. of *Pamela*	FM XVI, I, f,. 14; Hill, I, 131–2
[9 Mar.?]	Duck to R	*Pamela* index says this refers to continuation of *Pamela*, but letter itself could at least as well refer to end of Part I; either R made an error in index, or Sale (*Master Printer*, p. 167) is right and there was an unknown edn. of a Duck epistle in 1742. The letter, dated only Monday morning, incloses proof of an epistle, presumably *Every Man in His Own Way*, advertised 15 Mar., 1741	FM XVI, 1, f. 75
13 Apr.	Hill to R		FM XIII, 2, ff. 46–7; B, I, 66–9
21 Apr.	Hill to R		B, I, 70–5
15 May	Richard Newton to R	Extract only	FM XVI, 1, f. 49
25 May	Hill to R		FM XIII, 2, ff. 48–9

DATE	CORRESPONDENT	REMARKS	LOCATION
8 June	Ralph Courteville to R		FM XVI, 1, f. 50
22 June	'Philaretes' to R		FM XVI, 1, ff. 51–2
July	Anonymous to R	Same writer who earlier wrote to Rivington and was answered by Hill 6 Jan.	FM XVI, 1, f. 53
7 July	Cheyne to R	Rebecca Warner, *Original Letters*, p. 65, dates 14 Aug., but MS. clearly has 7 July	Edinburgh 42
29 July	Hill to R	Both printed versions cut	FM XIII, 2, ff. 51–2; Hill, II, 167–9; B, I, 75–8
Aug.	R to James Leake		FM XVI, 1, ff. 55–7; C, pp. 42–5
24 Aug.	Cheyne to R		Edinburgh 43
25 Aug.	Paul Bertrand to R		FM XVI, 1, f. 59
26 Aug.	Mary Barber to R		FM XVI, 1, f. 54
26 Aug.	James Leake to R		FM XVI, 1, f. 60
31 Aug.	R to Paul Bertrand	Draft—perhaps not sent	FM XVI, 1, f. 65
31 Aug.	R to Cheyne	Draft—perhaps not sent	FM XVI, 1, ff. 61–4; C, pp. 46–51
[Late summer or autumn?]	Alexander Gordon to R	Remarks on opera used in *Pamela* II	FM XVI, 1, f. 12
3 Sept.	R to Mary Barber		FM XVI, 1, ff. 66–7
22 Sept.	Cheyne to R		Edinburgh 44
8 Oct.	R to Ralph Allen		FM XVI, 1, f. 68; C, pp. 51–2
11 Oct.	Anonymous to R	Encloses letter from Lady Davers to Pamela	FM XVI, 1, ff. 69–72
14 Oct.	Duck to R		FM XVI, 1, f. 73
15 Oct.	Hill to R		Hill, II, 170–1; B, I, 79
22 Oct.	Hill to R		FM XIII, 2, ff. 52–3
24 Oct.	Cheyne to R		Edinburgh 45

DATE	CORRESPONDENT	REMARKS	LOCATION
31 Oct.	Cheyne to R		Edinburgh 46
[Oct.–Nov.?]	R to Duck	Draft answer to Duck's 14 Oct. 'Not sent'	FM XVI, 1, f. 74; C, pp. 52–3
Nov.	Hill to R		FM XIII, 2, f. 35
12 Nov.	Hill to R		FM XIII, 2, ff. 54–5
12 Nov.	A Dublin printer to R		Quoted in R's *Address to the Public* in 1st edn. of *Grandison*, VII
15 Nov.	Cheyne to R		Edinburgh 47
[Late Nov.]	Cheyne to R	N. d., but evidently out of order in numbering, since references to R's health show he is still considering Cheyne's cure and references to Strahan and Knapton clearly indicate 1741—probably 'my last' mentioned in Cheyne's of 2 Dec.	Edinburgh 62
2 Dec.	Cheyne to R		Edinburgh 48
7 Dec.	Cheyne to R		Edinburgh 49
8 Dec.	Hill to R		FM XIII, 2, f. 56
12 Dec.	Cheyne to R		Edinburgh 50
15 Dec.	Hill to R		FM XVI, 1, ff. 76–7
21 Dec.	Solomon Lowe to R		FM XVI, 1, f. 78
23 Dec.	Cheyne to R		Edinburgh 51
30 Dec.	Cheyne to R		Edinburgh 52
31 Dec.	Astræa Hill to R		FM XIII, 2, f. 60
[Late Dec. or early Jan. 1742]	Hill to R	No beginning, n. d.; index shows it is answer to R's answer to Hill's apology for correcting verses, referred to in Hill's 15 Dec.	FM XIII, 2, ff. 58–9
[Dec. or early 1742]	Morley to R	Discusses continuation of *Pamela*	FM XVI, 1, f. 15

DATE	CORRESPONDENT	REMARKS	LOCATION
[Dec. or early 1742]	David Mallet to R	Two notes on continuation of *Pamela* 1742	FM XVI, 1, f. 16
[Early Jan.]	R to Cheyne	Draft, not sent; answers Cheyne's 30 Dec.; C incorrectly says it answers Cheyne's 10 Jan.	FM XVI, 1, f. 58; C, pp. 54–5
[Jan.–Feb.?]	Six Reading Ladies to R	They have just read *Pamela* II	FM XVI, 1, ff. 17–18
7 Jan.	P. Delany to R	Dated 1741, but references to death of Mrs. Delany and *Pamela* II clearly indicate 1742	FM XVI, 1, f. 42
10 Jan.	Cheyne to R		Edinburgh 53
19 Jan.	John Swinton to R?	Extract	FM XVI, 1, f. 79
24 Jan.	Anonymous to R		FM XVI, 1, ff. 80–1
25 Jan.	Anthony Fulford to R		FM XVI, 1, f. 82
Recd. 26 Jan.	Anonymous to R		FM XVI, 1, ff. 83–4
27 Jan.	Anonymous to R		FM XVI, 1, ff. 85–6
2 Feb.	Cheyne to R		Edinburgh 54
25 Feb.	Hill to R	No ending	FM XIII, 2, f. 57
Feb.	Cheyne to R	Answers R's answer to Cheyne's 2 Feb.	Edinburgh 55
9 Mar.	Cheyne to R		Edinburgh 56
14 Mar.	Cheyne to R		Edinburgh 57
21 or 22 Mar.	'Philopamela' to R		FM XVI, 1, ff. 87–8
[c. Mar.]	Six Reading Ladies to R	Complain letter [Jan.–Feb.?] not answered	FM XVI, 1, f. 18
[c. Mar.]	R to Six Reading Ladies	Answer to above	FM XVI, 1, ff. 19–20
[c. Mar.]	Samuel Vanderplank to R	About Six Reading Ladies	FM XVI, 1, f. 21
2 Apr.	Cheyne to R		Edinburgh 58
10 Apr.	R to Hill		FM XIII, 3, f. 2
19 Apr.	Cheyne to R		Edinburgh 59
26 Apr.	Cheyne to R		Edinburgh 60

DATE	CORRESPONDENT	REMARKS	LOCATION
2 May	Cheyne to R		Edinburgh 61
Recd. 17 May	Cheyne to R		Edinburgh 63
22 June	Cheyne to R		Edinburgh 64
30 June	Cheyne to R		Edinburgh 65
7 July	Hill to R	Extract	FM XIII, 3, ff. 3–4
14 July	Cheyne to R		Edinburgh 66
[Late July–Aug.]	Cheyne to R	Remarks on R's illness like those in Cheyne's 14 July and 30 July, but could be after the latter	Edinburgh 67
30 July	Cheyne to R		Edinburgh 68
29 Aug.	Cheyne to R	N. y.; remarks on illness fit here	Edinburgh 69
5 Sept.	Cheyne to R		Edinburgh 70
17 Sept.	Cheyne to R		Edinburgh 71
24 Sept.	R to Hill		FM XIII, 3, f. 5
26 Sept.	Cheyne to R		Edinburgh 72
12 Oct.	Cheyne to R		Edinburgh 73
24 Oct.	Hill to R		B, I, 80–2
29 Oct.	R to Hill		Princeton; B, I, 83–6
2 Nov.	Cheyne to R		Edinburgh 74
17 Nov.	R to William Warburton	C has cut	FM XVI, 1, 89; C, pp. 55–6
19 Nov.	Cheyne to R		Edinburgh 74
18 Dec.	Cheyne to R		Edinburgh 76
28 Dec.	William Warburton to R		B, I, 133–5
		1743	
14 Jan.	Cheyne to R	Dated 1742, but refers to *New Dunciad*, Richard Newton's *Pluralities Indefensible*, Cheyne's illness	Edinburgh 78
21 Jan.	R to Cheyne	Extract	Berg; C, pp. 56–8
27 Jan.	Cheyne to R	Dated 1742, but refers to Cheyne's illness, his 14 Jan. letter, and Bertrand	Edinburgh 79

DATE	CORRESPONDENT	REMARKS	LOCATION
		translation, further discussed 7 Feb.	
7 Feb.	Cheyne to R		Edinburgh 80
4 Mar.	Cheyne to R		Edinburgh 81
24 Mar.	Cheyne to R	Dated 1742; further reference to Bertrand translation	Edinburgh 82
2 Apr.	Hill to R		B, I, 89–93
2 Apr.	R to Hill	Answer to preceding; C has cut	FM XIII, 3, f. 6; C, pp. 58–9
5 Apr.	Hill to R		B, I, 93–7
7 Apr.	R to Hill		FM XIII, 3, f. 8
11 Apr.	Hill to R		FM XIII, 3, ff. 9–10
[11 Apr.]	R to Hill	Monday night; refers to Hill's 11 Apr. on *Fanciad* and referred to in Hill's 15 Apr.	FM XIII, 3, f. 12
15 Apr.	Hill to R		FM XIII, 3, f. 13
21 Apr.	James Leake, Jr.?, to R	On death of Cheyne	Edinburgh (unnumbered)
25 Apr.	Hill to R		FM XIII, 3, ff. 13–15
28 Apr.	R to Hill		FM XIII, 3, f. 11
11 May	R to Samuel Lobb		Mrs. A. Cory-Wright
19 May	Hill to R		FM XIII, 3, ff. 20–1
21 May	Samuel Lobb to R		B, I, 173–6
21 May	Hill to R		FM XIII, 3, ff. 22–3
June	Pilkington to R		B, II, 113–16
15 July	Pilkington to R		B, II, 116–17
		1744	
19 Jan.	R to Hill	C has cut	FM XIII, 3, f. 16; C, p. 60
20 Jan.	Hill to R		B, I, 87–8
[Feb.?]	Hill to R	B gives only year; refers to rehearsal of *Alzira*, performed 30 Apr.	B, I, 108–11
22 Mar.	Hill to R		FM XIII, 3, ff. 24–5
3 Apr.	Hill to R		FM XIII, 3, f. 26

DATE	CORRESPONDENT	REMARKS	LOCATION
4 Apr.	R to Hill		FM XIII, 3, f. 17
6 Apr.	Hill to R		FM XIII, 3, ff. 18–19
20 June	Young to R	B dates only 1744	MM i; B, II, 4–6
9 July	Young to R	B's letter of this date includes paragraphs from four different MM letters; only her paragraph 3 is in MM of this date	MM iii; B, II, 3–4
24 July	Hill to R	Hill has one paragraph not in B; she has three paragraphs, including early reference to Clarissa, not in Hill	Hill, II, 239–41; B, I, 101–4
29 July	Young to R		MM ii
10 Sept.	Hill to R		B, I, 104–8
Nov.	Hill to R		FM XIII, 3, f. 27
8 Dec.	Young to R	MM includes first part of letter B dates 20 Apr. 1744	MM iv; B, II, 1–2
[c. 12 Dec.]	R to Young	N. d., but answers Young's 8 Dec.; B and C have cut	MM v; B, II, 6–8; C, p. 61
[c. 15 Dec.]	Young to R	N. d., but answer to above; proposes to be in town soon after Christmas; partly included in B's 20 Apr. 1744	MM vi; B, II, 1–2
21 Dec.	R to Birch		B.M. Sloan MS. 4317, f. 174
28 Dec.	R to Birch		B.M. Sloan MS. 4317, f. 176
		1745	
1745	Pilkington to R	B gives only year	B, II, 124–7
1745	Pilkington to R	B gives only year; seems an answer to answer to above	B, II, 134–5
1745	Pilkington to R	B gives only year	B, II, 131–3
7 Jan.	Hill to R		B, I, 99–101
12 Feb.	R to Birch		B.M. Sloan MS. 4317, f. 177

DATE	CORRESPONDENT	REMARKS	LOCATION
28 Feb.	Hill to R	Dated 1744; refers to MS. of *Clarissa*	FM XV, 3, ff. 5–6
13 Mar.	Pilkington to R		B, II, 118–21
4 Apr.	Hill to R		FM XIII, 3, f. 28
19 Apr.	Hill to R		FM XIII, 3, f. 31
[May–June?]	Hill to R	Dated in another hand 1745/6; refers to return of *Columella*, loan of which is mentioned 19 Apr., and vellum volumes of *Clarissa*	FM XIII, 3, f. 36; Hill, II, 300
[Mid–1745?]	Hill to R	N. d.; refers to volumes of *Clarissa*	Hill, II, 301–2
2 May	Young to R		*MM* ix
16 May	Pilkington to R		B, II, 121–2
27 May	Pilkington to R		B, II, 123–4
11 June	Young to R		*MM* x
29 June	Pilkington to R		B, II, 127–31
13 Aug.	Pilkington to R		B, II, 135–6
[Aug.–Sept.?]	Young to R	Dated only Saturday; refers to Young's visit to Tunbridge, to Capt. Cole and Mrs. Liston	*MM* xxviii
17 Sept.	Young to R		*MM* xi
[Nov.–Dec.]	Hill to R	N. d.; in R's hand 'With XI and XII Parts [of *Clarissa*] in MS Before I begun to prune 1745. Latter End of ye Year'	FM XIII, 2, ff. 61–2; B, I, 97–9
26 Nov.	Young to R	B includes *MM* letter of 17 Aug. 1746 under this date	*MM* xii; B, II, 11
3 Dec.	R to Young	C has cut	*MM* xiii; C, p. 62
10 Dec.	Young to R		*MM* xiv
19 Dec.	Young to R	The first part of letter B dates 10 Dec. is letter *MM* dates 19 Dec.	*MM* xv; B, II, 14
[19 Dec.?]	Pilkington to R	B dates only Dec. and Thursday; it	B, II, 137–8

DATE	CORRESPONDENT	REMARKS	LOCATION
		precedes her 23 Dec. letter	
23 Dec.	Pilkington to R		B, II, 138–9
28 Dec.	Pilkington to R		B, II, 140–1
		1746	
[1745–6]	Hill to R	Dated '1745/6' in another hand	FM XIII, 3, f. 37
11 Jan.	Hill to R		FM XIII, 3, ff. 35–6
20 Jan.	R to Hill		FM XV, 3, f. 7; C, pp. 62–4
28 Jan.	Pilkington to R		B, II, 142–4
29 Jan.	R to Hill		FM XIII, 3, f. 33
30 Jan.	R to Charles Acres		N&Q, N.S. II (1964), 299
[30 Jan.]	Hill to R	Dated Jan., 1745/6, in another hand; 30 Jan. referred to in letter; concerns revising *Clarissa*	FM XIII, 3, f. 34
[Late Jan.?]	Hill to R	Dated Jan., 1745/6 in another hand; on revising *Clarissa*— could be answer to R's 20 Jan.	FM XIII, 3, f. 32
[Jan.–Feb.?]	Young to R	N. d.; after reference to Young's stepdaughter on 19 Dec. 1745 and before 12 Mar., when Young proposes to be in town	*MM* xvii
6 Feb.	Hill to R		FM XIII, 3, ff. 38–9
18 Feb.	Young to R	Dated 1745, but references to Young's hæmorrhoids and to his stepdaughter indicate 1745/6; the last paragraph and P.S. of B's letter of this date are in *MM* letter of 4 Mar.	*MM* vii; B, II, 9–10
[Feb.–Mar.?]	Pilkington to R	References to son	B, II, 144–6

DATE	CORRESPONDENT	REMARKS	LOCATION
		and granddaughter fit this date; B gives only year	
Mar.	Hill to R	Date in another hand, but letter concerns *Clarissa*	FM XIII, 3, ff. 29–30
[Late Feb.– early Mar.]	Young to R	N. d., but refers to proposed trip to town on 12 Mar. (on 19 Mar. Young has recently seen R); references to reading *Clarissa* and to Young's step-daughter, whom R met before 2 May 1745, fit 1746; partly printed in B's 20 Apr. 1744 letter	*MM* xvii; B, I, 1–2
2 Mar.	P. Delaney to R		B, II, 146
4 Mar.	Young to R	Dated 1745, but refers to death of Capt. Cole. End of letter included in B's letter of 18 Feb.	*MM* viii; B, II, 10–11
19 Mar.	Young to R	B includes most of this letter in letter she dates 10 Dec. 1745	*MM* xvi; B, II, 14–15
3 Apr.	Pilkington to R		B, II, 147–9
11 Apr.	Hill to R		FM XIII, 3, f. 40
20 Apr.	Young to R	Partly included in B's letter of 20 Apr. 1744	*MM* xviii; B, II, 1–2
May	R to Young	Dated Sunday	*MM* xix
6 May	Pilkington to R		B, II, 149–51
16 May	R to Samuel Lobb		Mrs. A. Cory-Wright
13 June	Hill to R		FM XIII, 3, f. 41
25 June	R to Hill		FM XIII, 3, f. 42
[July]	Hill to R	Dated '1746' in another hand; refer-ences to Hill's work on Cæsar fit early July	FM XIII, 3, f. 54

DATE	CORRESPONDENT	REMARKS	LOCATION
4 July	Hill to R		FM XIII, 3, f. 43
4 July	R to Samuel Lobb		Mrs. A. Cory-Wright
7 July	R to Hill		FM XIII, 3, f. 46
10 July	Hill to R		FM XIII, 3, ff. 44–5
17 July	Young to R	Each version has some material not in the other	*MM* xx; B, II, 15–17
21 July	Hill to R		FM XIII, 3, ff. 47–8
29 July	Hill to R		FM XIII, 3, ff. 49–50
[July 1746–Mar. 1750]	R to William Lobb	After 4 July 1746, when their correspondence has not begun, and before 10 Apr. 1750, when it is well established	Mrs. A. Cory-Wright
4 Aug.	Hill to R		FM XIII, 3, ff. 51–2
5 Aug.	R to Hill		FM XIII, 3, f. 53
17 Aug.	Young to R	Included in B's letter dated 26 Nov. 1745	*MM* xxi; B, II, 12–13
22 Aug.	Wescomb to R	Her first extant letter	FM XIV, 3, ff. 9–10
3 Sept.	Wescomb to R		FM XIV, 3, ff. 5–6
15 Sept.	Hill to R		FM XIII, 3, ff. 55–6
15 Sept.	R to Wescomb	Part cut in B; not dated in B or Huntington, but reference to R's tour to Hants. and Wilts. makes FM date certain; C has cut	Huntington; FM XIV, 3. ff. 7–8; B, III, 250–5; C, pp. 67–9
[Late Sept.?]	R to Wescomb	N. d.; references to *Clarissa* and Ann Vanderplank make this date likely; formality of tone	B, III, 244–9; C, pp. 64–7

DATE	CORRESPONDENT	REMARKS	LOCATION
		indicates an early letter	
8 Oct.	Wescomb to R		FM XIV, 3, ff. 11–12
13 Oct.	R to Wescomb	C has cut	Berg; C, pp. 69–70
13 Oct.	Hill to R		B, I, 112–17
23 Oct.	Hill to R		FM XIII, 3, ff. 59–62
25 Oct.	Hill to R		FM XIII, 3, ff. 57–8
29 Oct.	R to Hill		FM XIII, 3, ff. 63–4; C, pp. 70–5
29 Oct.	R to Arthur Onslow?	Copied on top of Hill's 25 Oct., which refers to a letter from Onslow to R	FM XIII, 3, f. 57
5 Nov.	R to Wescomb		EM i
5 Nov.	Hill to R		FM XIII, 3, ff. 65–6
10 Nov.	Hill to R		Folger Shakespeare Library
11 Nov.	Young to R	B's letter includes also paragraphs from MM letters of 16 Nov. and 2 Dec.	MM xiii; B, II, 17–20
16 Nov.	Young to R	B prints only one paragraph, included in 11 Nov. letter	MM xxiii; B, II, 20–1
20 Nov.	Hill to R		FM XIII, 3, f. 67
Nov.	Hill to R	No day; reference to loan of £100 places it after 10 Nov.	B, I, 118
[Late 1746?]	Pilkington to R	B gives only year; reference to illness could be fever from which on 20 Feb. 1747 she has recently recovered	B, II, 151–4
2 Dec.	Young to R	Most of it included in B's 11 Nov. letter	MM xxiv; B, II, 19
22 Dec.	Hill to R		FM XIII, 3, f. 68;

DATE	CORRESPONDENT	REMARKS	LOCATION
			copy FM XV, 2, f. 6
24 Dec.	R to Young		*MM* xxv
[1746–1747?]	Mr. Bennet to R	Reference to Cibber's letter on *Clarissa* sounds as if novel has not yet been published	FM XV, 3, ff. 10–11
		1747	
5 Jan.	R to Wescomb		*EM* ii
5 Jan.	R to Hill		FM XIII, 3, f. 81; C, pp. 75–8
11 Jan.	Young to R		*MM* xxvi
23 Jan.	Hill to R		FM XIII, 3, ff. 82–5
24 Jan.	James Hervey to R		Morgan
26 Jan.	R to Hill	C has cut	FM XIII, 3, ff. 85–8; end FM XVI, 1, f. 36; C, pp. 78–84
27 Jan.	R to Wescomb		*EM* iii
27 Jan.	R to Wescomb		*EM* iv
28 Jan.	R to James Hervey		Morgan
28 Jan.	Hill to R		FM XIII, 3, f. 89
9 Feb.	Hill to R		FM XIII, 3, ff. 89–92
14 Feb.	R to Wescomb		*EM* v
20 Feb.	Pilkington to R		B, II, 154–5
27 Feb.	Wescomb to R		FM XIV, 3, f. 13
5 Mar.	Wescomb to R		FM XIV, 3, ff. 15–16
6 Mar.	R to Wescomb		FM XIV, 3, f. 4; B, III, 239–43
21 Mar.	Wescomb to R		FM XIV, 3, ff. 17–18
9 Apr.	Young to R	Printed by B as last two paragraphs of her 17 May letter	*MM* xxvii; B, II, 21–2
14 Apr.	Wescomb to R	Dated 1746, but references to *Clarissa* fit 1747, and R seems to have met her in Aug. 1746	FM XIV, 3, ff. 2–3

DATE	CORRESPONDENT	REMARKS	LOCATION
3 May	Young to R		*MM* xxix
17 May	Young to R	Only beginning in B; rest of her letter of this date is *MM* 9 Apr.	*MM* xxx; B, II, 21
21 May	Wescomb to R		FM XIV, 3, ff. 19–20
30 June	Wescomb to R		FM XIV, 3, ff. 21–2
13 July	Wescomb to R		FM XIV, 3, ff. 23–4
5 Aug.	Young to R		B, II, 23
[Autumn]	Joseph Highmore to R	Reference to Preface to *Clarissa* shows this is before publication	FM XV, 2, f. 86
[Autumn]	R. Smith to R	Comments on above	FM XV, 2, f. 87
3 Nov.	Hill to R	Extract	FM XIII, 3, f. 92
3 Nov.	James Hervey to R		B, II, 180–2
3 Nov.	Wescomb to R		FM XIV, 3, f. 25
12 Nov.	John Heylin to R		FM XV, 2, f. 3
19 Nov.	R to Young	C has cut	*MM* xxxi; B, II, 24–5; C, pp. 84–5
24 Nov.	Young to R	Part is in B's letter of 9 July 1744	*MM* xxxi *bis*; B, II, 4
24 Nov.	Mary Heylin to R		FM XV, 2, f. 3
26 Nov.	Hill to R		FM XIII, 3, f. 93
3 Dec.	Hill to R		FM XIII, 3, ff. 93–4
4 Dec.	R to Hill		FM XIII, 3, ff. 148–9
13 Dec.	Carter to R		*MM*
18 Dec.	R to Carter		Harvard; *MM*
21 Dec.	Anonymous to R		FM XV, 2, f. 4
31 Dec.	Carter to R		*MM*
		1748	
[Early 1748?]	'Philaretes' to R	On the first two vols. of *Clarissa*	FM XV, 2, f. 32
6 Jan.	Wescomb to R	Letter dated 6 Nov. 1747/8, but R has corrected to 6 Jan.	FM XIV, 3, ff. 26–7
12 Jan.	R to Samuel Lobb		Mrs. A. Cory-Wright

DATE	CORRESPONDENT	REMARKS	LOCATION
21 Jan.	Spence to R	Osborn copy is rough draft	Osborn; B, II, 319–27
[Feb.?]	Young to R	N. d.; refers to edn. of *Night-Thoughts* published in Feb.	*MM* xxxiii
9 Feb.	'John Cheale' [Duke of Richmond] to R		FM XVI, 1, f. 90
29 Feb.	James Hervey to R	Dated 1747, which was not a leap year	Facsimile, B, VI
1 Mar.	Samuel Lobb to R		B, I, 177–81
7 Mar.	R to Samuel Lobb		Mrs. A. Cory-Wright; B, I, 181–3
30 Mar.	Cibber to R		B, II, 167–70
6 Apr.	Anonymous (woman) to R		FM XV, 2, ff. 4–5
14 Apr.	R to William Warburton	Partial publications in sales catalogues and in C have misdated 19 Apr.	University of Indiana; C, pp. 85–6
25 Apr.	William Warburton to R		Facsimile, B, VI
30 Apr.	Young to R		*MM* xxxii
5 May	Hill to R		FM XIII, 3, ff. 95–6; Hill, II, 302–6
10 May	R to Hill	No addressee, but answers above letter of 5 May	FM XI, f. 1; C, pp. 86–8
20 May	Anonymous to R		FM XV, 2, ff. 5–6
23 May	Solomon Lowe to R		FM XV, 2, ff. 101–2, and (end) FM XVI, 1, f. 90
15 June	Wescomb to R		FM XIV, 3, ff. 28–9
18 June	M. Delany to R		FM XV, 2, f. 7
2 Aug.	R to S. Highmore	C has cut	B, II, 203–8; C, p. 88
4 Aug.	Wescomb to R		FM XIV, 3, f. 20
9 Aug.	H. Morgan to R		FM XV, 2, ff. 15–16

DATE	CORRESPONDENT	REMARKS	LOCATION
[Late Aug.]	R to Wescomb	N. d.; R at Tunbridge; refers to her 4 Aug. and is referred to in her 12 Sept.	B, III, 311–19
2 Sept.	Anonymous to R		FM XV, 2, f. 6
5 Sept.	Channing to R		B, II, 337–40
12 Sept.	Wescomb to R		FM XIV, 3, ff. 31–2
1 Oct.	Edward Moore to R		FM XV, 2, ff. 17–18
3 Oct.	R to Edward Moore	C has cut	FM XV, 2, ff. 19–20; C, pp. 88–9
4 Oct.	J. Collier to R		B, II, 61–5
10 Oct.	Lady Bradshaigh to R		B, IV, 177–82
11 Oct.	Wescomb to R		FM XIV, 3, ff. 33–4
15 Oct.	Henry Fielding to R		E. L. McAdam
[c. 20 Oct.]	Lady Bradshaigh to R	Answers R's answer to her 10 Oct.	B, IV, 182–4
22 Oct.	Hill to R		FM XIII, 3, ff, 150–1
26 Oct.	Channing to R		FM XV, 2, f. 24
26 Oct.	R to Lady Bradshaigh	B misdates 6 Oct.	FM XI, ff. 153–6, and (end) FM XV, 2, f. 27; B, IV, 185–94; C, pp. 89–97
27 Oct.	R to Hill	C has cut	B, I, 119–24; C, pp. 98–9
29 Oct.	Channing to R		FM XV, 2, f. 24
31 Oct.	Channing to R		B, II, 333–6
2 Nov.	Hill to R	Each version has passages not in the other	Hill, II, 324–30; B, I, 124–32
7 Nov.	R to Hill	C has cut	FM XIII, 3, f. 152; C, pp. 99–100
12 Nov.	Hill to R		FM XIII, 3, ff. 153–4; Hill, II, 331–2

DATE	CORRESPONDENT	REMARKS	LOCATION
13 Nov.	Lady Bradshaigh to R	End missing	FM XV, 2, f. 27
[17 Nov.?]	Lady Bradshaigh to R	N. d., but before her 20 Nov., refers to his 26 Oct.; her [early Dec. ?] mentions a letter of 17th of last month. Could be end of her 13 Nov.	B, IV, 194–201
18 Nov.	R to Hill	C has cut	FM XIII, 3, ff. 142–3; C, pp. 100–1
20 Nov.	Lady Bradshaigh to R		B, IV, 202–6
25 Nov.	Hill to R		FM XIII, 3, ff. 144–5
28 Nov.	Channing to R		FM XV, 2, ff. 25–6
29 Nov.	Hill to R		FM XIII, 3, ff. 146–7; Hill, II, 332–5
[Early Dec.?]	Lady Bradshaigh to R	N. d. but last vol. of *Clarissa* is out; FM has ending only	B, IV, 207–17; FM XI, f. 2
1 Dec.	R to Mrs. R		On flyleaf of *Clarissa* (owned by Jasper A. Peck); FM XV, 3, f. 9; C, p. 102
1 Dec.	Philip Yorke to R		FM XV, 2, f. 14
2 Dec.	Edwards to R		FM XII, 1, f. 4; Bodleian MS. 1011, p. 76
5 Dec.	John Read to R		FM XV, 2, ff. 28–9
12 Dec.	Garrick to R		*Some Unpublished Correspondence of David Garrick*, ed. George Pierce Baker (Boston, 1907), p. 73
13 Dec.	Astræa and Minerva Hill to R		FM XIII, 3, ff. 138–41
14 Dec.	R to Astræa and	C has cut	FM XIII, 3, ff.

DATE	CORRESPONDENT	REMARKS	LOCATION
	Minerva Hill		136–7; C, pp. 102–3
15 Dec.	R to Lady Bradshaigh	N. d. in B; 4 pp. missing in FM; quoted B, I, xlviii; C has cut	FM XI, ff. 3–10, 12; B, IV, 217–238; C, pp. 103–16
16 Dec.	Carter to R		FM XV, 2, f. 11; *MM*
17 Dec.	R to Carter	C has cut	*MM*; C, p. 117
19 Dec.	Hill to R		FM XIII, 3, ff. 134–5
20 Dec.	R to Grainger		Morgan
23 Dec.	Edward Moore to R		FM XV, 2, ff. 20–1
27 Dec.	Solomon Lowe to R	A. M.	FM XV, 2, f. 103
27 Dec.	Solomon Lowe to R	P. M.	FM XV, 2, f. 105
[Late Dec.]	R to Lady Bradshaigh	End only; R's note on her 11 Jan. (begun 6 Jan.) letter says his last letter had not been received when she wrote; in that letter she refers to his 15 Dec.	FM XI, f. 13
[Dec. or Jan. 1749]	R to Edward Moore	Appears to answer his 23 Dec.	FM XV, 2, f. 21, and (end) FM XIV, 2, ff. 76–7; C, pp. 118–22
		1749	
[1749–1750?]	R to [Lady Bradshaigh?]	A draft not sent or an extract from letter to R's 'Warrington Lady'	FM XV, 3, f. 12; C, pp. 167–9
2 Jan.	S. Highmore to R		FM XV, 2, f. 12
4 Jan.	Hill to R		FM XIII, 3, ff. 97–8
6 Jan.	R to Hill		FM XIII, 3, f. 98
8 Jan.	S. Fielding to R		B, II, 59–61
11 Jan.	Hill to R		FM XIII, 3, ff. 99–100
11 Jan.	Lady Bradshaigh	Begun 6 Jan.; end	FM XI, ff. 11,

DATE	CORRESPONDENT	REMARKS	LOCATION
	to R	and one other page missing in FM	13–16; B, IV, 238–49
12 Jan.	R to Hill		Folger Shakespeare Library; FM XIII, 3, ff. 101–2
13 Jan.	R to Thomas Birch		B.M. Sloan MS. 4317, f. 178
15 Jan.	Solomon Lowe to R	Or 13 Jan—one date on top, another on bottom	FM XV, 2, f. 106
16 Jan.	Hill to R		Hill, II, 341–3
17 Jan.	R to Hill		FM XIII, 3, f. 103
19 Jan.	Hill to R		FM XIII, 3, ff. 104–5
21 Jan.	R to Solomon Lowe	C has cut	FM XV, 2, ff. 106–8; C, pp. 123–5
[Mid-Jan.]	R to Lady Bradshaigh	N. d., but answers her 11 Jan.; no beginning or end in FM	FM XI, ff. 17–18; B, IV, 250–7
25 Jan.	M. Delany to R	P. S. by P. Delany	FM XV, 2, f. 13
26 Jan.	Edwards to R	Bodleian dates 25 Jan. 1748	FM XII, 1, ff. 5–6; Bodleian MS. 1011, pp. 103–4; B, III, 1–3
Jan.	Anonymous to R		FM XV, 2, f. 36
[Early 1749]	Channing to R	Written as 'Orthodoxus Anglicanus' about Elias Brand; on 28 Nov. 1748 Channing regretted omission of Brand letter; B dates 1748–9	B, II, 327–32
[Feb. 1 or 2]	Solomon Lowe to R	Forwarding letter of 1 Feb. from Thomas Cooper, just received —written in the evening	FM XV, 2, f. 109
3 Feb.	R. Smith to R	Commenting on above	FM XV, 2, f. 112
5 Feb.	Solomon Lowe to R		FM XV, 2, f. 114

DATE	CORRESPONDENT	REMARKS	LOCATION
7 Feb.	Hill to R		FM XIII, 3, ff. 107–8
9 Feb.	Young to R		*MM* xxxvi
28 Feb.	Hill to R		FM XIII, 3, f. 106
8 Mar.	Hill to R		FM XIII, 3, ff. 109–10
[Late Mar.]	Hill to R	N. d., but sending part of *Gideon*	FM XIII, 3, f. 113
13 Apr.	J. Collier to R		B, II, 65–8
22 Apr.	Hill to R		FM XIII, 3, f. 111
Recd. 8 May	Young to R		B, II, 25–7
9 May	Hill to R		FM XIII, 3, ff. 114–15
10 May	R to Hill		FM XIII, 3, f. 115
18 May	Hill to R		FM XIII, 3, ff. 116–17
18 May	Solomon Lowe to R		FM XV, 2, ff. 116–17
20 May	R. Smith to R		FM XV, 2, f. 118
24 May	Young to R		*MM* xxxvii
27 May	Skelton to R		B, V, 193–7
28 May	Pilkington to R		B, II, 156–7
8 June	R to Anonymous	On fire scene	Printed letter (copy in FM)
10 June	Skelton to R		FM XV, 2, ff. 47–8
13 June	James Harris to R		B, I, 161–2
30 June	Henry Home to R		Universiteits- Bibliotheek van Amsterdam
30 June	Miss Churchill to R		FM XV, 2, ff. 22–3
9 July	Young to R		*MM* xxxviii
9 July	J. Collier to R		FM XV, 2, ff. 8–9
10 July	Hill to R		FM XIII, 3, ff. 118–19; Hill, II, 372–4
10 July	Solomon Lowe to R		FM XV, 2, f. 120
11 July	R to Henry Home		Universiteits- Bibliotheek van Amsterdam
12 July	R to Hill	C has cut	FM XIII, 3, f. 112; another copy in FM XIII, 3, f.

DATE	CORRESPONDENT	REMARKS	LOCATION
			120; C, pp. 125–6
20 July	Hill to R		FM XIII, 3, ff. 121–2
27 July	Astræa and Minerva Hill to R		FM XV, 2, ff. 74–6
4 Aug.	R to Astræa and Minerva Hill	C has cut	FM XV, 2, ff. 78–9; C, pp. 127–8
11 Aug.	R to Countess of Pembroke		FM XV, 2, f. 37
11 Aug.	Hill to R		FM XIII, 3, f. 123
17 Aug.	Strahan to R		B, I, 136–9
18 Aug.	R to Hill		FM XIII, 3, f. 126; C, pp. 128–130
24 Aug.	Strahan to R		B, I, 139–42
25 Aug.	Wescomb to R		FM XIV, 3, ff. 38–9
2 Sept.	Strahan to R		B, I, 143–6
9 Sept.	R to Young		Morgan; *MM* xxxix
10 Sept.	Young to R		*MM* xl
12 Sept.	R to John Conybeare		FM XV, 2, f. 38
16 Sept.	Strahan to R		B, I, 147–51
[19 Sept.?]	J. Collier to R	Dated in another hand 'June 1749', but the letter refers to article in Aug. *Gentleman's Magazine*; probably sent with enclosure dated 19 Sept., FM XV, 2, f. 33	FM XV, 2, f. 49
21 Sept.	Strahan to R		B, I, 151–5
1 Oct.	Strahan to R		B, I, 156–7
5 Oct.	Strahan to R		B, I, 157–60
15 Oct.	Young to R		*MM* xli
28 Oct.	Young to R		*MM* xlii
29 Oct.	Lady Bradshaigh to R		B, IV, 257–61
30 Oct.	R to Spence		Osborn
[Late Oct.– early Nov.]	R to Young	Answers Young's 28 Oct.	*MM* xlviii

DATE	CORRESPONDENT	REMARKS	LOCATION
[Early Nov.?]	Lady Bradshaigh to R	N. d., answered in part by R's [late Nov.?], but both may be compounded of more than one letter, written any time during Jan.–Nov. 1749	B, IV, 262–83
5 Nov.	Young to R		B, II, 27–8
9 Nov.	R to [Grainger]		N&Q, 4 S. I (1868), 285–6
26 Nov.	R to S. Highmore	C has cut	B, II, 209–19; C, pp. 130–2
[Late Nov.?]	R to Lady Bradshaigh	Answers parts of both her 29 Oct. and her [early Nov.?] letters; is answered by her 16 Dec.; may be compounded of more than one letter; C has cut	B, IV, 284–94; C, 132–6
5 Dec.	R to Grainger		Hyde
12 Dec.	Young to R		MM xliv
16 Dec.	Lady Bradshaigh to R		B, IV, 294–311
21 Dec.	R to Grainger	C has cut	Historical Society of Pennsylvania; C, pp. 136–41
28 Dec.	Edwards to R		FM XII, 1, f. 7; Bodleian MS. 1011, p. 162
		1750	
[1750?]	Astræa and Minerva Hill to R	They have read R's correspondence with 'Belfour'	FM XV, 2, f. 39
1 Jan.	R to Young		MM xxxiv
1 Jan.	Wescomb to R		FM XIV, 3, ff. 35–6
7 Jan.	Young to R	Dated 1749, but answers R's 1 Jan.	MM xxxv
9 Jan.	R to Lady Bradshaigh		B, IV, 311–21
16 Jan.	Cibber to R		Berg; B, II, 171–2

DATE	CORRESPONDENT	REMARKS	LOCATION
22 Jan.	R to Grainger	C has cut	*N&Q*, 4 S. III (1869), 375–8; C, pp. 141–50
25 Jan.	Wescomb to R		FM XIV, 3, f. 37
28 Jan.	Lady Bradshaigh to R		B, IV, 322–33
[30 Jan.]	Edwards to R	Dated only '1749/50', but enclosure dated 30 Jan.	FM XII, 1, f. 9
1 Feb.	R to Grainger		Morgan
2 Feb.	John Read to R		FM XV, 2, f. 80
[2 Feb.]	R to Lady Bradshaigh	B dates 3 Feb., but reference to tomorrow's being fine shows letter was written on Friday—undoubtedly the Friday letter referred to in his [5 Feb.]	B, IV, 336–45
[5 Feb.]	R to Lady Bradshaigh	B dates 2 Feb., but references to Saturday in the Park and yesterday at North End show letter was written on Monday; the enclosure must be his (undelivered) letter of [2 Feb.]; answered by her 7 Feb.	B, IV, 333–6
7 Feb.	Lady Bradshaigh to R	N. y., but concerns their meeting	B, IV, 345–8
8 Feb.	R to Lady Bradshaigh		B, IV, 348
9 Feb.	Lady Bradshaigh to R		B, IV, 349–52
9 Feb.	Lady Bradshaigh to R	N. y., but refers to their meeting and her morning letter	B, IV, 353
10 Feb.	R to Lady Bradshaigh		B, IV, 354–6
10 Feb.	R to Skelton		B, V, 198–200
[12 or 19 Feb.]	R to [Charles Chauncy]	Dated only Monday A.M.; refers to	Huntington

DATE	CORRESPONDENT	REMARKS	LOCATION
		possibility of 'Belfour's' seeing picture of Clarissa	
14 Feb.	Lady Bradshaigh to R	N. y., but refers to meeting	B, IV, 357–9
15 Feb.	R to Lady Bradshaigh		B, IV, 359–65
21 Feb.	Lady Bradshaigh to R		B, IV, 366–70
22 Feb.	R to Lady Bradshaigh	Begun 21 Feb.	B, IV, 371–6
24 Feb.	Lady Bradshaigh to R		B, IV, 376–9
28 Feb.	R to Grainger		B.M. Add. MS. 33, 964
27 Mar.	Lady Bradshaigh to R	Begun 25 Mar.	B, VI, 1–9
29 Mar.	R to Grainger	Quotations only in *Edwards Cat.*	Morrison, V, 252–4; *Francis Edwards Cat.* No. 386 (Dec. 1919), item 385; C, pp. 150–7
31 Mar.	R to Lady Bradshaigh		B, VI, 10–14
31 Mar.	Wescomb to R		FM XIV, 3, ff. 40–1
3 Apr.	Lady Bradshaigh to R		B, VI, 14–19
5 Apr.	Urania Johnson to R		FM XV, 2, f. 40
6 Apr.	R to Wescomb		FM XIV, 3, f. 42
10 Apr.	R to William Lobb		Mrs. A. Cory-Wright
10 Apr.	Young to R	Misdated 1780	*MM* xlviii
22 Apr.	David Graham to R		FM XV, 2, ff. 81–4
24 Apr.	[John] Rivington to R	References to his wife identify the writer as John Rivington	Harvard
28 Apr.	Edwards to R	N. y., but number (iv) in R's index, content, and day of week (Saturday) fit 1750	FM XII, 1, f. 8

DATE	CORRESPONDENT	REMARKS	LOCATION
1 May	Edwards to R		FM XIII, 1, f. 11
3 May	R to David Graham	C has cut	FM XV, 2, f. 85; C, pp. 157–9
22 May	Gilbert Hill to R		FM XIII, 3, f. 127
29 May	Wescomb to R		FM XIV, 3, f. 44
29 May	Urania Johnson to R		FM XIII, 3, f. 128
3 June	Lady Bradshaigh to R		B, VI, 20–5
4 June	R to S. Highmore	C has cut	B, II, 225–7; C, pp. 160–1
15 June	Mrs. Jobson to R	P.S. by Wescomb	FM XIV, 3, f. 43
21 June	R to Urania Johnson		FM XIII, 3, f. 130
22 June	R to S. Highmore	C has cut	B, II, 237–50; C, pp. 161–2
24 June	Urania Johnson to R		FM XIII, 3, f. 131
27 June	Wescomb to R		FM XIV, 3, ff. 45–6; B, IV, 256–61
2 July	R to Wescomb		FM XIV, 3, ff. 47–9; B, III, 261–70
8 July	Young to R		*MM* xlix
8 July	Dewes to R		B, IV, 3–7
9 July	Astræa Hill to R		FM XIII, 3, ff. 132–3
13 July	R to Mulso		B, III, 159–62
14 July	Donnellan to R		B, IV, 7–11
20 July	R to Donnellan		B, IV, 11–14; C, pp. 163–5
20 July	R to Mulso		B, III, 162–6
20 July	R to S. Highmore	C has cut	Brotherton Collection, University of Leeds; B, II, 251–7; C, pp. 162–3
21 July	R to Grainger		Historical Society of Pennsylvania
22 July	R to Lady Bradshaigh		B, VI, 26–8
23 July	Urania Johnson to R		FM XIV, 1, ff. 1–2
24 July	R to Urania Johnson		FM XIV, 1, f. 3

DATE	CORRESPONDENT	REMARKS	LOCATION
26 July	Urania Johnson to R		FM XIV, 1, f. 4
26 July	Wescomb to R		FM XIV, 3, ff. 50–2; B, III, 271–5
31 July	R to Millar		Hyde
[Aug.?]	W. Duncombe to R	N. d., but forwarding letter from George Jeffreys of 29 July	FM XV, 2, f. 89
1 Aug.	R to Lady Bradshaigh		B, VI, 29–40
6 Aug.	R to Grainger		Hyde
6 Aug.	R to Wescomb		FM XIV, 3, ff. 53–4
8 Aug.	R to Millar	Quoted only	*Francis Edwards Cat.* No. 396 (Dec. 1919), item 213
9 Aug.	R to Cave		Nichols, *Literary Anecdotes*, V, 37; B, I, 164–6; C, p. 165
17 Aug.	Gilbert Hill to R		FM XIII, 3, f. 124
17 Aug.	Donnellan to R		B, IV, 15–19
20 Aug.	R to Sutton		B, IV, 120–4; C, pp. 166–7
20 Aug.	R to Dewes		B, IV, 20–2
23 Aug.	Cave to R		Nichols, *Literary Anecdotes*, V, 38; B, I, 166–70
4 Sept.	Wescomb to R		FM XIV, 3, f. 55
5 Sept.	R to Mary Hallows		*MM* xlv
7 Sept.	Wescomb to R		FM XIV, 3, f. 56
8 Sept.	R to Grainger		Harvard
16 Sept.	Young to R		*MM* l
24 Sept.	Dewes to R		B, IV, 23–8
25 Sept.	Donnellan to R		B, IV, 29–34
25 Sept.	Sutton to R		B, IV, 125–8
9 Oct.	Lady Bradshaigh to R		FM, XI, f. 24
12 Oct.	Mrs. Chapone to R		FM XII, 2, ff. 4–5

DATE	CORRESPONDENT	REMARKS	LOCATION
12 Oct.	Mulso to R		*Posthumous Works of Mrs. Chapone,* II, 29–34
15 Oct.	Wescomb to R		FM XIV, 3, ff. 57–8; B, III, 281–5
16 Oct.	Young to R		*MM* li
19 Oct.	R to Mrs. Chapone		FM XII, 2, f. 6
1 Nov.	R to Wescomb		FM XIV, 3, ff. 59–60; B, III, 285–93
2 Nov.	R to Grainger		Hyde
10 Nov.	Mulso to R		*Posthumous Works of Mrs. Chapone,* II, 37–85
23 Nov.	Wescomb to R		FM XIV, 3, ff. 61–2; B, III, 294–8
24 Nov.	Mrs. Chapone to R		FM XII, 2, ff. 16–18
25 Nov.	Lady Bradshaigh to R	FM has a gap; some of what is in B and not in FM is answered by R's [mid-Mar. 1751], which is answered by her 29 Mar. and thus may not belong to this letter	FM XI, ff. 19–20; B, VI, 40–8
[Dec.?]	C. Talbot to R	Returns R's correspondence with 'Belfour' through 9 Feb. 1750; discusses matter to be included in new edn. of *Clarissa* (published in 3rd edn., Apr. 1751); seems to have New Year's greeting	FM XV, 2, f. 39
5 Dec.	R to Wescomb		FM XIV, 3, ff. 63–4; B, III, 298–305
6 Dec.	R to Mrs. Chapone		FM XII, 2, ff. 7–8

DATE	CORRESPONDENT	REMARKS	LOCATION
10 Dec.	R to I. H. Browne		Hyde
10 Dec.	Young to R		*MM* lii
13 Dec.	Young to R		*MM* liii
15 Dec.	Mrs. Chapone to R		FM XII, 2, ff. 9–10
25 Dec.	Cibber to R		B, II, 174–5
[28 Dec.]	Lady Bradshaigh to R	Dates 27 Dec. and 28 Dec. are given in letter; n. y., but references to Young and her penitent seem to follow her 25 Nov.	B, VI, 49–57
[Dec.–Jan.]	R to Lady Bradshaigh	This letter appears to be a composite of several; the last two pages refer to correspondence with Miss Mulso on parental authority as in process (the last of her letters is 3 Jan.), and one sentence is answered in Lady Bradshaigh's 28 Dec., but another refers to her 28 Dec.	B, VI, 121–3; C, pp. 184–5

1751

DATE	CORRESPONDENT	REMARKS	LOCATION
[Jan.]	R to Lady Bradshaigh	N. d., but answers her 28 Dec., answered by her 9 Feb.	B, VI, 57–62
[Jan.]	R to Edwards	Quoted in Edwards to Arthur Onslow, 19 Jan.	Bodleian MS. 1011, pp. 207–8
[Jan.]	Young to R		*MM* lv
2 Jan.	R to Young		*MM* liv
3 Jan.	Mulso to R		*Posthumous Works of Mrs. Chapone,* II, 89–143
9 Jan.	R to Edwards	B dates 1750, but letter answered by Edward's 24 Jan.	B, III, 4–5
11 Jan.	R to Mrs.	C has cut	FM XII, 2, ff.

DATE	CORRESPONDENT	REMARKS	LOCATION
	Chapone		11–12; C, pp. 172–3
21 Jan.	R to de Freval	Dated '*Jan.* 21, 1750, *O. S.*'; answered by de Freval's 17 Apr.	B, V, 271–5; C, pp. 174–5
21 Jan.	Mrs. Chapone to R	Dated 1750, but her first letter to R is 12 Oct. 1750	FM XII, 2, ff. 13–15
24 Jan.	Edwards to R	FM dated '1750/ 51', others 1750	FM XII, 1, ff. 12–13; Bodleian MS. 1011, pp. 210–14; B, III, 5–10
25 Jan.	Wescomb to R		FM XIV, 3, ff. 65–8; B, III, 306–10
1 Feb.	R to Wescomb		FM XIV, 3, f. 69
8 Feb.	Edwards to R		FM XII, 1, ff. 14–15; Bodleian MS. 1011, ff. 223–6
9 Feb.	Lady Bradshaigh to R	B prints this as if it is the beginning of letter completed 17 Mar., but the first part of the letter is answered by R's [Feb.–Mar.] and the last (17 Mar. part) by his 24 Mar.; B must have combined two letters	B, VI, 69–75
13 Feb.	R to Edwards		Morgan
25 Feb.	Mrs. Chapone to R		FM XII, 2, ff. 19–20
[Feb.–Mar.]	R to Lady Bradshaigh	N. d., but answers her 9 Feb.; C has cut	B, VI, 78–84; C, pp. 177–9
5 Mar.	Lady Bradshaigh to R	Only the end	FM XI, f. 21
5 Mar.	Skelton to R	Dated 1750, but answered by R's 25 Mar.	B, V, 201–3

DATE	CORRESPONDENT	REMARKS	LOCATION
9 Mar.	Johnson to R		Morgan; B, V, 281–2
9 Mar.	Edwards to R	FM dates only Mar. 1750/51; Bodleian 9 Mar. 1750	FM XII, 1, ff. 18–19; Bodleian MS. 1011, pp. 131–3
10 Mar.	Young to R	Dated 1750, but Shotbolt reference continued in Young's 19 Mar.	*MM* xlvi
[Mid-Mar.??]	R to Lady Bradshaigh	Refers to a sentence in her 25 Nov. 1750, to the part in B and not in FM; not answered by her 28 Dec., referred to in her 29 Mar. 1751 —see under 8 Apr.	B, VI, 62–8; C, pp. 170–2
17 Mar.	Lady Bradshaigh to R	Printed as a continuation of her 9 Feb., but a separate letter; see 9 Feb. and intervening 5 Mar. letters	B, VI, 75–7
19 Mar.	Young to R	Dated 1750, but referred to in Young's 26 Mar.	*MM* xlvii
19 Mar.	R to Edwards	C has cut	FM XII, 1, ff. 16–17; C, pp. 176–7
20 Mar.	Mrs. Chapone to R		FM XII, 2, ff. 21–2
24 Mar.	R to Lady Bradshaigh	N. y., but answers her 17 Mar.; C has cut	B, VI, 85–9; C, pp. 179–80
25 Mar.	R to Mrs. Chapone	C has cut	FM XII, 2, ff. 23–4; C, pp. 180–1
25 Mar.	R to Skelton		B, V, 204–6
26 Mar.	Young to R		*MM* lvi
30 Mar.	Edwards to R		FM XII, 1, ff. 20–1; Bodleian MS. 1011, pp. 247–52; B, III, 11–18

DATE	CORRESPONDENT	REMARKS	LOCATION
[Apr.–Oct.]	Lady Bradshaigh to R	The part of her 29 Mar.–8 Apr. letter not in FM is probably another letter—most of B's letters of 1751 are in utter confusion. The subject of wicked women unites this with R's [Apr.–Oct.?] and her two [May–Nov.] letters	B, VI, 96–101
[Apr.–Oct.?]	R to Lady Bradshaigh	Refers to Balzac quotation in her [Apr.–Oct.]; referred to in R's 26 Dec. 1751. Certainly a composite of at least two letters	B, VI, 116–21; C, pp. 182–4
Apr.	Young to R		*MM* lvii
8 Apr.	Lady Bradshaigh to R	Begun 29 Mar.; P.S. 8 Apr.; end only in FM	FM XI, ff. 22–3; B, VI, 90–101
9 Apr.	Young to R	First paragraph in B as beginning of 30 Apr. letter	Wellesley College; B, II, 48
16 Apr.	Lady Bradshaigh to R		B, VI, 110–16
17 Apr.	de Freval to R		B, V, 275–81
23 Apr.	Mrs. Chapone to R		FM XII, 2, ff. 1–3
24 Apr.	M. Delany to R		B, IV, 35–40
[May–Nov.]	Lady Bradshaigh to R	Refers to *Rambler* essay (19 Feb.) and to composition of *Grandison*—the latter in a way which shows she knows more of the novel than when she wrote her 16 Apr. letter	B, VI, 101–9
[May–Nov.]	Lady Bradshaigh to R	References to story of wicked woman	B, VI, 123–7

DATE	CORRESPONDENT	REMARKS	LOCATION
		continue remarks in above	
2 May	R to Edwards		FM XII, 1, ff. 99–100
8 May	Edwards to R		FM XII, 1, ff. 23–6; Bodleian MS. 1011, pp. 268–72; B, III, 19–24
10 May	Skelton to R		B, V, 207–11
10 May	R to Mrs. Chapone		FM XII, 2, f. 26
27 May	R to Edwards		FM XII, 1, ff. 27–8
15 June	M. Delany to R		B, IV, 40–2
17 June	Mrs. Chapone to R		FM XII, 2, f. 28
19 June	Edwards to R	Bodleian dates 18 June	FM XII, 1, f. 29; Bodleian MS. 1011, pp. 280–2; B, III, 24–6
11 July	R to Mulso	C has cut	B, III, 166–70; C, pp. 185–6
27 July	R to Mulso	C has cut	B, III, 171–5; C, pp. 186–7
27 July	R to Edwards		FM XII, 1, f. 30
27 July	R to Mrs. Chapone		FM XII, 2, f. 29
30 July	Young to R		*MM* lviii
[Mid–1751??]	R to Edwards	Edwards is at Ember Court; would fit here, but date really quite uncertain	Brown University
1 Aug.	R to Young		*MM* lix
5 Aug.	Mrs. Chapone to R		FM XII, 2, ff. 30–1
7 Aug.	Young to R		Tinker Collection, Yale; *MM* lx
13 Aug.	Wescomb to R		FM XIV, 3, f. 70
16 Aug.	M. Delany to R		B, IV, 43–8
26 Aug.	Edwards to R		FM XII, 1, ff. 31–2; Bodleian MS. 1011, pp. 296–8

DATE	CORRESPONDENT	REMARKS	LOCATION
3 Sept.	R to Mulso		B, III, 175–81; C, pp. 187–90
28 Sept.	R to Grainger		Yale
30 Sept.	R to Mulso		B, III, 182–91; C, pp. 190–4
15 Oct.	J. Duncombe to R		B, II, 271–4
22 Oct.	R to W. Duncombe	Quoted in part	*Maggs Bros. Cat.* No. 411 (Autumn 1921), item 2215; C, pp. 194–5
24 Oct.	Donnellan to R		B, IV, 48–51
26 Oct.	Sutton to R		B, IV, 128–32
2 Nov.	R to [Samuel Johnson]	N. y., but refers to Charlotte Lennox's *Female Quixote*; reference to *Rambler* makes addressee certain	Harvard
7 Nov.	R to Sutton		B, IV, 132–5
7 Nov.	R to Wescomb		FM XIV, 3, f. 71
17 Nov.	J. Duncombe to R		B, II, 275–7
18 Nov.	Mrs. Chapone to R		FM XII, 2, ff. 32–4
21 Nov.	Charlotte Lennox to [R]	Quoted only; for the identification of R as the addressee, see T. C. Duncan Eaves, 'Dr. Johnson's Letters to Richardson', *PMLA*, LXXV (1960), 380	George Birkbeck Hill, ed., *Letters of Samuel Johnson* (Oxford, 1892), I, 26n–7n
22 Nov.	R to Mrs. Chapone	C has cut	FM XII, 2, f. 35; C, p. 195
23 Nov.	Young to R		*MM* lxi
23 Nov.	Wescomb to R		FM XIV, 3, ff. 72–3
[Late Nov. or Dec.]	R to Charlotte Lennox	Later than hers to him of 21 Nov.; dated only 'Friday morn.' An unsigned sheet of criticism of the	Harvard

DATE	CORRESPONDENT	REMARKS	LOCATION
		Female Quixote (also at Harvard) was probably forwarded with this letter	
[Late Nov. or Dec.]	Charlotte Lennox to R	Dated only 'Friday 4 0 clock'; a reply to the above letter	Morgan
9 Dec.	Mrs. Chapone to R		FM XII, 2, ff. 36–7
10 Dec.	Young to R		*MM* lxii
10 Dec.	Johnson to [R]	Summarized and quoted only	*Sotheby Cat.*, 10 May, 1875, item 83
12 Dec.	R to J. Duncombe		B, II, 278–9
14 Dec.	M. Delany to R		B, IV, 52–4
15 Dec.	Young to R		*MM* lxiii
18 Dec.	R to Young		*MM* lxiv
19 Dec.	Wescomb to R		FM XIV, 3, ff. 74–5
23 Dec.	Edwards to R		FM XII, 1, ff. 33–4; Bodleian MS. 1011, pp. 306–8
2[3] Dec.	Edwards to R	Last figure of date torn, but dated Monday night	FM XII, 1, f. 35
24 Dec.	Young to R		*MM* lxv
26 Dec.	R to Lady Bradshaigh		B, VI, 128–37
28 Dec.	R to Edwards	Another hand has written 30 Dec., which B follows, but date at end is clearly 28 Dec.	FM XII, 1, f. 36; B, III, 27–9
[1751–1752?]	Johnson to R	On MS. of *Grandison*	Robert H. Taylor
		1752	
3 Jan.	Lady Bradshaigh to R		B, VI, 137–46
9 Jan.	Young to R		*MM* lxvi
10 Jan.	Edwards to R		FM XII, 1, ff. 39–40; Bodleian MS. 1011, pp. 316–17

DATE	CORRESPONDENT	REMARKS	LOCATION
13 Jan.	R to Charlotte Lennox		Harvard
19 Jan.	James Harris to R		B, I, 162–3
11 Feb.	Donnellan to R		B, IV, 54–7
19 Feb.	Edwards to R		FM XII, 1, ff. 37–8; Bodleian MS. 1011, pp. 335–7; B, III, 30–2
19 Feb.	R to Skelton		B, V, 212–14
21 Feb.	R to Edwards	C has cut	FM XII, 1, ff. 41–2; B, III, 33–5; C, pp. 195–6
22 Feb.	R to Dewes		B, IV, 62–5
22 Feb.	R to Donnellan	C has cut	B, IV, 58–62; C, pp. 196–7
22 Feb.	Mrs. Chapone to R		FM XII, 2, ff. 58–61
23 Feb.	R to Lady Bradshaigh	C has cut	B, VI, 146–55; C, pp. 197–9
28 Feb.	Edwards to R		FM XII, 1, ff. 43–4; Bodleian MS. 1011, pp. 338–40; B, III, 35–8
2 Mar.	R to Mrs. Chapone		FM XII, 2, ff. 38–45; C, pp. 199–206
16 Mar.	R to Edwards		FM XII, 1, f. 46; B, III, 38–40
20 Mar.	Edwards to R	Begun 18 Mar.	FM XII, 1, ff. 47–9; Bodleian MS. 1012, pp. 1–6; B, III, 41–8
26 Mar.	Donnellan to R		B, IV, 66–70
[Mar.]	Mrs. Chapone to R	N. d., but answers his 2 Mar. and answered (after a delay) 18 Apr.	FM XII, 2, ff. 46–57
[Mar.]	Lady Bradshaigh to R	N. d., but answers his 23 Feb. and answered by his 22 Apr.	B, VI, 155–9
6 Apr.	R to Charlotte Lennox		Harvard

DATE	CORRESPONDENT	REMARKS	LOCATION
18 Apr.	R to Mrs. Chapone	C has cut	FM XII, 2, ff. 62–73; C, pp. 206–11
22 Apr.	R to Lady Bradshaigh	C has cut	B, VI, 160–76; C, pp. 211–15
19 May	Lady Bradshaigh to R		B, VI, 176–84
Recd. 4 June	Mrs. Chapone to R		FM XII, 2, ff. 75–80
20 June	R to Mulso		B, III, 191–7; C, pp. 215–18
21 June	R to Mary Hallows		*MM* lxvii
21 June	R to Dewes		B, IV, 71–3; C, pp. 218–19
24 June	Edwards to R		FM XII, 1, ff. 52–3; Bodelian MS. 1012, pp. 13–14
24 June	R to Lady Bradshaigh		B, VI, 185–91
28 June	R to Edwards		FM XII, 1, f. 54
2 July	Mary Hallows to R		*MM* lxviii
3 July	Wescomb to R		FM XIV, 3, ff. 76–7
4 July	R to Mary Hallows		B, II, 29–31
6 July	R to Wescomb		FM XIV, 3, f. 78
9 July	Edwards to R		FM XII, 1, ff. 55–6; Bodleian MS. 1012, pp. 16–18
15 July	Skelton to R		B, V, 215–20
22 July	Wescomb to R		FM XIV, 3, ff. 79–80
24 July	Mulso to R	Extract	*Posthumous Works of Mrs. Chapone,* II, 213–15
24 July	R to Sutton		B, IV, 136–8
28 July	Lady Bradshaigh to R		B, VI, 192–203
29 July	Thomas Wilson to R		Hyde

DATE	CORRESPONDENT	REMARKS	LOCATION
30 July	Wescomb to R		FM XIV, 3, ff. 81–2
17 Aug.	R to Lady Bradshaigh	Last part probably later—see [*c.* 25 Sept.]	B, VI, 203–11
20 Aug.	Edwards to R		FM XII, 1, f. 57
21 Aug.	R to Edwards		FM XII, 1, f. 58
28 Aug.	Wescomb to R		FM XIV, 3, ff. 83–4
1 Sept.	R to Wescomb		*EM* vi
[*c.* 1 Sept.]	Lady Bradshaigh to R	B's letters at this period seem confused; we are assuming that they are composites and that the last part of this letter, on Sir Charles's divided love, does not belong with the first but about a month earlier	B, VI, 215–17
14 Sept.	Stinstra to R		Amsterdam
14 Sept.	Wescomb to R		FM XIV, 3, ff. 85–6
24 Sept.	Wescomb to R		FM XIV, 3, ff. 107–8
[*c.* 25 Sept.]	R to Lady Bradshaigh	The last part of this letter dated by B 17 Aug. refers to her [*c.* 1 Sept.?], whereas the first part answers her 28 July	B, VI, 211–13
29 Sept.	Edwards to R		FM XII, 1, ff. 61–2; Bodleian MS. 1012, pp. 25–6
[Early Oct.]	Garrick to R	After 28 Sept., when R's fire took place; well before 30 Nov., when *Every Man in His Humour* was performed	Facsimile, B, VI
[Early Oct.?]	Lady Bradshaigh to R	See [*c.* 1 Sept.?]; the first part of this	B, VI, 214–15

DATE	CORRESPONDENT	REMARKS	LOCATION
		letter is answered, after a delay, by his 20 Nov.	
5 Oct.	R to Mulso	C has cut	B, III, 197–206; C, pp. 219–20
23 Oct.	Edwards to R	The Bodleian copy is dated 19 Oct. and is a shorter version of the FM letter	FM XII, 1, f. 63; Bodleian MS. 1012, p. 27
23 Oct.	Mrs. Chapone to R		FM XII, 2, f. 81
25 Oct.	R to Edwards	C has cut	FM XII, 1, f. 64; C, p. 220
9 Nov.	Donnellan to R		B, IV, 74–8
14 Nov.	Young to R		Historical Society of Pennsylvania; *MM* lxix
18 Nov.	W. Duncombe to R	R quotes Duncombe's description of Stinstra in a letter to Stinstra of 6 Dec.; his quotation contains part of what is printed in this letter and also additional information—printed version must be cut	*Letters by Several Eminent Persons Deceased* (1772), II, 205
20 Nov.	R to Lady Bradshaigh	C has cut	B, VI, 217–25; C, pp. 220–1
30 Nov.	[W. Duncombe to R]	Further description of Stinstra—see 18 Nov.	Quoted in letter to Stinstra, 6 Dec.
6 Dec.	R to Stinstra		Amsterdam
15 Dec.	Edwards to R		FM XII, 1, ff. 65–6; Bodleian MS. 1012, pp. 33–4
23 Dec.	R to Edwards		FM XII, 1, f. 67; B, III, 48–9
28 Dec.	Skelton to R		B, V, 221–3
		1753	
1 Jan.	Mrs. Chapone to R		FM XII, 2, ff. 84–5
1 Jan.	Edwards to R		FM XII, 1, ff.

DATE	CORRESPONDENT	REMARKS	LOCATION
			68–9; Bodleian MS. 1012, pp. 59–61; B, III, 50–3
[Jan.–Feb.]	Lady Bradshaigh to R	Answered by his 24 Feb.	B, VI, 226–9
7 Feb.	Wescomb to R	Dated in another hand 1753/4 (but new style of dating began Sept. 1753); answered by his 8 Feb.	FM XIV, 3, ff. 113–14
8 Feb.	R to Wescomb		*EM* vii
11 Feb.	Wescomb to R	Year in another hand, but answers above	FM XIV, 3, f. 115
15 Feb.	Edwards to R		FM XII, 1, ff. 70–1; Bodleian MS. 1012, pp. 64–5
20 Feb.	R to Edwards	C has cut	FM XII, 1, ff. 72–3; C, p. 221
24 Feb.	R to Lady Bradshaigh	At least the penultimate paragraph, referring to the runs of *The Earl of Essex* and *The Brothers* (closed 15 Mar. and 17 Mar.) is misdated. C has cut	B, VI, 235–46; C, pp. 221–4
[Mar.]	Lady Bradshaigh to R	Answers his 24 Feb.	B, VI, 230–4
5 Mar.	Edwards to R		FM XII, 1, f. 74; Bodleian MS. 1012, pp. 71–2; B, III, 53–5
14 Mar.	R to M. Delany		B, IV, 79–82
[Late Mar.]	R to Lady Bradshaigh	End of 24 Feb. letter—see above	B, VI, 246–7; C, pp. 224–5
31 Mar.	Edwards to R		FM XII, 1, ff. 76–7; Bodleian MS. 1012, pp. 84–6; B, III, 56–8
2 Apr.	Stinstra to R		Amsterdam; B, V, 241–53

DATE	CORRESPONDENT	REMARKS	LOCATION
6 Apr.	Clairaut to R	Quoted only	Morrison, I, 208; *Hist. MSS. Comm.* 9th Report, Pt. II (1883), p. 478a
13 Apr.	Wescomb to R		FM XIV, 3, 109–110
17 Apr.	Johnson to R		*Letters*, ed. Chapman, I, 49
21 Apr.	R to Edwards		FM XII, 1, f. 78; B, III, 59–62; C, pp. 225–7
30 Apr.	Stinstra to R		Amsterdam
2 May	R to Wescomb		*EM* viii
10 May	Edwards to R	B dates 1 May	Bodleian MS. 1012, pp. 102–3; B, III, 62–5
16 May	Wescomb to R		FM XIV, 3, ff. 87–8
20 May	Cibber to R		B, II, 175–6
[29?] May	Cibber to R	B dates 27 May, but MS. has Tuesday and the last part of date torn off; reference to reading *Grandison* in sheets makes year certain; could be 22 May	Robert H. Taylor; B, II, 172–4
June	Charles Chauncy to R	Dated on back	FM XV, 4, ff. 9–10
2 June	R to Stinstra	B prints part as P.S. to 20 Mar. 1754 letter; C prints from McKillop MS.	Amsterdam; MS. copy by Martha Bridgen owned by Alan Dugald McKillop; B, V, 269–70; C, pp. 228–35
2 June	R to Lady Bradshaigh	C has cut	B, VI, 248–54; C, p. 235
4 June	Wescomb to R		FM XIV, 3, ff. 89–90
6 June	Cibber to R		Facsimile in B, VI; B, II, 176
9 June	Carter to R		*MM*
12 June	Lady Bradshaigh to R	Begun 6 June	B, VI, 254–65

DATE	CORRESPONDENT	REMARKS	LOCATION
12 June	R to Stinstra		Amsterdam
12 June	R to Carter	C has cut	*MM*; C, pp. 235–6
21 June	Young to R		*MM* lxx
22 June	Carter to R		*MM*
23 June	Stinstra to R		Amsterdam
23 June	Lady Talbot to R		FM XV, 4, f. 3
4 July	R to Stinstra		Amsterdam
4 July	R to Carter		Hyde; *MM*
5 July	R to Clairaut		B.M. grangerized copy of Thomas Moore's *Letters and Journals of Lord Byron*, XLI, facing p. 396 (press mark C. 44.g); C, pp. 236–8
6 July	Lady Talbot to R		FM XV, 4, f. 4
6 July	Edwards to R		FM XII, 1, ff. 79–80; Bodleian MS. 1012, pp. 103–4
10 July	R to Sutton		B, IV, 139–40
[10 July]	Sutton to R	Dated only '*Tuesday*, 1753' but clearly an answer to his of same day	B, IV, 141–2
10 July	Charles B. Kaiser to R		Alan Dugald McKillop; printed McKillop, *Richardson*, pp. 254–5
14 July	Wescomb to R		FM XIV, 3, ff. 91–2
15 July	R to S. Highmore		B, II, 280–7
16 July	R to Edwards	C has cut	FM XII, 1, f. 81; C, pp. 238–9
20 July	R to Wescomb	C has cut	FM XIV, 3, f. 93; *EM* ix; C, 239–40
23 July	Wescomb to R		FM XIV, 3, ff. 94–5
30 July	Wescomb to R		FM XIV, 3, ff. 96–7
31 July	R to Wescomb		*EM* x

DATE	CORRESPONDENT	REMARKS	LOCATION
[Early Aug.]	Wescomb to R	Answered by his 15 Aug.	FM XIV, 3, ff. 98–9
1 Aug.	Skelton to R		B, V, 224–7
1 Aug.	John Birkbeck to R		FM XV, 4, f. 13
4 Aug.	Faulkner to R	Quoted only	*Address to the Public* in *Grandison*, 1st edn., VII
10 Aug.	R to Faulkner	Quoted only	*Address to the Public* in *Grandison*, 1st edn., VII
11 Aug.	Stinstra to R		Amsterdam
13 Aug.	Carter to R		*MM*
15 Aug.	R to Wescomb	C has cut	FM XIV, 3, f. 100; *EM* xi; C, pp. 240–1
15 Aug.	R to Edwards		FM XII, 1, f. 82
16 Aug.	R to Lady Talbot		FM XV, 4, f. 5
16 Aug.	Faulkner to R	Quoted only; begun 14 Aug.	*Address to the Public* in *Grandison*, 1st edn., VII
17 Aug.	R to Carter		State University of New York at Buffalo; *MM*
18 Aug.	Lady Talbot to R		FM XV, 4, f. 6
21 Aug.	Edwards to R		FM XII, 1, f. 83; Bodleian MS. 1012, pp. 112–13
24 Aug.	R to Faulkner	Quoted only	*Address to the Public* in *Grandison*, 1st edn., VII
28 Aug.	Wescomb to R		FM XIV, 3, ff. 102–3
3 Sept.	J[ames] Leake, [Sr.] to R	Forwarding letter from Warburton to Leake	Robert H. Taylor
4 Sept.	Garrick to R		Boston Public Library
8 Sept.	Mrs. Chapone to R		FM XII, 2, ff. 86–7
8 Sept.	Faulkner to R		*Address to the Public* in *Grandison*, 1st edn. VII
11 Sept.	R to Stinstra		Amsterdam

DATE	CORRESPONDENT	REMARKS	LOCATION
11 Sept.	R to Wescomb	C has cut	FM XIV, 3, f. 104; *EM* xii; C, pp. 241–2
14 Sept.	Edwards to R		FM XII, 1, ff. 84–5; Bodleian MS. 1012, pp. 118–19; B, III, 66–8
15 Sept.	Faulkner to R	Extracts	*Address to the Public* in *Grandison*, 1st edn., VII
19 Sept.	R to Mrs. Chapone		FM XII, 2, ff. 88–9
19 Sept.	R to Edwards		FM XII, 1, f. 86; B, III, 68–70
20 Sept.	Young to R		*MM* lxxi
Recd. 22 Sept.	Wescomb to R		FM XIV, 3, ff. 105–6
25 Sept.	Lady Bradshaigh to R	Begun 13 Sept.	FM XI, ff. 25–8
25 Sept.	Lady Talbot to R		FM XV, 4, f. 7
26 Sept.	Johnson to R		Huntington; B, V, 283–4
28 Sept.	Kennicott to R		Historical Society of Pennsylvania
29 Sept.	Carter to R		*MM*
2 Oct.	Faulkner to R	Summarized	*Address to the Public* in *Grandison*, 1st edn., VII
2 Oct.	R to Carter		Berg; *MM*
3 Oct.	J. Chapone, Sr. to R		FM XII, 2, ff. 90–1
5 Oct.	R to Lady Bradshaigh	C has cut	FM XI, ff. 29–32; C, pp. 242–7
6 Oct.	Carter to R		Berg; *MM*
8 Oct.	Edwards to R		FM XII, 1, f. 87
11 Oct.	R to Sharpe	Quoted	R to Grainger, 16 Oct.
13 Oct.	Carter to R		*MM*
14 Oct.	Lady Bradshaigh to R		FM XI, f. 33
16 Oct.	R to Faulkner	Begun 13 Oct; quotations from	*Address to the Public* in *Grandison*, 1st edn., VII
16 Oct.	R to Grainger	Dated 1743, but	Historical Society

DATE	CORRESPONDENT	REMARKS	LOCATION
		concerns Irish pirates	of Pennsylvania
19 Oct.	R to Lady Bradshaigh		FM XI, f. 35
20 Oct.	Faulkner to R		*Address to the Public* in *Grandison*, 1st edn., VII
22 Oct.	A Dublin friend to R	Quoted	*Address to the Public* in *Grandison*, 1st edn., VII
27 Oct.	A Dublin friend to R	Quoted	*Address to the Public* in *Grandison*, 1st edn., VII
28 Oct.	Urania Johnson to R		FM XV, 3, f. 13
30 Oct.	Anna Williams and Mary Masters to R		FM XV, 3, f. 17
Nov.	Lady Barbara Montagu to R	Thursday	Cornell University
1 Nov.	Lady Talbot to R		FM XV, 4, f. 8
4 Nov.	Lady Bradshaigh to R		FM XI, f. 37
6 Nov.	Wescomb to R		FM XIV, 3, ff. 111–12
8 Nov.	Urania Johnson to R		FM XV, 2, f. 95
9 Nov.	Lord Orrery to R		B, I, 171–2
9 Nov.	Nicholas Harris to R	N. y., but refers to vols. of *Grandison*	FM XV, 4, f. 14
10 Nov.	James Harris to R		Facsimile, B, VI
12 Nov.	Ann Allen to R		FM XV, 4, f. 16
12 Nov.	R to Lady Bradshaigh		FM XI, f. 39; C, pp. 247–8
19 Nov.	Cibber to R		B, II, 177–9
22 Nov.	Young to R		*MM* lxxii
24 Nov.	R to Lady Echlin		Berg
26 Nov.	R to J. Chapone, Sr.		FM XIII, 1, ff. 92–3
26 Nov.	R to Young		*MM* lxxiii
26 Nov.	William Webster to R		FM XV, 3, f. 18
27 Nov.	Lady Bradshaigh to R	Begun 28 Oct.	FM XI, ff. 41–8

DATE	CORRESPONDENT	REMARKS	LOCATION
[Late 1753]	P. Delany to R	Receiving vols of *Grandison*	FM XV, 4, f. 19
[Late 1753]	P. Delany to R	Another note on same	FM XV, 4, f. 19
[Dec.]	Urania Johnson to R	Poem on *Grandison*; reference to Hill's *Works*; sends Season's greetings	FM XV, 3, ff. 14–16
1 Dec.	Sarah Lowe to R		FM XV, 2, f. 100
2 Dec.	J. Chapone, Jr., to R		FM XV, 3, ff. 19–22
8 Dec.	R to Lady Bradshaigh	C has cut	FM XI, ff. 49–53; C, pp. 249–60
9 Dec.	Mrs. George Berkeley to R	N. y., but refers to *Grandison*	FM XV, 3, f. 23
10 Dec.	Mrs. Chapone to R		FM XIII, 1, ff. 94–7
11 Dec.	Lady Bradshaigh to R	Begun 30 Nov.	FM XI, ff. 54–7
11 Dec.	Young to R		*MM* lxxiv
13 Dec.	W. Duncombe to R		FM XV, 3, f. 24
18 Dec.	Young to R		*MM* lxxv
20 Dec.	Hildesley to R		B, V, 115–19
20 Dec.	P. Delany to R		B, IV, 82–4
22 Dec.	R to P. Delany	C has cut	FM XV, 4, ff. 17–18; C, pp. 260–3
24 Dec.	Stinstra to R		Amsterdam; B, V, 254–61
c. 26 Dec.	Anonymous to R	So dated on letter; concerns *Grandison*	FM XV, 3, ff. 25–6
29 Dec.	R to Mrs Chapone	C has cut	FM XIII, 1, ff. 98–9; C, pp. 263–5
[1753–1754?]	R to S. Highmore	Reference to North End places letter before the end of 1754; since her friends have 'affronted' Charlotte Grandison, letter is probably after publication of *Grandison*; C dates [1750?]	B, II, 220–4; C, pp. 159–60

DATE	CORRESPONDENT	REMARKS	LOCATION
		1754	
4 Jan.	R to Lady Bradshaigh	C has cut	FM XI, ff. 58–61; C, pp. 265–72
10 Jan.	R to S. Highmore	Quoted	*Catalogue of Sammlung Karl Geigg-Hagenbach*, Basel, 30–1 May, 1961
14 Jan.	Lady Bradshaigh to R	Begun 23 Dec.	FM XI, ff. 62–5
26 Jan.	Anonymous to R		FM XV, 3, f. 32
28 Jan.	Edwards to R		FM XII, 1, ff. 88–9; Bodleian MS. 1012, pp. 129–31; B, III, 70–3
30 Jan.	James Leake, Jr., to R		FM XV, 3, f. 33
30 Jan.	Anonymous to R		FM XV, 3, f. 34
30 Jan	R to Lady Echlin		Berg
31 Jan.	R to S. Highmore	Two versions vary	*Letters of Several Eminent Persons Deceased* (1773), III, 6–13; B, II, 288–93; C, pp. 272–5
31 Jan.	R to Edwards		FM XII, 1, f. 90; B, III, 73–4
2 Feb.	Mrs. Chapone to R		FM XIII, 1, ff. 100–1
5 Feb.	Lady Bradshaigh to R		FM XI, ff. 69–74
6 Feb.	Edwards to R		FM XII, 1, ff. 91–2; Bodleian MS. 1012, pp. 141–3; B, III, 75–7
8 Feb.	R to Lady Bradshaigh	End missing; C has cut	FM XI, ff. 66–8; C, pp. 276–82
14 Feb.	R to Lady Bradshaigh	C has cut	FM XI, ff. 75–82; C, pp. 282–94
16 Feb.	Wescomb to R	Dated 1753, but R's answer points out error	FM XIV, 3, f. 117
17 Feb.	R to Edwards	Begun 16 Feb.; C has cut	FM XII, 1, ff. 93–4; C, pp. 294–5

DATE	CORRESPONDENT	REMARKS	LOCATION
17 Feb.	R to Wescomb	N. y.; end missing in *EM*	FM XIV, 3, f. 118; *EM* xxiii
22 Feb.	Lady Bradshaigh to R		FM XI, ff. 83–6
23 Feb.	Lady Echlin to R		B, V, 1–5
25 Feb.	R to Lady Bradshaigh	C has cut	FM XI, f. 87; C, pp. 295–6
27 Feb.	Lady Bradshaigh to R	The end of a letter forwarded with hers of 1 Mar.	FM XI, f. 88
[Mar. ?]	Elvira, Philoclæa, and Honoria to R	Answered, after a delay, 10 Apr.	FM XV, 3, f. 36
[Mar.]	Cox Macro to R	Forwarded by William Smith, [18 Mar. ?]	FM XV, 3, f. 23; B.M. Add. MS. 32,557, f. 175
1 Mar.	Lady Bradshaigh to R		FM XI, ff. 88–9
1 Mar.	Edwards to R		FM XII, 1, ff. 95–6; Bodleian MS. 1012, pp. 157–8; B, III, 78–80
7 Mar.	R to Edwards		FM XII, 1, f. 75
10 Mar.	Charles Chauncy to R		FM XV, 4, f. 11
12 Mar.	R to Stinstra	Written for R by William R	Amsterdam
14 Mar.	Young to R		Morgan; *MM* lxxxvi; B, II, 32–3
14 Mar.	Julia[n Bere] to R		FM XV, 4, ff. 20–1
15 Mar.	Wescomb to R		FM XIV, 3, f. 119
15 Mar.	R to a lady	Printed letter on supplementary vol. of *Grandison*, written as answer to 'Julia's' 14 Mar.	Copy in FM
17 Mar.	R to Skelton		B, V, 227–31
[18 Mar. ?]	W[illiam] S[mith] to R	Forwards Cox Macro's letter [Mar. ?]; marked recd. 17 or 18 Mar., but in answer (22 Mar.) R says recd. Tuesday last (19th)	FM XV, 4, f. 22

DATE	CORRESPONDENT	REMARKS	LOCATION
19 Mar.	Skelton to R		B, V, 231–5
19 Mar.	R to Lady Echlin		B, V, 6–10
20 Mar.	R to Stinstra	B's P.S., V, 269–70, is really from 2 June 1753 letter; C has cut	Amsterdam; B, V, 261–8; C, pp. 297–8
22 Mar.	Lady Bradshaigh to R		FM XI, ff. 90–5
22 Mar.	R to Anonymous		FM XV, 4, f. 23
22 Mar.	R to Wescomb		FM XIV, 3, f. 120; *EM* xiii
22 Mar.	R to Cox Macro		B.M. Add. MS. 32,557, ff. 176–7; FM XV, 4, f. 23
25 Mar.	R to a friend	Printed letter on Catholic compromise; largely quotes from letter to Macro, above	Copy in FM
28 Mar.	Johnson to R		Hyde
28 Mar.	Wescomb to R		FM XIV, 3, ff. 122–3
Recd. 28 Mar.	K. L. to R		FM XV, 4, f. 24
29 Mar.	Julian Bere to R		FM XV, 4, f. 26
29 Mar.	Edwards to R		FM XII, 1, ff. 101, 138; Bodleian MS. 1012, pp. 161–2
3 Apr.	R to Skelton		B, V, 236–40
5 Apr.	R to Edwards	C has cut	FM XII, 1, ff. 102–3; C, pp. 298–9
6 Apr.	Mrs. Chapone to R		FM XIII, 1, ff. 102–3
8 Apr.	Stinstra to R		Amsterdam
8 Apr.	R to Lady Bradshaigh	C has cut	FM XI, ff. 96–7; C, pp. 299–301
10 Apr.	R to Julian Bere		FM XV, 4, f. 27
10 Apr.	R to Elvira, Philoclæa, and Honoria		FM XV, 3, f. 37
Recd. 17 Apr.	Anonymous to R		FM XV, 3, ff. 39–40
Recd. 23 Apr.	Celia and Aminta to R		FM XV, 4, f. 28

DATE	CORRESPONDENT	REMARKS	LOCATION
24 Apr.	R to Celia and Aminta		FM XV, 4, f. 29
2 May	B. F. to R		FM XV, 3, f. 41
10 May	Reich to R	FM is undated	FM XV, 3, f. 56; B, V, 297–8
13 May	$X \Omega$ to R		FM XV, 3, f. 42
17 May	R to Lady Echlin	C has cut	Boston Public Library; C, pp. 302–3
17 May	James Fitzgerald to R		FM XV, 3, ff. 43–5
[Late May]	Anne R to R	Comments on Fitzgerald's letter of 17 May	FM XV, 3, f. 51
21 May	Lady Bradshaigh to R	Begun earlier—a date in letter is 29 Apr.	FM XI, ff. 98–101
21 May	Mrs. Chapone to R		FM XIII, 1, ff. 104–5
23 May	Stinstra to R		Amsterdam
23 May	Anonymous to R		FM XV, 3, f. 52
23 May	G[rainger] to R	Answered by R's 29 May	FM XV, 3, ff. 46–9
27 May	Celia and Aminta to R		FM XV, 4, f. 30
28 May	R to Mrs. Chapone	C has cut	FM XIII, 1, ff. 106–7; C, pp. 304–5
29 May	R to Grainger		FM XV, 3, f. 50
29 May	Elvira, Philoclæa, and Honoria to R		FM XV, 3, f. 38
29 May	Edwards to R		FM XII, 1, ff. 104–5; Bodleian MS. 1012, pp. 174–5; B, III, 81–4
30 May	R to Lady Bradshaigh	C has cut	FM XI, ff. 102–105; C, pp. 305–9
6 June	Wescomb to R		FM XIV, 3, ff. 124–5
8 June	Mrs. Chapone to R		FM XIII, 1, ff. 108–9
9 June	Kennicott to R		B, II, 183–96
11 June	Anonymous to R		FM XV, 3, f. 53

DATE	CORRESPONDENT	REMARKS	LOCATION
12 June	R to Wescomb		FM XIV, 3, f. 128; *EM* xiv
12 June	R to Edwards		FM XII, 1, f. 106; B, III, 84–7
12 June	R to Charles Chauncy		FM XV, 4, f. 12
15 June	Mrs. Chapone to R		FM XIII, 1, ff. 110–11
15 June	Wescomb to R		FM XIV, 3, ff. 126–7; B, III, 320–1
23 June	R to Wescomb		*EM* xv
28 June	R to Stinstra		Amsterdam
29 June	R to M. Delany		B, IV, 85–90
30 June	Lady Bradshaigh to R	Begun earlier; a date in letter is 23 June	FM XI, ff. 106–9
6 July	S. Fielding to R		B, II, 68–70
9 July	R to Lady Bradshaigh		FM XI, ff. 110–12
11 July	Hildesley to R		B, V, 120–4
13 July	R to Hildesley		B, V, 125–8
14 July	Young to R		*MM* lxxvi
Recd. 15 July	A. B. to R		FM XV, 3, f. 54
15 July	R to Kennicott		B, II, 196–201
16 July	Wescomb to R		FM XIV, 3, ff. 129–30
18 July	Edwards to R		FM XII, 1, ff. 108–9; Bodleian MS. 1012, pp. 156b–8b; B, III, 88–92
20 July	M. Delany to R		B, IV, 90–2
21 July	Young to R		*MM* lxxvii
21 July	A. B. to R		FM XV, 3, f. 55
23 July	R to Wescomb		FM XIV, 3, ff. 131–2; *EM* xvi
24 July	R to Lady Echlin		State University of New York at Buffalo
24 July	R to Young		*MM* lxxviii
25 July	R to Edwards	C has cut	FM XII, 1, ff. 110–11; C, pp. 309–10
28 July	Young to R		*MM* lxxix
31 July	Mrs. Chapone to R		FM XIII, 1, f. 112

DATE	CORRESPONDENT	REMARKS	LOCATION
[Aug.?]	R to Watts	Beginning and end missing; Mrs. Watts and R have evidently only recently met again; R wants histories of her friends and herself—on 27 Sept. he has history of one of her friends, but not hers	Alan Dugald McKillop
1 Aug.	Young to R		*MM* lxxx
1 Aug.	Edwards to R		FM XII, 1, ff. 112–13; Bodleian MS. 1012, pp. 163b–4b; B, III, 94–6
5 Aug.	Young to R		*MM* lxxxi
5 Aug.	R to Mr. and Mrs. Chapone		FM XIII, 1, f. 113
5 Aug.	R to Young		*MM* lxxxii
5 Aug.	R to Reich	Partly burnt during Second World War	Deutsches Buch- und Schrift- museum, Leipzig
6 Aug.	Lady Bradshaigh to R	Begun earlier; 20 July is date in letter	FM XI, ff. 113–15
7 Aug.	Wescomb to R		FM XIV, 3, ff. 133–4
9 Aug.	R to Wescomb		FM XIV, 3, ff. 135–6
12 Aug.	Lady Echlin to R		B, V, 11–21
12 Aug.	Dr. Oliver to R		FM XV, 4, f. 33
12 Aug.	Young to R		Harvard, tipped in 1755 edn. of *Centaur Not Fabulous*; facsimile, B, VI
14 Aug.	R to Young		Harvard, tipped in 1755 edn. of *Centaur Not Fabulous*
15 Aug.	R to Kennicott	End of letter only	Morgan
16 Aug.	J. Duncombe to R		B, II, 294–6
Recd. 17 Aug.	Wescomb to R		FM XIV, 3, ff. 137–8

DATE	CORRESPONDENT	REMARKS	LOCATION
21 Aug.	R to Mulso	C has cut	B, III, 207–12; C, pp. 311–12
22 Aug.	Silvester to R		FM XIV, 4, ff. 1–2
24 Aug.	R to J. Duncombe		B, II, 297–9
28 Aug.	R to Lady Bradshaigh		FM XI, ff. 120–4
12 Sept.	R to Lady Echlin	FM lacks beginning	Hyde; FM XI, ff. 126–7; B, V, 21–8
21 Sept.	Mrs. Chapone to R	P.S. by J. Chapone, Sr.	FM XIII, 1, ff. 115–16
22 Sept.	Thomas Wilmot to R	Note on bottom of Silvester's 22 Aug.	FM XIV, 4, f. 2
24 Sept.	R to Silvester		FM XIV, 4, f. 3
24 Sept.	R to Mulso	C has cut	B, III, 213–19; C, pp. 312–14
27 Sept.	R to Watts		Morgan
27 Sept.	Lady Bradshaigh to R		FM XI, ff. 128–131
27 Sept.	Lady Echlin to R		B, V, 29–32
1 Oct.	R to Wescomb	*EM* dates 3 Oct.	FM XIV, 3, f. 139; *EM* xviii
6 Oct.	R to Mrs. Chapone	P.S. to J. Chapone, Sr.	FM XIII, 1, ff. 147–52
7 Oct.	Edwards to R		FM XII, 1, f. 114
9 Oct.	Wescomb to R		FM XIV, 2, ff. 9–10
9 Oct.	R to Lady Bradshaigh	C has cut	FM XI, ff. 132–5; C, pp. 314–15
10 Oct.	R to Lady Echlin	C has cut	Yale; B, V, 33–8; C, pp. 315–16
recd. 12 Oct.	Silvester to R		FM XIV, 4, ff. 4–5
17 Oct.	Edwards to R		FM XII, 1, f. 115
18 Oct.	R to Edwards	On bottom of above	FM XII, 1, f. 115
22 Oct.	R to Hildesley		B, V, 128–30
22 Oct.	R to Wescomb	*EM* dates 2 Oct.	FM XIV, 2, f. 8; B, III, 322–3; *EM* xvii
23 Oct.	Wescomb to R		FM XIV, 2, ff. 39–40
24 Oct.	R to Thomas Newcomb		FM XV, 4, f. 38
[Late Oct.]	Thomas Newcomb	Answer to above;	FM XV, 4, ff.

DATE	CORRESPONDENT	REMARKS	LOCATION
	comb to R	on back is written 'October latter End, 1754'	39–40
[Oct.–Nov.?]	R to Joseph Highmore	So dated by Mrs. Duncombe; about portrait of Young	*Gentleman's Magazine*, LXXXVII (1817), ii, 210
[Nov.]	R to Kennicott	Evidently before 26 Nov.	Osborn
19 Nov.	Lady Bradshaigh to R		FM XI, ff. 136–7
20 Nov.	Edwards to R		FM XII, 1, ff. 116–17; Bodleian MS. 1012, pp. 172b–3b; B, III, 96–8
26 Nov.	R to Kennicott		University of Pennsylvania
26 Nov.	R to Edwards		FM XII, 1, f. 118; B, III, 98–101
7 Dec.	R to Lady Echlin		Princeton
17 Dec.	R to Young		*MM* lxxxiii
19 Dec.	Edwards to R		FM XII, 1, ff. 121–2; Bodleian MS. 1012, pp. 178–9; B, III, 101–3
30 Dec.	R to Edwards	C has cut	FM XII, 1, ff. 123–4; B, III, 104–7; C, pp. 317–18
		1755	
15 Jan.	Edwards to R		FM XII, 1, ff. 128–9; Bodleian MS. 1012, pp. 181–3; B, III, 107–12
21 Jan.	R to Young		*MM* lxxxvii
22 Jan.	Lady Echlin to R		B, V, 39–41
[26 Jan.]	Young to R	Dated only Sunday, but answers in haste R's 21 Jan.	*MM* lxxxviii
27 Jan.	R to Edwards	C has cut	FM XII, 1, ff. 130–1; B, III, 112–15; C, pp. 307–8

DATE	CORRESPONDENT	REMARKS	LOCATION
[29 Jan.]	Young to R	Dated only Wednesday, but continues subject of *Centaur Not Fabulous* from R's 21 Jan. and Y's [26 Jan.]; returns last sheet which in [26 Jan.] Young expected tomorrow	*MM* lxxxix
3 Feb.	Johnson to R		Huntington
4 Feb.	Edwards to R		FM XII, 1, ff. 132–3; Bodleian MS. 1012, pp. 188–90; B, III, 115–19
8 Feb.	Hildesley to R		University of Iowa
18 Feb.	R to Lady Echlin	Begun 14 Feb.	Berg
21 Feb.	R to Hildesley		B, V, 130–4
23 Feb.	R to Edwards		FM XII, 1, ff. 134–5
[27 Feb.?]	Young to R	Dated only Thursday; subject of 2nd edn. of *Centaur*, continued 6 Mar., and reference to dentist makes this date probable	*MM* xc
6 Mar.	Young to R		*MM* xci
6 Mar.	Urania Johnson to R		FM XIV, 1, f. 5
19 Mar.	Edwards to R		FM XII, 1, ff. 136–7; Bodleian MS. 1012, pp. 197–9; B, III, 120–3
21 Mar.	Dewes to R		B, IV, 93–5
23 Mar.	Young to R	N. y., but concerns 2nd edn. of *Centaur*	*MM* xcii
26 Mar.	Urania Johnson to R		FM XIV, 1, ff. 6–7
29 Mar.	Lady Bradshaigh to R		FM XI, f. 138
30 Mar.	Young to R	N. y., but concerns *Centaur*	*MM* xciii

DATE	CORRESPONDENT	REMARKS	LOCATION
31 Mar.	[M. Collier to R]	Sender identified by note in a 'tremulous hand', presumably R's	J. Paul de Castro, 'Henry Fielding's Last Voyage', *Library*, 3 S. VIII (1917), 157–9
7 Apr.	R to Stinstra	Written by William R	Amsterdam
8 Apr.	Mrs. Chapone to R		FM XIII, 1, ff. 133–4
9 Apr.	R to Watts	Morrison says to Miss Mulso, 1753, but death of R's brother William fixes year, and Miss 'M.' in letter is Miss Mogg; reference to Jeronymo makes recipient certain. C (who cuts) dates 1753 and says to Miss Mulso	Morrison, V, 256–7; C, p. 225
10 Apr.	Lady Bradshaigh to R		FM XI, f. 139
18 Apr.	R to Mr. Scott		FM XIV, 1, f. 8
19 Apr.	R to Lady Echlin		Berg
[30] Apr.	Wescomb to R	Dated 31 Apr.—R in reply points out error	FM XIV, 2, f. 41
2 May	R to Wescomb		FM XIV, 2, f. 42; *EM* xix
14 May	R to Wescomb		*EM* xx
25 May	Lady Bradshaigh to R		FM XI, f. 140
27 May	R to Lady Bradshaigh	End only	FM XI, f. 141
28 May	Edwards to R		FM XII, 1, ff. 140–1; Bodleian MS. 1012, p. 210; B, III, 123–5
28 May	R to Lady Echlin		Yale; B, V, 42–5
30 May	R to Edwards		FM XII, 1, f. 139
31 May	Dewes to R		B, IV, 96–8
1 June	Lady Bradshaigh to R		FM XI, ff. 142–3
4 June	R to Dewes		B, IV, 98–105

DATE	CORRESPONDENT	REMARKS	LOCATION
9 June	R to Mrs. Ashurst		FM XI, f. 144
13 June	Stinstra to R		Amsterdam
18 June	Edwards to R		FM XII, 1, ff. 142–3; Bodleian MS. 1012, pp. 213–14
20 June	Lady Echlin to R		B, V, 46–7
21 June	Mrs. Ashurst to R		FM XI, ff. 145–6
23 June	Stinstra to R		Amsterdam
24 June	Lady Bradshaigh to R	Copy on back of Mrs. Ashurst's 21 June and fragment of original	FM XI, ff. 146–7
26 June	S. Fielding to R		B, II, 71–2
28 June	R to Lady Bradshaigh	Only beginning in FM	FM XI, f. 148; B, VI, 265–70
7 July	R to Lady Echlin		Yale; B, V, 48–51
14 July	R to Edwards		FM XII, 1, f. 144
24 July	R to Stinstra		Amsterdam
25 July	Lady Bradshaigh to R		FM XI, ff. 149–150; B, VI, 270–6
28 July	Edwards to R		Hyde; Bodleian MS. 1012, pp. 220–2; B, III, 126–30
[Aug.]	R to Edwards	Answers Edwards's 28 July; Edwards on 7 Oct. says he did not receive this letter for two months	FM XII, 1, ff. 145–6
13 Aug.	R to Lady Bradshaigh	C has cut	FM XI, ff. 151–2; C, pp. 318–19
15 Aug.	R to Mrs. Chapone		FM XIII, 1, f. 135
15 Aug.	R to Mulso	C has cut	B, III, 219–29; C, pp. 319–22
2 Sept.	Lady Echlin to R		B, V, 52–8
5 Sept.	Lady Bradshaigh to R		FM XI, ff. 157–8
12 Sept.	R to Clairaut		Liverpool Public Library
17 Sept.	Stinstra to R		Amsterdam
20 Sept.	Young to R		MM xciv; B, II, 34

DATE	CORRESPONDENT	REMARKS	LOCATION
22 Sept.	Mrs. Chapone to R		FM XIII, 1, ff. 136–7
22 Sept.	R to Lady Echlin	C has cut	Robert H. Taylor; B, V, 58–62; C, p. 322
[c. 1 Oct.]	R to Lady Bradshaigh	Answers her 5 Sept., referred to in her 18 Oct.	B, I, clix–x; C, pp. 322–3
1 Oct.	Wescomb to R		FM XIV, 2, f. 43
3 Oct.	R to Wescomb		FM XIV, 2, f. 43; EM xxi
3 Oct.	M. Collier to R		B, II, 72–9
6 Oct.	Wescomb to R		FM XIV, 2, f. 44
7 Oct.	Edwards to R		FM XII, 1, f. 147; Bodleian MS. 1012, p. 222
13 Oct.	Wescomb to R		FM XIV, 2, f. 45
17 Oct.	Edwards to R		FM XII, 1, f. 148
18 Oct.	Lady Bradshaigh to R		FM XI, ff. 159–60
20 Oct.	Wescomb to R		FM XIV, 2, f. 46
[22 Oct.]	Mary R to R	Dated only Wednesday evening, but she has just arrived for visit at Enfield	FM XIV, 2, f. 47
22 Oct.	R to Lady Bradshaigh	Begun 21 Oct.	FM XI, f. 161
30 Oct.	[Sally Righton] to R	Signed Anna Hickman but refers to herself in letter	FM XIV, 2, ff. 49–50
[Oct.–Nov.]	Wescomb to R	So dated by R on back; confirmed by Polly's visit to Enfield—she left by 15 Nov.	FM XIV, 2, f. 48
12 Nov.	Silvester to R		FM XIV, 4, ff. 7–8
15 Nov.	Wescomb to R		FM XIV, 2, f. 51
16 Nov.	Lady Bradshaigh to R		FM XI, f. 162
24 Nov.	R to Silvester	Copy on bottom of Silvester's 12 Nov.	FM XIV, 4, f. 8
26 Nov.	R to Stinstra		Amsterdam
29 Nov.	Dewes to R		B, IV, 105–9
3 Dec.	Edwards to R		FM XII, 1, f. 149

2A*

DATE	CORRESPONDENT	REMARKS	LOCATION
9 Dec.	Wescomb to R		FM XIV, 2, f. 52
15 Dec.	Silvester to R		FM XIV, 4, ff. 9–10
15 Dec.	R to Lady Echlin		Yale; B, V, 63–7
17 Dec.	R to Lady Bradshaigh		FM XI, ff. 163–4
17 Dec.	Edwards to R		FM XII, 1, f. 150
24 Dec.	R to M. Collier		B, II, 80–4
29 Dec.	R to William Lobb		B, I, 183–6
29 Dec.	R to Samuel Lobb		Robert H. Taylor
30 Dec.	Wescomb to R		FM XIV, 2, ff. 53–4
31 Dec.	M. Collier to R		B, II, 85–91
[1755?]	[Samuel] Lobb to R	B has signature as W. Lobb, but writer clearly refers to son in letter and to his successful try for degree (B.A. 1755, M.A. 1758)	B, I, 186–9

1756

Jan.	Betsy Jobson to R	Early in month; she refers to her recent visit to R	FM XIV, 3, ff. 60–1
2 Jan.	Righton to R		FM XIV, 2, f. 57
2 Jan.	R to Wescomb		FM XIV, 2, ff. 55–6; *EM* xxiv
5 Jan.	Edwards to R		FM XII, 1, ff. 151–2
5 Jan.	R to Righton		FM XIV, 2, f. 59
5 Jan.	R to M. Collier		B, II, 92–5
8 Jan.	R to Betsy Jobson		FM XIV, 2, f. 62
21 Jan.	Edwards to R		FM XII, 1, f. 153
23 Jan.	Lady Bradshaigh to R		FM XI, ff. 165–6
4 Feb.	[W.] Duncombe to R	Quoted in R to Stinstra, 21 Feb.	Amsterdam
5 Feb.	Mrs. Sheridan to R	MS. has '1746', but this must be an error; Patty is asked to help on her novel, and Mrs. Sheridan says she is almost	Robert H. Taylor; B, IV, 143–4

DATE	CORRESPONDENT	REMARKS	LOCATION
		twice the age when she wrote it (in 1746 Patty was 10, Mrs. Sheridan 22)	
5 Feb.	Peckard to R		B, V, 105–7
7 Feb.	Lady Echlin to R		B, V, 68–71
7 Feb.	Edwards to R		FM XII, 1, ff. 154–5
9 Feb.	R to Lady Bradshaigh		FM XI, ff. 167–8
10 Feb.	R to William Blackstone		Oxford University Press; I. G. Philip, *William Blackstone and the Reform of the Oxford University Press in the Eighteenth Century* (Oxford, 1957), pp. 39–42
11 Feb.	M. Collier to R		B, II, 96–100
15 Feb.	Silvester to R		FM XIV, 4, ff. 11–12
16 Feb.	R to Peckard		B, V, 108–10
19 Feb.	Peckard to R		B, V, 111–12
20 Feb.	R to Lady Echlin	C has cut	Berg; C, pp. 323–4
21 Feb.	R to Miss Colburn		*MM* xcv
21 Feb.	R to Stinstra		Amsterdam
22 Feb.	R to Edwards		FM XII, 1, f. 157
22 Feb.	R to Silvester		FM XIV, 4, f. 13
24 Feb.	Lady Bradshaigh to R	Begun 22 Feb.	FM XI, f. 169
28 Feb.	Silvester to R		FM XIV, 4, ff. 14–15
16 Mar.	R to Silvester		FM XIV, 4, f. 16
16 Mar.	Johnson to R		Hyde
[19 Mar.]	Johnson to R	B dates Tuesday, 19 Feb., which was a Thursday; day on facsimile and MS. is 'Fryday'; on back of MS. R has written Friday, 19	Hyde; B, V, 285, with facsimile facing

DATE	CORRESPONDENT	REMARKS	LOCATION
		Feb., evidently in error; reference to favour of two nights ago must be the money asked for in Johnson's 16 Mar.	
19 Mar.	Edwards to R		FM XII, 1, ff. 162–3; Bodleian MS. 1012, pp. 232–4; B, III, 130–2
20 Mar.	Silvester to R		FM XIV, 4, f. 18
22 Mar.	R to Lady Bradshaigh		FM XI, ff. 173–4
24 Mar.	R to Silvester		FM XIV, 4, f. 19
29 Mar.	R to Edwards		FM XII, 1, ff. 158–9
29 Mar.	Lady Bradshaigh to R		FM XI, f. 175
30 Mar.	Pennington to R		Robert H. Taylor
30 Mar.	Young to R		National Library of Scotland
3 Apr.	Silvester to R		FM XIV, 4, f. 20
4 Apr.	R to Lady Bradshaigh		FM XI, f. 176
4 Apr.	R to Pennington		Robert H. Taylor
15 Apr.	Edwards to R		FM XII, 1, ff. 160–1; Bodleian MS. 1012, pp. 240–1; B, III, 132–5
23 Apr.	Lady Bradshaigh to R		FM XI, f. 177
23 Apr.	R to Young		*MM* xcvi
24 Apr.	R to Edwards		FM XII, 1, f. 166
27 Apr.	Young to R	Partly in B letter of 21 July 1757	*MM* cv; B, II, 39
4 May	Edwards to R		FM XII, 1, ff. 167, 169; Bodleian MS. 1012, f. 261
4 May	R to Lady Echlin		Yale
6 May	R to Lady Bradshaigh		FM XI, ff. 170–2
12 May	Silvester to R		FM XIV, 4, f. 21

DATE	CORRESPONDENT	REMARKS	LOCATION
13 May	R to Watts		Yale
14 May	Peckard to R		B, V, 113–14
15 May	R to Silvester		FM XIV, 4, f. 22
23 May	Lady Bradshaigh to R		FM XI, ff. 178–9
25 May	R to Edwards	B has end of 12 July letter with beginning of this	FM XII, 1, ff. 170–1; B, III, 135–6
29 May	R to Lady Bradshaigh		FM XI, f. 180
[Mid–1756?]	Mr. and Mrs. Sheridan to R	Hope to call on R—therefore in London; they were back in Dublin by late Oct. Letter refers to Mr. Fraser, who left for America c. 14 July 1757 (see Mrs. Sheridan's 24 July 1757)	New York Historical Society
2 June	Edwards to R		FM XII, 1, ff. 168, 182; Bodleian MS. 1012, f. 267
22 June	R to Lady Echlin		Yale
26 June	Lady Bradshaigh to R		FM XI, ff. 181–2
1 July	Wescomb to R		FM XIV, 2, f. 63
5 July	R to Wescomb		EM xxv
6 July	Young to R		MM xcviii
10 July	R to Lady Bradshaigh	C has cut	FM XI, f. 183; C, pp. 325–6
11 July	Young to R		MM xcvii
12 July	R to Edwards	B has combined the end of this letter with the beginning of letter of 25 May	FM XII, 1, ff. 172–3; B, III, 136–7
13 July	Silvester to R		FM XIV, 4, ff. 23–4
20 July	R to Silvester		FM XIV, 4, f. 25
2[1] July	Wescomb to R	Dated Wednesday, 20 July (a Tuesday)	FM XIV, 2, f. 64
26 July	Silvester to R		FM XIV, 4, f. 26
30 July	Edwards to R		FM XII, 1, ff. 180–1; Bodleian MS. 1012, ff. 267–8

DATE	CORRESPONDENT	REMARKS	LOCATION
[Aug.–Nov.?]	S. Fielding to R	Dated only 'Friday'; reference to Parson's Green puts it after Oct. 1754; she is going to Bath —by Dec. 1756 she was there	Hyde
[c. 1 Aug.]	R to S. Highmore	References to Mrs. Watts and Anne R put this letter between 22 July and 30 Aug.; Miss Highmore went to Marlow about 20 July. C has cut	Gentleman's Magazine, LXXXVI (1816), i, 506–8; C, pp. 326–8
2 Aug.	Lady Echlin to R		B, V, 72–5
10 Aug.	Smollett to R		Historical Society of Pennsylvania; MM
10 Aug.	Silvester to R		FM XV, 1, ff. 29–31
12 Aug.	R to Silvester		FM XV, 1, ff. 32–4
12 Aug.	Silvester to R		FM XV, 1, f. 35
13 Aug.	Lady Bradshaigh to R		FM XI, f. 184
13 Aug.	R to Silvester		FM XV, 1, f. 36
13 Aug.	R to Smollett	C has cut	Historical Society of Pennsylvania; MM; C, pp. 328–9
15 Aug.	Silvester to R		FM XV, 1, f. 37
16 Aug.	Urania Johnson to R		Harvard
25 Aug.	R to Lady Echlin		Fales Collection, New York University
27 Aug.	Lady Bradshaigh to R	Begun 21 Aug.	FM XI, ff. 185–6
27 Aug.	R to Mulso	Extract	Posthumous Works of Mrs. Chapone, II, 215–16
30 Aug.	R to Lady Bradshaigh		FM XI, f. 187
30 Aug.	R to Mulso		B, III, 230–4

DATE	CORRESPONDENT	REMARKS	LOCATION
6 Sept.	Mrs. Scudamore to R		FM XIV, 2, f. 58
7 Sept.	R to Mrs. Scudamore		*EM* xxvi
11 Sept.	R to Edwards		FM XII, 1, f. 179
12 Sept.	Young to R		*MM* xcix
13 Sept.	Edwards to R		FM XII, 1, f. 178
15 Sept.	Edwards to R		FM XII, 1, ff. 176–7
18 Sept.	R to Edwards		FM XII, 1, f. 175
22 Sept.	John Scudamore to R		FM XIV, 2, f. 65
24 Sept.	Edwards to R		Bodleian MS. 1012, f. 279
28 Sept.	R to Edwards		FM XII, 1, f. 174
1 Oct.	Edwards to R		Bodleian MS. 1012, ff. 279–80
3 Oct.	Mrs. Scudamore to R		FM XIV, 2, f. 66
4 Oct.	R to Mrs. Scudamore		FM XIV, 2, f. 67; *EM* xxvii
5 Oct.	Lady Bradshaigh to R	Begun 3 Oct.	FM XI, ff. 188–9
9 Oct.	R to Lady Bradshaigh	C has cut	FM XI, f. 190–1; C, p. 329
9 Oct.	Pennington to R		Princeton
15 Oct.	R to Pennington		Hyde
16 Oct.	R to Lady Bradshaigh		FM XI, f. 192
18 Oct.	Sir Roger Bradshaigh to R	N. y., but dated by references to Bath and banking	FM XI, ff. 193–4
19 Oct.	Edwards to R		Bodleian MS. 1012, f. 287
20 Oct.	Mrs. Scudamore to R		FM XIV, 2, f. 68
25 Oct.	R to C. Talbot		B.M. Add. MS. 39,311, f. 81
30 Oct.	Lady Bradshaigh to R		FM XI, ff. 195–6
31 Oct.	Pennington to R		Robert H. Taylor
4 Nov.	R to Young		*MM* c
9 Nov.	Young to R		*MM* ci
9 Nov.	R to Lady Bradshaigh		FM XI, f. 197

DATE	CORRESPONDENT	REMARKS	LOCATION
9 Nov.	R to Lady Echlin		Berg
10 Nov.	R to Samuel Lobb		Morgan; B, I, 189–92
10 Nov.	R to Pennington		Robert H. Taylor
12 Nov.	Loftus to R		B,V, 155–8
20 Nov.	Mrs. Sheridan to R		B, IV, 145–50; Morrison, VI, 125
23 Nov.	R to Mrs. Scudamore		FM XIV, 2, f. 69
25 Nov.	John Scudamore to R		FM XIV, 2, f. 70
[Dec.]	Mrs. Scudamore to R	Asks for loan, for which she thanks him 31 Dec.	FM XIV, 2, ff. 15–16
2 Dec.	Pennington to R		Princeton
3 Dec.	Mrs. Scudamore to R		FM XIV, 2, f. 71
4 Dec.	Righton to R		FM XIV, 2, f. 1
5 Dec.	R to Mrs. Scudamore		FM XIV, 2, f. 72; *EM* xxviii
6 Dec.	Lady Bradshaigh to R		FM XI, f. 198
7 Dec.	R to S. Fielding	C has cut	B, II, 101–5; C, p. 330
13 Dec.	R to Loftus		B, V, 159–62
14 Dec.	R to Righton		FM XIV, 2, f. 2
15 Dec.	R to Dewes	C has cut	B, IV, 110–14; C, pp. 330–1
19 Dec.	R to Mrs. Sheridan		Historical Society of Pennsylvania
21 Dec.	Young to R		*MM* cii
21 Dec.	Loftus to R		B, V, 163–5
23 Dec.	R to Pennington		Hyde
27 Dec.	Silvester to R		FM XV, 1, f. 38
[Late Dec.]	R to Young	Answers Young's 21 Dec.	*MM* ciii
31 Dec.	R to Silvester	Written for R by William R	FM XV, 1, f. 38
31 Dec.	Mrs. Scudamore to R		FM XIV, 2, ff. 73–4
		1757	
[2 Jan.]	Young to R	Dated only Sunday, but refers to invalids at Parson's Green;	*MM* civ

DATE	CORRESPONDENT	REMARKS	LOCATION
		sends New Year's greeting	
3 Jan.	R to Mrs. Scudamore		FM XIV, 2, f. 75
7 Jan.	R to Young		*MM* cvi
8 Jan.	Miss Sack to R		B, V, 290–6
10 Jan.	R to [Lady Echlin]		B.M. Add. MS. 19,683, f. 59
13 Jan.	Young to R		*MM* cvii
14 Jan.	R to Young	C has cut	*MM* cviii; C, pp. 331–5
17 Jan.	R to S. Fielding		B, II, ff. 106–9
19 Jan.	Meades to R		B.M. Add. MS. 28,097, ff. 2–3
20 Jan.	Young to R		*MM* cviii *bis*
27 Jan.	Righton to R		FM XIV, 2, ff. 3–4
2 Feb.	R to Meades		B.M. Add. MS. 28,097, f. 3
4 Feb.	M. Collier to R		B, II, 109–12
6 Feb.	Anne R to [R and Mrs. R]		Alan Dugald McKillop
8 Feb.	Mrs. Sheridan to R		B, IV, 150–6
12 Feb.	Meades to R		B.M. Add. MS. 28,097, ff. 4–6
13 Feb.	Lady Bradshaigh to R		FM XI, f. 199
24 Feb.	Young to R		*MM* cix
19 Mar.	Mrs. Scudamore to R		FM XIV, 2, f. 17
22 Mar.	R to Mrs. Scudamore		FM XIV, 2, f. 18
26 Mar.	Young to R		*MM* cx
28 Mar.	Meades to R		B.M. Add. MS. 28,097, ff. 6–7
2 Apr.	R to Reich		A. S. I. Berard, *Isographie des hommes célèbres* (Paris, 1828–30), III, under R
10 May	R to Young		*MM* cxi
11 May	R to Mrs. Sheridan		B, IV, 156–9
12 May	Young to R		*MM* cxii

DATE	CORRESPONDENT	REMARKS	LOCATION
13 May	Lady Bradshaigh and Sir Roger to R		FM XI, f. 200
15 May	Young to R		*MM* cxiii
16 May	R to Meades		B.M. Add. MS. 28,097, f. 8
22 May	Lady Bradshaigh and Sir Roger to R	Begun 20 May; B omits P.S. 22 May and Sir Roger's signature	FM XI, ff. 201–2; B, VI, 276–9
22 May	Young to R		*MM* cxiv
27 May	R to Lady Bradshaigh		FM XI, ff. 203–4
28 May	Meades to R		B.M. Add. MS. 28,097, ff. 9–10
29 May	Young to R		*MM* cxv
31 May	Loftus to R		B, V, 166–9
5 June	R to [J.] Duncombe		B.M. Add. MS. 20,084; B, II, 300–7
11 June	Reich to R	Quoted in R to Lady Bradshaigh, 2 Jan. 1758	FM XI, f. 228
20 June	Loftus to R		B, V, 170–3
25 June	Lady Bradshaigh to R		FM XI, ff. 205–8; B, VI, 279–88
[July?]	R to Reich	Quoted in R to Lady Bradshaigh, 2 Jan. 1758; answers Reich's 11 June	FM XI, f. 228
8 July	Meades to R		B.M. Add. MS. 28,097, f. 11
12 July	R to Lady Bradshaigh		FM XI, ff. 209–12
14 July	R to J. Duncombe		Facsimile, B, VI
19 July	R to Young		*MM* cxvi
21 July	Young to R	B's first paragraph belongs here, her second in letter of 27 Apr. 1756	*MM* cvii; B, II, 38
Recd. 24 July	Mrs. Sheridan to R		Harvard; B, IV, 159–64
26 July	R to Young		*MM* cxviii
30 July	Young to R		*MM* cxix

DATE	CORRESPONDENT	REMARKS	LOCATION
31 July	Lady Echlin to R		B, V, 76–9
2 Aug.	R to Mulso		National Library of Scotland; B, III, 234–8
3 Aug.	Loftus to R		B, V, 174–6
12 Aug.	R to Lady Echlin		Yale; B, V, 80–2
12 Aug.	Lady Bradshaigh to R		FM XI, ff. 213–16
18 Aug.	Meades to R		B.M. Add. MS. 28,097, ff. 12–15
26 Aug.	Mrs. Scudamore to R		FM XIV, 2, ff. 35–6; B, III, 324–7
28 Aug.	R to Silvester		FM XV, 1, f. 39
2 Sept.	R to Lady Bradshaigh		FM XI, ff. 217–18
5 Sept.	R to Meades		B.M. Add. MS. 28,097, f. 15
7 Sept.	Reich to R	Quoted in R to Lady Bradshaigh, 2 Jan. 1758	FM XI, f. 228
12 Sept.	R to Mrs. Scudamore		Haverford College; FM XIV, 2. f. 7; B, III, 328–9
15 Sept.	Meades to R		B.M. Add. MS. 28,097, ff. 16–18
18 Sept.	Loftus to R		B, V, 177–9
19 Sept.	R to S. Highmor		Harvard; B, II, 308–11
20 Sept.	Mrs. Scudamore to R		FM XIV, 2, ff. 19–20
20 Sept.	Meades to R		B.M. Add. MS. 28,097, f. 18
2[9?] Sept.	Young to R	Dated Thursday, 27 Sept. which was a Tuesday	Osborn
2 Oct.	Lady Bradshaigh to R	N. y., but refers to Polly's marriage	FM XI, ff. 223–4
14 Oct.	R to Reich	Quoted in R to Lady Bradshaigh, 2 Jan. 1758	FM XI, f. 228
23 Oct.	Young to R		B, II, 40
24 Oct.	R to Young		B, II, 41–2
1 Nov.	Young to R		*MM* cxx
6 Nov.	Mrs. Scudamore to R		FM XIV, 2, f. 21

DATE	CORRESPONDENT	REMARKS	LOCATION
10 Nov.	Lady Echlin to R		B, V, 82–5
19 Nov.	R to Lady Bradshaigh	C has cut	FM XI, ff. 121–122; C, pp. 335–7
29 Nov.	M. Klopstock to R		B, III, 139–41; *Klopstock*, pp. 222–3
3 Dec.	R to Lady Echlin		B, V, 86–8
18 Dec.	Lady Bradshaigh to R		FM XI, ff. 225–6
18 Dec.	Mrs. Sheridan to R		B, IV, 165–7
22 Dec.	R to M. Klopstock		Freies Deutsches Hochstift, Frankfurt am Main; B, III, 141–4; *Klopstock*, pp. 250–3

1758

DATE	CORRESPONDENT	REMARKS	LOCATION
[1758?]	Silvester to R	Dated only Monday evening; Silvester in town, as he was in Mar., which would also fit position in R's file	FM XV, 1, f. 40
2 Jan.	R to Lady Bradshaigh	C has cut	FM XI, ff. 227–229; C, pp. 337–9
3 Jan.	Young to R	Each version has ending not in the other	*MM* cxxi; B, II, 43–5
Jan.	R to Young	The P.S. appears also in *MM* cxli (22 Dec. 1758), where it fits better— answers remark in Young's [*c.* 20 Dec.]	*MM* cxxii; B, II, 45–7
5 Jan.	Lady Echlin to R		B, V, 89–91
15 Jan.	Mrs. Scudamore to R		FM XIV, 2, f. 23
24 Jan.	Lady Bradshaigh to R		FM XI, ff. 230–1
24 Jan.	R to Lady Echlin		Morgan
1 Feb.	Mrs. Scudamore to R		FM XIV, 2, f. 22
10 Feb.	Loftus to R		B, V, 180–2

DATE	CORRESPONDENT	REMARKS	LOCATION
10 Feb.	R to Mrs. Scudamore		FM XIV, 2, f. 24
11 Feb.	R to Lady Bradshaigh		FM XI, f. 232
28 Feb.	R to Lady Bradshaigh		FM XI, f. 233
1 Mar.	R to Millar		Attached to R's will
1 Mar.	Millar to R	N. y.	Attached to R's will
12 Mar.	Mrs. Scudamore to R		FM XIV, 2, ff. 25–6; B, III, 330–2
14 Mar.	M. Klopstock to R		B, III, 144–9; *Klopstock*, pp. 224–8
16 Mar.	T. Sheridan to R		Harvard; B, IV, 167–74
20 Mar.	Silvester to R		FM XV, 1, f. 42
30 Mar.	Pennington to R		Robert H. Taylor
31 Mar.	Spence to R		Osborn
31 Mar.	Lady Bradshaigh to R	Begun 27 Mar.	FM XI, ff. 234–5
4 Apr.	R to Lady Bradshaigh		FM XI, f. 236
6 Apr.	Lady Echlin to R		B, V, 92–4
6 Apr.	R to Mrs. Scudamore		FM XIV, 2, f. 27
6 Apr.	R to Silvester		FM XV, 1, f. 42
7 Apr.	R to M. Klopstock		Maine Historical Society; *Klopstock*, pp. 253–8
9 Apr.	R to T. Sheridan		Morgan
[10 Apr.]	Psalmanazar to R	Dated Monday, forwarded to Swinton 11 Apr.	Hyde
11 Apr.	R to John Swinton	Forwarding above	Hyde
11 Apr.	Mrs. Sheridan to R		B, IV, 174–6
15 Apr.	Mrs. Scudamore to R		FM XIV, 2, ff. 28–9
18 Apr.	R to Lady Bradshaigh		FM XI, f. 237
21 Apr.	Lady Bradshaigh to R	Two letters of same date	FM XI, ff. 238–41

DATE	CORRESPONDENT	REMARKS	LOCATION
21 Apr.	Francis Gosling to R		Attached to R's will
30 Apr.	Young to R	B's first paragraph not in *MM* but in Young's 9 Apr. 1751	*MM* cxxiii; B, II, 49
2 May	R to Young		*MM* cxxiv; B, II, 50–2
3 May	Spence to R	Typescript copy	Osborn
6 May	M. Klopstock to R		B, III, 150–5; *Klopstock*, pp. 228–32
14 May	Young to R		*MM* cxxv; B, II, 53
16 May	Loftus to R		B, V, 183–5
21 May	Young to R		Berg
23 May	R to Lady Bradshaigh		FM XI, ff. 242–3
25 May	R to Loftus		B, V, 185–9
28 [May]	Young to R	No month or year, but dated Sunday, which fits date of month in May, and concerned with Young's *Argument*— Young says he will not wait till last fortnight of June	*MM* cxxix
30 May	Lady Bradshaigh to R		FM XI, ff. 244–5
3 June	Mrs. Chapone to R		FM XIII, 1, ff. 138–9; copy in ibid., ff. 129–30
4 June	Young to R		*MM* cxxviii
12 June	Reich to R		B, V, 299–300
23 June	R to M. Klopstock		'Sammlung Clodius', Universitätsbibliothek, Leipzig; *Klopstock*, pp. 259–65
23 June	R to Lady Echlin		Berg
27 June	R to Lady Bradshaigh		FM XI, f. 246

DATE	CORRESPONDENT	REMARKS	LOCATION
27 June	R to Mrs. Chapone		FM XIII, 1, ff. 117–18
9 July	Mrs. Scudamore to R		FM XIV, 2, ff. 37–8
18 July	R to Silvester		FM XV, 1, f. 42
18 July	Urania Johnson to R		FM XIV, 1, f. 9
21 July	Lady Bradshaigh to R		FM XI, f. 247
25 July	R to de Luc		Morgan
31 July	Silvester to R		FM XV, 1, f. 43
5 Aug.	R to Silvester		FM XV, 1, f. 44
16 Aug.	Urania Johnson to R		FM XIV, 1, ff. 11–12
17 Aug.	Meades to R		B.M. Add. MS. 28,097, f. 19
17 Aug.	Silvester to R		FM XV, 1, ff. 45–6
19 Aug.	M. Delany to R	B dates 1751, but answered 11 Sept.	B, IV, 114–16
19 Aug.	Urania Johnson to R		FM XIV, 1, ff. 13–14
23 Aug.	Mrs. Chapone to R		FM XIII, 1, ff. 140–3; copy in ibid., ff. 119–23
26 Aug.	R to de Luc		Hyde
26 Aug.	M. Klopstock to R		B, III, 155–7; *Klopstock*, pp. 233–4
27 Aug.	Mrs. Scudamore to Patty R		FM XIV, 2, ff. 30–1
30 Aug.	R to Mrs. Chapone	C has cut	FM XIII, 1, ff. 125–6; C, p. 340
1 Sept.	R to Mrs. Scudamore		FM XIV, 2, ff. 5–6
2 Sept.	Mrs. Chapone to R		FM XIII, 1, ff. 144–6; copy in ibid., ff. 123, 127–8
9 Sept.	Urania Johnson to R		FM XIV, 1, ff. 20–1
11 Sept.	R to Lady Echlin		Harvard
11 Sept.	R to M. Delany		B, IV, 117–19
11 Sept.	R to Mrs. Chapone		FM XIII, 1, ff. 131–2
27 Sept.	R to Miss Morris	Quoted only	*Anderson Gal-*

DATE	CORRESPONDENT	REMARKS	LOCATION
			leries Cat., 19–20 Apr. 1933, item 398; *Parke Bernet Cat.*, 8–9 Jan. 1946, item 472
8 Oct.	Young to R		*MM* cxxxi
11 Oct.	R to Young		*MM* cxxxii
2 Nov.	Lady Barbara Montagu to R		Cornell University
2 Nov.	Silvester to R		FM XV, 1, f. 47
7 Nov.	R to de Luc		Morgan
9 Nov.	R to Silvester	Copy on bottom of Silvester's 2 Nov.	FM XV, 1, f. 47
16 Nov.	Mrs. Scott to R		Cornell University
21 Nov.	R to Mrs. Scott		Harvard
23 Nov.	Lady Barbara Montagu to R		Cornell University
23 Nov.	Loftus to R		B, V, 190–2
4 Dec.	S. Fielding to R	N. y., but refers to Polly's baby and *Countess of Delwyn*	R. N. Carew Hunt, 'Letters from an Autograph Collection', *Cornhill Magazine*, LXXIII (1932), 474–5
5 Dec.	Dr. Oliver to R		Bath Municipal Libraries and Victoria Art Gallery
6 Dec.	Young to R		*MM* cxxxiii
8 Dec.	Carter to R		Robert H. Taylor
10 Dec.	Mrs. Scudamore to R		FM XIV, 2, ff. 33–4
[17 Dec.]	Young to R	Dated only Sunday; answered by R's 18 Dec.	*MM* cxxxiv
18 Dec.	R to Young		*MM* cxl
[*c.* 20 Dec.]	Young to R	Answers R's 18 Dec. and answered by R's 22 Dec.	*MM* cxxxv
21 Dec.	L. L. G. Major [Majes?] to R		B, III, 158
22 Dec.	R to Young		*MM* cxli
26 Dec.	R to Young		*MM* cxxxvi

DATE	CORRESPONDENT	REMARKS	LOCATION
		1759	
5 Jan.	R to Lady Barbara Montagu		Harvard
7 Jan.	Young to R		*MM* cxxxvii
11 Jan.	Young to R		*MM* cxxxviii
[16 Jan.]	Lady Barbara Montagu to R	Dated from R's list of their correspondence; William R's answer of 27 Jan. says recd. 19 Jan.	Cornell University
24 Jan.	R to Young		*MM* cxxxix
25 Jan.	Akenside to R	N. y., but refers to article in *Philosophical Transactions* of the Royal Society, 1758–9	B.M. Sloan MS. 4300
27 Jan.	William R to Lady Barbara Montagu		Cornell University
31 Jan.	Lady Barbara Montagu to R		Cornell University
[Late Jan.]	Young to R	Answers R's 24 Jan.	*MM* cxxx
14 Feb.	R to Thomas Osborne, Jr.		Harvard
15 Feb.	R to Peckard		Columbia University
17 Feb.	R to Lady Barbara Montagu		Hyde
17 Feb.	R to de Luc		Bodleian MS. Montagu d 18
[4 Feb.	Silvester to R		FM XV, 1, f. 48
228? Feb.]	R to Lady Echlin	Quoted and partial facsimile; dated 29 Feb.; whether error is in day or year is uncertain	*American Art Association Cat.*, 8–9 Feb. 1927, item 250
2 Mar.	Ann Scudamore to R		FM XIV, 2, f. 11
8 Mar.	R to Ann Scudamore		FM XIV, 2, f. 32
8 Mar.	R to Lady Barbara Montagu		Osborn
27 Mar.	R to Lady Barbara Montagu		Hyde

DATE	CORRESPONDENT	REMARKS	LOCATION
31 Mar.	Lady Barbara Montagu to R		Cornell University
[April?]	Young to R	On distribution of copies of *Conjectures*, published 12 May	*MM* cxlii
3 Apr.	William R to Lady Barbara Montagu		Cornell University
4 Apr.	Smollett to R	N. y., but answered by William R's 5 Apr.	*MM*
5 Apr.	William R to Smollett		*MM*
7 Apr.	Lady Barbara Montagu to William R	N. y., but fits context of other 1759 letters	Cornell University
21 Apr.	R to Silvester		FM XV, 1, f. 49
22 Apr.	Lady Barbara Montagu to William R		Cornell University
25 Apr.	William R to Lady Barbara Montagu		Cornell University
25 Apr.	Silvester to R		FM XV, 1, f. 49
29 Apr.	Lady Barbara Montagu to William R		Cornell University
1 May	William R to Lady Barbara Montagu		Cornell University
8 May	Lady Barbara Montagu to William R		Cornell University
[13 or 20 May]	Young to R	Dated only Sunday; referred to in R's 24 May; on new edn. of *Conjectures* (1st edn. 12 May; 2nd edn. 14 June)	*MM* cxliii
20 May	R to Lady Echlin		Lady Charnwood Autograph Collection (B.M. Loan 60/2, 676F); printed in Lady Charnwood's *Call*

DATE	CORRESPONDENT	REMARKS	LOCATION
			Back Yesterday (London, 1938), pp. 120–3
[22 May?]	Young to R	Dated only Tuesday; refers to same subjects as R's 24 May, but not as if either letter answered the other; perhaps R wrote before receiving it; reference to *Conjectures* makes approximate date certain	*MM* cxliv
22 May	Lady Bradshaigh to R		FM XI, ff. 257–8
24 May	R to Young		*MM* cxlv
25 May	Young to R		*MM* cxlvi
29 May	R to Young	Paragraph five in both versions is also in *MM* cxl (18 Dec. 1758), where reference to Addison's death fits better	*MM* cxlvii; B, II, 54–6
31 May	R to [John] Rivington		Hyde
[Early June]	Young to R	Answers R's 29 May	*MM* cxxvi
5 June	R to Lady Bradshaigh		FM XI, ff. 259–60
[Mid-June]	Young to R	Scott and Davey lacks P.S. Continues subject of Johnson's remarks on *Conjectures* from R's 29 May, but since that letter R has evidently told Young that he sent 'in vain' for Johnson's remarks	*MM* cxxvii; facsimile [Henry Thomas] Scott and Samuel Davey, *A Guide to the Collector* (London, 1891), Appendices, p. 95
20 June	Mrs. Chapone to R		FM XIII, 1, ff. 155–6
26 June	R to Mrs. Chapone		FM XIII, 1, f. 153
26 June	R to Silvester		FM XV, 1, f. 49

DATE	CORRESPONDENT	REMARKS	LOCATION
28 June	Lady Barbara Montagu to R		Cornell University
30 June	Silvester to R		FM XV, 1, f. 50
10 July	R to Lady Barbara Montagu		Wisbech and Fenland Museum
15 July	Lady Bradshaigh to R		FM XI, ff. 249–50
17 July	R to Silvester		FM XV, 1, f. 52
21 July	Silvester to R		FM XV, 1, ff. 53–4
24 July	Spence to R		Osborn
2 Aug.	R to Lady Echlin		University of Indiana
2 Aug.	R to Lady Bradshaigh		FM XI, f. 251
11 Aug.	Young to R		Tinker Collection, Yale; *MM* cxlviii
11 Aug.	J. Douglas to Silvester	Written for R	FM XV, 1, f. 55
13 Aug.	Silvester to R		FM XV, 1, ff. 56–7
21 Aug.	J. Douglas to Silvester	Two copies, one (draft?) in R's hand	FM XV, 1, ff. 57–8
2 Sept.	R to Lady Barbara Montagu		Cornell University
16 Sept.	Lady Barbara Montagu to R	N. y.; refers to book on Magdalen House	Cornell University
18 Sept.	Lady Bradshaigh to R		FM XI, ff. 253–4
24 Sept.	R to Catherine Lintot		Yale
27 Sept.	R to Lady Barbara Montagu		Cornell University
2 Oct.	S. Fielding to R	Summarized only; year (in parentheses) may be dubious	*Sotheby's Cat.*, 15 Dec. 1954, item 755
11 Oct.	Lady Barbara Montagu to R		Cornell University
15 Oct.	R to Lady Barbara Montagu		Cornell University
18 Oct.	R to Lady Bradshaigh		FM XI, f. 261
23 Oct.	Lady Barbara Montagu to R		Cornell University
3 Nov.	R to Lady Barbara Montagu		Cornell University

DATE	CORRESPONDENT	REMARKS	LOCATION
1 Dec.	Lady Barbara Montagu to R		Cornell University
2 Dec.	Lady Bradshaigh to R		FM XI, ff. 255–6
12 Dec.	R to Lady Barbara Montagu		Cornell University
13 Dec.	Lady Echlin to R		B, V, 95–8
		1760	
14 Jan.	Lady Barbara Montagu to R		Cornell University
4 Feb.	Smollett to R		*MM*
10 Mar.	Lady Bradshaigh to R	Date on envelope	FM XI, f. 262
12 Mar.	R to Lady Bradshaigh		FM XI, ff. 264–5
18 Mar.	R to Mills		Yale
28 Mar.	Lady Echlin to R		B, V, 99–101
1 Apr.	R to Lady Echlin	Addressing her as Mrs. Roberts	B, V, 102–3
1 May	Smollett to R		*MM*
10 May	Mrs. Scudamore to R		FM XIV, 2, ff. 13–14
31 May	Smollett to R		*MM*
8 June	Lady Bradshaigh to R	Begun 20 May	FM XI, ff. 266–7
20 June	R to Lady Bradshaigh		FM XI, ff. 268–9
28 July	R to Birch		B.M. Sloan MS. 4317, f. 180
10 Aug.	R to Lady Bradshaigh		FM XI, f. 271
23 Aug.	Lady Bradshaigh to R		FM XI, ff. 272–4
26 Aug.	Hildesley to R		B, V, 135–8
4 Sept.	Ethelinda, Charlotte, and Henrietta to R		Berg
8 Sept.	Young to R		Tinker Collection, Yale; B, II, 57–8
10 Sept.	R to Hildesley	*Anderson Galleries Cat.* quotes last two sentences only	B, V, 138–40; *Anderson Galleries Cat.*, 9–10 Dec. 1909, item 309
Oct.	R to [Catherine Lintot]		E. L. McAdam

DATE	CORRESPONDENT	REMARKS	LOCATION
12 Oct.	Smollett to R		*MM*
Nov.	Mrs. Scott to R		Cornell University
11 Nov.	Hildesley to R		B, V, 141–5

1761

[*c.* Mar.]	R to Hildesley	B dates 24 Sept., after R's death; answered by Hildesley's 1 Apr.; letter from [Martha?] R to Lady Bradshaigh of [early Mar.] says R has written Hildesley after a three months' silence; C has cut	B, V, 145–9; C, pp. 341–2
[Early Mar.]	[Martha?] R to Lady Bradshaigh	Draft in R's hand; requests her marked copies of *Pamela* and *Clarissa*; answered by Lady Bradshaigh's 13 Mar.	FM XI, f. 270
13 Mar.	Lady Bradshaigh to [Martha?] R	Answers the above but addresses R in letter	FM XI, f. 276
1 Apr.	Hildesley to R		B, V, 150–4
5 Apr.	R to Lady Echlin		Berg
4 May	R to Hildesley	Quoted only	*Sotheby's Cat.*, 22–3 Oct 1956, item 444

INDEX

We have tried in this index to be selective rather than complete, on the theory that references chosen with judgement are more useful to the reader than very long entries. Complete listings of references to Richardson's novels, for instance, or to some of his friends, would have been little better than a blanket *passim*.

Thus we have not included names referred to in passing, which have only peripheral connection with Richardson or his times—for example, Milton and Joyce on page 2 and Homer on page 19. Nor have we listed older books, periodicals, or newspapers cited only for confirmation of facts—for example, the journals in note 63, page 33. We have, however, aimed at a complete listing of all references to critics or scholars cited in connection with Richardson or his circle.

Entries for Richardson's works include only references which we believe of interest to persons studying the work in question, not passing mentions, brief and unrevealing opinions of Richardson's contemporaries, or quotations from the works cited in confirmation of Richardson's views on other subjects. Similarly we have not included the names of Richardson's correspondents when they are mentioned only because Richardson wrote to them about some other subject. With this exception, we have aimed at including all references to his contemporaries. Thus page 5 is listed under Johannes Stinstra because there is information about Richardson's autobiographical letter to him which might be of interest to someone interested in Stinstra; subsequent references to the letter in Chapter I are not listed. Page 8 is listed under Samuel and William Lobb because the quotation contains information about the Lobbs; page 16 is not listed under Samuel Lobb because the quotation from Richardson's letter to him casts no light on the correspondent.

We have no index to the APPENDIX. Anyone wanting to locate the letters to or from a particular correspondent should have no difficulty in scanning the list of letters. Italics are used to indicate main entries.

T.C.D.E.
B.D.K.